A Dakota-English Dictionary

STEPHEN RETURN RIGGS

Edited by
James Owen Dorsey

With a Foreword by
Carolynn I. Schommer

BOREALIS

MINNESOTA HISTORICAL SOCIETY PRESS

Published by the Minnesota Historical Society Press, St. Paul

First published in 1890 by the Department of the Interior, U.S. Geographical and Geological Survey of the Rocky Mountain Region, as Contributions to North American Ethnology, volume 7.

 For information, write to the Minnesota Historical Society Press, 345 Kellogg Blvd. W., St. Paul, MN 55102-1906. Borealis Books is an imprint of the Minnesota Historical Society Press.

www.mnhs.org/mhspress

Manufactured in the United States of America

10 9 8 7 6 5 4 3

♾ The paper used in this publication meets the minimum requirements of the American National Standard for Information Sciences–Permanence for Printed Library Materials, ANSI Z39.48–1984.

Front cover: Dakota camp at White Bear Lake (now Lake Minnewaska), Pope County, Minnesota, 1869 (Beal's Art Gallery, Minneapolis); back cover: Dakota camp, 1890—both photographs in Minnesota Historical Society collections

International Standard Book Number 0-87351-282-0

Library of Congress Cataloging-in-Publication Data

Riggs, Stephen Return, 1812–1883.
A Dakota-English dictionary/Stephen Return Riggs ;
edited by James Owen Dorsey : with a new foreword by Carolynn I. Schommer.
p. cm. — (Borealis books)
Originally published: Washington, D.C. : Govt. Print. Office, 1890.
ISBN 0-87351-282-0 (pbk. : alk. paper)
1. Dakota language—Dictionaries—English.
2. English language—Dictionaries—Dakota.
I. Dorsey, James Owen, 1848–1895.
II. Title.
PM1023.R55 1992
497′.5—dc20 92-28736

A Dakota-English Dictionary

FOREWORD

During the eighteenth century Dakota tribal groups moved south and west from the central Minnesota area that they had inhabited to the Minnesota River valley and present-day South Dakota. From that period forward the Dakota people identified themselves as belonging to the Oceti Sákowin (Seven Council Fires). The seven divisions are: Wah'petonwan (in English, Wahpeton), Dwellers among the Leaves; Mdewakantonwan (Mdewakanton), Dwellers of the Spirit Lake; Sisitonwan (Sisseton), Dwellers of the Fish Grounds; Wah'pekute (Wahpekute), Leaf Shooters; Ihanktonwan (Yankton), Dwellers at the End; Ihanktonwana (Yanktonais), Little Dwellers at the End; Titonwan (Teton), Prairie Dwellers.

This migration led to changes in the Dakota language, making it a diverse language with regional variations or dialects. Dialectic divisions in the Oceti Sákowin parallel the political divisions. The first four groups named above are called the Santee, and they speak what is called the D or Dakota dialect. This dialect is used predominantly by four communities in Minnesota in the 1990s. They are the Pejihutazizi or Pajutazee (Yellow Medicine), Upper Sioux Community, at Granite Falls; Cansayapi (Trees Marked Red), Lower Sioux Community, at Morton; Mde Maya To (Blue Bank Lake), Shakopee-Mdewakanton Community, at Prior Lake; Tinta Wita (Prairie Island), Prairie Island Community, near Red Wing.

The N or Nakota dialect is used by the Yankton and Yanktonais. It can be heard on the Sisseton (Fish Ground) Reservation in Sisseton, South Dakota. The L or Lakota dialect occurs among the Teton, who reside predominantly on the Pine Ridge,

Standing Rock, Cheyenne River, and Rosebud reservations in western South Dakota.

The Dakota language and culture are one and the same. The language is the foundation of the Dakota culture. Until the mid-nineteenth century, the Dakota language existed in oral form only. In 1834 missionaries Samuel W. and Gideon H. Pond, Stephen R. Riggs, and Dr. Thomas S. Williamson, operating in Minnesota under the auspices of the American Board of Commissioners for Foreign Missions, created a written form of Dakota and translated biblical texts into it. The missionaries wanted to teach the Dakota people to read and write in their own language first; later, after learning to speak English, the Dakota learned to read and write English.

Three Dakota speakers and one Nakota speaker cooperated closely with the missionaries on the language project, which lasted into the twentieth century. They were Michael Renville, son of fur trader Joseph Renville, Sr.; the Reverend David Grey Cloud; the Reverend James Garvie; and Walking Elk, a Yankton tribal leader.

The missionaries translated the Bible into Dakota with the help of Joseph Renville, Sr., whose father was French and mother Dakota and who was bilingual in his parents' native languages. Williamson read the Bible in French, Renville translated the verses into Dakota, and Riggs and the Pond brothers struggled to write the words down. Thereafter, various chapters of the Bible, prayer books, and hymnals were issued in the D dialect. The collection effort bore additional fruit in 1852 when the *Grammar and Dictionary of the Dakota Language*, edited by Riggs and sponsored by the Minnesota Historical Society, was published by the Smithsonian Institution. An expanded version of the dictionary, also the result of work by Riggs, appeared in 1892 as *A Dakota-English Dictionary* and is the version now reprinted.

Serious study of the Dakota language was hindered by the lack of a dictionary that translated from English to Dakota. This deficiency was finally remedied in 1902 with *An English-Dakota Dictionary* edited by John P. Williamson, son of Dr. Thomas Williamson. The younger Williamson grew up speaking both Dakota and English and also became a missionary, spending most of his career at Santee Reservation in northeastern Nebraska.

Other scholars were interested in preserving the Dakota language, a part of the Siouan linguistic family. In the early twentieth century, anthropologist Franz Boas and his colleagues in linguistics, ethnology, and anthropology were working and studying toward preservation of language and customs. Ella C. Deloria, a Yankton, a student of Boas, and a graduate of Columbia University, later became an associate and collaborator. She was proficient in the translation of older, written Dakota into English. A notable aspect of these various translation projects using the D, N, and L dialects is that they were accomplished prior to 1934. Until that year the federal government had worked vigorously to eradicate the languages and culture of the indigenous people. With passage of the Indian Reorganization Act in 1934, Congress modified its stance and allowed use of native languages.

Riggs, Williamson, and the Pond brothers were in the forefront among scholars, linguists, and anthropologists who were transforming an oral language into written form. Because many sounds in the Dakota language are not present in the English language and are not comparable, the missionaries used diacritics–modifying marks indicating the different phonetic sounds. They noted differences in sounds and compared various equivalencies between the English alphabet and Dakota. They borrowed sounds from other languages, such as the German guttural and the French "j" and nasal sound. The

Dakota language structure is much different from the English, and no literal translation can be made from either language into the other.

The reprint editions of *A Dakota-English Dictionary* and *An English-Dakota Dictionary* will be a great resource for the Dakota language courses at colleges and universities and to Indian education classes in elementary and secondary schools and community colleges. The spelling system developed by Stephen Riggs and subsequently adopted and improved by Dakota speakers works quite well in Dakota language courses, provided the instructor insists that the students acquire a speaking knowledge of Dakota expressions before they refer to the written form.

These language classes are crucial to the cultural survival of the Dakota people. The preservation of the language is the key to the revitalization of Dakota culture and traditions; it will help suppress the derogatory stereotyping to which, for generations, the Dakota have been subjected. Through the oral traditions the younger generation will gain knowledge of their culture, traditions, and self-determination.

WAH'PETONWIN (Leaf Dweller Woman)
CAROLYNN I. CAVENDER SCHOMMER

American Indian Studies Department
University of Minnesota

Bibliographic Note

Barton, Winifred W. *John P. Williamson: A Brother to the Sioux.* New York: Fleming H. Revell, 1919.

Pond, Samuel W. *The Dakota or Sioux in Minnesota as They Were in 1834.* St. Paul: Minnesota Historical Society, 1908, Borealis Books, 1986.

——. *Two Volunteer Missionaries among the Dakotas, or the Story of the Labors of Samuel W. and Gideon H. Pond.* Boston: Congregational Sunday-School and Pub. Soc., 1893.

Riggs, Stephen R. *Mary and I: Forty Years with the Sioux.* Boston: Congregational Sunday-School and Pub. Soc., 1887; Minneapolis: Ross and Haines, 1969.

List of Abbreviations

adj. = adjective
adj.red. = adjective reduplicated
adv. = adverb
adv.red. = adverb reduplicated
cont. = contraction
Ih. = Ihanktonwan (Yankton)
imp. = imperative
intj. = interjection
i.q. = *idem quod* (the same as)
n. = noun
n.dim. = noun diminutive
n.p. = noun plural
num.adj. = numeral adjective
part. = participle
prep. = preposition
pron. = pronoun
red. = reduplicated
Si. = Sisseton
T. or Ti. = Titonwan (Teton)
v. = verb
v.a. = verb active
v.col.pl. = verb collective plural
v.cont. = verb contraction
v.imperat. = verb imperative
v.n. = verb noun
v.pos. = verb possessive
v.recip. = verb reciprocal
v.red. = verb reduplicated
v.reflex. = verb reflexive

NOTE BY THE DIRECTOR.

The Dakota, commonly known as the Sioux, forms the leading and best known division of the Siouan linguistic family. The Dakota language now consists of three well defined dialects, the Santee, Yankton and Teton.

The earliest record of the Siouan languages mentioned by Mr. Pilling in his Bibliography[1] is that of Hennepin, compiled about 1680. The earliest printed vocabulary is that of the Naudowessie (i. e., the Dakota) in Carver's Travels, first published in 1778.

In 1852 the Smithsonian Institution published a grammar and dictionary of the Dakota language, prepared by S. R Riggs. In that work the following preface appeared:

The preparation of this volume is to be regarded as one of the contributions to science made by the great missionary enterprise of the present age. It was not premeditated, but has been a result altogether incidental to our work. Our object was to preach the Gospel to the Dakotas in their own language, and to teach them to read and write the same until their circumstances should be so changed as to enable them to learn the English. Hence we were led to study their language and to endeavor to arrive at a knowledge of its principles.

About eighteen years ago, Messrs. S. W. and G. H. Pond, of Washington, Conn., took up their residence among the Indians of the Minnesota Valley. In the summer following Dr. T. S. Williamson and his associates, from Ohio, under the direction of the American Board of Commissioners for Foreign Missions, reached the same country. They immediately commenced the labor of collecting and ascertaining the meaning of Dakota words.

In the summer of 1837 we joined the mission and engaged in the same labors. Others who reached the country at a later period have rendered much assistance, among whom it is but just to mention the late Rev. Robert Hopkins, of Traverse des Sioux.

In prosecuting this work we have at all times availed ourselves of the best native assistance; but during the first years of our residence among them the natives did not

[1] Bibliography of the Siouan Languages, by James Constantine Pilling. Washington: Government Printing Office, 1887. 8°, 87 pp.

know enough to give us the help we needed. If we required the meaning of a word, as, for example, kaśka (*to bind*), the reply generally was, "It means 'kaśka,' and can not mean anything else." It is related of Hennepin that, while a captive among these Indians, on a certain occasion he ran off a little distance, and then, running back again, inquired of the braves who sat near what they called *that*. In trying to learn the meaning of Dakota words we have often been obliged to adopt similar expedients.

The preparation of the Dakota-English part of the dictionary for the press, containing more than sixteen thousand words, occupied all the time I could spare from my other missionary employments for more than a year. The labor bestowed on the English-Dakota part was performed partly by Mrs. Riggs.

A manuscript grammar of the language, written by the Rev. S. W. Pond, was kindly furnished to aid in the preparation of this work; but as it was not received in New York until midwinter, it has been used only in the latter part. Since my arrival in this city the grammar has been entirely remodeled and rewritten, according to the suggestions and under the direction of Mr. William W. Turner, of the Union Theological Seminary of New York. Of this gentleman's labors in connection with this work I cannot speak too highly. Not only has he by his eminent literary qualifications been able to render valuable assistance in the way of suggestion and criticism, but he has also read with great care the proof-sheets, especially of the grammar, that nothing might be wanting to make the work, under the circumstances, as perfect as possible. It is proper also to mention the name of Mr. William H. Smith, of New York, who assisted in the revision of the latter half of the dictionary in the absence of Mr. Turner.

About the 1st of January, 1851, a prospectus was issued at Saint Paul, under the sanction of the Historical Society of Minnesota, to publish the work by subscription, and in this many of the most prominent citizens of the Territory manifested much interest. Among the larger subscriptions may be mentioned those of Governor Alexander Ramsey, Hon. H. H. Sibley, Hon. Martin McLeod, Rev. E. D. Neill, and H. M. Rice, esq. The prudential committee of the American Board of Commissioners for Foreign Missions also made an appropriation for the same object, besides another for defraying the necessary expenses of superintending the press.

These provisions, though liberal, considering the circumstances under which they were made, were not sufficient to warrant the commencement of the publication; and being informed, in answer to a letter addressed to Prof. Joseph Henry, LL. D., that the work, on certain conditions, might probably be accepted as one of the Contributions to Knowledge of the Smithsonian Institution, it was concluded to present it for that purpose. After passing the prescribed examination, it was accepted by the Institution and directed to be printed.

With the manner in which the work has been brought out its friends will, I trust, be fully satisfied. Neither pains nor expense has been spared in the publication. The plan had already been followed, in the books printed in the language, of using the vowels with the sounds which they have in Italian and German, and of representing each articulation by a single character. In the present work a few changes have been introduced into the orthography for the sake of expressing some of the sounds in a manner more perspicuous and consistent with analogy, and more in accordance with the system of notation which is now becoming general among scientific philologists in Europe. It was necessary in consequence to rearrange a great many of the articles in the manuscript dictionary, and to have a number of new punches made.

With the hope that it may be the means of interesting some in behalf of the Dakotas, of perpetuating memorials of their language, and affording, to some extent, the means of arriving at correct conclusions in regard to their origin, this work, the result of years of toil, is submitted to the kind regards of its generous patrons.

STEPHEN R. RIGGS.

NEW YORK CITY, 1852.

While the work of Mr. Riggs referred to in the preface quoted was styled a grammar and dictionary of the Dakota language, most of the entries in the dictionary were in the Santee dialect, as that was the dialect of those Dakota who had been reached by Mr Riggs and his associates. Only here and there were a few words in the Sisseton, Yankton, and Mdewakantonwan, though A. L. Riggs now shows that the Mdewakantonwan were the original Santee. As the years rolled by Mr. Riggs and his two sons were enabled to add many Santee words, which are given in the present volume Numerous Teton words have been inserted, furnished chiefly by W. J. Cleveland, who became a missionary to some of the Teton tribes in 1873. There will also be found more Yankton words, introduced by J. P. Williamson, a missionary to the Yanktons, though another Yankton missionary, J. W. Cook, has already gained thousands of Yankton words (not in this volume) which differ materially from their Santee equivalents. As the entire Bible and most of the books and newspapers printed in the Dakota have been published in Santee, that dialect has become the standard or literary dialect of the language. From a comparison of the Teton in this dictionary with that in the texts now in the possession of the Bureau of Ethnology, Mr. Dorsey has been led to suspect that there are provincial differences in the Teton—subdialects, if I may so term them.

It is still difficult to say whether the speech of the Assiniboin should be considered a dialect of the Dakota or a distinct language of the Siouan stock, though it is known that this people is an offshoot of the Yanktonnai Dakota, who speak the Yankton dialect. Whether there ever was a dialect known as the Sisseton is considered by Mr. Dorsey an open question, though Mr. Riggs gave several Sisseton examples in the introduction to his grammar.

By request of the Director, Mr. Riggs submitted his enlarged dictionary for examination, and its publication was ordered. Owing to the inability of the author to remain in Washington, the work of editing the new volume was assigned, with the consent of Mr. Riggs, to Mr. J. Owen Dorsey, of this Bureau, as Mr. Dorsey had been making a special study of the Siouan languages, including the Dakota, since 1871, and was eminently qualified for the work.

The original work of Messrs. Riggs and Dorsey, with other materials already published, will place the Siouan languages on record more thoroughly than those of any other family in this country.

The accompanying letter of transmittal gives the reasons for the publication of the dictionary before that of the grammar, texts, and ethnography.

J. W. Powell,

Director.

LETTER OF TRANSMITTAL.

SMITHSONIAN INSTITUTION, BUREAU OF ETHNOLOGY,
Washington, D. C., November 1, 1889.

SIR: I have the honor to transmit to you the copy for "Contributions to North American Ethnology, Vol. VII, A Dakota-English Dictionary."

This material was furnished to the Bureau in 1882 by the author, the Rev. S. R. Riggs, A. M., who died at Beloit, Wis., in August of the following year. Besides the material now transmitted, Mr. Riggs prepared the copy for another volume, to be entitled "Grammar, Texts, and Ethnography of the Dakota," which material is still in my possession.

As the English-Dakota dictionary of the edition of 1852 contained many inaccuracies, Mr. Riggs wished to furnish, as a companion volume to the present one, a revised and enlarged English-Dakota dictionary; but owing to his illness and death the preparation of that part of the work devolved on the Rev. J. P. Williamson, missionary at the Yankton Agency, Dakota. The following quotation is from Mr. Williamson's letter to me, dated May 11, 1883:

> I commenced my English-Dakota dictionary before Dr. Riggs made any arrangement to republish his work. . . . I do not know that any agreement has been made obligating me to submit it as a part of the Dakota series. Yet I would not refuse the Smithsonian Institution my manuscript if it were ready, and I think that it will be complete some time next winter.

During the last illness of Mr. Riggs, and while I was correcting proof for him, I received several letters, in which a few pertinent sentences occur, thus:

> I think best to trust the whole matter to you for the present. I send on Mr. Cleveland's Teeton[1] words. You know better than any one else how I have heretofore used them. If I should be taken away, A. L. Riggs and T. L. Riggs will have this matter to attend to.

[1] I am constrained to differ from Mr. Riggs in the spelling of the English equivalent for "Titonwan." The word "Teton," with the "e" pronounced as in "me," has been used for more than a quarter of a century in gazetteers and geographies, and to me it seems preferable to "Teeton." Besides, Messrs. A. L. and T. L. Riggs have recently furnished another variant, "Titon." Let us retain "Titonwan" as the Dakota word and "Teton" as its English equivalent.—J. O. D.

Rev. A. L. Riggs wrote subsequently:

My father wishes to acknowledge your favor of March 8, just received, and to say in answer that any changes he may find absolutely necessary he will make in the plates Please go on with the work and use your best judgment.

Since then there has been considerable correspondence with Messrs. A. L. Riggs and J. P. Williamson, but no definite reply has been received as to the time when the English-Dakota dictionary can be submitted. In March of this year, when it was determined to obtain a final answer respecting this, a letter was sent to the Rev. A. L. Riggs by the Director of the Bureau, eliciting the following reply:

DEAR SIR: Your favor of March 1 in regard to the progress made on the English-Dakota part of my father's dictionary is received. A good deal of work has been done on it, but the final revision is yet to be made. I cannot say whether we could furnish you the manuscript fast enough to warrant beginning on it until after I have conferred with Mr. Williamson. This I will do at once and report to you.

Nearly eight months have passed since the receipt of that letter, and it now seems probable that the revised English-Dakota dictionary will not be published in connection with the present work and the "Grammar, Texts, and Ethnography of the Dakota."

It was the original intention of the Director of the Bureau to publish simultaneously all of Mr. Riggs's works on the Dakota language, the Dakota-English dictionary appearing as the first volume, the English-Dakota dictionary as the second, and the Grammar, Texts, and Ethnography of the Dakota as the third; but on account of the delay referred to in this letter it has been found impossible to adhere to this plan.

It was finally decided to publish the Dakota-English dictionary without further delay, as the 665 pages of that work could not well be bound in one volume with the Grammar, Texts, and Ethnography. It was also decided to postpone the publication of the latter work.

All entries followed by "S. R. R." were contributed by the author. Those furnished by his son, Rev. Alfred L. Riggs, are signed "A. L. R." "T. L. R." stands for Rev. T. L. Riggs, and "J. P. W." for Rev. J. P. Williamson. Rev. W. J. Cleveland's articles are designated by "W. J. C.", and "J. O. D." marks those entries for which I am responsible.

Yours, respectfully,

J. OWEN DORSEY, *Ethnologist.*

To J. W. POWELL, *Director.*

A DAKOTA-ENGLISH DICTIONARY.

BY STEPHEN R. RIGGS.

THE ALPHABET.

VOWELS.

The vowels are five in number, and have each one uniform sound, except when followed by the nasal "ŋ," which somewhat modifies them.

a has the sound of English *a* in *father*.

e has the sound of English *e* in *they*, or of *a* in *face*.

i has the sound of *i* in *marine*, or of *e* in *me*.

o has the sound of English *o* in *go*, *note*.

u has the sound of *u* in *rule*, or of *oo* in *food*.

CONSONANTS.

The consonants are twenty-four in number, exclusive of the sound represented by the apostrophe (').

b has its common English sound.

ć is an aspirate with the sound of English *ch*, as in *chin*. In the Dakota Bible and other printing done in the language, it has not been found necessary to use the diacritical mark.*

ç̌ is an emphatic ć. It is formed by pronouncing "ć" with a strong pressure of the organs, followed by a sudden expulsion of the breath.†

d has the common English sound.

g has the sound of *g* hard, as in *go*.

ġ represents a deep sonant guttural resembling the Arabic *ghain* (غ). Formerly represented by *g* simply.‡

h has the sound of *h* in English.

ḣ represents a strong surd guttural resembling the Arabic *kha* (خ). Formerly represented by *r*.‡

* For this sound Lepsius recommends the Greek χ. † These are called *cerebrals* by Lepsius.

‡ These correspond with Lepsius, except in the form of the diacritical mark.

k has the same sound as in English.

ḳ is an emphatic letter, bearing the same relation to *k* that "ç" does to "ć." In all the printing done in the language, it is still found most convenient to use the English *q* to represent this sound.*

l has the common sound of this letter in English. It is peculiar to the Titoŋwaŋ dialect.

m has the same sound as in English.

n has the common sound of *n* in English.

ŋ denotes a nasal sound similar to the French *n* in *bon*, or the English *n* in *drink*. As there are only comparatively very few cases where a full *n* is used at the end of a syllable, no distinctive mark has been found necessary. Hence in all our other printing the nasal continues to be represented by the common *n*.

p has the sound of the English *p*, with a little more volume and stress of voice.

p̣ is an emphatic, bearing the same relation to *p* that "ç" does to "ć."*

s has the surd sound of English *s*, as in *say*.

ś is an aspirated *s*, having the sound of English *sh*, as in *shine*. Formerly represented by *x*.†

t is the same as in English, with a little more volume of voice.

ṭ is an emphatic, bearing the same relation to *t* that "ç" does to "ć."*

w has the power of the English *w*, as in *walk*.

y has the sound of English *y*, as in *yet*.

z has the sound of the common English *z*, as in *zebra*.

ź is an aspirated *z*, having the sound of the French *j*, or the English *s* in *pleasure*. Formerly represented by *j*.†

The apostrophe is used to mark an hiatus, as in s'a. It seems to be analogous to the Arabic *hamzeh* (ء).

NOTE.—Some Dakotas, in some instances, introduce a slight *b* sound before the *m*, and also a *d* sound before *n*. For example, the preposition "om," *with*, is by some persons pronounced *obm*, and the preposition "en," *in*, is sometimes spoken as if it should be written *edn*. In these cases, the members of the Episcopal mission among the Dakotas write the *b* and the *d*, as "ob," "ed."

---

* These are called *cerebrals* by Lepsius.

† These correspond with Lepsius, except in the form of the diacritical mark.

DAKOTA-ENGLISH.

A.

a, the first letter of the Dakota alphabet. It has but one uniform sound, that of *a* in father.

a, an inseparable preposition or prefix.

1. Prefixed to verbs and adjectives, it usually means *on* or *upon:* as, maġaźu, *to rain*, amaġaźu, *to rain on;* mani, *to walk*, amani, *to walk on;* haŋ, *to stand*, ahaŋ, *to stand on;* waśte, *good*, awaśte, *to be good on* or *in addition to; to become, to befit:* when, in addition to the prefix, ka *or* kaća is suffixed, the idea of *incredulity* or *contempt* is expressed: as, awaśteka, amaḳukaća.
2. In some cases it gives a causative meaning to the verb: as u, *to come*, au, *to bring;* ya, *to go*, aya, *to take.*
3. It forms a collective plural in the case of some verbs of motion: as, au, *they come;* aya, *they go;* ahi, *they have arrived.*
4. Prefixed to nouns, it sometimes makes adverbs: as, wanića, *none*, awanin *or* awaninya *in a destroying way;* paha, *a hill*, apahaya, *hill-like.*
5. It makes nouns of some verbs: as, bapta, *to cut off from*, abapte, *a cutting on*, ćaŋ abapte, *a cutting-board.*

a, *n.* *the arm-pit, under the arm:* as, a ogna wao, *I hit under the arm* or *foreleg.*

a, *v.* *imperat.* only; *hark, listen:* a, a wo, a ye; pl. a po, am, a miye.

a-a', *n.* *mold.*

a-a', *adj.* *moldy.*

a-a', *v. n.* *to mold, become moldy.*

a-a'-mna, *v. n.* (aa *and* omna) *to smell moldy.*

a-ba'-hda, *v. a.* *to shave off with a knife*, as the fat from guts—abawahda, abayahda.

a-ba'-hda-hda, *v.* *red.* of abahda.

a-ba'-ka, *v. a.* (a *and* baka) *to cut* or *split the feather from a quill; fig. to be straight* or *without wrong doing:* abakapi se wauŋ—abawaka.

a-ba'-ke-za, *v. a.* (a *and* bakeza) *to cut off smooth*, as a feather for an arrow—abawakeza, abayakeza.

a-ba'-kpa, *v. a.* (a *and* bakpa) *to pare off on*—abawakpa.

a-ba'-kpaŋ, *v. a* (a *and* bakpaŋ) *to cut fine on, make fine on*, as in cutting tobacco: ćaŋ abakpaŋ, *a tobacco board*—abawakpaŋ, abayakpaŋ.

a-b a'-k s a, *v. a.* (a *and* baksa) *to cut off*, as a stick, *on* anything, *with a knife*—abawaksa, abauŋksapi.

a-b a'-k s a-k s a, *v. red.* of abaksa.

a-b a'-k ś i ś, *v. cont.* of abakśiźa: abakśiś iyeya, *to double* or *shut up*, as a knife, *on* anything.

a-b a'-k ś i-ź a, *v. a.* (a *and* bakśiźa) *to shut upon*, as a pocket-knife—abawakśiźa, abayakśiźa.

a-b a'-ķ e-z a, *v. a.* (a *and* baķeza) *to split the feather end of a quill; to cut off*, as the ribs of an animal *on*—abawaķeza, abayaķeza, abauŋķezapi.

a-b a'-m d a, *v. a.* (a *and* bamda) *to cut in strips on*—abawamda.

a-b a'-m d a-y a, *v. a.* (a *and* bamdaya) *to smooth over by cutting with a knife, to shave off lumps on*—abawamdaya.

a-b a'-m d a-z a, *v. a.* (a *and* bamdaza) *to cut* or *rip open on*—abawamdaza, abayamdaza, abauŋmdazapi.

a-b a'-m d e-ć a, *v. a.* (a *and* bamdeća) *to break by cutting on* anything, *as something brittle; to cut up in pieces on*—abawamdeća, abayamdeća, abauŋmdećapi.

a-b a'-m d e n, *v. cont.* of abamdeća: abamden iyeya.

a-b a'-m n a, *v. a.* (a *and* bamna) *to rip on*, as with a knife—abawamna.

a-b a'-p e, *v. a.* (a *and* bape) *to cut off short on*, or *make stubbed*—abawape

a-b a'-p o n, *v. cont.* of abapota.

a-b a'-p o-t a, *v. a.* (a *and* bapota) *to cut in pieces on, destroy on* anything, by cutting *with a knife*—abawapota, abayapota, abauŋpotapi

a-b a'-p s a-k a, *v. a.* (a *and* bapsaka) *to cut off on*, as a cord or string, *with a knife*—abawapsaka, abayapsaka, abauŋpsakapi

a-b a'-p ś u ŋ, *v. a.* (a *and* bapśuŋ) *to unjoint with a knife on* anything—abawapśuŋ.

a-b a'-p t a, *v. a.* (a *and* bapta) *to cut off from*, as a piece; *to cut on*, as clothes on a board—abawapta, abayapta, abauŋptapi.

a-b a'-p t e, *n.* ćaŋ abapte, *a cutting-board.*

a-b a'-p t u ś, *v. cont.* of abaptuźa: abaptuś iyeya.

a-b a'-p t u-ź a, *v. a.* (a *and* baptuźa) *to split* or *crack by cutting on* anything; *to crack* or *split*, as a knife-handle, *in cutting on* anything—abawaptuźa, abayaptuźa.

a-b a'-s d e-ć a, *v. a.* (a *and* basdeća) *to split on*—abawasdeća.

a-b a'-s k i-ć a, *v. a.* (a *and* baskića) *to press out on*, as with a knife by cutting—abawaskića

a-b a'-s k i-t a, *v. a.* (a *and* baskita) *to press upon with a knife*—abawaskita.

a-b a'-s k u, *v. a.* (a *and* basku) *to pare on*, as an apple—abawasku.

a-ba'-smiŋ, *v. a.* (a *and* basmiŋ) *to cut* or *shave off close,* as meat from bones—abawasmiŋ.

a-ba'-so, *v. a.* (a *and* baso) *to cut off a string from; to cut a string on* anything—abawaso, abayaso.

a-ba'-so-so, *v. red.* of abaso: *to cut strings from; to cut into strings on*—abawasoso.

a-ba'-śda, *v. a.* (a *and* baśda) *to make bare on, shave off with a knife on; to cut,* as grass, *in addition to* what is already done—abawaśda, abayaśda, abauŋśdapi.

a-ba'-śdo-ka, *v. a.* (a *and* baśdoka) *to cut a hole in, on* anything—abawaśdoka.

a-ba'-śi-pa, *v. a.* (a *and* baśipa) *to cut off* or *prune upon* anything—abawaśipa.

a-ba'-śki-ća, *v. a.* (a *and* baśkića) *to press out upon,* as by cutting with a knife—abawaśkića.

a-ba'-śku, *v. a.* (a *and* baśku) *to cut off upon,* as corn from the cob—abawaśku.

a-ba'-śpa, *v. a.* (a *and* baśpa) *to cut off on,* as a piece of a stick—abawaśpa.

a-ba'-śpu, *v. a.* (a *and* baśpu) *to cut up on, cut in pieces*—abawaśpu.

a-ba'-śpu-śpu, *v. red.* of abaśpu.

a-ba'-tpaŋ, *v. a.* Same as abakpaŋ, which see.

a-ba'-źan, *v. cont.* of abaźata: abaźan ośtaŋ, *to sit astride, be placed on astride.*

a-ba'-źa-ta, *v. a.* (a *and* baźata) *to make a split on*—abawaźata.

a'-be-ki-ya, *adv. scattered, separately.*

a'-be-ya, *adv. separately, scattering*—abeya iyayapi.

a-blo', *n. Ti.* for amdo, which see.

a-bo'-ḣde-ća, *v. a.* (a *and* boḣdeća) *to split by shooting or punching on* anything—abowaḣdeća.

a-bo'-ḣdo ka, *v. a.* (a *and* boḣdoka) *to punch a hole in* one thing *on* something else—abowaḣdoka.

a-bo'-ḣpa, *v. a.* (a *and* boḣpa) *to make fall on by shooting*—abowaḣpa.

a-bo'-kpaŋ, *v. a.* (a *and* bokpaŋ) *to pound fine on*—abowakpaŋ.

a-bo'-ksa, *v. a.* (a *and* boksa) *to break off by shooting on; to break off by punching on*—abowaksa, aboyaksa, abouŋksapi.

a-bo'-ku-ka, *v. a.* (a *and* bokuka) *to shoot* or *punch to pieces on*—abowakuka, aboyakuka, abouŋkukapi.

a-bo'-ķe-ġa, *v. a.* (a *and* boķeġa) *to miss fire on,* as in trying to shoot; *to snap a gun on*—abowaķeġa, aboyaķeġa, abouŋķeġapi, abomaķeġa.

a-bo'-ķeḣ, *v. cont.* of aboķeġa; aboķeḣ iyeya.

a-bo'-mda-za, *v. a.* (a *and* bomdaza) *to tear open by shooting on* anything—abowamdaza, aboyamdaza.

a-bo'-mde-ća, *v. a.* (a *and* bomdeća) *to break in pieces by shoot-*

ing or *punching on*—abowamdeća, aboyamdeća, abouŋmdećapi.

a-bo′-mden, *v. cont.* of abomdeća: abomden iyeya.

a-bo′-mdu, *v. n.* (a *and* bomdu) *to blow up on*, as by the wind; *to bubble up on*, as water; said when a multitude gathers around one—abomamdu.

a-bo′-mdu-mdu, *v. red.* of abomdu; *to bubble up*, as water.

a-bo′-pa *and* a-bo′-paŋ, *v. a.* (a *and* bopa *or* bopaŋ) *to pound fine on*, as corn—abowapaŋ.

a-bo′-po-ta, *v. a.* (a *and* bopota) *to shoot to pieces on* anything—abowapota, aboyapota, abouŋpotapi.

a-bo′-psa-ka, *v. a.* (a *and* bopsaka) *to break off*, as a cord, *by shooting on*—abowapsaka, aboyapsaka.

a-bo′-pta, *v. a.* (a *and* bopta) *to punch off a piece*, by striking on anything, *with the end of a stick*—abowapta, aboyapta, abouŋptapi.

a-bo′-ptuś, *v. cont.* of aboptuźa: aboptuś iyeya.

a-bo′-ptu-źa, *v. a.* (a *and* boptuźa) *to split* or *crack*, as an arrow *by shooting against* anything; or, as a stick, *in punching*—abowaptuźa, aboyaptuźa, abouŋptuźapi.

a-bo′-sdan, *v. n. cont.* of abosdata: as, abosdan hde, *to place upright on;* a phrase used of the *mirage*, or *looming up* of things on a cold, clear morning.

a-bo′-sda-ta, *v. n. to stand upright on.*

a-bo′-sde-ća, *v. a.* (a *and* bosdeća) *to split by shooting upon*—abowasdeća.

a-bo′-so-ta, *v. a.* (a *and* bosota) *to use all up by shooting upon*—abowasota.

a-bo′-śda, *v. a.* (a *and* bośda) *to make bare on by punching*—abowaśda.

a-bo′-śde-ća, *v. a.* (a *and* bośdeća) *to split off on*, as a piece, *by shooting* or *punching*—abowaśdeća.

a-bo′-śdo-ka, *v. a.* (a *and* bośdoka) *to shoot off on; to empty the contents of a gun on* anything, *by shooting at it:* mazakaŋ abośdoka—abowaśdoka, aboyaśdoka, abouŋśdokapi.

a-bo′-śna, *v. a.* (a *and* bośna) *to miss fire on*, as of a gun—abowaśna.

a-bo′-śpa, *v. a.* (a *and* bośpa) *to shoot a piece off on*—abowaśpa.

a-bo′-śpu, *v. a.* (a *and* bośpu) *to knock off upon*, as anything stuck on, by *punching* or *shooting*—abowaśpu.

a-bo′-ta-ku-ni-śni, *v. a.* (a *and* botakuniśni) *to destroy by shooting* or *punching on* anything—abowatakuniśni, aboyatakuniśni, abouŋtakunipiśni.

a-bo′-ṭa, *v. a.* (a *and* boṭa) *to kill on* by *punching*—abowaṭa.

a-bo′-we-ġa, *v. a.* (a *and* boweġa)

to break on, as by *shooting* or *punching*—abowaweġa.

a-bo'-źu-źu, *v. a* (a *and* bożuźu) *to break all up on; to destroy upon*—abowaźuźu.

a-ća'-ġa, *v. n.* (a *and* ćaġa) *to freeze in, on*, or *upon; to become ice upon*—amaćaġa.

a-ća'-ġa-śda-ya, *adj. all smooth with ice, icy.* Same as aćaḣśdaya.

a-ćaḣ'-sna-sna, *v. n.* (a ćaġa *and* snasna) *to rattle, as icicles formed on* anything.

a-ćaḣ-śda-ya, *adj.* (a ćaġa *and* śdaya) *all icy, covered with ice*, as trees when rain is frozen on them.

a-ća'-kśiŋ, *v. a. to step over, pass over, jump over; to avoid, pass by, neglect; to transgress*—aćawakśiŋ, aćayakśiŋ, aćauŋkśiŋpi, aćamakśiŋ, aćaćikśiŋ, etc.; woaćakśiŋ, *passing over.*

a-ća'-kśiŋ-ya, *v. a. to cause to pass over*—aćakśiŋwaya, aćakśiŋmayaŋ.

a-ća'-kśiŋ-yaŋ, *adv. passing over.*

a-ća'-mni, *v. n.* (a *and* ćamni) *to sprout on.*

a-ćaŋ'-ćaŋ, *v. n.* (a *and* ćaŋćan) *to shake on account of*—amaćaŋćaŋ.

a'-ćaŋ-ćaŋ, *v. a. to apply oneself to intensely:* áćaŋćaŋ ḣiŋća; áćaŋćaŋ ećoŋpi, *i q.* akiptaŋ ećoŋpi—áwaćaŋćaŋ, áyaćaŋćaŋ.

a-ćaŋ'-ka-śka, *v. a.* (a ćaŋ *and* kaśka) *to bind wood on; to inclose on, fence in*—aćaŋwakaśka. See aćoŋkaśke.

a-ćaŋ'-ka-śka-ya, *v. a.* (a ćaŋ *and* kaśkaya) *to make a fence, to inclose*, as a fort; *to bind wood together on*—aćaŋkaśkawaya.

a-ćaŋ'-ku-ya, *v. a.* (a ćaŋku *and* ya) *to make a road on; to pass through on*—aćaŋkuwaya.

a-ćaŋ'-ku-ya, *adv. lying on*, as a road; *passing through.*

a-ćaŋ'-ni-yaŋ, *v. n.* (a *and* ćaŋniyaŋ) *to be angry for*—aćaŋmaniyaŋ, acaŋniniyaŋ, acaŋniuŋyaŋpi.

a-ćaŋ'-ni-ye-ya, *v. a. to be angry at* one *on account of* something—aćaŋniyewaya, acaŋniyeuŋyaŋpi.

a-ćaŋ'-nuŋ-pa, *v. a.* (a *and* caŋnuŋpa) *to smoke on* or *after*, as after eating—aćaŋnuŋmuŋpa. See ćaŋnuŋpa.

a-ćaŋ'-te-śi-ća, *v. n* (a ćaŋte *and* śića) *to be sad on account of.* See ićaŋteśića

a-ćaŋ'-te-śin-ya, *adv. sorrowfully for.*

a-ćaŋ'-te-śin-ya-ken, *adv. sadly for.*

a-ća'-pa, *v. a.* (a *and* ćapá) *to stab on, stick in; to take stitches in* or *on*—aćawapa, aćayapa.

a-ćem'-ya, *v. a.* of aćepa: *to make fat for* a certain purpose—aćemwaya.

a-ćem'-ya-ken, *adv. in a state of fattening for:* aćemyaken hde.

a-će′-pa, *v. n.* (a *and* ćepa) *to be fat for, be in good order; to be getting fatter: i. q.* kitaŋna ćepa.

a-će′-sdi, *v. a.* (a *and* ćesdi) *to* ćesdi *on* anything—aćewasdi, aćeyasdi. See ćesdi.

a-će′-sdi, *n. something to* ćesdi *on*, as *a diaper.*

a-će′-ti, *v. a.* (a *and* ćeti) *to make a fire on* or *at*, as a log; *to heat*, as a gun-lock, for the purpose of hardening; *to burn*, as stone or brick, *in a kiln*—aćewati, aćeyati, aćeuŋtipi.

a-će′-ya, *v. a.* (a *and* ćeya) *to cry for* anything, as a child does; *to mourn for*, as for one dead—awaćeya, ayaćeya, uŋkaćeyapi.

a-će′-ya-pi, *part. crying for, cried for.*

a-ćoŋ′-ka-śke, *n. a place fenced in, a fort.* See ćoŋkaśke and ćaŋkaśka.

a-ćo′-pa, *v. a.* (a *and* ćopa) *to wade into the water for* anything—aćowapa, aćoyapa, aćouŋpapi.

a-ćos′-ya, *adv. warmly.*

a-ćo′-za, *v. n.* (a *and* ćoza) *to be warm on, to be comfortable.*

a-ću′, *v. n.* (a *and* ću) *to dew on, bedew.*

a-ću′, *n.* and *prep. dew upon.*

a-ću′-wi-ta, *v. n.* (a *and* ćuwita) *to be cold upon*—amaćuwita.

a-ću′-ya, *v. a. to cause dew upon, to bedew*—aćuwaya.

a-de′-tka, *n. a branch* or *limb* of a tree; *a limb*, as of the body.

a-de′-źa, *v. a.* (a *and* deźa) *to urinate on* anything—awadeźa, ayadeźa, uŋkadeźapi.

a-de′-źa, *n. a diaper.*

a-di′, *v. a. to climb up, climb* a tree; *to climb over*, as a fence; *to ascend*, as a hill—awadi, ayadi, uŋkadipi.

a-di′-di, *v. red.* of adi.

a-di′-di-ya, *adv. red.* of adiya.

a-di′-di-ya-ken, *adv. in a climbing manner.*

a-di′-ki-ya, *v. a. to cause to climb*—adiwakiya.

a-di′-ya, *adv. climbing.*

a-di′-ya-ken, *adv. in a climbing way.*

a-do′-kso, *v. a.* (prob. of doksi) *to fold up the arms; to put the hand under the arm*—adowakso, adoyakso, adouŋksopi.

a-do′-kso-haŋ, *v. a. to fold in the arms; to put under the arm*, as one's cap—adowaksohaŋ: adoksohaŋ iću, *to fold in the arms*—adoksohaŋ iwaću.

a-dos′, *cont.* of adoza.

a-dos′-dos, *cont.* of adosdoza: adosdos mahiŋhda.

a-dos′-dos-ye-ća, *v. n to experience a burning sensation; to become angry*—adosdoswayeća. See adosya.

a-dos′-do-za, *v. n. red.* of adoza; *to be scorched, but not cooked*, as something held in the flame.

a-dos′-ya, *v. a. to scorch*, as meat held in the flame; *to have one's feelings touched* by any circumstance, *to be made angry;* adosyapi seksen hiŋhda, *to experience a burning sensation*, as in sickness; adosyapi se kiŋyaŋka, *to run just as fast as one can:* adosye ḣiŋća—adoswaya, adosyaya, adosuŋyaŋpi.

a-do′-waŋ, *v. a.* (a *and* dowaŋ) *to sing in praise of* any one; *to sing for*, as for the death of an enemy—this the Dakotas do when they go to war against their enemies, and desire to take their lives; wićaśta adowaŋ, *to sing to a man, to sing the praises of a man;* zitkadaŋ pa adowaŋ, *to sing over the heads of birds*—this expresses a custom which the Dakotas have, when a man takes some woodpeckers' heads and sings over them to another person, expecting to receive from him in return a horse, or some valuable consideration. In this case, the individual mentions the honorable deeds of the person to whom he gives the birds' heads, and sings his praise—awadowaŋ, ayadowaŋ, uŋkadowaŋpi. See wa′-dowaŋ.

a-do′-za, *v. n. to be scorched, but not cooked;* taŋćaŋ adoza se; adoza se hiŋhda, *to feel a scorched sensation pass over the body*, as in a fever.

a′-e-ta-hnag-ya, *adv. towards, through, among.*

a′-e-ta-hna-ka, *prep. towards.*

a′-e-to-o-pta, *prep. towards.*

a′-e-to-o-pte-ya, *adv. towards, in that direction.*

a′-e-to-pta, *prep. in the direction of* a certain object.

a′-e-to-pte-ya, *adv. in that direction, past* a certain point.

a-gla′, *v. a. Ti.*, same as ahda.

a-gle′-śka-na, *n. Ti., a lizard*—ahdeśkadaŋ.

a-gli′, *v. a. Ti.*, same as ahdi—awagli, ayagli, uŋkaglipi.

a′-ġa, *v. n. to make a splash*, as a fish jumping up in the water; *to fall or jump into water with a splash*—aġe iḣpaya, aġe iwaḣpamda, aġe uŋkiḣpayapi.

a′-ġe, *v. n.* See aġa.

a-ġi′, *v. n.* (a *and* ġi) *to be covered with rust, mildewed; to have a rusty* or *brown stain.*

a-ġu′, *v. n.* (a *and* ġu) *to burn on* anything; *to burn on account of* or *by reason of* anything.

a-ġu′, *part. burnt on.*

a-ġu′-ġu, *v. n. red. of* aġu.

a-ġu′-ġu-ya, *v. a. red.* of aġuya; *to cause to burn on.*

a-ġu′-ya, *v. a. to cause to burn on*—aġuwaya, aġuyaya, aġuuŋyaŋpi.

a-ġu′-ya-pi, *n.* (aġuya) *bread*, so called because *burned* or *baked; wheat bread* especially; *wheat;* wamnaheza aġuyapi, *corn bread.*

a-ġu′-ya-pi-hu, *n. wheat growing; wheat straw.*

a-ġu′-ya-pi-i-ća-paŋ, *n. a flail.*

a-ġu′-ya-pi-mdu, *n. flour.*

a-ġu′-ya-pi-su, *n. wheat not ground, the grain of wheat.*

a-ġu′-ya-pi-ća-ġu, *n. leav-*

ened bread, because like the lungs—ćaġu.

a-h a′-h a-y e-d a ŋ, *adv.* *not firmly, movably.* See hahayedaŋ.

a-h a′-k a m, *adv.* *after.* Not much used. See ohakam.

a-h a′-k a m-y e-d a ŋ, *adv* *not deep, shallow;* said of dipping up anything when it is shallow.

a-h a ŋ′, *v. n.* (a *and* haŋ) *to stand on, rest on*—awahaŋ, ayahaŋ, uŋkahaŋpi. Ahe ćiŋ, *a foundation.*

a-h a ŋ′, *v* *imperat.* only; *take care:* ahaŋ duśna kta, *take care, you will mistake.*

a-h a ŋ′, *intj.* *of assent:* from haŋ, *yes.*

a-h a ŋ′-h a ŋ, *v.* *red.* of ahaŋ, *to stand on;* and also of ahaŋ, *to take care.*

a-h a ŋ′-k e-t a, *adv* *at the end.* See ihaŋketa.

a-h a ŋ′-k e-y a, *adv.* *immediately, then, following, at the end of.*

a-h a ŋ′-m d e, *v. a.* (a *and* haŋmde) *to dream about something* wakaŋ—awahaŋmde.

a-h a ŋ′-m n a, *v. a.* (a *and* haŋmna) *to dream about* anything—awahaŋmna, ayahaŋmna.

a-h a ŋ′-z i, *v. n.* *to be shady upon, overshadowed*—amahaŋzi.

a-h a ŋ′-z i-y a, *v. a.* *to overshadow, cause shade upon, make dark upon; to screen from the sun; to reveal to* one, as the shadows of things going before; *to give a presentiment of*—ahaŋziwaya, ahaŋzimayaŋ.

a-h d a′, *v. a.* (a *and* hda) *to take home, carry* or *bear home*—awahda, ayahda, uŋkahdapi, amahda, aćihda, wićuŋkahdapi.

a-h d a′, *v.* *col. pl.* of hda; *they go home.*

a-h d a′-d a, *v. a.* *pos.* of akada; *to scatter one's own upon*—awaḥdada.

a-h d a′-ġ e-ġ e, *v. a.* *pos.* of akaġeġe; *to sew one's own upon.*

a-h d a′-h a ŋ, *v. a.* (ahda *and* haŋ) *to stand carrying home.*

a-h d a′-h a ŋ, *v. n.* *to bear up, be strong enough to bear,* as ice—amahdahaŋ, uŋkahdahaŋpi, awićahdahaŋ.

a-h d a′-h a ŋ, *v., col. pl.* *they keep going home one after another.*

a-h d a′-ḣ p a, *v.* *pos.* of akaḣpa; *to throw,* as a garment, *over one's own; to cover one's own*—awahdaḣpa.

a-h d a′-ḣ p e-k i-t o ŋ, *v.* *pos.* of akaḣpetoŋ; *to clothe* or *cover one's own*—ahdaḣpewakitoŋ, ahdaḣpeyakitoŋ.

a-h d a′-ḣ p e-t o ŋ, *v.* *pos.* of akaḣpetoŋ; *to clothe one's own*—ahdaḣpewatoŋ, ahdaḣpeyatoŋ.

a-h d a′-ḣ p e-y a, *v.* *pos.* of akaḣpeya; *to cover one's own*—ahdaḣpewaya, ahdaḣpeuŋyaŋpi: taku ahdaḣpeyapi, *clothes.* See aihdaḣpeya.

a-h d a′-k s a, *v. a.* *pos.* of akaksa; *to cut off one's own upon*—awahdaksa.

a-h d a′-k ś i ŋ ś, *or* a-h d a-k ś i ś:

aḣdakśiŋś waŋka, *to lie curled up on one side:* aḣdakśiŋś muŋka.

a-h d a′-m n a, *v. a.* *pos.* of akamna; *to gather one's own upon, to accumulate*—awahdamna.

a-h d a′-p a ŋ, *v. a.* *pos.* of akapaŋ; *to beat out* or *thresh one's own upon*—awahdapaŋ.

a-h d a′-p o-t a, *v. a.* *pos.* of akapota, *to beat in pieces one's own upon;* also, *v. n.* *to float upon.*

a-h d a′-p s i ŋ-t a, *v. a.* *pos.* of akapsiŋta; *to strike* or *whip one's own.*

a-h d a′-p s o ŋ, *v. a. pos.* *to spill one's own upon*—of akapsoŋ.

a-h d a′-p ś i n, *adv.* *bottom upwards,* said of a boat or anything turned up.

a-h d a′-p ś i ŋ-y a ŋ, *adv.* *bottom up:* ahdapśiŋyaŋ eḣpeya, and ahdapśiŋyaŋ iyeya. *to turn bottom side up*—ahdapśiŋyaŋ iyewaya.

a-h d a′-p ś u ŋ, *v. a.* *pos.* of a *and* kapśuŋ; *to put one's own out of joint on*—awahdapśuŋ.

a-h d a′-p t a, *v. n* (a *and* hdapta) *to cease to fall on,* as rain—amahdapta. See hdapta.

a-h d a′-p t a, *v. a.* (a *and* hdapta) *to dip* or *lade out from one's own* kettle, etc.—awahdapta. See kapta.

a-h d a′-s k i-ć a, *v. a.* *pos.* of akaskića; *to press down on one's own*—awahdaskića. *Part., face down, prone, headlong.*

a-h d a′-s k i n, *part.* *cont.* of ahdaskića; *on the face, prone:* ahdaskin eḣpeya, *to throw down on the face;* ahdaskin iḣpaya, *to fall down on the face*—ahdaskin iwaḣpamda, ahdaskin iyaḣpada.

a-h d a′-ś d a, *v. a.* *pos.* of akaśda; *to cut,* as grass, *on oneself*—amihdaśda.

a-h d a′-ś k i-ć a, *v.* *pos.* of akaśkića and ayaśkića; *to spit out on* something of one's own—awahdaśkića, ayahdaśkića.

a-h d a′-ś n a, *v. a.* *pos.* of ayaśna; *to make a mistake in speaking*—awahdaśna.

a-h d a′-ś p a, *v. a.* *pos.* of akaśpa; *to break a piece off one's own upon.*

a-h d a′-ś t a ŋ, *v.* *pos.* of akaśtaŋ and ayaśtaŋ; *to throw* or *spill,* as water, *on one's own;* *to cease speaking* or *eating.*

a-h d a′-t a, *v.* *pos.* of akata; *to hoe one's own,* as corn, etc.—awahdata, ayahdata.

a-h d a′-t a, *v. a.* *to chorus to, answer* or *respond to in music*—awićawahdata, *I respond to them.*

a-h d a′-t a-h e-n a, *adv.* of ahdata; *answeringly.*

a-h d a′-t k a ŋ, *v.* *pos.* of ayatkaŋ; *to drink one's own with* or *upon*—awahdatkaŋ.

a-h d e′, *v.* Same as ahda.

a-h d e′, *v. a.* (a *and* hde) *to place* or *make stand on*—awahde, ayahde, uŋkahdepi. See ahnaka, aŋpa, etc

a-h d e′-d a ŋ, *and* a-h d a′-d a ŋ, *n.* or *part.* *Standing on—placed on*

a-hde'-haŋ, *n.* *a foundation.*

a-hde'-he-ćiŋ, *n.* *a foundation.*

a-hde'-hi-ye-ya, *part.* *placed one after another.*

a-hde'-ki-ya, *v a.* (ahda *and* kiya) *to cause to take home*—ahdewakiya, ahdeyakiya, ahdeuŋkiyapi.

a-hde'-pa, *v. a.* (a *and* hdepa) *to vomit upon*—awahdepa.

a-hde'-śka-daŋ, *n.* *a lizard.*

a-hde'-ye-ya, *part.* *placed one after another.*

a-hde'-yus, *v.* *cont.* of ahdeyuza: ahdeyus kute, *to shoot, holding the gun against* the object, or *very near* it.

a-hde'-yu-za, *v.a.* *to hold against, hold near to; to come near to*—ahdemduza.

a-hdi', *v. a* *to bring* or *carry home*—awahdi, ayahdi, uŋkahdipi.

a-hdi', *v.* *col. pl.* of hdi; *they come home together.*

a-hdi'-i-ya-pe, *v.* (ahdi *and* iyape) *to wait for their coming home; to lie in wait by the way*—ahdiiyawape.

a-hdi'-psi-ća, *v. col.* *to come home and alight.*

a-hdi'-waŋ-ka, *v. col.* *to come home and sleep.*

a-hdi'-ya-haŋ, *v. n.* *to fly home and alight,* as fowls; *col. pl.* of hdiyahaŋ, *to come in sight and stop,* as on a hill, *coming home.*

a-hdi'-ya-hda, *v. a.* (ahdi *and* ahda) *to carry home again*—awahdiyahda, ayahdiyahda. See akiyahda.

a-hdi'-ya-hda, *v. col. pl.* *they pass home.*

a-hdi'-ya-hda-haŋ, *v. col. pl.* *they continue to pass home.*

a-hdi'-ya-ku, *v. a.* (ahdi *and* aku) *to start to bring home again*—awahdiyaku, ayahdiyaku.

a-hdi'-ya-ku, *v.* *col. pl.* of hdiću; *they start to come home together.*

a-hdi'-ya-pe, *v.* See ahdiiyape.

a-hdi'-ya-pe-pe, *v. n.* *to skip,* as something flat thrown along on the surface of the water.

a-hdi'-ya-pe-pe-ya, *v. a.* *to cause to skip along on the surface,* as a stone or chip on the water—ahdiyapepewaya.

a-hdi'-yo-hi, *v.* *col. pl.* of hdiyohi; *they reach home on returning.*

a-hdi'-yo-taŋ-ka, *v.* *col. pl.* of hdiyotaŋka; *they come home and sit down.*

a-hdi'-yu-ḣpa, *v. a.* *to lay down on the way coming home*—ahdimduḣpa. *Col. pl., they come home and lay down* their burdens.

a-hdi'-yu-kaŋ, *v. col. pl.* *to come home and remain,* as deer, in abundance: ahdiyukaŋpi, *they come home and remain.*

a-hdi'-źu, *v. a.* (ahdi *and* eźu) *to bring home and pile up*—ahdiwaźu, ahdiyaźu, ahdiuŋźupi.

a-hdo'-hda, *v.* *to carry home*—awahdohda.

a-hdo'-ni-ća, *v. a.* (a *and* hdonića) *to hold to one's own on* a point—awahdonića.

a-hdu′-ġa-ta, *v.* *pos.* of a *and* yuġata *to open out* as one's hand *on* anything—awahduġata.

a-hdu′-ha, *v.* *pos.* of ayuha; *to have* or *take one's own on account of; to provide for* some occasion, *to keep one's own for* a certain purpose—awahduha, ayahduha, uŋkahduhapi.

a-hdu′-ho-mni, *v.* *pos.* of ayuhomni; *to turn upon one's own*, as a gun—awahduhomni.

a-hdu′-ḣi-ća, *v.* *pos.* of ayuḣića; *to waken up one's own upon*—awahduḣića.

a-hdu′-kaŋ, *v. a.* *to leave unmolested*—awahdukaŋ, amahdukaŋ.

a-hdu′-ka-wa, *v.* *pos.* of a *and* yukawa; *to open upon one's own.*

a-hdu′-kćaŋ, *v.* *pos.* of a *and* yukćaŋ; *to understand one's own upon* or *in relation to*—awahdukćaŋ.

a-hdu′-maŋ, *v* *pos.* of a *and* yumaŋ; *to grind one's own upon*—awahdumaŋ.

a-hdu′-mdu, *v.* *pos.* of a *and* yumdu; *to plow one's own upon*—awahdumdu.

a-hdu′-so-ta, *v.* *pos.* of a *and* yusota; *to use one's own up on*—awahdusota.

a-hdu′-sto, *v.* *pos.* of a *and* yusto; *to smooth one's own down on*, as hair; *to stroke*—awahdusto.

a-hdu′-su-ta, *v.* *pos.* of a *and* yusuta; *to make hard one's own upon.*

a-hdu′-śki-ća, *v.* *pos.* of a *and* yuśkića; *to press out one's own upon.*

a-hdu′-śna, *v.* *pos.* of a *and* yuśna; *to make a mistake over.*

a-hdu′-śtaŋ, *v.* *pos.* of ayuśtaŋ; *to leave off* something *pertaining to oneself*—awahduśtaŋ, ayahduśtaŋ, uŋkahduśtaŋpi.

a-hdu′-śte, *v. n.* *to be numb on*—amahduśte.

a-hdu′-ta, *v.* *pos.* of a *and* yuta; *to eat one's own with* something or *upon* something.

a-hdu′-ti-taŋ, *v.* *pos.* of a *and* yutitaŋ; *to stretch one's own upon; to pull upon.*

a-hdu′-we-ġa, *v.* *pos.* of a *and* yuweġa; *to bend* or *break upon.*

a-hdu′-za, *v.* *pos.* of a *and* yuza; *to hold one's own to.*

a-he′-će-ća, *v. n.* *to be rather better*, as in recovering from sickness, *to be neither good nor bad, middling*—amahećeća, anihećeća, uŋkahećećapi.

a-he′-će-ća-ke, *adj.* *rather better*—amahećećake.

a-he′-ćen, *cont.* of ahećeća.

a-he′-ćen-ya, *adv.* *pretty well, middling.*

a-he′-ćiŋ, *n.* *a standing-place, foundation.*

a-he′-he-ye-daŋ, *adv.* *not firmly:* aheheyedaŋ yaŋka.

a-he′-ki-ya, *v. a.* (ahaŋ *and* kiya) *to cause to stand on*—ahewakiya.

a-he′-yuŋ, *v. a.* (a *and* heyuŋ) *to*

tie up a bundle on—ahemuŋ, ahenuŋ.

a-hi', *v. a.* *to bring to* a place—awahi, ayahi, uŋkahipi, aćihi, amahi, awićawahi.

a-hi', *v.* *col. pl.* of hi; *they have come.*

a-hi'-be, *v.* See ahimaŋ.

a-hi'-maŋ, *v. n.* *to come and hatch,* as birds of passage; *to lodge on*: *pl* ahimaŋpi.

a-hi'-mni-ći-ya, *v.* (ahi *and* mnićiya) *to assemble to; to keep coming in one after another.*

a-hi'-na-pa, *v. n.* (a *and* hinapa) *to come out on,* as sores or pimples on the skin; *to break out in sores* or *spots*—amahinapa. Sometimes written ahinaŋpa.

a-hi'-na-pa, *v.* *col. pl.* of hinapa; *they come in sight.*

a-hiŋ'-haŋ, *v. n.* (a *and* hiŋhaŋ) *to rain upon, fall on as rain*—amahiŋhaŋ, uŋkahiŋhaŋpi.

a-hiŋ'-he, *v. n.* Same as ahiŋhaŋ.

a-hiŋ'-he-ki-ya, *v. a.* *to cause to rain on*—ahiŋhewakiya.

a-hiŋ'-he-ya, *v. a.* *to cause to fall on,* as rain—ahiŋhewaya.

a-hiŋ'-ḣpa-ya, *v. n.* (a *and* hiŋḣpaya) *to fall on* anything—amahiŋḣpaya, anihiŋḣpaya, uŋkahiŋḣpayapi.

a-hiŋ'-ḣpa-ye-ya, *v a.* *to cause to fall on*: amahiŋḣpayeyaya, *you caused it to fall on me.*

a-hi'-ti, *v.* (ahi *and* ti) *to come and pitch one's tent*—ahiwati, ahiyati, ahiuŋtipi.

a-hi'-toŋ-waŋ, *v. a.* (ahi *and* toŋwaŋ) *to look towards* one; *to look upon; to look to, regard*—ahiwatoŋwaŋ, ahiyatoŋwaŋ, ahiuŋtoŋwaŋpi, ahimatoŋwaŋ.

a-hi'-toŋ-waŋ-yaŋ-pi, *v. pl.* *they come and make a village*—ahiuŋtoŋwaŋyaŋpi.

a-hi'-toŋ-we-ki-ya, *v a.* *to cause to look towards*—ahitoŋwewakiya.

a-hi'-toŋ-we-ya, *v. a.* *to cause to look to*—ahitoŋwewaya, ahitoŋwemayaŋ.

a-hi'-waŋ-ka, *v n.* (ahi *and* waŋka) *col. to come and sleep;* or *v. a. to bring and lie down*—ahimuŋka.

a-hi'-ya-haŋ, *v n.* *to come and alight on,* as a flock of birds in a field: zitkataŋka en ahiyahe. *Col. pl.*, as, paha ahiyahe, *they come up on the hill*

a-hi'-ya-haŋ-haŋ, *v.* *red.* of ahiyahaŋ.

a-hi'-ya-hde, *v. a.* *to bring home and place on; pl. they come and go on towards home.*

a-hi'-ya-hde-ya, *part.* *coming and going on*

a-hi'-ya-ka-siŋ-siŋ, *v. a. col. pl.* *to pass along, sometimes in sight, and sometimes out of sight.* See ahiyokasiŋsiŋ.

a-hi'-yaŋ-ka, *v. n* (ahi *and* yaŋka) *to bring one thing after another, keep bringing; to bring and remain*—ahimaŋka, ahinaŋka: *pl.* ahiyukaŋpi.

a-hi′-ya-ya, *v. col. pl.* of hiyaya; *they passed by.*

a-hi′-ya-ya, *v. a. to take or carry round; hand round to*, as a pipe; *to sing*, as a hymn or tune—awahimdamde, ayahidade, uŋkahiyayapi. Hence oahiyaye, *a tune.*

a-hi′-yo-ka-kiŋ, *v. to come and peep in and draw back the head*—ahiyowakakiŋ, ahiyoyakakiŋ.

a-hi′-yo-ka-siŋ, *v. to look in at a window* or *door, to peep in.* It does not appear to be quite synonymous with ahiyokakiŋ—ahiyowakasiŋ, ahiyouŋkasiŋpi.

a-hi′-yo-ka-siŋ-siŋ, *v. red.* of ahiyokasiŋ; *to appear and disappear; to peep and peep again.*

a-hi′-yu, *v. a. to start to bring*—ahibu.

a-hi′-yu, *col. pl.* of hiyu: *they come, start to come.*

a-hi′-yu-kaŋ-pi, *v. pl. they come and remain.*

a-hi′-źu, *v. a.* (ahi *and* źu) *to bring and pile up*—ahiwaźu.

a-hmi′-hbe-ya, *v. a. to cause to roll on* anything—ahmihbewaya.

a-hmi′-hma, *v. n to roll on:* ahmihma iyaya, *to go rolling on* anything

a-hmi′-yaŋ-yaŋ, *adv. round on* anything: ahmiyaŋyaŋ iyaya, *to move round*, as a ball in a socket; *to become round by turning* or *rolling.*

a′-hna *or* a-hna′, *prep. with, together with; upon.* For this last meaning, see wahna.

a′-hna-haŋ, *part. standing with.*

a-hna′-haŋ, *v. n.* of hnahaŋ; *to fall on*, as fruit on anything.

a-hn̄a′-hna, *prep. red.* of ahna.

a-hna′-ka, *v. a.* (a *and* hnaka) *to place on* anything; *to apply as medicine externally*, in the form of a poultice or plaster—awahnakna, ayahnaka, uŋkahnakapi. See ahde, aoŋpa, aźu, ehnaka, and ohnaka

a-hna′-na, *adv. only with; with so many only.*

a′-hna-wo-ta-pi, *n. a table; anything to eat on.* See wahnawotapi.

a-ho′-ćo-ka, *adv.* (a *and* hoćoka) *in the midst.*

a-ho′-ćo-ka-ya, *v. a. to surround*—ahoćokawaya.

a-ho′-ćo-ka-ya, *adv. around, surrounding*—ahoćokaya uŋyaŋpi.

a-ho′-ki-pa, *v. pos.* of ahopa; *to value as one's own; to take care of*—ahowakipa, ahouŋkipapi.

a-ho′-ki-pe-śni, *v. neg. not to value; to impair*—ahowakipeśni, ahouŋkipapiśni.

a-ho′-kśi-wiŋ-kta, *v. to get angry at*, as a child; *to act like a child towards* one—ahokśiwawiŋkta, ahokśimawiŋkta.

a-ho′-pa, *v. a. to honor, respect, reverence, stand in awe of; to keep* as a commandment, law, or custom—ahowapa, ahoyapa, ahouŋpapi.

a-ho′-pe-ki-ya, *v. a. to cause to respect* or *keep*—ahopewakiya.

a-ho′-pe-ya, *v. a. to cause to observe*—ahopewaya.

a-ho'-pe-ya, *part.* *honoring, respecting, observing.* *Adv., obediently.*

a-ho'-taŋ, *v. a.* *to make a noise around* one—ahowataŋ, ahomataŋ, ahouŋtaŋpi.

a-ho-taŋ'-ka, *n.* *one who makes a noise around.*

a-ho'-toŋ, *v. a.* (a *and* hotoŋ) *to cry out for,* as a bird for food.

a-ho'-toŋ-toŋ, *v.* *red.* of ahotoŋ; *to cry out for, bawl for* anything.

a-hu'-tkaŋ-yaŋ, *adv.* *branching, having many prongs* or *roots.* See hutkaŋ.

a-ḣam'-ya, *v.* (a *and* ḣamya) *to scare on,* as game—aḣamwaya.

a-ḣaŋ'-ḣaŋ, *v. a.* *to do* a thing *carelessly, not to have one's mind on* it—awaḣaŋḣaŋ.

a-ḣaŋ'-ḣaŋ-ka, *adj.* *careless, negligent.*

a-ḣa'-pa, *v.* See aḣamya.

a-ḣba'-ya, *adv.* *mildly.*

a-ḣba'-ye-daŋ, *adv.* *mildly, patiently:* aḣbayedaŋ wauŋ.

a-ḣćo', *n.* *the part of the arm above the elbow; that part of the wing of a fowl next the body.*

a-ḣdaḣ'-ye-će-śni, *v.* *to haunt about* a place: *i. q.* amaḣyeća.

a-ḣdo', *v. n.* (a *and* ḣdo) *to growl over* or *about* a thing, as a dog over a bone.

a'-ḣe, *v. n.* *to evaporate:* aḣe aya, *to decrease* or *fall,* as the water in a river, lake, etc.

a-ḣe'-waŋ-ka, *v. n.* (a *and* ḣewaŋka) *to be frost on* anything.

a'-ḣe-ya, *v. a.* *to cause to evaporate*—aḣewaya.

a'-ḣo, *v. n.* *to stand up* or *back,* as hair on the forehead: ite aḣo.

a-ḣpa'-ya, *v. n.* *to fall upon*—amaḣpaya. See ahiŋḣpaya.

a-ḣpe'-ya, *v. a.* *to throw upon; to throw away; to leave, forsake*—aḣpewaya, aḣpeuŋyaŋpi. See eḣpeya, which is more commonly used.

a-ḣta'-ni, *v.* (a *and* ḣtani) *to labor for* one; *to work on* anything; *to sin, break a law*—awaḣtani, ayaḣtani, uŋkaḣtanipi, aćiḣtani.

a-ḣta'-ta, *adj.* *languid, feeble.*

a-ḣta'-te-ća, *adj.* *weak, feeble.*

a-ḣtu'-daŋ, *n.* *something to be spit upon; i. q.* śićedapi.

a-ḣtu'-ta, *adj.* *a little thawed.*

a-ḣtu'-te-ća, *adj.* *a little thawed; thawing some.*

a-i', *v. a.* *to carry* or *take to* a place—awai, uŋkaipi; *to charge with* or *lay upon, accuse,* as en ai, en amai; *to visit upon,* as for a sin.

a-i', *v.* *col. pl.* of i; *they reached* a place.

a-i'-a, *v. a.* (a *and* ia) *to talk about, consult in regard to; to speak evil of, slander*—awaia, ayaia, uŋkaiapi, amaia, aniia, aćiia.

a-i'-a-pi, *n.* *consultation; slander.*

a-i'-ća-ġa, *v.* (a *and* ićaġa) *to grow on, yield, produce.*

a-i'-ćaḣ, *v.* *cont.* of aićaġa.

a-i′-ćaḣ-ya, *v. a.* *to cause to grow on, cause to produce*—aićaḣwaya.

a-i′-ćam, *cont.* of aićapa.

a-i′-ća-mna, *v. n.* (a *and* ićamna) *to storm upon—blow furiously on.*

a-i′-ća-pa, *v. a.* (a *and* ićapa) *to stab* one thing *through* or *on* another—aićawapa, aićayapa.

a-i′-ća-pa, *v. a.* (a *and* ikapa) *to open the mouth against* any one—aiwakapa.

a-i′-ća-pta, *v.* *to open the mouth on.* See ićapta.

a-i′-ća-ptaŋ, *v.* See the frequent. form, aićaptaŋptaŋ.

a-i′-ća-ptaŋ-ptaŋ, *v. n.* *to roll over and over on* anything—amićaptaŋptaŋ, anićaptaŋptaŋ.

a-i′-ća-zo, *v. a.* (a *and* ićazo) *to draw a line upon; to take credit on account of*—aiwakazo.

a-i′-ći-ma-ni, *v. n.* (a *and* ićimani) *to journey upon, to take a journey for* some purpose—aićimawani.

a-i′-ći-ta-ki-hna, *adv.* *one on the other, folded on, double.* Compare aitahnaka.

a-i′-ćo-ġa, *v. n.* (a *and* ićoġa) *to gather* or *drift on* anything.

a-i′-ćo-za, *v. n.* (a *and* ićoza) *to be warm on* or *with*—aimaćoza.

a-i′-ç̣i-ći-ta, *v.* *reflex.* of akita; *to seek oneself; to regard one's own interests*—amiç̣ićita, aniç̣ićita.

a-i′-ç̣i-ći-ya, *v.* *reflex.* (of aya) *to be diligent, make effort, bestir one's self*—amiç̣ićiya, aniç̣ićiya.

a-i′-ç̣i-ći-ya, *adj.* *diligent:* aiç̣ićiya wauŋ.

a-i′-ç̣i-ći-ya-ka, *v. reflex.* *to bestir himself, be diligent*—amiç̣ićiyaka, aniç̣ićiyaka.

a-i′-de, *v. n.* (a *and* ide) *to burn* or *blaze on.*

a-i′-de-śa-śa, *adv.* *in the red flame:* aideśaśa yuza, *to hold in the red flame.*

a-i′-de-śa-śa-ya, *v. a.* *to put in* or *hold in the red flame, to scorch*—aideśaśawaya.

a-i′-de-ya, *v. a.* *to cause to burn on* or *around; to set fire to*—aidewaya, aideuŋyaŋpi; aideiç̣iya, *to set fire around about himself*—aidemiç̣iya.

a-i′-de-ya, *part.* *setting fire to.*

a-i′-e. Same as aia.

a-i′-e-ki-ya, *v. a.* *to cause to talk about,* either in a good or bad sense; *to consult with:* woope aiekiyapi, *lawgivers, lawyers.*

a-i′-haŋ, *v. col. pl.* *they go and stand on* anything.

a-i′-haŋ-mna, *v. a.* *to dream about*—aiwahaŋmna. See ihaŋmna.

a-i′-hda-da, *v.* *reflex.* of ahdada; *to cast* or *throw upon himself.*

a-i′-hda-ḣpa, *v.* *reflex.* of akaḣpa; *to cover himself*—amihdaḣpa,

a-i′-hda-ḣpe-ya, *v. a.* *to cast about* one—aihdaḣpewaya: taku aihdaḣpeyapi, *clothes.*

a-i′-hda-śtaŋ, *v.* *reflex.* of akaśtaŋ; *to pour out* or *spill on himself*—amihdaśtaŋ, anihdaśtaŋ.

a-i′-hda-taŋ, *v.* *reflex.* of yataŋ;

to praise himself for some quality or capability—amihdataŋ.

a-i'-h d u-h a, *v. reflex.* of yuha; *to have* or *retain for one's own use;* 2, *to provide for himself, to be a citizen*—amihduha, anihduha.

a-i'-h d u-ḣ p a, *v. reflex.* of yuḣpa; *to cause to fall on himself,* as the limb of a tree—amihduḣpa.

a-i'-h d u-k s a, *v. reflex.* of yuksa; *to break off,* as a limb of a tree, *on himself*—amihduksa.

a-i'-h d u-p o-t a, *v. reflex.* of hdupota; *to tear* or *rend* as one's own garment *on himself.*

a-i'-h d u-ś d a, *v. reflex.* of yuśda; *to cut,* as grass, *and cover one's self with:* peźi amihduśda.

a-i'-h d u-ś i-ć a, *v. reflex.* of yuśića; *to get one's self into difficulty with*—amihduśića.

a-i'-h d u-t a ŋ, *v. reflex. to pull* the trigger of a gun *on himself; to besmear himself* with one's own emission. See ayutaŋ.

a-i'-h d u-z a, *v. reflex.* of hduza; *to dress* or *prepare one's self for* an occasion—amihduza.

a-i'-ḣ p a-y a, *v. n.* (a *and* iḣpaya) *to fall on,* as leaves do on anything.

a-i'-ḣ p e-y a, *v.a. to throw* or *place on; to leave with* one; *to charge with; to bequeath to* one—aiḣpewaya, aiḣpemayaŋ, aiḣpećiya: "wookiye aiḣpećiyapi," John xiv. 27.

a-i'-k a-p a, *v.a.* (a *and* ikapa) *to open the mouth upon, to scold*—aiwakapa.

a-i'-k o-y a g, *cont.* of aikoyaka; *sticking to.*

a-i'-k o-y a g-y a, *v. a. to cause to stick to; to link to* or *on*—aikoyagwaya.

a-i'-k o-y a-k a, *v. n. to stick to* or *on; to cleave to, be fastened to.*

a-i'-k p a-ġ a ŋ, *v. reflex.* of paġaŋ; *to part with one's self for* any purpose—amikpaġaŋ, anikpaġaŋ.

a-i'-k p a-ġ a ŋ-y a ŋ, *part. parting with himself for.*

a-i'-k p a-t a ŋ, *v. reflex.* of pataŋ; *to reserve for one's self; to reserve one's self for* any duty or purpose—amikpataŋ, anikpataŋ.

a-i'-k p a-t a ŋ-y a ŋ, *part. reserving himself for.*

a-i'-k ś i n-k i-y a, *v. a. to make faces at*—aikśinwakiya, aikśinyakiya, aikśinuŋkiyapi, aikśinmakiya.

a-i'-m n i-ć i-y a, *v. col. to gather together for a purpose.*

a-i'-n a-p a, *v. a.* (a *and* inapa) *to come in sight upon*—ainawapa.

a-i'-n i-h a ŋ, *v. n. to be afraid on account of*—aimanihaŋ.

a-i'-n i-h a ŋ-y a ŋ, *adv. excitedly, fearfully.*

a'-i-n i-n a, *adv. stilly* or *silently for,* as in approaching game.

a-i ŋ'-y a ŋ-k a, *v.* (a *and* iŋyaŋka) *to run on,* as a floor; *to run for, run to get*—awaimnaŋka, ayainaŋka, uŋkaiŋyaŋkapi.

a-i'-p o-ġ a ŋ, *v. a.* (a *and* ipoġaŋ) *to blow upon*—aiwapoġaŋ.

a-i′-siŋ-yaŋ, *adv. out of sight, behind something else:* aisiŋyaŋ iyaya.

a-i′-śta-ćen-ya, *v. to catch a side glimpse of* anything—aiśtaćenwaya, aiśtaćenyaya.

a-i′-śta-hnag, *cont.* of aiśtahnaka: aiśtahnag yanka, *to place the eyes on* anything, *keep looking at* it—aiśtahnag mayaŋka.

a-i′-śta-hnag-ya, *part. looking at intently.*

a-i′-śta-hnag-ya-ken, *adv. intently looking at.*

a-i′-śta-hna-ka, *v. a.* (iśta *and* hnaka) *to place the eyes upon, look at intently*—aiśtawahnaka, aiśtayahnaka.

a-i′-śta-hna-ke-śni, *v.* See aiśtahnaka. This also appears to be used affirmatively: *to fix the eyes on,* lit. *why does he not take his eyes off?*—aiśtawahnakeśni.

a-i′-śtiŋ-ma, *v. n.* (a *and* iśtiŋma) *to sleep on*—amiśtiŋma.

a′-i-ta-hda-ḣbe, *adv. with the wind*—aitahdaḣbe uŋyaŋpi.

a′-i-ta-hda-ḣbe-ya, *adv. with the wind*—aitahdaḣbeya mda.

a′-i-ta-hna-ka, *v. a. to place one on top of another,* as in carrying—aitawahnaka.

a-i′-tkoŋ, *v. n. to blaze upon, burn on,* as fire.

a-i′-to-kam, *adv. before* in time.

a-i′-toŋ-śni, *v. to tell lies on*—aiwatoŋśni.

a-i′-tpa-ġaŋ, *v. a.* Same as aikpaġaŋ.

a-i′-tpa-ġaŋ-yaŋ, *adv.* Same as aikpaġaŋyaŋ.

a-i′-tpa-taŋ, *v. a.* Same as aikpataŋ.

a-i′-tpa-taŋ-yaŋ, *adv.* Same as aikpataŋyaŋ.

a-i′-ya-hde, *v. n. to lead to, reach to,* as a road; *to lead to,* as a result of conduct.

a-i′-ya-hde-ya, *v. a. to lead to; to merit, deserve, bring upon one*—aiyahdewaya; aiyahdeiçiya, *to bring upon himself*—aiyahdemiçiya.

a-i′-ya-hde-ya, *adv. leading to, even to, until.*

a-i′-ya-ḣpa-ya, *v.* See iyaḣpaya.

a-i′-ya-ḣpe-ya, *v. a. to hand to; to put on; to throw over,* as a rope, in catching a horse; *to communicate to* one, as a disease—aiyaḣpewaya, aiyaḣpeuŋyaŋpi, aiyaḣpemayaŋ, aiyaḣpećiya; aiyaḣpeiçiya, *to throw one's self on,* as on a horse—aiyaḣpemiçiya.

a-i′-ya-kam, *cont.* of aiyakapa.

a-i′-ya-ka-pa, *v. to exceed, surpass.* Not much used.

a-i′-ya-ka-śka, *v. a. to tie* one thing *on* something else—aiyawakaśka, aiyayakaśka.

a-i′-ya-ka-śke-ya, *part. tying on to* something else

a-i′-ya-pe, *v. a.* (a *and* iyape) *to lie in wait for*—aiyawape.

a′-i-ya-pe-mni, *v. a.* (a *and* iyapemni) *to wrap around; wrap up with*—aiyawapemni.

a-i'-ya-sa-ka, *v. n.* *to stiffen* or *become hard on,* as raw hide—aiyamasaka.

a'-i-yog, *adv.* *cont.* of aiyoka, *out on one side;* aiyog yaŋka, *to be off one side;* aiyog iyeya, *to put aside.*

a'-i-yo-ħpe-ya, *adv.* *down hill;* *i. q.* apamahde.

a'-i-yo-ka, *adv.* *at one side; off from, in another place from; near to.*

a'-i-yo-ka, *n.* *a neighbor, one near to.*

a'-i-yo-ki-pi, *adj.* *pleasant, agreeable; i. q.* oiyokipi.

a'-i-yo-ki-pi-ya, *adv.* *agreeably.*

a-i'-yo-pte-ća, *adv.* *less than.*

a-i'-yo-pten, *adv. cont.* *less:* aiyoptenya, *diminishing.*

a-i'-yo-pte-tu, *adv.* *less.*

a-i'-yo-pte-tu-ya, *adv.* *less, in a less manner:* aiyoptetuyaken.

a'-i-yo-taŋ, *adv.* *more than, greater than, beyond:* aiyotaŋ iyekiya, *to have difficulty on account of.*

a-i'-zi-ta, *v. n.* (a *and* izita) *to smoke* or *burn,* as incense, *for* any purpose.

a-ka'-ćiŋs, *cont.* of akaćiŋza: akaćiŋswaćiŋ, *to desire a great deal*—akaćinswaćaŋmi.

a-ka'-ćiŋ-za, *v.* See akaćiŋs.

a-ka'-da, *v. a.* (a *and* kada) *to pour out on,* said of grain, not of liquids—awakada, ayakada, uŋkakadapi.

a-ka'-da-da, *v.* *red.* of akada: akadada iyeya, *to pour out on* anything.

a-ka'-ġa, *v. a.* (a *and* kaġa) *to make on* anything; *to make for* a purpose; *to make in addition, add to; to make* or *fabricate* on one, *tell a lie about; to blaspheme, speak evil of; to exaggerate*—awakaġa.

a-ka'-ġa-pi, *n.* *something made in addition; falsehood; exaggeration.*

a'-ka-ġa-tki-ya, *adv.* *stretched out,* as the arms: akaġatkiya uŋ.

a-ka'-ġe-ġe, *v. a.* (a *and* kaġeġe) *to sew on* or *to, to patch on* something else—awakaġeġe.

a-ka'-haŋ-yaŋ-ka, *n.* *a distant relative.*

a-ka'-hu-te, *v.* *to cut off from the little end to a stump; to think much of oneself, i. q.* iyotaniçida—awakahute, ayakahute.

a-ka'-ħa, *v.* *to desire more, i. q.* saŋpa ćiŋ—awakaħa.

a-ka'-ħam, *cont.* of akaħapa.

a-ka'-ħa-pa, *v.* (a *and* kaħapa) *to drive* or *whip on*—awakaħapa.

a-ka'-ħpa, *v. a.* *to cover, throw on* or *around; to cover up, conceal:* śina akaħpa, *to throw a blanket on*—awakaħpa, uŋkakaħpapi, amakaħpa.

a-ka'-ħpe, *n.* *a covering:* owinźa akaħpe, *a quilt, any covering for a bed.*

a-ka'-ħpe-ki-ći-ći-ya, *v.* *to cover up for* one; *to pass by* a matter, *forgive, cancel*—akaħpewećićiya

a-ka'-ḣpe-ki-ći-toŋ, *v. a.* *to cover for* one—akaḣpewećitoŋ, akaḣpemićitoŋ.

a-ka'-ḣpe-ki-toŋ, *v.* *pos.* of akaḣpetoŋ; *to cover one's own*—akaḣpewetoŋ.

a-ka'-ḣpe-ki-ya, *v. a.* *to cause to cover; to clothe, put on*—akaḣpewakiya, akaḣpemakiya.

a-ka'-ḣpe-toŋ, *v. a.* *to cover, throw on* as a covering; *to cover up* or *conceal*, as one's real opinions, when used with ia, as akaḣpetoŋ iwae—akaḣpewatoŋ, akaḣpeyatoŋ.

a-ka'-ḣpe-toŋ, *part.* *covered, concealed.*

a-ka'-ḣpe-toŋ-toŋ, *v.* *red.* of akaḣpetoŋ: akaḣpetoŋtoŋ ia, *to speak coveredly, to deceive.*

a-ka'-ḣtaŋ, *v. n.* *to soak into and come through on the other side*, as grease through a skin. See kaḣtaŋ.

a-ka'-ḣtaŋ-yaŋ, *v. a.* *to cause to soak into; to cut and make rough on*—akaḣtaŋwaya.

a-ka'-kaŋ, *v. a.* (a *and* kakaŋ) *to hew on* anything; *to counter-hew, hew over again*—awakakaŋ, ayakakaŋ, uŋkakakaŋpi.

a-ka'-kpaŋ, *v. a.* (a *and* kakpaŋ) *to pound fine on* anything; *to pound in addition to* what is already done—awakakpaŋ, ayakakpaŋ.

a-ka'-kpi, *v. a.* *to crack on*, as a nut on anything—awakakpi.

a-ka'-ksa, *v. a.* (a *and* kaksa) *to cut off on* something; *to cut off from; to cut off in addition to*—awakaksa, ayakaksa, uŋkakaksapi.

a-ka'-kśa, *v. a.* *to coil up on*, as a rope—awakakśa.

a-ka'-kśaŋ, *v. a.* *to go around*—awakakśaŋ.

a-ka'-kśaŋ, *adv.* *around, not in a straight course:* akakśaŋ iyaya, *to have gone around.*

a-ka'-kśaŋ-yaŋ, *adv.* *around.*

a-ka'-kśiś, *cont.* of akakśiźa: akakśiś iyeya.

a-ka'-kśi-źa, *v. a.* *to bend into* or *around*, as a piece of iron—awakakśiźa, ayakakśiźa.

a-ka'-ktaŋ, *v. a.* *to bend on to, bend around*—awakaktaŋ.

a-ka'-ku-ka, *v. a.* *to pound to pieces on*—awakakuka.

a-kam', *adv.* *out by one's self, out from, on the outside:* akam haŋ, *to stand on the outside*, as the one on the outside of a nest of tubs or kettles.

a-kam', *prep.* *over, upon, beyond:* akam iyeya, *to throw beyond.*

a-ka'-mda, *v. a.* (a *and* kamda) *to cut into thin slices* or *strips on* anything; *to slice in addition to*—awakamda.

a-ka'-mda, *n.* *fringe:* huŋska akamda, *fringe on leggins.*

a-ka'-mda-ġa, *v. n.* *to spread out over*, as wings.

a-ka'-mdaḣ, *cont.* of akamdaġa—akamdaḣ iyeya, *to spread over*, as a bird its wings.

a-ka'-mdas, *cont.* of akamdaza: akamdas iyaya.

a-ka'-mdaś, *cont.* of akamdaźa; *astride;* akamdaś inaźiŋ, *to stand astride of* anything.

a-ka'-mda-ya, *v. a. to make level on*—awakamdaya.

a-ka'-mda-za, *v. n. to tear open on,* as a bag on a horse.

a-ka'-mda-źa, *v. a. to straddle, spread the legs apart*—awakamdaźa.

a-ka'-mde-ća, *v. a.* (a *and* kamdeća) *to break,* as an instrument, *by striking* it *on* anything; *to break* one thing lying *on* another *by striking*—awakamdeća.

a-ka'-mden, *cont.* of akamdeća: akamden iyeya, *to break in pieces on:* akamden eḣpeya—akamden eḣpewaya.

a-ka'-mdu, *v. a.* (a *and* kamdu) *to break up fine upon*—awakamdu.

a-kam'-haŋ, *standing on the outside,* as the one on the outside of a nest of tubs or kettles.

a-ka'-mna, *v. a.* (a *and* kamna) *to acquire in addition to; to tear open on,* as a seam—awakamna.

a'-ka-mni: ákamni iyaya, *v. n. to separate with a splash,* as snow with water underneath when one steps on it.

a-kan', *prep. on upon.*

a-kan'-mna, *v. n.* (kata *and* omna) *to smell like something burning.*

a-kan'-ta, *adv. above;* used with taŋhaŋ.

a-kan'-taŋ-haŋ, *adv. above, overhead.*

a-kan'-ta-taŋ-haŋ, *adv. from above.*

a-kan'-tkan, *prep. red.* of akan.

a-kan'-tu, *adv. above.*

a-kan'-tu, *adj.* wićaśta akantu, *living men,* in distinction from dead men and spirits, *common men; men in authority.*

a-kan'-tu, *n. the top one.*

a-kan'-tu-ya, *adv. above, high up; on the outside, without.*

a-kan'-tu-ya-ken, *adv. above.*

a-kan'-tu-ye-daŋ, *adv. outside, on the surface; almost on the top; above, high up.*

a-kan'-ya, *v. a.* (a *and* kanya) *to cause to heat upon*—akanwaya.

a-kaŋ', *v. n. to become old on* or *with*—amakaŋ, anikaŋ, uŋkakaŋpi; kići amakaŋ, *I have become old with;* yuha amakaŋ, *having it, I have become old.*

a'-kaŋ-taŋ-ka, *n. the large tendon of the arm.*

a'-ka-pa, *n. the outside.*

a'-ka-pa-ta, *adv. on the outside, on the top, from above.*

a'-ka-pa-taŋ-haŋ, *adv. on the outside, from above, from another place.*

a'-ka-pe-ća, *adv. around about;* with kiŋ, used as a noun, as, ákapećakiŋ, *those around about, spectators; those without.*

a'-ka-pe-ya, *v. a. to throw beyond the bounds,* as in playing ball—ákapewaya, ákapeyaya.

a-ka′-pe-ya, *v. n.* *to exceed, go beyond.*

a′-ka-pon, *cont.* of ákapota; *afloat.*

a′-ka-pon-ya, *v. a.* *to cause to float*—ákaponwaya.

a′-ka-po-ta, *v. n.* *to float on,* as a buoy.

a-ka′-po-ta, *v. a.* (a *and* kapota) *to beat in pieces on* anything—awakapota, ayakapota.

a′-ka-pot-pon, *cont.* of ákapotpota.

a′-ka-pot-po-ta, *v. red.* of ákapota; *to float along in little waves.*

a-ka′-pṫa, *v. a.* (a *and* kapta) *to cut off on,* as part of a stick; *to lade out on*—awakapta.

a-ka′-pte-će-daŋ, *v. a.* *to make shorter, cut off a piece from* a stick—awakaptećedaŋ.

a-ka′-pte-ya, *v. a.* *to provoke beyond endurance*—akaptewaya.

a-ka′-pte-ya, *part.* *cut off on; provoked.*

a-ka′-sam, *adv.* *cont.* of akasaŋpa; *over* the river *from.*

a-ka′-saŋ-pa, *adv.* *opposite, across, on the other side,* as of a river or lake; itato akasaŋpa, *on this side.*

a-ka′-saŋ-pa-taŋ-haŋ, *adv.* *on the other side, from beyond, from the other side.*

a-ka′-ska, *v. a.* (a *and* kaska) *to eat up, to devour greedily, to eat after one is full*—awakaska, ayakaska: akaska yaŋka, *to continue eating.*

a-ka′-ski-ća, *v. n.* *to be pressing down; to press down:* akaskin waŋka.

a-ka′-sni, *v. a.* (a *and* kasni) *to extinguish on,* as fire—awakasni.

a-ka′-ṣo, (a *and* kaso) *to chop off a piece from*—awakaso.

a-ka′-stag, *cont.* of akastaka: akastag elipewaya.

a-ka′-stag-ya, *adv.* *sticking on* or *in.*

a-ka′-stag-ya-ken, *adv.* *sticking on.*

a-ka′-sta-ka, *v. a.* *to throw on* or *daub* with mud, *make stick; to plaster*—awakastaka, uŋkakastakapi.

a-ka′-sto, *v. a.* (a *and* kasto) *to smooth down on,* as hair on the head—awakasto, ayakasto, uŋkakastopi.

a-ka′-śda, *v. a.* (a *and* kaśda) *to cut* or *mow upon,* as grass—awakaśda.

a-ka′-śka, *v. a.* (a *and* kaśka) *to bind upon*—awakaśka.

a-ka′-śpa, *v. a* (a *and* kaśpa) *to cut* or *break off on*—awakaśpa.

a-ka′-śpa, *v. n.* *to be provoked beyond endurance*—amakaśpa, anićaśpa.

a-ka′-śpe-ya, *v. n.* *to remain longer than one can well endure; to be provoked*—amakaśpeya.

a-ka′-śpe-ya, *v. a.* *to provoke*—akaśpewaya, akaśpeyaya, akaśpemayaŋ.

a-ka′-śta-ka, *v. a* (a *and* kaśtaka) *to beat* one *on* another—awakaśtaka, ayakaśtaka.

a-ka'-śtaŋ, *v. a.* (a *and* kaśtan) *to pour out on; to spill on*, as water; *to baptize*, mini akaśtaŋ—awakaśtaŋ, ayakaśtaŋ, uŋkakaśtaŋpi, amakaśtaŋ: aćićaśtaŋ, *I pour out on you.*

a-ka'-ta, *v. n.* (a *and* kata) *to be hot on*—amakata, anikata.

a-ka'-ta, *v a. to hoe, dig about with a hoe, hill up*, as corn; *to cover with dirt*—awakata, ayakata, uŋkakatapi: wamnaheza akata, *to hoe corn.*

a-ka'-te-ya, *v. a. to cause to hoe*—akatewaya.

a'-ka-tiŋ, *v. a. to straighten on*, as the arms; *to measure with the arms stretched out on; to fathom*—áwakatiŋ, áyakatiŋ.

a'-ka-tiŋ-pi, *n. an ell; the length* or *distance between the ends of the fingers when the arms are stretched out.*

a-ka'-ṭiŋs, *cont.* of akaṭiŋza.

a-ka'-ṭiŋs-ya, *v. a. to press down on* anything *by means of weights*—akaṭiŋswaya.

a-ka'-ṭiŋ-za, *v. n.* (a *and* kaṭiŋza) *to press* anything *down tight*, as a weight does.

a-ka'-uŋ-yaŋ, *adv. lying across*, as a boy on a horse.

a-ka'-waŋg, *cont.* of akawaŋka: akawaŋg eḣpeya.

a-ka'-waŋ-ka, *v. a.* (a *and* kawaŋka) *to cut down*, as a tree, *on* anything; *to make fall on by cutting*—awakawaŋka.

a-ka'-we-ġa, *v. a.* (a *and* kaweġa) *to break* or *fracture by striking on* anything—awakaweġa.

a-ka'-weḣ, *cont.* of akaweġa: akaweḣ eḣpeya.

a-ka'-wiŋ, *v. a. to exaggerate, tell lies, try to exceed in telling lies; to exceed in length; to do more than:* akawiŋ ećon—awakawiŋ.

a-ka'-wiŋ-ġa, *v. n. to go round and round*, as an eagle; *make gyrations.*

a-ka'-wiŋḣ, *cont.* of akawiŋġa; *round and round:* akawiŋḣ iyeya.

a-ka'-wiŋś, *cont.* of akawiŋźa: akawiŋś iyeya.

a-ka'-wiŋ-yaŋ, *adv. hyperbolically; exceeding in falsehood.*

a-ka'-wiŋ-źa, *v. a. to bend down on*, as grass on anything—awakawiŋźa.

a'-ka-za-mni, *v. a.* (a *and* kazamni) *to open upon* one; *to throw open*, as one's blanket—áwakazamni, áyakazamni; ákazamni eḣpeya, *to set open;* ákazamni haŋ, *to stand open.*

a'-ka-za-mni-yaŋ, *part. opened on.*

a-kda'-ta-he-na, *Ih.* for ahdatahedaŋ.

a-kde'-śka-na, *n. Ih., a lizard.*

a-ke', *adv. again, repeated, a second time.*

a-ke'-nom, *cont.* of akenoŋpa.

a-ke'-noŋ-pa, *num. adj. twelve.*

a-keś', *adv. again, i. q.* ake.

a-ke'-śa-hdo-ġaŋ, *num. adj. eighteen.*

a-ke'-śa-ko-wiŋ, *num. adj.* *seventeen.*

a-ke'-śa-kpe, *num. adj.* *sixteen.*

a-ke'-tom, *cont.* of aketopa.

a-ke'-to-pa, *num. adj.* *fourteen.*

a-ke'-waŋ-źi, *num. adj.* *eleven.*

a-ke'-waŋ-źi-daŋ, *num. adj.* *eleven.*

a-ke'-waŋ-źi-na, *num. adj.* *Ih.*, *eleven.*

a-ke'-ya, *v. a.* *to place on, make a roof on; to place on the roof; to make* one *roof on* another—akewaya, akeyaya.

a-ke'-ya-mni, *num. adj.* *thirteen.*

a-ke'-za-ptaŋ, *num. adj.* *fifteen.*

a-ki', *v. a.* *to carry* or *bear home,* or *to one's own residence;* distinguished from ahda by the idea of *arriving at*—awaki, ayaki, uŋkakipi.

a-ki', *v* *col. pl.* of ki; *they reach home.*

a-ki'-a-gla, *v. a.* *Ti.*, *to carry home*—akiawagni, akiayagni, etc. T. L. R.

a'-ki-be-ya, *adv.* *around.*

a-ki'-ća-ġa, *v. a.* *to make on, add to; to be unreasonable, go too far*—awećaġa, ayećaġa, amićaġa.

a'-ki-ća-ġa, *v. n.* *to grow on, grow in addition to.*

a-ki'-ća-ġe-ća, *v. a.* *to overreach, cheat, want more than is right, be unreasonable*—awećaġeća.

a-ki'-ćaḣ, *cont.* of akićaġa; akićaḣya, *unreasonably.*

a-ki'-ća-śka, *v. a.* of kaśka; *to bind to* or *on; to bind together*—akiwakaśka, akiyakaśka.

a-ki'-ća-śka-śka, *v.* *red.* *to baste on, sew on,* as in basting—akiwakaśkaśka.

a-ki'-će-pa, *v. n.* of ćepa; *to become fleshy for* or *again*—amakićepa.

a-ki'-će-ya, *v.* *pos.* of aćeya; *to cry for one's own; to mourn for, weep over one's own,* as a dead relative—awakićeya, ayakićeya, uŋkakićo yapi.

a-ki'-ći-ća-ta, *v.* of akata; *to hoe for* one—awećićata, amićićata.

a-ki'-ći-ći-pa-pi, *v.* *pl.* of akipa; *they meet each other.*

a-ki'-ći-ći-ta, *v* of akita; *to hunt* a thing *for* another—awećićita, amićićita.

a-ki'-ći-çuŋ-çuŋ-ka, *v.* *to do* a thing *often for* one—awećiçuŋçuŋka, amićiçuŋçuŋka.

a-ki'-ći-kći-ta, *v.* *pos.* of akita; *to hunt one's own*—awećikćita.

a-ki'-ći-kta, *v.* of akta; *to receive* or *accept from* one; *to have respect unto*—awećikta, amićikta.

a-ki'-ći-kta-śni, *v.* of aktaśni; *to refuse, reject when offered by* one—awećiktaśni, amiciktaśni.

a-ki'-ći-pa, *v.* of apa; *to strike for* one—awećipa, ayećipa, uŋkakićipapi.

a-ki'-ći-pa-pi, *v.* *pl.* of akipa; *they meet each other.*

a-ki'-ći-pe, *v.* of ape; *to wait for* one; *to hope for*—awecipe, ayećipe, uŋkakićipepi.

a-ki'-ći-ta, *v.* of akita; *to hunt*

for another—awećita: heya aćićita, *I hunt lice for you.*

a-ki′-ći-ta, *n.* *a head warrior, one next to a chief; a warrior* or *soldier*—amakićita, anikićita: akićita hemaća, *I am a warrior.*

a-ki′-ći-ta-kte, *v.* (akićita *and* kte) *to punish officially, punish for the violation of a law;* this is done by those who have attained to the place of brave, and consists in killing a horse or dog, cutting up tents and blankets, breaking guns, etc.—akićitawakte, akićitamakte.

a-ki′-ći-ta-na-źiŋ, *v. n.* *to stand as a warrior* or *soldier, stand guard*—akićitanawaźiŋ.

a-ki′-ći-ta-taŋ-ćaŋ, *n.* *an officer, a chief warrior.*

a-ki′-ći-toŋ-waŋ, *v.* of atoŋwaŋ; *to look at for* one, *to have the oversight of for* one—awećitoŋwaŋ, amićitoŋwaŋ.

a-ki′-ȼuŋ-ȼuŋ, *v.* *to do* a thing *repeatedly; to glory in*—aweȼuŋȼuŋ, ayeȼuŋȼuŋ.

a-ki′-ȼuŋ-ȼuŋ-ka, *v.* *to do* a thing *repeatedly; to be proud of, glory in*—aweȼuŋȼuŋka.

a-ki′-ȼu-ya, *adv.* *much:* akiȼuya maḳu, *give me much.* See iyakiȼuya.

a′-ki-de-će-ća, *adj.* *like to, equal to*—ákidemaćeća, ákidenićeća, ákideuŋćećapi. See iyećeća.

a′-ki-de-ćen, *adv.* *like to, equal to.*

a′-ki-de-ćen-ya, *adv.* *equally.*

a′-ki-de-haŋ-haŋ-ke-ća, *adj.* *red.* of ákidehaŋkeća.

a′-ki-de-haŋ-haŋ-yaŋ, *adv.* *red.* of ákidehaŋyaŋ.

a′-ki-de-haŋ-ke-ća, *adj.* *of the same length,* used with kići; kići ákidemahaŋkeća, *I am of the same length as* some one else.

a′-ki-de-haŋ-ska, *adj.* *of the same length* or *height.*

a′-ki-de-haŋ-yaŋ, *adv.* *alike far, equally far.*

a′-ki-de-nag-na-ke-ća, *adj.* *red.* of ákidenakeća.

a′-ki-de-na-ke-ća, *adj.* *alike many, of equal number*—ákideuŋnakećapi. See iyenakeća.

a′-ki-de-na-na, *adj.* *alike few.*

a-ki′-ġe, *v. a.* (a *and* kiġe) *to scold about* anything—awakiġe, ayakiġe.

a-ki′-haŋ, *v. n.* of ahaŋ; *to grow on again.*

a-ki′-haŋ, *v. col. pl.* *they have all reached there.*

a-ki′-hdag, *cont.* of akihdaka.

a-ki′-hdag-ki-ći-toŋ, *v.* *to patch for* one—akihdagwećitoŋ.

a-ki′-hdag-ki-toŋ, *v.* *pos.* of akihdagtoŋ; *to patch one's own*—akihdagwetoŋ.

a-ki′-hdag-toŋ, *v.* *to put on a patch, to patch; patched, having a patch on*—akihdagwatoŋ.

a-ki′-hdag-ya, *v. a.* *to patch, put on a patch; to use for a patch*—akihdagwaya.

a-ki′-hda-ka, *v.* *to patch, sew on a patch.*

a-ki'-hda-ka, *n.* *a patch.* See wakihdaka.

a-ki'-hda-ski-ća, *adj.* *face downwards, prone.*

a-ki'-hda-skin, *cont.* of akihdaskića: akihdaskin eḣpeiçiya, *to throw oneself on one's face.*

a-ki'-hda-skin-ya, *adv.* *lying on the face, prone.*

a-ki'-hde, *adv.* *again, more than once, once again, times*: used with the numerals, noŋpa akihde, *twice.*

a-ki'-hde, *v.* *pos.* of ahde.

a-ki'-hde-hde, *adv.* *red.* of akihde.

a-ki'-hde-ya, *adv.* *repeatedly.*

a-ki'-he-ća, *adj.* *withered, nearly dead,* as a tree.

a-ki'-he-će-ća, *v. n.* *to become so on returning home, i. e.* to get sick or to get well on one's reaching home—akihemaćeća.

a-ki'-hen-he-ća, *adj.* *red.* of akiheća.

a'-ki-hiŋ-sko-ke-ća, *adj.* *of equal size with.*

a'-ki-hiŋ-sko-ya, *adv.* *of equal distance around.*

a-ki'-hna, *adv.* *one on* or *over another, in layers; through*: akihna iyaya, *to pass through one into another.*

a-ki'-hna, *v.* *to have a care for,* as for offspring; *take care of.*

a-ki'-hnag, *cont.* of akihnaka.

a-ki'-hnag-ya, *adv.* *placed on.*

a-ki'-hna-hna, *adv.* *red.* of akihna.

a-ki'-hna-ka, *v.* *pos.* of ahnaka; *to place one's own on*—awehnaka, ayehnaka.

a-ki'-hna-ya, *v. a.* *to cause to take care of*—akihnawaya.

a-ki'-ḣaŋ, *v. n.* *to be without food, hungry; to starve*—amakiḣaŋ, anićiḣaŋ, uŋkakiḣaŋpi.

a-ki'-ḣaŋ-pi, *n.* *a starving, famine*—wićaakiḣaŋ.

a-ki'-ḣaŋ-ši-ća, *v. n.* (kiḣaŋšića) *to be bad weather on, to storm on*—amakiḣaŋšića.

a-ki'-ḣaŋ-ṭa, *v.* *to starve to death, die of hunger*—akiḣaŋmaṭa.

a-ki'-ḣaŋ-ṭe-ya, *v. a.* *to cause to die of hunger*—akiḣaŋṭewaya.

a-ki'-ḣaŋ-yaŋ, *v. a.* *to cause to starve*: akiḣaŋiçiya, *to cause himself to fast*—akiḣaŋmiçiya.

a-ki'-ḣaŋ-yaŋ, *adv.* *in a fasting way.*

a-ki'-ḣo, *v. n.* *to be skillful, dexterous, to have acquired skill by practice*—awakiḣo, ayakiḣo, uŋkakiḣopi.

a-ki'-ḣo-ka, *n.* *one who is skillful.*

a-ki'-ḣo-pi, *n.* *dexterity, skill.*

a-ki'-ḣo-ya, *adv.* *skillfully, dexterously.*

a-ki'-ḣta-ta, *adv.* *many, very much; i. q.* ota ḣiŋća.

a-k'i'-i-a, *v.* *pos.* of aia; *to talk about* something *that concerns one's self; to consider; to talk against*—awakiia, ayakiia, uŋkakiiapi.

a-ki'-kši-źa, *v.* *pos.* of akšiźa;

to bend down as the hand *on: to retain* anything—awekśiźa.

a-ki'-kta, *v. pos.* of akta; *to give heed to*—awakikta: akiktaśni, *to disregard.*

a'-ki-kta, *v. n. to do* anything *with great determination*—áwakikta, áyakikta.

a'-ki-kta-daŋ, *adv. with much determination.*

a-ki'-ktoŋś, *cont.* of akiktoŋźa.

a-ki'-ktoŋś-ya, *v. a. to cause to forget*—akiktoŋśwaya.

a-ki'-ktoŋś-ya, *adv. in a forgetful manner.*

a-ki'-ktoŋ-źa, or a-ki-ktuŋ-źa, *to forget, not to remember*—awektoŋźa, ayektoŋźa, uŋkakiktoŋźapi, aćiktoŋźa, amiktoŋźa, aniktoŋźa.

a'-ki-le-će-ća, *adj. Ti., equal to, of equal size.* See akidećeća.

a'-ki-le-haŋ-ke-ća, *adj. of equal length.* See akidehaŋkića.

a-ki'-mna-yaŋ, *v. a. to collect* one thing *to* another—akimnawaya.

a-kin', *cont.* of akita: akin iyaya, *he is gone to hunt* something.

a-ki'-na-taŋ, *v. pos.* of anataŋ; *to rush for one's own; to reach* or *arrive at the goal*—akinawataŋ: kići akinawataŋ, *I arrived at the same time with him.*

a-ki'-ni-ća, *v. a. to dispute, debate about; to dispute with; to strive about*—awakinića, ayakinića, uŋkakinićapi.

a-ki'-ni-ća-pi, *n. a debating, disputation;* also *pl.* of akinića.

a-ki'-nin, *cont.* of akinića.

a-ki'-nin-ki-ya, *v. to cause to debate*—akininwakiya.

a-ki'-nin-ya, *adv. disputatiously.*

a-ki'-nin-ya, *v. a. to cause to dispute* or *debate about*—akininwaya.

a'-ki-ni-sko-ke-ća, *adj. of equal size with:* kići ákinimaskokeća, *I am of the same size with him.*

a'-ki-ni-sko-ya, *adv. equally far around.*

a-kiŋ'-yaŋ, *v. a.* (a *and* kiŋyan) *to fly over* or *on.*

a-ki'-oŋ, *v. a.* of aoŋ; *to place on,* as wood on one's own fire; *to place on for* one—awakioŋ, ayakioŋ.

a-ki'-oŋ-pa, *v. pos.* of aoŋpa; *to put on one's own,* as wood on the fire—awakioŋpa

a-ki'-pa, *v. to meet,* as anyone traveling, *come against; to come upon* one, *happen to* or *befall* one—awakipa, ayakipa, uŋkakipapi.

a'-ki-pam, *adv. divided, partaken of equally;* ákipam ehnaka, *to divide, separate:* ákipam iyeya, *to separate, divide.*

a-ki'-paś, *v. cont.* of akipaźa; akipaś iyeya, *to double over.*

a-ki'-pa-źa, *v. a. to fold on, to double over.*

a-ki'-pe, *v.* Same as akipa.

a-ki'-pe, *v. a. to wait for* one; *to wait for, expect, hope for*—awakipe, ayakipe, uŋkakipepi.

a-ki'-pśa-pśa, *adv. close together, standing thick,* as grain or grass;

jammed together, as men or animals; *full of*, as a lake of fish—akipśapśa hiyeya.

a-ki'-pśa-pśa-ya, *adv.* *thickly, close together.*

a-ki'-pśa-ya, *adv.* *close together.*

a-ki'-ptaŋ, *adv.* *together, joining forces;* akiptaŋ uŋyaŋpi: akiptaŋ ećoŋpi.

a-ki'-sni, *v.* *pos.* of asni; *to get well, recover from sickness; to recover from anger*, etc.—amakisni, anićisni, uŋkakisnịpi.

a-ki'-sni-yaŋ, *v. a.* *to cause to get well*—akisniwaya, akisnimayaŋ.

a-ki'-sni-yaŋ, *adv.* *getting well.*

a-ki'-ś'ag, *cont.* of akiś'aka.

a-ki'-ś'ag-ya, *adv.* *strewed thickly over.*

a-ki'-ś'a-ka, *adj.* *thick as leaves on the ground.*

a-ki'-śo-ka, *adj.* of śoka; *thick on, thick together*, as wheat growing in a field.

a-ki'-ta, *v. a.* *to seek for, hunt for*, as something lost; *to make effort to get*—awakita, ayakita, uŋkakitapi, aćićita, amakita: akitapi, *sought for.*

a-ki'-ta-ku-ni-śni, *v. n.* of atakuniśni; *to become nothing, be nothing*—amakitakuniśni.

a-ki'-to, *v.* *pos.* of ato; *to tattoo, make blue marks on the body*; this is generally done by pricking in powder—aweto, ayeto, uŋkakitopi.

a-ki'-to-pi, *n.* *the marks made by tattooing.* *Part., marked, tattooed.*

a-ki'-ṭa, *v. n.* *to die after getting home*, as a wounded man who is carried home—akimaṭa. Also said when grass or corn is so thick that a part dies.

a-ki'-ya, *v. a.* *to practice, give the mind to*—awakiya.

a-ki'-ya-hda, *v. a.* (aki *and* ahda) *to carry* or *take off home*—awakiyahda, ayakiyahda, uŋkakiyahdapi; eḣpeya makiyahda, *to have gone off home and left me;* eḣpeya makakiyahda, *to take off home from me.*

a-ki'-ya-ka, *v. n.* *to be a practitioner*—awakiyaka.

a'-ki-ye-će-ća, *adv.* *like, like to.*

a-ki'-ye-daŋ. *adv.* *near.* See ikiyedaŋ.

a-ki'-yu-ćaŋ-pi, *v. pl.* *to shake* anything *when several do it together.*

a-ki'-yu-ha-pi, *v. pl.* *to bear, carry, when several do it together:* akiyuha ayapi—amakiyuhapi.

a-ki'-yu-ḣpa, *v.* (aki *and* yuḣpa) *to carry home and throw down*—akimduḣpa, akiduḣpa.

a-ki'-yu-ski-ća, *v.* *to tie* or *fasten together, to attach one to another*—akimduskića.

a-ki'-yu-ti-taŋ-pi, *v. pl.* *to pull different ways.*

a-ki'-yu-za-pi, *v. pl.* said when *two* or *more seize and hold* anything *together; held by two or more.*

a'-ki-źan, *cont.* of ákiźata.

a'-ki-źan-ya, *v. n.* *to fork*, as a stream.

a'-ki-źan-ya, *adv.* *in a forked manner.*

a′-ki-źa-ta, *adj.* *forked*, as a stream.

a-ko′, *adv.* *beyond, on the other side of.*

a-ko′-i-to-he-ya, *adv.* *towards, with the face the other way, turned with the face from* one; akoitoheya naźiŋ, *to stand with the face from* one.

a′-ko-kam, *adv.* *across, by a near way;* ákokam ya, *to go across;* akokam mda, *I go by a near way.*

a′-ko-ka-pa, *adv.* *by a nearer way.* Not much used.

a′-kos, *adv* See akosaŋ.

a′-ko-saŋ, *adv.* *whilst, in the mean time.*

a-ko′-taŋ-haŋ, *adv.* *from beyond.*

a-ko′-ta-taŋ-haŋ, *adv.* *from beyond.*

a-ko′-wam, *adv.* See akowapa.

a-ko′-wa-pa, *adv.* *further on, beyond.*

a-ko′-wa-pa-taŋ-haŋ, *adv.* *from beyond.*

a-ko′-za, *v. a.* *to make a motion at, attempt to strike*—awakoza, ayakoza, amakoza.

a-ko′-źan, *adv.* *cont.* of akoźata; *straddling;* akoźan naźiŋ, *to stand over a thing, stand with a thing between one's feet.*

a-ko′-źan-ya, *adv.* *astride.*

a-ko′-źa-ta. Obsolete. See akoźan.

a-kpa′-ġaŋ, *v. a.* *pos.* of paġaŋ; *to give away one's own for* some purpose—awakpaġaŋ.

a-kpa′-ġaŋ-yaŋ, *adv.* *giving away for.*

a-kpas′, *cont.* of akpaza.

a-kpa′-spa, *v.* *to suffer patiently, to endure until it has passed off*—awakpaspa, ayakpaspa.

a-kpa′-spe-ća, *v.* *to suffer patiently until one's anger goes off*—awakpaspeća.

a-kpas′-ya, *v. a.* *to cause darkness on, darken*—akpaswaya.

a-kpas′-ya, *adv.* *benightedly.*

a-kpa′-taŋ, *v.* *pos.* of pataŋ; *to reserve one's own for* a purpose—awakpataŋ.

a-kpa′-taŋ-yaŋ, *adv.* *reserving for* a purpose.

a-kpa′-ya, See akpayeća.

a-kpa′-ye-ća, *v. n.* *to be lighter than its proper color*, as a child which will yet darken; *to be yellow*, as a mulatto—amakpayeća.

a-kpa′-ye-ća, *n.* *one who is neglected;* *i. q.* aktapiśni.

a-kpa′-za, *v. n.* (a *and* kpaza) *to come night on* one, *be benighted*—amakpaza, anikpaza.

a-kpa′-zo, *v.* *pos.* of pazo; *to point at one's own*—awakpazo.

a-kśa′, *adv.* *more, in addition to.* This word signifies that it is already well, but intimates a desire for more; it is usually followed by uŋkaŋś: akśa mayaḳu uŋkaŋś, *if you had given me more.*

a-kśa′-ken, *adv.* See akśa; waŋna maśte, akśaken maġaźu uŋkaŋś waśte kta, *it is now warm, if it would rain it would be good.*

a-kśaŋ′-kśaŋ, *adv.* *to and fro, across and back.*

a-kśi′-źa, *v. a.* *to double up on*, as the hand on anything; *to retain* anything not one's own; *i. q.* anića—awakśiźa, ayakśiźa.

a-kta′, *prep.* *of, about, concerning.*

a-kta′, *adv.* *again, over again;* akta eya, *to repeat, say again.*

a-kta′, *v. a.* *to have respect for, to regard, keep in mind, give heed to; to receive*—awakta, ayakta, uŋkaktapi. From this are formed akikta, akićikta, ihakta, wakta, etc.

a-kta′-kta, *adv.* *red.* of akta; *again and again, repeatedly.*

a-kta′-kta-ya, *adv.* *repeatedly.*

a-kta′-śni, *v.* of akta; *to reject, despise*—awaktaśni.

a-kta′-śni, *adv.* *not well:* aktaśni ećoŋ, *to do* a thing *badly.*

a-kta′-śni-yaŋ, *adv.* *badly, wrong, not right.* See ektaśniyaŋ.

a-ktoŋ′, *adv.* *more than;* wikćemna aktoŋ, *more than ten.* *Pl.*, aktoŋpi.

a-ktoŋ′-ktoŋś, *cont.* of aktoŋktoŋźa; aktoŋktoŋśya; aktoŋktoŋśmayaŋ, *it has made me forgetful.*

a-ktoŋ′-ktoŋ-źa, *adj.* *red;* waćiŋ maktoŋktoŋźa, *my memory is treacherous.* See ktoŋktoŋźa

a-ktonś′, *cont.* of aktoŋźa.

a-ktoŋ′-źa, *v.* *to forget.* See akiktoŋźa.

a-ktoŋ′-źa, *adj.* *forgetful.*

a-ku′, *v. a.* *to bring, to come bringing home*—awaku.

a-ku′, *v.* *col. pl.* of ku; *they are coming home.*

a-ku′-i-to-he-ya. See akoitoheya, the more correct form.

a-ku′-ka, *v. n.* *to become old* or *rotten on* one, as clothing—amakuka, anikuka, uŋkakukapi.

a-ku′-ta, *v.* *to watch for, look for, look out for* one's coming: akuta kuwa—akuta wakuwa.

a-ḳa′, *v* (a *and* ḳa) *to dig on:* maka aḳa—awaḳa, ayaḳa, uŋkaḳapi.

a-ḳiŋ′, *n.* (a *and* ḳiŋ) *something to pack on, a pack-saddle; a riding-saddle; a harness-saddle:* śuktaŋka aḳiŋ.

a-ḳo′. See oḳo.

am, *v.* *imperat. pl.* of a; *hark.*

a′-ma-ġa-ġa, *v.* This is said to be from ákaġaġa, *to fall on in drops, trickle on.* The *ma* is the pronoun.

a-ma′-ġa-ya, *v.* See amaḣya.

a′-ma-ġa-źu, *v. n.* (a *and* maġaźu) *to rain on*—amamaġaźu, animaġaźu, uŋkamaġaźupi.

a′-ma-ġa-źu-ki-ya, *v. a.* *to cause to rain on*—ámaġaźuwakiya.

a′-ma-ġa-źu-ya, *v. a.* *to cause to rain on*—ámaġaźuwaya.

a-ma′-ḣpi-ya, *v. n.* *to cloud over.*

a-ma′-ḣpi-ya, *adj.* *cloudy, clouded over.*

a-maḣ′-ya, *v. a.* *to plant at* a place, *make a field at; to be attached to*—amaḣwaya.

a-maḣ′-ye-ća, *v.* Same as amaḣya—amaḣwayeća.

a-ma′-ni, *v.* (a *and* mani) *to walk on*—amawani, amayani, amauŋnipi; ćaŋ amanipi, *a ladder.*

a-maŋ', *v.* (a *and* maŋ) *to sit on and hatch,* as fowls; *to hatch on*—amaŋpi.

a-ma'-śte, *v. n.* (a *and* maśte) *to be warm on*—amamaśte, animaśte, amauŋśtepi.

a-ma'-śte-na-pta-pta, *n. the glimmering of vapor in the sun heat;* the *burning appearance* on the prairie on a hot day, *mirage.*

a-ma'-śte-ya, *adv. exposed to the heat, in the sun.*

a-ma'-śte-ya-ken, *adv. hotly.*

a-mda'-ke-daŋ, *adj. calm, still, without wind.*

a-mda'-ke-daŋ, *n. a calm:* amdakedaŋ iću.

a-mda'-ke-na, *adj. Ih.*, same as amdakedaŋ.

a-mda'-ke-taŋ, *adj. Mde.*, same as amdakedaŋ.

a-mda'-ska-ya, *adv. level, without ridges.*

a-mda'-ya, *adj. level on.*

a-mde'-ća. See amdećahaŋ.

a-mde'-ća-haŋ, *part. scattered, fallen off,* as from a pile of rock, etc.

a-mdes', *cont.* of amdeza: amdes iyaya, *to become clear, become sober;* amdes aya—amdes amayaŋ.

a-mdes'-ya, *v. a. to make clear* or *sober*—amdeswaya.

a-mdes'-ya, *adv. clearly, soberly:* amdesya waŋmdaka, *I see clearly.*

a-mdes'-ya-ken, *adv. clearly.*

a-mde'-za, *v. a.* of mdeza; *to see clearly*—awamdeza, ayamdeza.

a-mde'-za, *v. n. to be clear, perspicuous; to be sober*—amamdeza, uŋkamdezapi.

a-mdo', *n. the shoulder, the scapula.*

a-mdo'-hu, *n. the shoulder bone* or *blade, scapula.*

a-mdo'-i-yo-ki-źu, *n. the part between the shoulders.*

a-mdo'-o-ki-ta-he-daŋ, *n. between the shoulders.*

a-mdo'-śa *and* amdośaśa, *n. the red-winged blackbird.* See wamdośa.

a-mi'-ç̣i-ći-ya, *v.* 1st pers. sing. of aiç̣ićiya (perhaps from aya); tokeŋ owakihi amiç̣ićiya, *I act as I am able.*

a-mi-ni'-he-ća, *v. n.* (a *and* miniheća) *to be industrious in regard to*—amaminiheća, animiniheća. See amniheća and its derivatives.

a-mi-ni'-hen-i-ç̣i-ya, *v. reflex. to make himself industrious about* anything—aminihemiç̣iya.

a-mi-ni'-hen-ya, *v. a. to cause to be industrious about* anything.

a-mi-ni'-hen-ya, *adv. industriously, stirringly.*

a-mi-ni'-taŋ, *v. n.* (a mini *and* taŋka) *to overflow.* See amnitaŋ.

a-mi-ni'-taŋ-ya, *v. a. to cause to overflow.* See amnitaŋya.

a-mna'-i-ç̣i-ya, *v. reflex.* of mnayaŋ; *to gather for himself, to be selfish*—amnamiç̣iya.

am'-na-ka-ha. See aŋpetu nakaha.

a-mna'-yan, *v. a.* (a *and* mnayaŋ)

to collect, gather together to, add to—amnawaya, amnayaya.

a-mni′, *v.* (a *and* mni) *to spread out* to dry *on* anything—awamni, ayamni, uŋkamnipi.

a-mni′-ći-ya, *v.* (a *and* mnićiya) *to assemble to, make an assembly; to assemble on account of*—amnimićiya, amninićiya, amniuŋkićiyapi.

a-mni′-ći-ya-keŋ, *adv. in the manner of assembling.*

a-mni′-mni, *v. a. to sprinkle on* anything, *sprinkle with* water, etc.—awamnimni, ayamnimni, uŋkamnimnipi: aćimnimni, *I sprinkle you.*

a-mni′-taŋ, *v.n. to flood, overflow.*

a-mni′-taŋ-ya, *v. a. to cause to overflow, to flood*—amnitaŋwaya.

a-mni′-taŋ-yaŋ, *adv. in an overflowing manner.*

a′-mo-mo-na, *n. a babe; a doll.*

a-na′-bu, *v. a.* (a *and* nabu) *to make a noise on* with the feet, *to stamp*—anawabu.

a-na′-bu-bu, *v. red.* of anabu.

a-na′-ġo-ptaŋ, *v. a. to listen to, hearken to; to obey*—anawaġoptaŋ, anayaġoptaŋ, anauŋġoptaŋpi, anamaġoptaŋ; anaćiġoptaŋ, *I obey you;* anauŋniġoptaŋpi, *we hearken to you.* See noġoptaŋ and naḣoŋ.

a-na′-ġo-ptaŋ-ya, *v.a. to cause to listen to*—anaġoptaŋwaya, anaġoptaŋmayaŋ.

a-na′-ġo-ptaŋ-yaŋ, *adv. obediently, attentively.*

a-na′-ha, *v. a. to kick out of the way*—anawaha.

a-na′-hdo-hdo, *v. n. to bubble up*, as in boiling.

a-na′-hdu-śte, *v. n. to be lame in the leg, limp; to break down,* as one's leg does sometimes: anahduśte iyaya.

a-na′-ḣa, *adj. rough, roughened up.*

a-na′-ḣbe, *v.* See anaḣma.

a-na′-ḣbe-ya, *adv. secretly, slyly, covertly.*

a-na′-ḣbe-ya-haŋ, *adv. secretly.*

a-na′-ḣda-ta, *v. a. to crawl up carefully on* anything—anawaḣdata.

a-na′-ḣdo-ka, *v.a.* (a *and* naḣdoka) *to wear a hole in,* as in a moccasin, *on* something—anawaḣdoka.

a-na′-ḣma, *v. a. to hide, conceal*—anawaḣbe, anayaḣbe, anauŋḣmaŋpi. From this comes woanaḣbe.

a-na′-ḣmaŋ-pi, *n. a concealing, concealment.*

a-na′-ḣpa, *v. a.* (a *and* naḣpa) *to kick down on* anything—anawaḣpa.

a-na′-ḣta-ka, *v. a.* (a *and* naḣtaka) *to kick* one *on* something else—anawaḣtaka, anamaḣtaka.

a-na′-i-ç̌i-psoŋ, *v. reflex.* of anapsoŋ; *to spill on one's self*—anamiç̌ipsoŋ.

a-na′-ke-ya, *adv. turned partly on one side.*

a-na′-ki-ći-ġo-ptaŋ, *v.* of anaġoptaŋ; *to heaken to for* one—anawećiġoptaŋ. *Pl.*, anakićiġoptaŋpi, *they hearken to each other*—anauŋkićiġoptaŋpi.

a-na'-ki-ći-ġo-ptaŋ-yaŋ, *adv.* *hearkening to each other.*

a-na'-ki-ći-pta-pi, *v. pl. recip.* of anapta; *they stop* or *hinder each other*—anauŋkićiptapi.

a-na'-ki-ġo-ptaŋ, *v. pos.* of anaġoptaŋ; *to hearken to, to obey,* as one's father—anawakiġoptaŋ.

a-na'-ki-ġo-ptaŋ-yaŋ, *adv. obediently.*

a-na'-ki-ḣbe, *v.* See anakiḣma.

a-na'-ki-ḣbe-ya, *v. a. to cause to conceal*—anakiḣbewaya.

a-na'-ki-ḣbe-ya, *adv. covertly, secretly,*

a-na'-ki-ḣbe-ya-haŋ, *adv. stealthily, privately.*

a-na'-ki-ḣma, *v. a. to hide, conceal, refuse to tell; to deny, affirm that it is not so*—anawakiḣbe, anayakiḣbe, anauŋkiḣmaŋpi.

a-na'-ki-ḣmaŋ-pi, *n. denying, concealing. Part., concealed.*

a-na'-ki-kśiŋ. *v. a. to stand over and defend* one; *to interpose for* one, when in danger; *to expose oneself for* another; *to work for* one, and give him an opportunity to rest—anawekśiŋ, anayekśiŋ, anaćićikśiŋ or anaćikśiŋ, anamikśiŋ.

a-na'-ksa, *v.* (a *and* naksa) *to break off* a thing *on* something *with the foot*—anawaksa, anauŋksapi.

a-na'-kśiś, *cont.* of anakśiźa; anakśiś iyeya.

a-na'-kśi-źa, *v.* (a *and* nakśiźa) *to bend down on with the foot,* as grass on the prairie—anawakśiźa.

a-na'-ktaŋ, *v.* (a *and* naktaŋ) *to bend on* or *over.*

a-na'-ḳe-za, *v. to make smooth by treading on.* See onaḳeza, which is more correct.

a-na'-mda-ġa, *v. n.* (a *and* namdaġa) *to open* or *spread out on.*

a-na'-mdas, *cont.* of anamdaza: anamdas iyeya, *to make burst by kicking.*

a-na'-mda-za, *v. a.* (a *and* namdaza) *to tear open with the foot, to burst open on*—anawamdaza.

a-na'-mde-ća, *v. n. to spread out on,* as grain when poured on anything.

a-na'-mden, *cont.* of anamdeća: anamden eḣpeya, *to scatter* by pouring down.

a-na'-mdu, *v. a.* (a *and* namdu) *to kick dust on*—anawamdu; anamamdu, *he kicks dust on me.*

a-na'-mna, *v. a* (a *and* namna) *to rip on* anything *with the foot;* haŋpa iŋyaŋ anamna, *to rip one's moccasin on a stone*—anawamna.

a-na'-mni, *v. n. to give way under the foot,* as snow when there is water under it; anamni iyewaya.

a-na'-pa, *v. a.* (a *and* napa) *to run to for refuge*—anawapa, anayapa, anauŋpapi.

a-na'-pća, *v.* (a *and* napća) *to swallow on* or *after* something else—anawapća, anauŋpćapi.

a-na'-po-pa; *v. n.* (a *and* napopa) *to burst on* anything—anamapopa.

a-na'-po-ta, *v. a.* (a *and* napota)

to wear out on, as one's moccasins on anything—anawapota.

a-na′-psa-ka, *v. a.* (a *and* napsaka) *to break a string with the foot on* something—anawapsaka.

a-na′-psoŋ *and* a-na-psuŋ, *v. a.* (a *and* napsoŋ) *to kick over and spill on* anything—anawapsoŋ, anamapsoŋ, anauŋpsoŋpi.

a-na′-psoŋ, *v. n.* *to boil over on* anything.

a-na′-pśa, *v. n.* anapśa hiŋhda, *to bubble up*, as foul water when disturbed; *to come up*, as bubbles on water.

a-na′-pśa-pśa, *v. n.* *red.* of anapśa; *to boil up, come up*, as bubbles on water.

a-na′-pśuŋ, *v. a.* (a *and* napśuŋ) *to dislocate, put out of joint on* anything—anawapśuŋ.

a-na′-pta, *v. a.* *to stop, hinder, cause to cease, to obstruct, forbid*—anawapta, anayapta, anauŋptapi, anamapta; anaiçipta, *to stop for one's self, to cease from one's self*—anamiçipta.

a-na′-pta, *v. n.* *to cease, stop.*

a-na′-pta-pi, *part.* *stopped, ceased:* oŋ anaptapi, *that which produces a stoppage*, the name given to *paregoric.*

a-na′-pte-ća, *v. n.* *to hinder, obstruct*—anamapteća.

a-na′-pte-ća, *adv.* *in an obstructed manner; less.*

a-na′-ptel, *adv.* *T.*, same as anapten.

a-na′-pten, *adv.* *less, less than*

a-na′-pten-ya, *adv.* *in a less manner.* *T.*, anaptelya.

a-na′-pten-ya-ken, *adv.* *less, in a lessened manner.*

a-na′-pte-toŋ, *v. a.* *to prohibit, lay a hindrance, lay an embargo*—anaptewatoŋ.

a-na′-pte-toŋ, *n.* *a prohibition, obstruction, hindrance.*

a-na′-ptu-źa, *v. a.* (a *and* naptuźa) *to crack* or *split with the foot on* anything—anawaptuźa.

a-na′-po, *v. n.* *to come all over* one, as ashes or steam; *to be fog on*—anamapo, ananipo.

a-na′-sa, *v. a* (a *and* nasa) *to hunt* or *go after*, as buffalo—anawasa. Nasa and wanasa are more generally used.

a-na′-sa, *v. n.* *to rise up on*, as a hog's bristles on his back; *to bristle up.*

a-na′-sda-ta, *v. a.* (a *and* nasdata) *to creep up to carefully*, as a hunter to game—anawasdata, anauŋsdatapi.

a-na′-sda-ta-pi, *n.* *a creeping up to* game.

a-na′-śdoka, *v.* *to kick off*, as one's moccasins; *to come in haste to*—anawaśdoka

a-na′-ta, *v.* *to bury with the foot, scrape dirt on with the foot*—anawata.

a-na′-taŋ, *v. a.* (a *and* nataŋ) *to rush on* any person or thing, *make an attack on*—anawataŋ, anayataŋ, anauŋtaŋpi, anamataŋ, anawićataŋ.

a-na′-taŋ-pi, *part. attacked.*

a-na′-ti-ća, *v. a.* (a *and* natića) *to scrape* snow *on* anything *with the foot*—anawatića.

a-na′-ti-pa, *v. n. to crisp, shrivel up on; burned.*

a-na′-ti-taŋ, *v.* (a *and* natitaŋ) *to push on with the foot; to pull back on account of*—anawatitaŋ.

a-na′-tpi, *v. a.* (a *and* natpi) *to crack,* as a louse, *with the foot, on* something—anawatpi.

a-na′-tu-ka, *v. a.* (a *and* natuka) *to wear off with the foot,* as the hair from a buffalo-skin moccasin—anawatuka.

a-na′-ṭa, *v. a.* (a *and* naṭa) *to kill with the foot on* something—anawaṭa, anayaṭa.

a-na′-ṭiŋs, *cont.* of anaṭiŋza.

a-na′-ṭiŋs-ya, *adv. firmly trodden.*

a-na′-ṭiŋ-za, *v. a.* (a *and* naṭiŋza) *to tramp down hard and tight*—anawaṭinza, anauŋṭiŋzapi.

a-na′-uŋ-yaŋ, *v. n. to go out of sight on* or *behind* something.

a-na′-wam, *adv. over against, beyond.*

a-na′-waŋg, *cont.* of anawaŋka.

a-na′-waŋg-ki-ya, *v. a. to cause to gallop on. T.*, anauŋgkiya.

a-na′-waŋ-ka, *v. a.* (a *and* nawaŋka) *to kick down on* anything—anawawaŋka.

a-na′-waŋ-ka, *v. n.* (a *and* nawaŋka) *to gallop,* as a horse, *on* anything. *T.*, anauŋka.

a-na′-we-ġa, *v.* (a *and* naweġa) *to break on* anything *with the foot,* but not to break off—anawaweġa, anayaweġa.

a-na′-weḣ, *cont.* of anaweġa: anaweḣ iyeya.

a-na′-wiŋ, *v.* (a *and* nawiŋ) *to fly around over; to tell round about; to tell what is not true, to lie; to conceal: T, to scrape the foot on*—anawawiŋ.

a-na′-wiŋś, *cont.* of anawiŋźa: anawiŋś iyeya.

a-na′-wiŋ-yaŋ, *adv. concealing by circumlocution; parabolically,* John x. 16.

a-na′-wiŋ-źa, *v. a.* (a *and* nawiŋźa) *to bend down on with the foot*—anawawiŋźa.

a-na′-źi-ća, *v. a.* (a *and* naźića) *to run away; to leave on account of*—anawaźića.

a-ni′, *v. n.* (a *and* ni) *to live on* or *for*—awani.

a-ni′-ća, *v. a. to withhold, keep back from, retain* something claimed by another; *to lay claim to; to forbid, oppose*—awanića, ayanića, uŋkanićapi. From this is formed akinića.

a-nin′, *cont.* of anića. *T.*, anil.

a-ni′-ni, *n. anything that collects on,* as soot, thick scum, etc.: anini se hiyeya, said of soot that hangs loosely.

a-ni′-waŋ, *v. a.* (a *and* niwaŋ) *to swim for; to swim on*—awaniwaŋ.

a-ni′-ya, *v. a.* (a *and* niya) *to*

breathe on—awaniya, ayaniya, uŋkaniyapi.

a-nog', *adv.* *cont.* of anoka; *on both sides;* anog ope, *sharp on both sides, two-edged.*

a-nog'-pa-ska, *n.* *the white-headed eagle:* from anokataŋhaŋ pa ska.

a-nog'-wa-ki-ća-śka, *n.* *T.* *saddle-bags:* literally, *something bound on both sides.*

a-no'-ġo-ptaŋ, *v. a.* *T. to obey, give ear to.* See anaġoptaŋ.

a-noḣ'-ke-ći-ya, *v.* *to lend an ear to, listen to;* anoḣkećiya maŋka, *I am listening to it.*

a-noḣ'-ki-ći-ya, *v.* Same as anoḣkećiya. Both are said to be correct.

a-no'-ka, *adv.* *on both sides.*

a-no'-ka-saŋ, *n.* *T. the white-headed eagle.*

a-no'-ka-taŋ-han, *adv.* *on both sides, from both sides, backward and forward.*

a-no'-wab-ya, *adv.* *T. off to one side.*

aŋp, *cont.* of aŋpa; *T.*, aŋp ićamna, *n.* *stormy day.*

aŋ'-pa, *n.* *day, light of day, daylight.* Opposed to otpaza. *Ih., i. e.*, aŋpetu.

aŋ'-pa-ka-mde-za, *n.* *day-breaking, daybreak.*

aŋ'-pa-o, *v. n.* *to dawn,* as the morning. Possibly the *o* is the verb o, *to shoot, to hit,* the reference being to the shooting up of light.

aŋ'-pa-o, *n.* *the dawn of morning, daylight:* aŋpao hinapa, *dawn appears;* aŋpao duta, *the redness of the dawn;* aŋpao waŋka, *during dawn;* aŋpao ska, *the first glimmer of day.*

aŋ'-pa-o-ho-toŋ-na, *n.* (aŋpa *and* hotoŋ) *domestic fowls,* so called from their crowing in the morning.

aŋ'-pa-wi, *n.* *Ih. the sun*—aŋpetu wi.

aŋ-pe', *n.* *day; space.*

aŋ-pe'-ćiŋ-haŋ, *adv.* *in a day, to-day.*

aŋ-pe'-ćo-ka-ya, *n.* *midday, noon.*

aŋ-pe'-ću-sa, *adv.* *during the day.* The idea is that of having a whole day before one—no need of haste. See the next word.

aŋ-pe'-ću-sa-ken, *adv.* Same as aŋpećusa: haŋḣaŋna aŋpećusaken uŋyaŋpi kta, *in the morning, with the day before us, we will go.*

aŋ-pe'-de-han, *adv.* *this day, to-day, now.*

aŋ-pe'-haŋ, *adv.* *to-day, to-day as past*—*the past part.*

aŋ-pe'-he-pi-ya, *n.* *the space between the earth and heavens; the day* or *part of the day yet to come.*

aŋ-pen', *adv.* (aŋpa *and* en) *by day:* aŋpen miśtiŋbe, *by day I slept.*

aŋ-pe'-tu, *n.* *a day,* either *a natural day,* the time between the rising and setting of the sun, or *a civil day,* the whole twenty-four hours.

aŋ-pe'-tu-he-pi-ye-la, *adv.* *T. before noon.*

aŋ-pe'-tu-ta-he-na, *adv. before the day is done.*

aŋ-pe'-tu-wa-kaŋ, *n. sacred day, the Sabbath.* Also, aŋpetu okiḣpapi.

aŋ-pe'-tu-wi, *n. the sun,* lit. *day-sun;* thus distinguished from haŋyetuwi, *the night-sun* or *moon.*

aŋ-po'-skan, *adv.* (aŋpa *and* oskan) *by day.*

aŋ-po'-skan-tu, *adv. by day, in the day-time.*

aŋ-po'-skan-tu-ya, *adv. by day.*

aŋ-po'-skan-tu-ya-ken, *adv. by day, in the day-time. T.,* anposkaŋtuyakel.

aŋ-pta'-ni-ya, *n. the breath of day,* i. e., *the very first glimmerings of morn; vapors raised by the sun.*

a-o'-ćiŋ, *v.* of oćiŋ; *to desire some of* a thing: aowaćiŋ kta tuka tonana, *I would desire some, but there is only a little.*

a-o'-ćo-ka, *adv. in the midst.* See ahoćoka, which is the correct form.

a-o'-ćo-ka-ya, *adv. surrounded by.*

a-o'-de, *v.* (a *and* ode) *to seek for* something *in addition to*—aowade, aoyade.

a-o'-gla-kiŋ, *v. a. T. to peep around at one's own.*

a-o'-haŋ-zi, *v. n.* (a *and* ohaŋzi) *to shade, overshadow*—aomahaŋzi.

a-o'-haŋ-zi, *adv. in the shade, shade upon.*

a-o'-haŋ-zi-ya, *v. a. to cause shade upon, to overshadow*—aohaŋziwaya, aohaŋzimayaŋ.

a-o'-haŋ-zi-ya, *adv. shadowy, in the shade.*

a-o'-hda-ka, *v. a.* (a *and* ohdaka) *to tell in regard to* or *in addition to.*

a-o'-hdu-ta, *v. n. to close up, fill up,* as a hole or wound, *to heal over*—aomahduta.

a-o'-hdu-te, *v. n.* Same as aohduta. *Part., closed up, healed over.*

a-o'-hdu-te-ya, *v. a. to close up, to cause to heal over; to press around, surround, throng, overwhelm*—aohduteWaya, aohdutemayaŋ, aohduteuŋyaŋpi.

a-o'-hdu-te-ya, *part. surrounding:* maka aohduteya, *around the earth.*

a-o'-hdu-te-ya, *adv. throngingly.*

a-o'-hi-yu, *v. n.* (a *and* ohiyu) *to come out upon, to leak upon.*

a-o'-hna-ka, *v. a.* (a *and* ohnaka) *to place upon,* as a cover—aowahnaka.

a-o'-ḣaŋ-haŋ-haŋ, *adv. very skillfully.*

a-o'-ḣaŋ-haŋ-haŋ-ken, *adv. very skillfully. T.,* aoḣaŋhaŋkel.

a-o'-ka-ġa, *v. a. to add to,* as in building, *make something in addition to; to do more than one ought to do; to exaggerate*—aowakaġa, aouŋkaġapi, aomakaġa.

a-o'-ka-ġa, *v. n. to drift down stream*—aomakaġa.

a-o'-ka-ġe-ća, *v. a.* *to add to, do* or *say more than is fitting, to be unreasonable*—aoyakaġeća.

a-o'-kaḣ, *cont.* of aokaġa.

a-o'-ka-ḣbog, *cont.* of aokaḣboka; *drifting* or *floating on*—aokaḣbog iyaya; aokaḣbog uŋyaŋpi.

a-o'-ka-ḣbo-ka, *v. n.* *to drift on, float down stream.* *T.*, aokaḣwoka.

a-o'-ka-ḣni-ġa, *v. a.* (a *and* okaḣniġa) *to understand about; to understand in consequence of*—aowakaḣniġa.

a-o'-kaḣ-ya, *adv.* *extravagantly*, as in talking.

a-o'-kaḣ-ya-ken, *adv.* *exaggeratingly.* *T.*, aokaḣyakel.

a-o'-ka-kiŋ, *v. a.* *to peep into*—aowakakiŋ, aoyakakiŋ.

a-o'-ka-kiŋ-yaŋ, *adv.* *peeping into.*

a-o'-ka-pon, *cont.* of aokapota; *floating on* a stream: aokapon iyaya.

a-o'-ka-po-ta, *v. n.* *to rise to the top*, as anything in water; *to float on*, as on water.

a-o'-ka-siŋ, *v. a.* *to look into, peep into*—aowakasiŋ, aoyakasiŋ, aouŋkasiŋpi.

a-o'-ka-siŋ-yaŋ, *adv.* *peeping in upon.*

a-o'-ka-sto, *v. a.* (a *and* okasto) *to smooth down upon*—aowakasto.

a-o'-ka-ta, *v. n.* *to be warm on*—aomakata.

a-o'-ka-ta, *v. a.* *to cover with earth*—aowakata.

a-o'-ka-taŋ, *v. a.* (a *and* okataŋ) *to nail* one thing *on* another—aowakataŋ, aoyakataŋ, aouŋkataŋpi.

a-o'-ka-ti-ća, *v. a.* *to draw* or *scrape* snow *on* anything—aowakatića.

a-o'-ka-ţiŋs, *cont.* of aokaţiŋza.

a-o'-ka-ţiŋs-ya, *adv.* *pressed in* or *on tight.*

a-o'-ka-ţiŋ-za, *v. a.* (a *and* okaţiŋza) *to press* or *pound in tight*, as in packing flour; *to hammer on tight*, as a hoop—aowakaţiŋza.

a-o'-ki-be, *v. a.* *to encircle, go around; to clasp, encircle with the arms*—aowakibe. *T.*, aokime.

a-o'-ki-be-ya, *v. n.* *to go round*, as the sun. *T.*, aokimeya.

a-o'-ki-be-ya, *adv.* *encircling.*

a-o'-ki-ći-pa-ġi, *v.* of opaġi; *to fill a pipe for* one *in addition to*—aowećipaġi.

a'-o-ki-haŋ-na, *n.* *something worn over* or *with* another garment, *a vest.*

a'-o-ki-hna, *n.* *a vest.* See áokihaŋna.

a-o'-ki-hna-ka, *v. a.* (a *and* okihnaka) *to put some in in addition to, to help* one to food *a second time*—aowehnaka. *T.*, aokignaka.

a-o'-ki-ḣpa, *v. a.* (a *and* okiḣpa) *to rest* or *lie by for*—aowakiḣpa.

a-o'-ki-ya, *v.* (a *and* ókiya) *to follow, come after; to help in regard to; to band together for* a purpose—aowakiya.

a-o'-kpa-ġi, *v.* *pos.* of aopaġi; *to fill one's pipe again*—aowakpaġi.

a′-o-kpa-ni, *v. n.* *to be wanting, not sufficient.*

a′-o-kpa-ni-yaŋ, *adv.* *insufficiently, less than.*

a-o′-kpas, *cont.* of aokpaza.

a-o′-kpas-ya, *v. a.* *to darken, make dark upon*—aokpaswaya, aokpasmayaŋ.

a-o′-kpas-ya, *adv.* *obscurely, darkened.*

a-o′-kpa-za, *v. n.* *to be dark on* any place or thing—aomakpaza.

a-o′-ķo, *v. n.* (a *and* oķo) *to be a fuss made about.*

a-o′-ķo-ya, *v. a.* *to buzz about, to make a noise* or *fuss about*—aoķowaya, aoķomayaŋ.

a-o′-mna, *v. a.* (a *and* omna) *to smell upon; smell in consequence of*—aowamna.

a-o′-na-ki-ta-ka, *v.* *pos.* of aonataka; *to fasten,* as a door, *on* one—aonawakitaka.

a-o′-na-pa, *v. a.* (a *and* onapa) *to flee to, take refuge at*—aonawapa.

a-o′-na-śdo-ka, *v. a.* *to run away from, leave*—aonawaśdoka. *T.*, aonaśloka, *to desert,* as a friend in danger.

a-o′-na-tag, *cont.* of aonataka: aonatag iyeya.

a-o′-na-ta-ka, *v. a.* *to fasten on* one; tiyopa aonataka, *to fasten the door on* one—aonawataka.

a-o′-na-ţiŋs, *cont.* of aonaţiŋza: aonaţiŋs iyeya.

a-o′-na-ţiŋ-za, *v. a.* *to press down tight in* a box or barrel—aonawaţiŋza.

a-oŋ′, *v. a.* *to lay* or *place* on, as wood on the fire—awaoŋ, ayaoŋ, uŋkaoŋpi.

a-oŋ′-pa, *v. a.* *to lay* or *place* wood *on* the fire. Same as aoŋ—awaoŋpa, ayaoŋpa, uŋkaoŋpapi.

a-oŋ′-pe-ća, *v.* *to have one's ability tested; to back out, not to do as one proposed*—awaoŋpeća.

a-oŋ′-śi-ya, *adv.* *more poorly, in a worse condition.*

a-oŋ′-śi-ya-ken, *adv.* *still worse, worse and worse.*

a-o′-pa, *v.* (a *and* opa) *to follow with*—aowapa.

a-o′-pa-ġi, *v.* (a *and* opaġi) *to fill the pipe again, to fill the pipe after* eating—aowapaġi.

a-o′-pe-mni, *v. a.* (a *and* opemni) *to roll up in*—aowapemni.

a-o′-pe-ya, *v. a.* *to add to, cause to follow with.*

a-o′-pe-ya, *adv.* *with, together with.*

a-o′-po-ġaŋ, *v. a.* (a *and* opoġan) *to blow on*—aowapoġaŋ.

a′-o-pte-ća, *adj.* *less, little.*

a′-o-pten, *adv.* *less than.* *T.*, aoptel.

a′-o-pten-ya, *v. a.* *to diminish*—aoptenwaya. *T.*, aoptelya.

a′-o-pten-ya, *adv.* *less.*

a′-o-pten-ya-ken, *adv.* *less, less than.*

a′-o-pte-tu, *adv.* *less.*

a′-o-pte-tu-ya, *adv.* *less, in a less manner.*

a-o'-ta-la-se, *adv. T., more;* aotalase maḳu ye, *give me more.*

a-o'-te-haŋ, *v. n. to be far.*

a-o'-te-haŋ-tu, *v. n. to be a long time; to be too late*—aomatehaŋtu.

a'-o-tpa-ni, *v. n. to be lacking, less than.*

a'-o-tpa-ni-yaŋ, *adv. less than.*

a-o'-tpas, *cont.* of aotpaza.

a-o'-tpas-ya, *v. a. to make dark on*—aotpaswaya; aotpasuŋyaŋpi, *they make it dark on us.*

a-o'-tpas-ya, *adv. darkly, in the dark.*

a-o'-tpa-za, *v. n.* (a *and* otpaza) *to be dark on*—aomatpaza.

a-o'-tpa-zaŋ, *v. a. to push into,* as an arrow into a quiver, or a feather into one's hair—aowatpazaŋ.

a-o'-tpa-zaŋ-ki-toŋ, *v. n. to have a sheath* or *case upon; be sheathed* or *pushed in.*

a-o'-ṭiŋs, *cont.* of aoṭiŋza.

a-o'-ṭiŋs-ya, *v. a. to crowd* or *press about, to beset*—aoṭiŋsmayaŋ, aoṭiŋsuŋyaŋpi.

a-o'-ṭiŋs-ya, *adv. crowding, besetting.*

a-o'-ṭiŋ-za, *v. n.* (a *and* oṭiŋza) *to be tight on,* as a garment; *to be tight in,* as anything inside of another—aomaṭiŋza.

a-o'-ṭo-hna-ka, *v. n. to be foolhardy, to dare, risk one's life*—aoṭowahnaka, aoṭouŋhnakapi. *T.,* aoṭognaka.

a-o'-uŋ-yaŋ, *v.* (a *and* ouŋyaŋ) *to be* or *abide on:* akan ouŋyaŋ.

a-o'-we-haŋ, *v. n. to jest, make fun, be ironical, make a false statement*—aowewahaŋ.

a-o'-we-haŋ-haŋ, *v. red.* of aowehaŋ; *to jest, make sport*—aowewahaŋhaŋ, aoweuŋhaŋhaŋpi.

a-o'-we-haŋ-haŋ-yaŋ, *adv. jestingly, in sport.*

a-o'-wiŋś-ki-ya, *v. a. to make a bed on for; e. g.,* to put a blanket down for a child to play on.

a-o'-ze-ze, *v. n. to dangle.*

a-o'-ze-ze-ya, *adv. danglingly.*

a-o'-zi-ća, *v. a. T., to reach out after.*

a-o'-zig-zi-ća, *v. a. to stretch up after* anything—aowazigzića.

a-o'-zig-zin, *cont.* of aozigzića: aozigzin naźiŋ, *to stand stretching up*—aozigzin nawaźiŋ. *T.,* aozigzil.

a-o'-zi-ya, *v. a. to cause to rest for*—aoziwaya.

a-o'-źaŋ-źaŋ, *v. n.* (a *and* oźaŋźaŋ) *to be light on* anything—aomaźaŋźaŋ.

a-o'-źaŋ-źaŋ-ya, *v. a. to cause to be light upon*—aoźaŋźaŋwaya.

a-o'-źaŋ-źaŋ-yaŋ, *adv. in an illuminated manner.*

a-pa', *n. some, a part,* as of a mass of anything.

a-p'a', *v. a. to strike* or *smite* a thing in any way—awap'a, ayap'a, uŋkap'api, amap'a, aćip'a; also a-pa'.

a-pa'-be, *v.* Same as apamaŋ. *T.,* apame.

a-pa'-bu, *v. a.* (a *and* pabu) *to*

drum or *make a noise on* anything—awapabu.

a-pa'-ćaŋ-ćaŋ, *v. a.* (a *and* paćaŋćaŋ) *to push and make tremble on* anything; *to make* one *tremble by pushing*—awapaćaŋćaŋ.

a-pa'-ćo-za, *v. a.* (a *and* paćoza) *to rub and make warm on* anything—awapaćoza.

a-pa'-daŋ, *n.* *dim.* of apa; *a small part.*

a-pa'-daŋ-ka, *n.* Same as apadaŋ.

a-pa'-gna, *v. a.* *T.*, *to shell*, as corn. See apahba.

a-pa'-ġan, *v. a.* (a *and* paġan) *to spare* or *give away for* a purpose—awapaġaŋ.

a-pa'-ġo, *v. a.* (a *and* paġo) *to carve* or *engrave on* anything—awapaġo.

a-pa'-ġu-ka, *v. a.* (a *and* paġuka) *to sprain by rubbing on* anything—awapaġuka.

a-pa'-ha, *v. a.* (a *and* paha) *to raise on* or *over*, as the hand to strike one: isaŋ apaha makuwa, *he follows me with his knife drawn*—awapaha.

a-pa'-ha, *adv.* *convexly; hill-like.*

a-pa'-ha-daŋ-ka, *adv.* *hill-like.*

a-pa'-ha-ya, *adv.* *convexly.*

a-pa'-hba, *v. a.* (a *and* pahba) *to shell off*, as corn, *on* anything—awapahba.

a-pa'-hdu-śte, *v. n.* *to be lame;* of huśte.

a-pa'-hi, *v. a.* (a *and* pahi) *to pick up* or *gather on* anything—awapahi.

a-pa'-hiŋ-ta, *v. a.* (a *and* pahiŋta) *to brush on* anything—awapahiŋta.

a-pa'-hmi-hma, *v. a.* (a *and* pahmihma) *to roll over on*—awapahmihma; apahmihma iyeya, *to turn over and over on.*

a-pa'-hmi-yaŋ-yaŋ, *v. a.* (a *and* pahmiyaŋyaŋ) *to make round*, as a ball, *on* anything.

a-pa'-hmoŋ, *v. a.* (a *and* pahmoŋ) *to twist* or *roll on* anything—awapahmoŋ.

a-pa'-ho-mni, *v. a.* (a *and* pahomni) *to push* or *shove around on* anything—awapahomni.

a-pa'-hu-hu-za, *v. a.* (a *and* pahuhuza) *to shake on* anything—awapahuhuza.

a-pa'-ḣa-tka, *adj.* *against the grain, rough.*

a-pa'-ḣa-tka-ya, *adv.* *roughly, against the grain.*

a-pa'-ḣda-ġaŋ, *v. a.* (a *and* paḣdaġaŋ) *to make large on* anything—awapaḣdaġaŋ.

a-pa'-ḣdan-toŋ, *v. a.* (apaḣdate *and* toŋ) *to bind* or *embroider with ribbon*—apaḣdanwatoŋ.

a-pa'-ḣda-ta, *v. a.* *to embroider.*

a-pa'-ḣda-te, *n.* *ribbon, ferret, binding.* See śina apaḣdate.

a-pa'-ḣde-ća, *v. a.* (a *and* paḣdeća) *to tear* or *rend on* anything; *to rend, by shoving* with the hand, as the coat on one's back—awapaḣdeća.

a-pa'-ḣdo-ka, *v. a.* (a *and* paḣdoka) *to pierce* or *make a hole in, on* anything—awapaḣdoka.

a-pa′-ḣpa, *v. a.* (a *and* paḣpa) *to throw down on*—awapaḣpa, uŋkapaḣpapi.

a-pa′-ḣpu, *v. a.* (a *and* paḣpu) *to pick off on*—awapaḣpu.

a-pa′-ḣta, *v. a.* (a *and* paḣta) *to bind* or *tie on* anything—apawaḣta, apauŋḣtapi.

a-pa′-ke-za, *v. a.* (a *and* pakeza) *to make a noise by filing* or *rubbing on.*

a-pa′-kiŋ-ta, *v. a.* (a *and* pakiŋta) *to wipe* or *rub off on* anything—awapakiŋta.

a-pa′-kpaŋ, *v. a.* (a *and* pakpaŋ) *to crush* or *make fine on*—awapakpaŋ.

a-pa′-kpi, *v. a.* (a *and* pakpi) *to crack on,* as a louse on anything.

a-pa′-ksa, *v. a.* (a *and* paksa) *to break off on*—awapaksa.

a-pa′-kśi-źa, *v. a.* (a *and* pakśiźa) *to bend* or *double up on* anything—awapakśiźa.

a-pa′-ku-ka, *v. a.* (a *and* pakuka) *to rub to pieces on* anything—awapakuka.

a-pa′-ḳe-za, *v. a.* (a *and* paḳeza) *to make smooth by scraping on*—awapaḳeza.

a-pa′-ḳo-za, *v. a.* (a *and* paḳoza) *to rub and make smooth on*—awapaḳoza.

a′-pa-ma-hde, *adj.* *down hill, descending.*

a′-pa-ma-hde-ya, *adv.* *down hill, in a descending manner:* ápamahdeya uŋyaŋpi.

a-pa′-maŋ, *v. a.* (a *and* pamaŋ) *to file, rub,* or *polish on*—awapamaŋ.

a-pa′-mda-ska, *v. a.* (a *and* pamdaska) *to make flat on* anything—awapamdaska.

a-pa′-mda-ya, *v. a.* (a *and* pamdaya) *to make level on* anything—awapamdaya.

a-pa′-mda-za, *v. a.* (a *and* pamdaza) *to burst open on, tear open on.*

a-pa′-mde-ća, *v. a.* (a *and* pamdeća) *to break* or *crush on* anything—awapamdeća.

a-pa′-mdu, *v. a.* (a *and* pamdu) *to crush to powder on* anything—awapamdu.

a-pa′-mni, *v. a.* (a *and* pamni) *to divide out on*—awapamni, ayapamni, uŋkapamnipi.

a-pa′-pa, *n.* *red.* of apa.

a-pa′-po-pa, *v. a.* (a *and* papopa) *to make pop* or *burst on* anything—awapapopa.

a-pa′-psa-ka, *v. a.* (a *and* papsaka) *to break in two,* as a cord, *on* anything—awapapsaka.

a-pa′-psoŋ, *v. a.* (a *and* papsoŋ) *to spill on* anything, as water—awapapsoŋ.

a-pa′-pśuŋ, *v. a.* (a *and* papśuŋ) *to put out of joint on* anything, as the arm—awapapśuŋ.

a-pa′-ptaŋ, *v. a.* (a *and* paptaŋ) *to roll over on* anything—awapaptaŋ.

a-pa'-ptaŋ-ptaŋ, *v. red.* of apaptaŋ; *to roll over and over on* anything.

a-pa'-ptu-źa, *v. a.* (a *and* paptuźa) *to make crack* or *split on* anything—awapaptuźa.

a-pa'-pu-za, *v. a.* (a *and* papuza) *to wipe dry on* anything—awapapuza.

a-pa'-sde-ća, *v. a.* (a *and* pasdeća) *to split by rubbing on* anything—awapasdeća.

a-pa'-sdo-haŋ, *v. a.* (a *and* pasdohaŋ) *to shove* or *push along on* anything—awapasdohaŋ.

a-pa'-si, *v. a.* (a *and* pasi) *to follow after, to follow on*—awapasi.

a-pa'-si-sa, *v. a.* (a *and* pasisa) *to stitch on to; to patch. T., to stick in* or *through,* as a pin—awapasisa.

a-pa'-si-sa-pi, *n. T., a pincushion.*

a-pa'-snoŋ, *v. a.* (a *and* pasnoŋ) *to roast on* or *over* anything—awapasnoŋ.

a-pa'-spa, *v. n. to pass off* or *over,* as clouds or anger; *to cover over,* as clouds or waves.

a-pa'-spe-ya, *adv. passing off,* as clouds.

a-pa'-sto, *v. a.* (a *and* pasto) *to make smooth* or *brush down on* anything—awapasto.

a-pa'-su-ta, *v. a.* (a *and* pasuta) *to make hard* or *stiff by kneading on* anything—awapasuta.

a-pa'-śbog, *v. cont.* of apaśboka: apaśbog iyaya. *T.,* apaświog.

a-pa'-śbo-ka, *v. n.* (a *and* paśboka) *to come up on* or *over,* as water; *to overflow. T.,* apaświoka.

a-pa'-śbu, *v. n.* (a *and* paśbu) *to come up on.*

a-pa'-śdi, *v. a.* or *n. to squeeze out on; to ooze out.*

a-pa'-śdi-ya, *adv. in an oozing way.*

a-pa'-śdo-ka, *v. a.* (a *and* paśdoka) *to pull* or *shove off on,* as one's coat—awapaśdoka.

a-pa'-śi-ća, *v. a.* (a *and* paśića) *to soil* or *injure by rubbing on* anything—awapaśića.

a-pa'-śi-pa, *v. a.* (a *and* paśipa) *to break off close on* anything; *to put out of joint on*—awapaśipa.

a-pa'-śpa, *v. a.* (a *and* paśpa) *to break off a piece on* anything—awapaśpa.

a-pa'-śpu, *v. a.* (a *and* paśpu) *to pull off on* anything; *to pick off* or *rub off,* as one thing sticking on another—awapaśpu.

a-pa'-śu-źa, *v. a* (a *and* paśuźa) *to mash* or *crush on* anything—awapaśuźa.

a-pa'-ta, *v. a.* (a *and* pata) *to cut up on,* as meat on a block—awapata.

a-pa'-taŋ, *v. a.* (a *and* pataŋ) *to reserve* or *take care of for* a purpose—awapataŋ.

a-pa'-taŋ, *v. a.* (a *and* pataŋ) *to push against*—awapataŋ.

a-pa'-te-pa, *v. a. to wear off short,* as a pencil on paper.

a-pa'-ti-ća, *v. a.* (a *and* patića)

to scrape off from, as snow from the ground—awapatiċa.

a-pa'-ti-taŋ, *v. a.* (a *and* patitaŋ) *to push* or *brace against*—awapatitaŋ.

a-pa'-tpi, *v.* Same as apakpi.

a-pa'-tuś, *v.* *cont.* of apatuźa: apatuś yaŋka, *to be in a stooping position.*

a-pa'-tuś-ya, *adv.* *stoopingly.*

a-pa'-tu-źa, *v. a.* (a *and* patuźa) *to stoop down on* or *over*—awapatuźa.

a-pa'-ṭa, *v. a.* (a *and* paṭa) *to kill by pressing on* anything—awapaṭa.

a-pa'-ṭa-ṭa, *v. n.* *T.* *to become numb*, as by freezing on.

a-pa'-ṭiŋ-za, *v. a.* (a *and* paṭiŋza) *to press tight on, to make stiff on*—awapaṭiŋza.

a-pa'-ṭo, *v. n.* *to obstruct, oppose, prevent progress*—amapaṭo.

a-pa'-ṭo-ya, *v. a.* *to obstruct, stop, hinder*—apaṭowaya, apaṭomayaŋ.

a-pa'-ṭo-ya, *adv.* *in an obstructing manner.*

a-pa'-waŋ-ka, *v. a.* (a *and* pawaŋka) *to push down on* anything—awapawaŋka. *T.*, apauŋka.

a-pa'-we-ġa, *v. a.* (a *and* paweġa) *to break partly*, as a stick, *on* anything—awapaweġa.

a-pa'-weḣ, *cont.* of apaweġa: apaweḣ iyeya.

a-pa'-wiŋ-ġa, *v. n.* *to go round in circles on* or *over.*

a-pa'-wiŋḣ, *cont.* of apawiŋġa: apawiŋḣ iyaya.

a-pa'-wiŋś, *cont.* of apawiŋźa: apawiŋś iyeya.

a-pa'-wiŋ-ta, *v. a.* (a *and* pawiŋta) *to rub on*—awapawiŋta.

a-pa'-wiŋ-źa, *v. a.* (a *and* pawiŋźa) *to bend* or *press down*, as grass, *on* anything—awapawiŋźa.

a'-pa-ye, *n.* *seasoning*, anything like *meat* or *grease* boiled with corn. See wapaye.

a'-pa-ye-ya, *v. a.* *to use* a thing *for seasoning*—apayewaya.

a-pa'-zo, *v. a.* (a *and* pazo) *to show* or *point to on* anything; *to point at:* nape amapazo, *he points his finger at me*—awapazo.

a-pa'-zuŋ-ta, *v. a.* (a *and* pazuŋta) *to stitch* or *run up in sewing on* anything—awapazuŋta.

a-pa'-źa-źa, *v. a.* (a *and* paźaźa) *to wash by rubbing on* anything—awapaźaźa.

a-pa'-źi-pa, *v. a.* (a *and* paźipa) *to prick* or *pinch on* anything—awapaźipa.

a-pa'-źu-źu, *v. a.* (a *and* paźuźu) *to rub out on* anything—awapaźuźu.

a-pće'-ya, *v. a.* (a *and* pćeya) *to cut and dry*, as meat, *on* anything—awapćeya.

a-pe', *v. a.* *to wait for, wait on; to hope for, expect:* u ape, *to wait for* one *to come;* ye ape, *to wait for* one *to go*, or *desire* one *to go along*—awape, ayape, uŋkapepi.

a-pe', *n.* *a leaf* of a tree, *leaves; a blade* of corn or grass; *a fin* of a fish, as in hoape.

a-p'e', *v.* Same as ap'a.

a-pe'-haŋ, *v.* (a *and* pehaŋ) *to fold on* anything—awapehaŋ.

a-pe'-ćo-ka-na, *n.* (ape *and* ćokadaŋ) *a species of fish*, without fins, as the name indicates.

a-pe'-ćo-kaŋ-he-daŋ, *n.* Same as above.

a-pe'-hiŋ, *n.* *the mane* of a horse.

a-pe'-ki-ya, *v. a.* *to cause to wait for*—apewakiya.

a-pe'-śa, *n.* *the red-fin*, a species of fish.

a-pe'-śa-śa, *n.* Same as apeśa.

a-pe'-ya, *adv.* *waiting for, hoping for.*

a-pe'-źa-ta, *n.* *the forked-fin*, a species of fish.

a-pe'-yo-haŋ, *n.* *T. the mane of a horse.*

a-piś', *cont.* of apiźa.

a-piś'-pi-źa, *v.* *red.* of apiźa; *to be wrinkled on.*

a-piś'-ya, *adv.* *in a wrinkled manner.*

a-pi'-ya, *v. a.* *to mend on*—apiwaya.

a-pi'-źa, *v. n.* *to be wrinkled on* anything—amapiźa.

a'-po, *v.* *pl. imperat.* of a.

a-po', *v. n.* (a *and* po) *to swell on*—amapo.

a-po'-ġaŋ, *v. a.* (a *and* poġaŋ) *to blow on*—awapoġaŋ.

a-po'-mna-mna, *v. a.* (a *and* pomnamna) *to shake* or *wag the head about*—apowamnamna.

a-po'-pa, *v. n.* *to burst on, break open.*

a-po'-pa-haŋ, *adv.* or *part.* *bursting open.*

a-po'-ptaŋ-ptaŋ, *v. a.* (a *and* poptaŋptaŋ) *to shake the head about, dissent from*—apowaptaŋptaŋ.

a-po'-śiŋ, *v.* *to make faces at*—apowaśiŋ.

a-po'-śiŋ-śiŋ, *v. a.* *to make faces at*—apowaśiŋśiŋ.

a-po'-tpo-ta, *v. n.* *to be worn out* or *ragged on.*

a-po'-tpo-ta-haŋ, *part.* *worn out on, ragged.*

a-po'-źaŋ, *v. a.* *to blow out on*, as from a tube—awapoźaŋ.

a-psi'-ća, *v. a.* *to jump over* anything; *to jump on*—awapsića.

a-psin', *cont.* of apsića: *T.*, apsil.

a-pśa', *v. a.* (a *and* pśa) *to sneeze on* anything—awapśa.

a-pśa'-pśa, *adj.* *thick, close together*, as grass, etc.

a-pśa'-pśa-ya, *adj.* *thickly set, in a close state; thick*, as mush.

a-ptaŋ'-ptaŋ, *v. n.* (a *and* ptaŋptaŋ) *to roll about on*—amaptaŋptaŋ.

a-ptaŋ'-yaŋ, *v. n.* *to roll over on, fall on; to fall from*—amaptaŋyaŋ, aniptaŋyaŋ.

a-ptu'-źa-haŋ, *part.* *cracked* or *split on.*

a-pus', *cont.* of apuza.

a-pu'-ski-ća, *v. a.* (a *and* puskića) *to press down tight upon*—awapuskića.

a-pu'-skin, *v.* *cont.* of apuskića.

a-pu'-skem-ya, *adv.* *in a filtering manner.* *T.*, apuskebya.

a-pu′-ske-pa, *v. n.* (a *and* puskepa) *to filter out on.*

a-pu′-spa, *v. a.* (a *and* puspa) *to stick on; to make stick on, scab*—awapuspa.

a-pu′-spa-pi, *n.* *mucilage, solder.*

a-pu′-spe-ya, *adv.* *in a sticking manner.*

a-pus′-pu-za, *v.* *red.* of apuza.

a-pus′-ya, *v. a.* (a *and* pusya) *to cause to dry on*—apuswaya.

a-pus′-ya, *adv.* *in the manner of drying on.*

a-pu′-tag, *cont.* of aputaka.

a-pu′-tag-ya, *v. a.* *to cause to touch.*

a-pu′-tag-ya, *adv.* *in the manner of touching.*

a-pu′-ta-ka, *v. a.* (a *and* putaka) *to touch, lay on,* as the hand, etc.: nape amaputaka, *he placed his hand upon me.*

a-pu′-ṭiŋs, *v.* *cont.* of apuṭiŋza.

a-pu′-ṭiŋs-ṭiŋs, *v.* *cont. red.*

a-pu′-ṭiŋs-ṭiŋs-ya, *adv.* *firmly; pressed upon.*

a-pu′-ṭiŋs-ṭiŋ-za, *v.* *red.* of apuṭiŋza.

a-pu′-ṭiŋs-ya, *adv.* *firmly.*

a-pu′-ṭiŋ-za, *v. a.* *to press down upon, make firm*—awapuṭinza.

a-pu′-za, *v. n.* (a *and* puza) *to dry on, become dry on* one, as clothes—amapuza.

a-po′, *v. n.* (a *and* po) *there is fog on* a thing.

a-sa′-ka, *v. n.* (a *and* saka) *to become dry* or *hard upon*—amasaka.

a-saŋ′, *v. n.* (a *and* saŋ) *to become whitish* or *grayish:* asaŋ eyaku, *to take a grayish stain.*

a′-saŋ, *adv.* Same as osaŋ.

a-saŋ′-pi, *n.* (aze *and* haŋpi) *milk* of any kind, *breast milk;* pte asaŋpi, *cow's milk.*

a-saŋ′-pi-i-hdi, *n.* *the oil of milk,* i. e., *cream, butter.*

a-saŋ′-pi-ni-ni, *n.* *thick milk; cream.*

a-saŋ′-pi-sa-mna, *n.* *T. cheese.*

a-saŋ′-pi-su-ta, *n.* *hard milk,* i. e., *cheese.*

a-saŋ′-pi-ta-sa-ka, *n.* *hardened* or *frozen milk,* i. e., *cheese.*

a-saŋ′-pi-wa-sna, *n.* *T. butter.*

a-saŋ′-pi-wi-gli, *n.* *T. butter; cream.*

a-sa′-pa, *v. a.* (a *and* sapa) *to become black on:* asapa eyaku, *to take a black stain.*

a-sas′-ya, *adv.* of asaza; *slowly, gently, stilly.*

a-sas′-ye-daŋ, *adv.* *gently, slowly.*

a-sa′-za, *adj.* *gently:* used mostly with the negative; asaze śni, *inconstant, unchaste:* asaze śni wauŋ, *I am inconstant.*

a-sba′-haŋ, *part.* *raveling on. T., worn off,* as the nap of cloth.

a-sbu′-haŋ, *part.* *crumbling on.* See sbuhaŋ.

a-sda′, *v. n.* (a *and* sda) *to be greasy on* anything.

a-sda′-ya, *v. a.* (a *and* sdaya) *to make greasy, to grease*—asdawaya.

a-sda′-ya, *adv.* *greasily.*

a-sdi′-pa, *v. a.* (a *and* sdipa) *to lick off, lick from,* as a dog does.

a-sdo′-haŋ, *v. n.* (a *and* sdohaŋ) *to crawl along on* anything—awasdohaŋ.

a-sdon′-ya, *v. a.* (a *and* sdonya) *to know about; to be wise about, know all about*—asdonwaya. *T.*, aslolya.

a-si′-ću-toŋ, *v. a.* *to sole, put on a sole,* as on a moccasin, shoe, etc.—asićuwatoŋ.

a-s'iŋ′, *v. n.* *to sponge, loaf, hang about* a place to get something to eat; *T., to covet, secretly long for*—awas'iŋ.

a-s'iŋ′-s'iŋ, *v.* *red.* of as'iŋ.

a-ska′, *v. n.* (a *and* ska) *to become white on.*

a′-skam, *cont.* of áskapa.

a-skam′-toŋ, *v. a.* *to make stick on, to seal*—askamwatoŋ. *T.*, askabtoŋ.

a′-skam-ya, *v. a.* *to make stick on, to seal*—áskamwaya.

a-skaŋ′, *v. n.* (a *and* skaŋ) *to melt* or *thaw on; to disappear from,* as snow.

as′-kaŋ, *n.* (aze *and* kaŋ) *the cords* and *veins of the breast.*

a′-ska-pa, *v. n.* *to stick to* or *on, adhere to*—amaskapa.

a-ske′-pa, *v. n.* (a *and* skepa) *to leak out on.*

a-smag′-ya, *adv.* (a *and* smaka) *in an indented manner:* asmagya waŋka.

a-sna′-sna, *v.* (a *and* snasna) *to ring* or *rattle on.*

a-sni′, *v. n.* *to recover* or *get well from* sickness; *to recover from* anger, etc.—amasni, anisni, uŋkasnipi.

a-sni′-ki-ya, *v. a.* *to heal, cause to get well*—asniwakiya. *T., to rest one's self,* as a horse part way up a hill.

a-sni′-yaŋ, *v. a.* *to cause to get well, to cure*—asniwaya, asniuŋyaŋpi.

a-sni′-ya-ken, *adv.* *in the way of recovering.*

a-soŋ′, *v. a.* (a *and* soŋ) *to plait* or *braid on* anything—awasoŋ.

a-so′-so, *v. a.* (a *and* soso) *to cut into strings on* any place—awasoso.

a-spaŋ′, *v. n.* (a *and* spaŋ) *to become soft* or *melt on,* as snow on anything.

a-spa′-ya, *v. n.* (a *and* spaya) *to become wet on; to sink* in water, as in drowning—amaspaya.

a′-spe-ya, *v. a.* *to cause to sink down,* as an anchor in water; *to buoy up; to weigh*—áspewaya: maza aspeyapi, *an anchor;* oŋ aspeyapi, *scales, a steelyard.*

a-spe′-ye-toŋ, *v. a.* *to weigh* anything; *to balance*—aspeyewatoŋ.

a′-staŋ, *v. n.* *to be purple on, become purple.*

a-staŋ′-ka, *adj.* *purple, made purple.*

a′-sto-ya, *v. a.* (a *and* stoya) *to smooth down upon.*

a-su′-ta, *v. n.* (a *and* suta) *to become hard* or *strong upon*—amasuta.

a-su′-toŋ, *v. n.* (a *and* sutoŋ) *to become ripe on* or *upon*, as seed.

a-śa′, *v. n.* (a *and* śa) *to become reddish; aśa eyaku, to take a red stain.*

a-ś'a′, *v. a.* (a *and* ś'a) *to shout at* or *on account of*—awaś'a.

a-śag′, *cont.* of aśaka.

a-śag′-ya, *adv.* *in a coated manner;* aśagya yaŋka.

a-śa′-ka, *v. n.* *to be coated* or *furred*, as the tongue in sickness; *to be dirty*, as a gun that needs cleaning out.

a-ś'a′-ko-wiŋ-na, *adv.* *mightily, strongly;* aś'akowiŋna ećoŋ.

a-śam′, *cont.* of aśapa.

a-śam′-ya, *v. a.* *to defile, make dirty*—aśamwaya.

a-śam′-ya, *adv* *dirtily, in a defiled manner.*

a-śa′-pa, *v. n.* (a *and* śapa) *to become black* or *dirty on* anything—amaśapa.

a-śbe′, *v. n.* Same as aśma.

a-śbe′-ya, *adv.* *deeply, in a deep manner.* *T.*, aśmeya.

a-śbu′, *v. n.* (a *and* śbu) *to drop*, as water, *on* anything.

a-śbu′-ya, *v. a.* *to cause to drop on*, as water—aśbuwaya

a-śda′, *v. n.* (a *and* śda) *to be bare on* anything.

a-śdo′, *v. n.* (a *and* śdo) *to fuse* or *melt*, as metals, *on* anything.

a-śdo′-ya, *v. a.* *to cause to melt on*—aśdowaya.

a-śdun′-ya, *v. a.* (a *and* śdunya) *to make slip on.*

a-śdu′-śdu-ta, *v. n.* (a *and* śduśduta) *to be slippery on.*

a-ś'e′, *v.* *T.* *to drop on; fall in drops on.*

a-śe′-ća, *v. n.* (a *and* śeća) *to become dry* or *seasoned on* anything.

a-ś'e′-ya, *v. a.* *T.* *to cause to drip on.*

a-śi′-ća, *v. n.* (a *and* śića) *to become bad* or *unpleasant on* or *for.*

a-śi′-ća-ho-wa-ya, *v. a.* *to cry out on account of*—aśićahowamda.

a-śi′-ća-ȟdo, *v. a.* *to growl about, complain of*—aśićawaȟdo.

a-śi′-ća-ya, *adv.* *badly, unpleasantly.*

a-śi′-ća-ya-ken, *adv.* *unpleasantly.*

a-śi′-će-ća-ke, *adj.* *unpleasant*, as the weather or country. See ośićećake.

a-śi′-ȟtiŋ, *v. n.* *to be poorly on account of; to be defective*—amaśiȟtiŋ.

a-śi′-ȟtiŋ-ya, *adv.* *poorly.*

a-śin′-ya, *adv.* *badly, sadly.* *T.*, aśilya.

a-śin′-ya-ken, *adv.* *badly, unpleasantly.*

a-śka′-daŋ, *adv.* *soon, presently; near, close by.*

a-śka′-daŋ-ȟiŋ, *adv.* *very near; very soon.*

a-śka′-ka, *adv.* *soon, near.*

a-śka′-na, *adv.* *Ih.* Same as aśkadaŋ.

a-śkaŋ'-śkaŋ, *v. n.* (a *and* śkaŋśkaŋ) *to move about on* anything.

a-śkaŋ'-śkaŋ-yaŋ, *adv.* *moving about on.*

a-śka'-ta, *v. n.* (a *and* śkata) *to play on* any place—awaśkata.

a-śka'-tu-daŋ, *adv.* *lately, not long since.*

a-śka'-tu-ya, *adv.* *not long ago.*

a-śka'-tu-ye-daŋ, *adv.* *lately, but a short time ago.*

a-śka'-ye-daŋ, *adv.* *for a little while, not enduring.* *T.*, aśkayela.

a-śke', *n.* *the tuft* or *bunch* of hair which some Dakotas wear on the side of their heads: aśke yuwipi, *the bunch* of hair *tied up.*

a-śke'-haŋ, *v. n.* (a *and* śkehaŋ) *to frisk* or *jump about on; to be changeable.*

a-śkom'-ya, *adv.* *crookedly, in an arched manner.*

a-śko'-pa, *v. n.* (a *and* śkopa) *to be crooked on* or *arched.*

a-śla'-ya, *adv.* *T. openly, plainly.*

a-śla'-ye-la, *adv.* *T. plainly.*

a-śma', *v. n.* (a *and* śma) *to be deep,* as water, *on* any place.

a-śni'-yaŋ-yaŋ, *v. n.* *T. to crawl* or *creep on,* as a bug on one.

a-śni'-yaŋ-yaŋ, *adv.* *creeping along, in a crawling manner.*

a-śni'-źa, *v. n.* (a *and* śniźa) *to be wilted* or *withered on* or *for.*

a-śo'-ka, *v. n.* (a *and* śoka) *to be thick,* as a board, *on* anything.

a-śo'-ta, *v. n.* (a *and* śota) *to be smoky on* or *at.*

a-śpaŋ', *v. n.* (a *and* śpaŋ) *to be cooked* or *burnt on* or *by* anything.

a-śtun'-ya, *v. a.* *to cause to thaw on*—aśtunwaya. *T.*, aśtulya.

a-śtu'-ta, *v. n.* (a *and* śtuta) *to thaw on* anything.

a-śuŋ'-pa, *v. n.* (a *and* śuŋpa) *to shed on,* as the quills of geese.

a-śu'-ta, *v. a.* (a *and* śuta) *to miss, fail of*—aśuwata.

a'-ta, *suffix prep.* *to, at, on.* When suffixed to nouns ending in a, it becomes ta alone, as máġa, *a field,* maġata, *at the field;* in other cases, a y is introduced for euphony, as ti, *a house,* tiyata, *to the house;* ćaŋ, *wood,* ćaŋyata, *at the woods.*

a-tab'-ye-la, *adj.* *T. thin; i. q.* zibzipela.

a-ta'-ġo-śa, *v. a.* (a *and* taġośa) *to spit on* anything—ataġowaśa.

a-ta'-kiŋ-yaŋ, *adv.* *leaning on, not perpendicular:* wi atakiŋyaŋ yaŋka, *the sun is declining.*

a-ta'-kpe, *v. a.* (a *and* takpe) *to make an attack on*—atawakpe.

a-ta'-ku-ni-śni, *v. n.* *to come to naught; to become enfeebled:* atakuniśni amayaŋ, *I am becoming feeble:* amatakuniśni. *T., to be ruined, spoiled.*

a-ta'-ku-ni-śni-yaŋ, *v. a.* *to bring to naught*—atakuniśniwaye.

a-taŋ', *v. a.* *to care for, have respect for*—awataŋ; ataŋśni, *to disregard, throw away.*

a-taŋ'-iŋ, *v. n.* (a *and* taŋiŋ) *to appear on, be manifest.*

a-taŋ'-iŋ-iŋ, *v. red.* of ataŋiŋ.

a-taŋ'-iŋ-śni-yaŋ, *adv. in a lost manner.*

a-taŋ'-iŋ-yaŋ, *adv. appearing, manifestly.*

a-taŋ'-ka, *v. n.* (a *and* taŋka) *to be large on* or *in addition to; to be larger.*

a-taŋ'-ka-daŋ, *dim.* of ataŋka.

a-taŋ'-ka-ya, *adv. widely, extensively.*

a-taŋ'-se, *adv. silently, stilly:* ataŋse yaŋka, *to be motionless.*

a-ta'-om, *cont.* of ataoŋpa: ataom iyaya, *to have gone past perpendicular. T.*, ataob.

a-ta'-om-ya, *adv. leaningly.*

a-ta'-oŋ-pa, *v. n. to lean,* as the sun does in the afternoon; *T., to lean over,* as a warrior on his horse.

a-ta'-pa, *v. n.* (a *and* tapa) *to follow after on* anything.

a-ta'-sa-ka, *v. n.* (a *and* tasaka) *to become stiff* or *hard on* as clothes—amatasaka.

a-taś'-ta-źa, *v. n. red.* of ataźa; *to be rough* or *in waves on* one, as water.

a-ta'-te-yaŋ-pa, *v. n.* (a *and* tateyaŋpa) *to blow upon* anything, as the wind does.

a-ta'-to-haŋ, *adv. to the windward.*

a-ta'-to-he-ya, *adv. on the windward side.*

a-ta'-tpe, *v.* Same as atakpe.

a-ta'-ya, *v. a. to go directly to* anything; *to be fortunate in reference to*—atawaya.

a'-ta-ya; *adv. wholly, altogether. all; universally; alone, separately.*

a'-ta-ye-daŋ, *adv. directly, without a medium:* atayedaŋ ećamoŋ, *I did it myself* or *personally;* atayedaŋ maḳu, *he gave it directly to me.*

a-ta'-źa, *v. n.* (a *and* taźa) *to be rough* or *in waves on* one—amataźa.

a-te', *n. father, my father;* niyate, *thy father;* atkuku, *his* or *her father.*

a-te', *v. n.* (a *and* te) *to become blue;* ate eyaku, *to take a blue stain.* Same as ato.

a-te'-ća, *v. n.* (a *and* teća) *to become new on.*

a-tem'-ya, *v. a.* (a *and* temya) *to cut up* or *devour on*—atemwaya.

a-te'-pa-haŋ, *part. worn off short on.*

a-te'-ya, *v. a. to have for a father; to sustain the relation of a child to* a man—atewaya, ateyaya, ateuŋyaŋpi. Among the Dakotas one's father's brothers are also called ate.

a-te'-ye-daŋ, *adv.* Same as átayedaŋ.

a-ti', *v. n.* (a *and* ti) *to build a house* or *put up a tent at* or *on; to pitch a tent* or *encamp at for* a certain purpose: psiŋ ati, *to camp at the rice.*

a-ti'-hnag-ya, *adv. near by.*

a-ti'-hna-ka, *adv. close by, near to.*

a-tiŋ', *adv. pretty well.*

a-tiŋ'-ka, *adv. well.*

a-ti'-pa-haŋ, *part. crisped* or *drawn up on.*

a-tkiŋ', *v. n.* (a *and* tkiŋ) *to be damp on.*

a-tku′-ku, *n.* *his* or *her father.*

a-to′, *v. n.* (a *and* to) *to become blue* or *green on; to tattoo;* see akito: ato eyaku, *to take a blue* or *green stain.*

a′-to-kaŋ, *adv.* *in another place, to another place.*

a-to′-ke-ća, *v. n.* *to become different:* atokeća śni, *it makes no difference.*

a-to′-kśu, *v. a.* (a *and* tokśu) *to carry* or *draw* anything *on; T., to pile up at* or *on,* as on horses' backs—atowakśu.

a-toŋ′-waŋ, *v. a.* (a *and* toŋwaŋ) *to look to* or *at*—awatoŋwaŋ, uŋkatoŋwaŋpi.

a-toŋ′-waŋ-yaŋ, *v. a.* *to cause to look at; to make a village at* or *on* a place, probably because by making a village people are *caused to look to* or *at* a place—atoŋwaŋuŋyaŋpi.

a-tpa′-ġaŋ, *v. a.* (a *and* tpaġaŋ) *to part with one's own for* a purpose—awatpaġaŋ. See akpaġaŋ.

a-tpa′-hi, *v. a.* (a *and* tpahi) *to gather up one's own on* something.

a-tpa′-mde-ća, *v. a.* (a *and* tpamdeća) *to break in pieces one's own on* something.

a-tpas′, *cont.* of atpaza.

a-tpa′-spa, *v. n.* (a *and* tpaspa) *to disappear, go out of sight, fade away,* as clouds, or as the sun disappears at night.

a-tpas′-ya, *v. a.* *to darken, overshadow*—atpaswaya.

a-tpas′-ya, *adv.* *darkly, obscurely.*

a-tpa′-ta, *v. a.* (a *and* tpata) *to cut up* or *carve one's own on* anything.

a-tpa′-taŋ, *v. a.* (a *and* tpataŋ) *to spare* or *keep one's own for* a purpose. See akpataŋ.

a-tpa′-za, *v. n.* (a *and* tpaza) *to bcome dark on*—amatpaza, anitpaza, uŋkatpazapi. See akpaza.

a-tu′-kta, *adv.* *well, fortunately:* atukta ećamoŋ kiŋ, *I did well to do it;* atukta de ćiŋhaŋ, *if you go, it will be well.*

a-ṭiŋs′, *cont.* of aṭiŋza.

a-ṭiŋs′-ya, *adv.* *tightly, in a squeezing manner.*

a-ṭiŋ′-za, *v. n.* (a *and* ṭiŋza) *to press on, be tight on*—amaṭiŋza.

a-ṭo′-za, *v n.* (a *and* ṭoza) *to become blunt* or *dull on.*

a-ṭuŋg′-ya, *v. a.* *to suspect* one, *have an inkling of*—aṭuŋgwaya. See ṭuŋgya.

a-ṭuŋ′-ka, *v, n.* See aṭuŋkeća.

a-ṭuŋ′-ke-ća, *v. n.* (a *and* ṭuŋkeća) *to be suspected of*—amaṭuŋkeća.

a-u′, *v. a.* (a *and* u) *to carry* or *bring* anything *towards.*

a-u′, *v. col. pl.* *they come.*

a-u′, *v. n.* (a *and* u) *to come out on; to ooze out* or *run,* as sap: mini au.

a-uŋ′, *v. a.* *to put wood on the fire.* See aoŋ.

a-uŋ′, *v. n.* (a *and* uŋ) *to be on*—awauŋ.

a-u ŋ'-h d a-k a, *v.* (a *and* uŋhdaka) *to move camp on account of; to decamp for* some reason: auŋhdaka uŋyaŋpi.

a-u ŋ'-y a ŋ, *v. n.* *to be on* or *over:* auŋyaŋ iyaya, *to pass over*, as a fence; auŋyaŋ kute, *to shoot on the wing*, or as it flies *over*.

a-u ŋ'-y e-y a, *v. a.* of auŋyaŋ; *to cause to be on.*

a-u ŋ'-y e-y a, *v. n.* *to approach from the windward.*

a-u ŋ'-y e-y a-p i, *n.* *a species of berry*, which if approached from the windward is said to be bitter, but if from the opposite direction, sweet; *sand berries.*

a-w a', *v. n.* (a *and* wa) *to snow upon; to be snow on* anything—amawa. See awahiŋhe *and* awapa.

a-w a'-ć i, *v. a.* (a *and* waći) *to dance on* anything—awawaći, awauŋćipi.

a-w a'-ć i ŋ, *v. a.* (a *and* waćiŋ) *to think on* or *of, meditate upon; to trust, believe in*—awaćaŋmi, awaćaŋni, awauŋćiŋpi and uŋkawaćiŋpi.

a-w a'-ć i ŋ-h a ŋ, *part.* *thinking upon.*

a-w a'-ć i ŋ-k e ŋ, *adv.* *thinking upon.* *T.*, awaćiŋkel.

a-w a'-ć i ŋ-p i, *n.* *a thinking upon, trusting in, faith.*

a w a'-ć i ŋ-y a ŋ, *adv.* *thinking upon.*

a-w a'-ć i ŋ-y a ŋ-k e n, *adv.* *in the manner of thinking on.*

a-w a'-h i ŋ-h e, *v. n.* (awa *and* hiŋhe) *to snow upon.*

a-w a'-h i ŋ-h e-y a, *v. a.* *to cause to snow upon*—awahiŋhewaya.

a-w a'-h i ŋ-h e-y a, *adv.* *snowing upon.*

a-w a'-ḣ p a-n i, *v. n.* *to be poor on account of.*

a-w a'-ḣ p a-n i-ć a, *v. n.* (a *and* waḣpanića) *to become poor on account of* or *by means of*—amawaḣpanića.

a-w a'-ḣ p a-n i y a, *v. a.* *to make poor by means of*—awaḣpaniwaya.

a-w a'-ḣ p a-n i-y a ŋ, *adv.* *poorly off.*

a-w a'-ḣ t a-n i, *v. a.* *to sin on, to transgress*—awawaḣtani.

a-w a'-ḣ t e-k a, *v. n.* (a *and* waḣteka) *to be bad* or *worthless.*

a-w a'-ḣ t e-ś n i, *v. n.* (a *and* waḣteśni) *to be worthless on* some account.

a-w a'-ḣ t e-ś n i-y a ŋ, *adv.* *worthlessly, vilely.*

a-w a ḣ'-w a-y e-l a, *adv.* *T.* *mildly, gently*—*Is.*, awaḣbayedaŋ. See waḣbayedaŋ.

a-w a'-k a ŋ, *v. n.* (a *and* wakaŋ) *to be sacred* or *incomprehensible on* some account.

a-w a'-k a ŋ-k a, *v. n.* Same as awakaŋ.

a-w a'-k a ŋ-k a, *n.* *a supernatural being.*

a-w a'-k a ŋ-y a ŋ, *adv.* *mysteriously, supernaturally.*

a-w a'-k e-y a, *v. a.* *to make a*

booth; to spread over, as tree branches; *to make a shade, to make an awning over*—awakewaye. See wakeya.

a-wa'-ke-ya-pi, *n. a booth.*

a-wa'-ki-ćiŋ, *v. a. pos.* of awaćiŋ.

a-wa'-ni-ća, *v. n.* (a *and* wanića) *to be* or *become nothing for* some reason.

a-wa'-nin, *cont.* of awanića; used adverbially, *in a destroying manner:* awanin iyeya. *T.*, awanil.

a-wa'-ni-ye-tu, *v. n.* (a *and* waniyetu) *to come winter on* one—amawaniyetu.

a-waŋg', *cont* of awaŋka: awaŋg mda. *T.*, ayuŋg.

a-waŋg'-ya, *v. to cause to lie on* or *for*—awaŋgwaya. See awaŋka.

a-waŋ'-hdag, *cont.* of awaŋhdaka.

a-waŋ'-hda-ka, *v. pos.* of awaŋyaka; *to oversee* or *take care of one's own*—awaŋwahdaka. *T.*, awaŋglaka.

a-waŋ'-ka, *v. n.* (a *and* waŋka) *to be* or *lie on; to lie in wait* or *spend the night out for*, as for the purpose of killing deer: taĥiŋća awaŋg mda, *I am going to lie in wait for deer.* *T.*, ayuŋka.

a-waŋ'-kam, *adv. above, overhead.*

a-waŋ'-ki-ći-ya-ka, *v* of awaŋyaka; *to watch* or *oversee for* one—awaŋwećiyaka.

a-waŋ'-yag, *cont.* of awaŋyaka: awaŋyag wauŋ.

a-waŋ'-yag-ki-ya, *v. a. to cause to attend to* or *oversee*—awaŋyagwakiya.

a-waŋ'-ya-ka, *v. a.* (a *and* waŋyaka) *to look upon; to see to, have the oversight of*—awaŋmdaka, awaŋdaka, awaŋuŋyakapi.

a-wa'-pa, *v. n.* (a *and* wapa) *to snow on.* See awahiŋhe.

a-wa'-śa-ka, *adj. cheap, easily purchased.*

a-wa'-śa-ka-daŋ, *adj. cheap*, as goods. *T.*, awaśakayela.

a-wa'-śte, *v. n.* (a *and* waśte) *to be good on* or *for; to become better than*—amawaśte.

a-wa'-śte-ka, *v. n. to be good for, befit.*

a-wa'-śte-ya, *adv. well, better than.*

a-wa'-śte-ya-ken, *adv. better, in a better manner:* awaśteyaken amayaŋ, *I am becoming better.*

a-wa'-taŋ-iŋ-śni, *adj. dark, obscure*, as in the dusk of the evening.

a-wa'-ṭe-ća, *adv.* See wawaṭeća.

a-wa'-ya-pi-ka, *v. n.* (a *and* wayapika) *to be eloquent about* anything; *to be more eloquent than* some one—awamdapika.

a-wa'-yu-pi-ka, *v. n.* (a *and* wayupika) *to be skillful about; to be more skillful than*—awamdupika.

a-wa'-yu-pi-ya, *adv. skillfully, well.*

a-we', *v. n.* (a *and* we) *to become lean*, as cattle do in the spring of the year; *to bleed on.*

a-we′-tu, *v. n.* (a *and* wetu) *to become spring on* one—amawetu.

a′-wi-ća-ka, *v. n. to be true, to tell the truth*—awicawaka.

a′-wi-ća-ke-haŋ, *adv. truly, of a truth.*

a′-wi-ća-ke-ya, *adv. truly.*

a′-wi-ća-ke-ya-haŋ, *adv of a truth.*

a′-wi-ća-śa, *n.* of aśa; *shouting.*

a′-wi-ća-ya-śpu-ya, *n. the itch, itching.*

a-wi′-hnu-ni, *v. n to come to naught; to be destroyed. T*, awignuni.

a-wi′-hnu-ni-ya, *v a. to destroy, to use up*—awihnuniwaye.

a-wiŋ′-ta, *v. a. to creep on*, as a child—awawiŋta.

a′-wi-tu-ka-daŋ, *adv familiarly, among themselves. Ih.*, awitukana.

a-wi′-ya-kpa, *v.n.* (a *and* wiyakpa) *to glisten on* anything.

a-wi′-ye-ya, *adv.* (a *and* wiyeya) *ready for* anything. See wiyeya.

a′-ya, *v. a. to take* or *carry* anything *along.*

a′-ya, *v. col. pl.* of ya; *they go together.*

a′-ya, *v. n. to become, to be, to be in* or *on:* maśte aya, *it is becoming warm;* asniyaŋken amayaŋ, *I am recovering* from sickness; waniyetu teća uŋkayapi, *we are in the new year.*

a-ya′-ba-ġa, *v. a.* (a *and* yabaġa) *to twist* or *turn with the mouth on* anything—amdabaġa. *T.*, ayawaġa.

a-ya′-ba-źa, *v to bite off on. T.*, ayawaźa.

a-ya′-bu, *v. a.* (a *and* yabu) *to growl about*—amdabu.

a-ya′-će-ya, *v. a.* (a *and* yaćeya) *to make cry by talking to*—amdaćeya.

a-ya′-ćo, *v. a* (a *and* yaćo) *to condemn on; to condemn for* or *on account of*—amdaćo. *T.*, ayasu.

a-ya′-ġa, *v. a.* (a *and* yaġa) *to peel off with the teeth on* anything—amdaġa. *T.*, ayaġo.

a-ya′-ġo-pa, *v. a.* (a *and* yaġopa) *to suck up on*—amdaġopa.

a-ya′-hba, *v. a.* (a *and* yahba) *to shell* or *bite off on*—amdahba. *T.*, ayagba.

a-ya′-hbe-za, *v. a.* (a *and* yahbeza) *to bite and make rough on* anything. *T.*, ayagbeza.

a-ya′-hiŋ-ta, *v. a.* (a *and* yahiŋta) *to brush off with the mouth*—amdahiŋta.

a-ya′-hna-yaŋ, *v. a.* (a *and* yahnayaŋ) *to deceive with the mouth, tell a falsehood about. T.*, ayagnayaŋ.

a-ya′-ḣda-ya, *v. a.* (a *and* yaḣdaya) *to bite* or *peel off with the teeth on* anything—amdaḣdaya.

a-ya′-ḣde-ća, *v. a.* (a *and* yaḣdeća) *to tear with the teeth on*—amdaḣdeća.

a-ya′-ḣdo-ka, *v. a.* (a *and* yaḣdoka) *to bite a hole in on* anything—amdaḣdoka.

a-ya'-ḣe-pa, *v. a.* (a *and* yaḣepa) *to drink up on*—amdaḣepa.

a-ya'-ḣpa, *v. a* (a *and* yaḣpa) *to throw down with the mouth on* anything—amdaḣpa.

a-ya'-ḣpu, *v. a.* (a *and* yaḣpu) *to bite off on*, one thing *on* another—amdaḣpu.

a-ya'-ḣta-ka, *v. a.* (a *and* yaḣtaka) *to bite* one thing *on* another.

a-ya'-ḣu, *v. a.* (a *and* yaḣu) *to peel off on.*

a-ya'-kća, *v. a.* (a *and* yakća) *to untie with the teeth on* anything—amdakća.

a-ya'-ko-ka, *v. a.* (a *and* yakoka) *to clatter* or *gnash the teeth on* or *for* anything—amdakoka.

a-ya'-koŋ-pi, *v. n. pl.* of ayaŋka; *they are in* such a condition.

a-ya'-kpa, *v. a.* (a *and* yakpa) *to bite out on*—amdakpa.

a-ya'-kpaŋ, *v. a.* (a *and* yakpaŋ) *to chew fine on*—amdakpaŋ.

a-ya'-kpi, *v. a.* (a *and* yakpi) *to crack with the teeth on* anything.

a-ya'-ksa, *v. a.* (a *and* yaksa) *to bite off on*—amdaksa.

a-ya'-kśaŋ, *v a.* (a *and* yakśaŋ) *to bend with the mouth on*—amdakśaŋ.

a-ya'-kśiś, *cont.* of ayakśiźa.

a-ya'-kśi-źa, *v. a.* (a *and* yakśiźa) *to double up with the teeth on* anything.

a-ya'-ktaŋ, *v. a* (a *and* yaktaŋ) *to bend with the mouth on*—amdaktaŋ.

a-ya'-ku-ka, *v. a.* (a *and* yakuka) *to bite* or *tear in pieces with the teeth on* anything—amdakuka.

a-ya'-ḳe-ġa, *v. a.* (a *and* yaḳeġa) *to gnaw on* anything.

a-ya'-ḳe-za, *v. a.* (a *and* yaḳeza) *to make smooth with the teeth on* anything.

a-ya'-ḳo-ġa, *v. a.* (a *and* yaḳoġa) *to bite* or *gnaw off on.*

a-ya'-ḳo-za, *v. a.* (a *and* yaḳoza) *to bite off smooth*, as a horse eating grass. *T.*, oyaḳoza.

a-ya'-ma, *v. a.* (a *and* yama) *to gnaw on.*

a-ya'-mda-ska, *v. a.* (a *and* yamdaska) *to make flat with the mouth on* anything. *T.*, ayablaska.

a-ya'-mda-ya, *v. a.* (a *and* yamdaya) *to make level with the teeth.*

a-ya'-mda-za, *v. a.* (a *and* yamdaza) *to tear open with the teeth.*

a-ya'-mde ća, *v. a.* (a *and* yamdeća) *to crush on* anything *with the teeth.*

a-ya'-mdu, *v. a.* (a *and* yamdu) *to chew fine on.*

a-ya'-mna, *v. a.* (a *and* yamna) *to gain on* or *for, by speaking.*

a-yaŋ'-ka, *v. n.* (a *and* yaŋka) *to be on* or *for, to be in* such a condition.

a-yaŋ'-pa, *v. n.* *to come light on; to come morning; to come morning on; to endure until the morning light*—amayaŋpa, uŋkayaŋpapi.

a-ya'-o-ni-haŋ, *v. a.* (a *and* yaonihaŋ) *to praise on* or *for.*

a-ya′-o-taŋ-iŋ, *v. a.* (a *and* ya-otaŋiŋ) *to make manifest on* or *for*—amdaotaŋiŋ.

a-ya′-pe-haŋ, *v. a.* (a *and* yapehaŋ) *to fold up with the mouth on* anything.

a-ya′-pe-mni, *v. a.* (a *and* yapemni) *to twist with the mouth on* anything.

a-ya′-po-ta, *v. a.* (a *and* yapota) *to bite in pieces on* anything—amdapota.

a-ya′-psa-ka, *v. a.* (a *and* yapsaka) *to bite off*, as a string, *on* anything—amdapsaka.

a-ya′-psoŋ, *v. a.* (a *and* yapsoŋ) *to spill with the mouth on* anything—amdapsoŋ.

a-ya′-pśuŋ, *v. a.* (a *and* yapśuŋ) *to pull out by the roots with the mouth on* anything—amdapśuŋ.

a-ya′-ptaŋ-yaŋ, *v. a.* (a *and* yaptaŋyaŋ) *to turn over on* anything *with the mouth.*

a-ya′-ptu-źa, *v. a.* (a *and* yaptuźa) *to crack* or *split with the mouth on* anything.

a-ya′-sba, *v. a.* (a *and* yasba) *to pick to pieces with the teeth on* anything.

a-ya′-sde-ća, *v. a.* (a *and* yasdeća) *to split with the teeth on* anything.

a-ya′-skab-toŋ, *v. a.* *T.* *to patch*, as clothes; *to put a stamp on* a letter. See askamtoŋ.

a-ya′-sku, *v. a.* (a *and* yasku) *to pull off on with the teeth:* mdo ha owaŋka amdasku, *I bite off potato-skins on the floor.*

a-ya′-smiŋ, *v. a.* (a *and* yasmiŋ) *to pick off with the teeth on, make bare with the teeth.*

a-ya′-sna, *v. a.* (a *and* yasna) *to make ring*, as a little bell, *with the mouth on* or *over* anything.

a-ya′-so-ta, *v. a.* (a *and* yasota) *to eat all up on*—amdasota.

a-ya′-spa-ya, *v. a.* (a *and* yaspaya) *to wet with the mouth on* anything.

a-ya′-staŋ-ka, *v. a.* (a *and* yastaŋka) *to moisten on* anything *with the mouth.*

a-ya′-sto, *v. a.* (a *and* yasto) *to lick smooth on.*

a-ya′-su, *v.* See ayaćo.

a-ya′-su-ta, *v. a.* (a *and* yasuta) *to make firm* or *establish with the mouth.*

a-ya′-śa-pa, *v. a.* (a *and* yaśapa) *to blacken* or *defile with the mouth.*

a-ya′-śdu-ta, *v. a.* (a *and* yaśduta) *to have the teeth slip on* anything.

a-ya′-śki-ća, *v. a.* (a *and* yaśkića) *to press with the mouth upon*, as in chewing tobacco—amdaśkića.

a-ya′-śko-pa, *v. a.* (a *and* yaśkopa) *to make crooked* or *twisted by biting on.*

a-ya′-śna, *v. a.* (a *and* yaśna) *to miss with the mouth, let fall on from the mouth*—amdaśna.

a-ya′-śpa, *v. a.* (a *and* yaśpa) *to*

bite a piece off on anything—amdaśpa.

a-ya′-śpu, *v. a.* (a *and* yaśpu) *to bite off on*, as one thing that adheres to another.

a-ya′-śtaŋ, *v. a.* (a *and* yaśtaŋ) *to cease from speaking* or *eating*—amdaśtaŋ, uŋkayaśtaŋpi.

a-ya′-śu-źa, *v. a.* (a *and* yaśuźa) *to bite* or *mash up on with the teeth.*

a-ya′-ta, *v. a.* *to guess, predict, foretell, divine, soothsay*—amdata, adata, uŋkayatapi.

a-ya′-ta-ku-ni-śni, *v. a.* (a *and* yatakuniśni) *to destroy with the mouth on* anything.

a-ya′-taŋ, *v. a.* (a *and* yataŋ) *to praise for.*

a-ya′-taŋ-iŋ, *v. a.* (a *and* yataŋiŋ) *to make manifest upon* or *for, by speaking.*

a-ya′-ta-pi, *n.* *guessing, prophecy, divination.*

a-ya′-ta-ya *and* a-ya′-ta-ya-keŋ, *adv.* *by guess.*

a-ya′-te, *n.* *a soothsayer, diviner, prophet.*

a-ya′-te-ya, *v. a.* *to cause to foretell*—ayatewaya.

a-ya′-ti-taŋ, *v. a.* (a *and* yatitaŋ) *to pull with the teeth on* anything.

a-ya′-tkaŋ, *v. a.* (a *and* yatkaŋ) *to drink*, as water, *on* or *after* eating, etc.—amdatkaŋ.

a-ya′-tkaŋ-yaŋ, *adv.* *drinking on* or *after.*

a-ya′-tog-ya, *v.* of yatokeća; *to conceal, to change in telling:* ayatogwaye and amdatogwaye.

a-ya′-tpaŋ, *v. a.* Same as ayakpaŋ.

a-ya′-waŋ-ka, *v. a.* (a *and* yawaŋka) *to throw down with the mouth on* anything. *T.*, ayauŋka.

a-ya′-wa-śte, *v. a.* (a *and* yawaśte) *to bless upon*—amdawaśte.

a-ya′-we-ġa, *v. a.* (a *and* yaweġa) *to fracture by biting on.*

a-ya′-za-mni, *v. a.* (a *and* yazamni) *to open* or *uncover with the mouth* or *by speaking.*

a-ya′-zaŋ, *v. n.* (a *and* yazaŋ) *to be sick on*—amayazaŋ.

a-ya′-zo-ka, *v. a.* (a *and* yazoka) *to suck out on.*

a-ya′-zuŋ-ta, *v. a.* (a *and* yazuŋta) *to connect* or *weave together*, as in talking.

a′-ye, *v.* Same as aya.

a-ye′-ġa, *v. n.* (a *and* yeġa) *to glisten* or *shine on.*

a-yeh′-ya, *adv.* *in a glistening manner.*

a-yu′-ba-ġa, *v. a.* (a *and* yubaġa) *to twist* or *turn on.*

a-yu′-be, *v.* Same as ayumaŋ.

a-yu′-bu, *v. a.* (a *and* yubu) *to make a drumming noise on* anything.

a-yu′-ćaŋ, *v. a.* (a *and* yućaŋ) *to sift* or *shake on* or *over*—amdućaŋ.

a-yu′-ćaŋ-ćaŋ, *v. a.* (a *and* yućaŋćaŋ) *to cause to shake* or *tremble on.*

a-yu′-će-ka, *v. a.* (a *and* yućeka) *to make stagger on* any place.

a-yu'-će-ya, *v. a.* (a *and* yućeya) *to make cry on.*

a-yu'-ćo, *adv.* *well, excellently:* ayućo kaġa.

a-yu'-ćo-ya, *adv.* *well.*

a-yu'-ćo-za, *v. a.* (a *and* yućoza) *to make warm on* any place.

a-yu'-e-će-tu, *v. a.* (a *and* yuećetu) *to fulfill* or *accomplish on.*

a-yu'-e-ći, *v. a.* (a *and* yueći) *to turn wrong side out on* anything.

a-yu'-ġa, *v. a.* (a *and* yuġa) *to husk on,* as corn—amduġa.

a-yu'-ġaŋ, *v. a.* (a *and* yuġaŋ) *to open,* as a door, *on* anything.

a-yu'-ġa-pa, *v. a.* (a *and* yuġapa) *to strip* or *pull off on,* as the skin of an animal.

a-yu'-ġa-ta, *v. a.* (a *and* yuġata) *to open out,* as the hand, *on* anything.

a-yu'-ġe, *v. a.* (a *and* yuġe) *to dip out on.* See ayuze.

a-yu'-ġe-ġe, *v. a.* (a *and* yuġeġe) *to take up by handfuls on* anything.

a-yu'-ġiŋ, *v. n.* *to slumber*—amduġiŋ.

a-yu'-ġo, *v. a.* (a *and* yuġo) *to make marks on.*

a-yu'-ġu-ka, *v. a.* (a *and* yuġuka) *to sprain on; to draw out,* as one's sword from the scabbard.

a-yu'-ha, *v. a.* (a *and* yuha) *to have* or *possess on; to hold* or *lift on; to have for*—amduha.

a-yu'-ḣba, *v. a.* (a *and* yuḣba) *to shell,* as corn, *on.* *T.,* ayugna.

a-yu'-ḣbe-za, *v. a.* (a *and* yuḣbeza) *to make rough on.* *T.,* ayugmeza.

a-yu'-ḣbu, *v. a.* (a *and* yuḣbu) *to make rattle on,* as in taking hold of shelled corn. *T.,* ayugmu, *to make a noise,* as of one drowning.

a-yu'-ḣda, *v. a.* (a *and* yuḣda) *to uncoil* or *untwist on.* *T.,* ayugla.

a-yu'-ḣiŋ-ta, *v. a.* (a *and* yuḣiŋta) *to sweep* or *rake off on.*

a-yu'-ḣmi-ḣma, *v. a.* (a *and* yuḣmiḣma) *to roll on.* *T.,* ayugmigma.

a-yu'-ḣmuŋ, *v. a.* (a *and* yuḣmuŋ) *to twist,* as a string, *on* anything. *T.,* ayugmuŋ.

a-yu'-ḣmu-za, *v. a.* *to shut upon,* as the hand upon anything—amduḣmuza. *T.,* ayugmuza.

a-yu'-ḣna, *v. a.* (a *and* yuḣna) *to shake off on,* as fruit. *T.,* ayugna.

a-yu'-ḣna-yaŋ, *v. a* (a *and* yuḣnayaŋ) *to miss in trying to catch hold of.* *T.,* ayugnayaŋ.

a-yu'-ḣnu-ni, *v. a.* (a *and* yuḣnuni) *to make wander on* any place. *T.,* ayugnuni.

a-yu'-ho-ho, *v. a.* (a *and* yuhoho) *to shake on,* as anything loose.

a-yu'-ho-mni, *v. a.* (a *and* yuhomni) *to turn around on,* as in bringing a gun round and pointing it at one—amduhomni, amayuhomni.

a-yu'-ḣu-ḣu-za, *v. a.* (a *and* yuḣuḣuza) *to shake on* or *over,* as a tree. *T.,* ayuḣuŋḣuŋza.

a-yu'-ḣa, *v. n.* *to become attached to; to stick to.*

A-yu'-ḣba, *n. pl.* (*sleepy ones*) *the Iowas.*

a-yu'-ḣda, *v. a.* (a *and* yuḣda) *to ring* or *rattle over.*

a-yu'-ḣda-ġaŋ, *v. a.* (a *and* yuḣdaġaŋ) *to make large upon; to leave, forsake. T.*, ayuḣlaġaŋ, *to slacken on*, as a noose.

a-yu'-ḣda-ta, *v. a.* (a *and* yuḣdata) *to scratch on.*

a-yu'-ḣda-ya, *v. a.* (a *and* yuḣdaya) *to peel off on*, as the skin of a potato.

a-yu'-ḣde-ća, *v. a.* (a *and* yuḣdeća) *to rend* or *tear on* one, as a garment—amduḣdeća.

a-yu'-ḣdo-ka, *v. a* (a *and* yuḣdoka) *to make a hole on; to open on*—amduḣdoka.

a-yu'-ḣe-pa, *v. n.* (a *and* yuḣepa) *to absorb on.*

a-yu'-ḣe-ya-ta, *v. a.* (a *and* yuḣeyata) *to push back on, push on one side.*

a-yu'-ḣi-ća, *v. a.* (a *and* yuḣića) *to waken* one *upon*—amduḣića.

a-yu'-ḣla-ġaŋ-śni, *v. T. not to leave* or *forsake, to be with constantly.*

a-yu'-ḣmiŋ, *v. a.* (a *and* yuḣmiŋ) *to sling* or *throw on one side*, as a stone, *on* anything; *to do crookedly*, as in writing.

a-yu'-ḣmiŋ-yaŋ, *adv.* *crookedly.*

a-yu'-ḣmuŋ, *v. a.* (a *and* yuḣmuŋ) *to make buzz on.*

a-yu'-ḣpa, *v. a.* (a *and* yuḣpa) *to throw down on; to shut*, as a window—amduḣpa.

a-yu'-ḣpu, *v. a.* (a *and* yuḣpu) *to make crumble on.*

a-yu'-ḣtu-ta, *v. a.* (a *and* yuḣtuta) *to mash* or *break on*, as one's skin; *to make rough on.*

a-yu'-ḣu, *v. a.* (a *and* yuḣu) *to peel off on*, as bark.

a-yu'-ḣu-ġa, *v. a.* (a *and* yuḣuġa) *to break a hole in, upon* anything.

a-yu'-ḣuŋ-ta, *v. a.* (a *and* yuḣuŋta) *to make soft on* by rubbing.

a-yu'-kaŋ, *v. a.* *to go around; to give place to.* See kiyukaŋ.

a-yu'-kaŋ-yaŋ, *adv.* *going around.*

a-yu'-ka-tiŋ, *v. a.* (a *and* yukatiŋ) *to straighten out on* with the hand.

a-yu'-ka-wa, *v. a.* (a *and* yukawa) *to cause to open on.*

a-yu'-kća, (a *and* yukća) *to unite on, disentangle on.*

a-yu'-kiŋ-ća, *v. a.* *to scrape off on*, as in cleaning a fish—amdukiŋća.

a-yu'-ki-pam, *adv.* *separately, divided.*

a-yu'-ki-pa-tuś-ya, *v. a.* *to make bow down*—ayukipatuśwaya.

a-yu'-ki-pa-tu-źa, *v. a.* *to cause to stoop or bow down on.*

a-yu'-kpaŋ, *v. a.* (a *and* yukpaŋ) *to grind* or *make fine on*—amdukpaŋ.

a-yu'-ksa, *v. a.* (a *and* yuksa) *to break off on*, as limbs or sticks, *with one's hand*—amduksa.

a-yu'-kśa, *v. a.* (a *and* yukśa) *to bend, fold*, or *double up on.*

a-yu'-kśi-źa, *v. a.* (a *and* yukśiźa) *to bend* or *double up on; to pull*, as the trigger of a gun, *on* one—amdukśiźa.

a-yu'-ktaŋ, *v. a.* (a *and* yuktaŋ) *to bend around on.*

a-yu'-ku-ka, *v. a.* (a *and* yukuka) *to make rotten on.*

a-yu'-ķe-ġa, *v. a.* (a *and* yuķeġa) *to scratch* or *scrape on* anything.

a-yu'-ķe-za, *v. a.* (a *and* yuķeza) *to make hard and smooth on; to shave off close*, as a mule's mane.

a-yu'-ķo-ġa, *v. a.* (a *and* yuķoġa) *to scratch up, make rough.*

a-yu'-ķo-za, *v. a.* (a *and* yuķoza) *to make hard and smooth on.*

a-yul'; *cont.* of ayuta; *T.* ayul yaŋka, *to continue looking at.*

a-yu'-maŋ, *v. a.* (a *and* yumaŋ) *to grind* or *file off on; to sharpen by grinding.*

a-yu'-mda-ska, *v. a.* (a *and* yumdaska) *to make flat on. T.*, ayublaska.

a-yu'-mda-ya, *v. a.* (a *and* yumdaya) *to spread out on, unroll on.*

a-yu'-mda-za, *v. a.* (a *and* yumdaza) *to burst open on, make an incision on.*

a-yu'-mde-ća, *v. a.* (a *and* yumdeća) *to break* or *crush on*—amdumdeća.

a-yu'-mdu, *v. a.* (a *and* yumdu) *to plow on, make mellow on*—amdumdu.

a-yu'-mni-mni-źa, *v. n.* *to ruffle, to curl.*

a-yu'-mni-mni-źa, *n.* *a ruffle.*

a-yu'-na-źiŋ, *v. a.* (a *and* yunaźiŋ) *to cause to stand on.*

a-yu'-o-ȟtal-ya, *adv.* *T. in a loose manner.*

a-yu'-o-ȟta-ta, *v.* *T. to loosen*, as a noose.

a-yu'-paŋ-ġa, *v. a.* (a *and* yupaŋġa) *to tie up loosely on.*

a-yu'-pe-haŋ, *v. a.* (a *and* yupehaŋ) *to fold up on.*

a-yu'-pe-mni, *v. a.* (a *and* yupemni) *to twist* or *turn to one side on.*

a-yu'-po-ta, *v. a.* (a *and* yupota) *to wear out on; to tear to pieces* or *destroy on*—amdupota.

a-yu'-psa-ka, *v. a.* (a *and* yupsaka) *to break* or *pull in two on* anything, as a string.

a-yu'-psoŋ, *v. a.* (a *and* yupsoŋ) *to pour out* or *spill on*, as water.

a-yu'-pśuŋ, *v. a.* (a *and* yupśuŋ) *to pull out by the roots* or *extract*, as teeth, *on* anything.

a-yu'-pta, *v. a.* (a *and* yupta) *to cut off on* or *pare*, as a garment—amdupta.

a-yu'-pta, *v. a.* *to answer, speak in return* or *opposition; to give* or *grant* a thing *when asked*—amdupta, adupta, uŋkayuptapi; aćiyupta, *I answer thee;* amayadupta, *thou answerest me.*

a-yu'-ptaŋ-ptaŋ, *v. a.* (a *and* yuptaŋptaŋ) *to turn* or *roll back and forth on.*

a-yu'-ptaŋ-yaŋ, *v. a.* (a *and* yuptaŋyaŋ) *to turn* or *roll over on*—amduptaŋyaŋ.

a-yu' ptu-źa, *v. a.* (a *and* yuptuźa) *to crack* or *split on* anything.

a-yu'-sba, *v. a.* (a *and* yusba) *to ravel out* or *pick in pieces on.*

a-yu'-sbu, *v. a.* (a *and* yusbu) *to make a rustling* or *rattling noise on* or *over.*

a-yu'-sde-ća, *v. a.* (a *and* yusdeća) *to split on.*

a-yu'-sdo-haŋ, *v. a.* (a *and* yusdohaŋ) *to drag* or *draw along on*—amdusdohaŋ: *to run over:* ćaŋpahmihma ayusdohaŋpi, *the wagon ran over him;* literally, *they dragged the wagon over him.*

a-yu'-sdu-ta, *v. a.* (a *and* yusduta) *to pull out on.*

a-yu'-ske-pa, *v. a.* (a *and* yuskepa) *to make evaporate on* or *from.*

a-yu'-ski-ća, *v. a.* (a *and* yuskića) *to press down tight on.*

a-yu'-ski-ta, *v. a.* (a *and* yuskita) *to bind* or *bandage on.*

a-yu'-sku, *v. a.* (a *and* yusku) *to peel* or *pare off on.*

a-yu'-sma-ka, *v. a.* (a *and* yusmaka) *to indent on.*

a-yu'-smiŋ, *v a. to make bare*—amdusmiŋ.

a-yu'-sna, *v.* (a *and* yusna) *to ring on* or *over,* as a bell.

a-yus'-o, *v. n. to wade after.*

a-yu'-so-ta, *v. a.* (a *and* yusota) *to use up* or *expend on.*

a-yu'-sto, *v. a.* (a *and* yusto) *to smooth down on, make smooth,* as hair, *on* the head.

a-yu'-su-ta, *v. a.* (a *and* yusuta) *to make firm upon.*

a-yu'-śa-pa, *v. a.* (a *and* yuśapa) *to blacken* or *defile on* anything.

a-yu'-śda, *v. a.* (a *and* yuśda) *to shave off on; to cut,* as grass, *to cover* one *with*—amduśda; amihduśda, *I cut on* or *for myself.*

a-yu'-śdo-ka, *v. a.* (a *and* yuśdoka) *to pull out on.*

a-yu'-śdu-ta, *v. a.* (a *and* yuśduta) *to draw* or *slip out on* anything.

a-yu'-ś'e, *v. n. T. to fall in drops on.*

a-yu'-ś'e-ya, *adv. T. in a dripping manner.*

a-yu'-śi-ća, *v. a.* (a *and* yuśića) *to spoil* or *make bad on*—amduśića.

a-yu'-śki-ća, *v. a.* (a *and* yuśkića) *to press out on.*

a-yu'-śko-pa, *v. a.* (a *and* yuśkopa) *to make twist* or *warp on* anything.

a-yu'-śna, *v. a.* (a *and* yuśna) *to drop* or *let fall on.*

a-yu'-śpa, *v. a.* (a *and* yuśpa) *to break off a piece on.*

a-yu'-śpi, *v. a.* (a *and* yuśpi) *to pick,* as fruit, *on* a place.

a-yu'-śpu, *v. a.* (a *and* yuśpu) *to pick* or *pull off on.*

a-yu'-śpu-ya, *v. a.* (a *and* yu-śpuya) *to scratch on*, when an itchy sensation is felt.

a-yu'-śtaŋ, *v. a.* (a *and* yuśtaŋ) *to stop* or *cease from, leave off* what one is doing; *to let go* or *let alone*—amduśtaŋ, aduśtaŋ, uŋkayuśtaŋpi; amayaduśtaŋ, *thou hast left me.*

a-yu'-śu-źa, *v. a.* *T. to sliver on*, by twisting.

a-yu'-śu-śu-źa, *v.* *red.* of ayu-śuźa.

a-yu'-ta, *v. a.* *to cover with earth; i. e.* akata: 2. of yuta, *to eat; to eat upon* or *in addition to*: 3. *T.*, *to look at, look steadily at;* amayaluta, *you are looking at me.*

a-yu'-ta-ku-ni-śni, *v. a.* (a *and* yutakuniśni) *to destroy* or *bring to naught on.*

a-yu'-taŋ, *v.* (a *and* yutaŋ) *to touch, put the hand upon*—amdutaŋ. *T.*, *to mix up*, as cherries and grease, *to mingle.*

a-yu'-taŋ-iŋ, *v. a.* (a *and* yu-taŋiŋ) *to make manifest upon.*

a-yu'-te-ća, *v. a.* (a *and* yuteća) *to renew upon.*

a-yu'-te-pa, *v. a.* (a *and* yutepa) *to wear off on.*

a-yu'-ti-ća, *v. a* (a *and* yutića) *to scrape* or *paw on.*

a-yu'-ti-pa, *v. a.* (a *and* yutipa) *to make cramp* or *draw up on.*

a-yu'-ti-taŋ, *v. a.* (a *and* yutitaŋ) *to pull on.*

a-yu'-to-kaŋ, *v. a.* *to shove away, put aside a little.*

a-yu'-tpaŋ, *v.* Same as ayukpaŋ.

a-yu'-wa-kaŋ, *v. a.* (a *and* yu-wakaŋ) *to consecrate* or *make sacred for*—amduwakaŋ.

a-yu'-waŋ-ka, *v. a.* *to make fall* on—amduwaŋka. *T.*, ayuyuŋka.

a-yu'-waŋ-kaŋ, *v a.* (a *and* yu-waŋkaŋ) *to exalt; make high for.*

a-yu'-wa-śte, *v. a.* (a *and* yu-waśte) *to make good on* or *for.*

a-yu'-we-ġa, *v. a.* (a *and* yuweġa) *to break down on* or *fracture.*

a-yu'-wi, *v. a.* (a *and* yuwi) *to wrap on.*

a-yu'-wi-ća-ka, *v. a.* (a *and* yu-wićaka) *to assure one; to asseverate.*

a-yu'-wiŋ-źa, *v. a.* (a *and* yu-wiŋźa) *to bend down on.*

a-yu'-za-mni, *v. a.* (a *and* yuza-mni) *to open on, set open on*, as a a door; *to unroll on.*

a-yu'-ze, *v. a.* (a *and* yuze) *to dip* or *skim out on.* *T.* ayuġe.

a-yu'-zi-ća, *v. a.* (a *and* yuzića) *to draw* or *stretch on.*

a-yu'-zuŋ-ta. *v. a.* (a *and* yu-zuŋta) *to connect* or *link together on.*

a-yu'-źa-źa, *v. a.* (a *and* yuźaźa) *to wash on.*

a-yu'-źi-pa, *v. a.* (a *and* yuźipa) *to pinch upon.*

a-yu'-źuŋ, *v. a.* (a *and* yuźuŋ) *to pull out by the roots on* anything.

a-yu'-źu-źu, *v. a.* (a *and* yuźuźu) *to destroy* or *take to pieces on.*

a-zaŋ', *adv.* See azaŋzaŋka.

a-zaŋ'-zaŋ-ka, *or* a-za'-za-**ka,**

adv. thinly, standing at a distance from each other.

a-z e', *n.* *the breasts* of a female; *the udder* of a cow, etc.

a-z e'-p i ŋ-k p a, *n.* (aze pa *and* iŋkpa) *the nipple* of the breast; *the teat* or *dug* of a cow, etc.

a-z e'-p i ŋ-t p a, *n.* Same as azepiŋkpa.

a'-z i, *v. n.* *to get aground* or *stick fast*, as a boat.

a'-z i-k i-y a, *v. a.* *to run aground, to cause to stick*—aziwakiya.

a-z i n'-k i-y a, *v. a.* *to burn incense, make a good smell by burning*, as cedar-leaves when one is sick, and in their religious ceremonies—azinwakiya.

a-z i n'-t o ŋ, *v. a.* *to make a pleasant smell by burning* leaves—azinwatoŋ. *T.*, aziltoŋ.

a-z i ŋ', *v. a.* *to suck*, as a child its mother, or the young of mammals—awaziŋ: aziŋ eḣpeya, *to leave off sucking;* aziŋ ayuśtaŋkiya, *to cause to leave off sucking, to wean.*

a-z i ŋ'-k i-y a, *v. a.* *to give suck to* or *nurse*, as a mother her child—aziŋwakiya. *T.*, azilkiya.

a-z i ŋ'-k i-y e, *n.* *a wet-nurse.*

a-z i'-t a, *v. n.* *to smoke upon, to burn*, as incense.

a'-z i-y a, *v. a.* (azi *and* ya) *to cause to get aground, to run aground*, as a boat—áziwaya.

a-z i'-y a, *v. a.* (a *and* ziya) *to make yellow on* anything. See aziyahaŋ.

a-z i'-y a-h a ŋ, *part.* *becoming yellow on.*

a'-z i-z i, *v.* *red.* of ázi: ázizi uŋyaŋpi, *we often get aground as we go.*

a-z u'-y a, *v. a.* (a *and* zuya) *to make war on* any one, *go to war against* a people—azuwaya; azuwićuŋyaŋpi, *we make war on them*

a-ź i'-ź i, *v.* *to whisper about* a person or thing—awaźiźi, ayaźiźi.

a-ź o', *v.* See aźoźo.

a-ź o'-k i-y a *or* a-ź o g-k i-y a, *v.* *to move the ears*, as a horse.

a-ź o ŋ'-t k a, *n.* *T.* *the kidneys.*

a-ź o'-ź o, *v.* *to whistle about; to call by whistling*, as a dog—awaźoźo.

a-ź o'-ź o-k i-y a, *v. a.* *to cause to whistle for*—aźoźowakiya: nakpa aźoźokiya, *to prick up the ears*, as a horse.

a'-ź u, *v. a.* *to lay up*, as rice or corn on a scaffold for drying; *to pile up*—awaźu, uŋkaźupi.

a-ź u'-k i-y a, *v. a.* *to cause to lay up* for drying.

a-ź u ŋ'-t k a, *n.* *Ih.* *the kidneys: i. e.*, pakśiŋ: this latter is applied by the Ihanktons to the fat that is on the kidneys; *i. e.*, pakśiŋ śiŋ. See aźoŋtka.

B.

b, *the second letter of the Dakota alphabet.* It has the same sound as in English.

ba, *a prefix* to a class of verbs, signifying that the action is done by *a sawing motion*, as in cutting with a knife or saw. The place of the pronoun is immediately after the prefix. In the Titoŋwaŋ dialect this prefix, with but few exceptions for the sake of euphony, is changed to wa.

ba, *v. a.* *to blame*—waba, yaba, uŋbapi; maba, niba; ćiba, *I blame thee;* wićawaba, *I blame them;* iç̣iba, *he blames himself*—miç̣iba.

ba-ćaŋ′-ksi, *v. a.* (ba *and* ćaŋksi) *to make angry by cutting.*

ba-će′-ya, *v. a.* (ba *and* ćeya) *to make cry by cutting*—bawaćeya.

ba-ći′-ḳa-daŋ, *v. a.* (ba *and* ćiḳadaŋ) *to shave small*—bawaćiḳadaŋ. *T.*, waćiḳala.

ba-ći′-stiŋ-na, *v. a.* (ba *and* ćistiŋna) *to make small by cutting*—bawaćistiŋna. *T.*, waćisćila.

ba-ćo′-ka, *v. a.* *to cut out* or *cut open*—bawaćoka.

ba-ġam′, *cont.* of baġapa; baġam iyeya, *to take off*, as the hide of an animal—baġam iyewaya. *T.*, waġab.

ba-ġan′, *cont.* of baġata; baġan iyeya. *T.*, waġal.

ba-ġan′-ġa-ta, *v.* *red.* of baġata; *to make marks*, such as cuts or saws, in anything; *to haggle*—bawaġanġata. *T.*, waġalġata.

ba-ġa′-pa, *v. a.* (ba *and* ġapa) *to take off*, as the skin of an animal, *with a knife, to flay*—bawaġapa.

ba-ġa′-ta, *v. a.* (ba *and* ġata) *to mark* or *cut with a knife, to carve, hack*—bawaġata.

ba-ġo′, *v. a.* *to make marks* or *gashes* in the flesh; *to mark, carve*, or *engrave, with a knife*, in wood—bawaġo, bayaġo, bauŋġopi. *T.*, waġo.

ba-ġo′-ki-ya, *v. a.* *to cause to carve*—baġowakiya.

ba-ha′, *adj* *aged.*

ba-ha′, *n.* *a middle-aged* or *oldish man.* Sometimes, but not often, applied to a woman.

ba-ha′-i-ye-ya, *v. a.* *to throw down* or *push aside.* See pahaiyeya.

ba-ha′-ka, *n.* *an aged person.*

ba-hba′, *v. a.* *to cut off*, as corn from the cob—bawahba: wabahba ohaŋ, *to boil* corn that is *cut off.* *T.*, wagba.

ba-hbe′-za, *v. a.* (ba *and* hbeza) *to carve, make rough with a knife*—bawahbeza. *T.*, wagbeza.

ba-hda′, *v. a.* *to take off*, as tallow from entrails, *with a knife*—bawahda. *T.*, wagla.

b a - h d a′ - h d a, *v. red.* of bahda.

b a - h d a′ - k a, *v. a.* (ba *and* hdaka) *to cut like the teeth of a coarse comb; to cut notches in*—bawahdaka. *T.*, waglaka.

b a - h n a′, *v. a.* (ba *and* hna) *to cut off*, as fruit from a tree, *to make fall off by cutting*—bawahna. *T.*, wagna.

b a - h n a′ - ś k i ŋ - y a ŋ, *v. a.* (ba *and* hnaśkiŋyaŋ) *to make crazy* or *frantic by cutting* or *stabbing.*

b a - h n a′ - y a ŋ, *v. a.* (ba *and* hnayaŋ) *to miss* in attempting to strike *with a knife*—bawahnayaŋ. *T.*, wagnayaŋ.

b a - h o ŋ′, *v. a.* *to cut across*, in one's flesh, or in meat of any kind; *to gash* or *cut* the flesh, as the Dakotas are accustomed to do for the dead—bawahoŋ, bayahoŋ, bauŋhoŋpi; baiçihoŋ, *to cut* or *gash one's self*—bamiçihoŋ.

b a - h o ŋ′ - h o ŋ, *v. a.* *red.* of bahoŋ; *to cut many gashes*—bawahoŋhoŋ.

b a - h u ŋ′, *v. a.* Same as bahoŋ.

b a - h u′ - t e, *v. a.* (ba *and* hute) *to cut off by the roots; to wear to a stump*, as an old knife—bawahute.

b a - h u′ - t e - d a ŋ, *v. a.* *dim.* of bahute; *to wear out*, as a knife—bawahutedaŋ.

b a - h u′ - t e - d a ŋ, *part.* *worn out*, as an old knife.

b a - ḣ a ŋ′ - h i, *v.* See baḣaŋhiya.

b a - ḣ a ŋ′ - h i - y a, *adv.* *slowly cutting:* baḣaŋhiya se ećoŋ wo, bayaḣdeće kta, *cut slowly, or you will tear it.*

b a - ḣ ć i′, *v. a.* (ba *and* ḣći) *to cut* or *break out notches by cutting*—bawaḣći.

b a - ḣ ć i′ - ḣ ć i, *v.* *red.* of baḣći; *to break out notches in* a knife *by cutting*—bawaḣćiḣći.

b a - ḣ d a′, *v. a.* (ba *and* ḣda) *to make rattle with a knife*—bawaḣda.

b a - ḣ d a′ - ġ a ŋ, *v. a.* (ba *and* ḣdaġaŋ) *to enlarge*, as a hole, *by cutting around*—bawaḣdaġaŋ. *T.*, owaḣlaġaŋ.

b a - ḣ d a′ - ḣ d a, *v. a.* (ba *and* ḣdaḣda) *to make rattle by cutting*—bawaḣdaḣda.

b a - ḣ d a′ - y a, *v. a.* *to pare off;* ha baḣdaya, *to peel, i. q.* basku—bawaḣdaya. *T.*, waḣlaya.

b a - ḣ d a′ - y e - d a ŋ, *v.* *dim.* of baḣdaya. *T.*, waḣlayela.

b a - ḣ d e′ - ć a, *v. a.* *to cut* or *break in pieces with a knife; to tear* or *rend in cutting*—bawaḣdeća. *T.*, waḣleća.

b a - ḣ d e′ - ḣ d e - ć a, *v. red.* of baḣdeća.

b a - ḣ d e n′, *cont.* of baḣdeća: baḣden iyeya. *T.*, waḣlel.

b a - ḣ d o g′, *cont.* of baḣdoka: baḣdog iyeya.

b a - ḣ d o′ - k a, *v. a.* (ba *and* ḣdoka) *to cut a hole in* anything *with a knife*—bawaḣdoka.

b a - ḣ d o′ - ḣ d o - k a, *v. red.* of baḣdoka.

b a - ḣ p a′, *v. a.* *to cut off* anything *and let it fall*—bawaḣpa.

b a - ḣ p u', *v. a.* *to cut off in small pieces*—bawaḣpu.

b a - ḣ p u' - ḣ p u, *v.* *red.* of baḣpu.

b a - ḣ u', *v. a.* *to cut the hull* or *rind off, to peel,* as an orange, *with a knife*—bawaḣu, bayaḣu.

b a - ḣ u' - ḣ u, *v.* *red.* of baḣu.

b a - i' - ç i - h o ŋ, *v.* *reflex.* of bahoŋ; *to cut* or *gash one's self*—bamiçihoŋ.

b a - k a', *v. a.* *to cut* or *strip,* as the feather from a quill; *to cut off,* as the ribs of an animal; *to split a quill in the middle*—bawaka. *T.*, waka.

b a - k a' - h a ŋ, *part.* *split,* as the feather end of a quill.

b a - k a ŋ', *v.* *T.* (ba *and* tokaŋ) *to saw* or *cut crookedly; to saw to one side of the mark.*

b a - k a ŋ' - y a ŋ, *adv.* *sawed crookedly.*

b a - k a' - t i ŋ, *v. a.* (ba *and* katiŋ) *to straighten with a knife, cut straight*—bawakatiŋ. *T.*, wakatiŋ.

b a - k ć a', *v. a.* *to cut straight; to remove tangles with a knife*—bawakća. *T.*, wakća.

b a - k e s', *cont.* of bakeza.

b a - k e s' - k e - z a, *v.* *red.* of bakeza.

b a - k e s' - y a, *part.* *scraping, striking* and *grating,* as a knife that strikes the bone.

b a - k e' - z a, *v.* *to strike* a bone, *cut* or *grate on* a bone, as in cutting meat—bawakeza. *T.*, wakeza.

b a - k i' - ć i - ġ o, *v.* of baġo; *to cut* or *carve for* one—bawećiġo, bauŋkićiġopi, bamićiġo, baćićiġo.

b a - k i' - ć i - h o ŋ, *v.* of bahoŋ; *to cut* or *gash for* one—bawećihoŋ.

b a - k i' - ć i - h o ŋ - h o ŋ, *v.* *red.* of bakićihoŋ.

b a - k i' - ć i - ḣ u, *v.* of baḣu; *to cut the rind* or *hull off for* another—bawećiḣu.

b a k i' ć i - k p a ŋ, *v.* of bakpaŋ; *to cut up fine,* as tobacco, *for* one—bawećikpaŋ.

b a - k i' - ć i - k s a, *v.* of baksa; *to cut off for* one—bawećiksa, bayećiksa, bauŋkićiksapi, bamićiksa, banićiksa, baćićiksa.

b a - k i' - ć i - k s a - k s a, *v.* *red.* of bakićiksa.

b a - k i' - ć i - m d a - z a, *v.* of bamdaza; *to cut open* or *cut lengthwise for* one—bawećimdaza. *T.*, wakićiblaza.

b a - k i' - ć i - p t a, *v.* of bapta; *to cut off* or *trim for* one—bawećipta.

b a - k i' - ć i - s d e - ć a, *v. a.* of basdeća; *to split with a knife* or *rip with a saw for* one—bawećisdeća. *T.*, wakićisleća.

b a - k i' - ć i - s k u, *v.* of basku; *to peel* or *pare for* one—bawećisku.

b a - k i' - ć i - ś d a, *v.* of baśda; *to cut* or *shave off with a knife for* one—bawećiśda.

b a - k i' - ć i - ś d o - k a, *v.* of baśdoka; *to cut out, cut a hole for* one; *to take out a piece for*—bawećiśdoka.

b a - k i' - ć i - ś p a, *v.* of baśpa; *to cut off a piece for* one—bawećiśpa.

ba-ki′-ći-śpu, *v.* of baśpu; *to cut off* something that was *stuck on, for* another—bawećiśpu.

ba-ki′-ġo, *v. pos.* of baġo; *to cut* or *carve one's own, engrave*—bawakiġo.

ba-ki′-hoŋ, *v. pos.* of bahoŋ; *to cut* or *gash one's own*—bawakihoŋ.

ba-ki′-hoŋ-hoŋ, *v. red.* of bakihoŋ.

ba-ki′-ksa, *v. pos.* of baksa; *to cut off one's own with a knife* or *saw*—bawakiksa and baweksa.

ba-ki′-ksa-ksa, *v. red.* of bakiksa.

ba-ki′-mde-ća, *v. pos.* of bamdeća; *to break one's own*, by attempting to cut, *with a knife*—bawakimdeća. *T.*, wakibleća.

ba-kiŋs′, *cont.* of bakiŋza: bakiŋs iyeya.

ba-kiŋs′-kiŋ-za, *v. red.* of bakiŋza.

ba-kiŋ′-za, *v. a.* (ba *and* kiŋza) *to make a scraping, squeaking noise, with a knife* or *saw*—bawakiŋza.

ba-ki′-pta, *v. pos.* of bapta; *to pare, cut off*, or *trim one's own*—bawakipta.

ba-ki′-pu-ski-ća, *v.* (ba *and* kipuskića) *to clap together* and *make fit* or *adhere by shaving*—bawakipuskića.

ba-ki′-pu-skin, *cont.* of bakipuskića: bakipuskin iyeya.

ba-ki′-sde-ća, *v. pos.* of basdeća; *to split* or *rip*, as a board or stick, *with a knife* or *saw*—bawakisdeća. *T.*, wakisleća.

ba-ki′-sde-sde-ća, *v. red.* of bakisdeća.

ba-ki′-sku, *v. pos.* of basku; *to pare one's own*, as an apple or potato—bawakisku.

ba-ki′-śda, *v. pos.* of baśda; *to cut off* and *make bare*, as in cutting *one's own* grass, *with a knife*—bawakiśda.

ba-ki′-śda-śda, *v. red.* of bakiśda.

ba-ki′-śki-ta, *v. pos.* of baśkita; *to cut across on one's own*—bawakiśkita.

ba-ki′-śpa, *v. pos.* of baśpa; *to cut off a piece from one's own*—bawakiśpa.

ba-ki′-śpa-śpa, *v. red.* of bakiśpa.

ba-ki′-śpu, *v. pos.* of baśpu; *to cut up one's own in pieces*—bawakiśpu.

ba-ki′-śpu-śpu, *v. red.* of bakiśpu.

ba-koŋ′-ta, *v. a.* (ba *and* koŋta) *to dig out with a knife, to hollow* or *groove*—bawakoŋta.

ba-koŋ′-tkoŋ-ta, *v. red.* of bakoŋta; *to make in grooves* or *ridges*—bawakoŋtkoŋta: ćaŋ bakoŋtkoŋta, *a wash-board.*

ba-kpa′, *v. a. to cut off, cut from; to cut out* or *cut into*—bawakpa: iśta bakpa, *to cut out the eye, make blind.* *T.*, wakpa.

ba-kpaŋ′, *v. a.* (ba *and* kpaŋ) *to cut up fine with a knife*, as tobacco—bawakpaŋ, bayakpaŋ, bauŋkpaŋpi.

b a - k p a ŋ' - k p a ŋ , *v. red.* of ba-kpaŋ.

b a - k p i', *v. a. to cut open*, as a nut, *with a knife; to crack with a knife*, as a louse—bawakpi.

b a - k p i' - k p i , *v. red.* of bakpi.

b a - k s a', *v. a.* (ba *and* ksa) *to cut off*, as a stick, *with a knife* or *saw; to separate* anything *by cutting cross-wise* bawaksa, bayaksa, bauŋksapi. *T.*, waksa.

b a - k s a' - k s a , *v. red.* of baksa; *to cut off in several places, cut in pieces, with a knife* or *saw*—bawaksaksa. *T.*, waksaksa.

b a - k ś i ś', *cont.* of bakśiźa: bakśiś iyeya.

b a - k ś i' - ź a , *v. a.* (ba *and* kśiźa) *to shut up*, as a knife-blade, *when in the act of cutting*—bawakśiźa.

b a - k t a ŋ', *v. a.* (ba *and* ktaŋ) *to make crooked by shaving*—bawaktaŋ.

b a - k t a ŋ' - k t a ŋ , *v. red.* of ba-ktaŋ.

b a - k u ŋ' - t a , *v. a.* Same as ba-koŋta.

b a - ķ e s' - y a , *part. cutting off:* baķesya aya, *to strip off clean*, as meat from bones—baķesya amda.

b a - ķ e' - z a , *v.* (ba *and* ķeza) *to smooth over by shaving*—bawaķeza.

b a - m d a', *v. a. to cut in slices*, as bread—bawamda, bayamda, bauŋmdapi. *T.*, wabla.

b a - m d a' - m d a , *v. red.* of bamda.

b a - m d a' - m d a - z a , *v. red* of ba-mdaza.

b a - m d a s', *cont.* of bamdaza: ba-mdas iyeya, *to rip open*—bamdas iyewaya.

b a - m d a' - s k a , *v. a.* (ba *and* mda-ska) *to make dull* or *flat on the edge*, as a knife, *by shaving*—bawa-mdaska.

b a - m d a s' - m d a - z a , *v. red.* of bamdaza.

b a - m d a' - y a , *v. a.* (ba *and* mdaya) *to make flat with a knife, to shave off lumps*, etc.—bawamdaya.

b a - m d a' - z a , *v. a.* (ba *and* mdaza) *to rip open, cut open lengthwise*, as in butchering an animal—bawa-mdaza.

b a - m d e' - ć a , *v. a. to break*, as brittle ware, *with a knife*—bawa-mdeća.

b a - m d e' - m d e - ć a , *v. red.* of bamdeća.

b a - m d e n', *cont.* of bamdeća: ba-mden iyeya. *T.*, wablel.

b a - m n a', *v. a to rip*, as a seam, *with a knife*—bawamna, bauŋmnapi.

b a - m n a' - m n a , *v. red.* of bamna.

b a - n i', *v. a. to shake in cutting*, as jelly; *to cut off*, as the fastenings of a skin stretched up; *to rip*—ba-wani. *T.*, wani.

b a - n i' - n i , *v. red.* of bani.

b a - o' - p o , *v. a. to push in with a knife, make a hole in*—bawaopo.

b a - o' - z e - z e , *v. a. to cut nearly off with a knife* and let swing—bawaozeze.

b a - o' - z e - z e - y a , *v. a. to cause to cut in strips* or *dangles*—baoze-zewaya.

b a - p a'- k o, *v. a.* (ba *and* pako) *to cut* or *saw crooked*—bawapako.

b a - p e', *v. a.* (ba *and* pe) *to sharpen with a knife*—bawape.

b a - p e'- m n i, *v. a.* (ba *and* pemni) *to make crooked* or *twisted by shaving*—bawapemni. *T.*, wapemni.

b a - p e'- m n i - y a ŋ, *part. shaved twisting.*

b a - p e'- s t o, *v. a.* (ba *and* pesto) *to shave to a point*—bawapesto.

b a - p o n', *cont.* of bapota; bapon iyeya, *to rip up* or *destroy with a knife.*

b a - p o'- t a, *v. a. to destroy by cutting; to cut to pieces,* as in cutting up a tent—bawapota, bauŋpotapi.

b a - p o'- t p o - t a, *v. red.* of bapota. *T.*, wapolpota.

b a - p s a g', *cont.* of bapsaka; bapsag iyeya, *to cut off suddenly with a knife,* as a string.

b a - p s a'- k a, *v. a. to cut off,* as a string or cord, *with a knife*—bawapsaka, bauŋpsakapi.

b a - p s a'- p s a - k a, *v. red.* of bapsaka.

b a - p ś u ŋ', *v. a.* (ba *and* pśuŋ) *to cut round a joint, to joint with a knife*—bawapśuŋ.

b a - p ś u ŋ'- p ś u ŋ, *v. red.* of bapśuŋ.

b a - p t a', *v. a. to cut off a piece, trim off the edge of* anything; *to cut out,* as a garment; *to cut through*—bawapta, bauŋptapi: baptapi se, *as it were cut off* or *trimmed;* bapta iyeya, *to trim off with a stroke. T.*, wapta.

b a - p t a'- p t a, *v. red.* of bapta.

b a - p t e'- ć e - d a ŋ, *v. a.* (ba *and* ptećedaŋ) *to cut short, cut too short*—bawaptećedaŋ. *T.*, waptećela.

b a - p t e m', *n. baptism.* This form was introduced from the French.

b a - p t e m'- ķ u, *v. a. to give baptism, baptize*—baptem waķu: baptem ćiçu, *I baptize you.*

b a - p t i'- s m a, *n. baptism.* This form is used by the Episcopal mission, and is the preferable form. It is now proposed to use the verb ećoŋ instead of ķu: baptisma ećaćićoŋ, *I do for you baptism,* or *I do to you baptism.* Also written baptizma.

b a - p t i'- z o, *v. to baptize,* introduced from the Greek. According to analogy, the pronoun should be inserted after the ba; but the Messrs. Pond in using it have prefixed the pronouns.

b a - p t u'- p t u - ź a, *v. red.* of baptuźa.

b a - p t u ś', *cont.* of baptuźa: baptuś iyeya, *to cause to crack suddenly with a knife*—baptuś iyewaya.

b a - p t u'- ź a, *v. a. to crack* or *partly split with a knife*—bawaptuźa.

b a - s d e'- ć a, *v. a. to saw, to slit* or *rip up,* by sawing—bawasdeća, bauŋsdećapi. *T.*, wasleća.

b a - s d e n', *cont.* of basdeća; basden iyeya, *to split with a knife* or *saw.*

b a - s d e'- s d e - ć a, *v. red.* of basdeća; *to saw up*, as a log, *into boards*—bawasdesdeća, bauŋsdesdećapi. *T.*, waslesleća.

ba-sde′-sden, *cont.* of basdesdeća.

ba-sdi′, *v. a.* *to press out with a knife* or *by cutting*—bawasdi.

ba-sdi′-sdi, *v.* *red.* of basdi.

ba-sdi′-tka, *v. a.* *to cut to a point, make taper*—bawasditka.

ba-ski′-ća, *v. a.* *to press out with a knife*—bawaskića. *T.*, waskića.

ba-skin′, *cont.* of baskića *and* baskita. *T.*, waskil.

ba-ski′-ta, *v. a.* *to press upon with a knife*—bawaskita.

ba-sku′, *v. a.* *to pare* or *shave off*, as the skin of a potato or apple, and as flesh from a hide—bawasku, bauŋskupi. *T.*, wasku.

ba-sku′-sku, *v.* *red.* of basku.

ba-sma′-ka, *v. a.* (ba *and* smaka) *to indent* or *make a hollow place by cutting with a knife*—bawasmaka.

ba-smiŋ′, *v. a.* *to cut* or *shave off clean*, as meat from a bone—bawasmiŋ, bauŋsmiŋpi.

ba-smiŋ′-na, *v.* *dim.* of basmiŋ.

ba-smiŋ′-smiŋ, *v.* *red.* of basmiŋ; *to pare* the meat *off clean and smooth* from the bones—bawasmiŋsmiŋ.

ba-smiŋ′-yaŋ, *part.* *cutting off smoothly.*

ba-so′, *v. a.* *to cut* or *pare around the edge; to cut off a string*—bawaso. *T.*, waso.

ba-so′-so, *v.* *red. to cut into strings.* *T.*, wasoso.

ba-śda′, *v. a.* (ba *and* śda) *to make bare by cutting with a knife; to shave* or *scrape off*, as the hair from a hide—bawaśda, bauŋśdapi.

ba-śda′-śda, *v.* *red.* of baśda.

ba-śdog′, *cont.* of baśdoka; baśdog iyeya.

ba-śdo′-ka, *v. a.* (ba *and* śdoka) *to cut a hole in, to cut out a piece, cut out*, as an eye; *to cut loose* something that is fast in, etc.—bawaśdoka.

ba-śdo′-śdo-ka, *v.* *red.* of baśdoka.

ba-śi′-ća, *v. a.* (ba *and* śića) *to spoil by cutting*—bawaśića.

ba-śi′-ća-ho-wa-ya, *v. a.* (ba *and* śićahowaya) *to cause to cry out by cutting*—bawaśićahowaya.

ba-śi′-ḣtiŋ, *v. a.* (ba *and* śiḣtiŋ) *to enfeeble by cutting*—bawaśiḣtiŋ. *T.*, waśiḣtiŋ, *to do poorly* with knife or saw.

ba-śi′-kśi-ća, *v.* *red.* of baśića.

ba-śim′, *cont.* of baśipa; baśim iyeya. *T.*, waśib.

ba-śim′-śi-pa, *v.* *red.* of baśipa.

ba-śi′-pa, *v. a.* *to cut off*, as a branch from a tree, *to prune; to cut off*, as a pin, *with a knife*—bawaśipa. *T.*, waśipa.

ba-śki′-ća, *v. a.* *to squeeze by cutting; to press out*, as water from a cloth, *with a knife; to scrape out*—bawaśkića.

ba-śkin′, *cont.* of baśkića *and* baśkita; baśkin iyeya. *T.*, waśkil.

ba-śki′-śki-ća, *v.* *red.* of baśkića.

b a - ś k i′ - ś k i - t a, *v. red.* of baśkita; *to cut much, gash*—bawaśkiśkita.

b a - ś k i′ - t a, *v. a. to cut across, gash; i. q.* bahoŋ—bawaśkita,

b a - ś k u′, *v. a. to cut off,* as corn from the cob—bawaśku, bauŋśkupi: wabaśku ohe, *to boil* corn *that is cut off*

b a - ś k u′ - ś k u, *v. red.* of baśku.

b a - ś p a′, *v. a.* (ba *and* śpa) *to cut off a piece, cut up*—bawaśpa, bauŋśpapi: baśpa iyeya.

b a - ś p a′ - ś p a, *v. red.* of baśpa; *to cut into many pieces,* as meat—bawaśpaśpa.

b a - ś p i′, *v. a. to cut off,* as fruit from a tree—bawaśpi.

b a - ś p i′ - ś p i, *v. red.* of baśpi.

b a - ś p u′, *v. a. to cut up, cut into pieces; to rip,* as a seam, *to rip up, cut,* as in ripping—bawaśpu.

b a - ś p u′ - ś p u, *v. red.* of baśpu; *to cut up into pieces*—bawaśpuśpu.

b a - t a′ - k u - n i - ś n i, *v. a.* (ba *and* takuniśni) *to cut to pieces, destroy by cutting*—bawatakuniśni.

b a - t a ŋ′ - k a, *v. a.* (ba *and* taŋka) *to cut large*—bawataŋka.

b a - t a ŋ′ - k a - y a, *adv. cut large.*

b a - t e m′, *cont.* of betepa; batem iyeya. *T.*, wateb.

b a - t e m′ - y a, *adv. cut short.*

b a - t e′ - p a, *v. a. to shorten by cutting off* at the end *with a knife, to cut short*—bawatepa. *T.*, watepa.

b a - t k o ŋ′ - t a, *v.* See bakoŋta, which is the proper form.

b a - t p a′, *v. a.* Same as bakpa.

b a - t p a ŋ′, *v. a.* Same as bakpaŋ.

b a - t p a ŋ′ - t p a ŋ, *v. red.* of batpaŋ.

b a - t p i′, *v.* Same as bakpi.

b a - t p u′, *v. a. to cut a very little off, cut fine*—bawatpu.

b a - t p u′ - t p u, *v. red.* of batpu; *to cut up fine*—bawatputpu.

b a - t u′ - k a, *v. a. to cut off,* as fur or hair; *to destroy,* as furs, *by cutting*—bawatuka. *T.*, watuka.

b a - t u′ - k a - k a, *v. red.* of batuka.

b a - t u′ - t k a, *v. a.* (ba *and* tutka) *to cut up into crumbs*—bawatutka. *T.*, watutka, *to cut into bits* or *scraps, to whittle.*

b a - ṭ a′, *v. a.* (ba *and* ṭa) *to kill with a knife*—bawaṭa.

b a - w i′ - ć i - ś n i - y a ŋ, *v.* bawićiśniyaŋ iyeya, *to run* the knife *out of the right course in cutting.*

b a - z a′. See yubaza.

b a - z a m′, *cont.* of bazapa; bazam iyeya. *T.*, wazab.

b a - z a m′ - z a - p a, *v. red.* of bazapa.

b a - z a′ - p a, *v. a. to skin, cut off; to cut,* as meat for drying—bawazapa.

b a - z a′ - z a, *v. to cut into fringe.*

b a - z a′ - z a, *adv. in dangles; i. q.* kasbupi.

b a - ź a g′ - ź a - t a, *v. red.* of baźata.

b a - ź a n′, *cont.* of baźata. *T.*, waźal.

b a - ź a n′ - y a, *v. a. to cause to cut forked, make forked*—baźanwaya.

b a - ź a n′ - ź a - t a, *v. red.* of baźata. *T.*, waźalźata.

ba-źa′-ta, *v. a.* (ba *and* źata) *to cut into a fork, make forked*—bawaźata.

ba-źu′-źu, *v. a.* (ba *and* źuźu) *to cut to pieces, cut up*, as an animal—bawaźuźu.

bdo, *n.* *potatoes;* more commonly written mdo.

bdo-ke′-tu, *n.* *summer.* See mdoketu, which is the more common pronunciation.

bdo′-ki-ṭa, *v. n.* *to be tired; i. q.* mdokiṭa.

be, *v. n.* *to hatch*, as fowls. Same as maŋ.

beś, *intj.* signifying *strong affirmation*, and *surprise* that it should be doubted. John vi, 42.

Be-śde′-ke, *n. p.* *the Fox Indians.*

be-yaŋ′-ke-ća, *v. n.* (be *and* yaŋkeća) *to remain at home and keep house*, as an old man does—bemaŋkeća, benaŋkeća.

bla-bla′-ta, *n.* *T.* *rolling prairie, hills and levels; i. q.* mdamdata.

bla′-ska, *adj.* *T.* Same as mdaska.

bla′-ye, *adj.* *T.* *level; i. q.* mdaya.

ble, *n.* *T.* *a lake.* Same as mde.

blo, *n.* *T.* Same as mdo.

blo-a′-li-ya, *adv.* *T.* *along the ridge.*

blo-taŋ′-huŋ-ka, *n.* *T.* *the leader of a war party.*

blo-waŋ′-źi-la, *n.* *T.* *a divide, a single upland plain* between streams.

bo, a prefix to verbs, signifying that the action is done by *shooting*, *punching*, *pounding* with the end of a stick, or by *blowing*. It is also used when the action of rain is expressed. The pronoun's place is after the prefix. In the Titoŋwaŋ dialect this prefix is uniformly wo.

bo-a′-kan-hi-yu-ya, *v. a.* *to cause to rise to the top*, as scum or froth, *by shooting in*, as in water—boakanhiyuwaya. *T.*, woakaŋlhiyuya.

bo-a′-śda-ya, *v. a.* (bo *and* aśdaya) *to make bare, lay open* or *expose by shooting in:* boaśdaya iyeya.

bo-ćaŋ′-ćaŋ, *v. a.* (bo *and* ćaŋćaŋ) *to make tremble by shooting*—bowaćaŋćaŋ.

bo-ćeg′, *cont.* of boćeka; boćeg iyeya.

bo-ćeg′-ya, *adv.* *staggeringly.*

bo-će′-ka, *v. a.* *to make stagger by shooting* or *punching*—bowaćeka.

bo-će′-kće-ka, *v.* *red.* of boćeka.

bo-ćo′-ka, *v. a.* (bo *and* ćoka) *to empty by shooting in* anything, *to make a great hole in*—bowaćoka.

bo-ćo′-ka-ka, *v.* *red.* of boćoka.

bo-ćo′-za, *v. a.* (bo *and* ćoza) *to make warm by punching.*

bo-ç̔o′, *v. a.* *to churn*—bowaç̔o, bouŋç̔opi.

bo-ç̔o′-ç̔o, *v.* *red.* of boç̔o.

bo-ġa′, *adv.* *spreading out, spraddling:* boġa se naźiŋpi.

bo-ġa′-ġa, *v. n.* *to shoot out in*

different directions, as rays of light or the branches of a tree. *T.*, yuġaġa.

b o - ġ a′ - ġ a - y a, *adv.* *spraddled*, as a tree-top when cut down; *shooting out from a center.*

b o - ġ a′ - y a, *adv.* *shooting out from a point.* *T*, yuġaya.

b o - h a′, *v.* boha iyeya, *to shoot* or *punch over.*

b o - h a′ - h a - y e - d a ŋ, *v.* *to make totter by shooting* or *punching.*

b o - h b a′, *v. a.* *to shell off by shooting* or *punching*—bowahba.

b o - h d a′, *v. a.* *to uncoil* or *make roll out*, as in blowing entrails—bowahda. *T.*, wogla.

b o - h d a′ - k i ŋ - y a ŋ (bo *and* hdakiŋyaŋ) bohdakiŋyaŋ iyeya, *to cause to glance*, as a bullet. *T.*, woglakiŋyaŋ.

b o - h i n′, *cont.* of bohiŋta; bohin iyeya, *to sweep all off*, as men in a battle-field; *to blow away.*

b o - h i ŋ′ - g l a, *v. n.* *T.* *to rush, to break and run*—bomahiŋgla, etc.

b o - h i ŋ′ - ḣ p a - y a, *v. a.* *to make fall by shooting* or *punching.* *T.*, wohiŋḣpaya.

b o - h i ŋ′ - t a, *v. a.* *to sweep off by shooting*, as men in a battle-field; *to blow away*—bowahiŋta.

b o - h n a′, *v. a.* *to shoot off*, as fruit from a tree—bowahna. *T.*, wogna.

b o - h n a′ - ś k i ŋ - y a ŋ, *v. a.* (bo *and* hnaśkiŋyaŋ) *to make crazy* or *furious*, as an animal, *by shooting* it—bowahnaśkiŋyaŋ. *T.*, wognaśkiŋyaŋ.

b o - h n a′ - y a ŋ, (bo *and* hnayaŋ) *to miss in shooting* or *striking with the end of a stick*—bowahnayaŋ. *T.*, wognayaŋ, *to shoot to one side of.*

b o - h o′ - h o, *v. a.* *to shake* or *loosen by shooting*—bowahoho.

b o - h o′ - t a, *adj.* *short and thick, chubby; i. q.* taku ptećedaŋ taŋka: bohota se.

b o - h o′ - t a ŋ - i ŋ, *v. a.* (bo *and* hotaŋiŋ) *to make cry out by punching*—bowahotaŋiŋ.

b o - h o′ - t o ŋ, *v. a.* (bo *and* hotoŋ) *to make bawl by shooting* or *punching*—bowahotoŋ.

b o - h u′ - h u s, *cont.* of bohuhuza; bohuhus iyeya. *T.*, wohuŋhuŋs.

b o - h u′ - h u s - y a, *part.* *shaken by shooting* or *punching*,

b o - h u′ - h u - z a, *v. a.* (bo *and* huhuza) *to shake*, as a tree, *by shooting* it—bowahuhuza. *T.*, wohuŋhuŋza.

b o - h u ŋ′ - k a, *v. a.* *T.* *to make fall*, as an animal when shot—bowahuŋka. Perhaps the *T.* is wohuŋka.

b o - ḣ a′, *v. a.* *to strike and cut* or *scrape along*, as a flint on a pan that is too soft; *to miss fire*—bowaḣa; boḣa iyewaya.

b o - ḣ a ŋ′ - h i - y a, *part.* boḣaŋhiya iyeya, *to let off a gun when it hangs fire* or "*makes long fire.*"

b o - ḣ ć i′, *v. a.* *to break out a piece by punching*, as from the edge of a chisel—bowaḣći.

b o - ḣ ć i′ - ḣ ć i, *v.* *red.* of boḣći.

b o - ḣ ć i′ - ḣ ć i, *n.* *a string of beads.*

bo-ḣći'-ḣći-ya, *adv.* *in dangles. dangling:* boḣćiḣćiya hiyeya.

bo-ḣći'-ya, *adv.* *in dangles, dangling:* hiyete boḣćiya, *an epaulet.*

bo-ḣda', *v. a.* *to make rattle by shooting*—bowaḣda.

bo-ḣda'-ġaŋ, *v. a.* (bo *and* ḣdaġaŋ) *to enlarge by shooting*—bowaḣdaġaŋ.

bo-ḣda'-ḣda, *v.* *red.* of boḣda.

bo-ḣda'-ya, *v. a.* *to peel off by shooting,* as the bark of a tree—bowaḣdaya.

bo-ḣde'-ća, *v. a.* *to break in,* as one's skull, *by shooting* or *punching*—bowaḣdeća. *T.*, woḣleća, *to tear through by shooting,* as cloth or skin.

bo-ḣde'-ḣde-ća, *v.* *red.* of boḣdeća.

bo-ḣden', *cont.* of boḣdeća; boḣden iyeya. *T.*, woḣlel.

bo-ḣdog', *cont.* of boḣdoka: boḣdog iyeya.

bo-ḣdo'-ḣdo-ka, *v.* *red.* of boḣdoka

bo-ḣdo'-ka, *v. a.* (bo *and* ḣdoka) *to shoot* or *punch a hole in*—bowaḣdoka. Maḣpiya-boḣdoka, *Hole-in-the-day,* a celebrated Ojibwa chief.

bo-ḣmiŋ', *v. a.* (bo *and* ḣmiŋ) *to make* a gun *crooked by shooting*—bowaḣmiŋ.

bo-ḣmiŋ'-yaŋ, *part.* *crooked by shooting.*

bo-ḣpa', *v. a.* *to make fall by shooting, to shoot down,* as birds on the wing—bowaḣpa.

bo-ḣpa'-ḣpa, *v.* *red.* of boḣpa.

bo-ḣtag', *v. a.* *cont.* of boḣtaka.

bo-ḣta'-ka, *v. a.* (bo *and* ḣtaka) *to pound, punch,* or *knock with the end* of anything—bowaḣtaka.

bo-ḣu', *v. a.* *to peel off,* as bark, *by shooting.* *T.*, woḣu, *to strike and scrape along.*

bo-ḣu'-ġa, *v. a.* *to break in* or *break open by shooting* or *punching*—bowaḣuġa.

bo-ḣuḣ', *cont.* of boḣuġa; boḣuḣ iyeya.

bo-ḣu'-ḣu-ġa, *v.* *red.* of boḣuġa.

bo-i'-de, *v. a.* (bo *and* ide) *to blow and make blaze,* as a fire—bowaide: boide iyewaya.

bo-i'-de-ya, *v. a.* *to cause to make blaze by blowing*—boidewaya.

bo-i'-pa-tku-ġa, *v. a.* *to make get into a line* or *row by shooting amongst*—boipatkuḣ iyewaya. *T.*, woipatkuġa, *to shoot and make get out from others.*

bo-i'-tkoŋ, *v. a.* (bo *and* itkoŋ) *to kindle* or *make burn by blowing*—bowaitkoŋ, boiuŋtkoŋpi.

bo-i'-tpi-ska, *v.* boitpiska eḣpeya, *to shoot* or *punch and knock over on its back.*

bo-i'-yo-was, *cont.* of boiyowaza; boiyowas iyeya, *to make an echo by shooting.*

bo-i'-yo-wa-za, *v. a.* *to make an echo by shooting*—bowaiyowaza.

bo-kaŋ', *v. a.* *to punch* or *shoot off*—bowakaŋ.

bo-ka'-tiŋ, *v. a.* (bo *and* katiŋ)

to make stretch or *straighten out by punching*—bowakatiŋ.

b o - k i'- ć i - ç o, *v.* of boço; *to churn for* one—bowećiço, bouŋkićiçopi, boćićiço, bomićiço.

b o - k i'- ć i - ḣ d o - k a, *v.* of boḣdoka; *to shoot* or *punch a hole for* another.

b o - k i'- ć i - ḣ p a, *v.* of boḣpa; *to shoot down* something *on the wing*, or *that is hanging up, for* another—bowećiḣpa.

b o - k i'- ć i - k p a ŋ, *v.* of bokpaŋ; *to pound for* one—bowećikpaŋ.

b o - k i'- ć i - k s a, *v.* of boksa; *to shoot* or *punch off*, as a limb or an arm, *for* one—bowećiksa, boyećiksa, bouŋkićiksapi.

b o - k i'- ć i - k s a - k s a, *v.* *red.* of bokićiksa.

b o - k i'- ć i - m d e - ć a, *v. a.* of bomdeća; *to break for* another *by shooting* or *punching*—bowećimdeća.

b o - k i'- ć i - p t a, *v.* of bopta; *to dig* or *pry up for* one, as in digging a turnip—bowećipta.

b o - k i'- ć i - s n i, *v.* of bosni; *to blow out*, as a candle, *for* one; *to blow and cool for* another, as hot food—bowećisni.

b o - k i'- ć i - s o - t a, *v.* of bosota; *to kill all off for* one *by shooting* as cattle—bowećisota.

b o - k i'- ć i - ś d o - k a, *v.* of bośdoka; *to shoot off a gun for* one—bowećiśdoka, bomićiśdoka.

b o - k i'- ć i - ś n a, *v.* of bośna; *to miss in shooting for* one—boweciśna.

b o - k i'- ć i - ś p a, *v.* of bośpa; *to shoot off a piece for* one; *to shoot for* one *and relieve from danger*, as from a wild animal: wićaśta waŋ waḣaŋksića bowećiśpa, *I delivered a man from a bear by shooting it*—bowećiśpa.

b o - k i'- ć i - w e - ġ a, *v.* of boweġa; *to break*, but not entirely off, *for* one, *by shooting* or *punching*—bowećiweġa.

b o - k i'- k s a, *v.* *pos.* of boksa; *to break in two one's own by shooting* or *punching*—bowakiksa.

b o - k i'- k s a - k s a, *v.* *red.* of bokiksa.

b o - k i'- k t a ŋ, *v.* *pos.* of boktaŋ; *to crook one's own by shooting*, as one's arrow—bowakiktaŋ.

b o - k i'- m d e - ć a, *v.* *pos.* of bomdeća; *to break one's own by pounding* or *shooting*—bowakimdeća. *T.*, wokibleća.

b o - k i'- m d e - m d e - ć a, *v.* *red.* of bokimdeća

b o - k i'- m d e n, *cont.* of bokimdeća; bokimden iyeya. *T.*, wokiblel.

b o - k i'- n u - k a ŋ, *v. a.* (bo *and* kinukaŋ) *to separate by shooting:* bokinukaŋ iyeya.

b o - k i ŋ'- ć a, *v. a.* *to scrape* or *scratch* in shooting. *T.*, wokiŋća; *red.*, wokiŋtkiŋća.

b o - k i'- p o - w a - y a, *v.* *pos.* of bopowaya.

b o - k i'- p u - s k i - ć a, *v. a.* (bo *and*

kipuskića) *to drive up close together, by punching, shooting,* or *raining on*—bowakipuskića.

bo-ki'-pu-skin, *cont.* of bokipuskića: bokipuskin iyeya.

bo'-ki-sa-pa, *v.* (bo *and* kisapa) *to shoot into* snow, *and make the bare ground appear; to rain on,* as on snow, *and make the ground bare.*

bo-ki'-śda, *v. pos.* of bośda; *to injure* or *lay bare by shooting*—bowakiśda.

bo-ki'-śda-ya, *v. a. to make bare* or *expose by shooting*—bowakiśdaya.

bo-ki'-śde-ća, *v. pos.* of bośdeća; *to split off a piece from one's own by shooting* or *punching*—bowakiśdeća.

bo-ki'-śdo-ka, *v. pos.* of bośdoka; *to shoot* or *punch a hole in one's own, shoot off one's own gun; to blow out and make clear,* as a tube—bowakiśdoka.

bo-ki'-śna, *v. pos* of bośna; *to miss in attempting to shoot one's own*—bowakiśna.

bo-ki'-śpa, *v. pos.* of bośpa; *to shoot off a piece from one's own*—bowakiśpa.

bo-ko'-ka, *v. a. to make rattle by shooting* or *punching*—bowakoka.

bo-ko'-ke-daŋ, *v. a.* (bo *and* kokedaŋ) *to make active* or *restless by shooting* or *punching*—bowakokedaŋ. *T.*, wokokela, *to make rattle,* by shooting in.

bo-kpa', *v. a.* (bo *and* kpa) *to shoot out, punch out*—bowakpa: iśta bokpa, *to make blind;* bokpa iyeya.

bo-kpaŋ', *v. pos.* of bopaŋ; *to pound one's own, pound fine,* as in a mortar, *with a pestle; to shoot to pieces*—bowakpaŋ, boyakapaŋ, bouŋkpaŋpi.

bo-kpaŋ'-kpaŋ, *v. red.* of bokpaŋ.

bo-kpi', *v. a. to crack by punching*—bowakpi.

bo-ksa', *v. a.* (bo *and* ksa) *to break off by punching* or *shooting,* as a stick, limb, etc.—bowaksa.

bo-ksa'-ksa, *v. red.* of boksa; *to break off in many places by shooting*—bowaksaksa.

bo-kśe'-ća, *v. a. to shoot and make keel over*—bowakśeća. *T.*, wokśeća, *to shoot and make double up.*

bo-kśen', *cont.* of bokśeća; bokśen iyeya. *T.*, wokśel.

bo-ktaŋ', *v. a.* (bo *and* ktaŋ) *to bend* or *make bend by punching*—bowaktaŋ.

bo-kte', *v. a.* (bo *and* kte) *to kill by punching*—bowakte.

bo-ku'-ka, *v. a.* (bo *and* kuka) *to shoot* or *punch all to pieces.*

bo-ḳe'-ġa, *v. a. to snap,* as a gun; *to miss fire,* as in firing off a gun; *to scrape,* as a gun missing fire—bowaḳeġa.

bo-ḳeh', *cont.* of boḳeġa: boḳeh hiŋhda, *to go off after a long time;* boḳeh iyaya, *to hang fire,* as a gun.

bo-ḳeh'-ya, *part. missing fire,* as a gun.

b o - m d a', *v. a.* *to shoot* or *punch off a piece*—bowamda. *T.*, wobla.

b o - m d a s', *cont.* of bomdaza; bomdas iyeya.

b o - m d a'- s k a, *v. a.* (bo *and* mdaska) *to flatten by punching; to flatten by shooting*, as in shooting a bullet against a stone—bowamdaska: bomdaska iyeya.

b o - m d a'- y a, *v. a.* (bo *and* mdaya) *to spread out by blowing* or *punching*—bowamdaya.

b o - m d a'- z a, *v. a.* *to tear open by shooting*, as the bowels of an animal—bowamdaza.

b o - m d e'- ć a, *v. a.* *to break in pieces by striking with a pestle*, or *by shooting*—bowamdeća. *T.*, wobleća.

b o - m d e'- m d e - ć a, *v.* *red.* of bomdeća.

b o - m d e n', *cont.* of bomdeća; bomden iyeya. *T.*, woblel.

b o - m d u', *v. a.* (bo *and* mdu) *to pound up fine, crush*—bowamdu.

b o - m d u', *v. n.* *to blow in fine particles, drift*, as snow, *to blow about*, as dust; *to boil up*, as water in a spring: bomdu hiyu; bomdu iyeya; wa bomdu, *the snow is blown about.* *T.*, woblu.

b o - m d u'- m d u, *v.* *red.* of bomdu.

b o - m d u'- y a, *part.* *blowing up*, as the wind blows dust or snow.

b o - m n i'- ġ a, *v. a.* *to full up*, as cloth, *by pounding, to cause to full up*—bowamniġa.

b o - m n i ḣ', *cont.* of bomniġa; bomniḣ iyeya.

b o - n a'- s u ŋ - s u ŋ, *v.* *to make struggle by shooting:* bonasuŋsuŋ iyeya.

b o - n i', *v. a.* (bo *and* ni) *to resuscitate by blowing*—bowani; boni iyewaya.

b o - n i'- n i, *v. a.* *to wake up by punching*—bowanini.

b o - n i'- y a, *v. a.* (bo *and* niya) *to resuscitate by blowing*—bowaniya.

b o - o'- ḣ a ŋ - k o, *v. a.* (bo *and* oḣaŋko) *to make lively by punching* or *shooting*—bowaoḣaŋko.

b o - o'- ḣ p a, *v. a.* *to break in*, as the skull, *by shooting* or *punching*—bowaoḣpa.

b o - o'- k s a, *v. n.* *to break off in*, as the bank of a river: booksa iyewaya.

b o - o'- k t a ŋ, *v. a.* *to bend into by punching*—bowaoktaŋ.

b o - o'- k t a ŋ - y a ŋ, *v. n.* *to become crooked*, as an arrow, *by being shot into anything:* booktaŋyaŋ iyeya.

b o - o'- z e - z e, *v. a.* *to shoot almost off and let swing*—bowaozeze.

b o - o'- z e - z e - y a, *adv.* *shot almost off and swinging;* boozezeya eḣpeya, *to make swing by shooting.*

b o - p a', *v. a.* *to pound*, as hominy in a mortar, *with a pestle*—bowapa, boyapa, bouŋpapi.

b o - p a'- k o, *v. a.* (bo *and* pako) *to knock crooked, by shooting* or *punching*—bowapako.

b o - p a ŋ', *v. a.* *to pound fine*, as corn in a mortar—bowapaŋ, bouŋpaŋpi.

b o - p a ŋ′ - p a ŋ , *v.* *red.* of bopaŋ.

b o - p a ŋ′ - p a ŋ - n a , *v. a.* (bo *and* paŋpaŋna) *to pound soft with the end of a stick*—bowapaŋpaŋna.

b o - p e′ - m n i , *v. a* (bo *and* pemni) *to turn aside* or *twist by blowing* or *shooting.*

b o - p e′ - m n i - y a ŋ , *part.* *twisting* or *turning aside by blowing* or *shooting.*

b o - p e′ - s t o , *v.* (bo *and* pesto) *to sharpen by punching.*

b o - p o′ - t a , *v. a.* (bo *and* pota) *to shoot* or *punch to pieces, destroy by shooting*—bowapota.

b o - p o′ - t p o - t a , *v.* *red.* of bopota. *T.*, wopolpota.

b o - p o′ - w a - y a , *v. a.* (bo *and* powaya) *to make soft by blowing up,* as nap or fur, also *by striking with the finger*—bowapowaya.

b o - p s a g′, *cont.* of bopsaka; bopsag iyeya.

b o - p s a′ - k a , *v. a.* (bo *and* psaka) *to break off,* as a cord, *by shooting* or *punching*—bowapsaka, bouŋpsakapi.

b o - p s a′ - p s a - k a , *v.* *red.* of bopsaka.

b o - p t a′, *v. a.* *to punch* or *dig with the end of anything:* tipsiŋna bopta, *to dig turnips*—bowapta, boyapta, bouŋptapi.

b o - p t a ŋ′ - y a ŋ , *v. a.* (bo *and* ptaŋyaŋ) *to make glance off, in shooting; to make turn over by shooting,* as a boat—bowaptaŋyaŋ. *T.*, woptaŋyaŋ.

b o - p t a′ - p t a , *v.* *red.* of bopta.

b o - p t u′ - p t u - ź a , *v.* *red.* of boptuźa.

b o - p t u ś′, *cont.* of boptuźa; boptuś iyeya.

b o - p t u′ - ź a , *v. a.* *to split* or *crack by shooting, pounding* or *punching*—bowaptuźa. *T.*, woptuźa.

b o - p u′ - s k i - ć a , *v. a.* (bo *and* puskića) *to ram in tight*—bowapuskića.

b o - p u′ - s k i n , *cont.* of bopuskića; bopuskin iyeya. *T.*, wopuskil.

b o - s d a n′, *adv.* *cont* of bosdata; *upright, straight up:* bosdan naźiŋ, *to stand erect.* *T.*, woslal.

b o - s d a′ - t a , *adv.* *on end, erect, perpendicularly.*

b o - s d a′ - t u , *n.* *height, perpendicularity.* See obosdatu.

b o - s d a′ - t u , *adv.* *perpendicularly.*

b o - s d a′ - t u - d a ŋ , *adv.* *straight up.* *T.*, woslalhaŋ.

b o s d a′ - t u - d a ŋ - ḣ i ŋ , *adv.* *exactly perpendicular.*

b o - s d a′ - t u - y a , *adv.* *perpendicularly.*

b o - s d e′ - ć a , *v. a.* *to split by shooting* or *punching*—bowasdeća.

b o - s d e n′, *cont.* of bosdeća; bosden iyeya. *T.*, woslel.

b o - s d e′ - s d e - ć a , *v.* *red.* of bosdeća.

b o - s d i′, *v. a.* *to push down in,* as in churning; *to squirt*—bowasdi.

b o - s k a ŋ′, *v. n.* *to cause to melt and flow off,* as rain does snow.

b o - s k i′ - ć a , *v. a.* *to press down tight by pounding*—bowaskića.

b o - s k i n′, *cont.* of boskića; boskin iyeya. *T.*, woskil.

b o - s n a′, *v. a.* (bo *and* sna) *to make ring by shooting;* said also of the noise made by the falling of leaves which have been shot down—bowasna.

b o - s n a′ - s n a, *v. red.* of bosna.

b o - s n i′, *v. a.* (bo *and* sni) *to extinguish, blow out,* as a candle; *to cool by blowing*—bowasni, bouŋsnipi.

b o - s n i′, *v. n. to put out,* as rain does fire on the prairie.

b o - s n i′ - s n i, *v. red.* of bosni.

b o - s o n′, *cont.* of bosota; boson iyeya. *T.*, wosol.

b o - s o n′ - s o - t a, *v. red.* of bosota.

b o - s o′ - t a, *v. a.* (bo *and* sota) *to kill all off, use all up by shooting*—bowasota, boyasota, bouŋsotapi. *T.*, wosota.

b o - s o′ - t s o - t a, *v. red.* of bosota.

b o - s p a′ - y a, *v. n.* (bo *and* spaya) *to wet by raining on.*

b o - s t a ŋ′ - k a, *v.* (bo *and* staŋka) *to moisten by raining on.*

b o - s u′ - k s u - t a, *v. red.* of bosuta.

b o - s u′ - t a, *v.* (bo *and* suta) *to make hard by punching* or *ramming; to make hard by raining on*—bowasuta, bouŋsutapi.

b o - ś a g′, *cont.* of bośaka.

b o - ś a g′ - ś a g - y a, *part. red.* of bośagya.

b o - ś a g′ - ś a - k a, *v. red.* of bośaka.

b o - ś a g′ - y a, *part. shooting with too little force.*

b o - ś a′ - k a, *v. a. to shoot with too little force to penetrate*—bowaśaka.

b o - ś d a′, *v. a.* (bo *and* śda) *to make bare by shooting, shoot off,* as hair, etc.—bowaśda.

b o - ś d a′ - ś d a, *v. red.* of bośda.

b o - ś d e′ - ć a, *v. a. to split off a little piece by shooting* or *punching*—bowaśdeća.

b o - ś d e n′, *cont.* of bośdeća; bośden iyeya. *T.*, woślel.

b o - ś d e′ - ś d e - ć a, *v. red.* of bośdeća.

b o - ś d o g′, *cont.* of bośdoka; bośdog iyeya.

b o - ś d o′ - k a, *v. a. to fire off* a gun, *shoot out* a load; *to blow out, clear out by blowing,* as a tube—bowaśdoka, bouŋśdokapi.

b o - ś d o′ - ś d o - k a, *v. red.* of bośdoka.

b o - ś d u n′, *cont.* of bośduta; bośdun iyeya, *to make glance,* as a bullet. *T.*, woślul.

b o - ś d u′ - t a, *v. n.* (bo *and* śduta) *to glance,* as a bullet.

b o - ś i′ - ć a, *v. a.* (bo *and* śića) *to injure* or *spoil by shooting* or *punching*—bowaśića.

b o - ś i′ - ć a - h o - w a - y a, *v. a.* (bo śića *and* howaya) *to make cry out by shooting* or *punching.*

b o - ś i m′, *cont.* of bośipa; bośim iyeya. *T.*, wośib.

b o - ś i m′ - ś i - p a, *v. red.* of bośipa.

b o - ś i′ - p a , *v. a.* *to shoot off*, as a branch or anything projecting from another body—bowaśipa.

b o - ś k i′, *v. a.* *to pound*, as corn not well dried—bowaśki.

b o - ś k i′ - ć a , *v. a.* *to squeeze out by ramming*—bowaśkića.

b o - ś k i n′, *cont.* of bośkića; bośkin iyeya. *T.*, wośkil.

b o - ś n a′, *v. a.* *to miss in shooting, miss the mark*—bowaśna, bouŋśnapi.

b o - ś n a - ś n a , *v.* *red.* of bośna.

b o - ś n a′ - y a , *v. a.* (bośna *and* ya) *to cause to miss*—bośnawaya.

b o - ś p a , *v. a.* *to punch* or *shoot off a piece*—bowaśpa.

b o - ś p a′ - ś p a , *v.* *red.* of bośpa; *to shoot* or *punch to pieces*—bowaśpaśpa.

b o - ś p a′ - y a , *part.* *shot* or *punched off.*

b o - ś p i′, *v. a.* *to shoot off*, as fruit—bowaśpi.

b o - ś p i′ - ś p i , *v.* *red.* of bośpi.

b o - ś p u′, *v. a.* *to shoot off a piece, to break* or *crack off by punching* or *shooting*—bowaśpu.

b o - ś p u′ - ś p u , *v.* *red.* of bośpu; *to punch to pieces*, as a cake of tallow—bowaśpuśpu.

b o - ś u ś′, *cont.* of bośuźa; bośuś iyeya.

b o - ś u′ - ś u - ź a , *v.* *red.* of bośuźa.

b o - ś u′ - ź a , *v. a* (bo *and* śuźa) *to crush by punching; to crush* or *mash up*, as a bullet does bones—bowaśuźa.

b o - t a′, *v* bota iyeya, *to blow off; i. q.* bohin iyeya.

b o - t a′ - k u - n i - ś n i , *v. a.* (bo *and* takuniśni) *to destroy by punching* or *shooting; to shoot all to pieces; to carry off*, as rain does snow—bowatakuniśni.

b o - t a ŋ′, *v. a.* *to pound*, as in washing clothes.

b o - t a ŋ′ - k i - y a , *v. a.* (botaŋ *and* kiya) *to cause to pound*—botaŋwakiya.

b o - t a′ - t a , *v. a.* *to knock* or *shake off by striking*, as in cleaning dust from clothes—bowatata.

b o - t' a′ - t' a , *v. a.* *to make dull*, as a pestle, *by pounding* in a mortar, or as an arrow, *by shooting.*

b o - t e m′, *cont.* of botepa; botem iyeya, *to wear off*, as the point of an arrow. *T.*, woteb.

b o - t e′ - p a, *v. a.* (bo *and* tepa) *to wear off short*, as an arrow, *by shooting*—bowatepa.

b o - t i′ - ć a , *v. a.* *to grab* or *snatch away a part.* *T.*, wotića, *to make spatter out*, as mud, *by shooting.*

b o - t i n , *cont.* of botića; botin iyeya

b o - t i ŋ′, *v. n.* *to stand upright, be stiff.*

b o - t i ŋ′, *adj.* *stiff, standing up*, as horses' ears.

b o - t i ŋ′ - t i ŋ , *adj.* *red.* of botiŋ; *stiff, standing up.*

b o - t i ŋ′ - t i ŋ - y a ŋ , *adv.* *red.* of botiŋyaŋ.

b o - t i ŋ′ - y a ŋ , *adv.* *stiffly.*

b o - t k u′ - ġ a , *v. a.* (bo *and* tkuġa)

to shoot off square, as a stick; *to shoot and break partly off; to strike and crack*, as a plate—bowatkuġa. *T.*, wotkuġa.

b o - t k u ḣ′, *cont.* of botkuġa.

b o - t o′, *v. a.* *to knock* or *pound on* anything—bowato. See iboto. *T.*, *to miss fire*, as a gun, because of faulty loading, or a poor cartridge.

b o - t o′ - k a, *adj.* *pounded off short, short.*

b o - t o′ - k a ŋ, *v. a.* (bo *and* tokaŋ) *to make change places by shooting at*—bowatokaŋ.

b o - t o′ - k e - ć a, *v. a.* (bo *and* tokeća) *to alter* or *make different by punching* or *shooting.*

b o - t o ŋ′, *v. n.* *to be unable to see, to grope about:* botoŋ wauŋ.

b o - t' o ŋ′, *v. n.* *to shoot well*—bowat'oŋ.

b o - t o ŋ′ - t o ŋ, *v.* *red.* of botoŋ; *to grope about*, said when one's eyes are very sore.

b o - t o ŋ′ - y a ŋ, *adv.* *in a groping manner.*

b o - t o′ - t o, *v.* *red.* of boto.

b o - t p a′, *v. a.* *to shoot into*, as into an eye; *to shoot through:* botpa iyeya.

b o - t p a ŋ′, *v. a.* Same as bokpaŋ.

b o - t p i′, *v. a.* *to shoot into*—bowatpi.

b o - t p i′ - t p i, *v.* *red.* of botpi.

b o - t u′ - k a, *v. a.* *to spoil*, as the fur of an animal, *by shooting*—bowatuka.

b o - t u′ - k a - k a, *v.* *red.* of botuka; *to spoil* or *hurt by shooting; to make smart by shooting*—bowatukaka. *T.*, *i. q.*, wokiŋtkiŋća.

b o - t u′ - k a - k a - k a, *v. a.* *to make smart* or *feel pain by shooting*—bowatukakaka.

b o - t u′ - t k a, *v. a.* (bo *and* tutka) *to shoot* or *punch off pieces*—bowatutka.

b o - ṭ a′, *v. a.* (bo *and* ṭa) *to kill by punching* or *shooting; to strike so as to endanger life, to stun*—bowaṭa; boṭa iyewaya; boiçiṭa, *to stun one's self by shooting; to shoot and kill one's self*—bomiçiṭa; mini boṭa, *to drown one out*, as when the water leaks through the roof. See iboṭa.

b o - ṭ i ŋ s′, *cont.* of boṭiŋza; boṭiŋs iyeya.

b o - ṭ i ŋ s′ - ṭ i ŋ - z a, *v.* *red.* of boṭiŋza.

b o - ṭ i ŋ s′ - y a, *adv.* *tightly.*

b o - ṭ i ŋ′ - z a, *v. a.* (bo *and* ṭiŋza) *to tighten, make tight by punching; to blow up tight*, as a bladder—bowaṭiŋza.

b o - ṭ i ŋ′ - z a, *v. n.* *T.*, woṭiŋza; ćaġa woṭiŋza, *the ice is firm.*

b o - ṭ o ś′, *cont.* of boṭoźa.

b o - ṭ o′ - ź a, *v. a.* *to make short* or *blunt by shooting*—bowaṭoźa.

b o - w a′ - n i - ć a, *v. a.* (bo *and* wanića) *to shoot* or *punch to nothing.*

b o - w a′ - n i n, *cont.* of bowanića; bowanin iyeya, *to shoot to pieces, destroy by shooting.*

b o - w e′ - ġ a, *v. a* *to break*, but not off, *by shooting*—bowaŵeġa, boyaweġa, bouŋweġapi.

b o - w e ȟ', *cont.* of boweġa; boweȟ iyeya.

b o - w e ȟ' - w e - ġ a, *v. red.* of boweġa.

b o - w e ȟ' - y a, *part. broken by shooting*, but not entirely off: boweȟya yaŋka.

b o - w o' - ṭ i ŋ - z a, *v. a. T.*, wowọṭiŋza, *to ram down tight in: i. q.*, bopuskića.

b o - y a', *adj.* boya se, *ragged, dangling.*

b o - y a' - y a, *n. T.*, woyaya, *a bunch, a skein:* śipto woya yamni, *three bunches of beads.*

b o - z a', *v.* boza hiŋhda, *to start up all at once*, as a company on hearing some startling intelligence

b o - z a ŋ', *v. a. to shoot well, to shoot so as to kill*—bowazaŋ. *T.*, wozaŋ, *to shoot in the heart* or *vital part; to stun.*

b o' - z a ŋ, *n.* miniboẓaŋ, *slow rain, mist. T.*, miniwozaŋ.

b o - ź a g' - ź a - t a, *v. red.* of bożata.

b o - ź a' - t a, *v. a.* (bo *and* źata) *to make forked by punching*, as a turnip-digger—bowaźata.

b o - ź a' - ź a, *v. n. to wash*, as the rain does.

b o - ź u' - ź u, *v. a.* (bo *and* źuźu) *to break to pieces* or *destroy by shooting: to knock* or *punch to pieces; to break*, as the rain does ice—bowaźuźu.

b u, *v. n. to make a noise; to low*, as a cow. See kabu, nabu, etc.

b u - b u' *v. red.* of bu.

b u - b u', *adj.* bubu se, said of one who has a large head and face. *T.*, bubukesa.

b u - b u' - y a, *adv. red.* of buya; *noisy, with a noise.*

b u - y a', *adv. noisy, in the manner of lowing:* buya apa, *to thump* or *strike*, making a hollow sound.

b u - y a' - k e n, *adv. in a noisy manner. T.*, buyakel.

b u - y e ȟ', *adv.* (buya *and* ȟiŋ) *with a loud noise:* buyeȟ hiŋȟpaya. *T.*, buyeȟćiŋ.

C.

ć, *the third letter of the Dakota alphabet.* It has the power of *ch* in *chain.*

ć a, *adv. when.* This word is used when a general rule or something customary is spoken of, and is generally followed by će or eće at the end of the member or sentence: yahi ća piwada će, *when thou comest I am glad;* waniyetu ća wapa eće, *when it is winter it snows.* See eća. *T.*, ćaŋ *and* ćaŋnahaŋ. In Titoŋwaŋ, as a particle, it is śka *and* śke lo, *they say.*

ć a, *n. a step, the distance which one steps:* ća nihaŋska, *thy step is long.*

ć a - d o' - k i - m n a, *adv.* (ćana *and* okimna) *between the knees.* Vulgar.

ća-do′-ta-he-daŋ, *adv.* (ćana *and* otahedaŋ) *between the knees* or *feet.* *T.*, ćanootahela.

ća-du′-za, *adj.* *swift, running swiftly,* as water: mini ćaduza. Same as kaduza.

ća′-e-će, *adj.* *many, a great many.*

ća-e′-hde, *v. n.* (ća *and* ehde) *to step, take a step*—ćaewahde. *T.*, ćaegle.

ća-e′-hde, *n.* *a step, a space.* *Pl.*, ćaehdepi, *steps.* *T.*, ćaegle.

ća′-ġa, *v. n.* *to freeze, become ice:* wakpa ćaġa, *the river freezes.*

ća′-ġa, *n.* *ice.*

ća-ġan′-ki-ya, *adv.* *iceward, out on the ice.*

ća-ġa′-ta, *adv.* *at* or *on the ice.*

ća-ġu′, *n.* *the lungs, lights.*

Ća-ġu′, *n. p.* *Burnt-thighs,* the designation of a clan of Yanktons. J. P. W.

ća-ġu′, *n.* See ćaġuka.

ća-ġu′-ka, *n.* *a fool;* *i. q.* waćiŋtoŋśni.

ća-hde′, *v. n.* *to step.* See ćaehde. *T.*, ćagle.

ća-hde′-pi, *n.* *steps.* Same as ćaehdepi.

ćaḣ, *cont* of ćaġa; ćaḣ kun, *under the ice;* ćaḣ iyaya, *the ice is gone;* ćaḣ hiyaya, *floating ice.*

ćaḣ-a′-hde-daŋ, *n.* or *adv.* (ćaġa *and* ahdedaŋ) *great and sudden, spreading rapidly* or *widely.*

1. *swift on glare ice.*
2. *standing on ice seen from afar.*
3. *a snag frozen in with much ice.*
4. *the shock of putting ice on the body.*
5. *the shock of bad news.*

A. L. R.

ćaḣ-a′-ki-haŋ, *adv.* said of the ice when it first became firm.

ća-ḣdi′, *n.* *charcoal; gunpowder*

ća-ḣdi′-o-pi-ye, *n.* *a powder-magazine.*

ća-ḣdi′-o-źu-ha, *n.* *a powder-flask, powder-horn*

ća-ḣdi′-ti-pi, *n.* *a powder-house.*

ća-ḣdo′-źu-ha, *n.* *a powder-horn* or *flask.* See ćaḣdioźuha.

ćaḣ-i′-ća-zo, *n.* *T. skates.*

ća-ḣli′, *n.* *T. gunpowder.* Same as ćaḣdi.

ća-ḣo′-ta, *n.* *ashes.*

ća-ḣta′-mna, *adj.* *rusty,* as old pork, *strong smelling.*

ćaḣ-to′-wa-ta, *adj.* *transparent,* as newly formed ice. *T.*, ćaḣowata.

ćaḣ-wo′-ṭiŋ, *n.* *the cracking of ice* by reason of the cold. See oṭiŋ.

ća′-i-a, *v.* (ćeya *and* ia) *to talk crying*—ćawaia.

ća′-i-a-a, *v.* *red.* of ćaia.

ća-ka′, *n.* *the palate, roof of the mouth, gills*—mićaka.

ća-ka′-ka, *n.* *a liar;* *i. q.* tuwe itoŋśni kiŋ. *T.*, ćakala.

ća-ki′-ći-pa, *v* of ćapá; *to stab for* one.

ća-ki′-pa, *v.* *pos.* of ćapá; *to stab one's own*—ćawakipa.

ća-ki′-yu-ḣu-ġe, *n* (ćaka *and* iyuḣuġe) *a fish-hook.*

ća ksu', *n.* *bare* or *smooth ice.*

ća-kśiŋ', *v.* *to step, bend the leg.* See aćakśiŋ.

ćam, *cont.* of ćapá. See ićam.

ća-mni', *n.* *a sprout, a germ* or *bud:* ćamni uya, *to sprout.*

ća-na', *n.* *the groin, inside of the thigh, the gland in the groin.*

ćan-ha'-ħa-daŋ, *adj.* (ćaŋte *and* hahadaŋ) *quick-tempered*—ćanmahahadaŋ.

ćan-ha'-ha-ka, *adj.* *quick-tempered, easily excited*—ćanmahahaka.

ćan-ha'-ha-ya, *v. a* *to irritate*—ćanhahawaya.

ćan-ha'-ha-ya, *adv.* *irritably.*

ćan-ha'-ha-ye-daŋ, *adv.* *in an excited state, irritably.*

ćan-i'-yu-taŋ-yaŋ, *n.* (ćaŋte *and* iyutaŋyaŋ) *temptation.*

ćan-ki'-ya, *v.* *cont.* of ćaŋtekiya.

ćan-psag'-ya, *v. a.* (ćaŋte *and* psaka) *to make sad, to grieve one*—ćanpsagwaya.

ćan-psag'-ya, *adv.* *in a broken-hearted manner.*

ćan-psa'-ke-ća, *adv.* *broken-hearted, without control over one's self.*

ćan-skem'-ya, *v. a.* (ćaŋte *and* skepa) *to make the heart melt* or *pass away; to disappoint*—ćanskemwaya.

ćan-skem'-ya, *adv.* *in a disappointed manner.*

ćan-ske'-pa, *adj.* (ćaŋte *and* skepa) *disappointed, angry, troubled*—ćanmaskepa.

ćan-śin', *cont.* of ćaŋte śića. *T.*, ćanśil.

ćan-śin'-ya, *v. a.* *to make sad*—ćanśinwaya. *T.*, ćanśilya.

ćan-śin'-ya, *adv.* *sadly, sorrowfully.* *T.*, ćanśilya.

ćan-śin'-ya-ken, *adv.* *sorrowfully.*

ćan-ţiŋs'-ya, *v. a.* *to embolden* or *encourage* one—ćanţiŋswaya.

ćan-ţiŋ'-za, *v. n.* (ćaŋte *and* ţiŋza) *to be of good courage*—ćanmaţiŋza.

ćan-waŋ'-ka, *n.* (ćaŋte *and* waŋka) *a coward.* *T.*, ćaŋlwaŋka.

ćan-waŋ'-ka, *v. n.* *to be a coward*—ćanwaŋmaka and ćanmawaŋka, ćanwaŋnika, ćanwaŋuŋkapi.

ćan-waŋ'-ka-ka, *v.* *red.* of ćanwaŋka.

ćan-waŋ'-ka-pi, *n.* *cowardice.*

ćan-wa'-śte, *v. n.* *to be happy, contented.* *T.*, ćaŋlwaśte.

ćan-za'-ni, *v. n.* (ćaŋte *and* zani) *to be well in heart, to be tranquil* or *of good cheer*—ćanmazani.

ćan-ze', *v. n.* *to be troubled, to have a load on the heart*—ćanmaze: ćanze hiŋgla, *T.* *to become angry.*

ćan-ze'-ka, *adj.* *troubled*—ćanmazeka.

ćan-ze'-ya, *v. a.* *to trouble, to make angry*—ćanzewaya.

ćan-ze'-ya, *adv.* *angrily.*

ćan-źan'-ya, *adv.* (ćaŋte *and* źata) *undecidedly, hesitatingly.*

ćan-źan'-ye-ća, *v. a.* *to make*

undecided, make hesitate—ćanźanwayeća.

ćan-źa'-te, *adj.* or *v. n.* (ćaŋte and źata) *heart forked; hesitating*—ćanmaźate.

ćaŋ, *n.* *a tree, trees; wood.*

ćaŋ, *n.* *a night* or *day.* This is always used *after* the numeral adjective, as noŋpa ćaŋ, yamni ćaŋ, etc. In this way it is distinguished from the preceding word. May not this meaning of the word have grown out of the fact, that the Indians when traveling calculate to reach *wood* at *night?*

ćaŋ, *adv.* *Ih., when: i. q.* ća. *T.,* ćaŋnahaŋ.

ćaŋ'-a-di-pi, *n.* See ćaŋiyadipi.

ćaŋ'-a-kan-yo-taŋ-ka, *n.* *something to sit on, a chair, a stool.* *T.,* ćaŋakaŋyaŋkapi.

ćaŋ'-a-kan-yo-taŋ-ka-pi-haŋ-ska, *n.* *any long thing to sit on, a bench, a form.*

ćaŋ'-a-ki-ṭa, *adv.* *much brush, many trees down.*

ćaŋ-a-ki'-yu-ha-pi, *n.* *a bier for the dead.* See ćaŋwiçihupa, said to be the better form.

ćaŋ'-a-ma-ni-pi, *n.* *stairs, a ladder.* See ćaŋiyamanipi, the better form. *T.,* ćaŋalipi.

ćaŋ-an', *adv.* See ćaŋnan.

ćaŋ ba'-kpa, *n.* (ćaŋ and bakpa) *a shingle;* ćaŋbakpapi, *shingles.*

ćaŋ-ba'-sde-ća, *v. a.* (ćaŋ and basdeća) *to saw lengthwise.* *T.,* ćaŋwasleća.

ćaŋ-ba'-sde-ća-pi, *n.* *wood sawed lengthwise; plank, boards; sawing; making boards.*

ćaŋ-ba'-sde-sde-ća, *v. a.* *to saw boards, saw lengthwise of the wood often*—ćaŋbauŋsdesdećapi.

ćaŋ-ba'-sde-sde-ća-ti-pi, *n.* *a saw-mill.* *T.,* ćaŋwaslećatipi.

ćaŋ-ćaŋ', *v. n.* *to shake, tremble, have the ague*—maćaŋćaŋ, nićaŋćaŋ, uŋćaŋćaŋpi.

ćaŋ-ćaŋ'-ki-ya, *v. a.* *to make tremble* or *shake*—ćaŋćaŋwakiya.

ćaŋ-ćaŋ'-pi, *n.* *the ague, trembling.*

ćaŋ-ćaŋ'-se, *adv.* *hastily, quickly.*

ćaŋ-ćaŋ'-ya, *v. a.* *to make tremble* or *shake; to hasten one*—ćaŋćaŋwaya.

ćaŋ-ćaŋ'-yaŋ, *adv.* *tremblingly.*

ćaŋ'-će-ġa, *n.* (ćaŋ and ćeġa) *a skin stretched over a hoop, a drum:* ćaŋćeġa apa, *to drum;* ćaŋćeġa kabu, *to drum.*

ćaŋ-de', *v. a.* *to get wood, get fire-wood*—ćaŋwade. Quite likely this is compounded of ćaŋ and ode, *to hunt wood.*

ćaŋ-de'-pi, *n.* *getting fire-wood; cutting up wood for a fire.*

ćaŋ-di', *n.* *tobacco:* ćaŋdi uŋpa. *to smoke tobacco*—ćaŋdi uŋmuŋpa; ćaŋdi yaśkića, *to chew tobacco.* *T.,* ćaŋli; ćaŋli yata, *to chew tobacco.*

ćaŋ-di'-a-ba-kpaŋ, *n.* (ćaŋdi and abakpaŋ) *a board to cut tobacco on.* *T.,* ćaŋliawakpaŋ.

ćaŋ-di'-a-ba-tpaŋ, *n.* Same as ćaŋdiabakpaŋ.

ćaŋ-di′-yu-hmuŋ, *v.* *to twist tobacco, to make tobacco into twists; to make cigars.* *Ih.*, ćaŋdiyukmuŋ.

ćaŋ-di′-yu-hmuŋ-pi, *n.* *cigars.* *Ih.*, ćaŋdiyukmuŋpi; *T.*, ćaŋliyugmuŋpi.

ćaŋ′-do-waŋ-ki-ya, *v.* (ćaŋ *and* dowaŋkiya) *to play on an instrument*, as the violin.

ćaŋ′-do-waŋ-ki-ya-pi, *n.* *a musical box; the organ.* *T.*, ćaŋlowaŋkiyapi.

ćaŋ-do′-źu-ha, *n.* (ćaŋdi *and* oźuha) *a tobacco-pouch.*

ćaŋ-du′-hu-pa, *n.* *a Dakota pipe, a pipe of any kind to smoke with.*

ćaŋ-du′-hu-pa-pa-hu, *n.* *the bowl of a pipe*, usually made of red pipe-stone by the Dakotas.

ćaŋ-du′-hu-pa-suŋ-ta, *n.* *a pipe-stem;* also, *the name of a kind of ash*, much used for making pipe-stems. *T.*, ćaŋnoŋpasuŋta.

ćaŋ-ha′, *n.* (ćaŋ *and* ha) *tree-skin*, i. e., *bark.*.

ćaŋ′-haŋ-pa, *n.* (ćaŋ *and* haŋpa) *shoes;* lit., *wooden moccasins.* Perhaps the Dakotas at first thought that shoes were made of wood.

ćaŋ′-haŋ-pa-haŋ-ska, *n.* *long shoes*, i. e., *boots.* *T.*, ćaŋhaŋpa iśkahu yukaŋ.

ćaŋ-haŋ′-pi, *n.* (ćaŋ *and* haŋpi) *sugar;* lit., *tree-sap.*

ćaŋ-haŋ′-pi-mdu, *n.* *powdered sugar.* *T.*, ćaŋhaŋpiblu.

ćaŋ-haŋ′-pi-mi-ni, *n.* *sugar-water, sap.*

ćaŋ-haŋ′-pi-śa-śa, *n.* *candy.*

ćaŋ-haŋ′-pi-ta-sa-ka, *n.* *cake sugar.*

ćaŋ-han′-pi-ti-kti-ća, *n.* *molasses.*

ćaŋ-ha′-saŋ, *n.* (ćanha *and* saŋ) *the sugar maple* or *rock maple;* so called from its *bark* being *whitish.* Also, *the white birch.*

ćaŋ-ha′-śa, *v.* (ćaŋha *and* śa) *cinnamon-bark.*

ćaŋ-hda′-ka, *n.* *large trees alone, without underbrush.* *T.*, ćaŋglaka.

ćaŋ-hde′-hde, *n.* *scattering trees, one here and there.* *T.*, ćaŋglegle.

ćaŋ-hde′-hde-ka, *n.* *trees that stand here and there.*

ćaŋ-hde′-śka, *n.* *a hoop, a wheel.*

ćaŋ-hde′-śka, *adj.* *round, wheel-like.* *T.*, ćaŋgleśka.

ćaŋ-hde′-śka-ku-te, *v.* *to play at shooting through a hoop* while it is rolling.

ćaŋ-hdu′-kaŋ, *v.* *pos.* of yukaŋ; *to shake off;* said of snow falling from trees.

ćaŋ-hmuŋ′-za, *n.* *the name of a small bush bearing little three-lobed red berries.*

ćaŋ-ho′-ta-daŋ, *n.* *a swing.* See hotadaŋ.

ćaŋ-ho′-ta-pi-śko, *n.* *a swing.*

ćaŋ-huŋ′, *n.* *the sturgeon*, a kind of fish.

ćaŋ-hu′-ta, *n.* *a stump.*

ćaŋ-ȟa′-ȟa-ke, *n.* *a vertebra, a buffalo's hump.*

ćaŋ-ȟa′-ȟa-ke-toŋ, *v. n.* *to be humped, having a hump.*

ćaŋ-ȟa′-ȟa-ya, *adv.* *brushy.*

ćaŋ-ȟa′-ka, *n.* (ćaŋ *and* ȟaka) *a brush, a bush.*

ćaŋȟ-ćaŋ′-ġa, *v. n.* *to crunch* or *make a noise in chewing anything hard,* as corn.

ćaŋ-ȟdo′-ȟu, *n.* *weeds, pig-weed, any large weed.* *T.*, ćaŋȟloġu

ćaŋ-ȟdo′-ka, *n.* (ćaŋ *and* ȟdoka) *a hollow tree* or *log.* *T.*, ćaŋȟloġeća.

ćaŋ-ȟe′-ta-źu, *v.* (ćaŋ *and* ȟetaźu) *to put wood ashore* from a boat. See ȟetaźu.

ćaŋ-ȟi′-ya, *v. a.* *to disappoint* one, either in a good or bad sense; *to lead on* or *tempt* one, as the presence of a wild animal leads one to desire to kill it—ćaŋȟiwaya, ćaŋȟimayaŋ.

ćaŋ-ȟlo′-ġa, *n.* *T. hollow stalks, sunflowers.*

ćaŋ-ȟo′-tka, *n.* *a kind of small bush:* ćaŋȟotka hu.

ćaŋ-ȟo′-tka, *adj.* *frosty, covered with frost.*

ćaŋ-ȟpaŋ′, *n.* *the coot* or *water-hen.*

ćaŋ-ȟpi′ *and* ćaŋ′-ȟpi, *n.* *a war-club, tomahawk.*

ćaŋ-ȟu′-na-ptaŋ, *n.* (ćaŋ *and* ȟunaptaŋ) *the side of a hill covered with trees.*

ćaŋ′-i-ba-kse, *n.* (ćaŋ *and* baksa) *a saw, hand* or *cross-cut saw.* See ćiŋbakse. *T.*, ćaŋiwakse.

ćaŋ′-i-ća-kaŋ, *n.* (ćaŋ *and* kakaŋ) *an adze, a broad-ax,* any instrument used in *hewing* or *adzing.*

ćaŋ′-i-ća-sde-će, *n.* (ćaŋ *and* kasdeća) *something to split wood with, a wedge.*

ćaŋ′-i-ća-źi-pe, *n.* (ćaŋ *and* kaźipa) *a drawing-knife; a plane.* See ćaŋwićaźipe.

ćaŋ-i′-ći-pa-we-ġa, *n.* *a cross.*

ćaŋ′-i-ćo-ġe, *n.* *drift-wood.*

ćaŋ′-iŋ-kpa, *n.* *the ends of branches, buds.* See ćiŋkpa.

ćaŋ′-iŋ-tpa, *n.* *buds.* Same as ćaŋiŋkpa.

ćaŋ′-i-pa-be, *n.* (ćaŋ *and* pamaŋ) *a wood-rasp.* *T.*, ćaŋipame.

ćaŋ′-i-pa-kiŋ-za, *n.* (ćaŋ *and* pakiŋza) *a fiddle*

ćaŋ-i′-ya-li-pi, *n.* *T. a ladder; stairs.*

ćaŋ′-i-ya-ma-ni-pi, *n.* (ćaŋ *and* amani) *pieces of wood to walk on, a ladder, stairs* or *steps, a bridge.*

ćaŋ′-i-yu-be, *n.* (ćaŋ *and* yumaŋ) *a wood-rasp.* See ćaŋipabe.

ćaŋ-i′-yu-ȟlo-ka, *n.* *T. an auger, gimlet.*

ćaŋ′-i-yu-mni, *n.* (ćaŋ *and* yumni) *an auger; a gimlet.* See ćiŋyumni *T.*, ćaŋiyuhomni.

ćaŋ′-i-yu-sdo-he, *n.* (ćaŋ *and* yusdohaŋ) *a sled, a sleigh.* See ćaŋwiyusdohe. *T.*, ćaŋwoslohaŋ.

ćaŋ-i′-yu-ski-ta-wo-hna-ka-pi, *n.* *T. a basket.*

ćaŋ′-i-yu-ta-pi, *n.* *a cord of wood.*

ćaŋ′-i-yu-te, *n.* (ćaŋ *and* iyuta) *a measure for wood, a square* or *rule.*

ćaŋ-i′-yu-wi, *n.* *curly wood, a vine.* See ćaŋwiyuwi.

ćaŋ-ka′, *n.* *a fire-steel.*

ćaŋ-ka′-ġa, *n.* *a log,* any *large piece of wood* on the ground.

ćaŋ-ka′-ġi-ća, *n.* *touchwood, spunk.*

ćaŋ-ka′-hu, *n.* (ćaŋka *and* hu) *the spine* or *backbone, the vertebræ.*

ćaŋ-kaȟ′-oŋ-pa, *v. a.* (ćaŋkaġa *and* oŋpa) *to lay* or *place logs* to walk on, *to bridge.*

ćaŋ-kaȟ′-oŋ-pa-pi, *n.* *logs laid* to walk on, *a bridge:* iŋyaŋ ćaŋkaȟoŋpapi, *a stone bridge.*

ćaŋ-ka′-ȟpa-ȟpa, *n.* *shingles; i. q.* ćaŋbakpa.

ćaŋ′-ka-i-de, *v.* *to make wood blaze by rubbing:* of ćaŋ *and* kaide.

ćaŋ′-ka-i-de-pi, *n.* *matches.*

ćaŋ-ka′-kiŋ-za, *v. n.* *to swing and creak,* as trees in the wind.

ćaŋ-ka′-suŋ-ta, *n.* (ćaŋka *and* suŋta) *the spinal marrow.* *T.*, ćaŋkaslute.

ćaŋ-ka′-śka, *v.* (ćaŋ *and* kaśka) *to bind wood together; to inclose with wood, to fortify*—ćaŋwakaśka; ćaŋkaśka yaŋka, *to be fortified.* *T.*, ćaŋiyakaśka.

ćaŋ-ka′-śka-pi, *n.* *a fence, a fortification.* See ćoŋkaśke.

ćaŋ-ka′-śko-kpa, *n.* (ćaŋ *and* kaśkokpa) *wood hewed out, a trough.*

ćaŋ-ka′-śko-tpa, *n.* Same as ćaŋkaśkokpa.

ćaŋ′-ka-wa-ći-pi, *n.* (ćaŋ *and* kawaći) *a top.*

ćaŋ′-ka-źi-pa, *v.* *to shave* or *plane wood.*

ćaŋ-ka′-źi-pe, *n.* (ćaŋ *and* kaźipa) *a carpenter.*

ćaŋ-ke′, *adv.* or *adverbial conjunction* used by Ihaŋktoŋwaŋ and Titoŋwaŋ; *because; therefore, i. q.*, nakaeś: osni ćaŋke wahi śni, *I came not because it was cold,* J. P. W.; *and so; and then; hence, therefore:* sometimes it is equivalent to nakaeś, sometimes to heoŋ, and sometimes to hehaŋ; the idea of *time* is often involved as well as of *cause.* It connects two complete sentences, and makes one subordinate to the other. T. L. R.

ćaŋ-ke′-da-ka, *adv.* *therefore:* waniyetu ćaŋkedaka osni, *it is winter, therefore it is cold.* *T.*, ćaŋkelaka.

ćaŋ-ko′-pa, *n.* *T. the back,* as of a book.

ćaŋ-ko′-ye, *n.* *the parts along the back.* *T.*, ćaŋkohaŋ.

ćaŋ-ko′-ye-śiŋ, *n.* *the fat along the back and sides.*

ćaŋ-ko′-źu-ha, *n.* (ćaŋka *and* oźuha) *a tobacco-pouch* or *bag,* so called because they carry in it their flint and steel; *a medicine-bag.*

ćaŋ-kpe′, *n.* *the tibia; the bone in the hind leg of animals below the knee;* ćaŋkpe huwaḳipe, *the fibula.* *Ih.*, *the knee-pan, the knees:* atkuku ćaŋkpe akan iyotaŋka, *he sits on his father's knees.*

ćaŋ-kpe′-ća-ka, *n.* *one who is furious;* *i. q.* tuwe ohitiiçida kiŋ.

ćaŋ-ksi′, *v. n.* *to be angry, irritated*—ćaŋwaksi.

ćaŋ-ksi′-ksi, *v.* *red.* of ćaŋksi.

ćaŋ-ksi′-ksi-ka, *n.* *one who is petulant.*

ćaŋ-ksi′-ksi-ya, *adv.* *red.* of ćaŋksiya.

ćaŋ-ksi′-ksi-ze-ća, *adj.* *petulant, irritable.*

ćaŋ-ksi′-ya, *adv.* *angrily, in a petulant manner.*

ćaŋ-ksi′-ya-haŋ, *adv.* *crossly.*

ćaŋ-ku′, *n.* *a road, way, path, trail.*

ćaŋ-ku′-lu-za-haŋ, *n.* *T.* *a railroad.* See duzahaŋ.

ćaŋ-ku′-ya, *v.* *to make for a road, have for a road*—ćaŋkuwaya.

ćaŋ-ku′-ye, *n.* *a row,* as of corn, etc.

ćaŋ-ku′-ye-toŋ, *v.* *to be in rows* or *furrows.*

ćaŋ-ku′-ye-toŋ-toŋ, *v.* *to make rows* or *furrows,* as a plough—ćaŋkuyetoŋtoŋ aya.

ćaŋ ku′-ye-toŋ-toŋ-yaŋ, *adv.* *in rows* or *furrows.*

ćaŋ-ma′-ko-pa-za, *n.* *wood, trees.* The sacred name.

ćaŋ′-mi-ni-ća-źo, *n.* *a sawyer* in the river.

ćaŋ-mi′-ni-yu-ha, *n.* *a wooden water-holder, a wooden buchet, water-bucket.*

ćaŋ-na′, *n.* See ćana, the better orthography.

ćaŋ′-na-haŋ, *adv.* *when, at such time, as;* wetu ćaŋnahaŋ maġa ahdi ẹćee, *when it is spring, the geese return;* *i. q.*, ćiŋnahaŋ.

ćaŋ-na′-ksa, *n.* *a war-club,* *i. q.* ćaŋḣpi; perhaps, *a club broken off with the foot.*

ćaŋ-nan′, *adv.* *out from the shore, in the middle of the river:* paćaŋnan iyeya, *to shove off* a boat.

ćaŋ-nan′-tki-ya, *adv.* *out from the shore, towards the middle of a stream.*

ćaŋ-nan′-wa-pa, *adv.* *out fr m the shore, further out.*

ćaŋ-ni′-ki-ya, *v. n.* *to be angry.* See ćaŋniyaŋ.

ćaŋ-ni′-yaŋ, *v. n.* *to be angry*—ćaŋmaniyaŋ, ćaŋniniyaŋ, ćaŋuŋniyaŋpi.

ćaŋ-ni′-ye-ki-ći-ya-pi, *v.* *to be angry with one another.* As a noun, *anger, malice.*

ćaŋ-ni′-ye-ki-ya, *v. a.* *to make angry*—ćaŋniyewakiya.

ćaŋ-ni′-ye-ya, *v. a.* *to be angry at, offended with*—ćaŋniyewaya, ćaŋniyeyaya, ćaŋniyeuŋyaŋpi, ćaŋniyećiya, ćaŋniyemayaya.

ćaŋ-ni′-ye-ya-pi, *n.* *an object of anger; anger.*

ćaŋ-noŋ′-pa, *v.* See ćaŋnuŋpa.

ćaŋ-no′-ma-slo-ye, *n.* *T.* *pewter, zinc.*

ćaŋ-num′, *cont.* of ćaŋnuŋpa; ćaŋnum mani, *to smoke as one walks.*

ćaŋ-nuŋ′-pa, *v. n.* (ćaŋdi *and* uŋpa) *to smoke tobacco:* ćaŋnuŋmunpa, *I smoke;* ćaŋnunuŋpa, *you smoke;* ćaŋnuŋkoŋpapi, *we smoke.*

ćaŋ′-o-hna-hna-ka-pi, *n.* (ćaŋ ohna *and* hnaka) *a coffin.* *T.*, ćaŋwognake

ćaŋ-o′-hna-ka, *n.* (ćaŋ *and* ohnaka) *a trunk, box.* See ćaŋwohnaka

ćaŋ-o′-ḣlo-ka, *n.* *T. a hollow tree.*

ćaŋ-o′-i-ya-li-pi, *n.* *T. stairs* in a house.

ćaŋ-o′-ka-ḣpa-ḣpa, *n.* (ćaŋ *and* kaḣpa) *chips.* *T.*, ćaŋokpaŋ.

Ćaŋ-o′-na, *n. p.* *a family* or *clan of the Yanktonais Dakotas:* the same as the Wazikute. The story is that long ago, some young men practiced shooting at a *pine tree;* whence the name Wazikute. And as they learned to hit the mark, they earned the name of Ćaŋ-o-na, *Wood-hitters.*

ćaŋ-o′-pa-mna, *n.* *sprouts growing up round a stump.*

ćaŋ-o′-pi-ye, *n.* (ćaŋ *and* opiye) *a dressing-case, a work-box.* See ćaŋwopiye. *T., a trunk.*

ćaŋ-o′-ti-daŋ, *n.* *the Dakota god of the woods*—an unknown animal said to resemble a man, which the Dakotas worship; *the monkey.*

ćaŋ′-o-ṭo-źa, *n.* (ćaŋ *and* ṭoźa) *a round stick.*

ćaŋ′-o-waŋ-ća-ya, *n.* *wood all over,* i. e., *a forest*

ćaŋ-pa′, *n.* *choke-cherries,* of the genus *prunus.* *T.*, ćaŋpakakaŋ.

ćaŋ-pa′-gmi-gma, *n.* *T.* See ćaŋpahmihma.

ćaŋ-pa′-gmi-yaŋ, *n.* *T. a wagon.*

ćaŋ-pa′-hmi-hma, *n.* (ćaŋ *and* pahmihma) *a cart, wagon, any vehicle.*

ćaŋ-pa′-hmi-hma-hu-noŋ-pa, *n.* *a cart, two-wheeled carriage*

ćaŋ-pa′-hmi-hma hu-to-pa, *n.* *a wagon, a four-wheeled carriage.*

ćaŋ-pa′-hu, *n.* *choke-cherry bushes.*

ćaŋ-pa′-kiŋ, *v.* (ćaŋ *and* pakiŋ) *to set up a stick* in the ground *to point the way* one is going—ćaŋwapakiŋ. *T.*, wasabgle.

ćaŋ-pa′-kiŋ, *n.* *the stick thus set up* pointing the direction one has gone. *T., a tree bent over.*

ćaŋ-pa′-kiŋ-za, *v.* (ćaŋ *and* pakiŋza) *to play on the violin*—ćaŋwapakiŋza.

ćaŋ-pa′-kiŋ-za-pi, *n.* *a violin.*

ćaŋ-pa′-kmi-kma, *n.* *Ih.* See ćaŋpahmihma.

ćaŋ-pa′-kmi-yaŋ, *n.* *Ih. a wagon.*

ćaŋ-pa′-ksa, *n.* (ćaŋ pa *and* ksa) *a stump.*

ćaŋ-pa′-mna, *n.* *the bunch of sprouts that grow at the root of a tree* or *stump.* See ćaŋopamna.

ćaŋ-pa′-nmi-nma, *n.* Mdewa. See ćaŋpahmihma.

ćaŋ-pa′-sa-pa-wi, *n.* (caŋpa sapa *and* wi) *the moon when choke-cherries are black, August.*

ćaŋ-pa′-sla-ta, *v.* *T. to set posts.*

ćaŋ-pa′-sla-te, *n.* *T. a post.*

ćaŋ-pe′-śka, *adv.* *on the knees:* ćaŋpeśka makehdeyainaźiŋ, *to stand on one's knees,* i. e., *to kneel.*

ćaŋ-pteḣ′, *adv.* *well, very well:* ćaŋpteḣ sdonya, *to know* a thing *well;* ćaŋpteḣ anaġoptaŋ.

ćaŋ-pteḣ′-ya, *adv.* *well.*

ćaŋ-sa′-ka-daŋ, *n.* (ćaŋ *and* saka) *a switch, a twig, a rod.*

ćaŋ-saŋ′, *n.* *a pillory; a pole.*

ćaŋ-saŋ′-se, *adv.* *quickly, in haste.* See ćaŋćaŋse.

ćaŋ-ska′, *n.* *the mulberry tree.*

ćaŋs-mna′, *adj.* *unpleasant to the taste,* as lean meat, *i. q.* mazamna sećeća.

ćaŋ-su′, *n.* (ćaŋ *and* su) *hickory-nuts, hickory-wood.*

ćaŋ-su′-hu, *n.* *the hickory-tree, the walnut* of New England; *Carya alba.*

ćaŋ′-su-sbe-ća, *n.* (ćaŋ *and* su-sbeća) *a wooden cross.* See su-sbeća. *T.*, ćaŋkaićiyopteya.

ćaŋ-śa′-śa, *n* *the bark which the Dakotas mix with their tobacco for smoking.* This they take from two or three bushes, one a species of dogwood and the others species of willow.

ćaŋ-śa′-śa-ḣiŋ-ća-ke, *n.* *a species* of *cornus* or *dogwood,* the bark of which is considered the best for smoking.

ćaŋ-śin′, *adj.* *cont.* of ćaŋteśica.

ćaŋ-śin′-ya, *adv.* *sorrowfully.*

ćaŋ-śiŋ′, *n.* (ćaŋ *and* śiŋ) *the gum* or *resin that oozes from trees, pitch-plaster; the pitch pine-tree,* from which the gum oozes.

ćaŋ-śiŋ′-ća-ḣpu, *n.* *a small species of bird.*

ćaŋ-śiŋ′-śiŋ-na, *n.* *a plant from which gum oozes when it is broken off;* perhaps a species of *camomile.* *T.*, ćaŋśiŋśiŋla.

ćaŋ-śka′, *n.* *a species of hawk.*

ćaŋ-śka′-waŋ-mdi-daŋ, *n.* *a species of kite* or *eagle.*

ćaŋ-śke′-du-ta, *n.* *the red bird.* *T.*, śkeluta.

ćaŋ-śko′-kpa, *n.* *T. a wagon-bed.*

ćaŋ-śu′-śka, *n.* (ćaŋ *and* śuśka) *the box-elder, Acer negundo.* See taśkadaŋ.

ćaŋt-a′-hde, *v. a.* (ćaŋte *and* ahde) *to desire, wish for, set the heart upon;* especially, *to set the heart on for evil, determine evil against* one—ćaŋtawahde, ćaŋtayahde, ćaŋtauŋhdepi, ćaŋtaćihde.

ćaŋt-a′-hde-pi, *n.* *a determining evil against.* *T.*, ćaŋtaglepi.

ćaŋt-a′-hde-ya, *v. a.* *to cause to set the heart against*—ćaŋtahdewaya. *T.*, ćaŋtagleya.

ćaŋ-te′, *n.* *the heart* of men and animals; *the seat of the affections:* ćaŋte yukaŋ, *to have a heart, to be kindly disposed;* ćaŋte wanića, *to have no heart;* mićaŋte, *my heart:* also *the eye* of corn, *the germinating part* of seeds.

ćaŋ-te′-a-sni, *v. n. to recover from anger* or *sorrow*—ćaŋteamasni.

ćaŋ-te′-a-sni-yaŋ, *v. a. to cause to recover from sorrow*—ćaŋteasniwaya.

ćaŋ-te′-en-a-i, *v. to take to heart, be displeased*—ćaŋteenawai.

ćaŋ-te′-en-yu-za, *v. to have* or *hold in the heart, to esteem*—ćaŋteenmduza.

ćaŋ-te′-ha-ha-daŋ, *adj. quick-tempered*—ćaŋtemahahadaŋ. See ćanhahadaŋ.

ćaŋ-te′-ha-ha-ye-daŋ, *adj. quick-tempered, irascible. T.*, ćaŋtehahayela.

ćaŋ-te′-ḣni-yaŋ-yaŋ, *v. n. to be disturbed*, or *distressed*, as when one's food hurts him—ćaŋtemaḣniyaŋyaŋ.

ćaŋ-te′-i-ki-çuŋ, *v. to sustain oneself, have command over oneself; to be resolute; i. q.* śagiçiya—ćaŋteiweçuŋ.

ćaŋ-te′-i-ki-çuŋ-yaŋ, *adv. resolutely, restraining one's self.*

ćaŋ-te′-ka-ze, *v. n. to be distressed*, as when one is thirsty while eating—ćaŋtemakaze.

ćaŋ-te′-ki-ći-ći-ya-pi, *n. loving each other.* See ćaŋtekiya.

ćaŋ-te′-ki-çuŋ, *v.* See ćaŋteikiçuŋ.

ćaŋ-te′-ki-ya, *v. a. to love, have an interest in* or *affection for*, which prompts to benevolent acts—ćaŋtewakiya, ćaŋteyakiya, ćaŋteuŋkiyapi, ćaŋtećićiya, ćaŋtemayakiya.

ćaŋ-te′-ki-ya-pi, *n. love, benevolence; one loved.*

ćaŋ-te′-ki-yu-za, *v. a. to hold in the heart* for good or ill; *to have an opinion of*, whether good or bad: taŋyaŋ ćaŋtewakiyuza, *I hold him in my heart for good.*

ćaŋ-te′-o-ki-çu-ni-ća, *v. n. to be offended; i. q.* ćaŋteptaŋyan: ćaŋteoweçunića, *I am angry at.*

ćaŋ-te′-o-ki-çu-nin, *cont.* of ćaŋteokiçunića. *T.*, ćaŋteokiçunil.

ćaŋ-te′-o-ki-çu-nin-ya, *v. a. to offend, make angry* by opposition—ćaŋteokiçuninwaya.

ćaŋ-te′-oŋ-śi-ka, *adj. low-spirited*—ćaŋteoŋmaśika.

ćaŋ-te′-o-yu-ze, *n. inclination, intention.* See ćaŋteoze.

ćaŋ-te′-o-ze, *n. the way the heart is affected, mind, thought, purpose*—mićaŋteoze.

ćaŋ-te′-o-ze-ya, *adv. with the whole heart. T.*, ćaŋteoyusya.

ćaŋ-te′-ptaŋ-yaŋ, *v. n. to be angry, be in a passion*—ćaŋtemaptaŋyaŋ, ćaŋteniptaŋyaŋ.

ćaŋ-te′-ptaŋ-yaŋ, *adj. angry.* From this comes woćaŋteptaŋye, *anger, wrath.*

ćaŋ-te′-ptaŋ-ye-ya, *v. a. to make angry, to provoke*—ćaŋteptaŋyewaya.

ćaŋ-te′-ske-p̣a, *v. n. to have the heart pass away; to be surfeited, sick.* See ćanskepa.

ćaŋ-te′-so-so-pi-se-ća, *v. n. to be terrified, miserable, have the heart cut into strings as it were*—ćaŋtemasosopiseća. See soso.

ćaŋ-te'-su-ta, *v. n.* *to be firm of heart; to be brave, not cowardly*—ćaŋtemasuta.

ćaŋ-te'-śi-ća, *v. n.* *to be sad, sorrowful*—ćaŋtemaśića, ćaŋteniśića, ćaŋteuŋśićapi.

ćaŋ-te'-śi-ća-ya, *adv.* *sadly, sorrowfully.*

ćaŋ-te'-śin-ya, *v. a.* *to make sad, sadden*—ćaŋteśinwaya.

ćaŋ-te'-śin-ya, *adv.* *sorrowfully.* *T.*, ćaŋteśilya.

ćaŋ-te'-śin-ya-ken, *adv.* *sadly.*

ćaŋ-te'-ṭiŋs-ya, *v. a.* *to strengthen the heart, encourage*—ćaŋteṭiŋswaya.

ćaŋ-te'-ṭiŋs-ya, *adv.* *courageously.*

ćaŋ-te'-ṭiŋ-za, *v. n.* *to be firm of heart, courageous*—ćaŋtemaṭiŋza.

ćaŋ-te'-wa-ni-ća, *v. n.* *to be heartless, unprincipled, mean, wicked*—ćaŋtemanića.

ćaŋ-te'-wa-śte, *v. n.* *to be glad, cheerful, joyful*—ćaŋtemawaśte.

ćaŋ-te'-wa-śte-ya, *v. n.* *to make glad, gladden*—ćaŋtewaśtewaya

ćaŋ-te'-wa-śte-ya, *adv.* *joyfully, cheerfully.*

ćaŋ-te'-ya-śi-ća, *v. a.* *to make sad by talking to, to dishearten*—ćaŋtemdaśića.

ćaŋ-te'-ya-śni-śni-źa, *v. n.* *T.* *to have a tickling in the throat.*

ćaŋ-te'-ya-ṭiŋs, *cont.* of ćanteyaṭiŋza.

ćaŋ-te'-ya-ṭiŋ-za, *v. a.* *to cheer up by words; to comfort, strengthen*—ćaŋtemdaṭiŋza.

ćaŋ-te'-ya-wa-śte, *v. a.* *to make happy by words*—ćaŋtemdawaśte.

ćaŋ-te'-ya-zaŋ, *v. n.* *T.* *to be heart-sick; to be very hungry.*

ćaŋ-te'-yu-kaŋ, *v. n.* *to have a heart, be benevolent*—ćaŋtemayukaŋ, ćaŋteniyukaŋ.

ćaŋ-te'-yu-za, *v. n.* *to think, form an opinion*—ćaŋtemduza: token ćaŋteduza he, *what is your opinion?*

ćaŋt-i'-ća-spe-ya, *v. a.* *to satisfy the desires of the heart,* whether good or bad; *to gratify one's desires*—ćaŋtićaspewaya. *T.*, ćaŋtićaŋpteya.

ćaŋt-i'-he-ya, *v. a.* *to set the heart upon, to desire very much, covet*—ćaŋtihewaya, ćaŋtiheyaya, ćaŋtiheuŋyaŋpi.

ćaŋt-iŋ'-yuŋ, *adv.* *voluntarily.*

ćaŋt-i'-ya-hde, *v. n.* *to be angry, meditate evil*—ćaŋtiyamahde. *T.*, ćaŋtiyagle.

ćaŋt-i'-ya-hde-pi, *n.* *malice, anger.* See woćaŋtiyahde.

ćaŋt-i'-ya-hde-ya, *v. a.* *to be angry at; to make angry*—ćaŋtiyahdewaya.

ćaŋt-i'-ya-hde-ya, *adv.* *angrily.*

ćaŋt-i'-yo-zi, *v. n.* *to get over one's anger*—ćaŋtiyomazi.

ćaŋt-ka'-spe-ya, *v. n.* *to be*

provoked, be emulous; to relieve one's self, gratify one's desires—ćaŋtkaspewaya. See ćaŋtićaspeya.

ćaŋt-ki'-ya, *v.* See ćaŋtekiya.

ćaŋt-o'-ç̇u-ni-ća, *v. n. to be irritated, angry.* See ćaŋteokiç̇unića.

ćaŋt-o'-ç̇u-nin-ya, *v. a. to make ashamed* or *angry*—ćaŋtoç̇uninwaya.

ćaŋt-o'-ġaŋ, *n. the pericardium.*

ćaŋt-o'-ġe, *n.* (ćaŋte *and* oġe) *the pericardium.*

ćaŋt-o'-ġiŋ, *n. the pericardium.*

ćaŋt-o'-hnag-ya, *v. a. to cause to place in the heart*—ćaŋtohnagwaya. *T.*, ćaŋtognagya.

ćaŋt-o'-hnag-ya, *adv. in a loving manner.*

ćaŋt-o'-hna-ka, *v. a.* (ćaŋte *and* ohnaka) *to place in the affections, to love*—ćaŋtowahnaka, ćaŋtouŋhnakapi.

ćaŋt-o'-hna-ka-pi, *n. love.*

ćaŋt-o'-ki-hna-ka, *v. pos.* of ćaŋtohnaka; *to place in one's heart*—ćaŋtowakihnaka.

ćaŋt-o'-kpa-ni, *v. a.* (ćante *and* okpani) *to desire, long for* anything—ćaŋtowakpani, ćaŋtouŋkpanipi.

ćaŋt-o'-kpa-ni-yaŋ, *v. a. to cause to long for*—ćaŋtokpaniwaya.

ćaŋt-o'-kpa-ni-yaŋ, *adv. longing for.*

ćaŋt-o'-tpa-ni, *v.* Same as ćaŋtokpani.

ćaŋt-o'-tpa-ni-yaŋ, *adv. longing for.*

ćaŋt-o'-źu-ha, *n. T. a tobacco bag.*

ćaŋ-uŋ'-kće-mna, *n. the root of the honeysuckle.*

ćaŋ-uŋ'-pa, *v. n. to smoke tobacco.* See ćaŋnuŋpa.

ćaŋ-wa'-ķiŋ, *n. T. a saddle.*

ćaŋ-waŋ'-ka, *adj. weak-hearted, cowardly.* See ćanwaŋka.

ćan-wan'-ka-la, *adj. T. cowardly.*

ćaŋ-waŋ'-źi-la-wa-ta, *n. T. a log canoe.*

ćaŋ-wa'-pa, *n. leaves, small branches.*

ćaŋ-wa'-po-śbe, *n. thick leaves* or *foliage, full leaf,* said of the woods after the leaves come to their growth and until they fall off. *T.*, ćaŋwapewoḣeśma.

ćaŋ-wap'-toŋ-wi, *n. the moon in which the leaves are green,* answering to *May.* Some say ćaŋwapatowi. *T.*, ćaŋwapenablećawi

ćaŋ-wa'-ta, *n. a log canoe; a skiff.*

ćaŋ-wa'-ta-taŋ-ka, *n. a boat* or *barge.*

ćaŋ-wi'-ća-źi-pe, *n. a drawing-knife.*

ćaŋ-wi'-ç̇i-hu-pa, *n. sticks to carry a dead person on, a bier. T.*, ćaŋwićakiyuha.

ćaŋ-wi'-du-du-ta, *n. wood with which red or scarlet is dyed, logwood. T.*, ćaŋwilulye.

ćaŋ-wi'-du-ta, *n. logwood.*

ćaŋ-wi'-pa-snoŋ, *n. a spit* or *stick to roast meat on.*

ćaŋ-wi′-sku-ye, *n.* *a sweet-smelling shrub; the honeysuckle.*

ćaŋ-wi′-ta, *n.* *a little grove* or *island of trees.*

ćaŋ-wi′-ya-pe, *n.* (ćaŋ *and* iyape) *a grape vine; any twining vine.* *T.*, ćuŋwiyape: also *grapes.*

ćaŋ-wi′-ya-wa, *n.* *T.* *a counting stick.*

ćaŋ-wi′-yu-sdo-he, *n.* *a sleigh* or *sled* of any kind; sometimes *a wagon.* *T.*, ćaŋwiyuslohaŋ.

ćaŋ-wi′-yu-te, *n* *a wood measurer, a cord stick.*

ćaŋ-wi′-yu-wi, *n.* *curled wood,* i. e. *a vine.*

ćaŋ-wo′-hna-ka, *n.* *a trunk, box.* *T.*, ćaŋwognaka.

ćaŋ-wo′-ka-źi-pe, *n.* *shavings.*

ćaŋ-wo′-sdo-he, *n.* *a sled.* *T.*, ćaŋwoslohaŋ.

ćaŋ-yag′, *cont.* of ćaŋyaka: ćaŋyag yaŋka, *to be groaning in pain:* ćaŋyag ayaŋpa, *to groan all night until the morning*—ćaŋyag amayaŋpa.

ćaŋ-ya′-ka, *v. n.* *to be heart sick, to groan.* *T.*, ćaŋblaka, ćaŋlaka, ćaŋuŋyakapi; ćaŋyaka yaŋka, *to be groaning.*

ćaŋ-ze′, *v. n.* *to be incensed, angry.*

ćaŋ-źe′-ka, *adj.* *T.* *angry.*

ćaŋ-ze′-ya, *v. a.* *to make angry.* See ćanzeya.

ćaŋ-zi′, *n.* *yellow wood,* i. e. *sumac.*

ćaŋ-źa′-ta, *n.* *a forked stick, a hay-fork.*

ća-o′-ki-ṭa, *v. n.* *T.* *to sob.*

ća′-pa, *n.* *the beaver.* Ćápa wakpa, *Beaver Creek.*

ća-p′a′, *v. a.* *to thrust into,* as a knife—ćawap′a.

ća-poŋg′-i-ću-wa, *n.* (ćapoŋka *and* kuwa) *a mosquito-bar.* *T.*, ćapoŋgwokeya.

ća-poŋ′-ka, *n.* *the mosquito, mosquitoes.*

ća-pta′-he-za, *n.* (ćapa ta *and* haza) *the black currant, Ribes floridum.* See taptaheza.

ća-pu′-ta, *n.* *alder-berries.*

ća-pu′-ta-hu, *n.* *the alnus* or *alder-tree.*

ća-ske′, *n.* *the name of the first-born child, if a son*—ćamaske, ćaniske.

ća-ske′, *v.* *T.* *to take by mistake,* as in supposing a thing was intended for him, when it was meant for another—ćawaske.

ća-smu′, *n.* *sand; i. q.* wiyaka.

ća-smu′-smu, *red.* of ćasmu; *sandy, much sand.*

ćaś-ki′-toŋ, *v.* *pos.* of ćaśtoŋ; *to give a name to one's own*—ćaświakitoŋ.

ćaś-toŋ′, *v. a.* *to name, give a name to*—ćaświaton, ćaśyatoŋ, ćaśuŋtoŋpi.

ćaś-toŋ′-pi, *part.* *named.*

ća′-ta, *n.* *hard ashes, cinders.*

ća-taŋ′, *n.* *the name of the fourth child, if a son*—ćamataŋ, ćanitaŋ.

ća-tka′, *n.* *the left hand:* mićatka *and* maćatka, *my left hand;* nićatka, *thy left hand.*

ća-tka′, *adj.* *left-handed*—ćamatka, ćanitka.

ća-tka′-taŋ-haŋ, *adv.* *at the left hand*—mićatkataŋhaŋ.

ća-tku′, *n.* *the back part of a tent* or *house, the part opposite the door;* the place of honor.

ća-tkun′, *adv.* *at the back of a house* or *tent:* ćatkun iyaya wo, *go to the back part of the house.* *T.*, ćatkul.

ća-tku′-ta, *adv.* *at the back of the tent.*

ća-tku′-taŋ-haŋ, *adv.* *at the back part of a tent.*

ća-źe′, *n.* *a name;* maćaźe, *my name.*

ća-źe′-hdan, *cont.* of ćaźehdata; *in the name of one's own.* *T.*, ćaźeglal.

ća-źe′-hda-ta, *v.* *pos.* of ćaźeyata; *to call one's own by name*—ćaźewahdata.

ća-źe′-i-hda-ta, *v.* *reflex.* *to speak one's own name*—ćaźemihdata.

ća-źe′-ka-ġa, *v.* *T.* *to name, make a name for.*

ća-źe′-ki-ya-ta, *v.* *to mention* or *speak of* anything *to* one—ćaźewakiyata, ćazećićiyata.

ća-źe′-yan, *cont.* of ćaźeyata; *in the name of.*

ća-źe′-ya-ta, *v. a.* (ćaźe *and* yata) *to call by name, speak the name of* a person or thing, *mention by name*—ćaźemdata, ćaźedata, ćaźeuŋyatapi; ćaźemayadata, *thou speakest my name.*

će, *a particle.* It is commonly used at the end of a sentence or paragraph, when a general truth is expressed, or a common course of action mentioned; also, when reference is made to what is past, especially in quoting the words of another or one's own. See ća and će. *T.* interrogative for ći, which see.

će, *n.* *the penis*—maće, niće.

će-a′-ktoŋ, *or* će-ag′-toŋ, *v.* *T.* *to make a bridge*—ćeagwatoŋ.

će-a′-ktoŋ-pi, *n.* *a bridge.* See ćeyaka.

će-blo′-hu, *n.* *T.* *the collar bone.*

će-ća′, *n.* *the thigh; the cock of a gun;* mazakaŋ ćeća, *the breech of a gun.*

će-ća′-kaŋ-taŋ-ka, *n.* *the femoral artery.*

će-ća′-o-wa-gle, *n.* *T.* *the femur bone, the hip-joint.*

će-ćo′-ktaŋ-ktaŋ, *adj.* *bandy-legged.*

će-ćuŋ′-te, *n.* *the thigh-bone, femur.*

će-ćuŋt′-o-śtaŋ, *n.* *the neck* or *head of the femur, the articulation of the femur.* *T.*, ćetuŋtośtaŋ.

će-di′, *n.* *a reed-like grass with long joints.*

će-di′-ćo-taŋ-ka, *n.* *a large kind of reed.*

će-di′-hu, *n.* *the reed stalk.*

će-e′, *a particle.* For its definition, see će.

ćeg, *cont.* of ćeka. See ćegya.

ćeg′-ya, *adv.* of ćeka; *stumblingly.*

će′-ġa, *n.* *a kettle, pot; a pail, bucket.*

će′-ġa-hu-ha-toŋ-na, *n.* *an iron kettle with feet.*

će′-ġa-i-ha, *n.* *the lid* or *cover for a kettle* or *bucket.*

će′-ġa-i-hu-pa-haŋ-śka, *n.* *a frying-pan; long-handled kettle.*

će′-ġa-i-hu-pa-toŋ, *n.* *a kettle,* or *bucket with a bail.* *T.*, ćeġaikaŋtoŋ.

će′-ġa-i-pśuŋ-ka-daŋ, *n.* *a sauce-pan; a kettle with a small mouth.*

će-ġaŋ′-stiŋ-na, *n.* (ćeġa *and* ćistiŋna) *a small kettle* or *bucket.* *T.*, ćeġisćila.

će′-ġa-pśuŋ-ka-dan, *n.* *a sauce-pan.*

će′-ġa-ska, *n.* *a white tin kettle.*

će-ġa′-te-zi-toŋ-na, *n.* *a tea-kettle, any kettle that bulges in the middle.*

će-ġiŋ′-stiŋ-na, *n.* See ćeġaŋstiŋna. *T.*, ćeġisćila.

će-ġu′-ġu, *v. n.* *to fry,* as meat.

će-ġu′-ġu-ya, *v. a.* *to fry* meat—ćeġuġuwaya.

će-hbe′-ća, *n.* *a kind of nuts* which the Dakotas take from the deposits made by ground-squirrels or mice. A very small root, in size and shape resembling a pea, collected by mice and eaten by the Dakotas.

će-hnag′, *cont.* of ćehnake

će-hnag′-ki-toŋ, *v.* *to put on* or *wear a breech-cloth.*

će-hna′-ke, *n.* *a breech-cloth,* a piece of cloth worn around the loins by Dakota men. *T.*, ćegnake.

će-hna′-ke-ki-toŋ, *v.* *to put on and wear a breech-cloth*—ćehnakewakitoŋ. *T.*, ćegnakekitoŋ.

će-hu′-pa, *n.* *the under jaw.*

će-hu′-pa-hda-hda, *v. n.* *to chatter,* as the teeth on account of cold—ćehupawahdahda. *T.*, ćehupaglagla.

ćeḣ, *cont.* of ćeġa; ćeḣ sapa, *a black kettle;* ćeḣ ska, *a white kettle.*

ćeḣ *and* ećeḣ, *adv.* *times:* noŋpa ćeḣ noŋpa, *twice two.*

ćeḣ-hu′-ha-toŋ, *n.* *a kettle having legs.*

ćeḣ-i′-kaŋ, *n.* *T. a kettle-bail.*

ćeḣ-iŋ′ *and* ećeḣiŋ, *adv.* *just so much, that alone:* he ćeḣiŋ mduha, *I have that alone.* *T.*, ećelaḣćiŋ.

ćeḣ-na′-ġi, *n.* (ćeġa *and* naġi) *soot; dead coals.*

ćeḣ-o′-ki-hde-toŋ, *n.* *a kettle,* such as *a tea-kettle.* *T.*, ćeḣokiyetoŋ.

će-ḣpi′, *n.* *flesh, muscular fiber*—mićeḣpi.

ćeḣ-pśuŋ′-ka, *n.* *T. a pail small at the top and large at the bottom.*

ćeḣ-p̣o′, *n.* *the steam of a kettle.*

ćeḣ-uŋ′, *v.* See ćeḣuŋka.

ćeḣ-uŋ′-ka, *v. n.* *to be the object of anger*—ćeḣwauŋka.

ćeḣ-wo′-ho-ta, *n.* *T. a low, wide kettle.*

će′-ka, *v. n.* *to stagger*—maćeka.

će-kćeg, *cont.* of ćekćeka.

će-kćeg′-ya, *adv.* *staggeringly, reeling:* ćekćegya mani.

će-kće′-ka, *v. n.* *to stagger, reel.*

će-ki′-ća-ti, *v.* of ćeti; *to make a fire for* one—ćewećati, ćeyećati.

će-ki′-ći-ti, *v.* of ćeti; *to make a fire for* one—ćewećiti, ćeyećiti, ćeuŋkićitipi.

će′-ki-ći-ya, *v.* of ćekiya; *to pray* or *supplicate for* another—ćewećiya, ćeyećiya, ćeuŋkićiyapi; ćemiyećiya, *thou prayest for me.*

će-ki′-ti-pi, *n.* *a feast, of which virgins and men who have not known women are said to partake; i. q.* wimna śni.

će′-ki-ya, *v.* of ćeya; *to pray to, beseech, entreat*—ćewakiya, ćeyakiya, ćeuŋkiyapi, ćećićiya; ćeuŋnićiyapi, *we pray you.*

će-kpa′, *n.* *the navel; a twin:* ćekpapi, *twins*—maćekpa.

ćem, *cont.* of ćepa. *T.*, ćeb.

ćem-će′-pa, *adj.* *red.* of ćepa; *fat.*

ćem-ki′-ya, *v. a.* *pos.* of ćemya; *to fatten one's own*—ćemwakiya, ćemuŋkiyapi.

ćem-ya′, *v. a.* *to make fat, fatten*—ćemwaya.

ćem-ya′, *adv.* *fatly; liberally.*

ćem-ya′-pi, *part.* *fatted.*

ćen, *adv.* *about, nearly:* wikćemna ćen, *about ten.* *T.*, ćel.

će-om′, *cont.* of ćeoŋpa. *T.*, ćeob.

će-oŋ′-pa, *v. a.* *to roast,* as corn on the cob, or as potatoes in the ashes—ćewaoŋpa. See ćeuŋpa.

će′-pa, *adj.* *fat*—maćepa, nićepa, uŋćepapi.

će′-paŋ-śi, *n.* *Ih., i. q.,* ićepaŋ.

će-pće′-pa, *adj.* *red.* of ćepa. See also ćemćepa.

će-sdi′, *n.* *the dung* of man or animals. *T.*, ćesli; *i. q.* tuŋkće.

će-sdi′, *v. n.* *to dung*—ćewasdi, ćeyasdi.

će-sdi′-o-śa-ka, *v. n.* *to be foul,* as a gun or pipe-stem. *T.*, ćesli-ośaka.

će-sli′-ślo-ślo, *v. n.* *T. to have diarrhœa.*

ćeś, *conj.* *although.* Same as keś.

će-śka′, *n.* *the part of the breast near the collar-bone.*

će-śki′-ća-te, *n.* *the collar-bone, clavicle.* *T.*, ćeblohu.

će-śki′-kaŋ, *n.* (ćeśka *and* ikaŋ) *Ih.* *a button.*

će-śki′-yu-taŋ, *n.* *T. suspenders; i. q.,* śina kaŋ.

će-śko′-ḣdo-ka, *n.* *the hollow place in the throat by the collar-bone.*

će-śpu′, *n.* *a wart, a scab:* hoćeśpu, *fish-scales.*

će-taŋ′, *n.* *the chicken-hawk, the pigeon-hawk.*

će-ta′-ta, *adv.* *T. in the center of a lodge, near the fire.*

će-te′, *n.* *the bottom* of a vessel.

će-te′-ta, *adv.* *at the bottom; in the center* of a lodge, near the fire.

će-te′-ta-he-daŋ, *n.* *a standing on the bottom; a saucer.*

će-ti′, *v. a.* *to build a fire, make a fire*—ćewati, ćeyati, ćeuŋtipi.

će-to′-we-daŋ, *adv.* *less than half full, having a little in.* *T.*, ćeteyela.

ć e - t o′ - w e - t a, *adv.* *having a little in*, as a vessel. *T.*, ćetetala.

ć e′ - t u, *adv.* *then, so much, just so.*

ć e - t u ŋ′ - t e, *n.* *T. the thigh bone: i. q.* ćećuŋte.

ć e - ţ u ŋ′ - h d a, *v. a.* *to doubt, disbelieve*—ćeţuŋwahda, ćeţuŋyahda, ćeţuŋuŋhdapi, ćeţuŋćihda. *T.*, ćeţuŋgla.

ć e - ţ u ŋ′ - h d a - y a, *v. a.* *to cause to doubt*—ćeţuŋhdawaya.

ć e - u m′, *cont.* of ćeuŋpa.

ć e - u ŋ′ - p a, *v. a.* *to roast*, as corn by the fire, or as potatoes in the ashes—ćewauŋpa. See ćeoŋpa.

ć e′ - y a, *v. a.* *to cry, to weep*—waćeya, yaćeya, uŋćeyapi; wićaćeya, *weeping.* From this word comes ćekiya, *to cry to, pray.*

ć e - y a′ - k a, *n.* *a dam, anything that stops the water.* Iŋyaŋ ćeyaka, *the Little Rapids.*

ć e - y a′ - k a - k a - ġ a - p i, *n.* *a mill-dam.*

ć e - y a′ - k a - t a, *n.* *mint*, the generic name of mints. *T.*, ćeyaka.

ć e′ - y a - o - k i - ţ a - ţ a, *v.* *to sob.*

ć e′ - y e - k t a - k t a, *v.* *to cry sobbingly*—waćeyektakta.

ć e′ - y e - n a - k a, *v. n.* *T. to twitch under the eyes* or *about the mouth*—ćeyemanaka.

ć e - y e′ - n i - y a ŋ, *v.* *to cry out aloud.*

ć e - ź i′, *n.* *the tongue*—mićeźi: ćeźi noŋpa, *double-tongued;* ćeźi źata, *forked-tongued, deceitful.*

ć e - ź i′ - n i - y a, *v. n.* *to have a sore mouth*—ćeźimaniya.

ć e - ź i ŋ′, *n.* See će *and* źiŋ.

ć e - ź ĭ′ - ź a l - y a, *adv.* *T. deceitfully.*

ć i, a double pronoun in composition, including the nom. *I* and the obj. *thee.*

ć i, *prep. in comp.* *for, with, in.* This is used after *e* or *i* in the place of *ki*, as the first ći in amićićita, from akita.

ć i, *interrog. particle.* This is always used at the end of a sentence, and has the force of demanding an immediate answer; as, yahi kta ći, *you will come, will you?*

ć i - ć a′, *a.* *rough, frizzled, curled up.*

ć i - ć a′, *v.* of ka; *I mean thee.*

ć i - h i ŋ′ - t k u, *n.* *his* or *her son.* See ćiŋhiŋtku.

ć i′ - k ć i - ķ a - d a ŋ, *adj.* *red.* of ćiķadaŋ; *pl.* ćikćiķapidaŋ.

ć i - k ć i′ - s t i ŋ - n a, *adj.* *red.* of ćistiŋna; *pl.* ćikćistiŋpidaŋ. *T.*, ćikćisćila.

ć i′ - ķ a - d a ŋ, *adj.* *little, very small; pl.* ćiķapidaŋ—maćiķadaŋ.

ć i′ - ķ a - y e - d a ŋ, *adv.* *small, pent up in a small place.*

ć i - ķ o ŋ′, *adv.* *of time.* It is used after verbs and sometimes adjectives, and marks past time, as epe ćiķoŋ, *I said.* Where the verb or adjective immediately preceding changes *a* or *aŋ* into *e*, ćiķoŋ is used instead of ķoŋ. *T.*, ćoŋ.

ć i ŋ, *adv.* *cont.* of ćiŋka; miye ćiŋ, *I alone.*

ćiŋ, *def. art. the.* It is used in the place of kiŋ, when the verb or adjective preceding has changed *a* or *aŋ* into *e.*

ćiŋ, *v. a. to desire, want*—waćiŋ, yaćiŋ, uŋćiŋpi.

ćiŋ′-a-haŋ, *conj. if.* Same as ćiŋhaŋ.

ćiŋ′-ba-kse, *n. a saw.* See ćaŋibakse. *T.*, ćiŋwakse.

ćiŋ-ća′, *n. a child; the young of animals, a whelp, cub, calf, foal*—mićiŋća, nićiŋća, uŋkićiŋćapi; tuwe ćiŋća taŋiŋ śni, *whose child is not manifest,* i. e., *a bastard.*

ćiŋ-ća′-ka-ġa, *v. to beget a child*—ćiŋćawakaġa.

ćiŋ-ća′-ki-ći-toŋ, *v. to bear a child to* or *for* one—ćiŋćawećitoŋ, ćiŋćamićitoŋ.

Ćiŋ-ća′-kiŋ-ze, *n. p. The Apaches.*

ćiŋ-ća′-toŋ, *v. a. to have* or *give birth to a child*—ćiŋćawatoŋ, ćiŋćayatoŋ, ćiŋćauŋtoŋpi.

ćiŋ-ća′-ya, *v. to have for a child, adopt as a child*—ćiŋćawaya, ćiŋćamayaŋ.

ćiŋ′-ću, *n. his elder brother.* See ćiŋye.

ćiŋ-ćuŋ′-kpa, *adj. with child, pregnant; i. q.* ihduśaka.

ćiŋ-ćuŋ′-tpa, *adj.* Same as ćiŋćuŋkpa.

ćiŋ-haŋ′, *conj. if, when.* Same as kiŋhaŋ.

ćiŋ-hiŋ′-tku, *n. his* or *her son.*

ćiŋ′-ka, *adv. voluntarily:* miye ćiŋka, *I myself,* without the suggestion or command of any one.

ćiŋ′-ka, *v. a. to want, desire.* Same as ćiŋ—waćiŋka.

ćiŋ′-ka-haŋ, *adv. voluntarily:* iye ćiŋkahaŋ.

ćiŋ-ki′-ya, *v. a. to cause to desire, persuade*—ćiŋwakiya, ćiŋuŋkiyapi.

ćiŋ′-kpa, *n.* (ćaŋ *and* iŋkpa) *buds; a twig; the top of a tree, end of a stick.*

ćiŋ′-kpa-ta, *adv. at the buds.*

ćiŋ-kśi′, *n. a son;* sometimes used for a child, whether male or female: mićiŋkśi, *my son;* uŋkićiŋkśipi, *our son* or *our sons.* Also *a man's brother's son,* or *a woman's sister's son.*

ćiŋ-kśi′-tku, *n. his* or *her son.*

ćiŋ-kśi′-ya, *v. to have for a son, to be a father to* one—ćiŋkśiwaya.

ćiŋś, *n. son, my son;* used only when an address is made to the person. *T.*, ćiŋkś, used by men in addressing their children, whether boys or girls; *my child.*

ćiŋ-śka′, *n. T. a spoon.*

ćiŋ-to′, *adv. T. yes; to be sure.*

ćiŋ′-tpa, *v.* Same as ćiŋkpa.

ćiŋ′-tpa-ta, *adv.* Same as ćiŋkpata.

ćiŋ-ya′, *v. a. to cause to desire, persuade*—ćiŋwaya.

ćiŋ′-yaŋ, *adv.* kitaŋna ćiŋyaŋ taniŋyaŋ yaŋka, *it is but just in sight.* See kitaŋ.

ćiŋ-ye′, *n. a man's elder brother,*

my elder brother. Male cousins by the father's side older than oneself are also called ćiŋye. *T.*, ćiye.

ćiŋ-ye′-ku, *n.* *his elder brother.* Same as ćiŋću. *T.*, ćiyeku.

ćiŋ-ye′-ya, *v.* *to have for an elder brother*—ćiŋyewaya.

ćiŋ′-yu-mni, *n.* *an auger; a gimlet.* See ćaŋiyumni.

ćis′-ći-na, *adj.* *Ih. small.* Same as ćistiŋna.

ćis-ćis′-tiŋ-na, *adj.* *red.* Same as ćikćistiŋna. *T.*, ćisćisćila.

ćis′-ti-la, *adj.* *T.* Same as ćistiŋna. Also, ćisćila.

ći′-stiŋ, *adj.* *small, little.*

ći′-stiŋ-na, *adj.* *small, little*—maćistiŋna, uŋćistiŋpidaŋ.

ći′-sti-ye-daŋ, *adj.* *narrow, pent up*, as a way.

ći′-sti-ye-daŋ, *adv.* *for a little while.*

ćo, *v.* *to call, invite.* See kićo.

ćo, *n.* *the kernel* or *meat* of grain, seeds, etc.; ćo aya, *to ripen, bear seed.*

ćo, *intj.* *bang!* Said of the report of a gun.

ćo. See yućo and ayućo.

ćo-ćo′, *adj.* *soft*, as mud, opposed to ṭiŋza and suta; *not well cooked, i. q.* śpaŋ śni.

ćo-ćo′-daŋ, *adj.* *soft.*

ćo-ćo′-ya, *adv.* ćoćoya śpaŋ, *not well cooked.*

ćo′-daŋ, *adj.* *destitute, without, not having*, as tawiću ćodaŋ, *without a wife; bare, naked*, as sićodaŋ, *barefooted*, taŋćodaŋ, *naked.* See ćokadaŋ for the pronoun's place. *Ih.*, ćona.

ćo′-ġa, *adj.* *not neat, slovenly.* See ćoġeća.

ćo′-ġe-ća, *adj.* *slovenly, with one's clothes not well put on:* maćoġeća, *I am slovenly.*

ćo-ġiŋ′, *n.* *the pith* or *core* of anything.

ćoḣ, *adv.* *when.*

ćoḣ-waŋ′-źi-ća, *n.* *the smaller kind of willow.*

ćo-ka′, *n.* *the middle.* See ćokaya.

ćo-ka′, *adj.* *empty, without anything:* ćoka wahdi, *I have come home empty.*

ćo-ka′-daŋ, *adj.* *naked, bare:* taŋćomakadaŋ, *I am without clothes;* sićomakadaŋ, *I am without shoes.*

ćo-ka′-daŋ, *adv.* *empty*, said of a cask, etc.: ćokadaŋ haŋ. *Ih.*, ćokana.

ćo-ka′-hnag, *cont.* of ćokahnaka.

ćo-ka′-hnag-ya, *adv.* *placed in the middle.* This is used by Mr. Renville for *the veil of the temple.*

ćo-ka′-hna-ka, *v.* See ćokayahnaka. *T.*, ćokagnaka.

ćo-ka′-ka, *v.* *red.* of ćoka.

ćo-ka′-ka-daŋ, *adv.* *red.* of ćokadaŋ.

ćo-kam′, *adv.* *cont.* of ćokata; *in the midst.* *T.*, ćokal.

ćo-kan′, *adv.* *long ago, in former times.*

ćo-kan′, *cont.* of ćoka and en; ćo-kan iyeya, *to shoot through* the bowels. *T.*, ćokal.

ćo-kaŋ′, *n.* *a low bottom*, where are lakes or marshes. *T.*, ćokaŋya.

ćo-ka′-pa, *adv.* *in the midst.*

ćo-ka′-pa-taŋ-haŋ, *adv.* *in the inside.*

ćo-ka′-ta, *n.* *the middle.*

ćo-ka′-ta, *adv.* *in the middle, in the midst.*

ćo-ka′-ta-wa-pa, *adv.* *out in the middle*, as of a stream.

ćo-ka′-ya, *n.* *the middle.*

ćo-ka′-ya, *adv.* *in the middle.*

ćo-ka′-ya-hna-ka, *v. a.* (ćokaya *and* hnaka) *to place across the middle, place in the middle*—ćokayawahnaka. *T.*, ćokayagnaka.

ćo-koŋ′, *v. a.* *to purpose evil against, desire to take the life of one*—ćowakoŋ, ćoyakoŋ, ćouŋkoŋpi, ćomakoŋ: waćokoŋpi, *purposing evil against.*

ćo-ku′, *n.* *the inside of the cuticle, the under side of the skin, the thickness* or *stripe of the skin; the under part of the chin.*

ćo-ḳiŋ′, *v. a.* *to roast on a spit*—ćowaḳiŋ, ćoyaḳiŋ, ćouŋḳiŋpi: ćoḳiŋpi, *roasting.* *T.*, *to roast on coals.*

ćom, *cont.* of ćopa.

ćo-mni′, *v. n.* *to be tired of staying*—ćomamni, ćonimni. See also ićomni.

ćo-mni′-hda, *v. n.* *to feel uneasy, become tired of staying*—ćomniwahda, ćomniuŋhdapi. *T.*, ićomnigla.

ćo-mni′-hda-zi, *v. n.* *to sigh, groan*—ćomniwahdazi, ćomniyahdazi, ćomniuŋhdazipi. *T.*, ćuwiokini.

ćom-ya′, *v. a.* of ćopa; *to cause to wade*—ćomwaya. See ćopekiya.

ćo′-na-la, *adv.* *T.* *a few; i. q.* tonana.

ćo-ni′-ća, *n.* *flesh, meat* of any kind; *the meat* or *kernel* of grain; *the wood that grows inside of the sap;* waćonića, *dried meat.*

ćoŋ, *for* ćaŋ. See ćoŋtaŋka.

ćoŋ-ćoŋ′-se, *adv.* See ćaŋćaŋse.

ćoŋ′-ka-śke, *n.* *a fence, an inclosure; a fort.*

ćoŋ′-ḳiŋ, *n.* *a backload of wood;* i. e., *as much as a woman could carry on her back.*

ćoŋ′-ḳiŋ-ta, *n.* *any place where they go for wood.*

ćoŋ′-na-kde, *n.* *Ih.* *a ladder.*

ćoŋ′-pe-śka, *n.* *glue.* The Dakotas generally obtain it by boiling buffalo heads, and use it in fastening on the points of their arrows.

ćoŋ′-śma, *n.* (ćaŋ *and* ośma) *dense woods, forest.* *T.*, ćoŋwoḣeśma.

ćoŋ′-taŋ-ka, *n.* (ćaŋ *and* taŋka) *high wood, groves of timber.*

ćoŋ′-te-ḣi, *n.* (ćaŋ *and* oteḣi) *thick woods*

ćo-pa′, *v. a.* *to wade, go in the water*—ćowapa, ćoyapa, ćouŋpapi.

ćo-pe′-ki-ya, *v. a.* *to cause to wade*—ćopewakiya.

ćos, *cont.* of ćoza.

ćos-a′, *adv.* *warmly, comfortably*—ćosa maŋka.

ćos-ćo′-za, *adj.* *red.* of ćoza.

ćos-ya′, *v. a.* *to cause to warm*—ćoswaya; ćosiçiya, *to warm one's self*—ćosmiçiya; *to put out to dry*, as cooked victuals; *to dry and smoke*, as meat.

ćos-ya′, *adv.* *warmly.*

ćos-ya′-ken, *adv.* *in a warm state* T., ćosyakel.

ćo′-taŋ-ka, *n.* (ćo *and* taŋka) *a fife, flute, any wind instrument.*

ćo-toŋ′, *adj.* (ćo *and* toŋ) *ripe, mature.*

ćo′-wa-he, *n.* *a scaffold*, such as the Indians make to dry corn on.

ćo-wo′-he, *n.* *the belly, lower part of the abdomen.*

ćo-wo′-he-a-ka-ḣpe, *n.* (ćowohe *and* akaḣpe) *an apron.*

ćo-ya′, *v. n.* *to ripen*, as grain, etc. T., ćo aya.

ćo-ya′-pi, *n.* *harvest.*

ćo′-za, *adj.* *warm, comfortable*, used both in regard to persons and things, as clothing, houses, etc.—maćoza, nićoza, uŋćozapi.

ću, *n.* *dew:* ću śma, *heavy dew.*

ću-ću′-śte, *n.* *the side below the ribs, the flank.*

ću-ḣćiŋ′, *adv.* T. Used with personal pronouns, miye, niye, etc.; sometimes with a numeral, but never alone, as niye ćuḣćiŋ ećoŋ wo, *do it yourself.*

ću′-kćaŋ, *n.* *a kind of duck.*

ću-kćaŋ′-pa-ġi, *n.* *a duck about the size of a mallard, with a gray head and white breast.*

ću-kćaŋ′-pa-sa-pa, *n.* *a species of duck, with a black head and neck.*

ću-kćaŋ′-ta-hu-sa-pe-daŋ, *n.* Same as ćukćanpasapa.

ću-kćaŋ′-taŋ-ka, *n.* *the large species of duck which they denominate* ćukćaŋ.

ću′-mni, *n.* *dew-drops.*

ću-mni′-śe, *n.* *dew standing in drops, dew-drops.* See aś'e.

ću-mni′-śe-śe, *n.* *dew-drops* all over anything.

ćuŋ, *n.* *a woman's elder sister*, used only with pronouns: mićuŋ *and* mićuŋwaye, *my elder sister;* nićuŋ, *thy elder sister.* T., ćuŋwe.

ćuŋ′-ku, *n.* *her elder sister.*

ćuŋ′-ku-ya, *v.* *to have for older sister.*

ćuŋkś′, *n.* *cont.* T. *my daughter;* used by the women in addressing their children, whether boys or girls; *my child.*

ćuŋ-kśi′, *n.* *a daughter:* mićuŋkśi, *my daughter;* nićuŋkśi, *thy daughter;* uŋkićuŋkśipi, *our daughters* Also, *a man's brother's daughter*, and *a woman's sister's daughter.*

ćuŋ-kśi′-tku, *n.* *his* or *her daughter.*

ćuŋ-kśi′-ya, *v.* *to have for a daughter, count as a daughter*—ćuŋkśiwaya.

ćuŋ′-kśu-daŋ, *n.* *a little bow*, such as small boys use.

ćuŋś, *n.* *my daughter;* used only when an address is made to the individual.

ćuŋ-we′, *n.* *Ih.* Same as ćuŋ.

ćuŋ-we′-ku, *n.* *Ih.* Same as ćuŋku.

ćuŋ-we′-ya, *v.* *Ih.* Same as ćuŋkuya and ćuŋya.

ćuŋ-wi′, *n.* *T. i. q.* mićuŋ, *my sister.* Also, ćuŋwe.

ćuŋ-wiŋ′-tku, *n.* *his* or *her daughter.*

ćuŋ wi′ ya po, *n.* *T. grapes.*

ćuŋ-wi′-ya-pe-i-yu-wi, *n.* *grape-vines.*

ćuŋ-ya′, *v.* *to have for an elder sister*—mićuŋwaya, ćuŋkuyaya.

ću-pe′, *n.* *marrow.*

ću-sni′, *adj.* *cool,* as dewy mornings and evenings.

ću-sta′-ka, *adj.* *damp, dewy, wet.*

ću-te′, *n.* *the side under the arm, pleura;* ćute pańdoka, *to make holes in one's flesh,* as one in mourning.

ću-ti′-ç̌iŋ, *v.* *to carry at the side* or *under the arm,* as a powder-horn or shot-pouch, strapped over the shoulder and coming down under the arm.

ću-ti′-ki-ç̌iŋ, *v.* *pos.* of ćutiç̌iŋ.

ću-tu′-hu, *n.* *a rib, the ribs.*

ću-wi′, *n.* *the side, pleura:* ćuwi mayazaŋ, *my side aches.*

ç̌u-wi′-hu, *n.* *the ribs.*

ću-wi′-pa-ha, *n.* *the prominent part of the side below the arms.*

ću′-wi-ta, *adj.* *cold, feeling cold,* used only of living things—maćuwita, nićuwita, uŋćuwitapi.

ću-wi′-yu-ksa-o-gle, *n.* *T. a vest.*

ću-wi′-yu-ski-te, *n.* *T. corsets.*

ću-wi′-zi, *n.* *a flower,* perhaps *the daisy.*

ću-ya, *v. a.* *to cause dew*—ćuwaya.

Ç̌.

ç̌, *the fourth letter of the Dakota alphabet.* It has the explosive or click sound of ć, which is made by pressing the end of the tongue against the palate, and at the moment of separation making the sound of Eng. *ch.*

ç̌a, *conj.* *and.* Same as ḳa.

ç̌a, *v.* of ḳa; *to dig.* See kiç̌a.

ç̌e-haŋ′, *adv.* *when.* Same as ḳehaŋ. *T.,* ç̌oŋhaŋ or ç̌ohaŋ, *when,* in the past.

ç̌eś, *conj.* *although.* Same as ḳeś.

ç̌e′-yaś, *conj.* *even if, although.* Same as ḳeyaś.

ç̌oŋ, *adv.* *T. i. q.* ḳoŋ.

D.

d, *the fifth letter of the Dakota alphabet.* This sound does not occur in the Titoŋwaŋ dialect; it uniformly becomes "l."

da, *v. a.* *to form an opinion of,* whether good or bad; *to think of* or *esteem* in any manner—wada, yada, uŋdapi. It is used often with waśte and śića, as waśte wada.

da, *v. a.* *to ask, demand*—wada, yada, uŋdapi; kida, *to ask of* one. *T.*, la.

da, *v.* 2d pers. sing. of ya, *to go; thou goest.*

da-ka′, *v. a.* *to have an opinion of,* whether good or bad. *T.*, laka.

da-ka′-eś, *adv.* Same as nakaeś.

da-kaŋ′-noŋ, *v.* 2d pers. sing.; *thou art.* *Pl.*, dakaŋnoŋpi. It is a defective verb, these being the only forms in use.

da-kon′, *cont.* of dakota.

da-kon′-ki-ći-ya-pi, *n.* *alliance, friendship;* dakonkićiya yakoŋpi, *they are in alliance.* *T.*, olakolkićiyapi.

da-kon′-ya, *v. a.* *to be friendly with, to have for a friend*—dakonwaya, dakonuŋyaŋpi.

da-ko′-ta, *adj.* *feeling affection for, friendly;* wadakota śni, *unfeeling, without natural affection.*

Da-ko′-ta, *n. p.* *the name of the Sioux Indians.* They are divided into seven principal divisions—Mdewakaŋtoŋwaŋs, Waḣpetoŋwaŋs, Waḣpekutes, Sisitoŋwaŋs, Ihaŋktoŋwaŋs, Ihaŋktoŋwaŋnas, and Titoŋwaŋs—Damakota, Danikota, Dawićakota. *T.*, Lakota.

dam-ya′, *adv.* *stiffly* or *thickly,* as in making mush; opposed to hdaheya: damya ećoŋ, *to make thick* or *stiff.* *T.*, labya, *very much so, intensely.*

daŋ, *a diminutive termination* of pronouns, nouns, adjectives, verbs, and adverbs. It is often changed to "na," which is in common use in the Sisitoŋwaŋ and Ihaŋktoŋwaŋ dialects, and to "la" in the Titoŋwaŋ. When suffixed to numeral adjectives, demonstrative pronouns, and adverbs, it signifies *only;* as waŋźidaŋ, *only one;* denana, *only these;* dehaŋna, *only so far.* See Grammar, in the chapter on Nouns.

da′-pa, *adj.* *sticky, adhesive,* as clay; *thick, stiff,* as mud.

da-za′-ta, *adv.* *back of, back from; i. q.* ḣeyata.

da-za′-taŋ-haŋ, *adv.* *back from, out from.*

de, *pron. dem.* *this; pl.* dena, *these.* *T.*, le.

de, *v. a.* *to go after; to cut* or *procure,* as firewood. See ćaŋde.

de′-ća, *adv.* *such as this.* *T.*, lećа.

de-ća′-ki-ćoŋ, *v. a.* *to do thus to*—dećawećoŋ, dećayećoŋ, dećauŋkićoŋpi. See ećakićoŋ.

de-ća′-ki-oŋ, *v. a.* *to do this to*—dećawakioŋ.

de′-ća-na, *adv.* *Ih.* *i. q.* aśkatudaŋ; *now, lately, soon.*

de′-će-ća, *adv.* *like this, as, such as; pl.* dećećapi: demaćeća, *I am such as this.* *T.*, lećeća.

de-će′-daŋ, *adv.* (de *and* ećedaŋ) *this alone.* *T.*, lećela.

de′-će-kće-ća, *adv.* *red.* of dećeća; *such as these.*

de′-će-kćen, *adv.* *red.* of dećen. *T.*, lećekćel.

de′-će-kćen-ya, *adv.* *red.* of dećenya. *T.*, lećekćelya.

de′-ćen, *adv.* *so, thus, after this manner.* *T.*, lećel.

de′-ćen-ya, *adv.* *so, thus.*

de′-će-tu, *adv.* *thus, so; right, this is right.* *T.*, lećetu.

de′-će-tu-ken, *adv.* *in this manner.*

de′-ći, *adv.* *here, in this place.* *T.*, lići.

de′-ći-ya, *adv.* *here, about here.*

de′-ći-ya-taŋ, *adv.* *from this.*

de′-ći-ya-taŋ-haŋ, *adv.* *from this place, on this side.*

de-ći′-yo-taŋ, *adv.* *in this direction.* *T.*, lećiyotaŋ.

de-ći′-yo-taŋ-haŋ, *adv.* *in this direction, this way.*

de′-ćoŋ, *v. a.* (de *and* ećoŋ) *to do this, act in this way*—dećamoŋ, dećanoŋ, dećoŋkoŋpi.

de′-e, *this is it.* This word, and also hee and ee, contain the substantive verb. *T.*, lee.

de′-ġa, *adj.* *loose, swinging.* See deḣdeġa.

de-ha′, *v.* 2d pers. sing. of deya.

de-han′, *adv.* *at this place, here; at this time, to-day, now*

de-han′-haŋ-ke-ća, *adv* *red.* of dehaŋkeća.

de-han′-haŋ-na, *adv.* *red.* of dehaŋna.

de-haŋ′, *adv.* *now; thus far.*

de-haŋ′-haŋ-yaŋ, *adv.* *red.* of dehaŋyaŋ.

de-haŋ′-ke-ća, *adv.* *so long, so high.* *T.*, lehaŋkeća.

de-haŋ′-na, *adv.* *thus far; now, just now, immediately, suddenly.*

de-haŋ′-na-ḣiŋ, *adv.* *just now, very lately.*

de-haŋ′-taŋ-haŋ, *adv.* *from this, i. q.* detaŋhaŋ.

de-haŋ′-tu, *adv.* *to this, thus far; now.* *T.*, lehaŋtu.

de-haŋ′-tu-ḣiŋ, *adv.* *just so far, just now.*

de-haŋ′-tu-ken, *adv.* *just so far, in this way; just now.*

de-haŋ′-tu-ya, *adv.* *to this extent, on this wise.* *T.*, lehaŋtuya.

de-haŋ′-tu-ya-ken, *adv.* *just now, on this wise.*

de-haŋ′-yaŋ, *adv.* *so far,* in *space; so long,* in time. *T.*, lehaŋyaŋ.

de-he′-tu-ya, *adv.* *just the time, i. q.* iyehaŋtu.

deḣ-de'-ġa, *adv.* *red.* of deġa; *loose, wrinkled, flabby; puffed out.*

de-kśi', *n.* *mother's brother, uncle, my uncle.* It is not applied to one's father's brothers, who are called ate: nidekśi, *thy uncle.* *T.*, lekśi.

de-kśi'-tku, *n.* *his* or *her uncle.*

de-kśi'-ya, *v.* *to have for uncle, call uncle*—dekśiwaya, dekśimayaŋ.

de-kta'-ya, *v. a.* *to have no regard for, to be dissatisfied with; i. q.* ćiŋśni and aktaśni—dektawaya.

dem-de'-pa, *adj.* *notched.*

den, *adv.* *here, in this place.* *T.*, lel, *and* leŋl.

de-na', *pron.* *pl.* of de; *these.* *T.*, lena.

de-nag'-na-ke-ća, *adv.* *red.* of denakeća.

de-na'-ke-ća, *adv.* *so many:* demanakeća, *I am so many;* deuŋnakećapi, *we are so many.* *T.*, lenakel.

de-na'-ke-seḣ, *adv.* *all these, so many.* *T.*, lenakeḣćiŋ.

de-na'-na, *adv.* *only so many, so few; pl.* denanaŋpidaŋ. *T.*, lenala.

de-na'-os, *adv.* *these two, both these:* denaosnana, *only these two.*

de-na'-o-za, *adv.* *both these.*

de-ni'-os, *adv.* See denaoza.

de-ni'-yos, *adv.* See denaoza.

de-pa', *v.* 1st pers. sing. of deya; *I said this.*

de-pća', *v.* 1st pers. sing. (de *and* epća) *I thought this.* No other forms in use.

de-peḣ', *n.* *a leper.* Introduced from the English.

deś-de'-źa, *v. n.* *red.* of deźa; *to urinate often.*

de-taŋ'-haŋ, *adv.* *from this place, from here, hence:* demataŋhaŋ, *I am from this place;* denitaŋhaŋ, *thou art from here; from this time, henceforth, hence.* *T.*, letaŋhaŋ.

de'-tu, *adv.* (de *and* etu) *to this, at this place* or *time; hither, here; hitherto, now.* *T.*, letu.

de'-tu-ḣiŋ-ća, *adv.* *just here.*

de'-tu-ya, *adv.* *here.*

de'-ya, *v.* (de *and* eya) *to say this*—depa, deha.

de'-źa, *v. a.* *to urinate*—wadeźa, uŋdeźapi.

de'-źa, *n.* *urine, chamber-lye;* wićadeźa, *urine, the bladder* of a person; tadeźa, *the bladder* of an animal.

di-di'-ta, *adj.* *very warm, hot;* said of the temperature of the weather, of a house, etc. *T.*, lilita, *and* luluta.

di-di'-ta-hda, *v. n.* *to become very warm; to regard as hot*—diditawahda.

do, *a particle,* used at the end of a phrase or sentence, for the sake of euphony or emphasis, as waśte do; "do" is used by the men alone; the women say "ye." *T.*, lo, *and* ye lo; *Ih.*, do *and* ye do.

do, *adj.* *soft, tender, moist,* as fresh meat, etc.; opposed to saka, *dried.* See tado, *fresh meat.*

do, *n.* *food.* *T.*, lo.

do-ćiŋ', *v.* *to want food, have an appetite.* *T.*, loćiŋ, *to be hungry.*

do-ćiŋ'-pi, *n.* *appetite.*

do-do', *adj.* *red.* of do; *soft, damp, fresh.*

do-dom'-ya, *adv.* *tenderly, very tender;* said of meat well cooked: dodomya śpaŋ, *cooked tender.* *T.*, lolobya, *and* lolobyela.

do-do'-pa, *adj.* *soft, miry.*

do-do'-pa, *n.* *a miry place.*

do-ḣde'-ska, *n.* *the gullet, œsophagus.* *T.*, logleska.

do-ḣe', *n.* *the parts of the cheeks and throat which are loose and not fastened to the bones.*

do-ksi', *n.* *the arm-pit:* doksi kaśe, *to chafe under the arm*, as a tight coat.

do-kśiŋ'-ća, *n.* *a mink, Mustela lutraola.* *T.*, ikusaŋ.

dom-ya', *adv.* domya śpaŋ. See dodomya. *T.*, lobya.

do'-pa, *adj.* *soft, miry.* See dodopa.

do'-pa, *v. n.* *to mire.* See dodopa, kadopa, etc. *T.*, lopa.

do-te', *n.* *food.*

do-te', *n.* *the throat, the whole fore-part of the neck.* *T.*, lote.

do-te'-hbe-za, *n.* *the wind-pipe, trachea.* *T.*, glogleska.

do-ti'-ćiŋ, *n.* See idotićiŋ.

do-tku', *n.* *the throat*, especially of animals; *the part immediately under the jaw.*

dot-o'-pi-ye, *n.* (dote *and* opiye) *a granary, pantry.* *T.*, lotopiye.

do-waŋ', *v. n.* *to sing*—wadowaŋ, yadowaŋ. *T.*, lowaŋ.

do-waŋ', *n.* *a song, hymn*—mitadowaŋ. See odowaŋ.

do-waŋ'-pi, *n.* *hymns; singing.*

do-ya', *adj.* *moist, not dry, fresh,* as meat.

do-ya'-ke, *adj.* *fresh, not dried.*

do-ya'-ken, *adv.* *in a moist condition.*

du-kaŋ'-pi, *v.* 2d pers. pl. of yukaŋ; *you are.*

dun, *cont.* of duta. *T.*, lul.

dun-ya', *v. a.* *to color red* or *scarlet*—dunwaya, dunyaya. *T.*, lulya.

dus, *adv.* *swiftly:* dus ya, *to go fast*—dus mda. *T.*, lus.

dus-du'-za-haŋ, *v.* *red.* of duzahaŋ. *T.*, lusluzahaŋ.

dus-ki'-ya, *v. a.* *to cause to be swift.*

dus-ya', *v.* *to make swift*—duswaya.

du'-ta, *adj.* *red, scarlet.* *T.*, luta.

du'-za, *v.* 2d pers. sing. of yuza; *thou holdest.*

du'-za-haŋ, *v. n.* *to be swift, fast running*—waduzahaŋ, yaduzahaŋ, uŋduzahaŋpi. *T.*, luzahaŋ.

E.

e, *the sixth letter of the Dakota alphabet*, with the long sound of English *a*, as in *late*, *fate*, etc.

e, *an inseparable preposition* or *prefix*.
1. Prefixed to verbs it commonly signifies *to*, *at*, and is equivalent to ekta, as eeḣpeya, *to throw away at* a place. It makes a *locative* form of the verb, and denotes that the action is done *at a place*, as, ebaksa, *to saw off at*. There are two other locative prefixes, namely, "a" and "o."
2. Of some verbs commencing with "i," it makes a collective plural form: as, inaźiŋ, *he stands*, enaźiŋ, *they stand*; iyaya, *he has gone*, eyaya, *they have gone*.

e, *intj.* *ah! well!* said when one misses his mark in shooting: *strange! why!*

e, *a particle*, used commonly after the sign of the future tense, when it is followed by a statement of the cause of what precedes, as, taŋyaŋ yauŋ kta e heoŋ hećamoŋ, *I have done this that it might be well with thee.* It also occurs in hee and dee, and seems to have the force of the substantive verb.

e-ća′, *adv.* *when.* See remarks under ća. It is also used, as in the cases which follow, to give emphasis.

e-ća′, *adv.* *permanently, truly;* eća waun, *I am usually.* With ka or ća at the end of the verb, *not truly, at random;* eća hećonka, *he did it in fun;* eća heyeća, *he said it in sport.* *T.*, *generally;* hel eća uŋpi, *they are generally there.*

e-ća′, *intj.* *Well! I declare! well done!*

e-ća′-ća, *adv.* *at all, by any means, so, entirely;* with śni following, *not at all:* ećaća yuhe kte śni, *he will not have it at all;* ećaća hi śni, *he did not come at all.*

e-ća′-ća-daŋ, *adv.* *red.* of ećadaŋ; *soon*, referring to more than one event. *T.*, ećakćal.

e-ća′-ća-ka-eś, *adv.* *indeed.*

e-ća′-daŋ, *adv.* *soon.* *T.*, ećala.

e-ća′-daŋ-ḣiŋ, *adv.* *very soon.* *T.*, ećalaḣćiŋ.

e-ća′-e-ćoŋ-ka, *v. n.* *to follow*, as a business; *to pretend; to do as one likes*—ećaećamoŋka. *T.*, *to do persistently against advice.*

e-ća′-eś, *adv.* *indeed, truly.*

e-ća′-haŋ-ke-ya, *adv.* *immediately, immediately after, at that time, continuously.* *T.*, ećahaŋkeyela, *incompletely.*

e-ća′-he-ćoŋ-ka, *v.* *to feign, pretend; not to do*—ećahećamoŋka, ećahećanoŋka. *T.*, *to do in spite of.*

e-ćaḣ', *adv.* *indeed, truly.* See ećaḣe.

e-ća'-ḣaŋ, *v. a.* *to kill; i. q.* kte: ahi ećaḣaŋ, *to come and kill one,* as a war party does—ećawaḣaŋ, ećauŋḣaŋpi.

e-ća'-ḣe, *adv.* *indeed, truly,* expressing impatience.

e-ća'-ḣiŋ, *adv.* *truly.*

e-ća'-ḣtiŋ, *adv.* *Si.* *indeed.* *T.,* ećaḣćiŋ.

e-ća'-i-ći-źe-haŋ, *adv.* *often.* See iźehaŋ.

e-ća'-ka-eś, *adv.* *at any rate.* *T.,* ećakaleś.

e-ća'-ka-tiŋ, *adv.* *directly.*

e-ća'-ka-tiŋ-yaŋ, *adv.* *directly, straight forward, without stoppage.*

e-ća'-ken, *adv.* *generally; naturally.* *T.,* ećakel.

e-ća'-ken-eś, *adv.* *at any rate.*

e-ća'-ki-ći-ćoŋ-pi, *v. pl.* *they do to each other.*

e-ća'-ki-ćoŋ, *v.* of ećoŋ; *to do to* one—ećawećoŋ, ećayećoŋ, ećauŋkićoŋpi, ećaćićoŋ, ećamiyećoŋ.

e-ća'-ki-oŋ, *v.* of ećoŋ; *to do to;* ećakićoŋ is the better form—ećawakioŋ, ećayakioŋ, ećauŋkioŋpi, ećamioŋ, ećanioŋ.

e-ća'-la, *T.;* e-ća'-na, *Ih.;* *soon, i. q.* ećadaŋ.

e-ća'-mna, *adj.* *having smell* or *taste, fragrant, savory.*

e-ćaŋ'-kiŋ, *v. a.* *to think so of, form an opinion of* one—ećaŋwakiŋ, ećaŋyakiŋ, ećaŋuŋkiŋpi, ećaŋćićiŋ: ećaŋmayakiŋ, *thou thinkest so of me.*

e-ćaŋ'-tu-daŋ, *adv.* *i. q.* ehaŋtudaŋ.

e-ća'-oŋ, *v.* *to do to* one—ećawaoŋ, ećayaoŋ.

e-ća'-o-waŋ-ća-ya, *adv.* *all over.*

e-ća'-o-wa-siŋ, *adv.* *all,* emphatically.

e-ća'-o-ya-ke-ya, *adv.* *telling, in the manner of relating.* *T.,* ećaoyagya.

e-ćaś', *adv.* *indeed.* Same as ećaeś.

e'-ća-ta, *v.* *to draw a bow*—éwakata, éyakata, éuŋkatapi.

e-ća'-wi-ći-śni-yaŋ, *adv.* *wrongly, entirely wrong.*

e-ća'-yaŋ-ke-ća, *v. n.* *to remain in one place*—ećamaŋkeća, ećauŋkaŋpika.

e-ća'-yaŋ-ke-ća, *n.* *something permanent, a fixture.*

e-ća'-yu-ḣi, *n.* *something that is all over buboes,* as a toad.

e-ća'-yu-ḣi, *adj.* *rough, uneven* on the surface.

e-će', *adv.* *only, usually, always:* kośka eće, *young men alone;* dehan waźuśteća yukaŋ eće, *at this time there are usually strawberries;* maġaźu eća maka spaya eće, *when it rains the ground is always wet.*

e-će', *intj.* *T.* *denotes doubt;* eće! tuwe kakeśa, *who would believe it!*

e-će'-ća, *adv.* *thus, so.*

e-će'-ća, *v. n.* *to be so, be affected*

with, as with a cold or disease of any kind; *to be like*—emaćeća, enićeća, uŋkećećapi.

e-će'-ća-ke, *adv.* *just so, even so, that alone.*

e-će'-će-daŋ, *adv.* *red.* of ećedaŋ.

e-će'-daŋ, *adv.* *only, alone, without anything extraneous.* *T.*, ećeela.

e'-će-daŋ-ya, *v. a.* *to purify, take away everything extraneous*—ééedaŋwaya.

e-će'-e-daŋ, *adv.* *only, that only.*

e-će'-hna, *adv.* *just so, without alteration* or *change:* ećehna haŋ, *remaining just so.*

e-će'-hna-hna, *v.* *red.* of ećehna.

e-će'-hna-na, *adv.* *only so, just so, nothing more.*

e-ćeḣ', *adv.* *times; well:* topa ećeḣ topa, *four times four;* ećeḣ tuka će, *well, so it is,* said when one is badly off for some particular thing, although well off in most respects.

e-će'-ḣiŋ, *adv.* *so, just so.*

e-će'-ḣćiŋ, *and* e-će'-ḣtiŋ, *adv.* *just so, exactly.*

e-će'-kćen, *adv.* *red.* of ećen; *in this manner* or *way; so and so, thus and thus.* *T.*, ećekćel.

e-će'-kćen-ya, *adv.* *thus and thus.*

e-ćel', *adv.* *T.* *so, thus:* *i. q.* ećen.

e-ćel'-ya, *v.* *T.* for ećel iyeya: tiyopa ećelya, *shut the door.*

e-ćen', *adv.* *so, thus, as it was, as it ought to be:* ećen iću, *to place as it was;* tiyopa ećen iću, *shut the door.*

e-ćeś', *intj.* *of unwillingness.*

e'-će-ti, *v.* (ekta *and* ćeti) *to build a fire to* or *at*—ééewati, ééeyati, ééeuŋtipi.

e-će'-tu, *adv.* *so, thus; just, right; about so many* or *so much:* yamni ećetu, *about three.*

e-će'-tu, *v. n.* *to be accomplished* or *fulfilled.* From this are formed ekićićetu, ekićetu, yuećetu, etc.

e-će'-tu-ki-ya, *v. a.* *to make so, to accomplish, fulfill*—ećetuwakiya.

e-će'-tu-ya, *v. a.* *to fulfill, accomplish, bring about*—ećetuwaya, ećetuyaya, ećetuuŋyaŋpi.

e-će'-wa-kta, *v.* *to attend to, to pursue such a course; to be accustomed to*—ećewawakta, ećewayakta, ećewauŋktapi.

e-će'-wa-kta-ya, *adv.* *attending to.*

e-će'-wiŋ, *adv.* *very much; i. q.* ota: ećewiŋ mayaḳu, *thou hast given me much.* See ićewiŋ. *T.*, ićewiŋś.

e-će'-wiŋ-yaŋ, *adv.* *bountifully, liberally.* *T.*, ićewiŋśya.

e-će'-ye-daŋ, *adv.* *only so.*

e-ći'-ći-ya, *v.* of ećiya; *I say to thee.*

e'-ći-na-kśiŋ, *v. col.* used only with the plural ending, either on itself or a following verb (of anakikśiŋ): *to stand up for each other, to shield each other, to help each other:* ećinakśiŋ yakoŋpi.

e-ćiŋ', *v. n.* *to think, suppose*—ećaŋmi, ećaŋni, uŋkećiŋpi.

e-ćiŋ', *adv.* *to-day, soon, now* always referring to the future; *then indeed.*

e-ćiŋ'-e-śta, *adv.* *even to-day, by and by.*

e-ćiŋ'-ka, *v.* Same as ećiŋ; *to think, to hesitate* or *waver in one's opinions*—ećaŋmika.

e-ćiŋ'-kta, *adv.* *falsely, not truly:* ećiŋkta eya, *to tell what is not so.*

e-ćiŋ'-na-ke-ćiŋ-haŋ, *adv.* *soon, presently, in a little while.*

e-ćiŋ'-śni, *adj.* *thoughtless, foolish, vain.*

e-ćiŋ'-śni-yaŋ, *adv.* *thoughtlessly, foolishly, wrong:* ećiŋśniyaŋ ećamoŋ, *I have done foolishly:* ećiŋśniyaŋ nawahoŋ, *I heard wrongly.*

e-ćiŋ'-to, *adv.* *what of it?* The "to" is probably a contraction of tokeća. *T.*, ćiŋto.

e'-ći-pa, *v. n.* of akipa; *to meet together,* as two ends of anything, or as two armies in battle—éćipapi.

e'-ći-pe-ya, *v. a.* *to cause to meet together,* as the two ends of anything—éćipewaya.

e'-ći-ptaŋ, *adv.* of akiptaŋ; *together:* éćiptaŋ ećoŋkupi, *we do it together.*

e'-ći-ta-pa, *adj.* *agreeing with each other, fitted to, all of the same length.*

e'-ći-to-o-pta, *adv.* *in the direction of, by* anything.

e'-ći-to-o-pte-ya, *adv.* *directly by, in the direction of.*

e-ći'-ya, *v. a.* of eya; *to say to one*—ewakiya, eyakiya, uŋkekiyapi, emakiya, enićiya, ećićiya, emayakiya; uŋkekićiyapi, *we say to each other.*

e-ći'-ya-pi, *v.* 3d pers. pl. of ećiya; also *part., called, named:* hećen ećiyapi, *he is so called.*

e-ći'-ya-taŋ, *adv.* *from, thence, hence.*

e-ći'-ya-taŋ-haŋ, *adv.* *from, of, on account of, concerning, hence.*

e'-ći-yu-pta, *v.* of ayupta; *to answer one another;* *i. q.* akićiyuptapi: éćiuŋyuptapi, *we answer one another.*

e-ćoŋ', *v. a.* *to do, to work*—ećamoŋ, ećanoŋ, ećoŋkupi and ećoŋkoŋpi. Of this are formed ećakićoŋ, ećakićićoŋ, and ećakioŋ.

e-ćoŋ'-ka-p'iŋ, *v.* *to be tired of doing, not to want to do*—ećoŋwakap'iŋ, ećoŋuŋkap'iŋpi. See kap'iŋ.

e-ćoŋ'-ki-ya, *v. a.* *to cause to do* anything.

e-ćoŋ'-na, *v.* *dim.* of ećoŋ.

e-ćoŋ'-na, *v. n.* *to gamble, play* where anything is staked—ećamoŋna, ećanoŋna, ećoŋkupidaŋ.

e-ćoŋ'-pi-ća, *v.* *it can be done, is possible:* ećoŋpića śni, *it is not possible, cannot be done.* Pića, when joined to verbs, denotes *possibility.*

e-ćoŋ'-pi-ća-ka, *v.* *it is possible.*

e-ćoŋ'-pi-daŋ, *n.* *gambling.* See oećoŋna. *T*, wayekiyapi.

e-ćoŋ'-śi-pi, *n.* *orders.*

e'-e, *v.* *it is, that is.* This, with hee, dee, etc., includes the substantive verb.

e'-e-ća-ḣaŋ, *v.* See ećaḣaŋ.

e'-e-ḣpe-ki-ya, *v. a.* *to take to and leave at, to throw away at*—ćeḣpewakiya.

e'-e-ḣpe-ya, *v. a.* *to take and leave*—ćeḣpewaya.

e'-e-ki-ya, *adv.* *instead of.*

e'-e-ki-ya, *v. a.* *to substitute for, put for another; to regard as being something:* taku samya waŋke ćiŋ he tataŋka eewakiya, *that black thing I take to be a buffalo.*

e-eś', *adv:* *indeed.* John i, 50; *that is it.*

e'-gla, *prep.* *among: T. i. q.*, ehna.

e'-gla-ka, *v.* *T.* Same as ehnaka.

e'-gla-ku, *v.* *T.* Same as ehdaku.

e'-gle, *v.* *T.* Same as ehde: tiyopa ecel egle, *put the door to.*

e'-gna, *prep.* *T.* Same as ehna.

e'-gna-ka, *v.* *T.* Same as ehnaka.

e-ha'-eś, *adv.* *indeed, truly;* used when one overdoes the matter; 2. *intj.* *Well! I declare.* *T.*, ehakaleś.

e-ha'-ha, *v.* *red.* 2d pers. of eya.

e-ha'-ha-daŋ-ka, *v.* 2d pers. of eyayadaŋka; *you don't say so.* *T.*, ehahalaka, *you lie.*

e-ha'-ke, *adv.* *yet, yet to come:* ehake waŋżidaŋ, *one yet.*

e-ha'-ke, *n.* *the last one.*

e-ha'-ke-daŋ, *n.* *the last.* *Ih.*, ehakena.

e-ha'-ke-daŋ, *adv.* *yet a little while.*

e-ha'-ke-daŋ-ka-se, *adv.* *a little more, yet a little.*

e-ha'-ke-daŋ-ke-ćiŋ-haŋ, *adv.* *soon.*

e-haŋ', *adv.* *then, at that time:* he ehaŋ, *at that time*, referring to past time alone; *there, at that place, to, thus far:* ehaŋ wai, *I have been there;* ehaŋ uŋkipi, *we have been there.*

e-haŋ', *intj.* *of assent; oh yes! yes; i. q.* haŋ. The last syllable is prolonged.

e-haŋ'-ke-ća, *adv.* *Ih. i. q.* ehaŋḳoŋ. J. P. W.

e-haŋ'-ḳe-haŋ, *adv.* *T. formerly.*

e-haŋ'-ḳoŋ, *adv.* *indeed.* This word is used when one is informed or convinced of something which he has doubted or disbelieved, or has been ignorant of. It is sometimes followed by huŋśte, as ehaŋḳoŋ wićakapi huŋśte, *well, that is true.*

e-haŋ'-na, *adv.* *long ago.*

e-haŋ'-na-taŋ-haŋ, *adv.* *from a long time ago.*

e-haŋ'-taŋ-haŋ, *adv.* *from, from that time* or *place:* hipi kin ehaŋtaŋhaŋ yamni ćaŋ, *it is three days since they came.*

e-haŋ'-tu, *adv.* *at that time.*

e-haŋ'-tu-daŋ, *adv.* *then.* *Ih.*, ehaŋtuna.

e-haŋ'-tu-daŋ-ḣiŋ, *adv.* *just then.* *T.*, ehaŋtulaḣćiŋ, *just there.*

e'-hda-ku, *v.* *pos.* of éyaku; *to take up again, take back again; to take up one's own*—éwahdaku, éyahdaku, éuŋhdakupi. *T.*, eglaku.

e'-hde, *v. a.* *to place, set* or *make stand* in a place—éwahde, éyahde, éuŋhdepi. *T.*, egle.

e'-hde-ġa, *v.* *to overtake*—éwahdeġa, éyahdeġa.

e'-hdu-za, *v.* *pos.* of éyuza; *to overtake and take one's own; to retaliate*—éwahduza.

e-he'-daŋ, *v.* *dim.* of eha; *thou saidst so.* Used when speaking to a child.

e-he'-daŋ, *intj.* *thou sayest so.* A by-word.

e'-hna, *prep.* *with, in, amongst, through, in the midst of:* wićehna, *amongst them.* *T.*, egna.

e'-hnag, *cont.* of éhnaka; éhnag aya, *to take and lay away.*

e'-hna-hna, *prep.* *red.* of éhna.

e'-hna-ka, *v. a.* *to lay down* or *place; to lay away, to put off* or *delay; to stop from, let rest, lay aside,* as some matter of business—éwahnaka, éuŋhnakapi, and uŋkehnakapi. *T.*, egnaka.

e'-hna-na, *adv.* *amongst.* *T.*, egnalaȟćiŋ.

e'-ȟa, *v. a.* of ȟa; *to take to and bury at* a place—éwaȟa.

e-ȟpa'-ya, *v. n.* See iȟpaya, the better orthography.

e-ȟpe'-ki-ći-ći-ya-pi, *n.* *throwing each other away, divorcement.*

e-ȟpe'-ki-ći-ya, *v.* taku eȟpekićiya aku, *they throw away things as they return.*

e-ȟpe'-ki-ya, *v. a.* *pos.* of eȟpeya; *to throw away, forsake, leave one's own:* winoȟiŋća eȟpekiya, *he has put away his wife*—eȟpewakiya, eȟpeuŋkiyapi.

e-ȟpe'-ya, *v. a.* *to throw away, put aside, leave, forsake:* toki eȟpeya, *to lose* anything—eȟpewaya, eȟpeuŋyaŋpi.

e'-i-hda-ku, *v.* *reflex.* of éhdaku; *to take away* or *deliver one's self*—émihdaku, énihdaku. *T.*, eiglaku.

e'-ka-ta, *v.* *to put the arrow to the string, draw the bow*—éwakata, éyakata, éuŋkatapi. See éćata, which is more correct.

e-ki'-će-tu, *v. n.* *pos* of ećetu; *to recover, become as before*—emakićetu, enikićetu, euŋkićetupi.

e-ki'-će-tu-ya, *v. a.* *to cause to recover, make right again; to restore, raise up from the dead*—ekićetuwaya, ekićetuyaya, ekićetuuŋyaŋpi.

e-ki'-ći-će-tu, *v. n.* *to become as before to* or *for* one—emićićetu, enićićetu, euŋkićićetupi.

e'-ki-ći-hda-ku, *v.* *pos.* *to take one's own from* another; *to take away what one has given*—éwećihdaku, éyećihdaku, éuŋkićihdakupi, émićihdakupi.

e'-ki-ći-hde, *v.* of éhde; *to place for* one—éwećihde, éyećihde, éuŋkićihdepi. *T.*, ekićigle.

e'-ki-ći-hdu-za, *v.* of éḥduza; *to take one's own from* another; *to retaliate*—éwećiḥduza.

e'-ki-ći-hna-ka, *v.* of éhnaka; *to lay away for* one, *put away and keep for* one—éwećihnaka, éyećihnaka, éuŋkićihnakapi, émićihnaka.

e'-ki-ći-oŋ-pa, *v.* of éoŋpa; *to place* or *set* as a trap *for* anything; *to lay away* or *place* something *for* another—éwećioŋpa, éyećioŋpa, éuŋkićioŋpapi.

e'-ki-ći-pa, *v.* of akipa; *to meet, launch out to*—éwećipa, éuŋkićipapi.

e'-ki-ći-pa-zo, *v.* of épazo; *to point to for* one—éwećipazo, éyećipazo, éuŋkićipazopi.

e-ki'-ći-ya, *v.* used only in the dual and plural: ekićiyapi, *they said to each other;* uŋkekićiya, *we two say to each other.* See ećiya.

e'-ki-ći-ya-ku, *v.* of éyaku; *to take from* one—éwećiyaku, éyećiyaku, éuŋkićiyakupi.

e'-ki-ći-źu, *v.* of eźu; *to pile up for* one; *to hand over to* another, as to one who wins in gambling—éwećiźu, éuŋkićiźupi.

e'-ki-hde, *v.* *pos.* of éhde; *to place* or *lay away one's own*—éwehde, éyehde, éuŋkihdepi.

e'-ki-hde-ġa, *v.* *to overtake* one—éwehdeġa, éyehdeġa, éuŋkihdeġapi, éćihdeġa, émihdeġa, énihdeġa; éwićuŋkihdeġapi, *we overtake them.*

e'-ki-hna-ka, *v.* *pos.* of éhnaka; *to lay away one's own*—éwehnaka, éuŋkihnakapi.

e'-ki-pa-zo, *v.* of épazo; *to show to* one, *point to for* one—éwakipazo, éyakipazo, éuŋkipazopi, émakipazo.

e'-kna, *prep.* *Ih.* Same as éhna.

e'-kna-ka, *v.* *Ih.* Same as éhnaka.

e-kta', *prep.* *at, to:* ekta mde kta, *I will go to.*

e-kta'-ki-ya, *adv.* *to, towards.*

e-kta'-kta, *prep.* *red.* of ekta.

e-kta'-śni-yaŋ, *adv.* *not according to.*

e'-ktoŋ-źa, *v.* *Ih.* Same as akiktoŋźa. *T., to forget one's own.*

e-ķe', *compound rel. pron.* *that which, that itself, even that.* It refers to some person or thing before mentioned.

e-ķeś', *pron.* Same as eķe. *T., adv., as for that one.*

en, *prep.* *in, at, to, of,* or *concerning;* en uŋ, *he is in;* en ai, *to charge upon* one, *lay to one's charge;* en au, *to bring upon* one; en aya, *to lay to one's charge;* en amda, *I take to* or *charge upon* one. *T.,* el *and* eŋl.

e-nag'-na-la, *adv.* *T. i. q.* enana.

e-na'-ki-ya, *v. a.* *to finish, quit, cease from*—enawakiya, enauŋkiyapi.

e-na'-na, *adv.* *here and there.*

e-na'-na-ki-ya, *adv.* *scattered, here and there:* enanakiya iyayapi.

e'-naŋ-pa, *v.* See énapa.

e'-na-pa, *v.* *col. pl.* of inapa; *they come in sight.*

e'-na-pe-ya, *adv.* *coming in sight, coming out of.*

e'-na-pe-ya, *v. a.* *to cause to come in sight; to cause to come out, bring forward; to speak audibly, tell, relate, make known*—énapewaya, énapeyaya, énapeuŋyaŋpi; ho énapeye śni, *he does not make his voice heard.* *T.*, *to come in sight, become visible.*

e'-na-źiŋ, *v. n.* *to stand at* a place—énauŋźiŋpi.

e'-na-źiŋ, *v. n.* *col. pl.* of inaźiŋ; *they stand there.*

e'-na-źiŋ-ya, *v. a.* *to cause to stand at; to bring to a stand,* as one following deer, when he overtakes it—énaźiŋwaya.

e-ni'-ći-ći-ya, *adv.* *scattered abroad; i. q.* enanakiya.

e-ni'-ći-ya, *v.* of ećiya; *he says to thee.*

en'-tu, *adv.* *there, in that place; at, in.* See etu.

e'-o-ka-siŋ, *v.* See éyokasiŋ, the better orthography.

e'-oŋ-pa, *v. a.* *to place, lay, to set* as a trap; *to lay* or *place carefully,* as a sick person on a bed—éwaoŋpa, éyaoŋpa, éuŋkoŋpapi.

e-pa', *v.* 1st. pers. sing. of eya; *I said.*

e'-pa-ḣpa, *v. a.* *to take to and lay down at*—éwapaḣpa, éyapaḣpa, éuŋpaḣpapi.

e'-pa-ni, *v. a.* *T.* *to crowd* or *shove, push with the elbow.*

e-pa'-pa, *v.* *red.* of epa.

e'-pa-zo, *v. a.* *to point at, point to*—éwapazo, éyapazo, éuŋpazopi.

e-pća', *v.* 1st pers. sing. *I think:* epće ćikoŋ, *I thought.* This is the only *person* used. See hepća and kepća.

e-pća'-ken, *adv.* *as I think.*

e-pće'-ća, *v.* *I think so.* See epća.

e-pe'-daŋ, *v.* *dim.* of epa.

e-pe'-daŋ, *intj.* *I said so, I told you so.*

eś, *particle.* John xi. 56.

e-śa' *and* e-śaŋ', *adv.* *T.* *though, although: i. q.* eśta.

e-śta', *conj.* *though, although, even if:* hećamoŋ eśta waśte kte śni, *although I should do that, it would not be well.* It is used singularly in some phrases, as, mayaku eśta śni, *why don't you give it to me?* mayaku śni eśta śni, *thou needest not give it to me;* maku śni eśta kta, *do not give it to me.*

e-śtaŋ'-haŋ, *conj.* *although:* hi eśtaŋhaŋ sdonwaye śni, *although he has come I do not know it.* *T.*, eśahaŋ *and* yeśahaŋ.

e-śtaś', *intj.* *indeed!* *T.*, eśaś.

e-taŋ', *adv.* an abbreviated form of etaŋhaŋ.

e-taŋ'-haŋ, *prep.* *from, on account of, concerning.*

e-taŋ'-haŋś-to-ke-ća, *adv.* *T.* *what difference does it make?*

e-ta'-pa, *n.* *the right hand*—ematapa and mietapa, enitapa and nietapa: etapa ećiyataŋhaŋ, *at the right hand;* taŋ etapaŋhaŋ, *at the right side.*

e-ta'-pa, *adj.* *right-handed*—ematapa, enitapa, euŋtapapi.

e-ta'-pa-taŋ-haŋ, *adj.* *at the right hand of*—ematapataŋhaŋ.

e'-ta-wa-pa, *v.* (e *and* tawapa) *to overtake.*

e'-ti, *v. a.* *to encamp at, pitch a tent at*—éwati, éyati, éuŋtipi.

e'-tki-ya, *adv.* *towards:* étkiya ya, *to go towards, to make a motion to go towards.*

e'-toŋ-waŋ, *v. a.* *to look to* or *towards*—éwatoŋwaŋ, éyatoŋwaŋ, éuŋtoŋwaŋpi, ématoŋwaŋ.

e-to'-o-pta, *adv.* *in the direction of, through* or *by* an object, *straight through without stopping.*

e-to'-o-pte-ya, *adv.* *by, through, straight through.* *T.*, etoopteyela.

e-to'-o-pte-ya-ken, *adv.* *in the direction of, by.*

e-to'-pte-ya, *adv.* *by, towards, through.*

e'-tu, *adv.* *to, at, in:* he étu, *at that place.* See entu.

e'-uŋ, *v.* *to go and dwell* or *be; to be* or *dwell at*—éwauŋ, éyauŋ.

e'-wa-ćiŋ, *v. a* *to think of* or *concerning; to set the mind to, turn the attention to*—éwaćaŋmi, éwaćaŋni, éwauŋćiŋpi.

e'-waŋ-ka, *v. a.* *to go and sleep at*—émuŋka, énuŋka. *T.*, eyuŋka.

e'-waŋ-ka, *v.* *col. pl.* of iwaŋka.

e'-ya, *adv.* *also, too:* miś eya, *I also.*

e'-ya, *v.* *to say* anything—epa, eha, uŋkeyapi, ehapi, eyapi. From this come heya, keya, ećiya, ekićiya, and éyaya. The Titons and Yanktons say eyiŋ when kta follows, as eyiŋ kta, ehiŋ kta, epiŋ kta.

e'-ya-ća-śtoŋ, *v.* *to give a name to.* See ćaśtoŋ.

e'-ya-haŋ, *v.* *col. pl.* of iyahaŋ.

e'-ya-he, *v.* Same as éyahaŋ.

e'-ya-hiŋ-hda, *v.* *to commence* or *burst out saying.* *T.*, eyahiŋgla.

e'-ya-ke, *adv.* *also, too.*

e'-ya-keś, *intj.* *T.* *well, oh! well.*

e'-ya-ku, *v. a.* *to take up, take away*—émdaku, édaku, éuŋyakupi.

e'-ya-ni-yaŋ, *v.* *to cry out, to say calling out.*

e'-yaŋ-pa-ha, *v.* *to herald, proclaim aloud; to stand out and make a speech in camp*—éyaŋwapaha, éyaŋyapaha, éyaŋuŋpahapi.

e'-yaŋ-pa-ha, *n.* *a crier, herald, one who proclaims the decisions of councils.*

e'-ya-pa-ṭo, *v. n.* *to strike against* one, *butt against*—eyamapaṭo, eyanipaṭo, eyauŋpaṭopi.

e'-yaś, *adv.* *T.* *so, even so, although.*

e'-ya-śiŋ, *adv.* *T.* *nevertheless.*

e-ya'-ya, *v.* *red.* of eya; *to say often, repeat*—epapa, ehaha, uŋkeyayapi. *T.*, eyayalaka, *to lie.*

e'-ya-ya, *v. a.* *to take* or *have taken with* one—émdamde, édade, éuŋyayapi: makeyaya, *he has taken* *away* something of *mine.* See keyaya.

e′-ya-ya, *v. col. pl.* of iyaya; *they have gone.*

e′-ye, *v. i. q.*, eya.

e-yiŋ′, *v. T.* See under eya.

e′-yo-ka-kiŋ, *v. a. to look round into*, as in at a door partly open; *to look out of*—éyowakakiŋ, éyouŋkakiŋpi.

e′-yo-ka-siŋ, *v. a. to peep in*, as at a keyhole; *to look in by stealth*—éyowakasiŋ, éyouŋkasiŋpi.

e′-yu-ħpa, *v. a. to take and lay down at, to take off* one's pack *and rest at*—émduħpa.

e′-yu-kaŋ, *v col. pl. they go and stay.* Same as iyukaŋpi.

e′-yuŋ-ka, *v. T., i. q.*, ewaŋka.

e′-yu-za, *v. a. to go and take at, seize and hold at* or *on the way; to hold to* or *at*—émduza.

e-ze′, *intj.* expressing *surprise* and *unbelief.*

e′-źu, *v. a. to pile up, lay up in a pile*—éwaźu. *T.*, ekśu.

e′-źu-pi, *part. piled up.*

G.

g, *the seventh letter of the Dakota alphabet.* It has the sound of *g* in *good, glad*, etc. It occurs in the Dakota language only at the end of a syllable, and as a contraction of "ka," except in the Titoŋwaŋ dialect, where "gl" is used in the place of "hd" and "hn" of the Waħpetoŋwaŋ and "kd" and "kn" of the Ihaŋktoŋwaŋ dialects.

gla, *v. pos. T. to go to one's home*—wagla. Same as hda.

gla′-pa, *adj. T. i. q.* hdapa.

gla-pe′, *v. T. to take up* when one wins in gambling.

gla-tkaŋ′, *v. pos. T. i. q.* hdatkaŋ, *to drink one's own.*

gla′-wa, *v. pos. T. to read one's own*—waglawa. Same as hdawa.

gla-ya′, *v. T. to sound*, as the depth of water—glawaya.

gla-za′-ta, *adv. T. by the side of;* miglazata, *by my side.*

gla′-źa, *v. n. T. to be sick* or *diseased; i. q.* kaŋheźa: distinguished from wayazaŋka, as that means an attack of sickness—this a confirmed state: maglaźa, niglaźa, unglaźapi. T. L. R.

glaź-uŋ′-ke *or* glaś-uŋ′-ke, *v. n.* or *adj.* (glaźa *and* uŋ) *T. to be a confirmed invalid*—glaśmuŋke, etc.

gli, *v. pos. T. to come home*—wagli. Same as hdi.

gli-ću′, *v. pos T. to start to come home*—wagliću. Same as hdiću.

gli-gla′, *v. n. T. to pass on going home*—wagligla. Same as hnihda.

gli-yo′, *v. T. pos.* of hiyo: *i. q.* hduwe: gliyo mni kta, *I will go for my own.*

glo-gla′, *v. pos. T. to carry back home*—waglogla. Same as hdohda.

glo-gle′-ska, *n. T. the gullet; i. q.* hdohdeska.

glo-gli′, *v. pos. T. to bring back home*—waglogli. Same as hdohdi.

glu-kćaŋ′, *v. pos. T. to form an opinion of what concerns one's self*—waglukćaŋ. Same as hdukćaŋ.

gna′-ka, *v. a. T. i. q.* hnaka.

gna-śkiŋ′-yan, *v. T. i. q.* hnaśkiŋyaŋ

gna′-yaŋ, *v. T. i. q.* hnayaŋ.

gnu′-ni, *v. n. T. i. q.* hnuni or nuni: *to wander, be lost, lose*—wagnuni, etc.

gnu-gnu′-śka, *n. T. the grasshopper; grasshoppers; i. q.* psipsićadaŋ.

NOTE.—These words are only given as examples of this peculiarity of the Titoŋwaŋ dialect.

Ġ.

ġ, *the eighth letter of the Dakota alphabet.* It represents a deep sonant guttural.

ġa. See yuġa.

ġa-ġa′, *adv. T. on the surface.*

ġa-ġa′-ya, *adv. T.* ġaġaya śpaŋ, *cooked on the outside.*

ġa-ġa′-ye-la, *adv. T.* ġaġayela śpaŋ, *well cooked.*

ġa-haŋ′, *adj. great, loud, harsh,* or *rough,* as the voice: ho maġahaŋ, *my voice is rough.*

ġa-he′-ća, *adj. harsh, rough, loud,* as the voice—maġaheća.

ġam, *cont.* of ġapa.

ġaŋ, *adj. open, full of little holes.*

ġaŋ-ġaŋ′, *adj. open,* as thin cloth.

ġaŋ-ġaŋ′-na, *adj. thin, open, full of small holes.*

ġaŋ-ġaŋ′-ye-daŋ, *adj. very sharp and thin,* as the blade or bit of an ax: ġaŋġaŋyedaŋ yumaŋ, *to grind sharp and thin.*

ġaŋ-ġa′-ta, *adj. forked, pronged; open,* as cloth. *T.*, ġalġata.

ġaŋ-ġe′-ća, *n. dandruff.* See ġiŋġiŋća.

ġa′-pa. See yuġapa.

ġa-pa′-wa-haŋ, *part. stripped off, come off of itself.* See yuġapa.

ġa′-ta, *adj. forked, pronged:* tahiŋća he yamni ġata, *a deer's horns have three prongs.*

ġe-ća. See ġuġeća.

ġe-ġe′-ya, *v. n. to swing,* as one's arms, like a drunken man—ġeġeićiya.

ġe-ġe′-ya, *adv. swinging, dangling.*

ġi, *adj. brown, dark-gray, rusty-looking.*

ġi-ġi′, *adj. red.* of ġi; *brown, rusty.*

ġi-ġi′, *n.* *rust.*

ġi-ġi′-taŋ-ka, *n.* *oranges, lemons.* *T.*, taspaŋġi.

ġiŋ′-ća, *v. n.* *to snivel, grunt, sob*—waġiŋća, yaġiŋća, uŋġiŋćapi.

ġiŋ-ġiŋ′-ća, *n.* *dross; quicksilver* of looking-glasses; pa ġinġiŋća, *dandruff* (see ḣeġiŋća); maḣpi ġiŋġiŋća, *certain webs*, like spiders' webs, *which are seen floating in the air in the fall of the year.*

ġiŋ-ġiŋ′-ća, *adj.* *smoky, hazy* as Indian summer.

ġi-tka′, *adj.* *brownish.*

ġi-tka′-daŋ, *adj.* *a little brownish.*

ġi-tka′-tka, *adj.* *red.* of ġitka; *reddish, brownish,* or *yellowish.*

ġi-ya′, *v a.* *to make brown*—ġiwaya, ġiyaya, ġiuŋyaŋpi; ġiiçiya, *to make one's self brown*—ġimiçiya.

ġi-ya′, *adv.* *brownly:* ġiya śpaŋ, *cooked brown.*

ġom-ġom′, *cont.* of ġomġopa: ġomġom niya, *to breathe with difficulty*, as one snoring. *T.*, ġobġob.

ġom-ġo′-pa, *v.* *red.* of ġopa.

ġom′-ya, *adv.* *in a snoring manner.*

ġoŋ′-ġa, *adj.* iśta ġoŋġa, *blind, one blind*—iśta maġoŋġa, iśta niġoŋġa, iśta uŋġoŋġapi.

ġo′-pa, *v. n.* *to snore*—waġopa, yaġopa, uŋġopapi.

ġu, *v. n.* *to burn, singe, scorch, be burnt*—maġu, niġu, uŋġupi.

ġu-ġe′-ća, *n.* *the soft, spongy part of bones* in which there is oil.

ġu ġu′, *v.* *red.* of ġu; *to be burnt in several places.*

ġu-ġu′-ya, *v.* *red.* of ġuya

ġu′-ka. See yuġuka.

ġu-ka′-haŋ, *part.* *stretched, strained, sprained.*

ġu-ka′-wa-haŋ, *part.* *strained.*

ġu-mna′, *adj.* (ġu *and* omna) *smelling burnt.*

ġuŋ′-ġa, *adj.* *T.* *proud.*

ġuŋ′-ġa-ġa, *adj.* *T.* *red.* of ġuŋġa.

ġuŋ-ġa′-ġa-ya, *adv.* *T.* *proudly.*

ġu-ya′, *v. a.* *to burn, cause to burn*—ġuwaya, ġuyaya, ġuuŋyaŋpi.

ġu-ya′, *adv.* *in a burnt manner.*

ġu-ya′-pi, *n.* *a brand* on an animal.

H.

h, *the ninth letter of the Dakota alphabet.* It is an aspirate, like the English *h* in *hymn.*

h a, *n.* *a flea, fleas.* *T.*, hala.

h a, *n.* *the skin* or *hide* of animal, man included; *the bark* or *rind* of anything, as trees, etc.

h a - a′ - k a m, *adv.* *on the outside, on the surface.* *T*, haakab.

h a - a′ - k a m - y e - d a ŋ, *adv.* *on the surface, shallow,* as in plowing, *skimming over the surface.*

h a - a′ - k a - p a, *adv.* *on the outside.*

h a - a′ - k a - p a - t a, *adv.* *externally.*

h a - a′ - k a - p a - t a ŋ - h a ŋ, *adv.* *on the outer surface.*

H a′ - d e s, *n.* *the place of the dead, hell.* Introduced from the Greek.

h a - h a′ - d a ŋ, *adv.* *tottering, moving, easily moved.*

h a - h a′ - y a, *v. a.* *to move, make a coward of;* *i. q.* ćaŋtewaŋkaya—hahawaya, hahauŋyaŋpi.

h a - h a′ - y a, *adv.* *totteringly, moving.*

h a - h a′ - y e - d a ŋ, *adv.* *moved, not firm:* ćaŋte hahayedaŋ mayaŋka, *my heart is in an excited state.*

h a - ḣ o ŋ′ - t a, *n.* *thread, twine, cord.*

h a - ḣ o ŋ′ - t a - i - y a - p e - h a ŋ - p i, *n.* *spool-thread.*

h a - ḣ o ŋ′ - t a - z i b - z i - p e - d a ŋ, *n.* *fine thread, silk thread.* *T.*, haḣoŋta ćiḳala.

h a - ḣ u ŋ′ - t a, *n.* See haḣoŋta.

h a′ - k a - h m o ŋ - p i, *n.* (ha *and* kahmoŋ) *a cord, rope, twisted bark rope.*

h a′ - k a - h m u ŋ - p i, *n.* Same as hakahmoŋpi.

h a - k a′ - k t a, *adj.* *last, the last; the youngest*—hamakakta and mahakakta, nihakakta, uŋhakaktapi.

h a - k a m′, *adv.* *afterwards, in the mean time.* *T.*, hakab.

h a - k a m′ - y a, *adv.* *afterwards.*

h a - k a′ - p a, *adv.* See hakapataŋhaŋ.

h a - k a′ - p a - t a ŋ - h a ŋ, *adv.* *on the external surface;* also, haḳapaŋtaŋhaŋ. *Ih.*, *afterwards.*

h a - k a′ - t a - y a, *v.* *T.* *to have for a sister.*

h a - k e′, *n.* *the name of the fifth child, if a son.* This with hapaŋ and hapistiŋna are not used by the Yanktons.

h a - k e′ - k e, *n.* *red.* of hake It is so used as a proper name.

h a - k i′ - k t a, *v. n.* *to look around, look behind, turn round to look*—hawekta, hayekta, hauŋkiktapi.

h a - k i′ - k t a - k t a, *v.* *red.* of hakikta; *to look back often.*

h a′ - l a, *n.* *T. fleas.*

h a - m d e′, *v.* See haŋmde, the correct orthography.

h a m - i′ - t a - k e, *n.* See haŋpaitake.

h a′-m n a, *adj.* *smelling of the skin, poor, lean, not smelling well*, as meat.

h a′-n a-ḣ p u, *v.* See hanaḣpuḣpu.

h a′-n a-ḣ p u-ḣ p u, *v.* Said of the *rough bark* of trees, that seems ready to fall off. See naḣpu.

h a′-n a-s k u, *v.* See hanaskusku.

h a′-n a-s k u-s k u, *v. n.* *to crack and peel off*, as the skin of potatoes by boiling. See nasku.

h a′-n a-s k u-y a, *v. a.* *to cause to crack and peel off*—hanaskuwaya.

h a ŋ, *adv.* *of affirmation; yes, yea.*

h a ŋ, *n* *cont.* of haŋyetu; *night:* haŋ waśte, *good night;* haŋ ićamna, *a stormy night.*

h a ŋ, *v. n.* *to stand, stand upright* or *on end; to remain:* ećen haŋ, *it stands* or *remains as it was.* From this are formed iyahaŋ, kićihaŋ, etc.

h a ŋ-a′-k e-ć i ŋ, *n.* *T.* *to-morrow.*

h a ŋ-b l e′-ć e-y a, *v. n.* *T.* *to cry in vision seeking.*

h a ŋ-ć o′-k a, *n.* *midnight.*

h a ŋ-ć o′-k a-y a, *n.* (haŋyetu *and* ćokaya) *midnight.*

h a ŋ-d o′-w a ŋ, *n.* (haŋyetu *and* dowaŋ) *a night-song.*

h a ŋ-d o′-w a ŋ-p i, *n.* *a night-song.*

h a ŋ-h e′-p i, *n.* *Ih.* and *T.* *night:* *i. q.* haŋyetu: *last night;* haŋhepi kiŋhaŋ, *to-night;* haŋhepi kiŋ le, *this night.*

h a ŋ-h e′-p i-w i, *n.* *T.* *the night-sun—moon:* *i. q.* haŋyetu wi.

h a ŋ-ḣ a ŋ′-n a, *n.* *morning, to-morrow.* *T.*, hihaŋna.

h a ŋ-ḣ a ŋ′-n a-ḣ i ŋ, *n.* *very early in the morning.* *T.*, hihaŋnaḣćiŋ.

h a ŋ-k a′, *n.* *a man's sister-in-law, his wife's sister* or *brother's wife; my sister-in-law.*

h a ŋ-k a′-k u, *n.* *his sister-in-law.*

h a ŋ-k a′-ś a-d a ŋ, *n.* *the ground-hog* or *woodchuck*, the American *arctomys.*

h a ŋ-k a′-ś i, *n.* *a man's female cousin, his mother's brother's daughter*, but not his father's brother's daughter; *my female cousin.*

h a ŋ-k a′-ś i-t k u, *n.* *his female cousin.*

h a ŋ-k a′-ś i-y a, *v. a.* *to have for* or *call* haŋkaśi, *to sustain the relation of male cousin to a woman*—haŋkaśiwaya.

h a ŋ-k a′-y a, *v. a.* *to have for* or *regard as a sister-in-law*—haŋkawaya, haŋkauŋyaŋpi.

h a ŋ-k e′, *n.* *half; a part.*

h a ŋ-k e′-d a ŋ, *n.* *a small half.*

h a ŋ-k e′-k e, *n.* *red.* of haŋke; *half and half.*

h a ŋ-k e′-y a, *v. a.* *to halve; to have reached the middle*—haŋkewaya.

h a ŋ-k e′-y a, *adv.* *by the half.* *T.*, haŋkeyela, *only half.*

h a ŋ-k i′-k t a, *v. n.* (haŋyetu *and* kikta) *to rise very early in the morning; to wake while it is yet night*—haŋwekta, haŋyekta, haŋuŋkiktapi.

h a ŋ-k o′-k i-p a, *adv.* *T.* *cowardly, fearing night.*

h a ŋ-k p a ŋ′, *n.* *moccasin-strings.*

Mr. S. W. Pond suggests, that perhaps the "k" and "p" in this word have changed places, and the word was originally haŋpkaŋ, that is, haŋpa and ikaŋ.

h a ŋ′- m a - n i, *v. to walk in the night; to be in the dark about* anything, *not to understand*—haŋmawani: haŋmanipi se uŋyakoŋpi, *we are in the dark about it.*

h a ŋ - m d e′, *v. n. to fast and dream, to have intercourse with the spiritual world*, used in regard to their superstitions—haŋwamde, haŋuŋmdepi. *T.*, haŋble.

h a ŋ - m d o′- h d a g - i - a, *v.* (haŋmdohdaka *and* ia) *to tell dreams and visions; to talk so that common people do not understand*—haŋmdohdagiwaa. *T.*, haŋbloglagia.

h a ŋ - m d o′- h d a g - i - a - p i, *n. talking mysteriously; preaching.*

h a ŋ - m d o′- h d a - k a, *v. a.* (haŋmde *and* ohdaka) *to tell of one's intercourse with the spirit world, relate visions; to speak unintelligibly*—haŋmdowahdaka, haŋmdoyahdaka, haŋmdouŋhdakapi. *T.*, haŋbloglaka.

h a ŋ - m n a′, *v.* See ihaŋmna.

h a ŋ - n a′- k a, *n.* (haŋyetu *and* nakaha) *this night.*

h a ŋ p, *cont.* of haŋpa.

h a ŋ′- p a, *n. moccasins;* tahaŋpe, *his moccasins;* haŋpa hduśdoka, *to pull off one's own moccasins.*

h a ŋ′- p a - a - p e, *and* h a ŋ′- p a - a - p e - e - ć o ŋ - p i, *n* a game in which a bullet is hid in one of four moccasins or mittens, and sought for by the opposite party.

h a ŋ′- p a - i - t a - k e, *n. the face* or *upper part of a moccasin.* Pronounced often haŋpitake.

h a ŋ p a′- p e *and* h a ŋ p - a′- p e e - ć o ŋ′- p i, *n.* Same as haŋpaape. See ap'a, ap'e.

h a ŋ - p e′, *n.* See haŋpa—mitahaŋpe, tahaŋpe. See also iśtamihaŋpe.

h a ŋ - p i′, *n. broth, soup, gravy; juice, sap,* etc. See wahaŋpi.

h a ŋ p - i′- t a - k e, *n.* See haŋpaitake.

h a ŋ p - o′- h a ŋ, *v. to put on* or *wear moccasins*—haŋpowahaŋ.

h a ŋ p - o′- h e - k i - ć i - ć i - y a, *v. a. to put moccasins on* one—haŋpohewećićiya.

h a ŋ p - o′- h e - k i - y a, *v. a. to cause to put on moccasins*—haŋpohewakiya.

h a ŋ p - o′- k i - h a ŋ, *v. pos.* of haŋpohaŋ; *to put on* or *wear one's own moccasins*—haŋpowakihaŋ.

h a ŋ′- s k a, *adj. long; tall.*

h a ŋ′- s k a - s k a, *adj. red.* of haŋska.

h a ŋ′- s k e - y a, *v. a. to make long, lengthen*—haŋskewaya,

h a ŋ′- s k e - y a, *adv. far, extending, long.*

h a ŋ′- ś n i, *intj. no! not yes; i. q.* hiya.

h a ŋ′- t a, *v. imperat. only; get away, begone, get out of the way*—haŋta wo, haŋta po.

h a ŋ′ - t a ŋ - h a ŋ ś, *adv.* *Ih. i. q.* kiŋhaŋ; *if, in case that.*

h a ŋ - t p a ŋ′, *n.* Same as haŋkpaŋ.

h a ŋ′ - t u, *adv.* *indeed.*

h a ŋ′ - t u - ḳ e, *adv.* *indeed, for once.* *T.*, hantuḳeś, *certainly.*

h a ŋ - w a′ - ć i - p i, *n.* *night-dance; the name of a Dakota dance.*

h a ŋ - w a ŋ′ - k a, *v. n.* *to remain over night*, as something killed and left until the morning. *T.*, haŋyunka.

h a ŋ - w i′, *n.* See haŋyetuwi.

h a ŋ - w i′ - y a ŋ - p a, *n.* *moonlight.*

h a ŋ - y a′ - ġ u, *n.* *T.* *a robe dried out of doors* in winter by freezing.

h a ŋ - y a′ - k e - ć i n - h a ŋ, *n.* *T.* *to-morrow.*

h a ŋ - y e′, *cont.* of haŋyetu.

h a ŋ - y e′ - ć o - k a, *n.* *midnight.*

h a ŋ - y e′ - ć o - k a - y a, *n.* (haŋyetu *and* ćokaya) *middle of the night, midnight.* *T.*, haŋćokaya.

h a ŋ - y e n′, *adv.* *by night, at night.* *T.*, haŋhepi el.

h a ŋ - y e′ - t u, *n.* *night.* *T.*, haŋhepi *and* hihaŋpi.

h a ŋ - y e′ - t u - d a ŋ, *n.* *dim.* of haŋyetu. The *black bear* is sometimes so nicknamed.

h a ŋ - y e′ - t u - w i, *n.* *night-sun,* i. e., *the moon.* *T.*, haŋhepi wi.

h a - o′, *adv.* See ho.

h a′ - o - y a - s a - k a, *adj.* *skin dried to the bone, very lean.*

h a′ - p a - ḣ d a - y a, *v.* *to throw off the skin,* as snakes. *T.*, hapaḣlaya.

h a′ - p a ŋ, *n.* *the name of the second child, if a daughter.*

h a′ - p i s - t i ŋ, *n.* See hapistiŋna, which is more commonly used

h a′ - p i s - t i ŋ - n a, *n.* *the name of the third child, if a girl.*

h a′ - s t a ŋ, *adj.* *dark-complexioned*—hamastaŋ; of ha *and* staŋ.

h a - s t a ŋ′ - h a ŋ - k a, *n.* *grapes* of all kinds. *T.*, ćuŋwiyape.

h a - s t a ŋ′ - h a ŋ - k a - h a ŋ - p i, *n.* *grape-juice.*

h a - s t a ŋ′ - h a ŋ - k a - i - y u - w i, *n.* *grape-vines*

h a s - t a ŋ′ - k a, *n.* (haza *and* taŋka) *a kind of berry,* which, it is said, is bitter if approached from the windward—if from the leeward, sweet. *Syn.*, auŋyeyapi.

h a - s t a ŋ′ - y a ŋ - k a, *n.* *grapes.* This is probably the most ancient form of hastaŋhaŋka.

h a - ś b e′, *n.* *nettles; flax.* *T.*, haśme.

h a - y a′, *v.* *T.* *to have for clothing*—hawaya.

h a - y a′ - k e, *n.* *Ih.* *clothes; i. q.* heyake. *T.*, hayapi.

h a - y o′ - w e - d a ŋ, *n.* *marks made in the snow,* as by children in play: hayowedaŋ kiçuŋ.

h a′ - y u - z a, *v. a.* *to skin, take off the skin* of anything—hamduza.

h a′ - z a, *n.* *the whortleberry, huckleberry.* The Dakotas specify several kinds, as the winoḣin tahaza and the waḣaŋksin tahaza.

h b a. See yuhba, etc. *T.*, gba.

h b a - h a ŋ′, *part.* *falling off, shelling off of itself,* as corn. *T.*, gbahaŋ.

h b e - h b e′ - z a, *adj.* *red.* of hbeza;

in rings around, *ring-streaked*, *appearing like the ribs of animals.*

h b e - h b e′ - z e - d a ŋ, *adj.* See hbehbeza.

h b e′ - z a, *adj.* *ring-streaked*, *rings running around*, *rough:* dote hbeza, *the wind-pipe*, because it appears in rings.

h b e′ - z e - d a ŋ, *adj.* *striped* or *ringed*, like a screw; *rough.*

h b u, *adj.* *clear* of everything else, *cleaned*, as grain. One's hair is said to be "hbu," when not curled.

h b u, *v. n.* *to burst open*, as boiled potatoes. *T.*, gbu.

h b u - y a′, *adv.* *cleaned*, *clear* of everything else, as grain clear of chaff.

h d a. See yuhda.

h d a, used to make the possessive form of verbs commencing with "ka" and "ya:" as kaksa, *to cut off*, yaksa, *to bite off* hdaksa, *to cut off* or *bite off one's own;* nape wahdaksa, *I cut off* or *bite off my hand.* The pronouns are prefixed.

h d a, *v.* *pos.* of ya; *to go home*—wahda, yahda, uŋhdapi. *T.*, gla.

h d a, *v. n.* *to feel*, *become sensible of*, as of heat or cold, pain, etc.: ćuwita hda, *to become cold;* wayazaŋ hda, *to become sick.*.

h d a - ć e′ - y a, *v.* *pos.* of kaćeya or yaćeya. *T.*, glaćeya.

h d a - ć o′, *v.* *pos.* of yaćo; *to judge* or *condemn one's own*—wahdaćo. *T.*, glasu. *Th*, kdasu.

h d a - ć o′ - z a, *v.* *pos.* of kaćoza.

h d a - d a′, *v.* *pos.* of kada; *to spill one's own*—wahdada.

h d a - ġ a′ - p a, *v.* *to tear* or *bruise a piece off.* *T.*, glaġapa.

h d a - ġ e′ - ġ e, *v.* *pos.* of kaġeġe; *to sew one's own*—wahdaġeġe, uŋhdaġeġepi.

h d a - ġ o′, *v.* *pos.* of kaġo.

h d a - h a ŋ′, *adj.* *very thin*, as mush or gruel; *i. q.* haŋpi ota.

h d a - h a ŋ′, *v. n.* *to ravel*, *to untwist.* *T.*, glahaŋ.

h d a - h e′, *adv.* *unrolled of itself.*

h d a - h e′ - y a, *adv.* *straight forward*, *without interruption*, as hdaheya ia, *to speak continuously;* *thin*, as mush or gruel, *i. q.* haŋpi ota: hdaheya ećoŋ, *to make thin*, as gruel. *T.*, glaheya.

h d a - h i ŋ′ - t a, *v.* *pos.* of kahiŋta

h d a - h n a′ - y a ŋ, *v.* *pos.* of yahnayaŋ.

h d a - h o′ - h o, *v.* *pos.* of yahoho or kahoho.

h d a - h o′ - m n i, *v.* *pos.* of yahomni or kahomni.

h d a - h o′ - t o ŋ, *v.* *pos.* of kahotoŋ.

h d a - h u′ - h u - z a, *v.* *pos.* of kahuhuza.

h d a - ḣ a′ - p a, *v.* *pos.* of kaḣapa.

h d a - ḣ d a′ - y a, *v.* *pos.* of yaḣdaya; *to bite off*, as the skin of anything; *to tell a lie*—wahdaḣdaya.

h d a - ḣ d e′ - ć a, *v.* *pos.* of kaḣdeća and yaḣdeća, *to break open one's own by smiting;* *to tear open one's own by biting*—wahdaḣdeća.

h d a - ḣ d e n′, *cont.* of hdaḣdeća; hdaḣden iyeya, *to break* or *smash open one's own suddenly.* *T.*, glaḣlel.

h d a - ḣ d o′ - k a, *v. pos.* of kaḣdoka and yaḣdoka.

h d a - ḣ e m′, *cont.* of hdaḣepa; hdaḣem iyeya. *T.*, glaḣeb.

h d a - ḣ e′ - p a, *v. pos.* of yaḣepa; *to drink up one's own*—wahdaḣepa.

h d a - ḣ i′ - ć a, *v. pos.* of yaḣića.

h d a - ḣ n i′ - ġ a, *v. pos.* of kaḣniġa; *to choose one's own.*

h d a - ḣ p a′, *v. pos.* of kaḣpa.

h d a - ḣ p u′, *v. pos.* of yaḣpu; *to pull* or *tear off with the teeth* something of *one's own* that adheres to something else—wahdaḣpu.

h d a - ḣ p u′ - ḣ p u, *v. red.* of ḣdaḣpu.

h d a - ḣ t a g′, *cont.* of hdaḣtaka; hdaḣtag iyeya. *T.*, glaḣtag.

h d a - ḣ t a′ - k a, *v. pos.* of yaḣtaka; *to bite one's own*—wahdaḣtaka.

h d a - ḣ u′ - ġ a, *v. pos.* of kaḣuġa and yaḣuġa. See hdaḣuḣuġa.

h d a′ - ḣ u ḣ, *cont.* of hdaḣuġa.

h d a - ḣ u′ - ḣ u - ġ a, *v. pos.* of kaḣuḣuġa and yaḣuḣuġa; *to smash* or *break in one's own,* as the skull of one's child, or as one's kettle, *by pounding; to break up one's own with the teeth,* as bones which belong to one's self.

h d ȧ - k a′, *adj. standing apart; standing alone, separated,* as large trees without underbrush; *large-toothed,* as a coarse comb. See ćaŋhdaka. *T.*, glake.

h d a - k a ŋ′, *v. pos.* of kakaŋ; *to hew one's own.*

h d a - k a′ - w a, *v. pos.* of yakawa.

h d a - k ć a′, *v. pos.* of kakća; *to comb one's own*—wahdakća, yahdakća, uŋhdakćapi.

h d a - k e′ - y a, *adv. separately, at a distance from each other.*

h d a - k i ŋ′ - ć a, *v. pos.* of kakiŋća.

h d a - k i ŋ s′ - k i ŋ - z a, *v. pos. red.* of yakiŋza. See hiḣdakiŋskiŋza.

h d a - k i ŋ′ - y a ŋ, *adv. across, crosswise, transverse:* Mde hdakiŋyaŋ, *Lake Traverse;* oḣaŋ hdakiŋyaŋ, *perverse;* oie hdakiŋyaŋ, *a liar.* *T.*, glakiŋyaŋ ia, *to speak what is not true.*

h d a - k p a ŋ′, *v. pos.* of kakpaŋ; *to wink:* iśta wahdakpaŋ, *I wink my eyes.*

h d a - k s a′, *v. pos.* of kaksa and yaksa; *to cut off one's own,* as one's own wood, with an ax; *to bite off one's own*—wahdaksa, yahdaksa.

h d a - k s a′ - k s a, *v. red.* of hdaksa; *to cut* or *bite one's own in many pieces*—wahdaksaksa.

h d a - k ś i′ - ź a, *v. pos.* of yakśiźa.

h d a - k u′ - k a, *v. pos.* of yakuka

h d a - ķ e′ - z a, *v. pos.* of yaķeza.

h d a - ķ o′ - ġ a, *v. pos.* of yaķoġa.

h d a - m d a′ - y a, *v. pos.* of kamdaya.

h d a - m d a′ - z a, *v. pos.* of kamdaza and yamdaza.

h d a - m d e′ - ć a, *v. pos.* of kamdeća and yamdeća; *to break in pieces one's own by striking,* as anything brittle; *to bite in pieces*—wahdamdeća. *T.*, glableća.

h d a - m d e n', *cont.* of hdamdeća: hdamden iyeya. *T.*, glablel.

h d a - m d u', *v. pos.* of kamdu and yamdu.

h d a - m n a', *v. pos.* of kamna and yamna; *to acquire* or *collect property; to acquire by talking*—wahdamna.

h d a - m n i', *v.* used with ya or i; hdamni ya, *to go after* something *one has left*, as provisions hid in the snow—wahdamni mda.

h d a - m n i' - y a ŋ, *v.* Same as hdamni: hdamniyaŋ wai, *I have been for* something *left.*

h d a - o' - k s a, *v. pos.* of kaoksa.

h d a - o' - n i - h a ŋ, *v. pos.* of yaonihaŋ; *to praise one's own*—wahdaonihaŋ

h d a - o' - t a, *v pos.* of yaota; *to count one's own many.*

h d a - o' - t a ŋ - i ŋ, *v. pos.* of yaotaŋiŋ; *to manifest* or *declare one's own*—wahdaotaŋiŋ.

h d a - p a', *v. pos.* of yapa; *to take hold of one's own with the mouth*—wahdapa.

h d a - p a ŋ', *v. pos.* of kapaŋ; *to beat* or *thresh out one's own,* as one's corn—wahdapaŋ, uŋhdapaŋpi.

h d a - p e' - h a ŋ, *v. pos.* of yapehaŋ; *to fold up one's own with the mouth*—wahdapehaŋ.

h d a - p o n', *cont.* of hdapota; hdapon iyeya.

h d a - p o' - p a, *v. pos.* of yapopa.

h d a - p o' - t a, *v. pos.* of kapota *and* yapota; *to beat one's own to pieces; to bite to pieces, destroy one's own by biting*—wahdapota, uŋhdapotapi.

h d a - p s a g', *cont.* of hdapsaka; hdapsag iyeya.

h d a - p s a' - k a, *v. pos.* of kapsaka *and* yapsaka; *to cut off one's own by striking,* as one's own string; *to bite off one's own*—wahdapsaka.

h d a - p s i ŋ' - p s i ŋ - t a, *v. pos.* of kapsiŋpsiŋta; *to whip one's own* child—wahdapsiŋpsiŋta.

h d a - p s i ŋ' - t a, *v. pos.* of kapsiŋta. See hdapsiŋpsiŋta.

h d a - p s u ŋ', *v. pos.* of kapsuŋ *and* yapsuŋ; *to spill one's own by striking* or *with the mouth*—wahdapsuŋ.

h d a - p ś u ŋ', *v. pos.* of kapśuŋ *and* yapśuŋ; *to knock out one's own by the roots,* as a tooth; *to knock out of joint,* as one's own leg; *to bite out* or *knock out one's own,* as a horse does in shedding his teeth—wahdapśuŋ, hdapśuŋ iyeya.

h d a - p t a', *v. n. to stop, cease,* as rain or snow: maġaźu hdapte kta, *the rain will cease.* Also *pos.* of kapta *to lade out. T.*, glapta.

h d a - p t a ŋ' - y a ŋ, *v. pos.* of kaptaŋyan.

h d a - p t e' - ć e - d a ŋ, *v. pos.* of kaptećedaŋ *and* yaptećedaŋ.

h d a - p t e' - y a, *v. a. to cause to cease*—hdaptewaya.

h d a - p t u' - ź a, *v. pos.* of kaptuźa.

h d a - s a ŋ', *v. pos.* of kasaŋ, *to*

shave off one's own beard: putinhin wahdasan, *I shave off my beard.*

hda-sde'-ća, *v. pos.* of kasdeća.

hda-sdo'-han, *v. pos.* of kasdohan *and* yasdohan.

hda-skam', *cont.* of hdaskapa.

hda-ska'-pa, *v. pos.* of kaskapa; *to clap, make strike together:* nape hdaskapa, *to clap one's hands*—wahdaskapa. *T.*, glaskapa.

hda-ske'-pa, *v. pos.* of kaskepa.

hda-ski'-ća, *v. pos.* of kaskića *and* yaskića; *to press one's own with the mouth*—wahdaskića. See hdaśkića.

hda-sku', *v. pos.* of yasku; *to bite* or *peel off one's own*—wahdasku.

hda-sni', *v. pos.* of kasni *and* yasni.

hda-son', *cont.* of hdasota; hdason iyeya.

hda-so'-ta, *v. pos.* of kasota *and* yasota; *to eat up one's own; to use up words* or *language*, i. e., *to finish speaking; to cut all off*, as one's own timber—wahdasota.

hda-sto', *v. pos.* of kasto.

hda-su', *v. pos.* of yasu; *to perfect, finish*—wahdasu. See hdaćo *and* yaćo. *T.*, glasu.

hda-su'-ta, *v. pos.* of yasuta; *to confirm one's own words.*

hda-śa'-pa, *v. pos.* of yaśapa.

hda-śda', *v. pos.* of kaśda *and* yaśda; *to mow one's own* meadow; *to graze off one's own* grass—wahdaśda. *T.*, glaśla, *to shave*, as one's own beard.

hda-śdo'-ka, *v. pos.* of kaśdoka.

hda-śdu'-ta, *v.* of kaśduta.

hda-śi'-ća, *v. pos.* of yaśića; *to speak evil of one's own.*

hda-śka', *v. pos.* of kaśka; *to bind one's own.*

hda-śki'-ća, *v. pos.* of yaśkića; *to press one's own with the mouth*, as in chewing tobacco—wahdaśkića. See hdaskića.

hda-śki'-pa, *v. pos.* of yaśkipa.

hda-śko'-pa, *v. pos.* of kaśkopa *and* yaśkopa.

hda-śna', *v. pos.* of kaśna *and* yaśna; *to blunder in speaking; to miss in taking one's food into the mouth; to miss in attempting to strike one's own*—wahdaśna. *T.*, glaśna; ie glaśna, *to talk incorrectly.*

hda-śna'-śna, *v. red.* of hdaśna.

hda-śna'-śna-yan, *adv. blunderingly*, as in talking, *incorrectly.*

hda-śpa', *v. pos.* of kaśpa *and* yaśpa; *to knock* or *bite off a piece from one's own*—wahdaśpa.

hda-śpu', *v. pos.* of kaśpu *and* yaśpu.

hda-śta'-ka, *v. pos.* of kaśtaka; *to strike* or *smite one's own:* tawiću hdaśtaka, *he beats his wife*—wahdaśtaka.

hda-śtan', *v. pos.* of kaśtan *and* yaśtan; *to pour out one's own; to spill with the mouth*, as one's own coffee; *to finish eating* or *speaking*—wahdaśtan.

hda-ta', *v. pos.* of yata; *to taste one's own; to chew over again*, as a cow her cud.

h d a - t a ŋ′, *v.* *pos.* of yataŋ; *to praise one's own; to suck out one's own* blood—wahdataŋ.

h d a - t a ŋ′ - k a, *v.* *pos.* of yataŋka.

h d a - t' a′ - t' a, *v.* *pos.* of kat'at'a *and* yat'at'a; *to knock and shake one's own* blanket; *to take in the mouth and shake*, as a dog does anything—wahdat'at'a.

h d a - t e m′, *cont.* of hdatepa; hdatem iyeya. *T.*, glateb.

h d a - t e′ - h a ŋ, *v.* *pos.* of yatehaŋ.

h d a - t e′ - p a, *v.* *pos.* of yatepa; *to wear off one's own* teeth *short*—wahdatepa.

h d a - t i′ - t a ŋ, *v.* *pos.* of yatitaŋ.

h d a - t k a ŋ′, *v.* *pos.* of yatkaŋ; *to drink one's own*—wahdatkaŋ, yahdatkaŋ, uŋhdatkaŋpi.

h d a - t o′ - k a ŋ, *v.* *pos.* of yatokaŋ; *to put one's own in another place with the mouth; to speak of one's own as in another place*—wahdatokaŋ.

h d a - t o′ - k e - ć a, *v.* *pos.* of yatokeća; *to speak of one's own as different*—wahdatokeća.

h d a - t o′ - n a - n a, *v.* *pos.* of yatonana; *to count one's own few.* See hdaota.

h d a - t o′ - t o, *v.* *pos.* of katoto; *to knock at one's own* door—wahdatoto.

h d a - t p i′, *v.* *pos.* of katpi *and* yatpi; *to break one's own* nut *by pounding* or *pecking*—wahdatpi.

h d a - ṭ a′, *v.* *pos.* of kaṭa *and* yaṭa; *to kill one's own by striking; to bite one's own to death*—wahdaṭa.

h d a - ṭ i ŋ s′, *cont.* of hdaṭiŋza; hdaṭiŋs iyeya.

h d a - ṭ i ŋ′ - z a, *v.* *pos.* of kaṭiŋza *and* yaṭiŋza; *to make one's own tight by driving; to press one's own tight with the teeth*—wahdaṭiŋza.

h d a′ - w a, *v.* *pos.* of yawa; *to read one's own, count one's own*—wahdawa, yahdawa, uŋhdawapi. *T.*, glawa, *to reckon, count, value* one's own; he tokel yaglawa he, *how much do you value this at?*

h d a - w a′ - k a ŋ, *v.* *pos.* of yawakaŋ; *to call one's own sacred*—wahdawakaŋ.

h d a - w a ŋ g′, *cont.* of hdawaŋka; hdawaŋg iyeya. *T.*, glayung.

h d a - w a ŋ′ - k a, *v.* *pos.* of kawaŋka; *to cut down* or *fell one's own* trees—wahdawaŋka. *T.*, glayuŋka.

h d a - w a ŋ′ - k a ŋ, *v* *pos.* of yawaŋkaŋ.

h d a - w a′ - ś' a - k a, *v.* *pos.* of yawaś'aka.

h d a - w a′ - ś t e, *v.* *pos.* of yawaśte; *to bless one's own.*

h d a - w e′ - ġ a, *v.* *pos.* of kaweġa *and* yaweġa; *to break* or *fracture by striking*, as one's own ax-handle; *to break partly off with the teeth*—wahdaweġa.

h d a - w e ḣ′, *cont.* of hdaweġa.

h d a - w e ḣ′ - w e - ġ a, *v.* *red.* of hdaweġa.

h d a - w i′ - ć a - k a, *v.* *pos.* of yawićaka.

h d a - z a′ - m n i, *v.* *pos.* of kazamni; *to open one's own*—wahdazamni.

h d a - z a′ - p a, *v. pos.* of kazapa; *to cut off the fat with the skin*, in skinning *one's own*—wahdazapa.

h d a - z e′, *v. pos.* of kaze; *to lade out one's own* food—wahdaze, uŋhdazepi. *T.*, glaze.

h d a - z o′ - k a, *v. pos.* of yazoka; *to suck one's own*, as a child its own finger—wahdazoka. *T.*, glazoka.

h d a - z u ŋ′ - t a, *v. pos.* of yazuŋta; *to connect one's words, to speak correctly*—wahdazuŋta. *T.*, glazuŋta, *to praise* or *speak well of one's own.*

h d a - ź a′, *adj. T.*, glaźa, *sickly.*

h d a - ź a′ - ź a, *v. pos.* of kaźaźa.

k d a - ź i m′, *cont.* of hdaźipa; hdaźim yuta, *to eat very slowly, to nibble off;* hdaźim iyeya.

h d a - ź i′ - p a, *v. a. pos.* of kaźipa and yaźipa; *to shave one's own* stick; *to bite off* or *nibble one's own* food—wahdaźipa.

h d a - ź o′, *v. pos.* of yaźo; *to blow on one's own* instrument—wahdaźo.

h d a - ź u′ - ź u, *v. a. pos.* of kaźuźu; *to blot out* or *erase one's own; to pay one's own* debts—wahdaźuźu.

h d e, *v. to go home.* See hda.

h d e, *v. a. to put* or *place, make stand*, usually applied to things that stand on end, as barrels, etc.; *to have by one*, as mini wahde, *I have water.* This may be regarded as a transitive of haŋ.

h d e′ - ġ a, *adj. spotted, figured*, as calico.

h d e - h d e′, *adj. scattered, here and there.* Hence ćaŋhdehde.

h d e - h d e′ - ġ a, *adj. red.* of hdeġa; *spotted, speckled, brownish.*

h d e - h d e′ - k a, *adj. scattered, separated, one here and one there.* Hence ćaŋhdehdeka.

h d e - h d e′ - z a, *adj. striped, streaked.*

h d e - h d e′ - z e - d a ŋ, *adj. dim.* of hdezedaŋ; *striped, streaked.*

h d e - k i′ - y a, *v. a. to cause to go home, send home*—hdewakiya.

h d e m, *cont.* of hdepa; hdem hiyuya, *to vomit. T.*, gleb.

h d e m - k i′ - y a, *v. a. to cause to vomit*—hdemwakiya, hdemuŋkiyapi, hdemmakiya. *T.*, glebkiya.

h d e′ - p a, *v. a. to vomit, puke*—wahdepa, yahdepa, uŋhdepapi; ihdepa, *to vomit up* what one has eaten—iwahdepa; on hdepapi, *tartar emetic.*

h d e - ś i′, *v. a. to command to go home*—hdewaśi.

h d e - ś k a′, *adj. speckled, spotted.*

h d e - ś k a′ - ś k a, *adj. red.* of hdeśka; *spotted, figured*, as calico.

h d e′ - z a, *adj. striped, in ridges* or *rows.*

h d e′ - z e - d a ŋ, *adj. striped, in stripes* of any kind.

h d i, *v. pos.* of hi; *to come* or *arrive at home*—wahdi, yahdi, uŋhdipi.

h d i - a′ - p e, *v. a. to await one's coming home*—hdiawape.

h d i - ć u′, *v. pos.* (hdi *and* ku) *to start to come home*—wahdiću, yahdiću, uŋhdićupi. *T.*, gliću, also *to get down from* or *away;* as ćaŋpagmi etaŋhaŋ gliću yo, *get out of the wagon.*

h d i - ć u′ - y a, *v. a.* *to cause to start home*—hdićuwaya.

h d i - h a ŋ′, *v. n.* *to fall down*, as something thrown up; *to fall on end*, as a stick; *to fall*, as water falls: mini hdihaŋ.

h d i - h d a′, *v.* See hnihda.

h d i - h u′ - n i, *v.* *pos.* of hihuni; *to come to land* or *come through in coming home*—wahdihuni. *T.*, glihuni, *to reach home.*

h d i - ḣ p a′ - y a, *v.* *pos.* of hiŋḣpaya; *to fall down again; to come home sick*—wahdiḣpaya.

h d i - n a′ - p a *or* h d i - n a ŋ′ - p a, *v.* *pos.* of hinapa; *to come in sight coming home; to come out of* or *through*, as through a wood, *to emerge from; to come up again*, as one diving—wahdinapa, uŋhdinapapi.

h d i - p s i′ - ć a, *v.* *pos.* of hipsića; *to alight at home, jump down again*—wahdipsića.

h d i - p s i n′, *cont.* of hdipsića.

h d i - w a ŋ′ - k a, *v.* *pos.* of hiwaŋka; *to come home and sleep; to camp on the way home*—wahdimuŋka, yahdinuŋka, uŋhdiwaŋkapi. *T.*, gliyuŋka.

h d i - y a′ - ḣ p a - y a, *v.* *pos.* of iyaḣpaya; *to come back home and fall upon* one—wahdiyaḣpaya.

h d i - y a′ - k u, *v.* *pos.* *to return, start to come home;* only the first and second persons used—wahdiyaku, yahdiyaku, uŋhdiyakupi. For the third person see hdiću.

h d i - y o′ - h i, *v.* *pos.* of hiyohi; *to come back, reach home*—wahdiyohi: ćihdiyohipi kta, *I will come again to you*, John xiv, 15. *T.*; gliyohi, *to go after one's own, i. q.*, hduwe: as, gliyohi mni kta, *I will go and get it.*

h d i - y o′ - t a ŋ - k a, *v.* *pos.* of hiyotaŋka; *to come home and sit down; to return to one's place*—wahdimdotaŋka, yahdidotaŋka. This is a compound verb which requires two pronouns.

h d i - y u′ - w e - ġ a, *v.* *pos.* of hiyuweġa; *to cross* a stream *by fording in coming home*—wahdiyuweġa.

h d o, *a prefix which forms the possessive of some verbs.*

h d o, *v.* *to grunt, make a noise*, as hogs and buffalo calves do.

h d o - e′ - y a - y a, *v. pos.* *to take* or *have taken one's own with one.* See hdoweyaya.

h d o - ġ a ŋ′, *v. pos.* See yuġaŋ, hduġaŋ, etc.

h d o - h d a′, *v. pos.* *to carry* anything *back home, carry one's own home*—wahdohda, uŋhdohdapi. *T.*, glogla, *to be carrying one's own home.*

h d o - h d e′ - s k a, *n.* *the gullet, œsophagus.* Same as dohdeska.

h d o - h d i′, *v. pos.* *to bring back home one's own*—wahdohdi.

h d o - h d o′, *v.* *red.* of hdo; *to grunt*, as hogs and buffalo calves, also as grouse.

h d o - h d o′ - d a ŋ, *v.* See hdohdodowaŋ.

h d o - h d o′ - d o - w a ŋ, *v.* *to sing a*

grunting song. The Dakotas do so sometimes in going to war.

hdo-hi', *v. pos.* *to bring one's own to* a place, as when one is beaten in gambling he goes and brings what he has staked—wahdohi, uŋhdohipi. *T.*, glohi.

hdo-i', *v. pos.* *to take* or *have taken one's own to* a place—wahdoi, yahdoi, uŋhdoipi.

hdo-iŋ', *v. pos.* of iŋ. See hdowiŋ. *T.*, glowiŋ.

hdo-ki', *v. pos.* *to have taken one's own home*—wahdoki, uŋhdokipi.

hdo-ki'-ni-ća, *v. pos.* *to dispute in regard to one's own*—wahdokinića, uŋhdokinićapi.

hdo-ki'-ni-ća-pi, *n.* *disputation.*

hdo-ki'-nin, *cont.* of hdokinića; hdokinin wauŋ.

hdo-ki'-ya-hda, *v. pos.* (hdoki *and* ahda) *to be carrying one's own home*—wahdokiyahda, yahdokiyahda, uŋhdokiyahdapi.

hdo-ku', *v. pos.* *to bring one's own towards home*—wahdoku, yahdoku, uŋhdokupi.

hdo-ni'-ća, *v. pos.* of anića; *to refuse to give up what one claims, to hold as one's own; to forbid the use of one's own;* tihdonića, *to forbid one's house*—wahdonića.

hdo-nin', *cont.* of hdonića.

hdo-nin'-ki-ya, *v. a.* *to cause to hold as one's own*—hdoninwakiya.

hdo-nin'-ya, *v. a.* Same as hdoninkiya.

hdo-u', *v. pos.* *to come bringing one's own*—wahdou, uŋhdoupi.

hdo-we'-ya-ya, *v. pos.* *to have taken one's own along*—wahdowemdamda, yahdowedada, uŋhdoweyayapi. See huwe.

hdo-wiŋ', *v. pos.* of iŋ; *to put around one his own* blanket or cloak—wahdowiŋ, yahdowiŋ, uŋhdowiŋpi. *T.*, glowiŋ.

hdo-ya', *v. pos.* *to carry one's own towards* a place—wahdomda and wahdoya, yahdoda, uŋhdoyapi.

hdu. Verbs commencing with "hdu" are formed from verbs in "yu;" which change denotes that the action is *to* or *for one's own.* The pronouns are prefixed.

hdu-a'-ki-pam, *v. pos.* of yuakipam; *to divide* or *separate one's own:* hduakipam ewahnaka, *I make a division of my own.* *T.*, gluakipab.

hdu-a'-o-pte-tu, *v. pos.* of yuaoptetu; *to make one's own less*—wahduaoptetu.

hdu-ba'-ġa, *v. pos.* of yubaġa.

hdu-ba'-za, *v. pos.* of yubaza.

hdu-bo'-sda-tu, *v. pos.* of yubosdatu; *to place upright* something of *one's own*—wahdubosdatu.

hdu-ćaŋ', *v. pos.* of yućaŋ; *to shake* or *sift one's own*—wahdućaŋ, uŋhdućaŋpi.

hdu-ćaŋ'-ćaŋ, *v. pos.* of yućaŋćaŋ.

hdu-će'-ka, *v. pos.* of yućeka.

hdu-će'-ya, *v. pos.* of yućeya.

hdu-ćo', *v. pos.* of yućo; *to per-*

fect, finish one's own; to arrange one's own—wahduća, uŋhdućopi.

hdu-ćo'-ćo, *v.* *red.* of hdućo; also, *pos.* of yućoćo, *to make soft one's own*—wahdućoćo.

hdu-ćo'-ka, *v.pos.* *to finish.* See hdućo.

hdu-ćo'-ka-ka, *v.* *pos.* of yućokaka; *to empty one's own barrel*—wahdućokaka.

hdu-ćo'-za, *v.* *pos.* of yućoza.

hdu-e'-će-tu, *v.* *pos.* of yuećetu; *to make one's own right* or *as it was*—wahduećetu.

hdu-e'-ći, *v.* *pos.* of yueći; *to turn one's own the other side out,* as one's own bag—wahdueći. *T.*, gluećiya.

hdu-ġa', *v* *pos.* of yuġa; *to pull off,* as the husk of *one's own* corn—wahduġa.

hdu-ġaŋ', *v.* *pos.* of yuġaŋ; *to open out one's own,* as one's blanket or one's door—wahduġaŋ.

hdu-ġa'-ta, *v.* *pos.* of yuġata; *to spread out one's own,* as one's hands in prayer—wahduġata: nape hduġan naźiŋ, *to stand with one's hands extended* in a supplicating manner.

hdu-ġe', *v.* *pos.* of yuġe; *to pick* or *gather up* scraps *from one's* floor—wahduġe.

hdu-ġe'-ġe, *v.* *red.* of hduġe; *to gather up one's own by handfuls*—wahduġeġe.

hdu-ġo', *v.* *pos.* of yuġo; *to make marks* or *creases in one's own.*

hdu-ha', *v.* *pos.* of yuha; *to have* or *possess one's own*—wahduha, yahduha, uŋhduhapi.

hdu-hba', *v.* *pos.* of yuhba.

hdu-he'-ki-ya, *v. a.* *to put one in possession of his own*—hduhewakiya.

hdu-hiŋ'-ta, *v.* *pos.* of yuhiŋta.

hdu-hmi', *v.* *pos.* of yuhmi.

hdu-hmi'-hma, *v.* *pos.* of yuhmihma.

hdu-hmuŋ', *v.* *pos.* of yuhmuŋ; *to twist one's own*—wahduhmuŋ. *T.*, glugmuŋ.

hdu-hna', *v.* *pos.* of yuhna.

hdu-hnu'-ni, *v.* *pos.* of yuhnuni.

hdu-ho'-ho, *v.* *pos.* of yuhoho; *to shake one's own,* as one's teeth—wahduhoho.

hdu-ho'-mni, *v.* *pos.* of yuhomni; *to turn one's own around*—wahduhomni, uŋhduhomnipi.

hdu-hu'-hus, *cont.* of hduhuhuza. *T.*, gluhuŋhuŋs.

hdu-hu'-hu-za, *v.* *pos.* of yuhuhuza; *to shake one's own* tree—wahduhuhuza.

hdu-ḣda', *v.* *pos.* of yuḣda; *to ring one's own* bell—wahduḣda.

hdu-ḣda'-ġaŋ, *v.* *pos.* of yuḣdaġaŋ; *to loosen a little,* as one's belt; *to leave,* as a wife her husband—wahduḣdaġaŋ. *T.*, gluḣlaġaŋ śni, *to be constant to, not to leave one's own.*

hdu-ḣda'-ya, *v.* *pos.* of yuḣdaya; *to peel off* the skin of *one's own* potato—wahduḣdaya.

h d u - ḣ d e′ - ć a, *v. pos.* of yuḣdeća; *to tear one's own,* as one's coat, etc.—wahduḣdeća.

h d u - ḣ d e′ - ḣ d e - ć a, *v. red.* of hduḣdeća.

h d u - ḣ d e n′, *cont.* of hduḣdeća.

h d u - ḣ d o g′, *cont.* of hduḣdoka.

h d u - ḣ d o′ - ḣ d o - k a, *v. red.* of hduḣdoka.

h d u - ḣ d o′ - k a, *v. pos.* of yuḣdoka; *to make a hole in one's own by boring*—wahduḣdoka, yahduḣdoka, uŋhduḣdokapi.

h d u - ḣ e m′, *cont.* of hduḣepa; hduḣem iyeya.

h d u - ḣ e′ - p a, *v. pos.* of yuḣepa; *to dry up, to soak up and wipe out,* as water, *from one's own* canoe—wahduḣepa.

h d u - ḣ e′ - y a - p a, *v. pos.* of yuḣeyapa; *to remove* or *take away one's own*—wahduḣeyapa.

h d u - ḣ i′ - ć a, *v. pos.* of yuḣića; *to wake up one's own*—wahduḣića.

h d u - ḣ p a′, *v. pos.* of yuḣpa; *to take down one's own,* as something hung up—wahduḣpa.

h d u - ḣ p a′ - ḣ p a, *v. red.* of hduḣpa.

h d u - ḣ p a ŋ′ - ḣ p a ŋ, *v. pos. to make soft one's own,* as one's moccasins by putting them into water—wahduḣpaŋḣpaŋ.

h d u - ḣ p u′, *v. pos* of yuḣpu; *to pull off one's own,* as one's seal, or anything sticking fast—wahduḣpu.

h d u - ḣ p u′ - ḣ p u, *v. red.* of hduḣpu.

h d u - ḣ u′, *v. pos.* of yuḣu; *to pull off one's own,* as bark with one's hands—wahduḣu.

hdu-kaŋ′, *v. pos.* of yukaŋ; *to shake off one's own* fruit—wahdukaŋ.

h d u - k a′ - p a, *v. pos.* of yukapa.

h d u - k a′ - t i ŋ, *v. pos.* of yukatiŋ.

h d u - k a′ - w a, *v. pos.* of yukawa; *to open one's own,* as one's mouth: i wahdukawa, *I open my mouth.*

h d u - k ć a′, *v. pos.* of yukća; *to untie one's own*—wahdukća. *T.*, glukća, *to undo* or *unbraid,* as a woman her hair.

h d u - k ć a ŋ′, *v. pos.* of yukćaŋ; *to comprehend one's own; to understand what belongs to one's self*—wahdukćaŋ, yahdukćaŋ, uŋhdukćaŋpi *T.*, glukćaŋ, *to decide about, form an opinion for one's self.*

h d u - k e′ - z a, *v. pos.* of yukeza; *to scrape, rub, make smooth one's own*—wahdukeza.

h d u - k i′ - n u - k a ŋ *or* h d u - k i ŋ′ - n u - k a ŋ, *v. pos.* of yukinukaŋ; *to divide one's own;* hence, *to distract,* John xiv. 1.

h d u - k i ŋ′ - ć a, *v. pos.* of yukiŋća; *to scrape off,* as dirt, *from one's own* clothes, with the hand—wahdukiŋća, uŋhdukiŋćapi.

h d u - k o′ - k a, *v. pos.* of yukoka.

h d u - k p a ŋ′, *v. pos.* of yukpaŋ; *to grind one's own* corn, etc.—wahdukpaŋ, uŋhdukpaŋpi.

h d u - k s a′, *v. pos.* of yuksa; *to break off one's own,* as a stick with the hands—wahduksa, yahduksa.

hdu-ksa'-ksa, *v. pos.* of yukśaksa.

hdu-kśa', *v. pos.* of yukśa.

hdu-kśaŋ', *v. pos.* of yukśaŋ.

hdu-kśi'-źa, *v. pos.* of yukśiźa.

hdu-ktaŋ', *v. pos.* of yuktaŋ; *to bend one's own*—wahduktaŋ.

hdu-ku'-ka, *v. pos.* of yukuka; *to wear out* or *make old one's own*—wahdukuka.

hdu-ḳe'-ġa, *v. pos.* of yuḳeġa; *to scratch one's own*—wahduḳeġa.

hdu-ḳes'-ḳe-za, *v. red.* of hduḳeza; *to shave off one's own close*, as the hair of one's head, one's dog, etc.—wahduḳesḳeza.

hdu-ḳe'-za, *v. pos.* of yuḳeza; *to rub and make smooth one's own*, as one's arrows—wahduḳeza.

hdu-ḳo'-ġa, *v. pos.* of yuḳoġa.

hdu-ḳo'-za, *v. pos.* of yuḳoza.

hdu-maŋ', *v. pos.* of yumaŋ; *to grind and make sharp one's own*, as one's ax or knife—wahdube, uŋhdumaŋpi.

hdu-mda'-ya, *v. pos.* of yumdaya; *to spread out one's own*, as one's blanket—wahdumdaya.

hdu-mda'-za, *v. pos.* of yumdaza

hdu-mde'-ća, *v. pos.* of yumdeća; *to open out, take in pieces one's own*—wahdumdeća.

hdu-mden', *cont.* of hdumdeća.

hdu-mdu', *v. pos.* of yumdu; *to plow* or *make mellow by plowing one's own* field—wahdumdu, yahdumdu, uŋhdumdupi.

hdu-mna', *v. pos.* of yumna: *to rip one's own*—wahdumna.

hdun, *cont.* of hduta; hdun wauŋ, *I am eating my own* food. *T.*, glul.

hdu-na'-źiŋ, *v. pos.* of yunaźiŋ; *to make one's own stand up*—wahdunaźiŋ.

hdu-o'-ḣda-ġaŋ, *v. pos.* of yuoḣdaġaŋ; *to loosen one's own a little.* as one's girdle.

hdu-o'-ḣdaḣ, *cont.* of hduoḣdaġaŋ; hduoḣdaḣ iću, *to loosen a little* or *untie a knot.*

hdu-o'-ki-ni-haŋ, *v. pos.* of yuokinihaŋ; *to make one's own honorable*—wahduokinihaŋ.

hdu-o'-koŋ-waŋ-źi-daŋ, *v. pos* of yuokoŋwaŋźidaŋ; *to place all one's own together, make one of* them.

hdu-o'-mde-ća, *v. pos.* of yuomdeća; *to scatter out one's own*—wahduomdeća.

hdu-o'-mden, *cont.* of hduomdeća.

hdu-o'-ni-haŋ, *v. pos.* of yuonihaŋ; *to honor one's own*—wahduonihaŋ.

hdu-o'-ta, *v. pos.* of yuota; *to multiply one's own*—wahduota, yahduota, uŋhduotapi.

hdu-o'-taŋ-iŋ, *v. pos.* of yuotaŋiŋ; *to manifest one's own*—wahduotaŋiŋ.

hdu-o'-tkoŋ-za, *v. pos.* of yuotkoŋza; *to make equal one's own; to do like*—wahduotkoŋza.

hdu-o'-waŋ-ća-ya, *v. pos.* of yuowaŋćaya; *to cause to spread all over; to make one's own go all over*—wahduowaŋćaya.

h d u - p e′, *v.* *pos.* of yupe.

h d u - p e′- h a ŋ, *v.* *pos.* of yupehaŋ.

h d u - p e′- m n i, *v.* *pos.* of yupemni.

h d u - p o n′, *v.* *cont.* of hdupota.

h d u - p o′- p a, *v.* *pos.* of yupopa.

h d u - p o′- t a, *v.* *pos.* of yupota; *to wear out one's own*—wahdupota, uŋhdupotapi.

h d u - p o t′- p o - t a, *v.* *red.* of hdupota.

h d u - p s a g′, *cont.* of hdupsaka.

h d u - p s a′- k a, *v.* *pos.* of yupsaka; *to break one's own with the hands*, as a string—wahdupsaka.

h d u - p s a′- p s a - k a, *v.* *red.* of hdupsaka.

h d u - p s i′- ć a, *v.* *pos.* of yupsića; *to make one's own jump*, as one's horse; *to pull up* with a hook and line *one's own* fish—wahdupsića.

h d u - p s i n′, *cont.* of hdupsića. *T.*, glupsil.

h d u - p s i′- p s i - ć a, *v.* *red.* of hdupsića.

h d u - p ś u ŋ′, *v.* *pos.* of yupśuŋ; *to pull out* or *extract one's own*, as one's teeth—wahdupśuŋ.

h d u - p t a′, *v.* *pos.* of yupta; *to cut out one's own*, as clothes.

h d u - p t a ŋ′, *v.* See hduptaŋyaŋ.

h d u - p t a ŋ′- y a ŋ, *v.* *pos.* of yuptaŋyaŋ; *to turn over one's own*—wahduptaŋyaŋ.

h d u - p t e′- ć e - d a ŋ, *v.* *pos.* of yuptećedaŋ; *to shorten one's own*—wahduptećedaŋ.

h d u - p t u′- p t u - ź a, *v.* *red.* of hduptuźa.

h d u - p t u ś′, *cont.* of hduptuźa.

h d u - p t u′- ź a, *v.* *pos.* of yuptuźa; *to crack* or *split* anything of *one's own*, by boring, etc.—wahduptuźa.

h d u s, *cont.* of hduza; hdus naźiŋ, *to stand holding one's own.*

h d u - s d e′- ć a, *v* *pos.* of yusdeća.

h d u - s d o′- h a ŋ, *v.* *pos.* of yusdohaŋ.

h d u - s d u′- t a, *v.* *pos.* of yusduta.

h d u - s k a′, *v.* *pos.* of yuska.

h d u - s k e′- p a, *v.* *pos.* of yuskepa; *to absorb one's own; to cause one's own to leak out* or *evaporate*—wahduskepa.

h d u - s k i′- ć a, *v.* *pos.* of yuskića.

h d u - s k i n′, *cont.* of hduskita. *T.*, gluskil.

h d u - s k i′- s k i - t a; *v.* *red.* of hduskita; *to wrap* or *tie up one's own*, as a Dakota woman does her baby—wahduskiskita.

h d u - s k i′- t a, *v.* *pos.* of yuskita; *to wrap* or *tie up one's own*—wahduskita.

h d u - s k u′, *v.* *pos.* of yusku; *to cut close one's own*, as the hair of one's child; *to pare off*, as the skin of *one's own* potato or apple—wahdusku.

h d u - s k u′- s k u, *v.* *red.* of hdusku.

h d u - s n a′, *v.* *pos.* of yusna.

h d u - s n i′, *v.* *pos.* of yusni.

h d u - s o n′, *cont.* of hdusota; hdu son iyeya.

h d u - s o n′ - s o - t a, *v.* *red.* of hdusota.

h d u - s o′ - t a, *v.* *pos.* yusota; *to use all one's own up*—wahdusota, uŋhdusotapi.

h d u - s t o′, *v.* *pos.* of yusto; *to smooth down*, as *one's own* hair: pa hdusto, *to smooth one's hair.*

h d u - s t o′ - s t o, *v.* *red.* of hdusto.

h d u - s u′ - k s u - t a, *v.* *red.* of hdusuta.

h d u - s u′ - t a, *v.* *pos.* of yusuta; *to make firm* or *establish one's own*—wahdusuta.

h d u - ś a′ - k a, *v.* *pos.* of yuśaka; *to be burdened with one's own*—wahduśaka.

h d u - ś a m′, *cont.* of hduśapa

h d u - ś a m′ - ś a - p a, *v.* *red.* of hduśapa.

h d u - ś a′ - p a, *v.* *pos.* of yuśapa; *to defile one's own*—wahduśapa, yahduśapa, uŋhduśapapi.

h d u - ś d a′, *v.* *pos.* of yuśda.

h d u - ś d o g′, *cont.* of hduśdoka; hduśdog iyeya.

h d u - ś d o′ - k a, *v.* *pos.* of yuśdoka; *to pull off*, as one's own clothes; *to pull out*—wahduśdoka.

h d u - ś d o′ - ś d o - k a, *v.* *red.* of hduśdoka

h d u - ś d u′ - t a, *v.* *pos.* of yuśduta.

h d u - ś i′ - ć a, *v.* *pos.* of yuśića; *to make bad* or *injure one's own*—wahduśića.

h d u - ś i′ - ḣ t i ŋ, *v.* *pos.* of yuśiḣtiŋ; *to weaken*, *enfeeble one's own*, as one's horse—wahduśiḣtiŋ. *T.*, gluśiḣtiŋ, *to wear out*, *spoil*, *make bad or injure one's own.*

h d u - ś i′ - k ś i - ć a, *v.* *red.* of hduśića.

h d u - ś k a′, *v.* *pos.* of yuśka; *to untie* or *let go one's own*—wahduśka, uŋhduśkapi.

h d u - ś k a ŋ′ - ś k a ŋ, *v.* *pos.* of yuśkaŋśkaŋ; *to make one's own move about*—wahduśkaŋśkaŋ.

h d u - ś k i′, *v.* *pos.* of yuśki; *to pucker*, *gather*, *plait one's own*—wahduśki.

h d u - ś k i′ - ć a, *v.* *pos.* of yuśkića; *to press with one's hands; to milk one's own* cow

h d u - ś k i n′, *cont.* of hduśkića.

h d u - ś k i′ - ś k i - ć a, *v.* *red.* of hduśkića.

h d u - ś k o′ - p a, *v.* *pos.* of yuśkopa.

h d u - ś n a′, *v* *pos.* of yuśna; *to miss in regard to one's own*—wahduśna, uŋhduśnapi.

h d u - ś n a′ - ś n a, *v.* *red.* of hduśna.

h d u - ś p a′, *v.* *pos* of yuśpa.

h d u - ś p i′, *v.* *pos.* of yuśpi.

h d u - ś p u′, *v.* *pos.* of yuśpu.

h d u - ś p u′ - y a, *v.* *pos.* of yuśpuya; *to scratch one's own* flesh—wahduśpuya.

h d u - ś p u′ - ś p u - y a, *v.* *red.* of hduśpuya.

h d u - ś t a ŋ′, *v.* *pos.* of yuśtaŋ; *to finish one's own*—wahduśtaŋ, yahduśtaŋ, uŋhduśtaŋpi.

h d u - ś t a ŋ′ - ś t a ŋ, *v.* *red.* of hduśtaŋ.

h d u - ś t e′, *adj.* *numb*, as one's foot

when it sleep: siha mahduśte, *my foot is asleep;* nape nihduśte, *thy hand is numb.*

hdu′-ta, *v.* *pos.* of yuta; *to eat one's own* corn, etc.—wahduta, yahduta, uŋhdutapi.

hdu-ta′-ni, *v.* *pos.* of yutani *or* yutaŋni.

hdu-taŋ′, *v.* *pos.* of yutaŋ; *to praise one's own; to touch one's own*—wahdutaŋ.

hdu-taŋ′-iŋ, *v.* *pos.* of yutaŋiŋ; *to make manifest one's own*—wahdutaŋiŋ.

hdu-taŋ′-ka, *v.* *pos.* of yutaŋka; *to make large, enlarge one's own*—wahdutaŋka.

hdu-t'a′-t'a, *v.* *pos.* of yut'at'a; *to shake one's own,* as one's clothes.

hdu-te′-ća, *v.* *pos.* of yuteća; *to make new one's own*—wahduteća.

hdu-te′-haŋ, *v.* *pos.* of yutehaŋ; *to make a long time, put off, defer*—wahdutehaŋ.

hdu-te′-pa, *v.* *pos.* of yutepa; *to make blunt, wear off one's own*—wahdutepa.

hdu-ti′-ća, *v.* *pos.* of yutića; *to scrape off* the snow *from one's own* place—wahdutića.

hdu-ti′-taŋ, *v.* *pos.* of yutitaŋ; *to pull at one's own*—wahdutitaŋ.

hdu-to′-kaŋ, *v.* *pos.* of yutokaŋ; *to remove one's own to another place*—wahdutokaŋ.

hdu-to′-ke-ća, *v.* *pos.* of yutokeća; *to make one's own different*—wahdutokeća.

hdu-tpaŋ′, *v.* *pos.* of yutpaŋ; *to grind one's own* corn, etc.—wahdutpaŋ. *T.*, glukpaŋ.

hdu-ṭa′, *v.* *pos.* of yuṭa; *to kill one's own* by hanging, etc.—wahduṭa. *T.*, gluṭa, *to kill one's own by choking.*

hdu-ṭiŋ′-za, *v.* *pos.* of yuṭiŋza.

hdu-wa′-ḣba-daŋ, *v.* *pos.* of yuwaḣbadaŋ.

hdu-wa′-ḣpa-ni-ća, *v.* *pos.* of yuwaḣpanića.

hdu-wa′-kaŋ, *v.* *pos.* of yuwakaŋ; *to make one's own sacred*—wahduwakaŋ.

hdu-waŋ′-kan, *v.* *pos.* of yuwaŋkan; *to lift* or *raise up one's own*—wahduwaŋkan.

hdu-wa′-ś'a-ka, *v.* *pos.* of yuwaś'aḳa; *to make strong one's own*—wahduwaś'aka.

hdu-wa′-śte, *v.* *pos.* of yuwaśte; *to make good one's own*—wahduwaśte.

hdu-we′, *v.* *pos.* of huwe; used always with "ya", "hi", etc., as hduwe ya, *to go for one's own*—hduwe mda, hduwe uŋyaŋpi. *T.*, gliyohi.

hdu-we′-ġa, *v.* *pos.* of yuweġa; *to break* or *fracture one's own*—wahduweġa.

hdu-weḣ′, *cont.* of hduweġa.

hdu-weḣ′-we-ġa, *v.* *red.* of hduweġa.

hdu-wi′, *v.* *pos.* of yuwi; *to wrap up one's own,* as with a string or thong—wahduwi, uŋhduwipi.

hdu-wi′-ća-ka, *v.* *pos.* of yuwićaka; *to make true* or *prove one's own*—wahduwićaka.

h d u - w i ŋ'- ġ a, *v.* *pos.* of yuwiŋġa.

h d u - w i ŋ' - t a, *v.* *pos.* of yuwiŋta; *to stretch out the hand to, implore, worship; to stroke one's own*—wahduwiŋta.

h d u - w i ŋ s', *cont.* of hduwiŋźa.

h d u - w i ŋ s' - w i ŋ - ź a, *v.* *red.* of hduwiŋźa.

h d u - w i ŋ' - ź a, *v.* *pos.* of yuwiŋźa; *to bend down one's own* grass, etc.—wahduwiŋźa.

h d u - w i' - t a ŋ, *v.* *pos.* of yuwitaŋ; *to make proud* or *glorify one's own*—wahduwitaŋ.

h d u - w i' - t a - y a, *v.* *pos.* of yuwitaya, of witaya, *together.*

h d u - w i' - y a - k p a, *v.* *pos.* of yuwiyakpa, of wiyakpa.

h d u - w i' - y e - y a, *v.* *pos.* of yuwiyeya, of wiyeya, *ready.*

h d u - w o' - h d u - z e, *v.* *pos.* of yuwohduze; *to consecrate one's own*—wahduwohduze.

h d u' - z a, *v.* *pos.* of yuza; *to take* or *hold one's own; to take again, take back again:* tawiću hduza, *to take again* or *take firmly one's own wife*—wahduza, uŋhduzapi.

h d u - z a' - m n i, *v.* *pos.* of yuzamni.

h d u - z e', *v.* *pos.* of yuze; *to dip* or *lade out,* as victuals from *one's own* kettle—wahduze.

h d u - z o' - k a, *v.* *pos.* of yuzoka.

h d u - ź a', *v.* *pos.* of yuźa; *to stir one's own, to make one's own* mush, etc.—wahduźa.

h d u - ź a g' - ź a - k a, *v.* *red.* of hduźaka.

h d u - ź a' - k a, *v.* *pos.* of yuźaka; *to pull open one's own,* as one's eyes—wahduźaka.

h d u - ź a' - ź a, *v.* *pos.* of yuźaźa; *to wash one's own:* nape hduźaźa, *he washes his hands*—wahduźaźa.

h d u - ź i m', *cont.* of hduźipa.

h d u - ź i ŋ' - ć a, *v* *pos.* of yuźiŋća; *to pull* or *blow one's own* nose—wahduźiŋća.

h d u - ź i' - p a, *v.* *pos.* of yuźipa; *to pinch one's own*—wahduźipa.

h d u - ź u ŋ', *v.* *pos.* of yuźuŋ; *to pull one's own out by the roots,* as one's own tree—wahduźuŋ.

h d u - ź u' - ź u, *v.* *pos.* of yuźuźu; *to pull down* or *destroy one's own*—wahduźuźu.

h e, *interrog. particle;* wićayada he, *dost thou believe?* hena mayaḳu kta he, *wilt thou give me those?*

h e, *dem. pron.* *that; pl.* hena, *those.*

h e, *n.* *a horn, the horns* of animals; he katiŋ *and* he katiŋtiŋ, *straight horns.*

h e, *intj.* *T.* *look here!*

h e - ć a', *n.* *the buzzard* (*Cathartes aura*).

h e' - ć a, *adj.* *such, such like, belonging to such* a class or description—hemaća, henića, heuŋćapi.

h e' - ć a - e - s t a, *adv.* *although it is such, notwithstanding.*

h e' - ć a - k i - ć o ŋ, *v. a.* of hećoŋ; *to do thus to* one—hećawećoŋ, hećauŋkićoŋpi.

h e - ć a ŋ' - k i ŋ, *v. a.* *to think so of*

one, *form such an opinion of* one—hećaŋwakiŋ, hećaŋyakiŋ, hećaŋuŋkiŋpi; hećaŋćićiŋ, *I have such an opinion of thee.*

he′-će-ća, *adj. like, such as, like that*—hemaćeća.

he′-će-ća, *adv. so, always so.*

he′-će-ća-e-śta, *adv. notwithstanding.*

he-će′-ća-ka, *n. such a one; a mean fellow, i. q.* tuwe kinihaŋpi śni. *T.*, hećećake lo is said of one who is highly prized, as of a child or friend: but hećećake ꞔoŋ is said of one who is disliked. W. J. C.

he′-će-daŋ, *adv.* (he *and* ećedaŋ) *that alone, only that.*

he′-će-daŋ-ki-ya, *adv. only that way, that alone.*

he′-će-daŋ-ya, *v. a. to regard that alone*—hećedaŋwaya.

he-će′-e-daŋ, *adv. that alone.*

he-će′-e-daŋ-ke, *adv. only that.*

he-će′-e-daŋ-ki-ya, *v. to have only that*—hećeedaŋwakiya.

he′-će-hna, *adv. thus, so; only; immediately. T.*, hećegla.

he′-će-hna-haŋ, *adv. all, entirely; immediately upon that.*

he′-će-hna-na, *adv. thus, just so, just as, only that; without alteration. T.*, hećeglala.

he′-će-ḣiŋ, *adv just so, only so; altogether.*

he′-će-ḣtiŋ, *adv.* See hećeḣiŋ *and* ećeḣtiŋ. *T.*, hećeḣćiŋ.

he′-će-kće-ća, *adj. red.* of hećeća.

he′-će-kće-ća-ka, *adj. always such; bearing this character.*

he′-će-kćen, *adv. red.* of hećen; *in this manner, so, thus, just as.*

he′-će-kće-tu, *adv. red.* of hećetu; *so, in this manner.*

he′-će-kće-tu-ya, *adv. after this manner.*

he′-ćen, *adv. thus, so, in this way; hence, therefore;* hećen oḣaŋke, *to do in this manner usually, be accustomed so to do. T.*, hećel.

he-će′-ni-će, *n. a yearling colt. T.*, hećenićala.

he′-ćen-ya, *adv. so, thus, in that manner. T.*, hećelya.

he′-će-tu, *adv. as, so, thus; right, well.*

he′-će-tu-ke, *adv. as is common, as is usual.*

he′-će-tu-waŋ-źi-ća, *adj. always the same.*

he′-će-tu-ya, *adv. so, well.*

he′-će-tu-ya, *v. a. to make so, cause to be so* or *right*—hećetuwaya, hećetuuŋyaŋpi.

he′-ći, *adv. in* or *at that place, there.*

he-ćiŋ′, *v.* (he *and* ećiŋ) *to think this, think that*—hećaŋmi, hećaŋni, heuŋkećiŋpi.

he′-ćiŋ-a-haŋ, *adv if, if it is so.*

he′-ćiŋ-haŋ, *adv. if, if it is so.*

he′-ćiŋ-śka-ya-pi, *n. T., the mountain goat;* so called because its horns are used for spoons. See hekiŋśka.

he-ći′-ya, *v.* of heya; *to say this*

to one: hewakiya, *I said this to him;* heyakiya, *thou saidst this to him;* heuŋkiyapi, *we say to him*, or *he says to us;* hemakiya, *he says to me;* hećićiya, *I say to thee;* hekićiyapi, *they say to each other.*

h e′ - ć i - y a, *adv. at that place, there.*

h e′ - ć i - y a - p a - t a ŋ - h a ŋ, *adv. T.*, *towards that* time or place; *on the side next to.*

h e′ - ć i - y a - t a ŋ, *adv. from that place, thence.*

h e′ - ć i - y a - t a ŋ - h a ŋ, *adv. from that place; therefore.*

h e - ć i′ - y o - t a ŋ, *adv. in that direction.*

h e - ć i′ - y o - t a ŋ - h a ŋ, *adv. in that direction.*

h e′ - ć o ŋ, *v.* (he *and* ećoŋ) *to do that*—hećamoŋ, hećanoŋ, hećoŋkupi *and* hećoŋkoŋpi.

h e′ - e, *that is it; it is he.* This with "dee" includes the substantive verb and demonstrative pronoun.

h e′ - e - h a ŋ, *adv. at that time,* referring to the past.

h e - e′ - k i - y a, *v. a. to call* or *count that the person* or *thing; to substitute, put one in the place of another*—heewakiya, heeuŋkiyapi: *adv. in the place of.*

h e - h a n′, *adv. at that time, then:* hehan ećamoŋ kta, *at that time I will do it*

h e - h a ŋ′, *adv. at* or *to that place, there, to that distance:* hehaŋ wai kta, *so far I will go.*

h e - h a ŋ′ - h a ŋ, *adv. red.* of hehaŋ.

h e - h a ŋ′ - h a ŋ - k e - ć a, *adv. red* of hehaŋkeća; *so long, each so long.*

h e - h a ŋ′ - h a ŋ - n a, *adv. red.* of hehaŋna.

h e - h a ŋ′ - h a ŋ - y a ŋ, *adv. red.* of hehaŋyaŋ.

h e - h a ŋ′ - k e - ć a, *adv. so long.*

h e - h a ŋ′ - n a, *adv. so far and no farther; just then.*

h e - h a ŋ′ - n a - ḣ i ŋ, *adv. just so far. T.*, hehaŋlaḣćiŋ.

h e - h a ŋ′ - p i, *n. Ih. night, i. q.* hāŋyetu. *T.*, *last night.*

h e - h a ŋ′ - p i - w i, *n. T. the moon.*

h e - h a ŋ′ - t a ŋ - h a ŋ, *adv. from that time; therefore.*

h e - h a ŋ′ - t u, *adv. at that time, then.*

h e - h a ŋ′ - t u - d a ŋ, *adv. then.*

h e - h a ŋ′ - t u d a ŋ - ḣ i ŋ, *adv. just then. T.*, hehaŋtulaḣćiŋ.

h e - h a ŋ′ - y a ŋ, *adv. so far,* referring to place; *so long,* referring to time.

h e - h a ŋ′ - y a ŋ - y a ŋ, *adv. red.* of hehaŋyaŋ.

h e - ḣ a ŋ′ - y e - l a, *adv. T. so far, only so far.*

h e′ - h e, *intj. alas!* hehe maṭa nuŋ seća, *alas! it seems as if I should die.*

h e′ - h e - h e, *intj. alas!*

h e - ḣ a′ - k a, *n.* (he *and* ḣaka) *the male elk, Cervus alces.* So called from his branching horns. The female is called "upaŋ."

h e - ḣ a′ - k a - ć a ŋ - t e - y a - ś n i - ś n i - ź a, *n.* (heḣaka ćaŋte *and* yaśniźa) *the cricket.*

he-ȟa'-ka-ta-pe-źi-hu-ta, *n.* (heȟaka ta *and* peźihuta) *elk-medicine,* a kind of *mint,* perhaps *catnip.*

he-ȟa'-ka-ta-wo-te, *n.* (heȟaka *and* tawote) *elk-food,* perhaps the same as the preceding word.

He-ȟa'-ka-wa-kpa, *n.* (Elk River) *The Yellowstone River.*

he-ȟak'-ta-pe-źi-hu-ta, *n.* Same as heȟakatapeźihuta.

he-ȟdo'-ġe-ća, *adj.* *hollow-horned.* *T.,* heȟloġeća.

he-ki'-ći-na-ke-ća, *v. n.* *to be all used up to* or *for* one: hemićinakeća, *I have no more.* *T.,* hekićinala. See henakeća.

he'-kiŋ-śka, *n.* *a horn spoon.*

he-kiŋ'-śka-ya-pi, *n.* *the mountain goat; the mountain sheep;* from which the horn spoon is made.

he'-kta, *n.* *that behind, what is past,* applied to both space and time

he'-kta, *adv.* *behind:* hekta u, *he comes behind;* hekta hda, *he goes back home;* hekta waćiŋ uye śni, *he does not turn his thoughts back.*

he'-ktam, *adv.* *behind, after.*

he'-kta-pa, *adv.* *behind, after.*

he'-kta-pa-ta, *adv.* *behind:* wa-hektapata, *the stern* of a boat.

he'-kta-pa-taŋ-haŋ, *adv.* *from behind.*

he'-kta-taŋ-haŋ, *adv.* *behind.*

he'-ḳe, *pron.* *that itself.* *T.,* heḳeś.

He-le'-nes, *n. p.,* introduced; *the Greeks.*

he-mni'-śa-ka-daŋ, *n.* *an unhatched louse, a nit.*

hen, *adv.* (he *and* en) *in that place, there.* *T.,* hel.

he'-na, *pron.* *pl.* of he; *those.*

he-nag'-na-ke-ća, *adv.* *red.* of henakeća; *so many of each.*

he'-na-ka, *adv.* *so many.* *T.,* henakel, *only so many.*

he-na'-ke-ća, *adv.* *so many; enough, sufficient; finished, all gone:* waŋna henakeća, *it is now all gone.* *T.,* henakća.

he-na'-ke-seȟ, *adv.* *all these, so great a quantity* *T.,* henakeȟćiŋ.

he-na'-ki-ya, *adv.* *in so many ways.*

he-na'-na, *adv.* *only so many* or *so much; none, all gone.* *T.,* henala: henamala, *mine all gone, I have none.*

he-na'-na-ki-ya, *adv.* *only in so many ways* or *places.* *T.,* henalakiya.

he-na'-naŋ-pi-daŋ, *adv.* *pl.* of henana.

he-naŋg'-na-ke-ća, *adv.* *red.* of henakeća; *so many each.* See henagnakeća.

he-naŋg'-naŋg, *cont.* otoiyohi henaŋgnaŋg yuhapi kta, *each one will have so many.*

he'-na-os, *pron.* See henaoza.

he'-na-o-za, *pron.* *those two:* henios, heniyos, and heniyoza are also used.

he-na'-o-za-ki-ya, *adv.* *those two, those two times.*

he-na'-pe-toŋ-na, *n.* (heya nape *and* toŋ) *a louse partly grown, a louse that has feet.*

hen'-tu, *adv. at that place.*

he-o'-le-la, *n. T. the louse hunter; the ape.* See ode.

he'-oŋ, *adv. for that, on that account, therefore.*

he'-oŋ-e-taŋ-haŋ, *adv. therefore.*

he-paŋ', *n. the name of the second child, if a son.* This and "hepi" are Santee only.

he-paŋ'-na, *n.* Same as hepaŋ.

he-pća', *v.* 1st pers. sing. *I think that, I thought that.* This is the only form used. See epća *and* kepća.

he-pi', *n. the name of the third child, if a son.*

he-pi'-daŋ, *n. dim.* of hepi.

he-pi'-na, *n. Si.* Same as hepidaŋ.

he-piŋ', *v.* 1st pers. sing. *Ih.* and *Si.* Same as hepa. See heya.

he-pi'-ya, *adv. in the mean time; before,* waniyetu hepiya, *before winter; during, in the course of,* aŋpetu hepiya, *during the day. T.,* hepiyela—waniyetu hepiyela, *during the winter: this side of, part way.*

hes, *intj.* expressing *impatience, unbelief, pride.*

he-sda'-tka-daŋ, *n. a young male elk.*

he-śki'-źu-pi, *n.* See hiŋśkiźupi

he-taŋ', *cont.* of hetaŋhaŋ.

he-taŋ'-haŋ, *adv. from that place:* hemataŋhaŋ, *I am from that place; from that time; therefore, on that account*

he-taŋ'-haŋ-to-ke-ća, *adv. what difference is it?* hetaŋhaŋ itokeća śni, *it is none of his business;* hetaŋhaŋ iwatokiyaka, *what does it concern him? T.,* hetaŋhaŋś tokaka *and* hetaŋhaŋś toka. See etaŋhaŋtokeća.

he-tka'-daŋ, *n. the common striped ground squirrel,* a species of *Sciurus.*

he'-tu, *adv. at that place, there.*

he'-tu-daŋ, *adv. there, then.*

he'-tu-daŋ-ȟiŋ, *adv. just at that place* or *time. T.,* hetulaȟćiŋ.

he'-ya, *n. a louse, lice; head louse.*

he'-ya, *v.* (he *and* eya) *to say that* or *this*—hepa, heha, heuŋkeyapi.

he-ya'-ke, *n. clothes, wearing apparel* of any kind. *T.,* hayapi.

he-ya'-ke-ćiŋ-haŋ, *n. to-morrow;* heyakećiŋhaŋ saŋpa *and* heyakećiŋhaŋ ićima, *the day after tomorrow. T.,* haŋyakećiŋhaŋ.

he'-ya-śa, *n. a red louse, small louse.*

he-ya'-ya, *v. red.* of heya; *to say much, keep saying*—hepapa, hehaha, uŋkeyayapi.

he-ya'-ya-la-ka, *v. T. to tell lies.* See eyaya.

he-ye'-ki-ya, *v. a. to cause to say that*—heyewakiya.

He-yo'-ka, *n. the name of a Dakota god,* called by some *the anti-*

natural god. Heyoka is represented as a little old man with a cocked hat on his head, a bow and arrows in his hands, and a quiver on his back. In winter he goes naked, and in summer he wraps his buffalo-robe around him. See Waziya.

He-yo′-ka-ti, *n. p.* *the house of Heyoka*, the name of a conical hill about ten miles east of Lac-qui-parle. The little hills on the prairie are also the houses of Heyoka.

he′-yu-ġa *and* he′-yu-ġa-ġa, *n.* *an appellation of all animals that have branching horns.*

he′-yu-ktaŋ, *adj.* *bent-horn.* *T.*, pte heyuktala, *n.*, *a heifer, a young cow.*

he-yuŋ′, *v. a.* *to tie up, wrap up a pack, pack up*—hemuŋ, henuŋ, heuŋyuŋpi.

he-yuŋ′-pi, *n.* *wrapping up; what is wrapped around.*

he′-źaŋ-źaŋ, *n.* *T.* *a body-louse.*

hi, *n.* *a tooth, teeth; the bit* or *edge* of an ax; *the point* of anything—mahi; wićahi, *human teeth.*

hi, *v. n.* *to come to, arrive at*—wahi, yahi, uŋhipi: en mahi, *he came to me.*

hi-a′-pe, *v.* *to await one's coming*—hiawape.

hi-gna′, *n.* *T.* *husband;* mihigna, nihigna, hignaku; *i. q.* hihna.

hi-gna′-ya, *v.* *T.*, *to have for a husband;* hignawaya.

hi-haŋ′-zi, *v. n.* *T.* *to become dark, to grow obscure:* tawaćiŋ hihaŋzi, *to lose consciousness.*

hi-hda′, *v.* See hiŋhda.

hi′-hda-kiŋs-kiŋ-za, *v.* *to grate the teeth.* See hihdaḳiŋsḳiŋza.

hi′-hda-ko-kog, *cont.* of hihdakokoka; hihdakokog wauŋ.

hi′-hda-ko-ko-ka, *v.* *to gnash the teeth*—hiwahdakokoka.

hi′-hda-ḳiŋs-ḳiŋs, *cont.* of hihdaḳiŋsḳiŋza; hihdaḳiŋsḳiŋs wauŋ, *I am grating my teeth.*

hi′-hda-ḳiŋs-ḳiŋ-za, *v.* *to grate the teeth*—hiwahdaḳiŋsḳiŋza.

hi-he′-ya, *v. n.* (hi *and* iheya) *to come and enter*, as a bullet or arrow.

hi-he′-ya, *v.* *col. pl.* *they collect together, assemble in one place.*

hi-hi′, *adj.* *soft*, as fur or down.

hi-hi′-daŋ, *adj.* *soft*, as mud, etc.; *mellow*, as ground. *T.*, hihiyela.

hi-hi′-se, *adj.* *nappy, furry.*

hi-hna′, *n.* *a husband;* mihihna, *my husband;* nihihna, *thy husband.* See higna.

hi-hna′-ku, *n.* *her husband.*

hi-hna′-toŋ, *v. n.* *to have a husband, be married*—hihnawatoŋ, hihnauŋtoŋpi.

hi-hna′-ya, *v. a.* *to have for a husband*—hihnawaya, hihnayaya, hihnauŋyaŋpi, hihnamayaŋ.

hi-hnu′, *v.* See hiŋhnu.

hi-huŋ′ni, *v.* *to come to land, to arrive at* any place—wahihuŋni, uŋhihuŋnipi.

hi-ḣ'a′-ki-ya, *v. n.* *to show one's teeth, to grin*—hiḣ'awakiya.

hi′-i-pa-śku-daŋ, *n.* (hi *and* ipaśku) *a pin.* Probably because the Dakotas may have seen pins used to pick the teeth with. See hipaśkudaŋ.

hi′-i-ya-ṭiŋ-za, *n.* *T.*, *cloves.*

hi-mni′-ći-ya, *v. col. pl.* *to come, assemble, to keep coming.*

hi′-na-haŋ-ka, *intj.* *stop, hold, wait a minute.*

hi-naḣ′, *adv.* *yet, as yet.* See hinaḣiŋ.

hi-na′-ḣiŋ, *adv.* *yet, as yet;* used with śni, *not yet.*

hi-na′-ḣiŋ-ke-śni, *adv.* *not yet the time.*

hi′-na-ka, *intj.* See hinahaŋka.

hi′-na-ka-ha, *adv.* See hiŋnakaha.

hi-na′-pa *or* hi-naŋ′-pa, *v. n.* *to come in sight, come out of, come up,* as something planted—wahinapa, uŋhinapapi.

hi-na′-pe-ya, *v. a.* *to cause to come in sight*—hinapewaya.

hi-na′-źa, *n.* *the jaws of an arrow which hold the point.*

hi-na′-źiŋ, *v. n.* (hi *and* naźiŋ) *to come and stand*—wahinawaźiŋ, yahinayaźiŋ, hinauŋźiŋpi.

hiŋ, *interrog. part.* equivalent to nuŋ he: wau hiŋ, *shall I come?* It is used commonly by women.

hiŋ, *n.* *hair, fur, down.*

hiŋ-a′-ka-ġa, *n.* *an owl.* See hiŋhaŋkaġa.

hiŋ-ćiŋ′-ća, *n.* (hiŋta *and* ćiŋća) *a small species of bass-wood.*

hiŋ-gla′, *v. n.* *T.* This is an auxiliary signifying *action* or *movement, i. q.* hiŋhda. See bohiŋgla, sliŋ hiŋgla, ćaŋze hiŋgla, etc.—mahiŋgla, nihiŋgla.

hiŋ-haŋ′, *v. n.* *to fall,* as rain or snow, *to rain* or *snow:* hiŋhe kta, *it will rain.*

hiŋ′-haŋ, *n.* *last night.*

hiŋ-haŋ′, *n.* *an owl.*

hiŋ-haŋ′-ći-ḳa-la, *n.* *T., a small species of owl; i. q.*, hiŋhaŋhetoŋna.

hiŋ-haŋ′-he-toŋ-na, *n.* *the horned owl,* probably the *Strix bubo.*

hiŋ-haŋ′-ka-ġa, *n.* *an owl.* *T.*, hiŋyaŋkaġa.

hiŋ-haŋ′-ka-ġa, *v.* *to hoot* or *shout as an owl,* as young men do at night; *to act like an owl.*

hiŋ-haŋ′-ke, *n.* *this end, the end this way.*

hiŋ′-haŋ-na, *n.* *T.* and *Ih.* *to-morrow morning; i. q.* haŋḣaŋna, hiŋhaŋna le, *this morning.*

hiŋ-haŋ′-saŋ, *n.* *the gray owl.*

hiŋ-haŋ′-sa-pa, *n.* *the black owl.*

hiŋ-haŋ′-ska, *n.* *a white owl*

hiŋ-haŋ′-śa, *n.* *the red owl.*

hiŋ-haŋ′-toŋ-waŋ, *n.* *fern, brake.*

hiŋ′-hda, *v. n.* *to become, commence,* implying *suddenness*—mahiŋhda, nihiŋhda, uŋhiŋhdapi: yazaŋ hiŋhda, *to become sick suddenly.*

hiŋ-he′, *v. n.* *to rain.* See hiŋhaŋ.

hiŋ-he′-ki-ya, *v. a.* *to cause to fall,* as rain or snow—hiŋhewakiya.

hiŋ-he′-ya, *v. a* *to cause to rain, etc.*—hiŋhewaya.

hiŋ-hiŋ′-se, *adj.* See hihise.

hiŋ-hnu′, *v. a.* *to singe off*, as the down of a duck, etc.—hiŋwahnu, hiŋyahnu. *T.*, hiŋgnu.

hiŋ-hnu′-pi, *part.* *singed off.*

hiŋ-ḣpa′-ya, *v. n.* *to fall, fall down*—mahiŋḣpaya, nihiŋḣpaya, uŋhiŋḣpayapi. See iḣpaya.

hiŋ ḣte′, *n.* *thick fur, hair,* or *nap.*

hiŋ-ḣte′-ya, *adj.* *furry, rough, the fur side out*—hiŋḣteya hiŋmi, *I wear the fur side out.*

hiŋ-kpi′-daŋ, *n.* *short hair* or *fur*, as that on robes taken in summer; *robes with short hair.*

hiŋ′-na-ka-ha, *adv.* *suddenly, immediately, upon that.*

hiŋ-se′, *intj.* denoting *impatience*, used when one is asked to tell a thing over again.

hiŋ-ska′, *adj.* *shed off*, said of animals that have a new coat of hair: literally, *hair-white.*

hiŋ-ske′, *n.* *the long upper* or *canine teeth* of animals such as are called wamanića: hence wahiŋske, *the long-grained corn;* in horses, *the teeth that fall out when they are three years old;* in man, some say *the molar teeth*, others say *the canine teeth*, are called hiŋske.

hiŋ′-sko, *adv.* *so big, so large.*

hiŋ′-sko-ke-ća, *adv.* *so large, so great.*

hiŋ′-sko-ki′-ni-ća, *v. n.* (hiŋsko *and* akinića) *to be doubtful which is the largest.*.

hiŋ′-sko-sko-ke-ća, *adv.* *red.* of hiŋskokeća.

hiŋ′-sko-sko-ya, *adv.* *red.* of hiŋskoya.

hiŋ′-sko-taŋ-ka, *adv.* *so great.*

hiŋ′-sko-ya, *adv.* *so far around, thus far.*

hiŋ-śka′, *n* *Ih.* *the string with which they pack.* See teḣmiso.

hiŋ-śki′-źu-pi, *n.* *a fish-hook.*

hiŋ′-śko-daŋ, *adv.* *so small.* Why this is not hiŋskodaŋ, corresponding with the rest of the family, I cannot tell; but in this tiŋśkodaŋ resembles it. *T.*, niśkola.

hiŋ′-ta See kahiŋta, etc.

hiŋ′-ta, *n.* *the bass, linden,* or *lime wood:* hiŋta ćaŋ, *bass-wood, Tilia.*

hiŋ-te′, *intj.* expressive of *disbelief.*

hiŋ-tka′, *n.* *T.* *a body-louse; an unhatched louse.*

hiŋ-tkaŋ′, *n.* *the common cat-tail* or *Typha.*

hiŋ-tkaŋ′-hu, *n.* *the Typha stalk.*

hiŋ′-tkaŋ-ḣa-ka, *n.* *water-moss.* Called also minihiŋtkaŋḣaka.

hiŋ-tka′-za-pi, *n.* (hiŋta *and* kaza) *the bundles of linden bark* which the Dakotas prepare for tying rice.

hiŋ-tkuŋ′, *v.* *i. q.* yuśda: peźi hiŋtkuŋ mda, *I go to get grass.* Not in general use.

hiŋ-tpi′-daŋ, *n.* *anything with short fur; a summer robe.* Same as hiŋkpidaŋ. *T.*, hiŋkpila.

hiŋ-ya'-ḣiŋ, *adv.* *yet, as yet;* with śni, *not yet,* as, hiŋyaḣiŋ ećamoŋ śni, *I have not yet done it.* See hinaḣiŋ. *T.*, nahaŋḣća.

hiŋ-ya'-ḣiŋ-ke-śni, *adv.* *not yet, the time is not yet.*

hiŋ-yaŋ'-ka-ġa, *n.* *an owl.* Same as hiŋhaŋkaġa.

hiŋ-yaŋ'-pa, *v. n.* *to come in sight, come up out of,* as one diving. See hinapa.

hiŋ-yaŋs'-gla, *v.* *T., to dislike, be afraid of,* as of an infectious disease

hiŋ-yaŋs'-ya, *v. a.* *to provoke*—hinyaŋswaya.

hiŋ-yaŋs'-ya, *adv.* *sternly, crossly.* *T.*, wohiŋyaŋsya.

hiŋ-yaŋ'-za, *v. n.* *to be stern, cross*—mahiŋyaŋza: tawaćiŋ hiŋyaŋza, *to be of a surly disposition.*

hiŋ-yaŋ'-ze-ća, *n.* *one who is stern* or *cross.*

hiŋ-ya'-ta-oŋ-pa, *v. a.* *to lay on the shoulder*—hiŋyatawaoŋpa. See hiyetaoŋpa.

hiŋ-ya'-ta-źu, *v. a.* *to put into one's blanket on the arm,* as an Indian does—hiŋyatawaźu. Also hiyetaźu.

hiŋ-ya'-źi-će, *n.* *fur, down, swan's down.*

hiŋ-ye'-te, *n.* *the shoulder, whole shoulder.* See hiyete.

hiŋ'-źi-źi-daŋ, *n.* *thin hair,* as that on one's hands and arms.

hi'-pa-śku, *v.* *to pick the teeth*—hiwapaśku.

hi'-pa-śku-daŋ, *n.* *a pin, pins.* See hiipaśkudaŋ. *T*, hiyopataka.

hi-psi'-ća, *v.* *to jump down,* as from a horse—wahipsića.

hi'-psoŋ-psoŋ-na, *n.* *teeth on edge.* See psoŋpsoŋna.

hi-ta'-kaŋ-yu-wi, *v.* (hi takaŋ *and* yuwi) *T* *to bind an arrowhead on the shaft.*

hi-ti'-hda, *v. a.* *to loathe, dislike,* as food—hitiwahda, hitiyahda, hitiuŋhdapi.

hi-ti'-hda-ya, *v. a* *to cause to loathe* or *dislike*—hitihdawaya.

hi-tung'-taŋ-ka, *n.* *Ih.* *a rat:* hituŋka taŋka, *large mouse.*

hi-tuŋ'-ka, *n.* *a mouse, mice.*

hi-tuŋ'-ka-daŋ, *n.* hi-tuŋ'-ka-na, *Ih.*; *and* hi-tuŋ'-ka-la, *T.* *mice.*

hi-tuŋ'-ka-kaŋ, *v* *to tell tales* or *traditions*—hituŋwakakaŋ, hituŋuŋkakaŋpi. *T.*, huŋkaŋkaŋ.

hi-tuŋ'-ka-kaŋ-pi, *n.* *tales, legends, traditions, myths:* the word is pronounced also, hituŋkaŋkapi *and* hituŋkaŋkaŋpi. These myths can be told only at night.

hi-tuŋ'-ka-saŋ, *n.* *the weasel, ermine;* of the genus *Mustela.*

hi-tuŋ'-ka-saŋ-na, *n.* *the weasel, ermine.*

hi-tuŋ'-psi-ća-daŋ, *n.* *the field-mouse.*

hi-tuŋ'-psi-psi-ća-daŋ, *n.* *the field-mouse*

hi-waŋ', *v. imp.* *look here, halloo.* See hiwo.

h i - w a ŋ′ - k a, *v. n.* *to come and camp* or *spend the night*—wahimuŋka, yaȟinuŋka, uŋhiwaŋkapi. *T.*, hiyuŋka.

h i - w o′, *v. imp.* *look here, halloo.*

h i - y a′, *adv. of negation; no.*

hi-ya′-daŋ, *intj* *not so!* A by-word.

h i - y a′ - h a ŋ, *v. n.* *to come and stand on*—wahiyawahaŋ, yahiyayahaŋ, uŋhiyauŋhaŋpi.

h i - y a′ - h d e, *v. n.* *to reach to, lead to,* as a road; *to come upon* one—mahiyahde, nihiyahde, uŋhiyahdepi.

h i - y a′ - h d e - y a, *v. a.* *to cause to reach to; to bring upon* one—hiyahdewaya, hiyahdeuŋyaŋpi.

h i - y a′ - h d e - y a, *adv.* *reaching to, leading to.*

h i - y a′ - k a - p t a, *v. n.* *to come over,* as a stream or hill—wahiyawakapta, yahiyayakapta.

h i - y a′ - n u ŋ, *adj.* *puny; T.*, le ehaŋna tuka hiyanuŋ, heoŋ ćistila, *this is a long time ago, but was puny, and so is small;* opposed to koyanuŋ.

h i′ - y a ŋ - k a, *v. n.* *to come again and again, to keep coming*—wahimaŋka, yahinaŋka. *T.*, *imp.* only, *wait, hold on.*

h i - y a′ - y a, *v. n.* *to come and pass along, go by, go past*—wahimdamde, yahidade, uŋhiyayapi.

h i - y a′ - y a ŋ - p a, *v.* (hi *and* ayaŋpa) *to come morning on* one.

h i - y e′ - t a - o ŋ - p a, *v. a.* *to place on the shoulder*—hiyetawaoŋpa. Also hiŋyataoŋpa.

h i - y e′ - t a - ź u, *v. a.* *to put into one's blanket on the arm*—hiyetawaźu. See also hiŋyataźu.

h i - y e′ - t e, *n.* *the shoulder.* See also hiŋyete.

h i - y e′ - y a, *v. n.* *to be:* hiyeye ćiŋ, *those who are, all;* taku hiyeye ćiŋ, *all things;* oyate hiyeye ćiŋ, *all people;* uŋhiyeyapi, *we are.*

h i - y e′ y a, *v. n.* *to become; to cause to be.* See iyeya.

h i - y o′, *v.* *Ih.* and *T.*, *i. q.* huwe: hiyo mni kta, *I will go for it.* hiyo i; hiyo iyaya, etc.

h i - y o′ - h i, *v. n.* *to come to, arrive at, reach to*—wahiyohi, yahiyohi, mahiyohi, uŋhiyohipi.

h i - y o′ - h i, *v.* *Ih.* *to come for; i. q.* huwe hi—hiyowahi, hiyoyahi, hiyouŋhipi. *T.*, *to go for;* hiyohi mni kta, *I will go for it.*

h i - y o′ - h i - k i - y a, *v. a.* *to cause to come* or *reach to*—hiyohiwakiya.

h i - y o′ - h i - y a, *v. a.* *to cause to reach*—hiyohiwaya, hiyohiuŋyaŋpi.

h i - y o′ - h i - y a, *adv.* *reaching to.*

h i - y o′ - ȟ p a - y a, *v. n.* *to fall into, come and fall in; to come into* a road; *to join,* as one road does another—wahiyowaȟpamda *and* wahiyoȟpaya, yahiyoyaȟpada *and* yahiyoȟpaya, uŋhiyoȟpayapi.

h i - y o′ - ȟ p e - y a, *v. a.* *to cause to fall into, cast into, bring and put into,* as food into a dish—hiyoȟpewaya.

h i - y o′ - p a - p s o ŋ, *v.* *to throw* or *dash,* as water *into* a boat.

hi-yo'-pa-ta-ka, *n.* *T.* *a pin, a toothpick.* See hipaśkudaŋ.

hi'-yo-taŋ-ka, *v. n.* (hi *and* iyotaŋka) *to come and sit down; to establish one's self at* a place—wahimdotaŋka, yahidotaŋka, uŋhiyotaŋkapi.

hi-yu', *v. n.* *to come forth,* as a child born; *to come, come toward*—hibu *and* wahihbu, hidu *and* yahihdu, uŋhiyupi, hidupi *and* yahihdupi

hi-yu'-ki-ći-ći-ya, *v. a.* *to hand to one his own*—hiyuwećićiya, hiyumićićiya.

hi-yu'-ki-ya, *v. a.* *to cause to come to; to hand to*—hiyuwakiya, hiyuyakiya, hiyuuŋkiyapi.

hi-yu'-ya, *v. a.* *to cause to come to, to send* or *hand to; to throw up* from the stomach, *vomit*—hiyuwaya, hiyuyaya, hiyuuŋyaŋpi.

hma, *n.* *the black walnut, black walnuts.* *T.*, gma.

hma-hu', *n.* *the black walnut-tree, Juglans nigra.*

hmi-hbe', *v. n.* Same as hmihma.

hmi-hbe'-ya, *adv.* *round and round, going round.*

hmi-hma', *v. n* *to go round,* like a wheel. *Ih.*, kmikma; *T.*, gmigme. See ćaŋpagmigma.

hmi-hmi'-yaŋ, *adj.* *round,* like a ball.

hmi-hmi'-yaŋ-yaŋ, *adj.* *red.* of hmihmiyaŋ.

hmi-yaŋ', *adj.* *round,* as a wheel. *T.*, gmigma.

hmi-yaŋ'-na, *adj.* *roundish,* Same as hmiyaŋ.

hmi-yaŋ'-yaŋ, *adj.* *red.* of hmiyaŋ.

hmi-yaŋ'-yaŋ-na, *n.* *any little round things.*

hmoŋ, *adj.* *twisted.* See hmu *and* hmuŋ.

hmu *or* hmuŋ, *adj.* *twisted.* See kahmuŋ, yuhmuŋ, etc.

hmuŋg, *cont.* of hmuŋka: śuŋktokeća hmuŋg wauŋ, *I am trapping wolves.*

hmuŋ-hmuŋ'-za, *adj.* *red.* of hmuŋza.

hmuŋ'-ka, *v. a.* *to set a trap, to trap* any thing, *to catch in a trap*—wahmuŋka, yahmuŋka, uŋhmuŋkapi.

hmuŋs'-mna, *adj.* *smelling like fish.*

hmuŋ-wa'-haŋ, *part.* See hmuwahaŋ.

hmuŋ'-za, *adj.* *slimy, fish-like, smelling strong,* like spoiled meat.

hmus, *cont.* of hmuza. See iohmus.

hmus'-ya, *adv.* *shut up.*

hmu-wa'-haŋ, *part.* *becoming twisted of itself.* *T.*, gmuwahaŋ, *becoming untwisted.*

hmu'-za, *adj.* *shut,* as the mouth, hand, etc. See ohmuza.

hna. See yuhna. *T.*, gna.

hnag, *cont.* of hnaka.

hna'-haŋ, *part.* *fallen off of itself,* as fruit.

hna-hna'-do-waŋ, *v.* *to sing a grunting song.* *T.*, gnagnalowaŋ. See hdohdodowaŋ.

hna'-ka, *v. a.* *to lay* or *place, lay*

away; to lay up, as the dead on scaffolds, hence, *to bury the dead; to have by one*, as takudaŋ hnake śni, *he has nothing laid by him*—wahnaka, uŋhnakapi. From this are derived ahnaka, ehnaka, kihnaka, *and* ohnaka.

hna'-ka-pi, *n.* *dead persons laid away;* hence *graves, tombs.*

hna-śka', *n.* *the common frog.* See also naśka.

hna-śka'-ćaŋ-di-daŋ, *n.* *a small kind of frog; the tree-frog.*

hna-śkiŋ'-yaŋ, *v. n.* *to be oppressed, overcome, possessed,* as of devils—mahnaśkiŋyaŋ. *T.*, gnaśkiŋyaŋ, *to be wild, crazy, frantic.*

hna-wa'-haŋ, *part.* Same as hnahaŋ.

hna'-yaŋ, *v. a.* *to deceive, cheat, take advantage of*—wahnayaŋ, yahnayaŋ, uŋhnayaŋpi, mahnayaŋ; ćihnayaŋ, *I deceive thee;* iç̣ihnayaŋ, *to deceive one's self*—miç̣ihnayaŋ. *T.*, gnayaŋ.

ḣni hda', *v. n.* *to pass by* a place *going home.* This is used only in the third person; the other persons are formed from the obsolete "hdiyahda," as, wahdiyahda, yahdiyahda, uŋhdiyahdapi. *T.*, gligla.

hni-na'-pa *or* **hni-naŋ'-pa**, *v. n.* *to come forth; to return; to come out of* any place *going home; to rise,* as from the dead—wahninapa. Same as hdinapa. *T.*, gninapa.

hnu'-ni, *v. n.* waćiŋhnuni, *to be bewildered, deranged*—waćiŋmahnuni: *to be bewildered* or *lost,* as in trying to follow tracks—wahnuni, yahnuni. *T.*, gnuni.

ho, *adv. of affirmation.* *yes, yea.*

ho, *n.* *the voice* either of a man or of any animal or thing; *sound* in general—maho, niho, uŋhopi, wićaho.

ho, *n.* *cont.* of hoġaŋ; *fish; a fish-net.*

ho, *v. n.* *imp.* only; *come on, come now*—ho wo, ho po, ho miye. See iho.

ho-a'-pe, *n.* (hoġaŋ *and* ape) *fish-fins.*

ho'-bu, *n.* *a rough, unpleasant voice*—homabu: *a wild young man,* one who goes around yelling at night. J. P W.

ho'-bu-ki-ya, *v. n.* *to speak with a gruff, unpleasant voice*—hobuwakiya.

ho-ća'-ka, *n.* (hoġaŋ *and* ćaka) *fish-gills.*

ho-će'-śpu, *n.* *fish-scales; warts.* See ćeśpu. *T.*, hoćośpu, *warts, scales.*

ho-će'-ta, *n.* *the road* or *entrance* to a hoćoka or *court-yard: the straight road* to a drove of buffaloes when a surround is made.

ho-ćo'-ka, *n.* *a court-yard, an area surrounded by tents* or *houses:* tahoćoka, *his court.*

ho-da'-za-ta, *adv.* *outside of a circle of tents.*

ho'-e-ća-ḣe, *adv.* See ḣoećaḣe, the correct form.

ho-ġa'-haŋ, *n.* *a rough, loud voice*—homaġahaŋ.

h o - ġ a ŋ', *n. fish;* the generic name.

h o - ġ a ŋ' - m n a, *adj.* (hoġaŋ *and* omna) *smelling like fish, fishy.*

h o - ġ a ŋ' - s t i ŋ - n a, *n.* (hoġaŋ *and* ćistiŋna) *little fish,* such as minnows. *T.*, hoġaŋsćila.

h o - ġ a ŋ' - t a ŋ - k a, *n. big fish,* the name given to *whales.*

h o - ġ a ŋ' - w i - ć a - ś t a - ś n i, *n. trout* or *salmon,* lit., *ill-behaved fish.*

h o' - ġ a - t a, *n. a rough voice*—homàġata.

h o' - ġ i - t a, *adj. hoarse,* as a person's voice when he has taken cold—homaġita, honiġita, houŋġitapi.

h o' - h d a - ġ i - t a, *v. pos.* of hoyaġita; *to make one's self hoarse by speaking*—howahdaġita. *T.*, hoiglaġita.

H o' - h e, *n. p. the Assiniboine Indians.* Long ago they belonged to the Dakota nation. Also a clan of the Blackfeet Dakotas.—J. O. D.

h o' - h o, *intj.* Used when there is something said which is not liked. *T.*, hohe, denoting *surprise, regret.*

h o - h o', *adj. loose,* as a tooth.

h o - h o' - d a ŋ, *adj. loose, that can be shaken* or *moved:* hi mahohodaŋ, *my teeth are loose.*

h o' - h o - h e, *intj. T. red.* of hohe. See hehehe.

h o - h o' - p i - ć a - ś n i, *adj. immovable.*

h o - h o' - p i - ć a - ś n i - y a ŋ, *adv. immovably.*

h o - h u', *n. T. a bone.* See huhu.

h o - h u ŋ' - k a, *n. a mother-fish,* i. e., *an old fish.*

h o ħ, *intj. T.* expresses *doubt, unbelief.*

H o - ħ n o' - ġ i - ć a, *n. p. a Dakota god,* a fabulous being: *a household god,* related to Ćaŋotidaŋ, by which mothers scare their children.

H o - ħ n o' - ġ i - ć a - d a ŋ, *n. p. dim.* of Hoħnoġića.

h o - ħ p a', *v. n. to cough*—howaħpa.

h o - ħ p a' - p i, *n. coughing, having a cold:* hoħpapi emaćeća, *I have a bad cough.*

h o - ħ p i', *n. a nest, bird's nest.*

h o - ħ p i' - y a, *v. a. to have for a nest, make a nest of*—hoħpiwaya.

h o - i' - ć u - w a, *n.* (hoġaŋ *and* kuwa) *a fish hook, fishing apparatus. T.*, hoićuwa maza.

h o - i - y o' - ħ p a - y a, *v. n. to become hoarse,* by the wind blowing on one and affecting the voice—hoiyomaħpaya.

h o' - i - y o - ħ p e - y a, *v. a. to cast a net* in fishing—hoiyoħpewaya.

h o - i - y o' - k i - s e, *n. half of a company, half of a camp.*

h o' - i - y u - p s i - ć e, *n. a fish-hook.*

h o - k a', *n. a kind of fish. T., the eel.*

h o - k ' a', *n. the heron,* of the genus *Ardea.*

h o - k ' a' - ġ i - ć a, *n. the snipe, a small kind of heron* of the genus *Scolopax.*

h o - k ' a' - ġ i - ć a - d a ŋ, *n. dim.* of hok'aġića.

h o′ - k a - p s a ŋ - p s a ŋ - i - a, *v. to whine*—hokapsaŋpsaŋiwaa.

h o - k ' a′ - s a ŋ - n a, *n. a kind of heron* or *snipe.*

h o - k ' a′ - t o, *n. the blue heron.*

h o - k ś i′ - ć a - l a, *n. T. a baby: i. q.* hokśiyoḳopa.

h o - k ś i′ - ć e - k p a, *n. a blue wild flower,* which appears first in the spring: *twin flower.*

h o - k ś i′ - ć e - k p a *or* h o - k ś i′ - ć e - k p a - p i, *n. twins.*

h o - k ś i′ - ć e - t p a, *n. a twin* or *twins; a blue flower,* which appears early in the spring. Same as hokśićekpa.

h o - k ś i′ - ç o - p a, *n. Si.* and *Ih. a child; i. q.* hokśiyoḳopa.

h o - k ś i′ - d a ŋ, *n. a boy*—homakśidaŋ, honikśidaŋ; houŋkśipidaŋ, *we are boys.*

h o - k ś i′ - k a, *adj. yet a boy, under age*—homakśika.

h o - k ś i′ - k e - ś n i, *adj. of age, not a boy;* John ix. 21—homakśikeśni, honikśikeśni.

h o - k ś i′ - k s u - y a, *v. n. to travail, be in childbirth*—hokśinwaksuya, hokśinyaksuya.

h o - k ś i′ - l a, *n. T* Same as hokśidaŋ.

h o - k ś i n′, *cont.* of hokśina *or* hokśidaŋ. *T.*, hokśil.

h o - k ś i′ - n a, *n. Ih.* Same as hokśidaŋ.

h o - k ś i n′ - ć a ŋ t - k i - y a - p i, *n. the beloved son, one universally esteemed; the heir to the throne.*

h o - k ś i n′ - i - k p i - h n a̧ - k a, *v. n. to be with child, be pregnant*—hokśinikpiwahnaka.

h o - k ś i n′ - i - t p i - h n a - k a, *v. n. to be pregnant.* Same as hokśinikpihnaka. *T.*, hokśilikpignaka.

h o - k ś i n′ - k a - ġ a, *v. a. to beget a child*—hokśinwakaġa.

h o - k ś i n′ - k a - ġ a - p i, *n. a doll, a made child.*

h o - k ś i n′ - ḳ i ŋ, *v. a. to carry* or *pack a child on the back*—hokśinwaḳiŋ.

h o - k ś i n′ - w i ŋ - k t a, *v. to be angry and act like a child, be pettish*—hokśinmawiŋkta.

h o - k ś i n′ - w i - t k o - d a ŋ, *v. to be childish, silly.*

h o - k ś i n′ - y u - h a, *v. to give birth to a child*—hokśinmduha.

h o - k ś i′ - w i ŋ, *n.* See hokśiwiŋna.

h o - k ś i′ - w i ŋ - n a, *n. a virgin, one who has not had a husband.*

h o - k ś i′ - y o - ḳ o - p a, *n.* (hokśidaŋ *and* oḳopa) *a baby, a very little child;* but figuratively applied to grown persons—homakśiyoḳopa, houŋkśiyoḳopapi.

h o - k ś i′ - y o - p a, *n. a child, boy* or *girl*—homakśiyopa, honikśiyopa, houŋkśiyopapi.

h o - k u′ - w a, *v.* (hoġaŋ *and* kuwa) *to fish, take* or *catch fish* in any way, either by hook, net or spear—howakuwa; hokuwa mda, *I go a fishing.*

h o′ - m n a, *adj. smelling like fish, fishy.* Same as hoġaŋmna.

h o′-m n a-y a ŋ, *v.* *to gather* or *collect fish* for a feast—homnawaya.

h o-m n i′, *adj.* *round, going round.* See ohomni, yuhomni, etc.

h o-n a′-ġ i-d a ŋ, *n.* *the common house-fly.*

h o-n a′-w i-t k a-l a, *n.* *T.* *tadpoles.*

h o ŋ, *n.* See huŋ.

h o ŋ′-h o ŋ-h e, *intj.* of *doubt* or *surprise.* See hohohe *and* hoho.

h o ŋ′-k u, *n.* See huŋku.

h o ŋ-p e′, *n.* *the stick used in digging* tipsiŋna or *Indian turnips; a pestle.*

h o ŋ-s o ŋ′-z a-h e, *adj.* *Ih.* *shaky, not firm: i. q.* huhuzahaŋ.

h o-p a′-ś k u, *n.* *T.* *fish-scales.*

h o-p a′-t a ŋ-k a-l a, *n.* *T.* a kind of fish like the *perch.*

h o′-p i ŋ s, *cont.* of hopiŋza.

h o′-p i ŋ s-k i-y a, *v. a.* *to make the voice squeak, to speak with a squeaking voice.*

h o′-p i ŋ-z a, *n.* *a small squeaking voice*—homapiŋza.

h o-p o ŋ′-k a, *n.* *a gnat, gnats,* of the genus *Culex.* See ćapoŋka.

h o-p o ŋ′-k a-d a ŋ, *n.* *a gnat, gnats.*

h o′-p s i-ć a, *v. a.* (hoġaŋ *and* yupsića) *to make fish jump, to take fish with a hook and line*—homdupsića. See hoyupsića.

h o′-p s i n, *cont.* of hopsića; hopsin ya, *to go a fishing*—hopsin mda.

h o-s a′-m n a, *adj.* *smelling like fish, fishy.*

h o-s e′-w i-m n a, *adj.* *smelling like fish.*

h o-ś i′, *v.* (ho *and* śi) *to command the voice,* i. e., *to tell news, take word to* one. It is always used with other verbs.

h o-ś i′-h d a, *v.* (hośi *and* hda) *to carry word home*—hośiwahda.

h o-ś i′-h d i, *v.* (hośi *and* hdi) *to bring word home.*

h o-ś i′-h d i-ć u, *v.* (hośi *and* hdića) *to start home with news*—hośiwahdiću.

h o-ś i′-h i, *v.* (hośi *and* hi) *to arrive with intelligence*—hośiwahi.

h o-ś i′-i, *v.* (hośi *and* i) *to have been at to carry word*—hośiwai.

h o-ś i′-i-y a-y a, *v.* (hośi *and* iyaya) *to have gone to carry word.*

h o-ś i′-k a-h d a, *v.* (hośi *and* kahda) *to carry home word to* one.

h o-ś i′-k a-h d i, *v.* (hośi *and* kahdi) *to bring word home to* one.

h o-ś i′-k a-h i, *v.* (hośi *and* kahi) *to bring word to* one.

h o-ś i′-k a-i, *v.* (hośi *and* kai) *to have taken word to* one.

h o-ś i′-k a-k i, *v.* (hośi *and* kaki) *to have taken word home to* one.

h o-ś i′-k a-y a, *v.* (hośi *and* kaya) *to take word to* one—hośiwakamda, hośiyakada.

h o-ś i′-k i, *v.* (hośi *and* ki) *to have reached home with news.*

h o-ś i′-k u, *v.* (hośi *and* ku) *to be coming home with a message.*

h o-ś i ŋ′-y a-ś e-ć a, *n.* *the sucker,* a kind of fish. See paȟteća.

ho-śi′-u, *v.* (hośi *and* u) *to come with a message.*

ho-śi′-ya, *v.* (hośi *and* ya) *to go to take a message.*

ho-śuŋ′-pe-śda, *n.* *tadpoles.*

ho′-ta-daŋ, *n.* *a small sharp-billed duck.*

ho′-ta-daŋ, *n.* *a swing,* as a grape-vine attached to a tree above. *T.*, hoh̔otola.

ho′-ta-daŋ-ki-ćuŋ, *v. n.* *to swing, swing round*—hotadaŋ wećuŋ, hotadaŋ uŋkićuŋpi.

ho′-taŋ-iŋ, *v. n.* *to have the voice heard*—homataŋiŋ.

ho′-taŋ-ka, *n.* *the sturgeon,* a kind of fish of the genus *Acipenser.*

ho′-taŋ-ka-ki-ya, *adv.* *with a great* or *loud voice:* hotaŋkakiya ia, *to speak with a loud voice.*

Ho-taŋ′-ke, *n. p.* *the Winnebago Indians.*

ho′-taŋ-ke, *n.* *a loud* or *great voice.*

ho′-ta-pi-śko, *n.* *a swing:* hotapiśko kićuŋ. *to swing.* Hotadaŋ is generally used.

Ho-ta′-wa, *n. p.* *the Otawas* or *Oto Indians.*

ho-toŋ′, *v.* *to cry out, put forth the voice, howl,* as animals; *to crow,* as a cock, hence aŋpaohotoŋna; *to thunder,* as wakiŋyaŋ hotoŋ, *it thunders.*

ho-toŋ′-ki-ya, *v. a.* *to cause to bawl* or *cry out*—hotoŋwakiya.

ho-ṭe′-ća, *n.* *dead fish,* such as are found in the spring, having been frozen in the ice.

ho′-u-ki-ya, *v. a.* *to make the voice go to,* i. e., *to cry out to one*—houwakiya, houuŋkiyapi, houmakiya: houćićiya, *I cry out to thee.*

ho-u′-ma, *or* ho-uŋ′-ma, *n.* *one of the sides of a surround,* on the buffalo hunt.

ho′-u-ya, *v. a.* *to send the voice to, cry out to* one—houwaya, houuŋyaŋpi.

ho-wa′-kaŋ, *n.* *the large spotted pike* is sometimes so called.

ho-wa′-mdu-śka, *n.* (hoġaŋ *and* wamduśka) *an eel,* so called from its being both *fish* and *snake.*

ho-wa′-mdu-śka-daŋ, *n.* *dim.* of howamduśka.

ho-wa′-mdu-śka-na, *n.* *Ih. an eel.*

ho′-wa-na-se-ki-ya-pi, *n.* *a large fish-net.* See nasa *and* wanasa.

ho-wa′-sa-pa, *n.* (hoġaŋ owasiŋ *and* sapa) *the cat-fish,* so called from its being all black.

ho-wa′-sa pa-daŋ, *n.* *a small species of cat-fish, the bull-head.*

ho-wa′-ya, *v. n.* *to cry out, groan*—wahowamda, yahowada: śićahowaya, *to cry out badly:* waśićahowamda.

ho-we′, *T.* *adv.* of assent—*yes.* The Teeton women also say "ho" for *yes.*

ho-wo′, *v. imp* *come on.* The women use "ho we" *and* "ho ye."

ho′-ya, *v.* *there is fish;* said when fish assemble in one place and die there: hoya kta, *there will be fish.*

h o - y a′, *v.* *to use the voice* of another, as to have another sing in one's stead—howaya, hoćiya.

h o′ - y a - ġ i - t a, *v.* (ho *and* yaġita) *to make the voice hoarse by speaking*—homdaġita.

h o - y e′, *v. imp.* Same as ho wo. "Ye" and "pe" are the precatory terminations of the imperative mood, and the forms used by the women.

h o′ - y e - k i - y a, *v. a.* (ho *and* yekiya) *to cry to, call to, pray to*—hoyewakiya, hoyeyakiya, hoyeuŋkiyapi.

h o′ - y e - y a, *v. a.* (ho *and* yeya) *to cause the voice to go to*—hoyewaya, hoyeuŋyaŋpi.

h o′ - y u - ḣ i, *n.* *a ring* in timber, *a year's growth; a line* or *wrinkle in the skin* of a person.

h o′ - y u - p s i - ć a, *v. a.* *to make fish jump.*, i. e., *to catch fish with a hook and line*—homdupsića, houŋyupsićapi.

h o′ - y u - s d e - ć a, *n.* *wrinkles.*

h o′ - y u - s d e - ć e - t o ŋ, *v. n.* *to have wrinkles, to become old*—hoyusdećewatoŋ.

h o - z i′ - z i - d a ŋ, *n.* (hoġaŋ *and* zizi) *the perch*, a kind of fish. See śiŋtaka.

h u, *v. a.* *to copulate, have intercourse with a female*—wahu, yahu, uŋhupi.

h u, *n.* *a bone, bones*—mihu, nihu, wićahu; *the leg, legs* of a person or animal, as hu mayukaŋ, *I have legs; the stock* or *stem* of anything, as of a plant, tree, etc.; *the wheel* of a wagon, etc. See huha and huhu.

h u - a′ - ḳ i - p e, *n.* See huwaḳipe.

h u - ć a ŋ′, *n.* (hu *and* ćaŋ) *the stock* of a gun; *the shaft* of an arrow.

h u - ć o′ - ġ i ŋ, *n* *T.* *the calf of the leg.* See ćoġiŋ *and* sićoġiŋ.

h u - h a′, *n.* *the limbs, members of the body*, as the legs and arms; *the legs* of anything, as of a kettle.

h u - h a′ - s a - p e - d a ŋ, *n.* (huha *and* sapa) *the black-legged fox.*

h u - h a′ - ś a - d a ŋ, *n.* (huha *and* śa) *the red-legged fox.*

h u - h a′ - t o ŋ, *v. n.* (huha *and* toŋ) *to have legs* or *limbs*—huhawatoŋ.

h u - h a′ - t o - p a, *n.* (huha *and* topa) *a quadruped, the wolf* in particular.

h u - h a′ - y a, *v. a.* *to have for members, use for legs*—huhawaya.

h u′ - h d e, *v. a.* (hu *and* hde) *to set out, plant out*, as a young tree or plant of any kind—huwahde, huuŋhdepi.

h u - h d e′ - p i, *n.* *things set out, plants.*

h u - h u′, *n.* *a bone, bones, of the bone kind:* maza huhu, *arm-bands*, probably because at first they were made of bone.

h u - h u s′, *cont.* of huhuza. *T.*, huŋhuŋs.

h u - h u s′ - y a, *v. a.* *to cause to shake, to shake*—huhuswaya.

h u - h u s′ - y a, *adv.* *in a shaking manner.* *T.*, huŋhuŋsya.

h u - h u′ - t o - p a - o - w a - h d e, *n.* *the*

large end of the thigh-bone. See owahde.

hu-hu′-za, *adj.* *shaking, trembling*—mahuhuza, nihuhuza. *T.*, huŋhuŋza.

hu-hu′-za-haŋ, *part.* *shaken, shaking.*

hu′-ḣ'a, *n.* *bones bare* or *stripped of flesh, a skeleton:* tihuḣ'a, *the skeleton of a house,* as when the poles of a lodge are left standing. *T.*, huḣ'aka.

hu′-ḣa-ka, *n.* *a spear* for killing muskrats.

hu-ḣ'a′-ka, *adj.* *T.* *lean, poor, nothing but bones.*

hu′-ḣ'a-pi, *n.* *a skeleton.*

hu′-ḣ'a-ya, *adv.* *skeleton-like,* as the poles of a tent: huḣ'aya haŋ, *to stand as a skeleton.* *T.*, huḣ'akaka.

hu-ḣba′, *n.* *a kind of large water-grass,* the stalks of which are eaten by the Dakotas. *T.*, hoḣba *and* hoḣwa.

hu-ḣna′-ġa, *v.* See ḣuḣnaġa, the more correct form.

hu-iŋ′-yuŋ, *adv.* See huiyuŋ.

hu-i′-yuŋ, *adv.* (hu *and* iyuŋ) *on foot:* huiyuŋ mda, *I go on foot.*

hu-i′-yuŋ-ken, *adv.* *on foot, walking.*

hu-ku′-hu, *intj.* When a deer is brought into camp, the children shout "Hukuhu!"—S. W. POND.

hu-kun′, *adv.* *under, beneath.*

hu-ku′-wa-śte-śte-ki-ćuŋ, *v.* *to hop:* the pronouns come in in kićuŋ, wećuŋ, yećuŋ. The word is easily analyzed: hu, *bone;* ku, *to come;* waśte, *good,* and kićuŋ, *to use.*

hu-ku′-ya, *adv.* *below, under, at the lowest place.*

hu-mdo′, *n.* *the shin-bone.*

hu-na′-pta, *v.* *to be lame:* sićoġaŋ nawapta, *I have sprained my ankle.* Said when the muscle is so injured as to make one lame.

hu-na′-śte, *v.* *to sprain* one's leg—hunawaśte.

hu-na′-ti-pa, *v. n.* *T.* *to have cramp in the leg.*

hu′-ni. See hihuni.

hu′-noŋ-pa, *n.* (hu *and* noŋpa) *a biped, man,* in the sacred language.

huŋ, *n.* *mother*—nihuŋ, *thy mother;* huŋku, *his* or *her mother.* See ina, *my mother.*

huŋ-he′, *T.* *intj.* of astonishment.

huŋ-huŋ′-he, *intj.* *alas!* *T.*, hohohe.

huŋḣ, *n.* *some, a part*

huŋḣ′-na-na, *adv.* *only a part.* *T.*, huŋḣnala.

huŋ-ka′, *n.* *a parent* or *ancestor; an elder brother* is often so called—mihuŋka; *one who has raised himself* or *herself in the estimation of the people so as to be considered as a kind of benefactor* or *parent of all; the sun* is sometimes so called from *his munificence.*

huŋ-ka′-do-waŋ-pi, *n.* a rite or ceremony of the Dakotas. *T.*, huŋkalowaŋpi When a person, because he thinks highly of them, or for other good reason, intends in a measure to adopt the children of another, or to become "ate" to them, or be regarded by them as a relative in Dakota fashion, he makes the "huŋka lowaŋpi" for and in honor of the children. The children thus become "huŋka," and are always after known as such by a red stripe across the side of forehead and cheek, which they are permitted to wear as a badge. The number of these stripes shows how many times the wearer has been made "huŋka."—W. J. C.

h u ŋ - k a′ - k e, *n.* *an ancestor*—mihuŋkake, nihuŋkake, wićahuŋkake.

h u ŋ - k a′ - k e - y a, *v. a.* *to have for an ancestor*—huŋkakewaya, huŋkakeuŋyaŋpi.

h u ŋ - k a ŋ′ - k a ŋ, *v.* *T.* *to tell stories* or *myths: i. q.*, hituŋkaŋkaŋ.

h u ŋ - k a ŋ′ - k a ŋ - p i, *n.* *T.* *stories, fables: i. q.*, hituŋkaŋkapi.

h u ŋ - k a′ - w a ŋ - ź i, *n.* *a brother, one of the same family*—mihuŋkawaŋźi, nihuŋkawaŋźi.

h u ŋ - k a′ - w a ŋ - ź i n - k i - ć i - y a - p i, *n.* *brethren.*

h u ŋ - k a′ - w a ŋ - ź i n - y a, *v. a.* *to have for a brother, count as brother*—huŋkawaŋźinwaya.

h u ŋ - k a′ - w a ŋ - ź i - t k u, *n.* *his brother.*

h u ŋ - k a′ - y a, *v.* *to consider and honor as a* huŋka—huŋkawaya, huŋkauŋyaŋpi.

h u ŋ - k a′ - y a - p i, *n.* *one who is called* huŋka. Used also for *deacon* or *elder; the sun.*

h u ŋ′ - k e - ś n i, *v. n.* *to be slow, not fast,* in walking or working—wahuŋkeśni, yahuŋkeśni, uŋhuŋkapiśni: ćaŋte huŋkeśni, *low-spirited.*

h u ŋ′ - k p a, *n.* *the entrance to a camp* when made in a circle or hollow square.

H u ŋ′ - k p a - p a, *n. p.* the name of *a clan* or *division* of the Teeton Sioux. In marching and camping, the prairie Indians did everything by rule—each family had its place in the circle. Hence those who camped *at the entrance*, came to be named Huŋkpapa *and* Hunkpatina *or* Hunkpatidaŋ.

H u ŋ′ - k p a - t i, *n. p.* the "Lower Yanktonais." Same as Huŋkpatina.

H u ŋ′ - k p a - t i - n a, *or* H u ŋ′ - k p a - t i - d a ŋ, *n. p.* *a clan of the Yanktonais Sioux.*

h u ŋ - k t i′ - y a, *v.* *imp.* only; *go away, go along, get out of the way*—huŋktiya wo.

h u ŋ′ - k u, *n.* *his* or *her mother.*

h u ŋ′ - k u - y a, *v. a.* *to call mother, have for a mother*—huŋkuwaya, huŋkuyaya.

h u ŋ - p e′, *n.* See hoŋpe.

h u ŋ - s k a′, *n.* *leggings;* huŋska otoŋ, *to wear leggings.*

h u ŋ - s k a′ - y a, *v. a.* *to have for*

leggings, make leggings of—huŋskawaya.

h u ŋ - s k i' - ć a - ḣ e, *n garters.*

h u ŋ ś, *Ih. intj.* of surprise.

h u ŋ - ś t e', *adv. well, at any rate;* ećamoŋ kta huŋśte, *I will do it at any rate;* hećotu kte huŋśte, *well, so it will be. T.*, huŋśe.

h u ŋ' - t k a, *n. a large water-fowl, the cormorant. T., the loon.*

h u ŋ - y a' - k o ŋ, *n. Ih.* and *T. stockings.*

h u - p a' - h u, *n. the knee; the knee-pan, patella. T.*, ćaŋkpe.

h u - p a' - z a - h d e, *v. to sit with the knees bent up.*

h u - p a' - z a - h d e - y a, *adv.* hupazahdeya waŋka, *to lie on the back with the knees sticking up.*

h u - s a ŋ' - h m i, *adj. very lean; i. q.* tamaheća ḣiŋća.

h u - s a ŋ' - n i, *n. one of a pair, an odd one; one leg.* See saŋni.

h u - s d i', *n. the lower part of the leg,* just above the ankle; *the ankle: Ih., the tibia.*

h u' - s t a g, *cont.* of hustaka.

h u' - s t a g - y a, *v. a. to enfeeble*—hustagwaya

h u' - s t a - k a, *v. n. to be faint, weak, weary, feeble, lame*—humastaka

h u - ś t e', *adj. lame*—humaśte, huniśte; huuŋśtepi.

h u - ś t e' - k e n, *adv. lamely:* huśteken mani.

h u - ś t e' - y a, *v. a. to make lame*—huśtewaya.

h u - ś t e' - y a, *adv. limpingly.*

h u - ś t e' - y a - k e n, *adv. lamely.*

h u' - t a, *n. the root* of a tree or plant: ćaŋhuta, *a stump with sprouts, the bottom of a tree.*

h u - t a', *n. the shore or margin* of a river or lake; *the edge* of a prairie or wood.

h u' - t a - h u, *n. the part on top of the leg-bone, the shin-bone. T.*, hublohu.

h u' - t a m, *adv. cont.* of hutapa: hutam yeye ćiŋ, *along the shore. T.*, hutab, *below, down stream.*

h u' - t a m - y a, *adv. by the edge* or *shore; at the time of need* or *extremity.* See hutamyaken. *T.*, hutabya, *down stream;* opposed to iŋkpatakiya.

h u' - t a m - y a - k e n, *adv. by the edge or shore; at the time of need, in one's extremity:* hutamyaken ómayakiye śni, *you did not help me when I was most in need.*

h u - t a' - n a - k u - t e, *v. n. to play with the* hutinaćute; *to throw a stick so as to make it slide along* on the snow—hutanawakute. *T.*, hutanaćute.

h u' - t a - p a, *adv. down stream, towards the root.*

h u - t a' - t a, *adv. at the shore* or *edge; to the shore; to the woods* or *interior:* hutata uŋyaŋpi.

h u - t a' - t a - k i - y a, *adv. towards the shore.*

h u - t a' - w a - p a, *adv. T. i. q.* hutata.

h u' - t e, *adj. worn, dull;* oŋspe hute, *a dull ax.*

hu′-te, *n.* *the bottom*, as of a tree, *the lowest part, root:* ćaŋhute, *the roots of a tree.*

hu′-te-la, *n.* *T.* *a pistol.*

hu-ti′-na-ću-te, *n.* *a long stick with a large head*, which the Dakotas make slide on the snow or ice.

hu-tkaŋ′, *n.* *a root, the roots of trees, plants*, etc.

hu-tkaŋ′-o-mdo-toŋ, *n.* (hutkaŋ *and* omdotoŋ) *the square root*, in arithmetic. *T.*, hutkaŋobłotoŋ, *a flat or square post.*

hut-o′-śke, *adj.* *broad at one end, tapering.*

hut-o′-tkoŋ-za, *adv.* *T.* *even with the roots.*

hut-o′-tkoŋ-za, *n.* *a bluff shore* with deep water below.

hu-wa′-ki-ś'a-ka, *adj.* *T.* *enduring, not easily tired.*

hu-wa′-ḳi-pe, *n.* *the smaller bones in the lower leg and forearm:* ćaŋkpe huwaḳipe, *the fibula;* iśpa huwaḳipe, *the ulna.*

hu-wa′-pa, *n.* *an ear of corn, corn* unshelled. See waḣuwapa.

hu-wa′-pa-ḣpe, *n.* See ḣuwapaḣpe.

hu-we′, *v.* *to bring, fetch* Used with other verbs, as, huwe ya, *to go to bring*—huwe mda; huwe i, *to have been for;* huwe hi, *to have come for.* *T.*, hiyo.

hu-ya′, *v.* *to have for a bone, have for a staff* or *leg*—huwaya.

hu-ya′-ta, *adv* *in the leg.*

hu-yo′-ka-ḣmiŋ, *n.* *the hollow behind the knee.*

hwo, *adv. interrogative.* Commonly used when the speaker is at a distance: toki da hwo, *where are you going?*

Ḣ.

ḣ, *the tenth letter of the Dakota alphabet.* It represents a deep surd guttural.

ḣa, *adj.* *curled, rough.* See yuḣa, *to curl.*

ḣa, *n.* *a curl.*

ḣa, *v. a.* *to bury*, as a dead person, or as corn in holes or caches—waḣa, uŋḣapi.

ḣ'a, *adj.* *gray* or *mixed*, as black and white, the black appearing under the white, as in the badger.

ḣa-ḣa′, *adj.* *red.* of ḣa; *curling, curled.* See yuḣaḣa.

ḣa-ḣa′, *n.* *waterfalls*, so called from the *curling* of the waters; especially *the Falls of St. Anthony* *T.*, iyoḣaḣa.

Ḣa-ḣa′-mdo-te, *n.* *the mouth of the Ṡt. Peter's* or *Minnesota River.*

Ḣa-ḣa′-toŋ-waŋ, *n. p.* *the Chippewa* or *Ojibwa Indians*, the name given to them by the Dakotas, as those who make their village at the falls. It is believed the name came from the Sault Ste. Marie and not the Falls of the Mississippi.

Ḣa-ha′-wa-kpa, *n.* *the Mississippi River*, lit. *river of the falls.*

ḣa′-ka, *adj.* *branching, having many prongs*, as some deer's horns. See heḣaka.

ḣa-ka′, *adj.* *ruffled, not smooth, made rough*, as a feather.

ḣa-ka′, *n.* *T.* *an instrument used for shooting at a mark in a game.*

ḣa-ka′-ku-te, *v.* *to play* or *shoot the* "ḣaka."

ḣa-kpa′, *adj.* *not straight* or *level, a little curved; ruffled.*

ḣam, *cont.* of ḣapa; ḣam hiŋhda *and* ḣam iyaya, *to start up*, as something scared. *T.*, ḣab.

ḣam-ḣam′-ya, *v. red.* of ḣamya.

ḣam-ḣa′-pa, *v. red.* of ḣapa.

ḣam-ḣa′-pe-daŋ, *n.* the name given to *silk cloth* of any kind, probably from the *rustling noise* made in handling it.

ḣa-mna′, *adj.* *smelling like stale meat, tainted.* *T.*, oḣamna.

ḣam-ya′, *v. a.* *to frighten or scare away* anything, as wild animals; *to drive off*—ḣamwaya. *T*, ḣabya.

ḣaŋ, *n.* *a scab:* ḣaŋ hiŋḣpaya, *the scab has fallen off.*

ḣaŋ, *v. n.* *to do, work, act*, in any way—waḣaŋ, uŋḣaŋpi: token yaḣaŋ he, *what are you doing?*

ḣaŋ-di′-ta, *v. n.* *to be active, make progress in work:* ḣaŋdita wauŋ, *I am active.*

ḣaŋ-di′-ta-ya, *v. a.* *to spur one up*—ḣaŋditawaya: ḣaŋditaiçiya, *to spur one's self up*—ḣaŋditamiçiya.

ḣaŋ-di′-ta-ya, *adv.* *actively.*

ḣaŋ-haŋ′-ska, *v. n.* (ḣaŋ *and* haŋska) *to be long-winded, not soon tired.*

ḣaŋ-hi′, *v. n.* *to be slow at work, advance slowly* or *leisurely*—ḣaŋwahi, ḣaŋuŋhipi.

ḣaŋ-hi′-ka, *n.* *one who is slow at work, one who is incapable*—ḣaŋwahika.

ḣaŋ-hi′-ki-ya, *adv.* *slowly, carefully*, as in finishing a piece of work.

ḣaŋ-hi′-ya, *adv.* *slowly, with difficulty.* *T.*, ḣaŋhiya wayazaŋka, *to to be sick of a slow disease.*

ḣaŋ-ḣi′, *adj.* *sloppy, slushy.*

ḣaŋ-i′-ṭa, *v. n.* *to give out at work, be laid up by work*—ḣaŋimaṭa.

ḣaŋ-i′-ṭe-ya, *v. a.* *to cause to give out at work*—ḣaŋiṭewaya.

ḣaŋ′-i-yo-kpa-ni, *v.* See ḣaŋokpani. *T.*, ḣuŋkpani.

ḣaŋ′-i-yo-tpa-ni, *v.* See ḣaŋotpani.

ḣaŋ-o′-kpa-ni, *v. n.* *to be unable to reach* or *to do, unable to accomplish;* ḣaŋokpani wauŋ, *I am unable to accomplish.*

ḣaŋ-o′-kpa-ni-yaŋ, *v. a.* *to cause to fail of accomplishing*—ḣaŋokpaniwaya, ḣaŋokpaniuŋyaŋpi.

ḣaŋ-o′-tpa-ni, *v. n.* Same as ḣaŋokpani.

ḣaŋ-o′-tpa-ni-yaŋ, *v.* Same as ḣaŋokpaniyaŋ.

ȟ a ŋ - p i′ - ć a, *v.* *that can be done:* token ȟaŋpića śni, *it cannot be done.*

ȟ a ŋ - t e′, *n.* *the cedar*, of the genus *Juniperus* and *Cupressus.*

ȟ a ŋ - t e′ - ś a, *n.* See ȟaŋteśadaŋ.

ȟ a ŋ - t e′ - ś a - d a ŋ, *n.* *the red cedar, Juniperus virginius.*

ȟ a ŋ - t k a ŋ′ - h u, *n.* *T.* *the upper arm bone.*

ȟ a ŋ - y a ŋ′, *v. n.* *to fail, decline, sink away*, as in sickness; *to be near death, i. q.* waŋna ṭe kta; *to be very tired*—ȟaŋwaya, ȟaŋuŋyaŋpi.

h a ŋ - y e′ - ć a, *v. n.* *to fail, decline, sink away*, as in approaching death—ȟaŋwayeća.

ȟ a′ - p a. See kaȟapa.

ȟ a′ - p a, *v. n.* *to make a rustling noise*, as in leaves or bushes, *to rustle.*

ȟ a - p a′, *adj.* *T.* *rough*, as the wind or voice; ho ȟapa, *i. q.* hoġita.

ȟ a - t p a′, *adj.* *ruffled*, as feathers or hair. See ȟakpa.

ȟ b a, *adj.* *sleepy, drowsy*—maȟba, uŋȟbapi, wićaȟba. *T.*, ȟwa.

ȟ b a′ - k a, *adj.* *sleepy, mild, gentle*—maȟbaka. See waȟbadaŋ *and* waȟbaka.

ȟ b a′ - y a, *v. a.* *to make sleepy*—ȟbawaya.

ȟ b a′ - y a, *adv.* *mildly, gently.*

ȟ b a′ - y e - d a ŋ, *adv.* *softly, gently, mildly:* ȟbayedaŋ wauŋ. *T.*, ȟwayela.

ȟ b o g′ - y a, *adv.* *collected, together.*

ȟ b o′ - k a. See kaȟboka.

ȟ b u, *v. n.* *to make a noise as in chewing snow* or *ice, to make a crunching noise.*

ȟ b u - ȟ b u′, *v.* *red.* of ȟbu.

ȟ b u - w a′ - h a ŋ, *part.* *crumbled*, as ice or snow in the spring.

ȟ ć a, *n.* *a flower, blossom.* See waȟća.

ȟ ć a, *v. n.* *to blossom;* ȟća aya, *to bloom* or *blossom.*

ȟ ć a, *adv.* *cont.* of ȟiŋća.

ȟ ć a′ - k a, *T.* *adv.-suffix.* *i. q.* ȟiŋća: waśtela ȟćaka, *very good.*

ȟ ć a - w a′ - h e - ć a, *adj.* *slovenly.* See ȟćoya.

ȟ ć a′ - y a, *v. n.* *to blossom.*

ȟ ć a′ - y a, *adv.* *blossoming.*

ȟ ć i, *adj.* *broken out in gaps.* See kaȟći.

ȟ ć i, *n.* *a gap*, as in the edge of an ax; *a gash, cut, scar.*

ȟ ć i - h a ŋ′, *part.* *broken out*, as a piece from the edge of an ax: *torn out*, as the ear by ear-rings.

ȟ ć i - ȟ ć i′, *red.* of ȟći; *gapped.*

ȟ ć i ŋ, *adv.* *Ih.* and *T.* *very; i. q.* ȟiŋća.

ȟ ć i - w a′ - h a ŋ, *part.* *broken out in gaps, gapped.*

ȟ ć o, *adj.* *slovenly, slatternly.*

ȟ ć o′ - k a, *adj.* *slovenly*—maȟćoka. See ȟdohaŋ *and* ȟdoheća.

ȟ ć o′ - y a, *adv.* *in a slovenly manner.*

ȟ ć o′ - y a - k e n, *adv.* *slovenly.*

ȟ d a, *v. n.* *to rattle.*

ȟ d a - h a ŋ′, *adv.* *loose, torn, dangling.* *T.*, ȟlahaŋ. See ȟnahaŋ.

ȟ d a - ȟ d a′, *v.* *red.* of ȟda. See mazaȟdaȟda.

ȟda-ȟda′, *n.* *a rattle.*

ȟda-ȟda′-ya, *adv.* *rattling, loosely.* *T.*, ȟlaȟlaya.

ȟda-ȟda′-ye-daŋ, *adv.* *not securely, loosely:* ȟdaȟdayedaŋ wahnaka, *I placed it loosely.* *T.*, ȟlaġaŋyela.

ȟda-ȟda′-yen, *adv.* *not securely:* ȟdaȟdayen hnake śni, *he has not placed it in securely.*

ȟdaȟ-ya′, *adv.* *to a distance, i. q.* tehaŋ; *removing.*

ȟdaȟ-ye′-ća, *v. n.* *to remove* or *go off to a distance:* ȟdaȟyeće śni, *it does not go off*, said of deer or other animals that stay about in the same place.

ȟda-ya′, *adv.* *rattling; not safely.* *T.*, ȟlaġaŋ.

ȟda-yen′, *adv.* *not securely* or *safely.*

ȟdi, *v. n.* *to break out in sores, be sore, raw*—maȟdi, uŋȟdipi: ćaŋkahu ȟdi, *to have a sore back*, as a horse.

ȟdi, *n.* *a running sore, a raw place.*

ȟdi, *adj.* *miry.* See kaȟdi.

ȟdi-ȟdi′, *adj.* *red.* of ȟdi; *broken out in sores; miring.*

ȟdi-ȟdi′-daŋ, *adj.* *miry, muddy.*

ȟdo, *v. n.* *to growl*, as a dog

ȟdo-ġe′-ća, *adj.* *hollow*, as a tree.

ȟdo-haŋ′, *adj.* *slovenly, not well put on*, as clothes. *T.*, ȟćoya. See ȟćoka.

ȟdo-he′-ća, *adj.* *slovenly.*

ȟdo-he′-ya, *adv.* *in a slovenly manner.* See ȟnaheya.

ȟdo-ȟdo′-ka, *adj.* *full of holes.* See ȟdoka.

ȟdo-ȟdo′-ka-haŋ, *part.* *full of holes.*

ȟdo-ȟdo′-ka-wa-haŋ, *part.* *having holes in.*

ȟdo′-ka, *n.* *a hole:* mini ȟdoka, *a spring of water.*

ȟdo′-ka, *part.* See kaȟdoka.

ȟdo-ka′-haŋ, *part.* *opened, having a hole in.*

ȟdo-ka′-wa-haŋ, *part.* *having a hole in.*

ȟdo-ki′-ya, *v. a.* *to make growl*—ȟdowakiya.

ȟdo-ya′, *v a.* *to cause to growl*—ȟdowaya.

ȟdo-ya′, *adv.* *growling.*

ȟe, *n.* *a high hill* or *ridge of hills, a mountain;* especially *the Coteau des prairies.*

ȟe-ġiŋ′-će, *n.* *dross:* pa ȟeġiŋće, *dandruff.* See also ġiŋġiŋća.

ȟe-he′-pi-ya, *adv.* *T.* *part way up the hill.*

ȟe-hu′-kul, *n.* *T.* *the bottom* or *foot of a hill.*

ȟ'e-ȟ'e′, *adj.* *dangling, ragged.*

ȟe′-i-mni-źa, *n.* (ȟe *and* imniźa) *a rocky ridge.*

ȟe-iŋ′-kpa, *n.* *the brink* or *brow of a hill, the end of a hill.* See ȟiŋkpa.

ȟe-iŋ′-tpa, *n,* Same as ȟeiŋkpa.

ȟe′-i-pa, *n.* *the brow of a hill;* especially *the head* or *commencement of the Coteau des prairies.*

ȟe-ku′, *n.* *the foot of a hill back*

from a river: ḣeku uŋyaŋpi, *we go at the foot of the hill.*

ḣe-ma'-ko-skaŋ, *adv.* *T.*, *i. q.* ḣewoskan.

ḣe-ma'-ni, *v.* *to walk on dry land.*

ḣe-ma'-ni, *n.* *a railroad; a train of cars.*

ḣe'-ma-ya-ćaŋ, *n.* *a wooded hill.*

ḣe'-mdo, *n.* *a hill-top, ridge; i. q.* mdamdata.

ḣe'-mdo-ka, *n.* Same as ḣemdo.

ḣe-mni'-ćaŋ, *n.* (ḣe mni *and* ćaŋ) *a hill that appears as if it were in the water; Red Wings' village,* a short distance above Lake Pepin, is so called.

ḣen, *adv.* (ḣe *and* en) *ashore:* ḣen eźu, *to put* anything *ashore,* as from a boat; ḣen ihaŋ, *to step ashore.*

ḣe-na'-ġi, *n.* *the shadow of a hill.*

ḣe-na'-ke, *n.* *a hill-side, slope.* See ḣuŋnaptaŋ.

ḣe-na'-ke-ya, *adj.* *sloping, sideling.*

ḣe-o'-ḣla-te, *n.* *T.* *the foot* or *bottom of a hill.*

ḣe-o'-ta-he-na, *adv.* *T.*, *i. q.* ḣewotahedaŋ.

ḣe'-pe-se, *adv.* ḣepese eḣpeya, *to make a splash,* as in throwing anything into water.

Ḣe-ska', *n.* *The Big Horn Mountains.*

ḣet-a'-źu, *v. a.* *to put ashore,* as the load of a boat. See waḣetaźu.

ḣe-uŋ'-na-ptaŋ, *n.* *a hill side.* See ḣonaptaŋ.

Ḣe-wa'-kto-kto, *n. p.* *the Arickaree Indians.*

ḣe-waŋ'-ke, *n.* *frost, hoar-frost* *T.*, ḣeyuŋke.

ḣe-wo'-skan, *n.* *an uninhabited, desert place.* *T.*, ḣemakoskan. See ḣowoskan.

ḣe-wo'-skan-tu, *adv.* *in a desert place.*

ḣe-wo'-skan-tu-ya, *adv.* *away from any dwelling, in a desert place, solitarily.*

ḣe-wo'-ta-he-daŋ, *adv.* *where no one lives, in a desert place.* *T.*, ḣeotahena.

ḣe-ya'-ka, *n.* *a hill, river hill, mountain.*

ḣe-ya'-ka-ta, *adv.* *at the hill.*

ḣe-yam', *cont.* of ḣeyapa; *by land, following the hill:* ḣeyam uŋyaŋpi, *we go by land: away, elsewhere:* ḣeyam ećoŋ, *go away.* *T.*, ḣeyab.

ḣe-yan', *cont.* of ḣeyata; *inland, in the interior.*

ḣe-ya'-pa, *v. n.* *to go by land, travel by land,* in distinction from going by water—ḣeyawapa.

ḣe-ya'-pa-ya, *adv.* *T.* *by land; i q.* ḣeyata.

ḣe-ya'-ta, *adv.* *back by the hill, back from* a river, *back from* a fire, *out back, back, behind:* ḣeyata ya, *to go out back, retire, withdraw*—ḣeyata mda; ḣeyata iyeya, *to shove aside* or *back, put out of office, reject.* This word and others like it are formed from the noun ḣe, *hill,* and the preposition ata, *at.* It might be called a prepositional noun. See iḣeyata.

ḣe-ya′-taŋ *and* **ḣe-ya′-taŋ-haŋ**, *adv. from behind.*

ḣi-ća′-haŋ, *v. n. to slip, misstep, stumble and fall*—maḣićahaŋ.

ḣi-ća′-he-ya, *v. a. to cause to slip and fall*—ḣićahewaya.

ḣiŋ, *adv. cont.* of ḣiŋća; *very.* See ḣćiŋ *and* ḣtiŋ.

ḣiŋ′-ća, *adv. very:* waśte ḣiŋća, *very good;* śiće ḣiŋća, *very bad.*

ḣiŋ-ća′-ke, *adv. very, indeed.*

ḣiŋ′-kpa, *n.* (ḣe *and* iŋkpa) *the brow of a hill.*

ḣiŋ′-kpa-ta, *adv. to* or *at the top of the hill;* ḣiŋkpata uŋyaŋpi kta, *we will go to the top of the hill.*

ḣiŋ′-kpa-taŋ-haŋ, *adv. at the hill-top, from the hill.*

ḣiŋ-tkaŋ′-hu, *n. the upper arm-bone.* Ḣiŋtkaŋ alone is said not to be used. *T.*, ḣaŋtkaŋhu.

ḣiŋ′-tpa, *n.* Same as ḣiŋkpa.

ḣiŋ′-tpa-ta, *adv.* Same as ḣiŋkpata.

ḣiŋ′-tpa-taŋ-haŋ, *adv.* Same as ḣiŋkpataŋhaŋ.

ḣiŋ-yaŋ′-taŋ, *n. the daisy,* which the Dakotas use in dyeing yellow.

ḣi-ya′-ya, *adv. bungled.* See yuḣiyaya.

ḣla′-ġaŋ, *adj. T. loose; i. q.* ḣdaġaŋ. See ḣdaya.

ḣmiŋ, *adj. crooked, misshapen:* siha ḣmiŋ, *a crooked foot.*

ḣmiŋ-ḣmiŋ′, *adj. red.* of ḣmiŋ.

ḣmiŋ-ḣmiŋ′-yaŋ, *adv. red.* of ḣmiŋyaŋ; *crookedly.*

ḣmiŋ′-yaŋ, *adv. crookedly.*

ḣmu′-ġa, *v.* See ḣmuŋġa.

ḣmuŋ, *v. n. to buzz, hum,* as the stones of a mill or the flapping of bird's wings; *to whistle,* as a bullet: ḣmuŋ hiŋhda, *to make a buzzing noise suddenly.*

ḣmuŋ′-ġa, *v. a. to cause sickness* or *death,* as the Dakotas pretend to be able to do, *in a supernatural way; to bewitch, kill by enchantment*—waḣmuŋġa, uŋḣmuŋġapi, maḣmuŋġa; kićiḣmuŋġapi, *bewitching each other.*

ḣmuŋ′-ġa, *adj. smelling strong, fishy, rancid, stinking,* as grease.

ḣmuŋḣ′-mna, *v. n. to smell rancid* or *fishy.* See homna.

ḣmuŋ-ḣmuŋ′, *v. red.* of ḣmuŋ; *to buzz.*

ḣmuŋ-ḣmuŋ′-ġa, *adj. red.* of ḣmuŋġa; *rancid.*

ḣmuŋ′-se, *adv. T. in a buzzing way,* as when many persons are talking together.

ḣmuŋ-ya′, *v. a. to cause to hum, make buzz*—ḣmuŋwaya.

ḣmuŋ-yaŋ′, *adv. buzzing.*

ḣna, *v. n. to snort,* as something dying; *to snicker: T.* ḣna mahiŋgla, *I snicker.*

ḣna-haŋ′, *adj. slovenly, not tidy, hanging,* as a horse's lip.

ḣna-he′-ya, *adv. loosely, slovenly:* ḣnaheya uŋ, *he is slovenly.* See ḣdoheya.

ḣni′-yaŋ, *v.* ćaŋte ḣniyaŋ, *to flutter* or *be troubled, be sick at the stomach,* as from eating too much—maḣniyaŋ.

ȟni'-yaŋ-yaŋ, *adj. afraid, quaking for fear*—maȟniyaŋyaŋ.

ȟni'-ye-ye-se, *adv. in haste, affrightedly:* ȟniyeyese mawani, *I walk hastily.*

ȟo, *v. n. to stand up on end,* as hair. See aȟo.

ȟo, *intj. of surprise.*

ȟo' e-ća, *intj.* expressing *dissatisfaction* or *dissent. T.,* ȟoȟ.

ȟo'-e-ćaȟ, *intj.* Same as ȟoećaȟe.

ȟo'-e-ća-ȟe, *intj. of disbelief* and *dissent. T.,* ȟoȟećaȟ.

ȟoȟ'-e-ćeś, *adv. T., i. q.,* ȟoećaȟe.

ȟo-ka', *n. the badger.*

ȟo-na'-ptaŋ, *n.* See ȟuŋnaptaŋ.

ȟoŋ'-hi-ki-ya, *v. a. to finish, perfect.* See ȟuŋhikiya.

ȟoŋ'-hi-ya; *v. a. to finish, perfect.* See ȟuŋhiya.

ȟoŋ'-ki-ṭa, *v. n. to become very tired.* See ȟuŋkiṭa. *T.,* watuka.

ȟoŋ'-kpa-ni, *v. n. to be in an unfinished state.* See ȟuŋkpani.

ȟoŋ'-kpa-ni-ki-ya, *v. to fail of finishing.* See ȟuŋkpanikiya.

ȟoŋ'-kpa-ni-yan, *v.* See ȟuŋkpaniyaŋ.

ȟoŋ'-tpa-ni, *v.* See ȟuŋtpani.

ȟoŋ'-tpa-ni-ki-ya, *v.* See ȟuŋtpanikiya.

ȟoŋ'-tpa-ni-yaŋ, *v.* See ȟuŋtpaniyaŋ.

ȟo'-pa, *adj. T. attractive, beautiful;* wiȟopawiŋ, *a pretty woman.*

ho'-pe-ća, *adj. T. beautiful, well formed.*

ȟo'-pi-daŋ, *intj. astonishing! wonderful!*

ȟo'-pi-daŋ-ni-ye, *intj. astonishing!*

ȟo'-pi-daŋ-śni, *intj. impossible!*

ȟo-pu'-za, *n.* (ȟe *and* opuza) *a dry country desert.*

ȟo'-śki, *adj. hilly, rough, uneven,* as a country.

ȟo'-śki, *n. the bad lands.*

ȟo'-śki-śki, *adj. red.* of ȟośki; *abounding in little hills, a hilly country.*

ȟo'-ta, *adj. gray, brown.*

ȟot-ȟo'-ta, *adj. red.* of ȟota. *T.,* ȟolȟota.

ȟo-ṭiŋ'-za, *n.* (ȟe *and* oṭiŋza) *hard ground, a desert.*

ȟo-wo'-skan, *n. an uninhabited country.* See ȟewoskan.

ȟpa, *part. thrown down.* See yuȟpa: *broken off.*

ȟpa, *v. n. to be wet* or *clogged,* as mosquitoes' wings with dew: ćapoŋka ȟpapi, *mosquitoes are wet with dew.*

ȟpa, *adv. together, in a bunch,* said of beans or potatoes which grow together.

ȟpa-haŋ', *part. thrown down, fallen down of itself.*

ȟpaŋ', *adj. soaked* with water, *wet;* ȟpaŋ ȟiŋgle, *T. to become softened.*

ȟpaŋ-yaŋ', *v. a. to soak* or *steep* in water—ȟpaŋwaya, ȟpaŋuŋyaŋpi.

ȟpa-wa'-haŋ, *part. thrown off, thrown down.*

ḣpa′-ya, *v. n.* *T.* *to lie down, recline;* kul ḣpaya, *he lies down;* ṭa ḣpaya, *he is dead:* ćaŋku kiŋ kal ḣpaya, *the road lies over there:* tohaŋ niḣpayiŋ kta, *where will you lie down?*

ḣpa′-ye-ya, *v. a.* *to cause to lie down; to kill,* as in battle.

ḣpe′-ća, *adj.* *faint, exhausted*—maḣpeća; ḣpeća śni, *untiring, strong to endure fatigue.* *T.*, ḣpećaka.

ḣpe-waŋ′-ka, *v. n.* *to stay with the young, hover over,* aṣ a hen does over her brood, *brood over*—ḣpemuŋka. *T.*, ḣpeyuŋka.

ḣpi′-ka, *adj.* *T.* *shaggy, bushy,* aṣ hair.

ḣpu. See yuḣpu.

ḣpu-ḣaŋ′, *part.* *crumbled off.*

ḣpu-ḣpu′, *red.* of ḣpu.

ḣpu-wa′-haŋ, *part* *crumbled off, come apart,* as things formerly stuck together.

ḣpu-ya′, *adv.* *crumbling off.*

ḣta, *cont.* of ḣtayetu.

ḣta-ću′-śni, *n.* *the cool of the evening.* *T.*, ḣtaćusni.

ḣta′-ka. See yaḣtaka.

ḣta-ki′-ya, *adv.* *towards evening.* *T.*, ḣtakiyaka.

ḣta′-ki-ya, *v. a.* *to cause to catch and hold,* as a trap. See mazaḣtakiyapi.

ḣta-ki′-ya-ken, *adv.* *towards evening.*

ḣtan, *cont.* of ḣtata; ḣtan iyaya, *to become weak.*

ḣta-ni′, *v. n.* *to labor, toil, work, do* such *labor* as the Dakota women do—ḣtawani, ḣtayani, ḣtauŋnipi.

ḣta′-ni-haŋ, *n.* *yesterday;* ḣtanihaŋ saŋpa *and* ḣtanihaŋ ićima, *the day before yesterday.* *T.*, ḣtalihaŋ.

ḣta-ni′-pi, *n.* *laboring;* *i. q.* wićoḣtani.

ḣtaŋ′-yaŋ, *adj.* *rough, made rough;* *i. q.* powaye. *T.*, ḣtaŋyela.

ḣta′-ta, *adj.* *languid, weak*—maḣtata.

ḣta′-te-ća, *adj.* *weak, feeble*—maḣtateća.

ḣta-yen′, *adv.* *in the evening;* generally *last evening.*

ḣta′-ye-tu, *n.* *the evening.*

ḣtiŋ, *Ih.* *adv.* or *particle,* intensive in force; *very.* See ḣćiŋ *and* ḣiŋ.

ḣu′-ġa, *part.* *broken in.* See kaḣuġa.

ḣu-ġa′-haŋ, *part.* *broken in.*

ḣu-ġa′-wa-haŋ, *part.* *broken in.*

ḣu-ġe′-ća, *n.* See ġuġeća.

ḣu-ha′, *n.* *the scrapings* or *shavings of hides,* taken off in making them thin enough for robes, and which are eaten by the Dakotas. See taḣuha.

ḣu-ḣna′-ġa, *v. n.* *to burn up, be consumed.* See huḣnaġa.

ḣu-ḣnaḣ′-ya, *v. a.* *to cause to burn up, to consume*—ḣuḣnaḣwaya.

ḣuŋ′-hi-ki-ya, *v. a.* *to finish, perfect.*

ḣuŋ′-hi-ki-ya, *adv.* *in a finishing way, perfectly:* ḣuŋhikiya ećamoŋ, *I do it by the way of finishing.*

ḣuŋ'-hi-ya, *v. a.* *to finish.*

ḣuŋ'-ki-ṭa, *v. n.* *to be tired, be weary and give out at work*—ḣuŋwakiṭa, ḣuŋuŋkiṭapi.

ḣuŋ'-kpa-ni, *v. n.* *to be unfinished.* See ḣoŋkpani.

ḣuŋ'-kpa-ni-ki-ya, *v. a.* *to leave in an unfinished state, to fail of accomplishing*—ḣuŋkpaniwakiya.

ḣuŋ'-kpa-ni-yaŋ, *v. a.* *to fail of finishing*—ḣuŋkpaniwaya.

ḣuŋ-na'-ptaŋ, *n.* *a hill-side.* See ḣenake *and* ḣeuŋnaptaŋ.

ḣuŋ-na'-ptaŋ-yaŋ, *adv.* *on the hill-side.*

ḣuŋ'-tpa-ni, *v. n.* *to be unfinished.* See ḣoŋtpani *and* ḣuŋkpani.

ḣuŋ'-tpa-ni-ki-ya, *v. a.* *to fail of accomplishing, leave unfinished*—ḣuŋtpaniwayakiya.

ḣuŋ'-tpa-ni-yaŋ, *v.* *to fail of finishing*—ḣuŋtpaniwaya.

ḣuŋ'-ṭa, *v. n.* *T.* *used up, exhausted*—ḣuŋmata. See ḣuŋkiṭa.

ḣuŋ'-ṭe-ya, *v. a.* *to cause to give out, to exhaust,* as one's strength.

ḣuŋ'-wiŋ, *v. n.* *to stink, become putrid,* as a dead body. See ḣwiŋ.

ḣuŋ-wiŋ'-mna, *adj.* *stinking, smelling putrid.*

ḣuŋ-wiŋ'-ya, *v. a.* *to cause to smell badly, make putrid*—ḣuŋwiŋwaya.

ḣu-pa'-hu, *n.* *the arm* of a person; *the wing* of a fowl—maḣupahu niḣupahu.

ḣu-pa'-hu-wa-ki-hda-ke-daŋ, *n.* *the bat,* lit., *little leather-wings.*

ḣu-pa'-ko-za, *v. n.* *to move* or *flap the wings, to fly.* See waḣupakoza. *T.*, ḣupaokoza.

ḣu-pa'-wa-ki-hda-ke-daŋ, *n.* *the bat.* *T.*, ḣupakiglaksla.

ḣu-piŋ'-yuŋ, *adv.* *by the arms, without instruments, by main strength.* See ḣupahu *and* iyuŋ.

ḣu-piŋ'-yuŋ-ken, *adv.* *by main strength.*

ḣu-wa'-pa-ḣpe, *n.* *the meat which is left sticking to a hide; the right side* of anything. See taḣuwapaḣpe.

ḣu-ya', *n.* *the common eagle:* ḣuya ćiŋća, *a young eagle.*

ḣwa, *v. n., i. q.* ḣba: The Titoŋwaŋs sometimes use "w" for "b," as in this case.

ḣwa'-ye-la, *adj.* *T.* *gently, slowly: i. q.* ḣbayedaŋ.

ḣwiŋ, *v. n.* *to stink, become putrid,* as a dead body. See ḣuŋwiŋ.

ḣwiŋ'-mna, *adj.* *stinking, smelling putrid.* See ḣuŋwiŋmna.

I.

i, *the eleventh letter of the Dakota alphabet.* It has the sound of English *ee*, or of *i* in *marine, machine.*

i, *an inseparable preposition* or *prefix.*

1. Prefixed to verbs and adjectives, it means *to, for, of* or *about; by means of, by reason of, on account of, in consequence of:* as, kićo, *to invite*, ikićo, *to invite to* eat any particular thing· ćekiya, *to pray to* one, ićekiya, *to pray to* one *for* something; wohdaka, *to tell news*, iwohdaka, *to tell about* some particular thing; ćaŋniyaŋ, *to be angry*, ićaŋniyaŋ *to be angry on account of* something; wayazaŋka, *to be sick*, iwayazaŋka, *to be sick in consequence of* something; ćepa, *fat*, ićepa, *fat by reason of.*
2. Prefixed to active verbs, it sometimes forms of them nouns of the instrument: as, kaźipa, *to shave*, ićaźipe, *a drawing-knife* or *plane;* kasdeća, *to split*, ićasdeće, *a wedge;* ćap'á, *to stab*, ićap'e, *a spear.*
3. Prefixed to the cardinal numbers, it forms of them ordinals: as, noŋpa, *two*, inoŋpa, *second;* yamni, *three*, iyamni, *third*, etc.
4. Prefixed to adverbs, it gives them the force of prepositions: as, tehaŋ, *far*, itehaŋ, *far from.*
5. Prefixed to nouns signifying time, it means *the next* or *succeeding* one: as, haŋhaŋna, *morning*, ihaŋhaŋna, *the next morning;* wetu, *spring*, iwetu, *the succeeding spring.*

i, *n. the mouth*—mii, nii, wićai: i en hde, *to cast up to one;* i en hiyeya, *to cast into one's teeth.*

i, *v. n. to have gone to, to have been at*—wai, yai, uŋkipi.

i-a', *v. n. to speak*—iwaa, iyaa, uŋkiapi.

i-a'-haŋ, *part. speaking.*

i-a'-kan, *prep.* (i *and* akan) *upon, on top of.*

i-a'-ka-p'iŋ or i-e'-ka-p'iŋ, *v. n. to be tired of speaking, unwilling to speak.* See kap'iŋ.

i-a'-ke, *adv. again, so many more.*

i-a'-ke-de-na-ke-ća, *adj. so many more than ten.*

i-a'-ke-de-na-na, *adj. only so many more than ten. T.*, iakelenala.

i-a'-ke-he-na-ke-ća, *adj. so many more than ten.*

i-a'-ke-ka-na-ke-ća, *adj. that number more than ten.*

i-a'-ke-noŋ-pa, *num. adj. twelfth.*

i-a′-ke-śa-hdo-ġaŋ, *num. adj.* *eighteenth.* *T.*, iakeśahloġaŋ.

i-a′-ke-śa-ko-wiŋ, *num. adj.* *seventeenth.*

i-a′-ke-śa-kpe, *num. adj.* *sixteenth.*

i-a′-ke-to-pa, *num. adj.* *fourteenth.*

i-a′-ke-waŋ-źi-daŋ, *num. adj.* *eleventh.*

i-a′-ke-ya-mni, *num. adj.* *thirteenth.*

i-a′-ke-za-ptaŋ, *num. adj.* *fifteenth.*

i′-a-ki-ća-ġe-ća, *n.* *one who is unreasonable in his demands; one who keeps asking for things after he should stop, an importunate person.* *T.*, aokaġeća.

i-a′-ki-ću-ni, *v.* *to desist from, grow tired and leave off.* See iyakićuni.

i-a′-ki-ç̌u-ya, *adj.* *much.* See iyakiç̌uya.

i′-a-ki-de-će-ća, *adv.* *alike, equal to.* See iyakidećeća.

i′-a-ki-de-ćen, *adv.* *like to, equal to.*

i′-a-ki-de-haŋ-haŋ-ke-ća, *adv.* *red.* of iakidehaŋkeća.

i′-a-ki-de-haŋ-haŋ-yaŋ, *adv.* *red.* of iakidehaŋyaŋ.

i′-a-ki-de-ḣaŋ-ke-ća, *adv.* *equal in length to;* kići iakidemahaŋkeća, *I am as tall as he.*

i′-a-ki-de-haŋ-yaŋ, *adv.* *alike in distance, as far as.*

i′-a-ki-de-na-ka, *adv.* *alike in number, as many as.*

i′-a-ki-de-na-ke-ća, *adv.* *as many as.*

i′-a-ki-he-će-ća, *adv.* *alike in kind.*

i′-a-ki-he-haŋ-ke-ća, *adv.* *alike in length.*

i′-a-ki-he-haŋ-yaŋ, *adv.* *alike in distance.*

i′-a-ki-he-na-ke-ća, *adv.* *of equal number with.*

i′-a-ki-p’a-p’a, *v.* (i *and* ap’a) *to strike on the mouth often,* as the young men do in shouting—iawakip’ap’a.

i′-aŋ-pe-tu, *n.* *the next day to, the day following.* *T.*, *the same day:* iaŋpetu haŋkeyela, *during that day.*

i-a′-pi, *n.* *talk, speech, language.*

i′-a-ś’a, *v.* *to halloo, make a loud inarticulate noise*—iawaś’a, iauŋś’api.

i′-a-ta-ye-la, *pronominal adv.* *T.* *that alone; personally, individually:* also iyatayela; iye iyatayela ećoŋ, *he did it himself.*

i-ba′-pe, *v.* *to make sharp by*—ibawape: ibapeśni, *to make dull on.* *T.*, iwape.

i-bo′-ç̌o, *n.* *a churn.* See boç̌o.

i-bo′-ḣta-ka, *v. n.* *to strike against*—ibomaḣtaka. *T.*, iwoḣtaka.

i-bo′-mdu, *v. n.* *to drift, blow up,* as snow or dust: wa ibomdu, *the snow is blown about; to storm.*

i-bo′-mdu-mdu, *v.* *red.* of ibomdu.

i-bo′-paŋ, *n.* *a pestle.* See bopaŋ.

i-b o′-p a ŋ, *v.* *to shoot in pieces*, *i. q.*, bokuka.

i-b o′-s d i, *n.* *a squirt*, *syringe; a squirt-gun.* This is made by Dakota boys of the common elder or box-wood, and is used for shooting water. See miniibosdi.

i-b o′-s d o-h a ŋ, *v.* *to blow along lengthwise:* ibosdohaŋ iyeya.

i-b o′-s d o-h a ŋ-h a ŋ, *v. red.*, of ibosdohaŋ.

i-b o′-ś a-k a, *v.* used with waćiŋ; waćiŋ ibośaka, *to be discouraged:* waćiŋ ibowaśaka, *I am discouraged.*

i-b o′-ś'a-k a, *v.* (i *and* boś'aka) *to hit with little force, not to penetrate*—ibowaś'aka.

i-b o′-ś t a-k e, *n.* (i *and* bośtaka) *a blunt-pointed arrow.* *T.*, wiwośtake.

i-b o′-t o, *v. n.* (i *and* boto) *to hit* or *strike against, to butt against*—ibomato, ibonito: siha iŋyaŋ ibomato, *I struck my foot against a stone;* pa en ibomato, *it struck my head.* See apaṭo, etc.

i-ć a′-b e-ć a, *v. n.* *to be pricked* or *have one's feelings injured* by some little thing. *T.*, ićameća. See ićama.

i-ć a′-b e-y a, *adv.* *pricked, injured in feelings;* ićabeya wauŋ, *my feelings are hurt.* *T.*, ićameya.

i-ć a′-b u, *n.* (i *and* kabu) *a drum-stick.*

i-ć a′-d u, *n.* (i *and* kadu) *a fan, wing* to fan one's self with. *T.*, ićalu.

i-ć a′-d u-ġ e, *n.* (i *and* kaduġa) *a fan* for wheat, something *to blow* or *clean with:* psiŋ ićaduġe, *a rice-blower.*

i-ć a′-g l a-l a, *prep.* *T.* *by the side of:* *i. q.* ićahda.

i-ć a′-ġ a, *v. n.* of kaġa; *to spring up, grow*, as grass, trees, etc.; *to grow from*, as a result from a cause; *to grow*, as a child, *become*, as a man or boy, in any respect—imaćaġa, inićaġa.

i-ć a′-ġ e, *n.* (i *and* kaġa) *something to make with, an instrument:* wowapi ićaġe, *a pen* or *pencil.*

i-ć a′-ġ e, *v.* of kaġe: ićaġe iću, *to take up* in a bucket, as water; *to take off* or *skim off*—ićaġe iwaću.

i-ć a′-ġ e-y a, *adv.* *together;* oyate ićaġeya tipi, *the people were camped together.*

i′-ć a-ġ e-ź u-y a, *v.* *to come up with* and *go along with* a company—ićaġeźuwićawaya, *I came up and went with them.*

i′-ć a-ġ e-ź u-y a, *adv.* *together with, in company.*

i-ć a′-ġ i, *v. n.* (i *and* kaġi) *to be hindered by, opposed by* an obstacle—imakaġi, inićaġi.

i-ć a′-ġ o, *n.* (i *and* kaġo) *a mark* or *line drawn.*

i-ć a′-ġ o, *v. a.* of kaġo; *to make a mark, draw a line, sketch*—iwakaġo, uŋkićaġopi.

i-ć a′-ġ o-y a, *v. a.* *to cause to mark*—ićaġowaya.

i-ć a′-ġ o-y a, *adv.* *marking, in the way of marking.*

i-ća′-h d a, *prep.* (i *and* kahda) *by the side of, near to.*

i-ća′-h i, *v. a.* (i *and* kahi) *to mix, stir up together*—iwakahi, iyakahi, uŋkićahipi.

i-ća′-h i, *v. n.* *to mix, mingle.*

i-ća′-h i-h i, *v. red.* of ićahi; *to mingle, mix together.*

i-ća′-h i-h i, *n.* *cement.*

i-ća′-h i-h i-y a, *adv.* *mixed up with, together with: i. q*, opepeya.

i-ća′-h i ŋ-t e, *n.* (i *and* kahiŋta) *a rake, a broom.*

i-ća′-h i-t o ŋ, *v. a.* *to mix together*—ićahiwatoŋ, ićahiyatoŋ, ićahiuŋtoŋpi.

i-ća′-h i-t o ŋ, *part.* *mixed.*

i-ća′-h i-y a, *v. a.* *to mix together, adulterate*—ićahiwaya, ićahiuŋyaŋpi.

i-ća′-h o-m n i, *n.* (i *and* kahomni) *something that is turned* or *turns, a wheel.*

i-ća ḣ′, *cont.* of ićaġa; icaḣ aya, *it keeps growing.*

i-ća′-ḣ a m-ḣ a-p e-d a ŋ, *v. n.* *to rustle,* as the grass in a gentle wind. See ḣamḣapedaŋ. *T.*, ićićaḣabḣapa.

i-ća′-ḣ a-p e, *n.* (i *and* kaḣapa) *something to drive with, a whip.*

i-ća ḣ′-k i-y a, *v. a.* *to cause to grow; to rear, raise,* as a child or domestic animal—ićaḣwakiya.

i-ća ḣ′-k o-k e-d a ŋ, *adj.* See oićaḣkokedaŋ.

i-ća′-ḣ o-t a, *n.* of ćaḣota; *drops* of rain, *flakes* of snow, so called because falling like *ashes.* *T.*, ićaḣolḣota.

i-ća′-ḣ t a g, *cont.* of ićaḣtaka.

i-ća′-ḣ t a g-e-y a, *v.* *to hint at, touch upon,* in speaking.

i-ća′-ḣ t a g-y a, *v. a.* *to cause to touch*—ićaḣtagwaya.

i-ća′-ḣ t a g-y a, *adv.* *touching, relating to, concerning.*

i-ća′-ḣ t a g-y a-k e n, *adv.* *relating to.*

i-ća′-ḣ t a-k a, *v. n.* *to touch, be near to*—imakaḣtaka, inićaḣtaka.

i′-ća-ḣ t a-k a, *n.* (i *and* kaḣtaka) *a place where a river touches* or *runs near a hill; a place where the prairie comes down to a river* or *lake.*

i-ća ḣ′-y a, *v. a.* *to cause to grow, raise,* as corn, etc.; *to rear, to train up,* as a child, etc.—ićaḣwaya, ićaḣmayaŋ.

i-ća ḣ′-y a, *adv.* *conformed to, made like.*

i-ća′-k a ŋ, *n.* (i *and* kakaŋ) *an adze.*

i-ća′-k a ŋ, *v. a.* of kakaŋ; *to strike and cut a piece out of*—iwakakaŋ, iyakakaŋ, uŋkićakaŋpi.

i-ća′-k i ś, *cont.* of ićakiźa; ićakiś wauŋ, *I am suffering for.*

i-ća′-k i ś-y a, *v. a.* *to cause to suffer for, to afflict*—ićakiświya.

i-ća′-k i ś-y a, *adv.* *in a suffering manner.*

i-ća′-k i-ź a, *v. n.* *to be in want of, lacking, suffering for*—imakakiźa, inićakiźa, uŋkićakiźapi: ićakiźe śni, *not in want of.*

i-ća′-ki-źe, *n.* (i *and* kakiźa) *affliction.* See iwićakakiźe.

i-ća′-ki-źe-śni-yaŋ, *adv. not in want of, plentifully.*

i-ćam′, *cont.* of ićapa; ićam iću, *to stick in and take out.*

i-ća′-ma, *adj. rough,* as cloth or the beard; *pricking,* as iron filings.

i-ća′-ma, *v. n. to hurt* or *prick,* as anything in the eye: taku iśta imakama, *something is pricking in my eye.*

i-ća′-ma-ma, *v. red.* of ićama; *to prick:* ićamama niuŋ he, *does it keep pricking you?*

i-ća′-mda-ska, *v. n.* (i *and* kamdaska) *to be flattened,* as a bullet that is shot into wood.

i-ća′-mna, *v. n. to blow, bluster, storm, drive,* as wind and snow; nina ićamna, *it is very blustering;* ićamna au, *a storm is coming: to be torn by* anything and lose the contents, as a bag of corn carried along. See kamna, *to rip.*

i-ćan′, *adv. whilst, in the meantime, just then.*

i-ća′-nan, *adv.* See ićaŋnan.

i-ćan′-ka-spe-ya, *v.* See ićaŋtkaspeya *and* ićantekaspeya.

i-ćan′-śi-ća, *v. n. to be sad for*—ićanmaśića. See ićaŋteśića.

i-ćan′-śi-ća-pi, *n. tribulation.*

i-ćan′-śin, *cont.* of ićanśića.

i-ćan′-śin-ya, *v. a. to make sad, grieve, disappoint* one *by means of* something—ićanśinwaya. See ićaŋteśinya.

i-ćan′-śin-ya, *adv. sadly, distressingly.*

i-ćan′-wa-śte, *v. n. to be glad for*—ićanmawaśte. See ićaŋtewaśte.

i-ćan′-wa-śte-ya, *adv. gladly for.*

i-ćaŋ′-a-ma-ni, *n. a ladder.* See ćaŋiyamanipi.

i-ćaŋ′-ćaŋ, *v. n.* (i *and* ćaŋćaŋ) *to tremble for, shake on account of* imaćaŋćaŋ, inićaŋćaŋ.

i′-ćaŋ-haŋ, *adv. leaning against. T.,* ićaŋyaŋ. See ićiŋhaŋ.

i′-ćaŋ-kćaŋ, *adv. making effort but not with much determination:* ićaŋkćaŋ ećamoŋ, *I did it, but not truly;* opposed to awićakehaŋ.

i′-ćaŋ-ksi, *v. n. to be angry* or *irritated at* or *in consequence of*—ićaŋwaksi, ićaŋyaksi.

i′-ćaŋ-ksi-ki-ya, *v. a. to cause to be angry for*—ićaŋksiwakiya.

i′-ćaŋ-ksi-ksi, *v. red.* of ićaŋksi.

i′-ćaŋ-ksi-ya, *adv. crossly, bluntly, roughly, angrily. T.,* ićaŋksiksiya.

i-ćaŋ′-nan, *adv. out from, out in the river* or *lake from.*

i-ćaŋt′, *cont.* of ićaŋte.

i-ćaŋt′-a-hde, *v. a. to determine evil against* one *for* some cause—ićaŋtawahde.

i-ćaŋ′-te, *adv. in* or *at the heart.* Used as in the following compounds.

i-ćaŋ′-te-ka-spe-ya, *v. to gratify one's self by avenging, make one's self cheerful by retaliating on* some relative of the one who has done the injury—ićaŋtekaspewaya.

i-ća ŋ'-te-ki-ç u ŋ, *v. n.* *to encourage one's self by reason of*—ićaŋteweçuŋ, ićaŋteyeçuŋ.

i-ća ŋ'-te-ki-ç u ŋ-y a ŋ, *adv.* *encouragingly.*

i-ća ŋ'-te-śi-ća, *v. n.* *to be sad on account of.* See ićanśića

i-ća ŋ'-te-śi-ća-ya, *adv.* *sadly on account of.*

i-ća ŋ'-te-śin-ya, *v. a.* *to render unhappy by.*

i-ća ŋ'-te-ţiŋs, *cont.* of. ićaŋteţiŋza.

i-ća ŋ'-te-ţiŋs-ya, *v. a.* *to encourage* one *by reason of*—ićaŋteţiŋswaya.

i-ća ŋ'-te-ţiŋs-ya, *adv.* *encouragingly.*

i-ća ŋ'-te-ţiŋ-za, *v. n.* *to be encouraged* or *sustained by*—ićaŋtemaţiŋza.

i-ća ŋ'-te-wa-śte, *v. n.* *to be glad on account of*—ićaŋtemawaśte.

i-ća n'-te-wa-śte-ya, *adv.* *gladly on account of.*

i-ća ŋ t'-i-ća-spe-ya, *v.* *to avenge one's self and thus become pleased*—ićaŋtićaspewaya. See ićaŋtekaspeya.

i-ća ŋ t'-ka-spe-ya, *v.* Same as ićaŋtekaspeya.

i-ća ŋ t'-o-hna-ka, *v. a.* *to place in the heart with reference to* something; *to purpose to give to* one—ićaŋtowahnaka.

i-ća ŋ t'-o-ki-ç u ŋ, *v.* *to strengthen* or *encourage one's self by*—ićaŋtoweçuŋ. See ićaŋtekiçuŋ.

i-ća ŋ t'-o-kpa-ni, *v.* *to long for in reference to*—ićaŋtowakpani.

i-ća ŋ t'-o-tpa-ni, *v.* Same as ićaŋtokpani.

i'-ća ŋ-y a ŋ, *adv.* *T.* *leaning against.* See ićaŋhaŋ.

i'-ća-pa, *v.* *to open the mouth*—iwakapa.

i-ća'-p'a, *v.* (i *and* ćap'a) *to stick into, take a stitch*—ićawap'a, ićayap'a, ićauŋp'api; *to stab with; to stick in,* as a thorn or stick: ćaŋ ićamap'a, *a splinter sticks in me.*

i-ća'-pa ŋ, *n.* of kapaŋ; *a thresher, threshing machine; something to pound with.*

i-ća'-p'e, *n.* (i *and* ćap'á) *something that sticks in, a spear, a splinter; a stitch.*

i-ća'-pe, *n.* (i *and* kapaŋ) *something to pound with.*

i-ća'-psa-ke, *n.* (i *and* kapsaka) *something used in cutting off strings;* pahiŋ ićapsake, *a porcupine-quill cutter, a small knife.*

i-ća'-psiŋ-te, *n.* (i *and* kapsiŋta) *something to whip with, a whip.*

i-ća'-pśiŋ-pśiŋ-ća, *n.* *a species of swallow.*

i-ća'-pśiŋ-pśiŋ-ća-da ŋ, *n.* *the common swallow.*

i-ća'-pśu ŋ, *n.* (i *and* kapśuŋ) *anything to pry out* or *pull up by the roots with.*

i'-ća-pta, *v. a.* (i *and* kapta) *to*

open the mouth at, scold—íwakapta, íyakapta.

i-ća'-pta, *v. n.* of kapta; *to break out*, as the hold of meat in carrying it.

i-ća'-ptaŋ-ptaŋ, *v. n.* of kaptaŋptaŋ; *to turn over much, roll about.*

i'-ća-pta-pta, *v. red.* of íćapta; *to be angry at, to scold*—iwakaptapta.

i-ća'-pte, *n.* (i *and* kapta) *something to dip out with, a ladle.* See also wićapte.

i-ća'-saŋ, *n.* (i *and* kasaŋ) *a razor.*

i-ća'-saŋ, *v. n. to become used to*, as to eating or doing anything—imakasaŋ, inićasaŋ. *T., v. a. to whiten by touching or striking*—iwakasaŋ.

i-ća'-sde-će, *n.* (i *and* kasdeća) *something to split with, a wedge.*

i-ća'-ski-ća, *v. n. to be pressed down*—imakaskića, inićaskića.

i-ća'-ski-će, *n.* (i *and* kaskića) *a press.*

i-ća'-ś'a-ka, *v. n.* of kaś'aka; *not to penetrate*, as an ax that is dull.

i-ća'-śda, *n.* (i *and* kaśda) *something to mow with:* peźi icaśda, *a scythe. T.*, ićaśla; putiŋ ićaśla, *a razor.*

i-ća'-śde-ća, *n. Ih. i. q.* ićasdeće.

i-ća'-śe, *n.* (i *and* kaśe) *something rubbing against, a hindrance.*

i-ća'-śe-ya, *v. a. to make a hindrance of, hinder by means of*—ićaśewaya.

i-ća'-śke, *n.* (i *and* kaśka) *something to tie* or *bind around with, a girdle, sash.*

i-ća'-śki-ća, *v. n. to cut a small gash, be gashed*—imakaśkića, inićaśkića.

i-ća'-śki-će, *n.* (i *and* kaśkića) *something to pound with, a beetle.*

i-ća'-śki-ta, *v. n. to cut a little gash in.*

i-ća'-śo-śe, *v. T. to mix* by shaking together—iwakaśośe.

i-ća'-śpe, *n.* (i *and* kaśpa) *an instrument for cutting off pieces:* mazićaśpe, *a cold chisel.*

i-ća'-śpu, *n.* (i *and* kaśpu) *something to knock off with.*

i-ća'-ta, *v.* ićata iheya, *to crowd together.* See kata iheya.

i-ća'-tka-taŋ-haŋ, *adv. to the left hand of*—mićatkataŋhaŋ. See ćatka.

i-ća'-tku-taŋ-haŋ, *adv. to* or *at the back part of the tent from* one. See ćatku.

i-ća'-zo, *v. a.* of kaźo; *to draw a mark* or *line; to take credit, to owe, be in debt*—iwakazo, iyakazo, uŋkićazopi. See also ikićazo.

i-ća'-zo, *n. a mark, line drawn.*

i-ća'-zo-ki-ya, *v. a. to cause to mark; to cause to take* things *on credit, give credit to*—ićazowakiya, ićazoyakiya, ićazouŋkiyapi, ićazomakiya, ićazoćićiya.

i-ća'-zo-pi, *n. credits.*

i-ća'-źa, *v. a. to think there is much* or *many; to do* a thing *much*, as to give away much; *to take more than is proper*—iwaćaźa, uŋkićaźapi.

i-ća′-źa-pi, *n.* *very much*, *i. q.* ota ȟiŋća.

i-ća′-źa-źa, *v. a.* *to wash by shaking*, as a bottle—iwakaźaźa.

i-ća′-źe, *adv.* of ćaźe; *in the name of.*

i-ća′-źe-ka, *n.* *a liar*, *i. q.* itoŋpiśni.

i-ća′-źe-ka, *v. n.* *to be named for* or *on account of.*

i-ća′-źe-yan, *adv.* *cont.* of ićaźeyata; *in the name of.*

i-ća′-źe-ya-ta, *adv.* *in the name of*, *in speaking the name of.*

i′-će-haŋ, *adv.* *leaning against:* ićehaŋ naźiŋ, *to stand leaning against.* See ićiŋhaŋ *and* ićiŋyaŋ.

i-će′-kiŋ, *v. a.* *to envy* any one—ićewakiŋ, ićeyakiŋ, ićeuŋkiŋpi, ićećićiŋ, ićemakiŋ.

i-će′-kiŋ-yaŋ, *adv.* *enviously.*

i-će′-ki-ya, *v. a.* of ćekiya; *to pray to* one *for* something—ićewakiya, ićeyakiya, ićeuŋkiyapi, ićećićiya: Woniya Wakaŋ ićeyakiya he, *dost thou pray for the Holy Spirit?*

i-će′-pa, *adj.* of ćepa; *fat on* or *by by*, *fat reason of*—imaćepa.

i-će′-paŋ, *n.* a woman's *husband's sisters* she calls ićepaŋ: ićepaŋku, *her sister-in-law.*

i-će′-paŋ-śi, *n.* a woman's *female cousin;* her *husband's brother's wife:* ićepaŋśitku, *her female cousin*, etc.

i-će′-paŋ-śi-ya, *v. a.* *to have for female cousin*—ićepaŋśiwaya.

i-će′-paŋ-ya, *v. a.* *to have for* or *count as sister-in-law*—ićepaŋwaya, ićepaŋmayaŋ.

i-ćeś′, *intj.* See ećeś.

i-će′-ti, *v.* of ćeti; *to make a fire to* or *at*—ićewati.

i-će′-wiŋ, *v. n.* *to give away much*—ićewawiŋ.

i-će′-wiŋ, *adv.* *much, very much:* ićewiŋ wićawaḳu, *I have given them very much.*

i-će′-wiŋȟ, *adv.* Same as ićewiŋ.

i-će′-wiŋ-wiŋ, *adv.* *red.* of ićewiŋ; *much, lavishly.*

i-će′-wiŋ-yaŋ, *adv.* *lavishly, bountifully.*

i′-ći, *a prefix.* Prefixed to verbs, it usually signifies *together:* as koyaka, *to put on*, íćikoyaka, *to fasten together;* waŋyaka, *to see*, íćiwaŋyaka, *to look at together, compare.* Prefixed to prepositions and adverbs, it conveys the idea of *space* or *time intervening* between the objects: as íćikiyedaŋ, *near to each other*, íćitehaŋ, *far apart.*

i-ći′, *a prefix to cardinal numbers which makes of them ordinals:* as yamni, *three*, ićiyamni, *the third.* See i, 3.

i′-ći-ća-hi, *v n.* *to mingle together, mix.*

i′ ći-ća-hi-ya, *v. a.* *to mix together, mingle, stir up together*—íćićahiwaya, íćićahiuŋyaŋpi.

i′-ći-ća-hi-ya, *adv.* *mingled.*

i′-ći-ća-hi-ya-pi, *part. mixed together.*

i′-ći-ća-ḣi-ḣa, *adj. connected, in links:* maza ićićaḣiḣa, *a chain.*

i′-ći-ća-śka, *v. to bind together.* See ićiyakaśka.

i′-ći-ća-wiŋ, *adv. back again by the same way:* ićićawiŋ hda, *to go home by the same way that one came;* anog ićićawiŋ, *back and forth.* See ićipaś.

i′-ći-ća-wiŋ-wiŋ, *adv. red.* of íćićawiŋ.

i′-ći-ća-wiŋ-yaŋ, *adv. back by the same way.*

i′-ći-ću-ya, *adv. passing by each other partly,* as two things placed thus ⚌; said of *twins,* if one is a boy and the other a girl.

i′-ći-hde-śka, *adj. speckled,* as corn of different colors.

i′-ći-hde-śka-śka, *adj. red.* of íćihdeśka.

i′-ći-he-haŋ-haŋ-yaŋ, *adv. red.* of íćihehaŋyaŋ.

í′-ći-he-haŋ-yaŋ, *adv. thus far apart.*

i-ći′-hni, *v. a. to beat* or *maltreat,* as a man his wife.

i′-ći-hnu-ni, *v. to be mixed up,* so as not to be distinguished

i′-ći-hnu-ni-ya, *v. a. to cause not to be distinguished*—íćihnuniwaya.

i′-ći-hnu-ni-yaŋ, *adv. mingled, mixed up.*

i′-ći-kaŋ-ye′-la, *adj. T. near to each other:* ićikiyena.

i′-ći-kde-kde-ġa, *adj. Ih. scattering, few.*

i′-ći-ki-ki-ye-daŋ, *adv. red.* of íćikiyedaŋ.

i′-ći-ki-ye-daŋ, *adv. near to each other.*

i′-ći-ko-yag, *cont.* of íćikoyaka; íćikoyag iyeya.

i′-ći-ko-yag-ya, *v. a. to fasten one to another*—íćikoyagwaya.

i′-ći-ko-ya-ka, *v. n. to be fastened one to another.*

i-ći′-ma, *adv. ever, again;* with śni, *never;* ḣtanihaŋ ićima, *the day before yesterday;* heyakećiŋhaŋ ićima, *the day after to-morrow;* ptiŋhaŋ ićima, *the fall before last.*

i-ći′-ma-na, *adv. ever;* śni always follows, making *never:* ićimana ećamoŋ kte śni, *I will never do it.*

i′-ći-ma-ni, *v. n. to travel, go on a journey without one's family; to visit*—íćimawani, íćimayani, íćimauŋnipi.

i′-ći-ma-ni-pi, *n. traveling; visiting.*

i-ći′-na-pćiŋ-waŋ-ka, *adj. the ninth.* This form is not much used. See inapćiŋwaŋka. *T.,* ićinapćiŋyuŋka.

i-ći′-noŋ-pa, *adj. the second. T., also, again; i. q.* ićimana.

i-ćiŋ′, *v. to desire one thing for another; to desire more of, in addition to*—iwaćiŋ.

i-ćiŋ′, *adv. T. of a truth; now: i. q.* ećiŋ.

i′-ćiŋ-haŋ, *adv.* *leaning against.*

i-ćiŋ′-iŋ, *v.* of kiŋiŋ; *to throw at, strike with*—iwakiŋiŋ.

i-ćiŋ′-yaŋ, *v. a.* *to cause to desire*—ićiŋwaya.

i′-ćiŋ-yaŋ, *adv.* *leaning against:* ićiŋyaŋ mayaŋka, *it is leaning against me.* *T.*, ićaŋyaŋ. See ićehaŋ *and* ićiŋhaŋ.

i′-ći-pa-si-sa, *v. a.* of pasisa; *to stick in one and another, sew together; to sew across*—ićiwapasisa.

i′-ći-paś, *cont.* of ićipaźa; *back by the same way;* ićipaś hdiću, *he started back by the same way.* See ićićawiŋ.

i′-ći-paś-ya, *adv.* *backwards and forwards, doubled on.* *T.*, ićipaśpaś.

i′-ći-pa-we-ġa, *v. n.* of paweġa; *to cross, lie across.*

i′-ći-pa-weḣ, *cont.* of ićipaweġa; *crosswise:* ićipaweḣ okataŋ, *to nail on crosswise,* as our Saviour when crucified; *to crucify.*

i′-ći-pa-weḣ-we-ġa, *v. red.* of ićipaweġa.

i′-ći-pa-weḣ-ya, *adv.* *crosswise, across.*

i′-ći-pa-źa, *adv.* *back by the same way, doubled back on, on the same track back.*

i′-ći-pu-kpe-ya, *adv.* *scattered, mixed up.* See kpukpeya.

i′-ći-pu-tpe-ya, *adv.* *mixed up, scattered about.*

i′-ći-sku-ya, *adj.* of skuya; *alike sour* or *sweet:* kići ićiskuya, *alike sweet with.*

i-ći′-śa-hdo-ġaŋ, *adj.* *the eighth.*

i-ći′-śa-kdo-ġaŋ, *adj.* *Ih.* *the eighth.*

i-ći′-śa-ko-wiŋ, *adj.* *the seventh.*

i-ći′-śa-kpe, *adj.* *the sixth.*

i′-ći-ta-ki-hna, *adv.* *in rows, in layers, one on another; double, stout,* as thick cloth.

i-ći′-taŋ, *adv.* *hardly; i. q.* kitaŋ se: ićitaŋ mduśtaŋ, *I have but just finished it;* ićitaŋ se ehaŋ wai, *I barely arrived at the place.*

i′-ći-taŋ-iŋ-śni, *v. n.* of taŋiŋ; *it is not manifest* between two or more *which is the one.*

i′-ći-te-haŋ, *adv.* of tehaŋ; *far apart.*

i′-ći-te-haŋ-haŋ, *adv.* *red.* of íćitehaŋ.

i′-ći-te-haŋ-haŋ-yaŋ, *adv.* *red.* of íćitehaŋyaŋ.

i′-ći-te-haŋ-yaŋ, *adv.* *far apart.*

i′-ći-tko-kim, *adv.* *meeting face to face, opposite each other.* See itkokim.

i′-ći-tko-ki-pa-pi, *v. pl.* of itkokipa; *they met face to face.*

i′-ći-to-haŋ, *adv.* *how long from?*

i′-ći-to-haŋ-haŋ, *adv. red.* of íćitohaŋ.

i′-ći-to-haŋ-haŋ-yaŋ, *adv.* *red.* of íćitohaŋyaŋ.

i′-ći-to-haŋ-yaŋ, *adv.* *how far apart?* John ii. 4.

i′-ći-toŋ-pe-ya, *adv.* of itoŋpa; *fearing each other, taking care for each other.*

i-ći-to-pa, *adj.* *the fourth.*

i-ći'-waŋ-ġa; *v.* of iwaŋġa; *I ask thee a question.* *T.*, ićiyuŋġa.

i'-ći-waŋ-ġa, *v. a.* *to cross-question, examine by cross-questioning*—ícimuŋġa, íćinuŋġa, uŋkićiwaŋġapi. *T.*, ićiyuŋġa.

i'-ći-waŋ-ġa-pi, *n.* *examination.* *T.*, ićiyuŋġapi.

i'-ći-waŋ-ya-ka, *v. a.* of waŋyaka; *to look at things together, compare*—íćiwaŋmdaka, íćiwaŋdaka, íćiwaŋuŋyakapi.

i'-ći-waŋ-ya-ka-pi, *n.* *comparison.*

i-ći'-wa-śte, *v. n.* *to be good with:* taku ićiwaśte he, *with what is it good? to be good for.*

i-ći'-wi-kće-mna, *adj.* *the tenth.* See iwikćemna.

i'-ći-wo-hdu-ze, *n.* *fellowship.*

i-ći'-ya, *v. a.* *to take sides with, assist* in a dispute or controversy, *assist* as an advocate—iwakiya, uŋkikiyapi, imakiya.

i'-ći-ya-ćiŋ, *v.* of iyaćiŋ; *to liken* several things *to each other, think equal*—íćimdaćiŋ, ićidaćiŋ.

i'-ći-ya-ćiŋ-yaŋ, *adv.* *likening to one another.*

i'-ći-ya-hda-skin, *adv.* *one above another, pressing on each other.* See ahdaskića.

i'-ći-ya-hda-śka, *v. pos.* *to unite together, tie one to another of one's own*—íćiyawahdaśka. See kaśka.

i'-ći-ya-hde, *v. n.* *to reach one to another.*

i'-ći-ya-hde-hde, *v. red.* of íćiyahde.

i'-ći-ya-hde-hde-ya, *adv. red.* of íćiyahdeya.

i'-ći-ya-hde-ya, *adv.* *reaching one to another.*

i'-ći-ya-hde-ya, *v. a.* *to cause one to reach to another, cause to meet*—íćiyahdewaya.

i'-ći-ya-ḣpa-ya, *v. a.* to catch from one another; *to communicate to others*, as an infectious disease. See aḣpaya.

i'-ći-ya-ḣpa-ya, *adj.* *contagious.*

i'-ći-ya-i-hda-śka-pi, *v. pl.* *to unite one to another, tie each other together*, as man and wife.

i'-ći-ya-ka-śka, *v. a.* *to tie* or *unite* things *together mutually*—íćiyawakaśka, íćiyayakaśka, íćiyauŋkaśkapi.

i-ći'-ya-mni, *adj.* *the third.*

i'-ći-ya-pu-spa, *v. a.* of iyapuspa; *to stick* two or more things *together*—íćiyawapuspa.

i'-ći-ya-skam, *cont.* of íćiyaskapa; *sticking to each other.*

i'-ći-ya-skam-ya, *v. a.* *to cause to adhere* or *stick to each other*—íćiyaskamwaya.

i'-ći-ya-skam-ya; *adv.* *adhering to each other:* íćiyaskamya waŋka, *they lie sticking together.*

i'-ći-ya-ska-pa, *v. n.* of iyaskapa; *to adhere* or *stick one to another.*

i'-ći-yas-ya-za, *adv. red.* of íćiyaza.

i'-ći-ya-wa, *v. a.* of iyawa; *to count up together*—íćimdawa, íćidawa, íćiuŋyawapi.

i'-ći-ya-za, *adv. red.* of iyaza; *in rows, in a range; from one to another*, as in passing a thing around.

i'-ći-yo-ki-he-ya, *adv. T. over again and again, repeatedly; one after another.*

i'-ći-yo-pe-ya, *v. a.* of iyopeya; *to barter, exchange one* thing *for another*—íćiyopewaya.

i'-ći-yo-pe-ya-pi, *n. barter, exchange:* íćiyopekićiyapi, *a market.*

i'-ći-yo-pta; *adv. in a range with, in the same direction.* See iyopta.

i'-ći-yo-pte-ya, *adv. in that direction, across, through.*

i'-ći-yo-ta-koŋs, *cont.* of íćiyotakoŋza; *opposite to each other. T.*, ićiyotatkoŋs.

i'-ći-yo-ta-koŋ-za, *adv.* of iyotakoŋza; *opposite to each other, equal to, even with. T.*, ićiyotatkoŋza.

i'-ći-yu-hmuŋ, *v. a.* of yuhmuŋ; *to twist together*—íćimduhmuŋ, ićiduhmuŋ.

i'-ci-yu-o-ta, *v. a.* of yuota; *to multiply together*—ícimduota, íćiuŋyuotapi.

i-ći'-za-ptaŋ, *adj. the fifth.*

i-ći'-źe-haŋ, *adv. often, repeatedly, frequently.*

i-ci'-źe-na, *adv. T. mingled, mixed up.*

i'-ćo-ġa, *v. n. to lodge on, drift and lodge on*, as a log of wood.

i-ćo'-i-ç̌i-oŋ, *v.* of ićokoŋ; *to determine evil against one's self; to be resolute.*

i-ćo'-kam, *adv. before, between* one and the fire—mićokam.

i-ćo'-kam-ya, *adv. before, between.*

i-ćo'-ka-pa, *adv.* of ćokapa; same as ićokam.

i-ćo'-ka-pa-taŋ-haŋ, *adv. before, in the midst, inside of.*

i-ćo'-koŋ, *v. a.* of ćokoŋ; *to determine evil against* one *for* any cause—ićowakoŋ.

i-ćo'-ma, *v. a. to draw up around the shoulders*, as one's blanket: śina iwaćoma, *I draw my blanket up.*

i-ćo'-mi, *v. a.* Same as ićoma; some use one form and some the other.

i-ćo'-mni, *v. n. to be tired of staying; weary, discontented*—ićomamni, ićonimni, ićouŋmnipi.

i-ćo'-pa, *v.* of ćopa; *to wade in*, as in one's moccasins—ićowapa, ićouŋpapi.

i-ćos', *cont.* of ićoza.

i-ćos'-ya, *v. a. to make warm with*—ićoswaya.

i-ćo'-za, *v. n.* of ćoza; *to be warm by means of*, as of clothing—imaćoza: takudaŋ inićoza śni, *you have nothing to keep you warm.*

i-ću', *v. a. to take, accept, receive, take up* anything—iwaću, iyaću, uŋkićupi; *to become*, as, otpas iću, *it has become dark.*

i-ćuŋ'-haŋ, *adv. whilst, during the time, in the mean time.*

i-ćuŋ'-haŋ-na, *adv.* *whilst, when.*

i-ćuŋ'-haŋ-nah, *adv.* *just at that time.*

i-ćuŋ'-om, *adv. cont.* of ićuŋoŋpa; *out at one side of;* tipi kiŋ ićuŋom mda, *I went off on one side of the house.*

i-ćuŋ'-oŋ-pa, *adv.* *off to one side, off from, out of the way:* ićuŋoŋpa waŋka, *it lies out of the way;* mićuŋoŋpa, *off from me.* *T.*, ićioŋpa.

i-ćuŋ'-oŋ-pa-taŋ-haŋ, *adv.* *out of the way, off to one side.*

i-ćuŋs', *cont.* of ićuŋza.

i-ćuŋs'-ya, *v.* *to be dilatory, not to do much, to have no mind to the work, work only for the pay; i. q.* taŋyeh ećoŋ śni—ićuŋswaya, icuŋsuŋyaŋpi.

i-ćuŋs'-ya-ken, *adv.* *not heartily, pretending.*

i-ćuŋs'-ye-ća, *n.* *one who is not faithful, one who does his duty not well.*

i-ćuŋ'-za, *v.* of kuŋza. Obsolete.

i-ću'-te, *n.* of kute; *something to shoot with,* as the *arrows* one uses in a game.

i-ću'-wa, *n.* of kuwa; *something with which to hunt* or *catch* anything; as, hoġaŋ ićuwa *and* hoićuwa, *a fish-hook, fishing-implements: farming-implements.*

i-ç̣e'-śi, *n.* a woman's *male cousin; her husband's sister's husband;* iç̣eśitku, *her male cousin,* etc. *T.*, śiç̣eśi.

i-ç̣e'-śi-ya, *v. a.* *to have for male cousin,* etc.—iç̣eśiwaya. *T.*, śiç̣eśiya.

i-ç̣i', *pron. reflexive.* It usually signifies that the action returns upon the actor; but sometimes, that the action is done *for* one's self. See Grammar, under compound pronouns, "iç̣i," "niç̣i," "miç̣i," and "uŋkiç̣i," which form the middle or reflexive of a large class of verbs.

i-ç̣i'-ća-ġa, *v.* *reflex.* of kaġa; *to make one's self; to make for one's self*—miç̣ićaġa, niç̣ićaġa.

i-ç̣i'-ća-śka, *v.* *reflex.* of kaśka; *to bind* or *tie one's self, to deliver up one's self* to the authorities—miç̣ićaśka.

i-ç̣i'-ći-ta, *adv.* *taking care, carefully; i. q.* itoŋpeyahaŋ: iç̣ićita aya wo, *take it along carefully.*

i-ç̣i'-ćoŋs, *v.* *cont.* of iç̣ićoŋza; iç̣ićoŋs opa, *to follow on one's own decision; to make a profession of religion.*

i-ç̣i'-ćoŋ-za, *v.* *reflex.* of koŋza; *to determine for one's self*—miç̣ićoŋza.

i-ç̣i'-ç̣u-ya, *adv.* of ḳu, *to give; giving one's self up to, devotedly:* iç̣ićuya ećoŋ, *he acts devotedly.*

i-ç̣i'-gla-lu, *v. reflex.* *T.* *to fan one's self.*

i-ç̣i'-hde, *v.* *reflex.* of hde; *to lay up for one's self*—miç̣ihde. Hence, taku iç̣ihdepi, *furniture.*

i-ç̣i'-hde-ka, *n.* *one who has*

much, one who is always accumulating.

i'-ç i-h n a-h n a, *adv.* *with care, pleasantly, politely:* içihnahna ećoŋ wo, *do it pleasantly.*

i-ç i'-h n a-k a, *v.* *reflex.* of hnaka; *to place* or *locate one's self; to lay up for one's self*—miçihnaka; taku içihnakapi, *furniture.* See içihde.

i-ç i'-h n a-y a ŋ, *v.* *reflex.* of hnayaŋ; *to deceive one's self*—miçihnayaŋ.

i-ç i'-h n i, *v.* *reflex.* of ihni; *to hunt,* as game, *for one's self*—miçihni. *T.*, iiçigni.

i'-ç i-ḣ a-ḣ a, *v.* *reflex.* of iḣa; *to make one's self a laughing-stock,* said of one who commits adultery—miçiḣaḣa. *T.*, iiçiḣaḣa.

i-ç i'-k ć u, *v.* *reflex.* of iću; *to help one's self, take what one is to have*—imiçikću. *T.*, iiçikću

i-ç i'-k s u-y a, *v.* *reflex.* of kiksuya; *to remember one's self, come to one's self*—miçiksuya.

i-ç i'-k t e, *v.* *reflex.* of kte; *to kill one's self, commit suicide.*

i-ç i'-k t o ŋ-ź a, *v* *reflex.* of akiktoŋźa; *to forget one's self, leave off* or *cease from one's* sorrow, etc.

i-d a g', *cont.* of idaka. *T.* wowilag.

i-d a g'-y a, *v. a.* *to cause to serve, have for a servant*—idagwaya.

i-d a'-k a, *v. a.* *to have for a servant, to control, govern, rule over*—iwadaka, uŋkidakapi. See wowidake.

i-d a'-z a-t a, *adv.* *back from, i. q.* iḣeyata. See dazata.

i-d a'-z a-t a ŋ-h a ŋ, *adv.* *in the rear of.*

i-d e', *v. n.* *to burn, blaze.*

i-d e', *n.* *a blaze, a burning, a prairie fire:* ide au, *a fire is coming.*

i'-d e-ć i-y a, *adv.* *on this side of.*

i'-d e-ć i-y a-t a ŋ, *adv.* *on this side of.*

i'-d e-ć i-y a-t a ŋ-h a ŋ, *adv.* *from this side of, on this side of, in this way from.*

i'-d e-ć i-y o-t a ŋ, *adv.* *in this direction from.*

i'-d e-ġ a, *n.* *pouting lips.* See deġa *and* deḣdeġa.

i'-d e-h a n, *adv.* *so far off.*

i'-d e-h a n-h a n, *adv.* *red.* of ídehan.

i'-d e-h a ŋ-n a, *adv.* *only so far off, near to.*

i'-d e-h a ŋ-y a ŋ, *adv.* *so far off.*

i-d e'-y a, *v. a.* *to burn, cause to burn, set fire to*—idewaya, ideyaya, ideuŋyaŋpi.

i-d i'-d i-t a, *adj.* *hot on account of.*

i-d i'-t a-k a, *v. n.* *to be animated for, brave for* or *on account of*—idimataka *and* imaditaka, iniditaka. See waditaka.

i-d o'-t i-ç i ŋ, *n.* (dote *and* ķiŋ) *a collar* for a horse.

i-d o'-w a ŋ, *v. a.* of dowaŋ; *to sing to* or *for, to sing the praises of, praise* one—iwadowaŋ, iyadowaŋ, uŋkidowaŋpi, imadowaŋ; ićidowaŋ, *I praise thee;* içidowaŋ, *to sing of one's self.*

i-e', *v.* Same as ia.

i-e'-a-ḣta-ni, *v.* *to sin in speaking, blaspheme.*

i-e'-hda-śna, *v.* *pos.* of ieyaśna; *to speak falsely of one's own,* as when one tells what is false in regard to his dreams or visions—iewahdaśna. *T.*, ieglaśna, *to blunder in speaking.*

i-e'-ka-ski-ska, *v. n.* *to stutter*—iemakaskiska, ienikaskiska.

i-e'-ki-ya, *v. a.* *to cause to speak, make speaker of; to have for interpreter*—iewakiya, ieyakiya.

i-e'-ksa-pa, *v. n.* *to be wise of speech, eloquent*—iemaksapa *and* iewaksapa.

i'-en-hde *and* i'-en-i-ye-ya, *v.* *to reproach, blame.*

i-e'-ska, *v. n.* *to be fluent, speak a language intelligibly*—iemaska, ieniska, ieuŋskapi.

i-e'-ska, *n.* *one who speaks well, an interpreter.*

i-e'-ska-ki-ya, *v. a.* *to have for interpreter, cause to interpret from one language to another*—ieskawakiya, ieskauŋkiyapi.

i-e'-śni, *v* *not to be able to speak, dumb; i. q.* iaokitpani.

i-e'-śni, *intj.* *not so!* *T.*, ieśnićaś. See iyeśni.

i-e'-wi-ća-ka, *v. n.* *to speak the truth*—iewićawaka, iewićayaka, iewićauŋkapi.

i-e'-wi-ća-ke-haŋ, *adv.* *truly, in truth.* *T.*, iewićakeya.

i-e'-yaŋ-pa-ha, *v.* *to proclaim, publish, make proclamation,* as the Dakota men do—ieyaŋwapaha, ieyaŋyapaha, ieyaŋuŋpahapi.

i-e'-yaŋ-pa-ha, *n.* *a public crier, herald, a man employed to proclaim with a loud voice the decisions of the principal men concerning any public matter,* such as the time when they will move, where they will encamp, etc.

i-e'-ya-śna, *v.* *to talk as one pleases, talk falsely*—iemdaśna, ieuŋyaśnapi.

i-e'-ya-śna-śna, *v.* *red.* of ieyaśna.

i-gla'-ho-mni, *v. reflex.* *T.* *to turn one's self around: i. q.* ihdamna.

i-gla'-ka, *v.* *T.* for ihdaka.

i-gla'-ye-ki-ya, *v.* *T.* *to push into,* as a straw to clear out a pipestem.

i-gla'-ye-ya, *n.* *T.* *a pipestem cleaner.*

i-gla'-za-ta, *adv.* *T.* *at one's side:* miglazata, *at my side.*

i-gla'-zuŋ-ta, *v. reflex.* *T.* *to praise one's self.*

i-glo'-ni-ća, *v.* *T.* for ihdonića.

i-glu'-ble-za, *v. reflex* *T.* *to make one's self see* or *think clearly.*

i-gmu', *n.* *T.* for inmu.

i-gmu'-gle-za, *n.* *T.* for inmuhdeza.

i-gmu'-gle-śka, *n.* *T.* for inmuhdeśka.

i-gmu'-ḣo-ta, *n.* *T.* for inmuḣota.

i-gmu'-śuŋ-ka, *n.* *T.* for inmuśuŋka.

i-g m u'-t a ŋ-k a, *n. T.* for inmutaŋka.

i-ġ a ŋ'-ġ a ŋ-h e-ć a, *n. a kind of swamp-grass.*

i-h a', *n.* (i *and* ha) *the lips; the lid* or *cover* of anything; as ćeġa iha, *a pot-lid; a stopper, cork; i. q.* iośtaŋpi.

i-h a', *adv.* signifying *doubt* or *want of knowledge* concerning what is affirmed or asked; as, iha, sdonwaye śni, *I do not know.*

i-h a'-i-s d a-y e, *n.* (iha *and* isdaye) *grease for the lips, ointment.*

I-h a'-i-s d a-y e, *n. p. the name of a Yankton clan.*

i-h a'-k a m, *adv. after* in place, *behind; after* in time—mihakam, nihakam; ćihakam wauŋ, *I am behind thee.*

i-h a'-k a m-y a, *adv. after, afterwards.*

i-h a'-k a-p a, *adv. after, behind.*

i-h a'-k a-pa-t a ŋ-haŋ, *adv. from behind.*

i-h a'-k i-ć i-k t a, *v. a.* of ihakta; *to accept of, take of* one—ihawećikta, ihamićikta.

i-h a'-k i-k t a, *v. pos.* of ihakta; *to have regard for one's own*—ihawekta *and* ihawakikta.

i-h a'-k t a, *v. a. to see to, be intent on; to watch over, guard; to have regard for, love; to obey, follow*—ihawakta, ihauŋktapi.

i-h a'-k t a-k t a, *v. red.* of ihakta.

i-h a'-k t a-y a, *v. a. to cause to have regard for*—ihaktawaya.

i-h a'-k t a-y a, *adv. having regard for.*

i-h a'-m n a, *v.* See ihaŋmna, which is the better spelling.

i-h a ŋ', *v. n. to stand in* or *at*—iwahaŋ; *to remain,* as ikićihaŋ, *to remain for* one. See haŋ.

i-h a ŋ'-b l a, *v T. to dream: i. q.* ihaŋmna.

i-h a ŋ g', *cont.* of ihaŋke.

i-h a ŋ g'-k i-y a, *v. a. pos. to destroy one's own; to destroy for* one—ihaŋgwakiya; ihaŋgkićićiyapi, *they destroy for each other.*

i-h a ŋ g'-y a, *v a. to destroy, bring to an end*—ihaŋgwaya; ihaŋguŋyaŋpi; ihaŋgiçiya, *to destroy one's self.*

i-h a ŋ'-ḣ a ŋ-n a, *n. the next morning, the morning following. T.,* ihiŋhaŋna.

i-h a ŋ'-k a-y e-t u, *n. the next day, day following.* This form is used by Mr. Renville. See ihaŋyaŋketu.

i-h a ŋ'-k e, *v. n. to end, come to an end.*

i-h a ŋ'-k e, *n. the end, termination; the border, boundary.*

i-h a ŋ'-k e-t a, *adv. at the end, at the last.*

i-h a ŋ'-k e-y a, *v. a. to make an end of, destroy.* See ihaŋgya.

i-h a ŋ'-k e-y a, *adv. at the end, at the last* or *lowest part:* kun ihaŋkeya, John viii. 23.

I-h a ŋ k'-t o ŋ-w a ŋ, *n. p.* (ihaŋke *and* toŋwaŋ) *the name of one of the divisions of the Dakota people; the Yanktons.*

I-haŋk'-toŋ-waŋ-na, *n. p.* (ihaŋke, toŋwaŋ *and* na) *another family* or *grand division of the Dakotas.* Perhaps originally these two were one band, but now they are distinct. These names signify those who have their *villages at the end. The Yanktonais.*

i-haŋ'-mde, *v.* See ihaŋmna.

i-haŋ'-mna, *v. to dream* in the ordinary way; *to have visions of what was known in a former state of existence; to have intercourse with spirits*—iwahaŋmna, uŋkihaŋmnaŋpi. *T.*, ihaŋbla. See haŋmde.

i-haŋ'-ya-ke, *n.* See ihaŋyaketu.

i-haŋ'-ya-ke-tu, *n. the next day. T.*, ihihaŋna.

i-hda', *a prefix,* used to make the reflexive form of verbs beginning with "ka" *and* "ya." *T.*, igla; *Ih.*, ikda.

i-hda'-ćiŋ, *v. pos.* of iyaćiŋ; *to liken one's own* or *one's self to*—iwahdaćiŋ, imihdaćiŋ, iyahdaćiŋ. *T.*, iglaćiŋ.

i-hda'-ćo, *v. reflex.* of yaćo; *to judge* or *condemn one's self*—mihdaćo, nihdaćo, uŋkihdaćopi. *T.*, iglaćo.

i-hda'-du, *v. reflex.* of kadu; *to fan one's self*—mihdadu *and* içihdadu.

i-hdag', *cont.* of ihdaka; ihdag uŋyaŋpi.

i-hda'-ka, *v. n. to move, start with one's family, to go camping, move about from place to place,* as the Dakotas do—iwahdaka, uŋkihdakapi.

i-hda'-ksa, *v. reflex.* of kaksa *and* yaksa; *to cut off* or *bite off one's own,* as one's arm—mihdaksa.

i-hda'-mna, *v. reflex.* of kamna *and* yamna; *to turn one's self around; to gain for one's self, to indemnify* or *remunerate one's self, get back one's own*—mihdamna, uŋkihdamnapi.

i-hda'-o-ni-haŋ, *v. reflex.* of yaonihaŋ; *to praise one's self*—mihdaonihaŋ.

i-hda'-o-taŋ-iŋ, *v. reflex.* of yaotaŋiŋ; *to manifest one's self, proclaim one's self*—mihdaotaŋiŋ.

i-hda'-su, *v. reflex.* of yasu; *to judge one's self. T.*, iglasu.

i-hda'-śi-ća, *v. reflex. to speak evil of,* or *blame one's self. T.*, iglaśića.

i-hda'-śka, *v. reflex.* of kaśka; *to bind one's self, to deliver one's self up to be punished*—mihdaśka.

i-hda'-śna *and* i-hda'-śna-śna, *v. reflex.* of yaśna; *to miss in biting one's self,* as a dog in trying to bite his own tail.

i-hda'-śpa, *v. reflex.* of yaśpa; *to bite one's self loose, break loose*—mihdaśpa.

i-hda'-taŋ, *v. reflex.* of yataŋ; *to praise one's self; to brag, boast, speak of one's self above what is true*—mihdataŋ, nihdataŋ, uŋkihdataŋpi.

i-hda'-taŋ-h, *intj. praise yourself very much! boast away!* A byword. See ihdataŋ.

i-hda'-to-kaŋ, *v. reflex.* of yatokaŋ; *to clear one's self, prove an alibi*—mihdatokaŋ.

i-h d a'-w a, *v. reflex.* of yawa; *to count one's self;* as, wićaśta ihdawa, *one who counts* or *esteems himself a man, i. e., a chief; to count one's own* or *what one is to have*—mihdawa.

i-h d a'-z o, *v. pos.* of ićazo; *to mark one's self; to mark one's own,* as a blanket—iwahdazo.

i-h d a'-ź i-ć a, *v. reflex.* of yaźića; *to speak of one's self as rich.*

i-h d a'-ź i-ć a-k a, *n. one who counts himself rich.*

i-h d e m', *cont.* of ihdepa.

i-h d e m'-k i-y a, *v. a. to cause* one *to vomit up* what he has eaten—ihdemwakiya.

i-h d e'-p a, *v. a. to vomit, throw up* what one has eaten—iwahdepa, iyahdepa, uŋkihdepapi.

i-h d i', *n. the soft fat of animals, grease, oil;* kukuśe ihdi, *lard;* pteasaŋpi ihdi, *butter:* also *vegetable oil.* See wihdi.

i-h d i'-y o-m d a-s i ŋ, *n. a looking-glass, mirror. T.,* miyoglasiŋ. See aokasiŋ *and* okasiŋ.

i-h d o'-h i, *v. reflex.* of hi; *to bring one's self to* a place, as a deer that might come to be shot—mihdohi.

i-h d o'-i, *v. reflex.* of i; *to take one's self to; to take one's own to*—mihdoi, nihdoi, uŋkihdoipi.

i-h d o'-k u, *v. reflex.* of ku; *to bring one's self towards home*—mihdoku.

i-h d o'-n i-ć a, *v. reflex. to forbid one's self, withhold one's self from* others; *to balk* as a horse—mihdonića. *T.,* iglonića.

i-h d o'-u, *v. reflex.* of u; *to bring one's self towards* a place—mihdou, nihdou, uŋkihdoupi.

i-h d o'-y a, *v. reflex.* of ya; *to take one's self to* a place; *to take to one's self*—said of using the personal pronouns in verbs: en ihdoyepića śni, *it cannot be applied to one's self*—mihdoya, nihdoya.

i-h d u', *a prefix* of verbs in "yu," making the reflexive form. *T.,* iglu; *Ih.,* ikdu.

i-h d u'-e-ć e-t u, *v. reflex.* of yuećetu, *to make one's self right; to reform, repent*—mihduećetu, uŋkihduećetupi.

i-h d u'-e-k i-ć e-t u, *v. reflex. to make one's self right* or *as before; to raise one's self from the dead,* as Christ did—mihduekićetu.

i-h d u'-h a, *v. reflex.* of yuha; *to possess one's self, be free; to restrain one's self, act well; to be able to carry one's* goods, etc.—mihduha, nihduha.

i-h d u'-h e-ć a, *v. to have all one's own with one*—mihduheća.

i-h d u'-h o-m n i; *v. reflex.* of yuhomni; *to turn one's self around*—mihduhomni. *T.,* igluhomni.

i-h d u'-h u-k u n, *cont.* of ihduhukuya, ihduhukun iyeiçiya, *to put one's self down.*

i-h d u'-h u-k u-y a, *v. reflex.* of yuhukuya; *to humble one's self*—mihduhukuya.

i-hdu′-ḣda-ḣda-ta, *v red. to scratch one's self much.*

i-hdu′-ḣda-ta, *v. reflex.* of yuḣdata; *to scratch one's self*—mihduḣdata. *T.*, igluḣlata.

i-hdu′-ḣdo-ka, *v. reflex.* of yuḣdoka; *to open* or *unbosom one's self; to open for one's self*—mihduḣdoka.

i-hdu′-ḣi-ća, *v. reflex.* of yuḣića; *to waken one's self up*—mihduḣića.

i′-hdu-ka-wa, *v. pos.* (i *and* hdukawa) *to open one's own mouth*—iwahdukawa. See hdukawa.

i-hdu′-kćaŋ, *v. reflex.* of yukćaŋ; *to have an opinion of one's self; to understand one's self; to examine one's self*—mihdukćaŋ. *T.*, iglukćaŋ, *to make up one's opinion.*

i-hdu′-ksa, *v. reflex.* of yuksa; *to break one's self away,* as a muskrat from a trap—mihduksa.

i′-hdu-kśaŋ, *adv. around, round about* anything—mihdukśaŋ, nihdukśaŋ, uŋkihdukśaŋ. *T.*, iglukśaŋ.

i′-hdu-kśaŋ-taŋ-haŋ, *adv. from all sides around.*

i′-hdu-kśaŋ-yaŋ, *adv. round about.*

i-hdu′-ku-ya, *v. reflex. to humble one's self.* See ihduhukuya.

i-hdu′-ķe-ġa, *v. reflex. to scratch one's self. T.* igluķeġa.

i-hdu′-mde-za, *v. reflex. to make one's self see* or *think clearly. T.*, iglubleza.

i-hdu′-noŋ-pa, *v. reflex.* of yunoŋpa; *to make two of one's self; to have two pursuits on hand at the same time*—mihdunoŋpa.

i-hdu′-o-ni-ḥaŋ, *v. reflex.* of yuonihaŋ; *to honor one's self*—mihduonihaŋ.

i-hdu′-o-ta, *v. reflex.* of yuota; *to multiply one's self; to do many things at the same time*—mihduota.

i-hdu′-o-taŋ-iŋ, *v. reflex* of yuotaŋiŋ; *to manifest one's self*—mihduotaŋiŋ.

i-hdu′-o-wo-taŋ-na, *v. reflex.* of yuowotaŋna; *to straighten one's self up, stand straight; to make one's self upright* or *righteous*—mihduowotaŋna.

i-hdu′-psi-ća, *v. reflex.* of yupsića; *to fish for one's own use; to prance* or *jump about,* as a frisky horse—mihdupsića.

i-hdus′, *cont.* of ihduza. Içihdus is also used. *T.*, iglus.

i-hdu′-so-ta, *v. reflex.* of yusota; *to use one's self up; to use up one's own*—mihdusota.

i-hdu′-su-ta, *v. reflex.* of yusuta; *to make one's self firm, establish one's self*—mihdusuta.

i-hdu′-ś'a-ka, *v. reflex.* of yuś'aka; *to be overburdened with one's self; to be pregnant*—ihdumaś'aka, ihduniś'aka.

i-hdu′-śa-pa, *v. reflex.* of yuśapa; *to blacken* or *defile one's self*—mihduśapa.

i-hdu′-śdo-ka, *v. reflex.* of yuśdoka; *to put off one's own, divest one's self of,* as one's garments; *to empty one's self* or *put off one's self*, as it is said of Christ, in Phil. ii. 7—mihduśdoka.

i-h d u'-ś i-ć a, *v. reflex.* of yuśića; *to make one's self bad, get one's self into difficulty*—mihduśića.

i-h d u'-ś i-ḣ t i ŋ, *v. reflex.* of yuśiḣtiŋ; *to enfeeble one's self, to injure one's self*, in any way.

i-h d u'-ś k a, *v. reflex.* of yuśka; *to untie* or *loose one's self*—mihduśka.

i-h d u'-ś p a; *v. reflex.* of yuśpa; *to break one's self away, deliver one's self*, as from a trap—mihduśpa.

i-h d u'-ś t a ŋ, *v. reflex.* of yuśtaŋ; *to finish* or *complete* the things *pertaining to one's self*—mihduśtaŋ, nihduśtaŋ, uŋkihduśtaŋpi.

i-h d u'-t a, *v pos.* of iyuta *and* yuta; *to measure one's self, measure* or *try one's own; to eat two things of one's own, one with the other*—iwahduta.

i-h d u'-t a-k u-n i-ś n i, *v. reflex.* of yutakuniśni; *to destroy one's self*—mihdutakuniśni.

i-h d u'-t a ŋ, *v. reflex.* of yutaŋ; *to paint one's self; to glorify one's self, praise one's self*—mihdutaŋ. *T.*, iglataŋ; *i. q.* ihdataŋ.

i-h d u'-t a ŋ-i ŋ, *v. reflex.* of yutaŋiŋ; *to manifest one's self*—mihdutaŋiŋ.

i-h d u'-t a ŋ-k a, *v. reflex.* of yutaŋka; *to make one's self great*—mihdutaŋka.

i-h d u'-t' a ŋ-t' a ŋ, *v. reflex.* of yut'aŋ; *to touch*, as with one's dirty hands; *touch often.*

i-h d u'-t e-ć a, *v. reflex.* of yuteća; *to make one's self new*—mihduteća.

i-h d u'-t o-k a ŋ, *v. reflex.* of yutokaŋ; *to remove one's self to another place*—mihdutokaŋ.

i-h d u'-t o-k e-ć a, *v. reflex.* of yutokeća; *to make one's self different*—mihdutokeća.

i-h d u'-w a-k a-ś o-t e-ś n i, *v. reflex. to purify one's self. T.*, igluska; *i. q.* ihduska.

i-h d u'-w a-ś' a-k a, *v. reflex.* of yuwaś'aka; *to strengthen one's self*—mihduwaś'aka.

i-h d u'-w a-ś t e, *v. reflex.* of yuwaśte; *to make one's self good, make reparation for* a wrong done.

i-h d u'-w i, *v. reflex.* of yuwi; *to wrap* or *tie on one's own*, as one's leggings—mihduwi.

i-h d u'-w i-y e-y a, *v. reflex.* of yuwiyeya; *to make one's self ready*—mihduwiyeya, uŋkihduwiyeyapi; ihduwiyeya maŋka, *I have made myself ready.*

i-h d u'-z a, *v. reflex.* of yuza; *to dress up, put on a dress, paint one's self up*—mihduza: Dakota ihduza, *to dress in Dakota style;* Waśićuŋ ihduza, *to dress like a Frenchman.*

i'-h d u-z e-z e, *v. reflex. to hold up one's self by; to cling to*—imihduzeze, uŋkihduzezepi: Nićiŋkśi ihduzeze uŋyakoŋpi, *we are clinging to thy Son.*

i'-h d u-z e-z e-y a, *adv. clinging to.*

i-hdu'-zi-ća, *v. reflex.* of yuzića; *to stretch one's self*—mihduzića.

i-hdu'-źa-źa, *v. reflex.* of yuźaźa; *to wash one's self*—mihduźaźa. *T.*, igluźaźa.

i-hdu'-źu-źu, *v. reflex.* of yuźuźu; *to take to pieces one's own*, as one's own bundle—mihduźuźu.

i-he'-ća, *n. something laid down to shoot at;* iheća kute, *to shoot arrows at a mark.* See owiŋheća. *T.*, oweheća, used only of arrows: one arrow is thrown first, and that becomes the *mark*, or oweheća, for the others to throw at.—W. J. C.

i'-he-ći-ya, *adv. in that way from.*

i'-he-ći-ya-taŋ, *adv. in that direction from.*

i'-he-ći-ya-taŋ-haŋ, *adv. on that side of.*

i-he-ći'-yo-taŋ, *adv. in that direction from.*

i'-he-haŋ-haŋ-yaŋ, *adv. red.* of ihehaŋyaŋ.

i'-he-haŋ-yaŋ, *adv. so far from.*

i-he'-ktam, *prep. behind, after one*—mihektam, nihektam; wićihektam, *behind them.*

i-he'-ktam-ya, *adv. behind.*

i-he'-kta-pa, *adv. behind:* mihektapa, *behind me.*

i-he'-kta-pa-ta, *adv. at the back, behind.*

i-he'-kta-pa-taŋ-haŋ, *adv. from behind.*

i-he'-pi, *n. head-oil, ointment for the hair. T.*, islaye.

i-he'-pi-o-pi-ye, *n. an oil-sack.*

i-he'-ya, *v. to go* or *pass through*, as iyoopta iheya, *to pass* or *discharge from the bowels*—ihewaya, iheyaya, iheuŋyaŋpi; *to shoot, hit*, as a mark; *to assemble, come together*, as, kata iheya; witaya iheya, waŋyag iheya. In these cases it is a collective plural: iheuŋyaŋpi is also used.

i-hi'-haŋ-na or i-hiŋ'-haŋ-na, *n. T. the day following, the next morning:* aŋpetu wakaŋ ihihaŋna, *the day after the Sabbath—Monday.* See ihaŋḣaŋna.

i'-hi-ya-ye, *n. semen; i. q.* oŋ hokšiyoḳopa kaǧapi.

i-hmuŋ'-ke, *n. a snare, a trap; poison* to trap with.

i-hna'-hna-yaŋ, *v. red.* of ihnayaŋ; *to sport with, deceive by*—iwahnahnayaŋ.

i-hna'-škiŋ-yaŋ, *v. n. to be possessed with, demonized; to be crazy for* or *by reason of*—imahnaškiŋyaŋ.

i-hna'-yaŋ, *v. a. to deceive with* or *for*—iwahnayaŋ, iyahnayaŋ, uŋkihnayaŋpi.

i-hni', *v. a. to hunt, seek for; to hunt* or *follow after*, as deer and such like game—iwahni, iyahni, uŋkihnipi. *T.*, igni. See wotihni.

i-hni'-hda, *v. a. to go for, take a journey for, procure; to have business*—iwahnihda, uŋkihnihdapi. *T.*, igniya

i-hnu', *v. a. to blame with, charge upon; to grumble, murmur about*—

iwahnu, uŋkihnupi; wikićihnupi, *they recriminate each other. T.*, ahoya.

i-h n u'-h a ŋ, *adv.* Used always with "kiŋ" *or* "ćiŋ," "kiŋhaŋ" *or* "ćiŋhaŋ" after it, and signifying *strong prohibition; beware:* ihnuhaŋ hećanoŋ kiŋ do, *see thou do it not. T.*, uŋgna *and* uŋgnahaŋ.

i-h n u'-h a ŋ-n a, *adv. suddenly, immediately. T.*, uŋgnahaŋla.

i-h o', *v.* iho wo, iho po, always *imp.; come on, come; be it so; see there.*

i-h o'-e-ć a, *adv. indeed. T.*, ihoećaś.

i-h o m'-e-ć a, *adv. now indeed.* This word is frequently used to introduce threatening expressions.

i-h o'-n i-ć a-t a, *n. T. a stone hammer, a pestle.*—T. L. R. See ihunićata.

i-h u'. This is an obscene by-word relating to copulation. See hu. It is much used by the Indians as an interjection denoting impatience—iwahu: oŋze ihu, *to commit sodomy;* iwićahu, *sodomy. T., to "hu" in the mouth.* See iaś'a.

i-h u'-d a ŋ, *intj.* Same as ihu.

i-h u'-k u-k u-y a, *adv. red.* of ihukuya.

i-h u'-k u n, *adv. under, beneath:* ihukun iyeya, *to put underneath.*

i-h u'-k u-y a, *adv. under, beneath* anything, *down below; inferior* in dignity or office—mihukuya, nihukuya.

i-h u'-n i, *v.* See ihuŋni.

i-h u'-n i-ć a-t a, *n. T. a stone to pound meat* or *cherries with.*

i-h u ŋ'-n i, *v. n. to land, reach the shore; to get through,* as a wood, *get across,* as a prairie; *to finish, to come to the end of*—iwahuŋni, iyahuŋni, uŋkihuŋnipi.

i-h u ŋ'-n i-k i-y a, *v. a. to go through with, finish, complete,* as the reading of a book—ihuŋniwakiya.

i-h u ŋ'-n i-y a, *v. a. to go through with, finish*—ihuŋniwaya, ihuŋniuŋyaŋpi.

i-h u ŋ'-n i-y a ŋ, *adv. clear through, entirely.*

i-h u'-p a, *n. the bail* or *handle* of anything; *the stem, shaft, thill,* etc.

i-h u'-p a-k i-ć i-t o ŋ, *v. a. to put in a handle,* etc., *for* one—ihupawećitoŋ.

i-h u'-p a-k i-t o ŋ, *v. pos. to bail* or *handle one's own*—ihupawetoŋ.

i-h u'-p a-t o ŋ, *v. to have a handle, be handled; to put a handle* or *bail to* anything—ihupawatoŋ.

i-h u'-w i-ć a-t a, *n. a stone for pounding meat.* A stick is fastened in a crease made round the middle, which serves for a handle. *T.*, ihunićata.

i-ḣ a', *v.* (i *and* ḣa) *to laugh; laugh at, make fun of*—iwaḣa, iyaḣa, uŋkiḣapi; imayaḣa, *thou laughest at me.*

i'-ḣ a d, *or* i'-ḣ a n, *adv. jestingly, laughingly.*

i-ḣ a'-h a, *n. the manyplies* or *omasum,* one of the stomachs of an animal. *T.*, tiḣaha. See tiḣaha.

i-ḣa′-ḣa, *v. red.* of iḣa; *to laugh at, make fun of, ridicule*—iwaḣaḣa. *T.*, iyoḣaḣa.

i′-ḣa-ḣa, *v. n.* *to bubble* and *curl* or *laugh along*, as rapid water.

i′-ḣa-ḣa, *n.* *the noise of water-falls* or *rapids.*

i-ḣa′-ḣa-ke, *n.* *one who is always jesting, a fool.*

i-ḣa′-ḣa-ya, *v. a.* *to cause to jest* or *laugh at*—iḣaḣawaya.

i-ḣa′-ḣa-ya, *adv.* *laughingly, jestingly.*

i-ḣa′-ke, *v.* *to laugh, jest*—iwaḣake.

i-ḣa′-ki-ya, *v. a.* *to cause to laugh*—iḣawakiya.

i′-ḣan, *adv.* *jestingly, in fun:* iḣan epeća, *I said it in fun.*

i-ḣaŋ′, *v. n.* of ḣaŋ; *to do, work, do in reference to:* tak iḣaŋ yahi he, *what didst thou come to do?*—iwaḣaŋ.

i-ḣ'aŋ′, *v. n.* *to graze, eat grass,* as an ox: peźi iḣ'aŋ, *to eat off the grass.* See wiḣ'aŋ.

i-ḣ'aŋ′-ki-ya, *v. a.* *to cause to feed* or *graze*—iḣ'aŋwakiya.

i′-ḣaŋ-yaŋ, *adv.* *temporarily.*

i-ḣa′-ṭa, *v.* *to laugh hard;* lit., *to die laughing.*

i-ḣa′-ṭa-ṭa, *v. n.* *to laugh immoderately*—iḣamaṭaṭa.

i-ḣa′-ya, *v. a.* *to cause to laugh, be the occasion of laughter*—iḣawaya, iḣamayaya.

i-ḣdaḣ′-ye-će-śni, *v. n.* *to stay, remain in a place.* *T.*, oyuḣlaġaŋ śni. See ḣdaḣyećeśni.

i′-ḣdi, *n.* *a sore mouth*—imaḣdi.

i-ḣdi′, *v. n.* *to have a sore* or *breaking out in consequence of*—imaḣdi, iniḣdi.

i-ḣ'e′, *n.* *gravel; a stony place.*

i-ḣe′-ya-ta, *adj.* of ḣeyata; *back from, behind*—miḣeyata: tipi kiŋ iḣeyata, *back of the house.* Perhaps this should be rather regarded as a preposition or postposition, formed of two prepositions and a noun, and taking the pronouns, as other prepositions. The two adverbial forms that follow take the pronouns also; as, miḣeyataŋhaŋ, *from behind me.*

i-ḣe′-ya-taŋ-haŋ, *adv.* *from behind.*

i-ḣe′-ya-ta-tàŋ-haŋ, *adv.* *from behind.*

i-ḣiŋ′-kpa, *n.* *the hill behind.* See ḣiŋkpa.

i-ḣiŋ′-kpa-ta, *adv.* *at the hill behind, back from.*

i-ḣiŋ′-kpa-taŋ-ḥaŋ, *adv.* *back from, towards the hill from.*

i-ḣiŋ′-tpa, *n.* Same as iḣiŋkpa.

i-ḣiŋ′-tpa-ta, *adv.* Same as iḣiŋkpata.

i-ḣiŋ′-tpa-taŋ-haŋ, *adv.* Same as iḣiŋkpataŋhaŋ.

i′-ḣna-haŋ, *v. n.* *to have the under lip hanging down*—imaḣnahaŋ. See ḣnahaŋ.

i-ḣni′-yaŋ-yaŋ, *v. n.* *to be troubled with, excited about*—imaḣniyaŋyaŋ: waśiŋ iḣniyaŋyaŋ, *to be distressed by eating fat.*

I′-ḣo-ka, *n.* *T.* *the name of a clan* or *band of Teetons.*

i-ḣ p a'-y a, *v. n.* *to fall, fall down; to become sick*—iwaḣpamda, iyaḣpada, uŋkiḣpayapi.

i-ḣ p e'-y a, *v. a.* *to throw down, throw away; to leave, forsake*—iḣpewaya, iḣpeuŋyaŋpi. See eḣpeya.

i-ḣ t a'-h e-p i, *n.* *Ih.* and *T.* *before night; before the day is out.*

i'-ḣ t a-y e-t u, *n.* *the next evening, the evening following* the time mentioned.

i-ḣ t i ŋ', *n.* *T.*, zeze. See iḣtiŋka.

i-ḣ t i ŋ'-k a, *n.* *anything that hangs down* or *dangles*, as ear-bobs, etc.

i-ḣ w i ŋ' *or* i-ḣ u ŋ'-w i ŋ, *v. n.* *to smell of, stink.* *T.*, iḣwiŋmna.

i-ḣ w i ŋ' *or* i-ḣ ú ŋ'-w i ŋ, *n.* *a bad smell, stink.*

i-i'-ć i-ḣ a-ḣ a, *v. reflex.* *to make one's self a laughing stock.*

i-i'-ć i-g n i, *v.* *T.* *to hunt for one's self: i. q.* ićihni.

i'-i-ç i-k ć u, *n* of iću; *one who takes without leave.* Perhaps this is for iye içikću.

i'-i-k i-y a, *v.* *T.* *to ask back what one has given.*

i'-i-k p u-t a-k a, *v. pos.* *to kiss one's own,* as one's relative—iiwakputaka.

i-i ŋ'-k p a-t a, *adv.* *at the point* of anything.

i-i ŋ'-t p a-t a, *adv.* Same as iiŋkpata.

i'-i-p u-t a-k a, *v.* *to touch mouths, to kiss*—iiwaputaka.

i'-i-t k o-p a-t a ŋ-h a ŋ, *adv.* See iyeitkopataŋhaŋ.

i'-i-t p u-t a-k a, *v.* *to kiss one's own.* Same as iikputaka.

i'-i-y u-w i, *n.* *a bridle:* śuŋg iiyuwi, *a halter* or *bridle for a horse.* *T.*, iteha *and* ipaḣte.

i-k a'-ġ i, *v.* See ićaġi—imakaġi.

i'-k a-h a n, *adv.* *so far from.*

i'-k a-h a ŋ-y a n, *adv.* *so far from.*

i'-k a-k i, *adv.* *on that side of.*

i'-k a-k i-y a, *adv.* *on that side of.*

i'-k a-k i-y a-t a ŋ-h a ŋ, *adv.* *in that way from, on that side.*

i-k a-k i'-y o-t a ŋ, *adv.* *in that direction from.*

i-k a ŋ', *n.* *a cord, a string, a rope; the bail* of anything.

i-k a ŋ'-k i-ć i-t o ŋ, *v. a.* *to put* or *tie a string* or *strap on for* one to carry by—ikaŋwećitoŋ.

i-k a ŋ'-k i-t o ŋ, *v. pos.* of ikaŋtoŋ; *to tie a string on one's own* pack, to carry it by—ikaŋwetoŋ.

i-k a ŋ'-t o ŋ, *v. a.* *to put a strap* or *string on* a bag, etc., to carry it by—ikaŋwatoŋ, ikaŋuŋtoŋpi.

i-k a ŋ'-y a ŋ, *v. a.* *to have for a handle* or *string*—ikaŋwaya, ikaŋuŋyaŋpi.

i-k a ŋ'-y e, *adv.* *towards the center,* as *towards* the fire, *towards* a river or lake, *down towards.*

i-k a ŋ'-y e-l a, *adv.* *T., near to.*

i-k a ŋ'-y e-t a *and* i-k a ŋ'-y e-t a ŋ, *adv.* or *n.* *in front of:* mikaŋyeta, *in front of me.*

i-k a ŋ'-y e-t a ŋ-h a ŋ, *adv.* *on the river* or *lake side of* an object, *in front of:* mikaŋyetaŋhaŋ, *in front of me.*

i′-ka-pa, *v. a.* (i *and* kapa) *to open the mouth on, scold*—iwakapa, imakapa. See ikapta.

i-ka′-pa, *v.* of kapa; *to pass by, go beyond, exceed*—ikawapa.

i′-ka-pa-s'a, *n.* *one who scolds, a scold.* *T.*, ikapaka *and* ikapakala.

i-ka′-pa-ya, *adv.* *more than, surpassing.*

i-ka′-pe-ya, *adv.* *beyond, more than.*

i′-ka-pta, *v.* (i *and* kapta) *to threaten, scold.* See ićapta, which is the better form.

i′-ka′-pta, *adv.* *through:* ikapta hiŋḣpaya, *to fall through.* See ićapta, the better form.

i′-ka-skam, *cont.* of ikaskapa.

i′-ka-skam-ya, *adv.* *smiting on the mouth.*

i′-ka-ska-pa, *v. a.* *to slap on the mouth*—iwakaskapa.

i-kća′-pta, *v. pos.* of ićapta; *to be angry and talk badly*—mikćapta.

i-kće′, *adj.* *common, wild, in a state of nature:* ikće haŋpa, or haŋpikćeka, *common moccasins*, that is, not ornamented; śuŋkikćeka, *a dog*, not a horse; Ikćewićaśta, *Indians*, not white men.

i-kće′, *adv.* *for nothing, freely, in the common way:* ikće maḳu, *he gave it to me for nothing.*

i-kće′-ka, *adj.* *common:* śuŋkikćeka, *a dog, a common dog*, not a horse, as they frequently call horses and oxen "śuŋka."

i-kće′-kće, *adv.* *red.* of ikće.

i-kće′-kće-ya, *adv.* *red.* of ikćeya.

i-kće′-wi-ća-śta, *n.* *common men, wild men, Indians*, not white men. *T.* and *Ih.*, ikćewićaśa.

i-kće′-ya, *adv.* *in a common manner, commonly, ordinarily, freely, wildly, naturally.*

i-kće′-ya-ken, *adv.* *ordinarily.*

i-ke′-kto-pa-wiŋ-ġe, *adj.* *the one thousandth.* *T.*, ikoktopawiŋġe.

i-ki′-ća-ġa, *v. n.* of ićaġa; *to become, grow to be*—imakićaġa, uŋkikićaġapi.

i-ki′-ća-zo, *v. a.* of ićazo; *to take credit of* one—iwećazo, iyećazo, uŋkićazopi, imićazo, inićazo.

i-ki′-ći-ća-ġa, *v. n.* of ićaġa; *to grow for* one—imićićaġa, uŋkićićaġapi.

i-ki′-ći-ću, *v.* of iću; *to take* or *get for* one—iwećiću, imićiću.

i-ki′-ći-do-waŋ, *v.* of idowaŋ; *to sing to* one, *to praise* one *for* another—iwećidowaŋ.

i-ki′-ći-haŋ, *v.* of haŋ; *to remain for* one—imićihaŋ, inićihaŋ, uŋkićihaŋpi.

i-ki′-ći-hni, *v.* of ihni; *to hunt* something, as deer, etc., *for* one—iwećihni.

i-ki′-ći-ḣa-ḣa-pi, *v. recipr.* *they laugh at each other.*

i-ki′-ći-ksa-pa, *v.* of iksapa; *to be wise for* one, *instruct* one *in the right way*—iwećiksapa.

i-ki′-ći-tu-ka, *v.* of ituka; *to beg of* one *for* another—iwećituka, imićituka. *T.*, wotikiya.

i-ki'-ći-uŋ, *v.* of iuŋ; *to rub on for*—iwećiuŋ.

i-ki'-ći-wi-śtaŋ, *v.* of yuśtaŋ; *to treat with kindness*, as a sick person, *do little things for* one—iwećiwiśtaŋ. See ikićiyuśtaŋ.

i-ki'-ći-yu-kćaŋ, *v.* of iyukćaŋ; *to judge of* or *form an opinion for* one—iwećiyukćaŋ, imićiyukćaŋ, uŋkićiyukćaŋpi, ićićiyukćaŋ.

i-ki'-ći-yu-śtaŋ, *v.* of iyuśtaŋ, *to take care of*, as of a sick person—iwećiyuśtaŋ.

i-ki'-ćo, *v. a.* *to invite to*, as to eat corn or meat—iwećo, iyećo, imićo: takudaŋ iwićawećo śni, *I have nothing to invite them to.*

i-ki'-hni, *v. pos.* *to hunt one's own.*

i-ki'-ḣa, *v. pos.* of iḣa; *to laugh at one's own*—iwakiḣa.

i-ki'-ḣa-ḣa, *v.* *red.* of ikiḣa; *to make fun of one's own*—iwakiḣaḣa.

i-ki'-kću, *v. pos.* of iću; *to take one's own; to take back* what one has given—iwekću, iyekću, uŋkikćupi.

i-ki'-ki-ye-daŋ, *adv.* *red.* of ikiyedaŋ.

i-ki'-ksam, *cont.* of ikiksapa.

i-ki'-ksam-ya, *v. a.* *to cause one to be wise in reference to his own*—ikiksamwaya; ikiksamiçiya, *to make one's self wise for one's self.*

i-ki'-ksam-ya, *adv.* *wisely, cautiously.*

i-ki'-ksa-pa, *v. n.* *to be wise for one's own; to consult*—iwakiksapa.

i-ki'-ni-ća, *v.* of akinića; *to dispute*, as about the division of anything—uŋkikinićapi.

i-ki'-nin, *cont.* of ikinića: ikinin ia, *to talk about in a displeasing way, to dispute about.*

i-ki'-paŋ, *v. a.* of kipaŋ; *to call to* one *for* something—iwakipaŋ.

i-ki'-pa-smi, *v. a.* *to provoke to anger*—iwakipasmi. *T.*, ćaŋzeya.

i-ki'-pa-źiŋ, *v. a.* of kipaźiŋ; *to quarrel with* one *for* or *on account of* anything—iwakipaźiŋ.

i-ki'-tu-ka, *v. n.* *to delight in* anything—imatuka, inićituka. *T.*, iyokipi.

i-ki'-uŋ, *v. pos.* of iuŋ; *to rub on one's self*—iwakiuŋ, iyakiuŋ, uŋkikiuŋpi.

i-ki'-ya, *v.* See ićiya.

i'-ki-ya-daŋ, *adv.* *near to, near at hand*—mikiyadaŋ, nikiyadaŋ, wićikiyadaŋ, ćikiyadaŋ.

i-ki'-yan-ya, *v.* *to have nearly finished*—ikiyanwaya,

i'-ki-ye-daŋ, *adv.* *nigh to*, referring both to time and place. Same as ikiyadaŋ.

i-ki'-yu-wi, *v. a.* *to bridle* or *put a rope in the mouth of* one's horse—iwakimduwi.

i-ko'-pa, *v. a.* *to be afraid of, to fear*, as some event—ikowapa, ikoyapa, ikouŋpapi.

i-ko'-pe-hda, *v. n.* *to be in a state of fear on account of*—ikopewahda.

i-ko'-pe-ki-ya, *v. a.* *to cause to be afraid of* or *for*—ikopewakiya.

i-ko'-yag, *cont.* of ikoyaka; ikoyag iyeya.

i-ko′-yag-ya, *v. a.* *to fasten to*, as a horse to a cart, *to join* one thing *to* another; *to clothe, put on*—ikoyagwaya, ikoyaguŋyaŋpi.

i-ko′-yag-ya, *adv.* *fastened to:* ikoyagya haŋ, *standing fastened to.*

i-ko′-yag-ya-ken, *adv.* *fastened to.*

i-ko′-ya-ka, *v. n.* *to adhere to, stick to*—ikomayaka: *to be fastened to*, as a horse to a cart.

i-kpa′-ġaŋ, *v.* *reflex.* of paġaŋ; *to spare one's self, yield up one's self*—mikpaġaŋ.

i-kpa′-ġe, *n.* *the notch in the end of an arrow.*

i-kpa′-hu-hu-za, *v. reflex. pos.* of pahuhuza.

i-kpa′-ḣdo-ka, *v.* *reflex.* of paḣdoka; *to pierce through, make a hole for one's self*, as the muskrat—mikpaḣdoka.

i-kpa′-ḣpa, *v.* *reflex.* of paḣpa; *to throw one's self off*, as from a horse—mikpaḣpa.

i-kpa′-ḣpe-ḣiŋ-ća, *n.* *one who throws away everything which he has, a squanderer, a spendthrift*—mikpaḣpeḣiŋća. *T.*, igluwaḣpanićala.

i-kpa′-kpi, *v. pos.* *to hatch out one's own.*

i-kpa′-ta-ka, *v. pos.* *T.* *to lean on one's own; to brace one's own.* See ipataka.

i-kpa′-ptaŋ, *v.* *reflex.* *to turn one's self over, roll over*—mikpaptaŋ, uŋkikpaptaŋpi. See ipaptaŋ.

i-kpa′-taŋ, *v.* *reflex.* of pataŋ; *to be careful of one's self*—mikpataŋ. *T.*, *to push along, as a boat with a pole; to steer a boat.*

i-kpa′-taŋ-yaŋ, *adv.* *taking care of one's self, carefully.*

i-kpa′-zo, *v. pos.* *to show one's self*—mikpazo.

i-kpi′, *n.* *the belly, abdomen.* Sometimes it may mean the *thorax* also; but that is more properly called "maku." See itpi.

i-kpi′-hnag, *cont.* of ikpihnaka: ikpihnag iyewaya.

i-kpi′-hnag-ya, *adv.* *placed in around the body.*

i-kpi′-hna-ka, *v. a.* *to place in the belly;* hokśin ikpihnaka, *to be pregnant*—ikpiwahnaka; *to place in* or *put around the body*, as in a blanket when tied around one. See itpihnaka.

i-kpi′-pa-taŋ-haŋ, *adv.* *in around the body.*

i-kpi′-ska-ya-waŋ-ka, *v.* *to lie with the belly turned up*, as a dog does.

i-kpi′-źu, *v. a.* (ikpi *and* oźu) *to put in around the body*—ikpiwaźu, ikpiuŋźupi. *T.*, ikpioźu.

i-kpu′-kpa, *adv.* *mixed up*, as people of different nations dwelling together, or as different kinds of corn growing together in the same field. *T.*, ikpukpeya.

i-ksam′, *cont.* of iksapa.

i′-ksam-ya, *v. a.* of iksapa; *to make* anything, *to do* anything, *i. q.* kićaŋyaŋ—iksamwaya.

i-ksam′-ya, *v. a.* of ksapa; *to*

make wise for or *concerning*—iksamwaya.

i-ksam′-ya, *adv.* *wisely.*

i-ksa′-pa, *v. n.* *to be wise about* anything—iwaksapa, iyaksapa, uŋkiksapapi.

i′-ksa-pa, *v. n.* *to be much engaged about; to be unfortunate, not to obtain*—imaksapa, iniksapa, uŋkiksapapi: ituḣ iksapa, *he has been working for naught.*

i-ksu′, *n.* *the beak* or *bill* of a bird; *i. q.* pasu.

i-ksu′-ya, *v. n.* *to see signs of an enemy; to be frightened by signs*—iwaksuya, uŋkiksuyapi. *T.*, wakiksuya—1st pers. sing., wamiksuya.

i-kśin′-ki-ya, *v. a.* *to make faces at*—ikśinwakiya, ikśinmakiya. *T.*, iteyukśilkiya.

i-kta′-he-la, *adv,* *T.* *moderately; carefully.*

i-kte′, *v.* of kte; *to kill with* anything—iwakte.

i-kte′-ka, *n.* *something to kill with,* as a gun: ikteka manića, *I have nothing to kill with.*

i-kto′-mi, *n.* *T.* *a spider; i. q.* uŋktomi.

i-ku′, *n.* *the chin; the lower jaw* of animals.

i-ku′-ka, *v. n.* *to be decayed by reason of, worn out by; to be boiled to pieces together with.*

i-ku′-ke-ya, *adv.* *rotten* or *boiled to pieces with:* ikukeya śpaŋ, *it is cooked all to pieces* *T*, kukeya.

i′-ku-saŋ, *n.* *a small kind of mink with a light-colored lower jaw.*

i′-ku-saŋ-na, *n.* Same as íkusaŋ.

i-ku′-śe-ya, *adv.* *in the way of.*

i-ku′-te, *n.* *ammunition; something to shoot with, a gun.* Ićute is the better form.

i-ku′-tku-te-ka, *v. n.* *to make trial, to endeavor beforehand to know how one can succeed,* for instance, in asking for anything—iwakutkuteka.

i-la′-za-ta, *adv.* or *n.* *T.* *at the side of;* milazata, *by my side.*

i-la′-za-taŋ, *and* i-la′-za-taŋ-haŋ, *adv.* *T.* *from the side of.*

i-le′-ġa, *v.* *T.* *to shine: i. q.* iyeġa.

i-leḣ′-le-ġa, *v.* *red.* of ileġa.

i-leḣ′-ya, *adv.* *T.* *in a shining manner.*

i-ma′-ġa-ġa, *v. n.* of maġaġa; *to be amused with, cheered by*—imamaġaġa, inimaġaġa.

i-ma′-ġa-ġa-ya, *v. a.* *to amuse with, enliven by, cheer* one—imaġaġawaya.

i′-ma-h̲en, *adv.* *within.*

i′-ma-h̄en-taŋ-haŋ, *adv.* *from within.*

i′-ma-hen-tu, *adv.* *within.*

i′-ma-hen-tu-ya, *adv.* *inwards, within.*

i′-ma-hen-tu-ya-ken, *adv.* *within, in the inside of.*

i′-ma-hen-wa-pa, *adv.* *towards the inside, inwards.*

i-ma'-ni, *v. a.* of mani; *to walk to* or *for* a thing—imawani, imauŋnipi.

i-mda'-mde, *v.* 1st pers. sing. of iyaya; *I went.*

i'-mna, *v. n.* *to be satisfied, have sufficient of*—imamna, inimna, iuŋmnaŋpi.

i'-mna-haŋ, *adv.* *satisfied, to satisfaction, enough, sufficiently:* imnahaŋ uŋtapi, *we have eaten sufficiently.*

i'-mna-haŋ-yaŋ, *adv.* *sufficiently.*

i'-mna-haŋ-yaŋ-ken, *adv.* *very much, a great deal, sufficiently*—imnahaŋyaŋken ećoŋ, *he has done enough.*

i'-mna-yaŋ, *v. a.* *to fill, satisfy*—imnawaya.

i'-mna-yaŋ, *adv.* *filled, satisfied.*

i-mna'-yaŋ, *v. a.* of mnayaŋ; *to gather together by means of*—imnawaya.

i-mni'-ći-ya, *v. n.* *to make an assembly to*—imnimićiya, imninićiya; *they assemble to* or *for some purpose.*

i'-mni-śtaŋ, *n.* *water running from the mouth:* imniśtaŋ au, *to drivel, slaver*—imniśtaŋ amau.

i-mni'-źa, *n.* *a rock, rocks.* *T.*, iŋyaŋȟe. See ȟeimniźa.

I-mni'-źa-ska, *n.* *The city of Saint Paul, Minn.:* so called from the white rocks on which the town is built.

I-mni'-źa-ska-daŋ, *n.* (imniźa *and* skadaŋ) the Dakota name for *Saint Paul; little-white-rock.*

iŋ, *and* iŋ'-ske, *T.* *intj.*, *i. q.* noŋ *or* noŋske, expressing *hesitancy* or *doubt.*

i-na', *n.* *mother, my mother.* It is used only in this form. For the second and third persons see "huŋ."

i-na', *or* i-naȟ', *intj.* *strange! surprising!* *T.*, hina *and* hinu.

i'-na-gna, *v.* *T.* *to move the lips*, as in reading to one's self.

i'-na-gna-gna, *v. red.* of inagna.

i-na'-ġu-ġe-ća, *adj.* *spongy* or *open*, like the soft part of bones. Said when the grease is all *boiled up* with the water or soup.

i-na'-ha-ya *and* i-na'-ha-ha-ya, *adv.* *T.* *loosely*, as wood corded badly.

i'-na-haŋ, *intj.* of assent; *truly! certainly! to be sure!* *T.*, ćiŋto.

i-na'-hda-ka, *v. n.* *to stand out*, as the ribs of a poor animal, *to be lean, very poor; to spread out*, as a moccasin. *T.*, naglaglake se.

i-na'-hi-na-hi-na, *intj.* of surprise; *indeed!* *T.*, hinuhinuhinu.

i-naȟ', *intj.* See inahinahina.

i-na'-ȟbe, *v.* See inaȟma.

i-na'-ȟbe-ki-ya, *v. a.* *to hide from, conceal from* one—inaȟbewakiya. *T.*, inaȟmekiya.

i-na.-ȟbe-ki-ya, *adv.* *in a concealed manner, secretly.*

i-na'-ȟbe-ya, *adv.* *secretly, slily, covertly.*

i-na'-ȟbe-ya-haŋ, *adv.* *in secret, secretly.*

i-na'-ȟći, *v. a.* *to pierce and have*

the hold break out of anything; *to have the hold break out*, as of a stirrup—inawaḣći.

i-na'-ḣćo, *v.* See naḣćo.

i-na'-ḣdo-ka, *v. a. to wear a hole with the foot by means of* something, as in one's moccasins or socks: haŋpa iŋyaŋ inawaḣdoka, *I have worn a hole in my moccasins on a stone*—inawaḣdoka.

i-na'-ḣma, *v. a. to hide, keep secret, conceal*—inawaḣbe, inauŋḣmaŋpi.

i'-na-ḣma, *v. a. to seduce, to commit fornication* or *adultery with* one—ínawaḣbe. See wiinaḣma.

i'-na-ḣmaŋ-pi, *n. seduction.*

i-na'-ḣni, *v. n. to be in haste, make haste, hurry*—inawaḣni, inauŋḣnipi.

i-na'-ḣni-ki-ya, *v. a. to cause to make haste, to hasten* one—inaḣniwakiya.

i-na'-ḣni-pi, *n. a hastening, haste, hurry.*

i-na'-ḣni-ya, *v. a. to hasten* one, *make hurry*—inaḣniwaya.

i-na'-ḣni-yaŋ, *adv. in haste, hastily; on an errand:* inaḣniyaŋ wahi, *I have come on an errand.*

i-na'-ḣpe, *n.* of naḣpa; *that which is stepped on and sets off a trap, the pan* of a trap.

i-na'-ḣpe-daŋ, *n. dim* of inaḣpe.

i-na'-keḣ-ya, *v. T. to make a scraping noise*, as a wagon brake: huinakeḣye, *a wagon brake.*

i'-na-ki-ḣbe, *v.* See inakiḣma.

i'-na-ki-ḣma, *v. pos.* of inaḣma; *to entice away one's own*, as a woman whom one has formerly had for a wife; tawiću inakiḣbe, *he has stolen away his old wife*—inawakiḣma.

i-na'-kim-ya, *adv.* of inamya; *taking refuge in, fleeing to for shelter.* or *refuge, trusting in:* Nićiŋkśi inakimya ćeuŋnićiyapi, *we pray to Thee, trusting in thy Son.*

i-na'-ki-pa, *v. pos.* of inapa: *to take refuge in one's own; to trust in* something that sustains some relation to one—inawakipa.

i-na'-ki-taŋ, *v. pos.* of inataŋ; *to go off and leave one's own in danger*—inawakitaŋ, inauŋkitaŋpi.

i-na'-ki-wi-zi, *v. pos.* of inawizi; *to be envious of one's own* relations; *to be jealous of one's own*—inawakiwizi.

i-na'-ku-ka, *v.* of nakuka; *to crush* or *destroy with the foot*—inawakuka.

i-na'-ķes-ya, *adv. T. near by, along side of.*

i-nam', *cont.* of inapa.

i'-na-ma, *intj. surprising! T.*, huŋhuŋhe.

i-na'-mni, *adv. T. beyond, over*, as over the hill from.

i-nam'-ya, *adv. taking refuge in, sheltered by:* tipi inamya wauŋ, *I am taking refuge in a house.*

i-naŋ'-pa, *v.* See inapa.

i-na'-pa, *v. a. to come out, come up out of*, as in diving; *to appear* or *come out on the other side; to get through, live through*, as through a winter; *to take shelter* or *refuge in*, from a storm or from any evil; *to trust in*—inawapa, inauŋpapi; inaćipa, *I take refuge in thee.*

i-na'-pćiŋ-waŋg-waŋ-ka, *adj. red.* of inapćiŋwaŋka; *every ninth* one.

i-na'-pćiŋ-waŋ-ka, *adj. the ninth. T.*, inapćiŋyuŋka.

i-na'-pe-ya, *v. a. to cause to come out of, cause to appear on the other side; to shoot through; to cause to live through*, as through a winter; *to cause to trust in*—inapewaya, inapeuŋyaŋpi.

i-na'-pe-ya, *adv. appearing; trusting in.*

i-na'-pi-śkaŋ-yaŋ, *v. to do little things to pass away time, to kill time*—inapiśkaŋwaya.

i-na'-pi-śkaŋ-yaŋ-pi, *n. toys, playthings.*

i-na'-pi-śtaŋ-yaŋ, *v.* Same as inapiśkaŋyaŋ.

i-na'-po-ta, *v. a.* of napota; *to wear out*, as one's moccasins, *by means of* something—inawapota.

i-na'-psa-ka, *v. a.* of napsaka; *to break off*, as a string, *with the foot, by means of* something—inawapsaka.

i-na'-pśa, *v. n. to make a noise*, as one walking with water in his moccasins—inawapśa.

i-na'-pta, *v. a. to wear out* a thing—inawapta: haŋpa inapta iyewaye, *I have worn out my moccasins.* See inapota.

i-na'-pṭe-ća, *v. n. to be prevented by;* used with śni: inapteća śni, *not to be prevented by* anything—inamapteća śni.

i-na'-pte-tu, *adv. prevented by; less.*

i-na'-śdog, *cont.* of inaśdoka; inaśdog iyaya.

i-na'-śdo-ka, *v. to pass on beyond; to wear through, wear out* a thing, as, haŋpa inawaśdoka, *I have worn through my moccasins; to get one's self away, escape*, as from danger—inawaśdoka. *T.*, inaśloka, *to slip off*, as a cover from anything. See inaȟdoka.

i-na'-śdo-ka, *adv. past:* wiyotaŋhaŋ inaśdoka, *a little past noon.*

i-na'-ta-ke, *n.* (i *and* nataka) *a fastener*, i. e., *a bolt, lock, bar; a fence, fort*, etc. See maȟinatake.

i-na'-taŋ, *v. a. to disregard, leave in danger*—inawataŋ, inamayataŋ. John xiii. 38.

i-na'-taŋ, *v. a. to press upon with the foot.* Hence, siinataŋ, *something on which the foot presses, stirrups.*

i-na'-tib-ya, *v. T. to roast hurriedly*, as meat on coals; *to make curl up.*

i-na'-wi-zi, *v. to be jealous; to be envious of*—inawawizi, inauŋwizipi.

i-na'-wi-zi-pi, *n. jealousy, envy.*

i-na'-wi-zi-ya, *v. a. to cause be jealous*—inawiziwaya. See nawizi.

i-na'-ya, *v. a. to call mother, have for mother*—inawaya, inauŋyaŋpi.

i-na'-źiŋ, *v. n.* *to rise up to one's feet, to stand, to go and stand at; to stop, come to a stand*—inawaźiŋ.

i-na'-źiŋ-ki-ya, *v. a.* *to cause to stand, to raise up*—inaźiŋwakiya.

i-ni', *v. n.* *to take a vapor-bath, steam one's self, to take a sweat*—iwani, iyani, uŋkinipi; *to make a kind of* wakaŋ. This consists in washing and steaming one's self four times over hot stones, accompanied with singing, etc. It is done after one has killed an enemy or a royal eagle.

i-ni'-haŋ, *v. n.* *to be scared, frightened, amazed, astonished*—imanihaŋ, ininihaŋ, uŋkinihaŋpi.

i-ni'-haŋ-pi, *n.* *amazement.* See wowinihaŋ.

i-ni'-haŋ-śni, *adv.* *fearlessly, persistently.*

i-ni'-haŋ-ya, *v. a.* *to frighten, scare, amaze, astonish* one—inihaŋwaya, inihaŋuŋyaŋpi.

i-ni'-haŋ-yaŋ, *adv.* *in amazement.*

i-ni'-ka-ġa, *v.* *to make* "ini."

i-ni'-la, *adj.* *T.* *still, silent; i. q.* inina.

i-ni'-na, *adv.* *still, silent:* inina yaŋka, *to be still* or *silent*—inina maŋka.

i-ni'-na-ya, *v. a.* *to cause to be silent, make still*—ininawaya.

i-nin'-ya, *v. a.* *to put to silence*—ininwaya.

i-ni'-pi, *n.* *a steaming, sweating.*

i-ni'-ti, *v.* *to take a vapor-bath, make a little house and sweat in it*—iniwati.

i-ni'-ti, *n.* *a sweat-house*

i-ni'-wo-ke-ya, *n.* *a sweat-house; i. q* initi. See wokeya.

i-ni'-ya, *v. a.* of niya; *to breathe from;* ćuwi iwaniya, *I breathe through a hole in my side.*

i-nma', *intj.* See inama.

i'-nmu, *n* *a cat,* the generic term for an animal of the cat kind. *T.*, igmu; *Ih.*, ikmu.

i-nmu'-hde-śka, *n.* *the spotted wild cat, the genet.*

i-nmu'-ḣo-ta, *n.* *the gray wild cat, catamount, lynx, Felis rufa* or *Felis lynx.*

i-nmu'-śuŋ-ka, *n.* (inmu *and* śuŋka) *the domestic cat.*

i-nṁu'-taŋ-ka, *n.* *the panther, Felis pardus.*

i-nom', *cont.* of inoŋpa.

i nom'-nom, *cont.* of inomnoŋpa.

i-nom'-noŋ-pa, *adj.* *every second* one.

i-noŋ'-pa, *adj.* *the second.*

i'-noŋ-pa, *n.* (i *and* noŋpa) *two mouths:* mazakaŋ ínoŋpa, *a double-barreled gun.*

i-nu', *adv.* *suddenly; i. q.* ihnuhaŋna. *T.*, uŋgnahaŋla.

i'-nuŋ. See ínunka.

i'-nuŋ-ka, *v. n.* *to grow well,* as grass, by reason of rain or any favorable circumstance, *to thrive.* See winuka.

i-nuŋ'-ka, *v.* 2d pers. sing. of iwaŋka; *thou liest down.*

i-n u ŋ' - k a, *v. n.* *to become large in the genital organs*—imanuŋka.

i ŋ, *a terminal* (*Ih.* and *T.*) of some verbs, as in "epiŋ kta," for "epe kta;" "ehiŋ kta," for "ehe kta;" "eyiŋ kta," for "eye kta." Also sometimes used by the Sisitoŋwaŋ.

i ŋ, *v. a.* *to wear around the shoulders*, as a blanket, shawl, or cloak—hiŋmi, hiŋni, uŋkiŋpi.

i ŋ - d e', *n.* *a flame, a blaze.* See ide, the better orthography.

i ŋ - k i' - y a, *v. a.* *to cause to wear*, as a shawl or blanket—iŋwakiya.

i ŋ' - k p a, *n.* *the end* of anything, *the small end; the head* or *source*, as of a stream, etc.

i ŋ' - k p a - t a, *adv.* *at the end, at the head* or *source:* wakpa iŋkpata yeye ćiŋ, *all along at the sources of a stream: above, up stream; i. q.* tatowam.

i ŋ' - k p a - ṭ a ŋ - h a ŋ, *adv.* *from the end.*

i ŋ' - s k a *and* i ŋ' - s k e, *T.* *intj.* of *hesitancy; let me see!* See iŋ.

i ŋ' - s k o - k e - ć a, *adv.* *so large.*

i ŋ ś, *pron.* *he, she, it.* Same as iś.

i ŋ' - t p a, *n.* Same as iŋkpa.

i ŋ' - t p a - t a, *adv.* Same as iŋkpata.

i ŋ' - y a ŋ, *n.* *a stone, stones.* Iŋyaŋtaŋkiŋyaŋyaŋ, *Big-Stone Lake.* Iŋyaŋćaŋgnahaŋ ohloka, *Pease Island* in the Missouri River.

i ŋ' - y a ŋ - ć e - ġ a, *n.* *a stone jar; earthen pot.*

i ŋ' - y a ŋ g, *cont.* of iŋyaŋka: iŋyaŋg mde kta, *I will go on a run.*

i ŋ' - y a ŋ - h a, *n.* *T.* *a sea shell.*

i ŋ' - y a ŋ - ḣ e, *n.* *a rocky hill.*

i ŋ' - y a ŋ - k a, *v. n.* *to run*—waimnaŋka, yainaŋka, uŋkinyaŋkapi.

i ŋ' - y a ŋ - k a - p e' - m n i, *n.* *T.* *a stone war-club.*

i ŋ' - y a ŋ - w a - a - n u - n u, *n.* *moss on stones, moss.* See waanunu.

i ŋ - y u ŋ', *intj.* *lo! behold!* iŋyuŋ ećoŋ yaśi koŋ ećoŋ śni, *behold! what thou commandest him to do he has not done.*

i - o' - b l u - l a, *n.* *T.* *a sheltered place, where the wind does not blow.*

i - o' - h d a - m n i - y a ŋ, *adv.* *following around the curves*, as of a stream.

i - o' - h m u s, *cont.* of iohmuza; iohmus maŋka, *I keep my mouth shut.*

i - o' - h m u s - y a, *v. a.* *to cause to shut the mouth.*

i - o' - h m u - z a, *n.* *a closed mouth.*

i - o' - k a - p a - z a, *v. n.* *to be pungent in the mouth*, as pepper—iomakapaza.

i - o' - k a - t a ŋ, *v. a.* *to nail* one thing *on* another; *to nail and hold* an ax *on the other side*—iowakataŋ.

i - o' - k a - w i ŋ ḣ, *adv.* *following around the circle.* See okawiŋġa.

i - o' - k p a - k a, *adv.* *with open mouth, furiously:* iokpaka iyaḣpaya, *to fall on one talking furiously*, as a drunken man, or as a dog barking attacks anything.

i - o' - k p a - k p a s, *adv.* *moving the lips:* iokpakpas yaŋka, *to be moving the lips*, as one talking to himself.

i - o ŋ' - ś i - d a, *v. a.* of oŋśida; *to*

have mercy or *compassion on* one *in reference to* something; *to grant, bestow*—ioŋśiwada, ioŋśiuŋdapi, ioŋśimada.

i-oŋ′-śi-da-ya, *adv. having compassion on one in reference to* something.

i-o′-pa-wiŋ-ġe, *adj. the one hundredth.*

i-o′-śtaŋ, *n.* of ośtaŋ; *a cork, stopper* for a vial, etc.

i-o′-śtaŋ-pi, *n.* Same as iośtaŋ.

i-o′-wa, *n.* of owa; *something to write* or *paint with, a pen* or *pencil.*

i-o′-źim-na-na, *adv. full, running over. T.*, ioźiblala. See iyuźimnana.

i-o′-źu-daŋ, *adj.* of oźudaŋ; *full to the brim.*

i-pa′, *n. the top* of anything: paha ipa, *the top of a hill;* ḣe ipa, *the head of the Coteau;* also, *a cape, promontory, projecting point.*

i-pa′-be, *v.* of pabe. Same as ipamaŋ.

i-pa′-be, *n. something to rub with;* as, ćaŋ ipabe, *a file;* waŋ ipabe, *a stone to rub arrows with.*

i-pa′-ġaŋ, *v.* of paġaŋ; *to push aside,* as a tent door, for the purpose of looking out: tiyopa ipaġaŋ inawapa, *I went out by pushing aside the door.*

i-pa′-ġe-ki-ya, *adv. shoving aside.*

i-pa′-ġo, *n.* (i *and* paġo) *something to carve* or *grave with, a carving* or *graving implement.*

i-pa′-ġo-ya, *adv. passing by, exceeding in length;* said when one thing is longer than another; *exceeding in speed,* as when one horse outruns another.

i-pa′-ha, *v.* ipaha iyeya, *to raise up,* as a curtain.

i-pa′-hdo-ka, *v. n. to run the head against, butt against*—imapahdoka. *T.*, ipagloka, *to be dislocated,* as a joint, *by anything.*

i-pa′-hiŋ, *v. n. to lean the head against, have for a pillow*—iwapahiŋ, iyapahiŋ, uŋkipahiŋpi.

i-pa′-hiŋ, *n. a pillow*—mitipahiŋ, nitipahiŋ.

i-pa′-hiŋ-ya, *v. a. to have* or *use for a pillow*—ipahiŋwaya.

i-pa′-ḣdan, *adv. through;* ipaḣdan iheya, *to shoot clear through.*

i-pa′-ḣdo-ka, *v. a. to make a hole in, punch through.*

i′-pa-ḣte, *n. T. a bridle,* of i, *mouth,* and paḣta, *to tie.*

i-pa′-ḣte, *n.* (i *and* paḣta) *something to tie up with, a string.*

i-pa′-ka, *v. n. to draw back,* as meat from ribs when cooked, or as husks of corn when ripe—ipaka iyeya.

i-pa′-kća, *n.* (i *and* pakća) *a comb. T.*, nasuŋpakća.

i-pa′-kća-daŋ, *n. a small comb.*

i-pa′-kća-sbu-daŋ, *n. a fine comb. T.*, nasuŋpakćeswula.

i-pa′-kća-taŋ-ka, *n. a dressing-comb.*

i-pa′-kiŋ-ta, *v. a. to wipe off*—iwapakiŋta.

i-pa′-kiŋ-te, *n.* (i *and* pakiŋta)

something to wipe with, a towel. Hence, napipakiŋte, *a napkin.*

i-pa'-ki-źa, *v.* *to rub*, as one's eyes, *with the hand*—iwapakiźa.

i-pa'-ko-te, *n.* *a probe.* Hence, ćaŋipakote *or* ćaŋwipakote, *a stick to probe with.*

i-pa'-kśaŋ, *n.* *a bend* in a river, etc. Mde ipakśaŋ, *Big-Stone Lake;* Wakpa ipakśaŋ, *the Big Sioux River.*

i-pa'-maŋ, *v. a.* of pamaŋ; *to rub, rub on*, as in filing—iwapabe, uŋkipamaŋpi. See ipabe

i-pa'-mna, *n.* *a setting-pole.*

i-pa'-mna-ki-toŋ, *v. a.* *to pole, to use a pole in boating*—ipamnawetoŋ. *T.*, ikpataŋ.

i-pa'-muŋg, *cont.* of ipamuŋka; ipamuŋg iću, *to dip up*, as water, *with a vessel*—ipamuŋg iwaću. *T.*, ipagmug.

i'-pa-muŋg, *cont.* ípamuŋg yatkaŋ, *to stoop down and drink from* a spring—ípamuŋg mdatkaŋ.

i-pa'-muŋ-ka, *v. n.* *to be capable of being dipped up with a bucket.* Thus it is asked, Miniyowe toketu hwo, *how is the spring?* Answer, Ipamuŋka, *it can be dipped up.* *T.*, ipagmuŋka.

i'-paŋ-ho-ye-ya, *adv.* *T.* *screamingly, above the natural voice.* See paŋ *and* hoyeya.

i-pa'-po-pe, *n.* *a pop-gun; the elder*, from which pop-guns are made.

i-pa'-psa-ke, *n.* *T. a small knife* for cutting porcupine quills; *i. q.* ićapsake.

i-pa'-ptaŋ, *v.* *to turn over:* ipaptaŋ eḣpeiçiya, *to turn one's self over.*

i-pa'-pu-za, *n.* (i *and* papuza) *something to wipe dry with, a towel.*

i-pa'-saŋ, *v. a.* *to put on white paint with the end of a stick, make white dots, to rub on and whiten with*—iwapasaŋ, imayapasaŋ.

i-pa'-sbu, *v.* ipasbu iyaya, *to pass through*, as through tall grass; ipa sbu iyeiçiya, *to force one's self into* a feast or company when not called.

i-pas'-haŋ, *n.* *anything that comes through and holds, the little iron that comes over and holds a trap* when set; *a screw.*

i-pa'-si-sa, *v. a.* *to stick in*, as a needle or pin; *to sew; to fasten*, as with a wiping screw—iwapasisa, iyapasisa, uŋkipasisapi.

i-pa'-si-se, *n.* (i *and* pasisa) *a stitch.* See ićap'e.

i-pa'-so-tka, *adj.* *conspicuous, extending up*, as a tall tree or steeple.

i-pa'-so-tka-ya, *adv.* *conspicuously.*

i-pa'-spa, *v.* *to drive in*, as tent-pins—iwapaspa. *T.*, okataŋ.

i-pa'-staŋ, *n.* *an instrument used in dressing skins, a rubbing instrument;* *i. q.* tahaipastaŋ. *T.*, ipaste.

i-pa'-śdog, *cont.* of ipaśdoka; ipaśdog iyeya.

i-pa'-śdo-ka, *v. a.* *to draw off over the head*, as a shirt; *to live through*, as through a winter or sickness: kitaŋ iwapaśdoka, *I have just lived through.*

i-pa'-ta, *v. a.* *to embroider, work quill-work, work with porcupine quills*—iwapata. See wipata.

i-pa'-tag, *cont.* of ipataka.

i-pa'-tag-toŋ, *v. a.* *to brace out* or *stretch,* as in drying hides and skins—ipatagwatoŋ.

i-pa'-tag-ya, *v. a* *to cause to brace out* or *up; to sustain, reinforce*—ipatagwaya, ipataguŋyaŋpi.

i-pa'-ta-ka, *v. a.* *to stretch out by means of cross-sticks; to have for a staff* or *support; to lean on, be dependent upon*—iwapataka, uŋkipatakapi.

i-pa'-ta-ke, *n.* (i *and* pataka) *a prop* or *brace, a stick to stretch* a skin *on;* siŋkpe ha ipatake, *a stick to stretch a muskrat-skin on.*

i-pa'-taŋ, *v. a.* *to mash up one* thing *with another*—iwapataŋ.

i-pa'-taŋ, *n.* *a prop* or *brace.*

i-pa'-tku-ġa, *adv.* *abreast, in a row, in a phalanx.*

i-pa'-tkuḣ-ya, *adv.* *in a row, abreast.*

i-pa'-ṭiŋ-za, *v. a.* *to make firm by means of*—iwapaṭiŋza.

i-pa'-ṭiŋ-za, *n.* (i *and* paṭiŋza) *anything that makes firm, sustenance, nourishment.*

i-pa'-we-ġa, *v. n.* *to bend across; to intersect, come into* or *cross,* as one road does another.

i-pa'-weḣ, *cont.* of ipaweġa: ipaweḣ iyaya, *to go across*—ipaweḣ imdamde.

i-pa'-weḣ-ya, *v. a.* *to cause to intersect*—ipaweḣwaya.

i-pa'-weḣ-ya, *adv.* *crossing, intersecting; aside, out of the way; incorrectly:* ipaweḣya waŋka, *it lies across.*

i-pa'-wiŋ-ta, *v. a.* *to rub on*—iwapawiŋta, iyapawiŋta, uŋkipawiŋtapi.

i-pa'-zi-ća, *adv.* *longer than* the rest; said of a tall tree, or anything relatively long; *bulged out,* as a tent when one leans against it.

i-pa'-źiŋ, *v. n.* *to be prevented by* something *from proceeding; to come to a stand, not to be able to go on*—imapaźiŋ: mde ipaźiŋ inaźiŋ, *he has come to a stand at a lake.*

i-pa'-źiŋ-yaŋ, *adv.* *prevented by, in opposition, opposing.*

i-pa'-źi-pa, *v. a.* *to stick in, to prick with*—iwapaźipa.

i-pa'-źi-pe, *n.* (i *and* paźipa) *something that pricks, a pricker.*

i-pe'-ġa, *v. n.* *to boil,* as water. See ipiġa, which is more commonly used.

i'-pi, *adj.* *full, satisfied; full of, satisfied with*—ímapi, ínipi, íuŋpipi, íwićapi. See wípi.

i-pi'-da, *v. a.* *to deny to, refuse to give to, withhold from*—ipiwada, ipiuŋdapi, ipamadi, ipićida: takudaŋ ipiuŋdapi śni, *he withholds from us nothing,* or *we refuse to give him nothing.*

i-pi'-ġa, *v. n.* *to boil,* as water, *to foam.*

i-pi'-ġa, *n.* *the foam of boiling water.*

i-pi'-ḣdag, *cont.* of ipiḣdaka.

i-pi'-ḣdag-ki-toŋ, *v. a.* *to put on one's girdle, gird one's self*—ipiḣdagwetoŋ.

i-pi'-ḣdag-toŋ, *v. a.* *to put on a girdle, girded*—ipiḣdagwatoŋ, ipiḣdaguŋtoŋpi. *T.*, ipiyagkitoŋ.

i-pi'-ḣda-ka, *v. pos.* of ipiyaka; *to put on one's own girdle*—ipiwaḣdaka, ipiuŋḣdakapi.

i-pi'-ḣda-ke, *n,* *a girdle.* See ipiyake.

i-piḣ', *cont.* of ipiġa.

i-piḣ'-ya, *v. a.* *to cause to boil*—ipiḣwaya, ipiḣuŋyaŋpi.

i-piḣ'-ya, *adv.* *boiling:* ipiḣya haŋ, *to stand boiling.*

i-piŋ'-ta, *v. n.* *to be defective in some part, too short* or *too little, not as is usual.* Said of one who is without a nose, or of a coat without skirts—imapiŋta, inipiŋta. See also iputaŋ *and* ipustaka.

i'-pi-ya, *v. a.* *to make full, to fill*—ípiwaya.

i-pi'-yag, *cont.* of ipiyaka.

i-pi'-yag-ki-ći-toŋ, *v. a.* *to put on a girdle for* one, *to gird* one—ipiyagwećitoŋ.

i-pi'-yag-ki-toŋ, *v. a. pos.* *to put on one's own girdle; to be girded*—ipiyagwetoŋ.

i-pi'-yag-toŋ, *v. a.* *to gird, put on a girdle; to be girded*—ipiyagwatoŋ, ipiyaguŋtoŋpi.

i-pi'-ya-ka, *v. a.* *to gird one's self, to put on a girdle*—ipimdaka, ipidaka, ipiuŋyakapi.

i-pi'-ya-ke, *n.* *a girdle, sash.*

i-pi'-ye, *n.* *something to repair with.*

i-po', *n.* *a swelling.* See iwićapo.

i-po'-ġaŋ, *v.n.* *to blow,* as the wind; *to breathe out, exhale*—iwapoġaŋ.

i-poḣ', *cont.* of ipoġaŋ: ipoḣ iyeya, *to blow on, blow in, blow away*—ipoḣ iyewaya.

i-poḣ'-ya, *v. a.* *to cause to blow*—ipoḣwaya

i-poḣ'-ya, *adv.* *blowing.*

i-psi'-ća, *v. n.* *to jump down from,* as from a horse; *to jump, jump over*—iwapsića, iyapsića, uŋkipsićapi.

i-psin', *cont.* of ipsića: ipsin iyaya.

i-psi'-psi-ća, *v. red.* of ipsića; *to hop,* as a grasshopper.

i-psi'-psi-ća-daŋ, *v. n. dim.* of ipsipsića; *to hop,* as do the psipsićadaŋ.

i-pte'-ġa, *n.* *the end of a lake where grass grows.*

i-pte'-ġa, *v. n.* ipteġa yaŋka, *to be sad about* anything.

i-pte'-ġa-ka, *v. n.* *to be sad about* anything; *i. q.*, ićaŋteśića—imapteġaka.

i'-pu-sdi, *v. n.* *to be close to, to press upon, to touch* anything, as the nose presses on the face; *to press upon, weigh down,* as sorrow—ímapusdi, ínipusdi.

i'-pu-sdi-ya, *v. a.* *to cause to press on*—ípusdiwaya.

i'-pu-sdi-ya, *adv.* *touching.* Hence, makipusdiya, *on the ground.*

i'-pu-ski-ća, *v. n.* *to be close to, to touch, press on*—ímapuskića.

i'-pu-ski-će-daŋ, *adv.* *pressed, close together.*

i'-pu-skin, *cont.* of ípuskića; *close together:* ípuskin iyotaŋkapi, *they sit close together.*

i'-pu-skin-ya, *v. a.* *to cause to press on*—ípuskinwaya.

i'-pu-skin-ya, *adv.* *pressed together.*

i'-pu-ski-skin, *cont.* ípuskiskin iyeya, *to shove up close together.*

i-pu'-spa, *v. a.* *to stick on*—iwapuspa.

i-pu'-spe, *n.* *anything that sticks to, a seal, a wafer.*

i-pu'-stag, *cont.* of ipustaka: makipustag eḣpeiçiya, *to throw one's self flat on the ground.*

i-pu'-sta-ka, *v. n.* *to be flat, wanting, defective;* one who has no nose is ipustaka—imapustaka. See ipiŋta *and* iputaŋ.

i-pu'-staŋ, *adv.* ipustaŋ yuza, *to clap up against,* as a coal of fire: peta ipustaŋpi se emaćeća, *it seems as if I was held up to the fire.*

i-pus'-ye, *n.* *T.* *something to dry on* or *with, a dryer.* See pusya.

i-puś'-iŋ, *n.* *the outside of a bend.*

i-pu'-tag, *cont.* of iputaka.

i-pu'-ta-ka, *v. a.* *to touch, to kiss*—iwaputaka, imaputaka. See iiputaka.

i-pu'-taŋ, *v. n.* *to be defective, wanting, flat, lower* or *shorter than usual*—imaputaŋ. See ipiŋta *and* ipustaka.

i'-pu-za, *v. n.* (i *and* puza) *to have the mouth dry, to be thirsty*—ímapuza, ínipuza, íuŋpuzapi.

i'-pu-za-ṭa, *v. n.* *to die* or *be dying of thirst; to be very thirsty, suffer from thirst*—ípuzamaṭa.

i-pu'-źi-ta, *v. a.* *to give when it is not wanted, to force upon* one—iwapuźita.

i-p̣o', *n.* of p̣o; *steam.*

i-p̣o'-za, *v.* See ip̣ozeća.

i-p̣o'-ze-ća, *v. n.* *to be out of humor about* anything—imap̣ozeća.

i-sa'-kim, *adv.* *both together, with.* *T.*, isakib, *along side of.* See sakim.

i-sa'-kim-tu, *adv.* *both together.*

i-saŋ', *n.* *a knife, knives:* this belongs to the eastern Dakotas; the Yanktons say miŋ'-na and the Teetons, mil'-la.

I-saŋ'-a-ti, *n.* (isaŋ *and* ati) *Isanties,* or *Esanties,* the name which is applied to the Dakotas of the Mississippi and Minnesota by those living on the Missouri. Why this name has been given to them by their brethren is still a matter of conjecture; perhaps, because they pitched their tents formerly at Isaŋtamde, or *Knife Lake,* one of those which go under the denomination of Mille Lacs; or, perhaps, it was given to them because they lived nearer the Isaŋtaŋka, or *Big-knives, i. e.,* the Americans.

i-saŋ'-na, *n. dim. a little knife.*

i-saŋ'-o-źu-ha, *n.* (isaŋ *and* oźuha) *a knife-case, knife-sheath. T.*, mioźuha.

i'-saŋ-pa, *adv. beyond that* place or time; *more than.*

i-saŋ'-pa-mi-ma, *n. round-pointed knives, table-knives. T.*, milapaksa.

i'-saŋ-pa-taŋ-haŋ, *adv. from beyond that.*

i-saŋ'-pe-sto-daŋ, *n. sharp-pointed knives.*

i-saŋ'-śko-pa, *n. a crooked knife,* i. e., *a sickle.*

I-saŋ'-ta-mde, *n. Knife Lake.* The name of a lake to the east of the Mississippi River.

I-saŋ'-taŋ-ka, *n.* (isaŋ *and* taŋka.) The name by which the Isaŋati Dakotas designate the people of the United States. It is said to have been given them because the first Americans who came among the Dakotas were officers with swords. The Yanktons say Miŋ'-na-haŋ'-ska, and the Teetons, Mil'-la-haŋ'-ska, *Long knives:* as Isaŋtaŋka is *Large knives.*

i-saŋ'-yaŋ, *v. a. to communicate the whiting from* one's robe *to another by rubbing against; to have for* or *use as a knife*—isaŋwaya.

I-saŋ'-ya-ti, *n.* See Isaŋati.

i-sa'-pa, *v. n. to be blackened by* anything—imasapa: taku inisapa he, *what has blackened you?*

i-sa'-pa, *n. the name of a stone used for blacking,* prob. *iron ore.*

i-sbu', *n. small stones.*

i-sbu'-daŋ, *n. dim.* of isbu; *gravel.*

i-sda'-ye, *n. ointment; i. q.*, taku oŋ sdayapi; *wagon grease.*

i-sdo'-ća, *v.* See isdonya.

i-sdon'-ya, *v. a. to know by means of*—isdonwaya, isdonyaya, isdonuŋyaŋpi. See sdonya.

i'-siŋ-yaŋ, *adv. out of sight, behind* something, *concealed:* ísiŋyaŋ iyaya, *he has gone out of sight.*

i'-sku-ya, *adj. sweet-mouthed, flattering; mouth watering for*—ímaskuya.

i'-sku-ya, *n. a flatterer.*

i'-sku-ya-hda, *v.n. to have one's mouth water for* anything, as for different kinds of food—ískuyawahda.

i'-sku-ye-ya, *v. a. to make one's mouth water for*—ískuyewaya, ískuyeuŋyaŋpi, ískuyemayaŋ.

i-sto', *n. the arm* of a person, *the fore-arm; the fore-leg* of an animal.

i-sto'-hdu-ka-tiŋ, *v. pos. to stretch out one's own arm. T.*, istoglukatiŋ.

i-sto'-hdu-kśaŋ, *v. pos. to bend one's arm. T.*, istoglukśaŋ.

i-sto'-i-yo-hi-ya, *v. to reach with the arm.*

i-sto'-ka-tiŋ-ki-ya, *v. a. to cause to stretch out the arm*—istokatiŋwakiya.

i-sto'-o-hi-ya, *adv. within arm's reach. T.*, istoiyohiya.

i-sto'-pa-kśaŋ, *n. the bend of the arm.*

i-sto′-pa-kśi-źa, *v.* *to bend up the arm; to bend up the leg,* as a lame dog—istowapakśiźa.

i-sto′-yu-kaŋ, *v.* *to have arms*—istomayukaŋ

i-sto′-yu-kśi-źa, *v.* *to bend up the arm*—istomdukśiźa.

iś, *pron.* *he, she, it:* iś iye, *he himself.* See iŋś.

i-śa′-hdo-ġaŋ, *adj.* *the eighth.*

i-śa′-hdo-hdo-ġaŋ, *adj. red.* *every eighth* one.

i-śa′-kdo-ġaŋ, *adj.* *Ih.* *the eighth.* *T.*, iśakloġaŋ.

i-śa′-ko-wiŋ, *adj.* *the seventh.*

i-śa′-k̇o-wiŋ-wiŋ, *adj. red.* *every seventh* one.

i-śa′-kpe, *adj.* *the sixth.*

i′-śa-kpe, *n.* *a six-shooter, a pistol.*

i-śa′-kpe-kpe, *adj. red.* *every sixth* one.

i-śi′, *n.* *Ih.* and *T.* *remuneration, pay; i. q.*, iyuŋwiŋ.

i-śi′-ća, *v. n.* See iśin; also, *to be bad on account of, to be injured by:* imaśića.

i-śi′-ća-wa-ćiŋ, *v. n.* *T.* *to be greedy about.*

i-śi′-hda, *v.* of śihda; *to be angry about*—iśinwahda.

i-śi′-ḣćiŋ, *adv.* *T.* *excitedly.*

i-śi′-ḣtiŋ, *v. n.* *to be enfeebled by; be injured by*—imaśiḣtiŋ.

i-śi′-ki-ćiŋ, *adv.* *angrily.*

i-śin′, *cont.* of iśića; iśinwaćiŋ, *to covet, desire more*—iśinwaćaŋmi, iśinwaćaŋni. *T.*, iśićawaćiŋ.

i-śi′-tki-hda, *v. n.* *to be angry on account of; to be sad about, be afflicted for*—imaśitkihda.

i-śi′-tki-hda-ya, *v. a.* *to make angry by; to torment, afflict for*—iśitkihdawaya.

i-śka′, *n.* *the ankle* or *tarsus*—miiśka. See iśkahu.

i-śka′-hu, *n.* *the ankle-bones* or *tarsus.* Hence haŋpiśkahu, *moccasin-tops.*

i-śka′-hu-toŋ, *v. a.* *to put tops on moccasins*—iśkahuwatoŋ.

i-śka′-kaŋ, *n.* *the large tendon extending from the heel up the leg; the large tendon in the back of the neck.*

i-śkaŋ′, *cont.* of iśkata; petiśkaŋ, *to come near the fire, draw up to the fire, to warm one's self*—petimaśkaŋ.

i-śka′-ta, *v. a.* *to play to* or *for* anything—iwaśkata, iyaśkata, uŋkiśkatapi.

i-śki′-źu-pi, *n.* *fish-hooks.* *T.*, hoićuwa maza. See hiŋśkiźupi.

i-śko′-na-ġi, *n.* *the small black bony substance on the inside of a horse's fore-leg, just above the knee, the web.*

i-ślo′-ya, *adj.* or *n.* *T.* *the right, the right hand.*

i-ślo′-ya-ta, i-ślo′-ya-taŋ, *and* i-ślo′-ya-taŋ-haŋ, *adv.* *T.* *at the right hand of.*

iś-na′-ka, *pron.* *he alone*—miśnaka.

iś-na′-la, *pron.* *T.* *he alone; i. q.* iśnana.

iś-na′-na, *pron.* *alone, he alone, she alone*—miśnana, niśnana; uŋkiśnaŋpidaŋ, *we alone.*

iś-na'-śna-na, *pron. red.* of iśnana.

iś-na'-ti, *v. n.* *to dwell alone* or *in a separate house; to have the menses.* This last, at present, appears to be the only meaning of the word; it is so used because, at such times, the Dakota women are not permitted to stay in the house with others, but put up a little one for themselves outside.

iś-na'-ti-pi, *n.* *dwelling alone; the menses.*

i-śni'-ka-eś, *adv.* *within a little, nearly:* iśnikaeś nikte śni, *it came near killing thee.* *T.*, iśnikaliś.

i'-śo-kśo-ka-pi-daŋ, *n.* *thick-lips*, a nickname for the Ojibwas.

i-ś'o'-ś'o, *adj.* *scampering, not easily restrained*—imaś'oś'o, iniś'oś'o.

i-śo'-śo-ka, *n.* *T.* *one who obeys cheerfully.*

i-śpa', *n.* *the lower part of the arm*—miiśpa. *T.*, *the elbow.* See isto.

i-śpa'-hu, *n.* *the bones in the lower part of the arm, the radius and ulna.*

i-śpa'-se, *the point of the elbow.*

i'-śpa-śpa, *v. n.* *to move the lips*, as some persons do when reading to themselves: iśpaśpa maŋka, *I am moving my lips.* *T.*, inagnagna. See inagna *and* iokpakpas.

i-śta', *n.* *the eye, eyes*—miiśta, niiśta, uŋkiśtapi.

i-śta'-ġoŋ-ġa, *v. n.* *to be blind; not to be able to see well*—iśtamaġoŋġa.

i-śta'-ġoŋ-ġe, *n.* *a blind person.*

i-śta'-ġoŋ-ġe-ya, *v. a.* *to make blind, to blind*—iśtaġoŋġewaya, iśtaġoŋġeuŋyaŋpi.

i-śta'-hda-kpa, *v. pos.* of iśtakakpa; *to put out one's own eye*—iśtawahdakpa.

i-śta'-ḣe, *n.* (iśta *and* ḣe) *the ridge above the eyes.*

i-śta'-ḣe-hiŋ, *n.* *the eye-brows.*

i-śta'-ḣe-pe *or* **i-śta'-ḣe-piŋ**, *n.* *the eye-lashes.*

i-śta'-ḣe-pe-hiŋ, *n.* *the eye-lashes.*

i-śta'-ḣmiŋ, *adj.* *cross-eyed.*

i-śta'-i-yo-hi-ya, *adv.* *as far as the eye can reach.*

i-śta'-ka-kpa, *v. a.* *to strike and put out an eye*—iśtawakakpa.

i-śta'-ka-kpaŋ, *v.* *to wink the eye*—iśtawakakpaŋ, iśtauŋkakpaŋpi.

i-śta'-ka-kpaŋ-kpaŋ, *v. red.* of iśtakakpaŋ.

i-śta'-ka-kpaŋ-pi se, *adv.* *in the twinkling of an eye.*

i-śta'-kpe, *v. n.* *to be blind, having the eye put out*—iśtamakpe. *T.*, iśtakpa.

i-śta'-kpe-ya, *v. a.* *to make blind*—iśtakpewaya.

i-śta'-kśiŋ, *v.* *to be squint-eyed* or *cross-eyed*—iśtamakśiŋ. *T.*, iśtaḣmiŋ. See iśtokśiŋ.

i-śta'-kśiŋ-ka, *n.* *a squint-eyed person.*

i-śta'-kśiŋ-kśiŋ, *v. n. red.* of iśtakśiŋ.

i-ś t a'-m d e s, *cont.* of iśtamdeza.

i-ś t a'-ṃ d e s-y a, *v. a.* *to make clear-sighted*—iśtamdeswaya.

i-ś t a'-m d e-z a, *v. n.* *to be clear-sighted*—iśtamamdeza.

i-ś t a'-m i-n i-ġ a-ġ a, *adv.* *in tears, with tears trickling down;* iśtaminiġaġa ia, *to speak with the tears dropping down.*

i-ś t a'-m i-n i-h a ŋ-p e, *n.* *tears;* iśtaminihaŋpe au, *to cry*—iśtaminihaŋpe amau.

i-ś t a'-m i-n i-o-ś d o-k a, *adj.* *with water standing in the eyes.* *T.*, iśtaminioślo.

i-ś t a'-n a-k a, *v. n.* *to have the eye twitch*—iśtamanaka, *my eye twitches;* "I shall see something nice."

i-ś t a'-o-h i-y a, *adv.* *as far as the eye can reach.* *T.*, iśtaiyohiya.

i-ś t a'-o-ź u-h a, *n.* *the eye-lids.* See iśtoźuha.

i-ś t a'-t p e, *v. n.* Same as iśtakpe.

i-ś t a'-w i-ć a-n i-y a ŋ, *n.* *T.* *sore eyes.*

i-ś t a'-w i-ć a-y a-z a ŋ-w i, *n.* *the moon in which sore eyes prevail;* a moon answering generally to the month of *March.*

i-ś t e'-ć a, *v. n.* *to be ashamed, ashamed of; to be bashful*—imaśteća, iniśteća, uŋkiśtećapi. See wiśteća.

i-ś t e n', *cont.* of iśteća.

i-ś t e n'-k i-y a, *v. a.* *to make* one *ashamed, to disappoint* one—iśtenwakiya, iśtenuŋkiyapi, iśtenmakiya.

i-ś t e n'-y a, *v. a.* *to make ashamed, dishonor*—iśtenwaya, iśtenuŋyaŋpi, iśtenmayaya.

i-ś t i', *n.* *the under lip.*

i-ś t i'-h a, *n.* *the skin of the under lip.*

i-ś t i'-m a, *v.* See iśtiŋma.

i-ś t i ŋ'-b e, *v. n.* Same as iśtiŋma.

i-ś t i ŋ'-m a, *v. n.* *to sleep*—miśtiŋbe, niśtiŋbe, uŋkiśtiŋmapi. Hence, oiśtiŋma, *sleep.*

i-ś t o'-ġ i ŋ-k i-y a, *adv.* *eyes partly closed.*

i-ś t o'-h d i-w a ŋ-ź i-d a ŋ, *n.* *a fixed look, a gaze.* *T.*, oiśtagliwaŋźila.

i-ś t o'-h m u s, *cont.* of iśtohmuza: iśtohmus maŋka, *I keep my eyes shut.* See ohmus.

i-ś t o'-h m u s-y a, *v. a.* *to cause to shut the eyes*—iśtohmuswaya.

i-ś t o'-h m u s-y a, *adv.* *having the eyes shut.*

i-ś t o'-h m u-z a, *v. n.* *to shut the eyes*—iśtowahmuza.

i-ś t o'-k ś i ŋ, *v. n.* *to partly close the eyes, to look askance*—iśtowakśiŋ.

i-ś t o'-k ś i ŋ-k i-y a, *v. a.* *to look askance at, look at with the eyes partly shut*—iśtokśiŋwakiya, iśtokśiŋmakiya.

i-ś t o'-ś n i-ź a, *v. n.* *to have the eyes blinded* or *dazzled* by the light—iśtomaśniźa. *T.*, iśtaiyośniźa.

i-ś t o'-ś n i ś-y a, *v. a.* *to dazzle the eyes*, as a light—iśtośniśmayaŋ.

i-ś t o'-ś n u-ź a, *v. n.* Same as iśtośniźa.

i-śto'-źu-ha, *n.* *the eye-lids.*

i-śun', *v.* iśun iyeya, *to do more than was requisite, to overdo.*

i-śu'-ta, *v. a.* *to fail of accomplishing, be unable to do* a thing—iśuwata. *T.*, *to miss in shooting at.*

i-śu'-te, *adv.* *at random, as it happens:* iśute otaka, *very much, i. q.* śtedapi. *T.*, ituśeś.

i-śu'-te-ka, *adv.* Same as iśute.

i-śu'-te-ya, *v. a.* *to cause to fail of*—iśutewaya, iśutemayaŋ.

i-ta'-ḣda-ḣbe, *adv.* *with the wind.* *T.*, itaglaḣwe.

i'-ta-ḣda-ḣbe, *adv.* *with the wind.* The word is accented in this way when used with a noun; as, paha ítaḣdaḣbe uŋyaŋpi, *we go to the leeward of the hill.*

i-ta'-ḣda-ḣbe-ki-ya, *adv.* *with the wind.*

i-ta'-ḣda-ḣbe-ya, *adv.* *with the wind.* *T.*, itaglaḣweya.

i'-ta-he-na, *adv.* *Ih.* *on this side of.*

i-ta'-he-na, *adv.* *Ih.* *on this side of; since.* See itato.

i-ta'-he-na-taŋ-haŋ, *adv.* *Ih.* *on this side of.*

i-ta'-he-pi, *adv.* *by the way, between* places. *T.*, itahepiyela.

i-ta'-hnag, *v. cont.* of itahnaka.

i-ta'-hnag-ya, *adv.* *placed one on top of another.*

i-ta'-hna-ka, *v. a.* *to place one on top of another*—itawahnaka.

i-ta'-hna-ka, *adv.* *placed one on another.* See ahnaka.

i-ta'-ka-ha, *n.* *the instep.* Hence, siitakaha, *the top of the foot, instep.*

i-ta'-ka-ḣpe, *n.* See iteakaḣpe.

i-ta'-ka-sam, *adv.* *over the river from, opposite to.* *T.*, koakata.

i-ta'-ka-saŋ-pa, *adv.* *over against, across the river* or *lake from* any place. *T.*, koakataŋhaŋ.

i-ta'-ka-saŋ-pa-taŋ-haŋ, *adv.* *on the other side from.*

i-ta'-ke, *n.* *the instep; the top* or *piece put in the instep of a moccasin.* See haŋpitake *and* haŋpaitake.

i'-ta-ki-hna, *adv.* *one over another, in layers.*

i'-ta-ki-hna, *n.* *something worn over* another garment, *a vest.*

i-ta'-ku-ni-śni, *v. n.* of takuniśni; *to come to naught.*

i'-tam, *adv.* *soon after:* ítam yaŋkeya, *to be after.*

i-taŋ', *adv.* of taŋ; *on the side:* itaŋ anog, *on both sides.* From this we have mitaŋtaŋhaŋ, *at my side;* mitaŋkiyedaŋ, *near me,* etc.

i-taŋ', *v. n.* *to be vain, proud of, to glory in*—imataŋ, initaŋ, uŋkitaŋpi Hence, iwićataŋ, *vain-glorying.* See witaŋ.

i-taŋ'-a-no-ka-taŋ-haŋ, *adv.* *on both sides of.*

i-taŋ'-ćaŋ, *n.* *a chief, ruler, head one; a lord, master; the principal* thing—imataŋćaŋ, initaŋćaŋ. See otaŋćaŋ *and* taŋćaŋ.

i-taŋ'-ćaŋ-ka, *n.* *chief one, lord, master.*

i-taŋ'-ćaŋ-ki-ya, *v. a.* *to have*

for or *acknowledge as chief* or *master; to make lord* or *chief*—itaŋćaŋwakiya, itaŋćaŋmakiya.

i-t a ŋ'-ć a ŋ-k i-y a, *adv. in a lordly manner, with authority.*

i-t a ŋ'-ć a ŋ-y a, *v. a. to have for chief* or *master*—itaŋćaŋwaya, itaŋćaŋuŋyaŋpi.

i-t a ŋ'-ć a ŋ-y a ŋ, *adv. with authority, chief-like.*

i-t a ŋ'-i-h d u-k ś a ŋ, *adv. round about* one.

i-t a ŋ'-k a n, *adv. without, outside of.*

i-t a ŋ'-k i-y e-d a ŋ, *adv. near to* one—mitaŋkiyedaŋ. See ikiyedaŋ,

i-t a ŋ'-o-k ś a ŋ, *adv. T. around about, on all sides;* itaŋokśaŋ eiçitoŋwaŋ, *he looked about himself.*

i-t a ŋ'-p i, *n. pride, vain-glorying.*

i-t a ŋ'-t a ŋ, *v. red.* of itaŋ.

i-t a ŋ'-t a ŋ-p i, *n. pride, glorying, arrogance.* See witaŋtaŋpi.

i'-t a ŋ-w a ŋ-k a ŋ-h d e, *adv. up hill, ascending:* itaŋwaŋkaŋhde ya, *to go up hill. T.*, itaŋwaŋkaŋgle.

i'-t a ŋ-w a ŋ-k a ŋ-h d e-y a, *adv. ascending. T.*, itaŋwaŋkaŋgleya, *up a very steep hill.*

i-t a ŋ'-y a ŋ, *v. n. to grow by reason of*, as by eating meat; *to be proud*—itaŋwaya.

i-t a ŋ'-y e-ś n i, *v. n. to receive no benefit from, to be of no use*—imataŋyeśni.

i-t a'-t o, *adv. on this side of, this side of;* used in reference to time, *since. T.*, itahena.

i-t a'-t o-k i-y a, *adv. on this side of.*

i-t a'-t o-t a ŋ-h a ŋ, *adv. on this side of, from this side of.*

i-t a'-t o-w a m, *adv. to the windward of, on this side of.*

i-t a'-t o-w a-p a, *adv. on this side of, to the windward of.*

i-t a'-t o-w a-p a-t a ŋ-h a ŋ, *adv. on this side of.*

i'-t a-w a ŋ-k a ŋ-h d e, *adv.* See ítaŋwaŋkaŋhde.

i-t a'-z i-p a, *n. a bow* to shoot with: mitinazipe, *my bow;* nitinazipe, *thy bow;* tinazipe, *his bow.*

i-t a'-z i-p a-i-k a ŋ, *n. a bow-string.*

i-t e', *v. n. to be made blue* or *bluish by, be made grape-colored*—imate.

i-t e', *n. the face*—miite, niite.

i-t'e', *n. the forehead. T.*, ituhu.

i-t e'-a-k a-ḣ p e, *n. a cover for the face, veil.*

i-t e'-a-n o g *or* i-t e'-a-n o-k a-t a ŋ-h a ŋ, *adv. on both sides of the face.*

i-t'e'-ć a, *adj. slightly warm, lukewarm, tepid.* Said of fluids only: mini it'eća, *lukewarm water. T.*, iteća *and* itećaka.

i-t e'-h a, *n. T. a halter.*

i'-t e-h a ŋ, *adv.* of tehaŋ; *far from.*

i'-t e-h a ŋ-h a ŋ, *adv. red.* of ítehaŋ.

i'-t e-h a ŋ-h a ŋ-y a ŋ, *adv. red.* of ítehaŋyaŋ.

i'-t e-h a ŋ-t a ŋ-h a ŋ, *adv. far away from.*

i'-t e-h a ŋ-y a ŋ, *adv. far away from.*

i-te'-hde-ġe-daŋ, *n.* *striped-face*, a name for *the raccoon*, *i. q.* wića. *T.*, wićitegleġa.

i-te'-hiŋ, *n.* *the forelock.* See itoyehiŋ.

i-te'-hna-ka-pi, *n.* *T.*, itognakapi. See itoḣnakapi.

i-t'e'-hu, *n.* *the frontal bone; the forehead.*

i-te'-ḣi, *v. n.* of teḣi; *to be difficult to get along with*—imateḣi.

i-te'-ka, *adv.* *T.* *time for; due,* as, waŋna li iteka, *now he ought to come.*

i-te'-la-za-taŋ-haŋ, *adv.* *T.* *behind the back.*

i-te'-na-śiŋ-śiŋ-ki-ya, *v.* *T.* *to make faces at.*

i-t'en'-ya, *v. a.* *to make slightly warm* or *tepid*, as water—it'enuŋyanpi. *T.*, iṭelya.

i-te'-o-wa-pi, *n.* *a photograph.* *T.*, wićiteowapi.

i-te'-o-yu-ḣo, *v. n.* *to have hair stand up on the head.*

i-te'-śin-ki-ya, *v.* *to frown; to grin*—iteśinwakiya, iteśinuŋkiyapi.

i-te'-śiŋ-śiŋ, *n.* *a wrinkled face*—itemaśiŋśiŋ.

i-te'-yu-ko-ki-ya, *v.* *T.* *to frown, scowl.*

i-te'-yu-śiŋ-ki-ya, *v. a.* *to draw up the face at* one; *to grin; to frown*—iteyuśiŋwakiya.

i-te'-yu-śiŋ-śiŋ, *adj.* *face wrinkled.*

i-ti'-ća-ġa, *v.* *to set up a tent for* a certain purpose—itiwakaġa.

i-ti'-ćaŋ-nan, *adv.* *away out on the prairie from, away from a house.* Tinćaŋnan is also used. *T.*, manil.

i-ti'-ma-ta, *v.* *to beg for:* he itimata wahi, *I have come to beg for that.*

i-tka', *n.* *a blossom, capsule; an egg; the seed* of anything; *the testicles*, *i. q.* susu.

i-tka'-ska, *n.* *the white of an egg.*

i-tka'-zi-će, *n.* *the yolk of an egg.*

i'-tko-kim, *cont.* of ítkokipa; *meeting; in presence of, before*—mitkokim; ítkokim ya, *to go to meet.*

i'-tko-ki-pa, *v. a.* *to meet, come together from opposite directions*—ítkowakipa, itkouŋkipapi.

i-tko'-kpa, *v. n.* *to be still-born*—itkomakpa. See also itkotpa.

i-tkom', *adv.* *again, back again, in return, in reply.*

i-tkom'-ya, *adv.* *in return.*

i-tkoŋ', *v. n.* *to burn, blaze,* as fire: peta itkoŋ, *the fire blazes.*

i-tkoŋ'-ya, *v. a.* *to make burn* or *blaze*—itkoŋwaya.

i-tkoŋ'-ya-haŋ, *part.* *burning, alive,* as coals.

i'-tkoŋ-za, *adv.* *even with.* See itkuŋza.

i-tko'-pa-taŋ-haŋ, *adv.* *in reply, back again.* See iyeitkopataŋhaŋ.

i-tko'-tpa, *v. n.* *to be still-born:* taku itkotpe ćiŋ, *an untimely birth, an abortion.*

i-tko'-tpe-ya, *v. a.* *to cause to abort* or *be aborted*—itkotpewaya.

i-tkuŋ′, *v. n.* *to burn, blaze.* See itkoŋ.

i′-tkuŋs, *cont.* of itkuŋza.

i-tkuŋs′-ya, *adv.* *even with.*

i′-tkuŋ-za, *adv.* *even with.* See itkoŋza.

i-to′, *adv.* *come, well:* ito mde kta, *well, I will go;* ito ećoŋ wo, *come do it.*

i-to′, *v. n.* *to become blue by means of.* See ite.

i-tog′-e-haŋ, *adv.* *at the first, formerly.*

i-tog′-to, *adv.* *T.* *alternately: i. q.* itokto.

i′-to-han, *adv.* *how far from? how long from?* See tohan.

i′-to-han-han, *adv.* *red.* of ítohan.

i′-to-haŋ-yaŋ, *adv.* *how far from?* See tohaŋyaŋ.

i-to′-he-ya, *adv.* *towards:* hekta itoheya, *backwards.*

i′-to-hna-ka-pi, *n.* *brooches,* such as are worn by the men on their hair and by the women on their gowns. *T.*, pegnakapi.

· i-to′-hna-ke, *n.* *the face, countenance, visage, appearance, presence*—mitohnake. *T.*, iteoyuze.

i-to′-ho-mni, *adj.* *dizzy, light-headed; drunk*—itomahomni, itonihomni. *T.*, itomni.

i-to′-ho-mni-ya, *v. a.* *to make dizzy* or *drunk*—itohomniwaya, itohomniuŋyaŋpi. *T.*, itomniya.

i-to′-i-yo-hi, *adj.* *each one.* See otoiyohi. *T.*, iyohila.

i-to′-ka-ġa, *n.* *the south.*

i-to′-ka-ġa, *adv.* *southward.*

i-to′-ka-ġa-taŋ-haŋ, *adv.* *to the south of, on the south side of, from the south.*

i-to′-kaḣ, *cont.* of itokaġa; *southward:* itokaḣ mda, *I am going south.*

i-to′-kaḣ-ki-ya, *adv.* *towards the south.*

i-to′-kaḣ-wa-pa, *adv.* *towards the south.*

i′-to-kam, *adv.* *before,* used either in reference to place or time, *in presence of*—mitokam, nitokam, wićitokam. *T.*, itokab.

i′-to-kam-tu, *adv.* *before.*

i′-to-kam-tu-ken, *adv.* *before, prior to.*

i′-to-kam-tu-ya, *adv.* *before.*

i-to′-ka-pa, *v. n.* *to be before one in birth, be older than*—mitokapa, *he is older than I.* See tokapa.

i-to′-ka-pa-taŋ-haŋ, *adv.* *before, from before, from the presence of*—mitokapataŋhaŋ.

i-to′-ka-tam, *adv.* *before the time of* a certain event.

i-to′-ke-ća, *v. n.* of tokeća; *to be altered, changed; to be affected by* in any way—imatokeća, initokeća.

i-to′-ke-ća-śni, *v.* etaŋhaŋ ítokećaśni, *it is none of his business,* or *it makes no difference to him*—imatokećaśni.

i′-to-ki, *adv* *where from? which way from?* See toki.

i-to′-ki-kta, *adv.* *face to face, facing each other.*

i′-to-ki-ya, *adv.* *which way from?*

i′-to-ki-ya-ka, *adv.* *which way from?*

i′-to-ki-ya-pa, *adv.* *which way from?*

i′-to-ki-ya-pa-taŋ-haŋ, *adv.* *which way from?*

i′-to-ki-ya-taŋ-haŋ, *adv.* *in what direction from?*

i-to′-kto, *adv.* See itoto.

i-to′-ḳe-haŋ, *adv.* *formerly, of old.*

i-to′-ke-yaś, *adv.* *T.* *let me see; wait a little.*

i-tom′-tom, *adj. cont.* of itomtopa.

i-tom′-to-pa, *adj red.* of itopa; *every fourth* one.

i′-to-na, *adv.* *of how many? which number?* See dena, hena, etc.

i′-to-na-ka, *adv.* *of how many?*

i′-to-na-ke-ća, *adv.* *of what number?* See kanakeća, etc.

i′-to-na-na, *adv.* *of a few:* de itonana en yaŋka, *this is one of a very few.* See denana, etc.

i-toŋ′, *v. n.* *to tell the truth.* Not in use. See itoŋśni.

i-toŋ′-ka, and i-toŋ′-ka-e, *v. n.* *to lie, tell a falsehood; i. q* itoŋśni. *T.*, owewakaŋ.

i-toŋ′-kam, *adv.* See ituŋkam.

i-toŋ′-ki-pa, *v. pos.* of itoŋpa; *to value, guard, take care of one's own*—itoŋwakipa, itoŋuŋkipapi; itoŋiçipa, *to take care of one's self*—itoŋmiçipa; itoŋiçipeśniyaŋ, *not taking care of one's self, neglectful of one's self.*

i-toŋ′-ki-pe-ya, *adv.* *carefully, guardedly.*

i-toŋ′-pa, *v. a.* *to guard, take care of; to refrain from, beware of*—itoŋwapa, itoŋuŋpapi, itoŋćipa, itoŋmapa.

i-toŋ′-pa, *adj.* *careful, prudent.*

i-toŋ′-pe-ya, *adv.* *carefully, prudently.*

i-toŋ′-pe-ya-haŋ, *adv.* *carefully.*

i-toŋ′-pi-śni, *n.* *untruth, lies.* *T.*, owowakaŋpi. See itoŋśni.

i-toŋ′-śni, *v. n.* *to tell an untruth, to lie*—iwatoŋśni, iyatoŋśni, uŋkitoŋpiśni. Hence, oitoŋśni, *a lie;* oimayatoŋśni, *thou liest about me.* This belongs to the eastern Dakotas. The Yanktons and Tetons say "owewakaŋ."

i-toŋ′-śni-śni, *v.* *red.* of itoŋśni; *i. q.* itoŋśni wanića.

i-toŋ′-śni-yaŋ, *adv.* *falsely.*

i-toŋ′-waŋ, *v. n.* of toŋwaŋ; *to look* or *see with,* as with one's eyes—iwatoŋwaŋ, iyatoŋwaŋ.

i-to′-o-pta, *adv.* *through, by,* as itoopta ya, *to go on past; from one to another,* as, itoopta wićaḳu, *he passes it on to others.* *T.*, iyopta.

i-to′-o-pta-i-ya-ya-pi, *n.* *a purge.* See iyooptaiyayapi.

i-to′-o-pte-ya, *adv.* *through, straight through, passing on.*

i-to′-pa, *adj.* *the fourth*—imatopa; *in* or *of the fourth,* as, itopa en zaptaŋ, or itopa zaptaŋ, *five in the fourth* ten, i. e. *thirty-five.*

i-top'-tom, *adj. red.* See itomtom.

i-top'-to-pa, *adj. red.* of itopa.

i-to'-to, *v. n. red.* of ito: *to be made blue by.*

i-to'-to, *adv. turn about, alternately:* uŋma itoto ećoŋkupi kta, *we will do it alternately. T.*, itogto.

i-to'-wi-ća-ho-mni, *n. a turning round, swimming,* as of the head; *drunkenness; something that turns round,* as a wheel. *T.*, itomnipi.

i'-to-ye, *n. the face, appearance*—mitoye, nitoye.

i'-to-ye-hiŋ, *n. the forelock.* See ītehiŋ.

i'-to-ye-ki-toŋ, *v. pos. to wear braids of hair* or *ornaments in front*—ítoyewetoŋ.

i'-to-ye-toŋ, *v. n. to have braids* or *ornaments dangling about one's face; to wear anything that makes one look frightful*—ítoyewatoŋ.

i-tpa'-ḣdo-ka, *v. reflex.* of paḣdoka; *to break up through,* as a muskrat under ice; *to hatch* as young birds, that is, *to break one's own shell.*

i-tpa'-ta-ka, *v. pos.* of ipataka; *to brace one's own.*

i-tpi', *n. the belly, abdomen; the chest.* See ikpi.

i-tpi'-hna-ka, *v. a. to put in* or *around the abdomen*—itpiwahnaka. See ikpihnaka.

i-tpu'-ta-ka, *v. pos.* of iputaka; *to kiss one's own*—iwatputaka. See iitputaka.

i-tpu'-tpa, *adv. mixed up.*

i-tu', *adv. wildly, without being planted* or *tamed,* as, itu ićaġa, *it has grown up of itself; for nothing,* as, itu ećamoŋ, *I have done it for naught.*

i-tu'-hu, *n. T. a stone used to break bones* or *pound berries; the frontal.* See it'e.

i-tu'-hu-wo-blu, *v. n. T. to have hair stand up.*

i-tuḣ', *adv. for nothing, gratuitously, without cause. T.*, ituḣćiŋ *and* otuḣćiŋ.

i-tu'-ḣaŋ, *v. a. to give, bestow; to give for nothing, give away,* as the Dakotas often do—ituwaḣaŋ, ituuŋḣaŋpi.

i-tu'-ḣaŋ, *adv. gratuitously, without reward.*

i-tu'-ḣiŋ, *adv. for nothing, gratuitously; without cause, falsely. T.*, ituḣćiŋ *and* utuḣćiŋ.

i-tu'-ka, *v. a. to beg, ask one for*—iwatuka, iyatuka, uŋkitukapi, imatuka, ićituka. *T.*, kićićiŋ.

i-tu'-ka-eś, *adv. truly, indeed. T.*, itukaleś.

i-tu'-ka-ġa, *v. a. to make up a lie on, tell a falsehood about* one; *to do for nothing*—ituwakaġa, ituuŋkaġapi, itumakaġa.

i-tu'-kaḣ, *cont.* of itukaġa.

i-tu'-kaś, *adv. truly, at any rate.*

i-tu'-ka-śta, *adv. for nothing. T.*, otuyaćiŋ. See itu, ituḣ, etc.

i-tu'-ki-ḣaŋ, *v. a.* of ituḣaŋ; *to make a present of to; to give to* one, as the Dakotas do when they expect to be praised for it—ituwakiħaŋ, ituuŋkiħaŋpi, itumakiħaŋ, itućićiħaŋ. *T.*, otukiħaŋ' *and* utukiħaŋ.

i-tuŋ′-kam, *adv.* *on the back:* ituŋkam waŋka, *he lies on his back;* ituŋkam iħpaya, *to fall backwards.*

i-tuŋ′-kam-tu, *adv.* *on the back.*

i-tu′-o-ćo-ka, *adv.* *in the middle, between.* See oćokam.

i-tu′-o-ćo-ka-ya, *adv.* *between, in the middle.* See oćokaya.

i-tu′-o-ki-ta-he-daŋ, *adv.* *in the middle, between.* *T.*, ituotahela.

i-tu′-śdi, *adj.* *abundant.*

i-tu′-śdi-ya, *adv.* *abundantly.*

i-tu′-śeś, *adv.* *T.* *indeed.*

i-tu′-tu, *adv.* *red.* of itu.

i-tu′-tu-ya, *adv.* *red.* of ituya.

i-tu′-uŋ, *v.* *to be in a wild state.* Hence, ituuŋpi, *wild beasts.* *T.*, otuyauŋ.

i-tu′-wo-ta-he-daŋ, *adv.* *far from any dwelling.* *T.*, makotahela.

i-tu′-ya, *adv.* *for nothing, without cause, gratuitously.* *T.*, otuya *and* utuya.

i-tu′-ya-ken, *adv.* *causelessly, gratuitously.* *T.*, ituyaćiŋ *and* otuyaćiŋ.

i-ţe′-ća, *adj.* *T.* *lukewarm,* as water.

i-ţel′-ya, *v. a.* *T.* *to make warm.*

i-ţiŋ s′, *cont.* of iţiŋza.

i-ţiŋ s′-ya, *v. a.* *to make firm by means of*—iţiŋswaya.

i-ţiŋ′-za, *v. n.* *to be firm by reason of.*

i-ţiŋ′-ze, *n.* (i *and* ţiŋza) *a strengthener, a tightener.*

i-ţuŋ g′-ki-ya, *v.* *to suspect concerning one's self.*

i-ţuŋ g′-ya, *v.* *T.* *to suspect.*

i-ţuŋ′-ke-ća, *v. n.* *to be suspected of*—imaţuŋkeća.

i-u′-ma-na-pći-waŋ-ka, *adj.* See iuŋmanapćiŋwaŋka.

i-uŋ′, *v. a.* *to rub on,* as ointment or soap—iwauŋ, uŋkiuŋpi.

i-uŋ′-ma-na-pćiŋ-waŋ-ka, *adj.* *the nineteenth.* *T.*, iakenapćiŋyuŋka. See iakenapćiŋwaŋka.

i-uŋ′-toŋ, *v. a.* *to put grease or brains on* a skin, in order to dress it—iuŋwatoŋ.

i-uŋ′-toŋ-pi, *part.* *greased, prepared for dressing.*

i′-wa-ćiŋ, *v.* *to think of going to*—íwaćaŋmi.

i-wa′-ćiŋ-ko, *v. n.* *to be impatient about, be out of humor on account of*—iwaćiŋmako, iwaćiŋniko, iwaćiŋuŋkopi.

i-wa′-ćiŋ-toŋ, *v.* *to be intelligent by reason of*—iwaćiŋwatoŋ.

i-wa′-ćiŋ-yaŋ, *v. a* *to trust in for* or *in reference to*—iwaćiŋwaya, iwaćiŋuŋyaŋpi.

i-wa′-ćiŋ-yaŋ, *adv.* *trustingly.*

i-wa′-ćiŋ-źa-ta, *v. n* *to be undecided about* anything—iwaćiŋmaźata.

i-wa′-hna, *adv.* *slowly.* *T.*, iwaśtela. See iwahnana.

i-wa′-hna-na, *adv.* *slowly, by short stages; carefully.*

i-wa'-ho-koŋ-ki-ya, *v. a. to instruct in regard to, to counsel* or *advise concerning*—iwahokoŋwakiya, iwahokoŋuŋkiyapi, iwahokoŋmakiya; wićoni owihaŋke wanića iwahokoŋćićiya, *I counsel thee in regard to eternal life.*

i-wa'-ho-koŋ-ki-ya-pi, *n. instruction, counsel.*

i-wa'-ho-ya, *v. a. to send word to concerning* anything; *to promise; to grant, give by promise; to permit*—iwahowaya, iwahouŋyaŋpi, iwahomayaŋ.

i-wa'-ḣaŋ-i-ç̣i-da, *v. reflex. to be proud of*—iwaḣaŋmiç̣ida.

i'-wa-ḣte-da, *v.* See íwaḣtedaśni.

i'-wa-ḣte-da-ka *and* **i'-wa-ḣte-da-ka-e**, *v. a. to dislike on account of* something—íwaḣtewadakae.

i'-wa-ḣte-da-śni, *v. a. to dislike on account of* something, *to dislike* something *in* one; *to disesteem, think lightly of for* something—íwaḣtewadaśni, íwaḣteuŋdapiśni.

i-wa'-i-ç̣i-ni-yaŋ, *v. reflex.* of iwakiniya; *to be dissatisfied with one's self.*

i'-wa-kaŋ, *adj. talkative, tattling, gabbling.*

i'-wa-kaŋ, *n. a babbler.*

i'-wa-kaŋ-yaŋ, *adv. in a babbling manner.*

i-wa'-kaŋ-yaŋ, *adv. supernaturally.*

i-wa'-ki-ći, *v. n. to dance the scalp-dance*—iwawakići, iwayakići, iwauŋkićipi.

i-wa'-ki-ći-pi, *n. the scalp-dance.* This dance follows the bringing home of the scalps of their enemies. A circle is formed, on one side of which stand the young men, with their bodies painted, with their feathers in their heads, and their drums, rattles, and other instruments of music in their hands; while on the other side stand the young women in their best attire, carrying the scalp or scalps stretched on a hoop. The war-song commences, and the women dance around, sometimes advancing towards the men, who are stationary, and then again retreating, and responding at intervals to the music in a kind of chorus. If the scalp is taken in the winter, the dance is kept up, frequently by day and night, until the leaves grow in the spring. If it is taken in the summer, they dance and rejoice over it until the leaves fall off, when it is buried.

i-wa'-ki-ćoŋ-za, *v. a.* of koŋza; *to influence* one, *command* one *in regard to*—iwawećoŋza.

i-wa'-ki-ćoŋ-ze, *n. a commandment, decree.*

i-wa'-ki-ni-ya, *v. a. to get out of humor with, to neglect*—iwawakiniya, iwayakiniya.

i-wa'-kta, *n. a mark, sign, pledge.*

i-wa'-kta, *v. n. to be on one's*

guard, to be on the look out; to guard—iwawakta, iwayakta.

i-wa′-kta-ya, *v. a. to put on one's guard, forewarn*—iwaktawaya, iwaktauŋyaŋpi.

i-wa′-kta-ya, *adv. guardedly.*

i-wa′-kte-hda, *v. n. to go home in triumph having taken scalps*—iwaktewahda, iwakteuŋhdapi.

i-wa′-kte-hdi, *v. n. to come home in triumph bringing scalps*—iwaktewahdi, iwakteuŋhdipi.

i-wa′-na-ġi-ye-ya, *v. a. to trouble* one *in regard to* or *with.* See naġiyeya.

i-wa′-na-pi-śtaŋ-yaŋ, *v. a. to kill, hurt,* or *do injury with*—iwanapiśtaŋwaya. See napiśtaŋyaŋ.

i-wa′-ni-ti, *v. n. to go and spend the winter at for* some purpose—iwaniwati.

i′-wa-ni-ye-tu, *n. the succeeding winter, next winter.*

i-waŋg′, *cont.* of iwaŋka; taḣiŋća iwaŋg mda, *I am going to lie out for deer. T.*, iyuŋg. See awaŋg.

i-waŋ′-ġa, *v. a. to inquire of* one, *ask* one *a question about, call to account*—imuŋġa, inuŋġa, uŋkiwaŋġapi, imawaŋġa, ićiwaŋġa. *T.*, iyuŋġa.

i-waŋ′-ġa-pi, *n. inquiry. T.*, iyuŋġapi. See wiwaŋġapi.

i-waŋ′-hdag, *cont.* of iwaŋhdaka; iwaŋhdag uŋyakoŋpi, *we are guarding our own.*

i-waŋ′-hda-ka, *v. pos.* of iwaŋyaka; *to look to* or *have regard for one's own*—iwaŋwahdaka. See itoŋkipa.

i-waŋḣ′, *cont.* of iwaŋġa; he iwaŋḣ wahi, *I have come to inquire about that. T.*, iyuŋḣ.

i-waŋ′-i-ç̌i-hda-ka, *v. reflex. to look at one's self; to guard one's self*—iwaŋmiç̌ihdaka, iwaŋuŋkiç̌ihdakapi. See itoŋiç̌ipa.

i-waŋ′-i-hdag, *cont.* of iwaŋihdaka: iwaŋihdag wauŋ.

i-waŋ′-i-hda-ka, *v. to look at one's self* in a glass; *to watch over, guard one's self, to set a guard*—iwaŋmihdaka, iwaŋnihdaka.

i-waŋ′-ka, *v. n. to lie down, go and lie down, go to bed*—imuŋka, inuŋka, uŋkiwaŋkapi. *T.*, iyuŋka.

i-waŋ′-kam, *adv. above*—miwaŋkam, niwaŋkam, uŋkiwaŋkam, wićiwaŋkam.

i-waŋ′-kam-tu, *adv. above, up.*

i-waŋ′-kam-tu-ya, *adv. up above.*

i-waŋ′-kam-tu-ya-ken, *adv. above.* Not much used.

i-waŋ′-kaŋ-pa, *adv. above* one.

i-waŋ′-kaŋ-pa-ta, *adv. up above, above* one.

i-waŋ′-kaŋ-pa-taŋ-haŋ, *adv. from above* one.

i-waŋ′-ki-ći-ya-ka, *v. to look to* or *watch over for* one—iwaŋwećiyaka. See waŋyaka.

i-waŋ′-ki-ći-ya-ka-pi, *v. pl. they look to* or *watch over one another*—iwaŋuŋkićiyakapi.

i-waŋ'-yag, *cont.* of iwaŋyaka; iwaŋyag wahi.

i-waŋ'-ya-ka, *v. a. to look to* or *at; to survey, examine; to spy out*—iwaŋmdaka, iwaŋdaka, iwaŋuŋyakapi.

i-waŋ'-ya-ka-pi, *n. spies, surveyors.*

i-waŋ'-ya-ke, *n. something by which to see, the sight* of a gun: *a telescope* or *field-glass.*

i-waŋ'-źi-ća, *adv. very much.*

i-wa'-pe-tog, *cont.* of iwapetokeća.

i-wa'-pe-tog-toŋ, *v. a. to mark* or *brand with*—iwapetogwatoŋ, iwapetoguŋtoŋpi.

i-wa'-pe-to-ke-ća, *n. a mark, sign.*

i-wa'-sa-za, *v. n. to take hardly, get sick over;* iwamasaza.

i-wa'-ś'ag, *cont.* of iwaś'aka.

i-wa'-ś'ag-ya, *v. a. to strengthen by means of*—iwaś'agwaya.

i-wa'-ś'a-ka, *v. n. to be strong by reason of* or *for*—iwamaś'aka, iwauŋś'akapi. See waś'aka.

i-wa'-ś'a-ka, *n. strength, the source of strength.*

i-wa'-śe-ća, *v. n. to be rich,* in provisions especially—iwamaśeća, iwauŋśećapi, iwawićaśeća.

i'-wa-śi-ćuŋ, *v. n. to be talkative, to talk badly*—ímawaśićuŋ, íniwaśićuŋ.

i-wa'-śte, *v. n.* of waśte; *to be better by means of*—imawaśte.

i-wa'-śte-daŋ, *adv. slowly, moderately, carefully; but little, not much:* iwaśtedaŋ yazaŋ, *he is not very sick. Ih.*, iwaśtena; *T.*, iwaśtela.

i-wa'-śte-ka, *v. n. to be none the better for:* he taku iniwaśteka, *thou art none the better for that.*

i-wa'-śte-ya, *adv. better.*

i-wa'-śte-ya-ken, *adv. a little better.*

i-wa'-to-ki-ya-ka-e, *v. n.* he etaŋhaŋ iwatokiyakae, *what matter is it to him? how does it concern him?*

i-wa'-to-ki-ya-pa-ka-e, *v. n.* Same as iwatokiyakae. *T.*, etaŋhaŋś toka.

i-wa'-to-ki-ya-pa-śni, *v. n. it does not concern* one—iwamatokiyapaśni. *T.*, iyowaźa śni.

i-wa'-to-ki-ya-śni, *v. n. to be none of one's business:* he etaŋhaŋ iwanitokiyaśni, *it is none of thy business.*

i-wa'-to-pe-ki-ya, *n. Ih. an oar* or *paddle; any thing to row a boat with.* See watopa.

i-wa'-tu-ka, *v. n. T. to be tired of* or *on account of* anything.

i-wa'-wi-ku-wa, *v. a. to do something to make* one *angry, to provoke* one—iwawiwakuwa. *T.*, iwakuwa.

i-wa'-ya-zaŋ, *v. n. to be sick in consequence of*—iwamayazaŋ.

i-wa'-yu-pi-ka, *v. n. to be skillful, handy on account of,* or *in doing*—iwamdupika; *i. q.* iwayupi kiçuŋ.

i-wa'-yu-pi-ya, *adv.* *handily, nicely, well.*

i-wa'-zi-ya-pa, *adv.* *to the north of.*

i-wa'-zi-ya-pa-taŋ-haŋ, *adv.* *to the north of.*

i-wa'-zi-ya-ta, *adv.* *at the north of.*

i-wa'-zi-ya-taŋ-haŋ, *adv.* *northward of.*

i-we', *v. n.* *to bleed by reason of*—iṃawe.

i'-we, *v. n.* *to bleed at the mouth*—íṃawe. *T.*, iwehiyu.

i-we'-će-ya, *v. a.* *to have regard for, do as one commands*—iwećewaya, iwećeuŋyaŋpi; iwećeyeśni, *to disregard*—iwećemayeśni. *T.*, wećeya.

i'-we-hi-yu-ya, *v.* *to raise blood, spit blood*—íwehiyuwaya.

i-we'-śde-ka, *v. n.* *to do something entitling to honor*, as the killing of an enemy—iwewaśdeka. *To wear* or *have as the evidence of bravery; insignia of honor.* The custom is to wear a split feather as a sign of having been wounded by the enemy.

i-wi'-ća-hna-yaŋ, *n.* of hnayaŋ; *deception.*

i-wi'-ća-hu-pi, *n.* of hu; *sodomy* This is now a vulgar byword.

i-wi'-ća-po, *n.* of po; *a swelling, inflation on account of.*

i'-wi-ća-pu-za, *n.* of ípuza; *thirst.*

i-wi'-ća-śte-ća, *n.* of iśteća; *shame.*

i-wi'-kće-mna, *adj.* *the tenth.* See ićiwikćemna.

i-wi'-kće-mna-mna, *adj. red.* of iwikćemna; *every tenth* one; *tithes.*

i-wiŋ'-kta, *v. n.* *to glory in, be proud of*—imawiŋkta, iniwiŋkta, uŋkiwiŋktapi.

i-wiŋ'-kta-kta, *v. red.* of iwiŋkta

i-wiŋ'-kta-pi, *n.* *a glorying in.*

i-wiŋ'-kta-ya, *v. a.* *to cause to glory in*—iwiŋktawaya.

i-wiŋ'-kta-ya, *adv.* *glorying, proudly.*

i-wi'-śtaŋ, *v. a.* *to treat well*, as a sick person—iwawiśtaŋ. See ikićiwiśtaŋ.

i-wi'-tko, *v. n.* of witko; *to be drunk on*—imawitko: taku iwitko, *something that makes drunk, liquor.*

i-wi'-tko-tko-ka, *v. n.* *to become foolish by means of.*

i-wi'-tko-ya, *v. a.* *to make drunk with*—iwitkowaya.

i'-wi-yo-hi-yaŋ-pa-ta, *adv.* *at the east of.*

i'-wi-yo-hi-yaŋ-pa-taŋ-haŋ, *adv.* *to the east of.*

i-wo'-blu, *v. n.* *T.* *to bluster; blowy, snowy: i. q.* ibomdu.

i-wo'-ġa-ġa, *n.* *T.* *a rifle.*

i-wo'-hda-ka, *v. pos* of iwoyaka; *to speak in reference to one's own*—iwowahdaka.

i-wo'-hdu-ze, *n.* *the cause of taboo.* See wohduze.

i-wo'-ḣta-ka, *v. n.* *T.* *to hit* or

strike against—iwomaħtaka; *i. q.*, iboħtaka.

i-wo′-mni-yaŋ, *adv. carefully, attentively:* iwomniyaŋ anaġoptaŋ, *he listened attentively. T.*, iktahela.

i-wo′-mni-yen, *adv. not hastily, leisurely, carefully:* iwomniyen ećamoŋ, *I did it carefully.*

i-wo′-mni-ye-tu, *adv. slowly, carefully.*

i-wo′-mni-ye-tu-ken, *adv. not in haste.*

i-wo′-so, *n. T. pouting lips.*

i-wo′-so-ki-ya, *v. T. to pout, push out the lips.* See iźokiya.

i-wo′-ya-ka, *v. a. to relate* or *tell of, to speak in reference to*—iwomdaka. See woyaka.

i-ya′, *intj. of surprise,* on meeting a friend unexpectedly.

I′-ya, *n. a fabulous creature worshipped by the Dakotas.*

i-ya′-be, *adv. individually, singly,* or *in little companies,* as the Dakotas go in hunting deer: iyabe uŋyaŋpi, *we are going separately. T.*, aweya.

i-ya′-be-ya, *adv. singly, separately, scattered,* as in hunting: iyabeya uŋyaŋpi, *we go separately. T.*, aweweya.

i′-ya-be-ya, *adv. scattering around, dispersedly:* íyabeya uŋkodepi, *scattering ourselves around we hunted.*

i-ya′-ći-ća, *adj. rough, ruffled up,* said of hair or feathers.

i-ya′-ćiŋ, *v. a. to liken to, compare with*—imdaćiŋ, idaćiŋ, uŋkiyaćiŋpi.

i-ya′-ćiŋ-ken, *adv. by way of comparison.*

i-ya′-ćiŋ-pi, *n. likeness, resemblance.*

i-ya′-ćiŋ-yaŋ, *adv. like to, in like manner, equal to; parabolically, metaphorically.*

i-ya′-ćiŋ-yaŋ-ken, *adv. somewhat like.*

i-ya′-ćo, *v. a.* of yaćo; *to judge of, judge on account of, to condemn for*—imdaćo, idaćo. *T.*, iyasu.

i-ya′-ćuŋ-ni, *v. n. to leave off, give up:* iyawaćuŋni. See iyakićuŋni.

i-ya′-di, *v. a.* of adi; *to climb up on*—iyawadi, iyayadi, iyauŋdipi. Hence, ćaŋ iyadipi, *stairs.*

i-yag′-toŋ, *v* of iyake; *to put a feather on an arrow*—iyagwatoŋ.

i-ya′-ġe, *n. a bunch, a cluster,* as as of grapes.

i-ya′-haŋ, *v. a.* of ahaŋ; *to go and stand on; to alight down in* or *on,* as birds in a cornfield or on a tree—iyawahaŋ, uŋkiyahaŋpi.

i′-ya-haŋ, *v. a. to put the foot on, step on* any thing—íyawahaŋ.

i′-ya-hda-pśiŋ-yaŋ, *adv.* of ahdapśiŋyaŋ; *bottom upwards.*

i-ya′-hda-pśiŋ-yaŋ, *v. a. to turn over upon* any thing—iyahdapśiŋwaya.

i-ya′-hda-ski-ća, *v. n.* of ahdaskića; *to lie on, press on, cover*—iyamahdaskića.

i-ya′-hda-skin, *cont.* of iyahdaskića; iyahdaskin mayaŋka, *it is pressing on me.*

i-ya'-hda-skin-ya, *v. a.* *to cause to press upon*—iyahdaskinwaya.

i-ya'-hda-śka, *v. pos.* of iyakaśka; *to tie one's own to*—iyawahdaśka, iyauŋhdaśkapi.

i-ya'-hde, *v. n* *to go* or *come to; to reach to, extend to; to lead to*, as a road; *to meet, come upon* one—iyamahde, iyauŋhdepi. See iyahdeya.

i-ya'-hde-haŋ-pa, *n.* (iyahde *and* haŋpa) *socks.* *T.*, huŋyakoŋ huha ptećela.

i-ya'-hde-huŋ-ska, *n.* (iyahde *and* huŋska) *socks, stockings.*

i-ya'-hde-toŋ, *v. a.* *to have on* or *over*, as, iyahdetoŋ ećoŋ, *he does it on* something else; *to knit.*

i-ya'-hde-toŋ-yaŋ, *adv.* *on* or *over, having something under:* iyahdetoŋyaŋ kaksa, *to cut* one stick *off on* another.

i-ya'-hde-ya, *v. a.* *to cause to reach to; to lead to, bring* one *to; to merit, deserve, bring upon* one—iyahdewaya, iyahdeuŋyaŋpi; iyahdeiçiya, *to bring on one's self*—iyahdemiçiya.

i-ya'-hde-ya, *adv.* *reaching to, even to.*

i'-ya-he, *n.* *the ball and heel of the foot.* *T.*, siyete iyahe.

i-ya'-hna, *prep.* *after, behind, following; with, together with:* iyahna ya, *to go with;* aŋpetu haŋyetu iyahna, *both day and night.*

i-ya'-hna-hna, *red.* of iyahna.

i'-ya-hna-hna-na, *adv.* *gently, carefully.* *T.*, iktahela; iwaśteglala.

i-ya'-hna-ken, *adv.* *in the manner of following.*

i-ya'-ȟpa-ya, *v. n.* *to fall upon, to seize, pounce upon, lay hold of violently*—iyawaȟpaya *and* iyawaȟpamda, iyayaȟpada, iyauŋȟpayapi. See aȟpaya.

i-ya'-ȟpe-ki-ći-ći-ya, *v. a.* *to put* or *throw on for* one, as in putting a load on a horse. See iyaȟpekiya.

i-ya'-ȟpe-ki-ya, *v. a.* *to give* or *hand to; to carry around to*, as the pipe is taken round on great occasions and held for each one to smoke; *to put on* or *throw over*, as in putting on the load of a horse—iyaȟpewakiya, iyaȟpeuŋkiyapi. *T.*, *to touch the ground with and then hold up to heaven*, as they do before smoking the pipe.—W. J. C.

i-ya'-ȟpe-ya, *v. a.* *to carry around to; to hand to; to throw over* or *on*—iyaȟpewaya. See iyaȟpekiya.

i-ya'-i-hda-śka, *v. reflex.* of iyakaśka; *to tie one's self; to give one's self up to be bound; i. q.* iyaiçihdaśka—iyamihdaśka, iyanihdaśka.

i'-ya-ka-ȟpe, *n.* of akaȟpa; *a cover* or *lid for the mouth* of any thing.

i'-ya-kam, *adv.* *beyond, surpassing.*

i'-ya-kam-tu, *adv.* *surpassingly.*

i'-ya-ka-pa, *v. n.* *to be larger than, to surpass*—íyamakapa.

i-ya'-ka-pa-taŋ-haŋ, *adv. T. afterwards; behind.*

i-ya'-ka-pe-i-çi-ya, *v. reflex. to go beyond one's self, to be intemperate.* See iyatahdeiçiya.

i'-ya-ka-pe-ya, *v. a. to pass, go beyond; to overcome; to persuade, succeed in persuading*—íyakapewaya, íyakapeuŋyaŋpi, íyakapemayaŋ.

i'-ya-ka-pe-ya, *adv. more than, surpassing.*

i-ya'-ka-pta, *v. a. to climb*, as a hill, *to reach the top; to pass over* or *beyond*—iyawakapta, iyauŋkaptapi, *and* uŋkiyakaptapi.

i-ya'-ka-pte-ya, *v. to cause to pass up* or *over*—iyakaptewaya.

i-ya'-ka-pte-ya, *adv. beyond, going over; going up hill.*

i-ya'-ka-saŋ-ni, *n. one side* or *half* of anything. See saŋni.

i-ya'-ka-saŋ-ni-na, *n. one side only*

i-ya'-ka-śka, *v. a.* of kaśkà; *to tie* one thing *to* or *on* another, *to bind to*—iyawakaśka, iyauŋkaśkapi.

i-ya'-ka-tiŋ, *v.*, of akatiŋ: *to measure by means of*, as with a yard-stićk—iyawakatiŋ.

i'-ya-ka-wiŋ, *v. n.* of akawiŋ; *to exceed, go beyond bounds, overflow*, as a river its banks.

i'-ya-ka-wiŋ, *adv. more than:* íyakawiŋ iyeya, *to surpass;* íyakawiŋ iyeya ećamoŋ, *I have done more than was needful. T.*, iyakab.

i'-ya-ka-wiŋ-yaŋ, *adv. surpassing.*

i-ya'-ke, *n. the feather end of a quill, the feather* on an arrow.

i-ya'-ke-noŋ-pa, *adj. the twelfth.* See iakenoŋpa. The ordinal numbers from this to *eighteen* will be found under "iake," and need not be repeated here, though by some they are all written with a *y* inserted.

i-ya'-ki-ći-yu-ha, *v. T. to be attached to*, as one horse to another.

i'-ya-ki-ćuŋ-ni, *v. n. to become tired and leave off, to cease from, give up pursuit*—íyawećuŋni, íyayećuŋni, íyauŋkićuŋnipi. See iyaćuŋni.

i'-ya-ki-ćuŋ-ni-ya, *v. a. to cause to leave off* or *cease from*—íyakićuŋniwaya.

i'-ya-ki-ćuŋ-ni-yaŋ, *adv. leaving off.*

i-ya'-ki-çu, *v. n. to be much, to increase.*

i-ya'-ki-çu, *adv. much, more than one needs:* iyakiçu wahnaka, *I have put away a great deal.*

i-ya'-ki-çuŋ-çuŋ-ka, *n. one who does more than is usual; one who keeps on begging.*

i-ya'-ki-çu-ya, *v. a. to have more than one needs*—iyakiçuwaya.

i-ya'-ki-çu-ya, *adv. much, a good deal, plentifully, in abundance:* iyakiçuya mduha, *I have a great deal.*

i'-ya-ki-de-će-ća, *adv. like, alike.* See iakidećeća.

i'-ya-ki-de-ćen, *adv. like.*

i′-ya-ki-de-haŋ-ke-ća, *adv.* *of the same length with.*

i′-ya-ki-de-haŋ-yaŋ, *adv.* *of equal distance.*

i′-ya-ki-de-na-ke-ća, *adv.* *of equal number.* See iakidenakeća.

i′-ya-ki-de-na-na, *adv.* *as few as.* See denana.

i-ya′-ki-gle-gle, *adv.* *T.* *over and over again, repeatedly.*

i-ya′-ki-hde, *v. n.* *to surpass, overlap, reach beyond* the time, as old corn lasting until the new comes. See akihde.

i-ya′-ki-hde, *adv.* *like to, as:* wetu iyakihde maśte, *it is as warm as spring.*

i-ya′-ki-hde-ġa, *v.* *to go on and overtake.*

i-ya′-ki-hdeh̔, *cont.* of iyakihdeġa; iyakihdeh̔ okihaŋ, *to keep following after but not overtake*—iyakihdeh̔ owakihaŋ.

i-ya′-ki-hde-ya, *v. a.* *to cause to reach round to; to make surpass*—iyakihdewaya

i-ya′-ki-hde-ya, *adv.* *surpassing.*

i′-ya-ki-he-će-ća, *adv.* *like to that.* See iakihećeća.

i-ya′-ki-he-haŋ-ke-ća, *adv.* *as long as.* See iakihehaŋkeća.

i′-ya-ki-he-na-ke-ća, *adv.* *as many as.* See iakihenakeća.

i′-ya-ki-he-na-na, *adv* *as few as.* See henana, etc.

i-ya′-ki-hna, *adv.* *in layers, one on another; i. q.* akihna.

i′-ya-ki-ni-sko-ke-ća, *adv.* *of the same size.*

i′-ya-ki-p'a-p'a, *v.* See íakip'ap'a.

i-ya′-ki-pe, *v. a.* *to wait for, wish to have go with* one; *to wait for, hope for; to befall, happen to*—iyawakipe, iyauŋkipepi, iyamakipe.

i-ya′-ki-pe-ya, *adv.* *waiting for.*

i′-ya-ki-ś'a, *v.* *T.* *to shout at one's own.*

i′-ya-ki-ś'a-ś'a, *v. red.* of iyakiś'a. See iyaś'a.

i′-ya-ki-ta, *v. a.* of akita; *to have an eye to, keep a watch on,* lest one commit some depredation; *to hunt for charges against* one—íyawakita.

i′-ya-ki-te-daŋ, *adv.* *together, familiarly, among themselves:* íyakitedaŋ hekićiyapi, *they say this among themselves.*

i′-ya-ko, *adv.* *beyond* anything. See ako.

i′-ya-kos, *adv.* See íyakosaŋ.

i′-ya-ko-saŋ, *adv.* *in addition, as an additional reason:* he íyakosaŋ dećen ećamoŋ, *I have done this in addition to that.* *T.*, iyakotaŋhaŋ.

i′-ya-ko-taŋ-haŋ, *adv.* *beyond, from beyond*

i-ya′-kta, *v.* Used only with śni. See iyaktaśni.

i-ya′-kta-śni, *v. a.* of aktaśni; *to disregard*—iyawaktaśni, iyauŋktapiśni.

i-yam′, *cont.* of iyapa; *striking against:* tiyopa iyam imdamde, *I struck against the door.*

i-ya'-mni, *adj.* of yamni; *the third.*

i-ya'-mni-mni, *adj. red. every third* one.

i-ya'-mni-mni, *or* i-a'-mni-mni, *v.* of amnimni, *to sprinkle,* as water on anything; *to sprinkle,* as clothes for ironing—iyawamnimni.

i-ya'-mni-na, *adj. only the third* one.

i-yam'-ya, *adv. butting* or *striking against.* See iyapa.

i-ya'-na-ka, *intj. of surprise* on meeting a friend.

i-ya'-na-pta, *v. a.* of anapta; *to detain, to go before and prevent from proceeding* — iyanawapta, iyanamapta.

i'-ya-ni-ća, *v. n.* of anića; *to be prevented, detained,* or *hindered by:* maġaźu kiŋ he iyamanića, *I am prevented by the rain*—íyamanića, íyauŋnićapi.

i-ya'-nuŋ-ġa, *v. n. to become hard, callous, unfeeling,* as a scarred place—iyamanuŋġa, iyaninuŋġa.

i-ya'-nuŋḣ, *cont.* of iyanuŋġa; iyanuŋḣ iyeya.

i-ya'-nuŋḣ-ya, *v. a. to cause to become callous*—iyanuŋḣwaya.

i-yaŋ'-pa, *v. a. to push out,* as an otter does his nose to breathe.

i-ya'-oŋ-pa, *v. a.* of aoŋpa; *to lay on, place on; to accuse of, blame with*—iyawaoŋpa, iyauŋḳoŋpapi, iyamaoŋpa.

i-ya'-oŋ-pa-pi, *n. an accusation.*

i-ya'-oŋ-pe-pi-ća-śni, *adj. blameless.*

i-ya'-oŋ-pe-pi-ća-śni-yaŋ, *adv. blamelessly.*

i-ya'-oŋ-pe-ya, *adv. in a blaming* or *accusing way.*

i-ya'-o-pta, *v.* See iyayupta.

i-ya'-p'a, *v. a.* of ap'a; *to beat, strike against; to beat,* as the heart or pulse, as, ćaŋte iyamap'a, *my heart beats; to strike* or *knock against,* as the foot—iyamap'a, iyauŋp'api; iyaiçip'a, *to strike one's self*—iyamiçip'a.

i'-ya-p'a, *v. n. to strike against,* as the wind against a hill.

i-ya'-pa, *v. n to be injured* or *wounded in one's feelings by* word or action. See iyapaka.

i-ya'-pa-ka, *v. n. to be injured* or *hurt in one's feelings by* something said—iyamapaka.

i-ya'-pa-spa, *v. n. to be obscured,* as the sun or moon by clouds. *T.,* taŋiŋśni. See apaspa.

i'-ya-pa-śtag, *cont.* of íyapaśtaka.

i'-ya-pa-śtag-ya, *v. a. to creep up and fall upon* before one is aware, *to take by surprise*—íyapaśtagwaya, íyapaśtagniyaŋpi, John xii, 35.

i'-ya-pa-śta-ka, *v. n. to be taken by surprise*—íyamapaśtaka, íyanipaśtaka.

i'-ya-pa-ṭo, *v. n. to butt against, be struck by; to press on* or *be cramped by,* as by a short moccasin—íyamapaṭo, íyauŋpaṭopi. See apaṭo.

i'-ya-pa-ṭo-ya, *v. a. to run*

against, press against; to hinder, prevent by—íyapaṭowaya.

i′-ya-pa-ṭo-ya-ken, *adv.* *in the manner of pressing against.*

i′-ya-pa-wo-haŋ-pi, *n.* *a certain sacred dance and feast.*

i-ya′-pa-ya, *v. a.* *to injure* or *hurt one's feelings by* what one says—iyapawaya. See iyapa.

i-ya′-pe, *v. a.* of ape; *to wait for; to lie in wait for, lie in ambush*—iyawape, iyauŋpepi, iyamape.

i-ya′-pe-haŋ, *v. a.* of pehaŋ; *to fold up with; to wind on,* as thread on a spool: haȟoŋta iyapehaŋpi, *spool-thread*—iyawapehaŋ, iyauŋpehaŋpi.

i-ya′-pe-haŋ-yaŋ, *adv.* *folding up.*

i′-ya-pe-la, *adv.* *T.* *near, close at hand; i. q.* ikiyela.

i-ya′-pe-mni, *v. a.* *to wrap around, wind up in*—iyawapemni, iyauŋpemnipi; *wrapped up in,* as, woaȟtani iyapemni uŋyakoŋpi, *we are enveloped in sin.*

i-ya′-pe-mni-yaŋ, *adv.* *wrapped up in.* See pemniyaŋ.

i-ya′-pe-ya, *v. a.* of iyape; *to cause to lie in wait for*—iyapewaya.

i-ya′-pe-ya, *adv.* *lying in wait for.*

i-ya′-pu-spa, *v. a.* *to glue, stick on with glue* or *paste*—iyawapuspa, iyauŋpuspapi.

i-ya′-pu-spa, *v. n.* *to stick to,* as wet clothes; *to be glued up,* as sore eyes—iyamapuspa. See puspa *and* askapa.

i-ya′-pu-spe-ya, *v. a.* *to cause to glue on*—iyapuspewaya.

i-ya′-pu-spe-ya, *adv.* *in a glued* or *sticking manner.*

i-ya′-sag, *cont.* of iyasaka.

i-ya′-sa-ka, *v. n.* of asaka; *to be dried hard on,* as skin garments on one—iyamasaka, iyauŋsakapi.

i′-ya-se, *n.* of íya; *a glutton.*

i-ya′-skam, *cont.* of iyaskapa; iyaskam waŋka, *it lies sticking on.*

i-ya′-skam-ya, *adv.* *sticking to.*

i-ya′-ska-pa, *v. n.* of askapa; *to stick to, stick on, adhere to*—iyamaskapa. See iyapuspa.

i-ya′-ski-ća, *v. a.* *to press* or *suck* one thing *on* another, as corn on the cob—imdaskića.

i-ya′-skin, *cont.* of iyaskića.

i-ya′-skin-ya, *adv.* *pressing* or *sucking on.*

i-ya′-ski-ska, *v. n.* *to be smoothed down,* as the hair of an animal by swimming in water—iyamaskiska. *T.*, stoyela.

i′-ya-sna-na, *adv.* *gently.* *T*, iwaśteglala.

i′-ya-sna-sna-na, *adv.* *carefully, gently.*

i-ya′-sni, *v. n.* of asni; *to become still,* as a noise ceasing: ećen iyasni, *so it became still; to recover from,* as from anger or sickness.

i-ya′-sni-ya, *v. a.* *to give to* one *unexpectedly; to make quiet*—iyasniwaya.

i-ya′-su, *v. a.* *T.* *to judge, condemn for;* *i. q.* iyaćo.

i′-ya-ś'a, *v.* of aś'a; *to shout at, shout against*—íyawaś'a, íyauŋś'api.

i′-ya-śla-ya, *adv.* *T.* *plainly, clearly:* *i. q.* aślayela.

i-ya′-ta, *v. a.* *to promise to give, betroth to* one, as a girl to a man—imdata, idata. *T.*, ḳu kta eya.

i′-ya-tab-ye-la, *adv.* *T.* *soon after.*

i-ya′-ta-hde, *v. n.* *to go beyond, surpass; to go beyond ordinary bounds, be excessive.*

i-ya′-ta-hde, *adv.* *full, running over.*

i-ya′-ta-hde-ya, *v. a.* *to go beyond, surpass; to do more than is right, exact too much; to cause to go beyond; to be intemperate*—iyatahdewaya, iyatahdeuŋyaŋpi; iyatahdeiçiya, *he is intemperate.*

i-ya′-ta-hde-ya, *adv.* *too much.*

i-ya′-ta-ku-ni-śni, *v. n.* *to come to nothing, come to naught.*

i′-ya-tam, *adv.* *soon, soon again.* See itam.

i-ya′-t'aŋ, *v. n.* *to touch with the mouth; to light,* as a pipe, which is done by drawing a few times when put to the fire—imdat'aŋ, idat'aŋ; ikićiyat'aŋ, *to light* a pipe *for* one.

i-ya′-ta-sag, *cont.* of iyatasaka.

i-ya′-ta-sag-ya, *adv.* *stiffly.*

i-ya′-ta-sa-ka, *v. n.* of tasaka; *to become hard* or *stiff on* one, as skin that has been wet and dried; *stiff* or *frozen on*—iyamatasaka, iyauŋtasakapi.

i′-ya-ta-ye-la, *adv.* *T.* *personally, it alone.* See atayedaŋ.

i-ya′-wa, *v. a.* of yawa; *to count by* or *according to, count together*—imdawa, idawa.

i-ya′-ya, *v. n.* *to have gone*—imdamde, idade, uŋkiyayapi: *to have gone down,* as, wi iyaya, *the sun has gone down; to be more than, go over; to be more than enough, be a surplus,* as, oŋġe iyaya, *there is some over;* ikićiyaya, *to remain for* or *stand to one's credit.*

i-ya′-ye-ya, *v. a.* *to cause to go* or *have gone, to send*—iyayewaya.

i-ya′-yu-ḣa, *v.* *T.* *to have an attachment for, be a follower of:* iyayuḣ wauŋ, *I am following him.*

i-ya′-yuḣ-ya, *adv.* *T.* *following.*

i-ya′-yu-pta, *v. n.* *to pass by without stopping*—iyamdupta, iyadupta, iyauŋyuptapi.

i-ya′-yu-pte-ya, *adv.* *passing by.*

i-ya′-yus, *cont.* of iyayuza; iyayus yuza, *to hold* anything *close to* another.

i-ya′-yu-stag, *cont.* of iyayuśtaka, *with, together with.*

i-ya′-yu-sta-ka, *v.* iyayustag heyuŋ, *to tie up one* thing *on another*—iyayustag hemuŋ.

i-ya′-yu-za, *v. a.* of yuza; *to hold to* or *at*—iyamduza.

i-ya′-yu-za, *n.* *a holder,* as a cloth to hold a hot iron with.

i-ya′-za, *adv.* *one after another:*

iyaza kaṭa, *to kill one after another;* ti iyaza wauŋ, *I go from house to house.*

i-ya'-zaŋ, *v. n.* of yazaŋ; *to be sck on account of* or *by means of; to be affected by sympathy with*—imayazaŋ, iniyazaŋ.

i-ya'-zi, *v. T. to be convalescent.*

i-ya'-zin, *cont.* of iyazita.

i-ya'-zin-ya, *v. a. to burn,* as sweet leaves, *to burn incense*—iyazinwaya.

i-ya'-zi-ta, *v. n. to burn,* as cedar leaves, *to smoke and make a pleasant smell.* See izita.

i-ya'-źu, *n.* of aźu; *something used to spread out and dry on:* ćaŋśaśa iyaźu, *a stick split partly, with others woven across, on which smoking-bark is placed to dry. T.,* ipusye.

i'-ye, *pers. pron. he, she, it. Pl.,* iyepi, *they.*

i-ye'-će-ća, *adv. like, like as, like to, such as, the same as.* See dećeća, hećeća, *and* kakeća.

i-ye'-će-ća, *v. n. to be like to*—iyemaćeća, iyenićeća, iyeuŋćećapi; *it is fitting, proper:* hećamoŋ kta iyećeća, *it is proper that I should do that.*

i-ye'-će-će-ȟiŋ, *adv. just like.*

i-ye'-će-kće-ća, *adv. red.* of iyećeća.

i-ye'-će-kćeŋ-ya, *adv. red.* of iyećenya.

i-ye'-ćen, *adv. like, in like manner.* See dećen *and* ećen.

i-ye'-ćen-ya, *adv. like; a little less, not much:* iyećenya se maḳu, *he gave me about so much.*

i-ye'-će-tu, *v. n. to be so, become so, to be as was expected; to come to pass, take place.* See ećetu, dećetu, hećetu, *and* kaketu.

i-ye'-će-tu, *adv. so, thus, right.*

i-ye'-će-tu-ya, *v. a. to make so, fulfill, accomplish*—iyećetuwaya.

i-ye'-će-tu-ya, *adv. so.*

i-ye'-će-tu-ya-ken, *adv. in this manner.*

i'-ye-ćiŋ, *adv.* (iye *and* ćiŋ) *voluntarily, of one's own accord, of one's self.*

i'-ye-ćiŋ-ka, *adv. of one's self, of one's own accord, without advice:* miyećiŋka ećamoŋ, *I did it of myself.*

i'-ye-ćiŋ-ka-haŋ, *adv. voluntarily.*

i-ye'-ću-ȟćiŋ, *pro. T. he himself.*

i'-ye-eś, *pron. he, she, it.*

i-ye'-ġa, *v n. to shine, sparkle, twinkle,* as the stars. *T.,* ileġa.

i-ye'-han, *adv. at* or *to the place; at the time appointed.* See dehan, hehan, *and* kahan.

i-ye'-ḥan-han-tu, *adv. red.* of iyehantu; *at the times* or *places referred to.*

i-ye'-han-tu, *adv. at the time, now, at the same time; it is now the time; there, thus far, so far.* See dehaŋtu *and* kahantu.

i-ye'-han-tu-daŋ, *adv. just at the time.*

i-ye′-han-tu-daŋ-ḣiŋ, *adv.* *exactly at the time.*

i-ye′-han-tu-śni, *adv.* *not time yet.*

i-ye′-han-tu-ya, *adv.* *at the time.*

i-ye′-han-wa-pa, *adv.* *towards the time.*

i-ye′-haŋ-haŋ-ke-ća, *adv.* *red.* of iyehaŋkeća.

i-ye′-haŋ-haŋ-yaŋ, *adv.* *red.* of iyehaŋyaŋ.

i-ye′-haŋ-ke-ća, *adv.* *so long, of the same length.*. See dehaŋkeća *and* hehaŋkeća.

i-ye′-haŋ-yaŋ, *adv.* *so far; at the proper time.* See dehaŋyaŋ, hehaŋyaŋ, *and* kahaŋyaŋ.

i-yeḣ′, *cont.* of iyeġa. *T.*, ileḣ.

i-yeḣ′-ya, *v. a.* *to cause to shine*—iyeḣwaya. *T.*, ileḣya.

i-yeḣ′-ye-ġa, *v.* *red.* of iyeġa; *to twinkle.* *T.*, ileḣleġa.

i-yeḣ′-yeḣ-ya, *v. a.* *to cause to twinkle*

i-ye′-i-ç̣i-ya, *v.* *reflex.* of iyeya; *to find one's self; to put* or *thrust one's self:* ohna iyeiç̣iya, *to push* or *crowd one's self in.*

i′-ye-i-tkom, *adv.* *T.*, iye śitkob. See iyeitkopataŋhaŋ.

i′-ye-i-tko-pa-taŋ-haŋ, *adv.* *returning the compliment;* as when one says to another what was fit should be said to himself.

i′-ye-ka-eś, *pron.* *even he.* *T.*, iyekaleś.

i-ye′-ki-ći-han-tu, *v. n.* *to be suitable for* one, *be befitting* or *belong to* one; *to be the time* or *opportunity for* one—iyemićihantu, iyeuŋkićihantupi. See iyehantu.

i-ye′-ki-ya, *v. a.* *pos.* of iyeya; *to find one's own; to recognise* any person or thing; *to experience,* as, iyotaŋhaŋ iyekiya, *to find it hard, have difficulty; to put* or *push one's own in,* as, ohna iyekiya—iyewakiya, iyeuŋkiyapi, iyemakiya.

i-ye′-kta-śni, *adv.* *T.* *incorrectly, not according to rule.*

i′-ye-ḳe, *pron.* *he himself, even he, she herself,* etc. *T.*, iyeśkalaka.

i′-ye-ḳeś, *pron.* Same as íyeḳe.

i-ye′-na, *adv.* *so many, as many as.* See dena, hena, *and* kana.

i-ye′-na-ka, *adv.* *as many as.*

i-ye′-na-ke-ća, *adv.* *so many, as many as, as much as*—iyemanakeća, iyeuŋnakećapi. *T.*, iyenakća. See denakeća, henakeća, *and* kanakeća.

i-ye′-naŋg-na-ke-ća, *adv.* *red.* of iyenakeća.

i-ye′-pe, *v. n.* *to lodge on,* as one tree on another in falling. *T.*, iyope.

i-ye′-pe-pe-ya, *adv.* *unsettled, without an abiding place, going from house to house:* iyepepeya wauŋ, *I am unsettled.*

i-ye′-pe-ya, *v. a.* *to make* one tree *lodge on* another—iyepewaya, iyepeuŋyaŋpi. *T.*, iyopeya.

i-ye′-pe-ya, *adv.* *lodging on*

i′-yeś, *pron.* See iyeeś.

i-ye'-śni, *intj* *you don't say so! it cannot be!*—iyepiśni. *T.*, iyeśnićaś.

i-ye'-śni-ća, *intj.* Same as iyeśni.

i-ye'-ya, *v. a.* *to find* anything; *to put, place,* or *thrust* into: ohna iyeya, *to thrust into*—iyewaya, iyeuŋyaŋpi. See iyeiçiya.

i-ye'-ya, *v. aux.* It is appended to verbs commencing with "ba," "bo," "ka," "pa," "ya," etc., and also to some adverbs; and generally gives *emphasis*, and expresses *quickness* or *suddenness of action*—iyewaya, iyeyaya, iyeuŋyaŋpi.

i-ye'-ya, *or* i-ye-ye, *v. n.* *to be, exist:* wićaśta iyeye ćiŋ, *all men.* See also hiyeye.

i-ye'-źa-ka, *adv* See iyeźakaken.

i-ye'-źa-ka-ken, *adv.* *unable, failing by a little;* said when one fails of doing what he has been accustomed to do: iyeźakaken temye śni, *he was unable to eat it up.*

i-yo', *prep. in comp.* compounded of *i* and *o*, with *y* introduced for euphony; *to, in, into.*

i-yo'-blu-la, *n.* *T.* *a sheltered place*

i-yo'-blu-la, *adv.* *T.* *sheltered.*

i-yo'-ća-hda, *adv* *rattling;* said of a noise made in the mouth: iyoćahda se iyaya, *to go down rattling,* as a bullet when put into a gun.

i-yo'-ćo-ka-ya, *adv* (i *and* oćokaya) *in the midst of; all put into the mouth; all swallowed up in;* wićoŋte kiŋ he woohiye kiŋ e oćowasiŋ iyoćokaya, *death is swallowed up in victory*

i-yo'-ćo-tka, *n.* *the two large lobes of the stomach.*

i-yog', *cont.* of iyoka; iyog iyeya, *to put on one side, to drive out*—iyog iyewaya, iyog iyeuŋyaŋpi.

i-yog'-ya, *adv.* *aside, away.*

i-yo'-ha-kam, *adv.* *after* in time, *subsequent to.* See ihakam *and* ohakam.

i-yo'-ha-kam-tu, *adv.* *afterwards*

i-yo'-ha-kam-tu-ya, *adv.* *afterwards.*

i-yo'-ha-kam-tu-ya-ken, *adv.* *a little after.*

i-yo'-ha-ka-pa, *adv.* *subsequent to.* See ihakapa.

i-yo'-ha-ka-pa-taŋ-haŋ, *adv.* *afterwards.* *T.*, iyakapataŋhaŋ.

i-yo'-haŋ, *v. a.* of ohaŋ; *to boil* one thing *with* another—iyowahe, iyouŋhaŋpi.

i-yo'-hda-hda, *adv.* *rattling;* iyohdahda se iyaya, *to make a noise,* as a bullet put into a gun, *to go down with a rattling noise.*

i-yo'-hda-mna, *adv.* *circuitously, round all the crooks and turns.*

i-yo'-hda-mna-yaŋ, *adv.* *circuitously, particularly:* iyohdamnayaŋ wohdaka, *to relate particularly.*

i-yo'-hda-mni-yaŋ, *adv.* *round about, circuitously.*

i-yo′-hdi, *n.* *a razor-strop; a hone, whetstone.* *T*, miyogli.

i-yo′-hdi-ya, *v. a.* *to rub back and forth*, as in whetting or stropping a razor—iyohdiwaya.

i′-yo-he, *n.* *something wrapped around the feet, socks, stockings.*

i-yo′-hi, *adj.* *each, every one; i. q.* otoiyohi.

i-yo′-hi-la, *adj.* *T.* *each one: i. q.* iyohi.

i-yo′-hi, *v. a.* *to reach, get to, arrive at*, a place—iyowahi: *to be sufficient for, reach to* one, as in a division of articles; *to be large enough for*, as a garment—iyomahi, iyouŋhipi, iyowićahi.

i-yo′-hi-ki-ya, *v. a.* *to cause to reach* or *arrive at; to give to each one, make go round*, as in dividing articles; *to pay one's debts entirely up*—iyohiwakiya, iyohiuŋkiyapi.

i-yo′-hi-śni, *v.* *not to reach to.* See iyohi.

i-yo′-hi-śni-yaŋ, *v. a.* *to cause not to reach to.* See iyohiya.

i-yo′-hi-ya, *v. a.* *to cause to reach* a place; *to extend the hand to; to make reach to all; to pay up one's debts*—iyohiwaya, iyohiuŋyaŋpi.

i′-yo-hmus, *cont.* of íyohmuza; íyohmus yaŋka.

i′-yo-hmus-ya, *v. a.* *to cause to shut the mouth.*

i′-yo-hmu-za, *v. n.* (i *and* ohmuza) *to have the mouth shut, lay the hand on the mouth*—íyowahmuza.

i-yo′-hnag, *cont.* of iyohnaka; iyohnag iyeya,

i-yo′-hnag-ki-ya, *v. a.* *to put into the mouth of* another; *to give to eat, cause to eat*—iyohnagwakiya.

i-yo′-hnag-ya, *v. a.* *to cause to put into the mouth, give food to*—iyohnagwaya.

i-yo′-hna-ka, *v. a.* (i *and* ohnaka) *to put into the mouth*, as food—iyowahnaka, iyouŋhnakapi.

i-yo′-hna-ka, *n.* *a mouthful.*

i-yo′-ḣa, *n.* *the lower part of the face, the side of the face; the jowl, lower jaw* of animals.

i-yo′-ḣa-ćaŋ-du-hu-pa, *n* *the common short-stemmed pipe.* *T.*, iyoḣaćaŋnoŋpa.

i-yo′-ḣa-hiŋ, *n.* *whiskers:* iyoḣahiŋśma *and* iyoḣiŋśma, *heavy whiskers.*

i-yo′-ḣa-ḣa, *n.* *T.* *water-falls.* See ḣaḣa.

i-yo′-ḣda-te-ya, *adv.* of oḣdateya; *underneath.*

i-yo′-ḣlo-ke, *n* *T.* *the mouth of a stream.*

i-yo′-ḣpa. See iyuḣpa.

i-yo′-ḣpa-ya, *v. a.* *to go in, fall into, alight in*, as ducks in a pond; *to join, become partakers of*, as in joining a church or society—iyowaḣpamda.

i-yo′-ḣpe-ki-ya, *v. a.* Same as iyoḣpeya.

i-yo′-ḣpe-ya, *v. a.* *to throw* or *cast into; to cause to fall into, to plant*, as corn or other grain—iyoḣpewaya: iyoḣpeiçiya, *to cast one's self into*—iyoḣpemiçiya.

i-yo'-ka, *adj.* *another*, as, wića-śta iyoka, *another man; in another place, elsewhere.*

i-yo'-ka-da, *v a.* of okada; *to empty* or *pour into*, as grain—iyo-wakada.

i-yo'-ka-da, *n.* *something into which anything is poured to measure with*: mazakaŋ iyokada, *a gun-charger.*

i-yo'-ka-du-za, *n.* *air in motion, a breeze.* See kaduza *and* okaduza.

i-yo'-ka-du-za, *adj.* *airy, cool.*

i'-yo-ka-ġa, *adv.* of okaġa; *down stream, south of, below.* *T.*, ihutab.

i'-yo-ka-ġa-taŋ-haŋ, *adv.* *from down stream, south of.*

i'-yo-kaḣ, *cont.* of íyokaġa.

i'-yo-kaḣ-ki-ya, *adv.* *down stream, south of.*

i'-yo-kaḣ-wa-pa, *adj.* *down stream, in a southerly direction.*

i-yo'-kan, *cont.* of iyokata.

i-yo'-kan-ya, *v. a.* *to warm, make hot in*—iyokanwaya, iyo-kanmayaŋ; *to heat with*, as a room by means of a stove.

i-yo'-ka-pa, *v.* of kapa; *to sur-pass*—iyowakapa.

i-yo'-ka-pas, *cont.* of iyokapaza.

i-yo'-ka-pas-ya, *v. a.* *to exert an evil influence upon*, as on a sick person by one's presence, *to make worse*—iyokapaswaya, iyokapas-mayaŋ.

i-yo'-ka-pas-ye-ća, *v. a.* Same as iyokapasya.

i-yo'-ka-pa-taŋ-haŋ, *adv.* *be-hind, after; younger than*—miyoka-pataŋhaŋ. Same as iyohakapa-taŋhaŋ. *T.*, iyakapataŋhaŋ.

i-yo'-ka-pa-za, *v. n.* *to be pun-gent, make smart*, as pepper or mus-tard seed in the mouth—iyomaka-paza.

i-yo'-ka-pte, *n.* of kapte; *some-thing to dip with, a dipper, ladle.*

i-yo'-ka-śke, *n.* of kaśka; *some-thing that connects, something to bind with.*

i-yo'-ka-ta, *v. n.* of okata; *to be warm in, warm by reason of.*

i-yo'-ka-taŋ, *v. a.* of okataŋ; *to drive in*, as a nail, *on* something—iyowakataŋ, iyouŋkataŋpi.

i-yo'-ka-tku-ġe, *n.* of katkuġa; *a nail, screw;* tiyopa iyokatkuġe, *nails;* maza iyokatkuġe, *nails.* *T.*, *a nut of a screw.*

i-yo'-ka-wiŋ-ġa, *v.* *to turn round and round.*

i-yo'-ka-wiŋḣ, *cont.* of iyoka-wiŋġa.

i-yo'-ka-zi-ća-hde, *adv.* *stretch-ing up, on tip-toe:* iyokazićahde waŋyaka, *to see by stretching up.* *T.*, igluzića.

i-yo'-ki, *v. a.* *to permit, encourage.* Not used except with "śni," or in a negative form. See iyokiśni *and* iyokika.

i-yo'-ki-ća-sde-ća, *v. a.* of ka-sdeća; *to split in two in the middle*—iyokiwakasdeća.

i-yo'-ki-ća-śka, *v. a.* of **kaśka**;

to tie together, as two strings—iyokiwakaśka.

i-y o'-k i-ć a-ś k e-y a, *adv. tied together, connected* or *following each other*, as the seasons, without any intervening time.

i-y o'-k i-ć a-ś p a, *v. a.* of kaśpa; *to divide in the middle*—iyokiwakaśpa.

i'-y o-k i-h e, *v. n. to be next to, be second*—íyowakihe.

i'-y o-k i-h e, *adj. second, next to.*

i-y o'-k i-h e, *n. a joint:* hu iyokihe, *the leg-joint.* See ókihe.

i'-y o-k i-h e-y a, *adv. lengthened out, added to, next to, following, succeeding.* See okiheya.

i-y o'-k i-h i, *v. a.* of okihi; *to be able for; to come upon, come up with*—iyowakihi, iyouŋkihipi.

i-y o'-k i-h i-y a, *v. a. to make able for*—iyokihiwaya. See okihiya.

i-y o'-k i-h i-y a, *adv. ably.*

i-y o'-k i-h n a g, *cont.* of iyokihnaka; iyokihnag hiŋhda, *at the same instant;* said of guns fired off at the same time.

i-y o'-k i-h n a-k a, *v. a.* of okihnaka; *to put* or *place in together; to put in one's own mouth*—iyowakihnaka.

i-y o-k i'-k a, *v. a. to forbid, hinder.* Same as iyokiśni.

i-y o'-k i-n i-h a ŋ, *adj.* of okinihaŋ; *honored for.*

i-y o'-k i-n i-h a ŋ-y a ŋ, *adv. honorably.*

i-y o'-k i-p i, *v. a. to please, be pleasing to*—iyowakipi, iyouŋkipipi, iyoćićipi.

i-y o'-k i-p i, *v. n. to be pleased with, to like; to be contented*—iyomakipi, iyonićipi, iyouŋkipipi.

i-y o'-k i-p i-y a, *v. a. to please, cause to be pleased*—iyokipiwaya, iyokipiuŋyaŋpi, iyokipimayaŋ.

i-y o'-k i-p i-y a, *adv. delightfully, pleasantly.*

i-y o'-k i-p t a, *v. pos.* of iyopta; *to go towards home; to advance, go on, make progress in* any business of *one's own*—iyomakipta, iyonićipta.

i-y o'-k i-s e, *n.* of okise; *the half* of anything cut in two.

i-y o'-k i-ś i-ć a, *v. n. to be sad, sorry, grieved*—iyomakiśića, iyonićiśića, iyouŋkiśićapi: waćiŋ iyokiśića, *to be displeased with, have one's mind made sad by*—waćiŋ iyowakiśića.

i-y o'-k i-ś i-ć a-p i, *n. sadness, sorrow.*

i-y o'-k i-ś i-ć a-y a, *v. a. to make sad, to sadden.* See iyokiśinya.

i-y o'-k i-ś i-ć a-y a, *adv. sadly.*

i-y o'-k i-ś i n, *cont.* of iyokiśića; iyokiśin wauŋ.

i-y o'-k i-ś i n-y a, *v. a. to sadden, grieve, displease, disappoint*—iyokiśinwaya, iyokiśinuŋyaŋpi, iyokiśinmayaŋ.

i-y o'-k i-ś i n-y a, *adv. in a manner producing sadness, sadly.*

i-y o-k i'-ś n i, *v. a. to forbid, prevent, hinder*—iyowakiśni, iyouŋkipiśni, iyomakiśni, iyoćićiśni. See iyokika, anića, etc.

i-yo'-ki-ta-he-daŋ, *adv.* *between.* See okitahedaŋ.

i-yo'-ki-taŋ-iŋ, *n.* of otaŋiŋ; *manifestation.*

i-yo'-ki-taŋ-iŋ-yaŋ, *adv.* *manifestly.*

i'-yo-ki-wiŋ, *v. a.* *to make a motion with the mouth, to gesture to* one *with the mouth*—íyowakiwiŋ.

i'-yo-ki-yu-sde-ća, *v. n.* of yusdeća; *to split in two, be divided in customs.*

i'-yo-ki-yu-sden, *cont.* of iyokiyusdeća; *divided in customs:* íyokiyusden uŋyakoŋpi, *we are in a divided state.*

i-yo'-ko-hnag, *cont.* See iyokihnag.

i'-yo-ko-pe-ya, *adv.* *opposite to, beyond, in sight:* mde íyokopeya waŋka, *it lies beyond the lake.*

i'-yo-kos, *adv.* *in the mean time.*

i'-yo-ko-saŋ, *adv.* *in the mean time.* See osaŋ.

i-yo'-kpa-ni, *v. n.* *to lack, be wanting; to be less than, not enough; to fail, not to reach in time, not to accomplish*—iyowakpani, iyouŋkpanipi.

i-yo'-kpa-ni-ya, *v. a.* *to cause to lack,* etc.—iyokpaniwaya.

i-yo'-kpa-ni-yaŋ, *adv.* *lacking, failing of.*

i-yo'-ḳo-pa, *n.* *the board on which a Dakota child is fastened.* See hokśiyoḳopa.

i-yo'-mda-ye, *n.* of omdaye; *a plain extending from,* as from a hill.

i-yo'-mni, *n.* *a sheltered place, a harbor.*

i-yo'-mni-na, *n.* *a sheltered place, a harbor.* *T.*, ioblula. See omnina.

i-yo'-mni-yaŋ, *adv.* *in a sheltered place; more particularly, over again;* iyomniyaŋ oćićiyake kte śni, *I will not tell it to you again.*

i-yo'-mni-yen, *adv* *leisurely.* *T.*, ḣaŋhiya. See iwomniyen.

i-yo'-mni-ye-tu, *adv.* *slowly, carefully.* See iwomniyetu.

i-yo'-na-ni-yaŋ *and* i-yo'-ka-ṅi-yaŋ, *v. n.* *T.* *to be jarred* or *shaken* by something heavy falling.

i-yo'-o-pta, *adv.* of opta; *through, beyond.* See iyopta.

i-yo'-o-pta-i-ya-ya, *v.* *to go by* or *beyond, go on further; to go through, pass through.* See iyoptaiyaya.

i-yo'-o-pta-i-ya-ya-pi, *n.* See iyooptaiyeyapi.

i-yo'-o-pta-i-ye-ya-pi, *n.* *a purge, a cathartic,* as rhubarb, salts, oil, etc.

i-yo'-o-pta-ya, *v. n.* *to pass on, go beyond.*

i-yo'-pa-ski-ća, *v. a.* *T.* *to press in, ram in,* as in loading a gun.

i'-yo-pa-śtag, *cont.* of íyopaśtaḳa; íyopaśtag wauŋ, *I am exciting.*

i'-yo-pa-śtag-ya, *adv.* *encouragingly.*

i'-yo-pa-śta-ka, *v. a. to excite, incite, encourage*—íyowapaśtaka, íyouŋpaśtakapi, íyomapaśtaka, íyoćipaśtaka.

i-yo'-pa-ta, *v. a. to patch, sew a piece on*—iyowapata, iyouŋpatapi.

i-yo'-pa-zaŋ, *v. a.* of opazaŋ; *to put into the mouth; to put in around the waist; to load*, as a gun—iyowapazaŋ.

i-yo'-pa-zaŋ, *n. something to bind* or *hold in*, as a ferrule; *the brass ring that holds in the ramrod of a gun; the ramrod itself; the bore* of a gun.

i-yo'-pe, *v. n. T. to fall and lodge on*, as one tree on another: *i. q.* iyepe.

i-yo'-pe-i-ç̣i-ya, *v. reflex.* of iyopeya; *to blame one's self, reprove one's self; to repent, change one's self; to sell one's self*—iyopemiç̣iya, iyopeuŋkiç̣iyapi.

i-yo'-pe-i-ç̣i-ya-pi, *n. a blaming one's self, repentance.*

i-yo'-pe-ki-ya, *v a. to reprove, chide, scold, to correct, punish; to change for* something else, *exchange*—iyopewakiya, iyopeuŋkiyapi, iyopemakiya, iyopećićiya.

i-yo'-pe-ya, *v. a. to chide, reprove; to correct, punish; to give in exchange for, barter*—iyopewaya, iyopeuŋyaŋpi.

i-yo'-pe-ya, *v. a. T. to make lodge on.*

i-yo'-pe-ya, *adv. T. lodging on.*

i-yo'-pe-ye, *n. the price paid: exchange.*

i-yo'-pśa-pśa, *v. n. T. to boil up in bubbles.*

i-yo'-pśa-pśa-ye, *adv. T. red.* of iyopśaye.

i-yo'-pśa-ye, *adv. T. close together; i. q.* akipśa.

i-yo'-pta, *v. n. to go on, move on*, as a cloud; *to go forward, advance, make progress in* anything—imayopta *and* iyomapta, iniyopta *and* iyonipta, uŋkiyoptapi *and* iyouŋptapi.

i-yo'-pta, *adv.* of opta; *through.* See iyoopta.

i-yo'-pta-i-ya-ya, *v. n. to pass through, pass on.* See iyooptaiyaya.

i-yo'-pta-i-ye-ya, *v. a. to cause to pass through.*

i-yo'-pta-i-ye-ya-pi, *n. a purge, cathartic; i. q.* iyooptaiyeyapi.

i-yo'-pte-ya, *v. n. to have acquired some skill, made some progress*—iyoptewaya.

i-yo'-pu-ḣdi, *n. wadding for a gun.*

i-yo'-pu-ḣdi-ya, *v. a. to use for gun-wadding.*

i-yo'-pu-ski-ća, *n. a ramrod. T.*, iyopazaŋ.

i-yo-pu-ski-ća, *v. a. to ram in tight: i. q.* iyopaskića.

i-yos'. See heniyȯs.

i-yos'-na-na. See heniyosnana.

i-yo'-śni-źa, *v. n. to be blinded by* the sun or snow—iyomaśniźa. See iśtośniźa.

i-yo'-śtaŋ, *n.* of ośtaŋ; *something*

pushed into the mouth of anything, *a vial-cork, a stopper.* See iośtaŋ.

i-yo'-śtaŋ-pi, *n.* *a cork, a stopper.*

i-yo'-ta-he-daŋ, *adv.* *between:* uŋkiyotahedaŋ, *between us.* See otahedaŋ.

i-yo'-ta-he-pi, *adv.* *between* one place and another. See otahepi.

i-yo'-ta-koŋs, *cont.* of iyotakoŋza; *opposite to, over against.* *T.*, iyotalkoŋs. See otakoŋs.

i-yo'-ta-koŋs-ya, *adv.* *even with, opposite to.*

i-yo'-ta-koŋ-za, *adv.* of otakoŋza; *opposite to, over against; even with.* *T.*, iyotalkoŋza.

i-yo'-taŋ, *adj.* *great, greater, greatest, chief;* used in comparing one thing with another—imayotaŋ, iniyotaŋ, uŋkiyotaŋpi.

i-yo'-taŋ, *adv.* *most, very:* iyotaŋ waśte, *very good, the best;* iyotaŋ ksapa, *the wisest;* iyotaŋ śića, *the worst.* See also iyotaŋiyekiya.

i-yo'-taŋ-da, *v.* See iyotaŋdaka.

i-yo'-taŋ-da-ka, *v. a.* *to esteem most, value most highly*—iyotaŋwadaka.

i'-yo-taŋg, *cont.* of íyotaŋka; íyotaŋg hiyeya.

i'-yo-taŋg-ki-ya, *v. a.* *to cause to sit down*—íyotaŋgwakiya.

i-yo'-taŋ-haŋ, *adv.* *very much.* Same as iyotaŋ. See iyotaŋhaŋiyekiya.

i-yo'-taŋ-haŋ-i-ye-ki-ya, *v. a.* *to have trouble, have a hard time, have difficulty; to trouble, make difficulty* or *hardship for* another—iyotaŋhaŋiyewakiya.

i-yo'-taŋ-ȟćiŋ, *adv.* *T.* *chiefly, most of all.*

i-yo'-taŋ-i-ye-ki-ya, *v. a.* *to find it difficult* or *hard, experience difficulty from; to trouble, make labor* or *difficult for* one—iyotaŋiyewakiya; iyotaŋiyemayakiya, *thou hast given me a hard time.*

i'-yo-taŋ-ka, *v. n.* *to sit, be sitting; to sit down; to sit up, get up*—ímdotaŋka, ídotaŋka.

i'-yo-taŋ-ka-haŋ, *part.* *sitting.*

i'-yo-taŋ-ke-haŋ, *part.* *sitting.*

i-yo'-taŋ-yaŋ, *v. a.* *to count the greatest*—iyotaŋwaya.

i-yo'-taŋ-yaŋ, *adv.* *greatly.*

i-yo'-tpa-ni, *v. a.* Same as iyokpani.

i-yo'-tpa-ni-yaŋ, *adv.* Same as iyokpaniyaŋ.

i-yo'-ṭo-hnag, *cont.* of iyoṭohnaka; iyoṭohnag mda, *I go at the risk of my life.*

i-yo'-ṭo-hna-ka, *v. n.* *to hazard life, risk one's life, go into danger.* See aoṭohnaka.

i-yo'-wa, *v. n.* *to gape, yawn*—iyowawa, iyouŋwapi. *T.*, iyoya.

i-yo'-wa, *n.* *writing materials.* See iowa.

i-yo'-waŋg, *cont.* of iyowaŋke; iyowaŋgićiya, *to be in the habit of, form a habit, take lessons from*—iyowaŋgmićiya. See owaŋgya.

i-yo'-waŋ-k'e, *n.* *habit.*

i-yo′-waś, *cont.* of iyowaźa; iyowaś waun śni *I am not near it.*

i-yo′-wa-źa, *adv.* of owaźa; *near to, equal to, relating to; concerned in.*

i-yo′-wa-źa-ka, *adv.* Used with the meaning of iyowaźaśni.

i-yo′-wa-źa-śni, *adv. not near to, not equal to, having nothing to do with:* iyowaźaśni waun, *and* iyowaś waun śni, *I am not near to him* or *it,* in any respect, *I am not concerned in it; i. q.* iwatokiyapaśni.

i-yo′-wa-źa-śni-yan, *adv. not near to.*

i-yo′-we-ḣa-dan, *and* i-yo′-wi-ḣa-dan, *adv. in jest, jestingly.*

i-yo′-wi-ća-ki-śi-će, *n.* of iyokiśića; *sorrow, sadness.*

i-yo′-wi-ća-ya-ka, *n.* of iyoyaka; *sorrow, sadness; sympathy, irritableness.*

i-yo′-wi-ḣan, *adv. in fun, in jest:* iyowiḣan epe śni, *I did not say it in jest.*

i-yo′-win, *v.* See iyokiwin.

i-yo′-win-ki-ya, *v. a. to permit, suffer, connive at; to receive, accept*—iyowinwakiya, iyowinunkiyapi, iyowinmakiya.

i-yo′-win-yan, *v. a. to bear, endure; to permit, connive at; to receive, accept; to be sufficient for, accomplish,* said of medicine in curing disease—iyowinwaya, iyowinunyanpi, iyowinmayan.

i-yo′-win-ye-śni, *adv. without leave, contrary to orders; insufficient, inoperative,* as medicine.

i-yo′-wo-tan-in, *n. a place from which one can see to a great distance,* as a hill. See owotanin.

i-yo′-ya, *v. n. T. to gape, yawn; i. q.* iyowa.

i-yo′-yag, *cont.* of iyoyaka; iyoyag waun.

i-yo′-yag-ya, *v. a. to displease, offend; to make sick*—iyoyagwaya, iyoyagunyanpi.

i-yo′-ya-ka, *v. n to be offended, displeased; to be made sick*—iyomayaka, iyounyakapi.

i-yo′-ya-ke-ća, *v. n. to be sorrowful, distressed*—iyomayakeća, iyoniyakeća.

i-yo′ yam, *cont.* of iyoyanpa.

i-yo′-yam-ya, *v. a. to shine on, illuminate, enlighten*—iyoyamwaya, iyoyamunyanpi, iyoyammayan

i-yo′-yam-ya, *adv. illuminated, in an illuminated manner.*

i-yo′-yan-pa, *v. n. to shine, give light.* See anpa *and* iyoźanźan.

i-yo′-yan-pa, *n. light.*

i-yo′-yan-pa-ya, *v. a. to enlighten, shine on*—iyoyanpawaya, iyoyanpamayan.

i-yo′-za. See heniyoza *and* oza.

i-yo′-zi, *n.* of ozi; *rest, repose.*

i-yo′-zi-ki-ya, *v. a. to cause to rest*—iyoziwakiya.

i-yo′-zi-ya, *adv. at rest.*

i-yo′-zi-zi-ya, *adv. red.* of iyoziya; *leisurely;* iyoziziya yatkan, *to sip, drink by draughts.*

i-yo′-źan-źan, *n.* of oźanźan; *light.* See iyoyanpa.

i-yo'-źaŋ-źaŋ-yaŋ, *v. n. to shine, shine into, give light to*

i-yo'-źaŋ-źaŋ-yaŋ, *adv. shining, giving light*

i-yo'-źib-na-la, *and* i-yo'-źib-ye-la, *adv. T. full to the brim.* See iyuźimnana.

i-yu'-be, *n. something to rub with:* maziyube, *a file.* See iyumaŋ *and* yube.

i-yu'-ćaŋ, *v. a. to sift, to shake,* as in sifting—imdućaŋ. See yućaŋ.

i-yu'-ćaŋ *and* wi'-yu-ćaŋ, *n. a sieve.*

i-yu'-e-će-tu, *v. a. to perfect. make right by means of*—imduećetu. See yuećetu.

i-yu'-ġe-ya, *adj. all, the whole;* iyuġeya dećena waśte, *all alone is good.*

i-yu'-ha, *adj. Ih.* and *T. all: i. q.* iyuḣpa.

i-yu'-ha-ya, *adv. T. loosely, slovenly.*

i-yu'-ha-ha-ya, *adv. T. red.* of iyuhaya.

i-yu'-hiŋ-he, *n. a harrow: i. q* iyuhiŋte.

i-yu'-hiŋ-te, *n.* of yuhiŋta; *any thing to rake with,* as maḣiyuhiŋte, *a rake.*

i-yu'-hmi-ḣma, *n.* of yuhmihma; *something that turns* a thing, *a turner,* as a water-wheel.

i-yu'-hna-yaŋ, *v. n.* of yuhnayaŋ; *to be deceived,* as in the prospect of receiving something—imayuhnayaŋ, iniyuhnayaŋ.

i-yu'-ho-ta, *n. the intestines, all the inside of an animal.*

i-yu'-ḣći, *v. a. to break out,* as the eye of a needle—imduḣći.

i-yu'-ḣda-ta, *v. a.* of yuḣdata; *to catch hold of with,* as with a hook; *to scratch with*—imduḣdata.

i-yu'-ḣda-te, *n.* (i *and* yuḣdata) *something to catch with, something to scratch with.*

i-yu'-ḣdo-ke, *n.* of yuḣdoka; *something to open with, something to make a hole with:* tiyopa iyuḣdoke, *a door-opener,* i. e., *a key: Ih. the mouth of a stream. T.,* iyuśloka.

i-yu'-ḣe-pe, *n.* of yuḣepa; *an absorber, a sponge.*

i-yu'-ḣmuŋ, *n.* of yuḣmuŋ; *a sling.*

i-yu'-ḣpa, *adj. all, the whole. T.,* iyuha.

i-yu'-ḣpe, *n.* of yuḣpa; *something to pull down with.*

i'-yu-kaŋ-pi, *v pl. they go and remain.* The singular of this is not so used. See yukaŋ.

i-yu'-kćaŋ, *v. a.* of yukćaŋ; *to understand, have an opinion* or *understanding of; to think, guess; to decide*—imdukćaŋ, idukćaŋ, uŋkiyukćaŋpi, ićiyukćaŋ; imayadukćaŋ, *thou understandest me.*

i-yu'-kćaŋ-ke, *n. one who forms an opinion.*

i-yu'-kćaŋ-ken, *adv guessing:* iyukćaŋken aya, *to go on guessing.*

i-yu'-kćaŋ-yaŋ, *v. n. to cause*

to understand—iyukćaŋwaya, iyukćaŋuŋyaŋpi.

i-yu'-kćaŋ-yaŋ, *adv.* *thinking, having understanding of.*

i-yu'-ke-ze, *n.* of yukeza; *a scraper.* *T.*, ićakoġe.

i-yu'-kiŋ, *v. a.* *to wrench, pry*—imdukiŋ, uŋkiyukiŋpi.

i-yu'-kiŋ-yaŋ, *adv.* *prying.*

i-yu'-ki-pam, *adv.* *divided.* Not much used.

i-yu'-kpaŋ, *v. a.* of yukpaŋ; *to rub up fine*, as with the fingers—imdukpaŋ.

i-yu'-kpaŋ, *n.* *something to make fine with, a mill.* See wiyukpaŋ.

i-yu'-kpu-kpa, *v. a.* of yukpukpa; *to break up fine and mingle together*—imdukpukpa.

i-yu'-ksa, *v. a.* of yuksa; *to break off with, cut off with*—imduksa, uŋkiyuksapi.

i-yu'-kse, *n.* *something to break* or *cut off with, snuffers.*

i-yu'-ķe-ġe, *n.* of yukeġa; *a grater.*

i-yu'-maŋ, *n.* of yumaŋ. See iyube.

i-yu'-mni, *n.* of yumni; *something that turns round:* tate iyumni, *a whirlwind;* ćaŋ iyumni, *an auger.*

i-yun', *cont.* of iyuta; *to eat with*, as one thing with another.

i-yun'-ki-toŋ, *n.* *something to eat with, sauce.*

i-yun'-toŋ, *n.* *something to eat with other things, sauce, condiment.*

i-yuŋ', *intj.* See iŋyuŋ.

i'-yuŋ, *v.* *to use:* hu íyuŋ, *to use one's legs, be on foot;* hu íyuŋ hiyu, *to come on foot.* *T.* *to rub on, apply,* as paint or grease. See iuŋ.

i-yuŋ'-ġa, *v.* *T.* *i. q.* iwaŋġa.

i-yuŋ'-ka, *v.* *T.* *i. q.* iwaŋka.

i'-yuŋ-ken, *adv.* hu iyuŋken, *on foot*

i-yuŋ'-wiŋ, *n.* *remuneration, something to pay with:* iyuŋwiŋ yukaŋ, *there is pay;* iyuŋwiŋ ćodaŋ, *without pay.*

i-yuŋ'-wiŋ-toŋ, *v.* *to have the means of paying, have something to give for*—iyuŋwiŋwatoŋ.

i-yuŋ'-wiŋ-yaŋ, *v. a.* *to have* or *use as pay*—iyuŋwiŋwaya.

i-yu'-pa-ġa, *v. a.* *to gather up in the hand*, as the mouth of a bag for tying; *to seize, lay hold of, arrest*, as a desperate fellow: as iyupaḣ iću—imdupaġa.

i-yu'-paḣ, *cont.* of iyupaġa; iyupaḣ yuza, *to clasp tight*, as the mouth of a bag. See yupaḣ.

i-yu'-pam, *adv.* *all together.* *T.*, ptayela.

i-yu'-paŋ, *v. a.* *to break* or *rub up*, as in the hand—imdupaŋ.

i-yu'-pi-źa, *adj.* *wrinkled.*

i-yu'-pse, *n.* *a steering-oar, the helm, rudder.* *T.*, wasiŋte.

i-yu'-pse-ki-ći-yu-za, *v. a.* *to hold the helm for* one, *steer a boat for* one; *to keep* one *from doing wrong, lead* him *to do right*—iyupsewećiyuza.

i-yu'-pse-pse-ya, *adv. red.* of iyupseya.

i-yu'-pse-ya, *adv. crookedly, zigzag.*

i-yu'-pse-yu-za, *v. to hold the helm, steer a boat, hold the paddle against the water* so as to turn the boat, *to back water*—iyupsemduza. *T.*, wasiŋte yuhomni.

i-yu'-pse-yu-ze, *n. a pilot, the one who holds the helm.*

i-yu'-pśa-ya, *adv. mixed up, all together* good and bad.

i'-yu-pśi-pśi-źa, *v. to have the lips quiver,* as from cold, etc.—ímayupśipśiźa. *T.*, pute gniyaŋyaŋ.

i'-yu-pśi-ẓa. See íyupśipśiźa.

i-yu'-pta, *v.* iyupta iću, *to take up with* a spade, *to dig and take up,* as in spading—iyupta iwaću.

I'-yu-pta-la, *n. p. T. a society like the Omaha dance society.*—W. J. C.

i-yu'-pu-za, *v. a.* of yupuza; *to make dry with*—imdupuza.

i-yu'-pu-ze, *n. something to make dry with, a towel.*

i-yu'-sa-ke, *n. T. a gad, a whip.*

i-yu'-sdo-he, *n.* of yusdohaŋ; *something to drag along, a sled.* Hence, ćaŋiyusdohe, *something to haul wood on, a wood-sled.*

i-yu'-sdo-he-toŋ, *v. to have a sled* or *team*—iyusdohewatoŋ.

i-yu'-sdo-he-toŋ-na, *n. something that trails.*

i-yu'-ski-te, *n. a bandage:* of yuskita.

i-yu'-son, *cont.* of iyusota; iyuson eyaya, *all passed by.*

i-yu'-so-ta, *v. a.* of yusota; *to use all up with, use up for*—imdusota, uŋkiyusotapi.

i-yus'-o-yaḣ, *adv. with difficulty, i. q.* kitaŋ ḣiŋ: iyusoyaḣ pakpi, *to pick open with difficulty. T.*, iyusoyaḣćiŋ.

i-yu'-śda, *n.* of yuśda; *scissors, shears.*

i-yu'-śdo-ka, *n.* of yuśdoka; *something to pull out with,* as a corkscrew.

i-yu'-śdo-ke, *n. Ih. a key.*—J. P. W. *T.*, iyuśloke. See iyuḣdoke.

i-yu'-śdu-śdu-ta, *n.* of yuśdusduta; *something to make smooth with, a rubber, polisher.*

i-yu'-śi-ća, *v.* of yuśića. *to injure by means of, make bad with*—imduśića.

i-yu'-śi-će, *n. something that makes bad* or *injures.*

i-yu'-śka, *n.* of yuśka; *something by means of which to untie a bundle; what is given in return on the occasion of untying a bundle of tobacco sent from another village or people.* This is a Dakota custom. A bundle of tobacco is sent to renew the bond of friendship between bands or villages. If it is untied, blankets, guns, kettles, etc., are sent back in return; if they have nothing to give, they cannot untie the bundle.

i-yu'-śki-ća, *v. a. to press on and*

cut ccidentally, as with a knife; *to wring out of*, as out of water—imduśkića.

i-yu′-śki-će, *n.* of yuśkića; *a press.*

i-yu′-śkin, *cont.* of iyuśkića *and* iyuśkita.

i-yu′-śkiŋ, *v. n.* *to rejoice, be glad; to rejoice in*—imduśkiŋ, iduśkiŋ, uŋkiyuśkiŋpi.

i-yu′-śkiŋ-ki-ya, *v. a.* *to cause to rejoice*—iyuskiŋwakiya.

i-yu′-śkiŋ-śkiŋ, *v. red.* of iyuśkiŋ.

i-yu′-śkiŋ-śkiŋ-yaŋ, *adv. red.* of iyuśkiŋyaŋ.

i-yu′-śkiŋ-yaŋ, *v. a.* *to make glad, to gladden, rejoice*—iyuśkiŋwaya, iyuśkiŋmayaŋ.

i-yu′-śkiŋ-yaŋ, *adv.* *gladly, rejoicingly.*

i-yu′-śki-ta, *v. a.* *to press upon and cut* with a knife—imduśkita, imayuśkita. See baśkita.

i-yu′-śla, *n.* *T.* *shears, scissors, i. q.* iyuśda.

i-yu′-ślo-ka, *n.* *T.* *something to pull out with; i. q.* iyuśdoka.

i-yu′-śna, *n.* of yuśna; *one that has lost its mate, an odd one.*

i-yu′-śpa, *v. a.* of yuśpa; *to pick off from*, as a scab—imduśpa.

i-yu′-śpu, *v. a.* of yuśpu; *to pick off from*, as corn from the strings—imduśpu.

i-yu′-śtaŋ, *v. a.* of yuśtaŋ; *to finish inside, to finish for*—imduśtaŋ: ekta waki ḳa owasiŋ wiyeya imduśtaŋ, *when I have gone home and prepared a place*—John xiv, 3.

i-yu′-ta, *v. a* *to measure, weigh; to try, attempt*—imduta, iduta, uŋkiyutapi: ćaŋ iyuta, *to measure with a stick.*

i-yu′-ta, *v.* *T.* of uta; *to taste.*

i-yu′-ta, *v.* of yuta; *to eat with*, as one thing with another—iwata, iyata.

i-yu′-taŋ, *v. a.* *to put in grease and mash up, to make pemmican*—imdutaŋ, idutaŋ, uŋkiyutaŋpi.

i-yu′-taŋ, *v.* *to tempt; to be tempted* or *tried*—imayutaŋ, iniyutaŋ, uŋkiyutaŋpi.

i-yu′-taŋ, *n.* *the trigger* of a gun.

i-yu′-t'aŋ-t'aŋ, *v. a.* of yut'aŋ; *to touch, feel in several places*—imdut'aŋt'aŋ, uŋkiyut'aŋt'aŋpi.

i-yu′-taŋ-yaŋ, *v. a.* *to tempt, try, prove*—iyutaŋwaya, iyutaŋuŋyaŋpi, iyutaŋmayaŋ.

i-yu′-taŋ-yaŋ, *adv.* *tempting, trying.*

i-yu′-ta-pi, *n.* *a measure; an acre; a mile; a bushel; a pound;* noġiyutapi, *a yard.*

i-yu′-te-ki-ya, *v. a.* *to cause to measure; to adjust, arrange, appoint*—iyutewakiya.

i-yu′-te-pa, *v. n.* of yutepa; *to be torn off by* anything.

i-yu′-te-ya, *v. a.* *to adjust*—iyutewaya, iyuteuŋyaŋpi.

i-yu′-te-ya, *adv.* *by measure.*

i-yu′-ti-taŋ, *v. a.* of yutitaŋ; *to pull by*—imdutitaŋ.

i-yu'-ti-taŋ, *v. n. to be stretched* or *pulled by.*

i-yu'-ti-taŋ-yaŋ, *adv. stretched by.*

i-yut'-ki-toŋ, *n.* See iyunkitoŋ.

i-yu'-tku-ġe, *n. T. something fasten* or *lock with, a key.*

i-yu'-tpu-tpa, *v. a.* Same as iyukpukpa.

i-yu'-wa-śte, *v.* of yuwaśte; *to make good* or *benefit by means of*—imduwaśte.

i-yu'-wa-śte, *n. something that benefits.*

i-yu'-we-ġa, *v. a. to pass through, cross, ford,* as a stream—imduweġa, iduweġa, uŋkiyuweġapi. Hence, oiyuweġe, *a ford.*

i-yu'-weḣ, *cont.* of iyuweġa; iyuweḣ iyaya, *to ford* a stream.

i-yu'-weḣ-ya, *adv. crossing, fording.*

i-yu'-wi, *v. a* of yuwi; *to tie,* as a halter or rope in a horse's mouth—imduwi.

i-yu'-wi, *v. n. to curl, twist,* like a vine or curled wood.

i-yu'-wi, *n. anything twisted* or *tied, a vine, a bridle.* See iiyuwi *and* wiyuwi.

i-yu'-wiŋ. See iyuŋwiŋ.

i-yu'-wi-ya, *adv. tangled, in a snarl,* as hair or thread.

i-yu'-za, *v. a.* of yuza; *to hold on* or *to, to put the hand on and hold*—imduza.

i-yu'-ze, *n.* of yuza *and* yuze; *something to hold with, a holder; something to take out food with, a ladle.*

i-yu'-zi-ya, *adv. partly in sight;* said of anything seen over a hill.

i-yu'-zi-zi-ya, *adv. in sight, i. q.* taŋiŋyaŋ: iyuziziya iyaya, *to pass along in sight.*

i-yu'-źa-źa, *v. a.* of yuźaźa; *to wash with, to be washed with*—imduźaźa.

i-yu'-źa-źa, *n. something to wash with,* as a wash-tub, wash-board, etc.

i'-yu-źi-mna-na, *adv. full, brim full,* as a vessel of water, *just about to run over; at the edge of,* as íyuźimnana kaġeġe, *to sew close to the edge. T.,* iyoźibnala *and* iyoźibyela. See ioźimnana.

i'-yu-źi-mna-yaŋ, *adv. by the edge of, full.*

i-yu'-źi-pe, *n.* (i *and* yuźipa) *the front lock* of a man's hair; *something to pinch* or *lay hold with,* as, maziyuźipe, *tongs, pincers.*

i-za'-ptaŋ, *adj. the fifth.*

i-za'-ptaŋ-ptaŋ, *adj. red. every fifth* one.

i-zin', *cont.* of izita.

i-zin'-toŋ, *v. a. to make a smoke, to smoke* any thing—izinwatoŋ.

i-zin'-ya, *v. a. to cause to smoke; to smoke,* as a deer-skin—izinwaya. See ziya.

i-zi'-ta, *v. n. to smoke,* as a fire-brand.

i-zo', *n. a peninsula.*

i-zu'-ya-pi, *n. what the Dakotas carry with them in going to war, the palladium of the expedition.* Sometimes this is a pipe, and sometimes the skin of an animal. See zuya.

i-zu′-za, *n.* *a grindstone, a whetstone.*

i′-źan-ya, *adv.* *deceitfully, i. q.* oie noŋpa. *T.*, ćeźiźalya. See iźata.

i-źaŋ′-źaŋ, *v. n.* *to give light,* as a candle. See źaŋźaŋ.

i-źaŋ′-źaŋ, *v. a.* *to light,* as a candle.

i-źaŋ′-źaŋ, *n.* *a light.* See oźaŋźaŋ *and* petiźaŋźaŋ.

i-źaŋ′-źaŋ-ya, *v. a.* *to light,* as a candle; *to cause to give light*—iźaŋźaŋwaya.

i-źaŋ′-źaŋ-yaŋ, *adv.* *giving light for:* taḣiŋća iźaŋźaŋyaŋ wićakute, *he shoots deer by a light.*

i′-źa-ta, *adj.* *forked-mouth, double-tongued;* said also of a gun which has the upper part of the stock cut off. This form of expression is said to have been introduced by white people. *T.*, ćeźiźata.

i-źe′-haŋ, *adv.* *often, frequently, repeatedly.*

i-źe′-haŋ-yaŋ, *adv.* *often.*

i-źe′-haŋ-yaŋ-ken, *adv.* *frequently.*

i-źe′-źe-ya, *adv.* *mixed up,* as different kinds together. *T.*, iźena.

i-źe′-źe-ya-ken, *adv.* *mixed up, all sorts together.*

i-źi′-ća, *v. n.* *to be rich in goods;* in distinction from waśeća *or* iwaśeća, *to be rich in provisions.* See źića.

i-źi′-mna, *v. n,* *to smell like something burning,* as fat or bones.

i-źin′-ya, *v. a.* *to cause to be rich*—iźinwaya. See źinya.

i-źin′-ya, *adv.* *richly.*

i′-źog, *cont.* of iźoka.

i′-źog-ki-ya, *v. a.* *to push out the lips at* one. *T.*, iwośokiya.

i′-źo-ka, *v. n.* *to have the lips pushed out.*

i′-źo-ki-ya, *v.* *to push out the mouth at; to twist the mouth; to whistle*—iźowakiya. See źo.

K.

k, *the twelfth letter of the Dakota alphabet.* It is sounded as in English.

k, *a prefix,* making the possessive form of verbs which commence with *p:* as, paġaŋ *to part with;* kpaġaŋ, *to part with one's own.*

ka, *dem. pron.* *that; he, she, it.* This pronoun is used to denote some person or thing farther off than is meant by "de" *and* "he."

ka, *adv.* *there, yonder.* See kan *and* kakiya.

ka, *adv.* Used interrogatively at the end of a phrase or sentence, as ećoŋpića ka, *can it be done?*

ka, *a suffix* to verbs and nouns. In most cases it does not seem materially to alter the signification: as, waśteda *and* waśtedaka, *to love* any thing; itaŋćaŋ *and* itaŋćaŋka, *a chief one.* In some cases it helps to form verbal nouns: as, o, *to hit* in shooting; waoka, *a good marksman;* in these cases it indicates frequency or a habit, and seems to be equivalent to će *or* eće.—T. S. W.

k a, *adv. suffix.* It is equivalent to śni, *not,* and is sometimes used ironically: as, waśte, *good,* waśteka, *not good.*

k a, *a prefix* to a class of verbs. It shows that the action expressed by the verb is performed by *striking,* as with the hand, or with an ax, club or other instrument; or by the action of the wind or water. The pronouns are prefixed.

k a, *v. a. to mean, signify*—waká, yaká, uŋkápi, ćićá, maká; uŋnićapi, *we mean you. T., to ask for, demand.*

k a - a′ - i - y o - ḣ p e - y a, *adv. T. down hill, down a steep descent.*

k a - a′ - o - p t e - ć a, *v.* of aopteća; kaaopteća kaġa, *to lessen.*

k a - a′ - o - p t e n, *v. cont.* of kaaopteća; kaaopten ećoŋ, *to do less than.*

k a - a′ - o - p t e - t u, *v. to lessen:* kaaoptetu ećamoŋ, *I do less,* or *I make it less.* The difference between "kaaoptetu" *and* "yuaoptetu" is the difference between the prefix "ka" and the prefix "yu."

k a - a′ - o - p t e - t u - y a, *adv. in the way of diminishing.*

k a - a′ - o - p t e - t u - y a - k e n, *adv. diminishingly.*

k a - a′ - p a - m a - h d e, *adv. sloping down hill, gently sloping;* kaapamahde ḣiŋća, *quite steep.*

k a - a′ - p a - m a - h d e - y a, *adv. down hill, sloping:* kaapamahdeya waŋka, *it is descending.* See ápamahde.

k a - a′ - t a - k i ŋ - y a ŋ, *adv. leaning.* See takiŋyaŋ *and* yutakiŋyaŋ.

k a - a′ - t a - k u - n i - ś n i, *v. a. T. to destroy by striking; i. q.* katakuniśni.

k a - b a s′, *cont.* of kabaza; kabas iyeya. *T.,* kawas. See yubas.

k a - b a ś′, *cont.* of kabaźa; kabaś yaŋka, *he keeps at it. T.,* kawaś.

k a - b a′ - z a, *v. a. to throw up,* as cattle do earth: maka kabaza, *to paw up dust. T.,* kawaza *and* yuwaza. See yubaza.

k a - b a′ - ź a, *v. a. to work at a difficult thing, keep at work at* a thing *though hardly able to do so*—wakabaźa, uŋkabaźapi.

k a - b l a′, *v. a. T. to cut meat thin for drying;* wakabla, yakabla, etc. See kamda.

k a - b l a′ - b l a - p i, *n. T. preparing meat for drying* by slicing thin. See wakablapi.

k a - b u′, *v. a. to beat,* as on a drum; *to knock,* as on a door—wakabu, uŋkabupi.

k a - b u′ - b u, *v. red.* of kabu; *to beat* or *knock often*—wakabubu.

ka-bu′-bu-ya, *adv. red.* of kabuya; *knocking.*

ka-bu′-ya, *adv.* *striking, knocking:* kabuya wauŋ, *I keep knocking.*

ka-ća′, *a negative suffix; not;* as, waśtekaća, *it is not good.* *T.*, kaćaś.

ka-ća′, *v. a.* of kata; *to warm, heat.* See kanya, which seems to be the preferable form. *T.*, kalya.

ka-ća′-eś, *intj.* of doubt; *is it possible!* See kaćaś.

ka-ćaŋ′, *v. a.* *to shake, clean by shaking* or *blowing*, as the Dakotas do ćaŋśaśa; *to sift*—wakaćaŋ.

ka-ćaŋ′-ćaŋ, *v. a. red.* of kaćaŋ and also of ćaŋćaŋ; *to make tremble* or *shake*—wakaćaŋćaŋ.

ka-ćaŋ′-ćaŋ, *v. n.* *T.* *to trot*, as a horse.

ka-ćaŋ′-ćaŋ-yaŋ, *adv.* *shaking.*

ka-ćaŋ′-ćaŋ-ye-daŋ, *adv.* *shaking, shivering* with cold.

ka-ćaŋ′-he, *v. T.* *to shake with the cold*—wakaćaŋhe.

ka-ćaŋ′-nan, *v. a.* *to push out from shore with a paddle*——wakaćaŋnan: kaćaŋnan iyeya, *to blow out into the river.* See paćaŋnaŋ.

ka-ćaś′, *intj.* of doubt or hesitation; *what then! what of it!*

ka-će′, *pron.* tuwe kaće, *any one.* *T.*, keśa.

ka-ćeg′, *cont.* of kaćeka; kaćeg iyeya, *to make stagger by striking.*

ka-ćeg′-ćeg-ya, *adv. red.* of kaćegya.

ka-ćeg′-ya, *adv.* *staggering, in a staggering manner:* kaćegya mani, *he walks staggeringly.*

ka-će′-ka, *v. a.* *to strike and make stagger*—wakaćeka.

ka-ćen′, *adv.* tuwe kaćen, *any one, no matter who;* tokiya kaćen; *no matter where; about that, somewhere near that*, as, opawiŋġe kaćen, *about one hundred.*

ka-ćen′-ya, *adv.* *about, nearly.*

ka-će′-ya, *v. a.* of ćeya; *to make cry by striking*—wakaćeya, uŋkaćeyapi, makaćeya.

ka-ći′-ḳa-daŋ, *v. a.* of ćiḳadaŋ; *to make small by chopping off*—wakaćiḳadaŋ.

ka-ći′-ḳa-ye-daŋ, *v. a.* of ćiḳayedaŋ; *to make small by striking*—wakaćiḳayedaŋ.

ka-ći′-stiŋ-na, *v. a.* of ćistiŋna; *to make small by cutting.* *T.*, kaćisćila.

ka-ćo′-ćo, *v. a.* *to mix up*, as mortar, *to make a noise*, as in mixing mortar; *to beat up*, as eggs—wakaćoćo. See ćoćo.

ka-ćo′-za, *v. a.* *to make warm by striking:* wakaćoza kta waśkaŋ hećen wakaćoza, *I struck him for the purpose of warming him, in this way I made him warm.* See ćoza.

ka-da′, *v. a.* *to spill, scatter, to pour* or *throw out; to throw broadcast, to sow*, as grain; not applied to liquids—wakada, yakada, uŋkadapi: kada iyeya, *and* kada eħpeya, *he goes on scattering.* *T.*, **kala.**

ka-da'-da, *v. red.* of kada; *to spill, scatter; to sow, throw broadcast,* as grain—wakadada: kadada eḣpeya, *and* kadada iyeya, *he scatters along. T.*, kalalala.

ka-de'-ća-na, *adv. Ih. soon, pretty soon.* See ećadaŋ.

ka-dem'-de-pa, *v. red.* of kadepa; *to notch by cutting*—wakademdepa.

ka-de'-pa, *v. a. to cut a notch in*—wakadepa. See kademdepa.

ka-do', *n. the diamond* in cards. It is the French word, *carreau. T.*, śapestola (śa *and* pesto).

ka-dom', *cont.* of kadopa; kadom iyaya, *to mire.*

ka-dom'-dom, *red.* of kadom; *miring, wading,* as a horse in mud: kadomdom iyaya, *he goes on wading.*

ka-dom'-do-pa, *v. red.* of kadopa.

ka-dom'-ki-ya, *v. a. to cause to mire*—kadomwakiya.

ka-dom'-ya, *v. a. to cause to mire*—kadomwaya.

ka-dom'-ya, *adv. miring.*

ka-do'-pa, *v. n. to mire, stick in the mud*—wakadopa. See kaḣdi.

ka-du', *v. a. to blow* or *brush away a little with the hand*—wakadu.

ka-du'-daŋ-ka, *v.* of kadu; *to blow a little;* also said of a child who walks with difficulty, and puffs and blows as he goes along—wakadudaŋka.

ka-du'-ġa, *v. a. to fan, winnow, clean by winnowing*—wakaduġa, uŋkaduġapi,

ka-duḣ', *cont.* of kaduġa; kaduḣ iyeya.

ka-duḣ'-ki-ya, *v. n. to cause to winnow*—kaduḣwakiya.

ka-duḣ'-ya, *v. a. to cause to fan* or *winnow*—kaduḣwaya.

ka-duḣ'-ya, *adv. winnowing.*

ka-dus', *cont.* of kaduza.

ka-dus'-ya, *v. a. to cause to flow*—kaduswaya.

ka-dus'-ya, *adv. flowing, swiftly:* kadusya waŋka, *it is flowing on.*

ka-du'-za, *v. n. to flow, run,* as water; *to run swiftly.* Hence, minićaduza, *swift-running water.* See duzahaŋ.

ka'-e, *pron. that is he:* tuwe kae, *that one, any one.* See dee, ee, hee.

ka-e'-ća-la, *adv. T. soon, presently, in a little while.* See ećadaŋ *and* kadećana.

ka-e'-će-tu, *v. a. to make right* or *accomplish by striking*—wakaećetu.

ka-e'-eś, *pron. that one: even such.*

ka'-eś, *pron. that one:* kaeś nakuŋ ope kta, *even he will go along.*

ka-gla', *and* **ka-gla'-la**, *adv. T. by, near by; i. q.* kahda.

ka-gli', *v. T. i. q.* kahdi.

ka-gmi', *v. a. T. to cut all down, clear away,* as timber or grass, *make bare*—wakagmi, yakagmi.

ka'-ġa, *v. a. to make, form; to cause to be, be the cause* or *author of;*

to execute—wakaġa, yakaġa, uŋkaġapi, makaġa, nićaġa, ćićaġa.

ka-ġam′, *cont.* of kaġapa; kaġam iyeya, *to make spread out* or *open by cutting.*

ka-ġam′-ya, *adv.* *gaping open,* as a wound.

ka-ġan′-ġa-ta, *adv.* *red.* of kaġata.

ka-ġaŋ′, *v. n.* *to open, make an opening in; to come through,* as the wind through one's clothes; kaġaŋ hiyumayaŋ, *it blows through my clothes.*

ka-ġaŋ′-ġaŋ-yaŋ, *adv.* *red.* of kaġaŋyaŋ.

ka-ġaŋ′-yaŋ, *adv.* *open, spread out.*

ka-ġa′-pa, *v. a.* *to cut, spread open by cutting; to spread open*—wakaġapa, uŋkaġapapi.

ka-ġa′-ta, *adv.* *spread out,* as the hands or fingers. See yuġata, kaźata, etc.

ka-ġat′-ki-ya, *adv.* *spread out, stretched out,* as the hand or arm. *T.*, kaġalkiya.

ķa′-ġe, *v. a.* Same as kaġa.

ka-ġe′, *v. a.* *to skim off,* as grease from a pot—wakaġe, uŋkaġepi: kaġe yuza, *to gather in the hand,* to hold in a bunch.

ka-ġe′-ġe, *v. a.* *to sew; to sew* or *mend together,* as an old kettle—wakaġeġe, uŋkaġeġepi.

ka-ġi′, *v.* *to stop one's progress, to be in one's way,* as a river; *not to be able to proceed*—wakaġi, unkaġipi, makaġi, nićaġi. See ićaġi.

ka-ġi′-śni, *adv.* *without obstruction:* kaġiśni iyaya, *to pass on without obstruction.*

ka-ġi′-ya, *v. a.* *to hinder, obstruct, make go slow*—kaġiwaya, kaġiuŋyaŋpi, kaġimayaŋ.

ka-ġi′-ya, *adv.* *hindering:* kaġiya wauŋ.

ka-ġo′, *v. a.* *to mark, to make marks, cuts,* or *gashes in one's flesh,* as in mourning; *to draw a line;* also *to vaccinate*—wakaġo. See also ićaġo.

ka-ġo′-pa, *v. a.* *to strike* one *asleep, to wake partly up and make snore*—wakaġopa. See ġopa.

ka-ġug′, *cont.* of kaġuka; kaġug iyeya.

ka-ġug′-ya, *adv.* kaġugya hnaka, *to lay up to dry.*

ka-ġu′-ka, *v. a.* *to lengthen a little by striking; to sprain, strain,* as a tendon—wakaġuka.

ka-ha′, *v.* kaha iyeya, *and* kaha eḣpeya, *to put out of the way, shove aside; to blow down, drive along,* as the wind does; *to turn up,* as the brim of one's hat.

ka-han′, *adv.* *to this, at this, thus far.* See dehan, ehaŋ, hehan, *and* iyehan.

ka-han′-han, *adv.* *red.* of kahan.

ka-han′-tu, *adv.* *to that, so far, so long.* See dehaŋtu, ehaŋtu, hehaŋtu, *and* iyehaŋtu.

ka-han′-tu-ķe, *adv.* *this once, now then.*

ka-han′-tu-ya, *adv.* *so far.* See dehaŋtuya *and* iyehaŋtuya.

ka-haŋ′-haŋ-ke-ća, *adv. red.* of kahaŋkeća. See dehanhaŋkeća, hehaŋhaŋkeća, *and* iyehaŋhaŋkeća.

ka-haŋ′-haŋ-yaŋ, *adv. red.* of kahaŋyaŋ.

ka-haŋ′-ke-ća, *adv. so long.* See dehaŋkeća, hehaŋkeća, *and* iyehaŋkeća.

ka-haŋ′-na, *adv. only so far, so long.* See dehaŋna, ehaŋna, *and* hehaŋna.

ka-haŋ′-yaŋ, *adv. thus far.* See dehaŋyaŋ.

ka-haŋ′-yaŋ-ka, *adv. some distance off,* as in counting relationship. See akahaŋyaŋka.

ka-ha′-ya, *v. a. to push down; to push* or *turn up.*

ka-hba′, *v. a. to pound out, thresh,* as grain—wakahba, uŋkahbapi. *T.* uses "nakaŋ."

ka-hda′, *v. a.* of ahda; *to take home to* one —wakahda, uŋkahdapi.

ka-hda′, *v. n. to stretch out at full length, uncoil,* as a snake: kahda waŋke, *he lies uncoiled.*

ka-hda′, *adv. by the side of, near to:* wakpa kahda, *by the river. T.*, kaglala.

ka-hda′-ya, *adv. by the side of.*

ka-hde′-ġa, *v. a.* of hdeġa; *to mark across, make in stripes* or *figures, make rough*—wakahdeġa.

ka-hde′-hde-ġa, *v. red.* of kahdeġa; *to make stripes across by cutting.*

ka-hde′-hde-za, *v. red.* of kahdeza.

ka-hde′-za, *v. a.* of hdeza; *to mark across* or *around by cutting, make in stripes* or *figures*—wakahdeza.

ka-hdi′, *v. a* of ahdi; *to bring home to* one—wakahdi, uŋkahdipi, makahdi.

ka-hdog′, *cont.* of kahdoka; kahdog iyeya.

ka-hdo′-ka, *v. a. to dislocate, put out of joint by striking*—wakahdoka.

ka-hi′, *v. a.* of ahi; *to bring to* one, *to have brought to* one—wakahi, uŋkahipi, makahi, nićahi, ćićahi.

ka-hi′, *v. a. to stir; to rummage*—wakahi.

ka-hin′, *cont.* of hahiŋta; kahin iyeya, *and* kahin ehpeya, *to brush* or *sweep off.*

ka-hiŋ′-ta, *v. a. to sweep* or *brush up,* as a floor—wakahiŋta, uŋkahiŋtapi: *to drive* or *sweep off,* as the wind does dust.

ka-hiŋ′-to-kam, *adv. forward, in advance,* as of a traveling party; kahiŋtokam hdi, *to come home before the rest;* kahiŋtokam mani, *to walk in advance;* kahiŋtokam ya, *to go before, prepare* or *break the way. T.*, kaitokab *and* kaitokabya. See itokam.

ka-hiŋ′-to-ka-pa, *n. one who walks before* See kahiŋtokam *and* tokapa.

ka-hmi′-hma, *v. a. to roll along, make roll by striking*—wakahmihma. *T.*, kagmigma. See kahomni.

ka-hmi′-yaŋ-yaŋ, *v. a. to make round by striking,* as a ball—wakahmiyaŋyaŋ. See kamima.

ka-hmuŋ′, *v.* *to spin* or *twist* with the extended hand; wakahmuŋ.

ka-hna′, *v. a.* *to shake off*, as fruit from a tree, *by striking*—wakahna, uŋkahnapi.

ka-hna′-yaŋ, *v. a.* of hnayaŋ; *to miss in attempting to strike*—wakahnayaŋ. See kaśna.

ka-ho′-ho, *v. a.* *to strike and knock loose*, as a tooth, or stick set in the ground—wakahoho.

ka-ho′-ho-daŋ, *v.* Same as kahoho.

ka-ho′-mni, *v. a.* *to turn around*, as a wheel, *by striking; to spin*, as a top—wakahomni, uŋkahomnipi: *to turn*, as water or wind does a mill-wheel. See kahmihma.

ka-ho′-toŋ, *v. a.* *to make bawl out by striking*—wakahotoŋ.

ka-hu′-hus, *cont.* of kahuhuza; kahuhus iyeya. *T.*, kahuŋhuŋs.

ka-hu′-hus-ya, *adv.* *shaking;* kahuhusya haŋ, *it stands shaking. T.*, kahuŋhuŋsya.

ka-hu′-hu-za, *v. a.* *to shake*, as a tree or house, *by striking*—wakahuhuza, uŋkahuhuzapi: *to shake*, as the wind does trees, etc. *T.*, kahuŋhuŋza.

ka-hu′-kun, *adv.* *down:* kahukun iyeya, *to put down by striking.*

ka-hu′-kun-wa-pa, *adv.* *down a little.*

ka-hu′-te, *v. a.* *to wear to a stump by striking*, as an ax—wakahute, uŋkahutepi.

ka-hu′-te-daŋ, *part.* *worn to a stump.*

ka-hu′-to-śka, *v. a.* *to make large at one end*, as a hutinaćute—wakahutośka. See hutośke.

kaḣ, *cont.* of kaġa; kaḣ aya, *to continue making.*

ka-ḣa′, *v. a.* *to curl, to knot; to make rough* or *notch by striking*—wakaḣa.

ka-ḣa′, *n.* *a curl, a knot.*

ka-ḣag′, *cont.* prob. of kaḣaka, which is not now used: kaḣagpićaśni, *untamable, ungovernable*, as a wild horse.

ka-ḣa′-ḣa, *v. n.* *red.* of kaḣa; *to curl up*, as flame; *to sparkle* or *send up sparks.*

ka-ḣ'a′-kpa, *v. a.* *to notch, make a hollow place by cutting with an ax*—wakaḣ'akpa.

ka-ḣam′, *cont.* of kaḣapa; kaḣam aya, *to drive along*, as cattle or horses.

ka-ḣam′-ḣa-pa, *v.* *red.* of kaḣapa; *to beat against and make a rustling noise*, as the wind blowing against grass.

ka-ḣaŋ′-hi-ya, *adv.* of ḣaŋhiya; *a little slower, slowly.*

ka-ḣa′-pa, *v. a.* *to drive along; to whip, drive by whipping*—wakaḣapa, uŋkaḣapapi.

ka-ḣ'a′-tpa, *v.* Same as kaḣ'akpa.

ka-ḣba′, *v. a.* (ka *and* ḣba) *to make sleepy by shaking*—wakaḣba.

ka-ḣbog′, *cont.* of kaḣboka; ka-ḣbog iyaya, *it has drifted off; blown off, carried along*, either by wind or tide.

ka-ḣbog′-ya, *v. a.* *to cause to drift; to wave*, as a flag—kaḣbogwaya.

ka-ḣbog′-ya, *adv.* *drifting, waving.*

ka-ḣbo′-ḣbo-ka, *v.* *red.* of kaḣboka.

ka-ḣbo′-ka, *v. n.* *to drift along*, as wood on water, *to be driven along by the current; to wave in folds*, as a flag.

ka-ḣbo′-ka, *n.* *a drift, a float.*

ka′-ḣći, *v. a.* *to gap, break a gap in*, as in the edge of an ax—wakaḣći, yakaḣći, uŋkaḣćipi. See kamni.

ka-ḣći′-ḣći, *v.* *red.* of kaḣći; *to break out gaps* from the edge of an ax—wakaḣćiḣći.

ka-ḣći′-ya, *v. a.* *to cause* one *to break a gap in* an ax—kaḣćiwaya.

ka-ḣda′, *v. a.* *to rattle*, or *make sound by striking; to ring*, as a bell—wakaḣda, uŋkaḣdapi.

ka-ḣda′-ġaŋ, *v. n.* *to lengthen out, become long, extend:* kaḣdaġaŋ yeya, *to give away what has been given* one.

ka-ḣdaḣ′, *cont.* of kaḣdaġaŋ; kaḣdaḣ aya, *it lengthens out.*

ka-ḣda′-ḣda, *v.* *red.* of kaḣda; *to rattle*—wakaḣdaḣda.

ka-ḣda′-ḣda-ġaŋ, *v.* *red.* of kaḣdaġaŋ.

ka-ḣda′-ḣdaḣ, *cont.* of kaḣdaḣdaġaŋ.

ka-ḣda′-ḣdaḣ-ya, *adv.* *lengthening out:* kaḣdaḣdaḣya aya, *to become long* or *lengthen out*, as the days.

ka-ḣda′-ta, *v. a.* *to dig under, undermine, make large at the bottom*, as a corn-hole; *to get* one's fish-hook *fast* on anything—wakaḣdata. *T.*, kaḣlateya.

ka-ḣda′-ya, *v. a.* *to cause* one *to ring* or *rattle*—kaḣdawaya.

ka-ḣda′-ya, *v. n.* *to fall off*, as a sticking plaster; *to come off*, as paint or plaster, *in scales, to scale off.*

ka-ḣde′-ća, *v. a.* *to tear open by smiting; to split open; to break in*, as the skull, *to fracture; to break* or *fracture* the skin *by striking*—wakaḣdeća, uŋkaḣdećapi. *T.*, kaḣleća.

ka-ḣde′-ḣde-ća, *v.* *red.* of kaḣdeća; *to break in*, as the skull, *to fracture*—wakaḣdeḣdeća.

ka-ḣden′, *cont.* of kaḣdeća; kaḣden iyeya.

ka-ḣden′-ya, *v. a.* *to cause to fracture*—kaḣdenwaya.

ka-ḣdi′, *v. n.* *to mire, stick in the mud*—wakaḣdi. See kadopa.

ka-ḣdi′-ḣdi, *v.* *red.* of kaḣdi.

ka-ḣdi′-ya, *v. a.* *to cause to mire*—kaḣdiwaya.

ka-ḣdog′, *cont.* of kaḣdoka; kaḣdog iyeya, *to knock a hole in, to shoot a hole in.*

ka-ḣdog′-o-śtaŋ-pi, *n.* *Ih.* *a vest.*

ka-ḣdog′-ya, *v. a.* *to cause to make a hole in*—kaḣdogwaya.

k a - ħ d o′ - ħ d o - k a, *v. red.* of kaħdoka.

k a - ħ d o′ k a, *v. a. to cut* or *break a hole in* anything *with an ax, club,* etc, or *by striking; to break open; to make a mortice, cut a hole with a chisel; to dress* an animal *by cutting* the flesh from the bones. Hence, takaħdoka, *the flesh of a deer without the bones. T.,* kaħloka. See kaśdoka.

k a - ħ e m′, *cont.* of kaħepa; kaħem eħpeya, *to empty by lading out,* used only of liquids.

k a - ħ e′ - p a, *v. a. to bail out, throw out,* as water until it is all gone—wakaħepa.

k a - ħ e′ - y a - t a, *adv.* of ħeyata; *back, on one side:* kaħeyata iyeya, *to shove* or *throw back* or *to one side.*

k a - ħ i′ - ć a, *v. a. to wake up by striking*—wakaħića.

k a - ħ i′ - ġ i - ć a, *n. T. one who does nothing well.*

k a - ħ i′ - ġ i - ć e - ć a, *n. T. one very unskillful; i. q.,* wayuśićeća.

k a ħ - i n′, *adv.* of kaħita; *bent forward, stooping down;* kaħin inaźiŋ, *to stoop down, dodge, to stand bent forward,* as a hunter does when approaching his game—kaħin inawaźiŋ. *T.,* patuś.

k a ħ - i′ - t a, *adv.* kaħita se mani, *to walk with the head down.* See patuśya.

k a ħ - i′ - t e - ć a, *adv. not well made, unfinished; i. q.* kaħiteśni. *T.,* kaħiġića.

k a ħ - i′ - t e - ś n i, *adv. not well:* taku kaġapi śoka śića ećoŋpi kiŋ he kaħiteśni, *what is made clumsily and badly is called* kaħiteśni.

k a ħ - k i′ - y a, *v. a. to cause to make*—kaħwakiya.

k a - ħ l i′, *v. T. to mire: i. q.* kaħdi.

k a - ħ l o g′ - o - ś t a ŋ, *n. T. a garment made without sleeves, a vest.* See kaħdogośtaŋpi.

k a - ħ m i ŋ′, *n. an inside corner; a bend in a river, a bay; a point* of land, etc.

k a - ħ m i ŋ′, *v. a. to bend by striking*—wakaħmiŋ.

k a - ħ m u ŋ′, *v. a. to make buzz, to whirl and cause to make a noise*—wakaħmuŋ. See kahmuŋ.

k a - ħ m u ŋ′ - ħ m u ŋ, *v. red.* of kaħmuŋ.

k a - ħ m u ŋ′ - ħ m u ŋ - y a ŋ, *adv. buzzing.*

k a - ħ m u ŋ′ - y a ŋ, *adv. whirring, buzzing.*

k a ħ - n i′ - ġ a, *v. a. to choose, make choice of, select, elect; to appoint*—wakaħniġa, yakaħniġa, uŋkaħniġapi, ćićaħniġa, makaħniġa.

k a ħ - n i ħ′, *cont.* of kaħniġa; kaħniħ iću, *to take one's choice.*

k a ħ - n i ħ′ - k i - y a, *v. a. to cause to choose*—kaħniħwakiya.

k a ħ - n i ħ′ - n i - ġ a, *v. red.* of kaħniġa.

k a ħ - n i ħ′ - n i ħ, *cont.* of kaħniħniġa.

k a ħ - n i ħ′ - y a, *adv. choosing.*

k a - ħ o n′, *cont.* of kaħota; kaħon

aya, *to make rough marks; to make prints*, as in walking on burnt prairie. *T.*, naḣol.

kaḣ-o′-ya, *v. n.* *to sail, glide in the air*, as a hawk. *T.*, kaśa kiŋyaŋ.

kaḣ-o′-ya, *adv.* *gliding:* kaḣoya iyeya, *to throw, toss, fling. T.*, kaḣol iyeya, *to toss* or *throw away.*

ka-ḣpa′, *v. a.* *to cover* (see akaḣpa); *to throw* or *knock down* anything hanging up; *to strike, take down*, as a tent—wakaḣpa, uŋkaḣpapi; wihdaḣpa.

ka-ḣpa′-ḣpa, *v.* *red.* of kaḣpa; *to strike* and *make pieces fly off*, as from wood or ice; *to make chips*—wakaḣpaḣpa.

ka-ḣpe′-ki-ya, *v. a.* *to cause to knock down*—kaḣpewakiya.

ka-ḣpu′, *v. a.* *to knock off*, as something sticking; *to knock down*, as swallows' nests; *to scale off*—wakaḣpu, uŋkaḣpupi.

ka-ḣpu′-ḣpu, *v.* *red.* of kaḣpu.

ka-ḣpu′-ya, *adv.* *scaling off, falling off.*

ka-ḣta′-ka, *v.* See ićaḣtaka.

ka-ḣtaŋ′, *v. n.* *to soak up; to soak in*, as grease in wood; *to spread*, as disease in the body—makaḣtaŋ: kaḣtaŋ iyaya, *it has penetrated.*

ka-ḣtaŋ′-ka, *v.* *to be attached to, have an affection for*, as one animal has for another. *T.*, iyakićiyuha.

ka-ḣtaŋ′-yaŋ, *v. a.* *to cause to spread*, as grease.

ka-ḣta′-ta, *v.* *to enfeeble, make unwell by striking*—wakaḣtata; *to be enfeebled*—makaḣtata.

ka-ḣtu′-te-śni, *adv.* *not well made; i. q.* kaḣiteśni. *T.*, kaḣiġića.

ka-ḣu′, *v. a.* *to peel*, as bark; *to peel off, take off the rind from* any hard substance—wakaḣu.

ka-ḣu′-ġa, *v. a.* *to break up* or *break in*, as the skull, *by striking; to stave* or *knock in*, as a barrel head; *to break* or *smash*, as an egg—wakaḣuġa: pa makaḣuġa, *he has broken in my skull.*

ka-ḣuḣ′, *cont.* of kaḣuġa; kaḣuḣ iyeya.

ka-ḣuḣ′-ki-ya, *v. a.* *to cause to break* or *knock in*—kaḣuḣwakiya.

ka-ḣu′-ḣu, *v.* *red.* of kaḣu; *to make rough by breaking the bark* or *skin in many places*—wakaḣuḣu.

ka-ḣu′-ḣu-ġa, *v. red.* of kaḣuġa; *to smash*, as eggs.

ka-ḣuḣ′-ya, *adv.* *breaking* or *staving in.*

kaḣ-ya′, *n.* of kaġa; *make, kind, sort.*

kaḣ-ya′, *adv.* *made like, like:* wakiyedaŋ kaḣya, *in the form of a dove.*

ka-i′, *v. a.* of ai; *to take to* one—wakai, uŋkaipi, makai, ćićai.

ka-i′-ćaŋ, *v. n.* *T.* *to lean against.*

ka-i′-ćaŋ-yaŋ, *adv.* *T.* *leaning against.* *i. q.* kaićiŋyaŋ.

ka-i′-ći-ću-ya, *adv.* *crossing each other; crookedly.*

ka-i′-ćiŋ-yaŋ, *adv.* of ićiŋyaŋ; *leaning against.*

k a - i′- d e, *v.* of ide; *to make blaze*, as the wind does fire.

k a-i′-ġ e-ź u-y a, *adv.* *crowding in.*

k a - i′- p a - t k u - ġ a, *v. a.* of ipatkuġa; *to strike into a line.*

k a - i′- p a - t k u ḣ - y a, *adv.* *in a line fronting:* kaipatkuḣya aya, *they go into a line.*

k a - i′- p u - s t a g - y a, *adv.* *T.* *crowding, pressing against.*

k a - i′- ś t a - m i - n i - o - ġ e - i - y e - y a, *v.* *to bring tears into one's eyes*, as the wind does—kaiśtaminioġe iyemayaŋ. *T.*, kaiśtaminioźu.

k a - i′- ś t o - m i - n i - i ś - i - y e - y a, *v.* *to bring tears into one's eyes*, as the wind does—kaiśtominiiś iyemayaŋ. *T*, kaiśtaminihaŋpihiyuya.

k a - i′- ś u - t a, *v.* kaiśuta hiŋhda, *to stumble, make a miss step*—kaiśuta mahiŋhda.

k a - i′- ś u - t a - t a, *v.* kaiśutata iyaya, *to slip, miss step, stumble*—kaiśutata imdamda.

k a - i′- t a ŋ - w a ŋ - k a ŋ - h d e, *adv.* *up hill, ascending.* See itaŋwaŋkaŋhde.

k a - i′- t a ŋ - w a ŋ - k a ŋ - h d e - y a, *adv.* *up hill;* kaitaŋwaŋkaŋhdeya waŋka, *it lies in an ascending manner.* *T.*, kaiyakapteya.

k a - i′- t e - k p a s, *cont.* of kaitekpaza; kaitekpas iyeya.

k a - i′- t e - k p a - z a, *v. a.* *to bring darkness over for a little while by smiting, to stun by striking*—wakaitekpaza.

k a - i′- t e m, *adv.* *diagonally, not straight.*

k a - i′- t e m - y a, *adv.* *crosswise, slanting, diagonally:* kaitemya kaksa, *to cut diagonally.*

k a - i′- t e - p a, *v. a.* *to cut diagonally*—wakaitepa.

k a - i′- t k o - k i m, *adv.* *with the face towards* one, *meeting.*

k a - i′- t k o - k i m - y a, *adv.* *facing* one. See itkokim.

k a - i′- t k o - k i - p a - t a ŋ - h a ŋ, *adv.* *opposite to, fronting* one.

k a - i′- t k o m, *adv.* *back again:* kaitkom hdiḣpaya, *to fall back again, rebound.* See itkom.

k a - i′- t k o m - y a, *adv.* *opposite but a little to one side, not looking quite straight at* one: wi kaitkomya yaŋka, *the middle of the forenoon.*

k a - i′- t o - k a b, *adv.* *T.* *before, in advance of; i. q.* kahiŋtokam.

k a - i′- t o - k a b - y a, *adv.* *T.* *in advance of.*

k a - i′- t o - k a ŋ, *adv.* *T.* *out one side; i. q.* kaiyog. See tokaŋ.

k a - i′- y a - k a - p e - y a, *adv.* *T.* *exceeding, a little more than.*

k a - i′- y a - k a - p t e - y a, *adv.* *T.* *up hill.* See iyakapteya.

k a - i′- y a - k i - ç u - y a, *adv.* *T.* *a little more.* See iyakiçuya.

k a - i′- y o g, *cont.* of kaiyoka; kaiyog iyeya, *to put out of the way, shove to one side.* *T.*, kaitokaŋ.

k a - i′- y o g - y a, *adv.* *out at one side.*

k a - i′- y o - k a, *adv.* See kaiyog.

k a - i′- y o - t a ŋ, *adv.* of iyotaŋ; *im-*

moderately: kaiyotaŋ yeya, *to make* one *do more by forbidding*—kaiyotaŋ yewaya.

ka-i'-yo-taŋg, *cont.* of kaiyotaŋka; kaiyotaŋg hdiȟpaya, *to fall down in attempting to be seated.*

ka-i'-yo-taŋ-ka, *v.* kaiyotaŋka hdiȟpaya, *to fall down when being seated.*

ka-i'-yo-was, *cont.* of kaiyowaza; kaiyowas iyeya, *to cause an echo by striking.*

ka-i'-yo-wa-za, *v. a.* *to make an echo by striking, make resound*—wakaiyowaza, uŋkaiyowazapi. See yaiyowaza.

ka'-i-yu-ze-ya, *adv.* *T.* *a little way off:* kaiyuzeya iću, *to reach for.*

ka-ka', *pron.* and *adv.* *that, there.*

ka'-ka, *adj.* *stiff, rattling,* as a stiff hide when beaten; *sounding dull,* as a bell sometimes does. See kakeća.

ka-kag', *cont.* of kakaka; kakag hiŋhda, *to sound, rattle,* like an old kettle when shaken with stones in it.

ka-kag'-ya *and* ka'-kag-ya, *adv.* *rattling,* as an old kettle when shaken; *rattling,* as an empty wagon.

ka-kag'-ya-ken, *adv.* *rattling.*

ka-ka'-ka, *v. a.* *to make a dull noise by beating* an old kettle or a stiff hide—wakakaka.

ka-kaŋ', *v. a.* *to hew,* as a log, *to adze; to knock off,* as fruit—wakakaŋ, uŋkakaŋpi. See kahna *and* kasna.

ka-kaŋ'-kaŋ, *v.* *T.* *to cut notches in* or *knobs on.*

ka-kaŋ'-pi, *n.* *the pigeon cherry.* *T.*, ćaŋpakakaŋ. See ćaŋpa.

ka-kaŋ'-pi-na *and* ka-kaŋ'-pi-daŋ, *n.* See kakaŋpi.

ka-ka'-tiŋ, *v. a.* *to straighten out by striking*—wakakatiŋ.

ka-ka'-wa, *v. a.* *to make open by striking*—wakakawa.

ka-kća', *v. a.* *to comb,* as hair, *to disentangle*—wakakća, yakakća, uŋkakćapi.

ka'-ke-ća, *adv.* *in this manner, thus, so:* kakeća epće śni, *I did not think it was so.* See dećeća, ećeća, hećeća, iyakidećeća, *and* iyećeća.

ka'-ke-ća, *adj.* *stiff, making a noise when felt* or *handled,* as parchment. See káka.

ka'-ken, *adv.* *so, thus:* kaken ećoŋ wo, *do it in this manner.* See dećen, ećen, hećen, iyakidećen, etc.

ka'-ken-ya, *adv.* *thus, so.*

ka-kes'-toŋ, *v. a.* *to make barbed,* as an arrow—kakeswatoŋ.

ka-keś', *adv.* uŋma tukte kakeś, *whatever one, no matter which;* toketu kakeś, *at random.*

ka'-ke-tu, *adv.* *in this way, so, thus.* See dećetu, ećetu, hećetu, *and* iyećetu.

ka'-ke-tu-ya, *adv.* *so, thus.*

ka-ki', *v. a.* of aki; *to have taken home to* one—wakaki, uŋkakipi.

ka'-ki, *adv.* *there, yonder.* See dići *and* hići.

ka-ki'-ki-ta, *v. a.* *to make tough*

by pounding—wakakikita. *T.*, kasuta *and* kasuksuta. See kikita.

k a - k i n′, *cont.* of kakiŋća *and* kakiŋta; kakin iyeya, *to scrape off.*

k a - k i ŋ′ - ć a, *v. a.* *to scrape*, as hair from a hog or scales from a fish—wakakiŋća, yakakiŋća, uŋkakiŋćapi.

k a - k i ŋ s′, *cont.* of kakiŋza; kakiŋs iyeya.

k a - k i ŋ s′ - k i ŋ - z a, *v. red.* of kakiŋza.

k a - k i ŋ′ - t a, *v. a.* *to scrape, clean.* See kakiŋća.

k a - k i ŋ′ - z a, *v.* *to make creak*, as the wind does trees; *to creak*, as a cart-wheel not greased.

k a - k i′ - p a, *v.* of kapa; *to surpass, excel* one—kawakipa, kauŋkipapi.

ka-ki′-paś, *and* ka-ki′-paś-paś, *adv.* *T.* *wrinkled, loose fitting.*

k a - k i ś′, *cont.* of kakiźa.

k a - k i ś′ - y a, *v. a.* *to inflict, make suffer; to punish, inflict punishment*—kakiśwaya.

ka-kiś′-ya, *adv.* *afflicted, suffering.*

k a - k i ś′ - y a - k e n, *adv.* *in a state of suffering:* kakiśyaken wauŋ, *I am suffering*

k a′ - k i - y a, *adv.* *yonder, there.* See dećiya *and* hećiya.

k a′ - k i - y a - t a ŋ - h a ŋ, *adv.* *from yonder place; on this wise, in this way, by this means.* See dećiyataŋhaŋ, ećiyataŋhaŋ *and* hećiyataŋhaŋ.

k a - k i′ - y o - t a ŋ, *adv.* *in that direction.* See dećiyotaŋ *and* hećiyotaŋ.

k a - k i′ - y o - t a ŋ - n a - i - y e - y a, *v.* *it stretches up in this way*, said of anything high, as a tall tree.

k a - k i′ - ź a, *v. n.* *to suffer, be afflicted; to be sick a long time*—makakiźa, nićakiźa.

k a - k i′ - ź a, *adj.* *suffering, afflicted.*

k a - k m i ŋ′, *v. a.* *Ih.* *to clear off*, as weeds from a field; *i. q.*, kamni.

k a - k o g′, *cont.* of kakoka; kakog hiŋhda.

k a - k o g′ - y a, *adv.* *rattling.*

k a - k o g′ - y a - k e n, *adv.* *rattling.*

k a - k o′ - k a, *v. a.* *to rattle*, as a cow-bell; *to make rattle by striking*—wakakoka. See kakaka.

k a - k o′ - k a m, *adv.* *around, across, before:* kakokam ya, *to go around, to hedge up the way*, as in chasing buffalo—kakokam mda. See akokam.

k a - k o′ - k o - k a, *v.* *red.* of kakoka.

k a - k o ŋ′ - k o ŋ - t a, *v. a.* *red.* of kakoŋta; *to hollow out in grooves* or *ridges*—wakakoŋkoŋta.

k a - k o ŋ′ - t a, *v. a.* *to cut in ridges*—wakakoŋta. See kakuŋta.

k a - k o′ - y a - ḣ a ŋ - n a, *adv.* *hurrying, hastening a little:* kakoyaḣaŋna ećamoŋ, *I have done it in somewhat of a hurry.* *T.*, kokoyela. See koyaḣaŋ *and* koyaḣaŋna.

k a - k p a′, *v. a.* *to shoot through*, as an arrow through an animal; *to strike, make a hole in*, as, kaŋkakpa, *to cut a vein, to bleed* a person.

k a - k p a ŋ′, *v. a.* *to beat fine, mash*

up; to wink, as the eye—wakakpaŋ. See iśtakakpaŋ.

ka-kpi', *v. a.* *to crack* or *break*, as a nut—wakakpi.

ka-ksa', *v. a.* *to cut off with an ax* or *by striking*—wakaksa, yakaksa, uŋkaksapi. See baksa, naksa, paksa, yaksa, *and* yuksa.

ka-ksa'-ksa, *v.* *red.* of kaksa; *to cut off often; to cut up*, as wood for the fire—wakaksaksa.

ka-ksi'-za, *n.* *a ravine, hollow, low place, gully*, with or without water. *T.*, opaȟći. See osmaka.

ka-kśa', *v. a.* *to wind*, as yarn; *to fold up*—wakakśa, uŋkakśapi.

ka-kśa', *adv.* *coiled up:* kakśa waŋka, *it lies coiled up.*

ka-kśa'-daŋ, *adv.* *coiled up.*

ka-kśa'-kśa, *adv.* *red.* of kakśa; *coiled up, in coils, rolled round.*

ka-kśaŋ', *v. a.* *to bend, bend up*—wakakśaŋ, uŋkakśaŋpi.

ka-kśaŋ'-kśaŋ, *adv.* *crookedly, in a zigzag manner:* kakśaŋkśaŋ iŋyaŋka, *he runs crookedly.*

ka-kśi'-kśi-źa, *v.* *red.* of kakśiźa.

ka-kśiś', *cont.* of kakśiźa; kakśiś iyeya, *to double up.*

ka-kśiś'-ya, *v. a.* *to cause to shut up*—kakśiśwaya.

ka-kśi'-źa, *v. a.* *to bend up, double up by striking; to shut up*, as a pocket-knife—wakakśiźa.

ka-ktaŋ', *v. a.* *to bend by striking*—wakaktaŋ.

ka-ktaŋ'-ktaŋ, *v.* *red.* of kaktaŋ.

ka-ktaŋ'-yaŋ, *adv.* *bending.*

ka-kti'-haŋ, *adv.* *stumbling, tottering.* *T.*, kaćekćel.

ka-kti'-haŋ-haŋ, *adv.* *red.* of kaktihaŋ; *stumbling, tottering:* kaktihaŋhaŋ mani, *to walk in a staggering manner.* See kaćegya.

ka-kti'-haŋ-haŋ-yaŋ, *adv.* *stumblingly.*

ka-kti'-haŋ-yaŋ, *v. a.* *to cause to stumble along*—kaktihaŋwaya.

ka-ku', *v. a.* of aku; *to start to bring home to* one—wakaku, uŋkakupi, makaku.

ka-ku'-ka, *v. a.* *to pound to pieces, make rotten by pounding*—wakakuka, uŋkakukapi.

ka-kuŋ'-kuŋ-ta, *v. a.* *to cut in ridges*—wakakuŋkuŋta.

ka-kuŋ'-ta, *v. a.* *to cut a groove in*—wakakuŋta. See kakoŋta.

ka-kuŋ'-tkuŋ-ta, *v. a.* Same as kakuŋkuŋta.

ka-ḳe'-ġa, *v. a.* *to make a grating noise*—wakaḳeġa.

ka-ḳes', *cont.* of kaḳeza; kaḳes iyeya, *to blow off and leave bare and hard*, as when the wind blows the snow from the ground.

ka-ḳe'-za, *v. n.* *to leave hard and bare*, as the wind does the ground. See kaḳoza.

ka-ḳo'-ġa, *v. a.* *to scrape*, as a turnip—wakaḳoġa.

ka-ḳoȟ', *cont* of kaḳoġa; tipsiŋna kaḳoȟ yutapi, *scraping turnips they eat them.*

ka-ḳos', *cont.* of kaḳoza; kaḳos iyeya.

k a - ḳ o′ - z a, *v. a.* *to make hard, to leave hard and bare*, as the wind does the ground; *to beat hard*—wakaḳoza. See kaḳeza.

k a - m d a′, *v. a.* *to make smooth by cutting; to slice up*, as meat for drying; *to cut up*, as bread—wakamda, uŋkamdapi. *T.*, kabla, *to open*, as, iśta wakabla, *I open my eyes.*

k a - m d a′ - ġ a, *v.* *to spread out*, as wings: ḣupahu kamdaġa, *he spread his wings.*

k a - m d a ḣ′, *cont.* of kamdaġa; kamdaḣ iyeya.

k a - m d a′ - p i, *n.* *something cut up in slices* or *thin pieces*, as meat for drying.

k a - m d a s′, *cont.* of kamdaza; kamdas iyeya.

k a - m d a′ - s k a, *v. a.* *to flatten by beating*—wakamdaska, uŋkamdaskapi. *T.*, kablaska.

k a - m d a s′ - k i - y a, *v. a.* *to cause to rip* or *burst open*—kamdaswakiya.

k a - m d a ś′, *cont.* of kamdaźa; kamdaś inaźiŋ, *to stand astride of* anything.

k a - m d a ś′ - y a, *v. a.* *to cause to straddle*—kamdaśwaya.

k a - m d a′ - y a, *v. a.* *to make level* or *smooth by beating; to spread out*, as a piece of cloth; *to open* or *spread out*, as the hand—wakamdaya. *T.*, kablaya.

k a - m d a′ - z a, *v. a.* *to make rip open* or *burst by striking* or *throwing down*, as a bag of corn—wakamdaza. See akamdaza.

k a - m d a′ - ź a, *v. a.* *to spread open*, as the legs; *to straddle*—wakamdaźa. See akamdaźa.

k a - m d e′ - ć a, *v. a.* *to break by throwing down* or *striking*, as glass, plates, etc.—wakamdeća, yakamdeća, uŋkamdećapi. *T.*, kableća.

k a - m d e′ - m d e - ć a, *v. a.* *red.* of kamdeća; *to break to pieces*—wakamdemdeća.

k a - m d e′ - m d e n, *cont.* of kamdemdeća.

k a - m d e n′, *cont.* of kamdeća; kamden iyeya, and kamden eḣpeya, *to throw down and break to pieces.*

k a - m d e n′ - k i - y a, *v. a.* *to cause to break*—kamdenwakiya.

k a - m d e n′ - y a, *v. a.* *to cause to break to pieces.*

k a - m d e s′, *cont.* of kamdeza.

k a - m d e s′ - y a, *v. a.* *to cause to be clear, cause to clear off*, as the wind does fog.

k a - m d e′ - z a, *v. n.* *to become clear, clear off*, as a fog clears away: aŋpao kamdeza, *when things are again visible, daylight, the dawn.*

k a - m d e′ - z e - ś n i, *v. n.* *to be unable to see;* said when there is a fog or darkness, and things are not visible: kamdeześni eḣpeya, *to stun, knock senseless.* *T.*, kableze śni, *to strike and make frantic.*

k a - m d u′, *v. a.* *to pound fine; to stir up and granulate*, as sugar, *to make fine by stirring*—wakamdu, uŋkamdupi. *T.*, kablu.

k a - m d u′, *v. n.* *to blossom, open out*,

as flowers; *to decrease*, as the moon after its full: kamdu iću, *it is decreasing*. *T.*, nableća.

ka-mdu′-ki-ya, *v. a.* *to cause to make fine*—kamduwakiya.

ka-mdu′-mdu, *v. red.* of kamdu.

ka-mdu′-pi, *n.* *something fine*, as powdered sugar.

ka-mdu′-ya, *v. a.* *to cause to make fine*—kamduwaya.

ka-mi′-ma, *v. a.* *to make round*, as a wheel, *with an ax*—wakamima. See kahmiyaŋyaŋ.

ka-mi′-ni-o-ġe-i-ye′-ya, *v.* *to bring tears in one's eyes*, as the wind does. See kaiśtaminioġeiyeya.

ka-mna′, *v. a.* *to collect, gather; to get, procure, obtain; to break out*, as a piece from the edge of an ax; *to rip*, as a seam, *come open*—wakamna, yakamna, uŋkamnaŋpi. See mnayaŋ *and* kaḣći.

ka-mna′-ki-ya, *v. a.* *to cause to get* or *obtain*—kamnawakiya.

ka-mna′-yaŋ, *v. a.* *to cause to get* or *obtain*—kamnawaya, kamnauŋyaŋpi.

ka-mni′, *v. a.* *to make level* or *clear away*, as a place to put a tent; *to break a piece out*, as from the edge of an ax—wakamni. *T.*, kagmi *and* kaḣći. See kapinźa.

ka-mni′-ki-ya, *v. a.* *to cause to clear away*, etc.

ka-mni′-mni, *v. n.* *to hang loosely, dangle, swing*, as a blanket on one's shoulders.

ka-mni′-mni-na, *n.* *ear-drops*, such as are always dangling, made of a triangular shape. *T.*, owiŋpi *or* oiŋpi.

kam-pe′-ska, *n.* *T.* *white ware, chinaware*. See kaŋpeska.

kan, *adv.* *there, yonder, i. e.* kakiya. See den *and* hen.

kan, *cont.* of kata; kan iću, *it becomes hot*.

ka′-na, *pron. pl.* *these, those* See dena *and* hena.

ka-na′-ke, *adv.* *leaning, likely to fall; i. q.* owotaŋna yaŋke śni.

ka-na′-ke-ća, *adv.* *so many, so much, all these*. See denakeća *and* henakeća.

ka-na′-ke-seḣ, *adv.* *so many*. *T.*, kanakeḣćiŋ.

ka-na′-ke-ya, *adv.* *likely to fall:* kanakeya hiyaya, *it has become leaning*. See panakeya, etc.

ka-na′-ki-ya, *adv.* *all these, so many, in so many ways*.

ka-na′-na, *adv.* *only these, only so many*. See denana *and* henana.

ka-ni′-ća, *v. a.* (ka *and* nića) *to cut off clean*, as limbs from a tree; wakanića. See kasota.

ka-nmi′-nma, *v. a* *to roll, make roll*, as a ball, *by striking*—wakanminma. *T.*, kagmigma. See kahmihma.

kan-ya′, *v. a.* of káta; *to warm* or *heat* by the fire—kanwaya: kaniçiya, *to warm one's self*.

kaŋ, *n.* *a vein, artery; a sinew, tendon, i. q.* takaŋ; *the nerves; a cord, string*. See ikaŋ.

k a ŋ , *adj.* *aged*—makáŋ, nikáŋ, uŋkáŋpi.

k a ŋ - d i′, *n.* *the buffalo-fish.*

k a ŋ - ġ i′, *n.* *the raven.*

k a ŋ - ġ i′ - k a - ġ a - p i , *n.* *a half-dollar*, so called from its emblem, *the eagle*, which the Dakotas thought was a raven. The Yanktons apply this to a 25-cent piece. *T.*, śokela.

k a ŋ - ġ i′ - t a - m e , *n.* *T.* *coal.*

K a ŋ - ġ i′ - w i - ć a - ś a , *n. p.* *the Crow Indians.*

k a ŋ - h a ŋ′, *adv.* *dangling, tattered, old.*

k a ŋ - h a ŋ′ - h a ŋ , *adv.* *dangling, tattered, ragged.*

k a ŋ - h e′, *v. n.* *to shell out*, as ripe grain.

k a ŋ - h e′ - ć a , *adj.* *ragged, tattered*, as one's clothes—makaŋheća.

k a ŋ - h e′ - ź a , *adj.* *poor, distressed, feeble, sick*—makaŋheźa. *T.*, oŋśika. See wakaŋheźa.

k a ŋ - h e′ - ź a - k a , *adj.* Same as kaŋheźa.

k a ŋ - i′ - ć a - k p e , *n.* (kaŋ *and* kakpa) *a lancet.*

k a ŋ - i′ - ć a - t p e , *n.* (kaŋ *and* katpa) *a vein-cutter, a lancet.*

k a ŋ - i′ - ṭ a , *v.* *to die of old age*—kaŋimaṭa.

k a ŋ′ - i - y a - p ' a , *n.* *the pulse, the beating of the pulse.* See iyap'a.

k a ŋ - k a′ - k p a , *v. a.* *to cut a vein, bleed* one—kaŋwakakpa.

k a ŋ - k a ŋ′, *adj.* *gouged, uneven.*

k a ŋ - k a′ - t p a , *v. a.* Same as kaŋkakpa.

k a ŋ - k e′ - t a ŋ - k a , *n.* *the large red-headed woodpecker.* *T.*, kaŋkeća

k a ŋ - k i′ - ć a - k p a , *v. a.* *to strike a vein for* one, *bleed* one—kaŋwećakpa, kaŋyećakpa, kaŋuŋkićakpapi, kaŋmićakpa, kaŋćićakpa.

k a ŋ - k i′ - ć a - t p a , *v. a.* Same as kaŋkićakpa.

k a ŋ′ - n a - h m u ŋ - k i - y a , *v. a.* *to draw up tight*, as a bow-string—kaŋnahmuŋwakiya.

k a ŋ′ - n a - t i - p a , *v. n.* *to draw up, to cramp*, as the nerves or muscles.

k a ŋ - p e′ - s k a , *n.* *round, white medals, slightly curved*, worn by the Indians on their necks; *Ih.*, kaŋpeska wakśića, *china ware; an excrescence growing on trees, fungus.* See ćaŋkaŋpeska. Kaŋpeska mde, *Kanpaska Lake*, on the Coteau des Prairies, at the head of the Big Sioux River; Kaŋpeska Wakpa, *Laramie River.*

k a ŋ - s u′, *n.* *plum-stones: i. q.* kaŋta su; *playing-cards; any small card* or *ticket.*

k a ŋ - s u′ - k u - t e , *v. a.* *to shoot plum-stones, to gamble; to play cards*—kaŋsuwakute.

k a ŋ - s u′ - k u - t e - p i , *n.* *shooting plum-stones, gambling; playing cards.* Hence miniḣuha kaŋsukutepi, *playing-cards.*

k a ŋ′ - t a , *n.* *a plum, plums.*

k a ŋ′ - t a - h u *and* k a ŋ - t u′ - h u , *n* *plum-bushes*

k a ŋ - y e′, *adv.* *inwards, towards*

the center, *towards a river* or *lake* or *fire from* one; opposed to ḣeyata.

kaŋ-ye′-haŋ, *adv.* See kayehaŋ.

kaŋ-ye′-ki-ya, *adv.* *inwards*, *below.*

kaŋ-ye′-la, *adv.* *T.* *near:* kaŋye: *i. q* kiyela, kiyena.

kaŋ-ye′-na, *adv.* *Ih.* *near.*

kaŋ-ye′-ta, *adv.* or *n.* *before*, *in front of:* mikaŋyeta, *in front of me.*

kaŋ-ye′-taŋ-haŋ, *adv.* *on the inside of.* See ikaŋyetaŋhaŋ.

kaŋ-ye′-wa-pa, *adv.* *within*, *towards the center.*

Kaŋ′-ze, *n. p.* *the Kansas* or *Kaws.*

ka-o′-ći-kpa-ni, *adv.* *unequal*, *of different sizes.*

ka-o′-ći-kpa-ni-yaŋ, *adv.* *unequally:* kaoćikpaniyaŋ kaġapi, *they are made not alike.*

ka-o′-ći-pte-ća, *adv.* *not equal.*

ka-o′-ći-pten, *adv.* *unequal*, *one large and one small*, *diminishing* or *increasing in size.*

ka-o′-ći-pten-ya, *adv.* *unequally.*

ka-o′-ći-pte-tu, *adv.* *unequal in size*, etc.

ka-o′-ći-tpa-ni, *adv.* Same as kaoćikpani.

ka-o′-hda-pśiŋ, *adv.* *bottom side up*, *turned over:* kaohdapśiŋ eḣpeya, *to turn bottom up.*

ka-o′-hda-pśiŋ-yaŋ, *adv.* *turned over*, *bottom side up.*

ka-o′-hmi-hma, *v.* *to make roll over and over by striking.* See kaonminma.

ka-o′-ḣaŋ-ko, *v. a.* of oḣaŋko; *to strike and make work fast*—wakaoḣaŋko. See kakoyaḣaŋna.

ka-o′-ḣmi, *v. a.* *to whirl*, *throw obliquely*—wakaoḣmi. Same as kaoḣmiŋ.

ka-o′-ḣmiŋ, *v. a.* *to cause to move obliquely*—wakaoḣmiŋ.

ka-o′-ḣmiŋ-yaŋ, *adv.* *obliquely:* kaoḣmiŋyaŋ iyeya, *to throw obliquely.*

ka-o′-ḣpa, *v. a.* *to break through by striking*, *break in*, as one's skull; *to cut a hole in*, as in making a canoe—wakaoḣpa.

ka-o′-ḣpe-ki-ya, *v. a.* *to cause to knock a hole in*—kaoḣpewakiya.

ka-o′-ḣpe-ya, *v. a.* *to cause to strike through.*

ka-o′-ḣpe-ya, *adv.* *in the manner of striking through.*

ka-oḣ′-ya, *adv.* *leaning*, *sloping*, *twisting:* kaoḣya ewahnaka, *I placed it sloping.* See yuoḣya.

ka-o′-ksa, *v. a.* *to cut* or *pound a hole in*, as into a corn-hole or in ice; *to break through*—wakaoksa.

ka-o′-ksa, *v. n.* *to fall off* or *over*, as a bank; *fall in:* *i. q.* kaosba.

ka-o′-kse-ya, *v. a.* *to cause to break in*—kaoksewaya.

ka-o′-ktaŋ, *v. a.* *to bend and pound into*—wakaoktaŋ.

ka-o′-ktaŋ-yaŋ, *v. a.* *to cause to bend into*—kaoktaŋwaya.

ka-o′-ktaŋ-yaŋ, *adv.* *bending into.*

ka-o′-mni, *n.* *a calm place* in a lake or river. See iyomni.

k a - o′- m n i - i - ć u - y a, *n.* *a whirling round.* Said of the wind eddying, or whistling, or whirling under a lee shore.

k a - o′- m n i - n a, *n.* of omnina. *a calm place; in a calm place.* See iyomnina.

k a - o′- n m i - n m a, *v. a.* *to roll, make roll*—wakaonminma. See kaohmihma.

k a - o ŋ′- s p e, *v.* of oŋspe; *to train* or *teach,* as a horse—wakaoŋspe.

k a - o ŋ′- s p e - ś n i, *adj.* *untrained, untaught.*

k a - o ŋ′- z e - b o - s d a n, *adv.* (ka oŋze *and* bosdan) *heels up:* kaoŋzebosdan iyeya *and* kaoŋzebosdan eḣpeya, *to knock the other end up.*

k a - o′- p̣ o, *v.* *T.* *to raise a dust,* as in sweeping. See kap̣o.

k a - o′- s b a, *v.* kaosba hiŋḣpaya, *to fall off,* as from a bank into a river.

k a - o′- s m a - k a, *v. a.* *to make an indentation by striking*—wakaosmaka: kaosmag iyeya. See osmaka.

k a - o′- s p a, *v. a.* *to strike and bruise in*—wakaospa: kaospaiyeya.

k a - o′- s p e - y a, *v.* *T.* *to weigh down: i. q.* aspeya. See kaspeya.

k a - o′- s p e - y e - t o ŋ, *v.* *T.* *to weigh* anything. See iyuta.

k a - o′- t a ŋ, *v. a.* *to pound tight*—wakaotaŋ.

k a - o′- t a ŋ - i ŋ, *v. a.* of otaŋiŋ; *to make manifest* or *apparent*—wakaotaŋiŋ.

k a - o′- ṭ i ŋ s, *cont.* of kaoṭiŋza; kaoṭiŋs iyeya.

k a - o′- ṭ i ŋ - z a, *v. a.* of oṭiŋza; *to drive* or *pound in tight,* as a pin—wakaoṭiŋza.

k a - o′- w o - t a ŋ - i ŋ, *v.* *to clear off, become so that things can be seen at a distance.* See owotaŋiŋ.

k a - o′- w o - t a ŋ - n a, *v. a.* of owotaŋna; *to straighten, make straight by striking* in any way—wakaowotaŋna.

k a - o′- z e - z e, *v. n.* *to swing, dangle.*

k a - o′- z e - z e - y a, *adv.* *swinging, dangling:* kaozezeya yaŋka, *it is swinging.*

k a - p ’ a′, *v. a.* *to beat* or *thresh off,* as corn; *to pound up,* as meat—wakap’a, uŋkap’api. See kapaŋ.

k a - p a′ *and* k a - p e′, *v. a.* *to pass by* in running, as kapa iŋyaŋka, *to run past* one; *to excel, surpass in* anything, as in height; *to go beyond, to transgress*—kawapa, kauŋpapi, kamayapa.

k a - p a′- k o, *v. n.* of pako; *to become crooked.*

k a - p a ŋ′, *v. a.* *to beat* or *thresh off*—wakapaŋ. See kap’a.

k a - p a ŋ′- p a ŋ, *v. a.* *to beat soft, make mellow*—wakapaŋpaŋ.

k a - p ’ a′- p ’ a, *v. red.* of kap’a; *to beat* or *thresh,* as grain.

k a - p e′, *v. a.* of pe; *to sharpen by pounding, to upset,* as an old ax—wakape.

k a - p e′- m n i, *v. a.* of pemni; *to make crooked* or *awry by striking*—wakapemni. See kaśkopa.

ka-pe'-mni-mni-yaŋ, *adv.* *dangling.*

ka-pe'-mni-yaŋ, *adv.* *crookedly; dangling, swinging,* as scissors tied by a string.

ka-p'e'-p'e. *v. n.* *T.* *to skip,* as anything on water.

ka-p'e'-p'e-ya, *v. a.* *to make skip.*

ka-p'e'-p'e-ya, *adv.* *skipping.*

ka-pe'-sto, *v. a.* of pesto; *to make sharp-pointed with an ax*—wakapesto.

ka-pe'-ya, *v. a.* of kapa; *to go* or *pass beyond, do more; to cause to surpass*—kapewaya.

ka-pe'-ya, *adv.* *beyond, further, greater than, surpassing:* Atewaye ćiŋ he mikapeya taŋka, "*My Father is greater than I,*" John xiv, 28.

ka-p'iŋ', *v. n.* *to be indisposed* or *unwilling* to do a thing; *to be tired:* mani kap'iŋ, *to be indisposed to walk;* ećoŋ wakap'iŋ, *I am unwilling to do it;* ie kap'iŋ, *he is tired of talking*—wakap'iŋ, uŋkap'iŋpi.

ka-piŋs', *cont.* of kapiŋza.

ka-piŋś', *cont.* of kapiŋźa.

ka-piŋ'-za, *v. a.* *to make squeak* or *squeal,* as a squirrel, *by striking*—wakapiŋza.

ka-piŋ'-źa, *v. a.* *to clear away,* as brush, grass, etc.—wakapiŋźa. *T.,* kagmi. See kamni.

ka-po', *v. n.* *to swell,* as one's flesh—makapo, nićapo.

ka-po'-ġaŋ, *v. n.* *to puff out, to swell and become tight,* as a bladder that is blown.

ka-poh', *cont.* of kapoġaŋ; kapoh iyeya.

ka-poh'-ya, *v. a.* *to make swell out,* as anything filled with air—kapohwaya.

ka-poh'-ya, *adv.* *rising, swelling out.*

ka-pom', *cont* of kapopa; kapom iyaya, *to burst with a noise;* kapom iyeya, *to cause to burst.*

ka-po'-pa, *v. a.* *to make a popping noise; to strike and make burst*—wakapopa.

ka-po'-ta, *v. a.* *to pound to pieces,* as a garment; *to rend, tear in pieces,* as wind does clothes—wakapota.

ka-po'-tpo-ta, *v. red.* of kapota.

ka-psag', *cont.* of kapsaka; kapsag iyeya, *and* kapsag ehpeya, *to break violently.*

ka-psag'-ya, *v. a.* *to cause to break*—kapsagwaya.

ka-psag'-ya, *adv.* *broken,* as a string.

ka-psa'-ka, *v. a.* *to break,* as a string, *by striking; to break of itself*—wakapsaka, uŋkapsakapi.

ka-psaŋ'-psaŋ, *v. n.* *to dangle, swing back and forth; to sway to and fro,* as a limb in water.

ka-psa'-psa-ka, *v. red.* of kapsaka.

ka-psi'-ća, *v. a.* *to make jump by striking*—wakapsića, uŋkapsićapi

ka-psin', *cont.* of kapsića; kapsin iyeya. Also used as a contraction of kapsiŋta.

ka-psiŋ'-psiŋ ta, *v. a.* *to whip,*

correct by whipping, chastise—wakapsiŋpsiŋta.

ka-psiŋ'-ta, *v. a.* *to whip, flog; to correct,* as a child, *by whipping*—wakapsiŋta, uŋkapsiŋtapi: kapsiŋtapi se uŋ, *he appears as if he had been whipped.*

ka-psi'-psi-ća, *v. red.* *to make jump much by striking*—wakapsipsića.

ka-psi'-psin, *cont.* of kapsipsića; kapsipsin iyeya, *to throw out and make skip about,* as in fishing.

ka-psoŋ', *v. a.* *to upset and spill,* as a vessel of water; *to overturn and fall out,* as from a canoe—wakapsoŋ.

ka-psoŋ'-psoŋ, *v. red.* of kapsoŋ.

ka-pśuŋ', *v. a.* *to knock out,* as a tooth; *to dislocate,* as a joint, *by striking*—wakapśuŋ; *to shed,* as a deer his horns. Hence, the *December moon* is called Tahećapśuŋ wi, *Moon when the deer shed their horns.*

ka-pśuŋ'-ka, *v. a.* *to make round* or *knob-like*—wakapśuŋka.

ka-pśuŋ'-pśuŋ, *v. red.* of kapśuŋ.

ka-pśuŋ'-yaŋ, *v. a.* *to cause to knock out of place*—kapśuŋwaya.

ka-pta', *v. a.* *to lade* or *bail out,* as water from a boat—wakapta, yakapta, uŋkaptapi. See kaġe.

ka-ptaŋ'-ptaŋ, *v. a.* *to turn over and over*—wakaptaŋptaŋ.

ka-ptaŋ'-yaŋ, *v. a.* *to cause to fall over; to turn over, upset,* as a canoe—wakaptaŋyaŋ, uŋkaptaŋyaŋpi.

ka-ptaŋ'-yaŋ, *adv.* *turning over.*

ka-ptaŋ'-ye-ya, *v. a.* *to cause to fall over, to overturn*—kaptaŋyewaya.

ka-pta'-pta, *v. n.* *to fall to pieces,* as something rotten.

ka-ptu'-ptuś, *cont.* of kaptuptuźa; kaptuptuś iyeya.

ka-ptu'-ptu-źa, *v. red.* of kaptuźa; *to crack often by striking.*

ka-ptuś', *cont.* of kaptuźa; kaptuś iyeya.

ka-ptuś'-ki-ya, *v. a.* *to cause to make crack*—kaptuśwakiya.

ka-ptu'-źa, *v. a.* *to split* or *crack by striking,* but not to split open—wakaptuźa, uŋkaptuźapi.

ka-p̣o', *v. a.* *to strike and make a smell,* whether good or bad; *to stop* or *cease from,* as in gambling, and distribute the articles staked—wakap̣o. *T.,* *to raise a dust,* as in sweeping.

ka-p̣oś'-p̣o-źe-daŋ, *adv. red.* of kap̣oźedaŋ.

ka-p̣o'-źa, *adj.* *light, not heavy.*

Ka-p̣o'-źa, *n. p.* those who traveled *unincumbered with much baggage:* the name of the *Little Crow's band* of Dakota Indians; *Kaposia,* or *Little Crow's village.*

ka-p̣o'-źe-daŋ, *adj. dim.* *light, not heavy.*

ka-p̣o'-źe-la, *T.,* and ka-p̣o'-źe-na, *Ih. adj.* *light, not heavy.*

ka-sa', *v. a.* *to bury in the snow, cover over with snow*—wakasa, uŋkasapi.

ka-s'a', *v. n.* *to whistle* or *moan*, as the wind. *T.*, *to sail* or *glide* in the air, as birds.

ka-sag', *cont.* of kasaka; kasag iyeya.

ka-sa'-ka, *v. a.* *to switch, whip*—wakasaka.

ka-sak'-sa-ka, *v. red.* of kasaka; *to whip*—wakasaksaka.

ka-sam'-ye-daŋ, *adv.* *heavily:* kasamyedaŋ hiŋȟpaya, *to fall heavily.*

ka-saŋ', *v. n.* *to whiten* or *wash off*, as the rain does paint. See kasepa.

ka-saŋ', *v. a.* *to shave off*, as the beard or hair; *to whiten by scraping*—wakasaŋ. *T.*, kasla.

ka-saŋ'-saŋ, *v. red.* of kasaŋ; *to scrape and whiten*—wakasaŋsaŋ.

ka-sba', *v. a.* *to make lint; to curry*—wakasba, uŋkasbapi.

ka-sba'-sba, *v. red.* of kasba.

ka-sbu', *v. a.* *to cut into small strips, cut into dangles, make fringe*—wakasbu, uŋkasbupi.

ka-sbu'-ki-ya, *v. a.* *to cause to cut into strips*—kasbuwakiya.

ka-sbu'-pi, *n.* *dangles, fringe.* See akamda.

ka-sbu'-sbu, *v. red.* of kasbu; *to cut into strings and let hang*—wakasbusbu.

ka-sda'-ta, *v.* *to steal up to by paddling*, as to ducks; *to paddle softly*—wakasdata.

ka-sde'-ća, *v. a.* *to split*, as wood, *with an ax*—wakasdeća, uŋkasdećapi.

ka-sdem', *cont.* of kasdepa.

ka-sdem'-ya, *adv.* *tapering, wedge-like.*

ka-sden', *cont.* of kasdeća; kasden iyeya.

ka-sden'-ki-ya, *v. a* *to cause to split*—kasdenwakiya.

ka-sden'-ya, *v. a.* *to cause to split*—kasdenwaya.

ka-sde'-pa, *v. a.* *to make tapering, to make like a wedge*—wakasdepa.

ka-sde'-sde-ća, *v. a. red.* of kasdeća; *to split up fine*, as wood—wakasdesdeća.

ka-sde'-sden, *cont.* of kasdesdeća.

ka-sdi', *v. a.* *to strike and force some out*, as from a bladder full of grease; *to sharpen*, as a stick, *with an ax*—wakasdi. See kapesto.

ka-sdi'-sdi, *v. red.* of kasdi.

ka-sdi'-tka, *v. a.* of sditka; *to cut in notches, make knobs on*—wakasditka. *T.*, kakaŋkaŋ.

ka-sdi'-tka-tka, *v. red.* of kasditka.

ka-sdi'-ya, *v. a.* *to cause* one *to press out*—kasdiwaya.

ka-sdo'-haŋ, *v. n.* of sdohaŋ; *to waft* or *drive along*, as the wind does clouds. *T.*, kaslohaŋ, *to slide down hill.*

ka-sdo'-haŋ-haŋ, *v. red.* of kasdohaŋ.

ka-se'-pa, *v. n.* *to wash off*, as the rain does paint. See kasaŋ.

ka-s'iŋ', *adv.* *appearing, in sight.* See aokasiŋ *and* okasiŋ.

k a - s ' i ŋ' - s ' i ŋ , *adv. red.* of kaś'iŋ; *appearing now and then.*

k a - s ' i ŋ' - s ' i ŋ - y a ŋ , *adv. appearing at times, occasionally seen:* kas'iŋs'iŋyaŋ iyaya, *he passes along in sight sometimes.*

k a - s ' i ŋ' - y a ŋ , *adv. in sight, partly visible, projecting,* as a cork in a bottle.

k a - s k a', *v. a. to bleach by striking* or *dragging*—wakaska.

k a - s k a', *v. n. to clear off,* as clouds, smoke, or fog; *to become clear.*

k a - s k a' - h a ŋ , *n. dregs.*

k a - s k a m', *cont.* of kaskapa; kaskam iyeya, *to strike off with the hand.*

k a - s k a' - p a , *v. a. to strike,* as with the hand, *strike* hands *together:* nape hdaskapa, *he strikes his hands together.*

k a - s k e m', *cont.* of kaskepa; kaskem iyeya.

k a - s k e m' - k i - y a , *v. a. to cause to bail out,* as water from a canoe—kaskemwakiya.

k a - s k e m' - y a , *v. a. to cause to bail out.*

k a - s k e' - p a , *v. a.* of skepa; *to paddle* or *bail out,* as water from a canoe: also *v. n. to leak,* as a vessel; *to go dry,* as a well—wakaskepa. See kuse, kaȟepa, *and* kaśkepa.

k a - s k i' - ć a , *v. a. to press, press down on; to embrace*—wakaskića, uŋkaskićapi: taha kaskića, *to press packs of furs.* See kaśkića.

k a - s k i n', *cont.* of kaskića; kaskin yuza, *to clasp in the arms*—kaskin mduza.

k a - s k i n' - y a , *v. a. to cause to settle down, to press down*—kaskinwaya.

k a - s k i' - t a , *v. to press, to clasp:* kaskita yuza, *to embrace.*

k a - s k u', *v. a. to peel off,* as bark with an ax; *blaze,* by cutting off bark from a tree: ćaŋ kasku ya, *to go blazing trees,* as in making a road through woods—wakasku.

k a - s m a g', *cont.* of kasmaka; kasmag iyeya.

k a - s m a' - k a , *v. a. to indent* or *make concave by striking*—wakasmaka; *to make a track,* as a wagon does. See kaosmaka.

k a - s m i ŋ' - y a ŋ , *v. to make bare; to blow all off and leave bare,* as the wind does in taking off the snow.

k a - s m i ŋ' - y a ŋ - y a ŋ , *v. red.* of kasmiŋyaŋ.

k a - s n a', *v. a. to make ring* or *sound by striking; to make ring,* as the wind; *to knock* or *shake off* fruit or leaves from a tree: *i. q.* kahna—wakasna, uŋkasnapi.

k a - s n a' - s n a , *v. red.* of kasna; *to make ring; to trim* or *cut off all the limbs* from a tree *and leave* it *bare*—wakasnasna. See snasnana.

k a - s n i', *v. a.* of sni; *to put out* or *extinguish* fire *by beating; to cool* food *by shaking* it—wakasni, uŋkasnipi.

k a - s n i' - s n i , *v. red.* of kasni.

k a - s o n', *cont.* of kasota; kason iyeya, *to use all up.*

k a - s o' - t a, *v. a.* *to use up by striking; to kill off,* as cattle; *to cut all off,* as trees, *to make prairie of woodland; to use up*—wakasota, uŋkasotapi. See kanića.

k a - s o' - t a, *v. n.* *to clear off,* as the sky, *be clear* from clouds: kasota au, *it is clearing off.* See kaska.

k a - s p a' - y a, *v. a.* of spaya; *to wet, moisten*—wakaspaya.

k a - s p e' - y a, *v. a* *to make sink; to balance, weigh*—kaspewaya: kaspeya elinaka, *to place in a balance, to balance* or *weigh; to put so as to hold to its place,* as something placed to hold a book open. See kaospeya.

k a-s p e' - y a, *adv.* *balancing, ready to sink;* kaspeya yaŋka, *it is in a balance.*

k a - s t a g', *cont.* of kastaka; kastag eḣpeya, *to throw on and make stick,* as mud.

k a - s t a' - k a, *v. a.* *to throw on,* as mud, *to throw so as to make stick*—wakastaka.

k a - s t a ŋ' - k a, *v. a.* *to moisten by pounding*—wakastaŋka.

k a - s t o', *v. a.* *to smooth down, to stroke, comb,* as hair or grass—wakasto, uŋkastopi: kasto iyaya, *to drag* or *trip along.*

k a -s t o' - s t o, *v. red.* of kasto; *to stroke, make smooth.*

k a - s t o' - y a, *adv.* *smoothly.*

k a - s u k' - s u - t a, *v. red.* of kasuta.

k a - s u' - t a, *v.* of suta; *to pound and make hard* or *tough.*

k a ś, *conj.* *if, although.* See kaeś.

k a - ś a', *conj.* (ka *and* eśa) *T.* and *Ih.* *though, although:* sometimes it has the form of *ever;* as, tuwe kaśa, *whoever,* taku kaśa, *whatever: i. q.* kaśta.

k a - ś ' a g', *cont.* of kaś'aka.

k a - ś ' a g' - y a, *v. a.* *to cause to strike feebly*—kaś'agwaya.

k a - ś ' a' - k a, *v. a.* *to strike with too little force to penetrate; to discourage*—wakaś'aka.

k a - ś ' a' - k a, *adj.* *overloaded.*

k a - ś d a', *v a.* *to cut off, make bare,* as, pa kaśda, *to shave the head; to mow,* as grass, *make bare by mowing*—wakaśda, uŋkaśdapi. See peźikaśda.

k a - ś d a' - ś d a; *v. red.* of kaśda.

k a - ś d a' - y a, *v. a.* *to cause to make bare*—kaśdawaya.

k a-ś d e' - ć a, *v. a.* *Ih.* *to split: i. q.* kasdeća.

k a - ś d o g', *cont.* of kaśdoka; kaśdog iyeya.

k a - ś d o' - k a, *v. a.* *to knock off* or *out,* as the helve from an ax—wakaśdoka, uŋkaśdokapi; *to fall out,* as an arrow that has been shot into an animal. *T.*, kaśloka, *to clean out,* as a pipe. See kaḣdoka.

k a - ś d u n', *cont.* of kaśduta; kaśdun iyeya, *to cause to glance off;* kaśdun iyaya, *to glance off,* as an ax.

k a - ś d u' - ś d u - t a, *v. red.* of kaśduta; *to polish; to smooth by striking, to planish*—wakaśduśduta.

k a - ś d u' - t a, *v. a.* *to strike and make glance off*—wakaśduta.

ka-śe′, *v. n.* *to strike* or *rub against*—makaśe, nićaśe.

ka-śe′-ća, *v. a.* *to make dead* or *dry by striking, to deaden by cutting around*, as a tree—wakaśeća.

ka-śen′-ki-ya, *v. a.* *to cause to deaden*—kaśenwakiya.

ka-śe′-ya, *v. a.* *to rub against, fend off; to obstruct*—kaśewaya.

ka-śe′-ya, *adv.* *hitting against, touching.*

ka-śi′-ća, *v. a.* of śića; *to spoil* or *make badly by striking*—wakaśića.

ka-śi′-ća-ho-wa-ya, *v. a.* *to cause to cry out by striking*—wakaśićahowaya.

ka-śim′, *cont.* of kaśipa; kasim iyeya.

ka-ś'iŋ′, *v. n.* *to bend backwards*—makaś'iŋ, nićaś'iŋ.

ka-ś'iŋ′-yaŋ, *adv.* *bent backwards:* kaś'iŋyaŋ uŋ, *he is bent backwards.*

ka-śi′-pa, *v. a.* *to knock* or *cut off close*, as branches from a tree, legs from a chair or pot, or rivets from a knife—wakaśipa; *to break off*, as the wind does limbs from a tree.

ka-śka′, *v. a.* *to tie; to bind, imprison*—wakaśka, uŋkaśkapi, ćićaśka, makaśka: kaśka hnaka, *to put in bonds* or *in prison*—kaśka wahnaka.

ka-śka′-haŋ, *part.* *tied, bound.*

ka-śke′-haŋ, *v. a.* of śkehaŋ; *to make skip about by striking*—wakaśkehaŋ.

ka-śkem′, *cont.* of kaśkepa; kaśkem eḣpeya, *to strike out, to press out by striking*, as water from anything.

ka-śke′-pa, *v. a.* *to strike and press out*, as water—wakaśkepa. See kaskepa.

ka-śki′-ća, *v. a.* *to press by striking, to pound* or *batter out*, as clothes—wakaśkića. See kaskića.

ka-śkin′, *cont.* of kaśkića; kaśkin iyeya.

ka-śki′-śka, *v. a.* *to make rough by striking*—wakaśkiśka.

ka-śko′-kpa, *v. a.* *to hollow out, make concave, cut out*, as a trough—wakaśkokpa, uŋkaśkokpapi. Hence, ćaŋkaśkokpa, *a trough.*

ka-śko′-kpa-kpa, *v. red.* of kaśkokpa.

ka-śkom′, *cont.* of kaśkopa; kaśkom iyeya.

ka-śko′-pa, *v. a* *to make crooked* or *twisted by striking* or *falling*—wakaśkopa. See kapemni

ka-śko′-śko-pa, *v. red.* of kaśkopa.

ka-śko′-tpa, *v. a.* Same as kaśkokpa.

ka-śko′-tpa-tpa, *v. red.* of kaśkotpa.

ka-śna′, *v. a.* *to miss in attempting to strike*—wakaśna, uŋkaśnapi.

ka-śna′-śna, *v. red.* of kaśna.

ka-śni′-śni-źa, *v. a. red.* of kaśniźa; *to strike*, as a fire, *and cause to send forth sparks*—wakaśniśniźa.

k a - ś n i′ - ź a, *v. a.* of śniźa; *to make wither by striking*—wakaśniźa.

k a - ś o′ - ś a, *v. a.* *to stir up, make turbid; make into batter*—wakaśośa.

k a - ś p a′, *v. a.* *to separate, cut loose from; to cut in two,* as a pair of blankets; *to cough and spit, to expectorate*—wakaśpa, uŋkaśpapi; kićaśpa, and kićićaśpa, *to wrestle.* *T.*, kićikśaŋ.

k a - ś p a′ - p i, *n.* See kaśpapidaŋ.

k a - ś p a′ - p i - d a ŋ, *n.* *a small piece of money, a ten-cent piece, dime.*

k a - ś p e′ - p i - ć a - ś n i, *adj.* *not capable of being separated.*

k a - ś p e′ - y a, *v. a.* *to cause to separate* or *break off; to cause to expectorate*—kaśpewaya. *T.*, toŋ kaśpeya.

k a - ś p u′, *v. a.* *to cut off a piece by striking, cut off,* as a bulge from a tree, etc.—wakaśpu, uŋkaśpupi.

k a - ś p u′ - ś p u, *v. red.* of kaśpu; *to break up in pieces,* as ice or tallow, *by striking*—wakaśpuśpu; *to break up,* as the wind does ice.

k a - ś p u′ - ś p u, *n.* *pieces of lead cut and rounded in the mouth, slugs.*

k a - ś t a′, *conj.* (ka *and* eśta) *though, although:* tuwe kaśta, *whoever* or *nobody;* taku kaśta, *whatever* or *nothing;* toketu kaśta, *at all events, at any rate;* hećetu kaśta, *let it be so.* *Ih.* and *T.*, kaśa; also keśa.

k a - ś t a g′, *cont.* of kaśtaka; kaśtag yeya, *to throw,* as a hutinaćute—kaśtag yewaya. *T.*, kahol yeya.

k a - ś t a′ - k a, *v. a.* *to strike, beat, whip; to kill*—wakaśtaka, yakaśtaka, uŋkaśtakapi.

k a - ś t a ŋ′, *v. a.* *to pour out; to throw away;* said of liquids only—wakaśtaŋ, uŋkaśtaŋpi. See kada.

k a - ś u ś′, *cont* of kaśuźa; kaśuś iyeya.

k a - ś u′ - ś u ś, *cont.* of kaśuśuźa; kaśuśuś iyeya, *to bruise* or *mash down.*

k a - ś u′ - ś u ś - y a, *adv.* *battered, bruised.*

k a - ś u′ - ś u ź a, *v. a. red.* of kaśuźa.

k a - ś u ś′ - y a, *v. a.* *to cause to batter* or *bruise*—kaśuśwaya.

k a - ś u ś′ - y a, *adv.* *bruisedly, batteredly.*

k a - ś u′ - ź a, *v. a.* *to bruise, to batter, to mash, to crush*—wakaśuźa. See kahuġa.

k a′ - t a, *adj.* *warm, hot;* applied both to persons and things—makata, nikata.

k a - t a′, *adv.* *together:* kata iheya, *to assemble together*—kata iheuŋyaŋpi.

k a - t a′ - ġ a, *v.* of taġe; *to make waves and foam,* as the wind does by blowing on water.

k a - t a ḣ′, *cont.* of kataġa; kataḣ toŋ, *to make waves.*

k a - t a′ - k i ŋ, *v. a.* of takiŋ; *to strike and cause to lean*—wakatakiŋ.

k a - t a′ - k i ŋ - y a ŋ, *adv.* of takiŋyaŋ; *leaning:* katakiŋyaŋ haŋ, *to stand leaning.*

k a - t a′ - k o - h a ŋ, *v.* katakohaŋ yuza, *to embrace*—katakohaŋ mduza.

k a - t a′ - k u - n i - ś n i, *v. a.* (ka *and*

takuniśni) *to beat to pieces, destroy*—wakatakuniśni.

k a - t a ŋ′, *v. a.* *to pound on*—wakataŋ, uŋkataŋpi: *to press on*, as water on a paddle or wind on a sail.

k a - t a ŋ′ - i ŋ, *v. a.* of taŋiŋ; *to make apparent, to clear off*, as anything covered up—wakataŋiŋ. See kaotaŋiŋ.

k a - t a ŋ′ - k a, *v. a* of taŋka; *to beat out large, to enlarge*—wakataŋka.

k a - t a ŋ′ - k a - y a, *v. a.* *to make large*—wakataŋkaya.

k a - t a′ - o m, *cont.* of kataoŋpa; *leaning at an angle of forty-five degrees. T.*, kataob.

k a - t a′ - o m - y a, *adv* *leaning.*

k a - t a′ - o ŋ - p a, *v.* *to lean.* See kataom *and* oŋpa.

k a - t a′ - p a, *v.* *T.* *to shake and make dry*, as the wind does clothes.

k a - t a′ - p s i s, *cont.* of katapsiza; katapsis iyeya.

k a - t a′ - p s i - z a, *v. a.* *to cause to rise*, as bubbles in water, by throwing something in—wakatapsiza. *T.*, katapśiźa.

k a - t a′ - t a, *v. a.* *to shake off*, as dust, etc., from a bed; *to brush off with the hand* or *a brush*—wakatata, uŋkatatapi.

k a - t a′ - t a - p a, *v. red.* of katapa.

k a - t′ a′ - t′ a, *v. a.* *to make blunt* or *batter by striking*—wakat′at′a.

k a - t a′ - ź a, *v.* of taźa; *to make waves*, as the wind does. See kataġa.

k a - t e′ - h a ŋ, *adv.* of tehaŋ; *far, at a distance.*

k a - t e′ - h a ŋ - y a ŋ, *adv.* *at some distance, a little distance off.*

k a - t e m′, *cont.* of katepa; katem iyeya.

k a - t e′ - p a, *v. a.* *to cut to a stump; to cut tapering*—wakatepa.

k a - t i′ - ć a, *v. a.* *to scrape off*, as snow—wakatića, uŋkatićapi.

k a - t i′ - ć a, *v. n.* *to be obstructed*, as the nostrils.

k a - t i k′ - t i - ć a, *v. a.* *to thicken by stirring*—wakatiktića.

k a - t i n′, *cont.* of katića; katin iyeya.

k a - t i ŋ′, *adj.* *straight, straightened out*, as the arm—makatiŋ. See botiŋ, natiŋ, *and* patiŋ.

k a - t i ŋ′, *adv.* *T.* *in the way of, obstructingly*, as, katiŋ yaŋka.

k a - t i ŋ′ - k i - y a, *v. a.* *to stretch out, straighten out:* isto katiŋwakiya, *I straighten out my arm.*

k a - t i ŋ′ - y a ŋ, *adv.* *directly, continuously, without stop.*

k a - t k a′, *v. n.* *to choke* or *be choked*, as in eating, *to stick in the throat*—makatka, nićatka.

k a - t k e′, *v.* Same as katka.

k a - t k e′ - y a, *v. a.* *to cause to choke*—katkewaya.

k a - t k i′ - t k a, *v n.* *to collect in little bunches* or *lumps*, as meal thrown in, in making mush.

k a - t k i′ - t k a - t k a, *v. n. red.* of katkitka; *to gather into bunches* or *lumps, be tangled*, as locks of hair.

k a - t k u′, *adj.* *cut short, short, rather short.*

k a - t k u′ - d a ŋ, *adj.* *short:* oŋhdoȟda katkudaŋ seća, *the coat seems to be very short.*

ka-tku′-ġa, *v. a. to cut short, cut into short pieces*—wakatkuġa. Hence, tiyopa iyokatkuġe, *nails. T.*, kaptuġa.

ka-tkuȟ′, *cont.* of katkuġa; katkuȟ iyaya, *to go round and get on the other side, to go by a short cut*—katkuȟ imdamda.

ka-tkuȟ′-ya, *adv. going around.*

ka-tkuŋs′, *cont.* of katkuŋza.

ka-tkuŋ′-tkuŋ-ta, *v.* See kakuŋtkuŋta.

ka-tkuŋ′-za. *v. a. to cut off square*—wakatkuŋza.

ka-tku′-tku-ġa, *v. red.* of katkuġa.

ka-to′, *v. a. to strike* and not make an indentation; *to knock* or *rap on* a door—wakato.

ka-to′-haŋ, *v.* (kato *and* haŋ) *to stand and tap*, as a woodpecker on a tree.

ka-to′-kam, *adv. before, ahead.* See kahiŋtokam.

ka-to′-kam-wa-pa, *adv. ahead, in advance of.*

ka-to′-ka-pa, *adv. ahead.* See kahiŋtokapa.

ka-to′-na-waŋg-ki-ya, *v. a. to make gallop slowly*—katonawaŋgwakiya. *T.*, katonauŋgkiya.

ka-to′-na-waŋ-ka, *v. n. to gallop slowly*, as a horse. *T.*, katonauŋka.

ka-to′-to, *v. red.* of kato; *to knock* or *beat on*, as on a door; *to clear off*, as bushes, trees, etc., from a field—wakatoto. See kasota.

ka-tpa′, *v. a. to strike and knock out*, as an eye; *to strike*, as in bleeding, *i. q.* kaŋkatpa; *to strike through*, as in shooting with an arrow, *i. q.* katpa iyeya—wakatpa, uŋkatpapi. See kakpa.

ka-tpaŋ′, *v. a. to bruise, mash up by beating; to wink*, as the eyelids—wakatpaŋ. *i. q.* kakpaŋ.

ka-tpaŋ′-tpaŋ, *v. red.* of katpaŋ.

ka-tpa′-tpa, *v. red.* of katpa; *to strike and knock out pieces*—wakatpatpa.

ka-tpi′, *v. a. to crack*, as nuts, *by striking*—wakatpi. *i. q.* kakpi.

ka-tu′-ka, *v. a. to knock off*, as fur; *to destroy by smiting*—wakatuka. *T.*, kaśla.

ka-tu′-tka, *v. a. to break in small pieces, pound up fine*—wakatutka.

ka-ṭa′, *v. a.* (ka *and* ṭa) *to kill by striking, strike dead, to stun*—wakaṭa, yakaṭa, uŋkaṭapi: kaṭa iyeya, *to shoot down, kill by shooting;* kaṭa eȟpeya, *to knock over dead.*

ka-ṭa′-ga, *v. a. to shake and make dry*, as the wind does a wet cloth. *T.*, katatapa.

ka-ṭiŋs′, *cont.* of kaṭiŋza; kaṭiŋs iyeya.

ka-ṭiŋ′-s'a, *adv.* of ṭiŋs'a; *at rest, firmly, solidly.*

ka-ṭiŋs′-ya, *v. a. to cause to be solid* or *at rest.*

ka-ṭiŋ′-za, *v. a.* of ṭiŋza; *to pound*

tight, make tight, make firm—wakaṭiŋza.

k a - ṭ o′ - ź à, *v. a.* *to dull* or *make blunt by striking*—wakaṭoźa.

k a - ṭ u ŋ′ - k e - ć a, *v.* See aṭuŋkeća.

k a - u′, *v. a.* of au; *to bring to* one, *to be in the act of bringing to*—wakau, uŋkaupi; ćićau, makau.

k a - w a′. See yukawa.

k a - w a′ - ć i, *v. a.* (ka *and* waći) *to cause to dance by striking, to spin by whipping,* as the boys do their tops—wakawaći.

k a - w a′ - h a ŋ, *part.* *opened.*

k a - w a ŋ g′, *cont.* of kawaŋka; kawaŋg eḣpeya. *T.*, kauŋg.

k a - w a ŋ′ - k a, *v. a.* *to cut down, fell,* as trees—wakawaŋka; *to blow down,* as the wind does trees, houses, etc. *T.*, kauŋka.

k a - w a ŋ′ - k a - k a, *v. n.* *T.* *to be jolted* or *bounced up and down,* as in a wagon; kawaŋkaka yemaya.

k a - w a ŋ′ - k a n, *adv.* kawaŋkan iyeya, *to knock upwards.* See waŋkan.

k a - w a ŋ′ - k a n - w a - p a, *adv.* *a little up.*

k a - w a′ - ś ' a - k a, *v. n.* of waś'aka; *to be made strong by packing* or *carrying loads*—makawaś'aka.

k a - w a′ - ś t e, *v. a.* *to make well by striking* or *cutting with an ax.*

k a - w e′ - ġ a, *v. a.* *to break by striking,* but not entirely off; *to break,* as an ax-helve; *to break down*—wakaweġa, uŋkaweġapi; *to break,* as the wind does trees.

k a - w e ḣ′, *cont.* of kaweġa; kaweḣ iyeya.

k a - w e ḣ′ - w e - ġ a, *v. red.* of kaweġa.

k a - w e ḣ′ - w e ḣ, *cont.* of kaweḣweġa; kaweḣweḣ iyeya, *to fracture* or *break in several places.*

k a - w e ḣ′ - y a, *v. a.* *to cause to break*—kaweḣwaya.

k a - w e ḣ′ - y a, *adv.* *breaking.*

k a - w i′ - h n u - n i, *v. a.* *to destroy by striking, to break in pieces*—wakawihnuni.

k a - w i ŋ′ - ġ a, *v. n.* *to turn* in one's course; kawiŋġa iyaya, *he went turning*—wakawiŋġa. See pawiŋġa, yawiŋġa, *and* yuwiŋġa.

k a - w i ŋ ḣ′, *cont.* of kawiŋġa.

k a - w i ŋ ś′, *cont.* of kawiŋźa; kawiŋś iyeya *and* kawiŋś eḣpeya, *to beat down, mat down.*

k a - w i ŋ ś′ - w i ŋ ś, *cont.* of kawiŋświŋźa.

k a - w i ŋ ś′ - w i ŋ ś y a, *adv.* *matted down*

k a - w i ŋ ś′ - w i ŋ - ź a, *v. red.* of kawiŋźa.

k a - w i ŋ ś′ - y a, *v. a.* *to cause to mat down*—kawiŋśwaya.

k a - w i ŋ ś′ - y a, *adv.* *beaten down, fallen down.*

k a - w i ŋ′ - ź a, *v. a.* *to beat down, mat down by striking,* as grass, etc.—wakawiŋźa.

k a - w i′ - t a - y a *adv.* of witaya; *together:* kawitaya iheya, *to assemble together, flock together.*

k a - w o′ - o - t a ŋ - i ŋ, *v. n.* *to be-*

come light; to clear away, as a storm or anything that obstructs vision. See kaowotaŋiŋ *and* kataŋiŋ.

k a′ - y a , *v. a.* of aya; *to take to one*—wakamda, yakada, uŋkayapi, niéaya.

k a - y e′ - ġ a , *v. a.* *to make shine by striking*, as a fire. *T.*, kaleȟya. See iyeġa.

k a - y e′ - h a ŋ , *adv.* *before, out in front:* kayehaŋ eéoŋ, *to do before* another; kayehaŋ naźiŋ, *to stand out in front;* kayehaŋ içihnaka *and* kayehaŋiçiya, *to put one's self forward.* *T.*, ikokab. See kaŋyehaŋ.

k a - y o′ - d a ŋ , *adv.* See kayowedaŋ.

k a - y o′ - l a - w a - ć i - p i , *n.* *T.* *a dance of the Winnebagos;* also called Hotaŋke waćipi; *i. q* kayowedaŋ waćipi

k a - y o′ - t a ŋ, *adv.* Same as kayodaŋ

k a - y o′ - w e - d a ŋ , *adj.* *zigzag, in all kinds of shapes:* kayowedaŋ kiçuŋ, *to make figures*, as children do when playing in the snow; kayowedaŋ waćipi, *a kind of dance.* *T.*, yuglaśkiŋśkiŋ.

k a - y o′ - y o , *adv.* *yielding, giving* when struck or pressed on: kayoyo se ap'a, *he strikes as if it yielded* under the stroke.

k a - z a′, *v. a.* *to pick to pieces*, as the takaŋ, or sinew, used by the Dakotas in sewing—wakaza.

k a′ - z a , *n.* *a unit, an atom, a particle, a grain;* káza waŋźidaŋ, *one grain* or *particle;* káza noŋpa, *two grains.* See sukaza.

k a - z a′ - m n i , *v. a.* *to uncover* or *open out*, as anything covered; *to open out*, as a door—wakażamni, yakazamni. See yuzamni.

k a - z a ŋ′, *v. a.* *to hurt, stun by striking, render motionless; to part, to separate*, as grass in passing through — wakazaŋ, uŋkazaŋpi. See kaġaŋ.

k a - z a ŋ′ - y a ŋ , *adv.* *parting.*

k a - z a′ - p a , *v. a.* *to cut off meat from bones;* said also when, in flaying an animal, the fat is left on the skin—wakazapa, uŋkazapapi. Hence, kazapapi, *meat cut off from the bones.* *T.*, *to strip meat off clean, strip bare, tear off the periosteum*, as they do from the ribs of animals. See kaġapa.

k a - z a′ - z a , *v. a.* *to cut in strips; to gash*—wakazaza, uŋkazazapi.

k a - z a′ - z a - p i , *n.* *the ermine, i. q.* hituŋkasaŋ; so called because the skin is cut up into strips to wear on the head.

k a - z e′, *v. a.* *to lade* or *dip out with a spoon* or *ladle*—wakaze, yakaze, uŋkazepi. See kaġe, kapta, etc.

k a′ - z e - d a ŋ , *adj.* *shallow*, as water: mini kazedaŋ, *the water is shallow; i. q.* puzedaŋ. *Ih.*, kazena.

k a - z i′, *v. n.* *to fill up*, as a pipe-stem with water, etc.; *to have the sense of fullness*, so as not to be able to swallow: éaŋte kazi, *the heart is full*—éaŋte makazi: kazitoŋ, *to protect a skin drying*, stretched in a tent, by hanging something before it. *T.*, kazaŋ; ćaŋte kazaŋ is used when one has swallowed too much smoke.

ka-zil'-ya, *v. T. to stretch out, straighten:* kaziliçiya, *he stretched himself out.* See pazića, yazića, yuzića, etc.

ka-zo', *v. a. to mark; to throw back the arms*—wakazo, uŋkazopi. See kaġo.

ka-zon', *cont.* of kazoŋta; *to weave in,* as in making baskets, etc.

ka-zoŋ'-ta, *v. a. to weave,* as cloth, *to twist in,* as in making baskets or snow-shoes, *i q.* yáŋka—wakazoŋta, yakazoŋta, uŋkazoŋtapi.

ka-zuŋ'-ta, *v.* Same as kazoŋta.

ka-źa', *v. a. to split a little, to make gape*—wakaźa.

ka-źa'-haŋ, *v. a.* of źahaŋ; *to make open out by striking; to press open*—wakaźahaŋ.

ka-źa'-haŋ-haŋ, *v. red.* of kaźahaŋ.

ka-źa'-ka, *v. a. to strain* or *knock open; to press open,* as a wound—wakaźaka.

ka-źan', *cont.* of kaźata; kaźan iyeya.

ka-źaŋ'-źaŋ, *v. n.* of źaŋźaŋ; *to become light,* as clouds after rain.

ka-źaŋ'-źaŋ-ka, *v. n.* Same as kaźaŋźaŋ.

ka-źa'-ta, *v. a. to make forked by cutting with an ax*—wakaźata. See kaġata.

ka-źa'-źa, *v. a. to wash by pulling back and forth*—wakaźaźa.

ka-źa'-źa, *adv. clearly:* kaźaźa waŋyaka, *to see clearly. T.*, źaźayela

ka-źim', *cont.* of kaźipa; kaźim iyeya, *to shave off quickly* or *by a stroke.*

ka-źim'-źi-pa, *v. red.* of kaźipa.

ka-źi'-pa, *v. a. to shave with a knife* or *drawing-knife, to plane*—wakaźipa, uŋkaźipapi.

ka-źo', *v. n. to purge, have a diarrhœa*—wakaźo.

ka-źo'-pi, *n. a purging, a diarrhœa.*

ka-źuŋ', *v. a. to pull up,* as birds do corn; *to come out* or *moult,* as the quills of geese, etc. See kapśuŋ.

ka-źu'-źu, *v. a. to blot out, efface; to pay off,* as one's debts; *to forgive; to knock to pieces; to come to pieces,* as a wagon, cart, etc., in hauling—wakaźuźu. *v. n. to break up,* as ice in the river.

kća, *adj. loose, disentangled, straight.* See kakća, etc.

kća-haŋ', *part. coming loose, untying of itself.*

kćaŋ. See yukćaŋ.

kćaŋ'-ka, *n. one who fails of doing what he said he would.*

kćaŋ'-kćaŋ-ka, *n. anything that is tall, i. q.* haŋska.

kća-wa'-haŋ, *part. come untied.*

kd. Santee words commencing with "hd" commence with "kd" in Yankton; as, kda, *i. q.* hda. They need not generally be repeated.

k d a'-y a, *v. n.* *Ih.* *to scratch, rub.*

k d i-y o', *v.* *i. q.* hduwe: *Ih.*, kdiyo mni kta, *I will go for my own.*

k e, *particle.* It is sometimes used as the sign of the future tense of the first person; as, ḣećamoŋ ke epća, *I thought I would do that.*

k e, *n.* *T.* *a turtle: i. q.* keya.

k e-ć a' *and* k e-ć a'-l a, *n.* *T.* *a long-haired dog.*—T. L. R.

k e-ć a ŋ'-k i ŋ, *v. a.* *to think of as such, to regard as*—kećaŋwakiŋ, kećaŋyakiŋ, kećaŋuŋkiŋpi, kećaŋmayakiŋ, kećaŋćićiŋ. See ećaŋkiŋ.

k e-ć i ŋ', *v.* *to think that*—kećaŋmi, kećaŋni, uŋkećiŋpi. See ećiŋ.

k e-ć i'-y a, *v. a.* *to say to* one *that* it is so and so—kewakiya, keuŋkiyapi, kemakiya, kećićiya, kenićiya. See ećiya.

k e-ć o ŋ', *v.* *to do that:* taŋyaŋ kećoŋ iḉidaća, *he thinks he has done that well.* See ećoŋ.

k e-g l e'-z e-l a, *n.* *T.* *a spotted* or *striped turtle.*

k e-h a', *v.* 2d pers. sing. of keya.

k e'-h a, *n.* (keya *and* ha) *a tortoise-shell.*

k e ḣ-ķ e'-ġ a, *v. n.* *to have a rattling in the throat,* as anything choked to death—wakeḣķeġa. See koḣķoġa.

k e-k t o'-p a-w i ŋ-ġ e, *adj.* *a thousand:* kektopawiŋġe wikćemna, *ten thousand.* See koktopawiŋġe *and* opawiŋġe. Probably koktopawiŋġe was the original form, from kokta *and* opawiŋġe.

k e-n u ŋ'-y a ŋ, *v.* *to know partly, to suspect; i. q.* ţuŋgya—kenuŋwaya.

k e-n u'-n u-ź a, *n.* *T.* *the soft-shell turtle: i. q.* kezoŋta.

k e-p a', *v.* 1st pers. sing. of keya.

k e'-p a, *n.* (keya *and* pa) *a tortoise's head.*

k e-p ć a', *v.* 1st pers. sing.; *I thought that:* hećeće kta kepća, *I thought that it would be so.*

k e s-t o ŋ', *v. n.* *to be barbed, have a barb,* as a fish-hook.

k e ś, *conj.* *although.* It is always used in reference to past time.

k e-ś a', *adv.* *T.* tuwe kaśa, *whoever: i. q.* kaśta.

k e-t a'-ġ i-k a, *n.* *T.* *a fool: i. q.* ćaġuka.

k e'-y a, *n.* *the large tortoise; a roof, i. q.* wakeya.

k e'-y a, *adj.* *sloping, like a roof:* keya haŋ, *it stands roof-like.* *T.*, keiŋyaŋhaŋ.

k e'-y a, *v a.* *to make a roof of*—kewaya.

k e-y a', *v.* *to say that*—kepa, keha, uŋkeyapi. "Keya," "kećiŋ," *and* "kećaŋkiŋ," are from "eya," "ećiŋ," *and* "ećaŋkiŋ." Those of the latter class indicate that the subject of the preceding verb is identical with the person who says or thinks, which those of the former class do not: as, mde kta eha, *I will go, thou saidst;* mde kta keha, *thou saidst that I would go;* ećamoŋ kta ećiŋ, *I will do it, thought he,* **or** *he* *thought he would do it;* ećamoŋ kta kećiŋ, *he thought that I would do it.*

k e'-y a-h a ŋ, *part.* *sloping, roof-like.* *T.*, keiŋyahaŋ.

k e'-y a-y a, *v.* *pos.* of eyaya; *to have taken* anything *to one's own home.*

k e-z e', *n.* *the barb of a fish-hook.*

k e-z o ŋ'-t a, *n.* *the soft-shelled tortoise.* *T.*, kenunuźa.

k e-z u ŋ'-t a, *n.* Same as kezoŋta.

k i, *prep. in comp.* *to, for, of.* It is often prefixed to verbs or incorporated in them: as, kte, *to kill*, kikte, *to kill for* one; kaġa, *to make*, kićaġa, *to make for* or *to* one; ećoŋ, *to do*, ećakićoŋ, *to do to* one. When prefixed to verbs of motion commencing with a vowel, the *i* is dropped: as, kau, from ki *and* au; keyaya is probably from ki *and* eyaya.

k i, *pron.* *pos. in comp.* meaning *one's own;* as, okide, *to seek one's own.*

k i, *a prefix* to some verbs, which indicates that the action is performed *through the middle* of the object; as, kibaksa, *to cut in two in the middle.*

k i, *v. n.* *to arrive at one's house* or *where one lives;* this is used when the person speaking is away from the home spoken of—waki, yaki, uŋkipi.

k i, *v. a.* *to take from* one *by force, to rob*—waki, yaki, uŋkipi, maki, nići, ćići.

k i-a'-p e, *v. a.* *to wait till one reaches home*—kiawape.

k i-b a', *v.* *pos.* of ba; *to blame one's self* or *one's own;* *to suffer in consequence of one's own* course—wakiba, uŋkibapi.

k i-b a'-k i-y a, *v. a.* *to cause to blame one's self*—kibawakiya.

k i-b a'-k s a, *v. a.* *to cut in two in the middle,* as a stick—kibawaksa, kibauŋksapi.

k i-b a'-p s a-k a, *v. a.* *to cut* a cord or string *in two in the middle*—kibawapsaka.

k i-b a'-s'a, *n.* *one who is lazy, gets along with difficulty and blames himself much.*

k i-b a'-s d e-ć a, *v. a.* *to slit* or *saw in the middle*—kibawasdeća. See okibasdeća.

k i-b a'-ś p a, *v. a.* *to cut in two in the middle,* as an apple—kibawaśpa.

k i-b l e'-z a, *adj.* *T.* *convalescent; i. q.* kamdeza.

k i-b o'-k s a, *v. a.* *to shoot in two in the middle*—kibowaksa.

k i-b o'-p s a-k a, *v. a.* *to shoot off in the middle,* as a cord.

k i-b o'-ś p a, *v. a.* *to shoot in two,* as an apple—kibowaśpa.

k i-ć a', *prep. in comp.* *for, from:* as, opetoŋ, *to buy;* opekićatoŋ, *to buy from.*

k i-ć a', *v.* *pos.* of ka; *to mean one's own;* *to ask for* or *demand one's own*—weća, yeća, uŋkićapi.

k i'-ć a-d a, *v. a.* of kada; *to spill,* as grain, *for* another—wećada, uŋkićadapi.

k i'-ć a-ġ a, *v. a.* of kaġa; *to make*

to or *for* one: wowapi kićaġa, *to write a letter to* one—wećaġa, yećaġa, uŋkićaġapi, mićaġa, ćićaġa.

ki-ća'-ġa, *v. pos.* of kaġa; *to make for one's self*—wećaġa, etc.

ki-ća'-ġa, *v. n.* of ćaġa, *to become ice again.*

ki-ća'-ġo, *v.* of kaġo; *to make a mark for one; to vaccinate.*

ki'-ća-hda, *v.* of kahda; *to full out* or *unroll for* one—mićahda, nićahda.

ki'-ća-hi, *v.* of kahi; *to rummage for* one—wećahi, uŋkićahipi, mićahi.

ki-ća'-kća, *v.* of kakća; *to comb* or *curry one's own*—wećakća.

ki'-ća-kiŋ-ća, *v.* of kakiŋća; *to scrape,* as a fish, *for* one—wećakiŋća, uŋkićakiŋćapi.

ki'-ća-kpa, *v.* of kakpa; *to strike into for* one: kaŋ kićakpa, *to cut a vein for,* i. e., *to bleed* one.

ki'-ća-ksa, *v.* of kaksa; *to cut in two for* one, as a stick, *with an ax*—wećaksa, uŋkićaksapi.

ki-ća'-ksa, *v. a.* *to cut in two in the middle with an ax* or *by striking; to break,* as a law, *to disobey*—kiwakaksa, kiuŋkaksapi.

ki'-ća-ku-ka, *v.* of kakuka; *to pound to pieces* or *destroy for* one, as clothing—wećakuka.

ki'-ća-mde-ća, *v.* of kamdeća; *to break for* one *by striking,* as brittle ware—wećamdeća. *T.,* kićableća.

ki'-ća-mna, *v.* of kamna; *to collect* or *gather together for* one; *to earn for* one—wećamna, mićamna.

ki-ćaŋ', *v.* *to call on the dead when wailing for them,* as in crying, "Mićiŋkśi, mićiŋkśi," *my son, my son!*—wećaŋ, uŋkićaŋpi.

ki'-ćaŋ-pta, *v. a.* *to comfort* one; *to take sides with, desire to help* one—wećaŋpta, uŋkićaŋptapi. Hence, wićakićaŋpte, *a comforter.*

ki-ćaŋ'-yaŋ, *v. a.* *to work; to till, cultivate,* as the ground—wakićaŋmda *and* wakićaŋyaŋ, yakićaŋda, uŋkićaŋyaŋpi. See aḣtani *and* ḣtani.

ki'-ća-psag, *cont.* of kićapsaka; kićapsag iyeya.

ki'-ća-psa-ka, *v.* of kapsaka; *to cut in two,* as a string, *for* one—wećapsaka, uŋkićapsakapi.

ki-ća'-psa-ka, *v. a.* *to cut in two,* as a string, *in the middle*—kiwakapsaka.

ki-ća'-psaŋ, *v. a.* *to shake for* or *to* one: pa kićapsaŋ, *to bow the head to* one—wećapsaŋ.

ki'-ća-psuŋ, *v.* of kapsuŋ; *to knock over and spill out,* as water *for* one—wećapsuŋ.

ki'-ća-pśuŋ, *v.* of kapśuŋ; *to strike* or *knock off,* as a horn, *for* one—wećapśuŋ.

ki'-ća-pta, *v.* Same as kićaŋpta.

ki'-ća-sde-ća, *v.* of kasdeća; *to split in two for* one—wećasdeća.

ki'-ća-śpa, *v.* of kaśpa; *to divide for* one—wećaśpa.

ki-ća'-śpa, *v. a.* *to cut in two in*

the middle, as an apple—kiwakaśpa, kiuŋkaśpapi.

k i'- ć a - t p a , *v.* Same as kićakpa.

k i'- ć a - w e - ġ a , *v.* of kaweġa; *to partly break* or *fracture for* one—wećaweġa.

k i'- ć a - w i - h n u - n i , *v.* of kawihnuni; *to destroy for* one—wećawihnuni.

k i - ć i', *prep.* *with, together with:* kići mda, *I go with him.*

k i'- ć i , *prep. in comp.* *for:* kićićahdi, *to bring home for* one.

k i - ć i', *prep. in comp.* *to each other.* This makes the reciprocal form of verbs: as, ećakićićoŋpi, *they do to each other;* waśtekićidapi, *they love each other.*

k i - ć i'- a - t a - y e - k i - ć i - y a , *v.* *T.* *to meet face to face; to meet squarely* — kićiatayewećiya. See itkokipa.

k i - ć i'- ć a , *v. n.* *to be with, together with, following with, on the same side with; to have for a companion:* kićića wota, *of the same age with*—wećića, uŋkićićapi, mićića.

k i - ć i'- ć a , *n.* *T.* *a friend,* or *his friend* or *companion.* See kićuwa.

k i'- ć i - ć a - d a , *v.* of kada; *to pour out* or *spill for* one—wećićada, mićićada.

k i'- ć i - ć a - ġ a , *v.* of kaġa; *to make* anything *for* another—wećićaġa, uŋkićićaġapi. In use there is a difference between "kićaġa" *and* "kićićaġa." If one writes a letter *to* another, he uses "kićaġa"; if he writes *for* or *in the place of* another, he uses "kićićaġa."

k i'- ć i - ć a - ġ e - ġ e , *v.* of kaġeġe; *to sew* anything *for* one—wećićaġeġe, uŋkićićaġeġepi, mićićaġeġe.

k i'- ć i - ć a - h d a , *v.* of ahda; *to take to one's home for* him—wećićahda, mićićahda, uŋkićićahdapi.

k i'- ć i - ć a - h d i , *v.* of ahdi; *to bring to one's home for* him—wećićahdi, uŋkićićahdipi.

k i'- ć i - ć a - h i , *v.* of ahi; *to bring to* a place *for* one—wećićahi, uŋkićićahipi.

k i'- ć i - ć a - h i ŋ - t a , *v.* of kahiŋta; *to sweep for* one—wećićahiŋta, uŋkićićahiŋtapi.

k i'- ć i - ć a ḣ - n i - ġ a , *v.* of kaḣniġa; *to choose* or *select for* one—wećićaḣniġa.

k i'- ć i - ć a - ḣ u - ġ a , *v.* of kaḣuġa; *to fracture for* one, *break in,* as the skull or a barrel-head, *for* one—wećićaḣuġa.

k i'- ć i - ć a - ḣ u - ḣ u - ġ a , *v.* *red.* of kićićaḣuġa.

k i - ć i'- ć a - i , *v.* of ai; *to take to* a place *for* one—wećićai, uŋkićićaipi.

k i'- ć i - ć a - k a ŋ , *v.* of kakaŋ; *to hew for* one—wećićakaŋ, mićićakaŋ.

k i'- ć i - ć a - k ć a , *v.* of kakća; *to comb,* as hair *for* one—wećićakća.

k i'- ć i - ć a - k i , *v.* of aki; *to have taken to one's home for* him—wećićaki, uŋkićićakipi.

k i'- ć i - ć a - k i ŋ - ć a , *v.* of kakiŋća; *to scrape for* one—wećićakiŋća.

k i'- ć i - ć a - k s a , *v.* of kaksa; *to cut*

off, as a stick, *for* one—wećićaksa, mićićaksa, ćićićaksa.

ki'-ći-ća-ksa-ksa, *v. red.* of kićićaksa; *to cut up*, as fire-wood, *for* another—wećićaksaksa.

ki'-ći-ća-ku, *v.* of aku; *to be bringing* something *home for* one—wećićaku, uŋkićićakupi.

ki'-ći-ća-ku-ka, *v.* of kakuka; *to pound to pieces for* one—wećićakuka, mićićakuka.

ki'-ći-ća-mde-ća, *v.* of kamdeća; *to break up for* one, as dishes, *by striking*—wećićamdeća. *T.*, kićićableća.

ki'-ći-ća-sde-ća, *v.* of kasdeća; *to split*, as wood *for* one—wećićasdeća.

ki'-ći-ća-sde-sde-ća, *v. red.* of kićićasdeća.

ki'-ći-ća-śda, *v.* of kaśda; *to cut* or *make bare for* one, as in mowing—wećićaśda.

ki'-ći-ća-śka, *v.* of kaśka; *to tie* or *bind for* one—wećićaśka, uŋkićićaśkapi.

ki'-ći-ća-śpa, *v.* of kaśpa; *to deliver from, to relieve* or *free from* one; *to separate for* one—wećićaśpa, uŋkićićaśpapi.

ki'-ći-ća-śta-ka, *v.* of kaśtaka; *to smite for* one—wećićaśtaka, uŋkićićaśtakapi.

ki'-ći-ća-śtaŋ, *v.* of kaśtaŋ; *to pour out* or *spill for* one—wećićaśtaŋ, uŋkićićaśtaŋpi.

ki'-ći-ća-u, *v.* of kau; *to bring for* one—wećićau, mićićau.

ki'-ći-ća-we-ġa, *v.* of kaweġa; *to break* or *partly break for* one—wećićaweġa, uŋkićićaweġapi.

ki-ći'-ća-wo-ta, *n.* *one of the same age.*

ki'-ći-ća-ya, *v.* of kaya: *to take* or *carry to* a place *for* one—wećićamda, yećićada.

ki-ći'-ća-ya, *v.* of kićića; *to have for a companion*—kićićawaya.

ki'-ći-ća-zuŋ-ta, *v.* of kazuŋta; *to weave for* one—wećićazuŋta, mićićazuŋta.

ki'-ći-ća-źu-źu, *v.* of kaźuźu; *to pay for* anything *for* another; *to erase for* one; *to forgive* one—wećićaźuźu, uŋkićićaźuźupi.

ki'-ći-ćiŋ, *v.* of ćiŋ; *to desire* or *ask for, for* another—wećićiŋ, mićićiŋ.

ki-ći'-ćiŋ-yaŋ, *v.* *to go with, be with, accompany*, as one's friend—wećićiŋyaŋ. *T.*, kićićaya.

ki-ći'-ćo-pi, *v. recip.* of kićo; *to call each other*—uŋkićićopi: kićićo wotapi, *a feast in which a general invitation is given.*

ki'-ći-ću-te, *v.* of kute; *to shoot* anything *for* another—wećićute, mićićute.

ki-ći'-ću-te-pi, *v. recip.* *to shoot each other*, as in the wakaŋ waćipi—uŋkićićutepi.

ki'-ći-ḉiŋ, *v.* of ḱiŋ; *to carry* or *pack for* one—wećiḉiŋ.

ki-ći'-ġe-pi, *v.recip.* of kiġe; *to quarrel with each other*—uŋkićiġepi, yećiġepi. *T.*, akoyekićiya.

ki'-ći-haŋ, *v.* of haŋ; *to be* or *remain for* one—mićihaŋ, nićihaŋ: mazaska zaptaŋ mićihaŋ, *five dollars are due me.* See ikićihaŋ.

ki'-ći-hde, *v.* of hde; *to place* or *set for* one—wećihde.

ki'-ći-hde-daŋ, *v.* *to revenge, punish*—wećihdedaŋ, mićihdedaŋ.

ki-ći'-hde-ya, *adv.* *one by one:* kićihdeya au, *they come one at a time* or *one after another.* *T.*, ićiyakigle *and* ićiyakiglegle.

ki'-ći-hdo-hi, *v.* of hdohi; *to bring one's own to* him, *return* it—wećihdohi.

ki'-ći-hdo-i, *v.* of hdoi; *to have taken one's own to* him—wećihdoi.

ki'-ći-hdo-ya, *v.* of hdoya; *to take one's own to* him—wećihdoya.

ki'-ći-hi-yo-hi, *v.* *T.* *to go and fetch for* one: *i. q.* kihuwe—wećihiyohi mda, *I go to bring for him.*

ki'-ći-hna-ka, *v.* of hnaka; *to lay away* or *lay up for* one—wećihnaka, uŋkićihnakapi.

ki-ći'-hna-na, *adv.* *alone with* any one or anything. *T.*, kićiśnala.

ki'-ći-ḣa, *v.* of ḣa; *to bury for* one—wećiḣa.

ki'-ći-ḣaŋ-yaŋ, *v.* of ḣaŋyaŋ; *to fail* or *become worse for* one, as one's sick child—mićiḣaŋyaŋ.

ki-ći'-ḣmuŋ-ġa-pi, *v.* *recip.* of ḣmuŋġa; *to bewitch each other*—uŋkićiḣmuŋġapi.

ki'-ći-kpa-mni, *v.* of pamni; *to divide among themselves.*

ki'-ći-ksu-ya, *v.* of kiksuya; *to recollect for* one—wećiksuya, mićiksuya

ki-ći'-kśaŋ, *v.* *T.* *to wrestle with.* See kikśaŋ *and* kiihduśpa.

ki-ći'-kte-pi, *v.* *recip.* *to kill each other*—uŋkićiktepi.

ki'-ći-ku-źa, *v.* *T.* of kuźa; *to be sick for* one, as one's child: *i. q.* kikaŋheźa.

ki-ćiŋ', *v* of ćiŋ; *to desire one's own; to desire for* one; *to desire of* one. See okićiŋ.

ki-ćiŋ'-iŋ, *v.* *pos.* of kiŋiŋ; *to throw,* as stones, *at one's own*—wećiŋiŋ, uŋkićiŋiŋpi.

ki'-ći-pa, *v. a.* *to assist* one, as with something to carry on a game in gambling; *to espouse, reserve,* as a girl with the intention of marrying her; *to keep for one*—wećipa. See kipa.

ki'-ći-pa-be, *v.* of pamaŋ; *to file for* one—wećipabe. *T.*, kićipame.

ki'-ći-pa-ġaŋ, *v.* of paġaŋ; *to part with for* one—wećipaġaŋ.

ki-ći'-pa-ġaŋ-pi, *v. recip.* *to part with each other,* as a man and his wife—uŋkićipaġaŋpi.

ki'-ći-p̣a-ġo, *v.* of paġo; *to carve for* one—wećipaġo.

ki'-ći-pa-hi, *v.* of pahi; *to pick* or *gather up for* one—wećipahi, uŋkićipahipi, mićipahi.

ki'-ći-pa-hmuŋ, *v.* of pahmuŋ; *to twist,* as a string, *for* one—wećipahmuŋ.

ki'-ći-pa-kća, *v.* of pakća; *to comb out straight for* one—wećipakća.

ki'-ći-pa-kiŋ-ta, *v.* of pakiŋta; *to wipe for* one—wećipakiŋta, uŋkićipakiŋtapi.

ki'-ći-pa-mde-ća, *v.* of pamdeća; *to break for* one—wećipamdeća. *T.*, kićipableća.

ki'-ći-pa-mni, *v.* of pamni; *to divide for* one—wećipamni, uŋkićipamnipi.

ki-ći'-pa-mni-pi, *v. recip. to divide among themselves*—uŋkićipamnipi, yećipamnipi. *T.*, kićikpamnipi. See kićikpamni.

ki'-ći-paŋ, *v.* of paŋ; *to call to* one *for* another—wećipaŋ, uŋkićipaŋpi.

ki'-ći-pa-psoŋ, *v.* of papsoŋ; *to spill* or *pour out for* one, as water—wećipapsoŋ.

ki'-ći-pa-snuŋ, *v.* of pasnuŋ; *to roast*, as meat, *for* one—wećipasnuŋ.

ki'-ći-pa-su-ta, *v.* of pasuta; *to knead* or *make stiff*, as bread, *for* one—wećipasuta.

ki'-ći-pa-ta, *v.* of pata; *to cut up* or *carve for* one—wećipata.

ki'-ći-pa-taŋ, *v.* of pataŋ; *to take care of for* one—wećipataŋ, uŋkićipataŋpi, mićipataŋ.

ki'-ći-pa-zo, *v.* of pazo; *to point to for* one—wećipazo, uŋkićipazopi.

ki'-ći-pa-źa-źa, *v.* of paźaźa; *to wash out for* one, as a gun—wećipaźaźa.

ki-ći'-pa-źiŋ-pi, *v. recip.* of kipaźiŋ; *they oppose each other*—uŋkićipaźiŋpi.

ki'-ći-pa-źu-źu, *v.* of paźuźu; *to erase for* one—wećipaźuźu.

ki'-ći-pe-haŋ, *v.* of pehaŋ; *to fold up for* one—wećipehaŋ, uŋkićipehaŋpi.

ki'-ći-pe-mni, *v. n.* of pemni; *to become crooked* or *twisted for* one—mićipemni.

ki-ćis', *cont.* of kićiza; kićis waćiŋpi, *they want to fight.*

ki-ćis'-ki-ya, *v. a. to cause to fight.*

ki'-ći-soŋ, *v.* of soŋ; *to braid for* one—wećisoŋ.

ki'-ći-su-ta, *v. n.* of suta; *to become hard* or *firm for* one—mićisuta, uŋkićisutapi.

ki'-ći-śi-ća, *v. n.* of śića; *to become bad to* or *for* one—mićiśića.

ki-ćiś'-na-na, *pron. with him, her*, or *it alone*—wećiśnana, yećiśnana.

ki-ći'-ti-daŋ, *v. to side with one, to be of the same opinion, to be on the same side of a question*—kićiwatidaŋ. *T.*, ićiya.

ki'-ći-toŋ, *v.* of toŋ; *to have* or *acquire for* one; *to bear* or *have* a child *to* or *for* one—wećitoŋ, mićitoŋ: kićitoŋpi, *born to* one.

ki'-ći-tu-ka, *v. to beg for* one—wećituka. *T.*, kićićiŋ.

ki'-ći-wa-śte, *v. n.* of waśte; *to be good* or *become good for* one—mićiwaśte.

k i - ć i′ - y a - ć o - p i, *v. recip.* of yaćo; *to judge* or *condemn each other*—uŋkićiyaćopi. *T.*, kićiyasupi.

k i′ - ć i - y a - ḣ d e - ć a, *v.* of yaḣdeća; *to tear in pieces with the mouth for* one—wećiyaḣdeća.

k i′ - ć i - y a - ḣ d e - ḣ d e - ć a, *v. red.* of kićiyaḣdeća.

k i′ - ć i - y a - ḣ e - p a, *v.* of yaḣepa; *to drink up for* one—wećiyaḣepa.

k i′ - ć i - y a - ḣ t a - k a, *v.* of yaḣtaka; *to bite for* one—wećiyaḣtaka.

k i′ - ć i - y a - m n a, *v.* of yamna; *to acquire for* one *by talking*—wećiyamna.

k i′ - ć i - y a ŋ - k a, *v. n.* of yaŋka; *to be* or *exist for* one—mićiyaŋka. See kićihaŋ.

k i′ - ć i - y a - o - n i - h a ŋ, *v.* of yaonihaŋ; *to praise for* one—wećiyaonihaŋ.

k i′ - ć i - y a - o - t a ŋ - i ŋ, *v.* of yaotaŋiŋ; *to make manifest for* one—wećiyaotaŋiŋ.

k i′ - ć i - y a - p a, *v.* of yapa; *to hold in the mouth for* one; *to suck for* one, as in conjuring—wećiyapa. See kiyapa. The Dakotas, in their *powwowing* or *conjuring*, shake their gourd-shell and other rattles over the sick person, singing with all their might as an accompaniment. When this ceases, they apply their mouths to that part of the body which seems to be more especially affected by the disease, and draw out, as they say, that which is the cause of the sickness, whether that be matter or spirit. Undoubtedly this process does often answer as good a purpose as cupping or leeching.

k i′ - ć i - y a - p o - t a, *v.* of yapota; *to tear up with the mouth for* one—wećiyapota, mićiyapota.

k i′ - ć i - y a - p s a - k a, *v.* of yapsaka; *to bite off*, as a string, *for* one—wećiyapsaka.

k i′ - ć i - y a - s u, *T. v.* of yasu; *to judge* or *condemn for* one.

k i′ - ć i - y a - ś p a, *v.* of yaśpa; *to bite off a piece for* one—wećiyaśpa, mićiyaśpa.

k i′ - ć i - y a - t a ŋ, *v.* of yataŋ; *to praise for* one—wećiyataŋ, mićiyataŋ.

k i′ - ć i - y a - t a ŋ - i ŋ, *v.* of yataŋiŋ; *to make manifest* or *declare for* one—wećiyataŋiŋ.

k i′ - ć i - y a - w a, *v.* of yawa; *to count for* one; *to account to* one—wećiyawa, uŋkićiyawapi.

k i′ - ć i - y u - ć a ŋ, *v.* of yućaŋ; *to sift for* one—wećiyućaŋ, mićiyućaŋ.

k i′ - ć i - y u - ġ a ŋ, *v.* of yuġaŋ; *to husk*, as corn, *for* one—wećiyuġaŋ.

k i′ - ć i - y u - ġ a - t a, *v.* of yuġata; *to open out*, as the hand, *for* one—wećiyuġata.

k i′ - ć i - y u - h a, *v.* of yuha; *to have for* one, *keep for* one—wećiyuha, uŋkićiyuhapi.

k i′ - ć i - y u - h m u ŋ, *v.* of yuhmuŋ; *to twist for* one.

k i′ - ć i - y u - h o - m n i, *v.* of yuhomni; *to turn round for* one—wećiyuhomni, mićiyuhomni.

ki'-ći-yu-hu-hu-za, *v.* of yuhuhuza; *to shake for* one—wećiyuhuhuza. *T.*, kićiyuhuŋhuŋza.

ki'-ći-yu-ȟde-ća, *v.* of yuȟdeća; *to tear for* one—wećiyuȟdeća.

ki'-ći-yu-ȟdo-ka, *v.* of yuȟdoka; *to open* or *make a hole for* one—wećiyuȟdoka.

ki'-ći-yu-kćaŋ, *v.* of yukćaŋ; *to form an opinion about* anything *for* another—wećiyukćaŋ.

ki'-ći-yu-kpaŋ, *v.* of yukpaŋ; *to grind*, as grain, *for* one—wećiyukpaŋ, mićiyukpaŋ.

ki'-ći-yu-ksa, *v.* of yuksa; *to break off for* one—wećiyuksa, mićiyuksa.

ki'-ći-yu-kśaŋ, *v.* of yukśaŋ; *to bend for* one.

ki'-ći-yu-maŋ, *v.* of yumaŋ; *to grind*, as an ax, *for* one—wećiyumaŋ.

ki'-ći-yu-mda-ya, *v.* of yumdaya; *to spread out for* one—wećiyumdaya.

ki'-ći-yu-mdu, *v.* of yumdu; *to plow* or *break up for* one—wećiyumdu, mićiyumda.

ki'-ći-yu-o-ta, *v.* of yuota; *to multiply for* one—wećiyuota, uŋkićiyuotapi.

ki'-ći-yu-o-wo-taŋ-na, *v.* of yuowotaŋna; *to straighten for* one—wećiyuowotaŋna.

ki'-ći-yu-po-ta, *v.* of yupota; *to wear out* or *destroy for* one—wećiyupota.

ki'-ći-yu-psa-ka, *v.* of yupsaka; *to break*, as a cord, *for* another—wećiyupsaka.

ki'-ći-yu-pśuŋ, *v.* of yupśuŋ; *to pull out* or *extract for* one, as a tooth—wećiyupśuŋ, mićiyupśuŋ.

ki'-ći-yu-saŋ-pa, *v.* of yusaŋpa; *to increase* or *extend for* one—wećiyusaŋpa.

ki'-ći-yu-sa-pa, *v.* of yusapa; *to blacken for* one.

ki'-ći-yu-ski-ski-ta, *v. red.* of kićiyuskita.

ki'-ći-yu-ski-ta, *v* of yuskita; *to bind* or *wrap up for* one—wećiyuskita.

ki'-ći-yu-so-ta, *v.* of yusota; *to use up for* one—wećiyusota, mićiyusota.

ki'-ći-yu-sto, *v.* of yusto; *to make smooth for* one—wećiyusto, mićiyusto.

ki'-ći-yu-su-ta, *v.* of yusuta; *to make firm for* one—wećiyusuta.

ki'-ći-yu-śa-pa, *v.* of yuśapa; *to defile for* one—wećiyuśapa.

ki'-ći-yu-śdo-ka, *v.* of yuśdoka; *to pull off for* one, as clothes—wećiyuśdoka.

ki'-ći-yu-śi-ća, *v.* of yuśića; *to make bad* or *spoil for* one—wećiyuśića.

ki'-ći-yu-śi-ȟtiŋ, *v.* of yuśiȟtiŋ; *to enfeeble for* one; *to injure for* one—wećiyuśiȟtiŋ.

ki'-ći-yu-śka, *v.* of yuśka; *to loosen for* one—wećiyuśka.

k i'-ć i-y u-ś n a, *v.* of yuśna; *to make a mistake for* one—wećiyuśna.

k i'-ć i-y u-ś p i, *v.* of yuśpi; *to gather* or *pick off*, as berries, *for* one—wećiyuśpi.

k i'-ć i-y u-ś t a ŋ, *v.* of yuśtaŋ; *to finish* or *perfect for* one—wećiyuśtaŋ.

k i'-ć i-y u-t a, *v.* of yuta; *to eat* anything *for* one—wećiyuta, mićiyuta.

k i-ć i'-y u-t a, *v.* *to eat with* one—kićiwata.

k i'-ć i-y u-t a-p i, *v. recip.* *to eat one another.*

k i'-ć i-y u-t a-k u-n i-ś n i, *v.* of yutakuniśni; *to destroy for* another—wećiyutakuniśni.

k i'-ć i-y u-t'a ŋ; *v.* of yut'aŋ; *to touch for* one—wećiyut'aŋ, mićiyut'aŋ.

k i'-ć i-y u-t a ŋ-i ŋ, *v.* of yutaŋiŋ; *to manifest for* one—wećiyutaŋiŋ.

k i'-ć i-y u-t a ŋ-k a, *v.* of yutaŋka; *to enlarge for* another—wećiyutaŋka.

k i'-ć i-y u-t e-ć a, *v.* of yuteća; *to make new for* one—wećiyuteća.

k i'-ć i-y u-t e-h a ŋ, *v.* of yutehaŋ; *to make a delay for* one—wećiyutehaŋ.

k i'-ć i-y u-t o-k a ŋ, *v.* of yutokaŋ; *to put in another place* or *remove for* one—wećiyutokaŋ.

k i'-ć i-y u-t o-k e-ć a, *v.* of yutokeća; *to make different for* one—wećiyutokeća.

k i'-ć i-y u-t p a ŋ, *v.* of yutpaŋ. Same as kićiyukpaŋ.

k i'-ć i-y u-w a-ś'a-k a, *v.* of yuwaś'aka; *to make strong for* one—wećiyuwaś'aka.

k i'-ć i-y u-w a-ś t e, *v.* of yuwaśte: *to make good for* one—wećiyuwaśte, mićiyuwaśte.

k i'-ć i-y u-w e-ġ a, *v.* of yuweġa; *to partly break for* one, as a stick—wećiyuweġa.

k i'-ć i-y u-z a, *v.* of yuza; *to hold for* one.

k i'-ć i-y u-z a-m n i, *v.* of yuzamni; *to open out* or *uncover for* one—wećiyuzamni, mićiyuzamni.

k i-ć i'-y u-z a-p i, *v. recip.* *to hold each other, to take each other*, as man and wife: wakaŋ kićiyuzapi, *marriage.*

k i'-ć i-y u-ź a, *v.* of yuźa; *to make mush for* one—wećiyuźa, mićiyuźa.

k i'-ć i-y u-ź a-ź a, *v.* of yuźaźa; *to wash for* one.

k i'-ć i-y u-ź u ŋ, *v.* of yuźuŋ; *to pull out by the roots for* one—wećiyuźuŋ.

k i'-ć i-y u-ź u-ź u, *v.* of yuźuźu; *to tear down* or *tear to pieces for* one—wećiyuźuźu.

k i-ć i'-z a, *v.* of kiza; kići kićiza, *to quarrel* or *fight with* one—kići wećiza.

k i-ć i'-z a-p i, *n.* *a fighting, fight.*

k i-ć o', *v. a.* *to call to a feast, invite; to call to* any assembly or *for* any purpose—wećo, yećo, uŋkićopi, mićo, nićo, ćićo.

ki-ćoŋ'-za, *v.* See kićuŋza.

ki'-cu, *v.* of ku; *to restore to* one, *give to* one *what belongs to him*—weću, yeću, uŋkićupi, miću, niću, ćiću. According to analogy this should be kiçu, but it is not.

ki-ćuŋ'-ni, *v.* *to leave off, abstain from* what one was about to do; *to give over, be discouraged; to excuse, not press any further*—wećuŋni. See iyaćuŋni *and* iyakićuŋni.

ki-ćuŋ'-ni-yaŋ, *adv.* *carelessly, not heartily:* kićuŋniyaŋ epa, *I said it but did not wish it.*

ki-ćuŋ'-ske, *adv.* *half full.*

ki-ćuŋ'-ske-haŋ, *adv.* *half full*, as a vessel.

ki-ćuŋ'-za, *v.* *to determine in regard to*—wećuŋza.

ki-ću'-wa, *n.* *a friend, i. q.* koda. Used chiefly by the Sissetons and some of the Teetons of the Missouri. See kićića.

ki-ću'-wa, *v.* *pos* of kuwa; *to follow up, pursue*, as in giving medicine to one's child—wećuwa.

ki-ça', *v.* *pos.* of ka; *to dig one's own; to dig for* one—weça.

ki'-çiŋ, *v.* *pos.* of kiŋ; *to carry* or *pack one's own*, as one's own child, or one's own corn, etc.—weçiŋ, uŋkiçiŋpi.

ki-çoŋ', *v.* Same as kiçuŋ.

ki-çuŋ', *v. a.* *to put on* or *wear* as clothes; *to use*—weçuŋ, yeçuŋ, uŋkiçuŋpi: tawaćiŋ kiçuŋ, *to have one's own way, be stubborn;* oie kiçuŋ, *to use language.*

ki-çuŋ'-ki-ći-ći-ya, *v. a.* *to put on for* one, *help* one *to put on*, as clothes—kiçuŋwećićiya.

ki-çuŋ'-ki-ya, *v. a.* *to cause to put on*—kiçuŋwakiya.

ki-çuŋ'-ya, *v. a.* *to cause to put on*—kiçuŋwaya.

ki-da', *v.* of da, *to ask; to ask* or *beg of* one—wakida, yakida, uŋkidapi, makida

ki-da', *v.* *pos.* of da, *to think, esteem.* See waśtekida.

ki-da'-ka, *v.* Same as kida. See waśtekidaka.

ki-de'-de, *adv.* *just as it happens:* kidede wohdaka, *he talks at random;* kidede omawani, *I walk without any purpose.* This appears to be used when one has no determination to do or not to do a thing.

ki-do'-waŋ, *v.* of dowaŋ; *to sing to*, as to a child—wakidowaŋ.

ki-gla', *v. n.* *T.* *to have gone home; i. q.* kihda.

ki-gni', *v. n.* *T.* *to go home;* wagni, *I go home;* yagni, *you go home.*

ki-gnu'-ni, *v.* *T.* *to lose one's own*—wegnuni.

ki'-ġe, *v. a* *to scold, vex, quarrel with*—wakiġe, yakiġe, uŋkiġepi, makiġe, ćićiġe.

ki-hbe', *v.* *to resemble.* Same as kihma.

ki-hda' *or* kiŋ-hda', *v. n.* *to have gone home.* It generally refers to past time, though it may be used in the future. In all the persons except the third, "ya" is inserted, as if from kiyahda—wakiyahda, yakiyahda, uŋkiyahdapi.

k i - h d a′ - p a, *v.* *to dress* or *paint*, as the face and body—wehdapa, uŋkihdapapi. *T.*, śaiçiya.

k i - h d e′, *v.* Same as kihda.

k i - h d e′, *v.* of hde; *to place for, make ready for* one; *to place* or *lay up one's own*—wehde, uŋkihdepi. See kihnaka *and* kioŋpa.

k i - h d e′ - ġ a, *v. a.* *to overtake* one—wehdeġa, yehdeġa, uŋkihdeġapi, mihdeġa. See ehdeġa *and* ekihdeġa.

k i - h d e′ - y a, *v. a.* *to send off home*—kihdewaya.

k i - h d u′ - ś p a, *v. pos.* *to break in two one's own*—kiwahduśpa, kiuŋhduśpapi.

k i - h i′, *v. n.* *to be fledged*, as young birds; *to become large enough to provide for one's self.* See uŋćihi.

k i - h i′ - y a, *v. a.* *to raise*, as a child, *train up to manhood*—kihiwaya, kihiuŋyaŋpi. *T.*, uŋćihiya.

k i - h i′ - y e - y a, *v. a.* *to shoot* an arrow *as far as one can*—kihiyewaya, kihiyeuŋyaŋpi. *T.*, kiiŋyeya.

k i - h i′ - y e - y a - p i, *n.* *a bow-shot.*

k i - h m a′, *v. n.* *to look like, resemble, i. q.* kinma—wehma, *and* wakihma, yehma.

k i - h n a′, *v a.* *to caress, fondle*, as a child; *to comfort*—wehna, yehna, uŋkihnapi. *T.*, kigna. See kihnayaŋ.

k i - h n a g′, *cont.* of kihnaka; kihnag wahi, *I came to lay away.*

k i - h n a g′ - y a, *v. a.* *to cause to lay up one's own*—kihnagwaya.

k i - h n a′ - h n a, *v.* *red.* of kihna.

k i - h n a′ - k a, *v. a.* of hnaka; *to lay up for, keep for* one; *to lay up one's own; to put off, stop proceedings*—wehnaka, yehnaka, uŋkihnakapi. *T.*, kignaka. See kihde.

k i - h n a′ - y a ŋ, *v. a.* *to caress, to fondle*—wakihnayaŋ. *T.*, kignayaŋ. See kihna.

k i - h n u g′, *cont.* of kihnuka; kihnug iyaya, *to go under water, dive*—kihnug imdamde.

k i - h n u g′ - k i - y a, *v. a.* *to cause to dive*—kihnugwakiya.

k i - h n u′ - k a, *v.* *to dive*—wehnuka, yehnuka.

k i - h n u′ - n i, *v. n.* of hnuni; *to be bewildered, not able to remember how* to do a thing—wakihnuni. *T.*, kignuni *and* waćiŋgnuni.

k i - h n u′ - n i - y a, *v. a.* *to bewilder, cause to make a mistake*—kihnuniwaya, kihnunimayaŋ.

k i - h u ŋ′ - n i, *v. n.* *to get through, reach home*—wakihuŋni, uŋkihuŋnipi. See ihuŋni.

k i′ - h u - w e, *v.* of huwe; kihuwe ya, *to go to bring* something *for* another—kihuwe mda. *T*, kićihiyohi.

k i - ḣ a ŋ′, *v.* of ḣaŋ; *to do to* one, *to treat* one in any way—wakiḣaŋ, makiḣaŋ. *T.*, okiḣaŋ. See kiśkaŋ.

k i - ḣ a ŋ′ - n a, *v.* *dim.* of kiḣaŋ; kiḣaŋna ḣiŋća, *to do only a little for* one.

ki-ḣaŋ′-śi-ća, *v. n.* *to be bad* or *stormy weather, to rain* or *snow.* *T.*, ośićećake.

ki-ḣaŋ′-śi-ksu-ya, *v.* *to know by one's feelings that unpleasant weather is coming*—kiḣaŋśiwaksuya.

ki-ḣaŋ′-yaŋ, *v.* of ḣaŋyaŋ; *to be likely to die to* or *for* one, as one's child—makiḣaŋyaŋ, nićiḣaŋyaŋ. *T.*, kićiḣaŋyaŋ.

ki-ḣdo′, *v.* *pos.* of ḣdo; *to growl over one's own,* as a dog over his bone.

ki-ḣo′, *v.* See akiḣo.

ki-i′-hda-ksa, *v.* *reflex.* of kićaksa; *to injure one's self*—kimihdaksa, kinihdaksa.

ki-i′-hdu-śpa, *v.* *reflex.* *to free one's self, to wrestle.* Perhaps this is only used in the plural; as, kiihduśpapi, *they wrestle at arms' length*—kiuŋkihduśpapi. *T.*, igluśpa. See kićikśaŋ.

ki-iŋ′-yaŋ-ka, *v. n.* of iŋyaŋka; *to run with* one; *to run with* some object in view.

ki-iŋ′-yaŋ-ka-pi, *n.* *a running, a race.*

ki-iŋ′-ye-ya, *v.* *T.* *to shoot* or *make fly an arrow:* *i. q.* kihiyeya.

ki-iŋ′-ye-ya-pi, *n.* *T.* *a bowshot.*

ki-kaŋ′-he-źa, *v. n.* *pos.* of kaŋheźa; *to be sick for* or *to* one, as one's child—makikaŋheźa. *T.*, kićikuźa

ki-ka′-taŋ-ka, *n.* *a species of duck,* about as large as the mallard, with a sharp bill.

ki-ki′-hda, *or* **ki-kiŋ′-hda**, *v. n.* *to go home and leave* one, as one's dog or horse—makikihda, nićićihda, uŋkikihdapi. *T.*, kićikigla.

ki-ki′-ta, *adj.* *tough, elastic.* *T.*, zigzića.

ki-ksam′, *cont.* of kiksapa.

ki-ksa′-pa, *v. n.* of ksapa; *to become wise; to consult*—wakiksapa.

ki-ksu′-ya, *v. a.* *to remember, recollect; to be conscious, have a feel-* or *sense of*—weksuya, yeksuya, uŋkiksuyapi, miksuya, niksuya, ćiksuya.

ki-ksu′-ye-ki-ya, *v. a.* *to cause to remember*—kiksuyewakiya.

ki-ksu′-ye-śni, *v. n.* *to be unconscious, to be numb;* as nape weksuyeśni, *my hand is numb.*

ki-ksu′-ye-ya, *v. a.* *to cause to remember*—kiksuyewaya.

ki-kśaŋ′, *v. a.* *to violate, commit a rape on; to take without leave*—wakikśaŋ, uŋkikśaŋpi. *T.*, kiśleya. See kićikśaŋ *and* kiśdeya.

ki-kśaŋ′-pi, *n.* *rape.* See wikikśaŋpi. *T.*, wikiśleyapi.

ki-kta′, *v. n.* *to awake from sleep; to be awake*—wekta, yekta, uŋkiktapi.

ki-kta′-haŋ, *part.* *awake:* kiktahaŋ uŋ, *to keep awake.*

ki-kte′, *v. a.* of kte; *to kill one's own; to kill for* one—wekte, yekte, uŋkiktepi, mikte.

ki-kto′, *v. a.* *to take a boat to, bring over* the river—wakikto, makikto.

ki-kto′-ya, *v. a.* *to cause to come*

over, ferry over—kiktowaya: kiktoiç̣iya, *to ferry one's self over.*

k i - k u′ - s e, *v. pos.* of kuse; *to leak out for* one—makikuse, nićikuse, uŋkikusepi.

k i - k u′ - t e, *v.* of kute; *to shoot* anything *for* another, as ducks—wakikute, uŋkikutepi, makikute.

k i - k u′ - ź a. *v. pos.* of kuźa; *to be sick for* one*; to have one sick,* as a child—makikuźa.

k i - m a′ - k a, *v. to be renewed,* as an old field that has become good again.

k i′ - m a - m a, *n. the butterfly. T.,* kimimela *and* gmimela.

k i′ - m a - m a - n a, *n.* Same as kimama.

k i - m d e′ - ć a, *v. n.* of mdeća; *to break up,* as a gathering of people. *T.,* kibleća.

k i - m d e′ - z a, *v. n.* of mdeza; *to become clear-headed again, to recover from a drunken fit*—wakimdeza *and* wemdeza. *T,* kibleza.

k i - m i′ - m e - l a, *n. T. the butterfly; i. q.* kimama.

k i - m n a′ - h a ŋ, *v. n. to fall off, to rip off for* one—makimnahaŋ. See mna *and* mnahaŋ.

k i - m n i′, *v.* of mni; *to spread out one's own to dry* in the sun—wemni, yemni, uŋkimnipi.

k i - n a - h a ŋ′, *conj. if, when.* See kiŋhaŋ.

k i - n a′ - k s a, *v. a.* of naksa; *to break in two with the foot, to break in the middle*—kinawaksa, kinauŋksapi.

k i - n a′ - p a, *v. to come* or *go forth out of; to have passed through in going home*—wakinapa. See inapa.

k i - n a′ - p s a - k a, *v* of napsaka; *to break in two in the middle with the foot,* as a string—kinawapsaka.

k i - n a′ - p t u - ź a, *v.* of naptuźa; *to split* or *crack in the middle with the foot* or *by frost*—kinawaptuźa.

k i - n a′ - ś p a, *v.* of naśpa; *to break off about half with the foot*—kinawaśpa.

k i - n a′ - ź i ŋ, *v.* (ki *and* naźiŋ) *to reach home and stand; to stand again in one's place, recover one's position*—wakinawaźiŋ, yakinayaźiŋ.

k i - n b e′, *v.* See kinma.

k i - n i′, *v. n.* of ni; *to live again, to return to life,* as one dead; *to revive, recover* from fainting, etc.—wakini, uŋkinipi.

k i′ - n i - h a ŋ, *or* k i - n i′ - h a ŋ, *v. a. to honor, respect, reverence, have confidence in*—wakinihaŋ, uŋkinihaŋpi.

k i′ - n i - h a ŋ - p i, *part. honored, respected.*

k i′ - n i - h a ŋ′ - ś n i - y a ŋ, *adv. dishonorably.*

k i′ - n i - h a ŋ - y a ŋ, *adv. honorably, respectfully*

k i - n i′ - k i - y a, *v. a. to cause to live again*—kiniwakiya.

k i - n i′ - w a ŋ, *v. n.* of niwaŋ; *to swim home, swim back again*—wakiniwaŋ. *T.,* kinowaŋ.

k i - n m a′, *v. a. to be like, to resemble* in any respect; *to look like in features* or *form; to be like in character*, as a child resembles its parents—wakinbe, uŋkinmaŋpi, makinbe, nićinbe: atkuku kinma, *he resembles his father*. See kihma.

ki-no′-waŋ, *v.* *T.* of nowaŋ; *to swim home, swim back.*

ki-nu′-kaŋ, *or* kiŋ-nu′-kaŋ, *adv.* *separately, between two, divided, each having a part:* kinukaŋ ehnaka, *to divide, place in two piles.*

ki-nu′-kaŋ-ki-ya, *adv.* *separately.*

ki-nu′-kaŋ-yaŋ, *adv.* *separately.*

ki-nuŋ′-ka, *v. n.* *to grow, flourish.*

ki-nuŋ′-ka, *v.* *T.* 2d per. sing. of kiyuŋka; *thou liest down.*

kiŋ, *def. art.* *the.* When "a" or "aŋ" changed to "e" precedes, kiŋ becomes ćiŋ.

kiŋ′-ća, *adj* *scraping.* See yukiŋća.

kiŋ-ća′-haŋ, *part.* *bare; fallen off*, as hair from a dead animal, or as scales.

kiŋ-ća′-wa-haŋ, *part.* Same as kiŋćahaŋ.

kiŋ-haŋ′ *conj.* *if, when.* After "a" or "aŋ" changed to "e," it becomes "ćiŋhaŋ." See kinahaŋ.

kiŋ-haŋs′, *adv.* *and yet, if.*

kiŋ-hda′, *v.* See kihda.

kiŋ-iŋ′, *v. a.* *to throw at:* iŋyaŋ oŋ kiŋiŋ, *to pelt with stones, to stone*—wakiŋiŋ, makiŋiŋ, nićiŋiŋ.

kiŋs, *cont.* of kiŋza.

kiŋs-kiŋ′-za, *v. red.* of kiŋza; *to grate* or *gnash*, as the teeth; *to squeak*, as shoes do.

kiŋ′-sko-ke-ća, *adv.* *so large.* See tiŋskokeća.

kiŋ′-sko-sko-ke-ća, *adv.* *red.* of kiŋskokeća.

kiŋ′-sko-sko-ya, *adv.* *red.* of kiŋskoya. See tiŋskoskoya.

kiŋ′-sko-ya, *adv.* *thus far around.*

kiŋ-sle′-ya, *adv.* *T.* *grating*, as a wagon on snow. See kiŋza.

kiŋ-śka′, *n.* *Ih.* and *T.* *a horn spoon; spoons; a large kind of tortoise.* See tukiha.

kiŋ-yaŋ′, *v. n.* *to fly*, as birds do: kiŋyaŋ iyaya, *it has flown.*

kiŋ-yaŋ′-pi, *n.* *those that fly, birds.*

kiŋ-ye′, *v.* Same as kiŋyaŋ: taku kiŋye ćiŋ, *birds.*

kiŋ′-za, *v. n.* *to creak, to grate.*

ki-oŋ′-pa, *v pos.* of oŋpa; *to lay* or *place on one's own.*

ki-pa′, *v. a.* *to keep for* one, as a puppy or girl, *to keep what one has bespoken for* him—wakipa, uŋkipapi, makipa. See kićipa.

ki-pa′-kiŋ-ta, *v a.* of pakiŋta; *to cleanse away for* one, *wipe off*—wakipakiŋta, uŋkipakiŋtapi.

ki-pa′-mni, *v. a.* of pamni; *to divide* or *distribute to*—wićawakipamni.

ki-paŋ′, *v.* of paŋ; *to call to* one—wakipaŋ, uŋkipaŋpi.

ki-pa′-ta, *v. pos.* of pata; *to cut up one's own*, as meat: *i. q.* kpata.

ki-pa′-taŋ, *v.* of pataŋ; *to keep for*

one; *to mash up*, as food—wakipataŋ.

ki-pa′-ti-taŋ, *v.* of patitaŋ; *to push with all one's might, i. q.* śagiçiyapi—wakipatitaŋ.

ki-pa′-ya, *v. n.* See kipayeća.

ki-pa′-ye-ća, *v. n.* *to rise up again, recover itself*, as grass bent down.

ki-pa′-zo, *v.* of pazo; *to point to for* one, *to show to* one—wakipazo, makipazo.

ki-pa′-źiŋ, *v. a.* of paźiŋ; *to stand up against, rebel against, oppose* one—wakipaźiŋ, makipaźiŋ.

ki-pa′-źiŋ-yaŋ, *adv.* *opposing.*

ki-pi′, *v. n.* *to hold, contain, carry*, as a vessel, cart, etc.; *to be large enough to admit* anything; *to be large enough for*, as a coat; *to be sufficient for*—makipi, nićipi, uŋkipipi. See okipi.

ki-pi′-ya, *v. a.* *to cause to fit*—kipiwaya; *to go down well*, as a bullet that fits the gun.

ki-pi′-ya, *adv.* *fittingly, fitly, properly:* kipiya ećamoŋ, *I have done it fitly.*

ki-psi′-ća, *v.* *to jump down from, alight from*, as from a horse—wakipsića. See psića.

ki-saŋ′, *v. n.* of saŋ; *to become whitish for* one—makisaŋ.

ki-sa′-pa, *v. n.* of sapa; *to become black* or *bare again*, as the ground by the disappearance of snow.

ki-sa′-pa, *n.* *bare ground.*

ki-sdi′-pa, *v.* of sdipa; *to lick up one's own again*, as a dog his vomit—wesdipa.

ki-sna′-haŋ, *v. n* *to break and fall off*, as beads from a strand, *for* one—makisnahaŋ.

ki-so′, *v. pos.* *to cut a string from a hide; to cut up one's own:* whence kićiso *and* kićisoso.

ki-soŋ′, *v. pos.* of soŋ: *to braid one's own*—wesoŋ *and* wakisoŋ, yesoŋ *and* yakisoŋ, uŋkisoŋpi.

ki-so′-ta, *v. n.* of sota; *to be used up for* one—makisota, nićisota. See bosota, yasota, yusota, sonkiya, etc.

ki-spa′-ya, *v. n.* of spaya; *to be* or *become wet for* one—makispaya: oŋḣdoḣda nićispaya, *thy coat is wet.*

ki-śde′-ya, *or* **ki-śden-ya**, *v. a.* *to annoy, vex, continue to press* or *urge* one; *to make ashamed, to offend, dishonor*—kiśdewaya. *T.*, kiśleya.

ki-śi′-ća, *v. a.* *to check, oppose, put a stop to; to forbid, command to stop; to drive* or *kick out*, as a dog from the house—wakiśića. See anića, iyokiśni, *and* kipaźiŋ.

ki-śkaŋ′, *v. a.* of śkaŋ; *to do to, act towards* one—wakiśkaŋ. See kiḣaŋ.

ki-śka′-ta, *v. a.* of śkata; *to play to* or *with; to play for*—wakiśkata.

ki-śle′-ya, *v.* *T* *to seduce; i q.* kiśdeya. See kikśaŋ.

ki-śto′, *adv.* *T.* *why: i. q* kto.

ki-taŋ′, *v. n.* *to stick to*, as an opinion, *continue to assert; to insist upon, not yield*—wakitaŋ, uŋkitaŋpi.

ki'-taŋ, *adv. scarcely, hardly.*

ki'-taŋ-e-ćiŋ-yaŋ, *adv. slightly, just able:* kitaŋećiŋyaŋ okihi, *he was just able to do it.*

ki-taŋ'-iŋ, *v.* of taŋiŋ; *to appear* or *be visible for*—makitaŋiŋ.

ki-taŋ'-iŋ-śni, *v. n. to be lost for* one—makitaŋiŋśni.

ki'-taŋ-na, *adv. a little, very little, in a slight degree:* kitaŋna waśte, *but a little good.*

ki'-taŋ-se, *adv. with difficulty.*

ki-taŋ'-yaŋ, *adv. continuously; insisting upon*

ki-taŋ'-ye-ḣćiŋ, *adv. T. poorly, not thoroughly.* See kitaŋ.

ki-ta'-ta, *v. a. to shake; i. q.,* katata.

ki-ta'-ta, *adv. T. near together, frequently, in close succession.*

ki-toŋ', *v. to put on,* as clothes; *to be clothed with, to wear,* as wapaha kitoŋ, *to wear a hat*—wetoŋ *and* wakitoŋ, uŋkitoŋpi; *to use,* as, oie kitoŋ, *to use words*

ki-tu'-ka, *v. a. to beg of, ask of*—wakituka, makituka, ćićituka. *T.,* kila.

ki'-ṭa, *v. n.* of ṭa; *to die* or *be dead for* one, as one's child—makiṭa.

ki-uŋ'-ni, *v. n. to be hurt.* See kiuŋniyaŋ.

ki-uŋ'-ni-ki-ya, *v. a. to hurt, injure* anything—kiuŋniwakiya, kiuŋnimakiya.

ki-uŋ'-ni-yaŋ, *v. a. to hurt, injure*—kiuŋniwaya, kiuŋniuŋyaŋpi, kiuŋnimayaŋ.

ki-uŋ'-yaŋ, *v. T. to lose for one, lose what belongs to another*—wakiuŋyaŋ.

ki-wa'-kaŋ-he-źa, *v. n. to desire to be with, to be on good terms* or *be intimate with*—wakiwakaŋheźa. See wakaŋheźa.

ki-wa'-ni, *v. n. to be winter anew;* said of snow squalls in the spring. See wanikisapa, waniyetu, etc.

ki-waŋ'-ka, *v. n.* (ki *and* waŋka) *to go home and lie down, go and sleep at home; to sleep going home* or *on the way home*—wakimuŋka, yakinuŋka. *T.,* kiyuŋka.

ki-wi'-ta-ya, *adv.* of witaya; *together, assembled together.*

ki'-ya, *v. aux. to cause, to make to be:* ećoŋ kiya, *to cause to do;* ṭe kiya, *to cause to die;* samkiya, *to make black.* The place of the pronoun is before the "kiya."

ki'-ya, *v. aux. pos.* of ya *or* yaŋ.

ki'-ya, *adv. towards,* as in ektakiya; *separately, in different ways, in different places,* as, yamnikiya yakoŋpi, *they are in three different places.*

ki'-ya-daŋ, *adv. near, near to.* See kiyedaŋ *and* ikiyadaŋ.

ki'-ya-hda, *v. to have gone home.* This is used only in the first and second persons—wakiyahda, yakiyahda, uŋkiyahdapi. See kihda.

ki-ya'-hda-pta, *v. pos.* of kiyakapta; *to have passed over,* as a hill, *in going home*—wakiyahdapta.

ki-ya'-ka-pta, *v. n. to have*

passed over, as a hill, *in going home*—wakiyakapta *or* wakiyawakapta.

ki-ya'-ksa, *v.* of yaksa; *to bite in two in the middle*—kimdaksa, kiuŋyaksapi.

ki'-ya-la, *T.; and* **ki'-ya-na**, *Ih.* *adv.* *near to, not far off; i. q.*, kiyadaŋ.

ki-ya'-mna, *v.* of yamna; *to acquire for* another *by talking*—wakiyamna, makiyamna. *T.*, kiċiyamna.

ki-yan'-ya, *v.* *to be nearly finishing*—kiyanmda. *T.*, kiyela ya. Compare ḣuŋhikiya *and* yuśtaŋ.

ki-ya'-pa, *v.* of yapa; *to suck for, take in the mouth and suck*, as the Dakota conjurers do in the case of a sick person—wakiyapa, makiyapa, uŋkiyapapi. See kiċiyapa.

ki-ya'-pa-pi, *n.* *drawing with the mouth.*

ki-ya'-taŋ-iŋ, *v. a.* of yataŋiŋ; *to make manifest to* or *for*—wakiyataŋiŋ.

ki-ya'-ya, *v. n.* *to go by* or *near* a place—kiyawaya, kiyayaya.

ki-ya'-ya, *v.* of iyaya; *to go by* or *pass. Part.*, *went, gone*—uŋkiyayapi.

ki'-ye-daŋ, *adv.* *near, near to.* See ikiyedaŋ, kiyadan, *and* kiyala.

ki-yo'-hi, *v.* (ki *and* iyohi) *to reach home*—wakiyohi, yakiyohi, uŋkiyohipi.

ki'-yo-ki-źu, *v. n.* *to unite.* See iyokiźu, kokiźu, *and* okiźu.

ki'-yo-ki-źu-ya, *v. a.* *to put together, cause to unite; to add together sum up*—kiyokiźuwaya.

ki'-yo-ki-źu-ya, *adv.* *together, unitedly.*

ki'-yo-taŋ-ka, *v. n.* (ki *and* iyotaŋka) *to arrive and remain at home.* Said, by the person who arrives or by another person, when away from the place—wakimdotaŋka, yakidotaŋka, uŋkiyotaŋkapi.

ki-yu'-ġaŋ, *v. a.* of yuġaŋ; *to open for* one, as a door—wakiyuġaŋ.

ki-yu'-ġa-ta, *v. a.* of yuġata; *to open* as the hand *to, to stretch out* the hand *to; to implore*, as in worship—wakiyuġata.

ki-yu'-ha, *v.* of yuha; *to have* or *keep for* one—wakiyuha, uŋkiyuhapi. *T.*, kiċiyuha.

ki-yu'-ḣa, *v. a.* *to copulate*, as the male and female of animals. Hence, Takiyuḣa wi, *the moon when the deer copulate*, answering to *November.*

ki-yu'-kaŋ, *v. a.* *to make room for*, as in a tent, *give place to; to pass by* or *away from, leave unmolested*—wakiyukaŋ, uŋkiyukaŋpi, makiyukaŋ, ćiċiyukaŋ. See tiyukaŋ *and* yukaŋ.

ki-yu'-ksa, *v.* of yuksa; *to break in two one's own; to break* or *violate*, as a law or custom—kimduksa *and* wakimduksa, kiduksa, uŋkiyuksapi.

Ki-yu'-ksa, *n. p.* *a band of Da-*

kotas, Wapasha's band. So called, it is said, from the intermarrying of relations among them.

ki-yu'-śe, *v. a. to hate* one, *do evil to* one—wakimduśe, yakiduśe, uŋkiyuśepi, makiyuśe, ćićiyuśe.

ki-yu'-śka, *v. a.* of yuśka; *to loose, untie, unharness; to release from prison* or *confinement*—wakiyuśka *and* wakimduśka, yakiduśka, uŋkiyuśkapi.

ki-yu'-śpa, *v. a.* of yuśpa; *to break into pieces, divide,* as bread; *to divide,* as in arithmetic; *to deliver* or *free,* as from a trap or evil of any kind—kimduśpa *and* wakimduśpa, kiduśpa *and* yakiduśpa, uŋkiyuśpapi, makiyuśpa.

ki-yu'-śpa-pi, *n. a dividing, delivering;* in arithmetic, *division.*

ki-yu'-śpa-pi-haŋ-ska, *n. long division.*

ki-yu'-śpa-śpa, *v. red.* of kiyuśpa.

ki-yu'-te, *n. a strait* or *channel; an isthmus.* See okiyute.

ki-yu'-we-ġa, *v.* of iyuweġa; *to cross,* as a stream, *in going home*—wakimduweġa.

ki-yu'-za, *v. a.* of yuza; *to hold to* one—wakiyuza.

ki-yu'-za-mni, *v. a.* of yuzamni; *to open to* or *for* one; *to uncover for* one—wakiyuzamni.

ki-yu'-źa-źa, *v.* of yuźaźa; *to wash one's own; to wash for* another—wakiyuźaźa.

ki'-za, *v. a. to fight, quarrel with*—wakiza, uŋkizapi, makiza, ćićiza. See okićize.

ki-źo', *v. a.* of źo; *to whistle for, call by whistling;* wakiźo. See iwośokiya *and* iźoka.

ki-źo'-źo, *v. to whistle for, to call one's own by whistling,* as one's dog—wakiźoźo.

kma, *n. Ih. walnuts: i. q.* hma. *T.,* gma.

kn. Yankton words beginning with "kn" will be found under "hn." *e. g.,* knaśka; *i. q.* hnaśka.

kni, *v. Ih. i. q.* hda. The sign of the future changes kda into kni; as, wakni kta, *I will go home.* See mni.

ko, *conj. and, too, also.* See kokta, koya, *and* nakuŋ.

ko, *in comp. quick:* waćiŋko, *quick tempered;* ohaŋko, *quick at work.* See kohaŋ, kohaŋna, kokedaŋ, *and* koyahaŋna.

ko-a'-ka-ta, *and* ko-wa'-ka-ta, *adv. Ih.* and *T. the other side, over* or *across,* as a river: *i. q.* akasaŋpa.

ko-a'-ka-taŋ-haŋ, *adv. T. over the river; from the other side.*

ko-da', *n.* the *particular friend* of a Dakota man. The Teetons say "kola" *and* "kićuwa"—mitakoda, nitakoda, takodaku.

ko-da'-ki-ći-ya-pi, *n. friendship.*

ko-da'-ya, *v. a. to have for a particular friend*—kodawaya, kodamayaŋ.

kog, *cont.* of koka; kog hiŋhda, *to make a sound, to rattle* or *ring.*

k o - h a ŋ', *adv.* *soon, quickly, now.* *T.*, koyaŋla.

k o - h a ŋ' - n a, *adv.* *soon, very soon, too soon, early.* See kokohaŋna *and* koyaȟaŋna.

k o - h a ŋ ś', *adv.* *since that, so that.*

k o - h d a' - m n a, *adv.* *around, over:* kohdamna iću, *to put* or *take around; surrounding.* See ihdukśaŋ *and* okśaŋ.

k o - h d a' - m n a - y a ŋ, *v. a.* *to surround, restrain, cut off retreat*—kohdamnawaya.

k o - h d a' - m n i, *adv.* *around, surrounding:* kohdamni ya, *to surround.*

k o - h d a' - m n i - y a ŋ, *v. a.* *to go around, surround; i. q.* kokamya—kohdamniwaya.

k o - h d i', *adj.* *clear, translucent.*

k o - h d i' - h d i, *adj.* *red.* of kohdi. The flint-corn is so called from its translucency.

k o' - k a, *n.* *the sound of a bell, a ringing.* See kokela.

k o - k a', *n.* *a keg, barrel, box:* ćaȟdi koka, *a powder-keg.*

k o - k a' - d a ŋ, *n.* *dim.* of koká; *a small keg.*

k o - k a' - l a, *n.* *T.* *a keg.*

k o - k a' - l a, *adv.* *T.* *empty; i. q.* ćokadaŋ.

k o - k a m', *adv.* *beyond, across, by a near way, before* one; *i. q.* ákokam.

k o - k a m' - t u, *adv.* *by a near way, across.*

k o - k a m' - y a, *v.* *to go across, go by a near way.*

k o - k a' - o - ź u - h a, *n.* *an empty barrel.*

k o - k a' - p a, *adv.* Same as kokam.

k o - k a' - p a - h m i - h m a, *n.* (koka *and* pahmihma) *a keg that is rolled,* i. e., *a barrel.* *T.*, kokapagmiyaŋ.

k o - k a' - p a - t a ŋ - h a ŋ, *adv.* *by a near way, across.* *T.*, akokabya.

k o' - k e - d a ŋ, *adv.* *quickly, rapidly:* oićaȟ kokedaŋ, *of quick growth;* oyaȟe kokedaŋ, *it boils away fast.* See ko *and* kokokaŋ.

k o' - k e - l a, *v.* *T.* *to make a noise, to rattle,* as dishes.

k o' - k i - ć a - ȟ d o - k a, *v. n.* *to be opened through on both sides:* kokićaȟdog iyaya.

k o' - k i - ć a - ś p a, *v.* *to dig two holes into one; to shoot twice in the same place*—kowećaśpa. See okićaśpa.

k o' - k i - ć i - w a - ś i ŋ, *adv.* See kokićiyasiŋ.

k o' - k i - ć i - y a - ȟ d a n, *adv.* *linked together,* as the links of a chain; *entangled,* as the horns of a deer in brush.

k o' - k i - ć i - y a - s i ŋ, *adv.* *uniting, coming together and flowing on,* as two streams in one; *stuck* or *fastened together,* as dogs after copulating; used also of potatoes *in a bunch.* See okićiyasiŋ.

k o - k i' - p a, *v. a.* *to fear, be afraid of* one—kowakipa, koyakipa, kouŋkipapi, komakipa, konićipa, koćićipa. See kopa.

k o - k i' - p a - p i, *part.* *feared.* Hence, wokokipe, *fear.*

k o - k i' - p e - k i - y a, *v. a.* *to cause to fear*—kokipewakiya.

k o - k i' - p e - y a, *v. a.* *to cause to fear, make afraid of*—kokipewaya.

k o - k i' - p e - y a - h a ŋ, *adv.* *fearing, fearful, afraid:* kokipeyahaŋ wauŋ, *I am fearful.*

k o' - k i - ś p a, *v. n.* *to join, unite.* *T.*, ićiyakaśka. See ośpaye.

k o' - k i - ś p e - y a, *v. a.* *to cause to join*—kokiśpewaya.

k o' - k i - ź u, *v. n.* *to come together* See iyokiźu, kiyokiźu, *and* okiźu.

k o' - k i - ź u - y a, *v. a.* *to cause to unite together.*

k o' - k i - ź u - y a, *adv.* *unitedly.*

k o' - k o, *adv. red.* of ko.

k o' - k o - d a ŋ, *adv.* *lively.* *T.*, kokoyela. See kokedaŋ.

k o - k o g' - y a, *adv.* of kokoka; *rattling.*

k o' - k o - h a ŋ - n a, *adv.* *lively.* See kohaŋna

k o - k o' - k a, *v. n.* *to rattle*, as a stiff skin.

k o - k o' - y a - ḣ a ŋ - n a, *n.* *Ih.* *a chicken, fowls; i. q.* aŋpaohotoŋna. *T.*, kokoyaḣaŋla.

k o - k o' - y a ŋ - n a, *adv. red.* of koyaŋna. See kokohaŋna.

k o - k o' - y e - l a, *adv.* *T.* *in quick succession.*

k o - k o' - ź u - h a, *n.* (koká *and* oźuha) *an empty cask, barrel*, or *keg.* *T.*, kokaoźuha.

k o' - k t a, *adv.* *also, besides.* See ko *and* koya.

k o - k t a' *and* k o - k t o', *adj.* *T.* *one thousand.*

k o' - k t a - y a, *adv.* *besides.*

k o - k t o' - p a - w i ŋ - ġ e, *adj.* *a thousand.* See kektopawiŋġe.

k o ŋ, *v.* *to desire, to covet*—wakoŋ, yakoŋ, uŋkoŋpi.

k o ŋ, *n.* *mother-in-law;* koŋku, *his* or *her mother-in-law.* See kuŋ.

k o ŋ' - k o ŋ - t a, Same as koŋtkoŋta. *T.*, kuŋtkuŋṭa.

k o ŋ' - t a - h a ŋ, *part.* *uneven, ridged.*

k o ŋ' - t k o ŋ - t a, *adj.* *uneven, with ridges.* Hence, ćaŋbakoŋtkoŋta, *a wash-board.*

k o ŋ - y a ŋ', *v. n.* *to start in sleep*—wakoŋyaŋ: koŋyaŋ hiŋhda, *he started suddenly.* *T*, śkaŋ hiŋgla.

k o ŋ' - z a, *v.* *to determine, influence; to pretend*, as, witko koŋza, *to pretend to be drunk*—wakoŋza, yakoŋza, uŋkoŋzapi.

k o' - p a, *n.* *a fearful place; fear.* *T.*, okope.

k o' - p a, *adj.* *insecure, exposed to be killed by an enemy; in fear:* kope wauŋ, *I am in fear.*

k o' - p e - h d a, *v n.* *to be afraid, be in fear*—kopewahda, kopeyahda, kopeuŋhdapi. See kokipa.

k o' - p e - y a, *v. a.* *to make afraid*—kopewaya. *T.*, wakokipekićaġa.

k o' - p e - y a, *adv.* *insecurely.*

k o s, *cont.* of koza; nape kos wauŋ, *I am beckoning with my hand.*

k o - s a ŋ' - t a, *adv.* *from one to another:* kosaŋta wićawaḳu, *I gave away what was given to me.*

k o s - k o' - z a, *v. red.* of koza.

k o s - y a', *v. a.* *to cause to wave* or *make a signal*—koswaya.

k o - ś k a', *n.* *a young man*—komaśka, koniśka, kouŋśkapi. *T.*, kośkala *and* kośkalaka.

k o - ś k a' - l a, *n.* *T.* *a youth, young man;* one younger than a kośka: *i. q.* kośkana *and* kośkadaŋ.

k o - ś k a' - n a, *n.* *Ih.* *a youth:* kośka taŋka, *a man in the prime of life.*

k o - ś k a' - ś k a - p i, *n. red.* of kośka.

k o ś k i ŋ' - y a ŋ, *n.* *one who begins to think himself a young man.*

k o - w a' - k a - t a, *adv.* *T.* and *Ih.* *over the river, across the river:* *i. q.* koakata.

k o - w a' - k a - t a ŋ - h a ŋ, *adv.* *from beyond the river.*

k o' - y a, *conj.* *and, too, also.* See ko *and* kokta.

k o - y a g', *cont.* of koyaka; koyag wauŋ, *I am wearing;* koyag haŋ, *standing clothed, hitched up, harnessed.*

k o - y a g' - k i - y a, *v. a.* *to cause to put on* or *wear*—koyagwakiya, koyagmakiya.

k o - y a ǧ' - y a, *v. a.* *to cause to put on; to attach to*—koyagwaya.

k o - y a' - ḣ a ŋ, *v. n.* *to be quick in doing* a thing, *to hasten, hurry*—koyawaḣaŋ, koyayaḣaŋ, koyauŋḣaŋpi.

k o - y a' - ḣ a ŋ - n a, *adv.* *quickly, immediately.* See ko, kokodaŋ, koyaŋna, etc.

k o - y a' - k a, *v. a.* *to put on* or *wear*, as clothes—komdaka, kodaka, kouŋyakapi, komayaka.

k o - y a' - k a - p i, *part.* *clothed:* taku koyakapi, *clothing.* See wokoyake.

k o - y a ŋ' - n a, *adv.* *quickly; i. q.* kohaŋna. See kokedaŋ *and* kokoyaŋna.

k o - y a' - n o ŋ, *or* k o - y a' - n u ŋ, *v. n.* *to be of quick growth, precocious*—koyamanoŋ, koyaninoŋ.

k o - y a ŋ' - n u ŋ, *adj.* *T.* *vigorous;* le lećala tuka koyaŋnuŋ heoŋ lila taŋka, *this is of not long ago, but is vigorous, and so is large.*—T. L. R.

k o - y e' - l a *and* k o - y a ŋ' - l a, *adv.* *T.* *promptly, quickly.* See kohaŋ *and* koyaŋna.

k o' - z a, *v. a.* *to strike at, shake at; to wave,* as a signal, *brandish,* as a sword—wakoza, uŋkozapi: śina koza, *to wave one's blanket;* nape koza, *to wave the hand.*

k o - ź a g' - ź a l, *adv.* *T.* *striking together:* koźagźal mani, *to walk striking the knees.*

k p a, *a pos. prefix.* Verbs that take "pa" as a prefix, make the possessive form by adding "k" or "t," as, paġaŋ *or* kpaġaŋ. See tpa.

k p a, *v. n.* *to swell,* as rice does, *in cooking.*

k p a, *adj.* *durable, lasting, not soon eaten up,* as some kinds of food; for instance, rice. See tpa.

k p a, *adj.* *punched out:* noġe kpa, *deaf:* iśta kpa, *blind.* See tpa.

kpa-ġaŋ', *v. pos.* of paġaŋ; *to spare* or *give away one's own*—wakpaġaŋ, uŋkpaġaŋpi. See tpaġaŋ.

kpa-ha'-ha-pi-ka, *n. one who is put forward in company*—makpahahapika.

kpa-hi', *v. pos.* of pahi; *to pick up one's own*—wakpahi, uŋkpahipi.

kpa-hmoŋ', *or* **kpa-hmuŋ'**, *v. pos.* of pahmoŋ; *to twist one's own*—wakpahmoŋ.

kpa-ḣde'-ća, *v. pos.* of paḣdeća; *to make a hole in one's own, to lance*—wakpaḣdeća.

kpa-ḣpa', *v. poss.* of paḣpa; *to lay down* or *put off one's own* load—wakpaḣpa.

kpa-kiŋ'-ta, *v. pos.* of pakiŋta; *to wipe one's own*—wakpakiŋta, uŋkpakiŋtapi.

kpa-kpi', *v. pos.* of pakpi; *to crack or break one's own*, as a chicken breaking its shell.

kpa-kśi'-źa, *v. pos.* of pakśiźa; *to double up one's own*—wakpakśiźa.

kpa-ku'-ka, *v. pos.* of pakuka; *to wear out one's own by rubbing*—wakpakuka.

kpa-maŋ', *v. pos.* of pamaŋ; *to file one's own*—wakpamaŋ.

kpa-mde'-ća, *v. pos.* of pamdeća; *to break in pieces one's own*—wakpamdeća. See tpamdeća.

kpa-mni', *v. pos.* of pamni; *to divide out one's own*—wakpamni, uŋkpamnipi.

kpa-mni'-pi, *n. a distribution.*

kpaŋ, *adj. fine*, as flour. See bakpaŋ, yukpaŋ, etc. See tpaŋ.

kpaŋ'-na, *adj. fine, soft.*

kpa-psoŋ', *v. pos.* of papson; *to spill over one's own*—wakpapson.

kpa-pta', *v. to leave a company before it breaks up, to free one's self and go away* while the others remain—wakpapta.

kpa-pu'-za, *v. pos.* of papuza; *to make one's own dry by wiping*—wakpapuza.

kpa-snoŋ', *v. pos.* of pasnoŋ; *to roast one's own* meat—wakpasnoŋ.

kpa-su'-ta, *v. pos.* of pasuta; *to make hard by kneading one's own* bread—wakpasuta.

kpa'-ta, *v. pos.* of páta; *to cut up* or *carve one's own* meat—wakpata. *T.*, kipata. See tpata.

kpa-taŋ', *v. pos.* of pataŋ; *to take care of one's own, think much of* so as to spare or not use it up—wakpataŋ, yakpataŋ, uŋkpataŋpi.

kpa-ṭa'-ṭa, *v. n. T. to be numb* or *asleep:* siha wakpaṭaṭa, *my foot is asleep.*

kpa'-za, *adj. dark.* See okpaza.

kpa-zaŋ', *v. pos.* of pazaŋ; *to part* or *separate one's own* —wakpazaŋ.

kpa-źa'-źa, *v. pos.* of paźaźa; *to wash out one's own*, as one's own gun—wakpaźaźa.

kpa-źu'-źu, *v. pos* of paźuźu; *to rub out one's own*—wakpaźuźu.

kpe, *adj.* See kpa *and* tpe.

kpe-haŋ', *v. pos.* of pehaŋ; *to fold up one's own*—wakpehaŋ.

k p u - k p a', *adv.* *mixed up*, as water and grease in soup. See pukpa *and* tputpa.

k p u - k p e' - y a, *adv.* *mixed up, all kinds together.*

k p u - s p a', *v. pos.* of puspa; *to glue* or *seal one's own*—wakpuspa.

k p u - t a' - k a, *v. pos.* of putaka; *to touch one's own.* See ikputaka.

k s a, *adj.* *separated.* See baksa, kaksa, yuksa, etc.

k s a' - h a ŋ, *part.* *broken in two of itself.*

k s a - k s a' - p a, *adj. red.* of ksapa.

k s a m, *cont.* of ksapa.

k s a m - y a', *v. a.* *to make wise*—ksamwaya.

k s a m - y a', *adv.* *wisely, prudently.*

k s a m - y a' - h a ŋ, *adv.* *wisely.*

k s a' - p a, *adj.* *wise, prudent, having understanding*—waksapa, yaksapa, uŋksapapi.

k s a - w a' - h a ŋ, *part.* *broken in two.*

k s i' - z e - ć a, *adj.* *grum, growling, i. q.* waćiŋko—maksizeća.

k s u' - w e, *v. n.* *to be hurt.* See ksuweya.

k s u' - w e - y a, *v. a.* *to hurt* or *injure* the flesh or body of any one—ksuwewaya, ksuwemayaŋ.

k s u' - y e - y a, *v. a.* *to hurt, injure, inflict pain upon*—ksuyewaya. Same as ksuweya.

k ś a, *adj.* *bent, rolled.* See yukśa.

k ś a' - d a ŋ, *adj.* *bent.*

k ś a' - k a, *adj.* *bent up*, as an aged person, *decrepit*—makśaka.

k ś a ŋ, *adj.* *crooked:* kśa *and* kśaŋ were probably the same root. See yukśaŋ.

k ś a ŋ - k ś a ŋ', *red.* of kśaŋ.

k ś a ŋ - k ś a ŋ', *v. n.* *to wriggle*, as a fish.

k ś a ŋ - k ś a ŋ' - y a ŋ, *adv.* *crookedly.*

k ś a ŋ - y a ŋ', *v. a.* *to make crooked, to crook, bend*—kśaŋwaya.

k ś a ŋ - y a ŋ', *adv.* *crookedly.*

k ś a - w a' - h a ŋ, *part.* *rolled up.*

k ś i - k ś a', *adj.* *numb, stiff with cold. T.*, kśikśeća.

k ś i - k ś a ŋ', *adj.* *crooked.* See pakśikśaŋ.

k ś i - k ś e' - ć a, *adj. T.* *numb;* nape makśikśeća, *my hands are numb.*

k ś i - k ś i' - ź a, *adj.* *red.* of kśiźa.

k ś i ś, *cont.* of kśiźa; kśiśiçidaka, *to regard one's self as bent up.*

k ś i' - ź a, *adj.* *bent, doubled up.* See yukśiźa, etc.

k ś i - ź a' - h a ŋ, *part.* *bent up, doubled up.*

k ś i - ź a' - w a - h a ŋ, *part.* *bent up.*

k t a *and* k t e, *v. aux.* *shall* or *will.* The usual sign of the future tense.

k t a, *v.* *to wait for, to neglect doing and expect* another to do—wakta, yakta. See akta, wakta, ape, etc.

k t a' - e, *adv.* of kta *and* e; *in order that;* used in the turning of a sentence, as, hećamoŋ ktae oŋ wahi, *I came that I might do this.*

k t a' - k a, *v.* *to wait, expect* another to act—waktaka.

k t a ŋ, *adj.* *crooked, curved.* See yuktaŋ.

k t a ŋ - k t a ŋ', *adj.* *crooked.*

k t a ŋ - k t a ŋ′ - k i - y a, *adv. crookedly, indirectly, zigzag.*

k t a ŋ - k t a ŋ′ - y a ŋ, *adv. crookedly*

k t a ŋ - y a ŋ′, *adv. crookedly.*

k t e, *v.* Same as kta.

k t e, *v. a. to kill* anything—wakte, yakte, uŋktepi, makte, nikte, ćikte: tin wićakte, *to kill one of one's own people, commit murder;* akićita kte, *to kill as a soldier,* that is, *to execute a sentence on* one, by breaking his gun, cutting up his blanket or tent, or killing his horse. See kaṭa.

k t e′ - d a ŋ, *v. a. to overcome, be victorious over; to win, beat in gambling*—waktedaŋ, uŋktepidaŋ; *to be overcome*—maktedaŋ. See ohiya.

k t e - k i′ - y a, *v. a. to cause to kill*—ktewakiya.

k t o, *adv. why? what of it?* This is chiefly used in answering questions; as, hećanoŋ he, *didst thou do it?* haŋ hećamoŋ, kto, *yes, I did it; why?—perhaps; indeed; yes;* miye kto, *it is I indeed. T.,* kiśto.

k t o′ - k a, *adv. T. indeed, surely: i. q.* kto.

k u, *suffix pron. his, hers,* etc.

k u, *v. n. to come towards home, to be coming home; to be coming back*—waku, yaku, uŋkupi. See u *and* hdi.

k u′ - ć e - d a ŋ, *adv. low, low down, near the ground:* wi̧ kućedaŋ, *the sun is low.* See kutaŋhaŋ.

k u′ - ć e - e - d a ŋ, *adv. low down: i. q.* kućedaŋ. *T.,* kućiyela.

k u′ - ć e - y e - d a ŋ, **k u′ - t e - y e - d a ŋ**, *and* **k u′ - ć e - y e - n a**, *adv. low down, low of stature, short*

k u - k a′, *adj. rotten, tender, worn out,* as clothes; *spoiled,* as meat.

k u - k e′ - y a, *v. a. to make rotten, to wear out*—kukewaya.

k u - k e′ - y a, *adv. rotten, spoiled, decayed, fallen to pieces:* kukeya śpaŋ, *to be cooked too much.*

k u - k u′ - ś e, *n. a hog, hogs; pork.*

k u - k u′ - ś e - i - h d i, *n. hog's lard.*

k u - k u′ - ś e - ś i ŋ, *n. fat pork, pickled pork.*

k u - k u′ - y a, *adv. red.* of kuya; *under, below.*

k u n, *adv. below, under, beneath, down:* kun ku, *come down.*

k u ŋ, *v. T. to covet: i. q.* koŋ.

k u ŋ, *n. mother-in-law:* nikuŋ, *thy mother-in-law;* kuŋku, *his* or *her mother-in-law.* See uŋći.

k u ŋ′ - k ś i - t k u *and* **k u ŋ′ - k i - ś i - t k u**. See kuŋśi.

k u ŋ′ - l a, *v. T. to desire, to covet*—wakuŋla.

k u ŋ s - y a′, *adv.* of kuŋza; *pretending.*

k u ŋ s - y a′ - k e n, *adv. pretending.*

k u ŋ′ - ś i, *n. grandmother:* nikuŋśi, *thy grandmother;* kuŋśitku, kuŋkśitku, *and* kuŋkiśitku, *his* or *her grandmother.* See uŋći.

k u ŋ′ - t k i - y a, *adv. downwards.* See kutkiya.

k u ŋ′ - t k u ŋ - t a, *adj. T. grooved.* See koŋtkoŋta.

k u ŋ - y a′, *v. a. to have for mother-in-law*—kuŋwaya.

kuŋ'-za, *v.* Same as koŋza.

ku-se', *v. n.* *to leak*, as a vessel.

ku-śde'-ća, *n.* *the king-fisher.*

Ku-śde'-ća-wa-kpa, *n. p.* *the Loup fork of the Platte River.*

ku-śe'-ya, *v. a.* *T.* *to put in the way of.*

ku-śe'-ya, *adv.* *T.* *in the way of:* *i. q.* kaśeya.

kuś-ku'-źa-pi, *adj.* *red. pl.* of kuźa.

ku'-taŋ-haŋ, *adv.* *low down.* See kućedaŋ *and* kuyataŋhaŋ.

ku-te', *v. a.* *to shoot* anything with a gun or arrow; *to shoot at;* wakute tuka wao śni, *I shot at it but did not hit it:* *to shoot* with the medicine-bag. When a person is introduced into the secret society called "the Sacred Dance," he is shot, or pretended to be shot, by the beads or claws which are contained in the medicine-bags of the members. When the missile is extracted by the same conjuring process, and not until then, do they live again. This is their story—wakute, uŋkutepi, ćićute: wićawakute, *I shoot them;* kikute, *to shoot for* one; kićićutepi, *they shoot each other.*

ku'-te-ye-daŋ, *adv.* Same as kućeyedaŋ. *T.*, kućiyela.

ku'-tki-ya, *adv.* *downwards.* See kuŋtkiya.

ku'-wa, *v. imp.* *come here:* kuwa wo, kuwa po. This is used in the imperative only.

ku'-wa, *v. a.* *to follow after, chase, hunt,* as, siŋkpe kuwa, *to hunt musk-rats; to chase, pursue,* as kuwa amau, *he chases me; to treat* or *act towards* one, as taŋyaŋ kuwa, *to treat well,* śićaya kuwa, *to treat ill, persecute; to pursue, prosecute,* as work—wakuwa, uŋkuwapi. See kićuwa.

ku-wa'-ćiŋ, *v.* *to think of coming home.*

ku-wa'-śte-śte, *v.* *to hop.* See ipsića *and* psipsića.

ku'-ya, *adv.* *below, beneath, under, underneath, down.* See kukuya *and* kun.

ku'-ya-taŋ-haŋ, *adv.* *from below.* See kutaŋhaŋ.

ku'-źa, *adj.* *lazy, idle*—makuźa, nikuźa.

ku'-źa, *v. n.* *T.* *to be dumpish, sick;* sometimes said of one about to die; waŋna kuźa, *now he is slow:* makuźa, *I am sick.*

ku-zi'-ṭa, *v.* *to die* or *be dying of laziness, to be very lazy*—kuźimaṭa.

Ḳ.

ḳ, *the thirteenth letter of the Dakota alphabet.* This sound is made by fixing the organs so as to make "k," and then pressing the back part of the tongue against the roof of the mouth and withdrawing it suddenly, which makes what may be denominated a *click.* The other consonants of this class are ç, p, ṭ.

ḳa, *conj.* *and* When "a" *or* "aŋ" final in words immediately preceding is changed into "e," "ḳa" becomes "ça." *T.*, na.

ḳa, *v. a.* *to dig,* as the ground—waḳa, yaḳa, uŋḳapi; içiça, *to dig for one's self*—miçiça; kiçiça, *to dig for* another—weçiça.

ḳa-aś', *adv.* *even if, indeed.* *T.*, ḳeyaś.

ḳa-eś', *adv.* *even if.*

ḳa-eś'-toś, *adv.* *at any rate.* *T*, ḳeyaśtoś.

ḳa'-iś, *conj.* *or.*

ḳaś, *adv.* *even:* hee ḳaś, *even that one.* *T.*, ḳeś.

ḳe, *v. a.* *to dig.* Same as ḳa.

ḳe, *adv.* *as for:* he ḳe, *as for that.* Perhaps it is used for emphasis. *T.*, ḳeś.

ḳe'-ća, *intj.* expressive of unbelief; *indeed!* *T.*, kakeśa.

ḳe'-ġa, *v.* *to grate, scrape.* See boḳeġa.

ḳe-haŋ', *adv.* *when.* This always refers to past time. It becomes çehaŋ after "e" which has taken the place of "a" or "aŋ." *T.*, ḳoŋhaŋ.

ḳeḣ, *cont.* of ḳeġa.

ḳeḣ-ḳe'-ġa, *v.* *red.* of ḳeġa; *scraping along.*

ḳeḣ-ḳeḣ', *cont.* of ḳeḣḳeġa; ḳeḣḳeḣ ya, *to go scraping along.*

ḳeḣ-ḳeḣ'-ya, *adv.* *in a scraping manner:* ḳeḣḳeḣya mda, *I go scraping along.*

ḳel, *adv.* *T.* *there; i. q.* kiŋ el: maḣpiya ḳel, *in the heavens.*

ḳes, *cont.* of ḳeza.

ḳes-ḳe'-za, *adj.* *red.* of ḳeza; *smooth, trodden down.* See onaḳeza.

ḳeś, *adv.* emphatic; miye ḳeś, *as for me.* See ḳe.

ḳe'-ya, *adv.* *even, all; that kind, i. q.* kiŋ eya: heća ḳeya maḳu, *he gave me of that kind.*

ḳe'-yaś, *adv.* *although, so, even so.* See ḳaaś.

ḳe-yaś'-toś, *adv.* *at any rate, even if.* See ḳaeśtoś.

ḳe'-za, *adj.* *hard, smooth, trodden hard.*

ḳiŋ, *v. a.* *to carry, bear, carry on the back,* usually with a strap round the head or breast—waḳiŋ, yaḳiŋ, uŋḳiŋpi; kiçiŋ, *to carry one's own:* kiçiçiŋ, *to carry for* another.

ḳiŋ-ki′-ya, *v. a.* *to cause to carry*—ḳiŋwakiya.

ḳiŋ′-na-pa, *v.* *T.* of ḳiŋ *and* napa; *to run away with*, as a horse with a wagon.

ḳo′-ġa, *v. n.* *to rattle, make a rattling noise.*

ḳoh, *cont.* of ḳoġa; ḳoh iyeya.

ḳoh-ḳo′-ġa, *v.* *red.* of ḳoġa.

ḳoh-ḳoh′, *cont.* of ḳohḳoġa.

ḳoh-ḳoh′-ya, *v.* *to cause a rattling noise*—ḳohḳohwaya.

ḳoh-ḳoh′-ya, *adv.* *rattling.*

ḳoŋ, *pron. dem.* *that.* Both ḳoŋ *and* ćiḳoŋ refer to the past, to something done or said before, or to some person or thing mentioned in a previous sentence: as, wićaśta ḳoŋ, *that man;* hepe ćiḳoŋ, *I said that.* *T.*, ćoŋ is used for ćiḳoŋ.

ḳoŋ′-haŋ, *adv.* *Ih.* and *T.*, *i. q.* ḳehaŋ; *when.*

ḳu, *v. a.* *to give* anything *to* one—waḳu, yaḳu, uŋḳupi, maḳu, niću, ćiću: wićawaḳu, *I have given to them;* kiću, *to give* one *his own.*

ḳu-ki′-ya, *v.* *to cause to give*—ḳuwakiya.

ḳuŋ, *pron. dem.* Same as ḳoŋ.

ḳu′-śi, *v.* *to command to give*—ḳuwaśi.

ḳu-wa′-ćiŋ, *v.* *to be disposed to give*—ḳu waćaŋmi.

L.

l, *the fourteenth letter of the Dakota alphabet.* This letter is found only in proper names introduced into the language, and in the Titoŋwaŋ dialect, where it is used altogether for "d" and sometimes for "n." A few examples are here given.

la, *dim. termination:* *i. q.* na *and* daŋ.

la, *v.* *to demand*, *i. q.* da; kila, *i. q.* kida—wala.

lab-ya′, *adv.* *hard, difficult; much, intensely:* labya ećoŋ, *he did with might.*

la′-ka, *v.* *i. q.* daka—walaka.

la-ka′-eś, *adv.* *indeed*, *i. q.* nakaeś.

La-ko′-ta, *n. p.* *Dakota.*

la′-pa, *adj.* *smooth, level.*

la′-pe-la, *adj.* *level*, as a floor.

la-tkaŋ′, *v.* *i. q.* datkaŋ—mlatkaŋ.

la-wa′, *v* *i. q.* dawa—mlawa.

la-za′-ta, *adv.* *T.* *by the side of, behind.*

la′-za-taŋ-haŋ, *adv.* *behind, back from;* *i. q.* dazataŋhaŋ. See ilazataŋhaŋ, which should be in accord with this in its meaning.

le, *pron.* *this*, *i. q.* de.

le, *i. q.* ye, the sign of the imperative. Not so used here: the women's form for imp. sing. is "na" *or* "ye": the precative form is "ye."—W. J. C.

le-ća′-la, *adv.* *lately, a little while;* *i. q.* dećana.

le′-će-ća, *adv.* *like this, i. q.* dećeća.

le′-ćel *and* le′-ćeŋl, *adv.* *thus,* *i. q.* dećen.

le′-ći-ya, *adv.* *here: i. q.* dećiya.

le-ći′-yo-taŋ, *adv.* *in this direction, i. q.* dećiyotaŋ.

le-han′, *adv* *thus far, now; i. q.* dehan.

le-haŋ′-ke-ća, *adv.* *so long, i. q.* dehaŋkeća.

le-haŋ′-yaŋg, *adv.* *somewhere else:* lehaŋyaŋg iyaya, *he has gone off.*

le-ħiŋ′-la, *v.* *to forbid, think much of; i. q.* teħiŋda.

le-kśi′, *n.* *uncle; i. q.* dekśi.

lel *and* leŋl, *adv.* *here; i. q.* den.

le′-na, *pro.* *these; i. q.* dena.

le-na′-kel, *adv.* *so many.*

le-na′-ke-ħćiŋ, *adv.* *all these.*

le-taŋ′-haŋ, *adv.* *from this, i. q.* detaŋhaŋ.

le′-tu, *adv.* *here, i. q.* detu.

li′-la, *adv.* *very, i. q.* nina.

li-li′-ta, *adj.* *warm, hot; i. q.* didita.

lo, *particle, i. q.* do.

lo, *n.* *food.*

lo-ćiŋ′, *v. n.* *to be hungry*—lowaćiŋ.

lo-ġu′-te, *n.* *the hollow of the flank: i. q.* niġute.

lo-ksi′, *n.* *i. q.* doksi.

lo-ksu′, *n.* *the opening of the ear*

lo-li′-ħaŋ, *v.* *to prepare food, cook.*

lo-lob′-ye-la, *adj.* *soft, very soft.*

lo-lo′-pe-la, *adj.* *withered, soft, pliant, flabby.*

lo-lo′-pi-ye, *n.* *a pantry, a warehouse.* See dotopiye.

lo-te′, *n.* *i. q.* dote.

lo-waŋ′, *v.* *to sing; i. q.* dowaŋ.

lu-ha′, *v.* 2d pers. *thou hast; i. q.* duha.

lu-lu′-ta *and* o-lu′-lu-ta, *adj.* *hot: i. q.* odidita.

lus, *adv.* *swiftly;* lus ya, *to go quickly: i. q.* dus.

lu′-ta, *adj.* *scarlet; i. q.* duta.

lu′-za-haŋ, *adj.* *swift; i. q.* duzahaŋ.

M.

m, *the fifteenth letter of the Dakota alphabet.*

ma, *pron. objective; me.* It is also used with a class of neuter and adjective verbs, when it is translated by the nominative *I;* and with some nouns it is used as the possessive, *my, mine.*

ma, *or* maħ, *intj.* of calling; *look here! attend!*

ma-ća′, *n.* *the red of the morning, the aurora.*

ma′-ġa, *n.* *a cultivated spot, garden, field.*

ma-ġa′, *n.* *a goose, geese.*

ma-ġa′-ġa, *v. n.* *to be amused.*

ma-ġa′-ġa-ki-ya, *v. a.* *to amuse, comfort* one—maġaġawakiya.

ma-ġa′-ġa-ya, *v. a.* *to amuse, divert* one—maġaġawaya; maġaġaiçiya, *to amuse one's self*—maġaġamiçiya.

ma′-ġa-hu, *n.* *cornstalks.*

ma-ġa′-ksi-ća, *n.* *a duck, ducks,* the generic name.

ma-ġa′-paŋ-paŋ-na, *n.* *the brand-goose* or *brant.* So called from its peculiar voice, *i. q.* maġaśekśećadaŋ. *T.*, maġaśekśećala.

ma-ġa′-ska, *n.* *Ih.* and *T.* *a swan.*

ma-ġa′-śa-pa, *n.* (maġá *and* śapa) *the common wild goose.*

ma-ġa′-śe-kśe-ća-daŋ, *n.* *the brant.* Same as maġapaŋpaŋna. Said to be two species of the small goose.—A. L. R.

ma-ġa′-ta, *adv.* *at* or *in the field*

ma-ġa′-taŋ-ka, *n.* (maġá *and* taŋka) *the swan, swans.* Maġataŋka-ota-mde, *Swan Lake.*

Ma-ġa′-wa-kpa, *n. p.* *The Laramie River.*

ma-ġa′-żu, *n.* *rain.*

ma-ġa′-żu, *v. n.* *to rain.*

ma-ġa′-żu-ki-ya, *v. a.* *to cause to rain*—maġażuwakiya.

ma-ġa′-żu-mi-ni, *n.* *rain-water.*

ma-ġa′-żu-ya, *v. a.* *to cause to rain*—maġażuwaya.

ma-ġi′-ća-hiŋ-te, *n.* (máġa *and* kahiŋta) *a rake; a harrow.* *T.*, maħićahiŋte.

ma-ġi′-ća-mna, *n.* (máġa *and* kamna) *a hoe, hoes.*

ma-ġi′-na-ta-ke, *n.* (máġa *and* nataka) *a fence, rails.*

ma-ġi′-yu-hiŋ-te, *n.* (máġa *and* yuhiŋta) *a rake; a harrow.*

ma-ġi′-yu-mdu, *n.* (máġa *and* yumdu) *a plow.*

ma-hen′, *prep.* *within, in, into.* *T.*, mahel *and* maheŋl: mahel eoŋpa, *to put* or *place in.*

ma-hen′-uŋ-pi, *n.* *something worn within, a shirt, chemise.*

ma-hen′-wa-pa, *adv.* *inward, towards the interior.*

ma-he′-taŋ-haŋ, *adv.* *from within; on the inside.*

ma-he′-ta-taŋ-haŋ, *adv.* *from within.*

ma-he′-tu, *adv.* *within, inward, deep; i. q.* temahetu.

ma-he′-tu-ya, *adv.* *within, deep; i. q.* temahetuya.

ma-he′-tu-ya-ken, *adv.* *within.*

maħ, *intj.* of calling attention; *look here! listen!* *T.*, ma!

maħ, *cont.* of máġa *and* maġá.

maħ-a′-ka-ta, *v.* *to hoe,* as corn—maħawakata.

maħ-a′-waŋ-gla-ke-la, *n.* *T.* *the locust, grasshoppers.*

maħ-ćiŋ′-ća, *n.* (maġá *and* ćiŋća) *the young of geese* and *ducks.*

maħ-i′-ća-hiŋ-te, *n.* (máġa *and* kahiŋta) *a rake; a harrow.* See maġićahiŋte.

maħ-i′-çe, *n.* *Ih.* *a plow.*

mah-i′-kće-ka, *n.* *land, soil, common land.* See makikćeka

mah-i′-kće-ya, *adv.* *on land*, as opposed to water. See makikćeya.

mah-i′-na-ta-ke, *n.* (máġa *and* nataka) *a fence, rails.* See maġinatake.

mah-i′-yu-hiŋ-te, *n.* (máġa *and* yuhiŋta) *a rake, a harrow.* See maġiyuhiŋte.

mah-i′-yu-hiŋ-he, *n.* *Ih.* *a harrow: i. q.* iyuhiŋhe.

mah-i′-yu-mdu *n.* (máġa *and* yumdu) *a plow.*

mah-ki′-ćaŋ-yaŋ, *v.* (máġa *and* kićaŋyaŋ) *to work* or *till a field.*

mah-pa′-źo, *n.* (máġa *and* paźo) *a corn-hill, potato-hill.*

ma-hpi′-hpi-ya, *n* *red.* of mahpiya; *scattering clouds.*

ma-hpi′-ya, *n.* *the clouds; the sky; heaven, the heavens.*

ma-hpi′-ya-śa-pa, *n.* *black clouds.*

ma-hpi′-ya-śo-ka, *n.* *thick clouds.*

ma-hpi′-ya-śpu-śpu, *n.* *long broken clouds.*

ma-hpi′-ya-taŋ-iŋ, *n.* *T.* *northern lights, aurora borealis.*

Ma-hpi′-ya-to, *n. p.* *The Arapahoes.*

ma-hpi′-ya-to, *n.* *the blue sky.*

ma-hpi′-ya-to-la, *n.* *T.* *clear sky, blue sky: i. q.* mahpiyatowaŋźića.

ma-hpi′-ya-to-waŋ-źi-ća, *n.* *the blue sky, the firmament.*

mah-ta′-ni, *n.* *an old field.* See taŋni, taŋnika, etc.

mah-te′-ća, *n.* (máġa *and* teća) *a new field; a breaking.*

ma-ka′, *n.* *ground, earth; the earth; a season, a half year*, as a summer or winter. See omaka. Considerable discussion has taken place in regard to the proper pronunciation of this word Some say it should be written maŋ-ka′; but it appears rather to be ma-k'a′.

ma-ka′, *n.* *the skunk* or *polecat, Viverra mephitis.* See maŋka.

ma-ka′-a-ma-ni, *adv.* *T.* *afoot: i. q.* huiŋyuŋ.

ma-ka′-ća-hli, *n.* *T.* *coal: i. q.* kaŋġitame.

ma-ka′-će-ġa, *n.* *an earthen vessel* or *pot*, such as the Dakotas are said to have made and used before their intercourse with white people.

ma-ka′-da-pa, *n.* *sticky clay.*

ma-ka′-ġi, *n.* *brown earth.* Makaġiyuzapi, the name of a stream emptying into the Minnesota from the west, below Big Stone Lake.

ma-ka′-hde, *adv.* *end on the ground.* Same as makehde.

ma-ka′-he-ya, *v. a.* *to have a desire to kill* or *destroy, to think that one will kill, have a presentiment of killing* or *destroying.* *T.* *to finally accomplish what one has long desired.* See ćaŋhiya.

ma-ka′-htaŋ-ya, *v. a.* *to kill* or *destroy very much*—makahtaŋwaya.

ma-ka′-i-wa-za, *v.* *T.* *to paw*

up the ground, as a horse or mad bull.

m a - k a′ - i - y u - t a, *v.* *to measure land, survey.*

m a - k a′ - i - y u - t a - p i, *n.* *a measuring-chain, surveyor's chain: an acre of ground.*

m a - k a n′, *adv.* (maka *and* akan) *on the ground:* makan iwaŋka, *to sleep on the ground.*

m a - k a ŋ′, *n.* *tamarack roots.*

m a - k a ŋ′ - o - p i - y e, *n.* *a basket* Probably so called because the Dakotas supposed that willow baskets were made of *tamarack roots. T.*, psawognake.

m a - k a′ - o - b a - ś p e, *n.* *an acre of ground. T.*, 160 *acres.*

m a - k a′ - o - b o - ḣ p e, *n.* *a survey mound.*

m a - k a′ - o - h a ŋ - z i, *n.* *the shading of the earth,* i. e. *dusk.*

m a - k a′ - o - i - y u - t e, *n.* *a quarter section of land. T., one acre of land.*

m a - k a′ - o - w a - k e - y a, *n* *the name of a sacred feast* and ceremonies connected with going to war; when, it is said, they carry into the tent pulverized earth, and make hills like the gophers.

m a - k a′ - p a, *n.* *a swamp*, where the surface of the earth lies on water. *T.*, wiwila kapaŋpaŋ.

m a - k a - p a′, *n.* *a skunk's head.*

m a - k a′ - s a ŋ, *n.* *whitish* or *yellowish clay.*

m a - k a′ - s a ŋ - p a, *n.* *next year, next season.*

m a - k a′ - s i ŋ - t o - m n i, *adv.* See makasitomni.

m a - k a′ - s i - t o - m n i, *adv.* *all the world over.* See makowaŋća.

m a - k a′ - s i - t o - m n i - y a ŋ, *adv.* *the world over.* See makowaŋćaya.

m a - k a′ - t a, *adv.* *at the ground, on the ground, on the floor:* makata muŋka, *I lie on the ground.*

m a - k a′ - t o, *n.* *blue earth.* Makatooze, *the Makato* or *Blue Earth River:* The original form was Makato-yuza.

m a - k a′ - w a - k ś i - ć a, *n.* *earthen plates* or *dishes.* See wakśića.

m a - k a′ - w a - s e, *n.* *T.* *red earth* used as paint.

m a - k a′ - w a - ś e - ś a, *n.* *red earth,* used by the Dakotas as a paint instead of vermillion; *i. q.* wase. *T.*, makawase.

m a - k e′ - h d e, *adv.* *on end:* ćaŋpeśka makehde inaźiŋ, *to kneel.* Same as makahde. *T.*, makagle.

m a - k e′ - h d e - y a, *v. n.* *to fall down*, as a long stick, *endwise:* caŋpeśka makehdeya inaźiŋ, *to kneel.*

m a - k i′ - ć i - m a, *n.* *T.* (maka *and* ićima) *last year; a yearling*, as a colt or other animal.

m a - k i′ - ć i - n o ŋ, *v.* of manoŋ; *to steal* anything *for* another—mawećinoŋ; mauŋkićinoŋpi, *they steal from each other.*

m a - k i′ - k ć e, *n.* See makikćeka.

m a - k i′ - k ć e - k a, *n.* *the land,* as opposed to water; *soil*, as opposed to clay or gravel. See maḣikćeka.

ma-ki'-kće-ya, *adv.* *on land.* See mahikćeya.

ma-ki'-na-śpe, *n.* *a spade.* See makipapte.

ma-ki'-noŋ, *v.* of manoŋ; *to steal* anything *from* one—mawakinoŋ, mayakinoŋ.

ma-ki'-pa-pte, *n.* *T.* *a spade.* See makinaśpe.

ma-ki'-pu-sdi, *adv.* (maka *and* ipusdi) *with the face on the ground, prostrate, prone.*

ma-ki'-pu-sdi-ya, *adv.* *bowed down to the ground.*

ma-ki'-pu-ski-ća, *v. n.* (maka *and* ipuskića) *to presson the ground, lie flat on the ground, lick the dust.*

ma-ki'-pu-skin, *cont.* of makipuskića; makipuskin ehpeićiya, *to throw one's self on the ground.*

ma-ki'-saŋ-pa, *n.* *the next season, i q.* makasaŋpa.

ma-ki'-waŋ-ya-ke, *n.* *a compass; a surveyor.*

ma-ki'-ya-ka-saŋ-ni, *n.* *a side* or *part of a country.* See iyakasaŋni.

ma-ki'-yu-taŋ, *n.* (maku *and* iyutaŋ) *a saddle girth.*

ma-ki'-yu-ṭiŋ-za, *n.* *a surcingle, girth.*

ma-ko'-će, *n.* *a country, a place:* makoćaźeyate wanića, *a place without a name;* mitamakoće, *my country.* *T.* also, *a season, a year, a time of year.*—W. J. C. See omaka.

ma-ko'-će-i-waŋ-ya-ka-pi, *n.* *T.* *surveyors.*

ma-ko'-će-o-wa-pi, *n.* *a map, maps.* See makowapi.

ma-ko'-hdo-ka, *n.* *a hole in the ground, a cave, cavern.*

ma-koŋ'-ća-ġe, *n.* *a season, the seasons.*

ma-ko'-skan, *n.* *a place where no one dwells, a desert place.* See hewoskan, etc.

ma-ko'-skaŋ, *adv.* *Ih.* and *T.* *for naught, in vain; i. q.* ituya. See otumakoskaŋ.

ma-ko'-skan-tu, *adv.* *in a desert place.*

ma-ko'-skan-tu-ya, *adv.* *away from any dwelling, away on the prairie.*

ma-ko'-skan-tu-ya-ken, *adv.* *in a desert place.*

ma-ko'-sma-ka, *n.* (maka *and* osmaka) *any low place, a ditch.*

ma-ko'-śi-ća, *n.* *any prevalent disease, an epidemic,* as the smallpox; *i. q.* makoće śića.

ma-ko'-ta-he-daŋ, *adv.* (maka *and* otahedaŋ) *away from any dwelling, in the desert, on the prairie.* See hewotahedaŋ.

ma-ko'-wa-ki-ċi-pa, *n.* *a place a little hollowing, a slight hollow* or *depression in the prairie.*

ma-ko'-waŋ-ća, *n.* *all the earth.* See makasitomni.

ma-ko'-waŋ-ća-ya, *adv.* *all over the earth.* See makasitomniyaŋ.

ma-ko′-wa-pi, *n.* *a map of a country, maps.*

ma-ku′, *n.* *the breast, the forepart of the thorax.*

ma-ku′-a-gna-ke, *n.* *T.* *an apron.* See ahnaka.

ma-ku′-a-ka-ȟpe, *n.* *an apron, a woman's kerchief.* *T.*, makuagnake.

ma-ku′-hu, *n.* *the breast-bone, sternum.*

ma-ku′-i-yu-ski-te, *n.* *a child's swaddling-band.*

ma-ku′-i-yu-taŋ, *n.* *a girth; i. q.* makiyutaŋ.

ma-ma′, *n.* *a woman's breast, milk; mamma* or *mother.* It is a singular fact that with the Dakotas, mama means *milk*, and papa, *meat.*

ma′-ni, *v. n.* *to walk*—mawani, mayani.

ma-ni′-ća, *n.* *the gopher, a species of Diplostoma.* *T*, wahiŋheya.

ma-ni′-ća, *v. n.* 1st pers. sing. of nića; *I have none*—ninića.

ma-ni′-ća-pa-mdu, *n.* *gopher-hills.* *T.*, wahiŋheya pablu.

ma′-ni-haŋ, *part.* *walking.*

ma′-ni-ken, *adv.* *walking.*

ma′-ni-ki-ya, *v. a.* *to cause to walk*—maniwakiya.

ma-nin′, *adv.* *abroad, away from the house.* *T.*, manil.

ma′-ni-ni-na, *n.* *bed-bugs, i. q.* taku mani nina. *T.*, wabluśkaśaśa.

ma′-ni-sku-ya, *n.* *a species of plant;* prob. *the honeysuckle.* *T.*, ćaŋwiskuye.

ma-noŋ′, *v. a.* *to steal* anything—mawanoŋ, mayanoŋ, mauŋnoŋpi. This is by some written manu.

ma-noŋ′-pi, *n.* *a stealing, theft.*

ma-nu′, *or* ma-nuŋ′, *v.* See manoŋ.

maŋ, *intj.* *look here!* See ma *and* maȟ.

maŋ, *v.* *to build a nest and hatch young ones*, as birds do; *to fly about, hover, sail around,* as birds over a carcass. See amaŋ *and* be.

maŋ, *adj.* *sharp, i. q.* pe. See yumaŋ.

maŋ-ća′, *n.* *the aurora.* *T.*, haŋwakaŋ. See maća.

maŋ-ka′, *n.* *a skunk.* See maka.

maŋ-ka′, *v. n.* 1st per. sing. of yaŋká.

mas′-ćaŋ-ya-pa, *n.* *T.* (maza, ćaŋ, *and* yapa) *bridle bits.*

mas-će′-ġa, *n.* See mazaćeġa.

mas-i′-gmuŋ-ke, *n.* *T.* *a trap: i. q.* mazaȟtakiyapi.

mas-wa′-kśi-ća, *n.* *tin plates: i. q.* mazawakśića.

mas-i′-waŋ-ya-ke, *n.* *T.* *a telescope, a microscope.*

ma-śte′, *adj.* *warm, hot,* applied to the weather; maśte ȟiŋća, *very warm:* maśte au, *it becomes warm,* said of the sky clearing off.

ma-śte′-a-gle-haŋ, *n.* *T.* *sunstroke.*

ma-śte′-i-ṭa, *v. n.* *to be killed by heat; to be struck by the sun.*

ma-śte′-na-pta-pta, *n.* *hot waving air,* as on a hot day.

m a - ś t e′ - o - s n i, *n.* *clear and cold; cold and bright.*

m a - ś t e′ - ś t e, *adj.* *red.* of maśte.

m a - ś t e′ - y a, *adv.* *in a warm state, warmly.*

m a - ś t e′ - y a - k e n, *adv.* *warmly, hotly.*

m a - ś t i ŋ′ - ć a, *n.* *the rabbit, Lepus cuniculus:* tinmaśtiŋća, *the prairie rabbit* or *hare.* *T.*, maśtiŋćala.

M a - ś t i ŋ′ - ć a, *n.* *the Cree Indians.*

m a - ś t i ŋ′ - ć a - l a, *n.* *T.* *the rabbit.*

m a - ś t i ŋ′ - p u - t e, *n.* *a bush bearing red edible berries*, the leaves of which are sometimes used by the Dakotas for tobacco: *the berries* themselves, *the buffalo berry*, or *rabbit berry.*

m a - t a′ - p i - ḣ a, *n.* *T.* *a toad.* See natapeḣa.

m a - t a′ - w a - z e - z e - ć a, *n.* *moss.*

m a - t e′ - t e, *n.* of tete; *the side* or *rim* of a boat, *the part near the edge; a brow* or *projection*, as of a hill. See watete.

m a - t k a′, *n.* *sticky earth.* See maka *and* tkapa.

m a - t k a′, *n.* *T.* *the opossum.*

m a - t k a′ - ś a, *n.* *red earth.*

m a - t o′, *n.* *the gray* or *polar bear, Ursus maritimus.*

m a - t o′ - ḣ o - t a, *n.* *the grizzly bear*, a species of the *Ursus Americanus.*

m a - t u′ - ś k a, *n.* *the craw-fish.*

M a - w a′ - t a - d a ŋ, *n.* *the Mandan Indians.* *T.*, Miwatani.

M a - w a′ - t a ŋ - n a, *n.* Same as Mawatadaŋ.

m a - y a′, *n.* *a steep place, a bank*, as of a river.

m a - y a′, *adj.* *steep:* maya ḣiŋća, *very steep.* *T.*, mayaḣćake.

M a - y a′ - w a - k a ŋ, *n.* *the Chippewa River* which joins the Minnesota, from the north, about fifteen miles below Lac-qui-parle.

m a′ - z a, *n.* *metal* of any kind; *goods, merchandise.*

m a′ - z a - a - s p e - i - ç i - y e, *n.* (maza *and* aspeya) *an anchor.* *T.*, wataićaspe.

m a′ - z a - b l a - s k a - p e - s t o - l a, *n.* *T.* (maza, mdaska, *and* pesto) *a sharp-pointed shovel.*

m a′ - z a - ć a ḣ - i - ć a - z o, *n.* *T.* (maza, ćaġa, *and* ićazo) *skates.*

m a′ - z a - ć e - ġ a, *n.* (maza *and* ćeġa) *an iron pot* or *kettle.* Generally ćeġa alone is used.

m a′ - z a - ć e ś - k i - k a, *n.* *T* *metal buttons.*

m a′ - z a - h u - h u, *n.* (maza *and* huhu) *bracelets, arm-bands.* *T.*, napoktaŋ.

m a′ - z a - ḣ d a - ḣ d a, *n.* *a bell.*

m a′ - z a - ḣ t a - k i - y a - p i, *n.* (maza *and* ḣtaka) *"biting iron": a trap, traps, steel-traps*, such as are used in catching the otter, etc. *T.*, ćabigmuŋke.

m a′ - z a - ć a ŋ - k u, *n.* *T.* (maza *and* ćaŋku) *a railroad.*

m a′ - z a - i - ć a - k o - k e, *n.* *a cow-bell.* Commonly used with the "maza." See ićakoke.

m a′ - z a - i - ć a - s n a, *n.* *a cow-bell.*

m a′-z a-i-ći-ća-ħi-ħ a, *n.* *iron in links, a chain.* *T.*, mazaićićaħaħa

m a′-z a-i-ću, *n.* *a gun-screw*, the spiral wire which is used to draw wadding from a gun.

m a′-z a-i-y o-k a-t a ŋ, *n.* (maza *and* iyokataŋ) *nails.*

m a′-z a-i-y o-k a-t k u-ġ e, *n.* *a nail, nails.* *T.*, *a nut, iron nuts for bolts.* See, also, tiyopa iyokatkuġe *and* iyokatkuġe.

m a′-z a-i-y u-t a-p i, *n.* (maza *and* iyuta) *a steel-yard; an iron square.* *T.*, mazawiyute.

m a′-z a-k a-ġ a, *n.* (maza *and* kaġa) *a worker in metal, a blacksmith.* *Ih.*, mazkape.

m a′-z a-k a ŋ, *n.* (maza *and* wakaŋ) *a gun* See mazawakaŋ.

m a′-z a-k a ŋ-ć e-ć a, *n.* *the butt of a gun:* also *the gun hammer.* *T.*, mazawakaŋ śupute See ćeća.

m a′-z a-k a ŋ-e-ć o ŋ *and* m a′-z a-k a ŋ-i-y e-y a, *v.* *to shoot a gun;* mazakaŋ bośdoka, *to fire off a gun.* *T.*, mazawakaŋ uta.

m a′-z a-k a ŋ-i-n o ŋ-p a, *n.* (mazakaŋ, i, *and* noŋpa) *a double-barreled gun.*

m a′-z a-k a ŋ-i-y o-p a-z a ŋ, *n.* *the tubes* or *ferrules which hold in the ramrod.; the ramrod.* See iyopazaŋ.

m a′-z a-k a ŋ-i-y o-p u-ħ d i, *n.* *gun-wadding.* See iyopuħdi.

m a′-z a-k a ŋ-i-y o-p u-s k i-ć e, *n.* *a ramrod.* *T.*, mazawakaŋ iyopazaŋ. See iyopuskića.

m a′-z a-k a ŋ-n a-w a-t e, *n.* *the plate of a gun-lock.* See nawate.

m a′-z a-k a ŋ-n o-ġ e, *n.* *a gun-lock*, especially the *pan; the nipple.* See noġe.

m a′-z a-k a ŋ-n o-ġ e-y u-ħ p a, *n.* (mazakaŋ, noġe, *and* iyuħpa) *the whole of a gun-lock.*

m a′-z a-k a ŋ-o-y u-w i, *n.* *the inside work of a gun-lock.* See yuwi.

m a′-z a-k a ŋ-p a-h u, *n.* *the breech of a gun.* See pahu.

m a′-z a-k a ŋ-p t e-ć e-d a ŋ, *n.* (mazakaŋ *and* ptećedaŋ) *a short gun, a pistol* *T.*, mazawakaŋ ptećela: also iśakpe *and* hutela.

m a′-z a-k a ŋ-t a ŋ-k a, *n.* (mazakaŋ *and* taŋka) *a great gun, a cannon.* *T.*, mazawakaŋ taŋka.

m a′-z a-k i ŋ-ś k a, *n.* *T.* *an iron spoon, spoons:* *i. q.* mazkiŋśka.

m a′-z a-m d a-s k a, *n.* (maza *and* mdaska) *flat iron; a spade, shovel*, etc. *T.*, mazablaska.

m a′-z a-n a-p ć u-p e, *n.* *finger-rings.* *T.*, maza napsioħli. See napćupe.

m a′-z a-o-ć e-t i, *n.* *an iron fire-place, a stove.* See oćeti.

m a′-z a-o-k a-z e-z e, *n.* *skates:* maza okazeze kiçuŋ, *to skate.* *T.*, mazaćaħićazo. See okaze.

m a′-z a-s a g-y e, *n.* *an iron cane, a sword.* *T.*, miwakaŋ *and* miwakaŋla.

m a′-z a-s a-p a, *n.* (maza *and* sapa) *black metal, iron.*

ma'-za-ska, *n.* (maza *and* ska) *white metal, silver; money; a dollar.*

ma'-za-ska-haŋ-ke, *n.* *a half-dollar.* *T.*, mazaska okise. See haŋke.

ma'-za-ska-ka-śpa-pi-daŋ, *n.* *a twelve-and-a-half* or *ten-cent piece, a shilling, dime.* *T.*, kaśpapi. See kaśpapidaŋ.

ma'-za-ska-mi-ni-ħu-ha, *n.* *bank notes.* *T.*, miniħuha mazaska. See miniħuha.

ma'-za-ska-taŋ-ka, *n.* *a dollar.* *T.*, mazaska waŋźina.

ma'-za-ska-wa-na-piŋ, *n.* *a silver medal.* See wanapiŋ.

ma'-za-ska-zi, or ma'-za-ska-ma-za-zi, *n.* *yellow silver, gold.*

ma'-za-su, *n.* *lead; a bullet, bullets.*

ma'-za-su-i-śdo-ye, *n.* (maza, su, *and* iśdoye) *something to melt lead in.* See śdoya.

ma'-za-su-i-yo-ka-śtaŋ, *n* (maza, su, *and* iyokaśtaŋ) *bullet-molds.* See okaśtaŋ.

ma-za-śa, *n.* *red metal, copper.*

ma'-za-śdo-ya-pi, *n.* *pewter,* so called because used for running on the bowls of Dakota pipes.

ma'-za-śkaŋ-śkaŋ, *n.* *T.* (maza *and* śkaŋśkaŋ) *a clock; a watch.*

ma'-za-śko-pa, *n.* (maza *and* śkopa) *a concave medal for the neck,* used as the badge of a soldier.

ma'-za-ta-śpu, *n.* *metal buttons.* *T.*, mazaćeśkika. See taśpu.

ma'-za-ta-śpu-daŋ, *n.* *metal buttons.* See taśpudaŋ.

ma'-za-tu-ki-ha, *n.* *an iron* or *metal spoon.* *Ih.* and *T.*, mazkiŋśka. See tukiha.

ma'-za-wa-kaŋ, *n.* *a gun.* See mazakaŋ.

ma'-za-wa-kaŋ-u-ta, *v.* *T.* *to shoot off a gun.*

ma'-za-wa-kśi-ća, *n.* *tin* or *iron pans.* See wakśića.

ma'-za-wi-yu-te, *n.* *a carpenter's square.*

ma'-za-ya-ho-toŋ-pi, *n.* (maza *and* yahotoŋ) *a trumpet.*

ma'-za-ya-piŋ-za-pi, *n.* *brass instruments.*

ma'-za-ya-źo-pi, *n.* *brass instruments.*

ma'-za-zi, *n.* *yellow metal, brass.*

maz'-ćaŋ-ya-pa, *n.* *T.* (maza, ćaŋ, *and* yapa) *bridle-bits: i. q.* masćaŋyapa.

maz-i'-gmuŋ-ke, *n.* *T.* *a trap.*

ma-zi'-pa-be, *n.* (maza *and* ipabe) *a file.* *T.*, mazipame.

maz-i'-pa-bla-pi *and* mas-i'-pa-bla-pi, *n.* *T.* *sad-irons, flat-irons.*

maz-i'-pa-mda-ye, *n.* *sad-irons.* See pamdaya.

ma-zi'-ya-p'e, *n.* (maza *and* iya-p'a) *a hammer.*

ma-zi'-yu-be, *n.* *a file: i. q.* mazipabe. *T.*, maziyume.

maz'-i-yu-wi, *n.* (maza *and* iyuwi) *T.* *bridle-bits.*

ma-zi'-yu-źi-pe, *n.* (maza *and* iyuźipe) *pincers; tongs.* *T.*, ima-soyuspe.

m a z - k a′ - p ' e, *n.* (maza *and* kap'a) *Ih. a blacksmith.* See mazakaġa.

m a z - k i ŋ′ - ś k a, *n. Ih.* and *T. an iron spoon.* See kiŋśka.

m a z - o ŋ′ - s p e, *n.* (maza *and* oŋspe) *an ax.*

m a z - o′ - p i - y e, *n. a store, a store-house.* See opiye.

m a z - y u′ - h a, *n. T. a chief.* See naća.

m d a, *v.* 1st pers. sing. of ya; *I go.*

m d a, *a prefix.* Verbs commencing with "ya" change it into "mda" to form the first person singular, and into "da" for the second; for which the corresponding Teeton words are "bla" *and* "la."

m d a. See kamda.

m d a - ḣ a′, *adj. broad at one end, tapering.*

m d a - m d a′ - t a, *n. high level land, the divide* or *high land between two streams. T.*, blowaŋźila.

m d a s, *cont.* of mdaza.

m d a - s k a′, *adj. flat,* as, ćaŋ mdaska, *boards; broad at one end. T.*, blaska. See omdaska.

m d a - s k a′ - s k a, *adj. red.* of mdaska.

m d a - s k a′ - y a, *adv. flatly, on the flat side.* See omdaskaya.

m d a′ - y a, *adj. level, plain. T.*, oblaya. See omdaya.

m d a′ - y e, *n. a plain. T.*, oblaye. See omdaye.

m d a′ - y e - d a ŋ, *adj. level, plain. T.*, oblayela.

m d a′ - y e - y a, *adv. evenly. T.*, oblayeya.

m d a - z a′, *adv. in strips.* See bamdaza.

m d a - z a′ - h a ŋ, *part. ripped open of itself, torn open.*

m d a - z a′ - w a - h a ŋ, *part.* Same as mdazahaŋ.

m d e, *n. a lake. T.*, ble.

m d e - ć a′, *adj. broken.* See kamdeća *and* ómdeća.

m d e - ć a′ - h a ŋ, *part. broken of itself.*

m d e - ć a′ - ḣ m i ŋ, *n.* (mde *and* kaḣmiŋ) *a bay. T.*, bleokaḣmiŋ.

m d e - ć a′ - w a - h a ŋ, *part. broken of itself.*

m d e′ - d a ŋ, *n. a little lake, a pond.*

m d e′ - ġ a, *n. the pelican.*

M d e′ - h d a - k i ŋ - y a ŋ, *n. p.* (mde *and* hdakiŋyaŋ) *Lac Travers, Lake Traverse;* so called from its lying in a direction crosswise to Big Stone Lake.

M d e - i - y e′ - d a ŋ, *n. Lac-qui-parle.* This word was evidently supposed by the French to mean *the talking lake.* If that be the meaning, it is not apparent why the name was given. It is suggested that it is "mde iyahde," changed into "mdeiyedaŋ," referring to the fact that the river *is connected by the lake.*

m d e - k i′ - y u - t e, *n.* (mde *and* kiyute) *an isthmus; a strait* or *channel* in a lake.

m d e - m d e′ - ć a, *adj. red* of mdeća.

m d e - m d e′ - ć a - h a ŋ, *part. red.* of mdećahaŋ.

m d e - m d e′ - ć a - w a - h a ŋ, *part. red.* of mdećawahaŋ.

m d e - m d e s' - y a, *v. red.* of mdesya; mdemdesiçiya, *to amuse* or *regale one's self.*

M d e - m i' - n i - s o - t a, *n. Clear Lake,* which lies about thirty-five miles from Traverse des Sioux, on the old road to Lac-qui-parle.

m d e s, *cont.* of mdeza.

m d e - s a', *adj. clear, not fuddled:* mdesa wauŋ, *I am not drunk.* See mdeza.

m d e - s a' - h a ŋ, *part. clear-sighted, clearly.*

m d e s - y a', *v. a. to make clear, cause to recover from stupidity*—mdeswaya.

m d e s - y a', *adv. clearly.*

m d e s - y a' - k e n, *adv. clearly.*

m d e - t a ŋ' - h u ŋ - k a, *n. a leader of a war party* or *any other party. T.,* blotaŋhuŋka. See zuyećiŋ.

m d e - y a', *n.* Mdeyataŋka, *Otter-tail Lake.*

m d e - y a' - t a, *adv. at the lake.* This is used by the Dakotas in referring to Lake Superior, which they used to visit.

m d e' - z a, *adj. clear; clear-sighted,* as, iśta mdeza; *sober*—mamdeza, nimdeza. See mdesa.

m d e' - z e - d a ŋ, *adj. clear,* as water: mini mdezedaŋ, *clear water.*

m d o, *n. an esculent root* eaten by the Dakotas, in appearance and taste something like sweet potatoes, the Dakota tamdo; *potatoes,* the Waśićuŋ tamdo. *T.,* blo.

m d o, *n. a ridge* or *range of hills: T.,* blo; Waziblo owakipamni, *Pine Ridge Agency.*

m d o g - y a ŋ' - k a, *v. n. to remain at home when others go out to hunt*—mdogmaŋka, mdognaŋka, mdoguŋyaŋkapi.

m d o' - h u, *n. potato-tops.*

m d o - k a', *n. the male of animals.*

m d o - k a', *adj. male,* used only of animals, birds, etc., not of men.

m d o - k a' - s k a, *v. n. to hickup*—mdowakaska.

m d o - k a' - t a, *adv. at the water, by the shore. T.,* bleyata; hutata.

m d o - k e' - ć o - k a - y a, *n. midsummer. T.,* blokećokaŋyaŋ.

m d o - k e' - h a ŋ, *n. last summer:* mdokehaŋ ićima, *summer before last T.,* blokehaŋ.

m d o - k e' - t u, *n. summer, this summer, next summer. T.,* bloketu.

m d o - k i' - h d a - k a, *v. n. to move in the summer*—mdokiwahdaka. *T.,* bloketu ehaŋ iglaka. See ihdaka.

m d o' - k i - ṭ a, *v. n. to be tired* or *weary,* as by walking—mdowakiṭa, mdouŋkiṭapi *T.,* watuka.

m d o' - k i - ṭ e - y a, *v. a. to make tired* or *weary, to tire, weary, fatigue*—mdokiṭewaya, mdokiṭemayaŋ.

m d o' - t e, *n. the mouth* or *junction of one river with another* (a name commonly applied to the country about Fort Snelling, or mouth of the Saint Peters; also the name appropriated to the establishment of the Fur Company at the junction of the rivers, written Mendota); *the outlet of a lake. T.*, iyoḣloke.

m d o - w a ŋ′ - ź i - d a ŋ , *n. high table land; the top of a ridge. T.*, blowaŋźila: *i. q.* mdamdata.

m d o′ - z a , *n. the loon. T.*, huŋtka.

m d u , *adj. powdered, pulverized, fine:* aġuyapi mdu, *flour;* maka mdu, *dust.*

m d u - m d u′, *adj. red.* of mdu; *mellow and dry,* as apples or turnips.

m d u - m d u′, *v.* 1st pers. sing. of yumdu.

m d u - w a′ - h a ŋ , *part. crumbled down, not hard.*

m i , *pron. pos. in comp. my* or *mine; me; for me* or *to me,* as in mikte, *he kills for me.* See ni.

m i - b e′, *adj. round, circular: i. q.* mima.

m i - ć a′, *pron.* and *prep. in comp.* of kića; as in opemićatoŋ, *he buys from me. T., for me;* opemićatoŋ, *he buys for me.*—W. J. C.

m i′ - ć a , *n. a small species of wolf: cont.* for mićaksića.

m i - ć a′, *n. the lean meat on the side of an animal near the rump, the small of the back; the lean meat of the thigh.*

m i - ć a′ - h u , *n. the bone near the hip-bone.*

m i′ - ć a - ġ a , *v.* of kićaġa; *to make to* or *for me.*

m i′ - ć a - k s i - ć a , *n. a small wolf.* See mića, miyaća, *and* miyaśleća.

m i′ - ć a - p e - ć a , *n. T. i. q.* wićapeća.

m i′ - ć i , *pron.* and *prep.* of kići; *with me, for me. T.* means only *for me: e. g.*, mići uŋ, is *in my stead* or *for me: with me* is "kići mauŋ."—W. J. C. See nići *and* íći.

m i - ç i′, *pron. reflex. myself,* as, miçikte, *I kill myself; for myself,* as, miçićaġa, *I make for myself,* or *I make myself.* See niçi *and* içi.

m i - h n a g′, *cont.* of mihnaka; mihnag wauŋ.

m i - h n a′ - k a , *v. a. to put in under the girdle,* as a knife or hatchet; *to wear round the loins*—miwahnaka. *T.*, mićignaka. See miuŋpa.

m i′ - h n a - k a , *v.* of kihnaka; *he lays up for me.*

m i′ - l a , *n. T. a knife.* M i′ - l a - h a ŋ - s k a , *n. T. i. q.* Minahaŋska. See isaŋ.

m i′ - l a - p a - k s a , *n. T. a case-knife.*

m i′ - l a - p i - ś l a , *n. T. a case-knife.*

m i′ - n a , *n. Ih. a knife.*

M i′ - n a - h a ŋ - s k a , *n. Ih. long knife, an American: i. q.* Isaŋtaŋka.

m i′ - n a - y u - k ś i - ź a - p i , *n. Ih. a pocket knife. T.*, miyukśiźa.

m i′ - n i , *n. water.*

m i′ - n i - a - p a - ḣ t a , *v. T. to carry water in a skin.*

m i′ - n i - a - p a - ḣ t a , *n. a skin bottle for water.*

m i′ - n i - b o - s d i , *n. a syringe.* See miniibosdi.

m i′ - n i - b o - ṭ a , *v. n. to be drenched with water.* Said also when water comes much into a tent—minibomaṭa. *T*, miniwoṭa.

mi′-ni-bo-ḣa, *n.* *Ih.* *a gulch, a ravine made by water.* *T.*, wakogla.

mi′-ni-bo-zaŋ, *n.* *mist, fine rain.* *T.*, miniwozela.

mi′-ni-ća-du-za, *n.* *rapid water, strong current.*

mi′-ni-ća-siŋ-yaŋ, *n.* *T.* *rippling water.*

mi′-ni-ća-hda, *adv.* *by the water.*

mi′-ni-ćo-ćo, *adv.* *T.* *slushy; i. q.* waspaŋla.

mi′-ni-ḉa-pi, *n.* (mini *and* ḳa) *T.* *a well of water: i. q.* mniḉapi.

Mi′-ni-du-za, *n.* *the Saskatchawan River.*

mi′-ni-he-ća, *v. n.* *to be smart* or *active*—maminiheća, niminiheća, uŋminihećapi. *T.*, biliheća.

mi′-ni-hen-he-ća, *v.* *red.* of miniheća.

mi′-ni-hen-ya, *adv* *actively, industriously.*

mi′-ni-he-ya, *v. a.* *to make active:* miniheiḉiya, *to make one's self active, to be industrious*—minihemiḉiya. See mniheya.

mi′-ni-hiŋ-tkaŋ-ḣa-ka, *n.* *water-moss, that which grows under water.*

mi′-ni-hi-ya-ya, *n* *T.* *a flood of water.*

mi′-ni-ḣdo-ka, *n.* *a fountain* or *spring of water, a well.*

mi′-ni-ḣu-ha, *n.* *linen* or *cotton cloth, calico; paper.*

mi′-ni-ḣu-ha-ćaŋ-noŋ-pa, *n.* *a cigarette.*

mi′-ni-ḣu-ha-i-pa-tiŋ, *n.* *T.* *starch.* See patiŋ.

mi′-ni-ḣu-ha-i-yo′-wa, *n.* *T.* *a pen, pencil.* See iyowa.

mi′-ni-ḣu-ha-kaŋ-śu-ku-te-pi, *n.* *playing-cards.* See kaŋsukutepi.

mi′-ni-ḣu-ha-ma-za-ska, *n.* *T.* *paper money*

mi′-ni-ḣu-ha-o-wa-pi, *n.* *painted cloth, calico; a letter, a book.* See owapi.

mi′-ni-ḣu-ha-ska, *n.* *white cotton* or *muslin; white paper, writing paper.*

mi′-ni-ḣu-ha-ska-śo-ka, *n.* *bed-ticking.*

mi′-ni-ḣu-ha-ska-zib-zi-pe-daŋ, *n.* *fine muslin.*

mi′-ni-ḣu-ha-to-ḣća, *n.* *blue cloth* as distinguished from green.

mi′-ni-ḣu-ha-wi-yu-ma, *n.* *sand-paper.* See yumaŋ.

mi′-ni-i-bo-sdi, *n.* *a syringe; a squirt-gun.*

mi′-ni-ka-a-ta-źa, *n.* *T.* of mini *and* taźa; *waves.*

Mi′-ni-kaŋ-ye-wo-źu, *n. p* the name of one of the bands of Teeton Sioux; the Minneconjoux: meaning *those who plant near the water.* Some of them pronounce their name thus: Mí-ni-ko′-o-źu.

mi′-nin, *adv.* (mini *and* en) *in the water.*

mi′-ni-na-ġa-ġa, *v.* *to struggle,* as anything shot in the water.

mi′-nin-ṭa, *v. n.* *to drown, be drowned*—mininmaṭa.

mi′-nin-ṭe-ya, *v. a.* *to drown, cause to drown*—minintowaya.

mi-ni-o′-ka-bla-ya, *n.* *T.* *water spread out.*

mi′-ni-o-mni, *n.* *an eddy.* See miniyomni. *T.*, owamniyomni.

mi′-ni-o-ṭa, *v. n.* *to drown, be drowned*—miniomaṭa.

mi′-ni-o-ṭe-ya, *v. a.* *to drown, cause to drown*—miniotewaya.

mi′-ni-o-waŋ-ća, *n.* *all over water, the ocean: i. q.* miniwaŋća.

mi′-ni-o-we, *n.* *a spring, fountain of water: i. q.* miniyowe. *T.*, ominiowe.

mi′-ni-sa-pa, *n.* (mini *and* sapa) *ink.*

mi-ni-sku′-ya, *n.* (mini *and* skuya) *salt*, probably so called because salt was first found by them in springs or lakes.

mi′-ni-sku-ya, *n.* *vinegar.*

mi-ni-sku′-ya-o-hna-ka-pi, *n.* *a salt-cellar.* See ohnaka.

Mi′-ni-so-ta, *n.* *the Minnesota* or *Saint Peters River.* It means *whitish water*, and is the name also of the lake called by white people *Clear Lake.*

mi′-ni-śa, *n.* *red water*, i. e., *wine, cider, ale.*

mi′-ni-ś'e-ś'e, *v. n.* *T.* *to sprinkle, rain gently.*

mi′-ni-śi-ća, *n.* *bad water*, i. e., *whisky.*

Mi′-ni-śo-śe, *n.* *turbid water*, i. e., *the Missouri River.*

mi′-ni-ta-ġa, *n.* *foam, froth, spittle.*

mi′-ni-taŋ, *v. n.* *to flood.*

mi′-ni-taŋ, *n.* (mini *and* taŋka) *a flood, high water.*

mi′-ni-taŋ-ka-ya, *adv.* *with water spread over.*

mi′-ni-taŋ-ya, *v. a.* *to cause to flood*—minitaŋwaya.

mi′-ni-wa-kaŋ, *n.* (mini *and* wakaŋ) *water-spirit*, i e., *whisky.*

mi′-ni-wa-kaŋ-ti-pi, *n.* *a whisky-shop, groggery.*

mi′-ni-wa-mnu-ḣa-daŋ, *n.* *snails, periwinkles.*

mi′-ni-waŋ-ća, *n.* *the sea, the ocean: i. q.* miniowaŋća.

mi′-ni-waŋ-ća-wa-ta, *n.* *T.* *a ship: i. q.* wita wata.

mi′-ni-wa-ti-ćo-ġa, *n.* *T.* *the scum on stagnant water; water-moss.*

mi′-ni-wi-to-ye, *n.* *frog-spittle*, the green that collects on stagnant water. *T.*, minitola.

mi′-ni-ya-tkaŋ, *n.* (mini *and* iyatkaŋ) *a drinking-vessel, a tin cup.*

mi′-ni-ya-tke, *n.* Same as miniyatkaŋ.

mi′-ni-yo-ḣpaŋ-yaŋ, *v.* *to soak in water.*

mi′-ni-yo-mni, *n.* *an eddy, whirlpool: i. q.* miniomni.

mi′-ni-yo-pa, *adj.* *wet, saturated with water*, as wet wood. *T.*, spaya.

mi′-ni-yo-waŋ-ća, *n.* *water spread all over*, i. e., *the ocean: i. q.* miniowaŋća.

mi'-ni-yo-we, *n.* *a spring, fountain of water:* *i. q.* miniowe

mi'-ni-yo-we-hde-pi, *n.* *a well of water.*

mi'-ni-yu-śpa-śpa-ye-la, *n.* *T.* *water holes.*

mi'-ni-yu-śpe-daŋ, *v.* *to perspire much:* miniyuśpedaŋ waśkaŋ, *I work perspiring much.* *T.*, miniyuśpala.

mi'-ni-zi, *n.* (mini *and* zi) *bile,* which accumulates in the stomach.

mi'-o-gla-siŋ, *n.* *T.* *a mirror.* See mniohdasiŋ.

mi'-o-gle, *n* *T.* *a whet-stone;* probably of mila, *knife*, and ogle *or* egle, *to place.* See mihnáka.

mi-o'-zu-ha, *n.* *T.* *a knife-sheath.*

miś, *pron* *I:* miś miye, *I myself.* See iś *and* niś.

miś-na'-ka, *pron.* *I alone.* See iśnaka.

miś-na'-ka-se, *pro.* and *adv.* *T.*, miśnakase iyuha bluhe kta, *as if I were the only one that I should have all:* niśnakase, iśnakase.

miś-na'-na, *pron.* *I alone, I only.* *T.*, miśnala See iśnana *and* niśnana.

miś-na'-sa-ni-ća, *adv.* *on my side.*

mi-ta', *pron. prefix;* *my, mine.*

mi-ta'-he, *n.* *Ih.* *a tomahawk.* See ćaŋhpi *and* oŋspedaŋ.

mi-ta'-wa, *pron.* *my, mine.* See tawa *and* nitawa.

mi-uŋ'-pa, *n.* *something laid on the back to keep a pack from hurting, a pad:* miuŋpa kitoŋ, *there is a pad under it.* *T.*, wagnagtoŋ.

mi-wa'-kaŋ, *n.* *Ih.* *a sword.*

Mi-wa'-taŋ-ni, *n.* *T.* *the Mandans:* *i. q.* Mawataŋna.

mi'-ya-ća, *n.* *T.* *the prairie wolf.* See mićaksića.

mi-ya'-śle-ća, *n.* *T.* *a small kind of wolf—the coyote.* See mićaksića.

mi'-ye, *pron.* *I; me.* See iye *and* niye.

mi-ye', *pl. imperat.* termination, as, ećoŋ miye, *do ye it.* *T.*, pi ye; that is the plural termination "pi" and the precative "ye." Mr. Cleveland thinks these were, probably, corrupted by the Santees into "miye"; Yanktons and others into "biye." In the Lord's Prayer, we say, "Wauŋhtanipi kiŋ uŋkićićażupi ye"; but we do not say, in next clause: "ḳa taku wawiyutaŋ kiŋ ekta uŋkayapi śni piye," but "uŋkayapi śni ye."—W. J. C

mi'-ye-ćiŋ. See miyećiŋka.

mi'-ye-ćiŋ-ka, *pron.* *I myself, I alone without aid* or *counsel.* *T.*, miyećuhćiŋ; miyećuhćiŋ ećamoŋ kta, *I will do it alone:* miyećuhćiŋ kaġa yo, *make it yourself*—iyećuhćiŋ.

mi'-ye-ćiŋ-ka-haŋ, *pron.* *I alone.*

mi'-ye-ḳe, *pron.* *even I, such a one as I.* See niyeḳe.

mi'-ye-ḳeś, *pron.* *I myself.*

mi'-yeś, *pron* *I.*

mi-yo'-gla-siŋ, *n.* *T.* *a mirror, looking-glass.* See mioglasiŋ.

mi'-yo-gli, *n.* *T.* *a razor-strop; whet-stone.*

Mi-yo'-glu-ze, *n. p.* *T.* *Whetstone Agency.*

mi-yo'-ka-śiŋ, *n.* *the small of the back.*

mi'-yu-kśi-źa, *n.* *T.* *a pocket-knife.* *Ih.*, minayukśiźapi.

mna. See yumna, etc.

mna, *n.* *black-haws.*

mna-haŋ', *n.* *a rip.*

mna-haŋ', *part.* *ripped of itself.*

mna-haŋ'-haŋ, *red.* of mnahaŋ.

mna'-hu, *n.* *black-haw bushes.*

mna-ḣća'-ḣća, *n.* *the prairie lily.*

mna-ki'-ya, *v. a.* *to take up a collection for* one; *to gather one's own.*

mnaŋ'-ka, *v.* 1st pers. sing. of yáŋka; *to braid, plait.*

mna-wa'-haŋ, *part.* *ripped.*

mna-yaŋ', *v. a.* *to gather together, collect*—mnawaya, mnauŋyaŋpi.

mna-yaŋ'-pi, *n.* *a collecting, collection; harvest.*

mna-ye'-ki-ya, *v. a* *to cause to collect*—mnayewakiya.

mna'-źa, *n.* *a lion; lioness.* It is doubtful to what animal this name properly belongs; but it is used by the Dakotas for lion, although they have never seen one. It may also be used for *wolverine.*

mni. See yumni.

mni, *v. a.* *to lay up to dry, spread out in the sun to dry*—wamni, yamni, uŋmnipi.

mni, *v.* . *Ih.* and *T.*, 1st pron. of ya, *to go;* mni kta, *I will go;* ni kta, *thou wilt go.*

mni, *n.* *Ih.* for mini.

mni'-ći-ya, *v.* *to assemble,* as to a feast, etc.; *to make a feast* or *call an assembly*—mnimićiya, mniničiya, mniuŋkićiyapi.

mni-ça'-pi, *n.* *a well.*

mni'-ġa. See yumniġa.

mni-he'-ća, *v. n.* See miniheća.

mni-hen'-ya, *adv.* See minihenya.

mni-he'-ya, *v. a.* See miniheya.

mni'-ya-pa-taŋ-haŋ, *adv.* *Ih.* *next to the river, by the water.*

mni-yo'-hda-siŋ, *n.* *a looking-glass; window glass.* See mioglasiŋ.

mnu'-ġa, *v.* *to crunch,* as a horse does in eating corn.

mnuḣ, *cont.* of mnuġa.

mnuḣ'-mnu-ġa, *v.* *red.* of mnuġa. See yamnumnuġa.

mnuḣ-ye'-la, *adv.* *T.* *in a crunching way.*

mnu-mnu'-ġa-ha, *adj.* *T.* *soft,* as bone not formed; *cartilagenous.*

N.

n, *the sixteenth letter of the Dakota alphabet.* It has the sound of English *n* in *name, not*, etc., and, except in a few cases, occurs only in the beginning or middle of a syllable.

na, *a prefix* to verbs. It commonly indicates that the action is done with the foot; but it is also used to express the effects of frost, heat, etc.

na, *v. imperat.* only; *take it:* na wo, na po. *T.*, used by women and children: *i. q.* ye.

na, *conj.* *T.* *and, moreover, also: i. q.* ḳa.

na, *suffix diminutive.* *Ih.*, *i. q.* daŋ.

na, *adverbial exclamation. here;* na, iću wo, *here, take it,* said when passing the pipe around. T. L. Riggs thinks it is not a verb as used by Teetons.

na-a'-ġa-ġa, *v.* *to plunge,* said of fish plunging in water: naaġaġa śkaŋ, *it plays plunging about*

na-a'-hda-pśiŋ, *v.* of ahdapśiŋ; *to kick over*—naawahdapśiŋ.

na-a'-hda-pśiŋ-yaŋ, *v.* of ahdapśiŋyaŋ; naahdapśiŋyaŋ iyeya, *to kick* anything *over.*

na-a'-hmus, *cont.* of naahmuza.

na-a'-hmu-za, *v. n.* *to draw up,* as a person dying—naawahmuza. *T.*, natib aya.

na-a'-ka-mni, *v.* naakamni iyeya, *to cause to burst* or *spread out,* as one's moccasins. *T.*, nabla iyeya *and* napota.

na-a'-ka-ś'iŋ, *v.* *to bend backwards:* naakaś'iŋ iyaya. *T.*, nakaś'iŋ. See kaś'iŋ.

na-a'-mda-ya, *v.* *to make level by trampling on*—naawamdaya; *to become level* or *plain; to swell out full* *T.*, naablaya. See amdaya.

na-a'-ṭiŋ-za, *v. a.* *to tread down hard*—naawaṭinza.

na-bag', *cont.* of nabaka; nabag iyeya, *to kick out the foot.* *T.*, nagwag.

na-bag'-ba-ka, *v. red.* of nabaka.

na-ba'-ka, *v. n.* *to kick out the foot; to struggle*—nawabaka. *T.*, nagwaka.

nab-kaŋ', *n.* *T.* (nape *and* kaŋ) *the cords of the wrist.*

na-bla'-ya, *v.* *T.* *i. q* namdaya.

na-bu', *v. a.* *to drum with the foot, beat on the ground, stamp*—nawabu, nauŋbupi.

na-bu'-bu, *v. red.* of nabu; *to make a noise by stamping*—nawabubu.

na-ća', *n.* *T.* *a chief.* See mazyuha *and* itaŋćaŋ.

na-ćam'-ćam. See naćapćam.

na-ćaŋ'-ćaŋ, *v.* of ćaŋćaŋ; *to make shake with the foot; to shake*—nawaćaŋćaŋ.

na-ćap′-ćam, *cont.* of naćapćapa; naćapćam yȧ, *to go on a trot.* *T.*, yućabćab.

na-ćap′-ćam-ya, *v. a.* *to cause to trot*—naćapćamwaya.

na-ćap′-ća-pa, *v. n.* *to trot,* as a horse. *T.*, yućabćapa.

na-će′, *adv.* *perhaps: i. q.* niće.

na-će′-ća, *adv* *perhaps, probably, it may be.*

na-ćeg′, *cont.* of naćeka; naćeg iyeya.

na-ćeg′-ćeg, *cont.* of naćegćeka.

na-ćeg′-će-ka, *v. red.* of naćeka.

na-će′-ka, *v. a.* *to make stagger by kicking*—nawaćeka.

na-će′-ki-śkuŋ, *v. n.* *to lie with one's back to the fire*—naćeweśkuŋ. *T.*, ćaŋkahu okaltkiya.

na-ćen′, *adv.* *perhaps, about that.*

na-ćen′-ya, *adv.* *probably.*

na-će′-ya, *v. a.* (na *and* ćeya) *to make cry by kicking*—nawaćeya.

na-ći′-ḳa, *v.* Same as naćiḳadaŋ.

na-ći′-ḳa-daŋ, *v.* of ćiḳadaŋ; *to make small by trampling*—nawaćiḳadaŋ; *to become less by drying.*

na-ći′-stiŋ-na, *v. a.* of ćistiŋna; *to make less by trampling on*—nawaćistiŋna. *T.*, naćisćila.

na-gla′-gla, *adj.* *T.* *moving,* as the ribs of a buffalo.

na-gmu′ *and* na-gmuŋ′, *v. n.* *T.* *to twist of itself.*

na-ġa′, *v. n.* *to gape open,* as a wound: naġa iyeya, *to cause to spread open.* *T.*, naźal.

na-ġa′-ġa, *v. red.* of naġa; *to splash with the foot*—nawaġaġa; *to spatter* or *fly out,* as grease on the fire. *T.*, *to be scorched* or *cooked on the outside.*

na-ġa′-ġa-ken, *adv.* *standing open,* as a wound. *T.*, naźalźakel.

na-ġa′-ġa-ya, *adv.* naġaġaya śpaŋ, *partly cooked.*

na-ġa′-ġa-ye-la, *adj.* *T.* *partially.*

na-ġam′, *cont.* of naġapa; naġam iyeya. *T.*, naġal.

na-ġan′, *cont.* of naġata; naġan iyeya. *T.*, naġal.

na-ġan′-ġa-ta, *v. red.* of naġata. *T.*, naġalġata.

na-ġa′-pa, *v. a.* *to strip off the skin* of anything *with the foot*—nawaġapa.

na-ġa′-ta, *v. n.* *to stretch out the foot*—nawaġata.

na-ġi′, *n.* *the soul, spirit* of a person; *manes, shades, ghosts* (the Dakotas suppose several to belong to one person); *the shadow* of anything—minaġi, ninaġi, uŋnaġipi, wićanaġi: naġi iyaya, *he is gone to the spirit-land.*

na-ġi′-ya, *v. n.* *to go to the spirit-world:* naġi mda, *I go to the land of spirits.*

na-ġi′-ya-ta, *or* wa-na-ġi′-ya-ta, *adv.* *at* or *in the spirit-land.*

na-ġi′-ye-ya, *v. a.* *to trouble, vex, bother* one—naġiyewaya, naġiyemayaŋ.

na-ġo′-ġo, *v.* *to scratch*, as a cat; *to stick on*, as mud on one's foot.

na-ġu′-ka, *v. a.* *to sprain*, as one's ankle.

naġ-wag′, *cont.* of naġwaka.

naġ-wa′-ka, *v.* *T.* *to swing* or *dangle the feet.*

na-haḣ′, *or* na-haŋḣ′, *adv.* *yet;* used with śni, *not yet.*

na-ha′-ḣiŋ, *adv.* See nahaŋḣiŋ.

na-ha′-i-ye-ya, *v.* *to kick out of the way:* naha iyewaya, *I kick out of the way.* *T.*, nakab iyeya.

na-haŋ′, *conj.* *T.* *and, then; also; besides;* of na *and* hehaŋ.

na-haŋ′-ḣćiŋ, *adv.* *Ih.* *yet.*

na-haŋ′-ḣiŋ, *adv.* *yet;* nahaŋḣiŋ śni, *not yet:* nahaŋḣiŋ ećamoŋ śni, *I have not yet done it.* *T.*, nahaŋḣća.

na-haŋ′-ḣiŋ-ke-śni, *adv.* *not yet, not time yet.* *T.*, nahaŋḣćeke śni.

na-hba′, *v. n.* *to fall off*, as quill-work or the feathers of an arrow. *T.*, naswa; nasba.

na-hda′, *v. n.* *to uncoil of itself.* *T.*, nagla.

na-hda′-ka. See inahdaka.

na-hda′-ka-ya, *adv.* *sticking out*, as the ribs of an animal: nahdakaya wipi, *it is so full that its ribs stick out.* *T.*, naglakeya.

na-hda′-kiŋ-yaŋ, *adv.* *set cross-wise* or *turned out*, as the foot: siha nahdakiŋyaŋ iyeya, *to turn the foot out.*

na-hda′-pśiŋ-yaŋ, *v.* nahdapśiŋyaŋ iyeya, *to turn bottom up with the foot.* See naohdapśiŋyaŋ.

na-hda′-ptus, *cont.* of nahdaptuza: nahdaptus iyaya.

na-hda′-ptu-za, *v. n.* *to fly back*, as a bow that is bent, or as a tree that is pulled and let go.

na-hde′-hde-za, *v. n.* *to be checkered* or *marked.*

na-hdo′-ka, *v. a.* *to knock and injure*, as the joint of one's leg—nawahdoka. *T*, nagloka, *to slip out of place*, as a joint.

na-hin′, *cont.* of nahiŋta; nahin iyeya, *to scrape off with the foot.*

na-biŋ′, *v. imperat.* See na.

na-hiŋ′-ta, *v. a.* *to wipe off with the foot*—nawahiŋta.

na-hmi′-hma, *v. a.* *to roll with the foot*—nawahmihma. *T.*, nagmigma. See naohṁihma.

na-hmi′-yaŋ-yaŋ, *v. a.* *to make round with the foot*—nawahmiyaŋyaŋ. *T*, nagmiyaŋyaŋ. See nahomni.

na-hmuŋ′, *v. n.* *to curl* or *crisp*, as bark or burnt leather. *T.*, nagmuŋ.

na-hmuŋ-hmuŋ′, *v. red.* of nahmuŋ. *T.*, nagmugmuŋ.

na-hmuŋ′-yaŋ, *adv.* *curled:* nahmuŋyaŋ waŋka, *it lies curled up.* *T.*, nagmuŋyaŋ.

na-hna′, *v. a.* *to knock off with the foot*, as fruit—nawahna. *T.*, nagna.

na-hna′-yaŋ, *v. a.* *to stumble, miss step; to miss in trying to kick*—nawahnayaŋ. *T.*, nagnayaŋ.

n a - h n u′ - h n u, *v. n.* *to swell up.* *T.*, nuȟnuġe.

n a - h o′ - h o, *v. a.* *to shake* or *make loose with the foot*—nawahoho.

n a - h o′ - m n i, *v. a.* *to turn round with the foot*—nawahomni. *T.*, nahmiyaŋyaŋ.

n a - h u′ - ȟ u s, *cont.* of nahuhuza; nahuhus iyeya. *T.*, nahuŋhuŋs.

n a - h u′ - h u - z a, *v. a.* *to shake* or *rock with the foot*—nawahuhuza. *T.*, nahuŋhuŋza.

n a - ȟ a′, *v. n.* *to become rough,* as one's hands when chapped by the wind—namaȟa; *to stand up on end,* as grains of corn when boiling.

n a - ȟ a m′, *cont* of naȟapa; naȟam iyeya, *to scare* or *drive away by stamping.* *T.*, naȟab.

n a - ȟ a m′ - ȟ a - p a, *v. red.* of naȟapa.

n a - ȟ a ŋ′ - h i - y a, *adv.* *slowly: i. q.* iwaśtedaŋ.

n a - ȟ a′ - p a, *v. a.* *to scare away by stamping*—nawaȟapa.

n a - ȟ b a′, *v. a.* *to put to sleep by rocking with the foot*—nawaȟba. *T*, naȟwa.

n a - ȟ b e′, *v.* See naȟma.

n a - h b e′ - y a - h a ŋ, *adv.* *secretly.* *T.*, naȟmalahaŋ.

n a - ȟ ć i′, *v. a.* *to break out a piece with the foot*—nawaȟći.

n a - ȟ ć o′, *v. n.* *to come loose* or *untied,* as one's moccasins or leggins. *T.*, naśka. See inaȟćo, *to pull up:* oŋzooġe inaȟćo iyeya wo, *pull up your pants.*

n a - ȟ ć o′ - k a, *v. n.* *to come loose,* as one's leggins. See naićoġa.

n a - ȟ ć o′ - y a, *adv.* *loose, untied,* as the strings that hold up one's leggins.

n a - ȟ d a′, *v. a.* *to rattle with the foot*—nawaȟda. *T.*, naȟla.

n a - ȟ d a′ - ġ a ŋ, *v. n.* *to open, spread out, be enlarged.* *T.*, naȟlaġaŋ.

n a - ȟ d a′ - ȟ d a, *v. red.* of naȟda.

n a - ȟ d a n′, *v. cont.* of naȟdata.

n a - ȟ d a′ - t a, *v. a.* *to scratch with the toes*—nawaȟdata.

n a - ȟ d a′ - y a, *v. n.* *to peel off, come loose, fall off,* as a sticking plaster.

n a - ȟ d e′ - ć a, *v. a.* *to rend, tear open with the foot*—nawaȟdeća, nauŋȟdećapi. *T.*, naȟleća. See onaȟdeća.

n a - ȟ d e′ - ȟ d e - ć a, *v. red.* of naȟdeća.

n a - ȟ d e n′, *cont.* of naȟdeća; naȟden iyeya. *T.*, naȟlel.

n a - ȟ d i′, *v.* *to trample in.*

n a - ȟ d o g′, *cont.* of naȟdoka; naȟdog iyeya.

n a - ȟ d o′ - ȟ d o - k a, *v. red.* of naȟdoka.

n a - ȟ d o′ - k a, *v. a.* *to make a hole with the foot; to wear a hole in the foot by walking*—nawaȟdoka. *T.*, naȟloka. See onaȟdoka.

n a - ȟ e′ - y a n, *cont.* of naȟeyata; naȟeyan iyeya.

n a - ȟ e′ - y a - t a, *v. a.* *to kick off to one side*—nawaȟeyata: naȟeyata iyeya.

n a - ȟ i′ - ć a, *v. a.* *to wake* one *up with the foot, by touching* or *by walking*—nawaȟića.

na-ḣin′, *cont.* of naḣića; naḣin iyeya.

na-ḣi′-ye-ya, *v.* naḣiyeya iyeya, *to kick to pieces, to destroy:* naḣiyeya iyewaya.

na-ḣma′, *v. a. i. q.* naḣbe; *to hide, conceal*—nawaḣbe, nauŋḣmaŋpi. See analıma, *to hide on*, as in speaking; and inaḣma, *to hide in*, as one's actions.

na-ḣma′-na, *adv. secretly, slyly, covertly. T.*, naḣmalahaŋ.

na-ḣmiŋ′, *v. a. to turn out* or *make turn out*, as one's moccasins—nawaḣmiŋ. Compare naoḣmiŋ.

na-ḣol′, *cont.* of naḣota; *T.*, oye naḣol iyaya, *he makes tracks as he goes.*

na-ḣoŋ′, *v. a. to hear* anything; *to listen to; to attend to, obey*—nawaḣoŋ, nayaḣoŋ, nauŋḣoŋpi; namayaḣoŋ, *thou hearest me.* See noġoptaŋ.

na-ḣoŋ′-ki-ya, *v. a. to cause to hear, relate, and make hear*—naḣoŋwakiya.

na-ḣoŋ′-ya, *v. a. to cause to hear*—naḣoŋwaya, naḣoŋmayaŋ.

na-ḣo′-ta, *v.* See naḣol.

na-ḣpa′, *v. a. to touch* or *set off* a trap *with the foot, throw down with the foot*—nawaḣpa.

na-ḣpaŋ′-yaŋ, *v. to moisten with the foot*—nawaḣpaŋyaŋ *and* naḣpaŋwaye.

na-ḣpe′-ya, *v. a. to cause to make fall with the foot*—naḣpewaya.

na-ḣpu′, *v. a. to knock off with the foot* anything sticking—nawaḣpu; *to fall off of itself.*

na-ḣpu′-ḣpu, *v. red.* of naḣpu; *to fall off*, as anything that has been stuck on.

na-ḣtag′, *cont* of naḣtaka; naḣtag iyeya.

na-ḣta′-ḣta-ka, *v. red.* of naḣtaka.

na-ḣta′-ka, *v. a. to kick* anything — nawaḣtaka, nayaḣtaka, nauŋḣtakapi, namaḣtaka.

na-i′-ćo-ġa, *v. n. to come loose, to slip down*, as one's leggins See naḣćoka.

na-i′-ćoḣ, *cont.* of naićoġa; naićoḣ iyeya, *to cause to come untied and slip down*, as one's leggins: opposed to inaḣćo—naićoḣ iyewaya.

na-i′-ç̣i-ḣbe, *v. reflex.* See naiç̣iḣma

na-i′-ç̣i-ḣma, *v. reflex.* of naḣma; *to hide one's self*—namiç̣iḣbe.

na-iŋś′, *conj. T. or; i. q.* ḳa is.

na-i′-pa-tku-ġa, *v.* naipatkuḣ iyeya, *to kick into a row* or *line.*

na-i′-tpi-ska, *v.* naitpiska eḣpeya, *to kick over*, as a dog, *on its back T.*, naikpiska.

na-i′-tuŋ-kam, *v.* naituŋkam eḣpeya, *to kick over backwards.*

na-i′-yo-was, *cont.* of naiyowaza; naiyowas iyeya.

na-i′-yo-wa-za, *v. a. to cause an echo by stamping*—nawaiyowaza.

na′-ka, *adv. now, lately, but a short time ago, to-day:* náka ećamoŋ, *I did it just now. T.*, lećala.

na′-ka, *v. n. to twitch*, as the eye or flesh sometimes does involuntarily: iśta manaka, *my eye twitches.* See wićanaka.

n a - k a′ - a ś, *adv.* *indeed, truly.*

n a - k a′ - e ś, *adv.* *truly, indeed, of course.* *T.*, lakaś.

n a - k a b′, *cont.* of nakopa; nakab iyeya.

n a - k a′ - h a, *adv.* *now, lately, to-day*, referring to the past. *T.*, lećala See náka.

n a - k a′ - h a - ḣ ć i ŋ, *adv.* *T.* *at this moment.*

n a - k a′ - h a ś, *adv.* *at last, after a long time.*

n a - k a ḣ′, *adv.* *just now, lately.*

n a - k a′ - ḣ ć i ŋ, *adv.* of náka; *T.* *just now.*

n a - k a ŋ′, *v.* *to pound* or *beat out, thresh.*

n a - k a′ - p a, *v.* *to kick*, as a ball—nawakapa.

n a - k a′ - p o - ġ a ŋ, *v. n.* *to rise, swell up*, as bread rises.

n a - k a′ - p o, *v.* *to swell*, as the stomach.

n a - k a ś′, *adv.* *indeed, truly.* *T.*, nakeś See nakaaś.

n a - k a′ - ś′ i ŋ, *v.* *T.* *to bend backward.* See naakaś′iŋ.

n a - k a′ - t i ŋ, *v.* *to straighten with the foot; to straighten the foot*—nawakatiŋ; *to become straight of itself.*

n a - k a′ - w a, *v.* *to spring open; to kick open*—nawakawa.

n a - k ć a′, *v.* *to untie* or *loosen with the foot*—nawakća; *to come loose of itself.* *T.*, nakśa. See naḣćo.

n a - k e′ - n u - n a, *adv.* *during a short time, a little while:* nakenuna wani, *I have lived but a little while.*

n a - k e ś′, *adv.* *Ih.*, *at last:* *T.*, *just now; indeed, truly.*

n a - k e′ - y a, *v. n.* *to slope.* See keya.

n a - k e′ - y a, *adv.* *sloping, leaning, not level.* See kanakeya, etc.

n a - k i′ - ć i - b u, *v.* of nabu; *to drum with the foot for* one—nawećibu.

n a - k i′ - ć i - h m u ŋ, *v.* of nahmuŋ; *to twist* or *become twisted for* one—namićihmuŋ. *T.*, nakićigmuŋ.

n a - k i′ - ć i - h u - h u - z a, *v.* of nahuhuza; *to shake for* one—nawećihuhuza. *T.*, nakićihuŋhuŋza.

n a - k i′ - ć i - h u - h u - z a - p i, *n.* *seesawing.*

n a - k i′ - ć i - ḣ m a, *v.* of naḣma; *to conceal for* one—nawećiḣbe, nauŋkićiḣmaŋpi.

n a - k i′ - ć i - ḣ o ŋ, *v.* of naḣoŋ; *to hear for* one—nawećiḣoŋ; nakićiḣoŋpi, *they hear each other.*

n a - k i′ - ć i - ḣ t a - k a, *v.* of naḣtaka; *to kick for* one—nawećiḣtaka; nakićiḣtakapi, *they kick each other.*

n a - k i′ - ć i - k s a, *v.* of naksa; *to break off with the foot for* one—nawećiksa.

n a - k i′ - ć i - k u - k a, *v.* of nakuka; *to wear out with the foot for* one—nawećikuka.

n a - k i′ - ć i - k ś i ŋ, *v.* of nakikśiŋ; *to stand up for* one *in danger, stand by* one—nawećikśiŋ.

n a - k i′ - ć i - m d a - y a, *v.* of namdaya; *to make level by trampling on for* one—nawećimdaya. *T.*, nakićiblaya.

n a - k i'- ć i - m d e - ć a, *v.* of namdeća; *to break*, as a plate, *for* one *with the foot*—nawećimdeća; *to break for* one *by freezing*, etc.—namićimdeća. *T.*, nakićibleća.

n a - k i'- ć i - p a, *v.* of napa; *to flee from* any person or thing—nawećipa, namićipa.

n a - k i'- ć i - p a ŋ, *v.* of napaŋ; *to trample* or *tread out*, as grain, *for* one—nawećipaŋ.

n a - k i'- ć i - p o - t a, *v.* of napota; *to wear out*, as moccasins, *for* one—nawećipota.

n a - k i'- ć i - p s a - k a, *v.* of napsaka; *to break*, as a cord, *with the foot for* one—nawećipsaka.

n a - k i'- ć i - s u - t a, *v.* of nasuta; *to tread hard for* one—nawećisuta, nauŋkićisutapi.

n a - k i'- ć i - ś p a, *v.* of naśpa; *to kick off for* one anything sticking—nawećiśpa.

n a - k i'- ć i - t a - k a, *v.* of nataka; *to fasten* or *lock for* one—nawećitaka.

n a - k i'- ć i - t a ŋ - p i, *v. recip.* of nataŋ; *to kick each other*, as boys in play—nauŋkićitaŋpi.

n a - k i'- ć i - w e - ġ a, *v.* of naweġa; *to break*, as an ax-handle, *for* one, *by treading on it*—nawećiweġa.

n a - k i'- ć i - w i - z i - p i, *v. recip.* of nawizi; *they are jealous of each other*—nauŋkićiwizipi.

n a - k i'- ć i - ź a, *v.* of naźa *or* nakiźa; *to tread out for* one; *to hull for* one, as rice, *by treading*—nawećiźa.

n a - k i'- ć i - ź i ŋ, *v.* of naźiŋ; *to stand for* one, *stand in one's place*—nawećiźiŋ.

n a - k i'- ć i - ź i ŋ - k a, *v.* *to stand up for* one, *stand by* one—nawećiźiŋka.

n a - k i'- h m u ŋ, *v.* of nahmuŋ; *to become twisted of itself for* one—namakihmuŋ. *T.*, nakićigmuŋ.

n a - k i'- ḣ b e, *v.* See nakiḣma.

n a - k i'- ḣ m a, *v a. pos.* of naḣma; *to hide* or *conceal one's own*—nawakiḣbe, nauŋkiḣmaŋpi.

n a - k i'- ḣ o ŋ, *v. pos.* of naḣoŋ; *to hear one's own*, as what one has said or is reputed to have said—nawakiḣoŋ *and* naweḣoŋ.

n a - k i'- k i ŋ - y a, *adv.* *tenderly, soft:* nakikiŋya śpaŋ, *it is well cooked. T.*, nakiŋtkilya.

n a - k i'- k i - t a, *v. n.* *to be made limber* or *tender by boiling; to trample and make limber*—nawakikita. *T.*, nakiŋtkiŋta.

n a - k i'- k s a, *v. pos.* of naksa; *to break one's own with the foot*—naweksa *and* nawakiksa.

n a - k i'- k ś i ŋ, *v. a.* *to defend one's self*—nawekśiŋ. See anakikśiŋ.

n a - k i'- m d a - y a, *v. pos.* of namdaya; *to trample one's own level*—nawakimdaya. *T.*, nakiblaya.

n a - k i'- m d e - ć a, *v. pos.* of namdeća; *to break one's own by treading on it*—nawakimdeća. *T.*, nakibleća.

n a - k i'- m n i, *v. pos.* of namni; *to turn back to one's home*—nawakimni.

n a - k i n', *cont.* of nakiŋća *and* nakiŋta; nakin iyeya, *to scrape off with the foot.*

n a - k i ŋ' - ć a, *v. a.* *to scrape off*, as hair, *with the foot*—nawakiŋća, nauŋkiŋćapi.

n a - k i ŋ' - t a, *v. a.* *to brush off with the foot*—nawakiŋta.

n a - k i ŋ t' - k i l - y a, *adv.* *T.* *tenderly.*

n a - k i ŋ t' - k i ŋ - t a, *v. n.* *T.* *to be made tender* by boiling; *to become limber: i. q.* nakikita.

n a - k i' - p a, *v. pos.* of napa; *to flee* or *retreat towards home, turn back for fear*—nawakipa.

n a - k i' - p a - y a, *v. n.* *to straighten up of itself*, as grass that has been trampled down.

n a - k i' - p ć a, *v. pos.* of napća; *to swallow down one's own*, as one's spittle—nawakipća.

n a - k i' - p s a - k a, *v. pos.* of napsaka; *to break with the foot one's own* string—nawakipsaka.

n a - k i' - p s o ŋ, *v. pos.* of napsoŋ; *to spill over one's own with the foot*—nawakipsoŋ.

n a - k i' - p u - s k i - ć a, *v. a.* *to press close together with the feet*—nawakipuskića. See kipuskića.

n a - k i' - ś d o - k a, *v. pos.* of naśdoka; *to extricate one's self from, kick off one's own* moccasins. *T.*, nakiśloka.

n a - k i' - ś n a, *v. pos.* of naśna; *to miss one's footing, to slip*—nawakiśna.

n a - k i' - t a - k a, *v. pos.* of nataka; *to fence, fasten, bolt* or *bar one's own*—nawakitaka.

n a - k i' - w e - ġ a, *v. pos* of naweġa; *to break* or *splinter one's own with the feet*—nawakiweġa.

n a - k i' - w i - z i, *v. a.* of ṅawizi; *to be envious of, jealoas of*—nawakiwizi, namakiwizi.

n a - k i' - ź a, *v. pos.* of naźa; *to tread out one's own* rice.

n a - k o g', *cont.* of nakoka; nakog iyeya.

n a - k o' - k a, *v. a.* *to rattle*, as a bell, *with the foot*—nawakoka.

n a - k o' - k o - k a, *adj.* *rough*, as a country: ḣe nakokoka, *a rough hill.* *T.*, ḣośkiśki.

n a - k p a', *n.* *the external ear, auricle; the ears* of animals: *i. q.* natpa.

n a - k p a', *v. n.* iśta nakpa, *to become blind.* *T.*, iśtaġoŋġa.

n a - k p a', *v.* *to crackle*, as fire. See nakpakpa.

n a - k p a' - a - ź o g - k i - y a, *v. n.* *to prick up the ears*, as a horse, at anything. *T.*, nakpa yuwaŋkaŋ ikiću.

n a - k p a' - a - ź o - k i - y a, *v.* See nakpaaźogkiya.

n a - k p a' - ġ i - ć a, *n.* *the marten: i. q.* natpaġića.

n a - k p a' - ġ i - ć a - d a ŋ, *n.* *a small marten: i. q.* natpaġićadaŋ.

n a - k p a' - i - y o - t a - h e - l a, *adv.* *T.* *between the ears.*

n a - k p a' - k p a, *v. n.* *to crackle*, as wood burning.

n a - k p a ŋ′, *n.* *the sinews of the wrist.* See napkaŋ.

n a - k p i′, *v. a.* *to crack*, as a nut, *with the foot*—nawakpi: *i. q.* natpi.

n a - k p i′- i - y u - t a - k e, *n.* *T.* *an ear wrapper, scarf, tippet.*

n a - k p i′- k p i, *v red.* of nakpi; *to make successive sounds*, as a gun sometimes does in hanging fire.

n a - k s a′, *v. a.* *to break off*, as a stick, *with the foot*—nawaksa, nauŋksapi.

n a - k s a′- k s a, *v. red.* of naksa.

n a - k s a′- y a, *v* *to cause to break with the foot*—naksawaya.

n a - k s i′- z a, *v. n.* *to split* or *crack of itself; i. q.* napsiza.

n a - k ś a′, *v. n.* *to coil, roll up*, as anything burnt.

n a - k ś a′- d a ŋ, *v. n.* See nakśa.

n a - k ś a ŋ, *v. a.* *to crook* or *bend with the foot*—nawakśaŋ.

n a - k ś a ŋ′- k ś a ŋ, *v. red.* of nakśaŋ.

n a - k ś i′- k ś i - ź a, *v. red.* of nakśiźa.

n a - k ś i ś′, *cont.* of nakśiźa; nakśiś iyeya, *to bend up*, as one's legs.

n a - k ś i′- ź a, *v.* *to double up* anything *with the foot, bend up the leg; to double up itself*—nawakśiźa.

n a - k t a ŋ′, *v. a.* *to bend with the foot*—nawaktaŋ. See naoktaŋ.

n a - k t a ŋ′- k t a ŋ, *v. red.* of naktaŋ.

n a - k t a ŋ′- y a ŋ, *v. a.* *to cause to bend with the foot*—naktaŋwaya.

n a - k t i′- h e - ć a, *v. n.* *to stumble, trip, miss step, knock the feet together in walking*—nawaktiheća. *T.*, ḣićahaŋ; siićiyapapa.

n a - k t i′- h e - y a, *adv.* *tripping, stumbling;* naktiheya mani, *to walk stumblingly.* *T.*, ḣićahaŋyaŋ.

n a - k u′- k a, *v. a.* *to wear out with the feet*—nawakuka.

n a - k u ŋ′, *conj.* *and, also.*

n a - l e′- ġ a, *v.* *T.* *to make shine by kicking: i. q.* nayeġa.

n a - l e ḣ′, *cont.* of naleġa.

n a - l e ḣ′- y a, *v.* *T.* *to make shine* or *sparkle with the foot.*

n a - m d a′, *v. n.* *to split off straight.*

n a - m d a′- ġ a, *v. n.* *to swell out, burst open*, as corn boiling. *T.*, nablaġa.

n a - m d a ḣ′, *cont.* of namdaġa; namdaḣ iyaya.

n a - m d a s′, *cont.* of namdaza; namdas iyeya.

n a - m d a′- s k a, *v. a.* *to flatten with the foot*—nawamdaska. *T.*, nablaska.

n a - m d a′- y a, *v.* *to make level* or *smooth with the foot; to become level, spread out*—nawamdaya. *T.*, nablaya.

n a - m d a′- z a, *v.* *to kick open, make burst by kicking*—nawamdaza; *to burst*, as a kettle, *by freezing, to burst open*, as hominy, by boiling, or as one's entrails, etc. *T.*, nablaza.

n a - m d e′- ć a, *v.* *to break*, as glass, etc., *with the foot*—nawamdeća; *to break*, as earthenware or glass, *by freezing.* *T.*, nableća, *to open out*, as flowers, *blossom; to crack open*, as seed.

n a - m d e′- m d e - ć a, *v. red.* of namdeća.

n a - m d e n′, *cont.* of namdeća; namden iyeya.

n a - m d e n′ - y a, *v. a.* *to cause to break with the foot*—namdenwaya.

n a - m d e′ - z a, *v. n.* *to hull*, as corn does, by being boiled in ashes. *T.*, naślaya.

n a - m d u′, *v. a.* *to pulverize, tread up fine*—nawamdu

n a - m d u′, *v. n.* *to become dry and fine*, as sugar stirred up; *to wear off*, as a gun-lock, so that it will not stand cocked.

n a - m d u′ - m d u, *v. red.* of namdu.

n a - m d u′ - y a, *v. n.* *to break* or *wear off*, as a gun-lock, so that it will not stand; *to be plain* or *manifest*, as tracks not long since made; *to blossom.*

n a - m d u′ - y a, *v. a.* *to cause to wear off*, as a gun-lock, so that it will not stand cocked—namduwaya. *T.*, natepa.

n a m - k a′ - w i ŋ, *v.* (nape *and* kawiŋ) *to beckon with the hand, wave the hand*—namwakawiŋ. *T.*, nape koza. See napkawiŋ.

n am - k i′ - ć a - w i ŋ, *v. a.* *to beckon to with the hand*—namwećawiŋ, nammićawiŋ. *T.*, nape kićoza.

n a - m n a′, *v.* *to rip*, as the sewing of one's moccasins—nawamna; *to rip of itself.*

n a - m n a′ - m n a, *v. red.* of namna.

n a - m n a′ - y a ŋ, *v. a.* *to cause to rip*, as one's moccasins—namnawaya.

n a - m n i′, *v. n.* *to turn back when going on a journey, to give out going*—nawamni.

n a - m n i′ ġ a, *v. n.* *to shrink, draw up, full up*, as cloth

n a - m n i ḣ′, *cont.* of namniġa; namniḣ iyaya.

n a - m n i ḣ′ - k i - y a, *v.* *to make shrink, to full up.*

n a - m n i ḣ′ - y a, *v. a.* *to cause to shrink, to full up*, as cloth—namniḣwaya.

n a - m n i′ - m n i, *v. red.* of namni; *to swing*, as one's blanket. *T*, kamnimni.

n a′ - n a, *intj.* This is said to be used by the women when running after a boy they are unable to catch, meaning, *well, well! I will do it some time!* used by women also in handing anything: *red.* of na, *take it; here it is.*

n a′ - n a, *adv.* *alone, only;* used with the pronouns miś, niś, iś, uŋkiś. *T.*, nala.

n a - n a′ - k e - y a, *v. a.* *to push and make slope* or *lean with the foot*—nawanakeya. See nakeya, etc.

n a - n i′, *v. a.* *to touch* or *jog with the foot, rouse up*—nawani.

n a - n i′ - n i, *v. red.* of nani; *to jog with the foot, wake up*—nawanini.

n a ŋ - k a′, *v.* 2d pers. sing. of yaŋká, *to be.*

n a ŋ′ - k a, *v.* 2d pers. sing. of yáŋka, *to weave.*

n a ŋ - k p a′, *n.* See nakpa.

n a - o′ - h d a - p ś i ŋ, *v.* naohdapśiŋ

eḣpeya, *to kick* anything *over bottom up*.

n a - o′ - h d a - p ś i ŋ - y a ŋ , *adv. kicking over:* naohdapśiŋyaŋ iyeya, *to kick over.* See nahdapśiŋyaŋ.

n a - o′ - h d u - t a , *v.* naohduta iyeya, *to close up* or *cover with the foot.*

n a - o′ - h m i - h m a , *v.* *to roll* anything *with the foot*—naohmihma iyeya. *T.*, naogmigma. See naonminma.

n a - o′ - h m u s , *cont.* of naohmuza; naohmus iyaya. *T.*, naogmus.

n a - o′ - h m u - z a , *v.* *to close up of itself; to close* or *shut up*, as a flower does; *to close up* or *cover with the foot*—naowahmuza, naouŋhmuzapi. *T.*, naogmuza.

n a - o′ - ḣ a ŋ - k o , *v. a.* *to quicken* one's movements *by kicking* him—naowaḣaŋko. See oḣaŋko.

n a - o′ - ḣ m i ŋ , *v. n.* *to glance off sideways*, as a hutinaćute: naoḣmiŋ iyaya.

n a - o′ - ḣ p a , *v. n.* *to press* or *sink down into*, as into mud or water; *to break through*, as into a corn-hole.

n a - o′ - ḣ p e - y a , *v. a.* *to cause to sink down into, to make break through*—naoḣpewaya.

n a - o′ - k i - y u - t e , *v.* *T.* *to close up* or *heal*, as a wound.

n a - o′ - k s a , *v.* *to break through*, as when walking on ice or crusted snow—naowaksa, naouŋksapi. See naksa.

n a - o′ - k ś i ŋ , *v. n.* *to turn in the toes*, as in walking—naowakśiŋ: naokśiŋ mani, *to walk with the toes turned in.* *T.*, naowiŋḣ mani.

n a - o′ - k t a ŋ , *v. a.* *to bend into with the foot*—naowaktaŋ. See naktaŋ.

n a - o′ - k t a ŋ - y a ŋ , *adv.* *bent in:* naoktaŋyaŋ waŋka, *it lies bent in.*

n a - o′ - m n u - m n u - z a , *v.* *red.* of naomnuza.

n a - o′ - m n u s , *cont.* of naomnuza: naomnus iyaya

n a - o′ - m n u - z a , *v. a.* *to make creak* or *sound*, as when one walks on newly formed ice—naowamnuza.

n a - o′ - n m i - n m a , *v. a.* *to roll*, as a ball, etc., *with the foot*—nawaonminma *and* naowanminma. See naohmihma.

n a - o ŋ′ - z e - b o - s d a n , *v.* naoŋzebosdan iyeya, *to kick bottom upwards;* naoŋzebosdan iyeiçiya, *to turn a somersault.* See oŋze *and* bosdan.

n a - o′ - p i - ź e - l a , *adv.* *T.* *loose fitting.*

n a - o′ - p o , *v. n.* *to warp; to draw together*, as a flower, *to shut up.*

n a - o′ - ś d i , *v. n.* *to press up around*, as when one sits down in soft mud.

n a - o′ - ś d i - y a , *adv.* *puffed up around:* naośdiya po, *swelled up full.*

n a - o′ - ś i ŋ , *v. a.* *to make into a hard knot by kicking*, as a horse his traces—naowaśiŋ.

n a - o′ - ś i ŋ - y a ŋ , *adv.* *in the manner of a hard knot:* naośiŋyaŋ iyaya, *to become a hard knot.*

n a - o′ - ṭ i ŋ s, *cont.* of naoṭiŋza; naoṭiŋs iyeya.

n a - o′ - ṭ i ŋ s - y a, *v. a.* *to cause to press down tight in,* as a horse's foot—naoṭiŋswaya.

n a - o′ - ṭ i ŋ - z a, *v. a.* *to press in tight with the foot*—naowaṭiŋza, naouŋṭiŋzapi.

n a - o′ - w i ŋ - ġ a, *v.* *to turn in the toes:* naowiŋḣ mani, *to walk with toes turned in.* See naokśiŋ *and* naśada.

n a - p a′, *v. n.* *to run away, flee*—nawapa, nayapa.

n a - p a′ - h d e, *v. a.* (nape *and* ahde) *to place the hand on, bear down on with the hand*—napawahde.

n a - p a′ - h u ŋ - k a *and* n a - p a′ - h u ŋ - k e, *n.* (nape *and* huŋka) *the thumb.*

n a - p a′ - k a - h a, *n.* *the back of the hand.*

na-pa′-ko, *v. n.* *to bend up of itself.*

n a - p a′ - k o - y a, *adv.* *rounded up:* napakoya po, *swelled up.*

n a - p a′ - n u ŋ - k i ŋ, *adv.* *with both hands:* napanuŋkiŋ yuza, *to take hold of with both hands.* *T*, nape nupiŋ.

n a - p a ŋ′, *v. a.* *to trample fine; to tread out,* as grain—nawapaŋ.

n a - p a ŋ′ - p a ŋ, *v.* *red.* of napaŋ.

n a - p a′ - p a - ġ a, *v. n.* *to snap* or *crackle,* as corn parching, or as sinews thrown into the fire.

n a - p a′ - p a ḣ, *cont.* of napapaġa; napapaḣ iyeya.

n a - p a′ - p a ḣ - y a, *v. a.* *to parch,* as corn—napapaḣwaya.

n a - p a′ - p a - ś d e - ć a - p i, *n.* of nape; *the distance from the end of the thumb to the end of the middle finger when stretched out, a span.*

n a - p a′ - t a, *adv.* *by the hand:* napata yuza, *to hold by the hand.*

n a - p a′ - t u - ź a, *v. a.* of patuźa; *to kick and make bend:* napatuś iyeya.

n a - p ć a′, *v. a.* *to swallow,* as food—nawapća, nauŋpćapi.

n a - p ć a′ - p ć a, *v.* *red.* of napća; napćapća iyeya.

n a - p ć a′ - y a, *v. a.* *to cause to swallow*—napćawaya.

n a - p ć i ŋ′ - w a ŋ g - w a ŋ - k a, *adj.* *red.* of napćiŋwaŋka; *nine and nine, by nines.* *T.*, napćiŋyuŋgyuŋka.

n a - p ć i ŋ′ - w a ŋ - k a, *num. adj.* *nine.* *T.*, napćiŋyuŋka.

n a - p ć o′, *n.* *the lean meat near the back bone, the longissimus dorsi.* See tanapćo.

n a - p ć o′ - k a, *n.* (nape *and* ćokaya) *the palm of the hand.*

n a - p ć o′ - k a - y a, *n.* *T.* *the middle finger.*

n a - p ć u′ - p e, *n.* *a finger, fingers:* maza napćupe, *finger-rings.* *T.*, napsu *and* napsuhu.

n a - p ć u′ - p e - o - ḣ d a, *n.* *Si.* *finger-rings.*

n a - p e′, *v.* See napa.

n a - p e′, *n.* *the hand; the fingers; the fore-foot* of animals.

n a - p e′ - a - p a - h a, *v.* *to raise the hand to strike* anything: napeapaha makuwa, *he follows me with his hand raised.*

na-pe′-hdu-źa-źa, *v.* *to wash one's own hands.*

na-pe′-ḣe-ya-ta-he-daŋ, *n.* (*little-far-back-hands*) *the mole.* There are no moles in the Dakota country.

na-pe′-i-pa-hiŋ, *v.* of nape *and* ipahiŋ; *to lie with the head on the hand*

na-pe′-ki-ćo-za, *v.* of napekoza; *to wave the hand to*—napewećoza.

na-pe′-ko-za, *v.* *to wave the hand*—napewakoza. See namkawiŋ *and* napkoza.

na-pe′-kśi-kśa, *v.* *to have the hands numb* or *stiff with cold*—napemakśikśa.

na-pe′-mni, *v. n.* of pemni; *to twist of itself.*

na-pe′-o-ćo-ka-ya, *n.* *the middle finger.* *T.*, napećokaya.

na-pe′-o-hna-ka, *n.* *a handful.*

na-pe′-o-śtaŋ-na, *n.* (nape *and* ośtaŋ) *a thimble.* *T.*, napośtaŋ. See napośtaŋna.

na-pe′-o-śtaŋ-pi-daŋ, *n.* *a thimble, thimbles.*

na-pe′-śni-ka-ġa-pi, *n.* (*make-no-flight*) *the name of a dance and feasts connected with it,* in which they covenant not to flee in battle.

na-pe′-to-ka-he-ya, *n.* *the fore-finger.* *T.*, waepazo.

na-pe′-ya, *v. a.* *to cause to flee, to drive off* or *away*—napewaya, napeuŋyaŋpi.

na-pe′-ye-ki-ya, *v.* *to stretch out the hand to.*

na-pe′-ye-ya, *v.* *to stretch out the hand*—napeyewaya.

na-pi′-ća-śka, *v.* (nape *and* kaśka) *to tie to the hands of* one. *T.*, napiićaśka.

na-pi′-ća-śke-ya, *adv.* *tied to the hand,* i. e., *always with* one, *following* one *about:* napićaśkeya uŋ, *to accompany constantly.*

na-pi′-ćo-za, *v.* See napekoza.

na-pin′, *adv.* *they two, both.* *T.*, nupiŋ

na-pin′-tu, *adv.* *alike, equal,* as two things. *T.*, nupiŋtu

na-piŋ′, *adj.* *satisfying, strong, rich, oily;* as some kinds of food. This word expresses that property in food which makes one soon satisfied.

na-piŋ′-kpa, *n.* (nape *and* iŋkpa) *mittens; gloves.*

na-piŋ′-kpa-yu-ga-ga, *n.* *gloves.*

na-piŋ′-piŋ, *adj.* *red.* of napiŋ.

na-piŋ′-tpa, *n.* *mittens.* Same as napiŋkpa.

na-piŋ′-yuŋ, *adv.* *with the hands* or *arms alone, without weapons:* napiŋyuŋ ćodaŋ, *without anything in the hand.*

na-piŋ′-za, *v. n.* *to creak, make a creaking noise.*

na-pi′-śkaŋ, *v. n.* *to put the hand to for evil, lay hands on; to move the hand about on; to touch with evil design.*

na-pi′-śkaŋ-ki-ya, *v. a.* *to cause to move the hands on*—napiśkaŋwakiya.

n a - p i′ - ś k a ŋ - y a ŋ , *v. a.* *to hurt* or *destroy* anything, *to kill*, especially what is not one's own—napiśkaŋwaya. See napiśtaŋyaŋ.

n a - p i′ - ś t a ŋ , *v. n.* Same as napiśkaŋ.

n a - p i′ - ś t a ŋ - k a , *n.* *T.* *one who accomplishes much.*

n a - p i′ - ś t a ŋ - y a ŋ , *v. a.* *to lay violent hands on, to hurt, injure,* or *destroy* aŋythiŋg—napiśtaŋwaya, napiśtaŋuŋyaŋpi.

n a - p i′ - w i - ć o s , *cont.* of napiwićoza.

n a - p i′ - w i - ć o - z a , *v.* *to beckon to with the hand, to make gestures.* *T.*, napekićoza.

n a - p i′ - y u ŋ , *adv.* See napiŋyuŋ.

n a - p i′ - y u - z e - ć a , *v.* *to take* a thing *into one's own hands, to do* it *one's self*—napimduzeća.

n a p - k a ŋ′ , *n.* (nape *and* kaŋ) *the sinews of the wrist: i. q.* nakpaŋ.

n a p - k a′ - w i ŋ , *v. n.* (nape *and* kawiŋ) *to beckon with the hand*—napwakawiŋ. *T.*, napkoza.

n a p - k i′ - ć a - w i ŋ , *v. a.* of napkawiŋ; *to beckon to* one—napwećawiŋ.

n a p - k i′ - ć o - z a , *v. a.* of napkoza; *to wave the hand to*—napwećoza.

n a p - k o′ - z a , *v.* *to wave the hand*—napwakoza.

n a - p o′ , *v. n.* *to swell,* as corn soaked.

n a - p o b′ - y a - p i , *n.* *T.* *fire-crackers.* See napopa.

n a - p o′ - ġ a ŋ , *v. n.* *to ferment,* as yeast.

n a - p o′ - h n a , *n.* *what is in the hand,* i. e., *a handful.*

n a - p o′ - ḣ n a - k a , *v. a.* *to put into the hand*—napowaḣnaka.

n a - p o′ - ḣ n a - k a , *n.* *a handful.* See napeoḣnaka.

n a - p o ḣ′ , *cont.* of napoġaŋ; napoḣ iyeya.

n a - p o ḣ′ - y a , *v. a.* *to cause to ferment, to leaven, make light*—napoḣwaya. Hence, oŋ napoḣyapi, *leaven.*

n a - p o′ - k a - ś k e , *n.* *the wrist.*

n a - p o′ - k a - ś k e - e n - i - y e - y a - p i , *n.* *wristlets.*

n a - p o′ - k t a ŋ , *n.* *T.* *a bracelet.*

n a - p o m′ , *cont.* of napopa; napom hiŋhda, *to burst with a noise;* napom iyeya, *to cause to burst and make a noise.* *T.*, napol.

n a - p o n′ , *cont.* of napota; napon iyeya. *T.*, napol.

n a - p o n′ - p o - t a , *v.* *red.* of napota.

n a - p o ŋ′ , *v. n.* *to become fine, crumble up of itself.*

n a - p o′ - p a , *v. n.* *to burst,* as a boiler, or as a gun.

n a - p o′ - p a - b a - ġ a , *v. a.* *to rub in the hands*—napowapabaġa.

n a - p o′ - ś t a ŋ , *n.* *T.* *a thimble, thimbles.*

n a - p o′ - ś t a ŋ - n a , *n.* (nape *and* ośtaŋ) *a thimble.* *T.*, napośtaŋ. See napeośtaŋna.

n a - p o′ - ś t a ŋ - p i - d a ŋ , *n.* *a thimble, thimbles.*

n a - p o′ - t a , *v. a.* *to wear out with*

the feet, as shoes, etc.—nawapota, nauŋpotapi.

n a - p o t′ - p o - t a , *v. red* of napota. *T.*, napolpota.

n a - p o′ - w a - y a , *v. n.* *to spread* or *open out*, as a flower.

n a - p s a g′, *cont.* of napsaka; napsag iyeya.

n a - p s a′ - k a , *v. a.* *to break*, as a cord, *with the foot*—nawapsaka, nauŋpsakapi.

n a p - s a ŋ′ - n i , *n.* (nape *and* saŋni) *the hand on one side, one hand* of a person.

n a - p s a′ - p s a - k a , *v. red.* of napsaka.

n a - p s i′ - ć a , *v. n.* *to skip* or *jump about*—nawapsića.

n a - p s i n′, *cont.* of napsića; napsin iyaya *T.*, napsil.

n a - p s i n′ - y a , *v. a.* *to make jump*—napsinwaya. *T.*, napsilya.

n a - p s i′ - p s i - ć a , *v. red.* of napsića; *to dance about*—nawapsipsića: *to spatter out*, as hot grease when water is dropped into it.

n a - p s i′ - p s i n , *cont.* of napsipsića; napsipsin iyaya

n a - p s i′ - p s i n - y a , *v. a.* *to make skip* or *dance about*—napsipsinwaya.

n a - p s i′ - y o - ḣ l i, *and* n a - p s i′ - o - ḣ l e , *n.* *T.* *a finger-ring, a ring.*

n a - p s i′ - z a , *v. n.* *to split* or *crack of itself.*

n a p - s k a′ - ś n i , *adj.* *of unclean hands; a sinner.*

n a - p s o ŋ′, *or* n a - p s u ŋ′, *v. a.* *to kick over and spill; to throw out of* a canoe; *to make* a canoe *dip water*—nawapsoŋ; naiçipsoŋ, *to throw one's self out.*

n a - p s u′, *and* n a - p s u′ - h u , *n.* *T.* *the fingers.*

n a - p s u′ - k a - z a , *n.* (nape *and* sukaza) *the fingers.*

n a - p s u ŋ′, *v. a.* See napsoŋ.

n a - p ś u ŋ′, *v. a.* *to put out of joint*, as a foot or leg—nawapśuŋ.

n a - p t a′, *v. a* *to sprain*, as one's leg; *to wear off*—nawapta. See hunapta.

n a - p t a′ - ḣ p a - y a , *adv.* naptaḣpaya waŋka, *to lie on the belly resting on the arms.* *T*,, nape ipahiŋ,

n a - p t a ŋ′ - y a ŋ , *v.* *to kick over*—nawaptaŋyaŋ; *to turn over of itself.*

n a - p t a ŋ′ - y a ŋ - k e n , *adv* *in the manner of turning over.*

n a - p t e′ - ć a , *adv.* *less.* *T.*, aopteća.

n a - p t e n′, *cont.* of napteća. *T.*, aoptel.

n a - p t e n′ - y a , *adv.* *less.* *T.*, aoptelya.

n a - p t e ṇ′ - y e - d a ŋ , *adv.* *less, diminished.* *T.*, aoptelyela.

n a p - t o′ - k a - h e - y a , *n.* *the forefinger.* *T.*, waepazo: *i. q.* napetokaheya.

n a - p t u′ - p t u - ź a , *v. red.* of naptuźa.

n a - p t u ś′, *cont.* of naptuźa; naptuś iyaya.

n a - p t u′ - ź a , *v. n.* *to crack, split of itself* or *by the action of heat* or *cold.*

n a - p̣ i ŋ′, *v. a.* *to wear around the*

neck, as a kerchief or neck ornament, beads, etc.—nawapiŋ.

n a - p i ŋ'- k i - y a, *v. a.* *to cause to wear on the neck*—napiŋwakiya. See wanapiŋ.

n a - p i ŋ'- p i, *n.* ćaŋ napiŋpi, *an ox-yoke.* See ptetawanapiŋ.

n a - s a' *and* n a - s e', *v a.* *to hunt buffalo, to surround and kill*, as they do in a buffalo hunt—nawasa. See wanase.

n a - s a', *v. n.* *to stand erect*, as hogs' bristles.

n a - s a', *adj.* *sharp, prickly.*

n a - s' a', *v. n.* *to simmer, make a slight noise*, as water before boiling.

n a - s a'- k i - y a, *v.* *to make stand erect; to bristle up.*

n a - s a'- t i ŋ, *v.* nasatiŋ iyeya, *to stretch out*, as an animal when dying; *to become straight.*

n a - s a'- t i ŋ - t i ŋ, *v. red.* of nasatiŋ; nasatiŋtiŋ iyaya, *to go straight*, as a hutinaćute.

n a - s b a', *v. n* *to fall off*, as quill work: *i. q.* nahba.

n a s - ć a ŋ'- w a - p a, *n.* *T.* *a bridle: i. q.* masćaŋyapa.

n a - s d a', *v. a.* *to grease with the foot*—nawasda.

n a - s d a n', *cont.* of nasdata; *without noise, stilly.* *T.*, naslal.

n a - s d a'- s d a n, *cont.* of nasdasdata.

n a - s d a'- s d a - t a, *v. red.* of nasdata.

n a - s d a'- t a, *v. a.* *to go softly up to* anything, *to crawl up to*—nawasdata.

n a - s d e'- ć a, *v. n.* *to crack* or *split of itself*, as wood. *T.*, nasleća.

n a - s d e n', *cont.* of nasdeća; nasden iyaya. *T.*, naslel.

n a - s d e n'- y a, *v. a.* *to cause to split* or *crack*—nasdenwaya.

n a - s d e'- s d e - ć a, *v. red.* of nasdeća.

n a - s d i', *v. n.* *to hiss*, as wet wood burning.

n a - s d i'- s d i, *v. red.* of nasdi.

n a - s e m', *cont.* of nasepa; nasem iyaya, *to go scraping along, cleaning off, brushing off.* *T.*, naskeb.

n a - s e m'- s e - p a, *v. red.* of nasepa.

n a - s e'- p a, *v. n.* *to leak out, escape of itself.*

n a - s k a', *v. n.* *to bleach, become white.*

n a - s k e m', *cont.* of naskepa. *T.*, naskeb.

n a - s k e'- p a, *v.* of skepa; *to leak out.*

n a - s k i'- ć a, *v.* *to press down with the foot*—nawaskića; *to go down* or *become less of itself.*

n a - s k i n', *cont.* of naskića; naskin iyaya, *to abate* or *go down*, as a swelling. *T.*, naskil.

n a - s k i'- t a, *v. a.* *to tread on and press down*—nawaskita.

n a - s l i'- y a, *adv.* *T.* *oozing out*, as sap from a tree.

n a - s m i ŋ'- y a ŋ, *v. a.* *to scrape off with the foot*—nawasmiŋyaŋ.

n a - s m i ŋ'- y a ŋ - y a ŋ, *v. red.* of nasmiŋyaŋ; *to scrape* or *wear off with the feet and leave bare*—nawasminŋyanŋyanŋ.

na-sna', *v.* *to make a rattling noise with the feet; to shake off with the foot*—nawasna: *to fall off of itself*, as rice when the tying breaks.

na-sna'-sna, *v. red.* of nasna; nasnasna mani, *to make a tinkling as one walks.*

na-son', *cont.* of nasota; nason iyeya. *T.*, nasol.

na-soŋ' *or* na-suŋ', *v. n.* *to stretch out the feet and legs*—nawasoŋ, nauŋsoŋpi.

na-soŋ'-soŋ, *v. red.* of nasoŋ; *to struggle*—nawasoŋsoŋ.

na-soŋ'-yaŋ, *adv.* *in a struggling manner.*

na-so'-ta, *v. a.* *to use up; to destroy with the feet*—nawasota, nauŋsotapi.

na-spa'-ya, *v. a.* *to wet with the feet; to wet the feet*—nawaspaya.

na-staŋ'-ka, *v. a.* *to moisten with the feet*—nawastaŋka.

na-su', *n.* *the upper part of the head; the brain.*

na-su'-ćiŋ-ća, *n.* *the brain*, or *that part of it which communicates with the spinal marrow.*

na-su'-daŋ, *n. dim.* of nasu; *the cerebrum; the cerebellum.* *T.*, nasula. See naźute.

na-su'-hu, *n.* *the skull, cranium.* *T.*, natahu.

na-sul'-pa-kća, *n.* *T.* *a comb: i. q.* ipakća.

na-sul'-pa-kća-swu-la, *n.* *T.* *a fine comb.*

na-suŋ', *v.* See nasoŋ.

na-su'-su-za, *v. red.* of nasuza; *to snap*, as ice forming.

na-su'-śda, *adj.* *bald-headed.*

na-su'-ta, *v. a.* *to trample hard*—nawasuta.

na-su'-za, *v. n.* *to splinter* or *fly off*, as a piece of a bone; *to snap*, as water freezing.

na-swa', *v.* *T.* *to fall off*, as feathers.

na-śa', *v. n.* (na *and* śa) *to become red, to blush:* ite naśa hiŋhda, *his face colored up.*

na-śa'-da, *v.* *to turn out the toes*, as in walking; naśada mani, *to walk turning out the feet*—nawaśada.

na-śam', *cont.* of naśapa; naśam iyeya. *T.*, naśab.

na-śam'-ya, *v. a.* *to cause to soil with the feet*—naśamwaya. *T.*, naśabya.

na-śa'-pa, *v. a.* *to soil, blacken, defile with the feet*—nawaśapa.

na-śbe', *v.* See naśma.

na-śda', *v. a* *to make bare with the feet*—nawaśda.

na-śda'-ya, *v. n.* *to come off*, as the hull from corn when boiled.

na-śdi', *v. n.* *to ooze out*, as sap from trees, or juice from meat roasting. See nasliya.

na-śdog', *cont* of naśdoka; naśdog iyaya, *to run* or *flee away;* naśdog hdiću, *he starts off home in haste.*

na-śdo'-ka, *v. a.* *to pull off*, as one's pantaloons; *to escape, fly out*, as the cork of a bottle—nawaśdoka.

n a - ś d u n', *cont.* of naśduta; naśdun iyeya. *T.*, naślul.

n a - ś d u'- ś d u n, *cont.* of naśduśduta. *T.*, naśluślul.

n a - ś d u'- ś d u - t a, *v.* *to slip often; to make smooth with the foot*—nawaśduśduta.

n a - ś d u'- t a, *v. n.* *to slip, slide, slip down*—nawaśduta. *T.*, naśluta.

n a - ś e'- ć a, *v. a.* *to make wither by trampling on*, as grass—nawaśeća.

n a - ś e n'- y a, *v. a.* *to cause to trample on and make wither*—naśenwaya.

n a - ś i'- ć a, *v. a.* *to defile, spoil with the feet*—nawaśića, nauŋśićapi.

n a - ś i'- ć a - h o - w a - y a, *v. a.* *to make cry out by kicking*—nawaśićahowaya.

n a - ś i m', *cont.* of naśipa; naśim iyaya. *T.*, naśib.

n a - ś i m'- ś i m, *red.* of naśim; naśimśim iyeya. *T.*, naśibśib.

n a - ś i ŋ'- ś i ŋ, *v. n.* *to pace*, as a horse.

n a - ś i ŋ'- ś i ŋ, *n.* *a scar, a burn.*

n a - ś i ŋ'- ś i ŋ - y a, *adv.* *crisped:* naśiŋśiŋya śpaŋ, *cooked to a crisp.*

n a - ś i'- p a, *v. a.* *to break off*, as branches of a tree, *by stepping on* them; *to put out of joint*, as one's knee—nawaśipa.

n a - ś k a', *v. a.* *to untie with the foot*—nawaśka.

n a - ś k a', *v. n.* *to come untied of itself.*

n a - ś k a', *n.* *a frog.* See also hnaśka.

n a - ś k a'- ć a ŋ - d i'- d a ŋ, *n.* *the tree-frog.*

n a - ś k a'- h a ŋ *and* n a - ś k a'- w a - h a ŋ, *part.* *untied, loose.*

n a - ś k a ŋ'- ś k a ŋ, *v. a.* *to shake* or *move about with the foot*—nawaśkaŋśkaŋ.

n a - ś k a'- t o ŋ - t o ŋ - t a ŋ - k a, *n* *the bull-frog.* *T.*, gnaśkataŋka. See toŋtoŋtaŋka.

n a - ś k i'- ć a, *v. a.* *to press with the foot, press out by trampling on*—nawaśkića. See naskića.

n a - ś k i'- ć u - t e, *n.* (naśka *and* ićute) *little arrows*, used in shooting frogs. *T.*, gnaśkaićute.

n a - ś k i n', *cont.* of naśkića; naśkin iyeya. *T.*, naśkil.

n a - ś k i'- ś k a, *v. a.* *to make rough*, as ground, *by trampling on* it—nawaśkiśka.

n a - ś k o'- k p a, *v. a.* *to indent, make a hollow place with the foot*—nawaśkokpa.

n a - ś k o'- p a, *v.* *to twist with the foot*—nawaśkopa; *to twist* or *become crooked of itself.*

n a - ś k o'- ś k o - p a, *v. red.* of naśkopa.

n a - ś k o'- t p a, *v. a.* Same as naśkokpa.

n a - ś m a', *v. a.* *to hollow out* or *deepen with the feet*—nawaśbe. See naśbe.

n a - ś n a', *v. n.* *to slip, miss one's footing*—nawaśna.

n a - ś n a'- ś n a, *v. red.* of naśna.

n a - ś n i'- ź a, *v. a.* *to trample on and kill.* as grass—nawaśniźa.

n a - ś n u ŋ'- ź a, *v. n.* *to become injured of itself; to become withered.*

na-śo′-śa, *v. a.* *to foul* or *make turbid*, as water, *with the feet*—nawaśośa.

na-śpa′, *v. a.* *to break off* anything *with the foot; to take* anything *from a trap*—nawaśpa.

na-śpa′-śpa, *v. red.* of naśpa.

na-śpe′-ya, *v. a.* *to cause to break off with the foot; to break off a piece by shooting*, as from a gun—naśpewaya

na-śpi′, *v. a.* *to break off*, as fruit, *with the foot*—nawaśpi.

na-śpu′, *v. a.* *to break off with the foot*, as pumpkins—nawaśpu.

na-śpu′-śpu, *v. red.* of naśpu; *to break off pieces, break in pieces with the foot*, as tallow—nawaśpuśpu; *to come to pieces*, as in boiling.

na-śuś′, *cont.* of naśuźa; naśuś iyeya.

na-śu′-śuś, *cont.* of naśuśuźa.

na-śu′-śu-źa, *v. red.* of naśuźa; *to bruise* or *mash by trampling on*—nawaśuśuźa.

na-śu′-źa, *v. a.* *to bruise* or *crush with the foot; to crack off a piece*, as from a leg-bone—nawaśuźa.

na-ta′, *n.* *T.* *the head.* See pa.

na-ta′, *v.* nata iyeya, *to kick out of the way; to kick up.*

na-ta′-ćo-ku-ḣpu-ḣpu, *n.* *T.* *dandruff: i. q.* natakpuḣpu.

na-tag′, *cont.* of nataka; natag iyeya, *to fasten;* natag haŋ, *to stand fastened.*

na-ta′-ġu, *v. n.* *T.* *to be bald-headed.*

na-ta′-ha-la, *n.* *T.* *the scalp.*

na-ta′-hu, *n.* *T.* *the skull, cranium: i. q.* nasuḥu.

na-ta′-ka, *v. a.* *to fasten*, as a house, *to bolt, bar* or *barricade; to fence*, as a field—nawataka.

na-ta′-kpu-ḣpu, *n.* *T.* *dandruff.*

Na-ta′-mde-ća, *n. p.* *The Flatheads. The Bannocks.*

na-t'aŋ′, *v. a.* *to touch with the foot*—nawat'aŋ; *to make an attack, go after and rush upon*, as on enemies. See anataŋ

na-taŋ′-iŋ-śni, *v. a.* *to walk* or *run off, to go off*, as fatigue or partial sickness: nataŋiŋśni iyeya—nawataŋiŋśni.

na-taŋ′-ka, *v. n.* *to enlarge, become larger.*

na-t'aŋ′-t'aŋ, *v. a.* *red.* of nat'aŋ; *to feel after with the feet*—nawat'aŋt'aŋ: also, *to rush upon.*

na-ta′-om, *adv.* *leaning, inclined. T.*, nataob.

na-ta′-om-ya, *adv.* *leaning:* nataomya haŋ, *it stands leaning.*

na-ta′-pe-ḣa, *n.* *a toad.* *T.*, natapiḣa *and* matapiḣa. See naśka.

na-ta′-śla, *adj.* *T.* *bald-headed.*

na-ta′-ta, *v. a.* *to shake off*, as dust from one's feet or blanket—nawatata.

na-tem′, *cont.* of natepa; natem iyeya. *T.*, nateb.

na-tem′-ya, *v. a.* *to cause to wear off*, as one's horse's hoof—natemwaya. *T.*, natebya.

na-te'-pa, *v. a.* *to wear off with the foot, wear short,* as a hoof or shoe; *to wear out*—nawatepa.

na-te'-pa, *adj.* *worn off; worn out.*

na-ti'-ća, *v. a.* *to scrape with the foot; to paw,* as a horse—nawatića.

na-ti'-kti-ća, *v. n.* *to thicken by boiling; to trample, make thick by tramping.*

na-tim', *cont.* of natipa; natim iyaya. *T.*, natib; natib aya, *to draw up,* as a hide in drying.

na-tim'-ti-pa, *v.* *red.* of natipa.

na-tim'-ya, *v. a.* *to cause to draw up*—natimwaya. *T.*, natibya.

na-tin', *cont.* of natića; natin iyeya. *T.*, natil.

na-tiŋ', *v. n.* *to become stiff,* as a dead person. *T.*, wotiŋ.

na-ti'-pa, *v. n.* *to draw up,* as leather, meat, etc., when put on the fire, *to crisp; to cramp, contract,* as muscles.

na-ti'-taŋ, *v. a.* *to pull, pull backwards* or *forwards by bracing the feet,* as a horse in pulling—nawatitaŋ, nauŋtitaŋpi.

na-tku', *v. a.* *to break square off with the foot*—nawatku: hu nawatku seća, *it seems as if I had broken my leg.*

na-to'-to, *v. a.* *to make a noise by knocking with the foot; to clear off,* as brush, etc.—nawatoto.

na-tpa', *n.* *the external ear, the ear* of animals. Same as nakpa.

na-tpa', *v.* noġe natpa, *to become deaf* by sickness.

na-tpa'-ġi-ća, *n.* *the marten, Mustela martes.* Same as nakpaġića.

na-tpa'-ġi-ća-daŋ, *n.* *the marten.*

na-tpaŋ', *v. a.* *to bruise* or *mash up fine with the feet*—nawatpaŋ.

na-tpaŋ'-tpaŋ, *v.* *red.* of natpaŋ.

na-tpi', *v.* *to crack by treading on*—nawatpi; *to crack of itself,* as fire snapping: *i. q.* nakpi.

na-tpi'-tpi, *v.* *red.* of natpi; *to crack* or *snap,* as fire burning. Said also of many guns fired off about the same time.

na-tpi'-yo-ta-he-daŋ, *adv.* of natpa; *between the ears.* See iyotahedaŋ.

na-tpo'-ta, *v.* *pos.* of napota; *to wear out one's own* moccasins, etc.—nawatpota.

na-tpu'-tpa, *v. n.* *to mix together,* as in boiling.

na-tu', *n.* *corn-silk; the hair on the side of the head.*

na-tu'-ka, *v. a.* *to stamp off and destroy,* as fur—nawatuka.

na-tu'-ta, *v. n.* *to smart,* as one's feet by traveling: siha namatuta, *my feet smart.*

na-tu'-tka, *v. a.* *to knock pieces off with the foot*—nawatutka.

na-ṭa', *v. a.* *to kill by kicking*—nawaṭa

na-ṭe'-ki-ni-ća, *v.* of naṭa *and* kinića; *to annoy, to vex, to worry; to beg to death.*

na-ṭiŋs', *cont.* of naṭiŋza; naṭiŋs iyeya.

n a - ṭ i ŋ' - z a, *v. a.* *to press hard with the foot*—nawaṭiŋza.

n a - ṭ u ŋ' - k a, *v. n.* *to refuse to go, hesitate, hold back,* as a horse unwilling to go—nawaṭuŋka.

n a - ṭ u ŋ' - k i - y a, *v. a.* *to make afraid, make hesitate*—naṭuŋwakiya.

n a - w a' - n i - ć a, *v. a.* *to trample to nothing, to destroy by trampling on*—nawawanića.

n a - w a' - n i n, *cont.* of nawanića; nawanin iyeya, *to walk* or *run off* sickness or fatigue; *to destroy* or *annihilate,* as by the bursting of a boiler.

n a - w a ŋ g', *cont.* of nawaŋka: nawaŋg iyaya. *T.*, nayuŋg.

n a w a ŋ g' - k i - y a, *v a.* *to cause to gallop,* as a horse—nawaŋgwakiya.

n a - w a ŋ' - k a, *v. n.* *to gallop,* as a horse does. *T.*, nayuŋka.

n a - w a ŋ' - k a n, *v.* nawaŋkan hiyu, *to spring up,* as the boards of a floor.

n a - w a' - t e, *n.* *the temples; the ends* of a house; *the lock* of a gun.

n a - w a' - t e - s k a - d a ŋ, *n.* *a kind of small duck with a white spot on each side of the head.*

n a - w e' - ġ a, *v. a.* *to break,* as a stick, *with the foot,* but not entirely off—nawaweġa.

n a - w e ḣ', *cont.* of naweġa; naweḣ iyeya.

n a - w e ḣ' - y a, *v. a.* *to cause to break with the foot*—naweḣwaya.

n a - w i' - ć a - ś l i, *n.* *T.* *the measles* or *rash.*

n a - w i' - ć a - t i - p a, *n.* *cramping, cramps.*

n a - w i' - h n u - n i, *v. a.* *to destroy with the foot*—nawawihnuni.

n a - w i ŋ', *v. n.* *to scrape the foot; to sail around,* as an eagle.

n a - w i ŋ ś', *cont.* of nawiŋźa; nawiŋś iyeya.

n a - w i ŋ ś' - w i ŋ - ź a, *v.* *red.* of nawiŋźa.

n a - w i ŋ ś' - y a, *v. a.* *to cause to trample down*—nawiŋśwaya.

n a - w i ŋ' - ź a', *v. a.* *to trample down,* as grass, *to mat down*—nawawiŋźa.

n a - w i' - z i, *v.* *to be jealous, envious*—nawawizi.

n a - w i' - z i - s'a, *n.* *a jealous person.*

n a - y e' - ġ a, *v. a.* *to make shine* or *sparkle by kicking,* as when one pushes up the fire with his foot—nawayeġa. *T.*, naleḣya.

n a - y e ḣ', *cont.* of nayeġa; nayeḣ iyeya. *T.*, naleḣ.

n a - y e ḣ' - y e - ġ a, *v.* *red.* of nayeġa; *to kick* or *punch up* the fire *with the foot.* *T.*, naleḣleġa.

n a - z a ŋ', *v.* *to hurt; to stun by kicking.*

n a z - o ŋ' - s p e, *n.* *T.* *an ax.* See mazoŋspe.

n a z - o ŋ' - s p e - ć i - ḳ a - l a, *n.* *T.* *a hatchet.*

n a z - o ŋ' - s p e - i - h u - p a, *n.* *T.* *an ax-helve.* See ihupa.

n a z - o ŋ' - s p e - o - p e - t a ŋ - k a, *n.* *T.* *a broad-ax.* See ope.

n a - ź a', *v. a.* *to mash up* or *crush by trampling on*—nawaźa. See nakiźa. *T.*, inaȟuȟuġa.

n a - ź a n', *cont.* of naźata; naźan iyeya. *T.*, naźal; naźal iyeya, *to spread* or *gape open*, as a wound.

n a - ź a' - t a, *v. a.* (na *and* źata) *to make forked by kicking*—nawaźata.

n a - ź a' - t a - k a - h u, *n.* *a small bush*, something like the ćaŋśaśa.

n a - ź a' - ź a, *v. a.* *to wash out with the feet, trample out; to wash out by boiling*—nawaźaźa.

n a - ź i' - ć a, *v. n.* *to run away, flee, retreat.*

n a - ź i' - ć e - y a, *v. a.* *to cause to flee*—naźićewaya.

n a - ź i m', *cont.* of naźipa; naźim iyeya. *T.*, naźib.

n a - ź i n', *cont.* of naźića; naźin iyaya. *T.*, naźil.

n a' - ź i ŋ, *v. n.* *to stand, rise up; to stand still, stop; to stand on the ground, to get down, alight*, as from a horse—nawaźiŋ, nauŋźiŋpi.

n a' - ź i ŋ - h a ŋ, *part.* *standing:* naźiŋhaŋ naźiŋ, *to rise up and stand.*

n a' - ź i ŋ - k i - y a, *v. a.* *to cause to stand, to raise up, lift up*—naźiŋwakiya.

n a - ź i' - p a, *v. a.* *to prick* or *pinch with the toes*; *to punch* or *touch with the foot.*

n a - ź u' - t e, *n.* *the occipital bone; base of the skull; the back of the head; the cerebellum:* *i. q.* nasudaŋ.

n a - ź u' - t e - o - ś k o - k p a, *n.* *the hollow of the neck behind.*

n a - ź u' - ź u, *v. a.* *to kick to pieces*—nawaźuźu; *to come to pieces of itself.*

n i, *pron. in comp.* *thee, thou; thy, thine, your, yours.* See ma *and* mi.

n i, *v. n.* *to live*—wani, yani, uŋnipi, wićani. Hence, wićoni, *life.*

n i' - ć a, *v. n.* *to be destitute of, have none of*—manića, ninića, uŋnićapi, wanića.

n i - ć a', *v.* of ka; *he means thee.*

n i - ć e', *adv.* *perhaps.* See naće. Niće is objected to, as it is so often used obscenely.

n i - ć e' - ć a, *adv.* *Ih.* *probably: i. q.* naćeća.

n i' - ć i, *pron. and prep.* *with thee; for thee.* *T.* *for thee*, but not *with thee*, as, nićiyaŋka, *it remains for thee:* kići niuŋ, *it is with thee.* See kići *and* mići.

n i - d e', *n.* *water*, in the sacred language; *i. q.* mini.

n i' - e n *or* n i' - y e n, *adv.* *anew:* teća nien toŋpi, *born again, regenerated.*

n i - ġ e', *n.* *the paunch, stomach.*

n i - ġ u' - t e, *n.* *the flank:* niġute ośkokpa, *the hollow of the flank.* *T.*, loġute.

n i - h a ŋ', *adv.* *fearful;* nihaŋśni, *not afraid.* See inihaŋ.

n i - h a ŋ' - y a ŋ, *v. a.* *to scare*—nihaŋwaya. *T.*, inihaŋyaŋ.

n i - h i ŋ' - ć i - y a, *v. n.* *to be frightened, scared: to cry* or *scream*, as in fright; *to hurry*—nihiŋmićiya, nihiŋnićiya, nihiŋuŋkićiyapi.

ni-hiŋ′-ći-ya-ken, *adv.* *in fright.*

ni-ki′-ya, *v. a.* of ni; *to cause to live*—niwakiya. See niyaŋ.

nin, *cont.* of nića; tuwe nin uŋ kiŋ, *he who has none.* *T.*, lil.

ni′-na, *adv.* *very, very much,* always intensive. *T.*, lila.

ni′-naḣ, *adv.* See ninaḣiŋ. *T.*, lilaḣ.

ni′-na-ḣiŋ, *adv.* *exceedingly.* *T.*, lilaḣćiŋ.

ni′-na-na, *adv.* *very:* ninana ia, *to speak loud and fast, speak earnestly.* *T.*, liglila.

ni-ni′, *adj.* *coagulated, curdled, quivering,* said of thick sour milk: asaŋpi nini, *curdled milk, curds.*

niŋ, *intj.* *T.* *may it be, would that it were* Nitokićoŋze u niŋ, *Thy Kingdom come:* *i. q.* nuŋwe.

niŋ-tpa′-hu, *n.* *the haunch* or *hip-bone.* See nitpahu.

ni-po′, *adj.* *dead.* This is probably Ojibwa, but frequently used by the Dakotas when speaking with white people who do not understand their language.

ni-se′-hu, *n.* *the hip-bone, os ilium.*

ni′-sko, *adv.* *so large.* See niskokeća, hiŋsko, *and* tiŋsko.

ni′-sko-ke-ća, *adv.* *so large.* See hiŋskokeća *and* tiŋskokeća.

ni′-sko-sko-ke-ća, *adv.* *red.* of niskokeća.

ni′-sko-taŋ-ka, *adv.* *so large.* See hiŋskotaŋka.

ni′-sko-taŋ-ka-daŋ, *adv.* *so small.*

ni′-sko-ya, *adv.* *so far around.* See hiŋskoya *and* tiŋskoya.

niś, *pron.* *thou, thee:* niś niẏe, *thou thyself.* See iś, miś, *and* uŋkiś.

ni′-śko-daŋ, *adv.* *small, only so large.* *T.*, niśkola. See hiŋśkodaŋ *and* tiŋśkodaŋ.

ni′-śko-śko-daŋ, *adv.* *red.* of niśkodaŋ.

ni-śko-ye-daŋ, *adv.* *only so far around.*

niś-na′-na, *pron.* *thou alone;* niśnaŋpidaŋ, *you alone.* *T.*, niśnala. See iśnana, miśnana, *and* uŋkiśnana.

ni-śtu′-śte, *n.* *T.* *the rump, the heavy part near the tail:* *i. q* nite.

ni-ta′, *pron in comp.* *thy, thine; your, yours:* nitaśuŋke, *thy dog.* See ta, mita, *and* uŋkita.

ni-ta′-wa, *pron.* *thy, thine; your, yours.* See tawa, mitawa, *and* uŋkitawa.

ni-te′, *n.* *the lower part of the back, the rump.* *T.*, niśtuśte.

ni-te′-he-pi, *n.* *T.* *a petticoat.*

ni-te′-hu, *n.* *the os sacrum.*

ni-to′-śke, *n.* *a white woman's dress, long gown:* nitośke kitoŋ, *to put on white woman's clothes.* *T.*, ćuwignaka.

ni-tpa′-hu, *n.* *the hip-bone.* Same as nisehu.

ni′-uŋ, *v.* *to be living:* ni wauŋ, *I am alive.*

ni-waŋ′, *v. n.* *to swim*—waniwe, uŋniwaŋpi. *T.*, nowaŋ.

n i - w e′ - k i - y a, *v. a.* of niwaŋ; *to cause to swim*—niwewakiya. *T.*, nowaŋkiya.

n i - y a′, *v. n.* *to breathe*—waniya, yaniya, uŋniyapi: niya śni iyaya, *to die;* niya śni maṭa nuŋ seća, *I am out of breath.* See ni.

n i - y a′, *n.* *breath, life.* See oniya.

n i - y a′ - k e, *adj.* *alive;* niyake yuza, *to take alive;* niyake kte, *to strike but not kill*, as an enemy: niyake kte gli, *he came home, having struck an enemy.*—W. J. C.

n i - y a′ - k e n, *adv.* *alive, in a living manner.*

n i - y a ŋ′, *v. a.* of ni; *to cause to live, make live, revive*, as a sick person; *to let live, miss* or *fail of killing*, as an enemy or game—niwaya, niuŋyaŋpi, nimayaŋ. See nikiya.

n i - y a ŋ′, *adv.* *audibly, with a loud voice:* eya niyaŋ, *to say with a loud voice.*

n i - y a ŋ′ - ḣ i ŋ, *adv.* *yet.* See hinaḣiŋ. *T.*, nahaŋḣća.

n i - y a ŋ′ - ḣ i ŋ - k e - ś n i, *adv.* *not yet time, too soon.* *T.*, nahaŋḣćeke śni.

n i - y e′, *v.* *to cause to live.* See niyaŋ.

n i′ - y e, *pron.* *thou, thee;* niyepi, *you.* See iye, miye, *and* uŋkiye.

n i′ - y e - ć u - ḣ ć i ŋ, *pro.* *T.* *you at any rate.*

n i′ - y e - e ś, *pron.* emphatic; *thou, thee, you.* See iyeeś.

n i′ - y e - k a - e ś, *pron.* *even thou.* *T.*, niyekaleś. See iyekaeś.

n i′ - y e - ḳ e, *pron* emphatic; *thee thyself, you yourself, even you.* *T.*, niyeḳeś. See iyeḳe, miyeḳe, *and* uŋkiyeḳe.

n o′ - ć e. See nuŋće.

n o′ - ġ e, *adj.* *scabbed; swollen, enlarged*, and *hardened.* See nuŋġa.

n o′ - ġ e, *n.* *the ear; the sense of hearing*, as noġe ninića, *thou hast no ears* (in this sense it is used in reference to other things as well as men and animals); *the pan* of a gun-lock, as, mazakaŋ noġe—minoġe.

n o′ - ġ e - a - ź o g - k i - y a, *v.* *to prick up the ears*, as a horse, at any sound *T.*, noġe yuwaŋkaŋ ikikću.

n o′ - ġ e - i - y u - t a - p i, *n* *the distance from the ear to the end of the fingers when the arm is stretched out, a yard.* This is the common yard-stick of the traders.

n o′ - ġ e - k p a, *adj.* *deaf, hard of hearing*—noġemakpa.

n o′ - ġ e - k p e - y a, *v. a.* *to make deaf*—noġekpewaya.

n o′ - ġ e - o - ḣ d o - k a, *n.* *the orifice of the ear; the touchhole* of a gun.

n o′ - ġ e - t p a, *adj.* See noġekpa.

n o′ - ġ e - t p e - y a, *v.* See noġekpeya.

n o - ġ i′ - y u - t a - p i, *n.* *a yard* See noġeiyutapi.

n o′ - ġ o - p t a ŋ, *adj.* (noġe *and* ptaŋ) "turning the ear towards:" *listening, attending to;* noġoptaŋ maŋka, *I am attending to it.*

nog̈-su′-hu-te, *n.* *T.* *base of the ear.*

noḣ-no′-g̈e, *adj. red.* of nog̈e.

noḣ-paŋ′, *n.* of nog̈e *and* paŋ; *the ringing of the ear;* lit. *the calling of the ear,* i. e. *the sound;* noḣ mapaŋ, noḣ nipaŋ: when one has a ringing of the ear, they say, "He will soon hear from afar."—W. J. C.

nom, *cont.* of noŋpa; *two.* *T.*, nob.

nom′-na-na, *adj.* *two alone, only two.* *T.*, nobnala. See tomnana, yamnina, etc.

nom′-nom, *adj.* *two and two, by twos.* See tomtom.

nom′-noŋ-pa, *red.* of noŋpa; *by twos.* See toptopa.

noŋ. See nuŋ.

noŋ. See noŋske *and* nuŋske. *T.*, iŋske.

noŋ-će′. See nuŋće.

noŋ′-pa, *adj.* *two, twice.* See topa.

noŋ′-pa-ki-ya, *adv.* *twice, in two ways.* See topakiya, yamnikiya, etc.

noŋ′-ske *or* nuŋ′-ske, *intj.* expressing ignorance or want of recollection; *let me see! what do you call it?* *T.*, iŋske; iŋ.

no-waŋ′, *v. n.* *T.* *to swim: i. q.* niwaŋ—wanowaŋ.

nu′-g̈e, *adj.* *T.* *swollen, enlarged,* and *hardened.* See nog̈e.

nu-ksi′, *n.* *ears,* as the long ears of a dog. See nakpa.

nu′-ni, *v.* *to wander, miss the road and wander about, get lost; to be mistaken about* a thing—wanuni, yanuni, uŋnunipi. See hnuni *and* waćiŋhnuni.

nu′-ni-ya, *v. a.* *to cause to wander*—nuniwaya, nuniuŋyaŋpi.

nu′-ni-yaŋ, *adv.* *wandering, lost.*

nuŋ, *v.* 2d pers. sing. of uŋ, *to use.*

nuŋ, *cont.* of nuŋwe; *let it be so,* expressive of desire; *so be it, amen.* It is often equivalent to the sign of the future tense; as, mda nuŋ he, *shall I go?* token ećamoŋ nuŋ taŋiŋ śni, *what I shall do is not apparent* See niŋ.

nuŋ′-g̈a, *adj.* *callous.* Said of any hard place, formed by a burn or otherwise, on the skin—manuŋg̈a. *T.*, iyanuŋg̈a: *i. q.* nog̈e.

nuŋ′-ka, *v.* 2d pers. sing. of waŋka; *thou liest down.* *T.*, 2d pers. sing. of yuŋka.

nuŋ-kas′, *n.* *a step-son* or *step daughter:* nuŋkasku, *his* or *her step-son* or *step-daughter.* This is said to be used only by the generation passing away, that is, by old people. *T.*, tawag̈aŋ; tawag̈aŋku.

nuŋ-kas′-ya, *v. a.* *to have for* nuŋkas—nuŋkaswaya *T.*, tawag̈aŋya.

nuŋ-se′, *adv.* *almost, nearly;* ṭa nuŋse, *about to die.*

nuŋ′-ske. See noŋske. *T.*, iŋ; iŋske.

n u ŋ - w e′, *v.n.* *let it be so*, expressive of desire; *may it be so, amen.* *T.*, niŋ.

n u ŋ - y a ŋ′, *v. a.* *to tame, domesticate*, as animals—nuŋwaya. Hence, wanuŋyaŋpi, *tame cattle.* *T.*, niyaŋ: waniyaŋpi, *tame cattle.*

n u - p i ŋ′ - ć a - s k a, *adv.* *T.* *both together.*

n u - p i n′, *adj.* *T.* *both: i. q.* napin.

n u - ś n u ŋ′ - ź a, *adj.* *wrinkled pitted, not smooth.* *T.*, piśpiźa.

Ŋ.

ŋ, *the seventeenth letter of the Dakota alphabet.* It occurs only *after a vowel*, and has the sound of the French nasal *n* in *bon.*

O.

o, *the eighteenth letter of the Dakota alphabet*, with the sound of English *o* in *no.*

o, *a prefixed prep.* It is a contraction of ohna, okna, *and* ogna, meaning *in, into*, and prefixed to verbs makes the locative form in o′: as kaśtaŋ, *to pour out*, okaśtaŋ, *to pour into;* haŋ *to stand*, ohaŋ, *to stand in.* 2d. As a contraction of oŋ, *for*, it is prefixed to verbs, meaning *for, for the purpose of;* as, okuwa waśte, *it is good for following;* that is, *easily followed.*

o, *a prefix*, forming nouns of verbs; as, baśpa, *to cut off*, obaśpe, *a piece.*

o, *v. a.* *to shoot, to hit* when shooting—wao, yao, uŋḳopi: wakute eća wao eće *when I shoot I hit.*

o - a′ - a, *v. n.* *to mold; i. q.* aa.

o - a′ - a, *n.* *mold.*

o - a′ - d e, *n.* *a load* of wood in the arms. *T.*, oakśu.

o - a′ - g l e, *n.* *T.* *the end of the pipe-stem which is put in the pipe.*

o - a′ - h d e, *n.* *a place of holding* or *resting against*, as the shoulder where the gun is held. *T.*, oagle. See ahde.

o - a′ - h e, *n.* *something to stand on.* *T.*, owahe.

o - a′ - h e - ć e - c a, *adj.* *better, pretty well*, said *of* one sick. See ahećeća.

o - a′ - h e - h d e, *n.* *a foundation.* *T.*, owaheglepi.

o - a′ - h i - y a - y e, *n.* of ahiyaya; *a going* or *taking round; a tune, the air of a tune*

o - a′ - ḣ t a - n i, *n.* of aḣtani; *transgression.* See woaḣtani.

o - a′ - i - e, *n.* of aia; *counsel; slander.*

o - a′ - i - e - t i - p i, *n.* *a council-house.* *T.*, owoglake tipi.

o - a′ - k i - ḣ a ŋ, *n.* of akiḣaŋ; *starving.* See akiḣaŋpi.

o - a′ - k i - n i - ć a, *n.* of akiniċa; *disputing.*

o-a′-ki-ye-daŋ, *adv.* of akiyedaŋ; *near, not far: e. g.*, yapi kiŋ otehaŋ, kupi kiŋ oakiyedaŋ, *the going is far, the coming is near.*

o-a′-kśu, *n.* *T.* *a load*; *an armful: i. q.* oade.

o-a′-p'e, *n.* of ap'a; *strokes, stripes, beatings; the striking of a clock, an hour.*

o-a′-śi-ća, *adj.* of aśića; *unpleasant, disagreeable*, as a country, the weather, etc. *T.*, oiyokiśića.

o-a′-śi-ća-ya, *adv.* of aśićaya; *unpleasantly.*

o-a′-śi-ća-ya-ken, *adv.* of aśićayaken; *disagreeably.*

o-a′-śi-će-ća, *adj.* See oaśićećaka.

o-a′-śi-će-ća-ka, *adj.* *unpleasant, disagreeable*, as the appearance of a country, etc. See aśićećake *and* ośićećake.

o-a′-śin-ya, *adv.* of aśinya; *not satisfied* or *pleased with, unpleasantly:* oaśinya uŋyakoŋpi, *we are uncomfortably situated.* *T.*, oiyokiśilya.

o-a′-śin-ya-ken, *adv.* of aśinyaken; *unpleasantly.*

o-a′-śka-daŋ, *adv.* of aśkadaŋ; *near, short*, as a road; *short*, as time; aŋpetu oaśkadaŋ, *the days are short.* *T.*, akokabya.

o-a′-ya-śtaŋ, *n.* of ayaśtaŋ; *a stop, stopping*, as in talking.

o-a′-ya-te, *n.* of ayate; *a guess.*

o-a′-yu-śtaŋ, *n.* of ayuśtaŋ; *a stop, cessation from.*

o-ba′-hoŋ *or* o-ba′-huŋ, *n.* of bahoŋ; *a cut, gash.* *T.*, owahoŋ.

o-ba′-ḣda-ye, *n.* of baḣdaya; *something to peel off in.*

o-ba′-ḣdo-ka, *v. a.* *to cut a hole in*, when shaving, as in making a dish—obawaḣdoka. *T.*, owaḣloka.

o-ba′-ḣdo-ke, *n.* of baḣdoka; *a hole cut* or *made with a knife.*

o-ba′-po-te, *n.* of bapota; *a cutting up, destroying by cutting.*

o-ba′-sde-će, *n.* of basdeća; *a split, splitting.* *T.*, owasleće.

o-ba′-sden, *cont.* of obasdeća: obasden waśte, *good to split.* *T.*, owaslel.

o-ba′-sku, *v.* *to pare in* anything—obawasku.

o-ba′-sku, *n* of basku; *a paring.*

o-ba′-smiŋ, *n.* of basmiŋ; *something to shave off into.*

o-ba′-śpe, *n.* of baśpa; *a piece cut off:* obaśpe waŋźidaŋ, *one piece*, as of pork or meat of any kind.

o ba′-tu-tka, *v.* *to make chips* or *shavings in* a place—obawatutka.

o-be′, *n.* *a litter, brood; a division, class, sort.* Compare optaye *and* ośpaye. *T.*, owe.

o-bla′-ya, *adv.* *T.* *level.* See omdaya.

o-bla′-ye, *n.* *T.* *a plain, a level place.* See omdaye.

o-bla′-ye-la, *adv.* *T.* *level.*

o-blo′-toŋ, *adj.* *T.* *cornered.*

o-blo′-toŋ, *n.* *T.* *a corner: i. q.* omdotoŋ.

o'-b l u - l a, *n.* or *adj.* *T.* *calm, sheltered, protected:* waŋna oblula, *now it is calm:* le oblula, *this is a sheltered place:* *i. q.* omnina.

o - b o' - h a, *v.* oboha iyeya, *to knock into.* *T.*, owoha.

o - b o' - ḣ ć i - ḣ ć i, *n.* *a string* or *bunch of beads; any bunch that dangles:* *i. q.* boḣćiḣći. *T.*, opaḣte.

o - b o' - ḣ d o - k e, *n.* of boḣdoka; *a hole made by punching.*

o - b o' - p o - t a, *v. a.* of bopota; *to shoot to pieces in* anything—obowapota.

o - b o' - s d a n, *n.* *height.* *T.*, owoslal. See bosdan.

o - b o' - s d a - t a, *n.* *height.* *T.*, owoslata. See bosdata.

o - b o' - s d a - t u, *n.* *height, perpendicularity.* See bosdatu.

o - b o' - s k i - ć a, *v. a.* of boskića; *to punch* or *ram hard in* a hole—obawaskića.

o - b o' - s k i n, *cont.* of oboskića; oboskin iyeya.

o - b o' - ś k i, *v.* *to make faint, obliterate,* as the rain does tracks.

o - b o' - ś p e, *n.* of bośpa; *a piece shot* or *punched off.*

o - b o' - t a ŋ, *v.* of botaŋ; *to ram* or *pound hard in* a hole—obowataŋ.

o - b o' - ṭ a, *v. a.* of boṭa; *to punch to death in,* as in a hole—obowaṭa.

o - b o' - ṭ e, *n.* *a killing* or *punching to death in.*

o - b o' - ṭ i ŋ - z a, *v. a.* of boṭiŋza; *to pound in hard and tight*—obowaṭiŋza.

o - b o' - y a - y a, *n.* *a bunch of beads.* *T.*, woyaya, *a string of beads.*

o - b o' - z a, *v.* oboza hiŋhda, *to rise up with a rush,* as in case of an excitement. See boza.

o - b o' - z a - k a, *v.* *to rush:* ituḣ obozaka, *the rush was for naught.*

o - ć a' - ġ a, *v. n.* of ćaġa; *to freeze* or *become ice in.*

o - ć a' - h d e, *n.* of ćahde; *a step.* *T.*, ćagle; ćagle yuta, *to pace, measure by stepping.*

o - ć a ŋ' - k u, *n.* *a road, street, way.* See ćaŋku.

o - ć a ŋ' - w a - n i - ć a, *n.* *place where there is no timber, prairie.*

o - ć a ŋ - z e, *v. n.* oćaŋze kokela, *easily made angry.*

o - ć a' - ź e, *n* of ćaźe; *kind, sort, species, name.*

o - ć e' - s d i, *v.* of ćesdi; *to* ćesdi *in:* oćesditipi, *a privy.*

o - ć e' - t i, *n.* of ćeti; *a fire-place, place where the fire is made; a chimney:* maza oćeti, *a stove.*

o' - ć i - ḣ i ŋ - y a ŋ - p i, *v. recip.* of oḣiŋyaŋ; *they are offended at each other, they feel themselves slighted.*

o' - ć i - k a ŋ, *adv.* *having room, roomy:* óćikaŋ śni, *without room, crowded.*

o' - ć i - k p a - k p a - n i, *adj. red.* of oćikpani; *some longer and some shorter.* *T.*, aoćikpakpani.

o' - ć i - k p a - n i, *adj.* *not equal in length.* *T.*, aoćikpani.

o - ć i' - ḳ a - d a ŋ, *adj.* of ćiḳadaŋ; *small within:* ti ociḳadaŋ, *a small room.*

o-ći'-ḳa-ye-daŋ, *adj.* of ćiḳayedaŋ; *small inside, of small dimensions.*

o'-ćim, *adv.* *afterwards, after awhile, at length.*

o'-ći-mda-ġa-he, *adv.* *abreast, in a line.* *T.*, oćiblaġahe.

o-ći-mda-ġaŋ, *adv.* *abreast.*

o'-ći-mda-ġe-haŋ, *adv.* *in a row, abreast.* *T.*, oćiŋblaġehaŋ.

o'-ći-mdah, *cont.* of oćimdaġaŋ.

o-ćiŋ', *n.* of ćiŋ; *desire, wish, disposition.*

o-ćiŋ', *v. a.* *to desire, beg, ask for:* taku oćiŋ wahi, *I have come to ask for something*—owaćiŋ. See woćiŋ.

o-ćiŋ'-bla-ġe-haŋ, *adv.* *T.* *abreast.*

o-ćiŋ'-i-yu-li, *n.* *T.* *a ladder.*

o-ćiŋ'-śi-ća, *v. n.* *to be cross, bad-tempered, ill-disposed*—oćiŋmaśića.

o-ćiŋ'-śi-ća-ya, *adv.* *evilly disposed.*

o-ćiŋ'-yo-pe-ya, *v. a.* *to please, make glad* by giving to or in any other way, *to reward.* It is said to be used in case one is appointed to a difficult service, and well rewarded for it—oćinyopewaya, oćiŋyopeuŋyaŋpi, oćiŋyopemayaŋ.

o-ćiŋ'-yo-pe-ya, *n.* *a reward* of honor or service. *T.*, iyuŋwiŋ.

o'-ći-pte-ća, *adj.* *shorter than.*

o'-ći-pten, *adv.* *not equal to, lacking.*

o'-ći-pte-tu, *adv.* *unequal* in length, or otherwise. *T.*, aoćiptetu, *smaller than*

o-ći'-sti-la, *adv.* *T.* *little, for a little while.*

o-ći'-sti-ye-daŋ, *adv.* of ćistiyedaŋ; *for a little while.* *T.*, oćisćiyela

o'-ći-tkoŋs, *cont.* of oćitkoŋza; wićaśta oćitkoŋs waćiŋpi, *men think alike.*

o'-ći-tkoŋ-za, *adj.* *equal, alike, of the same size* or *length:* ćaŋ oćitkoŋza, *trees of the same height.*

o'-ći-tpa-ni, *adj.* *unequal.*

o'-ći-ṭiŋ-za, *v. n.* *to be crowded together; i. q.* óćikaŋ śni.

o'-ći-ya-ka-pi, *v. pl.* of oyaka; *i. q.* okićiyakapi.

o-ći'-yo-pe-ya, *v.* See oćiŋyopeya.

o'-ći-yu-śtaŋ, *v.* of oyuśtaŋ; *to be one in another,* as kettles; *to be doubled,* as a blanket.

o'-ći-yu-śṭaŋ-śtaŋ, *v. red.* *to be placed one inside of another,* as kettles.

o-ćo'-ka-ka, *v. n.* of ćoka; *to be empty, not full,* as a house, of persons; *there is room.* *T.*, okaŋ.

o-ćo'-kam, *adv.* of ćokam. *in the middle.*

o-ćo'-kam-tu, *adv.* *in the midst.* *T.*, ćokabtu.

o-ćo'-ka-ya, *adv.* of ćokaya; *in the middle:* ti oćokaya, *in the middle of the house.*

o-ćos', *cont.* of oćoza; oćos maŋka, *I am in a warm place.*

o-ćos'-ya, *adv.* *in a warm condition.*

o-ćo'-wa-siŋ, *adv.* *all, the whole, all together.* *T.*, ataya. See owasiŋ.

o-ćo'-za, *adj.* *warm in:* ti oćoza, *a warm house.*

o-ćo'-za, *n.* of ćoza; *warmth, heat.*

o-ću', *v. n.* of ću; *to become damp in; to have drops of water inside.*

od *or* on, *cont.* of yuta; od waśte, *good to eat, good to taste.* *T.*, oyul.

o-da'-kon, *cont.* of odakota. *T.*, olakol.

o-da'-kon-ki ći-ya-pi, *n.* *friendship, peace.* See dakonkići-yapi.

o-da'-kon-ya, *adv.* *friendly, peaceably.* *T.*, olakolya.

o-da'-ko-ta, *n.* *friendship, alliance, fraternity.* *T.*, olakota. See dakota.

o-de', *v. a.* *to seek for, hunt for* anything—owade, oyade, uŋkodepi. *T.*, ole; taku ole yahi he, *what have you come for?*

o-de'-źa, *v.* of deźa; *to urinate in* anything—owadeźa. *T.*, oleźa.

o-de'-źa, *n.* *the bladder; a chamber-pot.* *T.*, wićaleźa *and* taleźa: oleźapi.

o-di'-di-ta, *v. n.* of didita; *to be warm in,* as in a house where it is uncomfortably hot: ti odidita, *a hot house.* *T.*, oluluta.

o-di'-di-ta, *n.* *heat.*

o-don', *cont.* of odota; taku odon wahi, *I have come to borrow something* *T.*, olol.

o-do'-ta, *v. a.* *to borrow* anything—owadota, oyadota, uŋkodotapi. *T.*, olota.

od'-o-ta, *adj.* *red* of ota; *much of various kinds.*

o-do'-waŋ, *n.* of dowaŋ; *a song, hymn, tune.*

o-du'-te, *n.* *the large muscle* or *flesh on the thigh.*

o-du'-za-haŋ, *n.* of duzahaŋ; *swiftness.*

o-e'-će-ća, *v. n.* *to be a little better; i. q.* ahećeća.

o-e'-će-ća-ka, *v. n.* *to be like* one, as a son is like his father, in appearance, demeanor, etc.; *to be better,* as a sick person—oemaće-ćaka. *T.*, ahećeća *and* iyećeća. See owećećaka.

o e'-ćen-ya, *adv.* *so, however.* *T.*, eśa *and* yeśa.

o-e'-ćoŋ, *n.* of ećoŋ; *doing, work:* oećoŋ waśte, *good doing it.*

o-e'-ćoŋ-ka, *n.* *one who does* a thing *very much.*

o-e'-ćoŋ-la, *v.* *T.* *to do frequently at* some place; *to go often for* a special purpose; as to frequent a bawdy-house.

o-e'-ćoŋ-na, *n.* *gambling, a lottery.* Sometimes written oećona. *T.*, yekiyapi.

o-e'-ha-ke, *n.* of ehake; *the last.*

o-e'-hde, *v. a* of ehde; *to set* or *place in*—oewahde.

o-e'-hde, *n.* of ehde; *a setting down; a saying, a verse, a sentence.*

o-e'-hna-ka, *n.* of ehnaka; *a placing down, a stop, period.*

o-e'-ti, *n.* of eti; *an encampment ahead.*

o-e′-ya-ke-ya, *n.* *the act of telling a story, a relation.*

o-e′-ye, *n.* of eya; *a saying, verse, sentence.*

o-e′-yu-ḣpa, *n.* of yuḣpa; *a place of resting* or *throwing down burdens.*

O-gla′-la, *n.* *T.* The name of one of the clans of Teeton Sioux: *i. q.* ohdada, *to scatter one's own.* *Ih.*, Okdada.

o-gla′-ya, *v.* *T.* *to thrust into,* as a stick into a tube.

o-gla′-ye-ya, *v.* *T.* *to shove into.*

o′-gle, *n.* *T.; and* o′-kde, *Ih.* *a shirt* or *coat:* *i. q.* oŋḣohda *and* oŋḣdoḣda.

o′-gle-i-sto-wa-ni-ća, *n.* *T.* *a vest,* that is, *a coat without arms.*

o-glu′, *v. n.* *T.* *to befall one*—owaglu.

o-glu′, *n.* *T.* *luck, fortune;* oglu waśte, *good fortune.*

o-gmuŋ′, *v.* *T.* *to gurgle,* as a bad egg.

o′-gna, *prep.* *T.* *in:* *i. q.* ohna: ognapasi, *to follow after in:* *i. q.* opasi.

o-gna′-ka, *v. a.* *T.* *to place in:* *i. q.* ohnaka—owagnaka.

o′-ġaŋ, *n.* *something that is open,* as open cloth. *T.*, ġaŋġaŋla.

o-ġaŋ′-ġaŋ, *v. n.* *to be full of holes.* *T.*, ġaŋġaŋla.

o′-ġe, *n.* *clothes, covering; a sheath.*

o′-ġe-ki-ći-toŋ, *v.* *to clothe for one*—oġewećitoŋ.

o′-ġe-ki-toŋ, *v. pos.* of oġetoŋ; *to put clothes on one's own*—oġewetoŋ.

o′-ġe-pi, *n.* *clothes.* *T.*, heyapi. See heyake *and* wokoyake.

o′-ġe-toŋ, *v. a.* *to put on clothes, have clothes on*—oġewatoŋ, oġeuŋtoŋpi: oġeiçitoŋ, *to clothe one's self.*

o′-ġe-źu-ya, *v.* oġeźuya yuza, *to take hold of one's clothes*

o′-ġe-źu-ya, *adv.* *together with; among.*

o′-ġiŋ-ġiŋ, *v. n.* *to nod:* oġiŋġiŋ yaŋka, *he is nodding.* See pakapsaŋ.

o-ġi′-ya, *v.* of ġi; *to paint yellow.*

o-ġu′, *v. n.* of ġu; *to burn in,* as in a kettle.

o-ġu′, *n.* *scraps, cracknels; dregs,* as coffee *grounds.*

o-ġu′-ġu-ye, *n.* *a brand, mark burnt in.*

o-ġu′-ke, *n.* *tallow-scraps.*

o-ġuŋ′-ġa, *v. n.* *to be half asleep and awake, to slumber, doze*—omaġuŋġa, oniġuŋġa.

o-ġu′-ya, *v. a.* *to cause to burn in,* as meat—oġuwaya.

o′-ha, *v. n.* *to stick to, adhere,* as feathers—omaha.

o′-ha, *n.* of yuha; *a straight place in a river, the distance between two bends, a reach:* óha haŋska, *a long straight place.*

o-ha′-kam, *adv.* *afterwards.* See ihakam.

o-ha′-kam-ya, *adv.* *after.* See ihakamya

o-ha'-ka-pa, *adv.* *afterwards.* See ihakapa.

o-ha'-ka-pa-taŋ-haŋ, *adv.* *afterwards* See ihakapataŋhaŋ.

o-ha'-mna, *adj.* *smelling of the skin.*

o-haŋ', *intj.* *oh, yes!* See ahaŋ *and* haŋ.

o-haŋ', *adv.* *when,* in the past, *at what time.*

o-haŋ', *v. n.* (ohna *and* haŋ) *to stand in.*

o-haŋ', *v. a.* *to put on* socks or moccasins, *to wear; to boil,* as corn, meat, etc.—owahaŋ, oyahaŋ, uŋkohaŋpi.

o'-haŋ, *v.* *to try, attempt; to apply one's self, study*—ówahe, óyahaŋ, óuŋhaŋpi.

o'-haŋ, *n.* *a straight place in a river.* See óha.

o'-haŋ-haŋ, *v.* *to speak lightly of, to jest.*

o-haŋ'-haŋ, *adv. red.* of ohaŋ.

o'-haŋ-hde, *v.* See óhaŋhdeya.

o'-haŋ-hde-ya, *v. a.* *to keep near* one, *follow about,* as a colt its mother; *to love*—ohaŋhdewaya, ohaŋhdemayaŋ.

o'-haŋ-ḣaŋ-na, *n.* *the morning; i. q.* haŋḣaŋna. *T.*, ohihaŋla.

o'-haŋ-gle-la, *adv.* *T.* *in the middle; through the middle.*

o-haŋ'-ke-ta, *adv.* *T.* *at the last, finally; i. q.* uŋhaŋketa.

o-haŋ'-pi, *part.* *boiled.*

o-haŋ'-ska, *n.* of haŋska. *length.*

o-haŋ'-ska-ya, *adv.* *in length.*

o'-haŋ-zi, *n.* *shade, defense from the heat; shadow.*

o'-haŋ-zi, *v. n.* *to be shade on*—omahaŋzi.

o'-haŋ-zi-hde-pi, *n.* *something set up for a shade,* as the branches of trees or bushes; *an arbor; a porch; an umbrella.*

o'-haŋ-zi-ya, *v. a.* *to shade, make a shade on*—ohaŋziwaya, ohaŋziuŋyaŋpi.

o-hba'-haŋ, *part.* *fallen to pieces in,* as a barrel in a corn-hole.

o-hda'-da, *v. pos.* of okada.

o-hdag', *cont.* of ohdaka: he ohdag wahi, *I have come to tell that.*

o-hdaḣ'-ni-ġa, *v. pos.* of okaḣniġa; *to understand one's own affairs*—owahdaḣniġa. *T.*, okiglaḣniġa—okiweglaḣniġa.

o-hdaḣ'-niḣ, *cont.* of ohdaḣniġa: ohdaḣniḣ maŋka.

o-hda'-ka, *v. pos.* of oyaka; *to tell of one's own*—owahdaka, uŋkohdakapi.

o-hda'-kiŋ-yaŋ, *n.* of hdakiŋyaŋ; *width, breadth.*

o-hda'-pśiŋ-yaŋ, *adv.* *bottom upwards, turned over.* *T.*, oglapśiŋyaŋ. See ahdapśiŋyaŋ.

o-hda'-pta, *v pos.* of oyapta *and* okapta; *to leave some of one's own*—owahdapta.

o-hde', *v. a.* of hde; *to set* or *place in*—owahde. See ohnaka, oźu, etc.

o'-hde, *n.* *a coat; suspenders.* *T.*, ćeśkiyutaŋ, *suspenders.*

o-hdi'-haŋ, *v. n.* *to fall in* anything *endwise.*

o-hdi'-he-ya, *v. a.* *to cause to fall in endwise*—ohdihewaya.

o-hdu'-ġe, *v. pos.* of oyuġe; *to put on, wear one's own*—owahduġe. *T.*, ogiçitoŋ *and* kiçuŋ.

o-hdu'-so-ta, *v. n.* *to go off, leave, be all gone,* as ducks in the fall of the year. *T.*, óglusota. See yusota.

o'-hdu-ta, *v. n.* *to be closed up.*

o'-hdu-te-ya, *v. a.* *to close up*—óhdutewaya.

o-hdu'-ze, *v. pos.* of oyuze; *to dip out from into one's own* dish—owahduze.

o-he', *v.* Same as ohaŋ.

o-he', *n.* *a place; a niche, a bed; the old* or *former place*—mitóhe.

o'-he, *n.* of yuha; *a having:* óhe waśte, *it is good having;* óhe waśtekae, *useful.* *T.*, oyuha.

o'-he, *n.* of ohaŋ; *a boiling:* óhe waŋźidaŋ, *one boiling.* *T.*, owehe.

o-he'-hde-pi, *n.* *a bedstead, bed.* *T.*, oyuŋke *and* oyuŋke ihupa.

o-hem'-ya, *adv.* *not quite full, almost full.*

o-he'-yuŋ, *v. a.* *to wrap up in*—ohemuŋ, ohenuŋ. See heyuŋ.

o-he'-yuŋ, *n.* *a wrapper:* oheyuŋpi, *wrappers.*

o'-hi, *v. n.* *to hang over,* as hair over one's face, or grass over a path: *i. q.* ćaŋku peźi kaohduteyapi. *T.*, okahi.

o'-hi, *v. a.* *to be able to reach to, tall enough to reach up to, long enough to reach down to*—ówahi, óuŋhipi; *to reach to* one, *be large enough for*—ómahi.

o'-hi-daŋ, *v. dim.* of óhi.

o'-hi-haŋ-la, *n.* *T.* *the morning, during the forenoon.*

o'-hi-ka, *n.* *one whose hair is always hanging over his face.* *T.*, okahika.

o-hi'-ka, *n.* *one who has ability, one who is able to accomplish.*

o-hi'-ki-ya, *v. pos.* of ohiya; *to win back one's own; to give* something *to* another of *what one has won, to win for* another—ohiwakiya.

o'-hi-na-pe, *n* of hinapa; *a place of egress.*

o-hiŋ'-ḣpa-ya, *v.* (o *and* hiŋḣpaya) *to fall into; to fall from, forsake*—omahiŋḣpaya.

o-hiŋ'-ḣpa-ye-ya, *v. a.* *to cause to fall into*—ohiŋḣpayewaya.

o'-hi-ni, *adv.* See óhiŋni.

o'-hiŋ-ni, *adv.* *always.*

o'-hiŋ-ni-ki-ya, *v. a.* *to cease from, to finish*—óhiŋniwakiya. *T.*, ihunikiya.

o'-hiŋ-ni-ya, *v. a.* *to finish*—óhiŋniwaya. *T.*, ihuniya.

o'-hiŋ-ni-yaŋ, *adv.* *always, all along, all through.*

o-hi'-ti-da, *v. a.* *to consider furious*—ohitiwada: ohitiiçida, *to think one's self terrible, to bluster, to swagger, to bully*—ohitimiçida. *T.*, ohitilaka, *to consider brave.*

o-hi′-ti-ka, *v. n.* *to be furious, terrible, brave*—omahitika, onihitika. See wohitika.

o-hi′-ti-ya, *adv.* *furiously, terribly, savagely.*

o-hi′-ya, *v. a.* *to get the better of* one in any way, *to overcome; to gain, win, acquire in a game*—ohiwaya, ohiuŋyaŋpi.

o′-hi-ya, *v. a.* *to cause to reach to*—óhiwaya.

o′-hi-ya, *adv.* *reaching to; hanging over*, as hair.

o′-hi-ya, *n.* *the hair that hangs down on the face.* *T.*, okahiya.

o′-hi-ye, *n.* *a string* or *strand of beads; one length of* anything.

o-hi′-ye-ya, *and* o-hi′-ye-ki-ya, *v. a.* *to cause to win*—ohiyewaya.

o-hi′-yu, *v.* of hiyu; *to come through*, as water through a roof, *to leak; to come into, come through on*—omahiyu

o-hmuŋ′, *adj.* *faint, not very apparent*, as tracks in snow on which more has fallen.

o-hmuŋ′-hmuŋ, *adj. red.* of ohmuŋ; *indistinct*, as conversation not plainly heard.

o-hmuŋ′-hmuŋ-yaŋ, *adv.* *indistinctly.*

o-hmuŋ′-yaŋ, *adv.* *faintly, not apparent.*

o-hmuŋ′-ye-ća, *adj.* *partly visible*, as a chicken peeping out of its shell.

o′-hmus, *cont.* of óhmuza; i ohmus wauŋ, *my mouth is shut.* *T.*, ogmus; lotogmus yuza, *to hold by the throat.*

o′-hmus-ya, *v. n.* *to shut, cause to shut*—óhmuswaya.

o′-hmu-za, *v. n.* *to be shut* or *closed:* iśta ohmuza, *eyes shut.*

o-hna′, *prep.* *in, into, on, upon.* *T.*, ogna; *Ih.*, okna. See ahna *and* ehna.

o-hnag′, *cont.* of ohnaka; ohnag waśi, *I told him to put it in.*

o-hna′-hna, *prep. red.* of ohna.

o-hna′-hna-ka, *v. red.* of ohnaka.

o-hna′-hna-ka-pi, *n.* *something in which things are put* or *laid away, a chest; a coffin.* See ćaŋohnahnakapi. *T.*, ćanwogna.

o-hna′-ka, *prep.* *in, upon:* nape ohnaka, *in the hand.*

o-hna′-ka, *v. a.* *to put in, place in* anything. *T.*, ognaka. See ahnaka, ehnaka, hnaka, ouŋpa, etc.

o-hna′-ka-pi, *n.* *a placing in.*

o-hna′-na, *adv.* napohnana, *only a handful.*

o-hni′-hda, *v. n.* (o *and* hnihda) *to go on a journey, travel from place to place*—owahnihda, uŋkohnihdapi. *T.*, ognigla.

o-hni′-hde, *part.* *going from place to place:* ohnihde ya, *to go from place to place.*

o-hni′-hde-ki-ya, *v. a.* *to cause to go from place to place*—ohnihdewakiya. *T.*, ogniglekiya.

o-hni′-hde-ya, *v. a.* *to send hither and thither*—ohnihdewaya.

o-hni′-hde-ya, *adv.* *going from one place to another:* ohnihdeya wauŋ, *I am going about.*

o-hni'-hde-ya-pi, *n.* *those sent, messengers, apostles.*

o-ho'. See ohoka.

o-ho'-da, *v. a.* *to respect, honor, worship*—ohowada, ohouŋdapi.

o-ho'-da-ka, *v. a.* *to respect, honor, worship*—ohowadaka, ohouŋdapika.

o-ho'-ḣpa, *v. a.* of hoḣpa; *to cough and spit into*—ohowaḣpa. *T.*, otaḣośe.

o-ho'-ka, *n.* *one who is respectable* or *honorable. T.*, oholapi.

o-ho'-ki-da, *v.* *pos.* of ohoda; *to honor one's own. T.*, ohokila.

o-ho'-mni, *adv.* *around, round about:* ohomni ya, *to go around.*

o-ho'-mni-ku-wa, *v.* *to hint at; go round about* in regard to—ohomni makuwa.

o-ho'-mni-yaŋ, *adv.* *around, round about.*

o-huŋ'-kaŋ-kaŋ, *n.* *stories; myths; i. q.* hituŋkaŋkapi.

o'-hu-ta, *n.* *the place where the water meets the land, the edge* or *shore.* See huta.

o'-hu-tam, *adv.* *at the shore. T.*, ohuta. See hutam.

o'-hu-ta-pa, *adv.* *at the edge* or *shore.* See hutapa

o'-hu-ta-ta, *adv.* *at the shore.* See hutata

o-hu'-te, *n.* of hute; *the root, the bottom. T.*, hute.

o-ḣ'a', *adj.* *gray, black and white, white specks on a black ground. T.*, ḣota.

o-ḣ'a'-ka, *adj.* *gray, black appearing through the white, all colors intermingled.*

o-ḣa'-ka, *v. n.* *to be stuffed with food, surfeited; to be injured* or *made sick by food*—omaḣaka.

o-ḣa'-ka, *adj.* *hurtful, injurious,* as some kinds of food.

o-ḣa'-ka, *adj.* *T.* *forked,* as a stream.

o-ḣa'-ka, *n.* *the forks of a stream.*

o-ḣa'-mna, *v. n.* *to smell moldy; i. q.* aamna.

o-ḣaŋ', *v.* *to do, to work*—owaḣaŋ, uŋkoḣaŋpi. See ośkan.

o-ḣaŋ', *n.* *work, action, custom*—mioḣaŋ, nioḣaŋ, uŋkoḣaŋpi.

o'-ḣaŋ, *v. n.* *to be slow, to be long in doing*—omaḣaŋ.

o-ḣaŋ'-haŋ-haŋ, *v. n.* *to do odd things, to play pranks, cut capers; to do badly*—oḣaŋwahaŋhaŋ.

o-ḣaŋ'-haŋ-haŋ-ka, *v.* Same as oḣaŋhaŋhaŋ.

o-ḣaŋ'-ki-haŋ-haŋ, *v.* *to play pranks upon* one, *to do badly to*—oḣaŋwakihaŋhaŋ.

o-ḣaŋ'-ko, *v. n.* *to be quick in doing* anything, *handy*—oḣaŋmako, oḣaŋniko.

o-ḣaŋ'-ko-ya, *adv.* *quickly.*

o-ḣaŋ'-ko-ye-daŋ, *adv.* *quickly, suddenly.*

o-ḣaŋ'-pi, *v. n.* (oḣaŋ *and* pi) *to be generous, liberal*—oḣaŋmapi. See oḣaŋwaśte.

o-ḣaŋ'-pi-ya, *adv.* *generously, liberally.*

o-ḣaŋ'-sda-ta, *v. n.* (oḣaŋ *and* sdata) *to be slow in one's movements, to work slowly and deliberately*—oḣaŋmasdata. *T.*, oḣ'aŋslate.

o-ḣaŋ'-śi-ća, *v. n.* *to be stingy* or *illiberal; to be of a mean* or *cross disposition*—oḣaŋmaśića. See oḣaŋwaśte.

o-ḣaŋ-śi'-ća, *v. n.* *to be ill-behaved.*

o-ḣaŋ'-śi-ća-ya, *adv.* *badly.*

o-ḣaŋ'-śin-ya, *adv.* *badly, wickedly.*

o-ḣaŋ'-śin-ya, *v. a.* *to make stingy, make bad*—oḣaŋśinwaya, oḣaŋśinuŋyaŋpi.

o-ḣaŋ'-śuŋ-ke-ća, *v. n.* (oḣaŋ *and* śuŋka) *to behave ill, act like a dog; to eat up* or *destroy provisions,* or anything that is valued or stored up for use, and to which one has no right; *to be selfish*—owaḣaŋśuŋkeća, uŋkoḣaŋśuŋkećapi. *T.*, oḣ'aŋśuŋkeća, also when *one who is much trusted in dies,* he is said to be oḣ'aŋśuŋkeća.

o-ḣaŋ'-te-haŋ, *v. n* (oḣaŋ *and* tehaŋ) *to be long in doing* a thing—oḣaŋmatehaŋ.

o-ḣaŋ'-wa-śte, *v. n.* *to behave well, be good, be generous*—oḣaŋmawaśte. See oḣaŋśića.

o-ḣaŋ'-yaŋ, *v. n.* *to do, work, act*—owaḣaŋmda, oyaḣaŋda, uŋkoḣaŋyaŋpi.

o'-ḣaŋ-yaŋ, *v. a.* *to cause to be slow, to hinder*—oḣaŋwaye.

o-ḣaŋ'-ye-ya, *v. a.* *to cause to do*—oḣaŋyewaya.

o'-ḣa-ya, *v. a.* *to fill up,* as a hole with brush, etc.—oḣawaya, oḣauŋyaŋpi. *T.*, oḣáya.

o-ḣ'a'-ya, *adv.* *in a grayish* or *mixed manner.* Said of putting paint on the face. *T*, ḣolya.

o-ḣći'-ḣći, *adv.* *hanging, dangling.*

o-ḣći'-ḣći-ya, *adv.* *in bunches.*

o-ḣći'-ḣći-ya, *v.* *T.* *to make dangle.*

o-ḣda'-ḣda, *adj.* *loose, rattling,* as a small bullet in a gun. *T.*, oḣlaġaŋ. See oḣdaġaŋ *and* oḣtaḣtadaŋ.

o-ḣda'-ḣda-ye-daŋ, *adv.* *loosely,* as knitting; *not stretched,* as a cord. *T.*, oḣlaġaŋla.

o-ḣda'-te, *adv.* *under, beneath.* See oḣlate.

o-ḣda'-te-ya, *adv.* *beneath, under:* oḣdateya iyaya, *it has gone underneath.* *T.*, oḣlateya.

o-ḣda'-te-ya-taŋ-haŋ, *adv.* *from beneath.*

o'-ḣdo-ḣda, *n.* See oŋḣdoḣda.

o-ḣdo'-ka, *n.* *a hole* in anything, *an aperture.* *T.*, oḣloka.

o-ḣe', *n.* *a hill:* oḣeyahe and oḣeyawaḣe, *a hill that is much visited,* as Pilot-knob near Fort Snelling. See paha *and* ḣe.

o'-ḣe-ya, *v. n.* *to have but little in.* See aḣe.

o-ḣiŋ'-yaŋ, *v.* *to pout, be out of humor about, to be dissatisfied with* one's portion or treatment; *to slight, refuse*—owaḣiŋyaŋ, uŋkoḣiŋyaŋpi.

o-ḣla′-ġaŋ, *adj.* *T.* *not fitting, loose.* Said of a small thing in a large place.

o-ḣla′-ġaŋ-la, *adv.* *T.* *loosely.*

o-ḣla′-ġaŋ-ye-la, *adv.* *T.* *loosely.*

o-ḣla′-te, *adv.* *T.* *i. q.* oḣdate; *under*, as, maya oḣlate ćaŋku iyaya, *the road goes under the hill* or *bank.*

o-ḣla′-te-ya, *adv.* *T.* *under, beneath:* *i. q.* oḣdateya.

o-ḣle′, *and* o-ḣli′-se, *adv.* *T.* *crowded about*, as people around a tent to see a dance.

o-ḣlo′-ka, *n.* *T.* *a hole:* *i. q.* oḣdoka

o-ḣmi′-ḣmi-yaŋ, *adj.* *crooked.*

o-ḣmi′-yaŋ, *adj.* *crooked.*

o-ḣno′-ġa, *n.* *the corners that are usually fenced off on each side of the door in a Dakota lodge.* *T.*, uŋgnaġa.

o-ḣno′-ġa-ta, *adv.* *in the corners of the tent* near the door; *down at the side of a tent, close under.* *T.*, uŋgnaġata.

o-ḣno′-ġi-ća-daŋ, *n.* *a bird like a small owl.*

O-ḣno′-ġi-ća-daŋ, *n.* *an imaginary being worshipped by the Dakotas.* Same as Ćaŋotidaŋ. See Hoḣnoġićadaŋ. *T.*, Uŋgnaġićala.

o-ḣo′, *intj.* expressive of disbelief; *not so!* *T.*, hoḣ.

o-ḣpa′, *v. n.* *to gather together, flock together*, as geese, etc.

o-ḣpaŋ′, *v. n.* *to be wet* or *moist in.*

o-ḣpaŋ′-ki-ya, *v. a.* *to dip into, sop* or *soak in; to wet* or *soak*, so as to take off the hair—oḣpaŋwakiya.

o-ḣpaŋ′-yaŋ, *v. a.* *to cause to moisten* or *soak in; to soak*, as a skin for dressing—oḣpaŋwaya.

o-ḣta′-ḣta-daŋ, *adj.* *loose, not stretched tight*, as a slackened bowstring.

o-ḣta′-ḣta-ye-daŋ, *adv.* *loosely, not stretched.* Same as oḣdaḣdayedaŋ.

o-ḣta′-ni, *n.* of ḣtani; *work, labor*—mitoḣtani, nitoḣtani: toḣtani, *his work.* *T.*, wowaśi.

o′-ḣta′-ye-tu, *n.* of ḣtayetu; *the evening.*

oḣ′-ya, *adv.* *obliquely, from corner to corner, sloping*, as the characters in writing See kaoḣya, yuoḣya, etc.

o-i′-ća-ġa, *v. n.* of ićaġa; *to grow in* anything; *to grow up*—oimaćaġa, oinićaġa.

o-i′-ća-ġe, *n.* of ićaġa; *a growing, creation; interest* on money lent.

o-i′-ća-hi-toŋ, *v. a.* of ićahi; *to mingle, mix together in*, as tobacco and bark, in anything—oićahiwatoŋ. *T.*, ićahitoŋ.

o-i′-ća-hi-ye, *n.* of ićahiya; *a mixture, a mixing:* oićahiye waŋźidaŋ, *one mixing.*

o-i′-ćaḣ, *cont.* of oićaġa; oićaḣ kokedaŋ, *of quick growth;* oićaḣ tehaŋ, *of slow growth.*

o-i′-ćaḣ-waŋ-ka-la, *adj.* *T* *growing easily.*

o-i′-ćaȟ-ya, *v. a.* *to yield, produce; to make grow; to cause to produce*, as interest—oićaȟwaya.

o-i′-ća-zo, *n.* of ićazo; *a marking, a mark; credits, taking* things *on credit, giving credit.*

o-i′-ći-ma-ni, *n.* of ićimani; *traveling, a traveler;* oićimani waniéa, *there is no one traveling; a company of travelers.*

o-i′-ću-wa, *n.* of kuwa; *tools of* all kinds.

o-i′-ću-wa-śte, *adj.* of iću *and* waśte; *good to take, acceptable.*

o-i′-ḉi-hde, *n.* of hde; *what one has laid up, property.* *T.*, wakigle; wakignaka.

o-i′-ḉi-hi, *v. reflex.* of okihi; *to be able for one's self, be rich; to get for one's self, be selfish*—omiḉihi.

o-i′-ḉi-kpa-ni, *v.* Same as oiḉitpani.

o-i′-ḉi-tpa-ni, *v. reflex.* of okitpani; *not to be able to take care of one's self* or *family, to be poor*—omiḉitpani.

o′-i-ḉi-ṭiŋ-za, *v. reflex.* of oṭiŋza; *to have command of one's self*—omiḉiṭiŋza.

o-i′-ḉi-wa, *v. reflex.* of owa; *to write one's self:* ćaźe oiḉiwa, *to sign one's own name.*

o′-i-ḉi-ya, *v. reflex.* of okiya; *to help one's self.*

o-i′-de, *v. n.* of ide; *to blaze in.*

o-i′-de, *n.* *a flame.*

o-i′-e, *n.* of ia; *a word; a saying* or *speech.*

o-i′-e-ki-ća-toŋ, *v. a.* *to speak to,* John x, 6—oiewećatoŋ.

o-i′-e-ki-ḉuŋ, *v. n.* *to command, enforce obedience*—oieweḉuŋ.

o-i′-e-ki-toŋ, *v n.* *to use language, speak*—oiwetoŋ.

o-i′-e-ya, *v. n.* *to use words, to speak*—oiewaya.

o-i′-glag, *cont.* of oiglaka; oiglag uŋpi, *they are moving.*

o-i′-gla-ka, *v.* *T.* *to move; be moving,* as a family or camp. See ihdaka *and* uŋhdaka.

o-i′-gla-ke, *n.* *T.* *a moving party.*

o-i′-glu-śkaŋ, *v. n.* *T.* *to have a relapse, become sick again.*

o-i′-hda-ka, *v. reflex.* of oyaka; *to make one's self known, tell one's own* name; *to confess*—omihdaka. *T.*, oiglaka.

o-i′-hdo-ye. See ihdoya.

o-i′-hdu-ġe, *v. reflex.* *to put on one's self*—omihduġe.

o-i′-hdu-ha, *v. pos.* *to have one's self;* to be a citizen—omihduha. *T.*, oigluha.

o-i′-hdu-ha-pi, *n.* *citizenship.* *T.*, oigluhapi.

o-i′-hdu-so-ta, *v. reflex.* *to use one's self up, to go all away,* said of the ducks all leaving. See ohdusota *and* ihdusota. *T.*, oiglusota.

o-i′-hdu-śi-ća, *v. reflex.* *to injure one's self* in the estimation of others, *get one's self into difficulty*—omihduśića. *T.*, ogluśica. See ihduśića.

o-i'-hdu-ze, *n.* of ihduza; *what one puts on, clothing.*

o-i'-he-ya, *v. a.* of iheya; *to shoot into*—oihewaya.

o-i'-he-ye, *n.* *the place where the shot is sent.*

o-i'-huŋ-ni, *v. a.* of ihuŋni; *to land in* or *at*—oiwahuŋni.

o-i'-huŋ-ni, *n.* *a landing, harbor, port:* oihuŋni waśte, *a good landing.*

o-i'-kpa-ṭa, *v. n.* of ikpi *and* ṭa; *to be still-born.*

o-i'-kpa-ṭa, *n.* *T* *an abortion.*

o-i'-le-le-ke, *n.* *T.* *a thief.*

o-i'-na-pa, *v.* of inapa; *to go* or *come out into*—oinawapa.

o-i'-na-pe, *n.* *a place of coming out.*

o-i'-na-pe-daŋ, *n.* *dim.* of oinape.

o-i'-na-pe-ya, *adv.* *appearing,* as the summits of hills that first become bare of snow.

o-i'-na-ta-ka, *v.* of nataka; *to lock in,* as in a house—oinawataka.

o-i'-na-źiŋ, *n.* of inaźiŋ; *a standing place, starting place.*

o-i'-na-źiŋ-ta, *n.* *the place of standing, the goal.*

o-iŋ', *v.* *to wear,* as rings, *in the ears* or *nose*—owaiŋ, oyaiŋ, uŋkoiŋpi. *T.*, owiŋ.

o-iŋ', *n.* *an ear* or *nose jewel.* *T.*, owiŋ.

o-iŋ'-ki-ya, *v. a.* *to cause to wear,* as jewels—oiŋwakiya. *T.*, owiŋkiya.

o'-iŋ-kpa, *n.* *the end* of anything. See iŋkpa.

o'-iŋ-kpa-ta, *adv.* *at the end.* See iŋkpata.

o'-iŋ-kpa-ya, *adv.* *at the beginning, in the first place.*

o-iŋ'-na, *n.* *ear-jewels.* *T.*, owiŋla. See oiŋ.

o-iŋ'-pi, *n.* *ear-rings, jewels.* *T.*, owiŋpi.

o-iŋ'-pi-daŋ, *ear-drops, jewels.*

o-iŋ'-taŋ-ka, *n.* *a large ear-drop.*

o'-iŋ-tpa, *n.* *the end* of anything; *i. q.* oiŋkpa.

o'-iŋ-tpa-ta, *adv.* *at the end;* *i. q.* oiŋkpata.

o-i'-pa-kśaŋ, *n.* *a bend, crook, angle.* See ipakśaŋ.

o-i'-pa-ktaŋ, *n.* *T.* *a bend in a stream*: *i. q.* oiyuktaŋ.

o-i'-pe-ya, *n.* *T.* *a sheltered place; a warm place* out of the wind: *i. q.* oblula.

o-i'-pi-ya-ke, *n.* of ipiyaka; *the place around which the girdle is put, the waist.*

o-i'-pu-ta-ke, *n.* of iputaka; *a kiss.*

o-i'-se, *n.* *the outer corner,* as of a house.

o-i'-śta-waŋ-źi-la, *n.* *T.* *a steady gaze, a fixed look.*

o-i'-śtiŋ-be, *n* of iśtiŋbe; *a place to sleep in, a bed-room.* *T.*, oiśtiŋme.

o-i'-śtiŋ-ma, *n.* of iśtiŋma; *a bed-room.*

o-i'-toŋ-śni, *v.* of itoŋśni; *to lie, tell a lie respecting* one—oiwatoŋśni. *T.*, owewakaŋ; owewakaŋkaŋ.

o-i'-toŋ-śni, *n.* *a lie, falsehood.* *T.*, owewakaŋkaŋ.

o-i'-toŋ-śni-yaŋ, *adv.* *lying, falsely.* *T.*, owewakaŋkaŋyaŋ.

o-i'-ya-be, *n* of iyabe; *a dispersion, a hunting.*

o-i'-ya-be-ya, *v. a.* *to make a hunting excursion*—oiyabewaya.

o-i'-ya-be-ye, *n.* *a hunting, hunting-ground.*

o-i'-ya-haŋ, *v. n.* of iyahaŋ; *to alight down in.*

o-i'-ya-hde, *v. n.* of iyahde; *to reach to, reach from* one to another.

o-i'-ya-hde-ya, *v. a.* *to cause to reach to*—oiyahdewaya See iyahdeya.

o-i'-ya-hde-ya, *adv.* *reaching to.*

o-i'-ya-he, *n.* of iyahaŋ; *a lighting down in.*

o-i'-ya-ḣpe-ya, *v.* *T.* ćaŋnoŋpa oiyaḣpeya, *to hold up the pipe to,* as the Dakotas do to the Great Spirit before smoking.

o-i'-ya-ḣpe-ye, *n.* *what can be thrown over* the back of a horse, as, oiyaḣpeye waŋźidaŋ, *one load:* ćaŋduhupa oiyaḣpeye, *the end of the pipe-stem that is held in the mouth.* *T.*, oyape. See iyaḣpeya.

o-i'-ya-ka-śka, *v. a.* *to tie into*—oiyawakaśka. See iyakaśka.

o-i'-ya-ka-śke, *n.* *a tying into, a knot.*

o-i'-yam, *cont.* of oiyaŋpa.

o-i'-ya-ni-ća, *v. n.* *to be prevented in*—oiyamanića. See iyanića.

o-i'-ya-ni-će, *n.* *prevention; costiveness.*

o-i'-ya-nin, *cont.* of oiyanića. *T.*, oiyanil.

o-i'-ya-nin-ya, *v. a.* *to prevent, be the cause of prevention:* oiyaniniçiye śni wo, John xx, 27, *do not be yourself prevented, do not stand in your own way,* "*be not faithless.*" *T*, oiyanilya.

o-i'-yaŋ-pa, *v.* of iyaŋpa; *to breathe out of,* as an otter out of a hole; oiyam waŋka, *he lies breathing out of* the hole. *T.*, oniya yuŋka.

o-i'-yaŋ-pe, *n.* *a hole* or *breathing place.* *T.*, oniya oḣloka.

o-i'-yaŋ-pe-daŋ, *n.* *a hole,* as of a muskrat.

o-i'-ye-ki-ye, *n.* of iyekiya; *recognition.*

o-i'-ye-ya, *v.* See oieya.

o-i'-yo-blu-ya *and* o-i'-yo-blu-ye-la, *adj.* or *n.* *T.* *a calm;* oiyobluya hiyeya, *it grows calm.* See ioblula *and* iyoblula.

o-i'-yo-hnag, *cont.* of oiyohnaka; oiyohnag tonana, *a few mouthfuls.*

o-i'-yo-hna-ka, *n.* of iyohnaka; *a mouthful, very little.*

o-i'-yo-ḣlo-ka, *n.* *T.* *the mouth of a stream; an opening into.* See iyoḣloke.

o'-i-yo-ḣpa-ya, *v.* *to fall into*—oiyowaḣpamda. See iyoḣpaya.

o'-i-yo-ḣpe-ya, *v. a.* *to throw* or *cast into, to go into,* as into a river at a ford—oiyoḣpewaya. See iyoḣpeya.

o′-i-yo-ḣpe-ye, *n.* *a place of going into, a ford.* *T.*, oiyoḣpaya.

o′-i-yo-ki-pi, *adj.* *pleasant, agreeable.*

o′-i-yo-ki-pi, *v. n.* *to be pleased with*—oiyomakipi, oiyonićipi. See iyokipi.

o′-i-yo-ki-pi-ya, *adv.* *pleasantly, agreeably.*

o′-i-yo-ki-śi-ća, *adj.* *T.* *disagreeable,* as the weather; *unhappy, feeling badly*—oiyomakiśića.

o-i′-yo-kpa-za, *n.* *T.* *darkness.* See okpaza.

o-i′-yo-kpas-ya, *adv.* *darkly.*

o-i′-yo-kpas-ya, *v. a.* *to make dark.*

o-i′-yo-pe-ye, *n.* of iyopeya; *payment* for anything; *what is given in exchange; money,* as, oiyopeye manića, *I have no money.*

o-i′-yo-taŋ-ke, *n.* of iyotaŋka; *a seat, a sitting place.*

o-i′-yu-ktaŋ, *n.* of yuktaŋ; *a bend.* *T*, oipaktaŋ.

o-i′-yu-ski-te, *n.* of iyuskita; *a place where a band goes round.*

o-i′-yu-we-ġe, *n.* of iyuweġa; *the place of crossing* a stream, *a ford;* the name of *Traverse des Sioux.*

o-ka′-ća-ġi *and* o-ka′-ća-ġu, *v.* See okadya. *T.*, oġu.

o-ka′-da, *v. a.* *to lay eggs,* as fowls do: Maġáokada wi, *the moon when the geese lay eggs, April* and sometimes *May; to pour out into,* as grain of any kind; *to scatter in* or *on, sow, plant*—owakada, uŋkokadapi. *T.*, witka toŋ, *to lay eggs.*

o-ka′-da-da, *v.* *red.* of okada.

o-ka′-da-i-he-ya, *v.* *to load* a gun *in haste without a wad*—okadaihewaya.

o-ka′-dus, *cont.* of okaduza.

o-ka′-dus-ya, *adv.* *airy.*

o-ka′-du-za, *v. n.* *to blow through* or *into, blow on* one—omakaduza. See kaduza.

o-ka′-du-za, *n.* *air in motion, a draught of wind.*

o-kad′-ya *or* o-kan′-ya, *v.* okadyaġi *and* okadyaġu, *to be scorched in.* *T.*, oġu.

o-ka′-gla-ye-la, *adv.* *T.* *near to, close by.*

o-ka′-ġa, *n.* *things made* in the same manner, *kinds; a bundle of arrows made alike.*

o-ka′-ġa, *v. a.* *to make after a model, copy*—owakaġa, uŋkokaġapi.

o-ka′-ġa, *v. n.* *to stick into,* as something sharp: wićape omakaġa, *a prickle sticks in me.*

o′-ka-ġa, *n.* *the south.* *T.*, itokaġa.

o′-ka-ġa, *adv.* *southwards; down stream,* since the streams in the Dakota country run southwards. *T.*, itokaġa; hutabya.

o-ka′-ġa-pi, *n.* *a copy, model, image.*

o′-ka-ġa-taŋ-haŋ, *adv.* *from the south; from below, down stream.* *T.*, itokaġataŋhaŋ.

o-ka′-ġe, *n.* of kaġa; *something that is made.*

o-ka′-ġe-ġe, *n.* of kaġeġe; *a place where anything is sewed, a seam.*

o-ka'-ġe-źu-ya, *adv.* *whilst, between, beyond:* maḣpiya okaġeźuya, *among* or *beyond the clouds.* See iċaġeźuya.

o'-ka-hda, *adv.* of kahda; *by the side of;* okahda mda. *T.*, okagla *and* iċagla; okaglayela, *near to, close by.*

o-ka'-hi, *v. n.* *T.* *to hang over,* as the hair over the face.

o-ka'-hi-ka, *n.* *T.* *one whose hair hangs over the face; one who has bangs.*

o-ka'-hi-ya, *v. a.* *T.* *to make hang over.*

o-ka'-hi-ya, *adv.* *T.* *hanging over.*

o-kaḣ', *cont.* of okáġa: okaḣ waśte, *of good form.*

o'-kaḣ, *cont.* of ókaġa; *to the south;* ókaḣ uŋyaŋpi, *we go southwards.* *T.*, itokaḣ.

o'-ka-ḣbog, *cont.* of ókaḣboka. *T.*, kaḣwog.

o'-ka-ḣbog-ya, *v. a.* *to cause to float down stream*—ókaḣbogwaya. *T.*, kaḣwogya, *to make float in the air.*

o'-ka-ḣbo-ka, *v. n.* of kaḣboka; *to float along, to be borne on* the water or *in* the air. *T.*, kaḣwoka, *to float on the air.* See okaḣpa.

o'-ka-ḣbo-ka, *n.* *a drift, a float; a waif.* *T.*, kaḣwoka.

o-ka'-ḣde-ċa, *v. a.* of kaḣdeċa; *to tear a hole in, tear in pieces, to fracture*—owakaḣdeċa.

o-ka'-ḣde-ċe, *n.* *a rent, a fracture.*

o-ka'-ḣden, *cont.* of okaḣdeċa; okaḣden iyeya.

o-ka'-ḣdog, *cont.* of okaḣdoka; okaḣdog iyeya.

o-ka'-ḣdo-ka, *v. a.* *to make its way through,* as water through cloth, *to come through*—omakaḣdoka.

o-ka'-ḣdo-ke, *n.* of kaḣdoka; *a hole broken through.*

o'-kaḣ-hi-ya-ya, *v.* *T.* *to float by; to drift.*

o'-kaḣ-ki-ya, *adv.* *southwards, down stream.* *T.*, itokaḣkiya.

o-ka'-ḣmiŋ, *n.* *a corner; a bay.* See mdeċaḣmiŋ.

o-ka'-ḣni-ġa, *v. a.* *to understand, comprehend*—owakaḣniġa, oyakaḣniġa, uŋkokaḣniġapi; omayakaḣniġa, *thou comprehendest me.* See okiċaḣniġa.

o-ka'-ḣniḣ, *cont.* of okaḣniġa; okaḣniḣ waśte, *easy to understand;* okaḣniḣpiċa, *comprehensible;* okaḣniḣpiċa śni, *not capable of being understood.*

o-ka'-ḣniḣ-ki-ya, *v. a.* *to cause to understand*—okaḣniḣwakiya.

o-ka'-ḣniḣ-ya, *v. a.* *to make to comprehend, explain to* one—okaḣniḣwaya.

o-ka'-ḣo, *v. n.* *to travel around much, wander about*—owakaḣo, uŋkokaḣopi. *T.*, okaḣwoka.

o-ka'-ḣpa, *v. a.* of kaḣpa; *to make fall into by striking*—owakaḣpa.

o-ka'-ḣpa, *v. n.* *to float down on,* as on a river. See okaḣboka.

o-k a'-ħ p a-ħ p a, *n.* ćaŋ okaħpa-ħpa, *chips.*

o-k a'-ħ p u, *v. a.* of kaħpu; *to knock* or *brush off into*—owakaħpu.

o-k a'-ħ t a ŋ, *v. n.* of kaħtaŋ; *to soak in, become soaked.*

o-k a'-ħ t a ŋ-y a ŋ, *v. a. to dip in, sop up, sponge*—okaħtaŋwaya: *to soak in, absorb.* See okapon.

o-k a'-ħ t a ŋ-y e, *n. a sponge; i. q.* mini iyuħepe.

o'-k a ħ-w a-p a, *adv. southwards.*

o-k a'-ħ w o-k a, *v n. T. to float in the air.* See okaħboka *and* okaħo.

o'-k a ħ-y a, *v. a. T. to cause to float down stream.*

o'-k a ħ-y a, *adv. T. floating.*

o-k a'-k a ŋ, *v.* of kakaŋ; *to hew in* anything—owakakaŋ.

o-k a'-k a-p a, *v. a. to catch,* as a ball in a ball-club or in the hand—owakakapa.

o-k a'-k i ŋ, *v. to peep into.* See aokakiŋ *and* aokasiŋ.

o-k a'-k i ś-y a, *adv. T. abusively.*

o-k a'-k p a ŋ, *v. n. to be broken up in*

o-k a'-k s a, *v. a.* of kaksa; *to cut a hole into* or *through,* as in ice; *to break through in, to fall in*—owakaksa.

o-k a'-k s e, *n. pieces cut out, cuttings; a notch cut in.*

o-k a'-k ś a ŋ, *adv. around about, by a roundabout way.*

o-k a'-k ś e, *n.* of kakśa; *a roll* of ribbon or cloth, *a skein* of thread.

o-k a'-m d a, *n.* of kamda; *a piece cut off broad and flat,* as meat cut for drying; *a slice.*

o-k a'-m d a-y a, *adv.* of kamdaya; *without obstruction, expanded; plain, level; freely,* as in discoursing.

o-k a'-m d a-y e, *n. a level place, a plain. T.,* oblaye.

o-k a'-m d e-ć a, *v. a.* of kamdeća; *to break to pieces in* anything—owakamdeća.

o-k a'-m d e-ć a, *v. n. to break forth, spread out,* as in freshets: mini okamdeća, *the water has spread out.*

o-k a'-m d e-ć a-h a ŋ, *part. broken in.*

o-k a'-m d e-ć e, *n. a breaking in.*

o-k a'-m d e n, *cont.* of okamdeća: okamden iyeya, *to break* or *crush to pieces in.*

o-k a'-m d u, *v. n. to blow into,* as the wind does. Compare kamdu.

o-k a'-m d u-y a, *adv. airy, admitting air:* okamduya haŋ, *standing open* so as to admit air, as a door, etc.

o-k a'-m n a, *v. to avoid, to go around;* okamna ećoŋ, *to do in a crowd.*

o-k a'-m n a, *adv. T. avoiding, eschewing*

o-k a'-m n a, *adj. open,* as a wood where there is no underbrush

o-k a'-m n a, *n.* of kamna; *a gathering, collection:* okamna waśte, *it is good gathering.*

o-ka′-mna-yaŋ, *adv.* *going round, avoiding, taking care, picking one's steps*, as in walking: okamnayaŋ mani, *he walks carefully.*

o-kan′, *cont.* of okata. *T.*, okal.

o-kan′-ya, *v. a.* *to heat in*—okanwaya. See kanya.

o-kan′-ya, *adv.* *by the heat, heating:* okanya śpaŋyaŋ, *to toast, cook by the heat;* okanya ġi, *to scorch in* anything; okanya ġu, *to be scorched by holding near the fire.* *T.*, iyokalya.

o-kaŋ′, *v. n.* *there is room, room for; it is not crowded*—omakaŋ, uŋkokaŋpi: okaŋ śni, *there is no room.* See oćikaŋ, kiyukaŋ, etc.

o-kaŋ′, *n.* of kaŋ; *old age.* *T.*, kaŋ.

o-kaŋ′-o-hi, *v.* *to live to be old, reach old age*—okaŋowahi. *T.*, kaŋ ihuni.

o-kaŋ′-ta, *adv.* *at old age; at the last, at the end:* okaŋta waśte, *good in the end.*

o-kaŋ′-te-haŋ, *v. n.* (okaŋ *and* tehaŋ) *to be long becoming old, bear old age well.*

o-kaŋ′-te-ḣi, *v. n.* (okaŋ *and* teḣi) *to be long becoming old.*

o-ka′-pa, *v. n.* *to be spoiled* by standing in a vessel.

o-ka′-paŋ, *v.* of kapaŋ; *to pound in*—owakapaŋ.

o-ka′-paŋ, *n.* *something used for pounding in*, as a mortar.

o-ka′-pa-za, *v.* *to make smart*, as pepper does the mouth—omakapaza.

o-ka′-pe, *n.* *what is pounded at once.*

o′-ka-pe, *n.* *the mark* or *boundary*, as in ball playing. *T.*, wasabglepi. See kapa *or* kape.

o′-ka-pe-ya, *v. a.* *to throw over the mark*—okapewaya. *T.*, ekapeẏa.

o-ka′-po, *v.* *to make swell in by striking.*

o-ka′-pon, *cont.* of okapota; *to float on:* waḣpaya mini okapon iyaya, *the household stuff has floated off.* *T.*, okapol, *to soak in water.* See okaḣtaŋyaŋ.

o-ka′-pon-ya, *v. a.* *to cause to float on*—okaponwaya. *T.*, okapolya, *to put in water to soak.*

o-ka′-po-ta, *v. n.* *to be borne upon, float on* water; *to soak.*

o-ka′-pta, *v. a.* 1. *to leave, reserve; to pass over, miss.* See oyapta, oyupta, etc. 2. *to dip out into, lade out.* See kapta—owakapta, uŋkokaptapi.

o-ka′-pta-pi, *n.* *what is left, leavings, remnants.*

o-ka′-pte, *v.* *to lade out into.* See okapta.

o-ka′-sbu, *n.* of kasbu; *T. fringe:* śina kasbupi, *a shawl with fringe.*

o-ka′-sda-će-daŋ, *adj.* *gentle, mild.* See waḣbadaŋ.

o-ka′-sda-ta, *v. n.* *to stick in*, as a splinter.

o-ka′-sde-ća, *v. a.* of kasdeća; *to split within* anything—owakasdeća.

o-ka'-sdo-haŋ, *v. n.* of kasdohaŋ; *to make a trail by being dragged along in* *T.*, oyuslohaŋ.

o-ka'-sdo-he, *n.* *a mark of anything dragged along, a trace, a trail.* *T.*, ićaġo; oyuslohe.

o-ka'-sdo-sdo, *v. a.* *to bruise, mash* or *crush in*—owakasdosdo.

o'-ka-siŋ, *v.* *to look into.* See aokasiŋ, kas'iŋ, *and* okakiŋ.

o ka'-slo-he, *adj.* *T.* *bold; immodest.*

o-ka'-spe-ya, *v.* *to make sink into; to immerse.*

o-ka'-stag, *cont.* of okastaka; okastag iyeya *and* okastag eḣpeya, *to throw on* or *in*, as mud.

o-ka'-sta-ka, *v. a.* of kastaka; *to throw on* or *in*, *make stick on*, as in daubing a house—owakastaka.

o-ka'-sto, *n.* of kasto; *a trail* in the grass as that made by an otter.

o-ka'-ś'ag-ya, *adv.* *hindering, preventing, prevented by;* ókaś'agya wauŋ, *I am hindered* See kaś'agya.

o'-ka-ś'a-ka, *v. n.* *to be prevented by, have to stop and remedy*—ómakaś'aka. *T.*, iwaś'akeśni.

o-ka'-śa-ka, *v. n.* *to be accustomed to, to be hardened by, not affected by,* as by annoyances—omakaśaka. *T.*, wakiś'agkiçuŋ.

o'-ka-śe, *v. n.* *to touch.* See ókaśeya. *T.*, ipuskića.

o'-ka-śe-ya, *adv.* *touching, near to:* ti okaśeya, *near the house.* *T.*, ikaŋyela.

o'-ka-śe-ye-daŋ, *adv.* *close to:* okaśeyeyedaŋ okataŋ, *to drive a nail up to the head.* *T.*, ipuskilya; uhutaglezela.

o-ka'-śka, *v. a.* of kaśka; *to tie into*, as a scalp in a hoop; *to fasten up*, as a green hide to dry—owakaśka, uŋkokaśkapi.

o-ka'-śkaŋ, *v. n.* *to be injured internally*, as a woman during pregnancy—omakaśkaŋ: oihdaśkaŋ, *to hurt one's self inwardly.* See oyuśkaŋ.

o-ka'-śkaŋ-toŋ, *v. a.* *to bring forth before its time*—okaśkaŋwatoŋ.

o-ka'-śkaŋ-toŋ-pi, *n.* *an abortion.*

o-ka'-śke, *n.* of kaśka; *a binding, tying, fastening up:* okaśke waśte, *good to tie, good to catch.*

o'-ka-śke, *adj.* *large at one end and small at the other.*

o'-ka-śke, *n.* *T.* *the large end* of a thing.

o-ka'-śki, *v. n.* *to be mashed in,* or *become jelly*, as berries carried in a vessel; *to pound* or *mash in.*

o-ka'-śki-će, *v. n.* *T.* *to be mashed in, made jelly of.*

o-ka'-śna, *v. a.* of kaśna; *to miss, to pass over,* as a day; aŋpetu okaśna śni yahi, *thou comest every day*—owakaśna, uŋkokaśnapi.

o-ka'-śpa, *v. a.* of kaśpa; *to strike a piece off in; to expectorate in*—owakaśpa.

o-ka'-śpe, *n.* *a piece struck off.*

o-ka′-śta-ka, *v. a.* of kaśtaka; *to smite* one *in* a place, as in a house—owakaśtaka.

o-ka′-śta-ke, *n* *a smiting, punishment.*

o-ka′-staŋ, *v. a.* of kaśtaŋ; *to pour into, fill into,* said of liquids—owakaśtaŋ, uŋkokaśtaŋpi.

o-ka-ta′, *v. a.* *to cover up in,* as fire in a stove—owakata. See akata.

o-ka′-ta, *v n.* of kata; *to be warm inside:* tiokata, *a warm house.* See iyokata.

o-ka′-ta, *n.* *heat.*

o-ka′-taŋ, *v. a.* *to drive in,* as a nail or pin, *to nail, make fast with nails*—owakataŋ See iyokataŋ *and* kataŋ.

o-ka′-tkaŋ, *v.* See okatkiŋ.

o-ka′-tkiŋ, *v. n.* of tkiŋ; *to become damp, contract dampness,* as a pack of furs; said also of damp warm weather, as, haŋ okatkiŋ, *the night is damp.* *T.*, oću; ospaye.

o-ka′-tku, *v.* *to break through,* as through ice—owakatku. *T.*, kaoksa. See katku.

o-ka′-tku-ġe, *n.* *something that turns and makes fast, a screw, a nut of a bolt; a screw-driver:* okatkuġe nahomni, *he has screwed his legs,* said when one is very tired. See katkuġa.

o-ka′-toŋ, *v. n.* *to abound; to enlarge* in one's operations.

o-ka′-ṭe, *n.* of kaṭa; *to beat to death in;* okaṭe śića, *it is difficult beating him to death,* as anything in a hole.

o-ka′-ṭiŋs, *cont.* of okaṭiŋza; okaṭiŋs iyeya.

o-ka′-ṭiŋ-za, *v. a.* *to pound in tight, make tight, fill up*—owakaṭiŋza. See kaṭiŋza.

o-ka′-wiŋ-ġa, *v. n.* of kawiŋġa; *to go round and round at a distance:* okawiŋġa wauŋ ḳa wahdi, *I have been round and come home.*

o-ka′-wiŋh, *cont.* of okawiŋġa; okawiŋh ya, *to go round and round.* as the sun does.

o-ka′-wiŋh-ya, *adv.* *round and round.*

o-ka′-za, *n* of kazá; *an atom, a particle, a string* or *thread,* as of takaŋ. See káza.

o-ka′-ze, *v. n.* okaze kiçuŋ, *to skate, slide on the ice*—okaze weçuŋ. *T.*, ćahićaze kiçuŋ.

o-ka′-ze, *v. a.* of kazé; *to dip out into*—owakaze, uŋkokazepi.

o′-ka-ze-ze, *v. n* *to swing,* as anything suspended from a cord,

o′-ka-ze-ze-ya, *adv.* *swinging, dangling.* See kazezeya.

o′-ka-zi-ća-hde, *adv.* *some distance off, far off:* okazićahde iću, *to take by reaching* or *stretching one's arms to.* *T.*, kaiyuzeya. See iyokazićahde.

o′-ka-zi-ća-hde-ya, *adv.* *some distance off.*

o-ka′-źa-ya, *adv* *between, in the forks of.* See kaźa.

o′-kćaŋ, *n.* of yukćaŋ; *comprehending, understanding;* okćaŋ waśte, *easy of comprehension.* *T.*, iyukćaŋ.

o-k d e', *v.* *Th.* *i. q.* ohdé.

o'-k d e, *n.* *Th.* *a shirt, a coat:* *i. q.* oŋȟohda. See óhde.

o-k i', *a prefix* to verbs, signifying *through the middle:* this is made up of two prepositional particles from ohna *and* ki.

o-k i'-b a-k s a, *v. a.* of baksa; *to cut with a knife through the middle*—okibawaksa.

o-k i'-b a-m d a-z a, *v. a.* of bamdaza; *to rip open in the middle*—okibawamdaza.

o-k i'-b a-m d e-ć a, *v. a.* of bamdeća; *to break through the middle,* as a plate by cutting on it—okibawamdeća.

o-k i'-b a-p t u-ź a, *v. a.* of baptuźa; *to crack in the middle with a knife*—okibawaptuźa.

o-k i'-b a-s d e-ć a, *v. a.* of basdeća; *to slit, rip down,* as a log or board, *in the middle, with a saw*—okibawasdeća.

o-k i'-b a-ś p a, *v. a.* of baśpa; *to cut in two in the middle,* or *halve with a knife,* as an apple—okibawaśpa.

o-k i'-b a-ś p u, *v. a.* of baśpu; *to halve,* as a potato, etc., *with a knife*—okibawaśpu.

o'-k i-b e, *n.* *a seam, a joint.* *T.,* okime. See ókihe.

o'-k i-b e, *v. n.* *to join, meet, go round, encircle.*

o'-k i-b e-y a, *v. a.* *to cause to go round* or *encircle*—okibewaya.

o'-k i-b e-y a, *adv.* *encircling.*

o-k i'-b o-p t u-ź a, *v. a.* of boptuźa; *to split in the middle by shooting* or *punching*—okibowaptuźa.

o-k i'-ć a-ȟ a, *v. a.* *to tie* one thing *to* another—okiwakaȟa.

o-k i'-ć a-ȟ n i-ġ a, *v. a.* of okaȟniġa; *to understand, to comprehend*—okiwakaȟniġa.

o-k i'-ć a-k s a, *v. a.* of kaksa; *to cut in two in the middle,* as a stick, *with an ax*—okiwakaksa

o-k i'-ć a-m d a-z a, *v. a.* of kamdaza; *to cut* or *rip open in the middle*—okiwakamdaza.

o-k i'-ć a-m d e-ć a, *v. a.* of kamdeća; *to break in two in the middle,* as a plate, etc., *by striking*—okiwakamdeća.

o-k i'-ć a ŋ-y e, *n.* of kićaŋyaŋ; *work; tillage, cultivation:* okićaŋye ota, *complicated,* as a piece of mechanism.

o-k i'-ć a-p t u ś, *cont,* of okićaptuźa: okićaptuś iyeya.

o-k i'-ć a-p t u-ź a, *v. a.* of kaptuźa; *to crack* or *split in the middle by striking*—okiwakaptuźa.

o-k i'-ć a-s d e-ć a, *v. a.* *to split in two,* as a log, *in the middle*—okiwakasdeća *T.,* okićasleća. See iyokićasdeća

o-k i'-ć a-s d e n, *cont.* of okićasdeća; okićasden iyeya. *T.,* okićaslel.

o-k i'-ć a-ś k a, *v. a.* of kaśka; *to tie into, knot, tie knots*—okiwakaśka. See iyokićaśka.

o-ki'-ća-śpa, *v. a.* of kaśpa; *to smite in two in the middle*—okiwakaśpa. See iyokićaśpa.

o-ki'-ća-śtaŋ, *v.* of okaśtaŋ; *to pour one's own into: to pour into for* one—owećaśtaŋ.

o-ki'-ći-ća-śtaŋ, *v.* of okaśtaŋ; *to pour into for* one, as into a vial, etc.—owećićaśtaŋ.

o-ki'-ći-ćiŋ, *v.* of oćiŋ; *to desire of* one *for* another—owećićiŋ: okićićiŋpi, *they desire of each other.*

o-ki'-ći-ći-ya, *v.* of okiya; okićićiyapi, *they talk together, make peace.*

o-ki'-ći-ćo, *n.* of kićo; *inviting each other, feasting.*

o-ki'-ći-de, *v.* of ode; *to seek* anything *for* another—owećide, omićide. *T.*, okićile.

o-ki'-ći-do-ta, *v.* of odota; *to borrow of* one *for* another—owećidota: onićidota, *he borrows of thee; okićidotapi, they borrow of each other. T.*, okićilota.

o-ki'-ći-ġe-pi, *n.* of kiġe; *scolding each other; mutual recrimination. T.*, ahoyekićiyapi.

o-ki'-ći-haŋ, *v.* of ohaŋ; *to boil* anything *for* another—owećihaŋ.

o-ki'-ći-hna-ka, *v. a.* of ohnaka; *to put* or *place in for* one—owećihnaka, omićihnaka.

o-ki'-ćiŋ, *v.* of oćiŋ; *to ask* or *desire of* one, *beg something of* one—owakićiŋ, omakićiŋ, uŋkokićiŋpi.

o-ki'-ći-pa, *v.* of opa; *to follow for* anything, *obey*, as commands—owećipa, uŋkokićipapi.

o-ki'-ći-wa, *v.* of owa; *to write for* one—owećiwa.

o-ki'-ći-wa-śte, *adj.* of waśte; *good together*, as two things eaten together.

o'-ki-ći-ya, *v.* of ókiya; *to help another:* ókićićiyapi, *they help each other.*

o-ki'-ći-ya-pta, *v.* of oyapta; *to leave* a part of one's food *for* him.

o-ki'-ći-ya-siŋ, *v. n.* *to cling to each other*, as several potatoes hanging together; said also of dogs *fastened together* after copulation. See okiyasiŋ.

o-ki'-ći-yu-siŋ-pi, *v. recip.* of oyusiŋ; *to fall out with one another, quarrel.*

o-ki'-ći-yu-śtaŋ, *v.* of oyuśtaŋ; *to put one into another for* one, as one kettle into another—owećiyuśtaŋ, omićiyuśtaŋ.

o-ki'-ći-yu-ze, *n.* of yuza; *taking each other*, as in marriage. See oyuze.

o-ki'-ći-ze, *n.* of kićiza; *war, fighting a battle.*

o-ki'-ći-źi, *v.* *to whisper to one another.*

o-ki'-ći-źi-pi, *n.* *whispering.*

o-ki'-ći-źi-ya, *adv.* *whisperingly.*

o-ki'-ći-źu, *v. a.* of oźu; *to fill for* another, *plant for* another—owećiźu

o-ki'-ću-ni-ća, *v. n.* *to be made angry, to be offended:* ćaŋte owećunića, *my heart is disturbed.*

o-ki'-ç̇u-nin, *cont.* of okiç̇uniċa.

o-ki'-ç̇u-nin-ya, *v. a.* *to provoke to anger, to offend*—okiç̇uninwaya; ćaŋte okiç̇uninmayaya, *thou hast made me angry.*

o-ki'-ç̇uŋ, *v.* *to put paint on one's self:* maka okiç̇uŋ, *to daub one's self with earth*—oweċuŋ. *T.*, kiç̇uŋ.

o-ki'-de, *v.* *pos.* of ode; *to seek for one's own*—owakide, uŋkokidepi.

o-ki'-do-ta, *v.* of odota; *to borrow* anything *of* one—owakidota, uŋkokidotapi, oćićidota.

o-ki'-gla-ḣni-ġa, *v.* *reflex.* *T.* *i. q.* okihdaḣniġa—oweglaḣniġa.

o-ki'-haŋ, *v.* *pos.* of ohaŋ; *to put on, wear one's own,* as one's own moccasins—owakihaŋ.

o-ki'-haŋ, *v.* *pos.* of ohaŋ; *to boil one's own; to boil for* one—owakihe. See okićihaŋ.

o'-ki-haŋ, *v. a.* *to follow* or *be after* one, in traveling; *to follow* in years, *be younger than*—owakihaŋ, ouŋkihaŋpi: waniyetu yamni omayakihaŋ, *thou art three years younger than I.* See ókihe.

o'-ki-haŋ, *v. n.* *to grow again,* as anything cut off.

o-ki'-hda-ḣni-ġa, *v. reflex.* *to know* or *understand what pertains to one's self*—owehdaḣniġa. See ohdaḣniġa *and* okaḣniġa.

o-ki'-hde, *v.* *pos.* of ohde.

o-ki'-hde-toŋ-toŋ, *adv.* *in layers.* *T.*, okignagtoŋtoŋ. See okimdahaŋ.

o'-ki-he, *n.* *a joint,* as of a finger, etc. See ókibe.

o'-ki-he, *adj.* *next to, following, second.* See iyokihe *and* ókihaŋ.

o'-ki-he-ya, *adv.* *secondly, after.*

o-ki'-hi, *v. a.* *to be able, to be able for, able to accomplish*—owakihi, uŋkokihipi, omakihi. See óhi *and* ohika.

o-ki'-hi-daŋ, *v.* *dim.* of okihi.

o-ki'-hi-ka, *v. n.* *to be able;* okihika hećiŋhaŋ ećoŋ śni, *if he is able to do it, why does he not?*

o-ki'-hi-ki-ya, *v. a.* *to make able for*—okihiwakiya.

o-ki'-hi-pi-ća, *adj.* *that can be done, possible:* okihipića śni, *impossible.*

o-ki'-hi-ya, *v. a.* *to render able, cause to be able for*—okihiwaya, okihiuŋyaŋpi.

o-ki'-hi-ya, *adv.* *according to ability.*

o-ki'-hna-ka, *v.* *pos.* of ohnaka; *to place one's own in.*

o-ki'-hnuŋ-ka, *v n.* of kihnuŋka *or* kihnuka; *to dive* or *put one's head under water in* a vessel or bath.

o-ki'-ḣaŋ, *v.* of oḣaŋ; *to do to* one, commonly used in a bad sense—owakiḣaŋ.

o-ki'-ḣaŋ-śuŋ-ke-ća, *v. a.* *to do badly to, treat like a dog; to destroy what one has depended on,* as food; *not to give food to*—owakiḣaŋśuŋkeća, uŋkokiḣaŋśuŋkećapi.

o-ki'-ḣaŋ-yaŋ, *v.* of oḣaŋyaŋ; *to do to, act towards*—owakiḣaŋyaŋ, uŋkokiḣaŋyaŋpi.

o-ki'-ḣp̣a, *v.* *to rest, remain in the same place, not to remove*—owakiḣpa̧, uŋkokiḣpapi.

o-ki'-ḣpa-pi, *n.* *a resting, a rest:* aŋpetu okiḣpapi, *the day of rest, the Sabbath.*

o-ki'-ḣpe-ki-ya, *v. a.* *to cause to lie by* or *rest*—okiḣpewakiya.

o-ki'-ḣpe-ya, *v. a.* *to cause to lie by* or *rest*—okiḣpewaya.

o-ki'-kpa-ni, *v. a.* *to be unable for* a thing, *be impotent*—owakikpani, uŋkokikpanipi: *i. q.* okitpani.

o-ki'-kpa-ni-ya, *v. a.* *to render unable*—okikpaniwaya.

o-ki'-kpa-ni-yaŋ, *adv.* *not being able, incompetently:* okikpaniyaŋ wauŋ, *I am unable.*

o-ki'-ksam, *cont.* of okiksapa.

o-ki'-ksam-ya, *adv.* *wisely:* okiksamya wauŋ, *I am acting wisely.*

o-ki'-ksam-ya, *v. a.* *to cause to experience* or *know*—okiksamwaya: okiksamiçiya, *to make one's self wise.*

o-ki'-ksa-pa, *v. n.* of ksapa; *to be wise in respect to; to have gained wisdom by experience*—owakiksapa.

o-ki'-ksu-ye, *n.* *remembrance.*

o-ki'-ksu-ye, *v. a.* of kiksuya; *to remember;* okiksuye waśte, *it is easily remembered.*

o-ki'-kśu, *v. pos.* *to fill one's own; to put into one's own,* as into one's pocket.

o-ki'-kśu, *v.* *pos.* of oźu; *to plant* or *sow one's own,* as a field—owekśu, uŋkokikśupi. *T*, okiźu. See okśu.

o-ki'-mda-haŋ, *adj.* *many-coated,* as an onion; *in layers* or *leaves,* as a book. *T.*, okignagtoŋtoŋ. See okihdetoŋtoŋ.

o-ki'-mda-wa-haŋ, *adj.* Same as okimdahaŋ. See yumda.

o-ki'-mdo-toŋ-toŋ, *adj.* of omdotoŋ; *having many corners, angular.* *T.*, oblotoŋtoŋ.

o-ki'-mi-ni-he-ća, *v. n.* of miniheća; *to be smart* in doing anything. *T.*, okibliheća—owakibliheća.

o'-ki-na-haŋ, *adv.* *Ih.* *perhaps.* It occurs at the *beginning* of a clause. See ókini *and* naćeća.

o-ki'-na-ksa, *v. a* of naksa; *to break* anything *in two in the middle with the foot*—okinawaksa.

o-ki'-na-mda-ġa, *v. n.* of namdaġa; *to burst open,* as corn in boiling.

o-ki'-na-mda-za, *v. n.* of namdaza; *to burst,* as corn in boiling

o-ki'-na-mde-ća, *v. a.* *to break in two,* as a plate, etc., *by trampling on it*—okinawamdeća. See namdeća.

o-ki'-na-mden, *cont.* of okinamdeća; okinamden iyeya.

o-ki'-na ptuś, *cont.* of okinaptuźa.

o-ki'-na-ptu-źa, *v. n.* of naptuźa; *to crack* or *burst open.*

o-ki'-na-sde-ća, *v. n.* of nasdeća; *to split* or *burst open lengthwise.*

o-ki'-na-śpa, *v. a.* of naśpa; *to divide in the middle, break off*—okinawaśpa.

o'-ki-ni, *adv. perhaps, possibly. T.*, owekinahaŋś. Used at the *beginning* of a clause. See okinahaŋ *and* naćeća. The latter word is used at the *end* of a clause.

o-ki'-ni, *v. a. to share, receive a part in a division; to obtain a share,* in any way, *where there is a small amount*—owakini, uŋkokinipi.

o-ki'-ni-haŋ, *v. a. T. to single out,* either for praise or blame—owakinihaŋ.

o-ki'-ni-haŋ, *adj.* of kinihaŋ; *honorable.*

o-ki'-ni-haŋ-yaŋ, *adv. honored; honorably;* okinihaŋyaŋ uŋ, *to be honored; selected, singled out;* okinihaŋyaŋ makuwa.

o'-ki-niħ, *adv. suddenly T.*, ignuhaŋla

o'-ki-ni-ħiŋ, *adv. suddenly.*

o-ki'-ni-ki-ya, *v. a. to give a share of, cause to partake*—okiniwakiya, okinimakiya.

o-ki'-ni-ya, *v. n.* of niya; *to gasp, breathe as one dying*—owakiniya, uŋkokiniyapi. *T.*, ćuwi okiniya.

o-ki'-ni-ya, *v. a.* See okinikiya.

o-ki'-ni-ya, *n. the breast,* as that part from which one breathes. *T.*, maku.

o-kiŋ'-haŋ, *v. n. to cease from:* okiŋhaŋ wanića, *without rest, unceasing.*

o-kiŋ'-yaŋ, *v. n.* of kiŋyaŋ; *to fly in.*

o-kiŋ'-yaŋ, *adj.* okiŋyaŋ waśte, *docile, gentle. T.*, okuŋ.

o-ki'-pa, *v. pos.* of opa; *to go in one's own* boat, *to follow* or *obey one's own, to follow,* as one does the habits or trade of his father: atkuku oħaŋ okipa, *he follows his father's business*—owakipa.

o-ki'-pa-kśa, *n. a band; a division* or *bar,* as in music.

o-ki'-pa-ta, *v. a.* of patá; *to join* one *to* the other, *to patch on*—okiwapata. *T.*, oyaskabtoŋ.

o-ki'-pa-ta-pi, *n. patch-work.*

o-ki'-pe, *v.* Same as okipa.

o-ki'-pe-ća, *v. n. to do as one has been accustomed to do*—owakipeća.

o-ki'-pe-ki-ya, *v. a. to cause to follow one's own*—okipewakiya.

o-ki'-pe-mni, *v. pos.* of opemni; *to wrap around one's own*—owakipemni.

o-ki'-pe-ya, *v. a. to cause to follow one's own*—okipewaya.

o-ki'-pe-ya, *adv. following:* okipeya wauŋ.

o-ki'-pi, *v.* of kipi; *to be large enough for, to hold, admit, receive*—omakipi, onićipi, uŋkokipipi.

o-ki'-pi, *adj. capacious, holding much.*

o-ki'-pi-ya, *adv. admitting, receiving.*

o-ki'-sa-pa, *v. n.* of kisapa; *to become bare,* as a spot of ground, while the snow remains around.

o-ki'-se, *n.* *a part, the half, half* of anything cut in two, as a potato. See iyokise.

o-ki'-se-le-ya, *adv.* *T.* *sidewise:* okiseleya yaŋka, *to sit sidewise,* as a white woman rides.

o-ki'-so-ta, *v. n.* of sota; *to be used up, all gone.*

o-ki'-sta-ka, *v. n.* *to be enfeebled by* or *on account of:* witko okistaka, *to be enfeebled by debauch;* iśtiŋma okistaka, *to be feeble* or *listless,* as when just awakened from sleep.

o-ki'-ta-he-daŋ, *adv.* *between.* *T.,* okogna. See iyokitahedaŋ, ituokitahedaŋ, *and* otahedaŋ.

o-ki'-ta-he-pi, *adv.* *between* one place and another. *T*, iyokogna. See okootahela *and* otahepi.

o-ki'-taŋ-iŋ, *v. n.* *to appear, be conspicuous,* as a hill. See otaŋiŋ.

o-ki'-taŋ-iŋ, *n.* *manifestation, perspicuity:* okitaŋiŋ waśte, *a good manifestation.*

o-ki'-taŋ-iŋ-yaŋ, *adv.* *manifestly, gloriously.*

o-ki'-tpa-ni, *v.* Same as okikpani.

o-ki'-tpa-ni-ya, *v.* *to cause to be unable.* Same as okikpaniya.

o-ki'-tpa-ni-yaŋ, *adv.* Same as okikpaniyaŋ.

o-ki'-ṭa, *v. n.* *to be tired with, fatigued* or *worn out by; to be made sick by*—owakiṭa.

o-ki'-ṭe-ye-la, *adv.* *T.* *too large, bulky.*

o-ki'-uŋ-ni-yaŋ, *v.* of kiuŋniyaŋ; *to be injured internally.* *T.,* kiuŋniyaŋ.

o-ki'-uŋ-ni-ye, *n.* *an injury, a wound.*

o-ki'-wa, *v.* *pos.* of owa; *to write one's own,* as one's name—owakiwa, uŋkokiwapi. *T.,* oiçiwa.

o-ki'-waŋ-ka, *v.* *pos.* of owaŋka; *to resemble one's own.* See owaŋgya.

o-ki'-waŋ-źi-la, *adv.* *T.* *uniform, alike.*

o'-ki-ya, *v. a.* *to help, assist* one in anything—ówakiya, óuŋkiyapi, ómakiya, óćićiya.

o-ki'-ya, *v a.* *to talk with; to court,* as a man courts a woman; *to make peace with*—owakiya, uŋkokiyapi, oćićiya.

o-ki'-yag, *cont.* of okiyaka; he okiyag wahi, *I have come to tell him that.*

o-ki'-ya-ka, *v. a.* of oyaka; *to tell* anything *to* one—owakiyaka *and* owakimdaka, oyakidaka, uŋkokiyakapi, omakiyaka, oćićiyaka.

o-ki'-ya-pta, *v.* of oyapta; *to leave,* as food, *for* one—owakiyapta.

o-ki'-ya-siŋ, *v n* *to stick together,* as potatoes growing on the same root. See okićiyasiŋ.

o-ki'-ya-ska-pa, *v. n* *to stick on, stick together, cleave to, to fall in and become flat,* as an animal that is poor. See askapa *and* oskapa.

o-ki'-ya-ta-ke-ća, *adj.* *lean*, *i. q.* stodaŋ *or* ćistiŋna. Compare ostake śni.

o-ki'-yu-te, *v. n.* *T.* *to heal up*, as a wound; *to grow over*, as bark cut on a tree. See ohduta.

o'-ki-yu-te, *n.* *a strait* or *channel*.

o-ki'-zi, *v. n.* *to heal up, recover from a hurt* or *wound*—omakizi, onićizi, uŋkokizipi. See ozí, asni, etc

o-ki'-zi-ki-ya, *v. a.* *to cause to heal up*—okiziwakiya.

o-ki'-zi-ya, *v. a.* *to cause to heal, make well*—okiziwaya, okizimayaŋ.

o-ki'-źa-te, *n.* *the dividing* or *forks*, as of rivers: Wakpa okiźate, *the junction of the Yellow Stone and the Missouri Rivers.*

o-ki'-źu, *v.* of oźu; *to sow* or *plant one's own; to plant for* one; *to fill up*, as a bag; *to meet*, as two parties—owakiźu. See okićiźu *and* okikśu.

o'-ki-źu, *v. n.* *to be united.* See kokiźu. Iyokiźu is also used *T.*, ićikoyaka.

o'-ki-źu-ya, *v. a.* *to cause to unite*—ókiźuwaya. *T.*, ićikoyagya.

o'-ki-źu-ya, *adv.* *unitedly, together* *T.*, kokiźuya. See ićaġeźuya *and* okokiźuya.

o-ko', *n* *a crack, a hole, an aperture*, as in a house.

o-ko'-da-ki-ći-ye, *n.* *a league, covenant, communion, fellowship; a church, society, community.* *T.*, okolakićiye See koda *and* takoda.

o-ko'-gna, *adv.* *T.* *between* See okitahedaŋ.

o-ko'-ki-pe, *n.* *danger, fear.* See wokokipe.

o-ko'-ki-pe-ya, *adv.* *in fear.* *T.*, okokipeyakel; okokipeyakel ia, *to speak insultingly.*

o-ko'-ki-źu-ya, *adv.* *in the aggregate, collectively.* See okiźuya.

o-ko'-la-ya, *v.* *T.* *to have for a friend: i. q.* kodaya.

o-koŋ', *n.* *desire.* See koŋ.

o-koŋ'-ka, *n.* *one who desires* or *is covetous.* *T.*, okoŋ s'a.

o' koŋ-waŋ-źi-daŋ, *adj.* *unchanging, always the same*, expressive of *oneness*, as being of one mind—okoŋmawaŋźidaŋ. *T.*, okoŋwaŋźila.

o-koŋ'-ze, *n.* *a rule, a law.* *T.*, wowasukiye. See wokoŋze.

o-ko'-o-ta-he-la, *adv.* *T.* (oko *and* otahela) *between.* See okogna *and* otahedaŋ.

o-ko'-pe, *adj.* *T.* *afraid.*

o-ko'-pe, *n.* of kope; *fear.* See okokipe.

o-ko'-pe-ya, *adv.* *seen through a hole*, as one seen through an opening in the bushes; *in danger:* okopeya naźiŋ, *he stands in danger.* See oko.

o-ko'-toŋ, *v.* *there is a hole.*

o-ko'-toŋ-yaŋ, *n.* *an opening* or *communication; expanse, space.* This word is used for the expanse of the heavens or the firmament.

o-kpa'-ġi, *v. pos.* of opaġi; *to fill one's own pipe with one's own tobacco*—owakpaġi: *i. q.* otpaġi.

o′-k p a - n i, *v. n.* *to be lacking; less than.* See otpani *and* iyotpani.

o′-k p a s, *cont.* of okpaza; okpas iću, *to become dark.* See otpas.

o′-k p a s - y a, *v. a.* *to darken, make dark*—okpaswaya. *T.*, oiyokpasya. See otpasya.

o′-k p a s - y a, *adv.* *darkly, in the dark;* okpasya wanka, *it lies in the dark.* *T.*, oiyokpasya.

o′-kpa-za, *v. n.* *to be dark:* okpaze ḣiŋća, *it is very dark.*

o′-k p a - z a, *n.* *darkness, night: i. q.* otpaza.

o′-k p e, *v.* *to meet and assist in carrying a load:* okpe ya, *to go to assist* one; *to go to meet;* wićokpe uŋyaŋpi, *and* okpe wićuŋyaŋpi, *we go to their assistance: i. q.* ótpe.

o-k p u′-k p e, *n.* of kpukpa. *T. dregs, lees.*

o′-k s a, *v. n.* *to break off*, as a stick, *in* a hole. See oyuksa.

o-k s a′-h a ŋ, *part.* *broken off in, fallen in,* as a corn-hole.

o-k s a′-h e, *part.* Same as oksahaŋ.

o′-k s a - k a, *v.* See oksa.

o′-k s e, *n.* *anything broken off short.*

o′-k ś a ŋ, *adv.* *around, round about:* nitaŋ okśaŋ, *around thee.*

o-k ś u′, *v. pos.* of oźu. *T.* *to load,* as one's gun—owekśu See okikśu *and* okiźu.

o-k t e′-t o ŋ, *n.* *a flaw, something flawed.*

o-k u ŋ′, *adj.* *T.*, okuŋ waśte, *gentle, mild.* See okiŋyaŋ.

o-k u ŋ s′-t o ŋ, *adv.* *openly, manifestly.* *T.*, taŋiŋyaŋ.

o-k u ŋ s′-t o ŋ - y a ŋ, *adv.* *openly, manifestly, according to custom:* okuŋstoŋyaŋ tawiću toŋ, *to take a wife according to the custom.*

o-k u′-t e, *n.* of kute; *a shooting, a shot;* okute waŋźidaŋ, *one shot;* okute waśte, *a good shot.*

o-k u′-w a, *v. a.* of kuwa; *to chase, follow after* anything—owakuwa.

o-k u′-ź a, *v. n.* of kuźa; *to be lazy* or *sick on account of*—omakuźa. See ikuźa, *to be sick on account of.*

o-k u′-ź e, *n.* *laziness.* See wićokuźe.

o-ķ a′, *v. a.* of ķa; *to dig into, dig through*—owaķa, uŋkoķapi.

o-ķ a′-p i, *n.* *a digging into.*

o-ķ e′, *n.* *a digging, a mine.*

o-ķ i ŋ′, *n.* of ķiŋ; *a pack, load; something to carry* or *pack in,* as a blanket or sack.

o-ķ i ŋ′, *v.* of ķiŋ; *to carry in*—owaķiŋ.

o-ķ i′-p e, *n.* *something staked, the prize.*

o′-ķ o, *v.* *to stick to* or *on,* as feathers or down: pa maġá hiŋ ómaķo, *feathers stick to my head; to gather around for something to eat,* as crows about a carcass—ómaķo, óniķo.

o-ķ o′, *n.* *a noise, hum, buzz, bustle*

o-ķ o′-s e, *n.* *T.* *disturbance, tumult: i. q.* owodutatoŋ.

o-ķ o′-y a, *v. n.* *to make a noise* or *bustle*—oķowaya, oķouŋyaŋpi.

o-ḳu', *v. a.* *to lend* anything *to* one—owaḳu, uŋkoḳupi, omaḳu, oćiçu, oniçu.

o-ḳu', *v. a.* of ḳu; *to give to*, as food; *give a portion to;* dot oḳu, *to give something to eat*—owaḳu.

o-lab'-ya, *adv.* *T.* *very much.*

o-lab'-ya-kel, *adv.* *T.* *exceedingly.*

o-la'-kol, *cont.* of olakota; olakol kaġa, *to make a treaty.*

o-la'-kol-ya, *v.* *T.* *to have for a friend:* *i. q.* kodaya.

o-la'-ko-ta, *n.* *T.* *a covenant, treaty; peace.*

o-le', *v.* *T.* *to hunt, seek for; i. q.* ode.

o-li'-li-ta, *adj.* *T.* *warm, hot inside*, as a room: *i. q.* odidita.

o-li'-li-ta, *n.* *T.* *heat.*

o-lu'-lu-ta, *n.* *T.* *heat:* *i. q.* olilita.

om, *prep.* of opa; *with, together with.* "Kići" is used when speaking of *one*—om, when *more than one* is spoken of; as, he kići wauŋ, *I was with him;* hena om wauŋ, *I was with them.* *T.*, ob.

O-ma'-ha, *n. p.* *the Omaha Indians:* formerly called "Mahas" by white men: *i. q.* Oyatenoŋpa.

o'-ma-ka, *n.* *a season, half a year; winter* or *summer; a year.*

o-ma'-kiŋ-ća, *n.* *T.* *a deer's lair.*

o-ma'-ni, *v.* of mani; *to walk in* or *according to*, as in a road or according to a command, *to travel; to ride* as well as to walk—omawani, omauŋnipi, *and* uŋkomanipi.

o-ma'-ni, *n.* *a walk;* omani haŋska, *a long walk.*

o-ma'-ni-ken, *adv.* *walking:* omaniken wauŋ, *I am out walking.* *T.*, omaniyakel.

o-ma'-wa-he-toŋ, *n.* *the parents of a man and woman who are united in marriage* call each other omawahetoŋ.

o-ma'-wa-he-toŋ-ki-ći-ya, *v. reflex* *T.* *to have each other for* omawahetoŋ.

o-ma'-wa-he-toŋ-ya, *v. a.* *to call one* omawahetoŋ—omawahetoŋwaya.

o'-ma-śte, *v. n.* of maśte; *to be hot in.*

o'-ma-śte, *n.* *heat, warmth; the sunshine; where the sun shines.*

o-mda'-ska, *n.* of mdaska; *the flat side* of anything. *T.*, oblaska.

o-mda'-ska-ya, *adv.* *on the flat side, flat:* omdaskaya waŋka, *it lies flat.* *T.*, oblaskaya. See mdaskaya.

o-mda'-ya, *adj.* of mdaya; *level.*

o-mda'-ye, *n.* *a level place, a plain, a valley.* *T.*, oblaye.

o-mde'-ća, *adj.* *cornered, edged*, as a board. See omdetoŋ *and* omdotoŋ.

o-mde'-ća, *n* *the edge*, as of a board or blanket, *the edge* or *bit* of an ax, etc. *T.*, obleća.

o'-mde-ća, *v n.* *to be scattered* or *distributed here and there.* See oyumdeća.

o-mde'-ća-haŋ, *part. broken into fragments; scattered,* as a people.

o-mde'-ća-he-ya, *v. a. to scatter*—omdećahewaya.

o-mde'-ća-ya, *adv. on the side, with the sharp part up,* not on the flat surface: omdećaya waŋka, *it lies on the side. T.,* oblećaya.

o'-mden, *cont.* of ómdeća. *T.,* oblel.

o'-mden-ya, *adv. scattered. T.,* oblelya.

o'-mden-ya-ken, *adv. in a scattered condition.*

o-mdes', *cont.* of omdeza.

o-mdes'-ya, *adv. clearly, brightly, soberly. T.,* oblesya.

o-mde'-toŋ, *adj. square-edged.* See omdotoŋ. *T.,* oblotoŋ.

o-mde'-za, *v. n.* of mdeza; *to be clear, sober*—omamdeza.

o-mdo'-toŋ, *adj. cornered, having corners:* yamni omdotoŋ, *three-cornered, a triangle;* topa omdotoŋ, *a square.* See omdéća *and* omdetoŋ.

o-mdo'-toŋ, *n. a corner* of anything, *an angle;* hutkaŋ omdotoŋ, *square root:* omdotoŋ topa, *something with four corners, a square. T.,* oblotoŋ *and* omlotoŋ.

o-mi'-ni-o-we, *n. T. a spring of water, a fountain: i. q.* miniowe.

o-mlo'-toŋ, *adj. T. i. q.* omdotoŋ.

o'-mna, *v. a. to smell*—owamna, ouŋmnapi.

o'-mna, *n. smell:* omna waśte, *an agreeable smell.*

om'-na-na, *adv.* (om *and* nana) *alone with. T.,* obnala.

o-mna'-yaŋ, *v.* of mnayaŋ; *to gather into*—omnawaya, omnauŋyaŋpi.

o'-mni, *n.* mini omni, *an eddy. T.,* owamniomni. See iyumni.

o'-mni, *adv. round and round:* ómni wauŋ. *T.,* ohomni.

o-mni'-ća, *n. beans.* See oŋmnića, which is said to be the proper orthography.

o-mni'-ća-hmi-yaŋ-yaŋ, *n. "round beans": peas. T.,* omnićagmigmela. See oŋmnića.

o-mni'-ći-ye, *n.* of mnićiya; *an assembly, a feast:* omnićiye kaġa, *he makes a feast.*

o-mni'-he-ća, *v. n. to be active in doing* anything—omamniheća, onimniheća. *T.,* okibliheća. See mniheća.

o-mni'-he-ća, *n. activity, industry. T.,* wobliheća.

o-mni'-mni, *n.* of omni; *something that goes round and round, a whirlpool. T.,* wamniyomni.

o'-mni-mni, *n. T. a place where the wind whips around.*

o'-mni-mni, *adv. round and round:* omnimni wauŋ ḳa wahdi, *I have been round and come home. T.,* oyumnimni.

o'-mni-mni-ka, *v. n. to be destitute of undergrowth* or *brush; i. q.* woḣiŋśbe śni. *T.,* woḣeśmaśni.

o'-mni-na, *n. a calm place, a shelter:* ómnina akitapi, *they are seeking for shelter. T.,* oblula. See ioblula, iyomni, *and* iyomnina.

o'-mni-na, *adv.* *calmly, in a calm place* where the wind blows not, *sheltered:* ómnina uŋyakoŋpi, *we are in a sheltered place.*

o m - om', *prep. red.* of om. *T.*, obob.

o'-na, *n.* *Ih.* *a flame, a blaze; i. q.* ide.

o-na'-glo-ġe, *v. n.* *T.* *to rattle in the throat*, as one about to die.

o-na'-ḣda-te, *n.* of naḣdata; *a scratch.*

o-na'-ḣde-ća, *v. a.* *to tear a hole in a hole*—onawaḣdeća.

o-na'-ḣde-će, *n.* of naḣdeća; *a rent.*

o-na'-ḣdo-ka, *v. a.* *to make a hole* either in the ground *with the foot* or *in the foot by walking*—onawaḣdoka.

o-na'-ḣdo-ke, *n.* of naḣdoka; *a hole made in the foot* or *with the foot.*

o-na'-ḣoŋ, *v.* of naḣoŋ; *to hear what is reported; to hear of* or *concerning*—onawaḣoŋ, onauŋḣoŋpi.

o-na'-ḣoŋ, *n.* *hearing:* onaḣoŋ waśte, *it is good hearing.*

o-na'-ḣoŋ-ki-ya, *v. a.* *to cause to hear of, to communicate to concerning*—onaḣoŋwakiya.

o-na'-ḣoŋ-pi, *n.* *hearing.*

o-na'-ḣoŋ-ya, *v. a.* *to cause to hear; to communicate to;* onaḣoŋmayaye, *you have told me.*

o-na'-ḣta-ka, *v.* of naḣtaka; *to kick in*—onawaḣtaka.

o-na'-ḣta-ke, *n.* *a wound made by kicking.*

o-na'-kaŋ, *v. a.* *to strike* and *knock off into*, as into a canoe, *to tread off in*—onawakaŋ.

o-na'-ki-kśiŋ, *v. a.* of nakikśiŋ; *to take shelter* or *refuge in* or *behind*, as behind a tree in battle—onawekśiŋ, onauŋkikśiŋpi. *T.*, inakikśiŋ.

o-na'-kpa, *v. n.* of nakpa; *to burst within* something.

o-na'-ksa, *v. a.* of naksa; *to break into* or *through*, as in walking on ice—onawaksa.

o-na'-kse, *n.* *a breaking in.*

o-na'-kśaŋ, *n.* of nakśaŋ; *a bend, crook.*

o-na'-kśiŋ, *v.* See onakikśiŋ.

o-na'-ktaŋ, *v. n.* *to bend into of itself.* See naktaŋ *and* naoktaŋ.

o-na'-ktaŋ, *n.* *a bend.*

o-na'-ḳes, *cont.* of onaḳeza. *T.*, onaṭos.

o-na'-ḳes-ḳe-za, *v. red.* of onaḳeza. *T.*, onaṭosṭoza.

o-na'-ḳe-za, *v. a.* *to make smooth by stamping on*—onawaḳeza. *T.*, onaṭoza.

o-na'-ḳos, *cont.* of onaḳoza.

o-na'-ḳos-ḳo-za, *v. red.* of onaḳoza.

o-na'-ḳo-za, *v. n.* *to trample on and make hard*—onawaḳoza.

o-nam', *cont.* of onapa; onam iyaya, *it has taken refuge in.* *T.*, onab.

o-na'-pa, *v. a.* of napa; *to flee to, take refuge in*—onawapa, onauŋpapi. See onakikśiŋ.

o-na'-poḣ-ya, *v. n.* *T.* *to swell out, puff up*, as bread rising.

o-n a′-p o ḣ-y e, *n.* *leaven.* See oŋnapoḣyapi. Inapoḣye is also used *T.*, winapoḣye.

o-n a′-p o-p a, *v. n* of napopa; *to burst within* something.

o-n a′-p t a ŋ. See oŋnaptaŋ *and* uŋnaptaŋ.

o-n a′-s e, *n.* *the buffalo chase:* onase waŋźidaŋ, *one chase.* See wanase.

o′-n a-ś d o g, *cont.* of ónaśdoka; ónaśdog iyaya.

o′-n a-ś d o-k a, *v. n.* of naśdoka; *to leave behind, run off and leave*—ónawaśdoka, ónauŋśdokapi.

o-n a′-ś d o-k a, *v. a.* *to pull off in,* as shoes in the mud—onawaśdoka.

o-n a′-ś k a ŋ, *v. n.* *to become sick again, to relapse*—onawaśkaŋ. See okaśkaŋ *and* oyuśkaŋ.

o-n a′-ś'o, *v. n.* *T.* *to pace,* as a horse.

o-n a′-ś'o-l a, *n.* *T.* *a pacing horse.*

o-n a′-ś'o-ś'o, *v.* *red.* of onaś'o.

o′-n a-t a g, *cont.* of ónataka; ónatag iyeya.

o′-n a-t a-k a, *v. a.* of nataka; *to fasten, bar, bolt, lock,* as a door, *to fasten,* as a fence; *to fasten up in*—onawataka, onauŋtakapi.

o-n a′-t a-k e, *n.* *a cage, a pen.*

o-n a′-ṭ i ŋ s, *cont.* of onaṭiŋza; onaṭiŋs iyeya.

o-n a′-ṭ i ŋ-z a, *v. a.* of naṭiŋza; *to make firm by treading on*—onawaṭiŋza, onauŋṭiŋzapi.

o-n a′-ṭ o s, *cont.* of onaṭoza.

o-n a′-ṭ o s-ṭ o-z a, *v. red.* of onaṭoza.

o-n a′-ṭ o-z a, *v.* *T.* *to make smooth by stamping on:* *i. q.* onaḳeza.

o-n a′-ź a-ź a, *v. n.* of naźaźa; *to cleanse* or *wash out,* as clothes, by boiling.

o-n a′-ź i ŋ, *v.* of naźiŋ; *to stand in; to take refuge in* or *at*—onawaźiŋ.

o-n i′, *n.* of ni; *life;* toni, *his life.*

o-n i′-h a ŋ, *v. n.* *to remain, be remaining.*

o-n i′-h a ŋ-ś n i-ś n i, *adv.* *T.* *remaining:* onihaŋśniśni hel yaŋka, *he stays there constantly.*

o-n i′-h a ŋ-y a ŋ, *adv.* *remaining.*

o-n i′-s k o-k e-ć a, *adj.* *so large.* See iŋskokeća.

o-n i′-y a, *v.* of niya; *to breathe into; to breathe out of*—owaniya.

o-n i′-y a, *n.* *breath, breathing, life:* oniya waśte, *good breathing.*

o-n i′-y a-o-ḣ l o-k a, *n.* *T.* *a breathing hole.*

o-n i′-y e-t o ŋ, *v. n.* *to be affected by some internal hurt* or *disease; to have the lungs affected,* as in pulmonary consumption—oniyewatoŋ.

o n′-o-t a, *adj. red.* of ota. *T.*, olota: *i. q.* odota.

o-n u′-n i, *v. n.* of nuni; *to wander in*—owanuni.

o-n u′-n i-y a, *v. a.* *to cause to wander in* a place—onuniwaya.

o-n u′-n i-y a ŋ, *adv.* *wanderingly, lost.*

o-n u′-n i-y a-t a, *adv.* *wandering.*

oŋ, *prep.* *for, on account of; of,* as, maza oŋ kaġapi, *it is made of iron; with,* when used with the cause or instrument.

oŋ, *pron.* 1st pers. sing. *we.* See uŋ. Formerly some of the members of the Dakota mission wrote this "oŋ," and many of the Indians do so still.

oŋ-ćiʹ, *n.* *a grandmother.* See uŋći.

oŋʹ-ći-hi, *v. n.* *to be able to take care of one's self, be grown up, of age*—oŋmaćihi. See uŋćihi.

oŋʹ-ći-hi-śni, *v.* *not to be able to take care of one's self; to be lazy.*

oŋʹ-ći-hi-ya, *v. a.* *to bring up to self support*—oŋćihiwaya.

oŋ-ćiʹ-śi, *n.* *a mother-in-law.* See uŋćiśi.

oŋ-ćiʹ-śi-ća-daŋ, *n.* *a crow.* See uŋćiśićadaŋ. *T.*, oŋćiśićala.

oŋʹ-ç̣i-kpa-ni, *v. n.* *to be poor, not able to sustain one's self; i. q.* takudaŋ okihi śni; *to be lazy*—óŋmiç̣ikpani *and* óŋmaç̣ikpani, óŋniç̣ikpani, óŋuŋç̣ikpanipi.

oŋʹ-ç̣i-kpa-ni-yaŋ, *adv.* *in a destitute condition:* óŋç̣ikpaniyaŋ wauŋ, *I am badly off; lazily.*

oŋʹ-ç̣i-tpa-ni, *v. n.* Same as oŋç̣ikpani.

oŋʹ-ç̣i-tpa-ni-yaŋ, *adv.* Same as oŋç̣ikpaniyaŋ.

oŋʹ-ç̣uŋ-ni-ća, *v. n.* *to be delayed, be prevented; to wait until* the thing *cannot be done*—oŋmaç̣uŋnića, oŋniç̣uŋnića: *i. q.* uŋç̣oŋnića.

oŋʹ-ç̣uŋ-nin-ya, *v. a.* *to stop, keep from doing, prevent, hinder*—oŋç̣uŋninwaya: *i. q.* uŋç̣oŋninya. *T.*, oŋç̣unilya.

oŋʹ-e-ći-ya-taŋ-haŋ, *adv.* *by means of; on account of.*

oŋʹ-e-taŋ-haŋ, *adv.* *therefore; for that cause.* See heoŋetaŋhaŋ.

onʹ-glo-ġe, *n.* *T.* *a shirt.*

oŋʹ-ġeʹ, *n.* *some, a part, portion off,* applied to liquids and things which come under the denomination of dry measure. The Yanktons apply this *to persons*, as the Santees use "apa," which the former do not use.—J. P. W. *T.*, yuġe.

oŋ-ġeʹ-daŋ, *n.* *a little part, a small quantity.* *T.*, yuġela.

oŋʹ-haŋ-ke-ta, *adv.* See uŋhaŋketa.

oŋʹ-ḣdo-ḣda *and* oŋʹ-ḣdo-hda, *n.* *a coat, mantlet, shirt.* *T*, oŋgloġe. See óhde, ókde, *and* oŋwiḣdoḣda.

oŋ-kaŋʹ, *conj* *T.*, yuŋkaŋ. See uŋkaŋ.

oŋ-kaŋsʹ, *conj.* *T.*, yuŋkaŋś See uŋkaŋś.

oŋʹ-ki-ći-śka-ta-pi, *v. recip.* of oŋśkata; *to jest, joke,* or *banter each other*, as persons within certain degrees of affinity are at liberty to do among the Dakotas.

oŋʹ-ki-śka-ta, *v. a.* of oŋśkata; *to talk as one pleases with, boast, brag, joke with* one—oŋwakiśkata. This privilege is allowed only between brothers-in-law and sisters-in law.

o ŋ - m n i'- ć a, *n.* *Dakota beans; tuberous roots of the wild pea vine: i. q.* omnića. They grow wild in the valleys and low grounds, having a vine-like top. The beans grow on the roots, and are dug up in the fall and spring; *beans* of all kinds.

o ŋ - m n i'- ć a - g m i - g m e - l a, *n.* *T. peas.*

o ŋ - m n i'- ć a - h m i - y a ŋ - y a ŋ, *n.* *round beans; peas: i. q.* omnićahmiyaŋyaŋ.

o ŋ'- n a - p o ḣ - y a - p i, *n.* of napoḣya; *leaven.*

o ŋ - n a'- p t a ŋ, *adj.* *sideling:* ḣeoŋnaptaŋ, *or* ḣoŋnaptaŋ, *a side hill.* See uŋnaptaŋ.

o ŋ'- p a, *v. a.* *to place* or *lay* any *long object in a reclining attitude:* ćaŋkaḣoŋpapi, *a log laid across, a bridge*—waoŋpa, uŋk̇oŋpapi: *to keep* or *reserve,* as a puppy or girl, etc. See uŋpa, ohdé, ohnaka, *and* oźu.

o ŋ - s e'- y a - k a - d a ŋ, *n.* *a kind of small duck, the teal.* *T.*, śiyaka.

o ŋ - s p e', *v. n.* *to know how to do* a thing, *know how to* read or write, etc—oŋmaspe, oŋnispe, uŋkoŋspepi. See oŋwićaspe *and* wooŋspe.

o ŋ - s p e', *n.* *an ax.*

o ŋ - s p e'- a - p a - t a ŋ - h a ŋ, *adv.* *Ih.* *at the right hand; i. q.* etapataŋhaŋ. This would seem to be from oŋspe, *to know how.* *T.*, iślo-yataŋhaŋ. It is curious that while the name for *left-hand* (ćatka) is the same in all the three dialects, that for *right-hand* is different in each.

o ŋ - s p e'- ć a ŋ - d u - h u - p a, *n.* (oŋspe *and* ćaŋduhupa) *a pipe-hatchet.* *T.*, oŋspećanoŋpa.

o ŋ - s p e'- ć i - k a - l a, *n.* *T.* *a hatchet.*

o ŋ - s p e'- d a ŋ, *n. dim.* *a small ax, a hatchet.* *T.*, oŋspećik̇ala.

o ŋ - s p e'- d a ŋ, *v. dim.* of oŋspe.

o ŋ - s p e'- i - h u - p a, *n.* (oŋspe *and* ihupa) *an ax-handle.* *T.*, nazoŋspeihupa.

o ŋ - s p e'- k a, *v.* Same as oŋspe. Sometimes this is used in the sense of onspe śni, *not to know how.*

o ŋ - s p e'- k i - y a, *v. a.* *to cause to know how, to teach* one anything—oŋspewakiya, oŋspeuŋkiyapi, oŋspemakiya, oŋspenićiya, oŋspećićiya: oŋspeiçićiya, *to teach one's self, to learn*—oŋspemiçićiya, oŋspeniçićiya, oŋspeuŋkiçićiyapi.

o ŋ'- ś i, *adj.* *poor, miserable*—oŋmaśi, oŋuŋśipi. See oŋśika *and* oŋśiyeća.

o ŋ'- ś i - d a, *v. a.* *to have mercy on, to pity*—oŋśiwada, oŋśiuŋdapi, oŋśimada, onśićida.

o ŋ'- ś i - d a, *intj.* used by women to infants; *poor thing!*

o n'- ś i d a - k a, *v. a.* *to have mercy on, to pity*—oŋśiwadaka, oŋśiuŋdakapi: *i. q.* oŋśida.

o ŋ'- ś i - ḣ a ŋ, *v. n.* (oŋśi *and* ḣaŋ) *to be humble, to act humbly*—oŋśiwaḣaŋ.

o ŋ'- ś i - ḣ a ŋ - k a, *v. n.* *to be humble, to try to excite compassion, to fawn*—oŋśiwaḣaŋka: *i. q.* oŋśiḣaŋ.

o ŋ'- ś i - ḣ a ŋ - p i, *n.* *humility.*

oŋ′-śi-ka, *adj.* *poor, destitute, miserable*—oŋmaśika, oŋniśika, oŋuŋśipika: *i. q.* oŋśi.

oŋ′-śi-ki-da, *pos.* of oŋśida; *to have mercy on one's own*—oŋśiwakida, oŋśiuŋkidapi.

oŋ′-śi-ki-da-ka, *v. pos.* Same as oŋśikida—oŋśiwakidaka.

oŋ′-śi-ki-ḣaŋ, *v. a.* of oŋśiḣaŋ; *to humble one's self to* another, *act humbly towards*—oŋśiwakiḣaŋ.

oŋ′-śi-ya, *adv.* *poorly, miserably.*

oŋ′-śi-ye-ća, *adj.* *miserable*—oŋśimayeća. See oŋśi.

oŋ′-śka-ta, *v. n.* *to talk as one pleases, brag, jest,* as brothers-in-law and sisters-in-law are privileged to do among the Dakotas—oŋwaśkata, oŋćiśkata. See oŋkiśkata *and* uŋśkata.

oŋ-śpa′, *n.* *a piece* of anything.

oŋ-śpa′-daŋ, *n. dim.* *a little piece.*

oŋ-śpa′-śpa, *n. red.* of oŋśpa; *pieces, little pieces, crumbs.*

oŋ′-toŋ, *v. n.* *T.* *to be injured*—oŋmatoŋ. See toŋ.

oŋ′-toŋ-yaŋ, *v. a.* *T.* *to hurt, to wound, to injure.*

oŋ-we′-ya, *n.* *T.* *provisions:* *i. q* waŋeya.

oŋ′-wi-ća-spe, *n.* of oŋspe; *learning.*

oŋ-wi′-ḣdo-ḣda, *n.* *a coat.* See oŋḣdoḣda.

oŋ-wi′-yu-ta-pi, *n.* (oŋ *and* iyuta) *something to weigh* or *measure with.*

oŋ-ze′, *n.* *the rump, buttocks, the anus.*

oŋ-ze′-hu, *v.* *to copulate.*

oŋ-ze′-i-hu, *v.* *to commit sodomy.*

oŋ-ze′-kna-ka-taŋ-haŋ, *adv.* *Ih.* *from behind.* See dazataŋhaŋ.

oŋ-ze′-kte, *v.* *T.* *to give birty to another child while still nursing one.* See oŋzeṭa.

oŋ′-ze-o-ġe, *n.* *pantaloons:* *i. q.* oŋzooġe.

oŋ-ze′-o-ka-śtaŋ, *v.* *to give an injection*—onzeowakaśtaŋ.

oŋ-ze′-o-ka-śtaŋ-pi, *n.* *an injection.*

oŋ-ze′-o-ki-ća-śtaŋ, *v. a.* *to give an injection to* one—oŋzeowećaśtaŋ.

oŋ-ze′-pi-źe-la, *v.* *T.* *to be the oldest of two infants, one of which was born before the other was weaned.*

oŋ-ze′-ṭa, *v. n.* (oŋze *and* ṭa.) This word is used in reference to a child whose mother has again become pregnant—oŋzemaṭa. What can have originated the use of this coarse but curious form of speech? A. Renville says that it probably arose from the fact that children weaned under such circumstances are likely to become emaciated: *seat dead;* said of a woman who becomes pregnant while she has an unweaned child. Perhaps it was because it was considered necessary in this case to procure an abortion. She would be unable to walk and carry two children at the same time.—T. S. W.

oŋ-ze'-yu-hmu-za, *v. a.* *to shut up* or *hold shut* the oŋze.

oŋ-zi'-bo-sdan, *adv.* *head over heels:* oŋzibosdan naźiŋ, *and* onzibosdan yaŋka, *to turn a somersault, stand with the heels up; to be wrong end up; to be in a flurry, not know what one is about.* *T.*, oŋziwoslal. See kaoŋzebosdan.

oŋ-ziŋ'-tka, *n.* *musk.* *T.*, siŋkpe oŋzemna.

oŋ-ziŋ'-tka-mna, *v. n.* *to smell of musk.*

oŋ'-zo-o-ġe, *n.* *i. q.* oŋzeoġe. *T.*, oŋzoġe.

oŋ-źiŋ'-źiŋ-tka, *n.* *the rose, roses, rose-buds.* *T.*, also *tomatoes.*

oŋ-źiŋ'-źiŋ-tka-hu, *n.* *rose-bushes.*

o-o', *n.* of o; *a wound, a place where one is shot.*

o-o'-he, *n.* of ohaŋ; *a boiling, enough to boil at once,* as, oohe waŋźidaŋ, *one boiling.*

O-o'-he-noŋ-pa, *n. p.* the name of a clan of Teeton Sioux. *The Two Kettles—two boilings.* It is said to have originated in a boy's asking for meat enough to fill two kettles.

o-o'-hi-ye, *n.* of ohiya; *victory.* See woohiye.

o-o'-ki-ye, *n.* of ókiya; *an assistant, a servant.* *T.*, taokiye.

o-o'-ki-ye-ya, *v. a.* *to have for an assistant* or *servant*—ookiyewaya. *T.*, taokiyeya.

o-o'-kśu, *n.* *T.* *a load;* ookśu waŋźila, *one load:* *i. q.* oade. See okśu.

o-oŋ'-pa, *v.* of oŋpa; *to put* or *place in*—owaoŋpa, ouŋkoŋpapi. *T.*, mahel eoŋpa.

o-o'-o-ka-śtaŋ, *n.* of okaśtaŋ; *the Balsam of Life,* so called because poured into wounds; *i. q.* wićoni peźihuta.

o-o'-ṗe-toŋ, *n.* of opetoŋ; tiyopa oopetoŋ, *a toll-gate.*

o-o'-taŋ-iŋ, *v. n.* of otaŋiŋ; *to be manifest through.*

o-o'-wa, *n.* of owa; *a letter, character,* as the letters of the alphabet, *a figure* or *mark* of any kind: oowa yukaŋ, *and* owapi, *figured,* as calico

o-o'-wa-pta-ya, *n.* (oowa *and* ptaya) *the alphabet.*

o-o'-ya-ke, *n.* of oyaka; *the act of telling a story, a relation, a narrative.* *T.*, woyake.

o-o'-źu, *v.* of oźu; *to plant in*—oowaźu.

o-o'-źu, *v. n.* *to fall in,* as the sides of very old people sometimes do.

o'-pa, *v. n.* *to go with, follow; to pursue,* as, opa aya; *to go to, attend,* as a school or meeting, *to be present at; to be a member of,* as of an association or church; *to go in,* as in a canoe—owapa, oyapa, ouŋpapi, and uŋkopapi; omapa, onipa.

o-pa'-ba-ġa, *v. a.* of pabaġa; *to roll over* anything *in the hands, rub in the hands*—owapabaġa.

o-pa'-ġi, *v. a.* *to fill* or *cram a pipe with tobacco*—owapaġi, uŋkopaġipi.

o'-pa-ġi, *n.* *a pipeful of tobacco;* opaġi waŋźidaŋ, *one pipeful.*

o-pa'-ha, *n.* *a swelling, a protuberance.* *T.*, noġe; nuġe.

o-pa'-ha, *v.* *to push;* maya opaha, *to push over a bank*—owapaha.

o-pa'-hi, *v.* of pahi; *to gather* or *pick into* owapahi, uŋkopahipi.

o-pa'-ḣći, *n* *T.* *a ravine, a hollow; the heads of creeks* among the hills.

o-pa'-ḣde-ća, *v.* of paḣdeća; *to tear in*—owapaḣdeća.

o-pa'-ḣde-će, *n.* *a rent.*

o-pa'-ḣdo-ka, *v.* of paḣdoka; *to pierce in; to wear holes in,* as a sick man's bones do when they come through the flesh—owapaḣdoka, omapaḣdoka.

o-pa'-ḣdo-ke, *n.* *a hole.*

o-pa'-ḣta, *v.* of paḣta; *to tie* or *bind in*—opawaḣta.

o-pa'-ḣta, *v. a.* *to gaze at, look at steadfastly*—opawaḣta, opauŋḣtapi: opaḣta kuwa, *to keep gazing at.* *T.*, ayuta: ayul kuwa.

o-pa'-ḣte, *n.* *a package, a bundle; a bale* of blankets; *a bunch* of beads.

o-pam', *cont.* of opapa; opam ya *and* opam iyaya, *to crawl out from under the edge* of a tent *T.*, paġaŋ iyaya.

o-pa'-mna, *n.* *a clump,* as of bushes or weeds. *T.*, wapamna.

o-pa'-mna, *v. n.* *T.* *to rip,* as a seam.

o-pa'-mna, *n.* *T.* *a rip* or *rend.*

o-pa'-mni, *n.* of pamni; *a distribution.* *T.*, kpamnipi. See wopamni.

o-paŋ'-ġa, *v. n.* *to be bulky; to hinder* or *impede* one, as cumbersome clothes do—omapaŋġa.

o-paŋ'-ġe-ća, *v. n.* *to be hindered by bulky articles, to be bulky*—omapaŋġeća.

o-paŋ ḣ'-ya, *v. a.* *to hinder, impede*—opaŋḣwaya.

o-paŋ ḣ'-ya, *adv.* *bulky, not compressed.*

o-paŋ ḣ'-ya-kel, *adv.* *T.* *bulkily.*

o-paŋ ḣ'-ye-la, *adv.* *T.* *not well arranged; bulkily.*

o-pa'-pa, *n.* *the lower edge of a tent.* *T.*, opapuŋ. See opepa.

o-pa'-pa-taŋ-haŋ, *adv.* *from under the bottom of a tent;* opapataŋhaŋ manoŋ, *to steal from under the side of a tent.* *T.*, opapuŋtaŋhaŋ. See opepataŋhaŋ.

o-pa'-poŋ, *n.* *the border* of anything, *the stripe* of a blanket. See opapuŋ.

o-pa'-psoŋ, *v.* of papsoŋ; *to pour out into, spill into*—owapapsoŋ.

o-pa'-psuŋ, *v.* See opapsoŋ.

o-pa'-ptaŋ, *v.* of paptaŋ; *to turn over;* opaptaŋ iyeya.

o-pa'-ptaŋ-ptaŋ, *v. n.* *to roll over and over in* anything.

o-pa'-ptaŋ-yaŋ, *v. a.* *to roll* anything *on* or *into*—owapaptaŋyaŋ.

o-pa'-puŋ, *n.* *the border* or *edge* of anything, as of a blanket, book, etc.; *the list* or *selvage* of cloth; *the stripes* or *points* that are put into white blankets to show their size; opapuŋ ḣota, *gray list;* opapuŋ ska, *white list;* ḣe opapuŋ, *the edge of the Coteau des Prairies.* See opapoŋ.

o-pa'-puŋ-taŋ-haŋ, *adv.* *from under the edge.*

o-pa'-sem, *cont.* of opasepa; opasem hnaka, *to lay away with care.*

o-pa'-se-pa, *v a.* *to keep with care*—owapasepa.

o-pa'-si, *v.* of pasi; *to follow after in,* as to follow one in a road—owapasi. *T.*, ogna pasi.

o-pa'-spa, *v.* *to push under,* as in the water; *to press down into the water.*

o-pa'-śbo-ka, *v.* *to push in,* as a stick, *and stir.*

o-pa'-śu-śu-źa, *v.* *to mash up in.* See paśuźa.

o-pa'-taŋ, *v. a.* *to push into; to mash up in*—owapataŋ. See okataŋ.

o-pa'-ti-ća, *v. a.* *to stick* or *push in* or *under,* as a handspike—owapatića. See paġopatića.

o-pa'-tin, *cont.* of opatića; opatin iyeya, *to push under,* as a crow-bar. *T.*, opatil.

o'-pa-tkoŋs-ye-la, *adv.* *T.* *in line, fronting one way, facing one way.*

o-pa'-wiŋ-ġe, *num. adj.* *one hundred.*

o-pa'-wiŋ-ġe-ġe, *adv.* *by hundreds.*

o-pa'-wiŋḣ-wiŋ-ġe, *adv.* *by hundreds.*

o-pa'-wi-wi, *adv.* *T.* *tangled together, in a mass.* See pawiwi.

o-pa'-wi-wi-se, *adv.* *T.* *shaking as a mass* of anything. See pawiwise.

o-pa'-wi-ya, *adv.* *T.* *many together,* as a herd.

o-pa'-ya, *adv.* *T.* *along in;* ćaŋku opaya, *along in the way;* wakpa opaya, etc.

o-pa'-zaŋ, *v. a.* *to put into* or *under,* as into a sheath or belt; *to put under and over, to interlace,* as in making baskets—owapazaŋ.

o-pa'-zaŋ-yaŋ, *adv.* *running under.*

o-pa'-zaŋ-zaŋ, *v.* *red.* of opazaŋ; *to weave into*—owapazaŋzaŋ.

o-pa'-zo, *n.* *a protuberance: i. q.* opaha.

o-pa'-zoŋ-ta, *v. a.* *to wrap around, wind up in,* as a dead body in a winding sheet—owapazoŋta.

o'-pe, *v.* Same as ópa.

o-pe', *n.* of pe; *the edge, the sharp part* of anything, as the edge of a knife or ax.

o-pe'-han, *n.* *the outside* or *lower border* of a tent: opehan iyaya, *he went out under the bottom.*

o-pe'-han-taŋ-haŋ, *adv.* *from under the bottom of* a tent: opehantaŋhaŋ iću, *he took it out from under the bottom.*

o-pe′-haŋ, *v.* of pehaŋ; *to fold up in*—owapehaŋ, uŋkopehaŋpi: opehaŋ ehnaka, *to lay away folded up in.*

o-pe′-he, *n.* of pehaŋ; *a fold; a bolt* of cloth.

o-pe′-ki-ća-toŋ, *v.* of opetoŋ; *to buy* anything *from* one; *to buy for* one—opewećatoŋ, opeuŋkićatoŋpi. *T. to buy for one* only.

o-pe′-ki-ći-toŋ, *v.* of opetoŋ; *to buy for* another—opewećitoŋ, opemićitoŋ.

o-pe′-ki-toŋ, *v. pos.* of opetoŋ; *to buy* or *purchase one's own, redeem*—opewakitoŋ, opeuŋkitoŋpi.

o-pe′-ki-toŋ-pi, *part. redeemed, redeeming.*

o-pe′-ki-toŋ-yaŋ, *v. a. to cause to redeem*—opekitoŋwaya.

o-pe′-mni, *v. a. to wrap around,* as a garment—owapemni, uŋkopemnipi: *to be wrapped up in.* See pemni.

o-pe′-mni-yaŋ, *adv. wrapped around.*

o-pe′-pa. See opapa.

o-pe′-pa-taŋ-haŋ, *adv. from under the bottom* of a tent: *i. q.* opapataŋhaŋ. *T.*, opapuŋtaŋhaŋ.

o-pe′-toŋ, *v. a. to buy, purchase* anything; *to hire*—opewatoŋ, opeuŋtoŋpi: opetoŋpi, *purchased, hired.*

o-pe′-toŋ-yaŋ, *v. a. to cause to buy*—opetoŋwaya.

o′-pe-ya, *v. a. to cause to go with*—ópewaya.

o′-pe-ya, *adv. with, together.*

o-pi′-i-ç̌i-ya, *v. reflex. to form an opinion and act for one's self, get ready:* token opimiç̌iye kta he, *how shall I do?*

o-pi′-ki-da, *v. n. to be satisfied with,* as with food—opiwakida, opiuŋkidapi. This word is used also when mosquitoes bite severely and fill themselves with blood. See pida.

o-pi′-ki-da-ka, *v.* Same as opikida—opiwakidaka.

o-pi′-ye, *v. n.* of piya: opiye śića, *bad to doctor* or *make well.*

o-pi′-ye, *n. a place where things are put away and kept,* as, mazopiye, *a store-house;* dotopiye, *a granary: a roll* of anything, as of cloth, ribbon, etc.; also *a box, case,* or *crate,* anything for packing goods in.

o-pi′-źe-ća, *adj. wrinkled,* as an old person.

o-po′, *v. n. to be swelled*—omapo.

o′-po, *v. n. to be warped, to be shrunken.*

o-po′-ġaŋ, *v. a. to blow in upon, to blow out from*—owapoġaŋ. See poġaŋ.

o-poḣ′, *cont.* of opoġaŋ; opoḣ iyeya, *to blow away, blow from* the mouth.

o-po′-ḣdi, *v. a. to stuff* anything *into,* as an old coat into a broken window. See opuġi.

o′-psoŋ-psoŋ, *v. a. to draw back and forth in the water, to rinse. T*, miniyoḣpaya. See oyupsoŋpsoŋ.

o′-psuŋ-psuŋ, *v.* See opsoŋpsoŋ.

o′-pta, *adv.* *through, across.* See aetoopta, iyoopta, etc.

o′-pta-pta, *adv.* *red.* of opta; *through and through.*

o-pta′-ye, *n.* *a flock,* as of geese or ducks; *a herd* or *drove* of animals; *a company* of men. See ośpaye.

o′-pte, *n.* of yupta; *what is left, leavings.* *T.*, okaptapi.

o-pte′-ća, *adv.* *less.* *T.*, aoptetu.

o′-pte-he-ća, *adv.* *almost empty,* said of vessels.

o-pten′, *adv.* *less.* *T.*, aoptel.

o-pteṅ′-i-ç̣i-ya, *v.* *reflex.* *to cease from,* as from anger or strife, *become gentle*—optenmiç̣iya.

o-pte′-tu, *adv.* *less than.* *T.*, aoptetu, *less in size.*

o-pu′-ġi, *v. a.* *to push into,* as hay into moccasins; *to stuff, fill,* as with hay, etc.—owapuġi. See opoḣdi.

o-pu′-ġi-toŋ, *v. a.* *to put in stuffing,* as in moccasins—opuġiwatoŋ.

o-pu′-ḣdi, *v.* See opoḣdi.

o-pu′-ski-ća, *v. a.* *to press down in*—owapuskića. See kipuskića.

o-pu′-skin, *cont.* of opuskića. *T.*, opuskil.

o-pu′-ta-ka, *v.* of putaka; *to touch in*—owaputaka. See yut'aŋ.

o-pu′-tkaŋ, *v. a.* *to dip into, put in,* as the fingers; *sop,* as bread, etc.—owaputkaŋ.

o-p̣o′, *n.* *fog, steam.*

o-p̣o′-sa, *adj.* *clear and cold,* with particles of snow in the air. *T.*, op̣osya.

o-p̣os′-ya, *adv.* *T.* *clear and cold.*

o-p̣o′-za, *adj.* Same as op̣osa.

os, *n.* of oze *or* yuza; *a hand's breadth.*

o-s'a′-mna, *adj.* *sour smelling; i. q.* śićamna.

o′-saŋ, *adv.* *all, through the whole:* aŋpetu osaŋ, *all the day.* *T.*, ataya.

o-saŋ′-ka, *adj.* *without leaves,* as a tree. *T.*, osmismika.

o-saŋ′-ka-ka, *adj.* *red.* of osaŋka.

o′-saŋ-saŋ, *adv.* *red.* of ósaŋ. *T.*, alataya.

o-sda′, *v.* of sda; *greased in anything.*

o-sdo′-ća, *v.* *to know;* takudaŋ osdoće śni wauŋ, *I know nothing about it,* or *I am innocent of it.* *T.*, oslolya. See osdonya.

o-sdo′-haŋ, *v. n.* *to slide;* osdohaŋ kiç̣uŋ, *to slide on a board* or *sled* or *one's feet*—osdohaŋ weç̣uŋ. See sdohaŋ, yusdohaŋ, etc.

o-sdo′-haŋ, *n.* *a drawing* or *sliding in.*

o-sdon′-ya, *v. a.* *to know, be acquainted with* or *privy to* anything—osdonwaya. *T.*, oslolya.

o-sdoṅ′-ye, *n.* *knowledge.*

o-se′-ya-ka-daŋ, *n.* *i. q.* oŋseyakadaŋ. *T.*, śiyaka.

o′-siŋ, *v.* *to hate.* *T.*, oyusiŋka. See oyusiŋ.

o-siŋ′-siŋ, *v. n.* *to leave a mark,* as tears drying on one. See yuosiŋsiŋ.

o-ska′-ka, *adj* *bare*, as a tree whose leaves are fallen off; *open*, as a country without thickets. *T.*, osmismika.

o′-skam, *cont.* of óskapa.

o′-skam-ya, *adv.* *sticking to, adhering.*

o′-skan, *adv.* *desert-like:* tiŋta oskan, *an uninhabited place.* *T.*, makoskaŋ. See ȟewoskan.

o′-skan tu, *adv.* *desert-like, away from trees* or *dwellings.* *T.*, makoskaŋtu.

o′-ska-pa, *v. n* *to stick in, adhere to; to climb up*, as up a pole; *i. q.* otkapa. See adi.

o′-ska-pi, *n.* *ornamental work*, such as is put on *pipe-stems.* See ipatapi.

o′-ski-ća, *adj.* of yuskića; *tight, drawn around*, as a garment. *T.*, oṭiŋza.

o′-ski-će-daŋ, *adj.* *tight, well fitting.*

o′-ski-ski-ta, *v. red.* of óskita.

o′-ski-ta, *v.* *to bind up in*, as a child. See oyuskita.

o-sku′-ya, *adj.* *sour, turned sour*, as milk.

o-slol′-ya, *v.* *T.* *to know of: i. q.* osdonya

o′-sma-ka, *n* *a ditch, a hollow, a ravine.*

o-smi′-smi-ka, *adj.* *T.* *bare*, as trees, of leaves.

o-sna′-ze, *n.* *a scar:* also o-sna′-ze-ća.

o-sni′, *n.* *cold weather.*

o-sni′, *adj.* *cold in*, as, ti osni, *cold in the house.*

o-sni′-ke, *adj.* *cold.*

o-sni′-sni, *red.* of osni; *very cold.*

o-sni′-ta-wa-na-piŋ, *n.* *T.* (osni *and* wanapiŋ) *a tippet, scarf.*

o-so′, *v.* *T.* *to cut open*, as the skin of an animal, in preparing to skin it—owaso.

o-so′-ta, *v. col.* of yusota; *to be all gone*, as a company starting away.

o-spaŋ′-spaŋ-he-ća, *n.* See uspaŋspaŋheća.

o-spa′-ya, *v.* of spaya; *to become damp in.*

o′-stag, *cont.* of óstaka.

o′-stag-ya, *v. a.* *to make stick on*—óstagwaya.

o′-sta-ka, *v. n.* *to stick on* or *in*, as dirt on a plow or mud in a house; *to stick on*, as flesh—ómastaka; takudaŋ ostake śni, *very lean.* *T.*, otkapa.

o-sta′-ka, *v* of staka; *to be feeble on account of, to be debilitated;* iśtiŋma ostaka, *he is feeble by reason of sleep.*

o-staŋ′-mna, *n.* *the smell of a carcass* soon after the animal has died; *the smell of tainted meat.*

o-su′-kal-yu-za, *v.* *T.* *to take one's choice, take the best.*

o-su′-kan, *adv.* *taking* a thing *without having bestowed labor on it*, or *acquired a proper right:* osukan mduza, *I took it without permission.*

o-śbe′, *n.* *depth.* *T.*, osme. See wośbe.

o-śbu′, *v. n.* *to drop in*, as water. *T.*, oś'e.

o-śbu′, *n.* *a drop.* *T.*, oś'e.

o-śbu′-śbu, *v. n. red.* of ośbu. *T.*, oś'eś'e.

o-śbu′-ya, *v. a.* *to cause to drop into*, as water—ośbuwaya. *T.*, oś'eya.

o-śbu′-ye, *n.* *something into which* water, etc., *is made to drop, a trough*, etc.

o-śdo′-ḳa-haŋ, *part.* *pulled off in*, as an arrow point; *coming off, peeling off*, as bark.

o-śdo′-ḳa-he, *part.* Same as ośdokahaŋ.

o-ś'e′, *v. n.* *T.* *to drop into: i. q.* ośbu.

o-ś'e′-ya, *v. n.* *T.* *to make drop in*, as water.

o-śi′-ća, *adj.* *bad with*, as one kind of food with another.

o-śi′-će-ća, *adj.* or *v. n.* *stormy; it storms.*

o-śi′-će-ća-ka, *adj.* *unpleasant*, as rainy weather, *not pleasing*, as a country. See ośićeća.

o-śi′-će-ća-ki-ksu-ya, *v.* *to know by one's feelings when bad weather is coming.*

o-śil′-ye-o-ḣaŋ, *v.* *T.* *to act badly*

o-śin′-ḣaŋ-ka, *v. n.* *to do badly, steal*, etc., *act wickedly*—ośinwaḣaŋka. *T.*, ośilyeoḣaŋ. See oḣaŋśića.

o-śi′-tki-hda, *v. n.* of śitkihda; *to be angry with.* See ćaŋniyeya.

o-śi′-tki-hda-ya, *v. a.* *to make angry, cause to suffer*—ośitkihdawaya.

o′-śkan, *n.* *motion, movement.* See oḣaŋ.

o′-śkan-śin-ya, *v. a.* *to impede one's progress, prevent from moving freely*—ośkanśinwaya.

o-śka′-ta, *v.* of śkata; *to play in*—owaśkata.

o-śka′-te, *n.* *play, diversion.* See wićośkate.

o-śkiŋ′-ći-ya, *v.* *T.* *to busy one's self about*—ośkiŋmićiya. See ośkan.

o-śkiŋ′-ći-ye, *n.* *T.* *an occupation.*

o-śki′-śka, *adj.* of śkiśka; *complicated, intricate, confused, difficult.*

o-śki′-śken-ya, *adv.* *confusedly.*

o-śki′-śke-ya, *v. a.* *to make complicated* or *confused, create difficulty, perplex*—ośkiśkewaya.

o-śki′-śke-ya, *adv.* *crookedly, with difficulty.*

o-śki′-śki, *n.* *broken land, bad country.*

o-śko′-kpa, *n.* *a concavity.*

o-śku′-mna, *adj.* *sour, spoiled*, as food.

o-śme′, *n.* *T.* *depth: i. q.* ośbe.

o′-śna, *n.* of yuśna; *a piece that is dropped, a scrap, a crumb.*

o′-śna-pi, *n.* *crumbs, scraps.*

o-śni′-yaŋ-yaŋ, *v. n.* *to move about*, as worms in the stomach.

o-śog′-ya, *adv.* of śogya; *thickly.*

o-śo′-ka, *adj.* of śoka; *thick.*

o-śo′-ka, *n.* *thickness.*

o-śo′-ta, *adj.* of śota; *smoky, filled with smoke*, as a tent.

o-śpa′-ye, *n.* *a drove, a herd* consisting of different kinds of animals; *a company* separated from the main body. See obe *and* optaye.

o-śpa′-ye-toŋ-toŋ, *adv.* *T.* *in droves.*

o-śpe′, *n.* of yuśpa; *a breaking off: a piece, a part* of a section of land. *T.*, oyuśpe.

o′-śtaŋ, *v. a.* *T.* *to put in place of; to put in,* as a cork—owaśtaŋ, oyaśtaŋ.

o′-śtaŋ, *v. n.* *to be on,* as a hoop, or *in,* as a stopper; *to be in agreement with; to be in place of.* See oyuśtaŋ.

o′-śtaŋ-haŋ, *part.* *being in* or *on.*

o-śtaŋ′-haŋ, *n.* *a running, watery sore.*

o-śtaŋ′-haŋ, *v. n.* *T.* *to ooze out,* as water from a sore.

o-śte′, *adj.* *deformed*—omaśte, oniśte. See ośteka.

o-śte′, *intj.* *T.* *of surprise, incredulity.*

o-śte′-daŋ, *adj.* *deformed.*

o-śte′-hda, *v. a.* (ośte *and* hda) *to mock, speak evil of, call bad names, revile*—ośtewahda.

o-śte′-hda-pi, *n.* *contempt, opprobrious language.*

o-śte′-ka, *adj.* *defective in some part, deformed*—omaśteka.

o-śte′-ya, *adv.* *imperfectly, clumsily; by chance, accidentally;* ośteya ećoŋ, *he did it imperfectly.*

o-śte′-ya-ken, *adv.* *deformedly.*

o-śti′, *intj.* *T.* *oh, ah, alas;* it expresses strong disappointment and regret; as, ośti, waŋźini yuspiŋ kte śni, *alas! he will not catch a single one.*

o-śuŋg′-ye; *adv.* *very much, violently.* *T.*, ośuŋgyela.

o-śuŋ′-ke-ća-daŋ-ka, *n.* *a very little thing.*

o′-ta, *adj.* *much; many*—uŋkotapi: wićota, *a great company.*

o-tab′, *cont.* *T.* of otapa: otabaya, *to trail, follow tracks.*

o-tab′-tab, *red.* of otab.

o-ta′-ġo-śa, *v.* of taġośa; *to spit into* anything—otaġowaṡa, otaġouŋśapi. *T.*, otaḣośa *and* otaśośa.

o-ta′-he-daŋ, *adv.* *between.* See iyotahedaŋ *and* tahedaŋ.

o-ta′-he-la, *adv.* *T.* *off to one side; away from* others, said of one who has deserted his company and gone off alone. With this meaning it is not proper to apply the word to our Savior, as Mediator or daysman, as Mr. Cleveland says. But with us it appears quite proper to say of Him, "otahedaŋ yaŋka."

o-ta′-he-pi, *adv.* *between* places. *T.*, iyokogna. See iyotahepi *and* tahepi.

o-ta′-ḣo-śa, *n.* *T.* *a spittoon*

o′-ta-ka, *adj.* *many, much.* See ota.

o′-ta-ki-ya, *adv.* *oftentimes, frequently.*

o′-ta-koŋs, *adv.* *opposite to, over against.* See iyotakoŋs.

o'-ta-koŋ-za, *adv.* *over against, opposite to.* See iyotakoŋza.

o-ta'-ku-ye, *n.* of takuye; *brotherhood, relationship, friendship.*

o'-t'aŋ, *v.* *to touch, lay hold of, seize.* See oyut'aŋ.

o-taŋ'-ćaŋ, *n.* of taŋćaŋ; *the chief, the greatest.* See itaŋćaŋ.

o-taŋ'-ćaŋ-ke, *n.* *the greatest* in numbers, as the greatest herd, the largest war-party.

o-taŋ'-ćaŋ-ke-ya, *adv.* *in the greatest numbers.*

o-taŋ'-da, *v.* *to have, to keep:* otaŋda śića, *bad to keep;* otaŋda waśte, *good to keep.* *T*, oyuha.

o-taŋ'-hda-kiŋ-yaŋ, *n.* *breadth.* *T.*, oglakiŋyaŋ. See taŋhdakiŋyaŋ.

o-taŋ'-iŋ, *v. n.* of taŋiŋ; *to be manifest:* taku otaŋiŋ, *something that is manifest.*

o-taŋ'-iŋ-ka, *v. n.* *to appear, be manifest:* taku otaŋiŋka, *something is manifest:* sometimes this is used in the sense of otaŋiŋ śni, as, taku otaŋiŋka, *or* takudaŋ otaŋiŋ śni, *there is no news.*

o-taŋ'-iŋ-yaŋ, *adv.* *manifestly.*

o-taŋ'-ka, *n.* of taŋka; *greatness, largeness.*

o-taŋ'-ka, *adj.* *large, broad.*

o-taŋ'-ka-da. *v. a.* *to have in the greatest estimation*—otaŋkawada. *T.*, taŋkala.

o-taŋ'-ka-da-ka, *v. a.* *to esteem most highly*—otaŋkawadaka. *T.*, taŋkalaka.

o-taŋ'-ka-ya, *adv.* *largely, extensively,*

o-taŋ'-ka-ya-ka, *n.* *greatness.*

o-taŋ'-na, *v. n.* *to be proud, vain*—omataŋna. *T.*, witaŋtaŋ. See itaŋ.

o-taŋ'-toŋ-ka, *adj.* *large, prodigious.*

o-taŋ'-toŋ-yaŋ-kel, *adv.* *T.*, otaŋtoŋyaŋkel ia, *to speak in a dissatisfied way.*

o-taŋ'-yaŋ, *n.* *well being.*

o-ta'-pa, *v.* of tapa; *to follow after* one, as *in* a road—otawapa, otauŋpapi.

o-ta'-śo-śa, *v.* *T.* *to spit in, to expectorate in*—otawaśośa. See otaġośa.

o-ta'-śo-śe, *n.* *T.* *a spittoon.*

o-ta'-tkoŋ-za, *adj.* *T.* *square; equal to; parallel.* See otkoŋza.

O-ta'-wa, *n. p.* *the Otos* or *Otawas.* See Hotawa.

o-ta'-waŋ-źi-daŋ, *n.* *two alike, a pair of one kind.*

o-ta'-wa-ṭe-ća, *v. n.* *to be willing to do.* *T.*, otawaṭelya. See otawaṭenya.

o-ta'-wa-ṭel-śi-ća, *adj.* *T.* *unendurable.*

o-ta'-wa-ṭel-śil-ya, *adv.* *T.* *exceedingly bad.*

o-ta'-wa-ṭel-ya, *v.* *T.* *to be willing.*

o-ta'-wa-ṭen, *cont.* of otawaṭenya: otawaṭen waśte, *it is pleasant to do;* otawaṭen śića, *it is unpleasant to decide on doing.*

o-ta'-wa-ṭen-ya, *v. n.* *to be willing to do*—otawaṭenwaya.

o-ta'-wa-ṭe-śi-ca, *adj.* *great, fearful, numberless.*

o-ta'-źa, *n.* of taźa: *waves.* *T.*, kaataźa.

o-te'-haŋ, *adv.* *far, a long distance:* yapi kiŋ otehaŋ, kupi kiŋ oakiyedaŋ, *the going is far, the coming back is near.* See tehaŋ.

o-te'-haŋ, *v. n.* *to be long about* anything, *long in doing*—omatehaŋ kta.

o-te'-haŋ-ya, *v. a.* *to hinder, cause to be long* about a thing—otehaŋwaye.

o-te'-ḣi, *n.* *a thicket* of bushes or brush; *misery, difficulty.*

o-te'-ḣi-ka, *adv.* *very hard to endure; trying, difficult.*

o-ti', *v. n.* *to dwell in*—owati, uŋkotipi.

o-ti', *n.* *a house, dwelling.*

o-tiŋt'-o-ska, *n.* *T.* *an open place in the woods.*

o-ti'-wi-ta, *n.* *an old encampment,* where there has been a cluster of tents. *T.*, otiwota.

o-ti'-wo-ta, *n.* *an old encampment.* See otuwita.

o'-tkam, *cont.* of ótkapa.

o'-tkam-ya, *v. a.* *to make stick on, daub,* as with pitch—ótkamwaya.

o'-tka-pa, *v. n.* *to stick on,* as pitch, snow, or mud—ómatkapa. See oskapa *and* ostaka.

o-tke', *v. n.* *to hang from, be lodged on, be suspended from* anything, as a tree. See tke.

o-tke'-ya, *v. a.* *to hang up, suspend* anything—otkewaya, otkeuŋyaŋpi.

o-tke'-ya-haŋ, *part.* *hanging up.*

o-tkiŋ', *v. n.* *T.* *to become damp in.*

o-tkoŋs', *cont.* of otkoŋza: otkoŋs yuksa, *to break off even.*

o-tkoŋ'-se-la, *adv.* *T.* *evenly.*

o-tkoŋ'-za, *adj.* *even, equal, parallel.* See otatkoŋza.

o-to', *adj.* *cont.* of otoiyohi; *each one: i q.* owasiŋ.

o to'-i-yo-hi, *adj.* *each one, every one.* *T.*, otoiyohila; iyohila.

o-to'-ka-he, *n.* *the beginning:* otokahe ekta, *at the beginning.*

o'-to-ka-he, *n.* *that which goes first.*

o-to'-ka-he-ya, *n.* *the first, the beginning.* See tokaheya.

o-to'-ka-he-ya, *adv.* *at the beginning.*

o'-to-ka-ta, *adv.* *before, foremost.*

o-to'-ki-he, *adj.* *Ih.* *the next.* *T.*, iyokihe.

o-to'-kśu, *v.* of tokśu; *to haul* or *transport in,* as in a cart—otowakśu, ótouŋkśupi.

o-to'-kśu, *n.* *hauling, transporting:* otokśu waśte, *it is good hauling.*

o-toŋ', *v. a.* *to put on and wear,* as leggings or pantaloons—owatoŋ.

o-toŋ'-waŋ, *v.* of toŋwaŋ; *to look into*—owatoŋwaŋ, uŋkotoŋwaŋpi.

o-toŋ'-we, *n.* *a cluster of houses* or *tents, a village, a town, a city.* See toŋwaŋyaŋ.

o-toŋ'-yaŋ, *adv.* of toŋyaŋ; *suppurating.*

o-to'-sa, *adj.* *blunt, round, not cut up:* otosa śpaŋ, *cooked whole;* said of anything cooked without drawing the entrails. *T.*, otosya. See otoza.

o-tos'-ya, *adj.* *T.* *blunt, round.*

o-to'-to, *adv.* *red.* of oto.

o-to'-to-daŋ, *adv.* *clear of brush, long grass,* etc.

o-to'-za, *adj* *blunt, round, cylindrical, anything round and long; not split,* as, ćaŋ otoza, *a round stick.* See oṭoza.

o-tpa'-ġi, *v.* *pos.* of opaġi; *to fill one's own pipe*—owatpaġi: *i. q.* okpaġi.

o'-tpa-ni, *v. n.* *to lack, be wanting.* Hence, ćaŋtotpani, *to long for*: *i. q.* okpani.

o'-tpa-ni-yaŋ, *adv.* *less, lacking; not yet, beforehand:* otpaniyaŋ wahi, *I have come too soon.*

o'-tpas, *cont.* of otpaza: otpas iću, *to become dark:* *i. q.* okpas. *T.*, oiyokpas.

o'-tpas-ya, *v. a.* *to make dark*—otpaswaya: *i. q.* okpasya. *T.*, oiyokpasya.

o'-tpas-ya, *adv.* *darkly, obscurely.*

o'-tpa-za, *v. n.* *to be dark.* *T.*, oiyokpaza.

o'-tpa-za, *n.* *darkness, night.* Same as okpaza.

o'-tpe, *v.* Same as okpe.

o-tu'-ȟaŋ, *v.* *T.* *i. q.* ituȟaŋ; *to give away, make a present.*

o-tu'-ki-ȟaŋ, *v.* *T.* *to make a present to* one—otuwekiȟaŋ: *i. q.* itukiȟaŋ.

o-tu'-ma-ko-skaŋ, *adv.* *T.* *in vain; without cause.* See otuyaćiŋ, ituȟ, etc.

o-tu'-tka, *n.* *crumbs, fragments.*

o-tu'-wi-ta, *n.* *an old encampment.* See otiwita *and* otiwota.

o-tu'-ya, *adv.* *T.* *in vain.*

o-tu'-ya-ćiŋ, *adv.* *Ih* *at random:* *i. q.* ituyaćiŋ. *T.*, *a.* *in vain, for naught.*

o-ṭa', *v. n.* of ṭa; *to die in* any place; *to have the stomach overloaded, to die of a surfeit*—omaṭa.

o-ṭe', *v. n.* *to die, be dying:* oṭe teȟi, *hard to die, tenacious of life.*

o-ṭiŋ', *v. n.* *to roar,* as thunder; *to make a noise,* as the ice cracking.

o-ṭiŋs', *cont.* of oṭiŋza; oṭiŋs yaŋka.

o-ṭiŋs'-ṭiŋ-za, *red.* of oṭiŋza.

o-ṭiŋs'-ya, *adv.* *tightly, firmly.*

o-ṭiŋs'-ya-kel, *adv.* *T.* *firmly, tightly.*

o-ṭiŋ'-za, *v n.* *to be tight* or *fast in,* said of clothes that are too small and of food that sticks in the throat; *to be too little* or *too large*—omaṭiŋza. See iṭiŋza.

o-ṭo'-hnag, *cont.* of oṭohnaka.

o-ṭo'-hnag-ya, *adv.* *at the risk of life.*

o-ṭo'-hna-ka, *v. n.* *to risk life, be foolhardy, be willing to die*—oṭowahnaka. See oṭoohnaka.

o-ṭo'-o-hna-ka, *v. a* *to be willing to die, to dare, risk life*—oṭoowahnaka.

o-ṭo'-za *or* o-ṭo'-źa, *adj. blunt, stubbed; cylindrical.* See otoza.

o-uŋ', *v. n.* of uŋ, *to be; to be in*—owauŋ.

o-uŋ', *n.* of uŋ; *to be; condition, state; place.*

o-uŋ', *n.* of uŋ, *to use; a load* of a gun; *a dose* of medicine; *what is used at once; ammunition.*

o-uŋ'-ća-ġe, *n. likeness, form, kind, growth*—ouŋmaćaġe, ouŋnićaġe.

o-uŋ'-hda-ka, *v. n.* of uŋhdaka; *to be moving:* ouŋhdaka uŋpi, *they are moving* or *camping. T.*, oiglaka.

o-uŋ'-hda-ke, *n. a moving party. T.*, oiglake.

o-uŋ'-pa, *v. a. to lay in and bind up,* as an infant on a board—owauŋpa. See uŋpa, aoŋpa, oźu, etc.

o-uŋ'-pa, *n. T. one bound in, an infant.*

o-uŋ'-yaŋ, *v. n. to be* or *exist in, dwell in; to reign over, govern*—ouŋwaya, ouŋuŋyaŋpi.

o-uŋ'-ye-ki-ya, *v. a. to cause to dwell in; to cause to rule over*—ouŋyewakiya.

o-uŋ'-ye-ya, *v. a. to cause to dwell in, give power to*—ouŋyewaya, ouŋyeuŋyaŋpi.

o-u'-ye, *n.* of uya; *the coming, springing up,* as of the grass; *a quarter of the heavens:* tate ouye topa, *the four quarters of the wind.*

o-wa', *v. a. to paint, sketch, figure, write*—owawa, uŋkowapi.

o-wa'-će-ki-ya, *v.* of waćekiya; *to pray in.*

o-wa'-će-ki-ye-ti-pi, *n. a prayer-house, a church.*

o-wa'-ći, *v.* of waći; *to dance in*—owawaći, owauŋćipi.

o-wa'-ći, *n. a dance.*

o-wa'-ćiŋ-ksam, *cont.* of owaćiŋksapa.

o-wa'-ćiŋ-ksam-ya, *adv. intelligently.*

o-wa'-ćiŋ-ksa-pa, *adj.* of waćiŋksapa; *intelligent, wise, understanding*—owaćiŋmaksapa.

o-wa'-hde, *n. the set of a gun-cock.* See oahde.

o-wa'-he, *n.* of ohaŋ, *v. n.*; *T. something to stand on: i. q.* oahe.

o-wa'-he-gle-pi, *n. T. a foundation.* See oahehde.

o-wa'-hi-na-pe, *n.* of ahinapa; *the springing up* of vegetables, water, etc.

o-wa'-hi-na-pe-ya, *v. a. to cause to spring up*—owahinapewaya.

o-wa'-ḣam-ya, *v.* (owasiŋ *and* ḣamya) *to scare all away*—owaḣamwaya.

o-wa'-ḣam-ya, *n. one who scares away.*

o-wa'-ḣla-ġaŋ, *v. T. to enlarge,* as by cutting a hole with a knife: *i. q.* waḣdaġaŋ.

o-wa'-ḣla-ye, *n. T. parings,* as of an apple. See obaḣdaye.

o-wa′-ħpa-ni, *adj.* of waħpani; *poor, miserable.*

o-wa′-ħpa-ni-ća, *adj.* of waħpanića; *poor*—omawaħpanića.

o-wa′-ħpa-ni-ya, *v. a.* *to make poor*—owaħpaniwaya.

o-wa′-ħpa-ni-yaŋ, *adv.* *poorly, miserably.*

o-wa′-kaŋ-kaŋ, *v.* *T.* *i. q.* owewakaŋ

o-wa′-ki-be, *n.* *a seam, a joint.* *T.*, wakime: *i. q.* okibe *and* okihe.

o-wa′-ki-ćoŋ-ze, *n.* *a law, a rule.* *T.*, wowasukiye. See wokićoŋze *and* woope.

o-wa′-ki-ya, *v. a.* of owa; *to cause to write,* etc.—owawakiya, owauŋkiyapi.

o-wa′-ki-ye, *v. a.* of okíya; *to speak to* or *with; to speak harshly to, to reprimand; to offend*—owawakiye, owauŋkiyepi, owamakiye, owaćićiye.

o-wa′-koŋ-ze, *n.* of koŋza; *determination.* See wokoŋze, wokićoŋze, etc.

o-wa′-kpa-mni, *n.* *an Indian agency; place of distribution.* *T*, owakipamni.

o-wa′-ma-noŋ, *v.* of manoŋ; *to steal in* or *from* any place—owamawanoŋ.

o-wa′-ma-noŋ, *n.* *a thief.*

o-wa′-mni-yo-mni *or* o-wa′-mni-o-mni, *n.* *T.* *an eddy, a whirlpool.*

o-wa′-na-sa-pi, *n.* *T.* *a place of chasing buffalo.*

o-wa′-na-se, *n.* of nasa; *a place of chasing buffalo; the buffalo-chase.*

o′-wa-ni-ye-tu, *n.* *winter.* See waniyetu.

o′-waŋ-ća, *adv.* *all over.*

o′-waŋ-ća-ya, *adv.* *everywhere, all over; all together.*

o-waŋg′, *cont.* of owaŋka.

o-waŋg′-i-ća-hiŋ-ta, *n.* *T.* *a broom: i. q.* owaŋkaićahiŋte.

o-waŋg′-ya, *v. a.* *to resemble, imitate, take lessons from* one; *to follow the example of*—owaŋgwaya, owaŋguŋyaŋpi: owaŋgiçiya, *to form a habit, be in the habit of.*

o-waŋg′-ya, *adv.* *through all, through the middle.* *T.*, ohaŋglela *and* ohaŋgleyela.

o-waŋ′-ka, *v. n.* *to resemble, be like*—omawaŋka, oniwaŋka.

o-waŋ′-ka, *v. n.* of waŋka; *to lie in a place*—omuŋka, uŋkowaŋkapi. *T.*, oyuŋka.

o-waŋ′-ka, *n.* *a place to lie on, a place where persons sleep; a floor; a place of pitching a tent, the ground.* *T.*, oyuŋke *and* owaŋka.

o-waŋ′-ka-i-ća-hiŋ-te *and* o-waŋ′-ki-ća-hiŋ-te, *n.* *something to sweep with, a broom.* See ićahiŋte.

o-waŋ′-ka-i-hu-pa, *n.* *T.* *a bedstead.*

o-waŋk′-i-pa-kiŋ-te, *n.* *a mop, floor-cloth.* See ipakiŋte.

o-waŋk′-i-yu-hiŋ-te, *n.* *a broom.* *T.*, owaŋgićahiŋte. See iyuhiŋte.

o-waŋ'-yag, *cont.* of owaŋyaka: owaŋyag waśte, *beautiful;* owaŋyag śića, *ugly. T.*, ówaŋyag.

o-waŋ'-ya-ka, *v. a.* of waŋyaka; *to look upon*—owaŋmdaka: owaŋyake waśte, *good to look upon, handsome. T.*, ówaŋyaka.

o-waŋ'-ya-ke, *n. a sight, a show; a vision. T.*, ówaŋyake.

o-waŋ'-ya-ke-ka, *n. something delightful to be seen.*

o-waŋ'-ye-ye, *n. a place to look out at, a window. port-hole, a loophole.*

o-waŋ'-ye-ye-toŋ, *v. to have windows, having port-holes.* See toŋ, *v. a.*

o-waŋ'-źi, *adv. at rest, at leisure:* owaŋźi yaŋka, *to be at rest.* See owaŋźidaŋ.

o-waŋ'-źi-daŋ, *adv. at rest, disengaged, unemployed:* owaŋźidaŋ yaŋka, *to be unemployed;* owaŋźidaŋ maŋke śni, *I am not at leisure.*

o'-waŋ-źi-la, *adv. T. alike, the same: i. q* okoŋwaŋźila.

o-wa'-pi, *part. figured, written.*

o-wa'-siŋ, *adj. all, every one; the whole, the greater part. T.*, oyasiŋ.

o-wa'-siŋ-siŋ, *adj. red.* of owasiŋ. *T*, óyasiŋsiŋ.

o-waś', *cont.* of owaźa: owaś wauŋ śni, *I am not near to, not affected by.*

o'-wa-ś'ag, *cont.* of ówaś'aka.

o'-wa-ś'ag-la-ka, *v. T. to esteem easy of accomplishment.*

o-wa'-śag-toŋ, *adj. easily purchased. T.*, ówaśakela.

o'-wa-ś'ag-ye-la, *adv. T. almost finished, nearly complete.*

o-wa'-ś'a-ka, *v. n.* of waś'aka; *to be strong for* the accomplishment of anything—owamaś'aka. *T.*, ówaś'aka.

o-wa'-śa-ka-daŋ, *adj. cheap, easily purchased. T.*, ówaśakela.

o-wa'-śte, *n.* of waśte; *something good with* another thing. *T.*, iwaśte.

o-wa'-śte-ća, *adj.* See owaśtećaka.

o-wa'-śte-ća-ka, *adj. pleasant,* as a pleasant place, pleasant weather.

o'-wa-śte-kal, *adv. T. picking, choosing;* owaśtekal iću, *to take the pick of.*

o-waś'-ya, *v. a.* of owaźa; *to bring near to, cause to be near:* commonly use with the negative, as, owaśwaye śni.

o-wa'-ṭe-ća, *adv. almost.* See wawaṭeća.

o-wa'-u-ye, *n.* of uya; *the growing, springing up* of things.

o-wa'-ya-tpaŋ, *n.* of yatpaŋ; *what is chewed fine,* as the muskrat's food. *T.*, owayakpaŋ.

o-wa'-yu-hi. See wayuhi.

o-wa'-yu-śna, *v.* of yuśna; *to sacrifice in* any place—owamduśna. *T.* owauŋyaŋ *or* owayuȟtata, according to the kind of sacrifice.

o-wa'-yu-śna, *n. a place of sacrifice, an altar, a propitiatory. T.*, owauŋyaŋ *and* owayuȟtata.

o-wa'-yu-tpaŋ, *n.* of yutpaŋ; *what is ground up fine.* *T.*, owayukpaŋ.

o-wa'-źa, *v. n.* *to be near to; to be concerned in:* owaźa śni, *not near.* See iyowaźa śni.

o-we', *n.* *a foot-print, track, trail*—miowe, uŋkowepi. *T.*, oye.

o'-we, *n.* *a spring* or *well:* mini owe, *a well* or *spring of water.* See miniyowe.

o-we', *n.* *T.* *a class; division; order:* *i. q.* obe.

o-we'-će-ća-ka, *v. n.* *to be like* another in demeanor, appearance, etc.—owemaćećaka: *i. q.* oećećećaka.

o'-we-ćiŋ-haŋ, *adv.* *in succession, in Indian file, in an extended line.*

o'-we-ćiŋ-haŋ-haŋ, *adv. red.* of ówećiŋhaŋ.

o'-we-ćiŋ-haŋ-yaŋ, *adv.* *in Indian file.*

o'-we-haŋ-haŋ, *v. n.* *to jest, make fun*—ówewahaŋhaŋ. See aowehaŋ.

o'-we-haŋ-haŋ-yaŋ, *adv.* *jestingly.*

o-we'-he, *n.* *T.* *a boiling:* *i. q.* ohe.

o-we'-he-ća, *n.* *T.* *i. q.* iheća: *an arrow thrown for a mark for others to shoot at.*

o-we'-he-ća-ku-te, *v.* *T.* *to play* oweheća.

o-we'-kiś, *adv.* *T.* *perhaps, it may be.*

o-we'-ki-niś, *adv.* *T.* *perhaps.* See okinahaŋ.

o-we'-ki-na-haŋś, *adv.* *T.* *perhaps.*

o-we'-ki-wa-kaŋ, *v.* of owewakaŋ; *Ih.* and *T.* *to lie about one.*

o-we'-na-pe, *n.* *the place of egress; coming out of:* of inapa.

o-we'-śde-ke, *n.* *a war-prize,* as a pipe; *a badge of honor.* The Teetons give no war prizes, but the victor on his return must give away all his property.—W. J. C.

o-we'-śte, *v. n.* *to use a by-word*—owewaśte, oweuŋśtepi.

o-we'-śte, *n.* *a cant phrase.*

o-we'-śte-ka, *n.* *a by-word.*

o-we'-śte-pi, *n.* *by-words, cant phrases*

o-we'-śte-ya, *adv.* *in the manner of a by-word*—oweśteya ia.

o-we'-śuŋ-ke-ća, *v. n.* *to be unable to escape, unable by any effort to extricate one's self*—owewaśuŋkeća, oweuŋśuŋkećapi. *T.*, *to do badly and persist in denying it, after it is known; to protest innocence in the face of discovery.* See ohaŋśuŋkeća *and* uŋćoŋnića.

o-we'-wa-kaŋ, *v. n.* *Ih.* *to lie, to tell an untruth; i. q.* itoŋśni—owemawakaŋ. See hituŋkakaŋ *and* iewićaka.

o-we'-wa-kaŋ-kaŋ, *v. n.* *T.* *to lie, tell a falsehood; to pursue a crooked course*—owewawakaŋkaŋ: *i. q* ie wakaŋkaŋ.

o-wi'-ćah-ko-ke-daŋ, *adj.* *precocious,* as a child who walks early. See oićahkokedaŋ.

o-wi'-ćaḣ-te-haŋ, *adj.* *of slow growth* or *development*—owićaḣmatehaŋ. See oićaḣtehaŋ.

o-wi'-ća-ku-źa, *n.* of kuźa; *laziness, debility.* *T.*, *an unhealthy locality.*

o'-wi-ća-zi, *n.* of ozi; *rest.* *T.*, oziiçiyapi.

o-wi'-haŋ-ke, *n.* of ihaŋke; *the end* of time, *the end* of space; *the end* of anything, as of a lake.

o-wi'-haŋ-ke-śni-yaŋ, *adv.* *endlessly, eternally.*

o-wi'-haŋ-ke-ta, *adv.* *at the end.*

O'-wi'-haŋ-ke-wa-ni-ća, *n.* (*no end, without end*), *the Eternal One, Jehovah.*

o-wi'-haŋ-ke-wa-ni-ća, *adj.* *endless.*

o-wi'-haŋ-ke-wa-nin, *adv.* *always, ever; interminably.*

o-wi'-haŋ-ke-ya, *v. a.* *to bring to an end, destroy*—owihaŋkewaya, owihaŋkeuŋyaŋpi.

o-wi'-he-ća, *n.* *an arrow laid down* or *placed to shoot at; a mark to shoot at, a target.* *T.*, oweheća. See owiŋheća.

o-wi'-ḣaŋ, *v. n.* *to graze in*, as cattle in a field.

o-wi'-ke, *v.* Used only with śni. See owikeśni.

o-wi'-ke-śni, *v. n.* *to be strong, not to fail*, as the strength of a person; *to accumulate without being used*, as property—omawikeśni. *T.*, yuowi śni: wakiś'aka.

o-wiŋ', *v. n.* *T.* *to wear as an ornament: i. q.* oiŋ.

o'-wiŋ-ġe, *n.* *a curl*, as of hair: pesdete ówiŋġe, *the curl on the top of the head.* See yuwiŋġa.

o-wiŋ'-he-ća, *n.* *an arrow shot as a mark to shoot at; a target.* *T.*, oweheća.

o-wiŋ'-ki-ya, *v.* *T.* *to cause to wear jewels: i. q.* oiŋkiya.

o-wiŋ'-pi, *n.* *T.* *ear-rings.*

o-wiŋś', *cont.* of owiŋźa.

o-wiŋś'-ki-ća-toŋ, *v. a.* *to lay* or *place down a bed for* one—owiŋśwećatoŋ, owiŋśmićatoŋ.

o-wiŋś'-ki-ya, *v. a.* *to make a bed of, strew* or *spread down for a bed*—owiŋśwakiya.

o-wiŋś'-toŋ, *v.* *to have a bed*—owiŋśwatoŋ.

o-wiŋś'-ya, *v. a.* *to make a bed of*—owiŋśwaya. See owiŋśkiya.

o-wiŋ'-źa, *n.* *something spread to lie down* or *sit on, a bed; a floor.* See owaŋka.

o-wiŋ'-źa, *v. a.* *to make a bed of, use for a bed*—omiŋźa, oniŋźa, uŋkowiŋźapi.

o-wiŋ'-źa-a-ka-ḣpe, *n.* *a bed-quilt.*

o-wiŋ'-źa-o-ki-pa-ta-pi, *n.* *T.* *a bed-quilt of patchwork.*

o-wi'-tko, *v. n.* of witko; *to be drunk with*—omawitko.

o-wi'-tko-tko, *adj.* *foolish.*

o-wi'-tko-tko-ya, *adv.* *foolishly.*

o'-wi-tko-ya, *adv.* *acting foolishly from choice, playing the fool.*

o′-wi-tko-ya-ken, *adv. foolishly.*

o-wo′-bo-pte, *n.* of bopta; *the place from which a* tipsiŋna or *Dakota turnip has been dug.* Owobopte wakpa, *the river Pomme de Terre,* a branch of the Minnesota, which joins it from the north, a few miles above Lac-qui-parle. *T.*, owopte.

o-wo′-du-ta-toŋ, *v. n. to make a noise* or *bustle. T.*, oķoya.

o-wo′-du-ta-toŋ, *n. noise, bustle, clamor. T.*, oķose.

o-wo′-du-ta-toŋ-yaŋ, *adv. clamorously. T.*, oķoyase.

o-wo′-gla-ke, *n. T. a place of counciling.*

o-wo′-gla-ke-ti-pi, *n. T. a council-house.*

o-wo′-pte, *n. T. the place from which a turnip is dug.*

o-wo′-śma, *n. dense leaves. T.*, ćaŋwapewoȟeśma.

o-wo′-taŋ-iŋ, *adj.* of taŋiŋ; *clear, manifest:* owotaŋiŋ śni, *not clear, foggy, hazy, smoky.*

o-wo′-taŋ-iŋ, *n. clearness, appearance:* owotaŋiŋ śni au, *a haziness is coming on.*

o-wo′-taŋ-iŋ-ka. Same as owotaŋiŋ.

o-wo′-taŋ-la, *adj. T. straight: i. q.* owotaŋna.

o-wo′-taŋ-na, *adj. straight, not crooked; right, just; having done no wrong, upright*—omawotaŋna *and* omaowotaŋna, oniwotaŋna, uŋkowotaŋpidaŋ. *T.*, owotaŋla.

o-wo′-taŋ-taŋ-na, *adj. red.* of owotaŋna.

o-wo′-te, *n.* of yuta; *a place to eat in.*

o-wo′-te-ti-pi, *n. a hotel.*

o-ya′, *v. n.* and *v. a. to stick to, come off on,* as whitewash; *to stain, sully*—omaya; owicaya; *i. q.* owa.

o-ya′, *n. Ih. the arms; the legs, limbs.*

o-ya′-ġi, *v. a. to impede,* as high grass does in walking; *to scratch; to affect, as choke-cherries do the throat*—omayaġi.

o-ya′-ġi-ya, *v. a. to cause to impede,* as by sending one into the brush—oyaġiwaya.

o-ya′-ġi-ye-la, *adv. T. impeded by.*

o-ya′-hdo-hdo, *v. n. to rattle in the throat, have a rattling in the throat*—omdahdohdo. *T.*, onaglo-glo.

o-ya′-ȟdo-ȟdo-ka, *v. to begin to speak,* as a child—omdaȟdoȟdoka.

o-ya′-ȟdo-ka, *v. a.* of yaȟdoka; *to bite a hole in* anything; *to use language*—omdaȟdoka. *T.*, oyaȟloka, *to make a mark with the teeth, to bite in.*

o-ya′-ȟdo-ka, *n. a hole bitten in.*

o-ya′-ȟe, *v. n. to dry up, evaporate,* as water; *to fall* or *diminish,* as water in a stream; said also of a vessel when a little is taken out.

o-ya′-ȟe-ko-ke-daŋ, *adj. boiling away fast;* said of a pot or kettle. See kokedaŋ.

o-ya'-ħe-ya, *v. a.* *to cause to boil away* or *evaporate*—oyaħewaya.

o-ya'-ħlo-ħlog, *cont.* *T.* oyaħloħlog ia, *to talk like a baby.*

o-ya'-ħlo-ka, *v.* *T.* *to make a mark in with the teeth; to indent.*

o-ya'-ka, *v. a.* *to relate* anything, *tell*, as a story; *to introduce* one, *tell his name*—omdaka, odaka, uŋkoyakapi, oćiyaka.

o-ya'-koŋ-pi, *v. pl.* of yakoŋpi; *they are in* a place. *T.*, ouŋyaŋpi.

o-ya'-ksa, *v. a.* of yaksa; *to bite* anything *off in*—omdaksa.

o-ya'-ksa-ksa, *v. red.* of oyaksa.

o-ya'-kse. *n.* *a biting off.*

o-ya'-ḳo-ġa, *v.* *T.* *to bite or gnaw off in.*

o-ya'-ḳo-za, *v.* *T.* *to bite off short*, as a horse does.

o-ya'-ma, *v.* *T.* *to gnaw in.*

o-yaŋ'-ka, *n.* of yaŋká; *a place, seat; a place of residence.* *T.*, oyaŋke.

o-ya'-pe, *n.* of yapa; *the small end of a pipe-stem which is taken into the mouth.*

o-ya'-pe, *v.* *T.* *to put* or *take in the mouth*, as a pipe—blapa, lapa, oyapapi.

o-ya'-pta, *v. a.* *to leave, have over and above* what one eats—omdapta, uŋkoyaptapi.

o-ya'-pta-pi, *n.* *remnants, crumbs.*

o-ya'-sa-ka, *adj.* *dried hard on* or *in, withered.*

o-ya'-siŋ, *adj.* *T.* *all: i. q.* owasiŋ.

o-ya'-siŋ-siŋ, *adj.* *T.* *red.* of oyasiŋ.

o-ya'-ska, *v. a.* *to clean off by passing through the mouth*—omdaska: pahiŋ oyaska, *to draw porcupine quills through the mouth.*

o-ya'-śi-ća, *v a.* of yaśića; *to speak ill of, give a bad character to*—omdaśića. *T.*, śićaya oyake.

o-ya'-śiŋ-śiŋ, *v. n.* *T.* *to itch; to feel as if it wanted to be rubbed*—omayaśiŋśiŋ.

o-ya'-śki-śka, *v.* of yaśkiśka; *to speak unintelligibly*—omdaśkiśka.

o-ya'-tag, *cont.* of oyataka.

o-ya'-tag-ya, *v. a.* *to cause to stick* or *drag heavy*, as a sled on bare ground—oyatagwaya.

o-ya'-ta-ka, *v. n.* *to stick* or *drag heavily.*

o-ya'-t'aŋ, *v. a.* *to bite* or *press on with the teeth*—omdat'aŋ. *T.*, oyaħloka.

o-ya'-taŋ-iŋ, *v. n.* *to show, manifest, testify*—omdataŋiŋ, uŋkoya taŋiŋpi.

o-ya'-t'aŋ-t'aŋ, *v. red.* of oyat'aŋ.

o-ya'-te, *n.* *a people, nation, tribe, band.*

O-ya'-te-noŋ-pa, *n. p.* *The Omahas:* lit. "*two nations.*" They camped at times in two concentric circles.—J. O. D.

O-ya'-te-ya-mni, *n. p.* The name given to *the Ponkas:* lit. "*three nations.*" The Ponkas sometimes camped in three concentric circles.—J. O. D.

o-ya′-tkaŋ, *v. a.* of yatkaŋ; *to drink in* anything—omdatkaŋ.

o-ya′-tkaŋ-tkaŋ, *v. T. to come to a head*, as a sore.

o-ya′-tka-pa, *v. n.* of otkapa; *to stick on* or *in* anything.

o-ya′-tke, *n. drink; a draught* or *drink* of anything.

o-ya′-to-to, *v. T. to eat off clean*, as a horse does the grass.

o-ya′-ṭa, *v. a.* of yaṭa; *to bite to death in*—omdaṭa.

o-ya′-ṭa-ġe, *adj.* of yaṭaġa; *rough, roughened.*

o-ya′-ṭe, *n. a biting to death.*

o-ya′-wa, *v. a.* of yawa; *to count, to read; to read* or *count in*—omdawa. Hence, oyawa tipi, *a school-house.*

o-ya′-ya, *v. red.* of oya; *to be musty, moldy*, as hay. See oaa.

o-ya′-za, *n.* of yaza; *things strung on together, a string* of beads, *a bunch* of fish.

o-ya′-za, *v. T. to string*, as beads—oblaza.

o-ya′-zaŋ, *v. n. to be sick for, sick in consequence of*—omayazaŋ. See yazaŋ.

o-ye′, *n. a track, foot-print, mark* or *track left* by anything: *i. q.* owé.

o-yu′-bla-ye, *n. T. a page of a book: i. q.* yumdapi.

o-yu′-ćo-ka-ka, *v. T. to take all out of*, as the load of a gun.

o-yu′-ġe, *v. a. to put on* or *wear* anything—omduġe. *T.*, kićuŋ. See oġe.

o-yu′-ha, *v.* of yuha; oyuha waŝte, *good to have.*

o-yu′-hi, *v. to impede; i. q.* ćaŋku peži aohduteyapi. *T*, oyaġi. See óhi.

o-yu′-hi, *v. T. to scatter about, to spread*, as hay, for many horses to eat.

o-yu′-hi-hi, *v. red.* of oyuhi: oyuhihi eḣpeya yo.

o-yu′-ḣda, *v. a.* of yuḣda; *to ring*, as a bell, *in* a place—omduḣda. Hence, mazaḣdaḣda oyuḣda, *a belfry.*

o-yu′-ḣda-ḣda, *v. red.* of oyuḣda

o-yu′-ḣda-ta, *v. a.* of yuḣdata; *to scratch in*—omduḣdata.

o-yu′-ḣda-te, *n. a scratch.*

o-yu′-ḣde-ća, *v. a.* of yuḣdeća; *to tear in*, as in an old hole—omduḣdeća.

o-yu′-ḣde-će, *n. a rent.*

o-yu′-ḣdo-ka, *v. a.* of yuḣdoka; *to bore* or *make a hole in, to make holes in*, as hard snow does in horses' legs—omduḣdoka.

o-yu′-ḣdo-ke, *n. an opening.*

o-yu′-ḣi, *n.* of yuḣi; *a pimple, a rough place.*

o-yu′-ḣpa, *v. a.* of yuḣpa; *to put* or *pull down in*—omduḣpa.

o-yu′-ḣpe, *n. a throwing down.*

o-yu′-kpu-kpa, *v. to crumble in.*

o-yu′-ksa, *v. a.* of yuksa; *to break off*, as a stick, *in a hole*—omduksa, uŋkoyuksapi.

o-yu'-ktaŋ, *v. a.* of yuktaŋ; *to bend* anything *into* something else—omduktaŋ.

o-yu'-ktaŋ. *n.* *a bend, a crook.*

o-yu'-ktaŋ-yaŋ, *adv.* *bent into.*

o-yu'-kuŋ-ta, *v.* *T.* *to pick in,* as in nose or ears. Compare pakota.

o-yul', *cont.* of oyuta; *T.*, oyul waśte, *good to eat.*

o-yu'-mde-ća, *v. a.* of yumdeća; *to divide out, scatter, break to pieces within* something—omdum̄deća. *T.*, oyubleća.

o-yu'-mde-će, *n.* *a breaking in.*

o-yu'-mden, *cont.* of oyumdeća; oyumden iyeya: oyumden ehnaka, *to open out.* *T.*, oyublel.

o-yu'-mni-mni, *adv.* *round and round: i. q.* ómnimni.

o-yuŋg', *cont.* of oyuŋka.

o-yuŋ'-ka, *v.* *T.* *to lie down in*—omuŋka.

o-yuŋ'-ka, *n.* of yuŋka; *T.* *a place to lie down: i. q.* owaŋka.

o-yuŋ'-ka-i-hu-pa, *n.* *T.* *a bed with legs, a bedstead.*

o-yu'-paŋ-ġa, *adj.* of yupaŋġa; *loose, not tied tight.* *T.*, nagla, *untied.*

o-yu'-po-ta, *v. a.* of yupota; *to tear to pieecs in*—omdupota.

o-yu'-po-te, *n.* *a torn place, a rent.*

o-yu'-psoŋ-psoŋ, *v.* *to spill* or *sprinkle,* as water on a floor.

o-yu'-pta, *v. a.* *to cut out in: to cut out of*—omdupta. See yupta.

o-yu'-pta-pta-pi, *n.* *scraps, remnants.*

o-yu'-pte, *n.* *pieces left in cutting out* a garment, *scraps, remnants.*

o-yus', *coat.* of oyuza.

o-yu'-siŋ, *v. a.* *to fall out with* one, *hate, not to be on speaking terms with*—omdusiŋ, uŋkoyusiŋpi. See osiŋ.

o-yu'-siŋ-ka, *v.* *T.* *to hate.*

o-yu'-siŋ-yaŋ, *adv.* *out of humor with.*

o-yu'-ski-ta, *v. a.* of yuskita; *to wrap up in,* as a babe in its blankets—omduskita.

o-yu'-spa, *v. a.* *Ih.* and *T.* *to hold, to catch, to take hold of: i. q.* yuza—omduspa *and* omluspa, oduspa *and* oluspa. See yuspa.

o-yu'-spa-ya, *v. a.* of yuspaya; *to make wet with the hands in* anything—omduspaya.

o-yu'-spe-ki-ya, *v. a.* *to cause to lay hold of* one—oyuspewakiya.

o-yus'-ya, *adv.* *laying hold of.*

o-yu'-śi-ća, *v. a.* of yuśića; *to do wrong in respect of*—omduśića.

o-yu'-śi-će, *n.* *that which injures.*

o-yu'-śkaŋ, *v.* *to relapse*—omihduśkaŋ. See okaśkaŋ.

o-yu'-śna, *v. a.* of yuśna; *to let drop* or *fall into; to waste*—omduśna.

o-yu'-śna, *n.* *something dropped, crumbs, scraps.*

o-yu'-śtaŋ, *v. a.* of yuśtaŋ; *to finish within,* as a house; *to put* one *into* another, as buckets, or as a cork into a bottle—omduśtaŋ, uŋkoyuśtaŋpi. See ośtaŋ.

o-yu'-t'aŋ, *v. a. to touch, feel*—omdut'aŋ.

o-yu'-t'aŋ-t'aŋ, *v. red.* of oyut'aŋ; *to feel*—omdut'aŋt'aŋ.

o-yu'-te, *n eating, food. T.*, oyul; woyute. See woyute.

o-yu'-te, *n. T. the parts just above the hips*

o-yu'-tko-ġa, *v. a. T. to fasten*, as a horse, in a stall; *to lock*, as a door—oblutkoġa. See nataka.

o-yu'-tko-ġa-haŋ, *part. fastened, locked.*

o-yu'-tkoŋ-za, *v. a. to make equal, break off and make equal with* something else—omdutkoŋza. *T.*, otkoŋza yuksa. See yutkuŋza.

o-yu'-tkoŋ-ze, *n. something that makes equal.*

o-yu'-tpu-tpa, *v. a.* of yutputpa; *to crumble and scatter about in*—omdutputpa. *T.*, oyukpukpa.

o-yu'-ṭa, *v. a.* of yuṭa; *to kill in*—omduṭa.

o-yu'-ṭiŋ-za, *v. a.* of yuṭiŋza; *to make firm in*—omduṭiŋza.

o-yu'-ṭiŋ-ze, *n. a strengthener.*

o-yu'-wi, *adj. T. vine-like.*

o-yu'-zaŋ, *v a. to spread out*, as a curtain—omduzaŋ.

o-yu'-ze, *v. a.* of yuze; *to take* or *dip out* food *into*—omduze.

o-yu'-ze, *n.* of yuza; *a taking, catching*; oyuze waśte, *good catching.* See oze.

o-yu'-ze-ki-ya, *v. to cause to lay hold of.*

o-yu-źuŋ-ta, *v. to thrust into*, as the hand into a pail.

o'-za, *adj. both. T.*, deniyoza *and* heniyoza. See denaoza *and* henaoza.

o'-zaŋ, *n. a curtain:* ózaŋpi, *curtains*, as bed-curtains.

o'-ze, *v.* of yuza; *to catch:* oze waśte, *good to catch;* oze śića, *bad to catch: to take* or *get.* Hence, Makatooze (earth-blue-take), *the Blue Earth River. T.*, oyus; oyuze.

o'-ze, *n.* of yuza; *a hand's breadth:* oze waŋźidaŋ, *one taking hold of;* ćaŋte oze, *the feeling of the heart, purpose.*

o'-ze-ki-ya, *adv. taking hold of:* ćaŋte ozekiya, *the heart taking hold, thought. T.*, oyusya.

o'-ze-ya, *adv. in the manner of holding:* ćaŋte ozeya. *T.*, oyusya.

o'-ze-ye-ki-ya, *v. to cause to hold the mind* John xiii, 2. Perhaps this should have been ózekiya. *T.*, oyuskiya.

o-ze'-ze, *v. n. to swing, be hanging:* ozeze hiyeya. *T.*, zeze.

o-ze'-ze-ya, *adv. swinging. T.*, zezeya.

o'-zi, *v. n. to rest*—omazi, uŋkozipi.

o'-zi, *n. rest.* See owićazi.

o-zi'-ki-ya, *v. n. to rest, take rest*—oziwakiya. See asnikiya.

o-zin'-ya, *v. a. to make a smoke, to fumigate*—ozinwaya. *T.*, ozilyå. See zinya.

o-ziŋ'-tka, *n.* See oŋziŋtka.

o-zi′-ta, *v. n. to smoke.* See izita.

o′-zi-wa-nin, *adv. continually, without rest.*

o-zi′-ya, *v.* of ozi: *to rest, take rest:* oziiçiya, *to rest one's self*—ozimiçiya.

o-zo′, *n a cape* or *headland; a peninsula: i. q.* izo

o-zuŋ′-te, *n.* of zuŋta; *what is connected, connection.*

o-zu′-ye, *n.* of zuya; *war; a war-party, an army.*

o′-źaŋ-źaŋ, *n. light, a light.*

o′-źaŋ-źaŋ-hde-pi, *n. a window, windows; a looking-glass. T.,* oźaŋźaŋglepi.

o-źa′-te, *n.* of źata; *a fork, the forks* of a road or stream.

o-źi′, *v. a. to whisper about*—owaźi.

o-źiŋ′-źiŋ-tka, *n.* See oŋźiŋźiŋtka.

o-źi′-źi, *v. red* of oźi; *to whisper about*—owaźiźi, uŋkoźiźipi. See źiźi.

o-źi′-źi-ya, *adv. in a whispering manner.*

o-źi′-źi-ya-haŋ, *adv. whispering.*

o-źu′, *v. a. to plant* or *put in* the ground, as corn, etc., *to sow; to load,* as a gun—owaźu. See aźu, eźu, ouŋpa, etc.

o′-źu, *v. n. to be full of days, to be old, about to die of old age*—ómaźu, óniźu. *T.,* kaŋ.

o-źu′, *n. ammunition.*

o-źu′-daŋ, *adj. full, filled full*—omaźudaŋ: iśta maka oniźudaŋ, *thine eye is full of dust. Ih.,* oźuna. *T.,* oźula.

o-źu′-daŋ-ya, *v. a. to fill full*—oźudaŋwaya.

o-źug′-źu-daŋ, *adj. red.* of oźudaŋ; used in reference to vessels.

o-źu′-ha, *n. a sheath* or *case for* anything, as, isaŋ oźuha, *a knife-sheath; an empty bag; something that contains* or *covers, a box, barrel,* etc.: ćaḣdi oźuha, *a powder-flask;* tasusu oźuha, *a bullet-pouch;* kokoźuha, *an empty cask.*

o źu′-ki-ći-toŋ, *v.* of oźutoŋ; *to fill a bag for* one—oźuwećitoŋ.

o-źu′-ki-toŋ, *v. pos.* of oźutoŋ; *to fill up one's own* bags, etc.—oźuwakitoŋ *and* oźuwetoŋ, oźuuŋkitoŋpi.

o-źu′-la, *adv. T., i. q.* oźudaŋ: oźula nuŋ se, *almost full.*

o-źu′-pi, *part. filled; planted; loaded,* as a gun.

o-źu′-pi, *n. something to plant* or *sow, seed.*

o-źu′-śni, *adv. not full.*

o-źu′-toŋ, *v. a. to fill up* into sacks, etc.—oźuwatoŋ.

o-źu′-toŋ-pi, *n. filled bags.*

o-źu′-ya, *v. a. to fill; load,* as a gun; *to cause to fill* or *plant*—oźuwaya.

o-źu′-źu, *v n. to fall to pieces in* any place. See źuźu, kaźuźu, yuźuźu, etc.

o-źu′-źu-haŋ, *part. fallen to pieces in.*

o-źu′-źu-wa-haŋ, *part. fallen to pieces in.*

P.

p, *the nineteenth letter of the Dakota alphabet.* It has the same sound as in English.

pa, *a prefix* to verbs denoting that the action is done by *pushing* or *drawing, rubbing* or *pressing* with the hands or arms. The pronouns are prefixed.

pa, *n. the head* of man or beast—mapa, wićapa: *the principal part* of anything: *the nose,* as pa we hiyu, *the nose bleeds.* See nata, natahu, nasu, etc.

pa, *v. n. to fall,* as snow: wapa, *it snows.* See wa *and* hiŋhaŋ.

pa, *v. a. to bark at,* as a dog does: śuŋka mapa, *a dog barks at me;* śuŋka papi, *the dogs bark. T.,* papa.

p'a, *adj. bitter.*

pa-a'-hda-pśiŋ, *adv.* paahdapśiŋ eḣpeya, *to turn bottom upwards by pushing,* etc. See ahdapśiŋ, naahdapśiŋ, etc.

pa-a'-hda-pśiŋ-yaŋ, *adv. bottom upwards, overturned by pushing,* etc: paahdapśiŋyaŋ iyeya, *to turn bottom upwards.* See ahdapśiŋyaŋ, naahdapśiŋyaŋ, paohdapśiŋyaŋ, etc.

pa-a'-ḣo, *adv.* paaḣo iyeya, *to brush up,* as the hair from the forehead. *T.,* ipaḣo. See aḣo.

pa-a'-wa-ķiŋ, *n. Ih. a saddle, pack-saddle.* See aķiŋ *and* śuktaŋkaaķiŋ.

pa-a'-zi, *adv.* paazi iyeya, *to push aground.* See azi.

pa-ba'-ġa, *v. a. to roll* or *twist in the hand*—wapabaġa, uŋpabaġapi. *T.,* pawaġa.

pa-ba'-za, *v. a. to annoy* or *vex by pushing*

pa-be', *v. to file.* Same as pamaŋ. *T.,* pame.

pa-bo'-tu-ka, *n.* See paŋbotuka. *T.,* haḣoŋta opiye.

pa-bu', *v. a. to drum on with the fingers*—wapabu.

pa-bu'-bu, *v. red.* of pabu.

pa-bu'-ya, *v. a. to cause to make a drumming noise with the hand*—pabuwaya.

pa-ćaŋ'-ćaŋ, *v. a. to push and make tremble,* as one's arm by hard pushing—wapaćaŋćaŋ

pa-ćaŋ'-nan, *adv. shoved off:* paćaŋnan iyeya, *to shove out,* as a boat from the shore.

pa-ćeg', *cont.* of paćeka; paćeg iyeya.

pa-ćeg'-ćeg, *cont.* of paćegćeka; paćegćeg iyeya, *to push aside and make stagger.*

pa-ćeg'-će-ka, *v. red.* of paćeka; *to make stagger*—wapaćegćeka.

pa-će'-ka, *v. a.* of ćeka; *to push and make stagger*—wapaćeka, uŋpaćekapi.

pa-ći'-ķa-daŋ, *v. a.* of ćiķadaŋ; *to make small by rubbing*—wapaćiķadaŋ.

pa-ćiś'-ći-la, *v. T. i. q.* paćistiŋna.

pa-ći'-stiŋ-na, *v. a.* of ćistiŋna; *to make small by rubbing* or *pressing*—wapaćistiŋna. *T.*, paćisćila.

pa-ćo'-ćo, *v. a.* of ćoćo; *to rub soft*, as mortar—wapaćoćo.

pa-ćo'-ka-ka, *v. a. to empty, push* or *draw all out*—wapaćokaką. See ćoka.

pa-ćo'-za, *v. a.* of ćoza; *to make warm by rubbing*—wapaćoza.

Pa-da'-ni, *n. p. the Pawnee* or *Pani Indians.*

pa-dom', *cont.* of padopa; padom iyeya. *T.*, palob.

pa-dom'-dom, *red.* of padom; padomdom iyeya. *T.*, paloblob.

pa-do'-pa, *v. a.* of dopa; *to push into the mud, bemire*—wapadopa. *T.*, palopa.

pa-e'-će-tu, *v. a.* of ećetu; *to adjust as it was* or *should be, push into the right place*, as a dislocated joint—wapaećetu.

pa-e'-ze, *v. a. T. to rival, seek to supplant.*

pa-glo'-ka, *v. T. i. q* pahdoka.

pa-gmi'-gma, *v. T., i. q.* pahmihma.

pa-gna', *v. T. to shell off by rubbing: i q.* pahna.

pa-gna'-yaŋ, *v. T. to miss in pushing: i. q.* pahnayaŋ.

pa-ġam', *cont.* of paġapa; paġam iyeya. *T.*, paġab.

pa-ġaŋ', *v. a. to part with, give away, spare; to open*, as a door, *with the hand*—wapaġaŋ, uŋpaġaŋpi.

pa-ġaŋ'-ġaŋ, *v. red.* of paġaŋ.

pa-ġaŋ'-ya, *v. a. to cause to give away; to cause to open*—paġaŋwaya.

pa-ġaŋ'-yaŋ, *adv. parting with; opening.*

pa-ġa'-pa, *v. a. to push off with the hand*, as the skin of an animal—wapaġapa. See yuġapa, etc.

pa-ġe', *n. the diaphragm; the abdomen.* See ikpi, niġe, *and* tezi.

pa-ġo', *v. a. to carve, engrave*—wapaġo.

pa-ġo'-ki-ya, *v. a. to cause to carve* or *engrave*—paġowakiya.

pa-ġoŋ'-ta, *n. the mallard duck, Anas boschas;* also *the common tame duck.*

pa-ġo'-pa-ti-ća, *v.* (paġe *and* opatića) *to put in under a girdle*, as a knife.

pa-ġo'-pa-tin, *cont.* of paġopa tića; paġopatin iyeya.

pa-ġug', *cont.* of paġuka; paġug iyeya.

pa-ġu'-ka, *v. a. to sprain by rubbing*, etc.; *to rub down*, as in dressing skins—wapaġuka.

pa-ġuŋ'-ta, *n.* See paġoŋta.

pa'-ha, *n. the hair of the head; the scalp. T.*, pehiŋ. See páhiŋ.

pa-ha', *n. a mound, hill.*

pa-ha', *v. a. to raise to strike*—wapaha. See apaha.

pa-ha'-i-ća-sto, *n. a hair brush. T.*, pehiŋićasto.

p a - h a'-i - y e - y a, *v. a. to push aside; to oppose, reject. T.*, patokaŋ iyeya.

p a - h a'- p a - ź o - d a ŋ, *n. a prominent* or *conspicuous hill.*

p a - h a'- t a, *adv. at* or *on the hill, to the hill:* pahata mde kta, *I will go on the hill.*

p a - h a'- y a, *adj. piled up, projecting, prominent.*

p a - h a'- y e - l a, *adv. T. abundantly.* See iyakićuya.

p a - h b a', *v. a. to shell off,* as corn, *with the hands*—wapahba, uŋpahbapi. See pahna.

p a - h b e'- z a, *v. a. to make somewhat rough by rubbing*—wapahbeza. See pahdeza.

p a - h b u', *v. to push into, bury,* as in a barrel of corn: pahbu iyeya. *T.*, pasbu *and* paswu

p a - h d a'- k a - y a, *adv. spreading out, scattering,* as a herd of buffaloes when chased. *T.*, abebeya *and* aweweya. See hdakeya, nahdakaya, yuhdaka, etc.

p a - h d a'- k i ŋ - y a ŋ, *adv. pushing* or *crowding* to one side. *T.*, paglakiŋyaŋ.

p a - h d e'- z a, *v. a.* of hdeza; *to make spotted* or *ringed by rubbing*—wapahdeza. See pahbeza *and* dotehbeza.

p a - h d o'- k a, *v. a. to dislocate, push out of joint. T.*, pagloka.

p a - h i', *v. a. to pick up, gather up, gather together*—wapahi, uŋpahipi.

p a - h i n', *cont.* of pahiŋta: pahin iyeya, *to brush off quickly and completely*—pahin iyewaya. *T.*, pahiŋl.

p a'- h i ŋ, *n. the hair of the head. T.*, pehiŋ. See páha.

p a - h i ŋ', *n. the porcupine, the quills of the porcupine,* used by the Dakotas in ornamental work.

p a - h i ŋ'- t a, *v. a. to rub, brush,* or *wipe off*—wapahiŋta, uŋpahiŋtapi. *T.*, pakiŋta. See pawiŋta.

p a'- h i - y u, *v. T. to bleed at the nose: i. q.* pa we hiyu.

p a - h m i'- h m a, *v. a. to roll with the hand; to roll by pushing against*—wapahmihma Hence, ćaŋpahmihma. *T.*, pagmigma. See panminma.

p a - h m i'- y a ŋ, *v. a. to make round,* like a ball, *with the hands*—wapahmiyaŋ. See hmiyaŋ.

p a - h m i'- y a ŋ - y a ŋ, *v. a. to make a ball with the hands*—wapahmiyaŋyaŋ

p a - h m o ŋ', *v. a.* of hmoŋ; *to twist with the hand; to twist,* as yarn, *with a wheel*—wapahmoŋ, uŋpahmoŋpi.

p a - h m o ŋ'- k a, *v. to twist.* See pahmoŋ.

p a - h m o ŋ'- p i, *n. a hank* or *skein* of yarn.

p a - h m u ŋ', *v. a.* See pahmoŋ.

p a - h n a', *v. a. to shake off,* as fruit, *with the hand; to shell off,* as corn, by rubbing—wapahna. *T.*, pagna.

p a - h n a'- ś k i ŋ - y a ŋ, *v. a.* of hnaśkiŋyaŋ; *to make furious by pushing about*—wapahnaśkiŋyaŋ.

pa-hna′-yaŋ, *v. a.* of hnayaŋ; *to deceive with the hand, make deceptive gestures*—wapahnayaŋ. *T.*, pagnayaŋ.

pa-ho′-ho, *v. a.* *to shake* or *move, make loose by pushing*, as a tooth—wapahoho: pahoho śni, *immovable.*

pa-ho′-śni-yaŋ, *adv.* *immovably.*

pa-ho′-mni, *v. a.* *to push* anything *round*—wapahomni.

pa-ho′-toŋ, *v. a.* of hotoŋ; *to cause to make a noise*, as iron by filing, or an animal by stabbing—wapahotoŋ.

pa′-hu, *n.* *the skull-bone.* See nasuhu *and* natahu.

pa-hu′, *n.* *the large part* or *head* of anything; as, ćaŋduhupa pahu, *the bowl of a pipe;* mazakaŋ pahu, *the breech of a gun;* oŋspe pahu, *the pole of an ax;* mdo pahu, *the root of a Dakota potato;* tipsiŋna pahu, *the upper part of the* tipsiŋna; wamnaheza pahu, *the butt-end of a corn-cob.* See ipa.

pa-hu′-hus, *cont.* of pahuhuza; pahuhus iyeya. *T.*, pahuŋhuŋs.

pa-hu′-hus-ya, *v. a* *to cause to shake with the hand*—pahuhuswaya *T.*, pahuŋhuŋsya.

pa-hu′-hu-za, *v. a.* of huḣuza; *to shake by pushing*, as a tree—wapahuhuza. *T.*, pahuŋhuŋza.

pa-hu′-kun, *adv.* (pa *and* hukun) *down:* pahukun iyeya, *to bow the head, push the head down*; *to push* or *shove down.* *T.*, pahukul. See pakućedaŋ, pamahdedaŋ, etc.

pa-hu′-te, *n.* *the ridge of the nose at the base, between the eyes.*

pa-hu′-wa-te-zi, *n.* *the butt-end of a gun, when very large.* *T.*, pahutaŋka.

pa-ḣa′, *v. a.* *to make rough by rubbing*—wapaḣa.

pa-ḣa′, *v. n.* *to bud:* ćaŋwapa paḣa, *buds.*

pa-ḣa′-ḣa, *v. n.* *to be rough*, as ice sometimes is.

pa-ḣa′-tka, *v. a.* *to make rough, rub against the grain*—wapaḣatka.

pa-ḣći′, *v. a.* *to tear out a piece, pick out a piece*—wapaḣći.

pa-ḣći′-ḣći, *v. red.* of paḣći.

pa-ḣda′-ġaŋ, *v. a.* *to enlarge, to cause to lengthen out*—wapaḣdaġaŋ.

pa-ḣda′-ġo-źu, *n.* *the internal parts of the nose, the nasal fossæ.* *T.*, paḣlate.

pa-ḣdan′, *cont.* of paḣdata: paḣdan iyaya, *to go scratching* or *scraping along.*

pa-ḣda′-ta, *v. a.* *to scratch* or *scrape along*—wapaḣdata.

pa-ḣda′-te, *n.* *the root of the nose:* *i. q.* paḣdaġoźu. *T.*, paḣlate.

pa-ḣda′-ya, *v. a.* *to peel off, pull off*, as the skin of a potato—wapaḣdaya *T.*, yuḣlaya

pa-ḣde′-ća, *v. a.* *to tear, pull to pieces*—wapaḣdeća.

pa-ḣde′-ḣde-ća, *v. red.* of paḣdeća.

pa-ḣden′, *cont.* of paḣdeća; paḣden iyeya. *T.*, paḣlel.

pa-ḣdi′, *v. a.* *to stick in the ground*, as a stake or stick—wapaḣdi. *T.*, paḣli.

p a - ḣ d i′, *n.* *the excretion of the nasal fossæ.*

p a - ḣ d i′ - ḣ d i , *v. red.* of paḣdi.

p a - ḣ d i′ - y a , *v. a.* *to cause to push into the ground*—paḣdiwaya. *T.*, paḣliya.

p a - ḣ d o g′, *cont.* of paḣdoka; paḣdog iyeya.

p a - ḣ d o′ - h a ŋ , *v.* paḣdohaŋ iyeya, *to push down*, as one's coat sleeve: *i. q.* pasdohaŋ.

p a - ḣ d o′ - ḣ d o - k a , *v. red.* of paḣdoka.

p a - ḣ d o′ - k a , *v. a.* *to make a hole in, pierce, run through, bore*, as the ears—wapaḣdoka. *T.*, paḣloka.

p a - ḣ e′ - y a m , *cont.* of paḣeyata: paḣeyam iyeya, *to push aside.* *T.*, paḣeyab.

p a - ḣ e′ - y a - p a , *v.* *to shove aside.* See paḣeyata.

p a - ḣ e′ - y a - t a , *v.* paḣeyata iyeya, *to push back* or *out to one side.*

p a - ḣ i′ - y a - y a , *adv.* *roughly, not well made, not smooth*, as anything rasped.

p a - ḣ l a′ - t e , *n.* *T.* *the internal parts of the nose: i. q.* paḣdate.

p a - ḣ l a′ - y a , *v.* *T.* *to peel off of itself: i q.* paḣdaya.

p a - ḣ l a′ - ź i ŋ - ć a , *v.* *T.* *to sniff* or *snuff the nose.* See yuźiŋća.

p a - ḣ m i ŋ′ - s e , *adj.* *left-handed.* *T.*, ćatka.

p a - ḣ p a′, *v. a.* *to throw*, as a horse his rider; *to take down*, as anything hanging up; *to lay down* or *put off*, as one's load; *to scrape off*, as the flesh that sticks to a hide—wapaḣpa, uŋpaḣpapi.

p a - ḣ p a′ - ġ a , *v.* *to pop, to burst open*, as pop-corn: *i. q.* papaġa.

p a - ḣ p e′ - y a , *v. a.* *to cause to throw down*—paḣpewaya.

p a - ḣ p u′, *v. a.* *to pick off, break off in small pieces; to tear down*, as birds' nests—wapaḣpu

p a - ḣ p u′ - ḣ p u , *v. red.* of paḣpu.

p a - ḣ p u′ - y a , *v. a.* *to cause to pick off*—paḣpuwaya.

p a - ḣ t a′, *v. a.* *to tie up, make into bundles* or *packs*—pawaḣta, pauŋḣtapi. The "pa" in this word is not a prefix.

p a - ḣ t a′ - k a , *v. a.* *to bind in bundles*—pawaḣtaka. See heyuŋ.

p a - ḣ t a′ - p i , *n.* *a bundle, a pack, packs of furs.*

p a - ḣ t e′ - ć a , *n.* *the sucker*, a kind of fish.

p a - ḣ t e′ - y u - k o - k i - y a , *v.* *T.* *to frown.*

p a - ḣ u′ - ġ a , *v. a.* *to break through* or *push a hole in*, as in a kettle—wapaḣuġa.

p a - ḣ u ḣ′, *cont.* of paḣuġa; paḣuḣ iyeya.

p a - ḣ u′ - ḣ u - ġ a , *v.* *red.* of paḣuġa.

p a - i ŋ′ - y a ŋ - k a , *v. a.* of iŋyaŋka; *to shoot* or *throw a stick through a hoop when rolling, push through with the hand*—wapaiŋyaŋka: paiŋyaŋka kiçuŋpi, *the game of shooting through a hoop.*

p a - i′ - p u - s k i - ć a , *v. a.* of ipuskića; *to press down on with the hand*—wapaipuskića.

pa-i′-pu-skin, *cont.* of paipuskića; paipuskin iyeya. *T.*, paipuskil.

pa-i′-tkoŋs, *cont.* of paitkoŋza.

pa-i′-tkoŋ-za, *v. a. T. to make even by pressing; to strike off level*, as a measure of grain: *i. q.*, paotkoŋza.

pa-i′-tpi-ska, *adv.* paitpiska eḣpeya, *to throw over on the back belly up*, as a dog. *T.*, paikpiska.

pa-i′-wa-ś te-daŋ, *adv.* of iwaśtedaŋ; *slowly:* paiwaśtedaŋ iyeya, *to shove along slowly. T.*, paiwaśtela

pa-i′-wa-ś te-ya, *adv. slowly, gently.*

pa-i′-ya-pa-ṭo, *v. n.* of iyapaṭo; *to be pushed by:* paiyapaṭo ihemiçiye.

pa-i′-ya-pa-ṭo-ya, *v. a. to obstruct, push against*—paiyapaṭowaya.

pa-i′-yo-wa-za, *v. a. to make echo by striking with the hand*—wapaiyowaza.

pa-ka′, *v. a. to split* or *cut a slit in* for an arrowhead.

pa-ka′, *v.* paka iyeya, *to push down* or *break down*, as the ribs of an animal.

pa-ka′-huŋ-ka, *v. n. T. to nod, bow the head.* See pahukuŋ, etc.

pa-kam′, *cont.* of pakapa: pakam iyeya, *to throw* or *toss*, as a ball. *T.*, pakab.

pa-kaŋ′, *v. a. to respect, honor*—wapakaŋ. *T.*, ohola. See ohoda.

pa′-kaŋ, *v. n. to prevent:* mini pákaŋ, *to be prevented by water*, as in a journey.

pa-kaŋ′-ka, *v. to honor, respect*—wapakaŋka.

pa-kaŋ′-yaŋ, *adv. prevented by, impassable:* pakaŋyaŋ ya, *to go round*, as a lake.

pa-ka′-pa, *v. a. to toss, strike a ball that is thrown and send it back; to strike and stab before falling; to push away*—wapakapa. *T.*, kakapa.

pa′-ka-psaŋ, *v. a.* (pa *and* kapsaŋ) *to nod* or *bow the head, nod assent*—pawakapsaŋ. *T.*, pakahuŋka. See oġiŋġiŋ.

pa-ka′-tiŋ, *v. a.* of katiŋ; *to straighten out*, as the arm when bent at the elbow—wapakatiŋ.

pa-ka′-wa, *v. a. to open out with the hand*, as a gun-pan—wapakawa.

pa-kća′, *v. a. to comb, disentangle, untie*—wapakća, uŋpakćapi. *T.*, kakća.

pa-kes′, *cont.* of pakeza: pakes pamaŋ, *to make a noise by filing* anything. *T.*, paḳes.

pa-ke′-za, *v. a. to make a noise by rubbing*, as in filing—wapakeza. *T.*, paḳeza.

pa-ki′-ća-psaŋ, *v. a.* of pakapsaŋ; *to bow* or *nod the head to* one—pawećapsaŋ. *T.*, pakićahuŋka, which is from pakahuŋka.

pa-ki′-hnuŋg, *cont.* of pakihnuŋka; pakihnuŋg iyeya.

pa-ki′-hnuŋ-ka, *v. to push under water, make dive. T.*, opaspa. See kihnuka.

p a - k i'- ḣ t a, *v. pos.* of paḣta: *to tie up* or *bind together one's own, to pack up*—pawakiḣta, payakiḣta, pauŋkiḣtapi.

p a - k i n', *cont.* of pakiŋta; pakin iyeya, *to wipe* or *brush all off*—pakin iyewaya. *T.*, pakil.

p a - k i ŋ', *v. a.* *to set up slanting*, as a stick pointing in the direction one is going—wapakiŋ. Hence, ćaŋpakiŋ, *a stick thus set up, a guide-stick.*

p a - k i ŋ', *v. n.* *to stand leaning:* pakiŋ iyaya, *to bow down the head*—pakiŋ imdamda. See yukiŋ.

p a - k i ŋ s', *cont.* of pakiŋza.

p a - k i ŋ s'- k i ŋ - z a, *v. red.* of pakiŋza.

p a - k i ŋ'- t a, *v. a.* *to wipe*, as dishes, *rub off, cleanse*—wapakiŋta, uŋpakiŋtapi. See pahiŋta.

p a - k i ŋ'- y a ŋ, *adv.* *T.* *bent over:* pakiŋyaŋ mani.

p a - k i ŋ'- z a, *v. a.* *to make creak by rubbing*—wapakiŋza.

p a - k i'- p u - s k i - ć a, *v. n.* *to be pressed tight together.* See pakipuskita *and* yukipuskića.

p a - k i'- p u - s k i n, *cont.* of pakipuskića: pakipuskin iyeya, *to press together;* pakipuskin ehnaka, *to lay on for the purpose of pressing down.* *T.*, pakipuskil.

p a - k i'- p u - s k i - t a, *v. n.* *to be pressed together.*

p a - k o', *adj.* *crooked, bent round.*

p a - k o', *n.* *the outside of a bend.* See kaḣmiŋ.

p a - k o n', *cont.* of pakota; pakon iyeya.

p a - k o'- t a, *v. a.* *to dig* or *take out marrow from a bone, to probe*—wapakota. *T.*, pako. See oyukuŋta.

p a - k o'- z a, *v.* *to push back and forth.* *T.*, paslo iyeya na yutahena ića.

p a - k p a', *v. a.* *to pierce, gouge out*, as an eye—wapakpa: *i. q.* patpa.

p a - k p a ŋ', *v. a.* *to crush, make fine by pressing*—wapakpaŋ.

p a - k p a ŋ'- k p a ŋ, *v.* *red.* of pakpaŋ.

p a - k p i', *v. a.* *to pick a hole, break a hole*, as a young chicken in its shell; *to hatch; to crack open; to mash*, as a louse or flea: *i. q.* patpi.

p a - k p i'- k p i, *v.* *to prick holes in*, as in bread before baking.

p a - k s a', *v. a.* *to break off*, as a stick, *with the hand, break in two*—wapaksa.

p a - k s a'- k s a, *v.* *red.* of paksa.

p a - k ś a', *v.* *to fold*, as a blanket. See kakśa.

p a - k ś a', *adj.* *bent down*, like an old person—mapakśa.

p a - k ś a ŋ', *v. a.* *to bend, make bend by striking* or *pushing*—wapakśaŋ.

p a - k ś a ŋ'- k ś a ŋ, *v.* *red.* of pakśaŋ.

p a - k ś a'- y e - l a, *adv.* *T.* *in a bent condition.*

p a - k ś i'- k ś a ŋ, *adj.* *crooked, zigzag.*

p a - k ś i'- k ś i - ź a, *v.* *red.* of pakśiźa.

p a - k ś i ŋ', *n.* *the kidneys, reins*—mapakśiŋ, wićapakśiŋ. *Ih.*, *the fat that is on the kidneys.* See aźoŋtka *and* aźuŋtka.

p a - k ś i ŋ' - ś i ŋ , *n. kidney-fat, leaf-lard. Ih.*, pakśiŋ.

p a - k ś i ś', *cont.* of pakśiźa; pakśiś iyeya.

p a - k ś i' - ź a , *v. a. to bend* or *double up*, as the arm at the elbow; *to double up* anything—wapakśiźa.

p a - k t a ŋ', *v. a. to bend around with the hand*—wapaktaŋ.

p a - k t a ŋ' - k t a ŋ , *v. red.* of paktaŋ.

p a - k t a ŋ' - y a ŋ , *v. a. to cause to bend.*

p a - k t a ŋ' - y a ŋ , *adv. bent around.*

p a' - k u - ć e - d a ŋ , *adv. head down:* pakućedaŋ yuza, *to hold the head down, to apply one's self diligently.* See pahukun.

p a - k u' - k a , *v. a. to rub to pieces, wear out by handling*—wapakuka.

p a - k u' - ś k e , *n. T. the whip-poor-will:* in Lakota it seems to say, wo-ko-gli, wo-ko-gli, *clearness, translucency!*

p a - k u' - w i - ś k a , *n. the whip-poor-will. T.*, pakuśke.

p a - ḳ e' - g a , *v. a. to scrape with the hand, with glass,* etc.—wapaḳeġa.

p a - ḳ e ḣ', *cont.* of paḳeġa; paḳeḣ iyeya.

p a - ḳ e ḣ' - ḳ e - g a , *v. red.* of paḳeġa.

p a - ḳ e s', *cont.* of paḳeza; paḳes iyeya.

p a - ḳ e s' - ḳ e - z a , *v. red.* of paḳeza.

p a - ḳ e' - z a , *v. a. to scrape, make smooth by scraping*—wapaḳeza.

p a - ḳ o s', *cont.* of paḳoza; paḳos iyeya.

p a - ḳ o s' - ḳ o - z a , *v. red.* of paḳoza.

p a - ḳ o' - z a , *v. a. to rub and make smooth and hard*—wapaḳoza.

p a - m a' - h d e - d a ŋ , *adv. head bowed down, prone:* pamahdedaŋ uŋ, *to go with the head down,* as in sorrow.

p a - m a' - k o m , *adv. head down, prone, headlong:* pamakom yaŋka. See ahdaskin.

p a - m a ŋ', *v. a. to file, rub, polish*—wapabe, yapabe, uŋpamaŋpi. See pabe.

p a - m d a s', *cont.* of pamdaza; pamdas iyeya.

pa'-mda-ska, *adj. flat-head:* oŋspe pámdaska, *a flat-headed ax,* in distinction from the club-heads used by the Dakota women. *T.*, pablaska.

p a - m d a' - s k a , *v. a.* of mdaska; *to press out flat, to flatten*—wapamdaska.

p a - m d a' y a , *v. a.* of mdaya; *to spread out, make level; to iron,* as clothes; *to make smooth*—wapamdaya, uŋpamdayapi. *T.*, pablaya.

p a - m d a' - z a , *v. a. to burst open, tear open,* as a bag, *by sitting on* it—wapamdaza. See mdaza.

p a - m d e' - ć a , *v. a. to crush, break,* as brittle ware, *by pressing*—wapamdeća *T.*, pableća.

p a - m d e' - m d e - ć a , *v. red.* of pamdeća.

p a - m d e n', *cont.* of pamdeća; pamden iyeya. *T.*, pablel.

p a - m d e n'- y a, *v. a. to cause to crush*—pamdenwaya.

p a - m d u', *v. a. to bruise fine, crush to powder*—wapamdu, uŋpamdupi. *T.*, pablu.

p a - m i'- m a, *v. a. to make round by filing* or *rubbing*—wapamima. See pahmihma.

p a'- m i - m a, *adj.* (pa *and* mima) *round pointed:* isaŋ pámima, *a case-knife.* See mibe.

p a - m n a', *v. a. to rip*, as one's coat-sleeve—wapamna.

p a - m n i', *v. a. to divide, make a division, distribute* anything—wapamni, uŋpamnipi.

p a - m n i'- m n i, *v. red.* of pamni.

p a - n a'- k e, *adv.* panake iyeya, *to push over on one side.* Same as

p a - n a'- k e - y a, *adv.* of nakeya; *lying on one side after being pushed over:* panakeya iyeya.

p a - ṅ i', *v. a. to push* or *jog* one *with the elbow*—wapani.

p a - n i'- n i, *v. a. to push* or *jog with the elbow* or *hand; to wake out of sleep by jogging*—wapanini.

p a - n m i'- n m a, *v.* This form is used by the Mdewakaŋtoŋwaŋs. See pahmihma.

p a - n u ŋ'- ġ a, *v. a. to sprain*, as the arm or hand—wapanuŋġa.

p a ŋ, *v. n. to cry aloud, call, yell, halloo*—wapaŋ, uŋpaŋpi. See kipaŋ.

p a ŋ - b o'- t u - k a, *n. an Indian woman's bag*, in which she keeps her sewing apparatus; *a work-bag, a reticule. T.*, haȟoŋta opiye.

p a ŋ'- ġ a, *adj. bulky*, as buffalo-robes, *stuffed, filled full.*

p a ŋ'- ġ e - ć a, *adj. bulky, puffed out*—mapaŋġeća.

p a ŋ - ġ i', *n. the artichoke, Helianthus tubcrosus.*

p a ŋ - ġ i'- h u, *n. the stalk of the artichoke.*

P a ŋ'- k a, *n. p. the Ponkas.* See Oyate yamni.

p a ŋ - k e'- s k a, *n. T.*, *i. q.* panpeska: *crockery, China-ware.*

p a ŋ'- p a ŋ, *v. red* of paŋ; *to yell, make a noise, shout*, as the Dakota young men do—wapaŋpaŋ.

p a ŋ - p a ŋ'- n a, *adj. soft*, as a deer-skin or cloth. This may be from "paŋna," which is not now used.

p a ŋ - p e'- s k a, *n. round white ornaments for the neck, slightly curved:* ćaŋ paŋpeska, *the excrescences that grow on trees.* Same as kaŋpeska. *T.*, paŋkeska, *large shells; white ware.*

p a ŋ - p e'- s k a - d a ŋ, *n. dim.* of paŋpeska.

p a ŋ - p e'- s k a - w a - k ś i - ć a, *n. white-ware, China-ware.*

p a ŋ ś - p a ŋ'- ź a, *adj. soft, bunchy.*

p a ŋ ś - p a ŋ'- ź e - d a ŋ, *adj. soft*, as furs, *bulky.*

p a ŋ ś'- y a, *adv. bulky, bunchy.*

p a ŋ'- y a ŋ, *adv. crying out.*

p a ŋ - y a ŋ'- h a ŋ, *adv. crying out, yelling:* paŋyaŋhaŋ eya.

p a ŋ'- ź a, *adj. puffed up, soft, bunchy; one who is lazy*—mapaŋźa.

p a ŋ' - ź e - l a, *adj.* *T.* *puffed out, bulky.*

p a - o' - g l a - y a, *adv.* *T.* *singly, one by one.*

p a - o' - h d a - p ś i ŋ, *adv.* *rolled over, scattered about:* paohdapśiŋ eḣpeya, *to turn* an object *bottom up by pushing* it. See paahdapśiŋ.

pa-o'-hda-pśiŋ-yaŋ, *adv.* *tumbled over, topsy-turvey:* paohdapśiŋyaŋ iyeya. See ahdapśiŋyaŋ, ohdapśiŋyaŋ, etc.

p a - o' - h d u - t a, *v. a.* of ohduta; *to close up* or *over,* as a hole, *by rubbing*—wapaohduta.

p a - o' - h d u - t e - y a, *v. a.* *to cause to close up by rubbing*—paohdutewaya.

p a - o' - k a - g l a - l a, *adv.* *T.* *to an extraordinary degree.*

p a - o' - k a - ġ a, *adv.* *T.* *exceedingly, extravagantly.*

p a - o' - k i - h e, *n* (pa *and* okihe) *T.* *the bridge* or *ridge of the nose,* bone and cartilege.

p a - o' - k i - y a - s k a - p a, *v. n.* *to be bent in, jammed in.*

p a - o' - p o, *v. n.* *to warp; to push and make a hollow place.* *T.*, naopo.

p a - o' - p u - s k i - ć a, *v. a.* *to press down into.* See pakipuskića.

p a - o' - p u - s k i n, *cont.* of paopuskića; paopuskin iyeya.

pa-o'-spe, *v. a.* *to push under,* as in water—wapaospe: paospe iyeya, *to push under, push out of sight.*

p a - o' - t k o ŋ s, *cont.* of paotkoŋza. *T.*, paitkoŋs.

p a - o' - t k o ŋ - z a, *v. a.* *to press in full, make even full, strike off level,* as in measuring grain—wapaotkoŋza. *T.*, paitkoŋza. See tkoŋza.

p a - o' - ṭ i ŋ s, *cont.* of paoṭiŋza; paoṭiŋs iyeya.

p a - o' - ṭ i ŋ - z a, *v. a.* of oṭiŋza; *to press in hard and tight*—wapaoṭiŋza.

p a - o' z e - z e, *v. n.* *to swing, dangle, hang,* as berries. *T*, kaozeze.

p a - o' - z e - z e - y a, *adv.* *swinging, dangling.* See ozezeya.

p a - p a', *v.* T. *to bark,* as dogs; *to bark at one:* śuŋka mapapa. See pa.

p a' - p a, *n.* *Ih.* and *T.* *dried meat; i. q.* wakablapi. See mama *and* waćonića.

p a - p a' - ġ a, *v. n.* *to pop,* as corn in parching: *i. q.* paḣpaġa.

p a - p a ḣ' - y a, *v. a.* *to parch,* as corn—papaḣwaya, papaḣuŋyaŋpi. Hence, wapapaḣyapi, *parched corn.*

pa-piŋ'-kpa, *n.* *T.* (pa *and* iŋkpa) *the point of the nose.*

p a - p i ŋ' - z a, *v.* *to prick, prick* or *dot all over:* papiŋzapi se. *T.*, pakpikpi.

p a - p o m', *cont.* of papopa; papom iyeya, *to make burst.* *T.*, papob.

p a - p o' - p a, *v. a.* *to make burst* or *pop by squeezing* or *pressing*—wapapopa: papopapi se, said of quilting that is puffed up in little bunches.

p a - p o' - w a - y a, *v. a.* of powaya; *to rub* or *brush up,* as fur or nap on a hat or blanket—wapapowaya.

p a - p s a g′, *cont.* of papsaka; papsag iyeya.

p a - p s a g′ - y a, *v. a.* *to cause to break*, as a cord—papsagwaya.

p a - p s a′ - k a, *v. a.* *to break in two with the hand*, as a cord—wapapsaka, uŋpapsakapi.

p a - p s o ŋ′, *v. a.* *to pour out, spill, throw out*, as a liquid—wapapsoŋ.

p a - p s u ŋ′, *v.* See papsoŋ.

p a - p s u ŋ′ - p s u ŋ - l a, *v.* *T.* *to rub and make smooth and round*, as an arrow shaft.

p a - p ś u ŋ′, *v. a.* *to put out of joint* or *dislocate*, as one's arm—wapapśuŋ.

p a - p t a ŋ′, *v. a.* *to turn over*—wapaptaŋ.

p a - p t a ŋ′ - p t a ŋ, *v.* *red.* of paptaŋ; *to roll over, wallow about*—wapaptaŋptaŋ.

p a - p t a ŋ′ - p t a ŋ - y a ŋ, *adv.* *wallowing about.*

p a - p t a ŋ′ - y a ŋ, *adv.* *rolling about:* paptaŋyaŋ iyeya, *to roll over, roll away.*

p a - p t u′ - p t u - ź a, *v.* *red.* of paptuźa.

p a - p t u s′, *adv.* *curled up;* paptus iwaŋka.

p a - p t u ś′, *cont.* of paptuźa; paptuś iyeya.

p a - p t u ś′ - y a, *v. a.* *to cause to crack* or *split*—paptuśwaya.

p a - p t u′ - ź a, *v. a.* *to split, to crack by working with the hands*—wapaptuźa.

p a - p u s′, *cont.* of papuza; papus iyeya.

p a - p u′ - z a, *v. a.* of puza; *to rub dry, wipe dry*—wapapuza.

p a - s b u′, *v. a.* *to cut into strings; to make rattle*, as corn, *by pushing in*—wapasbu.

p a - s b u′ - p i, *n.* *fringe.*

p a - s b u′ - s b u, *v. red.* of pasbu.

p a - s b u′ - y a, *v. a.* *T.* *to make rattle by pushing.*

p a - s b u′ - y a, *adv.* *rattling.*

p a - s d a n′, *cont.* of pasdata. *T.*, paslal.

p a - s d a′ - t a, *v. a.* *to set up a pole in the ground, to drive in*, as a stake or tent-pins—wapasdata. *T.*, paslata. See paȟdata.

p a - s d e′ - ć a, *v. a* *to split by striking* or *rubbing*—wapasdeća. *T.*, pasleća See paȟdeća.

p a - s d e n′, *cont.* of pasdeća; pasden iyeya. *T.*, paslel.

p a - s d e′ - s d e - ć a, *v.* *red.* of pasdeća.

p a - s d o′ - h a ŋ, *v. a.* *to push* or *shove along*—wapasdohaŋ. *T.*, paslohaŋ. See paȟdohaŋ.

p a - s d o′ - h a ŋ - h a ŋ, *v.* *red.* of pasdohaŋ.

p a - s e m′, *cont.* of pasepa; pasem iyeya. *T.*, paseb.

p a - s e′ - p a, *v a.* *to rub off*, as white-wash—wapasepa.

p a - s i′, *v. a.* *to follow after* one, *follow in Indian file, follow*, as a leader; *to chase*—wapasi.

p a - s i′ - p i - k a, *n.* *one who is followed, a leader; a spokesman*—mapasipika.

pa-si'-sa, *v. a.* *to pin together; to stick in*, as a needle or pin—wapasisa.

pa'-ska, *adj.* *white-headed.*

pa-ska', *v. a.* *to bleach; to rub and make white*—wapaska. *T.*, naska.

pa-ski'-ća, *v. a.* *to press down on with the hand*—wapaskića. See paśkića.

pa-skin', *cont.* of paskića; paskin iyeya.

pa-slo'-haŋ-pi, *n.* *T.*, *i. q.* hutinaćute.

pa-slul', *cont.* *T.* of pasluta.

pa-slu'-slu-ta, *red.* of pasluta.

pa-slu'-ta, *v.* *T.* *to push out of*, as dirt from a pipe-stem.

pa-slu'-ta, *v. a.* *T.* *to commit masturbation*—wapasluta.

pa-slu'-ka, *n.* *T.* *masturbation; onanism.*

pa-smag', *cont.* of pasmaka; pasmag iyeya.

pa-sma'-ka, *v. a.* *to make a hollow in by pushing, to indent*—wapasmaka.

pa-smi', *v. a.* *to do little things to irritate, provoke, pick a quarrel with*—wapasmi, uŋpasmipi. *T.*, yuśigla kta kuwa.

pa-smi'-ka, *v. a.* Same as pasmi.

pa-smiŋ'-yaŋ, *v.* See pasmiŋyaŋyaŋ.

pa-smiŋ'-yaŋ-yaŋ, *v. a.* *to rub* or *scrape off, make smooth* or *clean; to make smooth*, as a gun-bore—wapasmiŋyaŋyaŋ.

pa-sna', *v. a.* *to make rustle; to shake down and make rustle*, as leaves—wapasna. *T.*, yusna.

pa-sni', *v. a.* *to extinguish*, as a fire-brand, *by pushing* it into the ashes—wapasni.

pa-snoŋ', *v. a.* *to roast*, as meat, *on a spit* or *stick*—wapasnoŋ, uŋpasnoŋpi.

pa-snuŋ', *v. a.* See pasnoŋ.

pa-spa'-ya, *v. a.* *to make wet, to sponge*—wapaspaya, uŋpaspayapi. This word is also used with the vulgar meaning of tawiŋtoŋ.

pa-staŋ', *v. a.* *to soak and take the hair off*, as from a hide—wapastaŋ. *T.*, oȟpaŋyaŋ.

pa-staŋ'-ka, *v. a.* *to moisten;* in a vulgar sense, tawiŋtoŋ. See paspaya.

pa-staŋ'-ki-ya, *v. a.* *to cause to take off the hair*, as in dressing a skin—pastaŋwakiya.

pa-sto', *v. a.* *to smooth, brush down*, as hair—wapasto, uŋpastopi. *T.*, kasto.

pa-sto'-sto, *v. red.* of pasto; *to brush down:* pastosto iyaya, *to go dragging along and brushing down*, as a wounded animal brushes down the grass. *T.*, kastosto.

pa-sto'-ya, *v. a.* *to cause to brush down*—pastowaya.

pa-sto'-ya, *adv.* *brushing down*

pa-su', *n.* *the nose* or *snout* of animals, sometimes also of man; *the beak* or *bill* of birds; *the external nose.*

pa-su′-mda-śka, *n.* (pasu *and* mdaśka) *a broad-billed duck.*

pa-su′-ško-pa, *n.* (*crooked-bill*) *the snipe; the prairie curlew,* a bird with a very long bill, which in one species is crooked, and hence the name.

pa-su′-ta, *v. a.* of suta; *to make stiff and hard by kneading,* as dough—wapasuta. *T.*, paṭiŋza

pa-śa′, *v. a.* of śa; *to make red by rubbing*—wapaśa.

pa-ś'a′-ka, *v. a.* *to push* or *strike with too little force to penetrate*—wapaś'aka.

pa-śbo′-ka, *v. n.* *to come up, overflow.* *T.*, apaśwoka.

pa-śbu′, *v. n.* *to come up* or *out.*

pa′-śda, *adj* (pa *and* śda) *bald-headed.* *T.*, nata śla.

pa-śda′, *v. a.* of śda; *to make bare, rub off,* as hair—wapaśda.

pa-śda′-ya, *v. a.* *to hull,* as corn in making hominy, *to make hominy*—wapaśdaya, uŋpaśdayapi.

pa-śda′-ya-pi, *n.* *corn hulled by boiling in ashes, hominy.*

pa-śdo′-ka, *v. a.* *to push* or *shove off,* as one's coat sleeve—wapaśdoka.

pa-śi′-ća, *v. a.* of śiča; *to spoil with the hands* or *by rubbing, soil, injure*—wapaśića.

pa-śi′-ća-ho-wa-ya, *v. a.* of śićahowaya; *to make cry out by pushing with the hand; to push* or *punch and make cry out*—wapaśićahowaya.

pa-śi′-ḣtiŋ, *v.* *to make badly; to do incorrectly.*

pa-śim′, *cont.* of paśipa; paśim iyeya. *T.*, yuśib

pa-śim′-śim, *red.* of paśim.

pa-śim′-śi-pa, *v. red.* of paśipa.

pa-śiŋ′, *n.* *a bunch on a tree.* *T.*, ćaŋ nuġe.

pa-śi′-pa, *v. a.* *to break off with the hand,* as the branches of a tree, close to the body, or as pins; *to push out of joint*—wapaśipa.

pa-śke′-pa, *v.* *T.* *to rub off,* as water.

pa-śki′-ća, *v. a.* *to press out with the hand*—wapaśkića. See paskića.

pa-śki′-śka, *v. a.* *to disarrange by rubbing*—wapaśkiśka.

pa-śki′-ta, *v. a.* *to press, squeeze out by pressing*—wapaśkita.

pa-śpa′, *v. a.* *to break off a piece, cut off a piece; to take out the dirt,* as in washing; *to wash out,* as a stain—wapaśpa, uŋpaśpapi: paśpe śni *and* paśpapi śni, *indelible,* as a stain.

pa-śpa′-śpa, *v. red.* of paśpa.

pa-śpe′-ki-ya, *v. a.* *to cause to break off; to cause to come out,* as a stain—paśpewakiya.

pa-śpe′-ya, *v. a.* *to cause to come out,* as a stain, etc.—paśpewaya.

pa-śpu′, *v. a.* *to break off,* as a bulb or excrescence, *break off,* as something bulbous—wapaśpu.

pa-śpu′-śpu, *v. a. red.* of paśpu; *to break* or *cut in pieces,* as a cake of tallow—wapaśpuśpu.

pa-śuś', *cont.* of paśuźa; paśuś iyeya.

pa-śu'-śu-źa, *v. red.* of paśuźa: *to mash up, break in pieces,* as bones—wapaśuśuźa.

pa-śu'-źa, *v. a.* *to crush with the hand; to break* or *mash by punching*—wapaśuźa.

pa-ta', *v. a.* *to cut out and sew up,* as in making a tent—wapata.

pa'-ta, *v. a.* *to cut up* or *carve,* as meat; *to cut in pieces,* as an animal—wapata, uŋpatapi.

pa'-ta, *n.* *a grove* of timber; *i. q.* taśkoźu.

pa-ta', *adv.* *together, crowded:* pata iheya, *they crowd together.* *T.,* witaya.

pa-tag', *cont.* of pataka; patag inawaźiŋ, *I stand, unable to proceed on account of* something.

pa-ta'-ka, *v.* *T.* *to dodge about; to run here and there; to come to a stop and then dart off in another direction,* as a wild horse; *to come to a stand; to touch:* hence, ipatake, *a brace: to be hindered.* See putaka.

pa-taŋ', *v. a.* *to esteem highly; to take care of; to be unwilling to part with*—wapataŋ.

pa-t'aŋ', *v. a.* *to push against with the hand; to feel for by pushing* with anything, other than the hand: the idea in the prefix "pa" is that of *pushing.*—W. J. C.—wapat'aŋ.

pa-t'aŋ'-haŋ, *part.* *pushing against.*

pa-taŋ'-iŋ, *v. a.* *to rub and make appear*—wapataŋiŋ.

pa-taŋ'-iŋ-śni, *v. n.* *to rub off, to obliterate*—wapataŋiŋśni.

pa'-taŋ-ka, *adj.* *large-headed.* *T.,* nata taŋka.

pa-taŋ'-ka, *v. a.* *to push out, make larger by pushing*—wapataŋka.

pa-t'aŋ'-t'aŋ, *v. red.* of pat'aŋ; *to feel for by punching.*

pa-t'aŋ'-t'aŋ-yaŋ, *adv.* *punching for,* as for turtle eggs in the sand; pat'aŋt'aŋyaŋ kuwa. See pazi.

pa-taŋ'-yaŋ, *adj.* *reserving, keeping.*

pa-t'aŋ'-yaŋ, *adv.* *pushing against.*

pa'-ta-pi, *n.* *a cutting up* of meat, *carving.*

pa'-ta-waŋ-źi-daŋ, *adv.* *directly, in one path, with one purpose, unchangeable.* *T.,* pat'aŋwaŋźila.

pa-te'-ća, *v. a.* *to make new, rub up and make new again*—wapateća.

pa-te'-pa, *v. a.* *to wear off by rubbing*—wapatepa.

pa-ti'-ća, *v. a.* *to scrape off,* as snow from the ground; *to work up by pressing on,* as dough when sticky and soft; *to shove, to push*—wapatića.

pa-tin', *cont.* of patića; patin iyeya. *T.,* patil; patimahel patil iyeya, *to shove into the house.*

pa-tiŋ', *adj.* *stiff,* as a new ribbon, *firm, not springing* or *yielding; stiffened* with the cold—mapatiŋ. See katiŋ *and* satiŋ.

pa-tiŋ'-ya, *v. a.* *to cause to become stiff*—patiŋwaya.

pa-ti'-taŋ, *v. a.* *to push against, push along*—wapatitaŋ.

pa-ti'-taŋ-yaŋ, *adv. pushing against.*

pa-tka'-śa-daŋ, *n a small species of tortoise.* See keya, etc.

pa-tku', *v. a. to break off square*—wapatku.

pa-tku'-ġa, *v. a. to break in two by striking; to break in two by pushing* or *punching*—wapatkuġa.

pa-tkuḣ', *cont.* of patkuġa; patkuḣ iyeya.

pa-tku'-tku-ġa, *v. red.* of patkuġa.

pa-to'-kaŋ-i-ye-ya, *v. T. to push aside.*

pa-tpa', *v. a.* Same as pakpa.

pa-tpi', *v. a. to break out of the shell,* as anything being hatched: *i. q.* pakpi.

pa-tuś', *cont.* of patuźa; patuś inaźiŋ, *to stand bent forward.*

pa-tuś'-ya, *v. a. to cause to bend forward* or *stoop, to make bow down*—patuśwaya.

pa-tu'-źa, *v. n. to bend over, lean forward, stoop down*—wapatuźa. See pakućedaŋ, pamahdedaŋ, etc.

pa-ṭa', *v. a. to press to death, kill by lying on*—wapaṭa.

pa-ṭa'-ṭa, *v. n T. to be numb; to be asleep,* as a limb. See kpaṭaṭa.

pa-ṭiŋs', *cont.* of paṭiŋza; paṭiŋs iyeya.

pa-ṭiŋs'-ṭiŋ-za, *v. red.* of paṭiŋza.

pa-ṭiŋ'-za, *v. a. to make stiff by kneading,* as in mixing up bread; *to press down tight*—wapaṭiŋza.

pa-uŋ'-ka, *v. T. to push and make fall down: i. q.* pawaŋka.

pa-waŋ'-ka, *v. a. to push down*—wapawaŋka. *T.,* pauŋka.

pa-waŋ'-kan, *adv.* pawaŋkaniću, *to shove up.*

pa'-we, *v. to bleed at the nose.*

pa-we'-ġa, *v. a. to break with the hand,* as a stick, but not entirely off; *to break by pushing against; to break by falling on*—wapaweġa: *to intersect,* as one road another. See ipaweġa.

pa-weḣ', *cont.* of paweġa; paweḣ iyeya.

pa-weḣ'-we-ġa, *v. red.* of paweġa.

pa-weḣ'-ya, *v. a. to cause to break; to break by pushing against*—paweḣwaya.

pa-wi', *adv. many,* as a great many maggots. *T.,* opawiwi. See pawise.

pa-wi'-hnu-ni, *v. a. to rub to pieces, to destroy*—wapawihnuni.

pa-wi'-ka, *adv. many:* itu pawika.

pa-wiŋḣ'-ya, *adv turning out of a straight direction.*

pa-wiŋś', *cont.* of pawiŋźa; pawiŋś iyeya.

pa-wiŋś'-wiŋ-źa, *v. red.* of pawiŋźa; *to bend down, to make shake.*

pa-wiŋ'-ta, *v. a. to rub*—wapawiŋta. See pahiŋta *and* pakiŋta.

pa-wiŋ'-źa, *v. a. to bend* or *press down,* as grass.

pa-wi'-se, *adv many,* as maggots. This word seems to convey the idea of crawling over each other, as a moving mass. See pawiwi and pawiwise. *T.,* opawiwi.

pa-wi′-ta-ya, *v. a.* of witaya; *to assemble, collect*—wapawitaya.

pa-wi′-wi, *adv. red.* of pawi; *in crowds.* See opawiwi.

pa-wi′-wi-se, *adv. shaking:* pawiwise iyaya, *to shake*, as the hair of a badger when walking. The idea of motion seems to be implied. See opawiwise.

pa-wi′-ya-kpa, *v. a.* of wiyakpa; *to rub and make shine, to polish*—wapawiyakpa.

pa-wi′-ya-tpa, *v. a.* Same as pawiyakpa.

pa-wo′-slal, *cont.* of pawoslata; pawoslal iyeya, *to run up*, as a flag.

pa-wo′-sla-ta, *v.* *T.* *to push up straight: i. q.* pabosdata.

pa-ya′-ta, *adv.* *in* or *at the head:* payata o, *to shoot in the head:* payata ićakśa, *to gather in a roll around the neck*, as an Indian sometimes does his blanket. *T.*, nata ekta.

pa-ye′-ġa, *v. a.* *to make shine by rubbing*—wapayeġa. *T.*, paleħya.

pa-yes′, *cont.* of payeza.

pa-ye′-za, *v. a* *to rub, to scour*—wapayeza.

pa-za′, *v. a* *to stick up bushes*, as the Dakotas do to sleep under when on a journey; *to make a booth*—wapaza. *T.*, initi yuktaŋ.

pa-za′, *n.* the sacred name for *wood.*

pa′-za, *adj.* *bitter*, as gall.

pa-zaŋ′, *v. a.* *to part* or *separate*, as in running the fingers or a comb through the hair; *to spread out* or *divide*, as the hair—wapazaŋ. See paġaŋ.

pa-zaŋ′, *v. a.* *to hurt* or *kill by striking*—wapazaŋ.

pa-zaŋ′, *adv.* *T.* *with the head only concealed*, as a hen in the bushes; pazaŋ ħpaya.

pa-zaŋ′-yaŋ, *v. a.* *to hurt* or *kill by striking*—wapazaŋyaŋ

pa-zaŋ′-yaŋ, *adv.* *spread out*, as curtains; *spread over*, as a booth: pazaŋyaŋ iwaŋka, *to sleep under a booth.* *T.*, pazaŋyaŋ iyuŋka, *to sleep under the brush;* the idea is, *not concealed.*

pa′-ze-ća, *adj.* *bitter.*

pa′-ze-ze, *v. n.* *to swing, nod.* See ozeze *and* paozeze.

pa′-ze-ze-daŋ, *adv.* *swinging, nodding, letting the head drop*, as in sleep.

pa′-ze-ze-ya, *adv.* *swinging.* See ozezeya.

pa′-ze-ze-ye-daŋ, *adv.* *nodding*, as in sleep.

pa′-zi, *n.* *yellow-head.* *T.*, natazi.

pa-zi′, *v. a.* *to push into*, as a stick into the sand in hunting for tortoise eggs—wapazi. *T.*, pat'aŋt'aŋ.

pa-zi′-ća, *v. a.* *to rub, roll out* or *stretch with the hand; to stretch by pressing against*—wapazića.

pa-zig′-zi-ća, *v. red.* of pazića.

pa-zo′, *v. a.* *to show, present* anything *to view*—wapazo, uŋpazopi.

p a - z o′ - k i - y a, *v.* *to cause to show*—pazowakiya.

p a - z u n′, *cont.* of pazuŋta; pazun owatoŋ, *I wear it only run up.* *T.*, pazul.

p a - z u ŋ′ - t a, *v. a.* *to sew* or *run up at the sides some distance from the edge*, as leggings—wapazuŋta.

p a - ź a′ *or* p a - ź a ŋ′, *adv.* *through:* paźa ćap'a, *to stab through.* *T.*, ihuŋniyaŋ.

p a - ź a l′. *T.* *cont.* of paźata.

p a - ź a l′ - ź a - t a. *T.* *red.* of paźata.

p a - ź a ŋ′, *adv.* See paźa.

p a - ź a ŋ′ - y a, *adv.* *through and through.*

p a - ź a′ - t a, *v. a.* *to make forked by punching* or *thrusting something into*—wapaźata.

p a - ź a′ - ź a, *v. a.* *to wash*, as a gun, *by pushing and pulling*—wapaźaźa.

p a - ź i m′, *cont.* of paźipa; paźim iyeya. *T.*, paźib.

p a - ź i m′ - ź i - p a, *v.* *red.* of paźipa.

p a - ź i ŋ′, *v.* *to prevent.* See ipaźiŋ, kipaźiŋ, wipaźiŋ, *and* wapaźiŋ.

p a - ź i′ - p a, *v. a.* *to prick* with a pin; *to press against and make penetrate.* See yaźipa *and* yuźipa.

p a - ź o′ - d a ŋ, *n.* *a high knoll* or *hill, the top of a hill.*

p a - ź o′ - y a, *adv.* *hill-like, swelled up.*

p a - ź u ŋ′, *v. a.* *to push down and pry up*, as a root; *to pull up*, as ducks do grass roots in water—wapaźuŋ.

p a - ź u′ - ź u, *v. a.* *to rub out, cross out, erase*—wapaźuźu.

p ć e′ - ć e - n a, *adj.* *Ih.* *short:* *i. q.* ptećedaŋ. *T.*, pćećela.

p ć e l - y e′ - l a, *adv.* *T.* *briefly, for a little time.*

p ć e - p ć e l′ - y e - l a, *adv.* *red.* of pćelyela.

p ć e - y a′, *v. a.* *to cut and dry meat* of any kind—pćewaya. *T.*, kablaya. See wapćeya.

p e, *adv.* *modal, plural ending*, old form for "pi."

p e, *the precatory plur. imp.* termination of verbs, used commonly by women, as, ećoŋ pe, *do ye do it.*

p e, *n.* *the top of the head.*

p e, *adj.* *sharp*, as edged tools; *pointed.*

p e - a′ - g l a - t a - t a, *v.* *T.* *to use all up, to exhaust one's supply by giving to others:* *i. q.* woźuha glatata—peawaglatata. See hdatata.

p e - ć o′ - k a ŋ - y a ŋ, *n.* *T.* *the scalp-lock.*

P e - ć o′ - k a ŋ - y a ŋ - h a ŋ - s k a, *n. p.* *the Chinese; a Chinaman.*

p e′ - ć o - k a - y a k i - s o ŋ - p i, *n.* *the scalp-lock.* *T.*, pećokaŋyaŋ.

p e - ć u s′, *cont.* of pećuza: wi pećus waŋka, *there are sun dogs.* *T.*, wi aćeiçiti, *the sun builds his own fires.*

p e - ć u s′ - y a, *adv.* wi pećusya waŋka; said when mock suns are observed.

p e - ć u′ - z a, *n.* *sun-dogs, mock-suns.*

pe′-gna-ka, *v. T. to wear in the hair* or *on the head: i q.* pehiŋ gnaka.

pe′-gna-ka-pi, *v. T. ornaments worn in the hair* or *on the head*, as *brooches*, *feathers*, etc.

pe-ġe′, *n. the side* or *height* of a vessel. *T.*, ćuwi.

pe-haŋ′, *v. a. to fold up* anything—wapehaŋ: pehaŋ ehnaka, *to fold up and lay away.*

pe-haŋ′, *n. the crane*, of several species.

pe-haŋ′-ġi-daŋ, *n. the gray* or *sand-hill crane.*

pe-haŋ′-haŋ, *v. red.* of pehaŋ; *to writhe* or *move about*, as one does with the stomach-ache—wapehaŋhaŋ

pe-haŋ′-ka-daŋ, *n. a small slender bird* which frequents the water. Same as siyukaŋśaśa.

pe-haŋ′-saŋ, *n. the large white crane.*

pe-hiŋ′, *n. T. the hair of the head: i. q.* pahiŋ.

pe-hiŋ′-i-ća-sto, *n. T. a hair brush.*

pe-hiŋ′-i-sla-ye, *n. T. hair-oil; grease for the hair.*

pe-ȟni′-ġa, *v. n. to be red hot, heated to a white heat.*

pe-ȟni′-ġa, *n. that which is heated to a red heat.* Compare peśniźa.

pe-ȟniȟ′, *cont.* of peȟniġa.

pe-ȟni′-ȟni-ġa, *v. red* of peȟniġa.

pe-ȟniȟ′-ya, *v. a. to heat red hot*—peȟniȟwaya.

pe-ksu′, *n. a kind of acorn. T.*, uta.

pe-ksu′-daŋ, *n. a species of acorn; a kind of grass with a red flower.*

pel, *cont.* of peta; *n. T. fire.*

pel-i′-le-ya-pi, *n. T. something to light a fire with; kindlings.*

pel-kaŋ′, *adv. T. near the fire.*

pe-mna′, *v. n. to smell of fire;* as if pet mna.

pe-mna′, *adj. smelling of fire, smelling burnt.*

pe-mni′, *adj. warped, twisted, crooked.*

pe-mni′, *v. n. to warp, twist; to become crooked, become entangled.*

pe-mni′-mni, *v. red.* of pemni.

pe-mni′-yaŋ, *adv. crookedly, perversely, twisting.*

pe-mnu′-mnu-ġa, *n. the pit of the stomach.* See also pimnumnuġa. *T.*, śipute.

pe-na′-kpa-kpa, *v. n.* (peta *and* nakpakpa) *to crackle*, as a fire.

pe-na′-tpa-tpa, *v. n. to crackle, emit sparks*, as fire. This and the preceding word may perhaps be used as nouns, meaning *small sparks.*

pe-pe′, *adj. red.* of pe; *prickly, jagged.*

pe-pe′-ya, *adv. prickly, sharp*, or *rough*, as a frozen road: pepeya hiyeya.

pe-sde′-te, *n. the top of the head; the comb of a rooster. T.*, peslete.

pe-sde'-te-o-wiŋ-ġe, *n. the curl of hair on the top of the head.*

pe-sle'-te, *n. T. i. q.* pesdete.

pe-sle'-te-śa, *n. T. the red comb of a chicken cock.*

pe'-sto, *adj. sharp-pointed.*

pe'-sto-daŋ, *adj. sharp-pointed. T.*, pestola.

pe'-sto-la, *n. T. the diamond in cards.*

pe'-sto-ya, *adv. in a sharp-pointed manner.*

pe'-sto-ye-la, *adv T. i. q.* pestoya

Pe'-śa, *n. p. the Kwapas.*

pe-śka', *n. the air-bladder of a fish.* This is sometimes used for making *glue*, hence the name ćoŋpeśka.

pe-śni'-źa, *n. sparks of fire.*

pet, *cont.* of peta, as in petiśkaŋ, etc. *T.*, pel.

pe'-ta, *n. fire.*

pe-ta'-ġa, *n. burning coals.*

pe-ta'-ġa-i-će-oŋ-pa, *v. to broil on the coals*—petaġa ićewaoŋpa.

pe-tan', *adv. on the fire:* petan elipeya, *to throw on* or *in the fire. T.*, petaŋl.

pe-tan'-na, *adv. in the fire.*

pet-i'-śkaŋ, *v. n. to draw near the fire, warm one's self*—petimaśkaŋ. *T.*, peliśkaŋ.

pet'-i-źaŋ-źaŋ *and* pe-ta'-i-źaŋ-źaŋ, *n. a torch, candle, lamp T.*, peliźaŋźaŋ.

pet-i'-źaŋ-źaŋ-i-hu-pa, *n. a candlestick, lamp. T.*, peliźaŋźaŋ ihupa.

pet-i'-źaŋ-źaŋ-i-yu-kse, *n. candle-snuffers. T.*, peliźaŋźaŋ iyukse.

pet-ka'-hda, *adv.* (peta *and* kahda) *near the fire, by the fire. T.*, pelkaŋye *and* pelićagla.

pet-ki'-ye-daŋ, *adv.* (peta *and* kiyedaŋ) *near the fire. T.*, pelkaŋyela.

pe-tu'-spe, *n. a fire-brand.*

pe-tu'-ste, *n. a fire-brand.*

pe'-wi-wi-la, *n. T. the soft spot in the cranium of infants.*

pe-yo'-haŋ, *n. a line running over the middle of the head from the forehead, the parting of the hair. T.*, peyohaŋla.

pe-yo'-haŋ-la, *n. T. i. q.* peyohaŋ.

pe-yo'-zaŋ, *n. the place which is left on the head by separating the hair: i. q.* peyohaŋ.

pe-źi', *n. grass, herbs, hay.*

pe-źi'-hiŋ-kpi-la, *n. T. moss.*

pe-źi-hu'-ta, *n. grass-roots, herbs; medicines* of all kinds. *T.*, peźuta.

pe-źi-hu'-ta-i-ya-tke, *n. something to drink medicine out of; teacups. T.*, peźuta iyatke. See yatkaŋ.

pe-źi-hu'-ta-i-yo-ka-śtaŋ, *n. something to pour medicine into; a coffee-pot, tea-pot; a syringe.*

pe-źi-hu'-ta-sa-pa, *n. black medicine,* i. e. *coffee. T.*, peźuta sapa.

pe-źi-hu'-ta-śi-ća, *n. bad medicine,* i. e. *poison. T.*, peźuta śića.

pe-źi-hu'-ta-wi-ća-śta, *n. a medicine man; a physician. T.*, peźuta wićaśa.

pe-źi-hu'-ta-zi, *n. yellow medicine; rhubarb. T.*, peźutazi.

Pe-źi-hu'-ta-zi-ḳa-pi-wa-kpa, *n. p. the Yellow Medicine River*, which joins the Minnesota from the Coteau des Prairies, about thirty miles below Mdeiyedaŋ. See ḳa *and* wakpa.

pe-źi'-ħo-ta, *n. a kind of grass* or *herb of a whitish* or *grayish appearance*, which grows abundantly on the prairies; *wild sage.* In our translations this word is used for *hyssop.*

pe-źi'-i-ća-śda, *n.* (pezi *and* kaśda) *a scythe.*

pe-źi'-i-na-kse, *n. T. a mowing machine.*

pe-źi'-i-to-kśu, *n.* (peźi *and* tokśu) *a hay-rack.*

pe-źi'-i-yu-hiŋ-te, *n. a hay-rake.*

pe-źi'-ka-śda, *v. to cut hay* or *grass, to mow*—peźiwakaśda. *T*, peźikaśla.

pe-źi'-o-ka-śla, *n. T. a place to cut hay, a meadow.*

pe-źi'-o-na-kse-ya-pi, *n. T. a place to cut hay in.*

pe-źi'-uŋ-kće-la, *n T.* (peźi *and* uŋkće) *the sand burr*

pe-źi'-uŋ-kće-kće-la, *n. T. sand burrs.*

peź'-o-wiŋ-źa, *n.* (peźi *and* owiŋźa) *grass-bedding* in a tent.

pe-źu'-ta-gmi-gme-la, *n. T. "round medicine," pills.*

pi, *the common plural termination* of verbs, nouns, pronouns, adjectives, and sometimes adverbs and prepositions. In the Titoŋwaŋ dialect the "pi" often becomes "pe" before "ye lo," when the "ye" is lost: *e. g.* "hećoŋpe lo" for "hećoŋpi ye lo"—W. J. C.

pi, *adj. good.* This word is probably obsolete, but words formed from it are in use, as, yupi, etc.

pi, *n. the liver*—mapi, wićapi: tapi, *the liver of animals.*

pi'-ća, *an auxiliary verb* with the force of *can.* It conveys the idea of *power* or *possibility*, as ećoŋpića, *that can be done.*

pi-ća', *adj. good.*

pi-ća'-ka, *an auxiliary verb*, sometimes with the force of pića, and sometimes with that of pića śni. The "ka" may in some cases be interrogative.

pi-ća'-ka, *adj. a little good: i. q.* kitaŋna waśte: *a little better than* some other.

pi-ća'-la-ke, *adj. T. more perfect than* some other; pićalake ćiŋ he ićuyo, *take the best one.*

pi-ća'-śni, *v. it cannot be, it is impossible.*

pi-ća'-ya, *adv. well.*

pi-da', *v. n. to be glad, thankful; to rejoice*—piwada, piuŋdapi. *T*, pila

pi-da'-da, *v. red.* of pida.

pi-da′-ki-ya, *v. a. to make glad, make thankful*—pidawakiya, pidauŋkiyapi: pidamakiya, *he has made me glad, I am thankful. T.*, pilakiya.

pi-da′-ya, *v. a. to make glad*—pidawaya, pidauŋyaŋpi. *T.*, pilaya.

pi-da′-ya, *adv. gladly.*

pi′-ġe-se, *adv. T. with a noise,* as one in diving into water.

pi-i′-ḉi-ya, *v. reflex.* of piya; *to prepare one's self, get ready*—pimiḉiya, piuŋkiḉiyapi.

pi-ki′-ći-da, *v. to give thanks to, be glad for*—piwećida. *T.*, pikićila, *to be glad* or *thankful with* or *for* another; *to take part with one in his thankfulness.* There seems to be no word for "to give thanks to", *to thank.* "Wopila" is not used, so the forms wopila ḳu, ećiya, etc., are not understood. The only expression of this idea is in the full form, pilayapi oglaka. However, it is contained in such forms as, pilamayaya, *you make me thankful,* i. e. *I thank you.*—W. J. C.

pi-ki′-ći-ya, *v.* of piya; *to mend for one*—piwećiya.

pi-ki′-da, *v. n. to be thankful, glad*—piwakida.

pi-ki′-ya, *v. a. to conjure, to pow-wow over the sick,* as the Dakotas do; *to mend* or *make new one's own*—piwakiya, piuŋkiyapi, pimakiya.

pi-ki′-ya-pi, *part. conjured, conjuring; mended. T.*, wapiyapi.

pi-ksu′-daŋ, *n. a kind of acorn.* See peksudaŋ.

pi-ksu′-ta, *n. a species of prairie grass—the blue joint.*

pil-i′-ḉi-ya, *v. reflex. T. to make one's self thankful.*

pi-mnu′-mnu-ġa, *n. the pit of the stomach. T.*, śipute.

piŋs-piŋ′-za, *n. the prairie dog,* an animal about the size of a mink or a large ground squirrel, which is found near the Missouri, and is said by the Dakotas to plant its own field.

piŋs-piŋ′-za, *v. red.* of piŋza; *to squeal,* as a ground squirrel when caught.

pi-śle′-ća, *n. T. the spleen: i. q.* piśniźe.

piŋś-piŋ′-źe-daŋ, *adj. thin, scattering,* as hair or grass.

piŋ′-za, *v. n. to creak,* as a shoe. *T.*, kiŋza; kiŋskiŋza.

piŋ′-ze-daŋ, *n. the prairie dog.*

piŋ′-źa, *adj. destitute of hair: i. q.* śmi.

pi-pi′-ya, *adv. red.* of piya; *well, anew, thoroughly.*

pis-pi′-za, *v. T. to make a noise with the lips,* as in whistling for a dog.

pi-śka′-te, *n. a small species of cranberry.*—S. W. P. See potpaŋka.

pi′-śko, *n. the night-hawk.*

pi′-śko-ta-haŋ-pe, *n.* lit. "the night-hawk's moccasin," *the lady's-slipper,* a flower; *mushrooms, fungus: i. q.* wićaŋhpi hiŋhpaya. *T.*, makaćaŋnakpaŋ.

pi-śni′-źe, *n.* *the spleen.* See tapiśniźe. *T.*, piśleća; tapiśleća.

piś-pi′-źa, *adj.* *red.* of piźa; *wrinkled*—mapiśpiźa.

piś-pi′-źe-daŋ, *adj.* *wrinkled* or *shrivelled*, as one's hands from being long in water, *withered*—mapiśpiźedaŋ.

pi-ya′, *v. a.* of pi, *good; to make anew, mend up, repair*—piwaya, piuŋyaŋpi. *T.* *to conjure the sick.* See pikiya.

pi′-ya, *adv.* *well, anew:* piya hduha, *to have again, recover one's own;* piya kaġa, *to mend, make anew.*

pi′-ya-e-haŋ-ke-ća, *adv.* *taller, longer than.*

pi′-ya-e-haŋ-na-ke-ćiŋ-haŋ, *adv.* *presently:* *i. q.* ehakedaŋke ćiŋhaŋ, *soon, again: after a pause; resting and then going on afresh.*

pi-ya′-e-haŋ-na-se, *adv.* *a little longer.*

pi′-ya-i-yu-kćaŋ, *v.* *to take another view of; to change one's mind.*

pi-ya′-ya, *v. n.* *to run well*, as a canoe or hutinaćute.

pi-ye′. *v.* See piya.

pi-ye′-deś, *adv.* *notwithstanding; heedlessly:* *i. q.* iyowinyeśni. Said of one who does not listen to what is said to him. See inihaŋ śni.

pi-ye′-pi-ća, *adj.* *reparable:* piyepića śni, *that cannot be repaired.*

pi-zi′, *n.* *the gall*—mapizi. See tapizi.

pi′-źa, *adj.* *wrinkled*—mapiźa.

po, *the plural termination* of verbs in the imperative mood. This is probably formed from "pi" *and* "wo."

po, *v. n* *to swell, puff out*—mapo, wićapo.

po-ġan′, *adv.* *on the nose.*

po′-ġaŋ, *v. n.* *to spread out*, as a bladder when blown; *to blow*, as with the mouth.

po-ġa′-śke, *n.* *the external part of the nose, the sides of the nostrils:* *i. q.* poḣaśke *T.*, poġe osmaka.

poġ-ćaŋ′-te, *n.* *T.* *the septum* or *partition of the nose:* *i. q.* poḣćaŋte.

po′-ġe, *n.* *the nose*—mapoġe, nipoġe: *nostril;* used also for outside of nose.

Po′-ġe-ḣdo-ke, *n. p.* *the Nez Percé Indians.*

po′-ġe-o-ḣdo-ka, *n.* *the nostrils.*

po′-ha-ha-se, *adv.* *shaking.* Said of a buffalo shaking his head; pohahase iŋyaŋka, *he runs shaking his head.*

po′-hdi-ćo-daŋ, *adv.* (pa *and* ohde) *head covered:* *i. q.* pośmićodaŋ: śina pohdićodaŋ hiŋmi, *I wear my blanket over my head.* *T.*, pośmićola.

po′-hmi-ćo-daŋ, *adv.* Same as pohdićodaŋ.

poḣ-a′-śke, *n.* (poġe *and* aśke) *the outside of the nostrils*: *i. q.* poġaśke.

poḣ′-ćaŋ-te, *n.* *the cartilage between the nostrils*: *i. q.* poġćaŋte.

p o ḣ - i′ - y a, *adv.* *T.* *crouching down:* poḣiya yaŋka, *to sit doubled up with hands over the knees.*

p o ḣ - y u′ - ś k i, *n.* *the inside of the nose, the nostrils.*

p o′ - k i - m n a - m n a, *v. a.* of pomnamna; *to shake the head at* one—powakimnamna.

p o - k p a ŋ′ - k a, *n.* See potpaŋka.

p o l - p o′ - t a, *adj.* *T.* *red.* of pota; *worn out.*

p o l - p o′ - t a ŋ - h a ŋ, *part.* *T.* *full of holes.*

p o m, *cont.* of popa; pom iyaya *and* pom hiŋhda, *to burst out, snap suddenly.* *T.*, pob.

p o′ - m n a - m n a, *v.* *to shake the head*—powamnamna.

p o′ - m n a - m n a - k i - y a, *v. a.* *to shake* or *wag the head at; to cause to wag the head*—pomnamnawakiya. See poptaŋptaŋkiya.

p o m - y a′, *adv* *snapping, popping.*

p o m - y e ḣ′, *adv.* *with a snap:* pomyeḣ iheya, *to shoot and kill immediately:* pomyeḣ iyeya.

p o m - y e′ - ḣ i ŋ, *adv.* *snapping.*

p o n, *cont* of pota. *T.*, pol.

p o ŋ - p o ŋ′, *adj.* *rotten,* as wood.

p o ŋ - p o ŋ′ - n a, *adj.* *rotten, soft,* as rotten wood. *T.*, puŋpuŋla.

p o′ - p a, *v n.* *to burst.* See napopa.

p o - p o′, *v. n.* *red.* of po; *to swell, puff out.*

p o - p o′ - p a, *adj.* *full of pith:* tipsiŋna popopa, *a stringy turnip.*

p o - p o′ - p e - s e, *adv.* Said of nap on a blanket and of fine fur on a robe.

p o - p o′ - t k a, *n.* *the screech-owl.*

p o - p o′ - t k a - d a ŋ, *n.* *the screech-owl.*

p o′ - p t a ŋ - p t a ŋ, *v. n.* *to shake the head, signify dissent*—powaptaŋptaŋ. See pomnamna.

p o′ - p t a ŋ - p t a ŋ - k i - y a, *v. a.* *to shake the head at; to cause to wag the head at*—poptaŋptaŋwakiya. See apoptaŋptaŋ.

p o′ - s k i - ć a, *v.* *to clasp around the neck.* See pośkin.

p o′ - s k i n, *cont.* of poskića; *by the neck.* *T.*, poskil.

p o′ - s k i n - i - y a ̧ - k a - ś k a, *v. a.* *to tie round the neck,* as a halter.

p o′ - s k i n - k t e, *v.* *to kill by choking*—poskinwakte. *T.*, yuṭa.

p o′ - s k i n - ṭ a, *v.* *to die by being strangled.*

p o′ - s k i n - y u - ṭ a, *v.* *to put to death by hanging.* *T.*, panakseya.

p o′ - s k i n - y u - z a, *v.* *to take by the throat; to put the arms around the neck of* one, *to embrace*—poskinmduza. *T.*, lotogmus yuza See adokso *and* kaskita yuza.

p o′ - ś d i - ś d i, *v.* *to have one's face always covered:* pośdiśdi wauŋ. *T.*, pośliśli. See pohdićodaŋ *and* pośmićodaŋ.

p o - ś d i′ - ś d i - k a, *n.* *one who keeps his face covered with his blanket:* *i. q.* pośliśli s'a.

p o′ - ś i ŋ, *v. n* *to sniff, snuff up the nose; make a face at*—powaśiŋ. See paḣlaźiŋća *and* iteyuśiŋkiya.

p o'- ś i ŋ - ś i ŋ , *v.* *red.* of pośiŋ; *to make faces at.*

p o'- ś l i - ś l i - s' a , *n.* *T.* *one who keeps his face covered.*

p o'- ś m i - ć o - d a ŋ, *adv.* *head covered,* as with a blanket: śina pośmićodaŋ hiŋmi, *I wear my blanket over my head.* See pośdiśdika.

p o'- ś t a ŋ , *v.* *T.* *to wear as a hat or head covering*—powaśtaŋ.

p o'- ś t a ŋ , *n.* *a hood, a child's cloak with a hood.* See tapośtaŋ.

p o' t a, *adj.* *worn out; spoiled.* See bapota, yupota, etc.

p o'- t a - h a ŋ, *part.* *worn out, full of holes.* *T.*, potahe.

p o - t a'- w a - h a ŋ, *part.* *full of holes.*

p o - t k a ŋ'- k a, *n.* *cranberries.* Same as potpaŋka. See piśkate.

p o - t p a ŋ'- k a, *n.* *cranberries, the Oxycoccus macrocarpus.*

p o - t p a ŋ'- k a - h u, *n.* *the cranberry-stalk.*

p o - t p o'- t a, *red.* of pota; *worn out.* *T.*, polpota.

p o - t p o'- t a - h a ŋ, *part.* *red.* of potahaŋ; *full of holes, torn, ragged,* as a worn-out garment. *T.*, polpotahaŋ.

p o - w a'- y a, *n.* *nap, fur.*

p o - w a'- y a, *adj.* *having nap.*

p o - w a'- y e - d a ŋ, *adj.* *having nap;* śa powayedaŋ, *red flannel.*

p o'- ź a ŋ - ź a ŋ, *v.* *to snuff up,* as an animal snuffs the wind; *to snuff* or *scent,* as a dog does. See pośiŋ.

p s a, *n.* *a kind of rush* or *water grass,* sometimes used in making mats: Psa-mde-waŋke-ćiŋ-wakpa, *the little stream* that empties into the Minnesota just below Little Rock.

p s a'- k a, *adj.* *broken.* See yupsaka.

p s a - k a'- h a ŋ, *part.* *broken,* as a string; said also of the heart.

p s a - k a'- w a - h a ŋ, *part.* *broken,* as a string.

p s a'- o - w i ŋ - ź a, *n.* *rush mats.*

p s a - p s a'- k a - h a ŋ, *part.* *red.* of psakahaŋ.

p s a - p s a'- k a - w a - h a ŋ, *part.* *red.* of psakawahaŋ.

p s a'- w a - p a - h a, *n.* *palm* or *chip hats.* *T.*, psawapośtaŋ.

p s a - w o'- g n a - k a, *n.* *T.* *a basket.*

p s e, *n.* *snow-shoes.* *T.*, psohaŋpi.

p s e'- ḣ t i ŋ, *n.* *the ash*

p s e - p a'- t o ŋ - n a, *n.* *sharp-toed snow-shoes.* *T.*, psohaŋpi pespestola.

p s e - y a'- p i, *n.* *the water-ash,* so called because used for making snow-shoes.

p s i'- ć a, *adj.* *jumping.* See yupsića, ipsića, etc.

p s i n, *cont.* of psića: psin iyaya, *to jump* or *hop away.* *T.*, psil.

p s i ŋ, *n.* *rice, wild rice:* psiŋ ati, *to pitch a tent at the rice;* psiŋ ska, *white rice, barley.*

p s i ŋ - ć a', *n.* *a bulbous esculent root which grows in marshes,* about the size of a black walnut with the hull on.

psiŋ-ćiŋ′-ća, *n. a bulbous esculent root* much used by the Dakotas of the lower Minnesota. It is about as large as a hen's egg, and grows on the margin of rivers and lakes. *T.*, śiptola.

psiŋ-ska′, *n. white rice; barley.*

psi-psi′-ća, *v. red.* of psića; *to jump much, to skip.*

psi-psi′-ća-daŋ, *n. the grasshopper. T.*, gnugnuśka.

psi-psi′-ća-la-sa-pa, *n. T. the black jumper; the field cricket.*

psi-psin′, *cont.* of psipsića; psipsin ya, *to go jumping* or *skipping along. T.*, psipsil.

pso′-haŋ, *v.* (pse *and* ohaŋ) *to put on* or *wear snow-shoes*—psowahaŋ, psouŋhaŋpi. *T.*, psohaŋpi kićuŋ.

pso′-haŋ-pi, *n. T. snow-shoes.*

pso-ka′, *n. a species of fish* somewhat resembling the pike.

pso′-kśaŋ, *n. a kind of round-toed snow-shoes.*

psoŋ-psoŋ′, *adj. rounded off, having the corners taken off; loose, not firm. T.*, psoŋpsoŋla.

psoŋ-psoŋ′-na, *adj. rounded, having the corners taken off;* said also of teeth on edge, as, hi psoŋpsoŋna.

psoŋ-psoŋ′-ye-la. *adv. T. loosely, not securely; likely to fall,* as a lamp placed on the edge of a table.

psuŋ-psuŋ′-na, *adj.* Same as psoŋpsoŋna. *T.*, psuŋpsuŋyela.

pśa, *v. n. to sneeze*—wapśa, uŋpśapi.

pśa-pśa′, *adv.* pśapśa se, *huddled together;* pśapśa se iyaya, *to make a noise* as when anything is poured into a vessel. See apśapśa.

pśa-ya′, *v. a. to cause to sneeze*—pśawaya.

pśiŋ, *n. leeks, onions.*

pśiŋ-ća′, *n. the flying-squirrel.*

pśuŋ, *adj. shed, fallen off,* as horns; *drawn out.* See yupśuŋ, kapśuŋ.

pśuŋ-haŋ′, *part. fallen off, dislocated. T.*, pśuŋwahaŋ.

pśuŋ-ka′, *adj. round, short, and thick.*

pśuŋ-ka′, *n. a bulge, a knot* on a tree; *a pill.*

pśuŋ-ka′-daŋ, *n. any tiny round thing.*

pśuŋ-ka′-ka, *n. tiny round things, pills.*

pśuŋ-ka′-ya, *adv. in a bunch, in a heap,* as an animal curled up; pśuŋkaya waŋka: *i q.* puśki.

pśuŋ-ka′-ya-ken, *adv. in a bunch, drawn up together.*

pśuŋ-ka′-ye-la, *adv. T. in a bunch.*

pśuŋ-wa′-haŋ, *part. dropped out, fallen off.* See pśuŋhaŋ.

pta. See yupta.

pta-haŋ′, *part. cut off, cut out.*

ptaŋ. See yuptaŋ.

ptaŋ, *n. the otter.* In the sacred dialect it is called "hepaŋ"

ptaŋ-ha′, *n an otter skin.*

ptaŋ-ptaŋ′, *adj. unsteady, rocking,* as a canoe.

p t a ŋ - p t a ŋ' - n a, *adj.* *unsteady, tottering.*

P t a ŋ - s i ŋ' - t a, *n. p.* *the name of the village at the upper end of Lake Traverse.* Lit. *Otter's tail.* By a rule, the reason of which is not apparent, the "siŋte" becomes "siŋta." So, also, in Ćapsiŋta.

p t a ŋ' - t a - ć a ŋ - k u, *n.* *an otter's trail; the trails of small animals in general.*

p t a ŋ' - y a ŋ, *adv.* *flurried.* See ćaŋteptaŋyaŋ.

p t a ŋ - y e' - t u, *n.* *autumn.* To summer and winter the Dakotas count five months each, and to spring and autumn but one each.

p t a - w a' - h a ŋ, *part.* *cut off, fallen off.* Same as ptahaŋ.

p t a' - y a, *adv.* *together, collectively:* ptaya uŋyaŋpi kta, *we will go together.* See witaya *and* optaye.

p t a' - y e - l a, *adv.* *T.* *together.*

p t e, *n.* *a cow, the female buffalo.* The bison or buffalo is colloquially termed "pte," irrespective of sex. The counterpart is "tataŋka."

p t e' - a - s a ŋ - p i, *n.* *cow's milk.*

p t e' - a - s a ŋ - p i - i - h d i, *n* *butter.*

p t e' - a - s a ŋ - p i - n i - n i, *n.* *thick milk, curdled milk.* *T.*, asaŋpinini.

p t e' - a - s a ŋ - p i - t a - s a - k a, *n.* *cheese.* *T.*, asaŋpisamna.

p t e' - a - s a ŋ - p i - w i - g l i, *n.* *T.* *butter; oil of milk.*

p t e' - ć e - d a ŋ, *adj.* *short*—maptećedaŋ. *Ih.*, pćećena; *T.*, ptećela *and* pćećela.

p t e' - ć e - y e - d a ŋ, *adv.* *for a short time.* *T.*, pćelyela.

p t e' - g l e - ś k a, *n.* *T.* *cattle, tame cattle,* so called from being of different colors.

p t e' - ġ a, *n.* *a marsh, a low place, a swampy place.* *T.*, wiwila.

p t e - ġ a ŋ' - n i - ć a - d a ŋ, *n.* *the wren.*

p t e - ġ o' - p e - ć a, *n.* *a kind of hawk,* so called because it frequents marshes. See ćetaŋ, etc.

p t e - h a' h i ŋ - ś m a, *n.* *Ih.* and *T.* *a buffalo robe; buffalo skin; hair thick.*

p t e - h a' - ś l a, *n.* *T.* *a hide with the hair taken off.* See śda.

p t e - h e' - ć a - l a, *n.* *T.* *a calf.* See pteźićadaŋ.

p t e - h i ŋ' - ć a - l a, *n.* *T.* *a calf: i. q.* ptehećala.

p t e - h i ŋ' - p a - ḣ p a, *n.* *T.* *tags of buffalo hair; old matted hair* fallen from buffalo See paḣpa.

p t e - h i ŋ' - ś m a, *n.* *T.* *a thick or long haired buffalo.*

p t e - h i ŋ' - ś m a - h a, *n.* *T.* *a buffalo robe.*

p t e ḣ - w i' - t a, *n.* (pteġa *and* wita) *firm land surrounded by a marsh, a swamp-island.*

p t e n - y e' - d a ŋ, *adv.* *for a short time.* *T.*, pćelyela.

p t e - p t e' - ć e - d a ŋ, *adj.* *red.* of ptećedaŋ.

p t e - t a' - m a - k a, *n.* *a lean cow.*

p t e - t a' - w a - n a - p i ŋ, *n.* *T.* *an ox-yoke.*

pte'-ta-wo-te, *n.* lit. "*buffalo's food*": *a prairie plant which bears juicy berries*

pte-wa'-ḳiŋ, *n.* *T.* *work-oxen.*

pte-wa'-nuŋ-yaŋ-pi, *n.* *tame cattle.* See nuŋyaŋ, *to tame.* *T.*, pte-waŋ'-ni-yaŋ-pi.

pte-wo'-ya-ka, *n.* *T.* *the large grasshopper without wings*, sometimes found in the west. It would seem that they tell of buffalo.

pte-wi'-ye, *n.* *a cow.*

pte-wi'-ye-na, *n.* *Ih.* and *T.* *a cow.*

pte-źi'-ća-daŋ, *n.* (pte *and* ćiŋćadaŋ) *a calf.* *T.*, ptehećala *and* ptehiŋćala

pte-źi'-će-na, *n* *Ih.* *a calf.*

ptiŋ'-haŋ, *n.* *last autumn:* ptiŋhaŋ ićima, *the fall before last.* See ptaŋyetu.

ptu-ḣa', *v. n.* *to crumble down.* *T.*, kaoksa.

ptu-ḣa'-ḣa, *v.* *red.* of ptuḣa.

ptu-ptu'-źa, *red.* of ptuźa.

ptu-ptu'-źa-haŋ, *part.* *red.* of ptuźahaŋ.

ptu-ptu'-źa-wa-haŋ, *part.* *red.* of ptuźawahaŋ.

ptu'-źa, *adj.* *split, cracked.* See yuptuźa.

ptu-źa'-haŋ, *part.* *cracked of itself.*

ptu-źa'-wa-haŋ, *part.* *cracked of itself.*

pu'-ġa, *v. n.* *T.* *to snort*, as a horse when frightened.

pu-kpa', *adj.* *boiled up, not clear, mixed up*, said of water or soup which contains floating particles. See kpukpa.

puŋ-puŋ'-la, *adj.* *T.* *rotten*, as wood.

pu-sa', *adj.* *dry:* pusa elınaka, *to lay aside to dry* or *season:* *i. q.* puza.

pu-skem', *cont.* of puskepa: puskem okaśtaŋ, *to strain* or *filter*—puskem owakaśtaŋ.

pu-ske'-pa, *v. a.* *to strain* or *filter*—wapuskepa. *T.*, *to pour all out, to empty.*

pus-ki'-ya, *v. a.* *to dry* or *cause to dry*, as wet clothes or fruit—puswakiya, pusuŋkiyapi: puskićićiya, *to dry for* one—puswećićiya.

pu-spa', *v. a.* *to stick on, glue; to seal*—wapuspa.

pu-spe'-ki-ya, *v. a.* *to cause to glue* or *seal*—puspewakiya.

pu-spe'-ya, *v. a.* *to cause to seal* or *glue.*

pus-pu'-za, *adj.* *red.* of puza.

pu-stag', *cont.* of pustaka; pustag iwaŋka, *to squat down;* pustag elıpeiçiya, *to get down so as to hide, bow down, squat down.*

pu-stag'-tu-ken, *adv.* *squatting down.*

pu-sta'-ka, *v. n.* *to squat down*—wapustaka. See patuźa.

pus-ya', *v. a.* *to dry, cause to dry*—puswaya, pusuŋyaŋpi.

pus-ya', *adv.* *in a drying manner.*

pus-ya'-kel, *adv.* *T.* *in a drying manner.*

pu-śki', *adv.* *in a bunch:* *i. q.* pśuŋkaya yaŋka. *T.*, pśuŋkayela.

pu-śki'-ća, *v. a.* *to press* or *rub out with the hand*—wapuśkića.

pu-śki'-daŋ, *adv.* *dim.* of puśki.

pu-śkin', *cont.* of puśkića; puśkin yaŋka. *T.*, puśkil.

pu-śkin'-ya, *adv.* *pressed, squeezed*

pu-tag', *cont.* of putaka; putag iḣpaya, *to fall down with the hands on the ground.*

pu-ta'-ka, *v. a.* *to touch,* as with the hand when one falls—waputaka. See pataka.

pu-te', *n.* *the upper lip; the snout* or *nose* of an animal.

pu-te'-hiŋ, *n.* *T.* *the mustache.*

pu-te'-ḣni-yaŋ-yaŋ, *v. n.* *to have the lips quiver with cold.*

Pu'-te-wa-ta, *n p.* *the Potowatomies.*

Pu'-te-wa-ta-daŋ, *n. p.* Same as Putewata.

pu-tiŋ', *n.* See putiŋhiŋ.

pu-tiŋ'-hiŋ, *n.* *the beard,* especially what grows on the upper lip, *the mustache.* *T.*, putehiŋ.

pu-tiŋ'-i-ća-śla, *n.* *T.* *a razor.*

pu-tpa', *adj.* Same as pukpa.

pu-tpe'-ya, *adv.* *scattering, scattered over.* *T.*, pukpeya.

pu'-za, *adj.* *dry, thirsty; dry,* as cloth, ground, etc., *not wet; shallow,* as a stream, *run dry;* puza sni, *dry cold.* See puzedaŋ *and* ipuza.

pu-zan', *cont.* of puzata; puzan iyaya: puzan iyayeya, *to run* one *ashore; to show that one has told a falsehood.* *T.*, puzal.

pu-zan'-zan, *red.* of puzan; puzanzan iyekićićiyapi *and* puzanzan iyayekićiyapi, *they run each other aground.*

pu-za'-ta, *adv.* *on dry land.*

pu'-ze-daŋ, *adj.* *shallow,* as a stream of water; *nearly dry.*

pu'-ze-na, *adj.* *Ih.* *shallow,* as a stream of water: *i. q.* kazedaŋ.

P̣.

p̣, *the twentieth letter of the Dakota alphabet.* It has a *click* or *explosive* sound like that of ç, ḳ, and ṭ.

p̣e, *n.* *the elm;* p̣e ćaŋ, *elm-wood;* p̣e ikćeka, *the common water-elm;* p̣e itazipa (*bow-elm*) *the rock-elm;* p̣e tutupa, *slippery-elm.*

p̣e-i'-kće-ka, *n.* *the common elm.*

p̣e-tuŋ'-tuŋ-pa, *n.* *T.* *the slippery-elm: i. q.* p̣etutupa.

p̣e-tu'-tu-pa, *n.* *the slippery-elm.*

p̣o, *n.* *fog, mist.*

p̣o, *adj.* *foggy, misty.*

p̣o'-p̣o, *adj.* *red.* of p̣o; *foggy.*

p̣o-sa', *adj.* *foggy, not clear;* said when the air is filled with particles of snow.

p̣o'-ze-ća, *v. n.* *to be out of humor*—map̣ozeća. *T.*, iśikćiŋ.

S.

s, *the twenty-first letter of the Dakota alphabet*, having the soft sound of the English *c*. When marked thus (s'), the sound is prolonged.

s'a, *an auxiliary suffix* to verbs, signifying frequency of action, or a habit formed, as, wai s'a, wakaġe s'a. It frequently gives verbs the force of nouns of the agent; as, wamanoŋ, *to steal;* wamanoŋ s'a, *a thief.*

s'a, *v. n.* *to hiss*, as a serpent; s'a waŋka, *lies hissing.*

s'a, *v. n.* *to roar*, as the waves: s'a waŋka. *T.*, s'ayela.

sab, *cont.* of sapa.

sab-ya', *adv* *T.* *darkly, blackly;* sabya yuŋka.

sab-ya', *v. a.* *to blacken*—sabwaya.

sab-ya'-pi, *n.* *T.* *a target, a mark to shoot at; something blackened and set up for a guide:* sabyapi kutepi.

Sag-da'-śiŋ *and* Sag-da'-śa, *n.* *the English*, the name which the Dakotas give to *the British, the inhabitants of Red River*, etc. This word is probably from some other Indian language. *T*, Ṡaglaśa.

sag-ye', *n.* *something used in walking, a staff:* ćaŋ sagye, *a cane;* maza sagye, *a sword.* *T.*, miwakaŋ.

sag-ye'-ki-toŋ, *v.* *to use a staff in walking*, as an old person—sagyewetoŋ

sag-ye'-toŋ, *v.* *to use a staff*—sagyewatoŋ.

sag-ye'-ya, *v. a.* *to use* anything *for a staff*—sagyewaya.

sak, *cont.* of saka; sakowasiŋ yutapi, *eaten raw.*

sa'-ka, *adj.* *raw, uncooked; hard, dried;* as, waćoni saka, *dried meat.* See tasaka.

sa'-ka-daŋ, *adj.* *green, limber.* Hence, ćaŋ sakadaŋ, *a switch.*

sa'-ka-yu-ta-pi, *n.* *what is eaten raw*, i. e., *melons, cucumbers.* *T.*, śpaŋ śni yutapi.

sa-kim', *adv.* *both, two, both together.* *T.*, sakib; nupiŋ sakib, *two side by side.*

sa-kim'-tu, *adv.* *two together.* *T.*, sakibtu.

sa-kim'-tu-ken, *adv.* *both together.*

sak'-o-wa-siŋ, *adv.* *entirely raw.* *T.*, śpaŋ śni.

sam, *adv.* *cont.* of saŋpa; *more, beyond, more than:* sam iyaya, *to go beyond, surpass;* sam iyeya, *to make go over* or *beyond.*

sam, *cont.* of sapa. *T.*, sab.

sam'-i-ye-ya, *adv.* *more than.*

s'a-mna', *adj.* *T.* *smelling sour; stinking.*

s a m - s a m', *adv.* *red.* of sam.

s a m - s a ŋ' - p a, *adv.* *red.* of saŋpa.

s a m - y a', *v. a.* of sapa; *to blacken, color black*—samwaya, samuŋyaŋpi. *T.*, sabya.

s a m - y a', *adv.* *beyond, further; black, dark; T.*, sabya: samya waŋka, *it lies darkly; T.*, sabya yuŋka.

s a m - y a' - h a ŋ, *adv.* *dark, blackish*, as water at a distance. *T.*, sabyahaŋ.

s a m - y a' - k e n, *adj.* *blackish; in sight, far off.*

s a ŋ, *adj.* *whitish* or *yellowish:* maka saŋ, *white earth:* hi saŋ, *to show the teeth.*

s a ŋ - k s a ŋ' - k i - t o ŋ, *v. n.* *to wear* or *put on a skirt*—saŋksaŋwetoŋ: *T.*, ćuwignakakiçuŋ.

s a ŋ - k s a ŋ' - n i - ć a, *n.* *a Dakota woman's skirt. T.*, ćuwignaka.

s a ŋ - k s a ŋ' - y a, *v. a.* *to use for a skirt, make a skirt of*—saŋksaŋwaya. *T.*, ćuwignagya.

s a ŋ - n i', *adj.* *of one side, on one side:* nape saŋni, *one hand;* si saŋni, *one foot.*

s a ŋ - n i' - ć a, *adv.* *on one side.*

s a ŋ - n i' - n a, *adv.* *of only one side. T.*, sanila.

s a ŋ - n i' - n a - t a ŋ - h a ŋ, *adv.* *from only one side.*

s a ŋ - o' - k p u - k p a, *adj.* *T.* *gray; black and white mixed: i. q.* saŋopapa.

s a ŋ' - o - p a - p a, *adj.* *gray hairs here and there* in one's head, *turning gray. T.*, saŋokpukpa.

s a ŋ' - p a, *adv.* *more, more than, over; beyond:* wikćemna saŋpa noŋpa, *two more than ten,* i. e., *twelve;* kitaŋna saŋpa, *a little more;* saŋpa waśte, *better.*

s a ŋ' - p a - t a ŋ - h a ŋ, *adv.* *from beyond.*

s a ŋ p' - s a ŋ - p a, *adv* *red.* of saŋpa.

s a ŋ - t o' - h u, *n.* *a species of grass with a hard round stalk and strong blade.*

s a ŋ - y a ŋ', *v. a.* *to whiten, whitewash*—saŋwaya.

s a ŋ - y a ŋ', *adv.* *whitish:* anpao saŋyaŋ hinapa, *the dawn appears brightly.*

s a' - p a, *adj.* *black*—masapa, nisapa.

s a' - p a - t a ŋ - k a, *n.* *T.* *the spade in playing-cards.*

S a' - p a - w i - ć a - ś a, *n. p.* *the Ute Indians.*

s a' - p a - y u - ġ a - ġ a, *n.* *T.* *the club in playing-cards.*

s a p - s a' - p a, *adj.* *red.* of sapa.

s a' - t a, *n.* *the horizontal stick placed in a tent on which the kettle is hung. T.*, ćeġiyokaśke.

s a - t i ŋ', *adj.* *stretched out straight,* as in death. See botiŋ, katiŋ, etc.

s a - t i ŋ' - t i ŋ, *adj.* *red.* of satiŋ.

s a - t i ŋ' - y e - l a, *adv.* *T* *stretched out,* as one dead.

s a t - i' - y a - k a - ś k e, *n.* *that which ties up* the sata: also sata oiyakaśke.

s' a - y e' - l a, *adv.* *T.* *roaring,* as waves: mini kaataźa s'ayela, *the waves roar.* See s'a wanka.

s b a. See yusba. *T.*, swa

sba-haŋ′, *part.* *ravelled.* *T.*, swahaŋ.

s b a - k a′, *adj.* *T.* *ragged: i. q.* swaka.

s b a - w a′ - h a ŋ, *part.* *ravelled out*

s b u. See kasbu. *T.*, swu.

s b u, *adv.* sbu se ihaŋ, *to fall down with a rushing sound,* as corn poured out

s b u′ - d a ŋ, *n.* *a grain, a small piece, a particle.*

s b u - h a ŋ′, *part.* *crumbling.* *T.*, swuhaŋ.

s b u′ - l a *and* s w u′ - l a, *adj.* *T.* *small, fine.*

s b u - s b u′, *red.* of sbu.

s b u′ - s b u - l a *and* s w u′ - s w u - l a, *adj* *T.* *red.* of sbula.

s b u - w a′ - h a ŋ, *part.* *crumbling, crumbled.*

s ć e - p a ŋ′, *n.* *T.* *i. q.* ićepaŋ.

s ć e - p a ŋ′ - k u, *n.* *T.* *her sister-in-law.*

s ć e - p a ŋ′ - y a, *v.* *T.* *to have for sister-in-law.*

S ć i′ - l i, *n. p.* *T.* *the Pawnee Indians.* The Pawnee Loups call themselves "Ski′-di." See Śćili.

s d a, *n.* *grease, oil, ointment, salve,* etc. *T.*, sla.

s d a - k i′ - y a, *v. a.* *pos.* of sdaya; *to grease, anoint*—sdawakiya, sdauŋkiyapi. *T.*, slakiya.

s d a′ - o - ź u - h a, *n.* *an oil-bag.* *T.*, islaye oźuha.

s d a′ - t a, *adj.* *slow, feeble:* ohaŋ sdata, *slow at work;* oie sdata, *slow of speech.*

s d a′ - t e - ć a, *adj.* *feeble*—masdatećа.

s d a - y a′, *v a.* *to grease* anything, *to anoint*—sdawaya, sdauŋyaŋpi. *T.*, slaya.

s d a - y a′ - o - ź u - p i, *n.* *a rifle-gun,* so called from its greased wads. *T.*, iwoġaġa.

s d e′ - ć a. See kasdeća.

s d e - ć a′ - h a ŋ, *part* *split of itself.*

s d e - ć a′ - w a - h a ŋ, *part.* *split of itself.*

s d i, *adj.* *tapering.*

s d i, *v. a* *to hiss,* as wet wood on the fire, a snake, etc. See nasdi *and* śdi.

s d i m, *cont.* of sdipa; sdim iyeya. *T.*, slib.

s d i m - k i′ - y a, *v. a.* *to cause to lick*—sdimwakiya. *T.*, slibkiya.

s d i m - y a′, *v. a.* See sdimkiya.

s d i′ - p a, *v. a.* *to lick, lick up* anything—wasdipa, uŋsdipapi. *T.*, slipa.

s d i - s d i′, *v* *red.* of sdi.

s d i - s d i′ - p a, *v.* *red.* of sdipa.

s d i - s d i′ - y a, *adv.* *red.* of sdiya; sdisdiya apa, *to strike with a switching sound.*

s d i - t k a′, *adj.* *tapering; rounded off.*

s d i - t k a′ - t k a, *adj.* *red.* of sditka; *knobbed, having knobs* or *grooves running round.*

s d i - y a′, *adv.* *hissing.*

s d o - ć a′, *v. n.* *to know.* *T.*, slolya. See sdonya.

s d o - h a ŋ′, *v. n.* *to crawl*—wasdohaŋ, uŋsdohaŋpi. *T.*, slohaŋ.

sdo-haŋ′-haŋ, *v. red.* of sdohaŋ; *to crawl along*, as in getting near ducks: sdohaŋhaŋ iħpaya mda, *I go creeping along.*

sdon-ki′-ya, *v. pos.* of sdonya; *to know one's own*—sdonwakiya, sdonuŋkiyapi. *T.*, slolkiya.

sdon-ki′-ye-ya, *v. a.* See sdotkiyeya.

sdon-ya′, *v. a. to know, have knowledge of* any thing or person—sdonwaya, sdonyaya, sdonuŋyaŋpi, sdonmayaŋ, sdonćiya. *T.*, slolya.

sdon-ye′-ki-ya, *v. a. to cause to know*—sdonyewakiya, sdonyeuŋkiyapi. *T.*, slolyekiya.

sdon-ye′-ya, *v. a. to cause to know*—sdonyewaya. *T.*, slolyeya.

sdo-sdo′-daŋ, *adj. soft*, as grease. See śdośdodaŋ.

sdot-ki′-ya, *v.* See sdonkiya.

sdot-ki′-ye-ya, *v. a. to cause* one *to know* something *that pertains to himself; to alarm*, as an enemy or game; *to put on one's guard*—sdotkiyewaya. *T.*, slolkiyeya.

sdot-ya′, *v.* See sdonya.

se, *a particle*, used at the end of sentences to give emphasis to what is said. Perhaps it should be regarded as an impersonal verb, *it appears so, it seems to me so, I thought:* hećetu se, *so it seems.*

se, *adv. like, as though.*

se′-ća, *adv. as though, seemingly, I thought so.*

se-će′-ća, *adv. it seems as, as if it was. T.*, selećeća.

se′-će-ći-ḳoŋ, *adv. I had thought so. T.*, selećeće ḉoŋ.

se′-e-će-ća, *adv. as if it was, it seems as if. T.*, selećeća.

se′-hiŋ-gla, *adv. T.*, waŋlaka sehiŋgle ćiŋhaŋ, *if you happen to see him.*

se′-kson, *adv. like.*

se-le′, *adv. T. like; as though.*

se-le′-ća, *adv. T. like as.*

se-le′-će-ća, *adv. T. as if, it seems so.*

se-le-će-će-ḉoŋ, *adv. T. I had thought so.*

sen-ya′, *adv. like, as though. T.*, sele.

sen-ya′-ken, *adv. as though, like.*

se′ wa-ćaŋ-mi, *v. I think it is so.* This form is used when speaking of something that is not distinctly recollected.

so-wi′-mna, *adj. rancid*, as fat that has stood long.

se-ya′, *adv. like as. T.*, se; sele.

se-ya′-ken, *adv. like as.*

si, *cont.* of siha; as siksa, *club-footed.*

si-ćaŋ′, *n. the outside of the thigh.*

Si-ćaŋ′-ġu, *n. p. the Brules; burnt thighs.*

si-ćaŋ′-o-pi-ye, *n.* of sićaŋ; *a side pocket*, as in one's pantaloons or coat; *any pocket.*

si-ća′-psaŋ, *v. to shake the foot*—siwakapsaŋ. See kapsaŋpsaŋ.

si-ćo′-ćo-daŋ, *adj. red.* of sićodaŋ.

si-ćo′-daŋ, *adj.* *bare-footed.* See sićokadaŋ.

si-ćo′-ġaŋ, *n.* *the calf of the leg.*

si-ćo′-ġiŋ, *n.* *T.* *i. q.* sićoġaŋ.

si-ćo′-ka-daŋ, *adj.* *bare-footed*—sićomakadaŋ.

si-ćo′-ka-ka-daŋ, *adj.* *red.* of sićokadaŋ.

si-ću′, *n.* *the sole* or *bottom* of anything: siću wanića, *without a bottom, bottomless, unfathomable.*

si-ću′-ha, *n.* *the sole of the foot, shoe* or *moccasin.*

si-ću′-psaŋ-psaŋ, *v. n.* *to wag the tail,* as a dog. *T.*, siŋtupsaŋpsaŋ.

si-ću′-ta, *adv.* *at the bottom* or *lower part* of anything.

si-ću′-toŋ. See asićutoŋ.

si′-gla-psaŋ-psaŋ, *v.* *T.* *to swing the feet.* See kapsaŋpsaŋ *and* sićapsaŋ.

si-ha′, *n.* *the foot, feet* of man; *the feet* of animals, but especially *the hind feet,* the fore feet being "nape"—misiha, nisiha, uŋsihapi.

Si-ha′-sa-pa, *n. p.* *the Blackfeet Sioux.*

si-hi′-yo-taŋ-i-ye-ki-ya, *v. n.* *to be troubled about the feet, to have no moccasins.* See iyotaŋiyekiya.

si-hu′, *n.* *the bones of the foot; the toes.*

si-ȟa′-pe, *n.* *the hollow of the foot.* *T.*, sioȟape.

si-i′-ći-ya-pa, *v.* *T.* *to strike the feet together in walking.*

si-i′-ći-ya-pa-pa, *v. red.* of siićiyapa. See ap'a.

si-i′-na-taŋ, *n.* *stirrups; pantaloon straps.*

si-i′-pu-śiŋ, *n.* *the ball of the foot.*

si-i′-ta-ka-ha, *n.* *the top of the foot, the instep.*

si-i-yu′-ta, *n.* *a foot measure.*

si-i′-yu-taŋ, *n.* *stirrups.*

si-ksa′, *adj.* *club-footed.*

si-ma′-za-i-na-ȟta-ke, *n.* *T.* *spurs.*

sin-wa′, *v. n.* *Ih.* *to have the temper stirred up.*—J. P. W.

sin-wa′-pa-ki-ya, *v.* *to paddle a canoe by one's self,* as in hunting muskrats—sinwapawakiya.

siŋ-kpe′, *n.* *the muskrat, Mus zibethicus:* *i. q.* siŋtpe.

siŋ-kpe′-i-ća-pe, *n.* *a muskrat spear.*

siŋ-kpe′-i-ću-wa, *n.* *spears, traps, axes,* etc.; *anything used in killing muskrats.*

siŋ-kpe′-on-ze-mna, *n.* *musk.*

siŋ-kpe′-ta-wo-te, *n.* *calamus, sweetflag, the Acorus calamus.*

siŋ-siŋ′, *adj.* *besmeared, slimed,* as with fish; *dried on, glued* or *glazed over.* See sisiŋ.

siŋ-te′, *n.* *the tail* of an animal.

siŋ-te′-haŋ-ska, *n.* *T.* *a young buck, a rowdy.*

siŋ-te′-ȟda, *n.* *the tail-rattler,* i. e. *the rattlesnake.*

Siŋ-te′-ȟda-wi-ća-śa, *n. p.* *the Snakes: the Comanches.*

siŋ-te′-ȟla, *n.* *T.* *i. q.* siŋteȟda.

si-ŋ-te′-po-ȟa, *n.* *Ih.* *a species of wolf.* See śuŋktokeća.

siŋ-te′-sa-pe-na, *n.* *the black-tailed deer; the prince of American deer.*

siŋ-te′-ska, *n.* *white-tail; deer, rabbits,* etc., are sometimes so called.

siŋ-te′-śda, *n.* *the opossum; rats.* *T.*, hituŋktaŋka.

siŋ-to′-mni, *adv.* See sitomni.

siŋ-toŋ′-pa-hu, *n.* *the tail bone; the os coccyx* in man.

siŋ-tpe′, *n.* *the muskrat.* Same as siŋkpe.

siŋ-tpe′-ta-wo-te, *n.* Same as siŋkpetawote.

si-o′-ȟa-pe, *n.* *T.* *the hollow of the foot.*

si-o′-ka-zuŋ-te, *n.* *T.* *the spaces between the toes.* *T.*, siyokaźa.

si-pa′, *n.* *the toes, the end of the big toe.*

si-pa′-huŋ-ka, *n.* *the great toe.* The Titoŋwaŋ use sipahuŋka for *the toes* in general. Sipahuŋka taŋka, *the big toe;* sipahuŋka ćiķala, *the little toe;* sipahuŋka iyokihe, *the toe next the great toe:* sipahuŋka ćokaya, *the middle toe;* and sipahuŋka ćiķala iyokihe, *the toe next the little one.*—W. J. C.

si-pa′-ksi-ze, *n.* *the lower part of the leg of animals: the hind toes* of animals.

si-piŋ′-kpa, *n.* (sipa *and* iŋkpa) *the toes; the jointsof the foot.*

si-piŋ′-tpa, *n* Same as sipiŋkpa.

si-pu′-te, *n.* *the breech* or *lower part* of a gunstock, *the end of the* pahu; *the screw in the end of the barrel, the breech-screw.*

si-saŋ′-ni, *n.* *one foot, the foot on one side.*

si-siŋ′, *n.* Mr. Renville considers this word synonymous with "wiwi," *a swamp,* and as the source whence the Sisitoŋwaŋs derived their name. But more recent authority makes "sisiŋ" to be *i. q.* hoğaŋmna or sićamna. Thus the Sisitoŋwaŋ villages were "sisiŋ" on account of the old fish-bones and putrid fish lying about They lived chiefly on fish. See siŋsiŋ.

Si-si′-toŋ-waŋ, *n. p.* *a band of the Dakotas* living at Swan Lake, Little Rock, at the Two Woods on the Coteau, and at Lake Traverse. They probably number about three thousand.

si-śa′-śte, *n.* *the little toe* of animals and man.

si-to′-mni, *adv.* *all over, throughout: i. q.* siŋtomni. See oćowasiŋ.

si-to′-mni-yaŋ, *adv.* *all over*

si-toŋ′-pa-hu, *n.* *the tail bone.* See siŋtoŋpahu.

si-ye′-te, *n.* *the heel.*

si-ye′-te-i-ya-he, *n.* *the ball of the heel.*

si-yo′-ka-źa, *n.* *T.* *the spaces between the toes: i. q.* siokazuŋte.

si-yo′-źaŋ, *n.* *between the toes: i. q.* siokazuŋte.

si-yu'-kaŋ, *n.* *the tendon of the heel.*

si-yu'-kaŋ-śa-śa-daŋ, *n* *a bird having slender reddish legs;* the pehaŋkadaŋ.

si-yu'-ka-za, *n.* *the toes.* See sipa *and* sipahuŋka.

ska, *adj.* *white; clear,* as, mini ska, *clear water: clean, new,* as, hiŋ ska, *new hair; pure in any respect:* taku ska, *nothing.*

skad, *cont.* of skadaŋ; taku skad.

ska'-daŋ, *adj. dim.* of ska; *white:* taku skadaŋ, *nothing:* Skadaŋ-ti, a common name for *Traverse des Sioux,* Skadaŋ having been the Dakota name of Mons. Provençalle, an early trader in that place. *T.,* skala.

skaŋ, *v. n.* *to dissolve, disappear, melt away,* as snow: wa skaŋ.

skaŋ'-yaŋ, *v. n.* *to melt, thaw.*

ska-ska', *v. red.* of ska.

ska-ska'-daŋ, *n.* *white beads.* *T.,* śipto skaska.

ska-ya', *v. a* *to whiten, make* anything *white.*

ska'-ya, *adv.* *white;* wa skaya waŋka, *the snow lies white.*

ska-ya'-kel, *adv.* *T.* *purely, undefiled;* skayakel uŋ, *to be pure; chaste,* as a saintly person.

ska-ye'-la, *adv.* *purely; whitish.*

skem, *cont.* of skepa. *T.,* skeb.

skem-ya', *v. a.* *to draw all out,* as a fluid, *to exhaust*—skemwaya. *T.,* skebya.

ske'-pa, *v. n.* *to leak out slowly, escape, pass away by evaporation,* as fluids.

ske-ske'-pa, *v.* *red.* of skepa.

ski'-ća. See kaskića.

ski-ća'-haŋ, *part.* *pressed down, close.*

ski-ća'-wa-haŋ, *part.* *pressed.*

ski-ska', *n.* *the wood-duck*

ski-ski'-ća, *red.* of skića.

ski-ski'-ća-haŋ, *part.* *all pressed together.*

ski-ski'-ća-wa-haŋ, *part.* *pressed together.*

ski-ski'-ta, *red.* of skita; *to be marked,* as a log by worms under the bark. See yuskiskita.

ski-ski-ta, *n.* *a strip of land pressed* or *hemmed in, an isthmus.*

ski'-ta, *adj.* *tied, bound, fastened,* as a child on a board. See yuskita.

sku, *adj.* *broken out a little.* See basku.

sku'-mna, *adj.* *sourish; savory; smelling badly* or *sour,* as the scalp when dirty.

sku'-sku, *red.* of sku; *shaved off:* pa skusku.

sku-sku'-ya, *adj. red.* of skuya.

sku'-ya, *adj.* *sweet; sour; salt.* The radical idea may be that of *having taste* or *savor.*

sku'-ye-ya, *v. a* *to make salt, give taste to*—skuyewaya, skuyeuŋyaŋpi.

sla-ki'-ya, *v.* *T.* *to anoint one's own.*

sla-ki'-ya-pi, *n.* *T.* *ointment; grease for greasing.*

sla'-ya, *v.* *T.* *to grease; to anoint:* *i. q.* sdaya.

sli-hiŋ'-gle, *n.* *T.* *the report of a gun.*

sliŋ'-hiŋ-gla, *v.* *T.* *to fire a shot;* sliŋ wahiŋgla. *n.* *a shot fired, report of a gun.*

slol-i'-çi-ya, *v. reflex.* *T.* *to know one's self.*

slol-ya', *v.* *T.* *to know:* *i. q.* sdonya.

slol-ye'-i-çi-ya, *v.* *T.* *to make one's self known.*

smag, *cont.* of smaka.

smag-smag'-ya, *adv.* *red.* of smagya.

smag-ya', *adv.* *indented, concave:* smagya waŋka.

smag-ya'-ken, *adv.* *indented.*

sma'-ka, *adj.* *hollow, concave.*

sma'-ka, *n.* *a hollow, a sunken place.* See osmaka.

smi, *adj.* See smismi.

smiŋ. See basmiŋ.

smi-smi', *adj.* *clear of limbs,* as a tree, *stripped.* See smiyaŋ.

smi-smi'-yaŋ, *adv.* *T.* *destitute, deprived of everything.*

smi-wa'-haŋ, *part.* *fallen off bare.*

smi'-yaŋ. See smiyaŋyaŋ

smi-yaŋ'-yaŋ *or* smiŋ-yaŋ-yaŋ, *adj.* *clean, nothing extraneous sticking to, bare, smooth,* as a worn blanket: taŋ smiyaŋyaŋna, *alone, having no relatives.*

sna, *v. n* *to ring.* See kasna.

sna-haŋ', *part.* *ringing, rustling;* as leaves falling in autumn.

sna-haŋ'-haŋ, *red.* of snahaŋ; *falling off, rustling.*

sna-sna', *red.* of sna; *to ring, rattle.*

sna-sna'-na, *adj.* *bare,* as a tree when its leaves have all fallen off.

sna-sna'-wa-haŋ, *part.* *red.* of snawahaŋ.

sna-wa'-haŋ, *part.* *ringing, rattling.*

sna'-za, *v. n* *to draw up,* as burnt skin; *to be scarred.*

sna' za, *n.* *a scar*

sni, *adj.* *cold,* as the weather, or as ice; *gone out,* as a fire: peta sni, *the fire is out;* sni kaeś, *although it is cold.*

sni, *n* *cold;* sni au, *cold is coming;* sni aya, *it grows cold.*

sni-sni', *adj.* *red.* of sni; haŋ snisni, *cold nights.*

sni'-ya-ho-ta, *v. n.* *to take cold, draw in the cold by breathing*—snimdahota, snidahota, sniuŋyahotapi.

sni-yaŋ', *v.* sniyaŋ uya, *to become cold, grow cold,* said of the weather changing to cold.

sni'-yaŋ-ṭa, *v.* *to die without apparent cause; to die suddenly.*

so. See soso.

so, *adv.* *T.* a question-mark; *i. q.* he, hwo; hee so, *is that it?*

sok-so'-ta, *adj.* *red* of sota: iśta soksota, *clear eyes.* This word is used in reference to the clear blue eyes of some children.

sol, *cont.* of sota; *T.*

son, *cont.* of sota; son iyeya. *T.*, sol.

son-ki'-ya, *v. a.* from the root sota, *used up, expended; to use up* or *destroy for* one, as to burn up fence-rails or wood for one—sonwakiya, sonmakiya. *T.*, solkiya. See kasota, yusota, etc.

son-ya', *adv* of sota; sonya iyaya, *to become a little whitish* or *clouded.*

soŋ, *v. a.* *to plait* or *braid*, as hair; *to braid*, as corn in strings—wasoŋ, uŋsoŋpi.

soŋ'-pi, *n.* *braids, strings* of corn.

so-so', *v. a.* *to cut into strings*, as a hide—wasoso, uŋsosopi: ćaŋte masosopi seća, *it seems as if my heart was cut into strings*, i. e., *I am greatly afflicted.*

so-so'-pi, *n.* *a strip* or *string cut from a hide.*

so'-ta, *adj.* *clear*, but not perfectly so; *slightly clouded*, but not turbid; *of a milky whitish appearance; sky-colored:* Wakpa minisota, *the Minnesota River;* Mde minisota, *Clear Lake: used up.* See kasota, yusota, *and* sonkiya.

so-tka'-zi, *adj.* *smoked*, as an old tent. See śotkazi.

spaŋ, *adj.* *soft*, as melting snow.

spaŋ, *v. n.* *to become soft, melt*, as snow: wa spaŋ. See śpaŋ.

spaŋ-yaŋ', *v. a.* *to cause to thaw*, as snow—spaŋwaya.

spa-spa'-ya, *red.* of spaya.

spa'-ya, *v. n.* *to be wet*, as clothes, *wet with water, moist, damp*—maspaya, uŋspayapi: *to sink in water, to drown:* spaya iyaya. See staŋka.

spa'-ye-ya, *v. a.* *to wet, cause to be wet* or *moist*—spayewaya.

spe'-ya, *v. a.* *to sink, make sink.* See aspeya.

stag, *cont.* of staka

stag-ya', *v. a.* *to make feeble*—stagwaya.

stag-ya', *adv.* *feebly, languidly.*

stag-ya'-ken, *adv.* *feebly:* stagyaken wauŋ.

stag-ye'-la, *adv.* *T.* *feebly.*

sta'-ka, *adj.* *feeble, languid, without appetite, weary, not able to walk*—mastaka. See ḣpeća *and* stusta; *also* śtaśta.

sta'-ka, *v. n.* *T.* *to be sick: i. q.* wayazaŋ—mastaka.

staŋ, *adj.* *moist, wet.* See pastaŋ. *T*, spaya.

staŋ, *adj.* *purple, grape-colored:* śa staŋ, *dark red;* ha staŋ, *dark complexioned.*

staŋ'-ka, *adj* *purple.* See staŋ.

staŋ-ka', *adj.* *moist.*

sto, *adj.* *smooth, lying smooth*, as hair. See kasto.

sto'-daŋ, *adj.* *small and neat*—mastodaŋ. See ćistiŋna *and* okiyatakeća.

sto-sto', *adj.* *red.* of sto; *smooth, lying flat.*

sto-ya', *v. a.* *to make smooth, smooth down*—stowaya.

sto-ya', *adv.* *smoothly.*

sto-ya'-ken, *adv.* *smoothly.*

sto-ye'-la, *adv.* *T* *smoothly.*

stu-sta', *adj.* *tired, weary, unable to move*—mastusta. See staka.

s t u - s t e' - y a, *v. a.* *to cause fatigue, to weary*—stustewaya.

s u, *n.* *the seed* of anything, *grain; bullets:* su waŋźidaŋ, *a bullet;* mazasu, *lead.*

s u, *adj.* *good.* Probably obsolete. See yasu, suya, ćo, *and* pi.

s u - ć i' - k ć i - ḳ a - d a ŋ, *n.* *shot.* *T.*, sukpaŋla

su-ći'-kći-ḳa-daŋ-se-ća, *n.* *pepper, allspice.* *T.*, yamnumnuġapi.

s u - k a' - z a, *n.* *a grain* of anything, *a particle, one, the smallest part.* Hence, napsukaza, *the fingers.*

s u - k p a' - l a *or* s u - k p a ŋ' - l a, *n.* *T.* *shot:* *i. q.* sućikćiḳadaŋ.

s u - k p a' - n a, *n.* *Ih.* *shot.*

s u - k s u' - t a, *adj.* *red.* of suta.

s u - m a' - n i - ć a, *n.* *any kind of wood that has become dead and very hard.* *T.*, ćaŋ śeća.

s u ŋ, *n.* *cont.* of suŋka; misuŋ, *my younger brother*, used in addressing him.

s u ŋ, *v.* *to braid.* See soŋ.

s u ŋ' - k a, *n.* *a younger brother* either of a man or woman. Certain cousins are likewise so called—misuŋka, nisuŋka.

s u ŋ - k a' - k i - ć i - y a - p i, *n.* *brethren, those related as brothers*—suŋkauŋkićiyapi.

s u ŋ - k a' - k u, *n.* *his* or *her younger brother.*

s u ŋ - k a' - y a, *v. a.* *to have for younger brother*—sunkawaya, suŋkauŋyaŋpi.

s u ŋ' - t a, *n.* *a stem:* ćaŋduhupa suŋta, *a pipe-stem;* ćaŋkasuŋta, *the spinal marrow.* *T*, suŋte.

s u ŋ - z i ŋ' - ć a *or* s u ŋ - z i' - ć a, *n.* *T* *the yellow hammer:* *i. q.* zuŋziŋća.

s u - s b e' - ć a, *n.* *the ant-eater, the mosquito-hawk.* *T.*, susweća.

s u - s b e' - ć a - k a - ġ a - p i, *n.* *a cross.* See ćaŋsusbeća.

S u - s o' - n i, *n. p.* *the Shoshones.* Perhaps Su-su'-ni is better.

s u - s u', *n.* *the testicles:* susu eḣpeya *and* susu baśdoka, *to castrate.*

s u - t a', *adj.* *hard, not yielding to the touch; strong, capable of endurance; firm; strong,* as coffee or tobacco—masuta, nisuta, uŋsutapi: ćaŋte suta, *courageous; stubborn.*

s u - t a' - y a, *adv.* *firmly, hard.*

s u - t a' - y a - k e n, *adv.* *firmly.*

s u - t o ŋ', *v. n.* *to ripen, have seed; to be ripe, fit for use,* as corn, etc.

s u - y a', *adv.* of su; *rightly, well.* *T.*, taŋyaŋ. See ayucoya *and* piya.

s w a - k a', *adj.* *T.* *ragged:* *i. q.* sbaka.

Ś.

ś, *the twenty-second letter of the Dakota alphabet*, with the sound of *sh* in English. When marked thus (ś') its sound is prolonged.

ś, *intj. hist! i. q.* śi; but the sibilant, with no vowel sound, is used.

śa, *adj. red*

śa, *conj. Ih.* and *T. i. q.* eśta *and* eśa.

ś'a, *v. n. to shout*—waś'a, yaś'a, uŋś'api.

śag-i'-ç̣i-ya, *v. reflex. to restrain one's self*—śagmiç̣iya.

Śa-gla'-śa, *n. p. T. an Englishman; the English: i. q.* Sagdaśiŋ.

śa-glo'-ġaŋ, *num. adj. T eight.*

ś'ag-ś'a'-ka, *n. corn boiled without hulling. T.*, ćatipaslaye śni ohaŋpi.

śag-ya', *v.* See śagiç̣iya.

śa-hdo'-ġaŋ, *num. adj. eight. T.*, śagloġaŋ. *Ih.*, śakdoġaŋ

śa-hdo'-ġaŋ-na, *adv. only eight.*

śa-hdo'-hdo-ġaŋ, *adv. by eights. T.*, śagloġaŋġaŋ.

ś'a'-hiŋ-hda, *v. to burst out with a shout.*

Śa-hi'-ye-na, *n. p. the Cheyennes.*

śa'-i-a, *v. n to speak a strange language*—śaiwaa.

śa'-i-a-pi, *n. a foreign* or *unknown language.*

śa'-ka, *adj. easy.* See bośaka, kaśaka, waśakadaŋ

ś'a'-ka, *adj. strong.* See waś'aka, yuś'aka.

ś'a'-ka, *adj. difficult, hard.* See ś'akeća. *T.*, teȟika

śa-ke', *n. the nails* of the fingers and toes; *the claws* of birds and beasts; *the hoofs* of animals.

ś'a'-ke-ća, *adj. hard to deal with, severe, austere*—maś'akeća, uŋś'akapika. *T.*, teȟika.

śa-ke'-haŋ-ska, *n. long-claws*, a name given to *the grizzly bear.*

śa-ki'-ya, *v. a to paint red, to redden*, as the Dakotas do scalps—śawakiya, śauŋkiyapi. 2. *to make glad by gifts.*

śa-ko'-wiŋ, *num. adj. seven.*

śa-ko'-wiŋ-na, *adv. only seven.*

śa-ko'-wiŋ-wiŋ, *adv. by sevens.*

śa'-kpe, *num. adj. six.*

Śa'-kpe-daŋ, *dim.* of śakpe; *Little Six*, the name of a Dakota chief at Tiŋtatoŋwe.

śa'-kpe-kpe, *adv. by sixes.*

ś'ak-ś'a'-ka, *n.* of ś'aka, *hard; corn boiled without being hulled.* See ś'agś'aka.

śam-ya', *v. a* of śapa; *to soil, to defile*—śamwaya. *T.*, śabya.

śam-ya', *adv. dirtily.*

śaŋ, *n. the vagina.*

śaŋ'-haŋ, *conj.* *Ih.* *i. q.* eśtaŋhaŋ, *although.*

śaŋ-haŋś', *adv.* *T.* *well; oh well!* oȟaŋkoya maḳu śaŋhaŋś, *well, hurry and give it me.* See śehaŋś.

śaŋ-ke', *n.* *a step-mother; a father's other wife.*

śaŋ-ke'-ya, *v. a.* *to have for* śaŋke—śaŋkewaya.

śa'-pa, *adj.* *dirty, defiled, blackened*—maśapa: nape niśapa, *thy hands are dirty.*

śa-pe' sto-la, *n.* of pesto; *the diamond in cards.* See kado.

śap-śa'-pa, *adj. red.* of śapa.

śa-śa', *adj.* *red.* of śa; *red.*

śa-śa'-ya, *v. a.* *to dye* or *paint red*—śaśawaya.

śa-śa'-ya, *adv.* *redly.*

śa-śte', *n.* *the little finger:* siśaśte, *the little toe; the little toe* or *nail* of birds and beasts

śa-śte'-i-yo-ki-he, *n.* *that which is next to the little finger, the third finger.*

śa-ta'-ćaŋ-te, *n.* *T.* *the heart in playing-cards.* See taćaŋta.

Śa-wa'-la, *n. p.* *the Shawnees.*

śa-ya', *v. a.* *to make red, to paint red*—śawaya.

śa-ya', *adv.* *redly.*

śa-ye'-daŋ, *adv.* *reddish:* śayedaŋ naźiŋ.

śbe, *adj.* *deep,* as water; *dense,* as foliage; *thick set,* as hair. *T.*, śme. See śma.

śbe'-ya, *adv.* *deeply, densely.* *T.*, śmeya.

śbe-ya'-ta, *adv.* *in the deep.* *T.*, śmeyata.

śbu, *v. n.* *to drop,* as water or any other liquid. *T.*, ś'e.

śbu-śbu', *v. red.* of śbu. *T.*, ś'eś'e.

śbu-ya', *v. a.* *to drop* or *cause to drop,* as water—śbuwaya, śbuuŋyaŋpi. *T.*, ś'eya.

śbu-ya'-pi, *n.* *a drop, drops.* *T.*, ś'eyapi.

Śći'-li, *n. p.* *the Pawnees,* so called by the Teeton Sioux, as distinguished from the Rees—probably meaning *incorporated.* See Sćili.

śda, *adj.* *bald, bare, naked:* nasu śda, *bald-headed;* paśdayapi, *corn made bald,* i. e., *hominy.* See kaśda. *T.*, śla.

śda-śda', *adj.* *red.* of śda. *T.*, ślaśla.

śda-ya', *v. a.* *to make bare*—śdawaya, śdauŋyaŋpi. *T.*, ślaya.

śda-ya', *adv.* *nakedly, without covering.*

śda-ya'-ta, *adv.* *in an open place.*

śda-ye'-hna, *adv.* *openly, exposed, in full view, uncovered, without a house, defenseless:* śdayehna haŋ, *standing out, unsheltered;* śdayehna waŋka, *to sleep out.* *T.*, ślayegna, also *clearly, so as to be easily understood.*

śda-ye'-hna-yaŋ, *adv.* *unsheltered.* *T.*, ślayegnayaŋ.

śdi, *adj.* *many.* *T.*, ota.

śdi, *adv.* *hissing, fizzing.* Said of the noise sometimes made by fish in water. See sdi.

ś d o, *v. n.* *to fuse, melt,* as metals. *T.*, ślo.

ś d o - k a', *n.* *a kind of spotted duck.*

ś d o' - k a. See kaśdoka.

ś d o - k a' - h a ŋ, *part.* *out of place,* as an ax-head off the handle, or an eye out of its socket.

ś d o - k a' - w a - h a ŋ, *part.* Same as śdokahaŋ.

ś d o - ś d o', *v.* *red.* of śdo. *T.*, śloślo.

ś d o - ś d o', *adj.* *soft,* as fat, *melted.*

ś d o - ś d o' - d a ŋ, *n.* *the soft fat parts* in an animal. *T.*, pakśiŋ. See sdosdodaŋ.

ś d o' - ś d o - d a ŋ, *n.* *the meadow-lark:* śdośdodaŋ kiźo, *to whistle to the meadow-lark.*

ś d o - y a', *v. a.* *to fuse, melt,* or *smelt* metals—śdowaya, śdouŋyaŋpi. *T.*, śloya.

ś d o - y a' - p i, *n.* *that which is melted:* śdoyapidaŋ *and* maza śdoyapi, *pewter.*

ś d u n - y a', *v. a.* *to cause to slip.* *T.*, ślulya.

ś d u - ś d u' - t a, *adj.* *slippery,* as a road; *smooth,* as ice, etc. *T.*, śluśluta.

ś d u' - t a, *adj.* *slipping.* See yuśduta, naśduta.

ś' e, *v. n.* *T.* *to drop,* as water. See śbu.

ś e' - ć a, *adj.* *dry, dead,* as wood, *rotten.*

ś e - h a ŋ ś', *adv.* *T.* denoting *impatience:* luha hećiŋhaŋ maku yo śehaŋś, *if you have it, give it to me at any rate.* See śaŋhaŋś.

ś e - h a ŋ ś' - k a, *adv.* *T.* *at any rate:* śehaŋśka hihaŋna ećamoŋ kte lo, *at any rate I will do it to-morrow.*

ś e - h a ŋ ś' - k a - l a - k a, *adv.* *T.*, śehaŋśkalaka oḣaŋkoya mayaku śni wamatehaŋ, *it is a long time, so now give it me quickly.*

ś e - h a ŋ ś' - t u - k a, *adv* *T.* *well, but.*

ś e - k ś e' - ć a, *adj.* *red.* of śeća.

ś e n - y a', *adv.* *withered; dried* or *drying, seasoning:* śenya hiyeya. *T.*, śelya.

ś e n - y a', *v. a.* *to make dry, cause to wither*—śenwaya: śenya eḣnaka, *to lay up to season.* *T.*, śelya.

ś e' - p a ŋ, *n.* *Ih.* *i. q.* ićepaŋ. See sćepaŋ.

ś i, *v. a.* *to command, bid; to ask.* This word is always preceded by another verb, as, ećoŋ śi, eye śi, etc.—waśi, yaśi, uŋśipi.

ś i, *v. imperat.* *stop, be still.*

ś i, *intj.* *hist! hark!* Used to call attention *privately.* See ś.

ś i' - ć a, *adj.* *bad, ugly; bad, wicked*—maśića, niśića, uŋśićapi.

ś i - ć a' - h o - w a - y a, *v. n.* *to scream out, to moan*—śićahowamda, śićahowada.

ś i - ć a' - h o - w a - y a, *adv.* *T.* *moaning, screaming:* śićahowaya wauŋ.

ś i - ć a' - k i - ḣ o, *v. a.* *to do one's work badly*—śićawakiḣo.

ś i - ć a' - m n a, *adj.* *bad smelling.*

ś i - ć a' - w a - c i ŋ, *adv.* *thoughtlessly, hurriedly:* śićawaćiŋ wau, *I came in haste* or *thoughtlessly.*

śi-ća'-wa-ćiŋ, *v. n.* T. *to be frightened; to hurry overmuch; to scream out.*

śi-ća'-ya, *adv.* *badly, not well.*

śi-ća'-ya-ken, *adv.* *badly.*

śi-će'-ća, *n.* *children, family*—mitaśićeća. *T.*, wakaŋheźa.

śi'-će-da, *v. a.* *to esteem as bad, to hate*—śićewada, śićeuŋdapi. *T*, śićela. See waȟtedaśni.

śi'-će-da-ka, *v.* *to think bad, to hate*—śićewadaka, śićeyadaka, śićeuŋdakapi, śićećidaka.

śi'-će-ki-ći-da-pi, *v. recip.* *hating each other.*

śi'-će-ki-da, *v.* *pos.* of śićeda; *to hate one's own*—śićewakida. *T.*, śićekila.

śi'-će-ki-da'-ka, *v.* *pos.* of śićedaka; *to hate one's own*—śićewakidaka.

śi-ći'-taŋ-ka, *adj.* *passionate*—śićimataŋka. *T.*, waćiŋke.

śi-ći'-ṭe, *adj.* *T.* (śića *and* iṭa) *very bad; worthless;* lit. *dead of badness.*

śi-ći'-ya, *v. n.* *to be angry*—śićiwaya. *T*, ćaŋzeka.

śi-ći'-ye-ki-ya, *v.* *to mourn for*—śićiyewakiya. *T.*, waśigla; aćeya.

śi-ćo'-ki-ya, *v. a.* of śića *and* okiya; *to speak evil to.*

śi-ḉe', *n.* *a woman's brother-in-law;* a woman calls her husband's brother and her sister's husband, śiḉe: śiḉeću *and* śiḉeku, *her brother-in-law.*

śi-ḉe'-ku, *n.* See śiḉe.

śi-ḉe'-śi, *n.* *a woman's male cousin;* śiḉeśitku, *her male cousin.*

śi-ḉe'-śi-ya, *v. a.* *to have for* or *call* śiḉeśi—śiḉeśiwaya.

śi-ḉe'-ya, *v. a.* *to have for* śiḉe—śiḉewaya.

śi-hda', *v. n.* *to be* or *become angry, take offense at*—śinwahda, śinyahda, śinuŋhdapi. In this word an *n* is introduced before the pronouns. See sinwa.

śi-hda'-pi, *n.* *anger, wrath.*

śi-hda'-ya, *v.a.* *to make angry, provoke*—śihdawaya, śihdauŋyaŋpi.

śi-ȟaŋ', *v. n.* *to behave badly*—śiwaȟaŋ. *T.*, śilȟaŋ.

śi-ȟaŋ'-yaŋ, *adv.* *behaving badly.* *T.*, śilȟaŋyaŋ.

siȟ-ćiŋ'-yaŋ, *adv.* *T.* *sternly, severely.*

śiȟ-ćiŋ'-yaŋ kel, *adv.* *T.* *crossly.*

śi'-ȟtiŋ, *adj.* *feeble, stupid, lazy, sick*—maśiȟtiŋ, uŋśiȟtiŋpi. *T.*, śiŋȟtiŋ, *bad; poorly made, imperfect.*

śi-ȟtiŋ'-ya, *v. a.* *to enfeeble*—śiȟtiŋwaya, śiȟtiŋmayaŋ.

śi-ȟtiŋ'-yaŋ, *adv.* *feebly.* *T.*, śiŋȟtiŋyaŋ.

śik-śi'-ća, *adj.* *red.* of śića.

śik-śi'-ća-ya, *adv.* *badly.*

śik-śil', *cont. red.* *T.* *badly:* śikśil iś taku tokoŋka, *he does very badly.*

śik-śil'-o-ȟaŋ, *v.* *T.* *to act badly; do wickedly.*

śik-śil'-o-ȟaŋ-ka, *n.* *T.* *one who does badly*

śik-śiŋ'-ya, *adv.* *red.* of śiŋya; *badly.*

śil-la', *v.* *T.* *to esteem bad*—śilwala. See śićeda.

śil-ya', *adv.* *T.* *badly.*

śil-ya'-kel, *adv.* *T.* *badly.*

śil-ye'-la, *adv.* *T.* *sadly, badly.*

śi-na', *n.* *a blanket, a cloak* or *shawl, anything worn as a blanket.* Henok thinks this should be written śiŋna, but, as A. Renville does not agree with him, the shorter orthography is preferred.

śi-na'-a-pa-ḣda-te, *n.* *ribbon, ferret.*

śi-na'-a-pa-ḣda-te-śok-śo-ka, *n.* *cotton ferret.*

śi-na'-a-pa-ḣda-te-zib-zi-pe-daŋ, *n.* *silk ribbon.*

śi-na'-ćaŋ-ko-he, *n.* *T.* *a blanket with bead-work across the middle.*

Śi-na'-gle-gle-ġa, *n. p.* *the Navajos.*

śi-na'-hiŋ-śma, *n.* *Ih.* *a buffalo robe.*

śi-na'-ḣo-ta, *n.* *the common white blanket.*

śi-na'-i-kće-ka. *n.* *T.* *a buffalo robe.*

śi-na'-i-pa-ta-pi, *n.* *T.* *a robe ornamented with quill-work.*

śi-na'-ka-su-pi, *n.* *T.* *a fringed shawl.*

śi-na'-o-ki-pa-ta, *n.* *T.* *a quilt made of pieces.*

śi-na'-o-pa-puŋ-ći-stiŋ-na, *n.* *a blanket with a small border, savelist cloth.*

śi-na'-o-pa-puŋ-ḣo-ta, *n.* *gray-list cloth.*

śi-na'-o-pa-puŋ ska, *n.* *white list* and *stroud.*

si-na'-o-pe-he, *n.* *T.* *a bale of blankets.*

śi-na'-o-pi-ye, *n.* *a bale of blankets.* *T.*, śina opehe.

śi-na'-śa, *n.* *a red blanket.*

śi-na'-to, *n.* *blue skirt cloth; a blue* or *green blanket.*

śi-na'-to-zib-zi-pe-daŋ, *n.* *blue broadcloth.*

śi-na'-wa-to-pe-ki-ya, *v.* *to go by sails, to sail*—śinawatopewakiya.

śi-na'-wa-to-pe-ki-ya-pi, *n.* *sails.*

śi-na'-zib-zi-pe-daŋ, *n.* *broadcloth.*

śi-na'-źaŋ-źaŋ, *n.* *a red blanket.* *T.*, sina ḣota śa.

śin-ya', *adv.* *badly, sadly.* *T.*, śilya.

śin-ya'-ken, *adv.* *badly, sadly:* ćaŋte śinyaken. *T.*, śilyakel.

ś'iŋ, *intj.* *T.* *begone!*

śiŋ, *n.* *the fat part* of animals, especially *fat meat,* as, kukuśe śiŋ, *fat pork; the sappy part* of wood.

śiŋ-ḣtiŋ', *adj.* *T..* *bad, imperfect.*

śiŋ-ḣtiŋ'-ya, *v.* *T.* *to injure.*

śiŋ-ḣtiŋ'-yaŋ, *adv.* *T* *badly, imperfectly.*

śiŋ-hda', *adj.* See śihda.

śiŋ-kpaŋ'-ka, *n.* See śiŋkpaŋkahu.

śiŋ-kpaŋ'-ka-hu, *n.* *the name of a root that,* it is said, *grows in low grounds.*

śiŋ-ta′, *n.* *the tamarack* or *hackmatack, the American larch.* This is probably so called because *the gum is hard, i. e.*, śiŋ tasaka. The original name seems to have been "makaŋ."—S. W. P.

śiŋ-ta′-ka, *n.* *the striped bass.*

śiŋ-tka′-hu, *n.* *the hip-bone, the os ilium.* *T.*, śiŋtkaŋhu.

śiŋ-tpaŋ′-ka, *n.* *a root that grows*, it is said, *in low ground:* śiŋtpaŋkahu, *the stalk and root* above referred to.

śiŋ-śiŋ′, *adj.* *wrinkled.*

śiŋ-yaŋ′-ta-ka-daŋ, *n.* *the name of a small bird* which frequents the rice lakes.

śi-pa′. See kaśipa, yuśipa.

śi-pa′-haŋ, *part.* *broken off close*, as the limbs of a tree, the teeth of a comb, pins, etc.

śi-pa′-wa-haŋ, *part.* Same as śipahaŋ.

śi-pto′, *n.* *beads.*

śi-pto′-la, *n.* *T.* *i. q.* psiŋćiŋća.

śi-pto′-pto, *n.* *beads.*

śi-pu′-te, *n.* *T.* *the pit of the stomach*, i. e., *below the navel.*

śi-śo′-ka, *n.* *the robin.*

śi-tki′-hda, *v. n.* *to be angry; to be afflicted;* śitkihda wauŋ.

śi-tki′-hda-ya, *v.* *to make angry; to afflict, to punish*—śitkihdawaya.

śi-tki′-hda-ya, *adv.* *in trouble, angrily, vexed:* śitkihdaya wauŋ.

śi-u′-ta-ka-ḣpe *or* śi-yo′-to-a-ka-ḣpe, *n.* *an apron.*

śi-ya′-ka, *n.* *the teal*, a kind of duck. The śiyaka are divided into śiyaka taŋka, mde śiyaka, *and* wakpa śiyaka.

śi-ya′-ka, *n.* *a boil:* śiyaka o, *hit by the* śiyaka, which results in a *boil*—śiyaka mao. We have not been able to ascertain the origin of this expression.

śi′-yo, *n.* *the grouse* or *prairie hen, the Tetrao cupido.*

śi-yo′-te, *n.* *T.* *the knees; the lap.*

śi yo′-to, *n.* *the knees, the front part of the legs; the lap*—maśiyoto. *T.*, śiyote.

śka. See yuśka

śka, *conj.* *T.* *but:* *i. q.* tuka; eśta.

śka, śke, *and* śket, *adv.* or *v. n.* *T.* eya śke, *though he says;* or more likely as a verb, *it is said that he says.*—T. L. R. See śkeli.

śka-haŋ′, *part.* *come untied of itself.*

śkal, *T.* *cont.* of śkata.

śkal′-wa-yu-pi-ka, *adj.* *T.* *skillful at games.*

śkan, *cont.* of śkata; śkan uŋpi. *T.*, śkal.

śkan-ki′-ya, *v.* *to cause to play*—śkanwakiya. *T.*, śkalkiya.

śkaŋ, *v. n.* *to do, to act; to move about:* token yaśkaŋ he, *what art thou doing?*—waśkaŋ, uŋśkaŋpi: śkaŋ hiŋhda, *to jump* or *flutter about*, as a bird when caught. See ḣaŋ.

śkaŋ′-ka-piŋ, *adj.* *lazy, unwilling to move about.*

śkaŋ′-ka-piŋ-pi, *n.* *laziness.*

ś k a ŋ - k i' - y a, *v. a.* *to cause to move about*—śkaŋwakiya.

ś k a ŋ - ś k a ŋ', *v.* *red.* of śkaŋ; *to stir, move about, change place.*

ś k a ŋ - ś k a ŋ' - y a ŋ, *v. a.* *to cause to move about*—śkaŋśkaŋwaya.

ś k a ŋ - ś k a ŋ' - y a ŋ, *adv.* *moving, in motion.*

ś k a ŋ - y a ŋ', *adv.* *moving.*

ś k a' - t a, *v. n.* *to play*—waśkata, uŋśkatapi.

ś k a - w a' - h a ŋ, *part.* *come untied of itself.*

ś k e *and* ś k e - l o', *v. n.* *T.* *they say; it is reported:* tawiću toŋ kta śke lo, *they say he is going to marry.* See śka *and* śkeli.

ś k e - ć a', *n.* *the fisher.*

ś k e - ć a' - t a ŋ - k a, *n.* *the wolverine.*

ś k e - d u' - t a, *n.* *the name of a small red bird.*

ś k e' - h a ŋ, *adj.* *wild, prancing,* as a horse; *ambitious.*

ś k e' - h a ŋ - h a ŋ, *adj.* *red.* of śkehaŋ; *jumping round, frolicsome.*

ś k e' - h e, *adj.* Same as śkehaŋ.

ś k e - h e' - ć a, *n.* *an animal that is wild* or *unsteady.*

ś k e' - h e - ś n i, *adj.* *gentle.*

ś k e - h e' - y a, *v. a.* *to make wild, make prance about*—śkehewaya.

ś k e' - h e - y a, *adv.* *ambitiously.*

ś k e' - l i, *adv.* *T.* *i. q.* śkelo.

ś k i - ć a'. See yuśkića.

ś k i - ć a' - h a ŋ, *part.* *squeezing, pressed.*

ś k i - ć a' - w a - h a ŋ, *part.* *pressing, squeezed.*

ś k i ŋ - ć i' - y a, *v.* *to move one's self, be industrious:* *i. q.* miniheićiya—śkiŋmićiya. See śkaŋ.

ś k i - ś k a', *adj.* *rough, not smooth and level.*

ś k i - ś k e' - y a, *v. a.* *to make rough*—śkiśkewaya.

ś k i - ś k e' - y a, *adv.* *roughly.*

ś k o - k p a', *adj.* *hollowed out, concave.*

ś k o m, *cont* of śkopa; śkom iyaya. *T.*, śkob.

ś k o m - y a', *v. a.* *to make crooked*—śkomwaya *T.*, śkobya.

ś k o m - y a', *adv.* *crookedly;* śkomya waŋka.

ś k o' - p a, *adj.* *crooked, warped; concave.*

ś k o - ś k o' - p a, *adj.* *red.* of śkopa.

ś k o - t p a', *adj.* *hollowed out, concave.*

ś k u, *v. n.* *to be wholly* or *partially roasted; to be covered with red spots,* as one who lies too close to the fire in cold weather—maśku, niśku.

ś k u - m n a', *adj.* *tainted,* as meat; *sour.*

Ś k u' - t a - n i, *n. p.* *the Kootenai.*

ś l i, *v. n.* *T.* *to ooze out,* as gum, under the action of the sun. See ḣdi.

ś l i' - y e - l a, *adv.* *T.* *whizzing,* as a bullet in the air.

ś m a, *adj.* *deep,* as water; *dense,* as foliage; *thickly set,* as hair.

ś m a - ś m a', *adj.* *red.* of śma.

ś m i, *adj.* *bare;* *i. q.* hiŋ wanića: pa śmi; said of a head with only a few scattering hairs. See smi.

śna. See yuśna.

śna, *adv.* *T.* *here, now;* used with other adverbs; as, dehaŋ śna, *here now;* lehaŋ śna, letu śna, etc., aŋpetu waŋźi śna, *some days,* i. e., *occasionally.*

śna-haŋ', *part.* *dropped, missed.*

śna-wa'-haŋ, *part.* *dropped.*

śni, *adv.* of negation; *not, no.* It follows verbs, nouns, pronouns, adjectives, adverbs, etc.

śni-śni'-źa, *adj.* *red.* of śniźa.

śniś-ya', *v. a.* *to make wither* or *dry up*—śniśwaya, śniśuŋyaŋpi.

śniś-ya', *adv.* *withered.*

śni-yaŋ'-yaŋ, *adv.* *abundantly.*

śni'-za, *adj.* *withered, dead, dried up,* as leaves by the sun; *blurred, indistinct:* iśtomaśniźa.

śnuŋ-śnuŋ'-źa, *adj.* *red.* of śnuŋźa

śnuŋ'-źa, *adj.* *blurred, indistinct,* as, iśtośnuŋźa. *T.*, śniźa.

śog, *cont.* of śoka.

śog-śog'-ya, *adv.* *red.* of śogya.

śog-ya', *adv.* *strongly, firmly, thickly:* śogya awaćiŋ, *to think intently.*

śog-yeḣ', *adv.* *strongly, firmly; greatly, much.*

śo'-ka, *adj.* *thick,* applied to solids.

śo'-ka-la, *n.* *T.* *a quarter of a dollar:* lit. *a small thick piece.*

śo-kśaŋ'-ka-daŋ, *n.* *a species of duck,* much smaller than the mallard duck, *the teal.*

śo-kśaŋ'-ka-taŋ-ka, *n.* *a large species of the teal.*

śo-kśo'-ka, *adj.* *red.* of śoka.

śol, *T.* *cont.* of śota.

śol-a'-ni-ni, *n.* *T.* *soot, smut.*

śol-na'-ġi, *n.* *T.* *soot.*

śol-ya', *v.* *T.* *to make smoky.*

śon, *cont.* of śota.

śon-na'-ġi, *n.* (*smoke-ghost*) *soot.* See śotkazi.

śon-ya', *v. a.* *to smoke, make smoky*—śonwaya. *T.*, śolya.

śoŋg-źo'-ya-ka, *n.* See śuŋźoyaka for the better orthography of this word.

śoŋ-ġi'-daŋ, *n.* See śuŋġidaŋ.

śoŋ'-ka, *n.* See śuŋka.

śoŋ-pa', *n.* See śuŋpa.

śoŋ-śoŋ'-la, *n.* *T.* *a mule.*

śoŋ-śoŋ'-la-i-kpi-ska, *n.* *T.* *a white-bellied mule,* i. e., *a donkey.*

śoŋ'-śoŋ-na, *adj.* *long-eared, hanging down,* as the ears of many dogs do; *dogs whose ears hang down.* Hence, śuktaŋka śoŋśoŋna, *a mule.* *T.*, śoŋśoŋla.

śoŋ-te', *n.* *the hole by which a beaver goes in and out.* *T.*, waśoŋ; ćaboti oḣloka.

śo'-śa, *adj.* *turbid, muddy,* as water.

śo'-śe, *adj.* Same as śośa: Miniśośe, *the Missouri River.*

śo-śe'-ya, *v. a.* *to make turbid* or *muddy, to stir up*—śośewaya.

śo-śe'-ya, *adv.* *turbidly.*

śo-śka', *n.* *a species of pine; a small kind of fish:* *i. q.* hośka.

śo'-ta, *n.* *smoke.*

śo'-ta, *v. n.* *to smoke,* as a fire.

ś o - t k a′ - z i, *n.* *soot.* See śonnaġi.

ś o - t k a′ - z i, *adj.* *smoked black, sooty.* See sotkazi.

ś o t - o′ - ź u, *adj.* *smoky, full of smoke,* applied to a hazy atmosphere.

ś p a. See yuśpa.

ś p a - h a ŋ′, *part.* *broken off.*

ś p a ŋ, *adj.* *cooked,* as food; *burnt* or *frozen,* as the face or parts of the body, by heat or cold: noġe maśpaŋ, *my ears are frozen;* siha niśpaŋ, *thy feet are frozen.* See spaŋ.

ś p a ŋ - k a′ - ġ a - p i, *n.* *Ih.* *green corn dried: i. q.* waskuya.

ś p a ŋ - k i′ - ć i - ć i - y a, *v. a.* *to cook for* one—śpaŋwećićiya.

ś p a ŋ - k i′ - y a, *v. a. pos.* *to cook one's own* food; *to cook for* another—śpaŋwakiya, spaŋuŋkiyapi.

ś p a ŋ′ - ś n i, *adj.* *T.* *raw, not cooked: i. q.* saka.

ś p a ŋ′ - ś n i - y u - t a - p i, *n.* *Ih.* and *T.* *anything eaten raw: i. q.* sakayutapi, *melons.*

ś p a ŋ - y a ŋ′, *v. a.* *to cook,* as food—śpaŋwaya, śpaŋuŋyaŋpi.

ś p a - w a′ - h a ŋ, *part.* *broken off.*

ś p e. See śpa.

ś p i. See yuśpi.

ś p i - h a ŋ′, *part.* *fallen off,* as berries.

ś p i - w a′ - h a ŋ, *part.* Same as śpihaŋ.

ś p u. See yuśpu.

ś p u - h a ŋ′, *part.* See śpuwahaŋ.

ś p u - w a′ - h a ŋ, *part.* *fallen off of itself,* as anything that adhered.

ś t a, *conj.* *although.* *T.* śa, eśa, *and* yeśaŋ. See eśta.

ś t a g, *cont.* of śtaka.

ś t a g - y a′, *v. a.* *to mash up; to make preserves*—śtagwaya.

ś t a g - y a′, *adv.* *free from ice:* śtagya waŋka.

ś t a′ - k a, *adj.* *free from ice,* as a river or lake when the ice has broken up and run out: *beaten, broken.* See kaśtaka.

ś t a ŋ. See kaśtaŋ, yuśtaŋ.

ś t a ŋ, *adj.* *blackish, dark-colored.* *T.,* sabya. See staŋ.

ś t a ŋ, *v. n.* *to become black,* as berries, by the heat of the sun.

ś t a ŋ′ - h a ŋ, *conj.* *although:* hi śtaŋhaŋ sdonwaye śni, *though he may have come I do not know it.* *T.,* yeśaŋ.

ś t a ŋ - h a ŋ′, *v. n.* *to ooze out,* as water from a sore, *to be sore and exude water.* *T.,* ośtaŋhaŋ. See ḣdi

ś t a - ś t a′, *adj.* *weak, brittle: i. q* waŋkadaŋ. See staka.

ś t a - ś t a′ - d a ŋ, *adj.* *brittle.*

ś t a - ś t a′ - k a, *adj.* *red.* of śtaka.

ś t e, *adj.* *deformed.* See ośteka, ośteḣda, waśte, etc. Śte *and* ḣte have good meanings as well as bad ones in Dakota, Ponka, Winnebago, and other cognate languages. See waḣtedaśni.

ś t e - d a′, *v.* of śte; *to think there is much* or *many, to rate high*—śtewada, śteuŋdapi.

ś t e - d a′ - p i, *n.* *a great many, much.*

ś t e - i′ - ç i - d a, *v. reflex* *to think much of one's self.*

śte-ya', *adv.* *deformedly.*

śtu-ća', *v. n.* *to thaw*, as anything that has been frozen. *T.*, śtulya. See śtunya *and* śtuta.

śtul-ya', *v.* *T.* *to thaw out: i. q.* śtuŋya.

śtun-ya', *v. a.* *to thaw, cause to thaw*—śtunwaya: śtuniçiya, *to thaw* or *warm one's self*—śtunmiçiya.

śtuŋ-ka', *adj.* *unripe*, as fruit.

śtuŋ-ka'-la, *adj.* *T.* *soft, mellow; not ripe yet*, as corn in the milk.

śtu-śta', *adj.* *soft*, as the flesh of an animal when hard chased, *wanting flavor.* See śtaśta, etc.

śtu-śte'-ya, *v. a.* *to chase so as to make weary* and render the meat flavorless—śtuśtewaya.

śtu'-ta, *adv.* *thawed, warmed:* nape maśtuta, *my hands are warmed.* See śtuća.

śuk-ćiŋ'-ća, *n.* *a young wolf.* See śuŋkćiŋća.

śuk-ćiŋ'-ća-daŋ, *n.* *a colt.* See śuŋkćiŋćadaŋ.

śuk-taŋ'-ka, *n.* (śuŋka *and* taŋka) *the horse, horses.* *Ih.* and *T.*, śuŋkawakaŋ.

śuk-taŋ'-ka-a-ķiŋ, *n.* *a saddle for a horse; a pack-saddle.* *T.*, ćaŋwaķiŋ. See śuŋgaķiŋ.

śuk-taŋ'-ka-i-i-yu-wi, *n.* *a horse-bridle, a rope for a horse's mouth.*

śuk-taŋ'-ka-śoŋ-śoŋ-na, *n.* *a mule, a jackass.*

śuk-taŋ'-ka-wa-na-piŋ, *n.* *a horse-collar.*

śuŋ, *n.* *the large feathers of birds' wings.*

śuŋg, *cont* of śuŋka.

śuŋg-a'-ķiŋ, *n.* *a saddle; a saddle blanket.* See śuktaŋkaaķiŋ.

śuŋg-hu'-daŋ, *n.* *a short-legged horse, a pony, a small horse.*

śuŋg-hu'-pte-pte-će-daŋ, *n.* *a short-legged dog* or *horse.*

śuŋg-i'-ća-psiŋ-te, *n.* *a horse-whip.*

śuŋg-i'-ća-śke, *n.* *a picket-pin; anything to fasten a horse with.*

śuŋg-i'-kte, *n.* lit. *that by means of which a wolf is killed: poison; strychnine.* See śuŋkigmuŋke.

śuŋg-i'-na-ḣta-ke, *n.* *T.* *a spur.*

śuŋg-i'-na-źi-pa, *n.* *T.* *a spur.*

śuŋg-i'-kaŋ, *n.* *harness.*

śuŋg-i'-pa-ḣte, *n.* *a bridle.*

śuŋ-gle'-śka, *n.* *T.* *a spotted horse.*

śuŋg-ma'-ki-ći-ma, *n.* *T.* *a young horse.*

śuŋg-ma'-ni-tu, *n.* *T.* *a wolf.*

śuŋg-mdo'-ka, *n.* *the male of the horse* or *dog.*

śuŋg-naḣ'-po-ġe, *n.* *T.* *a brown-eared horse.*

śuŋg-o'-i-na-źiŋ, *n.* *a stable.*

śuŋg-o'-na-śiŋ, *n.* *a pacing horse.*

śuŋg-wa'-ķiŋ-i-hu-pa, *n.* *the apparatus for packing on a horse* or *dog*, pronounced often śuŋgwaķuŋhupa *and* śuŋgwaķiŋhupa. It is made by placing the ends of two or more poles (usually tent-poles) together, and inclining them at an angle of some forty or fifty degrees. The ends fastened together are placed on the back of the horse or dog, with a strap around the breast. Behind the horse's tail cross-pieces are tied, on which loads are packed and children placed. The Sisitoŋwaŋs *and* Ihaŋktoŋwaŋs of the prairie keep large dogs for the purpose of packing. *T.*, hupaheuŋpi.

ś u ŋ g - w i'- y e, *n.* *a mare; a bitch.*

ś u ŋ g - w i'- y e - d a ŋ, *n.* *dim.* of śuŋgwiye.

ś u ŋ g - w i'- y e - l a, *n.* *T.* *a mare.*

ś u ŋ - ġ i'- d a ŋ, *n.* *the fox.*

śuŋ-ȟpa'-daŋ, *n.* *a puppy, a little dog.*

ś u ŋ'- k a, *n.* *a dog,* commonly; *a horse; an ox* or *cow,* occasionally. This latter use obtains only in the language of the braves or warriors of the nation—mitaśuŋke, nitaśuŋke, taśuŋke. See śoŋka.

ś u ŋ - k a'- k i - i - n a - ȟ t a - k e, *n.* *T.* *a spur.*

ś u ŋ'- k a - w a - k a ŋ, *n.* *Ih.* and *T.* *a sacred dog* or *spirit-dog,* i. e., *a horse: i. q.* śuŋktaŋka.

ś u ŋ'- k a - w a - k a ŋ - t a - w a - n a - p i ŋ, *n.* *a horse collar.*

ś u ŋ - k ć e', *n.* *a bulbous esculent root* that grows in swamps.

ś u ŋ k - ć i ŋ'- ć a, *n.* *a young wolf.* See śukćiŋća.

ś u ŋ k - ć i ŋ'- ć a - d a ŋ, *n.* *a colt.*

ś u ŋ k - i'- ć a - p s i ŋ - t e, *n.* *a horse-whip.*

ś u ŋ k - i'- g m u ŋ - k e, *n.* *T.* *poison; anything to use in trapping wolves: i. q.* śuŋgikte.

ś u ŋ k - o'- n a - ś o - l a, *n.* *T.* *a pacing horse.*

ś u ŋ k - p a'- d a ŋ, *n.* See śuŋȟpadaŋ.

ś u ŋ k - t a ŋ'- k a, *n.* (śuŋka *and* taŋka). See śuktaŋka.

ś u ŋ k - t a'- w a - n a - p i ŋ, *n.* *T.* *a horse collar: i. q.* śuŋkawakaŋtawanapiŋ.

ś u ŋ k - t a'- w a - n a - p i ŋ - n a, *n.* *the name of a small bird.*

ś u ŋ k - t o'- k e - ć a, *n.* *the other dog,* i. e., *the wolf.* *T.*, śuŋgmanitu.

ś u ŋ k - w i'- y e, *n.* *a mare: i. q.* śuŋgwiye. *T.*, śuŋgwiyela.

ś u ŋ - p a', *v. n.* *to moult, shed,* as geese their feathers: *i. q.* śoŋpa.

ś u ŋ - p a'- ȟ d i - ȟ d i, *v.* *to have the feathers partly grown.* Said of geese, etc., when their feathers have grown so that they are almost able to fly; *i. q.* ećadaŋ kihipi kta. *T.*, śuŋtoto.

ś u ŋ - t o'- t o, *v. n.* *T.* *to have the feathers partly grown.*

ś u ŋ - ź o'- y a g, *cont.* of śuŋźoyaka; śuŋźoyag iću, *to make a loop, noose,* or *lasso;* śuŋźoyag iyakaśka, *to tie a noose* or *running knot.*

ś u ŋ - ź o'- y a - k a, *n.* *a noose: i. q.* śoŋgźoyaka. *T.*, źoźoyagtoŋ.

ś u - p e', *n.* *guts, intestines.*

ś u - p e′ - ć o - w o - ź u, *n.* *a species of duck*, so called because its entrails are always full.

ś u - p e′ - o - ś i - ć a, *adj.* *T.* *hard to digest; disagreeing with one.*

ś u - p e′ - o - ś i - ć a, *n.* *T.* *anything hard to digest.*

ś u - p u′ - t e, *n.* *T.* *a gun-stock.*

ś u p - t a ŋ′ - k a, *n.* (śupe *and* taŋka) *the large intestines.*

ś u - ś k a′, *adj.* *slow, tardy, good for nothing, worthless*—maśuśka, niśuśka. *T.*, śkaŋkapiŋ.

ś u - ś k a′ - k a, *n.* *a worthless fellow.*

ś u - t a′, *v.* *to miss, fail of, to be unable to obtain*—śuwata, śuuŋtapi: *to miss*, as in shooting at anything; *to fail of getting*, śuwate, etc.

ś u - t e′ - y a, *v. a.* *to cause to fail* or *miss*—śutewaya.

T.

t. *the twenty-third letter of the Dakota alphabet.*

t a, *n.* *the moose.* This may properly be considered as the generic term for all ruminating animals, since it enters into the composition of the names of most of them; as, taḣiŋća, *deer;* tataŋka, *buffalo*, etc.

t a, *a prefix* to such nouns as signify the various members of the body, limiting them to the corresponding parts in ruminating animals; as, ćeźi, *the tongue*, taćeźi, *a buffalo tongue;* pa, *the head*, tapa, *a deer's head.*

t a, *prep. in comp.* *at, to, on;* suffixed to nouns it gives them the force of adverbs; as, maka, *the earth;* makata, *on the ground.* See also "ata" *and* "yata."

t a, *pron. in comp.* *his, hers, its;* with "pi" at the end of the noun, *theirs.*

t a, *adj.* *one of, a pair:* tawaŋźidaŋ, *one pair;* tanoŋpa, *two pairs.*

t a b, *cont.* of tapa.

t a b - i′ - ć a - k a - p e, *n.* *T.* *a ball-club.*

t a b - i′ - ć a - p s i - ć e, *n.* *T.* *a ball-club.* See takićapsića.

t a - b l o′ - h u, *n.* *T.* *i. q.* tamdohu.

t a - ć a ŋ′ - t a, *n.* (ta *and* ćaŋte) *the heart of the buffalo, the ox*, etc.

t a - ć e′ - s d i, *n.* *the dung of ruminating animals*, especially the buffalo; *the "Bois de vache"* of the French.

t a - ć e′ - ź i, *n.* *the tongue of ruminating animals*, especially the buffalo.

t a - ć i ŋ′ - ć a, *n.* *the young of deer, a fawn.* *T.*, taćiŋćala.

t a - ć i ŋ′ - ć a - d a ŋ, *n.* *a fawn, a lamb.*

t a - ć i ŋ′ - ć a - h a, *n.* *a fawn-skin, calf-skin.*

ta-ćiŋ'-ća-la, *n.* *T.* *the young of deer.*

ta-do', *n.* *fresh meat, the fresh meat* of ruminating animals, as the deer and buffalo.

ta-do'-hde-ska, *n.* *the windpipe of the buffalo.* *T.*, taglogleska *and* taglogloska.

ta-do'-ta-hu, *n.* *the neck; neck-bone* of animals.

ta-glo'-gle-ska *and* ta-glo'-glo-ska, *n.* *T.* *the windpipe in animals.*

ta'-ġa, *n.* mini taġa, *froth, foam*

ta-ġe', *n.* *froth, foam, spittle, scum:* taġe eḣpeya, *to skim, throw off the scum.*

ta-ġi'-ća, *n.* *a species of tortoise.* 2. *the hump of the buffalo; the buffalo itself.*

ta-ġi'-ća-ha, *n.* *a buffalo robe;* chiefly used by the Sisitoŋwaŋs and Ihaŋktoŋwaŋs: *i. q.* ptehaśina. So called from the hump. *T.*, śina ikćeka.

ta-ġo'-śa, *v. n.* *to spit, expectorate*—taġowaśa, taġouŋśapi. *T.*, taḣośa *and* taśośe.

ta-ġu', *n.* *an old buffalo bull, a poor scabby bull,* whether old or not, *a singed bull.*

ta-ha', *n.* *a deer-skin.*

ta-ha'-ba-ḣdo-ke, *n.* *the slits cut in a hide by which it is stretched.*

ta-ha'-daŋ, *adv.* *i. q.* hahadaŋ, ćante tahadaŋ śni.—A. L. R.

ta-ha'-ka-la-la, *n* *T.* (taha *and* kalala, *to dangle*) *a woman's buckskin dress,* usually ornamented with fringe, etc.

ta-haŋ', *n.* *a man's brother-in-law, a wife's brother,* and *a man's sister's husband; my brother-in-law:* nitahaŋ, *thy brother-in-law.*

ta-haŋ'-ki-ći-ya-pi, *n.* *brothers-in-law.*

ta-haŋ'-ku, *n.* *his brother-in-law.*

ta-haŋ'-śi, *n.* *a man's male cousin, my cousin.* This does not include a father's brother's sons, who are brothers—nitahaŋśi.

ta-haŋ'-śi-tku, *n.* *his male cousin.*

ta-haŋ'-śi-ya, *v. a.* *to sustain the relation of male cousin to* one—tahaŋśiwaya.

ta-haŋ'-ya, *v. a.* *to have for brother-in-law, sustain the relation of* tahaŋ *to* one—tahaŋwaya.

ta-ha'-sa-ka, *n.* *dried skin, parchment; a skin with the hair taken off,* but not yet dressed.

ta'-hdo-hu, *n.* *the soft maple, Acer rubrum.*

ta-he'-ća-psuŋ-wi, *n.* *the moon in which the deer shed their horns; December.* See kapsuŋ.

ta-he'-daŋ, *adv.* *on this side of.* See otahedaŋ.

ta-he'-daŋ-taŋ-haŋ, *adv.* *on this side of.*

ta-he'-na, *adv.* *Ih.* *on this side:* *i. q.* itato; *this way;* tahena u wo, *come this way.* See tahepi.

ta-he'-na-taŋ-haŋ, *adv.* *Ih.* *from this side of.*

ta-he'-pi, *adv.* *by the way, on the road, between* one place and another. *T.*, tahena. See otahepi.

ta-he′-pi-ya, *adv. between places, in the space between the earth and heaven.*

ta-hiŋ′, *n. buffalo* or *deer's hair.*

ta-hiŋ′-i-pa-kiŋ-će, *n. T. an instrument for scraping skins.*

ta-hiŋ′-i-pa-staŋ, *n. an instrument for scraping* or *currying skins.*

ta-hiŋ′-pa-ġu-ke, *n. pemmican; the knee-bone used as a pemmican stone.*

ta-hiŋ′-śpa, *n. an awl, awls.*

ta-hiŋ′-śpa-ći-ḳa-daŋ, *n. a needle, needles.*

ta-hiŋ′-śpa-ći-ḳa-la, *n. T. a needle.*

ta-hiŋ′-ye-te, *n.* of hiŋyete; *the shoulder of animals.*

ta-hiŋ′-yo-ki-be, *n. the joints of animals. T.*, okihe. See okibe.

ta-ho′-ćo-ka, *n. a court* or *open place.* See hoćoka.

ta-ho′-ka-śke, *n. cross bars* inside of a tent on which *a skin is fastened to dry.*

ta-ho′-ka-ta, *n. a spider's web; the pins used in stretching a skin;* of taha *and* okataŋ. *T.*, uŋktomi taokaśke.

ta-ho′-ka-taŋ, *v.* (taha *and* okataŋ) *to stretch out,* as a hide, with pins—tahowakataŋ.

ta-ho′-mni, *n. the hoop on which a scalp* or *hide is stretched.*

ta-hu′, *n. the back of the neck.*

ta-hu′-a-ka-ȟpe, *n. T. a cape for the neck.*

ta-hu′-am, *adv. with outstretched neck.*

ta-hu′-hu-te, *n. T. the nape of the neck*

ta-hu′-i-ćos-ya, *n. a scarf* or *comforter.* See ićosya.

ta-hu′-ka, *n. the hide of a buffalo, a green hide.*

ta-hu′-ka-wa-ta, *n. a bull-hide boat.*

ta-huŋ′-ske, *n. T. stockings: his* or *her stockings*

ta-hu′-o-gle, *n. T. a cape* or *ruffle.* See ogle.

ta-hu′-ska, *n. a shirt-collar; paper collars.*

ta-hu′-ska-i-na-piŋ, *n. a neck-tie*

ta-hu′-to-śtaŋ, *n. the nape, the prominent articulation of the neck behind. T.*, tahuhute.

ta-ȟaŋ′-hiŋ-hda, *v. n.* of taġe; *to froth* or *foam,* as when anything is thrown into water.

ta′-ȟća, *n. cont.* of taȟiŋća.

ta′-ȟća-śuŋ-ka, *n. Ih. sheep:* lit. *deer-dogs. T.*, taȟća śuŋkala.

ta′-ȟiŋ-ća, *n. the common deer, Cervus capreolus.*

ta′-ȟiŋ-ća-ha, *n. a deer-skin.* See taha. *T.*, taȟćaha.

ta′-ȟiŋ-ća-ska, *white deer,* i. e., *sheep. T.*, taȟća śuŋkala.

ta′-ȟiŋ-ća-śaŋ-la, *n. T. the antelope.*

ta′-ȟća-wa-ni-yaŋ-pi, *n. T. sheep.*

ta′-ȟiŋ-ća-wa-nuŋ-yaŋ-pi, *n. tame deer,* i. e., *sheep.*

ta′-ȟiŋ-wa-ṅuŋ-yaŋ-pi, *n. sheep. T.*, taȟćawaniyaŋpi.

t a - ḣ o′ - ś a, *v.* *T.* *to expectorate; i. q.* taġośa.

t a - ḣ p a′, *n.* *the lower part of the neck and breast* of animals; *the part between the shoulders* of a man; *the muscle across the abdomen.*

t a - ḣ p a′ - p a - y a - t a, *n.* *T.* *between the shoulders.*

t a - ḣ p i′ - y o - ġ i ŋ, *n.* *ground-cherries.* *T.*, auŋyeyapi.

t a - ḣ p i′ - y o - ġ i ŋ, *adj.* *ripe, fully ripe: i. q.* sutoŋ; taḣpiyoġiŋ śni, *not ripe.*

t a ḣ - t o ŋ′, *v.* of taġe; *to have scum.*

t a - ḣ u′ - h a, *n.* *the scrapings of hides* or *skins.*

t a - ḣ u′ - ś d a - h a, *n.* *a summer robe.* *T.*, tawelaha.

t a - ḣ u′ - w a - p a - ḣ p e, *n.* *the flesh that sticks to a hide.*

t a′ - k a, *v. a.* *to roast off the hull,* as of rice; *to roast,* as coffee—watáka, uŋtákapi.

t a - k a b′ - k a b, *cont.* of takabkapa; takabkab iyeya, *to play ball by striking and knocking.*

t a - k a ŋ′, *n.* *the sinew taken from the back of the deer and buffalo,* which is used by the Dakotas for thread, making bows, etc.

t a - k a ŋ′ - ġ i, *n.* *the knee-pan, the patella.* *T.*, ćaŋkpehu

t a - k a ŋ′ - h e - ć a, *n.* *raspberries.*

t a - k a ŋ′ - h e - ć a - h u, *n.* *raspberry bushes.*

t a - k a ŋ′ - i - t a - z i - p e, *n.* *a bow the back of which is overlaid with sinew.*

t a - k a′ - p o - p a - p i, *n.* *playing ball by striking.* *T.*, tabkabkab iyeyapi.

t a - k a′ - p s i - ć a, *v.* *to play ball* by taking up the ball in the club and throwing it—tawakapsića.

t a - k a′ - p s i - ć a - p i, *n.* *ball-playing.*

t a - k i′ - ć a - p o - p e, *n.* *a ball-club for striking.* *T.*, tabićakape.

t a - k i′ - ć a - p s i - ć a, *n.* *a ball-club,* a stick with a hoop at the end, interlaced so as to hold and carry the ball in readiness to be thrown. *T.*, tabićapsića, *a shinny stick with crook on the end for catchimg the ball.*

t a k - i′ - ḣ a ŋ, *v.* (taku *and* iḣaŋ) takiḣaŋ yahi he, *what have you come to do?* *T.*, takole.

t a - k i ŋ′, *v. n.* *to lean:* takiŋ iyaya, *to dodge.* *T.*, pakiŋ iyaya.

t a - k i ŋ′ - y a ŋ, *adv.* *leaning, not perpendicular:* wi takiŋyaŋ ya, said of the sun when it is half way up to the meridian. *T.*, wi kiŋ atakiŋyaŋ ya.

t a - k i′ - y u - ḣ a - w i, *n.* *the moon when the deer copulate; November.* See kiyuḣa.

t a - k o′ - d a, *n.* Used with the pronouns; as, mitakoda, *my friend;* nitakoda, *thy friend;* takodaku, *his friend.* See koda.

t a - k o′ - d a - k i - ć i - y a - p i, *n.* *particular friends.*

t a - k o′ - d a - k u, *n.* *his particular friend.*

t a - k o′ - d a - y a, *v. a.* *to have* one *for a particular friend*—takodawaya.

t a k′ - o - l e, *v.* *T.* (taku *and* ole) tak ole yahi he, *what have you come for?*

ta-ko'-mni, *adv.* *nevertheless, still, always, at any time, ever:* with śni following, *at no time.*

ta-koś', *n.* *a son-in-law* or *daughter-in-law, my son-in-law,* etc.; *nephews* and *nieces by marriage.*

ta-koś'-ku, *n.* *his* or *her son-in-law* or *daughter-in-law.*

ta-koś'-ya, *v. a.* *to have for son-in-law* or *daughter-in-law*—takośwaya.

ta-ko'-źa, *n.* *a grandchild, my grandchild*—mitakoźa, nitakoźa.

ta-ko'-źa-kpa-ku, *n.* *his* or *her grandchild.* Takoźakpa is not used alone.

ta-ko'-źa-tpa-ku, *n.* *his* or *her grandchild.*

ta-ko'-źa-ya, *v. a.* *to have for grandchild*—takoźawaya, takoźauŋyaŋpi.

ta-kpe', *v. a.* *to come upon, attack;* sometimes used in good sense, *to visit*—tawakpe, tauŋkpepi: takpe hi, *to come to attack;* takpe i, *to have been to attack;* takpe ya, *to go to attack;* takpe u, *to be coming to attack.*

ta-kpe'-ya, *adv.* *attacking.*

ta'-ku, *n.* *something.*

ta'-ku, *interrog. pron.* *what?* taku yaćiŋ he, *what dost thou want?*

ta-ku', *n.* *a relative, kindred.* See takuya.

ta'-ku-ća, *pron. interrog.* *what?*

ta'-ku-daŋ, *n.* *dim.* of táku; *a trifle, nothing,* mostly followed by śni, as, takudaŋ waćiŋ śni, *I want nothing.* *T.*, takuni.

ta'-ku-da-śni, *v. a.* *to count as nothing, not to regard; to be patient, submissive in suffering*—takuwadaśni. *T.*, takuni śni.

ta-ku'-ki-ći-ya-pi, *n.* *relatives, relationship.*

ta'-ku-ku, *n.* *red.* of táku; *small articles, trinkets.*

ta'-ku-ma-ni-ni-na, *n.* *moths* and other *small grubs.*

ta-ku'-mna, *v. n.* *to have taste* or *smell;* takumna śni, *to be without smell, taste,* or *aroma; unpalatable.*

ta'-ku-ni, *n.* *T.* *a trifle, nothing;* generally followed by śni.

ta'-ku-ni-śni, *n.* *nothing.*

ta'-ku-ni-śni, *v. n.* *to come to nothing, fail, perish*—matakuniśni. *T.*, atakuni śni.

ta'-ku-ni-śni-yaŋ, *adv.* *gone to nothing, perishing.*

ta'-ku-śa-śa, *n.* *bed-bugs; any red thing.* *T.*, wabluśkaśaśa.

Ta'-ku-śkaŋ-skaŋ, *n.* *one of the Dakota gods, the moving god* or *god of motion.* *T.* *a familiar spirit:* Takuśkaŋśkaŋ mitawa, *my familiar spirit:* *i. q.* Waśićuŋ; which see.

ta'-ku-śni, *n.* *nothing.*

ta'-ku-śni-śni, *n.* *small articles: trifles,* as, takuśniśni omdaka, *I tell little things.*

ta-ku'-ya, *v. a.* *to have* one *for a relation*—takuwaya, takuuŋyaŋpi, takumayaŋ, takućiya.

ta-ku'-ye, *n.* *a relative*—mitakuye, uŋkitakuyepi.

ta-le'-źa, *n.* *T.* *i. q.* tadeźa.

ta′-ma-he, *n.* *the pike*, a kind of fish.

ta′-ma-he-ća *or* ta-ma′-he-ća, *adj.* *poor, lean, not fat*—matamaheća, uŋtamahećapi.

ta′-ma-hen, *adv.* See taŋmahen. *T.*, tamahel.

ta′-ma-hen-he-ća, *adj.* *red.* of tamaheća.

ta′-ma-hen-ya, *adv.* *poorly, not in a fat state.*

ta′-ma-ka, *adj.* *poor, lean:* pte tamaka, *a lean cow.*

ta-mda′, *n.* See taŋmda.

ta′-mdo-hu, *n.* *the shoulder-blade of animals.* *T.*, tablohu.

ta-mdo′-ka, *n.* *the male of the common deer, a buck.* *T.*, tabloka.

tam-ki′-ya, *v. a.* *to say much to* one *about* anything, *to blame, talk roughly to*—tamwakiya, tamuŋkiyapi, tammakiya. The Titoŋwaŋ does not change the "m" in this and tamya: lila wahokoŋkiya.

ta-mni′, *n.* *the womb; the after birth* or *sack which envelopes the fœtus.*

ta-muŋ′-ka, *v.* 1st pers. sing. of tawaŋka.

tam-ya′, *v. n.* *to talk earnestly, vociferate; to complain, murmur, blame* one—tamwamda, tamyada, tamuŋyaŋpi.

ta-na′-ġi-daŋ, *n.* *a species of humming-bird.*

ta-na′-kpa-he-ća, *n.* *a species of flag* with a large root growing in water.

ta-na′-kpaŋ, *n.* *the fleshy part on the leg below the knee* of an animal; *the cords in the legs of animals.*

ta-na′-su-daŋ, *n.* *the brain of animals.*

ta-na′-tpa-he-ća, *n.* Same as tanakpaheća.

ta-na′-tpa-hu-te, *n.* Same as tanakpaheća.

ta-na′-wi-ti-će, *n.* *the little bulbous piece of meat on the fore-leg.*

ta-ni′, *adj.* *old.* See taŋni.

taŋ′-i-će-la, *n.* *T.* (taŋćaŋ nićala); *small insects; gnats, mosquitoes*, etc.

ta-ni′-ġe, *n.* *the paunch of a buffalo*, etc.

ta-ni′-ġe-mi-ni-a-ye, *n.* *T.* *a pouch for carrying water*, made of the paunch of the buffalo.

ta-ni′-haŋ, *adv.* *long ago.* See taŋnihaŋ.

ta-niḣ′-yu-sku, *v.* *to empty the paunch of a buffalo*, etc.

ta-ni′-ka, *adj.* *old.* See taŋnika.

ta-ni′-ya, *n.* *his* or *her breath* or *life.* See woniya.

taŋ, *cont.* of taŋćaŋ; as, taŋtoŋ.

taŋ, *cont.* of taŋka; as, minitaŋ.

t'aŋ. See yut'aŋ, pat'aŋ, etc.

taŋ, *prep.* or *adv.* *suffixed;* as in hećiyataŋ.

taŋ, *n.* *the side of an animal, the meat taken off the ribs:* taŋ waŋźidaŋ, *one piece of meat.* *T.* *a side of the beef*, including the bones; taŋ waŋźila, *one side* or *half the animal* cut down the middle of the backbone.—W. J. C.

taŋ-a′-ta-ye-daŋ, *adv.* *individually, directly, in person:* taŋatayedaŋ hdaźuźu, *to pay each one for himself.* *T.*, iyatayela.

taŋ-ćaŋ′, *n.* *the body*—mitaŋćaŋ, uŋtaŋćaŋpi; *the body* or *principal part* of anything, as of a tree, etc. See itaŋćaŋ, otaŋćaŋ, etc.

taŋ-ćaŋ′-ka, *n.* *the chief, the principal* *T.*, naća; itaŋćaŋ.

taŋ-ćaŋ′-ki-ya, *v. a.* *to make great; to prefer, consider chief*—taŋćaŋwakiya.

taŋ-ćaŋ′-toŋ, *v.* *to have a body; to be ripe, full grown.*

taŋ-ćo′-ćo-daŋ, *adj.* *red.* of taŋćodaŋ.

taŋ-ćo′-daŋ, *adj.* *naked, nearly naked, poorly clad:* taŋćodaŋ wauŋ. See sićodaŋ.

taŋ-ćo′-ka, *adj.* See taŋćokadaŋ.

taŋ-ćo′-ka-daŋ, *adj.* *naked, without clothing*—taŋćomakadaŋ, taŋćouŋkapidaŋ.

taŋ-ćo′-la, *adj.* *T.* *naked:* *i. q.* taŋćodaŋ.

taŋ-da′, *v. a.* *to love, honor, respect; to be patient*—taŋwada, taŋuŋdapi. *T.*, ohola; kinihaŋ. See ohoda.

taŋ-da′-ka, *v. a.* Same as taŋda.

taŋ-haŋ′, *prep.* *from;* as, hećiya taŋhaŋ. See etaŋhaŋ.

taŋ-hda′-kiŋ-yaŋ, *adv.* *crosswise, across* something else.

taŋ-hdu′-s'a-s'a-se-ća, *v.* *to be frightened*, as at a ghost, *frightened at* anything; *to be made sick by* seeing anything—taŋmahdus'as'a seća.

taŋ-hdu′-s'a-s'a-ya, *adv.* *in a state of fright.*

taŋ-iŋ′, *v. n.* *to appear, be manifest, be visible*—mataŋiŋ.

taŋ-iŋ′-iŋ, *v. n.* *red.* of taŋiŋ; *to appear occasionally*, as one passing under a hill, or as the sun through clouds.

taŋ-iŋ′-iŋ-yaŋ, *adv.* *red.* of taŋiŋyaŋ; *appearing occasionally:* taŋiŋiŋyaŋ iyaya.

taŋ-iŋ′-śni, *v. n.* *to be lost, to have disappeared.* See, also, kitaŋiŋśni.

taŋ-iŋ′-śni-yaŋ, *adv.* *out of sight, lost.*

taŋ-iŋ′-yaŋ, *adv.* *manifestly, openly, without concealment.*

taŋ-i′-yo-hi-daŋ, *adv.* *each one, every one.* *T.*, taŋiyohila.

taŋ′-i-yo-hi-na, *adv.* *Ih.* *each.*

taŋ′-ka, *adj.* *large, great* in any way—mataŋka, nitaŋka, uŋtaŋkapi. *T.*, also pronounced tȟaŋ′-ka.

taŋ′-ka, *n.* *a woman's younger sister*—mitaŋka, nitaŋka, taŋkaku.

taŋ-ka′-ki-ći-ya-pi, *n.* *they who are sisters.*

taŋ′-ka-ki-ya, *adv.* *largely:* ho taŋkakiya, *with a loud voice.*

taŋ-ka′-ku, *n.* *her younger sister.*

taŋ-kal′, *adv.* *T.* *without, out of doors:* *i. q.* taŋkan.

taŋ′-ka-la, *v.* *T.* *to consider great.*

taŋ-kan′, *adv.* *without, out of doors:* taŋkan iyaya, *to go out;* taŋkan iyeya, *to turn out, put out of doors.* *T.*, taŋkal.

t a ŋ - k a′ - t a, *adv.* *out of doors, outside.*

t a ŋ - k a′ - y a, *v. a.* *to have for a younger sister*—taŋkawaya.

t a ŋ′ - k a - y a, *v. a.* *to consider great*—taŋkawaya. *T.*, taŋkala.

t a ŋ′ - k a - y a, *adv.* *greatly, to a great extent:* taŋkaya wauŋ.

t a ŋ - k e′, *n.* *a man's older sister; my older sister*—mitaŋke, nitaŋke.

t a ŋ - k e′ - k u, *n.* *his older sister.*

t a ŋ - k e′ - y a, *v. a.* *to have for older sister*—taŋkewaya.

t a ŋ - k i ŋ′ - k i ŋ - y a ŋ, *adj.* *red.* and *pl.* of taŋka and taŋkiŋyaŋ; *very large.*

t a ŋ - k i ŋ′ - y a ŋ, *adj.* *very great, large.*

t a ŋ - k i ŋ′ - y a ŋ - y a ŋ, *adj.* *red.* of taŋkiŋyaŋ.

t a ŋ - k i′ - y a - d a ŋ, *adv.* *near to one*—mitaŋkiyadaŋ. *T.*, taŋkiyela.

t a ŋ - k i′ - y e - l a, *adv.* *T.* *near to one.* See kiyala.

t a ŋ - k ś i′, *n.* *a man's younger sister; my younger sister*—mitaŋkśi, nitaŋkśi.

t a ŋ - k ś i′ - t k u, *n.* *his younger sister.*

t a ŋ - k ś i - y a, *v. a.* *to have for younger sister*—taŋkśiwaya.

t a ŋ′ - k t a ŋ - k a, *adj.* *red.* of taŋka.

t a ŋ′ - k t a ŋ - k a - y a, *adv.* *red.* of taŋkaya; *largely.*

t a ŋ′ - k u, *n.* Same as taŋkeku.

t a ŋ′ - m a - h e l, *adv.* *T.* *i. q.* taŋmahen.

t a ŋ′ - m a - h e l - t a ŋ - h a ŋ, *adv.* *T.* *from within the body.*

t a ŋ′ - m a - h e n, *adv.* *in the body, within.* *T.*, taŋmahel.

t a ŋ′ - m a - h e n - t a ŋ - h a ŋ, *adv.* *from within.*

t a ŋ - m d a′, *n.* *round snow-shoes:* taŋmdohaŋ, *to put on* or *wear round snow-shoes.* *T.*, psohaŋpi.

t a ŋ - m d a s′, *cont.* of taŋmdaza; taŋmdas waŋka, *to lie on the side,* as animals.

t a ŋ - m d a′ - s k a - y a, *adv.* taŋmdaskaya waŋka, *to lie on the side, lie flat.*

t a ŋ - m d a′ - z a, *v.* *to spread the knees apart.* *T.*, kablaźa. See taŋmdas.

t a ŋ - n a′ - k e - k i - y a, *adv.* *on the side; with the head on one side:* taŋnakekiya waŋka, *it lies on its side.*

t a ŋ - n a′ - k e - y a, *adv.* *on the side; with head turned to one side,* as a drowsy person: taŋnakeya waŋka. See nakeya.

t a ŋ′ - n a - p a, *v. n.* *to twitch,* as the flesh of an animal, *jerk involuntarily.* *T.*, nagnaka.

t a ŋ′ - n a - p a - k i - y a, *v. a.* *to shrug up,* as the shoulders—taŋnapawakiya.

t a ŋ′ - n a - p a - p a, *v.* *red.* of taŋnapa.

t a ŋ - n i′, *adj.* *old, worn out.*

t a ŋ - n i′, *adv.* *of old:* taŋni hećeće kta epća, *I long thought it would be so; before; already.*

t a ŋ - n i′ - ć i ŋ - ć a, *n.* *a yearling calf.* *T.*, hećenićela.

t a ŋ - n i′ - h a ŋ, *adv.* *long ago, of old.* *T.*, ehaŋna.

taŋ-ni'-haŋ-taŋ-haŋ, *adv.* *of old, a long time ago.* *T.*, ehaŋnataŋhaŋ.

taŋ-ni'-ka, *adj.* *old, worn out, ancient.*

taŋ-ni'-la, *adj.* *T.* *old.*

taŋ-ni'-na, *adj.* *old.* *T.*, taŋnila.

taŋ-ni'-na, *adv.* *long ago, of old.* *T.*, ehaŋna.

taŋ-ni'-na-ka, *adv.* *of old, formerly.*

taŋ-ni'-ni, *adj.* *red.* of taŋni; *worn out.*

taŋ-o'-kśaŋ, *adv.* *around about, surrounding;* uŋkitaŋokśaŋpi, *around us.*

taŋ-o'-wa-siŋ, *n.* *the whole body.* *T.*, taŋćaŋ ataya.

taŋ-pa', *n.* *the white birch, Betula populifolia; the bark of the birch.* *T.*, ćaŋhasaŋ.

taŋ-pa'-ćaŋ-ka-ġi-ća, *n.* *spunk taken from the birch.*

taŋ-pa'-hu, *n.* *the white birch tree.*

taŋ-pa'-śa-śa-daŋ, *n.* *a small species of birch.*

taŋ-pa'-wa-kśi-ća, *n.* *dishes made out of the* taŋpa.

taŋ-pa'-wa-ta, *n.* *a birch-bark canoe.* *T.*, ćaŋhawata.

taŋ-sag', *cont.* of taŋsaka, which is not used: taŋsag ṭa, *to die of fright; to be much alarmed, to faint*—taŋsag maṭa: taŋsag ṭa eḣpeya, *to frighten very much.*

taŋ-sag'-ṭe-ya, *v. a* *to frighten very much*—taŋsagṭewaya.

taŋ-saŋ'-ni, *n.* *one side of the body.*

taŋ'-si-to-mni, *n.* *the whole body.*

taŋ'-si-to-mni-yaŋ, *adv.* *all over the body.*

taŋ-smi'-yaŋ-yaŋ, *adv.* *alone, deprived of everything:* taŋsmiyaŋyaŋ maŋka, *I am deprived of all.* *T.*, smismiyaŋ.

taŋ-smi'-yaŋ-yaŋ-ka, *n.* *one who is alone, without relations.* *T.*, wableniċa.

taŋ-śi'-ća, *adj.* *ugly, deformed*—taŋmaśića. *T.*, ośteka.

taŋ-śiŋ', *n.* *the fat on the ribs.*

taŋ-śna', *adj.* *alone, single, unmarried, without one's family:* taŋśna wauŋ, *I am alone;* wićataŋśna, *an unmarried man;* witaŋśna, *a single woman, a virgin*

taŋ-śna'-na, *adj.* *alone, without one's family:* taŋśnana uŋhipi, *we have come alone.*

taŋ'-taŋ-haŋ, *adj.* *from the body; near to* one.

taŋ-taŋ'-yaŋ, *adv. red.* of taŋyaŋ.

taŋ-te'-ća, *n.* *a species of red berry* that grows on a climbing plant.

taŋ-te'-ća-hu, *n.* *the vine producing the* taŋteća.

taŋ-toŋ', *v. n.* *to have a body, be in the body; to be substantial,* as some kinds of food. *T.* *to be ripe,* as fruit.

taŋ-toŋ'-ka, *adj.* *increasing in bulk,* as rice, etc., by cooking; *furnishing much nourishment for the quantity; very much so; exceedingly; exceptionally good.*

t a ŋ - t o ŋ′ - ś n i, *v. n.* *to have no body*, as a spirit; *to be unsubstantial*, as some kinds of food.

t a ŋ - t o ŋ′ - ś n i - y a ŋ, *v. a.* *to annihilate*—taŋtoŋśniwaya.

t a ŋ - t o ŋ′ - ś n i - y a ŋ, *adv.* *without body, unsubstantially; destitute*, as after giving away property on the death of one.

t a ŋ - t o ŋ′ - y a ŋ, *adv.* *visibly, bodily:* taŋtoŋyaŋ haŋ, *it stands visibly; a great deal.*

t a ŋ - t o ŋ′ - y a ŋ - k e l, *adv.* *T.* *excessively; intemperately:* taŋtoŋyaŋkel ia, *to speak angrily.*

t a ŋ - w a′ - ś t e, *adj.* *of fine form, handsome*—taŋmawaśte.

t a ŋ - y a m′, *adv.* taŋyam ia, *to take one's part, speak for* one; *i. q.* ićiya.

t a ŋ′ - y a ŋ, *adv.* *well:* taŋyaŋ uŋ, *to be well;* taŋyaŋ ećoŋ, *to do* anything *well;* taŋyaŋ iyeiçiya, *to be fortunate.*

t a ŋ′ - y a ŋ - k e n, *adv.* *well.*

t a ŋ - y a′ - t a - k i - y a, *adv.* *towards* one: taŋyatakiya hiyu, *to come towards* one.

t a ŋ - y e ḣ′, *cont.* of taŋyeḣiŋ.

t a ŋ - y e′ - ḣ ć i ŋ, *adv.* *T.* *very well, exceedingly well:* *i. q.* taŋyeḣiŋ.

t a ŋ - y e′ - k e l, *adv.* *T.* *whole, without injury.*

t a ŋ - y e′ - l a, *adv.* *T.* *well.*

t a ŋ - y e′ - ḣ i ŋ, *adv.* *very well.* *T.*, taŋyeḣćiŋ.

t a ŋ - z a′ - n i, *adj.* *healthy, in health, sound, not injured in body.*

t a ŋ - z a′ - n i - k e, *adv.* *T.* *well, in good health.*

t a ŋ - z a′ - n i - y a - k e, *adv.* *without injuring:* taŋzaniyake kaṭa, *to kill without injuring the skin* or *flesh.*

t a ŋ - z a′ - n i - y a ŋ, *adv.* *whole, not wounded.*

t a - o′, *v. a.* *to wound by shooting, wound*, but not kill—tawao.

t a - o m b′, *cont.* of taoŋpa. *T.* *leaning to one side.*

t a - o′ - k i - y e, *n.* *his disciple* or *assistant*—mitaokiye: taokiyeya, *to have for one's servant* or *helper.*

t a - o ŋ′ - p a, *v.* *to lean to one side.* See ataoŋpa.

t a - o′ - p i, *part.* *wounded; a wounded person* or *animal.*

t a - o′ - p i, *n.* *T.* *a wound.*

t a - o′ - u ŋ - y e, *n.* *his dwelling.*

t a - o′ - y a - t e, *n.* *his people*—mitaoyate.

t a′ - p a, *n.* *a deer's head.*

t a - p a′, *v. a.* *to follow after* one who has gone; *to follow*, as game; *to pursue*, as an enemy—tawapa.

t a′ - p a, *n.* *a ball*, such as the Dakotas use in playing.

t a - p a′ - ġ a, *n.* *the diaphragm of deer*, etc.

t a - p a′ - ḣ d o - ġ e - ź u, *n.* *the holes in an animal's head communicating with the nostrils; an edible plant having a pod* somewhat like that of the *Datura stramonium* or Jamestown weed *T.*, tapaḣlate.

t a - p a′ - ḣ l a - t e, *n.* *T.* *i. q.* tapaḣdoġeźu.

t a - p a' - k ś i ŋ, *n. the kidneys of buffalo*, etc. *T.*, taźoŋtka.

t a - p a' - z a - h u, *n. a species of plant having a pod.*

t a - p e' - t e, *n. the upper part of the back across the shoulders. T.*, tapetu.

t a - p e' - t e - p a, *adv. at the back. T.*, tapetupa.

t a - p e' - t e - p a - t a ŋ - h a ŋ, *adv. at* or *on the back. T.*, tapetupataŋhaŋ *and* tapetutaŋhan. See ilazataŋhaŋ, which is, *i. q.* tapetutaŋhaŋ, but incorrectly given as meaning "*from the side of.*"

t a - p e t' - o - g n a - k a, *v. T. to put* or *place on the back.*

t a - p e' - t u, *n. T. the back, the upper part of the back.*

t a - p e' - t u - o - g n a - k a, *v. T. i. q.* tapetognaka.

t a - p e' - t u - o - g n a g - y a, *and* t a - p e t' - o - g n a g - y a, *adv. T. placed on the back.*

t a - p e' - t u - p a, *adv. T. at the back.*

t a - p e' - t u - t a, *adv. T. on the back.*

t a - p i', *n. the liver of animals.*

t a - p i' - ś l e - ć a, *n. T. the spleen of animals.*

t a - p o', *n. the duodenum; one of the stomachs of ruminating animals; the crop of fowls.* See tatapo.

t a - p o ŋ', *n. the cheek*

t a - p o ŋ' - h u, *n. the cheek-bone.*

t a - p o' - p o - s k a, *n. T. tadpoles.*

t a - p o' - p u - s k a, *n. tadpoles. T.*, tapoposka.

t a - p o' - ś k o - h n a - k a, *v. n. to put* anything *on one's back under the blanket*—tapośkowahnaka. *T.*, tapetu ognaka.

t a - p s i' - p s i - z a, *v. red.* of tapsiza.

t a - p s i s', *cont.* of tapsiza; tapsis hiŋhda, *to bubble up*, as water when anything is thrown in, or spontaneously.

t a - p s i' - z a, *v. n. to bubble up, come up*, as bubbles on water.

t a - p t a' - h e - z a, *n. black currants, Ribes floridum.* See ćaptaheza.

t a - p u ŋ', *n.* See tapoŋ.

t a - s a g', *cont.* of tasaka; tasag hnaka, *to expose for the purpose of hardening.*

t a - s a g' - y a, *v. a. to cause to harden*—tasagwaya.

t a - s a g' - y a, *adv. in a hardened state:* tasagya hnaka, *to lay away in a hard state.*

t a - s a' - k a, *adj. stiff, hard, frozen, hardened by cooling*, whether at a temperature above or below the freezing point; *hard*, as tallow; *cold*, as, nape matasaka, *my hands are cold.*

t a - s a' - k a - ć a ŋ, *n. a kind of wood, a species of hard pine.*

t a - s a' - p a, *n. the black bear*, in the sacred dialect.

t a - s e', *intj. of contradiction* or *discredit*, as, tase, wimatko śni, *why no, I am not drunk:* tase hepe kaćaś, *that I said so is absurd:* it is followed by ka, kakeća, *or* kaćaś.—W. J. C.

ta-ska', *n.* taska wanuŋyaŋpi *and* taȟiŋća ska wanuŋyaŋpi, *sheep.* *T.*, taȟća śuŋka.

ta-ska'-kpa, *n.* *the woodlouse.*

ta-ska'-tpa, *n.* *the woodlouse.*

ta-spaŋ', *n.* *the red haw; apples.* So used now by the Yanktons and Teetons.—J. P. W.

ta-spaŋ'-ġi, *n* *lemons; oranges.*

ta-spaŋ'-hu, *n.* *the hawthorn; an apple tree.*

ta-spaŋ'-sdo-sdo-daŋ, *n.* *the dwarf red haw.*

ta-spaŋ'-taŋ-ka, *n.* *the crab apple, Pyrus coronaria; the common apple, Pyrus malus.*

ta-spaŋ'-taŋ-ka-hu, *n.* *the crab tree; the apple tree.*

ta-su'-su-o-źu-ha, *n.* *a shot-pouch.*

ta-śa'-ka, *n.* *the hoofs* or *nails of deer.* *T.*, taśake.

ta-śi'-śa-ke, *n.* *the nails* or *hoofs of animals*, used by the Dakotas for rattles. This was probably tasiśake originally.

ta-śi'-ya-gnoŋ-pa, *n.* *T.* *i. q.* taśiyakapopopa.

ta-śi'-ya-ka, *n.* *the pylorus* or *lower orifice of the stomach of ruminating animals; the large intestines.*

ta-śi'-ya-ka-po-po-pa, *n.* *a species of bird.* *T.*, taśiyagnoŋpa.

ta-śka'-daŋ, *n.* *the box-elder, Acer negundo.* Same as ćaŋśuśka.

ta-śko'-źu, *n.* *a grove of timber, thickly timbered land.*

ta-śna'-he-ća, *n.* *the prairie ground-squirrel.*

ta-śna'-he-ća-ȟo-ta, *n.* *the gray ground-squirrel.*

ta-śpu', *n.* *the stem*, as of a pumpkin; *a knob, a button.* See mazataśpu. *T.*, ćeśkika.

ta-śpu'-daŋ, *n.* *a knob, a button, the head* of a pin.

ta-śo'-śe, *v.* *T.* *to spit:* *i. q.* taġośa.

ta'-ta *or* ta-ta', *adj.* *dull, blunt, bruised up.*

ta-ta'-ȟpa, *n.* *the breast and neck of animals:* *i. q.* taȟpa.

ta-ta'-mni, *n.* *that which surrounds the fœtus, the womb of animals:* *i. q.* tamni.

ta-taŋ'-ka, *n.* *the male buffalo, the Bos,* or *Bison americanus; the common ox.*

ta-ta'-po, *n.* *the duodenum of ruminating animals; the omasum* or *third stomach.* See tapo.

ta-ta'-wa-mdu-śka, *n.* *the horse-fly.*

ta-ta'-wa-mdu-śka-daŋ, *n.* *the horse-fly.*

ta-te', *n.* *air in motion, wind.*

ta-te'-daŋ-se-ća, *n* *the essence of peppermint.*

ta-te'-i-yu-mni, *n.* *a whirlwind.*

ta-te'-ka-s'a, *v.* *the wind whistles.*

ta-te'-oŋ-na-ho-mni, *n.* (tate, oŋ, nahomni) *T.* *a wind-mill.*

ta-te'-o-u-ye, *n.* *a quarter of the heavens:* tate ouye topa, *the four quarters of the heavens.*

ta′-te-ya, *v.* *T.* *to hunt;* táte aya, *to go on a hunt with a large party;* used when a whole camp is moved along.—W. J. C.

ta-te′-yaŋ-pa, *v. n.* *it blows; the wind blows.*

ta-te′-yaŋ-pa, *n.* *wind.*

ta-tiŋ′-gle-ska, *n.* *T.* *intestinal worms.*

ta′-to, *n.* *cumfrey,* a root with a long branching stalk, the stem of which is eaten by the Dakotas; possibly also the *ginseng* root.

ta-to′-haŋ, *adv.* *up stream.* *T.*, tatowab. See tatowam.

ta-to′-he-ki-ya, *adv.* *against the wind,* or *current, up stream.*

ta-to′-he-ya, *adv.* *against the wind, up stream:* tatoheya uŋyaŋpi, *we go up stream,* or *against the wind.*

ta-to′-ka, *n.* *the big horned antelope.* Perhaps *the goat* of the Rocky Mountains, or *the Antelope rupicapra.*

ta-to′-ka-daŋ, *n.* *the gazelle* or *prairie antelope, the Antelope dorcas,* somewhat smaller than the common deer. They go in companies, and are very fleet.

ta-to′-wam, *cont.* of tatowapa; *up stream:* tatowam uŋyaŋpi. *T.*, tatowab.

ta-to′-wa-pa, *adv.* *up stream, up the river.*

ta-to′-wa-pa-taŋ-haŋ, *adv.* *from above, from up stream.*

ta-tpe′, *v.* *to come to, come upon, attack, make an attack on*—tawatpe, tauŋtpepi. *T.*, takpe.

ta-tpe′-hi, *v.* *to come to attack*—tatpewahi. See takpe hi, etc.

ta-tpe′-i, *v.* *to have been to attack*—tatpewai.

ta-tpe′-ya, *v.* *to go to attack*—tatpemda: tatpe iyaya, *to have gone to attack;* tatpe u, *to come to attack.*

ta-tpe′-ya, *adv.* *attacking.*

ta-uŋ′-ka, *v.* *T.* *to be be willing to do:* *i. q.* tawaŋka.

ta′-wa, *pron.* *his, hers, its*—mitawa, nitawa.

ta-wa′-ćiŋ, *n.* *the mind, will, understanding, disposition, purpose, thought*—mitawaćiŋ.

ta-wa′-ćiŋ-haŋ-ska, *adj.* *T.* *patient, long suffering.*

ta-wa′-ćiŋ-haŋ-ske-ya, *adv.* *patiently.*

ta-wa′-ćiŋ-hiŋ-yaŋ′-za, *adj.* *morose.*

ta-wa′-ćiŋ-ki-ç̇uŋ, *v. n.* *to be resolute, obstinate, have a mind of one's own*—tawaćiŋweç̇uŋ.

ta-wa′-ćiŋ-ki-ç̇uŋ′-yaŋ, *adv.* *resolutely.*

ta-wa′-ćiŋ-su-ta, *adj.* *firm, resolute, not easily influenced.*

ta-wa′-ćiŋ-su-ta-ya, *adv.* *resolutely.*

ta-wa′-ćiŋ-śi-ća, *adj.* *of a bad disposition*—tawaćiŋmaśića.

ta-wa′-ćiŋ-wan-ka-la, *adj.* *T.* *fickle, easily influenced.*

ta-wa′-ćiŋ-wa-śte, *adj.* *of a good disposition*—tawaćiŋmawaśte.

ta-wa′-ġaŋ, *n.* *a step-son; a step-father; any step relation.*

ta-wa'-ġaŋ-ku, *n.* *his step-son* or *step-father.*

ta-wa'-ġaŋ-ya, *v. a.* *to have for* tawaġaŋ—tawaġaŋwaya.

ta-wa'-ḣe-ća, *n.* *a swelling, a bubo; the groin.*

ta'-wa-i-ç̣i-ya, *v. reflex.* *to own one's self; to be free.*

ta'-wa-i-ç̣i-ya-pi, *n.* *freedom, liberty.*

ta-wa'-koŋ-ze, *n.* *his influence* or *purpose.* This is used for the Spirit of God—nitawakoŋze. *T.*, tawokoŋze.

ta-wa'-mni-pa, *n.* *the seven stars* in the constellation Taurus. *T*, tayamnipa.

ta-waŋ'-ka, *v. n.* *to be willing to undertake, disposed to do* or *attempt.* Generally this is used in the negative, as, tawaŋka śni, *not to be disposed to*—tamuŋka śni. *T.*, tauŋka. See tawaṭenya.

ta-waŋ'-źi, *n.* *one* of anything, *a pair:* tanoŋpa, *two* of anything, *two pairs;* tayamni, *three pairs.*

ta'-wa-śe, *n.* *T.* *a woman's female friend:* *i. q.* kola.

ta'-wa-śe-tku, *n.* *T.* *her female friend.*

ta'-wa-śe-ya, *v.* *to have for female friend.*

ta-wa'-ṭe-ća, *v.* See tawaṭenya.

ta-wa'-ṭel-śi-ća, *adj.* *T.* *unendurable, excessive.*

ta-wa'-ṭen-ki-ya, *v. a.* *to be willing to have* such a thing happen to one—tawaṭenwakiya, tawaṭenćićiya.

ta-wa'-ṭen-ya, *v. a.* *to be willing for* anything, *desirous to do* or *suffer*—tawaṭenwaya, tawaṭenuŋyaŋpi. See tawaŋka.

ta'-wa-śi, *n.* *a helper; a helpmate; a friend.* *T.*, tawowaśi.

ta'-wa-śi-tku, *n.* *his* or *her helper* or *friend.*

ta'-wa-śi-ya, *v. a.* *to have for helper*—tawaśiwaya. *T.*, tawowaśiya.

ta'-wa-ya, *v. a.* *to possess* anything, *have for one's own*—tawawaya, tawauŋyaŋpi.

ta-wa'-zu-zu-ḣe-ća, *n.* *intestinal worms, lumbrici.* *T*, tatiŋgleska.

ta'-we-la-ha, *n.* *T.* *a summer robe; a robe* from an animal killed in spring or summer: *i. q.* taḣuśdaha.

ta-wi'-ću, *n.* *his wife.* See tawiŋ.

ta-wi'-ću-toŋ, *v.* *to have a wife, be married*—tawićuwatoŋ, tawićuuŋtoŋpi.

ta'-wi'-na-pće, *n.* *the gullet of animals.*

ta'-wi-no-ḣćiŋ, *n.* *T.* *his wife.*

ta'-wi-no-ḣtiŋ, *n.* *a man's sister*—mitawinoḣtiŋ, nitawinoḣtiŋ. *T.*, taŋkśitku.

ta'-wi-no-ḣtiŋ-ya, *v. a.* *to have for* tawinoḣtiŋ—tawinoḣtiŋwaya.

ta-wiŋ', *n.* *a wife,* used only with the pronouns: mitawiŋ, *my wife;* nitawiŋ, *thy wife.*

ta-wiŋ'-ya, *v. a.* *to have sexual intercourse with a woman*—tawiŋwaya, tawiŋmayaŋ.

ta-wi′-toŋ, *or* ta-wiŋ′-toŋ, *v. a.* *to have sexual intercourse with a woman*—tawiwatoŋ, tawiuŋtoŋpi. The former orthography is preferred.

ta-wi′-ye-daŋ, *n.* *the female of the common deer, a doe* or *hind.*

ta-won′, *n.* *something to eat, food:* tawon manića: tawon toŋ, *to have food.* *T.*, tawoyute.

ta-wo′-koŋ-ze, *n.* *his influence* or *purpose.* See tawakoŋze.

ta-wo′-wa-śi, *n.* *T.* *his helper* or *servant:* *i. q.* tawaśi.

ta-wo′-wa-śi-ya, *v.* *to have for helper*, etc.: *i. q.* tawaśiya.

ta-wo′-yu-te, *n.* *his food.*

ta-ya′-mni-pa, *n.* *T.* *the seven stars in Taurus.* See tawamnipa.

ta-zu′-ka, *n.* *white walnuts, butternuts.*

ta-zu′-ka-hu, *n.* *the butternut tree, white walnut, the Juglans cinerea.*

ta′-źa, *n.* *waves.* *T.*, minikaataźa.

ta′-źa, *adj.* *rough*, as water agitated; nina taźa, *very rough.* *T.*, kaataźa.

ta-źoŋ′-tka, *n.* *T.* *the kidneys in animals:* *i. q.* tapakśiŋ.

ta-źo′-pa-wi-wi, *n.* *waves without white caps*

ta-źu′-śka, *n.* *the ant, ants, the emmet.*

te, *adj.* *blue stained.* See ate. *T.*, to.

teb-ki′-ći-ći-ya, *v.* *T.* *to eat up for one.* See temkiya.

teb-ki′-ći-ya-pi, *v.* *they eat each other up.*

teb-ki′-ya, *v. pos.* *T.* *to eat up one's own:* *i. q.* temkiya.

teb-ya′, *v.* *T.* *to eat up.* See temya, etc.

te′-ća, *adj.* *new*—mateća, niteća, uŋtećapi.

t′e′-ća, *adj.* *warm, lukewarm, tepid,* as water. See it′eća.

te′-ća-ya, *adv.* *newly.*

te′-ća-ya, *v. a.* *to make new, renew*—tećawaya.

te′-ća-ya-ken, *adv.* *newly.*

te′-haŋ, *adj.* *far; long*, used both in regard to time and place: tehaŋ wai, *I have been to a great distance;* tehaŋ waŋmdaka, *I saw it a long time.* See tȟaŋka.

te′-haŋ-haŋ, *adv.* *red.* of tehaŋ.

te′-haŋ-taŋ-haŋ, *adv.* *from afar.*

te′-haŋ-tu, *adv.* *far off, to* or *at a great distance.*

te′-haŋ-tu-ya, *adv.* *afar, far off.*

te′-haŋ-tu-ya-ken, *adv.* *far off.*

te-haŋ′-waŋ-kan, *adv.* *high up, very high.* *T.*, tehaŋwaŋkaŋl.

te′-haŋ-waŋ-kaŋl, *adv.* *T.* *high up.*

te-haŋ′-waŋ-kan-tu, *adv.* *very high.*

te-haŋ′-waŋ-kan-tu-ya, *adv.* *very high.* *T*, tehaŋwaŋkaŋltuya.

te-haŋ′-waŋ-kan-tu-ya-ken, *adv.* *loftily, high up.*

te-ḣi', *adj.* *difficult, hard to be done* or *endured*

te-ḣi'-ḣi-ka, *adj.* *red.* of teḣika.

te-ḣi'-ḣi-ya, *adv.* *red.* of teḣiya.

te-ḣi'-ka, *adj.* *hard to do* or *bear, difficult; dear, costly, valuable; hard to get along with, unreasonable*—mateḣika.

te-ḣi'-ke-da, *v. a.* *to think hard* or *difficult; to value very much*—teḣikewada, teḣikeuŋdapi.

te-ḣi'-ke-da-ka, *v.* Same as teḣikeda.

te-ḣi'-ke-ki-da, *v.* *pos.* of teḣikeda; *to value one's own*—teḣikewakida.

te-ḣi'-ke-ki-da-ka, *v.* Same as teḣikekida.

te-ḣi'-la, *v.* *T.* *to love, value very highly; to be unwilling to part with.*

te-ḣiŋ'-da, *v. a.* *to forbid* any one's doing or having a thing, *forbid* any course of conduct, *prohibit, hinder; to value very much, to be sparing of*—tewaḣiŋda, teyaḣiŋda, teuŋḣiŋdapi. *T.*, teḣila.

te-ḣi'-slol-ye-ki-ya, *v.* *T.* *to punish, to cause to suffer.* See sdonyekiya.

te-ḣi'-ya, *adv.* *hardly, with difficulty; badly:* teḣiya ećoŋ, *to do with difficulty, to do badly;* teḣi śni ećoŋ, *to do a thing easily.*

te ḣi'-ya-ken, *adv.* *with difficulty.*

te-ḣi'-ya-ku-wa, *v. a.* *to follow after for evil, to treat badly, to persecute.*

te-ḣmi'-so, *n.* *a leather string, a thong.* This is Santee; other bands or clans use "wikaŋ."

te-ḣpi, *n.* *a skin with the hair taken off worn as a blanket.* *T.*, ptehaśla.

te-ma'-hel, *adv.* *T.* *i. q.* temahen.

te-ma'-hen, *adv.* of mahen; *deep, far within.* *T.*, temahel.

te-ma'-hen-tu, *adv.* *far down, deep down.* *T.*, temaheltu.

te-ma'-hen-tu-ya, *adv* *deeply; deep down.* *T.*, temaheltuya.

tem-ki'-ći-ya, *v.* of temya, *to eat up provisions* of any kind *for* another—temwećiya.

tem-ki'-ya, *v. a.* *to eat up one's own; to eat up another's* or *for* another—temwakiya, temuŋkiyapi, temmakiya. *T.*, tebkiya.

te-mni', *v. n.* *to sweat; to pant, give out,* always including the idea of sweating—temamni, tenimni, teuŋmnipi.

te-mni'-ṭa, *v. n.* *to sweat very profusely, to die of sweating:* temni maṭa nuŋ seća, *it seems as if I should die of sweating.*

tem-te'-pa, *adj.* *red.* of tepa.

tem-ya', *v. a.* *to eat all up, to devour;* temwaya. *T.*, tebya.

te'-pa, *adj.* root form; *worn off,* as in batepa, katepa.

te-pa'-haŋ, *part.* *worn off.*

te-śdag', *cont.* of teśdaka.

te-śdag'-ki-toŋ, *v.* *to put on* or *wear a crown* or *fillet on the head*—teśdagwetoŋ.

te-śdag'-toŋ, *v.* (teśdag *and* toŋ) *to put on* or *wear a fillet around the head*—tesdagwatoŋ. See wateśdake.

te-śda'-ka, *v.* *to wear*, as a crown or fillet, *around the head*—tewaśdaka.

te-te', *n.* *the rim* of a kettle, *the rim* or *lip* of anything. *T.*, ićete.

te-te', *adj.* *red.* of te; *blue, grape-colored.* *T.*, tosapa.

te-te'-ni-ća, *n.* *the blue jay.* *T.*, zitkato.

te-waŋ'-haŋ-kan, *adv.* *high up.* *T.*, tehaŋwaŋkaŋl.

te-waŋ'-haŋ-kan-tu, *adv.* *up high.*

te-waŋ'-haŋ-kan-tu-ya, *adv.* *high up.*

te-waŋ'-haŋ-kan-tu-ya-ken, *adv.* *up high.*

te-waŋ'-kan, *adv.* *high up.* *T.*, tehaŋwaŋkaŋl.

te-waŋ-kan-tu, *adv.* *high up.*

te-waŋ'-kaŋ-tu-ya, *adv.* *high up.*

te-wa'-pa, *n.* *an esculent root*, growing in the water, which the Dakotas boil and eat.

te-wa'-pa-a-ȟe, *n.* *a plant somewhat like* the tewapa, but not eaten.

te-wa'-pa-hu, *n.* *the stalk* of the tewapa.

te-wi'-ća-mni, *n.* of temni; *sweating.*

te'-ya, *n.* *when a man has more than one wife, one calls the other* teya.

te'-ya-ki-ći-ya-pi, *n.* *those who stand in the relation of* teya *to each other.*

te'-ya-ku, *n.* *her* teya.

te'-ya-ya, *v. a.* *to have* one *for* teya—teyawaya, teyamayaŋ.

te-zi', *n.* *the stomach* or *paunch* of animals; *the gizzard* of fowls; *the belly.*

te-źig'-źi-će, *n.* *T.* *the fat around the paunch.*

te-źi'-kśi-źe, *n.* *the fat around the paunch.* *T.*, teźigźići.

tȟaŋ'-ka, *adj.* *T.* *i. q.* taŋka, *large.* The "ȟ" sound is introduced between "t" and its vowel quiet frequently by the Titoŋwaŋ; perhaps with the idea of giving emphasis. I am more inclined, however, to regard it as a conventionality. I give some examples: tȟo, *i. q.* to, *blue;* tȟokeća, *i. q.* tokeća, *different;* tȟehaŋ, *i. q.* tehaŋ, *far.*—W. J. C.

ti, *v. n.* *to live, dwell, abide*—wati, uŋtipi.

ti, *n.* *a house.* See tipi.

ti'-a-no-ka-taŋ-haŋ, *adv.* *on both sides of the house.*

ti-a'-waŋ-ya-ka, *v.* *to stand guard about a house; to stay at home and watch the house:* *i. q.* beyaŋkeća.

ti-blo', *n.* *T.* *i. q.* timdo.

ti-blo'-ku, *n.* *T* *i. q.* timdoku.

ti'-ća. See patića, *to scrape off.*

ti-ća'-bu-daŋ, *n.* *the pheasant.*

ti-ća'-ġa, *v.* *to put up a tent, pitch a tent; to build a house*—tiwakaġa, tiuŋkaġapi.

ti-ća'-haŋ, *part.* *scraped off; falling off of itself.*

ti'-ća-ni-će, *n.* See tićaniće-taŋka.

ti-'ća-ni-će-taŋ-ka, *n.* *a species of curlew.*

ti-ća′-tku, *n.* *the part of the tent* or *house opposite the door, the place of honor.*

ti-ća′-tku-ta, *adv.* *opposite the door.*

ti-ća′-wa-haŋ, *part.* *scraped off; falling off,* as hair from a soaked hide.

ti-će′, *n.* *the top of a tent* or *house, the comb; the hole where the smoke goes out:* tiće iyakaśka, *to tie up to the top of a tent.*

ti-će′-iŋ-kpa, *n.* *the top of a tent, the ridge of a house.*

ti-će′-śka, *n.* *the top of a tent, the ridge of a house.*

ti-će′-śka-o-ḣdo-ka, *n.* *the hole at the top of the tent* by which the smoke escapes.

ti′-daŋ, *v.* kići tidaŋ, *to take sides with one* on a question, *to be on the same side* in a game: miśnana watidaŋ, *I am alone,* that is, no one takes my side—uŋtipidaŋ. *T.,* tila.

ti′-haŋ-mde, *v.* See tihaŋmdeya.

ti′-haŋ-mde-ya, *v.* *to have been acquainted with in a former state of existence*—tihaŋmdewaya. *T.,* ćekpata uŋ slolya.

ti-hde′, *v.* *to have a family; to make a home.* *T.,* tigle.

ti-hdo′-ni-ća, *v.* *to forbid one's house, to prevent others from coming in*—tiwahdonića.

ti-gle′, *v.* *T.* *to be married; to have a house to live in.*

ti-hu′-ḣa, *n* *the poles of a tent left standing, the skeleton of a tent.*

ti-hu′-ḣa-ka, *n.* *T.* *the skeleton of a tent; the frame of a house.*

ti′-ḣa-ha, *n.* *the manyplies* or *omasum of animals.* *T.* tiḣamnamna.

ti′-ḣa-mna, *adj.* *T.* *having manyplies.*

ti′-ḣa-mna-mna, *n.* *T.* *the omasum* or *manyplies,* next in size to the taniġa. The four divisions are according to size, respectively, taniġa, tiḣamnamna, tatapo, *and* imnamnahića.—W. J. C.

tiḣ-muŋ′-ġa, *n.* *T.* *the house fly, flies.* See tuḣmaġa.

ti-kti′-ća, *adj.* *thick, stiff,* as mush; *sticky.* Hence, ćaŋhaŋpi tiktića, *molasses.*

til, *cont.* of ti en. *T.*

ti′-la, *v.* of ti. *T.* *to dwell;* hel watila, *I live there; to take sides with.* See tidaŋ.

ti-le′-haŋ-yag, *and* ti-le′-haŋ-yaŋk, *adv.* *T.* *i. q.* titokaŋ; tilehaŋyag iyaya, *he has gone to another house.*

tim, *cont.* *T.* for tin.

ti′-ma-hel, *adv.* *T.* *inside the house; within.*

ti′-ma-hen, *adv.* *within, in the house* or *inclosure.* *T.,* timahel.

ti′-ma-he-taŋ-haŋ, *adv.* *from within.*

ti′-ma-he-tu, *adv.* *within.*

ti-ma′-ta, *v.* *to ask for, beg:* timata hi, *to come begging.*

ti-mdo′, *n.* *a woman's elder brother, my elder brother:* nitimdo, *thy elder brother.* *T.,* tiblo.

t i - m d o' - k u, *n.' her elder brother.* *T.*, tibloku.

t i - m d o' - y a, *v. a. to have for elder brother*—timdowaya. *T.*, tibloya.

t i - m l o', *n. T. i. q.* timdo. See tiblo.

t i n, *adv. cont.* (ti *and* en) *in the house:* tin yaŋka, *he is in the house;* also, *cont.* of tiŋta, as, tinmaśtiŋća, *the hare* *T.*, til.

t i' - n a - z i - p e, *n.* of itazipe; *his bow*—mitinazipe, nitinazipe. *T.*, titazipe.

t i n' - ć a ŋ - n a n, *adv. out on the prairie.* *T.*, tiiheyapaya.

t i n' - k t e, *v. to kill in the house, to commit homicide,* in distinction from killing in war—tinwakte, tinwićakte. *T.*, tiokte.

t i n' - m a - ś t i ŋ' - ć a, *n. the hare, rabbit of the prairie, the Lepus timidus.* *T.*, maśtiŋska.

t i n' - w a - k i - y e - d a ŋ, *n. the house-pigeon; the turtle dove.* *T.*, wakiŋyela.

t i n' - w i - ć a - k t e, *v. a. to commit murder*—tinwićawakte. Also, *a murderer.* *T.*, tilwicakte.

t i n' - w i - ć a - k t e - p i, *n. murder.*

t i ŋ - g l e' - ś k a, *n. T. a fawn.*

t i ŋ' - ġ a, *v. n. to press, to be in labor,* as a woman in childbirth. See ṭiŋġa.

t i ŋ' - s k o, *adv. how large?* See hiŋsko.

t i ŋ' - s k o - k e - ć a, *adv. how big? how large?* See hiŋskokeća.

t i ŋ' - s k o - s k o - k e - ć a, *adv. red.* of tiŋskokeća.

t i ŋ' - s k o - s k o - y a, *adv. red.* of tiŋskoya.

t i ŋ' - s k o - y a, *adv. how far around? how extensively?* See hiŋskoya.

t i ŋ' - ś k o - d a ŋ, *adv. of what size? how small?* See hiŋśkodaŋ.

t i ŋ' - t a, *n. land without timber, the prairie.*

t i ŋ' - t a - m a - k o - b l a - b l a - y a, *adv. T. timbered land with open spaces.*

t i ŋ' - t a n, *adv. on* or *at the prairie.*

t i ŋ' - t a - o - s k a n, *adv. on the prairie, far from dwellings.*

t i ŋ' - t a - p a, *adv. belonging to the prairie;* as, tiŋtapa wićaśta, *men of the prairie;* tiŋtapa ia, *to speak as the men of the prairie do.*

t i ŋ' - t a - t a, *adv. at* or *on the prairie.*

t i ŋ' - t a - t a - p a, *adv. at the prairie.*

t i ŋ' - t a - w a - p a, *adv. on* or *towards the prairie.*

t i ŋ - o' - p t a, *adv. across the prairie.*

t i ŋ t - o' - s k a, *n. T. an opening in the woods.*

t i ŋ t - o' - s k a - s k a - y a, *adv. T. with open spaces*

t i ŋ t - o' - s k a ŋ, *adv. on the prairie; far from dwellings.*

t i ŋ' - z a, *adj. firm, tight:* otiŋza.

t i - o' - k o, *n. a house yard.*

t i - o' - k t e, *v. T. to kill; to commit murder: i. q.* tinkte.

t i - o' - t a - h e - l a, *adv. T. among the houses.*

t i - o' - l e, *v. T. to hunt a house for lodging or for a meal;* tiole mni kta.

t i - o' - n a - k i - p a, *v. to flee to the house.*

ti-o'-śpa-ye, *n* *T.* *a band; a clan; a party under one chief.*

ti'-pa. See yutipa.

ti-pa'-haŋ, *part.* *drawn up, cramped; crisped.*

ti'-pa-hiŋ, *n.* of ipahiŋ; *his pillow.*

ti-pa'-wa-haŋ, *part.* *drawn up, cramped.*

ti'-pi, *n.* *a tent, house, dwelling, abode.* See ti.

ti'-pi-wa-kaŋ, *n.* *a sacred house, a church.*

ti'-psiŋ, *n.* See tipsiŋna.

ti'-psiŋ-la, *n.* *T.*: *i. q.* tipsiŋna.

ti'-psiŋ-la-śa-śa, *n.* *T.* *radishes, beets.* See paŋġiśaśa.

ti'-psiŋ-na, *n.* *the Dakota turnip,* a bulbous root much eaten by the Dakotas in the beginning of summer. It grows on the high dry prairies. *T.*, tipsiŋla.

ti'-psiŋ-na-ska, *n.* *the white turnip.*

ti'-psiŋ-na-zi, *n.* *the rutabaga.*

ti'-śka-kaŋ, *n.* of iśkakaŋ; *the large sinew in the neck of animals.*

ti'-śko-na-ġi, *n.* of iśkonaġi (*the ghost of the leg*); *the bunch of hair growing on the inside of a deer's leg.*

ti'-śti, *n.* of iśti; *the lower lip of animals:* also, *his lower lip.*

ti-ta'-ku-ye, *n.* *T.* *a relative.* See takuye.

ti-ta'-zi-pe, *n.* *T.* *his bow.* See tinazipe.

Ti'-toŋ-waŋ, *n.* *i. q.* tiŋta-toŋwaŋ; *the name of the bands of Dakotas living on and beyond the Missouri, the Teetons.* They probably compose a majority of the whole nation. Their language differs from the dialects of the other bands, especially in their use of *l* for *d*.

ti'-toŋ-waŋ-se, *adj.* *proud, haughty,* because the Teetoŋs are thought to be so.

ti-uŋ'-na-ptaŋ-yaŋ, *n.* of uŋnaptaŋ; *the sides of a house, sides of the roof.*

ti-wa'-he, *n.* *a household,* including persons as well as things. See tiyohe.

ti-wo'-ta-he-daŋ, *adv.* of otahedaŋ; *away from any house.* *T.*, tiotahela.

ti-yaŋ', *cont.* of tiyata.

ti'-yaŋ-ka, *intj.* *T.* *wait! hold on!* *i. q.* hinyaŋkaha.

ti-ya'-ta, *adv.* *at the house, at home.*

ti-ya'-ta-ki-ya, *adv.* *towards the house:* tiyatakiya wahde kta, *I will go towards home.*

ti-ye'-pa, *n.* *T.* *a door:* *i. q.* tiyopa.

ti-ye'-pa-ta, *adv.* *T.* *at the door.*

ti-yo'-ble-ća *and* ti-o'-ble-ća, *n.* *T.* *an* A *tent,* or *a square tent;* not a Dakota tent.

ti-yo'-gna-ka, *n.* *T.* *i. q.* tiyohnaka.

ti-yo'-he, *n.* *a household; a place where a house once stood, a deserted house.* See tiwahe.

ti-yo′-hna-ka, *n.* (ti *and* ohnaka.) *the household.* *T.*, tiyognaka.

ti-yo′-ki-ta-he-daŋ, *adv.* *between houses.* See okitahedaŋ.

ti-yom′, *cont.* of tiyopa. *T.*, tiyob.

ti-yom′-i-na-ta-ke, *n.* *a door lock.* *T.*, tiyobinatake See nataka.

ti-yom′-ya, *v. a.* *to have* or *use for a door*—tiyomwaya.

ti-yo′-pa, *n.* *a door, the place of entrance; that which covers the entrance* in a Dakota tent, *a door.* *T.*, tiyepa.

ti-yo′-pa-gmi-gme-la *and* ti-ye′-pa-gmi-gme-la, *n.* *T.* *a door knob.*

ti-yo′-pa-i-yo-ka-tku-ġe, *n.* *a nail, nails.; screws.* So called perhaps from their being first used among the Dakotas only in making *doors.* *T.*, tiyepa iyokatkuġe.

ti-yo′-pa-ta, *adv.* *at the door.* *T.*, tiyepata.

ti-yo′-ślo-la, *n.* *T.* *a cricket, crickets.*

ti-yo′-śpa-ye, *n.* *a band, a division of a tribe: i. q.* tiośpaye.

ti-yo′-ti, *v.* *to set up a soldiers' lodge*—tiyouŋtipi.

ti-yo′-ti-pi, *n.* *a soldiers' lodge.* This is established for the purpose of making laws and providing for their execution. The object is generally to regulate the buffalo chase.

ti-yo′-toŋ-waŋ, *v.* (ti *and* otoŋwaŋ) *to look into a house.*

ti-yu′-kaŋ, *v.* of yukaŋ; *to leave the house.* Said when the women and children leave the tent for the men to feast in. See kiyukaŋ.

tka, *v. a.* *to scrape the hair off* a hide—watka, uŋtkapi.

tka, *adj.* *T.* *heavy: i. q.* tke.

tka, *conj.* *cont.* of tuk̇a; *but.*

tkab′-ya, *adv.* *T.* *stiffly: i. q.* damya.

tka′-eś, *conj.* *T.* *but, although.*

tka′-pa, *adj.* *adhesive, clammy.* See oskapa.

tke, *adj.* *heavy.*

tke′-i-yu-ta, *v a.* *to take up and feel the weight, to weigh*—tkeimduta. See tkeuta.

tke-tke′, *adj.* *red.* of tke.

tke-u′-ta, *v. a.* *to weigh* anything—tkeuwata.

tke-u′-ta-pi, *n.* *a pound; measures of weight; weights:* oŋ tkeutapi, *scales, a steel-yard.* *T.*, witkeyute.

tke′-ya, *adv.* *heavily:* tkeya ḳiŋ, *she carries heavily.*

tke′-ya-wa-ḳiŋ-ki-ya, *v.* *to load heavily, to overload.*

tkiŋ, *adj* *damp*, said of a less degree of wet than is denoted by "spaya."

tkiŋ′-yaŋ, *adj.* *damp*, as clothes.

tkiŋ′-tkiŋ, *red.* of tkiŋ.

tki-tka′, *adj.* *slushy*, as snow when soft.

tki-tka′-tka, *adj.* *red.* of tkitka.

tkoŋ-sa′, *n.* *a cipher*, in arithmetic.

t k o ŋ - s a′, *adj. even, just, exactly:* wikćemna nom tkoŋsa, *just twenty.* See tkoŋza, tkuŋsa, *and* otkoŋza.

t k o ŋ - s e′ - d a ŋ, *adj. even,* in numbers, as twenty, thirty, etc.

t k o ŋ s′ - y e - l a, *adv. T. evenly.*

t k o ŋ′ - z a, *adj even.* See tkoŋsa.

t k u. See yutku, natku, etc.

t k u′ - ġ a. See katkuġa.

t k u - ġ a′ - h a ŋ, *part. broken off.*

t k u - ġ a′ - w a - h a ŋ, *part. broken off.*

t k u ŋ - s a′, *adj even, just so much.* See tkoŋsa *and* tkuŋza.

t k u ŋ - s a′ - y a, *adv. evenly.*

t k u ŋ s - y a′, *adv. evenly.*

t k u ŋ′ - z a, *adj. even, square with.*

t k u - t k u′, *red.* of tku.

t k u - t k u′ - ġ a, *red.* of tkuġa.

t k u - t k u′ - ġ a - h a ŋ, *part. broken off in several places.*

t k u - t k u′ - ġ a - w a - h a ŋ, *part. broken off.*

t k u - w a′ - h a ŋ, *part. broken off,* as a spoon-handle, *flawed:* tkuwahe se mahiŋhda; said when one's legs are very tired and refuse further support.

t o, *adv. interrog. cont.* of tokeća; *why?* This is used at the end of the sentence; as, ećanoŋ śni to, *why don't you do it?*

t o *and* t o′ - i, *adv. T.: i. q.* toś, *yes;* used by men commonly.

t o, *adj. blue; green,* and the intermediate shades.

t o *for* t a, *pron.* Used in some cases when the noun commences with wo, as woćaŋniye, *anger;* toćaŋniye, *his anger.*

t o, *n. T. the noise made by a blow.*

t o′ - ć a ŋ - t e - p t a ŋ - y e, *n.* of woćaŋteptaŋye; *his wrath. T.,* toćaŋniye.

t o g, *cont.* of toki *and* tokeća.

t o g′ - e - ḣ p e - k i - y a, *v. a. to lose* anything, *throw away* one knows not where—togeḣpewakiya. *T.,* tokieḣpekiya.

t o g′ - e - ḣ p e - y a, *v. a. to lose* anything—togeḣpewaya, togeḣpeuŋyaŋpi.

t o g′ - g l a, *adj. T. dirty; indecent, unkempt.*

t o g - h d a′, *v. a. to count as a stranger, not to be familiar with, to be shy of*—togwahda, toguŋhdapi: toghda śni, *to be familiar with.*

t o g′ - i - a, *v. T. to talk a strange language: i. q.* śaia.

t o g - t o g′ - y e, *adv. red.* of togye; *in different ways.*

t o g - y e′, *adv. in a different manner, differently.*

t o - h a n′, *adv. when, at what time? T.,* tohaŋl. See dehan, dehaŋ, ehaŋ, iyehan, etc.

t o - h a n′ - h a n, *adv. red.* of tohan; *at what times? T.,* tohaŋlhaŋl.

t o′ - h a ŋ - ś n a, *adv. T. sometime.*

t o - h a n′ - t u, *adv. when? T.,* tohaŋltu. See dehaŋtu, ehaŋtu, kahantu, etc.

t o - h a n′ - t u - k a - ś t a, *adv. whenever, at any time. T.,* tohaŋltukaśa.

t o - h a n′ - t u - y a - k a - ś t a, *adv. whenever.*

t o - h a ŋ′, *adv.* *how far, to what place, where?* *T.*, tohaŋl. See dehaŋ, hehaŋ, kahaŋ, etc.

t o - h a ŋ′ - h a ŋ, *adv.* *red.* of tohaŋ; *at what places? how far?*

t o - h a ŋ′ - h a ŋ - k e - ć a, *adv.* *red.* of tohaŋkeća.

t o - h a ŋ′ - h a ŋ - y a ŋ, *adv.* *red* of tohaŋyan.

t o - h a ŋ′ - k e - ć a, *adv.* *how long?* usually referring to space. See dehaŋkeća, hehaŋkeća, etc.

t o - h a ŋ l′, *adv.* *T.* *when, where?*

t o - h a ŋ′ - t u - k e š, *adv.* *wherever, at any place.*

t o - h a ŋ′ - y a ŋ, *adv.* *how long, to what time? how far, to what place?* See dehaŋyaŋ, kahaŋyan, etc.

t o′ - h e, *n.* *his place, his camp; his office* or *position.*

t o′ - h i ŋ - g l a, *v. n.* *T.* *to resound.*

t o′ - h i ŋ - n i, *adv.* *when?* This word is an interrogative, always referring to past time; as, tohiŋni yahdi he, *when didst thou come home?* With "śni" following, it is used affirmatively, and means *never;* as, tohiŋni ećamoŋ śni, *I never did it.* *T.*, toŋwel. See ohiŋni.

t o′ - h o - w i ŋ - n i, *adv.* See tohiŋni, which seems to be the better orthography.

t o′ - ḣ a ŋ, *n.* *his acts.* See oḣaŋ.

t o′ - ḣ ć a, *adj.* *T* *blue,* as distinguished from *green.*

t o′ - ḣ t a - n i, *n.* *his* or *her work*—mitoḣtani, nitoḣtani. See wićoḣtani. *T.*, wowaśi tawa.

t o′ - i - y o - k i - t a ŋ - i ŋ, *n.* *his manifestation.*

t o - k a′, *adv.* *at the first.* See tokaheya.

t o′ - k a, *n.* *an enemy, one of a hostile nation.*

t o′ - k a, *adv.* See tókadaŋ: tóka ećamoŋ śni, *I cannot do it.*

t o′ - k a *and* t o′ - k a - e, *adv.* *Ih.* and *T.* *why? how is it?*

t o′ - k a - d a ŋ, *adv.* with śni following, *in no way;* as, tókadaŋ ećamoŋ śni, *I could do it in no way.* *T.*, tokani.

t o - k a′ - d a ŋ, *and* t o - k a′ - n a, *n.* *a small wolf—the swift.* *T.*, tokala.

t o - k a g′ - e - h a ŋ, *adv.* *at the first, formerly.* *T.*, tokagohaŋ.

t o - k a g′ - o - h a ŋ, *adv.* *T.* *at the first.*

t o - k a g′ - o - h e - e - h a ŋ, *adv.* *T.* *at the beginning.*

t o - k a′ - h a ŋ, *v. n.* *to travel foremost, to be foremost*—tokawahaŋ. *T.*, tokahe. See otokahe.

t o - k a′ - h e, *n.* *the first, the beginning.* See otokahe.

t o - k a′ - h e, *v.* *T.* *to be first; to go before.*

t o - k a′ - h e - k i - y a, *v. a.* *to cause to go before*—tokahewakiya.

t o - k a′ - h e - y a, *n* *the first.*

t o - k a′ - h e - y a, *adv.* *at the first, before:* tokaheya ya, *to go before.*

t o′ - k a - h u, *n.* *the thistle, Carduus lanceolatus.*

t o - k a ḣ′, *adv.* *at the first.*

t o - k a′ - ḣ ć i ŋ, *adv.* *T.* *at the first.*

to-ka'-ḣiŋ, *adv.* *at the first, the very first.* *T.*, tokaḣćiŋ.

to'-ka-ḣoŋ *or* to'-ka-ḣaŋ, *v. n.* *to lose, to suffer loss: what has become of it?*

to-ka'-ḣta, *n.* See tokaḣtayetu.

to-ka'-ḣta-ye-tu, *n.* *the first of the night, dusk.*

to'-ka-ḣuŋ, *adv.* *T.* *lost, misplaced.*

to'-ka-i-a-pi, *n.* *a foreign language; enemy's language.*

to'-ka-ki-ći-ya-pi, *n.* *enemies, those who are at variance with each other.*

to'-ka-ki-ćoŋ, *v.* of tokoŋ; *to do to, for* one: tokamiyećoŋ, *what hast thou done with it for me?*—tokawećoŋ, takaćićoŋ, John xiii, 12.

to'-ka-ki-ḣaŋ *and* to'-ka-ki-ḣoŋ, *v.* *to suffer injury or loss; to lose something:* tokamakiḣoŋ, tokanićiḣoŋ.

to-ka'-ķe-haŋ, *adv.* *at the first.* See tokagehaŋ.

to-ka'-la, *n.* *T.* *a small gray fox: i. q.* tokadaŋ.

to-kam', *cont.* of tokapa; kahin tokam ya, *to go before, break the road.* *T.*, tokab.

to'-ka-moŋ, *v.* 1st pers. sing. of tokoŋ.

to'-ka-no-ġe, *n.* (*enemies' ears*), *a species of red fungus growing on logs.*

to'-ka-noŋ, *v.* 2d pers. sing. of tokoŋ.

to-kaŋ', *n.* *another*, as, another person: tokaŋ tawa, *it is another's* See tokeća.

to-kaŋ', *adv.* *in another place, elsewhere; another way:* tokaŋ uŋ, *to be somewhere else;* tokaŋ elnaka, *to put somewhere else.*

to-kaŋ'-kaŋ, *red.* of tokaŋ.

to kaŋ'-taŋ-haŋ, *adv.* *from another source, place,* or *person.*

to-kaŋ'-yaŋ, *adv.* *having reference to another place.*

to-ka'-o-ḣdo-ka, *n.* See tokawoḣdoka *and* tokayuḣdokeća.

to-ka'-pa, *n.* *the first, first born, eldest*—matokapa, nitokapa, uŋtokapapi.

to-ka'-pa-taŋ-haŋ, *adv.* *ahead, before; i. q.* tokata taŋhaŋ.

to-kaś', *adv.* *T.* *perhaps.*

to'-ka-śni, *adv.* *T.* *for no reason; in vain.*

to-ka'-ta, *adv.* *before, ahead, forward; future, yet to come:* tokata ihaŋ, *to be yet future.* See toka

to-ka'-ta, *n.* *the future:* tokata ekta.

to-ka'-tam, *adv. cont.* of tokatapa: tokatam yeye ćiŋ, *in future, what is ahead.* *T.*, tokatab.

to-ka'-ta-pa, *adv.* *in advance, in future.*

to-ka'-ta-pa-taŋ-haŋ, *adv.* *ahead, future.*

to-ka'-ta-wa-pa, *adv.* *in advance, ahead.*

to-ka'-toŋ-pi, *n.* *first birth, one's birth*

to-ka'-wo-ḣdo-ka, *n.* *an inventor.* See tokaoḣdoka.

to'-ka-ya, *v. a.* *to count* one *as an enemy*—tókawaya, tókauŋyaŋpi, tókamayaŋ.

to-ka'-yu-ḣdo-ke-ća, *v.* *to invent* anything—tokamduḣdokeća.

tok'-ćel *and* tok'-ćeŋl, *adv.* *T.* *perhaps; I don't know.*

to'-ke, *adv.* *how?* John ix, 8.

to'-ke-ća, *adj.* *different, another:* wićaśta tokeća, *another man*—matokeća, nitokeća, uŋtokećapi: tomakeća, tonikeća, touŋkećapi—with this use of the pronouns it expresses the idea of *how am I?* etc. See tokaŋ *and* tokeća.

to'-ke-ća, *adv.* *why, wherefore?* tokeća hećanoŋ he, *why did you do it?* hetaŋhaŋ tokeća, *it makes no difference.* *T.*, toka (*why*) *and* ća (*and*): toka ća ećanon śni he? *why is it and* (that) *you have not done it?* Query—Is not the Santee the same, with the final "ća" gradually smoothed by use from "ça" to "ća"?—W. J. C.

to'-ke-ća-ća, *adv.* *T.* *slowly; unconcernedly.*

to'-ke-ća-će, *adv.* *why?*

to'-ke-ća-e, *adv.* *why?*

to'-ke-ća-ka-ćen, *adv.* *for no reason.*

to'-ke-ćiŋ, *adv.* *any how.*

to'-ke-ćiŋ-ćiŋ, *adv.* *any how, as one pleases:* tokećiŋćiŋ wauŋ, *I do just as I please.* See tokenćiŋćiŋ.

to'-ke-ćiŋ-ćiŋ-yaŋ, *adv.* *as pleases.*

to-keḣ', *adv.* *however, at any rate, at all events, any how:* tokeḣ da eśta ćiyahna wauŋ kta, *go where you will I will be with you;* tokeḣ ećanoŋ eśta duhe kte śni, *do as you will you shall not have it.*

to'-ke-ḣćiŋ, *adv.* *i. q.* tokeḣiŋ.

to'-ke-ḣiŋ, *adv.* *howsoever.* See tokeḣ. *T.*, tokeḣćiŋ.

to-kel', *adv.* *T.* *how?*

to'-ken, *adv.* *how, in what way?* *T.*, tokel.

to'-ken ćiŋ-ćiŋ, *adv* *in any way, as it happens:* *i. q.* tokećiŋćiŋ.

to'-ken-ken, *adv.* *red.* of token.

to'-ken-ken-tu, *adv.* *in whatever way.*

to'-ken-ken-tu-ya, *adv.* *in what way soever.*

to'-ken-tken, *adv.* See tokenken.

to'-keś, *adv.* *indeed.* See tokiŋś.

to'-keś, *adv.* tokeś he niye se waćaŋmi, *I thought that was you;* tokeś he miye miçića, *as though I meant myself,* that is, *I do not mean myself.*

to'-ke-śa, *adv.* *T.* *i. q.* tokeśta.

to'-ke-śke, *adv* *T.* *how; in whatsoever way.*

to'-ke-śta, *adv.* of assent; *presently, at any rate:* tokeśta ećamoŋ kta, *I will do it presently.* *T.*, tokeśa See tokśa.

to'-ke-tu, *adv.* *how is it? as it is:* toketu kiŋ ećen omdake kta, *I will tell it as it is;* toketu he, *how is it? what is the matter?* toniketu, *how is it with thee?* used in inquiring of one who is sick, *how are you?* toketu taŋiŋ śni, *how it is is not manifest*, an expression often used when a thing is doubtful: toketu kakeś, *as it happens;* toketu kaśta, *at all events, at any rate;* toketu kaśta mde kta, *whatever happens I will go.* *T.*, toketu kaćil. See tokeća.

to'-ke-tu-ya, *adv.* toketuya kaśta, *in whatever way;* toketuya keś, *at random:* toketuya kakeś.

to'-ki, *adv.* *where? somewhere:* toki skadaŋ, *nowhere.* See tokiya.

to-ki'-ći-ćoŋ, *v.* of tokićoŋ; *to take vengeance on for* one—towećićoŋ, touŋkićićoŋpi.

to-ki'-ći-kśu, *v.* of tokśu; *to transport for* one—towećikśu, touŋkićikśupi.

to'-ki-ćoŋ-ze, *n.* of wokićoŋze; *his law* or *determination.*

to-ki'-ćoŋ, *v. a.* *to revenge, take vengeance on*—towećoŋ, touŋkićoŋpi.

to'-ki-daŋ, *adv.* *where;* used with śni, *nowhere:* tokidaŋ mde kte śni, *I will go nowhere;* tokidaŋ wai śni, *I went nowhere* *T.*, tokiyala. See tokiskadaŋ.

to'-ki-e-ȟpe-ki-ya, *v. a.* (toki *and* eȟpekiya) *to drop somewhere, lose* anything—tokieȟpewakiya.

to'-ki-e-ȟpe-ya, *v. a.* (toki *and* eȟpeya) *to lose, drop somewhere*—tokieȟpewaya, tokieȟpeuŋyaŋpi. See togeȟpeya.

to'-ki-i-ya-ye-s'a, *n.* *one who is gone much; a strumpet:* *i. q* inaȟmaŋpi *T.*, tigleśni s'a: witkowiŋla.

to-kiŋ', *adv.* *oh that, I wish;* tokiŋ mduhen, *oh that I had it.* An "n" follows the use of this word, commonly at the end of the sentence or phrase, as in "mduhen" of the above example. In Titoŋwaŋ the "n" is "niŋ"; as, tokiŋ he bluha niŋ, ećaŋmi.

to-kiŋś', *adv.* *well, with difficulty:* tokiŋś maḳu: tokiŋś he niye se waćaŋmi, *I thought that was you.*

to-kiŋś'-eś-eś, *adv.* *T.* *at the first.*

to-kiŋś'-ya-kel, *adv.* *T.* *carelessly, without care.*

to'-ki-ska-daŋ, *adv.* *nowhere:* toki skad. See skad *and* tokidaŋ.

to'-ki-ya, *adv.* *where? in what place?* See toki.

to'-ki-ya-la, *adv.* *T.* *where?* when followed by śni, *nowhere.*

to'-ki-yam, *adv.* *cont.* of tokiyapa; *where? in what direction?* *T.* tokiyab.

to'-ki-ya-pa, *adv.* *where?*

to'-ki-ya-taŋ-haŋ, *adv.* *whence, from what place?* See dećiyataŋhaŋ, ećiyataŋhaŋ, hećiyataŋhaŋ, kakiyataŋhaŋ, *and* totaŋhaŋ.

to'-ki-ya-wa-pa, *adv.* *where, in what place?*

to-ki-yo'-pe-ki-ći-ya-pi, *n.* *barter, exchange.*

to-ki-yo'-pe-ki-ya. *v. a.* *to barter, exchange* one thing *for* another *with* one—tokiyopewakiya: tokiyopećićiya, *I exchange with thee.* See iyopekiya.

t o - k i - y o' - p e - y a, *v. a.* (toki *and* iyopeya) *to barter, exchange* one thing *for* another—tokiyopewaya, tokiyopeuŋyaŋpi.

t o - k i' - y o - t a ŋ, *adv.* *in what direction? how* or *in what manner it is* or *will be:* tokiyotaŋ taŋiŋ śni, *it does not appear how it is.* See dećiyotaŋ, hećiyotaŋ, *and* kakiyotaŋ.

to-ki'-yo-taŋ-haŋ, *adv.* *in what direction, from what course?* See dećiyotaŋhaŋ *and* hećiyotaŋhaŋ.

t o' - k o ŋ, *v. a.* *to do*—tokamoŋ, tokanoŋ, tokuŋkoŋpi: takudaŋ tokamoŋ śni, *I am doing nothing.*

t o - k o ŋ' - p i - ć a, *adj.* *T.* *useful, good for something.*

t o - k o' - y u - ś t a ŋ, *v. a.* *to displace, dislocate, put* one *in the place of* another—tokomduśtaŋ, tokomayuśtaŋ.

t o' - k s a - p e, *n.* of woksape; *his wisdom*—nitoksape.

t o k' - ś a, *adv.* *Ih.* and *T.* *presently, by and by, before long:* *i. q.* tokeśa.

t o k' - ś t a, *adv.* See tokeśta.

t o - k ś u', *v. a.* *to transport, carry, draw; to go back and bring*—towakśu, touŋkśupi.

t o k - t o g' - y e, *adv.* *red.* of togye; *in different ways.*

t o k - t o g' - y e - k e l, *adv.* *T.* *in different ways.*

t o k - t o' - k e - ć a, *adj.* *red.* of tokeća; *different.*

t o m, *cont.* of topa; *four.* *T.* tob.

t o m' - n a - n a, *adv.* *only four.* *T.*, tobnala.

t o m' - t o m, *adv.* *red.* of tom; *by fours, four and four:* *i. q.* toptopa. *T.*, tobtob.

t o' - n a, *adv.* *how many? which?* tona ee he, *which are they?* See dena, hena, iyena *and* kana.

t o' - n a g - n a, *adv.* *how many?* otoiyohi tonagna yuhapi kta, *how many shall each one have?*

t o' - n a g - n a g, *adv.* *how many?* tonagnag yuhapi kte.

t o' - n a g - n a - k e - ć a, *adv.* *red.* of tonakeća; *how many?*

t o' - n a g - n a - n a, *adv.* *red.* of tonana. *T.*, ćokćonala.

t o' - n a - k a, *adv.* *how many?* nitonakapi, *how many are there of you?* See henaka *and* iyenaka.

t o' - n a - k e - ć a, *adv.* *how many? how much?* See denakeća, henakeća, iyenakeća, *and* kanakeća.

t o - n a' - k e - ç e - y a ś, *adv.* *T.* *how many soever.*

t o' - n a - k i - y a, *adv.* *how many, how many times? in how many ways?* See henakiya *and* kanakiya.

t o' - n a - n a, *adv.* *a few:* tonana ḣiŋ, *very few;* uŋtonanaŋpidaŋ, *we are few.* *T.*, ćonala. See denana, henana, *and* kanana.

t o' - n a ŋ g - n a ŋ g, *cont.* See tonagnag.

t o ŋ, *v. a.* *to have, to give birth to,* as, ćiŋća toŋ, *to have a child, to possess, acquire*—watoŋ, uŋtoŋpi.

t o ŋ, *v. n.* *to form pus, to suppurate:* toŋ kta.

t o ŋ, *n.* *matter, pus:* toŋ yuke kta.

toŋ'-haŋ, *v. a.* *to be afraid of*—toŋwahaŋ, toŋuŋhaŋpi, toŋmahaŋ.

toŋ'-he-ća, *v. a.* *to be afraid of*, as of a person or animal—toŋwaheća.

toŋ'-ka-śpa, *v.* *to expectorate.* See kaśpa.

toŋ'-kće *or* tuŋ'-kće, *n.* *T.* *excrement: i. q.* ćesdi. See uŋkće.

toŋ'-la, *v.* *T.* *to have, possess: i. q.* toŋna.

toŋ'-na, *v.* *dim.* of toŋ; *to have;* used in speaking of children—watoŋna, yatoŋna *T.*, toŋla.

toŋ'-pi, *n.* *birth*—matoŋpi, uŋtoŋpi.

toŋ-śka', *n.* *a nephew, my nephew*—mitoŋśka, nitoŋśka. The women say "tośka."

toŋ-śka'-ku, *n.* *his nephew.*

toŋ-śka'-ya, *v. a.* *to have for nephew*—toŋśkawaya.

toŋ'-toŋ, *v.* *red.* of toŋ.

toŋ-toŋ'-taŋ-ka, *n.* *the bull-frog, Rana ocellata.* *T.*, gnaśkataŋka.

toŋ-waŋ', *v. n.* *to look, see*—watoŋwaŋ, uŋtoŋwaŋpi. See waŋyaka.

toŋ-waŋ'-haŋ, *part.* *looking, seeing:* toŋwaŋhaŋ maŋka.

toŋ-waŋ' yaŋ, *v. n* *to make a village, dwell at a place*—toŋwaŋuŋyaŋpi. *T.*, otoŋweya.

toŋ-wel', *adv.* *T.* *once on a time.* See tohiŋni.

toŋ-we'-ya, *v. a.* *to cause one to see, give sight to*—toŋwewaya.

toŋ-we'-ya, *v. n.* *to go to see, to go as a spy, go before* a war party to spy out the enemy—toŋwemda, toŋweuŋyaŋpi.

toŋ-we'-ya, *n.* *T.* *a spy; a guide.*

toŋ-yaŋ', *v. n.* *to suppurate.*

toŋ-źaŋ', *n.* *a man's niece: i. q.* tuźaŋ. The women say "toźaŋ."

to'-o-pe, *n.* *his law*—mitoope, nitoope. See woope.

to'-pa, *num. adj.* *four.*

to'-pa-ki-ya, *adv.* *in four ways, four times.* See koŋtakiya, etc.

top'-to-pa, *adj.* *red* of topa. See tomtom.

to-ska'-daŋ, *n.* *the common woodpecker.* See haŋketaŋka, etc.

to-sti'-ća-du, *n.* See tustićadu *and* tuskićadu. *T.*, ićalu.

toś, *adv.* *yes, yea.* Used by both men and women. See to *and* haŋ.

to-śe', *adj.* *T.* *dull, blunt.*

to-śe'-ya-kel, *adv.* *T.* *bluntly.*

to-śka', *n.* *a nephew, my nephew*—mitośka, nitośka. This form is used by the women. See toŋśka.

to-śka'-ku, *n.* *her nephew.*

to'-śkaŋ-śkaŋ, *n.* of wośkaŋśkaŋ; *his moving about; his kingdom*—nitośkaŋśkaŋ. See tokićoŋze.

to-śka'-ya, *v. a.* *to have for* tośka—tośkawaya

to-śu', *n.* *a tent-pole, tent-poles.* *T.* also has tuśu.

to-taŋ'-haŋ, *adv.* *whence, from what place? from what time?* See tokiyataŋhaŋ, detaŋhaŋ, etc.

to-to', *adj.* *red.* of to.

to-to'-daŋ, *n* *blue beads; green beads.* *T.*, śipto toto.

to'-wa-kaŋ, *n.* *his* wakaŋ or *spirit.* See wowakaŋ.

to-wa′-na-ke-ća, *adv. so many, how many soever; so much, by how much.* See tonakeća.

to-waŋ′-źi-ća, *n. the blue sky, all blue. T.,* maȟpiya tola.

to′-wa-oŋ-śi-da, *n.* of wowaoŋśida; *his mercy*—nitowaoŋśida.

to′-wa-ś'a-ke, *n.* of wowaś'ake; *his power* or *strength*—nitowaś'ake.

to′-wa-śte, *n.* of wowaśte; *his goodness*—nitowaśte.

to′-wi-ća-ke, *n.* of wowićake; *his truth*—nitowićake.

to′-wiŋ-źe, *n.* of owiŋźa; *his bed*—mitowiŋźe, nitowiŋźe.

to-ya′, *v. a. to dye* or *paint* anything *blue* or *green.*

to′-ya, *adv. in a blue* or *green manner.*

to-ya′-kel, *adv. T. i. q.* toyahen.

to-ya′-ken, *adv. in a blue* or *green form. T.,* toyakel.

to-źaŋ′, *n. a niece; my niece* when the person is addressed—mitoźaŋ, nitoźaŋ. This form is used by the women. See toŋźaŋ *and* tuźaŋ.

to-źaŋ′-ku, *n. her niece.* See toźaŋ.

to-źaŋ′-ya, *v. a. to have for a niece*—toźaŋwaya.

tpa, *pos. prefix* of some verbs, as, paġaŋ, tpaġaŋ; pataŋ, tpataŋ. See kpa.

tpa, *adj. durable; having the property of swelling;* said of things that increase in bulk by boiling, as corn, rice, etc. See kpa

tpa *and* tpe, *adj.* noġe tpa, *deaf;* iśta tpa, *blind.* This probably conveys the idea of *putting out* or *piercing.* See katpa *and* kpa.

tpa-ġaŋ′, *v. pos.* of paġaŋ; *to leave* or *separate from one's own; to spare* or *part with one's own*—watpaġaŋ, yatpaġaŋ, uŋtpaġaŋpi. Same as kpaġaŋ. *T*, kpaġaŋ; and so of all the rest.

tpa-hi′, *v. pos.* of pahi; *to gather* or *pick up one's own*—watpahi, uŋtpahipi. Same as kpahi.

tpa-mde′-ća, *v. pos.* of pamdeća; *to break in pieces one's own*—watpamdeća. *T.,* kpableća. Same as kpamdeća.

tpaŋ, *adj. soft,* as dressed leather; *fine,* as flour: *i. q.* kpaŋ.

tpaŋ′-na, *adj. soft, fine: i. q.* kpaŋna. *T.,* kpaŋla.

tpaŋ′-tpaŋ-na, *adj. red.* of tpaŋna; *soft.*

tpaŋ-yaŋ′, *v. a. to dress,* as skins, *make soft, tan,* as leather — tpaŋwaya, tpaŋuŋyaŋpi. Same as kpaŋyaŋ

tpa-spa′, *v. to put out of sight, push under,* as in water: *i. q.* paospa—watpaspa See atpaspa

tpas-ya′, *v. a. to make dark*—tpaswaya, tpasuŋyaŋpi.

tpa′-ta, *v. pos.* of páta; *to carve* or *cut up one's own,* as a slaughtered animal—watpata, uŋtpatapi: *i. q.* kpata.

tpa-ta′, *v. a. pos.* of patá; *to join together* as skins in making *one's own tent*—watpatá. *T.,* kipata.

t p a - t a ŋ', *v. a. pos.* of pataŋ; *to keep choice, set store by one's own, be sparing of* it—watpataŋ, uŋtpataŋpi. See kpataŋ.

t p a' - z a, *adj dark: i. q.* kpaza.

t p a' - z a, *n. darkness.* See otpaza.

t p e. Same as tpa.

t p e' - y a, *adv.* tpeya haŋ, said of a hole which runs in straight: tpeya ap'a, *to strike* anything *and make a sound.*

t p i, *adj. breaking open.* See patpi *and* pakpi.

t p i - h a ŋ', *part. cracked open of itself.*

t p i - t p i' - h a ŋ, *part. red.* of tpihaŋ.

t p u - t p a', *adj. mixed up, slightly turbid,* as water: *i. q.* mdezedaŋ śni. See kpukpa.

t p u - t p e' - y a, *adv. in a roiled manner.*

t p u - t p u' - w a - h a ŋ *and* t p u - w a' - h a ŋ, *part crumbled.*

t u ḣ - m a' - ġ a, *n. bees; wasps, hornets,* etc. *T.*, also tuḣmuŋġa.

t u ḣ - m a' - ġ a - ć a ŋ - h a ŋ - p i, *n. honey. T.*, tuḣmaġa toŋkće.

t u ḣ - m a' - ġ a - ć e - s d i, *n. beeswax; honey; molasses. T*, tuḣmaġa ćesli. See ćesdi.

t u ḣ - m a' - ġ a - t a ŋ - k a, *n. the humble-bee.*

t u ḣ - m u ŋ' - ġ a, *n. T. bees, wasps,* etc: *i. q.* tuḣmaġa.

t u - k a', *conj. but: i. q.* tka.

t u' - k a. See katuka.

t u - k a' - e ś, *adv. but. T.*, tkaeś.

t u - k a' - h a ŋ, *part. spoiled, destroyed,* said of furs.

t u - k a ŋ', *n.* See tuŋkaŋ.

t u - k a ś', *adv. but.* See tukaeś. *T.*, tkaeś.

t u - k a' - w a - h a ŋ, *part. spoiled,* said of furs. *T.*, tuktukawahaŋ.

t u - k i', *n. T. a shell.*

t u - k i' - h a, *n. a spoon, a ladle:* maza tukiha, *a metallic spoon. T. a shell.*

t u - k i' - h a - s a ŋ, *n. muscle shells; muscles, oysters.*

t u - k t a'. Same as tukte; not in common use.

t u - k t a' - d a ŋ, *adv.* See tuktedaŋ

t u - k t e', *pron. interrog. which?* uŋma tukte, *which of the two?* tukte ehaŋ, *when?* tukte e, *which is it?*

t u - k t e' - d a ŋ, *adv.* with the negative śni, *nowhere:* tuktedaŋ uŋ śni, *it is nowhere T.*, tukteni *and* tuktelna.

t u - k t e' - k t e, *pron. red.* of tukte.

t u - k t e' - k t e n, *adv. red.* of tukten; *sometimes, once in a while, now and then; in some places.*

t u - k t e l', *adv. T. somewhere.*

t u - k t e l' - n a, *adv. T.* with śni following, *nowhere.*

t u - k t e n', *adv.* (tukte *and* en) *where? in what place?*

tu-kte'-ni, *adv. T. i. q.* tuktedaŋ

t u - k t e' - t u, *adv. at what place?*

t u - k t u' - k a - w a - h a ŋ, *adj. T. spoiled,* as furs.

t u k t u ŋ' - m a, *adv. T. either one of two.*

t u - l a', *intj. T.* exclamation of *surprise* or *protest; for shame!*

tum, *n.* *the whistling* or *whizzing sound* made by a flying bullet.

tuŋ-kaŋ′, *n.* *a father-in-law:* nituŋkaŋ, *thy father-in-law;* tuŋkaŋku, *his father-in-law: a grandfather.* In the sacred language, *a stone*, and *the moon.* See tukaŋ, tuŋkaŋśi, *and* tuŋkaŋśidaŋ.

tuŋ-kaŋ′-ki-śi-tku, *n.* *his* or *her grandfather.* *T.*, tunkaŋśitku.

tuŋ-kaŋ′-kśi-tku, *n.* Same as tuŋkaŋkiśitku.

tuŋ-kaŋ′-ku, *n.* *his* or *her father-in-law.* See tuŋkaŋ.

tuŋ-kaŋ′-śi, *n.* *my father-in-law:* nituŋkaŋ, *thy father-in-law;* nituŋkaŋśi, *thy grandfather;* nituŋkaŋśipi, *your father-in-law.*

tuŋ-kaŋ′-śi-daŋ, *n.* *a grandfather, my grandfather:* nituŋkaŋśi, *thy grandfather: the President.* *T.*, tuŋkaŋśila.

tuŋ-kaŋ′-śi-daŋ-ya, *v. n.* *to have for grandfather*—tuŋkaŋśidaŋwaya.

tuŋ-kaŋ′-śi-la, *n.* *T.* *a grandfather; the President of the United States; the Supreme Being; God.*

tuŋ-kaŋ′-śi-na, *n.* *Ih.* Same as tuŋkaŋśidaŋ.

tuŋ-kaŋ′-śi-tku, *n.* *his* or *her grandfather.*

tuŋ-kaŋ′-śi-ya, *v. a.* *to have for* tuŋkaŋśi—tuŋkaŋśiwaya.

tuŋ-kaŋ′-ya, *v. a.* *to have for* tuŋkaŋ—tuŋkaŋwaya.

tuŋ-kće′, *n.* *T.* See toŋkće.

tuŋ-waŋ′, *n.* *a style of arrows*—mituŋwaŋ, nituŋwaŋ.

tuŋ-wel′, *adv.* *T.* *when;* tuŋwel yahi so, *when did you come?* See toŋwel.

tuŋ-wi′-ću, *n.* *his* or *her aunt.* See tuŋwiŋ.

tuŋ-wi′-ću-ya, *v. a.* *to have for one's aunt*—tuŋwićuwaya.

tuŋ-wiŋ′, *n.* *aunt, my aunt;* nituŋwiŋ, *thy aunt.* This word has the sense of *aunt* in English, though a mother's sisters are called "ina," *mother.*

tuŋ-wiŋ′-ya, *v. a.* *to have for aunt*—tuŋwiŋwaya.

tuŋ-źaŋ′, *n.* *a niece, my niece*—mituŋźaŋ, nituŋźaŋ. "Tuŋźaŋ" *and* "tuźaŋ" are both in good usage. A man's brother's children and a woman's sister's children are considered as children, and are not called "toŋśka" *and* "tuŋźaŋ."

tuŋ-źaŋ′-ku, *n.* *his niece.*

tuŋ-źaŋ′-ya, *v. a.* *to have for niece*—tuŋźaŋwaya.

tu-paŋ′-ka, *n.* *the black bass.*

tu-sda′, *n.* *the leech.*

tu-ski′-ća-du, *n.* *a fan.* *T.*, ićadu. See tustićadu.

tu-sti′-ća-du, *n.* *a fan; a wing.*

tu-śu′, *n* *T.* *a lodge-pole.* See tośu.

tu-ta′, *adj.* *smarting, chapped* by the wind: ite matuta, *my face is chapped.*

tu-tka′, *n.* *small insects.* See watutka.

tu-tka′-daŋ, *n.* *small insects.*

tu-tka′-tka, *n.* *small articles, trinkets.*

tu-tu'-pa, *adj.* *slippery, ropy, slimy.* Hence pe tutupa, *the slippery elm.*

tu'-wa, *pron.* *Ih.* and *T.* *who: i. q.* tuwe.

tu'-we, *pron. interrog.* *who?* rarely *which?*

tu'-we-daŋ, *pron.* used with śni following; *no one, nobody:* tuwedaŋ ećoŋ śni, *no one did it.* *T.*, tuweni.

tu'-we-ḣća, *pron.* *who indeed?*

tu'-we-ka-kśa *and* tu'-we-ka-ke-śa *and* tu'-wa-ka-kśa, *intj.* *T.* *oh pshaw! absurd!*

tu'-we-ka-leś *and* tu'-we-ka-śa, *pron.* *T.* *whoever.*

tu'-we-ka-śta, *pron.* *whoever.* *T*, tuwekaleś; tuwekeçeyas.

tu'-we-ni, *pron.* *T.* *nobody.*

tu'-we-ska *and* tu'-we-ska-daŋ, *n.* *nobody.* *T.*, tuweni śni.

tu'-we-ta-wa, *pron.* *whose?*

tu'-we-we, *pron.* *red.* of tuwe.

tu-źaŋ', *n.* *a niece, my niece*—mituźaŋ, nituźaŋ: tuźaŋku, *his niece.* See tuŋźaŋ.

tu-źaŋ'-ku, *n.* *his niece.* See tuźaŋ.

tu-źaŋ'-ya, *v. a.* *to have for niece*—tuźaŋwaya, tuźaŋuŋyaŋpi.

Ṭ.

ṭ, *the twenty-fourth letter of the Dakota alphabet.* It has the *click* or *explosive sound* of *t*, and corresponds to "ç," "ķ," and "p̧."

ṭa, *v. n.* *to die; to faint away, lose consciousness temporarily*—maṭa, niṭa, uŋṭapi.

ṭa'-ġa, *adj.* *rough: bitter, astringent,* as oak bark.

ṭa'-ḣi-yu-ya, *v. n.* *to be stillborn.*

ṭaḣ-ṭa'-ġa, *adj.* *red.* of ṭaġa; *rough, not smooth.*

ṭa'-nuŋ-se, *adv.* *about dead.*

ṭa-ṭa', *adj.* *palsied, withered, numb*—maṭaṭa.

ṭa-ṭa'-ka, *adj.* *palsied*—maṭaṭaka.

ṭe, *v. n.* *to die.* See ṭa.

ṭe-ća', *adj.* *dead:* ho ṭeća, *dead fish.*

ṭe'-ća-kiś *and* ṭe'-ća-kiś-ya, *adv.* *in a dying state.* See kakiśya.

ṭe'-ća-ya *and* ṭe'-ća-ya-ken, *adv.* *in a dead state.*

ṭe-ća'-źe-yaŋ, *adv.* *half dead.* *T.*, ṭanuŋse.

ṭe-ho'-wa-ya, *v. n.* *to cry out badly, to scream*—waṭehowamda.

ṭe-ho'-wa-ye-ya, *v. a.* *to cause to cry out*—ṭehowayewaya.

ṭe-ki'-ni-ća, *v. n.* *to contend with death; to be doubtful whether one dies* or *lives:* ṭemakinića.

ṭe-ki'-ya, *v. a* *to cause to die*—ṭewakiya.

ṭe-ko', *v.* See ṭekoŋ.

ţe-koŋ′, *v.* *to wish* one *dead, to imprecate*—ţewakoŋ. *T.*, ţekoŋza.

ţe-koŋ′-za, *v.* *T.* *to wish one dead; to determine one's death*, as a medicine man is supposed to do.

ţe-ya′, *v. a.* *to cause to die*—ţewaya.

ţe-ya′-su, *v.* *T.* *to condemn to die.*

ţe-ya′-su-pi, *part.* *T.* *condemned to die.*

ţiŋ, *v. n.* *Ih* and *T.* *to die: i. q.* ţa. This form usually, perhaps always and only, occurs when followed by "kta," the sign of the future, as, maţiŋ kta, niţiŋ kta, ţiŋ kta, for maţé kta, etc.

ţiŋ′-ġa, *v. n.* *to snivel, to grunt; to labor*, as a woman in travail—waţiŋġa, uŋţiŋġapi.

ţiŋ-s'a′, *adv.* *fast, tightly, fixedly, permanently.* See ţiŋza.

ţiŋ-s'a′-daŋ, *adv.* *firmly, permanently, established:* ţiŋs'adaŋ maŋke śni, *I am not established.*

ţiŋs-ya′, *v. a.* *to make firm*—ţiŋswaya: ţiŋsiçiya, *to restrain one's self*—ţiŋsmiçiya.

ţiŋs-ya′, *adv.* *firmly.*

ţiŋs-ya′-kel, *adv.* *T.* *firmly, bravely.*

ţiŋ′-za, *adj.* *stiff*, as mud; *firm, hard, fast; brave*, as ćaŋte ţiŋza. See ţiŋs'a.

ţoś′-ya, *adv.* of ţoźa; *bluntly.*

ţo′-źa, *adj.* *dull, pointless.*

ţuŋg-ya′, *v. a.* *to suspect, have a suspicion of* a thing—ţuŋgwaya, ţuŋguŋyaŋpi.

ţuŋ′-ka, *v.* See ţuŋkeća.

ţuŋ′-ke-ća, *v. n.* *to be suspicious; to be suspected*—maţuŋkeća.

ţuŋ-ki′-ya, *v.* *T.* *to suspect concerning one's self.*

U.

u, *the twenty-fifth letter of the Dakota alphabet*, with the sound of English "oo," as in *moon.* When preceded by "y," or followed by a nasal "ŋ," it is somewhat modified.

u, *v. n.* *to come, to be coming*—wau, yau, uŋkupi.

u-gna′-he-la, *adv.* *T.* *suddenly: i. q.* ihnuhaŋna. See uŋknuhaŋna *and* uŋgnahaŋla.

u-ġe′, *n.* *T.* *some: i. q.* oŋġe.

u-ħla′-gla, *v. n.* *T.* *to be torn* or *broken; to be ragged.*

u-ka′, *n.* *the skin, hide*, especially the skin of a living animal

u-ki′-ta, *v.* *pos.* of uta; *to try, prove*, as any new thing—uwakita, uuŋkitapi. *T.*, igluta.

u-ki′-ya, *v. a.* *to cause to come*—uwakiya.

u-ku′-hu, *intj.* When a deer is brought into camp, the children shout "ukuhu"*: i. q.* **wáhdiaś'api.**

u-ku′-hu-hu, *intj.* When an elk is brought in they sing "ukuhuhu."—S. W. POND.

u′-ma, *n.* *hazel-nuts.*

u′-ma-hu, *n.* *hazel-bushes.*

u-maŋ′, *adj.* *the one, the other.* See uŋma.

u-maŋ′-na, *adj.* See uŋmana.

u-maŋ′-na-pćiŋ-waŋ-ka, *adj.* See uŋmanapćiŋwaŋka. *T.*, akenapćiŋyuŋka.

uŋ, *v. n.* *to be:* en uŋ, *to be in*—wauŋ, yauŋ, uŋyakoŋpi.

uŋ, *v. a.* *to use* anything, *have for use*—muŋ, nuŋ, uŋkuŋpi.

uŋ, *pron. in comp.* *we, us.*

uŋ′-ća, *v. a.* *to mock, imitate, ridicule* one—uŋwaća, uŋuŋćapi, uŋmaća.

uŋ-ći′, *n.* *a grandmother, my grandmother;* nkuŋśi, *thy grandmother:* kuŋkśitku, *his* or *her grandmother; the sun,* in the sacred language. A woman calls her mother-in-law "uŋći."

uŋ-ći′-daŋ, *n.* *dim.* of uŋći.

uŋ′-ći-hi, *v. n.* *to have attained one's growth; to be able to take care of one's self*—uŋmaćihi, uŋnićihi, uŋuŋćihipi: with the negative "śni," uŋćihiśni, *to be incapable, lazy, indolent.*

uŋ′-ći-hi-ya, *v. a.* *to cause to sustain one's self; to raise, train up to manhood*—uŋćihiwaya.

uŋ-ći′-śi, *n.* *a mother-in-law, my mother-in-law:* nikuŋśi, *thy mother-in-law.* This is said to be the proper word for mother-in-law, but shortened by the women into "uŋći."

uŋ-ći′-śi-ća-daŋ, *n.* *the crow, crows, the Corvus americanus.*

uŋ-ći′-śi-daŋ, *n.* *dim.* of uŋćiśi.

uŋ-ći′-śi-ya, *v. a.* *to have* one *for* uŋćiśi—uŋćiśiwaya.

uŋ-ći′-ya, *v. a.* *to have for* uŋći—uŋćiwaya.

uŋ′-ćoŋ-ni-ća, *v. n.* *to give up, yield, not try to escape; to be prevented, penned up*—uŋmaćoŋnića. See oŋćuŋnića.

uŋ-ćoŋ′-nil-ya, *v. a.* *T.* *to obstruct, prevent.*

uŋ′-ćoŋ-nin, *v. n.* *cont.* of uŋćoŋnića.

uŋ′-ćoŋ-nin-ya, *v. a* *to obstruct, prevent from escaping, frighten* so as to make unable to escape—uŋćoŋninwaya.

uŋ′-ćoŋ-nin-ya, *adv.* *prevented:* uŋćoŋninya naźiŋ. *T.*, uŋćoŋnilya.

uŋ′-ćuŋ-ni-ća, *v.* See uŋćoŋnića.

uŋ′-ćuŋ-nin-ya, *adv.* See uŋćoŋninya.

uŋ-gna′, *intj.* *T.* *beware lest.*

uŋ-gna′-ġa, *n.* *T.* *the place fenced off on each side the door of a Dakota lodge:* *i. q.* oḣnoġa.

uŋ-gna′-ġa-ta, *adv.* *T.* *at* or *in the* uŋgnaġa; *by the door:* *i. q.* oḣnoġata.

uŋ-gna′-ġi-ća-la, *n.* *T.* *a bird like a small owl.* See Hoḣnoġićadaŋ *and* Oḣnoġićadaŋ.

uŋ-gna′-haŋ, *adv.* *T.* *i. q.* ihuhaŋ. See iḣnuhaŋ.

uŋ-gna′-haŋ-ḣćiŋ, *adv.* *T.* *possibly, it may be so.*

uŋ-gna'-haŋ-la, *adv.* *T.* *suddenly;* *i. q.* iħnuhaŋna.

uŋ'-haŋ-ke-ta, *adv* *at length, after a while, at the end.* *T.*, ohaŋketa. See ihaŋketa *and* uŋnahaŋ.

uŋ'-hda-ka, *v. n.* *to move, be moving about; to travel about with a family, pitching one's tent at short stages:* uŋhdaka wauŋ, *I am moving;* uŋhdaka uŋyakoŋpi, *we are camping.* *T.*, iglaka.

uŋ-ħće'-ġi-la, *n.* *T.* probably *the mastodon,* or other large animal, whose petrified remains are found in Dakota Territory.

uŋ-ħće'-ġi-la-hu, *n.* *the bones* of the uŋħćegila. See uŋkteħi.

uŋ'-kaŋ, *conj.* *and.* *T.*, yuŋkaŋ. See oŋkaŋ.

uŋ'-kaŋś, *conj.* *if;* the sign of the subjunctive mood, and usually of past time. *T.*, yuŋkaŋś.

uŋ'-kćc, *v. n.* *to defecate; to break wind*—uŋwakće, uŋuŋkćepi.

uŋ'-kće, *n.* *fæces; breaking wind.* *T.*, tuŋkće.

uŋ-kće'-kće-na, *n.* *the cactus.*

uŋ-kće'-ħi, *n.* *Ih.* *i. q.* uŋkteħi.

uŋ-kće'-ki-ħa, *n.* *the magpie.*

uŋ-kće'-pa-gmi-gma, *n.* *T.* *the beetle.*

uŋ-kće'-pa-hmi-yaŋ-yaŋ, *n.* *the beetle, the tumble-bug.*

uŋ-ki', *pron. in comp.*, with "pi" at the end of the word; *we; us.*

uŋ-kiś', *pron.* *we, ourselves.* See iś, miś, *and* niś.

uŋ-kiś'-na-la, *pron.* *T.* *i. q.* uŋkiśnana.

uŋ-kiś'-na-na, *pron.* *dual; we two alone:* *plur.*, uŋkiśnaŋpidaŋ. See iśnana, miśnana, etc.

uŋ-ki'-ta, *pron.* *pos. in comp.*, with "pi" at the end of the word; *ours.*

uŋ-ki'-ta-wa, *pron.* *dual; ours,* that is, *thine* and *mine.*

uŋ-ki'-ta-wa-pi, *pron.* *plur.* *ours.* See tawapi.

uŋ-ki'-ye, *pron.* *we, we two; us.* See iye, miye, etc.

uŋ-ki'-ye-ḳe, *pron.* *we ourselves.*

uŋ-ki'-ye-pi, *pron. plur.* *we; us.*

uŋ-knu'-haŋ-na, *adv.* *Ih.* *suddenly:* *i. q.* ihnuhaŋna. See ugnahela.

uŋ'-kśu, *n.* *a woman's work-bag;* *i. q.* paŋbotuka. *T.*, uŋkśula.

uŋ'-kśu-daŋ, *n.* *dim.* of uŋkśu; *a reticule.*

uŋ-kśu'-la, *n.* *T.* *a reticule.*

uŋ'-kśu-la, *n.* *T.* *a hood* or *case for a baby.*

Uŋ-kte'-ħi, *n.* *the Dakota god of the waters; a fabled monster of the deep; the whale: an extinct animal,* the bones of which are said to be sometimes found by the Indians, probably the *mastodon.* See uŋħćeġila.

uŋ-któ'-mi, *n.* *the spider;* also *a fabulous creature, a Dakota god.*

uŋ-kto'-mi-ta-o-ka-śke, *n.* *a spider's web.*

uŋ-kuŋ'-pi, *v. pl.* *we are:* *i. q.* uŋyakoŋpi.

uŋ'-ma, *adj. the one, the other:* uŋma tukte, *which of the two?* uŋma itoto, *one after the other, turn about.* See umaŋ.

uŋ'-ma-e-će-tki-ya, *adv. on the contrary.*

uŋ'-ma-e-ći-ya-taŋ-haŋ, *adv. from the other side; on the contrary.*

uŋ'-ma-la, *adj. T. i. q.* uŋmana.

uŋ'-ma-na, *adj.* with "śni" following, *neither:* uŋmana iwaću śni, *I took neither. T.*, uŋmala.

uŋ'-ma-na-pćiŋ-waŋ-ka, *num. adj. nineteen. T.*, akenapćiŋyuŋka.

uŋ'-la, *v. dim. T. to be; to use.*

uŋ'-na, *v. dim.* of uŋ, *to be*, and uŋ, *to use. T.*, uŋla.

uŋ'-na-haŋ, *adv. at last; i. q.* uŋhaŋketa: *soon, shortly.*

uŋ'-na-ptaŋ, *adj. sideling:* ȟe uŋnaptaŋ *and* ȟuŋnaptaŋ, *a side hill.*

uŋ'-na-ptaŋ-yaŋ, *adv. slantingly.*

uŋ'-pa, *v. a. to place* or *leave*, as a boat; *to raise for one's self*, as a dog or girl—wauŋpa, uŋkuŋpapi. See oŋpa, ooŋpa, etc.

uŋ'-pa, *v. n. to smoke*, as tobacco—uŋmuŋpa, uŋnuŋpa, uŋḳuŋpapi See ćaŋnuŋpa.

uŋ-paŋ', *n. T. the female elk: i. q.* upaŋ.

uŋ-paŋ'-ha, *n. T. elk skin.*

uŋ-paŋ'-hiŋ-ske, *n. T. elk teeth.*

uŋ'-pi, *v. pl.* of uŋ; *they are.*

uŋ-pśi'-źa, *n. T. i. q.* upśiźa.

uŋ-pśiś-ya, *adv. muddy.*

uŋ-siŋ', *n. the small end of a porcupine quill; the large quills in the porcupine's tail.*

uŋ-śtaŋ', *v. imperat. stop, quit.* Used only in this form. *T.*, ayuśtaŋ.

uŋ-tkaŋ'-na, *adv. much. T.*, yutkaŋla. See utkaŋna.

uŋ-we'-ya, *n. Ih. provisions for a journey: i. q.* waŋeya.

uŋ-ya, *v. T. to lose*, wauŋbla, yauŋla.—T. L. R.

uŋ'-yaŋ, *adv. T. without*, as uŋyaŋ wahi, *I come without it; out of sight, lost;* uŋyaŋ iyaya, *it has gone.*

uŋ-ya'-koŋ *v. dual, we two live together*, especially as man and wife.

uŋ-ya'-koŋ-pi, *v.* 1st pers. plur. *we are.*

uŋ-źiŋ'-ća, *n. a fledgling; a bird before the tail has grown.*

u-paŋ', *n. the female of the elk*, or *Cervus alces. T.*, uŋpaŋ.

u-pi', *n. the tail* of a bird; *the lower border* of a garment.

u-pi'-hde-ġa, *n. a balmoral skirt.*

u-pi'-zi-ća, *n. a yellow-tailed hawk.*

u-pi'-źa-ta, *n. the forked-tailed swallow.*

u-pśiś'-ya, *adv. muddily:* upśiśya waŋka.

u-pśi'-źa, *n. mud. T.*, uŋpśiźa.

u-sku'-ye-ća, *n. the acorns of the white oak:* uskuyeća ćaŋ, *the white oak.*

u-sku'-ye-ća-hu, *n. the white oak, Quercus alba.* See utuhu.

u-spaŋ'-spaŋ-he-ća, *n. the iron wood* or *hornbeam*, perhaps the *Ostrya virginica.*

u-śdo'-ni-ya, *n.* *a mineral spring; mineral sediment deposited from water*, as sulphate of iron or copperas. This word would seem to be formed from "u," *to come*, "śdo," *to melt* or *liquefy*, as metals, and "niya," *to breathe*, as if the metal came out liquefied by the earth's breath.

u-śdo'-wi-wi, *n.* *a swamp with a yellow sediment.* See wiwi.

u-śi', *v. a.* (u *and* śi) *to command to come, send*—uwaśi.

u-śtaŋ', *v. imperat.* only; *stop.* See uŋśtaŋ.

u'-ta, *n.* *an acorn, acorns, black oak acorns.*

u'-ta, *v. a.* *to try, taste* anything, *to attempt, try to do* a thing—uwata, uŋkutapi: *to try*, as a gun *in firing it off; to fire off.* *T.*, iyuta.

u'-ta-hu, *n.* *an oak tree.* See utuhu.

u'-ta-hu-ćaŋ, *n.* *T.* *oak wood.*

u-tam', *n.* *a load* or *charge of a gun*, plural, utapi, *loads:* ota utam, *a gun of many charges—a repeater:* ota utapi.

u-tkaŋ'-na, *adv.* *much, a great deal.* *T.*, yutkaŋla.

u-tkaŋ'-tkaŋ-na, *adv.* *red.* of utkaŋna. *T.*, yutkaŋtkaŋla.

u-tu'-hu, *n.* *the black oak, Quercus nigra.* See uskuyećahu.

u-tu'-ȟaŋ, *v.* *T.* *i. q.* ituȟaŋ.

u-tu'-ȟćiŋ, *adv.* *T.* *in vain.*

u-tu'-ki-ȟaŋ, *v.* *T.* *i. q.* itukiȟaŋ.

u-tu'-ya, *adv.* *T.* *i. q.* ituya.

u-tu'-ya-ćiŋ, *adv.* *T.* *for naught.*

u'-wa, *v. imperat.* *come.* Used by women.

u-ya', *v. a.* *to cause to go; to send, to start*—uwaya, uyaya.

u-ya', *v. n.* *to come; to become:* sniyaŋ uya, *it is becoming cold; to grow, spring up*, as grass.

u-ye'-ki-ya, *v. a.* *to cause to grow* or *spring up*—uyewakiya.

u-ye'-ya, *v. a.* *to cause to come*—uyewaya.

W.

w, *the twenty-sixth letter of the Dakota alphabet*, having the same sound that it has in the beginning of words in English.

wa, *pron. in comp.* *I.*

wa, *n.* *snow.*

wa, *v. n.* *to snow.* See wapa.

wa, *an abbreviation* of waȟaŋksića.

wa, *a prefix.* When used with verbs it usually puts them in the absolute or intransitive state, that is, the verb is changed into an adjective, or neuter, or passive verb; as, waoŋśida, *merciful*, from oŋśida, *to have mercy upon.* In some cases it forms of them nouns denoting the agent or actor. Indeed, the absolute forms may all be so used; as, wanikiya, *a savior.* When prefixed to nouns, it makes their signification more general.

w a, *a prefix.* *T.* *i. q*, ba, *a prefix:* it indicates that the action is done by *a sawing motion*, as with a knife or saw.

w a - a′- b l e s, *cont.* of waableza.

wa-a′-bleza, *v.* *T.* *i. q.* waamdeza.

w a - a′- ć a ŋ - k s i, *v. n.* of ćaŋksi; *to be ill-tempered, out of humor; to be threatening* every one—waaćaŋwaksi. *T.*, waaćaŋzeka.

wa-a′-ća ŋ - kśi-y a, *adv.* *in a cross, surly manner.* *T.*, waaćaŋzeya.

w a - a′- ć a ŋ - z e - k a, *v. n.* *T.* *to be ill-tempered.*

w a - a′- ć a ŋ - z e - y a, *adv.* *T.* *in a surly manner.*

w a - a′- g l a, *v.* *T.* *i. q.* waahda.

w a - a′- h d a, *v.* of ahda; *to take home*—waawahda. *T.*, waagla.

w a - a′- h d e - ć a, *v.* *to take home; one who takes home*—waawahdeća.

w a - a′- h d i, *v.* See wáhdi.

w a - a′- h o - t a ŋ - k a, *n.* *one who bawls out, one who vociferates*—waahowataŋka. See hotaŋke

w a - a′- h o - t o ŋ, *n.* *something that makes a noise*, as thunder, etc.

w a - a′- h o - y e - y a, *v.* of hoyeya; *to reprove, scold.*

w a - a′- i - a, *v.* of aia; *to talk about, to slander; to try*, as a case in court—waawaia, waauŋkiapi.

w a - a′- i-a-p i, *n.* *a talking against, slander; consultation; a trial in court.*

w a - a′- i - a - t i - p i, *n.* *a council-house; a court-house.*

w a - a′- i - e - s'a, *n.* *a slanderer, a tattler.*

w a - a′- k a - ġ a, *v.* of akaġa; *to add to; to transgress; to make a lie on; to blaspheme*—waawakaġa.

w a - a′- k a - ġ a - p i, *n.* *making on, blasphemy.*

w a - a′- k a - ḣ p a, *v.* of akaḣpa; *to cover*—waawakaḣpa.

w a - a′- k a - ḣ p e, *n.* *a covering.* See woakaḣpe.

w a′- a - k a - t a, *v.* *to cover with snow: i. q.* kasa.

w a - a′- k i - ć a - ġ a, *v.* *T.* *to play jokes on; make sport of.*

w a - a′- k i - ć i - y a - t a ŋ - i ŋ, *n.* of kićiyataŋiŋ; *manifestation.*

w a - a′- k i - k t o ŋ - ź a, *v.* of akiktoŋźa; *to forget*—waawektoŋźa. See wákiktoŋźa.

w a - a′- k i - k t o ŋ - ź a - p i, *n.* *forgetfulness.* See wákiktoŋźapi.

w a - a′- k i n, *cont.* of waakita. *T.*, waakil.

w a - a′- k i - n i - ć a, *v.* of akinića; *to dispute; one who disputes*—waawakinića.

w a - a′- k i - n i - ć a - p i, *n.* *disputation.*

w a - a′- k i - n i n, *cont.* of waakinića; waakinin uŋpi, *they are disputing.* *T.*, waakinil.

w a - a′- k i - n i n - y a, *adv.* *in the way of disputing.* *T.*, waakinilya.

w a - a′- k i - t a, *v.* of akita; *to hunt, seek*—waawakita.

w a - a′- m d e s, *cont.* of waamdeza.

w a - a′- m d e - z a, *v.* *to be observing, to be clear sighted*—waawamdeza. *T.*, waableza.

wa-a'-na-ġo-ptaŋ, *v.* of anaġoptaŋ; *to listen to, obey, be obedient*—waanawaġoptaŋ. *T.*, also waanoġoptaŋ.

wa-a'-na-ġo-ptaŋ-yaŋ, *adv.* *obediently:* waanaġoptaŋyaŋ wauŋ, *I am obedient.* *T.*, waanoġoptaŋyaŋ

wa-a'-na-ki-kśiŋ, *v.* of anakikśiŋ; *to expose one's self for others, take the place of danger*—waanawekśiŋ, waanauŋkikśiŋpi.

wa-a'-na-ki-kśiŋ-yaŋ, *adv.* *exposing one's self for others.*

wa-a'-na-śa-pa, *v.* of anaśapa; *to defile, soil by trampling on*—waanawaśapa.

wa-a'-na-śdo-ka, *n.* *something that flies out* or *refuses to stay in*, as a cork, etc.

wa-a'-na-taŋ, *v.* of anataŋ; *to rush on, make an attack*—waanawataŋ.

Wa-a'-na-taŋ, *n.* (*one who makes an attack*); a distinguished Sisitoŋwaŋ chief who was killed in 1839; a county of Minnesota.

wa-a'-na-źiŋ, *v.* of anaźiŋ; *to stand and shoot the image of that which is supposed to be the cause of the disease.* This is a part of the ceremony of Dakota conjuring—waanawaźiŋ, waanauŋźiŋpi.

wa-a'-nu-nu, *n.* *moss.* *T.*, peźi hiŋkpila.

wa-a'-p'a, *v.* of ap'a; *to strike*—waawap'a.

wa-a'-pa-ṭo-ya, *v.* of apaṭoya; *to hinder, obstruct*—waapaṭowaya.

wa-a'-pe, *v.* of ape; *to wait, be in waiting*—waawape.

wa-a'-s'iŋ, *v.* of as'iŋ; *to covet, desire what is another's; to stay where others are eating, expecting to share*—waawas'iŋ.

wa-a'-skam, *cont.* of waaskapa. *T.*, waaskab.

wa-a'-skam-ya, *v.* of askamya; *to cause to stick on, make adhere*—waaskamwaya.

wa-a'-skam-ya-pi, *n.* *sticking plaster.*

wa-a'-ska-pa, *v.* of askapa; *to stick on.*

wa-a'-ska-pe, *n.* *something that sticks, a sticking plaster.*

wa-a'-sni-yaŋ, *v.* of asniyaŋ; *to heal, make well*—waasniwaya.

wa-a'-sni-yaŋ, *n.* *a healer, healing.*

wa-a'-ś'a-ka, *v. n.* *to be loaded with* or *coated*, as the tongue in sickness. See wáś'aka.

wa-a'-śa-pa, *v.* of aśapa; *to be defiled*—waamaśapa.

wa-a'-śa-pe, *n.* *a blotter.*

wa-a'-taŋ-ka. See wátaŋka.

wa-a'-ta-ya, *v.* of ataya; *to be lucky, fortunate*—waatawaya.

wa-a'-ta-ye-s'a, *n.* *a fortunate one*, as a good hunter.

wa-a'-toŋ-waŋ, *v.* of atoŋwaŋ; *to be observing*—waawatoŋwaŋ.

wa-a'-toŋ-we, *n.* *an observer.*

wa-a'-wa-ćiŋ, *v.* of awaćiŋ; *to think about, consider, be thoughtful*—waawaćaŋmi.

wa-a'-wa-ćiŋ-yaŋ, *v. a. to cause to think* or *consider; one who makes others think*—waawaćiŋwaya.

wa-a'-waŋ-hdag, *cont.* of waawaŋhdaka.

wa-a'-waŋ-hda-ka, *v.* of awaŋhdaka; *to watch over one's own*—waawaŋwahdaka. See wáwaŋhdaka.

wa-a'-waŋ-hda-ke, *n. one who watches over, a shepherd, a bishop.*

wa-a'-waŋ-yag, *cont.* of waawaŋyaka.

wa-a'-waŋ-yag-ki-ya-pi, *n. one who is employed to oversee, a steward.*

wa-a'-waŋ-ya-ka, *v.* of awaŋyaka; *to oversee, watch over, take care of*—waawaŋmdaka.

wa-a'-waŋ-ya-ka, *n. some spiritual being who watches the Dakotas to do them hurt.*

wa-a'-waŋ-ya-ke, *n. a watchman.*

wa-a'-ya, *v.* of aya; *to take* or *bear to*—waamda.

wa-a'-ya-ta, *v.* of ayata; *to guess, predict, foretell*—waamdata.

wa-a'-ya-taŋ-iŋ, *v.* of ayataŋiŋ; *to proclaim, make manifest, bear witness*—waamdataŋiŋ.

wa-a'-ya-taŋ-iŋ, *n. a witness.*

wa-a'-ya-taŋ-iŋ-yaŋ, *adv. testifying.*

wa-a'-ya-te, *n. a prophet.*

wa-a'-yu-pta, *v.* of ayupta; *to answer*—waamdupta.

wa-a'-yu-pte, *n. one who answers.*

wa-a'-zil-toŋ, *v. T. i. q.* waaziŋtoŋ.

wa-a'-zin-toŋ, *v.* of azintoŋ; *to burn incense to* or *for*—waazinwatoŋ. *T.*, waaziltoŋ.

wa-ba'-ġa-pa, *v.* of baġapa; *to skin animals, be in the habit of taking off skins*—wabawaġapa. *T.*, wawaġapa.

wa-ba'-ġo, *v.* of baġo; *to carve, engrave*—wabawaġo.

wa-ba'-hba, *v.* of bahba; *to cut off,* as in shelling corn with a knife—wabawahba. *T.*, wawagna.

wa-ba'-hbe-za, *v.* of bahbeza; *to make rough; to haggle*—wabawahbeza.

wa-ba'-hda, *v.* of bahda; *to make uncoil by cutting.*

wa-ba'-hna, *v.* of bahna; *to make fall off by cutting.*

wa-ba'-hna-yaŋ, *v.* of bahnayaŋ; *to miss in trying to cut*—wabawahnayaŋ.

wa-ba'-huŋ, *v.* of bahuŋ; *to cut, gash*—wabawahuŋ.

wa-ba'-huŋ-huŋ, *v. red.* of wabahuŋ; *to cut,* as a piece of meat nearly off, *in many places:* wabahuŋhuŋ waḳu, *I gave it to him to cut in pieces.*

wa-ba'-hu-te-daŋ, *v.* of bahutedaŋ; *to wear off to a stump,* as a knife—wabawahutedaŋ. *T.*, wawatepa. See wabatepa.

wa-ba'-ḣda-ġaŋ, *v.* of baḣdaġaŋ; *to make large, to cut so that it becomes larger*—wabawaḣdaġaŋ.

wa-ba'-ḣda-ya, *v.* of baḣdaya; *to pare, to cut off the rind* or *skin*—wabawaḣdaya. See wabasku.

wa-ba'-ḣda-ye-daŋ, *n.* *parings.*

wa-ba'-ḣde-ća, *v.* of baḣdeća; *to tear in attempting to cut*—wabawaḣdeća.

wa-ba'-ḣdo-ka, *v.* of baḣdoka; *to cut holes*—wabawaḣdoka. See wabaśdoka.

wa-ba'-ḣu, *v.* of baḣu; *to peel, pare*—wabawaḣu. See wabasku.

wa-ba'-ke-za, *v.* of bakeza; *to make smooth with a knife; to trim off the feather,* as in making arrows—wabawakeza. *T.*, wawaḳeza. See wabaḳeza.

wa'-ba-ke-ze, *n.* *a board on which to trim the feather* in making arrows.

wa-ba'-koŋ-ta, *v.* of bakoŋta. See wabakoŋtkoŋta.

wa-ba'-koŋ-tkoŋ, *adj.* *cut* or *notched,* as a piece of meat given to a child.

wa-ba'-koŋ-tkoŋ-ta, *v.* of bakoŋtkoŋta; *to cut* or *notch*—wabawakoŋtkoŋta.

wa-ba'-kpaŋ, *v.* of bakpaŋ; *to cut up fine*—wabawakpaŋ.

wa-ba'-ksa, *v.* of baksa; *to cut off*—wabawaksa, wabaunksapi.

wa-ba'-ktaŋ, *v.* of baktaŋ; *to cut so as to make crook*—wabawaktaŋ.

wa-ba'-ḳe-za, *v.* of baḳeza; *to make smooth by cutting*—wabawaḳeza. See wabakeza.

wa-ba'-mda, *v.* of bamda; *to cut in slices*—wabawamda.

wa-ba'-mda-mda-za, *v. red.* of wabamdaza.

wa-ba'-mda-za, *v.* of bamdaza; *to rip open* or *up*—wabawamdaza.

wa-ba'-mde-ća, *v.* of bamdeća; *to cut up, break to pieces with a knife*—wabawamdeća.

wa-ba'-mna, *v.* of bamna; *to rip with a knife*—wabawamna.

wa-ba'-pe-sto, *v.* of bapesto; *to shave to a point*—wabawapesto.

wa-ba'-po-ta, *v.* of bapota; *to destroy by cutting*—wabawapota.

wa-ba'-psa-ka *v.* of bapsaka; *to cut off,* as cords—wabawapsaka.

wa-ba'-pta, *v.* of bapta; *to cut out, pare around*—wabawapta.

wa'-ba-pte, *n.* *a cutting-board. T.*, awawapte.

wa-ba'-pte-će-daŋ, *v.* of baptećedaŋ; *to cut off short*—wabawaptećedaŋ. *T.*, wawaptećela.

wa-ba'-ptu-źa, *v.* of baptuźa; *to crack* or *split with a knife*—wabawaptuźa.

wa-ba'-sku, *v.* of basku; *to pare,* as potatoes—wabawasku, wabauŋskupi. See wabaḣu.

wa-ba'-smiŋ, *v.* of basmiŋ; *to make bare with a knife*—wabawasmiŋ.

wa-ba'-śda, *v.* of baśda; *to shave off*—wabawaśda.

wa-ba'-śdo-ka, *v.* of baśdoka; *to cut out of*—wabawaśdoka. See wabaḣdoka.

wa-ba'-śki-ta, *v.* of baśkita; *to cut, gash*—wabawaśkita.

wa-ba'-śpa, *v.* of baśpa; *to cut off pieces*—wabawaśpa.

wa-ba'-śpu, *v.* of baśpu; *to cut in pieces*—wabawaśpu.

wa-ba'-śpu-śpu, *v. red.* of wabaśpu; *to cut up in pieces*, as tallow—wabawaśpuśpu.

wa-ba'-ta-ku-śni, *v.* of batakuśni; *to destroy.*

wa-ba'-te-pa, *v.* of batepa; *to cut off short*—wabawatepa. See wabahutedaŋ.

wa-ba'-tpaŋ, *v.* Same as wabakpaŋ.

wa-ba'-ṭa, *v.* of baṭa; *to kill.*

wa-be', *n.* of be; *a hatching-place.*

wa-ble'-ni-ća, *n.* *T.* *an orphan; i. q.* wamdenića.

wa-blo'-śa, *n.* *T.* *i. q.* amdośa.

wa-blu'-śka, *n.* *T.* *a snake; a bug; an insect. i. q.* wamduśka.

wa-blu'-śka-śa-śa, *n.* *T.* *bed-bugs.*

wa-bo'-će-ka, *v.* wabośeg iyeya, *to make stagger by shooting.* *T*, wawoćeka. NOTE.—All words change in Titoŋwaŋ, the prefix "bo" to "wo."

wa-bo'-ço, *v.* of boço; *to churn*—wabowaço.

wa-bo'-ha-i-ye-ya, *v.* of bohaiyeya; *to make tumble over by shooting*

wa-bo'-hiŋ-ta, *v.* of bohiŋta; *to sweep all off by shooting*—wabowahiŋta.

wa-bo'-hna, *v.* of bohna; *to knock off*, as fruit, *by shooting*—wabowahna.

wa-bo'-hna-śkiŋ-yaŋ, *v.* of bohnaśkiŋyaŋ; *to make crazy by punching* or *shooting*—wabowahnaśkiŋyaŋ.

wa-bo'-hna-yaŋ, *v.* of bohnayaŋ; *to miss in shooting*—wabowahnayaŋ.

wa-bo'-ho-ho, *v.* of bohoho; *to make loose by shooting*—wabowahoho.

wa-bo'-hu-hu-za, *v.* of bohuhuza; *to make shake by shooting*—wabowahuhuza.

wa-bo'-ḣći, *v.* of boḣći; *to shoot* or *punch out pieces*—wabowaḣći.

wa-bo'-ḣdo-ka, *v.* of boḣdoka; *to shoot* or *punch holes*—wabowaḣdoka. *T.*, wawoḣloka. See wabośdoka.

wa-bo'-ḣmiŋ, *v.* of boḣmiŋ; *to make crook* by shooting—wabowaḣmiŋ. See waboktaŋ.

wa-bo'-ḣpa, *v.* of boḣpa; *to shoot on the wing.*

wa-bo'-kpaŋ, *v.* of bokpaŋ; *to pound fine*—wabowakpaŋ.

wa-bo'-ksa, *v.* of boksa; *to break off by shooting* or *punching*—wabowaksa. *T.*, wawoksa.

wa-bo'-ktaŋ, *v.* of boktaŋ; *to bend by shooting* or *pounding*—wabowaktaŋ. See waboḣmiŋ.

wa-bo'-ku-ka, *v.* of bokuka; *to destroy by pounding* or *shooting*—wabowakuka.

wa-bo'-mda-ya, *v.* of bomdaya; *to make spread out by shooting* or *punching*—wabowamdaya. *T.*, waoblaya.

w a - b o′ - m d a - z a, *v.* of bomdaza; *to tear open by shooting*, etc.—wabowamdaza. *T.*, wawoblaza.

w a - b o′ - m d e - ć a, *v.* of bomdeća; *to break in pieces by shooting* or *punching*—wabowamdeća. *T.*, wawobleća.

w a′ - b o - m d u, *v.* *the snow flies.* *T.*, wa′woblu.

w a - b o′ - m d u, *v.* of bomdu; *to pound fine, to pulverize*—wabowamdu. *T.*, wawóblu.

w a - b o′ - p a ŋ, *v.* of bopaŋ; *to pound fine*, as hominy—wabowapaŋ.

w a - b o′ - p a ŋ - p a ŋ, *v.* of bopaŋpaŋ; *to make soft by pounding.*

w a - b o′ - p e - m n i, *v.* of bopemni; *to twist by shooting*, etc.—wabowapemni.

w a - b o′ - p o - t a, *v.* of bopota; *to shoot* or *pound to pieces*—wabowapota.

w a - b o′ - p s a - k a, *v.* of bopsaka; *to shoot off*, as strings—wabowapsaka.

w a - b o′ - p t a, *v.* of bopta; *to dig up by striking with a stick endwise*, as in digging tipsiŋna—wabowapta. *T.*, wawopta.

w a - b o′ - p t u - ź a, *v.* of boptuźa; *to crack by pounding* or *shooting*—wabowaptuźa.

w a - b o′ - s d a - t a, *n.* *a kind of long beads, large in the middle*, worn by the Dakotas.

w a - b o′ - s d e - ć a, *v.* of bosdeća; *to split by shooting*—wabowasdeća.

w a - b o′ - s n i, *v.* of bosni; *to blow out, extinguish*—wabowasni.

w a - b o′ - s o - t a, *v.* of bosota; *to exterminate by shooting*—wabowasota. *T.*, wawosota.

w a - b o′ - ś a - k a, *v.* of bośaka; *to shoot* or *punch with too little force to penetrate*—wabowaśaka.

w a - b o′ - ś d a, *v.* of bośda; *to shoot off bare*—wabowaśda.

w a - b o′ - ś d o - k a, *v.* of bośdoka; *to shoot* or *punch out*, as an eye—wabowaśdoka. *T.*, wawośloka. See waboȟdoka.

w a - b o′ - ś k i, *v.* of bośki; *to pound*, as corn not well dried—wabowaśki.

w a - b o′ - ś n a, *v.* of bośna; *to miss in shooting*—wabowaśna. *T.*, wawośna.

w a - b o′ - ś p a, *v.* of bośpa; *to shoot off a piece*—wabowaśpa.

w a - b o′ - ś u - ź a, *v.* of bośuźa; *to shoot to splinters.*

w a - b o′ - t a - k u - n i - ś n i, *v.* of botakuniśni; *to shoot to pieces* or *destroy*—wabowatakuniśni.

w a - b o′ - t i - ć a, *v.* of botića; *to snatch away, rob*—wabowatića. *T.*, wamanoŋ.

w a - b o′ - t i - ć e, *n.* *a robber.* *T.*, wamanoŋ s'a.

w a - b o′ - t p a ŋ, *v.* of botpaŋ. Same as wabokpaŋ.

w a - b o′ - t p i, *v.* of botpi; *to crack*, as nuts, *by pounding with a pestle*—wabowatpi. *T.*, wawokpi.

w a - b o′ - ṭ a, *v.* of boṭa; *to kill by punching.*

w a - b o′ - ṭ i ŋ - z a, *v.* of boṭiŋza; *to pound tight*—wabowaṭiŋza.

wa-bo'-we-ġa, *v.* of boweġa; *to break* or *fracture by shooting,* etc.—wabowaweġa.

wa-bo'-źa-źa, *v.* of boźaźa; *to wash out by punching*—wabowaźaźa

wa-ćan'-ki-ya, *adj.* of ćaŋtekiya; *kind, benevolent.* See waćaŋtkiya.

wa-ćan'-śin-ya, *v. a.* of ćanśinya; *to make sad*—waćanśinwaya. *T.,* waćaŋśilya.

wa-ćaŋ'-ġa, *n.* *a species of sweet-smelling grass.*

wa-ćaŋ'-te-śi-ća, *adj.* of ćaŋteśića; *unhappy*—waćaŋtemaśića.

wa-ćaŋ'-te-śin-ya, *v. a.* *to make sad*—waćaŋteśinwaya.

wa-ćaŋt'-ki-ya, *adj.* of ćaŋtekiya; *benevolent*—waćanwakiya, waćanyakiya, waćanuŋkiyapi.

wa-ćaŋt'-ki-ya-pi, *n.* *benevolence.*

wa-ćaŋt'-o-hna-ka, *v.* of ćaŋtohnaka; *to be generous, affectionate*—waćaŋtowahnaka.

wa-ćaŋt'-o-hna-ka, *adj.* *generous; affectionate.*

wa-ćaŋt'-o-hna-ka-pi, *n.* *generosity; affection.*

wa-ćaŋt'-o-kpa-ni, *v.* of ćaŋtokpani; *to desire much, long for; to be impatient*—waćaŋtowakpani.

wa-ćaŋt'-o-tpa-ni, *v.* Same as waćaŋtokpani.

wa-ćaŋ'-ze-ya, *v.* of ćaŋzeya; *to make angry.*

wa-ćaŋ'-ze-ze-ka, *n.* *one easily made angry.*

wa-ćaś'-toŋ, *v.* of ćaśtoŋ; *to name, give names*—waćaśwatoŋ.

wa-ćaś'-toŋ, *n.* *a namer, one who names.*

wa-ća'-źe-ki-ya-ta, *v. a.* *to mention the names of deceased relatives* to one, *and beg for their sakes*—waćaźewakimdata.

wa-ća'-źe-yan, *cont.* of waćaźeyata.

wa-ća'-źe-ya-ta, *v.* of ćaźeyata; *to ask for* or *beg in the name of the dead*—waćaźemdata.

wa'-će-he, *n.* See waćiŋbe.

wa-će'-hiŋ, *n.* *the long slender feathers growing near the tail of an eagle,* etc.

wa-će'-ki-ya, *v.* of ćekiya; *to pray to, ask for help, pray for assistance* in war, etc.—waćewakiya, waćeuŋkiyapi.

wa-će'-oŋ-pa, *v.* of ćeoŋpa; *to roast,* as corn in the ear; *one who roasts* corn—waćewaoŋpa.

Wa-će'-uŋ-pa, *n. p.* the name of a clan of the Yanktons and Sićaŋġu.—J. O. D.

wa-će'-oŋ-pa-pi, *n.* *roasting-corn.*

wa-će'-ṭuŋ-hda, *v.* of ćeṭuŋhda; *to doubt, disbelieve; one who always doubts*—waćeṭuŋwahda.

wa-će'-ṭuŋ-hda-pi, *n.* *unbelief, doubting.*

wa-će'-ṭuŋ-hda-ya, *adv.* *doubtingly.*

wa-ći', *v. n.* *to dance*—wawaći, wayaći.

wa-ćiŋ', *v.* 1st pers. sing. of ćiŋ.

wa-ćiŋ′, *v. n. to think, purpose*—waćaŋmi, waćaŋni, wauŋćiŋpi. This word requires an other verb in the infinitive mood to precede, as ećoŋ waćaŋmi, *I thought to do.*

wa-ćiŋ′-ble-za, *v. n. T. to be clear-headed; smart; quick to comprehend: i. q.* waćiŋmdeza.

wa-ćiŋ′-ća-daŋ, *n. a young bear, a cub. T.*, mato ćiŋćala.

wa-ćiŋ′-ći-ḳa-ye-daŋ, *adj. fickle-minded*—waćiŋmaćiḳayedaŋ.

wa-ćiŋ′-ći-sti-ye-daŋ, *adj. fickle-minded*—waćiŋmaćistiyedaŋ. *T.*, waćiŋćisćiyela.

wa-ćiŋ′-ha-ha-daŋ, *adj. cowardly, easily alarmed*—waćiŋmahahadaŋ.

wa′-ćiŋ-he, *n. the head-dress of a Dakota man; anything standing up on the head,* as feathers; *a plume: i. q.* waćehe.

wa′-ćiŋ-he-sap-sa-pa, *n. black plumes, ostrich feathers.*

wa′-ćiŋ-he-ya, *v. a. to use for a plume*—waćiŋhewaya.

wa-ćiŋ′-hiŋ-yaŋ-za, *adj. cruel, morose* — waćiŋmahiŋyaŋza. See wahiŋyaŋza.

wa-ćiŋ′-hnu-hnu-ni, *adj. red.* of waćiŋhnuni; *wandering in mind, bewildered, oblivious*—waćiŋmahnuhnuni.

wa-ćiŋ′-hnu-ni, *adj. wandering, bewildered*—waćiŋmahnuni.

wa-ćiŋ′-hnu-ni-ya, *v. a. to cause one's mind to wander, to bewilder*—waćiŋhnuniwaya

wa-ćiŋ′-i-bo-śa-ka, *v. n. to be out of heart about, to be discouraged*—waćiŋibowaśaka. *T.*, waćiŋiwośaka.

wa-ćiŋ′-i-wo-śag, *cont.* of waćiŋiwośaka.

wa-ćiŋ′-i-wo-śag-ya, *v. T. to discourage.*

wa-ćiŋ′-i-wo-śa-ka, *v. n. T. to be discouraged, be out of heart.*

wa-ćiŋ′-i-yo-ki-pi, *v. n. to be contented, satisfied with*—waćiŋiyowakipi.

wa-ćiŋ′-i-yo-ki-pi-ya, *adv. contentedly.*

wa-ćiŋ′-i-yo-ki-śi-ća, *v. n. to be displeased with; to be sad on account of, to regret*—waćiŋiyowakiśića; waćiŋiyowićawakiśića, *I am displeased with them.*

wa-ćiŋ′-i-yo-ki-śin-ya, *adv. displeased with. T*, waćiŋiyokiśilya.

wa-ćiŋ′-ka, *v.* Same as waćiŋ.

wa-ćiŋ′-ki-ći-yu-za-pi, *v. recip. having regard for each other.* See waćiŋkiyuza.

wa-ćiŋ′-ki-ya, *v. pos.* of waćiŋyaŋ; *to trust in,* as in anything laid up for one's own use; *to trust to* or *have confidence in,* as a friend, Jesus Christ our Saviour, etc—waćiŋwakiya.

wa-ćiŋ′-ki-yu-za, *v. a. to think of, hold in the mind,* either for good or ill—waćiŋwakiyuza.

wa-ćiŋ′-ko, *adj.* (waćiŋ *and* ko) *easily made angry, ill-natured, passionate*—waćiŋmako, waćiŋuŋkopi.

wa-ćiŋ′-ko-ke-la, *adj. T. easily made angry.*

wa-ćiŋ′-ko-pi, *n. passionateness.*

wa-ćiŋ′-ko-ya, *adv. passionately; crossly.*

wa-ćiŋ′-ksam, *cont.* of waćiŋksapa. *T.*, waćiŋksab.

wa-ćiŋ′-ksam-ya, *adv. wisely, discreetly.*

wa-ćiŋ′-ksa-pa, *adj. intelligent, wise*—waćiŋmaksapa, waćiŋuŋksapapi.

wa-ćiŋ′-o-a-ye, *n. inclination:* waćiŋioaye manića, *I am discouraged.*

wa-ćiŋ′-o-ze, *n.* of waćiŋyuza; *thought, thinking.*

wa-ćiŋ′-pi-ya-hna-ka, *v.* (waćiŋ, piya, *and* hnaka) *to take another view of* a thing, *be of another mind.*

wa-ćiŋ′-śi-ća, *adj. bad dispositioned.*

wa-ćiŋ′-taŋ-ka, *adj. patient, magnanimous, long-suffering, enduring long*—waćiŋmataŋka.

wa-ćiŋ′-toŋ; *v. to have understanding, have a mind of one's own, be wise*—waćiŋwatoŋ.

wa-ćiŋ′-toŋ-hnag-ya, *v. a. to comfort,* usually by giving to the afflicted; *to cause to have a different view*—waćiŋtoŋhnagwaya.

wa-ćiŋ′-toŋ-hna-ke, *n.* (wa ćiŋ, toŋ, *and* hnaka) *a comforter. T.*, wakićaŋpte.

wa-ćiŋ-toŋ-śni, *v. n. to be foolish*—waćiŋwatoŋśni.

wa-ćiŋ′-ṭa, *v. n. to be feebleminded, forgetful.*

wa-ćiŋ′-ṭa-ṭa-ke, *n. one who is feeble-minded.*

wa-ćiŋ′-wi̧-ki-ç̧uŋ-śni, *v. n. to be indifferent about.*

wa-ćiŋ′-yaŋ, *v. a. to trust in, depend upon; to believe in;* originally, *to desire, to wish for*—waćiŋwaya, waćinuŋyaŋpi, waćiŋmayaŋ, waćiŋćiya. See waćiŋkiya.

wa-ćiŋ′-yaŋ, *adj. confiding:* waćiŋyaŋ wauŋ.

wa-ćiŋ′-yaŋ-pi, *n. trusting in, confidence, faith; trusted in, trustiness.*

wa-ćiŋ′-ye-ki-ya, *v. a. to cause to trust in*—waćiŋyewakiya.

wa-ćiŋ′-ye-pi-ća, *n. something that can be trusted in:* waćiŋyepića śni, *that cannot be trusted in.*

wa-ćiŋ′-ye-ya, *v. n. to purpose, set the mind to; to cause to trust in.*

wa-ćiŋ′-źa-ta, *adj. forked mind,* i. e., *undecided, hesitating*—waćiŋmaźata.

wa-ći′-pi, *n.* of waći; *dancing, the dance*

wa-ćo′-ka, *n. low land lying near a river* or *lake without timber.*

wa-ćo′-koŋ, *v.* of ćokoŋ; *to desire to take life*—waćowakoŋ, waćomakoŋpi.

wa-ćo′-koŋ-pi, *n. a desire of taking life.*

wa-ćo′-ni-ća, *n.* of ćonića; *dried meat,* especially *dried buffalo* or *deer meat; venison; wild meat of any kind, fresh* or *dried* wa-ćo'-ni-ća-ka, *n.* *T.* *wild meat dried.*

wa-ćo'-ni-sa-ka, *n.* *hard dried meat.*

wa-ću'-tu-hu, *n.* of ćutuhu; *the ribs* or *knees of a boat; the ribs of a bear.* *T.*, waltućuhu; matoćuhu.

wa-da', *v.* of da; *to ask, beg*—wawada: also 1st pers. sing. of da.

wa-da'-da, *v.* *red.* of wada.

wa-da'-da-ka, *n.* *a beggar.*

wa-da'-ko-ta-śni, *adj.* of dakota; *not caring for relations, without natural affection*—wadamakotaśni. *T.*, olakolwićaye śni

wa-di'-ta, *adj.* *brave*—wamadita. See waditaka.

wa-di'-ta-ka, *adj.* *brave, courageous*—wamaditaka *and* wadimataka, wadinitaka, wadiuŋtakapi. *T.*, ćaŋte ṭiŋza.

wad-i-yo'-pe-ya, *v. a.* *to accuse* one *of doing what another has done*—wadiyopewaya.

wa' do waŋ, *v. abs.* See adowaŋ.

wa-dun'-ya, *v.* of dunya; *to dye red* or *scarlet*—wadunwaya. *T.*, walulya.

wa-dun'-ye, *n.* *a dyer of scarlet.* *T.*, walulye.

wa-du'-ta, *n.* *a red root used for dyeing scarlet.*

wa-e'-kta-śni, *adv.* waektaśni iću, *to take the wrong one; to accuse falsely.*

wa-e'-kta-śni-yaŋ, *adv.* *improperly, falsely.*

wa-e'-pa-zo, *n.* *T.* *the fore-finger.*

wa-gla'-mni, *v.* *T.* *to go after what one has left.* See hdamni.

wa-gle'-kśuŋ, *n.* *T.* *the wild turkey.*

wa-gli'-yo-ya, *v.* *T.* *to go after one's own; i. q.* wahduwe.

wa-glu'-ha-ha-ka, *adj.* *T.* *saving, frugal, parsimonious.*

wa-glu'-ha-ha-ke-ćiŋ, *n.* *a parsimonious person.*

wa'-glu-ḣe, *v. n.* *T.* *to be a hanger on with one's relations.*

Wa'-glu-ḣe, *n. p.* *the Loafer Band* of the Oglalas.

wa-glu'-la, *n.* *T.* *maggots, worms: i. q.* wamdudaŋ.

wa-glu'-śna, *v.* *T.* *for to drop one's own: i q.* wahduśna.

wa-glu'-za, *v.* *T.* *to take back what one has given.*

wa-gme'-za, *n.* *T.* *corn: i. q.* wamnaheza.

wa gme'-za-hu, *n.* *T.* *corn-stalks.*

wa-gmu', *n.* *T.* *pumpkins: i. q.* wamnu. See wakmu.

wa'-gna-wa-uŋ-yaŋ-pi, *n.* *T.* *an altar; a place on which offerings are made.*

wa'-gna-wa-yu-ḣta-ta-pi, *n.* *T.* *an altar for sacrifice;* especially *a place on which living ones are offered*

wa'-ġa, *n.* *the cotton-wood:* waġa ćaŋ, *the cotton-wood tree, the Populus canadensis.*

wa-ġi'-yo-ġi, *n.* There are two birds bearing this name, one of which is probably *a species of thrush;* both are so called from their song.

wa-ġi′-yo-ġiŋ, *n.* *ground cherries.*

wa′-ġoŋ, *n.* *rush mats; Chippewa tents.* *T.*, psa owiŋźa.

wa-ġu′-ġe-ća, *n.* *round heavy snow; sharp snow, crusted; hardened snow.*

wa-ġu′-ġu-ya, *v. a.* *to cause to burn, to scorch*—waġuġuwaya.

wa-ġu′-ya, *v. a.* *to scorch*—waġuwaya.

wa-ha′. *n.* *a bear-skin* *T.*, matoha.

wa-ha′-ćaŋ-ka, *n.* *a shield.*

wa-ha′-ćaŋ-ka-ska-ķiŋ, *v.* *T.* *to be generous; liberal; benevolent;* especially *to give much away when one cannot well spare it.* In old times the one most ohitika in the matter of *giving* to the poor, etc, was said to have the "ska" or *unsullied shield:* wahááaŋka ska waķiŋ, *I give freely,* &c.

wa-ha′-ka-kta, *n.* *the last, the youngest* *T*, hakakta. See wohakakta..

wa-haŋg′-ya, *v. a.* *to destroy*—wahaŋgwaya, wahaŋguŋyaŋpi. See ihaŋgya.

wa-haŋg′-ye-ća, *n.* *one who destroys* everything.

wa-haŋ′-pi, *n.* of haŋpi; *broth, soup* of any kind

wa-ha′-pa-ḣpa, *v.* *to flesh a robe* or *skin*—wahawapaḣpe, etc.

wa-hda′-ta, *v.* of hdata; *to steal up to,* as to game—wawahdata: also the 1st pers. sing. of hdata.

wa-hda′-ta-pi, *n.* *stealing* or *crawling up to,* as to game.

wa-hde′-ća, *v.* *to be in sympathy with,* as the Dakotas say a mother is with her absent children, when they think about her. The Indians assert that mothers feel peculiar pains in their breasts when anything of importance happens to their absent children, or when about to hear from them. This feeling is regarded as an omen—wawahdeća, wauŋhdećapi. See wakihdeća.

wa-hde′-ća-pi, *n.* *the sympathy that is said to exist between a mother and her absent children,* producing peculiar sensations in the breast.

wa-hdi′, *v.* 1st pers. sing. of hdi.

wa′-hdi, *v.* of ahdi; *to bring home*—wáwahdi, wáuŋhdipi.

wa′-hdi-a-ś'a-pi, *n.* *the shout that is made by the children when meat, etc., is brought into the camp.*

wa-hdu′-ha, *v.* of hduha; *to have one's own, to keep*—wawahduha: also the 1st pers. sing. of hduha.

wa-hdu′-ha-ha-kte-ća, *adj.* *parsimonious*—wawahduhahakteća. *T*, wagluhahaka.

wa-hdu′-ha-ha-kte-će-ćiŋ, *n.* *one who is parsimonious:* wahduhahapikteććećiŋ, *parsimony.*

wa-hdu′-we, *v.* of hduwe; wahduwe ya, *to go to bring one's own,* without specifying what.

wa-he′-ḣa-ka, *n.* the "heḣaka" and "uŋkteḣi" are sometimes so called.

wa-he'-ki-ç̣uŋ, *v. pos.* *to pack up* or *tie one's own*—waheweç̣uŋ. See waheyuŋ.

wa-he'-ktam, *cont.* of wahektapa; *at the stern.* *T.*, walhektab.

wa-he'-kta-pa, *v.* *to pilot* or *steer a boat* of any kind—wahektawapa. *T.*, walsiŋte yuhomni.

wa-he'-kta-pa, *n.* *a pilot, helmsman.*

wa-he'-kta-pa-taŋ-haŋ, *n.* *the stern of a boat, at the stern.* *T.*, walhektapataŋhaŋ.

wa-he'-sdo-ye, *n.* *a smooth shining horn.*

wa-he'-yuŋ, *v.* of heyuŋ; *to pack up in bundles*—wahemuŋ, wahenuŋ.

wa-he'-yuŋ-pi, *n.* *packing up.*

wa-hi', *n.* See waŋhi.

wa-hi'-bu, *v.* Same as hibu, *I come.* *T.*, hibu.

wa-hi'-hbu, *v.* 1st pers. sing. of hiyu. Same as wahibu.

wa-hi'-na-wa-pa, *v.* 1st pers. sing. of hinapa; double pronoun.

wa-hiŋ', *n.* *hairs:* wahiŋhdapi, *the hair that is sometimes attached to a pipe-stem.*

wa-hiŋ'-ća-ći-će, *n.* *a smoothing instrument used in dressing hides.*

wa-hiŋ'-he, *v.* *T.* of hiŋhaŋ; *it snows:* future, wahiŋhiŋ kta.

wa-hiŋ'-he-ya, *n.* *T.* *the gopher:* *i. q.* manića.

wa-hiŋ'-he-ya-pa-blu, *n.* *T.* *gopher hills.*

wa-hiŋ'-pa-ḣpa, *n.* *T.* *a fleshing-knife* or *chisel* used in preparing green hides for drying.

wa-hiŋ'-pe-ya, *n.* *cobwebs.*

wa-hiŋ'-ske, *n.* *the long-grained* or *southern corn;* so called because the grains resemble the canine teeth of animals: *i. q.* hiŋske.

wa-hiŋ'-tka, *n.* *an instrument used in scraping hides; a bit of steel fastened to an elk-horn handle and used as a hoe on the flesh side, making it the same thickness.*

Wa-hiŋ'-wa-kpa, *n.* *the Arkansas River.*—J. P. W.

wa-hiŋ'-yaŋ-za, *adj.* *morose*—wamahiŋyaŋza. *T.*, wawahiŋyaŋzeća. See waćiŋhiŋyaŋza.

wa-hiŋ'-ya-źi-će, *n.* *down, fur,* such as is used by the Dakotas in their sacred ceremonies.

wa-hiŋ'-yuŋ-toŋ, *v.* See waiŋyuŋtoŋ.

wa-hiŋ'-yu-za, *n.* *T.* *a bracelet.* See napoktaŋ.

wa-hi'-pa-spe, *n.* *T.* *tent-pins:* *i. q.* hutipaspe.

wa-hi'-śna-he-ća, *n.* *soft new snow.* See waġuġeća.

wa-hi'-ti-hda, *v.* of hitihda; *to be fastidious, to loathe; a fastidious person*—wahitiwahda.

wa-hi'-yo, *v. abs.* of hiyo; *T.:* *i. q.* wahuwe.

wa-hi'-yo-hi, *v.* *T.* *to go for; go to get,* without mentioning what.

wa-hi'-yu, *v.* of hiyu; *to start to come*—wahihbu. *T.*, hiyu.

w a - h m u', *n.* *Sis.* Same as wamnu, wagmu, *and* wakmu.

w a - h m u ŋ g', *cont* of wahmuŋka: wahmuŋg mda, *I am going trapping.*

w a - h m u ŋ' - k a, *v.* of hmuŋka; *to trap, hunt with traps*—wawahmuŋka: also 1st pers. sing. of hmuŋka.

w a - h m u ŋ' - k a - p i, *n.* *trapping.*

w a' - h n a g, *cont.* of wáhnaka.

w a' - h n a g - t o ŋ, *n.* *something put with* another thing: wahnag ćodaŋ, *one thing alone;* wahnag toŋ ḳu, *to give,* as a blanket, *with* a gun; *a pad,* as on a horse's back when sore.

w a' - h n a - k a, *v.* of ahnaka; *to place on, put on,* as poultices on sores, etc.—wawahnaka. See wákićihnaka

w a - h n a' - k a, *v.* 1st pers. sing. of hnaka.

w a' - h n a - w o - ś n a - p i, *n.* (ahna *and* wośna) *an altar for sacrifice. T.,* wagnawauŋyaŋpi, *or* wagnawayuȟtatapi, according as the sacrifice is *inanimate* or *animate.*

w a' - h n a - w o - t a p i, *n.* (ahna *and* wotapi) *something to eat from, a table.*

w a - h n a' - y a ŋ, *v.* of hnayaŋ; *to deceive*—wawahnayaŋ: also 1st pers. sing. of hnayaŋ.

w a - h n i' - h d a, *v.* of hnihda; *to travel; to go about from place to place:* wahnihda wauŋ, *I am traveling.*

w a - h n i' - h d e - ć a, *n.* *one who is always traveling.*

w a - h n u ŋ' - k a, *n.* *the red-headed woodpecker.* See kaŋketaŋka *and* ṭoskadaŋ.

w a - h o' - ć o - k a, *n.* *an area surrounded by tents.* Probably not used by the Indians generally. This hoćoka *or* wahoćoka was formerly used by the Dakotas, according to what men of different tribes have told me. I have the order in which each camped. The Winnebagoes did not have it. The Omahas, Ponkas, Iowas, and kindred tribes observed it during the summer hunt.—J. O. D. See hoćoka.

w a - h o' - ȟ p i, *n.* *nests.* See hoȟpi.

w a - h o' - k i - y a, *v. a.* *to send word to*—wahowakiya, wahouŋkiyapi. See wahoya.

w a - h o' - k o ŋ - k i - y a, *v. a.* *to instruct, counsel, advise* one—wahokoŋwakiya, wahokoŋuŋkiyapi

w a - h o' - k o ŋ - k i - y a - p i, *n.* *instruction, counsel, advice; counselled.*

w a - h o' - ś i, *v.* of hośi; *to carry word;* always used with another verb, as, wahośi i, wáhośi hi, wahośi ya, etc.; *to bring* or *carry news.*

w a - h o' - ś i - w a - k a ŋ, *n.* a formation used by some for *angel, messenger.* See ohnihde *and* ohnihdeyapi.

w a - h o' - ś i - y a - p i, *n.* *T.* *one sent with a message:* wahośiyapi wakaŋ, *sacred messengers, the apostles of Christ.*

w a - h o' - y a, *v. a.* *to send for* one, *to send word to* one, *to promise* something *to* one—wahowaya.

w a - h o' - y a - p i, *n.* *sending word to.*

wa-hu'-a-ta-ya, *v.* See wahuwataya.

wa-hu'-ke-za, *n.* *a spear*, such as is used in spearing muskrats; *a war-spear.* See huḣaka.

wa-hu'-noŋ-pa, *n.* *a biped;* an appellation of man, not much used.

wa-hu'-to-pa, *n.* *quadrupeds*, but used only for the dog and wolf, in the sacred dialect. See huhatopa.

wa-hu'-wa-pa, *n.* *corn, an ear of corn;* sometimes corn in bags. See wamnaheza.

wa-hu'-wa-ta-ya, *v. n.* *to find one's self all at once unable to proceed, to be unable to escape* from fright, or some other cause—wahuwatawaya

wa-hu'-wa-ta-ye-ya, *v. a.* *to frighten,* or in some way *make unable to escape*—wahuwatayewaya.

wa-ḣa', *v.* of ḣa; *to bury*—wawaḣa, wauŋḣapi: also 1st pers. sing. of ḣa.

wa-ḣam'-ya, *v.* of ḣamya; *to frighten* or *scare away*—waḣamwaya. *T.*, waḣabya.

wa-ḣaŋ'-da, *v. a.* *to esteem, think highly of* one—waḣaŋwada.

wa-ḣaŋ'-ḣaŋ-i-ç̌i-da, *v. reflex.* *to be self-sufficient, self-important*—waḣaŋḣaŋmiç̌ida.

wa-ḣaŋ'-i-ç̌i-da, *v.* *reflex.* of waḣaŋda; *to think highly of one's self, be proud*—waḣaŋmiç̌ida.

wa ḣaŋ'-i-ç̌i-da-pi, *n.* *pride.*

wa-ḣaŋ'-i-ṭe-ya, *v. a.* *to tire one out*—waḣaŋiṭewaya.

wa-ḣaŋ'-ka, *v.* *to do difficult things well*—wawaḣaŋka.

wa-ḣaŋ'-ksi-ća, *n.* *the black bear, the Ursus americanus: i. q.* wasapedaŋ. See mato.

wa-ḣaŋ'-ksi-ća-ta-ha-za, *n.* *a kind of berry* growing on small bushes resembling the whortleberry.

wa-ḣaŋ'-la-se, *n.* *T.* *a proud* or *vain person.*

wa-ḣa'-pi, *n.* *burying; something buried.*

wa'-ḣba, *adj.* *mild, gentle.*

wa'-ḣba-daŋ, *adj.* *gentle*—mawaḣbadaŋ, niwaḣbadaŋ, uŋwaḣbapidaŋ. *T.*, waḣwala.

wa'-ḣba-ka, *adj.* *mild, gentle,*—mawaḣbaka: wićaśta waḣbaka, *a gentleman;* wiwaḣbaka, *a lady.* *T.*, waḣwaka.

wa'-ḣba-ya, *adv.* *mildly, gently.*

wa'-ḣba-ya, *v.* of ḣbaya; *to make sleepy*—waḣbawaya.

wa'-ḣba-ye-daŋ, *adv.* *mildly, gently:* waḣbayedaŋ wauŋ, *I am conducting mildly.* *T.*, waḣwayela.

wa-ḣća', *n.* the generic name for *flowers:* waḣća kamdu *and* waḣća namdu, *to unfold* or *blossom.*

wa-ḣća'-ḣća, *n.* *red.* of waḣća; *flowers, blossoms.*

wa-ḣća'-zi-zi, *n.* *yellow flowers, the sunflower.*

waḣ-ćiŋ'-ća, *n.* *the aspen* or *small cotton-wood, the Populus canadensis.*

wa-ḣe'-ća, *n.* *round white hail; snow-flakes, round like shot.*

wa-ḣet'-a-źu, *v. a.* *to discharge freight, unload,* as a vessel—waḣetawaźu.

wa-ḣet'-a-źu-pi, *n.* *unloading.*

wa-ḣe'-ya-ta-i-ye-ya, *v.* *to push back; one who pushes* others *back.*

wa-ḣna'-ḣna, *n.* *the coffee-nut.*

wa-ḣna'-ḣna-hu, *n.* *the coffee-nut tree.*

wa-ḣna'-wa-he-ća, *adj.* *lean, poor; ill-looking,* but much better than it looks: waḣnawaheća tuka waśte, *it is good although it looks badly.*

wa-ḣpa'-ḣo-ta, *n.* *T.* a brown bird that follows cattle: *the cow-bird.*

wa-ḣpa'-ḣo-ta, *n.* *T.* *a species of blackbird.*

wa-ḣpa'-ni, *adj.* *poor, destitute.*

wa-ḣpa'-ni-ća, *adj.* *poor, destitute, having no* waḣpaya—mawaḣpanića, uŋwaḣpanićapi.

wa-ḣpa'-ni-da, *v. a.* *to consider poor; to feel compassion for, have mercy on*—waḣpaniwada

wa-ḣpa'-ni-ya, *v. a.* *to make poor, cause to be poor*—waḣpaniwaya, waḣpanimayaŋ.

wa-ḣpa'-ni-yaŋ, *adv.* *poorly, in a destitute way.*

wa-ḣpaŋ'-yaŋ, *v.* *T.* *to soak and take off the hair: i. q.* wakpaŋyaŋ.

wa-ḣpa'-taŋ-ka, *n.* *T.* *the common blackbird: i. q.* zitkataŋka.

wa-ḣpa'-ya, *n.* *anything one has of movable goods, baggage.*

wa-ḣpa'-ye-ća, *n.* *baggage.*

wa-ḣpe', *n.* *a leaf, leaves; tea.*

wa-ḣpe'-ćaŋ-li, *n.* *T.* *a leaf used for tobacco: a small vine which runs on the ground like wintergreen, the leaf of which is used for tobacco.*

Wa-ḣpe'-ku-te, *n.* *the Leaf-shooters;* a band of the Dakotas who lived chiefly on the headwaters of the Blue Earth and Cannon rivers. They are now with the Mdewakaŋtoŋwaŋ at the Santee Reservation, Neb.

wa-ḣpe'-mda-ska-ska, *n.* *wintergreens.*

wa-ḣpe'-pe-źi-hu-ta, *n.* *leaf-medicine,* i. e., *tea.*

wa-ḣpe'-taŋ-ka, *n.* *large leaf,* i. e., *cabbage.*

Wa-ḣpe-toŋ-waŋ, *n.* *a band of the Dakotas,* who resided chiefly at the Little Rapids, at Lac-qui-parle, and at the lower extremity of Big Stone Lake, but are now on the Lake Traverse Reservation.

wa-ḣpo'-pa, *n.* *the large species of willow.*

wa'-ḣta-ni, *v.* of aḣtani; *to transgress a usage* or *custom, to omit a ceremony; to do wickedly; to sin*—wáwaḣtani, wáyaḣtani, wáuŋḣtanipi.

wa-ḣta'-ni-sa, *n.* *a transgressor; a sinner.*

wa'-ḣta-ni-ya, *v. a.* *to cause to transgress* or *sin*—waḣtaniwaya.

wa-ḣte', *adj.* *good.* See waḣteśni *and* waśte.

wa-ḣte′-da, *v.* *to esteem good;* used only in the negative.

wa-ḣte′-da-ka, *v. a.* *to dislike: i. q.* waḣtedaśni.

wa-ḣte′-da-śni, *v. a.* *to dislike, abominate*—waḣtewadaśni, waḣteuŋdapiśni, waḣtećidaśni.

wa-ḣte′-ka, *adj.* *bad: i. q.* waḣteśni.

wa-ḣte′-śni, *adj.* *bad, worthless, wicked*—mawaḣteśni.

wa-ḣuŋ′-te-ya, *v.* *T.* *to tire one out.*

wa-ḣu′-pa-ko-za, *n.* *wing-flappers,* i. e., *fowls, domestic fowls.*

wa-ḣwa′-ke-ća, *adj.* *T.* *mild, gentle: i q.* waḣbaka.

wa-ḣwa′-la, *adj.* *T.* *gentle, mild: i q.* waḣbadaŋ.

wa-ḣwa′-ya, *adv.* *T.* *gently: i. q.* waḣbaya.

wa-ḣwa′-ye-la, *adv.* *T.* *mildly, gently: i. q.* waḣbaye daŋ.

wa-i′-ća-ġa, *v.* of ićaġa; *to grow, produce.*

wa-i′-ćaḣ-ya, *v. a.* *to cause to produce, to create*—waićaḣwaya.

wa-i′-ćaḣ-ya-pi, *n.* *that which is created.*

Wa-i′-ćaḣ-ye, *n.* *the Creator.*

wa-i′-ći-a, *v.* of aia; *to slander. T.,* waaia.

wa-i′-ći-a-pi, *n.* *slander.*

wa-i′-ći-e-s'a, *n.* *a tattler, a slanderer.*

wa-i′-ći-ḣa-ḣa, *n.* *a jester, an insolent fellow; one who does evil to others, and laughs at the mischief he has done.*

wa-i′-ći-ḣa-ḣa-pi, *n.* *insolence.*

wa-i′-ći-waŋ-ġa-pi, *n.* *mutual inquiry.* *T.,* wikićiyuŋġapi. See ićiwaŋġa.

wa-i′-ći-ya, *v.* of ićiya; *to assist, take one's part; an advocate.* *T.,* wawićiya. See wawićiya.

wa-i′-ću, *v.* of ića; *to take*—waiwaću.

wa-i′-ću-ću-ka, *n.* *a pilferer.*

wa-i′-ću-ću-kte-ća, *v.* *to desire to take, to covet; one who covets.* *T.,* waićućukteḣćiŋ.

wa-i′-ću-ću-pi-kte-će-ćiŋ, *n.* *covetousness.* *T.,* waićućupiktećeḣćiŋ.

wa-i′-ç̣i-glu-ḣta-ta, *v.* *T.* *to offer a sacrifice for one's self.*

wa-i′-ç̣i-hdu-śna, *v.* *reflex.* of wayuśna; *to sacrifice one's self; to let one's self fall*—wamiç̣ihduśna. See waihduśna.

wa′-i-ç̣i-ḣta-ni, *v* *reflex.* of waḣtani; *to sin against one's self*—wamiç̣iḣtani. NOTE.—See awáiç̣iḣtani: *To transgress* any law or custom is to awaḣtani the law or custom, and the person so doing is said thereby to become awáiç̣iḣtani: *e. g*, if he vows to dance the sun-dance and fails to do it, he awaḣtani's the custom of his people, and, having broken his vow, is awaiç̣iḣtani; in consequence he may expect to suffer some misfortune, as retribution for his offense; and then he is said to be wóaḣtani akipa. Hence to break God's law is to awáḣtani the law of God, and having vowed in baptism to keep it, he is also thereby awaiçiḣtani, and any misfortune befalling him thereafter would be considered as a wóaḣtani, or *retribution* visited upon him in consequence of his having become awaḣtani as regards one of God's laws.—W. J. C.

wa-i'-el-gle, *n.* *T.*: *i. q.*, waienhde.

wa-i'-en-hde, *n.* of ienhde; *one who casts up to another; an accuser.* *T.*, waielgle.

wa-i'-en-hi-ye-ya, *v.* of ienhiyeya; *to cast up to*—waienhiyewaya. *T.*, waieliyeya, *to reply to one who is talking badly.*

wa-i'-glu-ḣta-ta, *v.* *T.* *to offer one's self in sacrifice,* as our Saviour did—wamigluḣtata.

wa-i'-hdu-śna, *v.* *reflex.* of wayuśna; *to sacrifice one's self*—wamihduśna.

wa-i'-hdu-śtaŋ, *v.* *reflex.* of yuśtaŋ; *to finish what pertains to one's self*—wamihduśtaŋ.

wa-i'-hdu-śtaŋ-ke, *n.* *one who has finished what pertains to himself.*

wa-i'-ḣpe-ya, *v.* of aiḣpeya; *to throw on, place on, impute to; to leave to,* when one dies, as property; *to give to others; to sacrifice; give to the gods*—waiḣpewaya.

wa-i'-ḣpe-ya-pi, *n.* *leaving to, bequeathing; an heir; a sacrifice.*

wa-i'-ḣpe-ye, *n.* *a testator.*

wa-i'-le-pi, *n.* *T.* of ile; *matches.*

wa-iŋ'-yuŋ-toŋ, *v.* of iŋyuŋtoŋ; *to rub brains, grease,* etc., on hides to prepare them for dressing. *T.*, wahiŋyuŋtoŋ.

wa-i'-pi-da, *n.* of ipida; *one who forbids* or *refuses to part with what he has.* *T.*, wawipila. See wawipida.

wa-i'-śte-ća, *adj.* *bashful.* See wiśteća.

wa-i'-śten-ya, *v. a.* *to put to shame*—waiśtenwaya. *T.*, wawiśtelya.

wa-i'-ya-pe, *v.* of iyape; *to lie in wait.* See wawiyape.

wa-i'-ya-pe-pi, *n.* *an ambush.* *T.*, wawiyapepi.

wa-i'-ya-ta-gle-i-çi-ya, *v.* *T. reflex.* *to be intemperate; to overdo one's self.*

wa-i'-ya-ta-hde, *v.* *to have exceeding much*—waiyamatahde. *T.*, wawiyakapeya. See wiyatahde.

wa-i'-ya-ta-hde-ya, *v.* *to exceed, go beyond; to be intemperate; to crowd from behind; to urge on over much*—waiyatahdewaya. *T*, iyatagleya. See wiyatahdeya.

wa-i'-ye-ki-ya, *v.* of iyekiya; *to recognize*—waiyewakiya.

wa-i'-ye-ya, *v.* of iyeya; *to find*—waiyewaya.

wa-i'-ye-ye-ća, *n.* *one who finds much.*

wa-ka'-a-śla, *v* *T.* *to uncover, lay bare.*

wa-ka'-a-źa-źa, *v.* *T.* *to lay bare, to uncover,* as by sweeping.

wa-ka'-bla-pi *and* wa-ka'-bla-ya-pi, *n.* *T.* *meat cut up for drying.* See wakamda.

wa-ka'-bla-ya, *v.* *T.* *to cut in thin slices*, as meat for drying.

wa-ka'-će-ya, *v.* of kaćeya; *to make cry by striking*

wa-ka'-daŋ, *n.* *the roach, sun-fish.*

wa-ka'-daŋ-hi-yu-za-pi, *n.* *a kind of fish*, perhaps *the perch.* So called because the teeth and some of the small bones of the head are put in gourd shells, which are used as rattles in their pow-wowing, and in making their sacred feasts and dances.

wa-ka'-du-ġa, *v.* of kaduġa; *to fan; fanning, blowing* — wawakaduġa: also 1st pers. sing. of kaduġa

wa-kad'-ya-pi, *n.* of kadya; *coffee* or *tea; anything to be warmed.*

wa-ka'-ġa, *v.* of kaġa; *to make*—wawakaġa: also 1st pers. sing. of kaġa

wa-ka'-ġa-pi, *n.* *an image, picture, something made; a brand*, as on an animal.

wa-ka'-ġe-ġe, *v.* of kaġeġe; *to sew*—wawakaġeġe, wauŋkaġeġepi: also 1st pers. sing of kaġeġe.

wa-ka'-ġi, *v.* of kaġi; *to hinder* or *prevent by one's presence*, as to keep one from speaking or from doing something; *to be feared; to be revered*—wawakaġi, wamakaġi; also 1st pers. sing of kaġi.

wa-ka'-ġi, *n.* *one who restrains by his presence.*

wa-ka'-ġi-ya, *v. a.* *to hinder, obstruct, keep others from going fast*—wakaġiwaya.

wa-ka'-ġi-ya, *adv.* *slowly, preventing, detaining.*

wa-ka'-ha-i-ye-ya, *v.* *to put out of the way; one who pushes* things *out of the way.* See kaha.

wa-ka'-hi, *v.* of kahi; *to rummage*—wawakahi: also 1st pers. sing. of kahi.

wa-ka'-hi-ka, *n.* *one who rummages.*

wa-ka'-hiŋ-ta, *v.* of kahiŋta; *to sweep*—wawakahiŋta: also 1st pers. sing. of kahiŋta.

wa-ka'-hmi-hma, *v.* of kahmihma; *to roll*—wawakahmihma: also 1st pers. sing. of kahmihma. *T.*, wakagmigma.

wa-ka'-hmi-yaŋ-yaŋ, *v.* of kahmiyaŋyaŋ; *to make round*—wawakahmiyaŋyaŋ; also 1st pers. sing. of kahmiyaŋyaŋ. *T.*, wakagmiyaŋyaŋ.

wa-ka'-hmoŋ, *v.* See wakahmuŋ.

wa-ka'-hmuŋ, *v.* of kahmuŋ; *to spin, twist*—wawakahmuŋ: also 1st pers. sing. of kahmuŋ. *T.*, wakagmuŋ.

wa-ka'-hmuŋ-pi, *n.* *spinning.*

wa-ka'-ho-ho, *v.* of kahoho; *to shake, make loose*—wawakahoho: also 1st pers. sing. of kahoho.

wa-ka'-ho-mni, *v.* of kahomni; *to make turn round*—wawakahomni: also 1st pers. sing. of kahomni.

w a - k a'- h u - h u - z a, *v.* of kahuhuza; *to shake by striking*—wawakahuhuza: also 1st pers. sing. of kahuhuza.

w a - k a'- h u ŋ - h u ŋ - z a, *v.* *T.:* *i. q.* wakahuhuza.

w a - k a'- ḣ a - p a, *v.* of kaḣapa; *to drive along*—wawakaḣapa: also 1st pers. sing. of kaḣapa.

w a - k a'- ḣ d a, *v.* of kaḣda; *to rattle; to rummage*—wawakaḣda: also 1st pers. sing of kaḣda.

w a - k a'- ḣ d a - k a, *n.* *one who pilfers much.* *T*, wakaḣlaka.

w a - k a'- ḣ d e - ć a, *v.* of kaḣdeća; *to break open, to fracture*—wawakaḣdeća: also 1st pers. sing. of kaḣdeća.

w a - k a'- ḣ d i - y a, *v.* of kaḣdiya; *to make mire*—wakaḣdiwaya.

w a - k a'- ḣ d o - k a, *v.* of kaḣdoka; *to make a hole in*—wawakaḣdoka: also 1st pers. sing. of kaḣdoka. *T.*, wakaḣloka.

w a - k a'- ḣ e - p a, *v.* of kaḣepa; *to bail out*—wawakaḣepa: also 1st pers. sing. of kaḣepa. *T.*, wakaskepa.

w a - k a'- ḣ i - ć a, *v.* of kaḣića; *to waken up by striking*—wawakaḣića: also 1st pers sing. of kaḣića

w a - k a ḣ'- n i - ġ a, *v* of kaḣniġa; *to choose*—wawakaḣniġa: also 1st pers. sing. of kaḣniġa.

w a - k a'- ḣ p a, *v.* of kaḣpa; *to throw down*—wawakaḣpa: also 1st pers. sing. of kaḣpa.

w a'- k a - ḣ p a, *v.* of akaḣpa; *to cover*—wáwakaḣpa.

w a - k a'- ḣ p u, *v.* of kaḣpu; *to tear down; to strike and make fall; to strike and loosen from its fastenings*—wawakaḣpu: also 1st pers. sing. of kaḣpu.

w a - k a'- ḣ t a - k a, *v. n.* *to be easily hurt, touchy, nervous*—wamakaḣtaka. *T.*, wakaḣteke.

w a - k a'- ḣ t a - k e - ć a, *n.* *one who is made sick by a little matter, one who is nervous*—wamakaḣtakeća.

w a - k a'- ḣ t a - k a - k a, *n.* *T.* *one who is nervous, fretful, dissatisfied* with everything.

w a - k a'- ḣ t e - k e, *v.* *T.:* *i. q.* wakaḣtaka.

w a - k a'- ḣ t a ŋ, *v. n.* of kaḣtaŋ; *to absorb.*

w a - k a'- ḣ t a ŋ - k a, *adj.* *absorbent, absorbing.*

w a - k a'- ḣ t a ŋ - y a ŋ, *adj.* *rough, roughened,* as corn pulled open by the birds.

w a - k a'- ḣ u, *v.* of kaḣu; *to peel off,* as bark—wawakaḣu: also 1st pers. sing. of kaḣu.

w a - k a'- ḣ u - ġ a, *v.* of kaḣuġa; *to break,* as the skull, kettles, etc.—wawakaḣuġa: also 1st pers. sing. of kaḣuġa.

w a - k a'- ḣ u - ġ e - ć a, *n.* *one who kills much game.* *T.*, wigni wayupika.

w a - k a'- ḣ u ŋ - t a, *v.* of kaḣuŋta; *to make rough,* as the birds do by tearing open the husks of corn.

w a - k a'- i - d e, *v.* of kaide; *to make blaze*—wawakaide.

wa-ka'-i-paŋ-paŋ, *n. T. a harrow.*

wa-ka'-kaŋ, *v.* of kakaŋ; *to hew; to beat* or *strike off*, as berries; *to hammer on, strike*, as in shaping a stone—wawakakaŋ: also 1st pers. sing. of kakaŋ.

wa-ka'-kća, *v.* of kakća; *to comb, to disentangle*—wawakakća: also 1st pers. sing. of kakća.

wa-ka'-kiŋ-ća, *v.* of kakiŋća; *to scrape*—wawakakiŋća: also 1st pers. sing. of kakiŋća.

wa-ka'-kiś-ya, *v.* of kakiśya; *to cause to suffer*—wakakiśwaya.

wa-ka'-ko-ka, *v.* of kakoka; *to make rattle*—wawakakoka: also 1st pers. sing. of kakoka.

wa-ka'-kpaŋ, *v.* of kakpaŋ; *to pound fine*—wawakakpaŋ: also 1st pers. sing. of kakpaŋ.

wa-ka'-ksa, *v.* of kaksa; *to cut off with an ax*—wawakaksa: also 1st pers. sing. of kaksa.

wa-ka'-kśa, *v.* of kakśa; *to roll up*—wawakakśa.

wa-ka'-kśaŋ, *v.* of kakśaŋ; *to bend*—wawakakśaŋ: also 1st pers. sing. of kakśaŋ.

wa-ka'-kśi-źa, *v* of kakśiźa; *to double up*—wawakakśiźa: also 1st pers. sing. of kakśiźa.

wa-ka'-ktaŋ, *v.* of kaktaŋ; *to make bend*—wawakaktaŋ: also 1st pers. sing. of kaktan.

wa-ka'-ku-ka, *v.* of kakuka; *to pound to pieces, destroy*—wawakakuka: also 1st pers. sing. of kakuka.

wa-ka'-mda, *v.* of kamda; *to slice*—wawakamda: also 1st pers. sing. of kamda. *T.*, wakabla. See wakablapi.

wa-ka'-mda-ya, *v.* of kamdaya; *to make level, spread out*—wawakamdaya; also 1st pers sing. of kamdaya. *T.*, wakablaya.

wa-ka'-mda-za, *v.* of kamdaza; *to rip open*—wawakamdaza: also 1st pers. sing. of kamdaza. *T.*, wakablaza.

wa-ka'-mde-ća, *v.* of kamdeća; *to dash to pieces*—wawakamdeća: also 1st pers. sing. of kamdeća. *T.*, wakableća.

wa-ka'-mdu, *v.* of kamdu; *to pulverize*—wawakamdu: also 1st pers. sing. of kamdu. *T.*, wakablu.

wa-ka'-mna, *v.* of kamna; *to collect, gather together*—wawakamna: also 1st pers. sing of kamna.

wa-ka'-mna-ka, *n. one who collects.*

wa-ka'-mnaŋ-pi, *n. gathering together, collecting.*

wa-ka'-mni, *v.* of kamni; *to make mellow, prepare*, as a field—wawakamni: also 1st pers. sing. of kamni *T.*, yupaŋpaŋ.

wa-kan', *adv. above.* See waŋkan. *T.*, wakaŋl.

wa-kaŋ', *adj. spiritual, sacred, consecrated; wonderful, incomprehensible;* said also of women at the menstrual period—mawakaŋ, niwakaŋ, uŋwakaŋpi. *T.* NOTE.—*mysterious: incomprehensible; in a peculiar state, which, from not being understood, it is dangerous to meddle with;* hence the application of this word to women at *the menstrual period*, and from hence, too, arises the feeling among the wilder Indians that if the Bible, the Church, the Missionary, etc., are "wakaŋ," they are to be *avoided*, or *shunned*, not as being *bad* or *dangerous*, but as wakaŋ. The word seems to be the only one suitable for *holy, sacred*, etc., but the common acceptation of it, given above, makes it quite misleading to the *heathen*.—W. J. C.

w a - k a ŋ', *n.* *a spirit, something consecrated:* Taku wakaŋ *and* Wakaŋ taŋka, *the Great Spirit.*

w a - k a ŋ' - d a, *v. a.* *to reckon as holy* or *sacred; to worship*—wakaŋwada, wakaŋuŋdapi. *T.*, wakaŋla.

w a - k a ŋ' - d a - k a, *v. a.* Same as wakaŋda.

w a - k a ŋ' - e - ć o ŋ, *v.* *to do tricks of jugglery*—wakaŋećamoŋ.

w a - k a ŋ' - e - ć o ŋ - p i - d a ŋ, *n.* *magic, tricks of jugglery.*

w a - k a ŋ' - h a, *n.* *a bear's skin.* *T.*, matoha.

w a - k a ŋ' - h d i, *n.* *the lightning.* *Ih.*, wakaŋkdi. *T.*, wakaŋgli.

w a - k a ŋ' - h e - ź a, *n.* *children:* *i. q.* śićeća.

w a - k a ŋ' - i - ç i - d a, *v.* *reflex.* of wakaŋda; *to esteem one's self holy* or wakaŋ; *to be proud*—wakaŋmiçida.

w a - k a ŋ' - i - ç i - d a - p i, *n.* *pride.*

w a - k a ŋ' - k a, *n.* *an old woman*—wamakaŋka.

w a - k a ŋ' - k a - d a ŋ, *n.* Same as wakaŋka. *T.*, wakaŋkala.

w a - k a ŋ' - k a - ġ a, *v.* *to make* wakaŋ, *perform acts of worship according to the ideas of the Dakotas*—wakaŋwakaġa.

w a - k a ŋ' - k a - t o - p a - s n o ŋ, *n.* *the lumbar vertebræ;* so called because the old women roast that part. See pasnoŋ.

w a - k a ŋ' - k i - ć i - y u - z a - p i, *n.* *taking each other sacredly*, i. e., *marriage* according to law.

w a - k a ŋ' - k i - d a, *v.* *pos.* of wakaŋda; *to regard one's own as sacred*—wakaŋwakida.

w a - k a ŋ l', *adv.* *T.: i. q.* waŋkan.

w a - k a ŋ' - l a, *v.* *T.* *to esteem sacred: i. q.* wakaŋda.

W a - k a ŋ' - ś i - ć a, *n.* *the Bad Spirit; the devil.*

w a - k a ŋ' - t a - ć a ŋ - p a, *n.* *a species of wild cherry.* See ćaŋpa.

w a - k a ŋ' - t a - k o - p a - z a, *n.* *wood*, of all kinds, in the sacred language. See paza.

w a - k a ŋ' - t a - k o - ź u, *n.* *water*, in the sacred language. See also "nide."

W a - k a ŋ' - t a ŋ - k a, *n.* *the Great Spirit, the Creator of all things and the god of war.*

w a - k a ŋ' - w a - ć i - p i, *n.* *the sacred dance.* This is the name of a secret society among the Dakotas which purports to be the depository of their sacred mysteries. The medicine-sack is the badge of membership. With the claws or beads contained in this they pretend to shoot mysteriously, and cause death. The making of a *sacred dance* is a great occasion. The high priests of the ceremonies spend the night previous in heating stones, in sweating and singing, and holding communion with the spirit world. In the dance, those who belong to the society appear in their best attire, gaily painted, and drum, sing, dance, and feast together.

wa-kaŋ′-wo-haŋ, *v. to make a sacred feast*—wakaŋwowahe.

wa-kaŋ′-wo-haŋ-pi, *n. a sacred feast.* This is made by such as belong to the wakaŋwaćipi, and is preceded and accompanied by drumming, singing, etc.

wa-kaŋ′-wo-ḣpa, *n. meteoric stones, a meteor.*

wa-kaŋ′-yaŋ, *adv. sacredly, holily, mysteriously:* wakaŋyaŋ yuza, *to take a wife or husband after the Christian mode.* See wakaŋkićiyuzapi.

wa-kaŋ′-yu-za, *v. to take a wife after the manner of Christians*—wakaŋmduza.

wa-ka′-o-ḣpa, *v.* of kaoḣpa: *to break through*—wawakaoḣpa; also 1st pers. sing. of kaoḣpa.

wa-ka′-pa, *v.* of kapa; *to excel, exceed, surpass*—wakawapa, wakauŋpapi.

wa-ka′-pa, *v.* of kapa; *to pound off*—wawakapa: also 1st pers. sing. of kapa. See wakapaŋ.

wa-ka′-paŋ, *v.* of kapaŋ; *to pound off,* as corn—wawakapaŋ; also 1st pers. sing. of kapaŋ.

wa-ka′-paŋ-pan, *v.* of kapaŋpaŋ; *to pound soft*—wawakapaŋpaŋ: also 1st pers. sing. of kapaŋpaŋ.

wa-ka′-paŋ-pi, *n. pounded meat mixed with marrow or fat, pemmican.*

wa-ka′-pa-pi, *n. pemmican.*

wa-ka′-pće-će-la, *v. T., i. q.* wakaptećedaŋ.

wa-ka′-pe-mni, *v.* of kapemni; *to twist*—wawakapemni: also 1st pers. sing. of kapemni. *T. to swing around,* as a rope in the hand before throwing it

wa-ka′-pe-sto, *v.* of kapesto; *to sharpen*—wawakapesto: also 1st pers. sing. of kapesto.

wa-ka′-pe-ya, *v. to excel, cause to excel*—wakapewaya.

wa-ka′-po-ġaŋ, *v.* of kapoġaŋ; *to make swell out; to enlarge by blowing.*

wa-ka′-po-pa, *v.* of kapopa; *to make burst*—wawakapopa; also 1st pers. sing. of kapopa.

wa-ka′-po-ta, *v.* of kapota; *to pound to pieces*—wawakatopa; also 1st pers. sing. of kapota.

wa-ka′-psa-ka, *v.* of kapsaka; *to break in two,* as a string—wawakapsaka: also 1st pers. sing. of kapsaka.

wa-ka'-psi-ća, *v.* of kapsića; *to make hop*—wawakapsića: also 1st pers. sing. of kapsića.

wa-ka'-psiŋ-psiŋ-ta, *v.* of kapsiŋpsiŋta; *to whip*—wawakapsiŋpsiŋta; also 1st pers. sing. of kapsiŋpsiŋta.

wa-ka'-psoŋ, *v.* of kapsoŋ; *to spill*—wawakapsoŋ: also 1st pers. sing. of kapsoŋ.

wa-ka'-pśuŋ, *v.* of kapśuŋ; *to dislocate*—wawakapśuŋ: also 1st pers. sing. of kapśuŋ.

wa-ka'-pta, *v.* of kapta; *to dip out*—wawakapta: also 1st pers. sing. of kapta.

wa-ka'-pte-će-daŋ, *v.* of kaptećedaŋ; *to cut off shorter*—wawakaptećedaŋ: also 1st pers. sing of kaptećedaŋ. *T.*, wakapćećela.

wa-ka'-ptu-źa, *v.* of kaptuźa; *to split or crack*—wawakaptuźa; also 1st pers. sing of kaptuźa.

wa-ka'-sa, *v.* of kasa; *to bury in the snow*—wawakasa

wa'-ka-saŋ-saŋ, *n.* See wakasaŋsaŋna.

wa'-ka-saŋ-saŋ-na, *n.* *the snow bird* *T.*, iśtanićataŋka.

wa-ka'-sbu, *v* of kasbu; *to cut in strips*—wawakasbu: also 1st pers. sing. of kasbu. *T.*, wakaswu.

wa-ka'-sbu-pi, *n.* *dangles.* *T.*, wakaswupi.

wa'-ka-sda-ta, *v.* *to do* a thing *slowly*—wáwakasdata. *T.*, wayuslata.

wa-ka'-sde-ća, *v.* of kasdeća; *to split*—wawakasdeća: also 1st pers. sing. of kasdeća.

wa-ka'-sdi, *v.* of kasdi; *to strike and make fly out; to make spirt out by striking*, as matter from a sore—wawakasdi.

wa-ka'-sdi-tka, *v.* of kasditka; *to make knobbed*—wawakasditka.

wa-ka'-sdo-haŋ, *v. n.* *to drive along*, as the wind does a boat.

wa-ka'-ska, *v.* 1st pers. sing. of kaska, *to whiten.*

wa'-ka-ska, *v.* of akaska; *to eat greedily, eat long*—wáwakaska.

wa-ka'-ske-pa, *v.* of kaskepa; *to bail out.*

wa-ka'-ski-ća, *v.* of kaskića; *to press* or *pound tight*—wawakaskića.

wa-ka'-sma-ka, *v.* of kasmaka; *to indent by pounding*—wawakasmaka.

wa-ka'-smiŋ-yaŋ-yaŋ, *v.* *to make bare*, as the wind does the ground by driving off the snow.

wa-ka'-sna, *v.* of kasna; *to make ring; to shake off*, as the wind does leaves from a tree: also 1st pers. sing. of kasna.

wa-ka'-sni, *v.* of kasni; *to extinguish*—wawakasni: also 1st pers. sing. of kasni.

wa-ka'-so-ta, *v.* of kasota; *to use up, expend, make an end of*—wawakasota: also 1st pers. sing. of kasota.

wa-ka'-sto, *v.* of kasto; *to smooth down.*

wa-ka'-śa-ka, *v.* of kaśaka; *to strike with too little force to penetrate*—wawakaśaka: also 1st pers. sing. of kaśaka.

wa-ka'-śa-pa, *v.* *to make black* or *dirty by smiting*—wawakaśapa.

wa-ka'-śdo-ka, *v.* of kaśdoka; *to knock off*, as an axe from the handle—wawakaśdoka; also 1st pers. sing. of kaśdoka.

wa-ka'-śdu-ta, *v.* of kaśduta; *to make glance*, as an axe—wawakaśduta: also 1st pers. sing. of kaśduta,

wa-ka'-śe-ća, *v.* of kaśeća; *to deaden*—wawakaśeća: also 1st pers. sing. of kaśeća.

wa-ka'-śe-ya, *v.* of kaśeya; *to obstruct*—wakaśewaya.

wa-ka'-śi-ća-ho-wa-ya, *v.* of kaśićahowaya; *to cause to cry out by smiting*—wawakaśićahowaya.

wa-ka'-śi-pa, *v.* of kaśipa; *to break off*, as limbs from a tree—wawakaśipa: also 1st pers. sing. of kaśipa.

wa-ka'-śka, *v.* of kaśka; *to bind*—wawakaśka: also 1st pers. sing. of kaśka

wa-ka'-śki-ća, *v.* of kaśkića; *to press, pound*—wawakaśkića: also 1st pers. sing. of kaśkića.

wa-ka'-śko-kpa, *v.* of kaśkokpa; *to hollow out*, as a trough—wawakaśkokpa: also 1st pers. sing. of kaśkokpa.

wa-ka'-śko-pa, *v.* of kaśkopa; *to cut crookedly*—wawakaśkopa; also 1st pers. sing. of kaśkopa.

wa-ka'-śko-tpa, *v.* Same as wakaśkokpa.

wa-ka'-śna, *v.* of kaśna; *to miss in striking*—wawakaśna: also 1st pers. sing. of kaśna.

wa'-ka-śo-ta, *adj.* *blackened with smoke.*

wa'-ka-śo-te-śni, *adj.* *clean, not defiled, pure:* wakaśoteśni wauŋ, *I am undefiled.*

wa' ka śo te śni yaŋ, *adv.* *purely, undefiledly.*

wa-ka'-śpa, *v.* of kaśpa; *to cut off a piece; to expectorate*—wawakaśpa: also 1st pers. sing. of kaśpa.

wa-ka'-śta-ka, *v.* of kaśtaka; *to smite*—wawakaśtaka: also 1st pers. sing. of kaśtaka.

wa-ka'-śtaŋ, *v.* of kaśtaŋ; *to pour out*—wawakaśtaŋ: also 1st pers. sing. of kaśtaŋ.

wa-ka'-śu-źa, *v.* of kaśuźa; *to crush by striking*—wawakaśuźa: also 1st pers. sing. of kaśuźa.

wa-ka'-taŋ-ni, *v.* of kataŋni; *to wear out by striking*—wawakataŋni: also 1st pers. sing. of kataŋni.

wa-ka'-ta-ta, *v.* of katata; *to shake*, as a bed—wawakatata: also 1st pers. sing. of katata.

wa-ka'-te-pa, *v.* of katepa; *to cut to a stump*—wawakatepa: also 1st pers. sing. of katepa.

wa-ka'-ti-ća, *v.* of katića; *to scrape off*—wawakatića. *T.*, *to mix up*, as mortar.

wa-ka'-tka, *v.* of katka; *to choke*—wamakatka.

wa-ka′-tku-ġa, *v.* of katkuġa; *to cut up short.*

wa-ka′-tkuŋ-za, *v.* of katkuŋza; *to cut off square*—wawakatkuŋza.

wa-ka′-to-to, *v.* of katoto; *to knock*, as on a door; *to clear off*, as land for plowing—wawakatoto.

wa-ka′-tu-ka, *v.* of katuka; *to spoil by striking*, as furs—wawakatuka.

wa-ka′-tu-tka, *v.* of katutka; *to break into small pieces*—wawakatutka.

wa-ka′-ṭa, *v.* of kaṭa; *to kill by striking*—wawakaṭa.

wa-ka′-ṭiŋ-za, *v.* of kaṭiŋza; *to pound in tight*—wawakaṭiŋza.

wa-ka′-uŋ-ka, *v.* *T.* *i. q.* wakawaŋka.

wa-ka′-waŋ-ka, *v.* of kawaŋka; *to chop down*, as timber; *to blow down*, as the wind does trees. *T.*, wakauŋka.

wa-ka′-we-ġa, *v.* of kaweġa; *to break* or *fracture*—wawakaweġa.

wa-ka′-wi-hnu-ni, *v.* of kawihnuni; *to destroy*—wawakawihnuni.

wa-ka′-wiŋ-źa, *v.* of kawiŋźa; *to bend down by striking*—wawakawiŋźa.

wa-ka′-zaŋ, *v.* of kazaŋ; *to strike and make sick*—wawakazaŋ.

wa-ka′-ze, *v.* of kaze; *to lade* or *dip out*, as food from a kettle; *to lade* or *dip out*, as meat or other solids—wawakaze.

wa-ka′-zoŋ-ta, v. *to weave*—wawakazoŋta: also 1st pers. sing. of kazoŋta.

wa-ka′-źa-źa, *v.* of kaźaźa; *to wash by drawing back and forth* in the water; *to see well*—wawakaźaźa: also 1st pers. sing. of kaźaźa.

wa-ka′-źi-pa, *v.* of kaźipa; *to shave*—wawakaźipa.

wa-ka′-źuŋ, *v.* of kaźuŋ; *to tear up by the roots.*

wa-ka′-źu-źu, *v.* of kaźuźu; *to pay off; to erase; to forgive*—wawakaźuźu: also 1st pers. sing. of kaźuźu.

wa-kćaŋ′-yaŋ, *v.* *to observe and report:* wakćaŋyaŋ ya, *to go to spy out;* wakćaŋyaŋ hdi, *to come home and make report* of what one has learned, as in the case of a man sent out by the hunters to discover where the buffalo are. *T.*, toŋweyagli.

wa-kćaŋ′-ye-ya, *v. a.* *to cause to go and spy out*—wakćaŋyewaya.

wa-kće′-ya, *v.* *T.* *to hang over the fire to roast.* See wapćeya

wa-kće′-ya-pi, *n.* *T.* *the ribs of an animal, the roasting piece;* because the ribs are generally so cooked. See wapćeyapi.

wa-kdu′-ha, *v. abs.* *Ih.* *i. q.* wahduha.

wa-kdu′-ḣe, *v. n.* *Ih.* *to live with one's wife's relatives:* wawakduḣe.

Wa-kdu′-ḣe, *n. p* *the loafer band of Brule Sioux; to live with connections by marriage; a band of Oglalas.* *T.*, Wagluḣe.

wa-ke′-ya, *n.* *a skin tent, a Dakota lodge.* See wokeya.

wa-ke'-ya, *v. a.* *to have for a tent*—wakewaya.

wa-ke'-ya-ska, *n.* *a linen* or *cotton tent.*

wa-ki', *v.* 1st pers. sing. of ki, *to arrive at home,* and of ki, *to rob.*

wa-ki', *v* of ki; *to rob*—wawaki.

wa-ki'-ćaŋ-pta, *v. a.* *to comfort, console*—wawećaŋpta: wawićakićaŋpta, *he comforts them.*

wa-ki'-ćaŋ-pta, *adj.* *compassionate.*

wa-ki'-ćaŋ-pte, *n.* *a comforter.*

wa-ki'-ći-glu-ḣta-ta, *v.* *T.* *to offer something of one's own,* as a sacrifice, *for another;* as God gave His Son for the world.

wa-ki'-ći-hna-ka, *v.* of hnaka; *to lay away for* one—wawećihnaka.

wa'-ki-ći-hna-ka, *v* of ahnaka; *to lay on for* one, *apply a poultice* or *cataplasm to* one—wáwećihnaka.

wa-ki'-ći-uŋ-yaŋ, *v.* *T.* *to offer sacrifice for one.*

wa'-ki-ći-źu, *v. a.* *to lay on a poultice for* one—wáwećiźu, wámićiźu.

wa-ki'-ćoŋ-za, *v. a.* *to purpose, determine for* one; *to resolve to do to* or *for* one—wawećoŋza.

wa-ki'-ćoŋ-za, *n.* *one who determines* or *decides.*

wa-ki'-ćoŋ-ze, *n.* *T.* *a leader* or *chief; one who decides.*

wa-ki'-çuŋ-pi, *n.* *what is taken and used by all, common property.*

wa-ki'-gle, *n.* *T.* *what one has laid up; stores.*

wa-ki'-glu-ḣta-ta, *v.* *T.* *to sacrifice one's own.*

wa-ki'-gna-ka, *n.* *T.* *i. q.* wakigle.

wa-ki'-ġe, *v.* of kiġe; *to scold*—wawakiġe: also 1st pers. sing. of kiġe.

wa-ki'-hda-ka, *n.* *dressed skin, leather,* such as is used to make and mend moccasins with.

wa ki' hdo ća, *v a.* *to have a fooling for,* or *be in sympathy with an absent friend,* that causes a nervous sensation in the breast or an involuntary twitching of the muscles, said to be premonitory of what is to happen to the person—wawehdeća, wawićawehdeća. See naka.

wa-ki'-hnag, *cont.* of wakihnaka; wakihnag wahi, *I have come to lay away.*

wa-ki'-hna-ka, *v.* of kihnaka; *to store away one's own*—wawehnaka, wauŋkihnakapi.

wa-ki'-hna-ka-pi, *n.* *what is laid up, an inheritance.*

wa'-ki-ḣta-ni, *v.* of wáḣtani; *to sin against.* *T.*, awaḣtani: See under waiçiḣtani.

wa-ki'-kaŋ-he-źa, *v. a.* of kaŋheźa; *to conciliate by presents* or *by fawning, to make friends with by submission to*—wakiwakaŋheźa.

wa-ki'-ksu-ya, *v.* of kiksuya; *to remember; to hold communion with and receive communications from supernatural beings,* as the Dakotas pretend to do; *to call to remem-*

brance a dead friend—waweksuya, waunkiksuyapi. *T., to see signs of enemies; to be frightened by signs.*

wa-ki'-ksu-ya-pi, *n. remembering the past; having dreams or visions.*

wa'-ki-ktoŋ-źa, *v.* of akiktoŋźa; *to forget*—wáwektoŋźa.

wa'-kil. *T. cont.* of wakita.

wa-ki'-la, *v. T. to ask* or *beg of* one—wawakila

wa-ki'-mna-yaŋ, *n.* of mnayaŋ; *one who has collected much, one who is rich.*

wa'-ki-ni-ća, *v.* of akinića; *to dispute*—wáwakinića, wáuŋkinićapi.

wa'-ki-ni-ća-pi, *n. disputation, contest.*

wa-ki'-ni-haŋ, *v.* 1st pers. sing. of kinihaŋ.

wa'-ki-nin, *cont.* of wákinića; wakinin uŋ.

wa-ki'-ni-ya, *v. n. to be touchy, get out of humor*—wawakiniya.

wa-kiŋ'-iŋ, *v.* of kiŋiŋ; *to throw at, to stone*—wawakiŋiŋ: also 1st pers. sing. of kiŋiŋ.

wa-kiŋ'-yaŋ, *v.* of kiŋyaŋ; *to fly,* as birds.

wa-kiŋ'-yaŋ, *n.* of kiŋyaŋ; *the thunder; the cause of thunder and lightning,* supposed by the Dakotas to be a great bird.

wa-kiŋ'-yaŋ-ho-toŋ, *v. the thunder utters his voice; to thunder.*

wa-kiŋ'-yaŋ-na, *n. birds, fowls.*

wa-kiŋ'-yaŋ-pi, *n.* of kiŋyaŋ; *those that fly, birds.*

wa-kiŋ'-yaŋ-toŋ-waŋ-pi, *n. T. heat lightning;* lit. *the thunder bird's look.*

wa-kiŋ'-ye-la, *n. T. the pigeon; a dove.*

wa-ki'-pa-źiŋ, *v.* of kipaźiŋ; *to oppose* — wawakipaźiŋ: also 1st pers. sing. of kipaźiŋ.

wa-ki'-pi, *n. robbery, spoiling.* See wawićakipi.

wa-ki'-pśa-pśa, *adv. thick, close together. T.,* itupśapśase. See akipśapśa.

wa'-ki-soŋ, *v.* of akisoŋ; *to put edging around quill work*—wáwakisoŋ. *T.,* okśaŋipata.

wa-ki'-ś'ag, *cont.* of wakiś'aka.

wa-ki-ś'ag-ya, *v. a. to make endure*—wakiś'agwaya.

wa-ki'-ś'ag-ya, *adv. enduring.*

wa-ki'-ś'a-ka, *adj. capable of endurance, strong to endure hardship* or *suffering, not easily exhausted* or *overcome, indefatigable*—wamakiś'aka, wanićiś'aka. See waś'aka.

wa-ki'-ś'a-ke, *n. strength.*

wa-ki'-śde-ya, *v.* of kiśdeya; *to annoy, vex; one who annoys*—wakiśdewaya *T.,* naġiyeya.

wa-ki'-śko-kpa, *n. a bucket made of bark, a basket, a pitcher,* etc.

wa-ki'-śko-tpa, *n.* Same as wakiśkokpa.

wa'-ki-ta, *v.* of akita; *to seek for; to look for*—wáwakita, wáuŋkitapi.

wa-ki'-taŋ, *v.* of kitaŋ; *to insist upon; to persist in doing*—wawakitaŋ: also 1st pers. sing. of kitaŋ.

wa-ki'-taŋ-ka, *n.* *one who insists upon.*

wa-ki'-te-ħi, *adj.* *stingy, covetous*—wamakiteħi.

wa-ki'-toŋ-toŋ-ka, *v. n.* *to be frugal, economical; one who is frugal,* etc.—wawakitoŋtoŋka. *T.*, wagluhahaka

wa-ki'-tu-ka, *v.* of kituka; *to beg of*—wawakituka: also 1st pers. sing. of kituka. *T.*, wakila.

wa-ki'-uŋ-ni-ya, *v.* of kiuŋniya; *to injure, hurt*—wakiuŋniwaya.

wa-ki'-uŋ-yaŋ, *v.* *T.* *to sacrifice* or *make an offering to* one; *to sacrifice one's own.*

wa'-ki-ya, *v.* *T.* *to talk about, discuss; try,* as a case in court.

wa'-ki-ya-pi, *n.* *T.* *a trial.*

wa'-ki-ya-ti-pi, *n.* *T.* *a court house; a council house.*

wa'-ki-ya-wi-ća-śa, *n.* *T.* *a lawyer; a Congressman.*

wa-ki'-ya-zaŋ, *v. pos.* of wayazaŋ; *to become sick for* one, as one's child — wamakiyazaŋ, wanićiyazaŋ, wauŋkiyazaŋpi.

wa-ki'-ye, *n.* *birds.* See wakiŋyaŋpi.

wa-ki'-ye-daŋ, *n.* *a pigeon, pigeons.*

wa-ki'-yu-śe, *v.* of kiyuśe; *to oppose, to hate.*

wa-ki'-yu-śka, *v.* of kiyuśka; *to loosen, release*—wawakiyuśka and wawakimduśka: also 1st pers. sing. of kiyuśka.

wa-ki'-yu-śna, *v. a.* *to sacrifice to, offer to in sacrifice*—wawakiyuśna, wauŋkiyuśnapi, waćićiyuśna. *T.*, *to drop for one.* See wakiyuħtata.

wa-ki'-yu-śna-pi, *n.* *sacrificing to.* *T.*, wakiyuħtatapi, *and* wakiuŋyaŋpi.

wa-ki'-yu-za, *v. a.* *to take away the clothes of one who comes home in triumph.* This is done when the braves first come home in triumph, and their blankets may afterwards be taken from them on each occasion of painting the scalps red, which ceremony is commonly performed four times. Hence *to take advantage of*—wawakiyuza, wawićakiyuzapi.

wa-kma'-he-za, *n.* *Ih.* *corn:* *i. q.* wamnaheza. *T.*, wagmaheza.

wa-kmu', *n.* *pumpkins.* *Ih.* *i. q.* wamnu. *T.*, wagmu.

wa-ko'-gla, *n.* *T.* *a gully,* made by the action of water in a ravine.

wa-ko'-ki-pa, *v.* of kokipa; *to be afraid, fearful*—wakowakipa.

wa-ko'-ki-pe-ki-ća-ġa, *v. a* (wakokipa *and* kićaġa) *to make afraid, frighten into a measure*—wakokipewećaġa, wakokipemićaġa.

wa-ko'-ni-ya, *n.* *a fountain* or *spring of water.* *T.*, miniyowe.

wa-koŋ', *v.* of koŋ; *to desire*—wawakoŋ: also 1st pers. sing. of koŋ

wa-koŋ'-la, *v.* *T.* *to covet.*

wa-koŋ'-za, *v* of koŋza; *to influence, to determine*—wawakoŋza: also 1st pers. sing. of koŋza.

wa-koŋ′-ze, *n.* *influence:* nitawakoŋze, *thy influence* or *spirit.*

wa-ko′-yag-ya, *v.* of koyagya; *to put on, to clothe; to cause to put on*—wakoyagwaya.

wa-ko′-ya-ka, *v.* of koyaka; *to put on clothes*—wakomdaka, wakouŋyakapi.

wa-ko′-ya-ke-ća, *n.* *one who puts on clothes, one who dresses up, a fop*—wakomayakeća.

wa-kpa′, *n.* *a stream of water, a river:* *i. q.* watpa.

wa-kpa′-daŋ, *n.* *a small stream, a rivulet, a creek:* *i. q.* watpadaŋ. *T.*, wakpala; also, *a ravine*, although there is no water.

wa-kpa′-la, *n.* *T.* *i. q.* wakpadaŋ.

wa-kpa′-la-ho-ġaŋ, *n.* *T.* *the sun fish.*

wa-kpa′-taŋ-ka, *n.* *T.* of kpataŋ: *one who is economical.*

wa-kpi′-ća-hda, *adv.* *by the side of a stream.* See watpićahda.

wa-kpo′-hna, *adv.* *on the stream.* *T.*, wakpa ogna.

wa-kpo′-pta, *adv.* *across the stream.*

wa-kpu′-kpa, *n.* *dust, motes of dust;* *i. q.* watuśekśeća *and* watputpa.

wa-kpu′-kpe-ća, *n.* *anything scattered about, dust.*

wa-kśi′-ća, *n.* *a dish, a bowl, a pan, a plate.*

wa-kśi′-ća-o-pi-ye, *n.* *a cupboard.*

wa-kśi′-ća-ska-daŋ, *n.* *earthen plates.*

wa-kśiŋ′-o-pi-ye, *n.* *a cupboard—dish cupboard.*

wa-kśi′-śko-kpa, *n.* *T.* *soup plates; saucers.*

wa-kta′, *n.* *a sign, a mark.* *T.*, waktawićaye. See wowakta.

wa-kta′, *v. n.* *to look out for, watch for, be on one's guard*—wawakta, wauŋktapi. See akta

wa-kta′-ken, *adv.* *on the look out for, guardedly.*

wa-kta′-ya, *v. a.* *to put on one's guard, to warn*—waktawaya, waktauŋyaŋpi.

wa-kta′-ya, *adv.* *on one's guard, warily, prudently.*

wa-kta′-ya-ken, *adv.* *on the look out.*

wa-kte′, *v.* 1st pers. sing. of kte.

wa-kte′, *v.* of kte; *to kill, to have killed and scalped, to triumph*—wawakte, wauŋktepi: wakte ahda, *they go home in triumph;* wakte aḣdi, *they come home in triumph;* wakte hi, *to come in triumph;* wakte ḣda, *to go home in triumph, having taken scalps;* wakte ḣdi, *to come home bringing the scalps of enemies;* wakte ki, etc.

wa-kto′-ḣdag, *cont.* of waktoḣdaka.

wa-kto′-ḣdag-ki-ya, *v. a.* *to cause to tell how many scalps one has taken*—wakdoḣdagwakiya.

wa-kto′-ḣda-ka, *v. pos.* (wakte *and* oḣdaka) *to tell over one's own warlike exploits, tell how many scalps one has helped to take*—waktowaḣdaka.

wa-kto'-ki-ći-ya-ka, *v.* (wakte *and* okićiyaka) *to tell to* one *the warlike deeds of another for* him—waktowećiyaka.

wa-kto'-ki-ya-ka, *v.* (wakte *and* okiyaka) *to tell to* one *of warlike exploits*—waktowakiyaka.

wa-kto'-ya-ka, *v.* (wakte *and* oyaka) *to tell what one has done in killing enemies*—waktomdaka.

wa-kuŋ'-za, *v.* See wakoŋza.

wa-ku'-te, *v.* of kute; *to shoot, to be shooting* wawakute, wauŋkutepi: wakute mde kta, *I will go shooting:* also 1st pers. sing. of kute, *to shoot,* as fowls.

wa-ku'-te-pi, *n.* *shooting.*

wa-ku'-wa, *v.* of kuwa; *to hunt, hunt for furs,* as those of muskrats, otters, etc.: *hunting*—wawakuwa, wauŋkuwapi: also 1st pers. sing. of kuwa.

wa-ku'-wa-pi, *n.* *hunting,* as for furs.

wa-ḳa', *v.* of ḳa; *to dig*—wawaḳa, wauŋḳapi: also 1st pers. sing. of ḳa.

wa-ḳe'-daŋ, *n.* *the places from which squirrels dig up food.*

wa-ḳiŋ', *v.* of ḳin; *to pack, carry on one's back*—wawaḳiŋ, wauŋḳinpi: also 1st pers. sing. of ḳin.

wa-ḳiŋ', *n.* *a pack, a burden.*

wa-ḳiŋ'-ćaŋ-ki-ća-śka, *n.* *a place of deposit* for meat, etc., in the woods.

wa-ḳiŋ'-ki-ya, *v. a.* *to cause to pack* or *carry on the back,* as a horse—waḳiŋwakiya.

wa-ḳiŋ'-ḳiŋ-na-se, *n.* *like a pack,* i. e. *a square.*

wa-kiŋ'-la-se, *n.* *T.* *like a pack;* i. e., *a square* or *cube.*

wa-ḳiŋ'-pi, *n.* *a burden, a pack.*

wa-ḳu', *v.* of ḳu; *to give*—wawaḳu, wauŋḳupi: also 1st pers. sing. of ḳu.

wa-ḳu'-pi, *n.* *giving; receiving.*

wal, *T.* *cont.* of wata; *a boat.*

wal-će'-te, *n.* *T.* *the bottom* or *keel of a boat.*

wal-he'-ktab, *cont.* *T.* *adv.* *at the stern.*

wal-he'-kta-pa, *n.* *T.* *the stern of a boat.*

wal-i'-ća-śke, *n.* *T.* *an anchor.*

wal-i'-ća-śpe, *n.* *T.* *a tool for hollowing out a canoe.*

wal-i'-to-pe, *n.* *T.* *an oar, a paddle.*

wal-o'-i-hu-ni, *n.* *T.* *a boat landing.*

wal-o'-i-na-źiŋ, *n.* *T.* *a boat landing.*

wal-pa', *n.* *T.* *the bow of a boat.*

wal-siŋ'-te, *n.* *T.* *the rudder of a boat.*

wal-siŋ'-te-yu-ho-mni, *v.* *T.* *to steer a boat.*

wal-siŋ'-te-yu-ze, *n.* *T.* *a helmsman.*

wal-te'-te, *n.* *T.* *the rim* or *gunwale.*

wal-tu'-ću-hu, *n.* *T.* *the ribs of a boat.*

w a - m a′ - k a - ś k a ŋ, *n. creeping things*, the generic name for *vermin*. The western Sioux use this word for *game*, especially *the buffalo*. I should rather conclude that it had been the generic word for the *animal kingdom—all things that move upon the earth.*—J. P. W.

w a - m a′ - k i - n o ŋ, *v.* of makinoŋ; *to steal from* one—wamawakinoŋ, wamauŋkinoŋpi.

w a - m a′ - k o - h n a - k a, *n.* of maka *and* ohnaka; *the contents of the world; the whole creation, animate and inanimate.*

w a - m a′ - n i - ć a, *n.* the generic name for *carnivorous animals*. *T.* wamakaśkaŋ.

w a - m a′ - n i - t i, *n. a bear's den.* *T.*, mato oti.

w a - m a′ - n o ŋ, *v.* of manoŋ; *to steal*—wamawanoŋ, wamauŋnoŋpi.

w a - m a′ - n o ŋ - p i, *n. stealing, theft.*

w a - m a′ - n o ŋ - s'a, *n a thief.*

w a - m a′ - n u, *v.* See wamanoŋ.

w a - m d e′ - n i - ć a, *n. an orphan, a fatherless* or *motherless child*—wamamdenića, wauŋmdenićapi: wamdenića eĥpećiyapi śni, "*I will not leave you orphans.*" *T.*, wablenića, *without relatives.*

w a′ - m d e - z a, *v. n. to see clearly*—wáwamdeza, wáyamdeza. *T.*, wableza.

w a′ - m d e - z a, *n. an inspector.*

w a - m d i*, *n.* See waŋmdi.

w a - m d o′ - k a, *n. the he-bear.* *T.*, mato bloka.

w a′ - m d o - s k a, *n. a species of blackbird with white on its wings;* the wapaġića.

w a′ - m d o - ś a, *n. a species of blackbird with red on its wings*

w a - m d u′ - d a ŋ, *n. maggots.* *T.*, waglula.

w a - m d u′ - ś k a, *n. snakes; serpents.*

w a - m d u′ - ś k a - d a ŋ, *n. snakes; worms; bugs.*

w a - m d u′ - ś k a - ś a - ś a, *n. red bugs*, i. e. *bed bugs.* *T.*, wabluśkaśaśa.

w a′ - m i - n i, *n. snow-water.*

w a - m i′ - n i - t u, *n.* *T. a whale*

w a - m n a′ - d a, *v. a. to honor, respect, fear; to consider brave* or *energetic*—wamnawada, wamnauŋdapi. See ahopa, akta, kinihaŋ, etc.

w a - m n a′ - d a - ś n i, *v. a. to have no respect for* one's ability—wamnawadaśni.

w a - m n a′ - h e - ć a, *n. an oar, a paddle.* *T.*, walitope.

w a - m n a′ - h e - z a, *n. maize, Indian corn.* See wakmaheza, etc. *T.*, wagmeza.

w a - m n a′ - h e - z a - h u, *n. cornstalks.*

w a - m n a′ - h e - z a - k i - ć i - i - ć a - ġ e, *n. a blue flower that appears about the time corn is ripe.*

w a - m n a′ - i - ç i - d a, *v. reflex.* of wamnada; *to be proud, to think much of one's own abilities*—wamnamiçida.

w a - m n a′ - i - ç i - d a - p i, *n. pride.*

wa-mna′-yaŋ, *v.* of mnayaŋ; *to gather, collect*—wamnawaya, wamnauŋyaŋpi.

wa-mna′-yaŋ, *n.* *a collector;* in the Dakota churches, *a deacon.*

wa-mna′-yaŋ-pi, *n.* *gathering, harvest; a collection.*

wa-mni′, *v.* of mni; *to dry by spreading out,* as shelled corn—wawamni: also 1st pers. sing. of mni.

wa′-mni-mni, *v.* of amnimni; *to sprinkle; one who sprinkles*—wáwamnimni.

wa′-mni-o-mni, *n.* *a small worm,* perhaps *a chrysalis; a whirl of wind, a hurricane.*

wa-mnu′, *n.* *gourds; pumpkins, squashes, etc.* See wakmu, etc. *T.*, wagmu.

wa-mnu′-ha, *n.* *gourd-shells.* The Indian rattle is usually made of a gourd-shell. *T.*, wagmuha.

wa-mnu′-hu, *n.* *pumpkin vines.*

wa-mnu′-ḣa, *n.* *large beads; small spiral shells; snails.*

wa-mnu′-ḣa-daŋ, *n* *large beads; snail-shells.*

wa-mnu′-śa-daŋ, *n.* *a kind of bird, the snipe.*

wa-mnu′-taŋ-ka, *n.* *pumpkins.* *T.*, wagmutaŋka.

wa-muŋ′-ta, *n.* *an ear of corn well filled and flat at the end.*

wa′-na, *adv.* See waŋna.

wa-na′-bag-i-ye-ya, *v.* of nabaka; *to kick away, kick out the foot.*

wa′-na-bu, *v.* of anabu; *to make a drumming noise with the foot* on the ground—wanawabu.

wa′-na-bu-bu, *v. red.* of wánabu.

wa-na′-ćaŋ-ćaŋ, *v.* of naćaŋćaŋ; *to shake with the foot*—wanawaćaŋćaŋ.

wa-na′-će-kće-ka, *v.* of naćekćeka; *to make stagger by kicking*—wanawaćekćeka.

wa-na′-će-ya, *v.* of naćeya; *to kick and make cry*—wanawaćeya.

wa-na′-će-ye-s'a, *n* *one who kicks and makes cry.*

wa-nag′-bag-i-ye-ya, *v.* *T.* *to kick out of the way.*

wa-nag′-ba-ka, *v.* *T.* *to kick out the foot.*

wa-na′-ġi, *n.* of naġi; *the soul when separated from the body; a ghost, the manes; a shadow.*

wa-na′-ġi-ta-ćaŋ-ku, *n.* *the milky way.*

wa-na′-ġi-ta-ġo-śa, *n.* *ghost-spittle; a kind of exudation found around some plants; cuckoo-spittle; heavy dew.* *T.*, wanaġitaḣośa.

wa-na′-ġi-ta-ma-ko-će, *n.* *the world of spirits.*

wa-na′-ġi-ti-pi, *n.* *the house of spirits, the abode of the dead, hades.*

wa-na′-ġi-ya-ta, *adv.* *in the world of spirits, at the spirit-land, to the abode of spirits:* wanaġiyata mde kta, *I will go to the spirit-land.*

wa-na′-ġi-ye-ya, *v.* of naġiyeya; *to annoy, trouble, vex*—wanaġiyewaya.

wa-na′-ġu-ka, *v.* of naġuka; *to sprain*—wanawaġuka.

wa-na′-ha-i-ye-ya, *v.* of naha iyeya; *to knock down with the foot, to kick aside.*

wa-na′-hiŋ-ta, *v.* of nahiŋta; *to scrape off with the foot*—wanawahiŋta.

wa-na′-hmuŋ, *v.* of nahmuŋ; *to curl* or *twist up.*

wa-na′-hna, *v.* *to kick off,* as fruit—wanawahna.

wa-na′-hna-yaŋ, *v.* *to slip, slide, deceive.*

wa-na′-hna-ye, *n.* *slipping, deception.*

wa-na′-ho-ho, *v.* of nahoho; *to make loose with the foot*—wanawahoho

wa-na′-ho-mni, *v.* of nahomni; *to turn round with the foot*—wanawahomni.

wa-na′-ho-toŋ, *v.* of nahotoŋ; *to cause to make a noise by kicking*—wanawahotoŋ.

wa-na′-hu-hu-za, *v.* of nahuhuza; *to shake with the foot*—wanawahuhuza. *T.*, wanahuŋhuŋza.

wa-na′-ħa-pa, *v.* of naħapa; *to scare away by walking; one who frightens* game—wanawaħapa.

wa′-na-ħbe, *v.* of anaħma; *to conceal*—wánawaħbe. *T.*, wanaħme.

wa-na′-ħća, *n.* *T.* *flowers,* especially *cultivated flowers.*

wa-na′-ħći, *v.* of naħći; *to break out a piece with the foot; to break out pieces,* as from a horse's hoof.

wa-na′-ħda, *v.* of naħda; *to rattle with the foot*—wanawaħda.

wa-na′-ħda-ta, *v.* of naħdata; *to scratch with the foot; one who scratches with the foot,* as a cat—wanawaħdata.

wa-na′-ħde-ća, *v.* of naħdeća; *to tear with the foot; one who tears*—wanawaħdeća.

wa-na′-ħdo-ka, *v.* of naħdoka; *to wear holes in the feet by means of* something—wanawaħdoka.

wa-na′-ħe-ya-ta, *v.* of naħeyata, *to kick out of the way:* wanaħeyata iyeya.

wa-na′-ħi-ća, *v.* of naħića; *to waken up with the foot*—wanawaħića.

wa-na′-ħma, *v.* of naħma; *to conceal*—wanawaħma.

wa′-na-ħma, *v.* of anaħma; *to conceal; to deny a charge* — wánawaħma. *T.*, wanaħme.

wa-na′-ħoŋ, *v.* of naħoŋ; *to hear, hearken, obey* — wanawaħoŋ. See anaġoptaŋ *and* akta.

wa-na′-ħoŋ, *adj.* *hearkening, obedient.*

wa-na′-ħoŋ-pi, *n.* *the act of listening, hearkening.*

wa-na′-ħoŋ-śni, *v.* *to be disobedient, not to hearken to*—wanawaħoŋśni.

wa-na′-ħoŋ-śni-yaŋ, *adv.* *heedlessly*

wa-na′-ħpa, *v.* of naħpa; *to knock* or *shake down,* as one may do by walking on an upper floor—wanawaħpa.

wa'-na-ȟpa, *v.* *to kick* or *cast about snow with the feet,* as buffaloes and horses do.

wa-na'-ȟpe-ća, *v.* Same as wanáȟpa.

wa-na'-ȟpu, *v.* of naȟpu; *to kick off pieces.*

wa-na'-ȟta-ka, *v.* of naȟtaka; *to be in the habit of kicking*—wanawaȟtaka.

wa-na'-i-ç̣i-ȟmaŋ-pi, *n.* *those who conceal themselves; hypocrites:* *i. q.* wanakiȟmaŋpi.

wa-na'-ka-ka, *v.* of nakaka; *to make rattle with the foot,* as icicles, stiff hides, etc—wanawakaka. *T.*, wanakakaka.

wa-na'-kaś, *adv. cont.* of wanakaźa; *long ago.* *T.*, ehaŋna.

wa-na'-kaś-wo-ta, *adj.* *aged*—wanakaśmawota.

wa-na'-ka-tiŋ, *v* of nakatiŋ; *to stretch out with the foot*—wanawakatiŋ.

wa-na'-ka-źa, *adv.* *long ago.* *T.*, ehaŋna.

wa-na'-ka-źa-taŋ-haŋ, *adv.* *long since, of old, of a long time.*

wa'-na-ki-ȟma *and* wa'-na-ki-ȟbe, *v.* of anakiȟma; *to conceal* — wánawakiȟbe, wánauŋkiȟmaŋpi.

wa'-na-ki-ȟmaŋ-pi, *n.* *hypocrites; i. q.* wanaiç̣iȟmaŋpi.

wa'-na-ki-kśiŋ, *v.* of anakikśiŋ; *to interpose and defend* one by taking his place in danger—wánawekśiŋ, wánamikśiŋ.

wa-na'-ki-źa, *v.* of nakiźa; *to tread out,* as rice—wanawakiźa.

wa-na'-ko-ka, *v* of nakoka; *to rattle with the foot*—wanawakoka.

wa-na'-kpa, *n.* *bears' ears: i. q.* wanatpa. *T.*, mato nakpa.

wa-na'-ksa, *v.* of naksa; *to break off with the foot*—wanawaksa, wanauŋksapi.

wa-na'-ksa-ksa, *v.* *red.* of wanaksa.

wa-na'-kse-ya, *v.* *T.* *to harvest grain; to mow grass.*

wa-na'-kśi-źa, *v.* of nakśiźa; *to double up with the foot*—wanawakśiźa.

wa-na'-ktaŋ, *v.* of naktaŋ; *to bend with the foot*—wanawaktaŋ.

wa-na'-ku-ka, *v.* of nakuka; *to wear out with the feet*—wanawakuka.

wa-na'-ku-ke-ća, *n.* *one who wears out moccasins badly.*

wa-na'-mda-ska, *v.* of namdaska; *to flatten with the foot*—wanawamdaska.

wa-na'-mda-ya, *v.* of namdaya; *to spread out with the foot*—wanawamdaya.

wa-na'-mda-za, *v.* of namdaza; *to burst open.*

wa-na'-mde-ća, *v.* of namdeća; *to break in pieces with the foot*—wanawamdeća.

wa-na'-mna, *v.* of namna; *to rip with the foot,* as moccasins—wanawamna.

wa-na'-mna-ka, *n.* *one who rips his moccasins much.*

wa′-naŋ, *adv.* See waŋna.

wa-na′-o-ḣpa, *v.* of naoḣpa; *to break into with the feet*—wanawaoḣpa.

wa-na′-o-ksa, *v.* of naoksa; *to break through,* as through ice in killing muskrats—wanawaoksa.

wa-na′-o-ktaŋ, *v.* of naoktaŋ; *to bend into with the foot*—wanawaoktaŋ.

wa-na′-o-ṭiŋ-za, *v.* of naoṭiŋza; *to tread in tight*—wanaowaṭiŋza.

wa-na′-pa, *v.* of napa; *to flee*—wanawapa.

wa-na′-paŋ, *v.* of napaŋ; *to tread out,* as grain—wanawapaŋ.

wa-na′-paŋ-paŋ, *v.* of napaŋpaŋ; *to make soft by treading*—wanawapaŋpaŋ.

wa-na′-pća, *v.* of napća; *to swallow*—wanawapća: wanapća iyeya.

wa-na′-pe-ya, *v. to drive off, cause to flee; one who makes flee*—wanapewaya.

wa-na′-pi-ća-ġe-yu-za, *v.* (wanapa, iċaġa, *and* yuza) *to have it in one's power to make all flee; to be feared by all*—wanapićaġemduza.

wa-na′-pi-śkaŋ-yaŋ, *n. Ih. a toy, a plaything; amusements, shows.*

wa-na′-pi-śkaŋ-yaŋ, *v. T. to play with,* as children with toys; *to exhibit, perform,* as a circus. See wanapiśtaŋyaŋ.

wa-na′-pi-śtaŋ-yaŋ, *v.* of napiśtaŋyaŋ; *to destroy* or *injure everything*—wanipiśtaŋwaya.

wa-na′-po-hna-ka, *v. to put* or *hold in the hands.*

wa-na′-poḣ-ya, *v.* of napoḣya; *to leaven, cause to rise*—wanapoḣwaya.

wa-na′-pom-ya, *v. to cause to burst*—wanapomwaya.

wa-na′-po-pa, *v.* of napopa; *to burst.*

wa-na′-po-ta, *v.* of napota; *to wear out with the feet*—wanawapota.

wa-na′-po-te-ća, *n. one who wears out with the feet*—wanawapoteća.

wa-na′-psa-ka, *v.* of napsaka; *to break,* as a string, *with the foot*—wanawapsaka.

wa-na′-psoŋ, *v.* of napsoŋ; *to spill by kicking, kick over*—wanawapsoŋ.

wa-na′-ptu-źa, *v.* of naptuźa; *to split* or *crack.*

wa-na′-p̣iŋ, *n. a medal; a necklace of beads; a handkerchief; anything worn around the neck, a comforter,* etc.

wa-na′-p̣iŋ-ki-ća-toŋ, *v. a. to put on,* as a wanap̣iŋ; *to cause to wear a necklace,* etc.—wanap̣iŋweċatoŋ.

wa-na′-p̣iŋ-mda-ska, *n. a necklace of beads interwoven.*

wa-na′-p̣iŋ-ya, *v. a. to have* or *use for a* wanap̣iŋ—wanap̣iŋwaya.

wa-na′-sa, *v.* of nasa; *to hunt by surrounding and shooting,* as buffalo; *to chase buffalo*—wanawasa, wanauŋsapi. See howanasekiyapi.

wa-na'-sa-pi, *n.* *the buffalo chase.*

wa-na'-sda-ta, *v.* of nasdata; *to crawl up to.*

wa-na'-sde-ća, *v.* of nasdeća; *to split.*

wa-na'-se-ya, *v.* *to go on a buffalo hunt; to make a surround.*

wa-na'-sna, *v.* of nasna; *to make ring with the feet*—wanawasna.

wa-na'-sni, *v.* of nasni; *to trample out*, as fire.

wa-na'-śa-pa, *v.* of naśapa; *to defile with the feet*—wanawaśapa.

wa-na'-śda, *v.* of naśda; *to make bare with the feet.*

wa-na'-śdo-ka, *v.* of naśdoka; *to pull off*, as pantaloons—wanawaśdoka.

wa-na'-śe-ća, *v.* of naśeća; *to trample and make dry*, as grass—wanawaśeća.

wa-na'-śi-ća, *v.* of naśića; *to injure with the feet*—wanawaśića.

wa-na'-śi-pa, *v.* of naśipa; *to break off with the feet*—wanawaśipa.

wa-na'-śki-ća, *v.* of naśkića; *to press with the foot; one who presses with the foot*—wanawaśkića.

wa-na'-śna, *v.* of naśna; *to miss with the foot;* wanaśna iyeye s'a, *one who kicks.*

wa-na'-śni-źa, *v.* of naśniźa; *to trample down*, as grass, and *make wither*—wanawaśniźa.

wa-na'-śo-śa, *v.* of naśośa; *to foul*, as water, *with the feet*—wanawaśośa.

wa-na'-śpa, *v.* of naśpa; *to break off with the feet*—wanawaśpa.

wa-na'-śpu, *v.* of naśpu; *to break off*, as in trampling on pumpkins—wanawaśpu.

wa-na'-śu-źa, *v.* of naśuźa; *to bruise with the feet*—wanawaśuźa.

wa-na'-ta-ka, *v.* of nataka; *to fasten up*—wanawataka.

wa'-na-taŋ, *v.* of anataŋ; *to run upon, to attack*—wánawataŋ.

wa-na'-te-pa, *v.* of natepa; *to wear off short with the foot*—wanawatepa.

wa'-na-ti-ća, *v.* of natića; *to scrape away*, as snow; *to paw*, as a horse—wanawatića.

wa-na'-ti-pa, *v.* of natipa; *to cramp.*

wa-na'-ti-taŋ, *v.* of natitaŋ; *to pull* or *push against*—wanawatitaŋ.

wa-na'-tpa, *n.* *a bear's ears: i. q.* wanakpa.

wa-na'-tu-ka, *v.* of natuka; *to stamp to pieces*, as furs; *one who destroys by stamping*—wanawatuka. *T.*, wanakuka.

wa-na'-ṭa, *v.* of naṭa; *to kick to death*—wanawaṭa.

wa-na'-uŋ-ka, *v.* *T.* *to kick and make fall down.*

wa-na'-waŋ-ka, *v.* of nawaŋka; *to kick down; to start off on the gallop*, as a herd of buffalo. *T.*, wanauŋka.

wa-na'-we-ġa, *v.* of naweġa; *to break with the foot*—wanawaweġa.

w a′-n a-w i ŋ, *v.* of anawiŋ; *to tell what is not true, to conceal*—wánawawiŋ. *T.*, anaȟme.

w a-n a′-w i ŋ-ź a, *v.* of nawiŋźa; *to bend down with the foot,* as grass—wanawawiŋźa.

w a-n a′-ź a-ź a, *v.* of naźaźa; *to wash by boiling,* as clothes.

w a-n a′-ź a-ź a-y a, *v. a. to cause to wash out* or *come clean by boiling*—wanaźaźawaya.

w a-n a′-ź i-p a, *v* of naźipa; *to pinch* or *scratch with the toes*—wanawaźipa.

w a-n a′-ź u-ź u, *v.* of naźuźu; *to kick down, kick to pieces: one who kicks to pieces*—wanawaźuźu.

w a-n i-ć a′, *n. meat of all kinds:* wanića waćiŋ, *I desire meat. T.*, waćonića. See ćonića.

w a-n i′-ć a, *adj.* of nića; *none, without any*—manića, ninića, uŋnićapi.

w a′-n i-ć a, *v.* of anića; *to refuse to give up*—wawanića.

w a-n i′-ć a-d a ŋ, *adj. none, very little.*

w a-n i g′-n i-ć a, *adj. red.* of wanića.

w a-n i′-h a ŋ, *n. last winter.*

w a-n i′-k i-s a-p a, *n. a winter in which the ground is not covered with snow. T.*, waniyetu kisapa

w a-n i′-k i-y a, *v.* of nikiya; *to save, cause to live*—waniwakiya.

w a-n i′-k i-y a, *n. one who makes live; the Saviour.*

w a′-n i-ḳ a-d a ŋ, *n. a very little. T.*, waniḳala.

w a′-n i-ḳ a-l a, *n T. i. q.* waniḳadaŋ.

w a-n i n′, *cont.* of wanića: owihaŋke wanin wićoni, *life without end.*

w a-n i ŋ g′-n i-ć a, *adj red.* of wanića. See wanignića.

w a′-n i-s t i ŋ-n a, *n. a little, very little.*

w a-n i′-t i, *v. to spend the winter, to winter.*

w a-n i′-t i-p i, *n. a winter encampment.*

w a-n i′-u ŋ, *v. to winter, spend the winter.*

w a-n i′-y a, *v.* of niya; *to cause to live*—waŉiwaya.

w a-n i′-y a-k a-t a ŋ-k a, *n. the hen hawk, a species of kite.*

w a-n i′-y a ŋ-p i, *n. T. domestic animals: i. q.* wanuŋyaŋpi.

w a-n i′-y e, *n. one who makes live; the Saviour.*

w a-n i′-y e-t u, *n. winter, a winter; a year.* See kiwani.

w a-n u′, *adv.* See wanuŋ.

w a-n u ŋ′, *adv. by chance, accidentally:* wanuŋ ećoŋ, *to do by accident;* wanuŋ ećoŋpi, *an accident.*

w a-n u ŋ ȟ′, *adv. by accident.*

w a-n u ŋ′-k e n, *adv. accidentally.*

w a-n u ŋ′-y a ŋ, *v.* of nuŋyaŋ; *to tame, domesticate*—wanuŋwaya.

w a-n u ŋ′-y a ŋ-p i, *n. tame animals, domestic cattle. T.*, waniyaŋpi. See woteća.

w a ŋ, *art. indef. a* or *an.*

w a ŋ, *intj. look! see!*

w a ŋ, *n. a large blackish snake* five or six feet long. *T.*, waŋto.

waŋ, *n. cont.* of waŋźu, *a quiver;* and of waŋhiŋkpe, *an arrow.*

waŋ-a′-pe-śni, *adv.* *T.* without *wounding:* waŋapeśni kte, *to kill without wounding.*

waŋ′-ća, *num adj.* *one; i. q.* waŋźidaŋ.

waŋ′-ća, *adv.* *once.*

waŋ′-ća-daŋ, *adv.* *only once.*

waŋ′-ćag, *cont.* of waŋćake.

waŋ′-ća-hna, *adv.* *at once, immediately.*

waŋ′-ća-kća-daŋ, *adv. red.* of waŋćadaŋ; *a few times; now and then once; once apiece.*

waŋ′-ća-ke, *adv.* *at once.*

waŋ′-ći, *adj.* *T.* *one: i. q.* waŋźi.

waŋ-e′-ya, *n.* *what is prepared for eating on a journey, provisions.* *T.*, oŋweya. See uŋweya.

waŋ-hda′-ka, *v. pos.* of waŋyaka; *to see one's own*—waŋwahdaka, waŋuŋhdakapi.

waŋ-hi′, *n.* (waŋ *and* hi) *a flint, flints:* perhaps so called from the fact that *arrow-heads* were formerly made of *flints.*

waŋ-hiŋ′-kpe, *n.* *an arrow, arrows*—tiwaŋhiŋkpe, nitiwaŋhiŋkpe, mitiwaŋhinkpe

waŋ-hiŋ′-kpe-ki-hi-ye-ya-pi, *n.* *a bow-shot.* *T.*, waŋhiŋkpe kiŋiŋ yeyapi. See kihiyeya.

waŋ-hiŋ′-kpe-o-i-na-źin, *n.* *T.* *the notch in the end of an arrow.*

waŋ-hiŋ′-tpe, *n.* Same as waŋhiŋkpe.

waŋ-hi′-śa, *n.* *gun caps.*

waŋ-hi′-śa-daŋ, *n.* *gun caps, percussion caps.*

waŋ-hi′-yu-za, *n.* *flat arm* or *wrist-bands.*

waŋ-i-ya′, *intj.* of surprise; *indeed!* used on meeting one unexpectedly. *T.*, hoŋhoŋhe!

waŋ′-i-ya-ȟpe-ya, *v. n.* *to shoot arrows.*

waŋ′-i-yu′-ke-ze, *n.* *an instrument for making arrows.*

waŋ-ka′, *v. n.* *to be; to lie,* as a lake, field, or log; *to lie down; to spend the night; to continue,* as, ya waŋka, *to keep going on*—muŋka, nuŋka, uŋwankapi. *T.*, iyuŋka.

waŋ′-ka. See ćaŋwaŋka.

waŋ′-ka-daŋ, *adj.* *weak, tender; soft, brittle, easily broken* or *torn*—mawaŋkadaŋ. *T.*, waŋkala; *Ih*, waŋkana

waŋ-ka′-haŋ, *part.* *lying down, fallen down.* *T.*, yuŋkahaŋ.

waŋ-ka′-he-ya, *v. a.* *to throw down, cause to fall*—waŋkahewaya. *T.*, yuŋkaheya.

waŋ′-ka-la, *adj.* *T.* *i. q.* waŋkadaŋ.

waŋ-kan′, *adv.* *above, up high.* *T.*, waŋkaŋl.

waŋ-kan′-taŋ-haŋ, *adv.* *from above.* *T.*, waŋkaŋltaŋhaŋ.

waŋ-kan′-ta-taŋ-haŋ, *adv.* *from above.*

waŋ-kan′-ti-pi, *n.* *an upper room, up stairs.* *T.*, waŋkaŋltipi.

waŋ-kan′-tki-ya, *adv.* *upwards.*

waŋ-kan′-tu, *adv.* *up above, high up.*

wan-kan'-tu-ya, *adv.* *high up.*

wan-kan'-tu-ya-ken, *adv.* *up high.*

wan-kanl', *adv.* *T.* *i. q.* wankan.

wan-kanl'-tu, *adv.* *T.* *i. q.* wankantu.

wan'-kan-ye-la, *adv.* *T.* *loose, free to turn.*

wan'-ka-pi, *n.* *a lying down, an encampment.* *T.*, yunkapi.

wan-ki'-ći-ya-ka-pi, *v. recip.* of wanyaka; *to see each other.*

wan-mdi', *n.* *the royal* or *war-eagle, the Falco imperialis* or *Aquila heliaca.* *T.*, wanbli.

wan-mdu'-dan, *n.* *T.*, waglula. See wamdudan, the better orthography.

wan-mdu'-śka, *n.* See wamduśka.

wan-mdu'-śka-dan, *n.* See wamduśkadan.

wan-mli', *or* wan-bli', *n.* *T.* *i. q.* wanmdi.

wan-mlu'-la, *or* wan-blu'-la, *n.* *T.* *i. q.* wanmdudan.

wan-mlu'-śka-la, *or* wan-blu'-śka-la, *n.* *T.* *i. q.* wanmduśkadan.

wan'-na, *adv.* *now, quickly; lately, already:* wanna ećamon, *I have now done it;* wanna ećamon kta, *I will now do it.*

wan'-naś, *adv.* *now.*

wan'-ske, *n.* *the family name of a fourth child, if a daughter.*

wan-ske'-pa, *n.* *an arrow-head not barbed.* *T.*, kestonśni.

wan-sma'-hi, *n.* *an iron arrow-head.*

wan'-to, *n.* *T.* *a blackish blue snake.* See wan.

wan-yag', *cont.* of wanyaka; wanyag hi, *to come to see;* wanyag iheya, *to see all at once, to perceive, discover.*

wan-yag'-ki-ya, *v. a.* *to cause to see* any thing—wanyagwakiya, wanyagmakiya.

wan-yag'-ya, *v. a.* *to cause to see* or *perceive*—wanyagwaya.

wan-ya'-ka, *v. a.* *to see* or *perceive* anything; *to have seen*—wanmdaka, wandaka, wanunyakapi, wanćiyaka. See tonwan.

wan-ye', *v.* wanye ya, *to go to see* or *examine;* *i. q.* wakćanyan.

wan-ye'-ća, *n.* *rushes; the lightning bug, the fire-fly.*

wan-ye'-ya, *v. a.* *to shoot arrows; to shoot in the sacred dance*—wanyewaya. *T.*, wanhinkpe yeya.

wan-yu'-ġo, *v. a.* *to make the crooked marks on arrows,* which are considered essential to their goodness. See yuġo.

wan-yu'-ġo-dan, *n.* *the striped lizard.* *T.*, agleśkala.

wan-yu'-ġu-ka, *v.* *to draw an arrow out of the quiver.*

wan'-yu-kpan, *v.* *to shoot an arrow.*

wan'-yu-kpan-han, *v.* *to shoot arrows one after another*—wanmdukpanhan.

wan-yu'-la-śa, *v.* *T.* *to draw and shoot a bow; to shoot arrows from a bow.*

waŋ′-yu-tpaŋ-haŋ, *v.* See waŋyukpaŋhaŋ.

waŋ-źi′, *num. adj.* *one;* also used for an indefinite number, *some.*

waŋ-źi′-ća, *adj.* *one.*

waŋ-źi′-ća, *adv.* *in one way;* as, hećetu waŋźića, *in the same state, without change.*

waŋ-źi′-daŋ, *num. adj.* *one*—mawaŋźidaŋ, uŋwaŋźipidaŋ: waŋźipidaŋ, *they are one.* *Ih.*, waŋźina. *T.*, waŋźila.

waŋ-źi′-daŋ-ken, *adv.* *in one manner.*

waŋ-źi′-daŋ-ki-ya, *adv.* *in one way.*

waŋ-źig′-źi, *adj.* *red.* of waŋźi; *some.*

waŋ-źig′-źi-daŋ, *adj.* *red.* of waŋźidaŋ; *some.*

waŋ-źig′-źi-la, *adj.* *T.* *one by one; singly; one apiece.*

waŋ-źi′-i-to-kto *or* waŋ-źi′-i-to-to, *adv.* *turn about, i. q.* uŋma itoto. *T.*, waŋźiitoktog.

waŋ-źi′-kśi, *adj.* *red.* of waŋźi; *some.* *T.*, waŋźigźi.

waŋ-źi′-la, *num. adj.* *T.* *i. q.* waŋźidaŋ.

waŋ-źi′-na, *num. adj.* *Ih.* *one.*

waŋ′-źu, *n.* *a quiver:* waŋźu ḳiŋ, *to carry a quiver.*

waŋ′-źu-ya-pi, *n.* a name given to the śkeća, *fisher, Mustela canadensis,* as the skin of that animal alone, it is said, was formerly used for making quivers; *any skin used to make a quiver.*

wa-o′, *v.* of o; *to hit in shooting*—wawao: also 1st pers. sing. of o.

wa-o′-ho-da, *v.* of ohoda; *to honor, worship*—waohowada.

wa-o′-ka, *n.* *a marksman; a good hunter*—wawaoka.

wa-o′-ki-hi, *v.* of okihi; *to be able, to have ability*—waowakihi.

wa-o′-ki-hi-ka, *n.* *one who is able*—waowakihika.

wa-o′-ki-hi-ya, *v. a.* *to make able*—waokihiwaya.

wa-o′-ki-hi-ya; *adv.* *ably, powerfully.*

wa-o′-ki-ya, *n.* *one who communicates with* or *commands.*

wa-o′-ki-ya, *v.* of ókiya; *to help, aid*—waowakiya. *T.*, wawokiya.

wa-o′-ki-ye, *n.* *a helper; a lawyer.*

wa-o′-ḳu, *v.* of oḳu; *to lend*—waowaḳu.

wa-oŋ′-spe, *v.* of oŋspe; *to know how*—waoŋmaspe, waoŋnispe.

wa-oŋ′-spe-ki-ya, *v.* of oŋspekiya; *to teach*—waoŋspewakiya.

wa-oŋ′-spe-ki-ya, *n.* *a teacher.*

wa-oŋ′-śi-da, *adj.* *merciful, gracious*—waoŋśiwada, waoŋśiuŋdapi.

wa-o′-ṗo, *n.* *T.* *light snow flying in the sunlight.*

wa-o′-śte-hda, *v.* of ośtehda; *to speak evil of, call bad names; to revile, to slander*—waośtewahda.

wa-o′-wa-ki-ye, *v.* of owakiye; *to speak with*—waowawakiye.

wa-o′-yu-siŋ, *v.* *T.* *to hate, to be out of humor with.*

w a - o′ - y u - s i ŋ - k e, *n.* *T.* *one who hates.*

w a - o′ - ź i - ź i, *v.* of oźiźi; *to whisper; a whisperer*—waowaźiźi.

w a - p a′, *v.* of pa; *to bark,* as a dog.

w a - p a′, *v. n.* *to snow; it is snowing.* *T.*, wahiŋhe.

w a - p a′, *adv.* *towards, at:* waŋkan wapa, *upwards;* tokata wapa, *forwards;* tiŋta wapa, *at the prairie.*

w a′ - p a, *n.* *a bear's head.* *T.*, mato pa.

w a′ - p a, *n.* *leaves;* ćaŋwápa, *foliage:* ćaŋwapatowi, *the month of May.*

w a - p a′ - b a - ġ a, *v.* of pabaġa; *to roll, twist:* also 1st pers. sing. of pabaġa.

w a - p a′ - b e, *v.* of pamaŋ; *to file*—wawapabe: also 1st pers. sing. of pabe. *T.*, wapame.

w a - p a′ - b u, *v.* of pabu; *to beat, drum*—wawapabu: also 1st pers. sing. of pabu.

w a - p a′ - ć a ŋ - ć a ŋ, *v.* of paćaŋćaŋ; *to make shake:* also 1st pers. sing. of paćaŋćaŋ.

w a - p a′ - ć a ŋ - n a n - i - y e - y a, *v.* *to shove out from the shore,* as a boat. See paćaŋnaniyeya.

w a - p a′ - ć e - k a, *v.* See wapaćekćeka.

w a - p a′ - ć e - k ć e - k a, *v.* of paćekćeka; *to push and make stagger*—wawapaćekćeka: also 1st pers. sing. of paćekćeka.

w a - p a′ - g m i - g m a, *v.* *T.* *i. q.* wapahmihma.

w a - p a′ - ġ a ŋ, *v.* of paġaŋ; *to part with; to open*—wawapaġaŋ: also 1st pers. sing. of paġaŋ.

w a - p a′ - ġ a - p a, *v.* of paġapa; *to push off,* as the skin of animals—wawapaġapa: also 1st pers. sing. of paġapa.

w a - p a′ - ġ o, *v.* of paġo; *to carve; one who carves* or *engraves*—wawapaġo: also 1st pers. sing. of paġo.

w a - p a′ - ġ o - y a, *v. a.* *to cause to carve.*

w a - p a′ - h a, *n.* *a hat, cap, bonnet; a covering for the head:* wapaha kiçuŋ, *to wear one's hat;* wapaha hdusdoka, *to take off one's hat.* *T.*, *a headdress of feathers.* See wapośtaŋ.

w a′ - p a - h a, *n.* *the shaft* or *pole on which are tied feathers of various colors,* used in the Dakota dances; *a standard, a banner, a flag.*

w a - p a′ - h a - i - y e - y a, *v.* of pahaiyeya; *to push down.*

w a - p a′ - h a - k a - m n i - m n i - l a, *n.* *T.* *a war bonnet with feathers dangling down the back.*

w a′ - p a - h a - k a - m n i - m n i - l a, *n.* *T.* *a standard with a tuft of feathers dangling.*

w a - p a′ - h a - k i - t o ŋ, *v.* *to wear a hat; one who wears a hat,* i. e. *a white man,* as distinguished from an Indian. *T.*, wapośtaŋ kiçuŋ.

w a - p a′ - h a - m i - m e - l a, *n.* *T.* *a round war-bonnet.*

w a - p a′ - h a - o - ġ e - d a ŋ, *n.* *a handkerchief,* commonly pronounced "wapaoġedaŋ." So called from being tied around the head.

Wa'-pa-ha-śa, *n.* of wápaha; *the hereditary name of the Dakota chief* at the lowest village on the Mississippi, commonly pronounced by the Dakotas Wápaśa; and as the name of a county in Minnesota, written, with some want of judgment and taste, Wabashaw.

wa-pa'-hba, *v.* of pahba; *to shell*, as corn—wawapahba.

wa-pa'-hbe-za, *v.* of pahbeza; *to make rough*—wawapahbeza: also 1st pers. sing. of pahbeza.

wa-pa'-hi, *v.* of pahi; *to gather* or *pick up*—wawapahi: also 1st pers. sing. of pahi.

wa-pa'-hiŋ-ta, *v.* of pahiŋta; *to brush off*—wawapahiŋta: also 1st pers. sing. of pahiŋta.

wa-pa'-hi-pi, *n.* *gathering, picking up.*

wa-pa'-hmi-hma, *v.* of pahmihma: *to roll*—wawapahmihma: also 1st pers. sing. of pahmihma. *T.*, wapagmigma.

wa-pa' hmiŋ-yaŋ-yaŋ, *v.* of pahmiŋyaŋyaŋ; *to make round*—wawapahmiŋyaŋyaŋ: also 1st pers. sing. of pahmiŋyaŋyaŋ.

wa-pa'-hmuŋ, *v.* of pahmuŋ; *to twist*—wawapahmuŋ: also 1st pers. sing. of pahmuŋ.

wa-pa'-hmuŋ-ka, *n.* *one who twists, a spinner.*

wa-pa'-hmuŋ-pi, *n* *twisted thread, yarn.*

wa-pa'-hna-śkiŋ-yaŋ, *v.* *to make crazy:* also 1st pers. sing. of pahnaśkiŋyaŋ.

wa-pa'-hna-yaŋ, *v.* of pahnayaŋ; *to miss*, as in attempting *to stab:* also 1st pers. sing. of pahnayaŋ. *T.*, wapagnayaŋ.

wa-pa'-ho-ho, *v.* of pahoho; *to shake* or *make loose.*

wa-pa'-ho-mni, *v.* of pahomni; *to turn round*—wawapahomni: also 1st pers. sing. of pahomni.

wa-pa'-ho-toŋ, *v.* of pahotoŋ; *to make cry out*—wawapahotoŋ: also 1st pers. sing. of pahotoŋ.

wa-pa'-hu-hu-za, *v.* of pahuhuza; *to shake with the hand*—wawapahuhuza: also 1st pers. sing. of pahuhuza. *T.*, wapahuŋhuŋza, *to shake by pushing against.*

wa-pa'-ḣa-tka, *v.* *to rub against the grain:* also 1st pers. sing. of paḣatka.

wa-pa'-ḣći, *v.* of paḣći; *to tear out pieces:* also 1st pers. sing. of paḣći.

wa-pa'-ḣda-ġaŋ, *v.* of paḣdaġaŋ; *to enlarge:* also 1st pers. sing. of paḣdaġaŋ.

wa-pa'-ḣda-ka, *n.* *one who is a good hunter*—wawapaḣdaka.

wa'-pa-ḣdan-toŋ, *v.* *to work with ribbon; to embroider*—wapaḣdanwatoŋ.

wa'-pa-ḣda-ta, *v.* of apaḣdata; *to embroider.*

wa-pa'-ḣde-ća, *v.* of paḣdeća; *to tear, rend*—wawapaḣdeća: also 1st pers. sing. of paḣdeća.

wa-pa'-ḣdi, *v.* of paḣdi; *to push into the ground*—wawapaḣdi: also 1st pers. sing. of paḣdi.

w a - p a′ - ḣ d o - k a, *v.* of paḣdoka; *to make holes, to pierce*—wawapaḣdoka: also 1st pers. sing. of paḣdoka.

w a - p a′ - ḣ m i n, *v.* of paḣmiŋ; *to make crooked.*

w a - p a′ - ḣ p a, *v.* of paḣpa; *to throw down*—wawapaḣpa: also 1st pers. sing. of paḣpa.

w a - p a′ - ḣ p u, *v.* of paḣpu; *to pick off*—wawapaḣpu: also 1st pers. sing. of paḣpu.

w a - p a′ - ḣ t a, *v.* of paḣta; *to tie in bundles*—wapawaḣta, wapauŋḣtapi.

w a - p a′ - ḣ t a, *n.* *a bundle, a pack.*

w a - p a′ - ḣ u - ġ a, *v.* of paḣuġa; *to break holes in*—wawapaḣuġa: also 1st pers. sing. of paḣuġa.

w a - p a′ - k a - t i ŋ, *v.* of pakatiŋ; *to straighten out.*

w a - p a′ - k a - w a, *v.* of pakawa; *to open out.*

w a - p a′ - k ć a, *v.* of pakća; *to comb*—wawapakća; also 1st pers. sing. of pakća.

w a - p a′ - k e - z a, *v.* of pakeza; *to make smooth and hard:* also 1st pers. sing. of pakeza.

w a - p a′ - k i ŋ, *v.* *to set up in the ground,* as a stick leaning in the direction one is going; *to set up a sign post*—wawapakiŋ: also 1st pers. sing. of pakiŋ.

w a - p a′ - k i ŋ - t a, *v.* of pakiŋta; *to wipe*—wawapakiŋta: also 1st pers. sing. of pakiŋta.

w a - p a′ - k i ŋ - z a, *v.* of pakiŋza; *to make creak.*

w a - p a′ - k o - t a, *v.* *to probe* or *dig out*—wawapakota: also 1st pers. sing. of pakota.

w a - p a′ - k p a, *v.* *to pierce*—wawapakpa: also 1st pers. sing. of pakpa.

w a - p a′ - k p i, *v.* *to pick open,* as eggs: also 1st pers. sing. of pakpi.

w a - p a′ - k s a, *v.* of paksa; *to break off with the hand*—wawapaksa: also 1st pers. sing. of paksa.

w a - p a′ - k ś i - ź a, *v.* *to make double up*—wawapakśiźa: also 1st pers. sing. of pakśiźa.

w a - p a′ - k t a ŋ, *v.* *to crook, make crook*—wawapaktaŋ: also 1st pers. sing. of paktaŋ.

w a - p a′ - ḳ e - ġ a, *v.* *to scratch:* also 1st pers. sing. of paḳeġa.

w a - p a′ - ḳ e - z a, *v.* *to make hard and smooth*—wawapaḳeza: also 1st pers. sing. of paḳeza.

w a - p a′ - m a ŋ, *v.* of pamaŋ; *to file*—wawapamaŋ: also 1st pers. sing. of pamaŋ.

w a - p a′ - m d a - s k a, *v.* *to make flat*—wawapamdaska: also 1st pers. sing. of pamdaska. *T.*, wapablaska.

w a - p a′ - m d a - y a, *v.* of pamdaya; *to make smooth, to iron,* as clothes—wawapamdaya: also 1st pers. sing. of pamdaya. *T.*, wapablaya.

w a - p a′ - m d a - z a, *v.* *to make burst by pressing*—wawapamdaza: also 1st pers. sing. of pamdaza.

w a - p a′ - m d e - ć a, *v.* *to crush, break to pieces*—wawapamdeća: also 1st pers. sing. of pamdeća. *T.*, wapableća.

wa-pa′-mdu, *v.* *to pulverize*—wawapamdu: also 1st pers. sing. of pamdu. *T.*, wapablu.

wa-pa′-mi-ma, *v.* *to make round*—wawapamima: also 1st pers. sing. of pamima.

wa-pa′-mna, *n.* *a bunch*, as of grass or shrubs.

wa-pa′-mna, *v.* 1st pers. sing. of pamna.

wa-pa′-mni, *v.* of pamni; *to serve out, to distribute*—wawapamni: also 1st pers. sing. of pamni.

wa-pa′-mni-pi, *n.* *a distribution.*

wa-pa′-na-ke-ya, *v.* 1st pers. sing. of panakeya.

wa-pa′-ni-ni, *v.* 1st pers. sing. of panini.

wa-pa′-o-ġe-daŋ, *n.* *a handkerchief.* *T*, itepakiŋte

wa-pa′-o-hda-pśiŋ-yaŋ, *v.* of paohdapśiŋyaŋ; wapaohdapśinyaŋ iyeya, *to turn bottom upwards.*

wa-pa′-o-hdu-ta, *v.* *to close up:* wapaohduta iyeya: also 1st pers. sing of paohduta.

wa-pa′-o-ksa, *v.* *to push* or *break through:* also 1st pers. sing. of paoksa.

wa-pa′-o-spa, *v.* *to push under*, as in water: also 1st pers. sing. of paospa.

wa-pa′-o-ṭiŋ-za, *v.* *to press in tight:* also 1st pers. sing. of paoṭiŋza.

wa-pa′-o-wo-taŋ, *v.* *to make straight:* also 1st pers. sing. of paowotaŋ. *T.*, wapaowotaŋla.

wa-pa′-paḣ-ya, *v.* of papaḣya; *to parch*, as corn—wapapaḣwaya.

wa-pa′-paḣ-ya-pi, *n.* of papaḣya; *parched corn.*

wa-pa′-po-pa, *v.* *to burst open*, as corn: also 1st pers. sing. of papopa.

wa-pa′-psa-ka, *v.* of papsaka; *to break*, as cords: also 1st pers. sing. of papsaka.

wa-pa′-psoŋ, *v.* of papsoŋ; *to spill*, as water—wawapapsoŋ; also 1st pers. sing. of papsoŋ.

wa-pa′-pśuŋ-ka, *n.* *a provision bag, a small bundle.*

wa-pa′-ptu-źa, *v.* *to split* or *crack:* also 1st pers. sing. of paptuźa.

wa-pa′-pu-za, *v.* of papuza; *to make dry by wiping*—wawapapuza: also 1st pers. sing. of papuza.

wa-pa′-sda-ta, *v.* *to set up*, as a pole in the ground—wawapasdata: also 1st pers. sing. of pasdata.

wa-pa′-sde-ća, *v.* of pasdeća; *to split*—wawapasdeća: also 1st pers. sing. of pasdeća.

wa-pa′-ska, *v.* *to make white by rubbing*—wawapaska: also 1st pers. sing. of paska.

wa-pa′-sma-ka, *v.* *to indent*—wawapasmaka: also 1st pers. sing. of pasmaka.

wa-pa′-smiŋ-yaŋ-yaŋ, *v.* *to make bare and clean:* also 1st pers. sing. of pasmiŋyaŋyaŋ

wa-pa′-snoŋ, *v.* of pasnoŋ; *to roast*, as meat—wawapasnoŋ, wauŋpasnoŋpi: also 1st pers. sing. of pasnoŋ.

wa-pa'-snuŋ, *v.* See wapasnoŋ.

wa-pa'-staŋ, *v.* *to soak off hair*—wawapastaŋ: also 1st pers. sing. of pastaŋ. *T.*, waȟpaŋyaŋ.

wa-pa'-staŋ-ka, *v.* of pastaŋka; *to moisten*—wawapastaŋka.

wa-pa'-sto, *v.* of pasto; *to brush down*—wawapasto.

wa-pa'-sto-ka, *n.* *one who is gentle*—wawapastoka.

wa-pa'-śa-ka, *v.* of paśaka; *to push* or *stab with too little force*—wawapaśaka: also 1st pers. sing. of paśaka.

wa-pa'-śa-pa, *v.* of paśapa; *to defile*—wawapaśapa.

wa-pa'-śi-pa, *v.* of paśipa; *to break off close*, as the limbs of a tree—wawapaśipa: also 1st pers. sing. of paśipa.

wa-pa'-śki-ća, *v.* of paśkića; *to press, squeeze*—wawapaśkića.

wa-pa'-śki-śka, *v.* of paśkiśka; *to make rough.*

wa-pa'-śko-kpa, *v.* of paśkokpa; *to make hollow, to cut* or *dig out.*

wa-pa'-śko-pa, *v.* of paśkopa; *to make twisting.*

wa-pa'-śko-tpa, *v.* Same as wapaśkokpa.

wa-pa'-śna, *v.* of paśna; *to miss*—wawapaśna.

wa-pa'-śpa, *v.* of paśpa; *to push away; to break off; to wash out*, as stains; *that which is capable of being washed out*—wawapaśpa: also 1st pers. sing. of paśpa.

wa-pa'-śpu, *v.* of paśpu; *to break off*—wawapaśpu.

wa-pa'-śu-źa, *v.* of paśuźa; *to crush*—wawapaśuźa: also 1st pers. sing. of paśuźa.

wa-pa'-ta, *v.* of páta; *to cut up*, as a butcher does an animal—wawapata: 1st pers. sing. of páta.

wa-pa'-taŋ, *v.* of pataŋ; *to push; to mash; to be saving of*—wawapataŋ: also 1st pers. sing. of pataŋ.

wa-pa'-taŋ-ka, *n.* *one who is saving.* *T.*, wakpataŋka.

wa-pa'-ta-pi, *n.* *meat cut up; the act of cutting up meat.*

wa-pa'-ti-ća, *v.* *to scrape away*, as snow—wawapatića: also 1st pers. sing. of patića. *T.*, wapahiŋta.

wa-pa'-ṭiŋ-za, *v.* *to press hard*—wawapaṭiŋza: also 1st pers. sing. of paṭiŋza.

wa-pa'-ṭo-ya, *v.* *to obstruct, bear down on*—wapaṭowaya.

wa-pa'-we-ġa, *v.* *to break* or *fracture*—wawapaweġa: also 1st pers. sing. of paweġa.

wa-pa'-wi-hnu-ni, *v.* *to destroy*—wawapawihnuni: also 1st pers. sing. of pawihnuni.

wa'-pa-wiŋ-ta, *v.* of apawiŋta; *to rub on, to plaster: what is put on as plastering*—wáwapawiŋta.

wa-pa'-wiŋ-źa, *v.* of pawiŋźa; *to bend down*, as grass: also 1st pers. sing. of pawiŋźa.

wa'-pa-ye, *n.* *grease, meat; seasoning* of any kind. *T.*, wićahiyayutapi.

wa'-pa-ye-ya, *v. a.* *to use for seasoning*—wapayewaya.

wa-pa'-ye-za-ha, *n. T. a rival; a jealous person.*

wa-pa'-zaŋ, *v. to separate, part,* as hair—wawapazaŋ: also 1st pers. sing. of pazaŋ.

wa-pa'-ze-ze, *v.* 1st pers. sing. of pazeze.

wa-pa'-zo, *v.* of pazo; *to show*—wawapazo: also 1st pers. sing. of pazo.

wa-pa'-zoŋ-ta, *v. to sew up with a running thread, to baste*—wawapazoŋta: also 1st pers. sing. of pazoŋta.

wa-pa'-zo-pi, *n. a show, an exhibition.*

wa-pa'-źa-źa, *v.* of paźaźa; *to wash*—wawapaźaźa: also 1st pers. sing. of paźaźa.

wa-pa'-źiŋ, *v. n. to be prevented, not to be able to accomplish*—wamapaźiŋ

wa-pa'-źi-pa, *v.* of paźipa; *to pinch*—wawapaźipa: also 1st pers. sing. of paźipa.

wa-pa'-źuŋ, *v.* of paźuŋ; *to dig up with the bill,* as ducks feeding under water.

wa-pa'-źu-źu, *v.* of paźuźu; *to erase; to demolish*—wawapaźuźu: also 1st pers. sing. of paźuźu.

wa-pće'-ya, *v.* of pćeya; *to cut and dry meat*—wapćewaya, wapćeuŋyaŋpi. *T.*, wakablaya.

wa-pće'-ya-pi, *n. drying meat* of any kind.

wa-pe', *v. to snow. T.*, ićamna. See wapa.

wa-pe'-haŋ, *v. to fold*—wawapehaŋ: also 1st pers. sing. of pehaŋ.

wa-pe'-pe-ka, *n. prickles, briers, thorns; the prickly ash.*

wa'-pe-tog-tog-ya, *adv. marvellously, miraculously.*

wa'-pe-tog-to-ke-ća, *n. signs, marks; miracles, wonders.*

wa'-pe-tog-toŋ, *v. a. to mark* any thing, *have a sign*—wapetogwatoŋ, wapetoguŋtoŋpi.

wa'-pe-tog-toŋ-pi, *n. marks, signs.*

wa'-pe-tog-ya, *adv. marvellously.*

wa'-pe-to-ke-ća, *n. a sign, a mark, a bound; a miracle.*

wa'-pi, *adj. lucky, fortunate*—wamapi, wanipi, wauŋpipi.

wa-pi'-da, *v. n. to be thankful, glad*—wawapida. See pida *and* wōpida.

wa-pi'-da-pi, *n. gratitude.*

wa-pi'-da-pi-śni, *n. ingratitude.*

wa-pi'-da-śni, *v. n. to be unthankful, ungrateful*—wawapidaśni.

wa'-pi-ka, *adj. skillful.*

wa'-pi-ke, *n. one who is fortunate.*

wa-pi'-ki-ya, *v. to put up and lay away* things *well, to rearrange*—wapiwakiya.

wa'-pi-śni, *adj. unfortunate.*

wa'-pi-ya, *adv. fortunately.*

wa'-pi-ya, *v. a. to make fortunate*—wápiwaya.

wa-pi'-ya, *v. to conjure the sick, to powwow in the Indian way*—wapiwaya. See pikiya.

wa′-pi-ya-pi, *n. conjuring.*

wa-pi′-ye, *n. a conjurer, an Indian doctor.*

wa-po′-ble-ća, *n. T.*, wapaha *and* oblećа; *a war bonnet with feathers standing out around the head and hanging down.*

wa-po′-ġe-hna-ka, *n. a nose jewel.*

wa-po′-śtaŋ, *n. Ih.* and *T.*, *a hat* or *cap; a bonnet.* See tapośtaŋ.

wa-po′-śtaŋ-gmi-gma, *n. T. a cap.*

wa-po′-śtaŋ-gmi-gme-la, *n T.*, *a cap.*

wa-pus′-a-śpaŋ, *adj. well cooked, well done, cooked dry. T.*, wapusyaśpaŋ.

wa-pus′-a-śpaŋ-yaŋ, *v. to cook thoroughly* — wapusaśpaŋwaya.

wa-pu′-ske-pa, *v. to filter:* also 1st pers. sing. of puskepa.

wa-pu′-spa, *v.* of puspa; *to glue, to seal*—wawapuspa: also 1st pers. sing. of puspa.

wa-pu′-sta-ka, *v.* of pustaka; *to stoop down*—wawapustaka: also 1st pers. sing. of pustaka.

wa-pus′-ya-śpaŋ, *adj. cooked thoroughly.*

wa-pus′-ya-śpaŋ-yaŋ, *v. T. to cook thoroughly.*

wa′-pu-ta-ka, *v.* of aputaka; *to touch with the hand, press upon*— wawaputaka.

wa-sab′-gle, *v. T. to place for a landmark.*

wa-sab′-gle-pi, *n. T.* (sapa *and* gle) *the mark* or *boundary*, as in playing ball, *i. q* ókape.

wa-sag′-kde, *v. n. Ih. to erect landmarks. T.*, wasabgle.

wa-sag′-kde-pi, *n. Ih. a landmark.*

wa-sam′-hde, *v. to place up something black for a sign* or *scarecrow*— wasamwahde.

wa-sam′-hde-ya, *adv. in the manner of a scarecrow.*

wa-sam′-ya, *v.* of samya; *to blacken*—wasamwaya.

wa-sam′-ya-hde-pi, *n. something placed for a scarecrow. T.*, wasabglepi.

wa-saŋ′-ka, *n. T. arrows before they are ready to be used.*

wa-saŋ′-yaŋ, *v.* of saŋyaŋ; *to whiten*—wasaŋwaya.

wa-saŋ′-yaŋ-hde-pi, *n. a scarecrow, any thing white put up to scare away birds.*

wa-sa′-pe-daŋ, *n. the black bear; i. q.* wahaŋksića. *T.*, mato sapa.

wa-sas′, *cont.* of wasaza.

wa-sas′-ki-ya, *v. T. to care for tenderly.*

wa-sas′-ye-la, *adv. T. mildly, gently.*

wa-sa′-za, *v. n. to be nervous, easily excited; to be convalescent*— wamasaza.

wa-sa′-ze-ća, *n. one who is easily made sick; one who is getting well; i. q.* wakahtakeća—wamasazeća.

wa-sda′-ya, *v.* of sdaya; *to oil, to grease*—wasdawaya.

wa-sdi′-pa, *v.* of sdipa; *to lick*—wawasdipa: also 1st pers. sing. of sdipa.

wa-sdo-ća, *v.* of sdoća; *to know.*

wa-sdon′-ya, *v.* of sdonya; *to know*—wasdonwaya, wasdonuŋyaŋpi. *T.*, waslolya.

wa-sdon′-ya-pi, *n.* *knowledge.* *T.*, waslolyapi.

wa-sdon′-ye, *n.* *one who knows.*

wa-sdon′-ye-ya, *v. a.* *to cause to know*—wasdonyewaya. *T.*, waslolyeya.

wa-se′, *n.* *red earth, vermilion:* Waseyuzapi, *Vermilion River.*

wa-se′-ki-çuŋ, *v.* *to paint red; to put on vermilion.*

wa-se′-yaŋ-ka, *v. n.* *to have a spot on one's face*, etc.—wasemayaŋka.

wa-se′-yaŋ-ka, *n.* *a pimple.*

wa-si′-ću, *n.* *the keel* or *bottom of a boat.*

wa-si′-ću-ha, *n.* *the bottom of a boat; the bottom of a bear's foot.*

wa-siŋ′-te, *n.* See walsiŋte.

wa-siŋ′-te-yu-ho-mni, *n.* *a steering oar.*

wa′-skam-ya, *v.* of askamya; *to make stick on,* as a plaster—waskamwaya. *T.*, waskabya

wa′-skam-ya-pi, *n.* *a pitch plaster.*

wa′-ska-pe, *n.* *sticking plaster.*

wa-sku′-ya, *n.* *Santee only.* *green corn boiled and afterwards shelled and dried; sweet corn.*

wa-sku′-ye-ća, *n.* *fruit* of all kinds. *T.*, watokeća.

wa-sna′, *n.* *lard, grease, tallow.*

wa-sna′-po-ȟdi, *n.* *pimples.*

wa-sna′-ta-sa-ka, *n.* *tallow; hardened grease.*

wa-so′, *v* *T.* *to cut a strip* or *string,* as from a hide.

wa-so′-so, *v.* *red.* *to cut in strips.*

wa-soŋ′, *v.* of soŋ; *to braid in strings,* as corn or hair—wawasoŋ: also 1st pers sing of soŋ.

wa-spaŋ′-la, *adv.* *T.* *slushy.*

wa-spaŋ′-ta-ha-za, *n.* *service berries.*

wa-spaŋ′-ta-he-ya, *n.* (wa spaŋ *and* heya) *small black bugs* or *grubs* which appear when *the snow melts off:* hence the name.

wa-stu′-ste-ya, *v.* *to weary* one —wastustewaya. *T.*, watukakiya. See waśtuśteya.

wa-su′, *n.* *hail.*

wa-su′-hu-la, *n.* *T.* *Iroquois,* used for necklaces.

wa-su′-ki-ya, *v. a.* *to hold sacred, to honor.* This is from su, *well,* and kiya, *to cause;* 2d, *to divine:* 3d, *to decree, make a decree.*—J. P. W.

wa-su′-toŋ, *v.* of sutoŋ; *to get ripe, ripens,* as grain or fruit.

wa-su′-toŋ-pi, *n.* *harvest.*

wa-su′-toŋ-wi, *n.* *the moon in which corn ripens,* answering to *August.*

wa-su′-ya, *v.* *T.* *to make a law; to judge, condemn.*

w a - ś'a g', *cont.* of waś'aka: waś'ag hiŋhda, *to become strong;* waś'agiçiya, *to strengthen one's self.*

w a - ś'a g' - y a, *v. a. to make strong*—waś'agwaya, waś'aguŋyaŋpi.

w a - ś'a' - k a, *adj. strong*—wamaś'aka, waniś'aka, wauŋś'akapi.

wa-ś'a'-ka, *adv. T. almost; nearly:* waś'aka ećoŋ tka, *he almost did it.*

w a - ś a' - k a - d a ŋ, *adj. cheap; easy,* opposed to teȟika.

w a - ś a' - k a - y e - d a ŋ, *adv. easily, cheaply.*

w a - ś e, *n. T., a woman's female friend;* corresponding to kola, *a man's male friend.*

w a - ś e' - k i - ć i - y a, *v. T. to have each other for special friends.*

w a - ś e' - y a, *v. T. to have for friend.*

w a - ś e' - ć a, *adj. rich,* especially in provisions—wamaśeća, waniśeća, wauŋśećapi.

w a - ś e' - ś a, *n. red paint, vermilion.* See wase.

w a - ś i', *v. n. Ih.* and *T. to do, to work: to command*—wawaśi: *i. q.* ȟtaṅi.

w a - ś i' - ć a - h o - w a - y a, *v. to cry out badly, to moan, to groan*—waśićahowamda.

w a - ś i - ć e - d a - k a, *v.* of śićedaka; *to dislike; one who dislikes*—waśićewadaka.

W a - ś i' - ć u ŋ, *n. Frenchmen,* in particular; *all white men,* in general. It is said that this word is nearly synonymous with "wakaŋ"—Wamaśićuŋ, Waniśićuŋ. See wićaśa, wićaśta, *and* ikćewićaśta. *T., a familiar spirit; some mysterious forces or beings which are supposed to communicate with men:* mitawaśićuŋ he omakiyaka, *my familiar spirit told me that; i. q.,* takuśkaŋśkaŋ.

W a - ś i' - ć u ŋ - ć i ŋ - ć a, *n. a half-breed.*

W a - ś i' - ć u ŋ - h o - k ś i - d a ŋ, *n. a French boy;* the common name for Canadians in the Dakota country; *any one who labors.*

W a - ś i' - ć u ŋ - ȟ i ŋ - ć a, *n. a Frenchman from France. T.,* Waśićuŋikćeka.

W a - ś i' - ć u ŋ - w a - k a ŋ, *n.* the name given to missionaries and ministers of the Gospel generally, including all who are not Indians. Same as wićaśtawakaŋ.

w a - ś i' - g l a, *v. T. i. q.* waśihda.

w a - ś i' - g l a - k e, *n T. one who gets angry easily.*

w a - ś i' - h d a, *v. to mourn for the dead, put on mourning; to paint one's self black,* as in mourning—waśinwahda, waśinuŋhdapi.

w a - ś i' - h d a, *n. mourning habiliments.*

w a - ś i' - h d a - k a, *n. one who gets angry at every thing* See śihda.

w a - ś i' - h d a - y a, *adv. in mourning.*

w a - ś i' - ȟ a ŋ, *v.* of śiȟaŋ; *to act wickedly*—waśiwaȟaŋ. *T.,* śikśiloȟaŋ.

w a - ś i' - k t e, *n. pulmonary consumption, any lingering disease.* See waśiŋkte.

wa-śiŋ', *n.* *fat not fried out, fat meat, pork.* *T.*, tallow.

wa-śiŋ-kte, *n.* *pulmonary consumption, a lingering disease.*

Wa-śiŋ'-wa-kpa, *n. p.* *the South Platte River.*

wa-śiŋ'-yaŋ-śe-ća, *n.* *a species of fish with red fins.*

wa-śi'-tki-hda, *v.* *to be angry.*

wa-śi'-tki-hda-ya, *v.* of śitkihdaya; *to distress* or *make angry; one who makes angry.*

wa-śkaŋ'-śkaŋ-yaŋ, *v.* of śkaŋ; *to cause to move; one who causes to move* or *live*—waśkaŋśkaŋwaya.

wa-śki'-ta, *v.* *T.* *to mark, cut, engrave; i. q.* bag̣o.

wa'-śna-he-ća, *n.* *soft snow, snow that falls in soft flakes.* See wahiśnaheća.

wa-śniś'-ya, *v.* *to cause to wither; one who causes to wither*—waśniśwaya.

wa-śni'-źa, *adj.* *withered.* See śniźa.

wa-śoŋ', *n.* See waśuŋ.

wa-śpaŋ'-ka, *n.* *cooked food.*

wa-śpaŋ'-yaŋ, *v.* of śpaŋyaŋ; *to cook,* as food—waśpaŋwaya.

wa-śpu', *v.* *T.* *i. q.* ḅaśpu.

wa-śpu'-śpu, *v.* *T.* *red.* *to cut off in small bits.*

wa-śte', *adj.* *good; pretty*—mawaśte, uŋwaśtepi. See ośte, waȟte, pi, etc.

wa-śte'-ća, *adj.* See waśtećaka.

wa-śte'-ća-ka, *adj.* *good, well disposed.*

wa-śte'-da, *v a.* *to esteem good, to love*—waśtewada, waśteuŋdapi, waśtećida. *T.*, waśtela.

wa-śte'-da-ka, *v. a.* *to love*—waśtewadaka. *T.*, waśtelaka.

wa-śte'-da-ka-pi, *n.* *love; one who is loved.*

wa-śte'-ȟiŋ-ća, *adj.* *very good.*

wa-śte'-i-ç̣i-da, *v. reflex.* of waśteda; *to love one's self, to be selfish; to be proud*—waśtemiç̣ida.

wa-śte'-ka, *adj.* *good—little good, doubtfully good.*

wa-śte'-ki-ći-da-pi, *v. recip.* *loving each other;* waśtekićidakapi, *loving one another.*

wa-śte'-ki-da, *v. pos.* of waśteda; *to love one's own*—waśtewakida.

wa-śte'-ki-da-ka, *v. pos.* of waśtedaka; *to love one's own*—waśtewakidaka.

wa-śte'-la-ka, *v. a.* *T.* *i. q.* waśtedaka.

wa-śte'-mna, *adj.* of waśte *and* omna; *sweet smelling, odoriferous.*

wa-śte'-mna-ya, *v. a.* *to perfume, to embalm*—waśtemnawaya, waśtemnamayaŋ.

wa-śte'-śte, *adj. red.* of waśte.

wa-śte'-śte-ya, *adv. red.* of waśteya.

wa-śte'-ya, *v. a.* *to make good*—waśtewaya.

wa-śte'-ya, *adv.* *well, in a good manner.*

wa-śte'-ya-ken, *adv.* *well.*

wa-śtu'-ća, *v.* *to thaw.* *T.*, waśtulya.

wa-śtun'-ya, *v.* of śtunya; *to thaw, cause to thaw,* as any thing frozen—waśtunwaya. *T.*, waśtulya.

wa-śtuŋ'-ka-la, *n. T. corn boiled and dried.*

wa-śtu'-śte-ya, *v.* of śtuśteya; *to weary out*—waśtuśtewaya.

wa-śuŋ', *n. the den* or *hole* of animals who live in water, as the beaver, etc.; *a bear's den.*

wa-śuŋ'-pa, *v.* of śuŋpa; *to moult* or *shed feathers.*

wa-śuŋ'-pa-wi, *n. the moon in which geese,* etc., *shed their feathers; July.*

wa-śu'-ta, *v. T. to shoot and miss.*

wa'-ta, *v.* of yuta; *to eat*—wawata, wayata, wauŋtapi: wota is the form used in the third person: also 1st pers. sing of yuta.

wa-ta', *n. old hard snow.* See wahiśnaheća, wateća, etc. *T.*, waġuġeća.

wa'-ta, *n. a canoe, a boat:* ćaŋ wata, *a dug-out;* wata taŋka, *a large boat;* peta wata, *a steam-boat;* wita wata, *a ship.*

wa-ta'-kpe, *v.* of takpe; *to attack, attempt to seize*—watawakpe; watakpe mda.

wa-tan', *adv.* (wata *and* en) *in the boat. T.*, wata el.

wa-tan'-o-pa, *v.* (wata en *and* opa) *to embark.*

wa-taŋ', *n. bait,* used in fishing, etc.

wa-taŋ'-iŋ-śni, *adj. lost.*

wa-taŋ'-ka, *n. one who is great* or *rich.*

wa-taŋ'-ka-da, *v. a. to esteem great*—wataŋkawada. *T.*, wataŋkala.

wa-taŋ'-ka-i-ç̣i-da, *v. reflex. to esteem oneself highly, to be proud*—wataŋkamiç̣ida. *T.*, wataŋkaiç̣ila

wa-taŋ'-ka-i-ç̣i-da-pi, *n. pride, haughtiness.*

wa'-taŋ-toŋ, *v. T. to be lucky* or *fortunate: i. q.* wapi.

wa'-taŋ-toŋ-śni-yaŋ, *adv. T. unluckily.*

wa-taŋ'-ya, *v. a. to use* a thing *for bait*—wataŋwaya.

wa-taŋ'-ye-ya, *v. T. to be skillful in shooting*—wataŋyewaya.

wa-ta'-pa, *v.* of tapá; *to pursue*—watawapa.

wa'-ta-pe-ta, *n. T. a steamboat: i. q* peta wata.

wa ta'-tpe, *v.* Same as watakpe.

wa-ta'-tpe-ya-pi, *n. attacking, an attack.*

wa-ta'-wa-ṭen-ya, *v.* of tawaṭenya; *to be willing to do* or *suffer*—watawaṭenwaya.

wa-ta'-wa-ya, *v.* of tawaya; *to own, possess*—watawawaya.

wa'-te-ća, *n. snow lately fallen.* See watá *and* waśnaheća.

wa-te'-ća, *n. a part of one's food:* wateća hduha, *he has food.*

wa-te'-ḣi-ka, *adj. difficult, hard,* as a man in his dealings; *dear,* as goods, etc.

wa-te′-ḣiŋ-da, *v.* of teḣiŋda; *to withhold what one has; not to give away; to be stingy: one who withholds*—watewaḣiŋda.

wa-te′-ḣiŋ-da-pi, *n. parsimony.*

wa-tem′-ki-ći-ći-ya, *v.* of temya; *to eat up for* one—watemwećićiya.

wa-tem′-ki-ya, *v. pos.* of watemya; *to eat up one's own; to eat up for* one—watemwakiya, watemmakiya.

wa-tem′-ya, *v.* of temya; *to eat all up, to devour: one who eats up*, as a wolf, etc.—watemwaya, watemuŋyaŋpi. *T.*, watebya.

wa-ten′, *v.* tokiŋ aġuyapi waten, *oh! that I had bread to eat.* See yuta *and* tokiŋ. *T.*, wata niŋ.

wa-te′-pa, *v. T. to wear off short:* worn out.

wa-te′-śdag-ki-toŋ, *v. n. to wear a fillet* or *garland around the head*—wateśdagweton.

wa-te′-śdag-toŋ, *v. n. to have* or *wear a garland* or *civic crown*—wateśdagwatoŋ.

wa-te′-śda-ke, *n. a fillet, a wreath, a civic crown, any thing wrapped around the head.*

wa-te′-te, *n. the rim* or *edge of a boat, the gunwale.* See matete.

wa-te′-zi, *n. the stomach of a bear.*

wa-te′-źi-kśi-źa, *n. the omentum fat; "fat that covereth the inwards."*

wa-tka′, *v.* of tka; *to scrape,* as hides—wawatka: also 1st pers. sing. of tka.

wa-to′, *n. grass, green grass, weeds.*

wa-tog′-hda, *adj. wild, hostile.* See watokda.

wa-to′-gla, *adj. T. wild, untrained, skittish: i. q.* śkehe.

wa-tog′-ya, *v. a. to take vengeance, to retaliate*—watogwaya.

wa-to′-ha, *n.* (wata *and* yuha) *a portage.*

Wa-to′-ḣta-ta, *n. p. the Otos: i. q.* Hotawa.

wa-to′-i-hu-ni, *v. n. to come to land with a boat.*

wa-to′-i-hu-ni, *n. a landing-place.*

wa-to′-ka, *n. the bow of a boat.* See watokapa *and* watopa.

wa-to′-ka-haŋ, *v. n. to stand in the bow of a boat: one who stands in the bow of a boat*—watokawahaŋ.

wa-to′-ka-pa, *n.* of tokapa; *the first-born; the birthright; the bow of a boat: one who sits in the bow of a boat*—watomakapa, watonikapa.

wa-to′-ka-pa-taŋ-haŋ, *adv. on* or *at the bow of a boat.*

wa-to′-kda, *adj. Ih. wild, hostile: i. q.* watoghda.

wa-to′-ke-ća, *n.* of tokeća; *a different kind of food from what one has been accustomed to. T. fruits; vegetables.*

wa-to′-ki-çoŋ, *v. abs.* of tokiçoŋ; *to take vengeance.*

wa-to′-ki-çoŋ, *n. an avenger.*

wa-to′-kśu, *v.* of tokśu; *to carry, transport*—watowakśu, watouŋkśupi.

wa-to'-kśu-pi, *n.* *transportation.*

wa-tom', *cont.* of watopa: watom mda.

wa-toŋ', *v.* of toŋ; *to have, possess*—wawatoŋ: 1st pers. sing. of toŋ.

wa-toŋ'-ka, *n.* *one who is rich.*

wa-to'-pa, *v.* *to paddle a canoe*—watowapa, watoaŋpapi: ite hekta watopa, *to row.* See watoka.

wa-to'-pa-pi, *n.* *rowing, paddling*

wa-to'-pa-pi-wi, *n.* *the moon in which the waters become navigable, April.* Same as magaokadawi.

wa-to'-pe-ki-ya, *v. a.* *to make paddle* or *row*—watopewakiya: śina watopekiya, *to sail.*

wa-to'-to-ya, *adv.* *grass-like, green.* See wato.

wa-to'-ya, *adv.* *greenly.*

wa-tpa', *n.* *a river, a stream, a creek; the bow of a boat,* compounded of wata *and* pa; *the outside and bottom of a canoe* or *boat: i q.* wakpa.

wa-tpa'-daŋ, *n.* *a brook, a rivulet.*

wa-tpi'-ća-hda, *adv.* *by the side of a stream.*

wa-tpo'-hna, *adv.* *on a stream, by a stream.*

wa-tpo'-ki-źu, *n.* *the junction of streams:* watpokiźu mdote, *the mouth of a river.*

wa-tpo'-ki-źu-ya, *v. a.* *to cause the junction of streams*—watpokiźuwaya.

wa-tpo'-pa, *adv.* *in a stream.* *T.*, wakpa opaya.

wa-tpo'-pta, *adv.* *across a stream: i. q.* wakpopta. *T.*, wakpa opta.

wa-tpu'-tpa, *n.* *dust: i. q.* wakpukpa. *T*, wakpukpa.

wa-tu'-ka, *adj.* *faint, weary, exhausted*—wamatuka.

wa-tu'-ka-ya, *v.* *to make tired, to weary.*

wa-tul'-ka, *n.* *T.* *sweepings; little bits.*

wa-tu'-śe-kśe-ća, *n.* *dust, dirt, sweepings; manure.* *T.*, watulka.

wa-tu'-tka, *n.* *small animals; little things.*

wa-tu'-tka-daŋ, *n.* *small animals.* *T.*, wamakaśkaŋ.

wa-tu'-tka-tka, *n.* *trifles.* See tutkatka.

wa-ṭe'-ća, *adj.* *gentle, mild, docile, tractable.* *T.*, wawaṭeća.

wa-ṭe'-ća-ka, *adj.* Same as waṭeća.

wa-ṭi'-yu-wi, *n.* *running vines.*

wa-ṭuŋg'-ya, *v. a.* *to try to prevent*—waṭuŋgwaya. Perhaps this word may also be used in the sense of "ṭuŋgya," *to suspect, have an indistinct knowledge of.* See iṭuŋkeća.

wa-u'-ka, *n.* *the skin of a bear.* *T.*, matoha.

wa-uŋ', *v.* of uŋ; *to be; to be well off*—wawauŋ: also 1st pers. sing. of uŋ.

wa-uŋ'-ća, *v.* of uŋća; *to mock, imitate*—wauŋwaća, wauŋuŋćapi.

wa-uŋ'-ća, *n.* *a mocker; a monkey.*

wa-uŋ'-ća-daŋ, *n.* *a mocker; a monkey.*

w a - u ŋ' - k a, *v.* *to live well; one who lives well*—wawauŋka.

w a - u ŋ' - u ŋ - k a, *n.* *one who wanders about, a vagabond.*

w a - u ŋ' - y a ŋ, *v.* *T.* *to offer sacrifice,* as money or other inanimate things: 2. *to lose*—wawauŋyaŋ.

w a u ŋ' - y a ŋ - p i, *n.* *T.* *a place for cutting up meat.*

w a' - w a - ć i ŋ, *v.* of awaćiŋ; *to think of*—wáwaćaŋmi.

w a - w a' - ć i ŋ - k t a - y u - z a, *or* w a - w a - ć i ŋ - e - k t a - y u - z a, *v. n.* *to be kind, forbearing, long-suffering*—wawaćiŋktamduza.

w a - w a' - g n a, *v.* *T.* of wagna; *to cut off,* as in shelling corn.

w a - w a' - ġ a - p a, *v.* *T.* *i. q.* wabaġapa.

w a - w a' - h a, *n.* *furs, peltries.*

w a - w a' - h a, *a.* *T.* *the "points" on a blanket:* this word originally meant *a buffalo robe,* and in trading with the whites a blanket which was valued at two robes was called wawaha noŋpa, etc., śina wawahe, *blanket points.*

w a - w a' - h i - y a ŋ s - k a - l a - k a, *adj.* *T.* *morose, cross.*

w a - w a' - h i - y a ŋ - z e - ć a, *n.* *T.* *a morose person.*

w a - w a' - ḣ p a - n i - y a ŋ, *v.* of waḣpaniyaŋ; *to make poor*—wawaḣpaniwaya.

w a - w a' - k i - p a - ź i ŋ, *v. n.* *to rebel against, oppose; to be a rebel*—wawawakipaźiŋ, wawauŋkipaźiŋpi.

w a - w a' - k i - p a - ź i ŋ - p i, *n.* *opposition, rebellion.*

w a - w a' - k i - p a - ź i ŋ - y a ŋ, *adv.* *rebelliously.*

w a - w a' - ķ e - z e, *n.* *T.* *a board on which to trim feathers.* See wabaķeze.

w a - w a' - k p a ŋ - ś n i, *adj.* *T.,* of kpaŋ, *fine, active, stirring,* as a man; *nervous, quick stepping,* as a horse; *fleet,* as a dog: wawamakpaŋ śni. This word appears to be and is in the negative form only.—T. L. R.

w a - w a' - m n a - d a, *v.* of wamnada; *to respect, honor, have a high opinion of; one who respects*—wawamnawada.

w a - w a' - m n a - d a - ś n i, *n.* *one who respects nothing.*

w a - w a' - n i - ć a, *n.* *one who is nothing, an insignificant fellow.*

w a - w a' - n i - ć e - ć a, *v.* *there is nothing.*

w a - w a' - t e - p a, *v.* *T.* *to wear off to a stump.*

w a - w a ŋ' - y a g, *cont.* of wawaŋyaka; wawaŋyag mde kta, *I will go to see.*

w a - w a ŋ' - y a - k a, *v.* of waŋyaka; *to look on, see*—wawaŋmdaka, wawaŋdaka, wawaŋuŋyakapi.

w a - w a ŋ' - y a - k e, *n.* *a looker-on.*

w a - w a' - p i - d a - k i - y a, *v.* of pidakiya; *to make glad; one who makes glad*—wawapidawakiya.

w a - w a' - ś i - ć u ŋ - k e, *n.* *T.* *one who imitates* or *tries to be like a white man.*

wa-wa'-śi-ćuŋ-yaŋ, *adv.* of waśićuŋ; *like a white man;* said of a good dog that finds much game.

wa-wa'-śi-ćuŋ-yaŋ-ka, *n. one who finds much,* as game.

wa-wa'-śi-tki-hda, *v. n. to be angry, vexed; one who is angry.* See śitkihda.

wa-wa'-śi-tki-hda-ya, *v.* of śitkihdaya; *to make angry*—wawaśitkihdawaya.

wa-wa'-ṭe-ća, *adj T. gentle; mild.*

wa-wa'-ṭe-ća-ka, *n. T. one who is kind,* as a gentle horse.

wa-wa'-ṭe-ća, *adv. nearly, almost, i. q.* iśnikaeś: wawaṭeća ećamoŋ kta, *I had almost done it. T.,* iśnikaleś.

wa-wa'-yu-śna, *v.* of wayuśna; *to sacrifice; one who sacrifices, a priest*—wawamduśna. *T.,* wauŋyaŋ *and* wayuḣtata

wa-wi'-ćaḣ-ya, *v.* of ićaḣya; *to cause to grow, to form; to create*—wawićaḣwaya.

Wa-wi'-ćaḣ-ye, *n. a maker, a former; the Creator.*

wa'-wi-ćaŋ-ksi, *v. n.* of ćaŋksi; *to be cross, ill-natured*—wáwićaŋwaksi.

wa'-wi-ćaŋ-ksi-ka, *n. a wrangler, a contentious person T.,* wawahiyaŋzeća.

wa'-wi-ćaŋ-ksi-ya, *adv. crossly, roughly. T.,* wawahiyaŋsyakel.

wa-wi'-ći-ḣa-ḣa, *n. one who commits adultery; one who sins against others and makes light of it.*

wa-wi'-ći-ḣa-ḣa-pi, *n. a laughing-stock; adultery:* wawićiḣaḣapi ećanoŋ kte śni, *thou shalt not commit adultery: making light of sin.*

wa-wi'-ći-ya, *n.* of ićiya; *an advocate.*

wa-wi'-da-ke, *n.* of idake; *a master, a king, a ruler; a kingdom.* See wowidake.

wa-wi'-haŋg-ya, *v.* of ihaŋgya; *to destroy*—wawihaŋgwaya.

wa-wi'-haŋg-ye, *n. a destroyer.*

wa-wi'-ḣa, *v.* of iḣa; *to laugh at*—wawiwaḣa.

wa-wi'-ḣa-ḣa, *v. red.* of wawiḣa.

wa-wi'-ḣa-ka, *n. one who makes sport, a jester.*

wa-wi'-ḣa-pi, *n. jesting, making sport.*

wa-wi'-ḣa-ya, *v. a. to cause to laugh at*—wawiḣawaya.

wa-wi'-na-ḣni, *v.* of inaḣni; *to be in haste.*

wa-wi'-na-ḣni-yaŋ, *v. to hasten, cause to hurry*—wawinaḣniwaya.

wa-wi'-na-ki-ḣni, *v. to be in haste, to do beforehand*—wawinawakiḣni.

wa-wi'-na-ki-ḣni-ka, *n. one who is in haste.*

wa-wi'-ni-haŋ, *adj.* of inihaŋ; *fearful, afraid; inspiring fear:* wawinihaŋ maŋka.

wa-wi'-ni-haŋ-yaŋ, *n. to make afraid*—wawinihaŋwaya.

wa-wi'-ni-haŋ-yaŋ, *adv. fearfully.*

wa-wi'-pi-da, *v* of ipida; *not to give, to refuse*—wawipiwada.

wa-wi'-pi-i-ç̣i-da, *v. reflex.* of wawipida; *to think more of one's self than of any one else,* said of a woman who is unwilling to marry—wawipimiç̣ida.

wa-wi'-śte-ća, *adj.* *modest, ashamed.* See wiśteća, the better form.

wa-wi'-śten-ya, *v.* *to make ashamed*—wawiśtenwaya.

wa-wi'-śten-ya, *adv.* *ashamedly; bashfully.*

wa-wi'-tko-ya, *v.* of witkoya; *to make drunk*—wawitkowaya.

wa-wi'-toŋ-pa, *v.* of itoŋpa; *to be careful*—wawitoŋwapa.

wa-wi'-toŋ-pa-pi, *n.* *carefulness.*

wa-wi'-toŋ-pa-pi-śni, *n.* *carelessness.*

wa-wi'-waŋ-ġa, *v.* of iwaŋġa; *to inquire, ask questions.* *T.*, wawiyuŋġa.

wa-wi'-waŋ-ġa-pi, *n.* *inquiring.*

wa-wi'-waŋ ḣ, *cont.* of wawiwaŋġa: wawiwaŋḣ mda, *I go to inquire.* *T.*, wawiyuŋḣ.

wa-wi'-waŋ ḣ-tu-ken, *adv.* *in an inquiring manner.*

wa-wi'-waŋ ḣ-ya, *adv.* *inquiringly.*

wa-wi'-ya-ç̣iŋ, *v.* of iyaćiŋ; *to liken to, to use parables*—wawimdaćiŋ.

wa-wi'-ya-ćiŋ-yaŋ, *adv.* *figuratively.*

wa-wi'-ya-ḣtag-i-a, *v.* *to find fault*—wawiyaḣtagiwaa. *T.*, wayaḣtagia.

wa-wi'-ya-ḣta-ka, *v.* of yaḣtaka; *to bite.*

wa-wi'-ya-ka-pa, *v. T.* *to overcome; to beat in an argument.*

wa-wi'-ya-ka-pe-ya, *v.* *T.* *to exceed, go beyond:* wawiyakapeiç̣iya, *to exceed one's self, to be intemperate.*

wa-wi'-ya-pe, *v.* of iyape; *to lie in wait*—wawiyawape.

wa-wi'-ya-yu-ḣa, *n.* *one who follows.*

wa-wi'-ya-yuḣ-ya, *adv.* *T.* *following.*

wa-wi'-ya-pe, *n.* *an ambush.*

wa-wi'-ya-yuḣ, *cont.* *T.* *following,* as a colt its mother.

wa-wi'-ye-ki-ya, *v.* of iyekiya; *to recognize*—wawiyewakiya.

wa-wi'-ye-ya, *v.* of iyeya; *to find*—wawiyewaya.

wa-wi'-ye-ye-ća, *n.* *one that finds much,* as a good dog.

wa-wi'-yo-hi, *v.* of iyohi; *to reach to, extend to, arrive at; to be sufficient for*—wawiyowahi.

wa-wi'-yo-hi-ya, *v. a.* *to cause to reach to*—wawiyohiwaya.

wa-wi'-yo-hi-ya, *adv.* *reaching to, arriving at.*

wa-wi'-yo-ki-pi, *v.* of iyokipi; *to be pleased with*—wawiyomakipi.

wa-wi'-yo-ki-pi-ya, *adv.* *joyfully, gladly, pleasingly.*

wa-wi'-yo-ki-śi-ća, *v.* of iyokiśića; *to be sad*—wawiyomakiśića.

wa-wi'-yo-ki-śin, *cont.* of wawiyokiśića; *sad:* wawiyokiśin wauŋ, *I am sad.*

wa-wi'-yo-ki-śin-ya, *v.* of iyokiśinya; *to make sad*—wawiyokiśinwaya.

wa-wi'-yo-ki-śin-ya, *adv. sadly, sorrowfully.*

wa-wi'-yo-pa-śta-ka, *v.* of iyopaśtaka; *to encourage; urge on.*

wa-wi'-yo-pe-ki-ya, *v.* of iyopekiya; *to sell; to reprove*—wawiyopewakiya.

wa-wi'-yo-pe-ya, *v.* of iyopeya; *to reprove*—wawiyopewaya.

wa-wi'-yu-ka-ki-źa, *v.* of yukakiźa; *to make suffer* wawimdukakiźa.

wa-wi'-yu-kćaŋ, *v.* of iyukćaŋ; *to judge, to examine*—wawimdukćaŋ.

wa-wi'-yu-kćaŋ-ka, *n. one who examines and judges.*

wa-wi'-yuŋ-ġa, *v. T. i. q.* wawiwaŋġa.

wa-wi'-yuŋ-ġa-pi, *n. T. inquiring.*

wa-wi'-yuŋḣ, *cont. T.*

wa-wi'-yuŋḣ-tu-kel, *adv. T. inquiringly.*

wa-wi'-yu-pi-ya, *adv. well, expertly.*

wa-wi'-yu-taŋ-yaŋ, *v.* of iyutaŋyaŋ; *to tempt:* taku wawiyutaŋyaŋ uŋ kiŋ, *the tempter; temptation.*

wa-wi'-yu-taŋ-ye, *n. one who tempts.*

wa-wo'-će-ka, *v. T. i. q.* wabo-ćeka

wa-wo'-ḣiŋ-yaŋ, *v.* of oḣiŋyaŋ; *to be dissatisfied with*—wawowaḣiŋyaŋ.

wa-wo'-ki-ća-ḣni-ġa, *adj. of quick understanding.*

wa-wo'-ki-hi, *v.* of okihi; *to be able*—wawowakihi

wa-wo'-ki-hi-ka, *n. one who is able:* wićaśta wawokihika, *a man of ability.*

wa-wo'-ki-hi-ya, *v. to make able*—wawokihiwaya.

wa-wo'-ki-ya, *v.* of ókiya; *to help; to be with, to accompany*—wawowakiya.

wa-wo'-ki-ye, *n. one who helps; help.* See ookiye.

wa-woŋ'-spe-ki-ya. See waoŋspekiya.

wa-wo'-paŋ, *v. T. to pound fine.*

wa-wo'-sla-ta, *n. T. hair-pipe,* used for ornament.

wa-wo'-śte-hda, *v.* of ośtehda; *to call bad names; one who speaks evil of*—wawośtewahda.

wa-wo'-ya-ka, *v.* of oyaka; *to relate; one who relates, a narrator*—wawomdaka.

wa-wo'-yu-spa, *v. T.* of oyuspa; *to seize; to arrest,* as a prisoner.

wa-wo'-yu-spa, *n. T. a policeman.*

wa-wo'-yu-spa-pi, *n. T. making arrests.*

wa-wo'-źi, *v.* of aźiźi; *to tell secretly:* wawowaźi.

wa-ya'-a-taŋ-iŋ, *v.* of yaataŋiŋ; *to make manifest, proclaim*—wamdaataŋiŋ.

wa-ya'-a-śda, *v.* of yaaśda; *to graze.*

wa-ya'-a-śda-ya, *adv.* of yaaśdaya; *explaining, unfolding.*

wa-ya'-a-śka-daŋ, *v.* of yaaśkadaŋ; *to speak of as near*—wamdáaśkadaŋ.

wa-ya'-ba-za, *v.* of yabaza; *to bite,* as dogs do in playing with one another. *T.*, wayawaza.

wa-ya'-ba-źa, *v.* of yabaźa; *to bite* or *gnaw at,* as dogs. *T.*, wayawaźa.

wa-ya'-ćaŋ-ćaŋ, *v.* of yaćaŋćaŋ; *to make shake with the mouth*—wamdaćaŋćaŋ.

wa-ya'-će-kće-ka, *v.* of yaćekćeka; *to make stagger by biting,* etc.—wamdaćekćeka.

wa-ya'-će-ya, *v.* of yaćeya; *to make cry by scolding,* etc.—wamdaćeya

wa-ya'-ći-ḳa-daŋ, *v.* See wayaćistiŋna.

wa-ya'-ćis-ći-la, *v.* *T.* *to underrate.*

wa-ya'-ći-stiŋ-na, *v.* of yaćistiŋna; *to speak of as small, to underrate*—wamdaćistiŋna. *T.*, wayaćisćila.

wa-ya'-ćo, *v.* of yaćo; *to judge, condemn*—wamdaćo. *Ih.* and *T.*, wayasu.—J. O. D.

wa-ya'-ćo, *n.* *a judge: i. q.* wayasu.

wa-ya'-ćo-ćo, *v.* of yaćoćo; *to make soft by biting, to chew*—wamdaćoćo.

wa-ya'-ćo-ćo-ka, *n.* *one who always gives his opinion.*

wa-ya'-ćo-ya, *adv.* *in the manner of judging.*

wa-ya'-ćo-za, *v.* of yaćoza; *to make warm by biting,* etc.—wamdaćoza.

wa-ya'-e-će-tu, *v.* of yaećetu; *to accomplish* or *bring to pass by speaking*—wamdaećetu.

wa-ya'-gmi-yaŋ, *v.* *T.* *i. q.* wayamima.

wa-ya'-ġa, *v* of yaġa; *to bite off,* as husks.

wa-ya'-ġa-pa, *v.* of yaġapa; *to bite off the skin* or *husk; one who bites,* as a horse.

wa-ya'-ha-ha-ke, *n.* *one who causes to waver by biting.*

wa-ya'-ha-ha-ye-daŋ, *v.* of yahahayedaŋ; *to make waver* or *to render unstable by biting*—wamdahahayedaŋ.

wa-ya'-ha-i-ye-ya, *v.* *to throw down by biting,* as one horse does another.

wa-ya'-hba, *v.* of yahba; *to shell off with the teeth*—wamdahba

wa-ya'-hda, *n.* of yahda; *to draw out* or *uncoil,* as a dog does when eating the fat from entrails.

wa-ya'-hda-he-ya, *adv.* of yahdaheya; *continuously, connectedly:* wayahdaheya ia.

wa-ya'-hdo-ka, *v.* of yahdoka: *to put out of joint with the teeth.*

wa-ya'-hiŋ-ta, *v.* of yahiŋta; *to brush away with the mouth: one who names every point in his speech and thus brushes it away*—wamdahiŋta.

w a - y a′ - h m i - h m a, *v.* of yahmihma; *to make roll with the mouth*—wamdahmihma. *T.*, wayagmigma See wayanminma.

w a - y a′ - h m i - y a ŋ - y a ŋ, *v. to make round with the mouth*—wamdahmiyaŋyaŋ.

w a - y a′ - h n a - ś k i ŋ - y a ŋ, *v. to make crazy by talking to*—wamdahnaśkiŋyaŋ. *T.*, wayagnaśkiŋyaŋ.

w a - y a′ - h n a - y a ŋ, *v. to miss with the mouth, to deceive, to tell a falsehood*—wamdahnayaŋ. *T.*, wayagnayaŋ.

w a - y a′ - h n u - n i, *v. to make wander in mind by talking to, to confuse*—wamdahnuni.

w a - y a′ - h o - h o, *v.* of yahoho; *to make loose by biting*—wamdahoho.

w a - y a′ - h o - m n i, *v.* of yahomni; *to turn* one *around by talking, persuade* one *to change his opinions*—wamdahomni.

w a - y a′ - h o - t a, *n. a species of wild rye; tares: oats.*

w a - y a′ - h o - t o ŋ, *v.* of yahotoŋ; *to make cry out by biting*—wamdahotoŋ.

w a - y a′ - h u - h u - z a, *v.* of yahuhuza; *to shake with the mouth*—wamdahuhuza. *T.*, wayahuŋhuŋza.

w a - y a′ - h u ŋ - h u ŋ - z a, *v. T. to shake with the mouth.*

w a - y a′ - h u - t e - d a ŋ, *v. to bite off short.*

w a - y a′ - ḣ a - p a, *v.* of yaḣapa; *to scare up by talking,* as game—wamdaḣapa.

w a - y a′ - ḣ b a, *v.* of yaḣba; *to make sleepy by talking to*—wamdaḣba.

w a - y a′ - ḣ ć i, *v.* of yaḣći; *to bite out a piece*—wamdaḣći.

w a - y a′ - ḣ d a, *v.* of yaḣda; *to rattle with the mouth.*

w a - y a′ - ḣ d a - t a, *v.* of yaḣdata; *to scratch with the teeth.*

w a - y a′ - ḣ d e - ć a, *v.* of yaḣdeća; *to tear with the teeth*—wamdaḣdeća.

w a - y a′ - ḣ d o - k a, *v.* of yaḣdoka; *to bite a hole in*—wamdaḣdoka.

w a - y a′ - ḣ e - p a, *v.* of yaḣepa; *to drink all up*—wamdaḣepa.

w a - y a′ - ḣ e - y a - t a, *v.* of yaḣeyata; *to put* one *back by talking; one who disparages others by what he says*—wamdaḣeyata.

w a - y a′ - ḣ i - ć a, *v.* of yaḣića; *to waken up, cause* one *to awaken by speaking to* him—wamdaḣića.

w a - y a′ - ḣ i - y a - y a, *v.* of yaḣiyaya; *to be awkward in doing any thing with the mouth,* as in singing, making a bullet round, etc.—wamdaḣiyaya.

w a - y a′ - ḣ p a, *v.* of yaḣpa; *to throw down with the mouth*—wamdaḣpa.

w a - y a′ - ḣ p u, *v.* of yaḣpu; *to bite off* any thing that had been *glued on*—wamdaḣpu.

w a - y a′ - ḣ t a - k a, *v.* of yaḣtaka; *to bite; to abuse by speaking evil of: one that bites,* as a dog—wamdaḣtaka.

w a - y a′ - ḣ u, *v.* of yaḣu; *to peel off with the teeth*—wamdaḣu.

w a - y a′ - ḣ u - ġ a, *v.* of yaḣuġa; *to crush with the teeth*—wamdaḣuġa.

wa-ya'-i-de, *v.* of yaide; *to blow and make blaze*—wamdaide. *T.*, waile.

wa-ya'-i-ḣa, *v.* of yaiḣa; *to make laugh by talking; one who jests and makes others laugh.*

wa-ya'-i-na-ḣni, *v.* *to hasten, make hurry*—wamdainaḣni.

wa-ya'-i-ni-na, *v.* of yainina; *to put to silence by speaking*—wamdainina.

wa-ya'-i-nin-ya, *adv.* *putting to silence:* wayaininya ia.

wa-ya'-i-śte-ća, *v.* *to make ashamed by talking to.*

wa-ya'-i-yo-ka, *v.* of yaiyoka; *to set aside by counter argument; one who in argument refutes what has been said by others.* *T.*, wawiyakapa

wa-ya'-i-yo-wa, *v.* of yaiyowa; *to make yawn by talking.* *T.*, iyoyaya.

wa-ya'-i-yo-wa-za, *v.* *to speak of as pertaining to.*

wa-ya'-ka, *n.* *a captive taken in war, a prisoner:* wayaka ahdi, *to bring home a captive.*

wa-ya'-ka-ka, *v.* of yakaka; *to champ*, as a horse. *T.*, wayatata.

wa-ya'-ka-pa, *v.* of yakapa; *to catch in the mouth*—wamdakapa.

wa-ya'-ka-tiŋ, *v.* *to straighten with the mouth.*

wa-ya'-ka-wa, *v.* of yakawa; *to open with the mouth.*

wa-ya'-kća, *v.* of yakća; *to untie with the mouth, to disentangle*—wamdakća.

wa-ya'-ke-za, *v.* *to make smooth with the mouth.*

wa-ya'-kiŋ-za, *v.* *to grit* or *grind the teeth*, as a cow. *T.*, higlakiŋza.

wa-ya'-ko-ke-daŋ, *v.* *to make active by talking to*—wamdakokedaŋ.

wa-ya'-ko-ko-ka, *v.* *to make the teeth rattle*—wamdakokoka.

wa-ya'-koŋ-tkoŋ-ta, *v* *to indent* or *notch with the teeth*—wamdakoŋtkoŋta.

wa-ya'-ko-ya-ḣaŋ-na, *v.* *to hasten* one *by speaking to* him. *T.*, wayainaḣniya.

wa-ya'-kpaŋ, *v.* of yakpaŋ; *to masticate*—wamdakpaŋ.

wa-ya'-kpi, *v.* of yakpi; *to crack with the teeth*, as a louse—wamdakpi.

wa-ya'-ksa, *v.* of yaksa; *to bite off*—wamdaksa.

wa-ya'-ksa-ksa, *v.* *red.* of wayaksa.

wa-ya'-ksa-pa, *v.* of yaksapa; *to make wise by instructing, to teach*—wamdaksapa.

wa-ya'-kśi-źa, *v.* of yakśiźa; *to double up with the teeth*—wamdakśiźa.

wa-ya'-ktaŋ, *v.* of yaktaŋ; *to bend with the teeth*—wamdaktaŋ.

wa-ya'-ktaŋ-yaŋ, *adv.* *bending with the teeth.*

waya'-ku-ka, *v.* of yakuka; *to bite to pieces*—wamdakuka.

wa-ya'-ķe-ġa, *v.* of yaķeġa; *to gnaw*—wamdaķeġa.

w a - y a'- ḳ e - z a, *v.* of yaḳeza; *to bite smooth*—wamdaḳeza.

w a - y a'- ḳ o - ġ a, *v.* of yaḳoġa; *to gnaw*—wamdaḳoġa.

w a - y a'- m d a - s k a, *v.* of yamdaska; *to make flat with the mouth*—wamdamdaska.

w a - y a'- m d a - y a, *v.* of yamdaya; *to make level with the mouth*—wamdamdaya.

w a - y a'- m d a - z a, *v.* of yamdaza; *to bite* or *tear open with the teeth*—wamdamdaza.

w a - y a'- m d e - ć a, *v.* of yamdeća; *to break, crush,* or *tear in pieces with the teeth*—wamdamdeća.

w a - y a'- m d e - z a, *v.* of yamdeza; *to cheer up by speaking*—wamdamdeza.

w a - y a'- m d u, *v.* of yamdu; *to chew fine*—wamdamdu.

w a - y a'- m d u - m d u, *v. red.* of wayamdu.

w a - y a'- m i - m a, *v.* of yamima; *to make round in the mouth*—wamdamima. *T*, wayagmiyaŋ.

w a - y a'- m n a, *v.* of yamna; *to rip with the teeth; to gain by talking*—wamdamna.

w a - y a'- m n u - ġ a, *v. to grind,* as in eating parched corn—wamdamnuġa.

w a - y a'- m n u - m n u - ġ a, *v. red.* of wayamnuġa; *to gnaw,* as a dog does bone. See yamnumnuġa.

w a - y a'- n m i - n m a, *v.* of yanminma; *to roll with the mouth*—wamdanminma. See wayahmihma.

w a - y a'- o - ć i - p t e - ć a, *v.* of yaoćipteća; *to lessen; to count less, to depreciate*—wamdaoćipteća.

w a - y a'- o - ć i - p t e n, *cont.* of wayaoćipteća.

w a - y a'- o - ć i - p t e n - y a, *adv. counting less.*

w a - y a'- o - ć i - p t e - t u, *adv. in a lessening manner.*

w a - y a'- o - ć i - t p a - n i, *v. to speak of as unequal; to make unequal with the mouth. T.*, wayáokpaniyaŋ.

w a - y a'- o - ġ a ŋ, *v. to bite a hole in. T.*, yaóħloka.

w a - y a'- o - h d a - p ś i ŋ - y a ŋ, *v.* of yaohdapśiŋyaŋ; *to root over,* as a hog does any thing: wayaohdapśiŋyaŋ iyeya. *T.*, wayáptaŋ iyeya.

w a - y a'- o - ħ a ŋ - k o, *v.* of yaoħaŋko; *to make quick by speaking to*—wamdaoħaŋko.

w a - y a'- o - k s a, *v.* of yaoksa; *to bite through*—wamdaoksa.

w a - y a'- o - k t a ŋ, *v.* of yaoktaŋ; *to bend into with the teeth*—wamdaoktaŋ.

w a - y a'- o - n i - h a ŋ, *v.* of yaonihaŋ; *to praise, to honor*—wamdaonihaŋ.

w a - y a'- o - n i - h a ŋ - y a ŋ, *adv. praising.*

w a - y a'- o - p t e l - y a, *v. T. to make less with the mouth.*

w a - y a'- o - t a ŋ, *v. to exhort*—wamdaotaŋ. *T.*, also *to praise; i. q.* yaonihaŋ.

w a - y a'- o - t a ŋ - i ŋ, *v.* of yaotaŋiŋ; *to make manifest; one who makes manifest*—wamdaotaŋiŋ.

w a - y a'- p a, *v.* of yapa; *to hold in the mouth*—wamdapa.

wa-ya'-pa-ko, *v.* of yapako; *to bend with the teeth*—wamdapako. *T.* wayaktaŋ.

wa-ya'-pe-mni, *v.* of yapemni; *to twist with the teeth*—wamdapemni.

wa-ya'-pe-sto, *v.* of yapesto; *to bite to a point*—wamdapesto.

wa-ya'-pi, *v.* See wayapika.

wa-ya'-pi-ka, *v. n.* *to be fluent, to speak a language well, to be eloquent*—wamdapika, wadapika.

wa-ya'-pi-ya, *adv.* *fluently.*

wa-ya'-po-pa, *v.* of yapopa; *to make burst by biting*—wamdapopa.

wa-ya'-po-ta, *v.* of yapota; *to tear in pieces with the mouth, to rend; one who tears in pieces with the teeth,* as a dog—wamdapota.

wa-ya'-psa-ka, *v.* of yapsaka; *to bite off,* as cords—wamdapsaka.

wa-ya'-psi-ća, *v.* of yapsića; *to make hop by biting*—wamdapsića.

wa-ya'-psoŋ, *v.* of yapsoŋ; *to spill with the mouth*—wamdapsoŋ.

wa-ya'-psuŋ, *v.* Same as wayapsoŋ.

wa-ya'-pśuŋ, *v.* of yapśuŋ; *to shed,* as a horse his teeth.

wa-ya'-ptaŋ-yaŋ, *v.* of yaptaŋyaŋ; *to turn over with the mouth, roll over*—wamdaptaŋyaŋ. *T., to root over,* as a hog the ground.

wa-ya'-pte-će-daŋ, *v.* of yaptećedaŋ; *to bite off short.*

wa-ya'-ptu-źa, *v.* of yaptuźa; *to split,* as a tooth—wamdaptuźa.

wa-ya'-sba, *v.* *to pick off with the teeth*—wamdasba.

wa-ya'-sde-ća, *v.* of yasdeća; *to split with the teeth.*

wa-ya'-sdo-haŋ, *v.* of yasdohaŋ; *to drag along with the mouth,* as a wolf or other animal does his prey.

wa-ya'-sdu-ta, *v.* *to pull out with the teeth,* as a dog does.

wa-ya'-ska-pa, *v.* ho wayaskapa, said of the creaking noise made by fish when they come to the top of the water. *T., to make a noise, as in kissing; to kiss.* See howaśkapa.

wa-ya'-ske-pa, *v.* of yaskepa; *to drink all out.*

wa-ya'-ski-ća, *v.* of yaskića; *to press on with the mouth*—wamdaskića.

wa-ya'-ski-ta, *v.* *to press on with the mouth, make tight*—wamdaskita.

wa-ya'-śku, *v.* of yaska; *to peel off with the teeth, bite off the skin* or *rind*—wamdasku.

wa-ya'-sku-sku, *v. red.* of wayasku; *to bite off the rind* or *hull*—wamdaskusku.

wa-ya'-sma-ka, *v.* of yasmaka; *to bite and make indentations.*

wa-ya'-smiŋ, *v.* of yasmiŋ; *to gnaw off,* as dogs do.

wa-ya'-smiŋ-yaŋ-yaŋ, *v.* *to be eaten off smooth.*

wa-ya'-sna, *v.* of yasna; *to make ring with the mouth; to ravel*—wamdasna.

wa-ya'-sni, *v.* *to make go out by talking, talk until the fire goes out.*

wa-ya'-so-ta, *v.* of yasota; *to eat all up*, as food; *to use up*, as words—wamdasota.

wa-ya'-so-te-ća, *n.* *one who eats up much.*

wa-ya'-spa-ya, *v.* of yaspaya; *to wet with the mouth*—wamdaspaya.

wa-ya'-staŋ-ka, *v.* of yastaŋka; *to moisten with the mouth.*

wa-ya'-sto, *v.* of yasto; *to lick down*, as one cow does the hair of another.

wa-ya'-su, *v.* of yasu; *to make good with the mouth, by speaking*, etc.—wamdasu. *T.*, *to judge; pronounce sentence; to condemn.*

wa-ya'-su, *n.* *T.* and *Ih.* *a judge.*

wa-ya'-su-ta, *v.* of yasuta; *to make firm with the mouth, to establish* or *decree*—wamdasuta.

wa-ya'-śa-pa, *v.* of yaśapa; *to soil with the mouth.*

wa-ya'-śda, *v.* of yaśda; *to graze off, make bare*, as cattle do by grazing.

wa-ya'-śdo-ka, *v.* of yaśdoka; *to bite out.*

wa-ya'-śi-ća, *v.* of yaśića; *to speak evil of, to curse*—wamdaśića, wauŋyaśićapi.

wa-ya'-śi-hda, *v.* of yaśihda; *to make angry by talking to.*

wa-ya'-śi-ḣtiŋ, *v.* of yaśiḣtiŋ; *to enfeeble by biting* or *talking to*—wamdaśiḣtiŋ. *T.*, *to spoil* or *make bad with the mouth; to talk badly about; to find fault with.*

wa-ya'-śi-ḣtiŋ-ka, *n.* *T.* *one who always finds fault.*

wa-ya'-śi-pa, *v.* of yaśipa; *to bite off close.*

wa-ya'-śka, *v.* of yaśka; *to untie with the mouth.*

wa-ya'-śkaŋ-śkaŋ, *v.* of yaśkaŋśkaŋ; *to cause to move with the mouth.*

wa-ya'-śki-ća, *v.* of yaśkića; *to chew and press with the mouth*, as in chewing tobacco—wamdaśkića.

wa-ya'-śki-śka, *v.* of yaśkiśka; *to bite and make rough; to get into difficulty by talking; to make difficulty by talking; to misrepresent*—wamdaśkiśka.

wa-ya'-śko-kpa, *v.* of yaśkokpa; *to gnaw out a hollow place*—wamdaśkokpa.

wa-ya'-śko-pa, *v.* of yaśkopa; *to make warp* or *twist with the mouth.*

wa-ya'-śko-tpa, *v.* Same as wayaśkokpa.

wa-ya'-śna, *v.* of yaśna; *to miss* or *let fall from the mouth; to make mistakes in talking; to stammer*—wamdaśna.

wa-ya'-śpa, *v.* of yaśpa; *to bite off pieces*—wamdaśpa.

wa-ya'-śpi, *v.* of yaśpi; *to pick off* fruit, as birds do.

wa-ya'-śpu, *v.* of yaśpu; *to pick off with the mouth* something that has been stuck on.

wa-ya'-śpu-ya, *v.* of yaśpuya; *to tickle by biting*, as lice or fleas.

wa'-ya-śtaŋ, *v.* of ayaśtaŋ; *to complete with the mouth*, as eating or speaking—wámdaśtaŋ.

wa-ya'-śu-źa, *v.* of yaśuźa; *to crush with the mouth.*

wa-ya'-ta, *v.* 2d pers. sing. of wota.

wa-ya'-ta, *v.* of wota; *to chew*—wamdata.

wa-ya'-ta-ta, *v.* *T.* *to champ*, as a horse.

wa-ya'-ta-ku-ni-śni, *v.* of yatakuniśni; *to destroy with the mouth*—wamdatakuniśni

wa-ya'-taŋ, *n.* *a blister, blister salve.*

wa-ya'-taŋ-iŋ, *v.* of yataŋiŋ; *to make manifest*—wamdataŋiŋ.

wa-ya'-taŋ-ka, *v.* of yataŋka; *to speak of as large*—wamdataŋka.

wa-ya'-te-haŋ, *v.* *to speak of as far.*

wa-ya'-te-haŋ-haŋ, *v.* *to speak slowly*—wamdatehaŋhaŋ.

wa-ya'-te-ḣi-ka, *v.* of yateḣika; *to speak of as difficult*—wamdateḣika.

wa-ya'-te-kon-za, *v.* (wayata *and* koŋza) *to chew the cud*, as cows.

wa-ya'-te-pa, *v.* of yatepa; *to wear off the teeth*—wamdatepa.

wa-ya'-ti-taŋ, *v.* of yatitaŋ; *to pull with the teeth*—wamdatitaŋ.

wa-ya'-tkaŋ, *v.* of yatkaŋ; *to drink*—wamdatkaŋ, wauŋyatkaŋpi.

wa-ya'-tke-ki-ya, *v. a.* *to cause to drink; to give medicine to*—wayatkewakiya.

wa-ya'-tkoŋ-tkoŋ-ta, *v.* See wayakoŋtkoŋta.

wa-ya'-tkoŋ-za, *v.* of yatkoŋza; *to make equal*—wamdatkoŋza.

wa-ya'-tkuŋ-za, *v.* See wayatkoŋza.

wa-ya'-tog-ya, *adv.* wayatogya ia, *to speak of other things.*

wa-ya'-to-kaŋ, *v.* of yatokaŋ; *to speak off as in another place*—wamdatokaŋ.

wa-ya'-to-ke-ća, *v.* of yatokeća; *to alter, change, speak of as different*—wamdatokeća.

wa-ya'-tpaŋ, *v.* of yatpaŋ; *to chew up fine*—wamdatpaŋ, wauŋyatpaŋpi. *T.*, wayakpaŋ.

wa-ya'-tpu-tpa, *v.* of yatputpa; *to bite up into crumbs*—wamdatputpa. *T.*, wayakpukpa.

wa-ya'-tu-ka, *v.* of yatuka; *to nibble off*, as hair, etc.—wamdatuka.

wa-ya'-tu-ta, *v.* *to make smart by biting*—wamdatuta.

wa-ya'-tu-tka, *v.* *to bite off in little pieces*—wamdatutka.

wa-ya'-ṭa, *v.* of yaṭa; *to bite to death*—wamdaṭa.

wa-ya'-ṭiŋ-za, *v.* of yaṭiŋza; *to make firm with the mouth; to establish, declare.*

wa-ya'-uŋ-ka, *v.* *to bite and make fall*, as a beaver does trees.

wa-ya'-wa, *v.* of yawa; *to read; to count*—wamdawa, wauŋyawapi.

wa-ya'-wa-hiŋ-yaŋ-za, *v.* of yawahiŋyaŋza; *to bite and make cross:* wayawahiŋyaŋsya kuwa, *to keep biting for the purpose of making cross.*

wa-ya'-wa-kaŋ, *v.* *to speak of as sacred*—wamdawakaŋ.

wa-ya'-waŋ-ka, *v.* *to bite down*, as a beaver does trees.

wa-ya'-wa-pi, *n.* *reading; numeration, arithmetic.*

wa-ya'-wa-ś'a-ka, *v.* *to call strong*—wamdawaś'aka.

wa-ya'-wa-śa-ka-daŋ, *v.* *to speak of as easy* or *cheap*—wamdawaśakadaŋ.

wa-ya'-wa-śte, *v.* of yawaśte; *to bless*—wamdawaśte, wadawaśte, wauŋyawaśtepi.

wa-ya'-we-ġa, *v.* of yaweġa; *to break partly off with the mouth*—wamdaweġa.

wa-ya'-wi-ća-ka, *v.* *to call true*—wamdawićaka.

wa-ya'-wi-ća-śta-śni, *v.* *to speak of as wicked*—wamdawićaśtaśni.

wa-ya'-wi-hnu-ni, *v.* of yawihnuni; *to destroy with the mouth*—wamdawihnuni.

wa-ya'-wiŋ-źa, *v.* *to bend down with the mouth*—wamdawiŋźa.

wa-ya'-za, *v.* *to string,* as beads—wamdaza.

wa-ya'-za-mni, *v.* of yazamni; *to uncover with the mouth.*

wa-ya'-zaŋ, *v.* of yazaŋ; *to be sick* — wamayazaŋ, waniyazaŋ, wauŋyazaŋpi: wayazaŋ hiŋhda, *to be taken sick suddenly.*

wa-ya'-zaŋ-hda, *v.* *to become sick, to feel sick*—wayazaŋwahda.

wa-ya'-zaŋ-ka, *v.* *to be sick*—wamayazaŋka: wayazaŋke ćiŋ, *one who is sick.*

wa-ya'-ze, *v.* of yaze; *to take out food with the mouth,* as a dog.

wa-ya'-zi-ća, *v.* *to stretch* anything *with the mouth*—wamdazića.

wa-ya'-zo-ka, *v.* of yazoka: *to suck,* as sugar or candy—wamdazoka.

wa-ya'-zoŋ-ta, *v.* of yazoŋta; *to connect,* as language—wamdazoŋta. *T., to praise an undeserving person.*

wa-ya'-źa, *v.* *to crush* or *bite up.*

wa-ya'-źa-źa, *v.* of yaźaźa; *to wash* or *make clean with the mouth,* as a wolf or dog does by licking bones

wa-ya'-źi-pa, *v.* of yaźipa; *to bite,* as mosquitoes do.

wa-ya'-źo, *v.* of yaźo; *to blow on instruments*—wamdaźo.

wa-ya'-źu-źu, *v.* of yaźuźu; *to demolish with the mouth,* as an argument by counter argument; *to tear in pieces,* as a dog does anything with his mouth; *one who demolishes with his mouth*—wamdaźuźu.

wa-ye', *v. a.* *T.* *to hunt:* waye omani, wayei, etc.

wa-ye'-ki-ya-pi, *n.* *T.* *gambling.* See oećoŋna.

wa-ye'-ki-ya-śka-ta, *v.* *T.* *to play for stakes, to gamble.*

wa-yu'-a-ki-ḣaŋ, *v.* of yuakiḣaŋ; *to make starve.*

wa-yu'-a-ki-pam, *adv.* *separately.* See yuakipam.

wa-yu'-a-mda-ya, *v.* of yuamdaya; *to make level.*

wa-yu'-a-śda-ya, *v.* of yuaśdaya; *to make manifest; to uncover*—wamduaśdaya.

wa-yu'-a-śka-daŋ, *v.* of yuaśkadaŋ; *to make near.*

wa-yu'-a-zi, *v* of yuazi; *to run aground,* as a boat.

wa-yu'-ba-za, *v.* of yubaza; *to trouble, annoy, vex; to twist, roll*—wamdubaza.

wa-yu'-bo-sda-ta, *v.* of yubosdata: *to set upright.*

wa-yu'-bu, *v.* of yubu; *to make a drumming noise.*

wa-yu'-bu-bu, *v. red.* of wayubu.

wa-yu'-ćaŋ, *v.* of yućaŋ; *to sift*—wamdućaŋ.

wa-yu'-ćaŋ-ćaŋ, *v. red.* of wayućaŋ; *to shake, sift.*

wa-yu'-će-ka, *v.* See wayućekćeka.

wa-yu'-će-kće-ka, *v* of yućekćeka; *to make stagger*—wamdućekćeka.

wa-yu'-će-ya, *v.* of yućeya; *to make cry.*

wa-yu'-ći-ḳa-daŋ, *v.* of yućiḳadaŋ; *to make small, to compress*—wamdućiḳadaŋ.

wa-yu'-ći-stiŋ-na, *v. to make small*—wamdućistiŋna. *T.*, wayućisćila.

wa-yu'-ćo, *adv.* of ayućo; *well, neatly:* wayućo śni, *carelessly.*

wa-yu'-ćo-ćo, *adv. red.* of wayućo.

wa-yu'-ćo-ka-ka, *v.* of yućokaka; *to take out, empty,* as the load from a gun—wamdućokaka. *T.*, oyúćokaka.

wa-yu'-ćo-ya, *adv. well.* See ayućoya.

wa-yu'-ćo-za, *v.* of yućoza; *to make warm by kindling a fire*—wamdućoza.

wa-yu'-e-će-daŋ, *v.* of yuećedaŋ; *to purify*—wamduećedaŋ.

wa-yu'-e-će-tu, *v.* of yuećetu; *to make right, fulfil, accomplish*—wamduećetu.

wa-yu'-e-ći, *v.* of yueći; *to turn wrong side out*—wamdueći.

wa-yu'-ġa, *v.* of yuġa; *to open out* or *pull off,* as in husking corn—wamduġa.

wa-yu'-ġaŋ, *v.* of yuġaŋ; *to open*—wamduġaŋ.

wa-yu'-ġa-pa, *v.* of yuġapa; *to take off the skin,* as from an animal, *to flay*—wamduġapa.

wa-yu'-ġa-ta, *v.* of yuġata; *to spread out,* as the hands—wamduġata.

wa-yu'-ġo, *v.* of yuġo; *to make crooked grooves,* as in arrows.

wa-yu'-ġo-daŋ, *n.* See waŋyuġodaŋ.

wa-yu'-gu-ka, *v.* of yuġuka; *to stretch, strain; to sprain*—wamduġuka.

wa-yu'-ha-ha-ka, *n.* of yuha; *one who possesses much*—wamduhahaka.

wa-yu'-ha-ha-ye-daŋ, *v.* of yuhahayedaŋ; *to make unsteady*—wamduhahayedaŋ; *to make unsteady*—wamduhahayedaŋ.

wa-yu'-ha-i-ye-ya, *v.* of yuha iyeya; *to throw* or *push down.*

w a - y u′ - h b a; *v.* of yuhba; *to shell off*—wamduhba.

w a - y u′ - h b e - z a, *v.* of yuhbeza; *to make rough.*

w a - y u′ - h d a, *v.* of yuhda; *to untwist, uncoil*—wamduhda.

w a - y u′ - h d o - k a, *v. to dislocate*—wamduhdoka.

w a - y u′ - h e - ć a, *n. one who possesses much*—wamduheća.

w a - y u′ - h i, *v.* of yuhi; *to drive off,* as game—wamduhi. *T., to arouse, startle,* etc.

w a - y u′ - h i - k a, *adj. T. disturbing; troublesome.*

w a - y u′ - h i ŋ - t a, *v.* of yuhiŋta; *to sweep off*—wamduhiŋta.

w a - y u′ - h m i - h m a, *v.* of yuhmihma; *to roll*—wamduhmihma.

w a - y u′ - h m i - y a ŋ - y a ŋ, *v.* of yuhmiyaŋyaŋ; *to make round*—wamduhmiyaŋyaŋ.

w a - y u′ - h m u ŋ, *v.* of yuhmuŋ; *to twist*—wamduhmuŋ.

w a - y u′ - h n a, *v.* of yuhna; *to shake off,* as fruit.

w a - y u′ - h n a - ś k i ŋ - y a ŋ, *v.* of yuhnaśkiŋyaŋ; *to make crazy*—wamduhnaśkiŋyaŋ.

w a - y u′ - h n a - y a ŋ, *v. to miss, deceive.*

w a - y u′ - h n u - n i, *v.* of yuhnuni; *to make wander.*

w a - y u′ - h o - h o, *v.* of yuhoho; *to catch and hold loosely,* as something too large to grasp—wamduhoho.

w a′ - y u - h o - m n i, *v.* of ayuhomni; *to turn round on.*

w a′ - y u - h o - t a, *v. to desire much*—as food—wamduhota.

w a - y u′ - h o - t o ŋ, *v. to cause to make a noise.*

w a - y u′ - h u - h u - z a, *v.* of yuhuhuza; *to shake*—wamduhuhuza. *T.,* wayuhuŋhuŋza.

w a - y u′ - h u - t e - d a ŋ, *v.* of yuhutedaŋ; *to make short, wear to a stump*—wamduhutedaŋ. *T.,* hute okaŋyela yutepa. See okaŋyela *and* otehaŋ.

w a - y u′ - ḣ a ŋ - d i - t a, *v. to make quick* or *active. T.,* wayuoḣaŋko. See yuḣaŋdita.

w a - y u′ - ḣ a ŋ - h i, *v. to make slow, to retard.* See yuḣaŋhi.

w a - y u′ - ḣ a - t k a, *v.* of yuḣatka; *to make rough.*

w a - y u′ - ḣ d a, *v.* of yuḣda; *to make rattle.*

w a - y u′ - ḣ d a - ġ a ŋ, *v.* of yuḣdaġaŋ; *to make larger, to enlarge.*

w a - y u′ - ḣ d a - t a, *v.* of yuḣdata; *to scratch; to dig under.*

w a - y u′ - ḣ d e - ć a, *v.* of yuḣdeća; *to tear*—wamduḣdeća.

w a - y u′ - ḣ d o - k a, *v.* of yuḣdoka; *to make a hole; to open*—wamduḣdoka.

w a - y u′ - ḣ e - p a, *v.* of yuḣepa; *to drain off; to absorb.*

w a - y u′ - ḣ e - y a - t a, *v.* of yuḣeyata; *to shove aside, push back.*

w a - y u′ - ḣ i - ć a, *v.* of yuḣića; *to waken one up, cause to awake*—wamduḣića.

w a - y u′ - ḣ i - y a - y a, *v.* of yuḣiyaya; *to be awkward, to bungle*—wamduḣiyaya.

wa-yu'-ḣi-ya-ya-ka, *n. a bungler.*

wa-yu'-ḣmi, *v.* of yuḣmi; *to make crooked.*

wa-yu'-ḣmiŋ, *v.* of yuḣmiŋ; *to throw off sideways.*

wa-yu'-ḣmuŋ, *v.* of yuḣmuŋ; *to make buzz.*

wa-yu'-ḣpa, *v.* of yuḣpa; *to lay down, throw down; to buy a wife*—wamduḣpa. See woḣpa. *T.*, "*to buy a wife*" is wiŋyaŋ ċiŋ.—W. J. C.

wa-yu'-ḣpu, *v.* of yuḣpu; *to pick off pieces.*

wa-yu'-ḣta-ta, *v. a. T. to offer sacrifice; to kill in sacrifice*—wabluḣtata: generally used of *animate* objects, as wauŋyaŋ is of *inanimate* ones.

wa-yu'-ḣta-ta, *n. T. a priest; one who offers sacrifice:* wayuḣtata itaŋċaŋ, *a chief priest.*

wa-yu'-ḣta-ta-pi, *n. T. sacrifices; animals* or *things offered in sacrifice.*

wa-yu'-ḣtaŋ-yaŋ, *v.* of yuḣtaŋyaŋ; *to make rough.*

wa-yu'-ḣtu-ta, *v.* of yuḣtuta; *to make rough, break the grain* of a skin in dressing—wamduḣtuta.

wa-yu'-ḣu, *v.* of yuḣu; *to peel*—wamduḣu.

wa-yu'-ḣu-ġa, *v.* of yuḣuġa; *to break holes in*—wamduḣuġa.

wa-yu'-ḣuŋ-ta, *v.* of yuḣuŋta; *to make soft* or *pliant,* as a skin by rubbing—wamduḣuŋta.

wa-yu'-ḣuŋ-wiŋ, *v.* of yuḣuŋwiŋ; *to cause to putrefy.*

wa-yu'-i-ċi-ċa-hi, *v.* of yuiċiċahi; *to mingle.*

wa-yu'-i-de, *v.* of yuide; *to make blaze.*

wa-yu'-i-na-ḣni, *v.* of yuinaḣni; *to cause to hasten*—wamduinaḣni.

wa-yu'-i-ś-te-ċa, *v.* of yuiśteċa; *to make ashamed.*

wa-yu'-i-yo-ka, *v.* wayuiyog iyeya, *to push aside, put out of the way. T.*, yuṭokaŋiyeya.

wa-yu'-i-yo-wa-za, *v.* of yuiyowaza; *to cause an echo.*

wa-yu'-ka-ki-źa, *v.* of yukakiźa; *to make suffer*—wamdukakiźa.

wa-yu'-kaŋ, *v.* of yukaŋ; *to shake off,* as dew.

wa-yu'-ka-pa, *v.* of yukapa; *to catch in the hand,* as a ball—wamdukapa.

wa-yu'-ka-tiŋ, *v.* of yukatiŋ; *to straighten out.*

wa-yu'-ka-wa, *v.* of yukawa; *to open out, push back*—wamdukawa.

wa-yu'-kċa, *v.* of yukċa; *to unfold, untie*—wamdukċa.

wa-yu'-kċaŋ, *v.* of yukċaŋ; *to examine, investigate*—wamdukċaŋ.

wa-yu'-ke-ċa, *v. n.* of yukaŋ; *there is some.*

wa-yu'-kiŋ-ċa, *v.* of yukiŋċa; *to scrape.*

wa-yu'-kiŋ-za, *v.* of yukiŋza; *to make creak*—wamdukiŋza.

wa-yu'-ki-pa-źa, *v.* of yukipaźa; *to double* or *fold up.*

wa-yu'-ki-pe-haŋ, *v.* of yukipehaŋ; *to fold up.*

wa-yu'-ko-ka, *v.* of yukoka; *to rattle.*

wa-yu'-ko-ke-daŋ, *v.* of yukokedaŋ; *to make active.*

wa-yu'-ko-ko-ka, *v.* of yukokoka; *to rattle.*

wa-yu'-ko-pe-hda, *v.* of yukopehda; *to frighten.*

wa-yu'-ko-ya-ḣaŋ-na, *v. to make hasten.*

wa-yu'-kpaŋ, *v.* of yukpaŋ; *to make fine, pulverize, grind,* as grain—wamdukpaŋ, wadukpaŋ, wauŋyukpaŋpi. See wokpaŋ *and* wayutpaŋ.

wa-yu'-ḳpi, *v.* of yukpi; *to crack.*

wa-yu'-ksa, *v.* of yuksa; *to break off*—wamduksa, waduksa, wauŋyuksapi. See woksa.

wa-yu'-kse, *v. a. T. to break off,* as ears of corn; *to harvest,* as corn.

wa-yu'-ksa-ksa, *v. red.* of wayuksa.

wa-yu'-ksa-pa, *v.* of yuksapa; *to make wise; one who makes wise, an instructor*—wamduksapa.

wa-yu'-kśa, *v.* of yukśa; *to roll up.*

wa-yu'-kśa-daŋ, *v.* of yukśadaŋ; *to bend up.*

wa-yu'-kśaŋ, *v.* of yukśaŋ; *to bend.*

wa-yu'-kśi-źa, *v.* of yukśiźa; *to double up.*

wa-yu'-ktaŋ, *v.* of yuktaŋ; *to bend*—wamduktaŋ.

wa-yu'-ku-ka, *v.* of yukuka; *to spoil, wear out.*

wa-yu'-ḳe-ġa, *v.* of yuḳeġa; *to scratch.*

wa-yu'-ḳe-za, *v.* of yuḳeza; *to make smooth.*

wa-yu'-ḳo-ġa, *v.* of yuḳoġa; *to scratch, make rough.*

wa-yu'-ḳo-za, *v.* of yuḳoza; *to make smooth.*

wa-yu'-ma-hen-i-ye-ya, *v. to put* or *push into.*

wa-yu'-maŋ, *v.* of yumaŋ; *to whet, file, grind,* as edged tools—wamdube.

wa-yu'-mda-ska, *v.* of yumdaska; *to make flat.*

wa-yu'-mda-ya, *v.* of yumdaya; *to spread out, make level*—wamdumdaya.

wa-yu'-mda-za, *v.* of yumdaza; *to rip open.*

wa-yu'-mde-ća, *v.* of yumdeća; *to crush, break in pieces*—wamdumdeća.

wa-yu'-mdu, *v.* of yumdu; *to make mellow; to plough*—wamdumdu, wadumdu. See womdu.

wa-yu'-mi-ma, *v.* of yumima; *to make round by grinding*—wamdumima.

wa-yu'-mna, *v.* of yumna; *to rip.*

wa'-yu-mni, *v.* of ayumni; *to turn round on.*

wa-yu'-mni-ġa, *v.* of yumniġa; *to make shrink* or *draw up.*

wa-yu'-na-ke-ya, *v.* of yunakeya; *to turn on one side.*

wa-yu'-na-źiŋ, *v.* of yunaźiŋ; *to cause to stand up*—wamdunaźiŋ.

wa-yu'-ni-ya-śni, *v.* of yuniyaśni; *to suffocate, to strangle*—wamduniyaśni.

wa-yu'-nmi-nma, *v.* of yunminma; *to roll. T.*, wayugmigma.

wa-yu'-o-ćiŋ-śi-ća, *v.* of yuoćiŋśića: *to make cross.*

wa-yu'-o-ći-pte-ća, *v.* of yuoćipteća; *to make of different lengths. T.*, wayuoptetu.

wa-yu'-o-ći-pten, *cont.* of wayuoćipteća. *T.*, wayuoptel.

wa-yu'-o-ći-pten-ya, *adv. diminishing in size.*

wa-yu'-o-ći-pte-tu, *v. to make longer and shorter, to lessen*—wamduoćiptetu.

wa-yu'-o-ći-tkoŋ-za, *v.* of yuoćitkoŋza; *to make equal. T.*, wayuotkoŋza.

wa-yu'-o-ći-tpa-ni, *v.* of yuoćitpani; *to make unequal. T.*, wayuoćikpani.

wa-yu'-o-hda-pśiŋ-yaŋ-i-ye-ya, *v. to turn bottom up.*

wa-yu'-o-ḣa-ḣa, *v.* of yuoḣaḣa; *to fill up*, as holes. *T.*, okáta, of o *and* katá.

wa-yu'-o-ḣaŋ-ko, *v.* of yuoḣaŋko; *to make hasten*—wamduoḣaŋko. See wayuḣaŋdita.

wa-yu'-o-ḣmiŋ, *v.* of yuoḣmiŋ; *to miss, to throw on one side* of the mark.

wa-yu'-o-ḣpa, *v.* of yuoḣpa; *to break through into.*

wa-yu'-o-ka-ḣbo-ka, *v.* of yuokaḣboka; *to cause to float.*

wa-yu'-o-ki-ni-haŋ, *v.* of yuokinihaŋ; *to make honorable.*

wa-yu'-o-koŋ-waŋ-źi-daŋ, *v.* of yuokoŋwaŋźidaŋ; *to make into one, to unite.*

wa-yu'-o-mde-ća, *v.* of yuomdeća; *to scatter abroad, to disperse*—wamduomdeća.

wa-yu'-o-ni-haŋ, *v.* of yuonihaŋ; *to honor; to be respectful*—wamduonihaŋ.

wa-yu'-o-ni-haŋ-yaŋ, *adv respectfully.*

wa-yu'-o-s'iŋ, *v.* of yuos'iŋ; *to hate*—wamduos'iŋ. *T.*, waóyus'iŋ.

wa-yu'-o-śiŋ, *v.* of yuośiŋ; *to tie in a fast knot*—wamduośiŋ. *T.*, wayúoseya.

wa-yu'-o-ta, *v.* of yuota; *to multiply*—wamduota.

wa-yu'-o-taŋ-iŋ, *v.* of yuotaŋiŋ; *to make manifest*—wamduotaŋiŋ.

wa-yu'-o-ṭiŋ-za, *v.* of yuoṭiŋza; *to make tight in*—wamduoṭiŋza.

wa-yu'-o-wo-taŋ, *v.* of yuowotaŋ; *to straighten, to make upright*—wamduowotaŋ.

wa-yu'-o-wo-taŋ-na, *v.* Same as wayuowotaŋ.

wa-yu'-pa-ko, *v.* of yupako; *to make crooked.*

wa-yu'-paŋ-ġa, *v.* of yupaŋġa; *to tie up loosely, make puff out*—wamdupaŋġa

wa-yu'-paŋ-ġe-ća, *n. one who ties nothing up well, one who ties so that it always puffs out*—wamdupaŋġeća.

wa-yu′-paŋ-paŋ, *v.* of yupaŋpaŋ; *to make soft*—wamdupaŋpaŋ.

wa-yu′-paŋ-paŋ-na, *v.* See wayupaŋpaŋ.

wa-yu′-pa-tu-źa, *v.* of yupatuźa; *to bend down*

wa-yu′-pe-haŋ, *v.* of yupehaŋ; *to fold up.*

wa-yu′-pe-mni, *v.* of yupemni; *to twist.*

wa-yu′-pi, *v. n. to be skillful, ingenious*—wamdupi, wadupi, wauŋyupipi.

wa-yu′-pi-ka, *v. n. to be expert, skillful, dexterous*—wamdupika, wadupika.

wa-yu′-pi-ya, *adv. skillfully, expertly, well.*

wa-yu′-pi-ya-haŋ, *adv. well, skillfully. T.*, wayúpiyakel.

wa-yu′-po-pa, *v.* of yupopa; *to cause to burst.*

wa-yu′-po-ta, *v.* of yupota; *to wear out, cut up*—wamdupota, wauŋyupotapi.

wa-yu′-po-te-ća, *n. one who wears out* or *uses up much.*

wa-yu′-po-wa-ya, *v.* of yupowaya; *to brush up*, as fur.

wa-yu′-psa-ka, *v.* of yupsaka; *to break*, as cords—wamdupsaka.

wa-yu′-psi-ća, *v.* of yupsića; *to make jump*—wamdupsića.

wa-yu′-psoŋ, *v.* of yupsoŋ; *to spill out*—wamdupsoŋ.

wa-yu′-pśuŋ, *v.* of yupśuŋ; *to pull out by the roots, to dislocate*—wamdupśuŋ.

wa-yu′-pta, *v.* of yupta; *to cut out*, as clothes—wamdupta.

wa′-yu-pta, *v.* of ayupta; *to answer*—wámdupta

wa-yu′-ptaŋ-yaŋ, *v.* of yuptaŋyaŋ; *to turn over*—wamduptaŋyaŋ.

wa′-yu-ptaŋ-yaŋ, *v.* of ayuptaŋyaŋ; *to turn back on* one, *redound on one's self* or *one's relatives.*

wa-yu′-pta-ya, *n.* of yuptaya; *one who collects.*

wa-yu′-pte-će-daŋ, *v.* of yuptećedaŋ; *to shorten. T.*, wayupćećela.

wa-yu′-ptu-ḣa, *v.* of yuptuḣa; *to pick to pieces.*

wa-yu′-ptu-źa, *v.* of yuptuźa; *to crack, split.*

wa-yu′-saŋ, *v.* of yusaŋ; *to whiten, to whitewash.* See wayuska.

wa-yu′-sa-pa, *v.* of yusapa; *to blacken.*

wa-yu′-sba, *v.* of yusba; *to pick in pieces.*

wa-yu′-sbu, *v.* of yusbu; *to make a noise*, as in handling shelled corn.

wa-yu′-sde-ća, *v.* of yusdeća; *to split*—wamdusdeća.

wa-yu′-sdo-haŋ, *v.* of yusdohaŋ; *to draw along*—wamdusdohaŋ.

wa-yu′-sdu-ta, *v.* of yusduta; *to pull out*—wamdusduta.

wa-yu′-se-pa, *v.* of yusepa; *to rub off*, as dirt or paint—wamdusepa. *T.*, wayutepa.

wa-yu′-ska, *v.* of yuska; *to whiten, make white; to clear one* who has been charged with a crime, *to acquit*—wamduska. See wayusaŋ.

wa-yu′-ska-pi, *n. one who has been cleared from charges laid against him.*

wa-yu′-ske-pa, *v.* of yuskepa; *to draw all out, to exhaust.*

wa-yu′-ski-ća, *v.* of yuskića; *to press; to be neat and tidy; to surpass all others: one who is feared by* or *restrains* others—wamduskića.

wa-yu′-ski-ta, *v.* Same as wayuskića; *to bind, press.*

wa-yu′-sku, *v.* of yusku; *to shear off close, pare, shave off*—wamdusku.

wa-yu′-sku-sku, *v. red.* of wayusku.

wa-yu′-sla-ta, *v. T. to do a thing slowly, deliberately.*

wa-yu′-sla-sla-ta, *v. red. T. to do a thing slowly, deliberately.* See wákasdata.

wa-yu′-sma-ka, *v.* of yusmaka; *to hollow out; to indent.*

wa-yu′-smiŋ, *v.* of yusmiŋ; *to pick off, make bare.*

wa-yu′-sna, *v.* of yusna; *to ring, to rustle,* as leaves falling; *to ravel out*—wamdusna.

wa-yu′-sni, *v.* of yusni; *to make cold, to extinguish.*

wa′-yus-o, *v.* of ayuso; *to wade after; to pare off*—wámduso. *T., to pare off, to cut in strips* or *strings.* But "*to wade after*" is ćopa hiyohi ya.—W. J. C.

wa′-yus-os-o, *v. red.* of wáyuso.

wa-yu′-so-ta, *v.* of yusota; *to spend, use up, consume*—wamdusota.

wa-yu′-sto, *v.* of yusto; *to smooth down*—wamdusto.

wa-yu′-sto-ka, *n. one who makes smooth.*

wa-yu′-su, *v.* of yusu; *to make good*—wamdusu. *T.*, yuwaśte.

wa-yu′-su-ta, *v.* of yusuta; *to make strong, to establish*—wamdusuta.

wa-yu′-śa, *v.* of yuśa; *to make red.*

wa-yu′-ś'ag-ya, *v. a. to overload,* as an animal—wayuś'agwaya. *T.*, tkeya wakiŋkiya.

wa-yu′-ś'a-ka, *v.* of yuś'aka; *to be overloaded*—wamduś'aka.

wa-yu′-śa-pa, *v.* of yuśapa; *to soil*—wamduśapa.

wa-yu′-śda, *v.* of yuśda; *to make bare, cut off*—wamduśda.

wa-yu′-śdo-ka, *v.* of yuśdoka; *to pull out.*

wa-yu′-śdu-śdu-ta, *v.* of yuśduśduta; *to make slippery.*

wa-yu′-śe-ća, *v. to make dry up* or *wither.*

wa-yu′-śi-ća, *v.* of yuśića; *to make bad, to spoil*—wamduśića.

wa-yu′-śi-ḣtiŋ, *v.* of yuśiḣtiŋ; *to enfeeble*—wamduśiḣtiŋ. *T., to make bad; to injure* in any way.

wa-yu′-śik-śi-će-ća, *n. T.* of wayuśića; *one who does nothing well.*

wa-yu'-śiŋ-śiŋ, *v.* of yuśiŋśiŋ; *to tickle*—wamduśiŋśiŋ.

wa-yu'-śiŋ-ye-ya, *v.* of yuśiŋyeya; *to frighten*—wayuśiŋyewaya.

wa-yu'-śi-pa, *v.* of yuśipa; *to break off close.* See wayutkuġa.

wa-yu'-śka, *v.* of yuśka; *to untie.*

wa-yu'-śkaŋ-śkaŋ, *v.* of yuśkaŋśkaŋ; *to cause to move* or *stir about*—wamduśkaŋśkaŋ.

wa-yu'-śke-haŋ, *v.* of yuśkehaŋ; *to make wild* or *unsteady, to cause to prance*—wamduśkehaŋ.

wa-yu'-śki, *v.* of yuśki; *to plait*—wamduśki.

wa-yu'-śki-śka, *v.* of yuśkiśka; *to make rough; to make difficult* or *confused; to make mischief*—wamduśkiśka.

wa-yu'-śko-kpa, *v.* of yuśkokpa; *to hollow out.*

wa-yu'-śko-pa, *v.* of yuśkopa; *to make twisting.*

wa-yu'-śko-tpa, *v.* Same as wayuśkokpa.

wa-yu'-śna, *v.* of yuśna; *to drop, let slip, make a mistake*—wamduśna.

wa-yu'-śna, *v. a. to sacrifice, offer sacrifice*—wamduśna, waduśna, wauŋyuśnapi. See wośna. *T.*, wauŋyaŋ *and* wayuȟtata.

wa-yu'-śna-pi, *n. sacrificing. T.*, wauŋyaŋpi *and* wayuȟtatapi.

wa-yu'-śo-śa, *v.* of yuśośa; *to make turbid.*

wa-yu'-śpa, *v.* of yuśpa; *to break off pieces*—wamduśpa.

wa-yu'-śpi, *v.* of yuśpi; *to pick off,* as berries—wamduśpi, waduśpi, wauŋyuśpipi. See wośpi.

wa-yu'-śpu, *v.* of yuśpu; *to pick off* anything stuck on—wamduśpu.

wa-yu'-śpu-ya, *v.* of yuśpuya; *to scratch*—wamduśpuya.

wa-yu'-śtaŋ, *v.* of yuśtaŋ; *to finish*—wamduśtaŋ.

wa-yu'-śtaŋ-ka, *n. one who finishes.*

wa-yu'-śu-źa, *v.* of yuśuźa; *to crush.*

wa-yu'-ta, *v.* of yuta; *to be eaten up,* as by wolves; *to eat up; one who eats all up*—wawata, wauŋtapi. See wota.

wa-yu'-t'aŋ, *v.* of yut'aŋ; *to touch.*

wa-yu'-taŋ, *n. a servant; a master of ceremonies. T., one who passes the food around.*

wa-yu'-taŋ-ćo-daŋ, *v.* of yutaŋćodaŋ; *to make naked.*

wa-yu'-taŋ-iŋ, *v.* of yutaŋiŋ; *to make manifest, to expose*—wamdutaŋiŋ.

wa-yu'-taŋ-ka, *v.* of yutaŋka; *to make large.*

wa-yu'-taŋ-ki-ya, *v.* of wayutaŋ; *to have for cook* or *master of ceremonies:* wayutaŋwićakiyapi, *servants.*

wa-yu'-taŋ-ni, *v.* of yutaŋni; *to wear out, make old*—wamdutaŋni.

wa-yu'-taŋ-ni-ka, *n. one who wears out much.*

wa-yu'-t'aŋ-t'aŋ, *v. red.* of yut'aŋ; *to feel all over.*

wa-yu'-taŋ-toŋ-śni, *v* of yutaŋtoŋśni; *to make an end of, destroy.*

wa-yu′-taŋ-ya, *v.* of wayutaŋ; *to make master of ceremonies at a feast*—wayutaŋwaya.

wa-yu′-te-ća, *v.* of yuteća; *to make new, to renew*—wamduteća.

wa-yu′-te-haŋ, *v.* of yutehaŋ; *to make long, to be slow.*

wa-yu′-te-haŋ-haŋ-ka, *v. to be always long in doing* a thing—wamdutehaŋhaŋka.

wa-yu′-te-ḣi-ka, *v.* of yuteḣika; *to make difficult*—wamduteḣika.

wa-yu′-te-pa, *v.* of yutepa; *to wear off. T.*, also *to rub off*, as paint, etc. See wayusepa.

wa-yu′-te-pe-ća, *n. one who wears off.*

wa-yu′-ti-ća, *v.* of yutića; *to scrape away*, as a horse does snow by pawing.

wa-yu′-ti-pa, *v.* of yutipa; *to cramp, draw up.*

wa-yu′-ti-taŋ, *v.* of yutitaŋ; *to pull.*

wa-yu′-tkoŋ-za, *v.* of yutkoŋza; *to make even*—wamdutkoŋza. *T.*, wayúotkoŋza.

wa-yu′-tku-ġa, *v.* of yutkuġa; *to break off square. T., to break off;* but "*to break off square*" is ótkoŋs yuksa.—W. J. C.

wa-yu′-to-kaŋ, *v.* of yutokaŋ; *to put in another place, to remove*—wamdutokaŋ.

wa-yu′-to-ke-ća, *v.* of yutokeća; *to make different, to alter*—wamdutokeća.

wa-yu′-tpaŋ, *v.* of yutpaŋ; *to make fine, to grind*—wamdutpaŋ, wauŋyutpaŋpi. *T.*, wayukpaŋ. See wotpaŋ *and* wayukpaŋ.

wa-yu′-tpu-tpa, *v.* of yuputpa; *to pick to pieces, to make crumble*—wamdutputpa. *T.*, wayukpukpa.

wa-yu′-tpu-tpe-ća, *n. one who crumbles up* or *makes fine.*

wa-yu′-tu-ta, *v* of yututa; *to make smart by rubbing*—wamdututa.

wa-yu′-tu-tka, *v.* of yututka; *to break into small pieces.*

wa-yu′-ṭa, *v.* of yuṭa; *to kill, choke to death*—wamduṭa.

wa-yu′-ṭiŋ-za, *v* of yuṭiŋza; *to make firm*—wamduṭiŋza.

wa-yu′-wa-ćiŋ-toŋ, *v.* of yuwaćiŋtoŋ; *to make intelligent.*

wa-yu′-wa-hiŋ-yaŋ-za, *v. to make morose* or *ill disposed.* See waćiŋhiŋyaŋza, yuwaćiŋhiŋyaŋza *and* wayawahiŋyaŋza.

wa-yu′-wa-ḣba-daŋ, *v.* of yuwaḣbadaŋ; *to make gentle* or *mild*—wamduwaḣbadan.

wa-yu′-wa-ḣpa-ni-ća, *v.* of yuwaḣpanića; *to make poor*—wamduwaḣpanića.

wa-yu′-wa-ḣte-ka, *v. to make unable to do well, to incapacitate; i. q.* oŋspeśni daka.

wa-yu′-wa-kaŋ, *v.* of yuwakaŋ; *to make sacred, to consecrate*—wamduwakaŋ.

wa-yu′-waŋ-ka, *v.* of yuwaŋka; *to throw down. T.*, wayúuŋka.

wa-yu′-waŋ-kan-i-ću, *v. to lift up:* wayuwaŋkan iyeya, *to raise* or *pry up.*

wa-yu′-wa-ś'a-ka, *v.* of yuwaś'aka; *to make strong, to invigorate*—wamduwaś'aka.

wa-yu′-wa-śa-ka-daŋ, *v.* of yuwaśakadaŋ; *to make cheap* or *easy*—wamduwaśakadaŋ.

wa-yu′-wa-ś'a-ke-śni, *v. to make weak*—wamduwaś'akeśni.

wa-yu′-wa-śte, *v.* of yuwaśte; *to make good, to improve*—wamduwaśte, waduwaśte, waunyuwaśtepi. See wayusu.

wa-yu′-we-ġa, *v.* of yuweġa; *to break partly off*—wamduweġa.

wa-yu′-wi, *v.* of yuwi; *to wrap around.*

wa-yu′-wi-ća-ka, *v.* of yuwićaka; *to make true.*

wa-yu′-wi-ća-śta-śni, *v.* of yuwićaśtaśni; *to make bad, debase, corrupt*—wamduwićaśtaśni.

wa-yu′-wi-ḣnu-ni, *v.* of yuwiḣnuni; *to destroy*—wamduwiḣnuni.

wa-yu′-wiŋ-ġa, *v.* of yuwiŋġa; *to turn around.*

wa-yu′-wiŋ-ġe-ća, *n. one who turns about.*

wa-yu′-wiŋ-ta, *v.* of yuwiŋta; *to spread out the hands to; to stroke*—wamduwiŋta. *T., to stroke; to spread out the hands to* one *in salutation* only (for any other purpose they use kiyuġata).

wa-yu′-wiŋ-źa, *v.* of yuwiŋźa; *to bend down.*

wa-yu′-wi-taŋ-taŋ, *v. to make proud.* See yuwitaŋ.

wa-yu′-wi-ta-ya, *v.* of yuwitaya; *to gather together, to collect*—wamduwitaya.

wa-yu′-wi-tko, *v.* of yuwitko; *to make drunk*—wamduwitko.

wa-yu′-wi-tko-tko-ka, *v. to make foolish.*

wa-yu′-wi-ye-ya, *v.* of yuwiyeya; *to make ready*—wamduwiyeya.

wa-yu′-za, *v.* of yuza; *to take; to take the clothes of those who come home in triumph*—wamduza. See wakiyuza.

wa-yu′-za-mni, *v.* of yuzamni; *to uncover*—wamduzamni.

wa-yu′-zaŋ, *v.* of yuzaŋ; *to part* or *separate,* as hair on the head.

wa-yu′-ze, *v.* of yuze; *to lade* or *dip out* from a kettle—wamduze.

wa-yu′-zi-ća, *v.* of yuźića; *to stretch*—wamduzića.

wa-yu′-zoŋ-ta, *v.* of yuzoŋta; *to make connected; to decide*—wamduzoŋta. *T.,* ićikoyagya, *to make connected;* but iyukćaŋ, *to decide.*

wa-yu′-zuŋ-ća, *v.* Same as wayuzoŋta.

wa-yu′-źa, *v.* of yuźa; *to stir up; to make mush* or *hasty pudding*—wamduźa.

wa-yu′-źa-ka, *v.* of yuźaka; *to pull open*—wamduźaka.

wa-yu′-źa-źa, *v.* of yuźaźa; *to wash,* as clothes; *to do a washing*—wamduźaźa, waduźaźa, waunyuźaźapi. See woźaźa.

wa-yu′-źiŋ-ća, *v.* of yuźiŋća; *to pull* or *blow*, as the nose—wamduźiŋća.

wa-yu′-źi-pa, *v.* of yuźipa; *to pinch; one who pinches*—wamduźipa.

wa-yu′-źuŋ, *v.* of yuźuŋ; *to pull out by the roots*—wamduźuŋ.

wa-yu′-źu-źu, *v.* of yuźuźu; *to tear down, to demolish*—wamduźuźu.

wa-za′-za, *v. n.* *to dangle; to be fringed.* See kazaza.

wa-za′-za-pi, *n.* *fringe, dangles.*

wa-zi′, *n.* *a pine, pines.*

Wa-zi′-ḣe, *n.* *the Cypress Mountains.*

wa-zil′-ya, *v. a.* *T., to burn*, as incense—wazilwaya. See zinya.

wa-zi′-sa-ka, *n.* (wazi *and* saka) *a species of pine*, perhaps *the pitch pine, the fir.*

wa-zi′-se, *n.* *like pines; giants.*

Wa-zi′-ya, *n.* *the northern god* or *god of the north; a fabled giant* who lives at the north and blows cold out of his mouth. He draws near in winter and recedes in summer. By some Waziya is confounded with Heyoka, but he seems to be a different being. This is now become the designation of *Santa Claus.*

wa-zi′-ya-pa, *adv.* *at the north, to the north.*

wa-zi′-ya-pa-taŋ-haŋ, *adv.* *northwards; from the north.*

wa-zi′-ya-ta, *n.* *at the pines, the north.*

wa-zi′-ya-taŋ-haŋ, *adv.* *at the north, from the north.*

wa-zi′-ya-ta-taŋ-haŋ, *adv.* *from the north.*

Wa-zi′-ya-wi-ća-śa, *n.* the name of a branch of the *Assiniboins.*

wa-źu′, *v.* 1st pers. sing. of źu.

wa′-źu, *v.* of aźu; *to lay up to dry*, as rice, etc.; *to apply externally*, as a poultice—wáwaźu, wáuŋźupi.

wa′-źu-daŋ, *n.* *the hoards* or *deposits* of squirrels, etc.

wa-źuŋ′-tka, *n.* *the name of a small yellow bird.*

wa-źuŋ′-tka-daŋ, *n.* Same as waźuŋtka.

wa′-źu-pi-wi *or* wi-wa-źu-pi, *n.* *the moon in which the Indians lay up rice*, answering nearly to *October.*

wa-źu′-śte-ća, *n.* *strawberries.*

wa-źu′-śte-ća-hu, *n.* *strawberry vines.*

wa-źu′-śte-ća-śa-wi, *n.* *the moon in which strawberries are ripe; June* or *July.*

we, *n.* *blood.*

we, *adj.* *bloody.*

we, *v. n.* *to bleed:* poġe mawe, *my nose bleeds.*

we, sign of the *imperat.* sing.; used by the women; as, ećoŋ we, *do thou it.*

we, *pron.* compounded of "wa" and "ki." See Grammar, Pronouns.

we′-će-ya, *v. a.* *to have regard for* one, *to consult one's wishes*—wećewaya, wećeuŋyaŋpi. *T., to follow*, as a leader.

we'-ġa, *adj. broken.* See yuweġa, etc.

we-ġa'-haŋ, *part. broken, but not entirely off.*

we-ġa'-wa-haŋ, *part. broken, but not off;* thus distinguished from ksawahaŋ.

we'-haŋ, *n. last spring:* wehaŋ ićima, *the spring before last.*

weh'-weh-weh, *intj T.* used by the women in *calling a dog.*

we'-hna, *prep. among.* See ehna.

we-i'-ç̧i-ya, *v. ref. T. to bleed himself.*

we ki'-ći ya, *v. a. T. to bleed each other.*

we-śde'-ka-pi, *n. the wearing of honors,* especially *the feathers, signs of honorable wounds.*

we'-tu, *n. spring, the spring of the year; next spring* See wehaŋ.

we-we', *adj. red.* of we; *bloody.*

We'-wi-ća-śa, *n. The Bloods.*

we-ya', *v. a. to shed blood, make bleed;* hence *to put to death*—wewaya, weuŋyaŋpi.

we'-yo-ta-ni-će *and* wo'-ta-ni-će, *n. a clot of blood.*

wi, *n. the sun; the moon:* wi hinapa, *the sun rises;* wi iyaya, *the sun has set;* aŋpetu wi, *the day-sun;* haŋyetu wi, *the night-sun* or *moon* (*T.*, haŋhepi wi).

wi, *n. a moon, a lunar month.* The names of the moons are as follows:

1. Wi-teȟi, *January; the hard moon.*
2. Wićata-wi, *February; the raccoon moon.*
3. Iśtawićayazaŋ-wi, *March; the sore-eye moon.*
4. Maġaokada-wi, *April; the moon in which the geese lay eggs:* also called Wokada-wi; and sometimes Watopapi-wi, *the moon when the streams are again navigable. T.,* Maġaksića-agli-wi, *the moon when the ducks come back.*
5. Woźupi-wi, *May; the planting moon.* See ćaŋwaptoŋ-wi.
6. Waźuśtećaśa-wi, *June; the moon when the strawberries are red. T.,* Tipsiŋla-itkaȟća-wi, *the moon when the seed-pods of the Indian turnip mature;* and Wipazoka-waśte-wi, *the moon when the* wipazoka (berries) *are good.*
7. Ćaŋpasapa-wi *and* Waśuŋpa-wi, *July; the moon when the choke-cherries are ripe,* and *when the geese shed their feathers. T.,* Ćaŋpasapa-wi *and* Takiyuȟa-wi, *the deer-rutting moon.*
8. Wasutoŋ-wi, *August; the harvest moon. T.,* Kaŋta-śa-wi, *the moon when plums are red.*
9. Psiŋhnaketu-wi, *September; the moon when rice is laid up to dry. T.,* Ćaŋwapeġi-wi (ćaŋwapa, ġi, *and* wi), *the moon in which the leaves become brown.*
10. Wi-waźupi, *October; the drying rice moon;* sometimes written Waźupi-wi. *T.,* Ćaŋwape-kasna-wi, *the moon when the wind shakes off the leaves;* and Wayuksapi-wi, *corn-harvest moon.*

11. Takiyuḣa-wi, *November; the deer-rutting moon. T.*, Waniyetu-wi, *the winter moon.*

12. Tahećapśuŋ-wi, *December; the moon when the deer shed their horns T.*, Wanićokaŋ-wi (waniyetu ćokaŋyaŋ wi), *the mid-winter moon* See ćokaya.

wi, *cont.* of wiŋyaŋ *or* winoḣiŋća; as in wihdaśtaka *and* wiinaḣma.

wi, some verbs commencing with "i" make the absolute form by prefixing "w," instead of "wa;" as, ihaŋmna, wihaŋmna.

wi'-a-će-i-ç̌i-ti (wi *and* aćeti). *n. T. sun-dogs; there are sun-dogs; a ring around the moon; there is a ring around the moon.*

wi'-a-hi-na-pa, *v. to have the sun rise on* one.

wi-a'-i-ći-i-ç̌i-ta, *n. T. sun-dogs.*

wi'-a-ta-om-ya, *adv. when the sun is leaning; afternoon.*

wi'-bo-pe, *n. a mortar, a hominy-block.*

wi'-bo-pe-i-hu-pà, *n. a pestle.*

wi-ća', *n. the raccoon, Procyon lotor.*

wi-ća', *n. a male of the human species, a man*—wimaća, winića, wiuŋćapi.

wi-ća', *adj. male,* pertaining to sex; *human.* This adjective is prefixed to nouns that have reference to man. When the noun begins with a vowel, the "a" in wića is dropped; as, iśta, *an eye,* wićiśta.

wi-ća', *pron. in comp.* With active verbs this represents the third pers. plur. objective, *them;* as, wićawakte, *I killed them:* but when used with neuter verbs and adjectives it generally forms what may be regarded as abstract nouns; as, ćaŋćaŋ, *to shake,* wićaćaŋćaŋ, *the ague;* waśte, *good,* wićowaśte, *goodness.*

wi-ća'-a-ki-ḣaŋ, *n. starving, famine.*

wi-ća'-a-tku-ku, *n. a father, their father.*

wi-ća'-ba-pi, *n. blame.*

wi'-ćab-wo-ta-pi, *n. T. a table-fork.* See wićape *and* wota.

wi'-ća-ćaŋ, *n. T.* of kaćaŋ; *a sieve.*

wi-ća'-ćaŋ-ćaŋ, *n. the ague.*

wi-ća'-ćaŋ-te, *n the human heart.*

wi-ća'-ćaŋ-te-o-ze, *n. the thought of the heart.*

wi-ća'-ća-źe, *n. names, names of persons.*

wi-ća'-će, *n. the penis.*

wi-ća'-će-ḣpi, *n. human flesh.*

wi-ća'-će-pa, *n. human fatness, obesity.*

wi-ća'-će-sdi, *n. the excrement of the raccoon:* also *the human excrement.*

wi-ća'-će-ya, *n. weeping, crying.*

wi-ća'-će-źi, *n. the human tongue.*

wi'-ća-ći-će, *n. an instrument used in brushing up the fur of skins.* See katića.

w i - ć a′ - ć i ŋ - ć a, *n.* *children.*

w i - ć a′ - ć u - w i - t a, *n.* *the sense of cold experienced by human beings.* See ćuwita.

w i - ć a′ - d a, *v. a.* *to believe, put confidence in; to agree to*—wićawada, wićayada, wićauŋdapi, wićamada.

w i - ć a′ - d a - k a, *v. a.* *to believe*—wićawadaka, wićauŋdapika.

w i - ć a′ - d a - p i, *n.* *belief, believing; faith.*

w i - ć a′ - d a - p i - ć a, *adj.* *worthy of belief.*

w i - ć a′ - d a - y a, *v. a.* *to cause one to believe; to persuade*—wićadawaya.

w i - ć a′ - d e - ź a, *n.* *human urine.*

w i′ - ć a - d u - ġ e, *n.* of kaduġa; *a fan to winnow with.*

w i - ć a′ - g n a - ś k a, *n.* *T.* *gooseberries;* wićagnaśkahu, *gooseberry bushes.*

w i - ć a′ - g l a - t a, *n.* *T.* *the women who follow the men in singing at the war dance* or *other like dances* See ahdata.

w i′ - ć a - ġ e, *n.* of kaġa; *an instrument to make with.*

w i′ - ć a - ġ e - ġ e, *n.* of kaġeġe; *anything to sew with—thread.*

w i′ - ć a - ġ o, *n.* of kaġo; *an instrument to mark with.*

w i′ - ć a - ġ u - k e, *n.* Same as wićaćiće.

w i - ć a′ - h d e - ś k a, *n.* *gooseberries.* *T.*, wićagnaśka.

w i - ć a′ - h d e - ś k a - h u, *n.* *the gooseberry bush, Ribes grossularia.*

w i - ć a′ - h i, *n.* *human teeth.*

w i′ - ć a - h i, *n.* *something to mix with,* as a mush-stick.

w i′ - ć a - h i ŋ - t e, *n.* of kahiŋta; *a broom, a rake.*

w i′ - ć a - h i - y a, *v.* of icahiya; *to mingle*—wićahiwaya.

w i′ - ć a - h i - y a - y u - t a - p i, *n.* *T.* *cucumbers; seasoning, spices,* etc.

w i - ć a′ - h n a - k a - p i, *v.* *dead bodies laid up; tombs; burial-places.* *T.*, wićagnakapi, *bodies laid up on top of the ground* or *on scaffolds.* See wićaȟapi.

w i - ć a′ - h n a - y e, *n.* of hnayaŋ; *deception.*

w i - ć a′ - h o, *n.* *the human voice.*

w i - ć a′ - h u, *n.* *human bones.*

w i - ć a′ - h u - h a, *n.* *the limbs of the body.*

w i - ć a′ - h u - h u, *n.* *a human skeleton.*

w i - ć a′ - h u ŋ - k a - k e, *n* *ancestors.*

w i - ć a′ - h u ŋ - k u, *n.* *a mother, mothers.*

w i - ć a - ȟ a - p i, *n.* *T.* of ȟa; *bodies interred; graves, tombs.* Not properly used of burial on the surface of the ground or on scaffolds.

w i - ć a′ - ȟ a ŋ - ȟ a ŋ, *n.* *T.* *the small-pox.* See ȟaŋ, *scab.*

w i - ć a′ - ȟ b a, *n.* of ȟba; *drowsiness.*

w i′ - ć a - ȟ b o - k e, *n.* *a paddle, i. q.* wamnaheća. *T.*, walitope.

w i - ć a - ȟ ć a - l a, *n.* *T.* *an old man; an old male* of any kind.

w i′ - ć a - ȟ d e - ć e, *n.* of kaȟdeća; *something to tear* or *bruise with.*

wi'-ća-ȟdo-ke, *n.* of kaȟdoka; *something to make holes with*, as *a gimlet.*

wi-ća'-ȟća, *n* See wićaȟiŋća.

wi'-ća-ȟe-pe, *n.* of kaȟepa; *a ladle.*

wi-ća'-ȟiŋ-ća, *n. an old man*—wimaćaȟiŋća *and* wićamaȟiŋća, winićaȟiŋća *and* wićaniȟiŋća, wiuŋćaȟiŋćapi. See wićaȟćala.

wi-ća'-ȟmuŋ-ġa, *v. T. to shoot* or *send by magic* something (as a knife, nail, or bullet) *into* one, as the Dakota wizards pretend to do. To *remove* such things *by magic* is wokab iyeya.

wi-ća'-ȟmuŋ-ġa, *n. T. one who practices such shooting, a magician.*

wi-ća'-ȟmuŋ-ġe-s'a, *n. T. one who practices such shooting, a magician.*

wi'-ća-ȟpe, *n. an instrument to throw down with.* See kaȟpa.

wi'-ća-ȟpu, *n.* of kaȟpu; *an instrument to pick off with.*

wi'-ća-ȟu-ġe, *n.* of kaȟuġa; *something to break in with.*

wi-ća'-ȟuŋ-wiŋ, *n.* of ȟuŋwiŋ; *putrefaction.*

wi-ća'-i, *n. the human mouth.*

wi-ća'-i-ha, *n. the human lips.*

wi-ća-ka', *v.* of ka, *to mean; he means them.*

wi-ća'-ka, *v. n. to speak truth, to be true*—wićawaka, wićauŋkapi.

wi-ća'-ka-hi-ya-ya, *v.* of kahiyaya; *to carry round to them, to sing to them.*

wi-ća'-ka-ȟa-pa, *n* of kaȟapa; *a driver, one who drives.*

wi'-ća-kća, *n.* of kakća; *a curry-comb.*

wi-ća'-ke-da, *v. a.* (wićáka *and* da) *to esteem true, to believe*—wićakewada; wićakeiçida, *to believe one's self true, to continue to affirm.*

wi-ća'-ki-ćaŋ-pte, *n.* of kićaŋpta; *one who consoles, a comforter.*

wi-ća'-ki-ći-ća-źu-źu-pi, *n. forgiveness.*

wi-ća'-ki-ći-lo-waŋ, *v. T.* of lowaŋ; *to wail* or *sing for*, as for those who have gone on the war path, etc. See wiwakoŋza.

wi-ća'-ki-ćo-pi, *n.* of kićo; *calling, inviting.*

wi-ća'-ki-ġe-pi, *n. T.* of kiġe; *quarreling.*

wi-ća-kiŋ-će, *n.* of kakiŋća; *something to scrape with, a scraper.*

wi-ća-ki'-pi, *n. robbery.*

wi'-ća-kiś-ya, *v. to cause to suffer*—wićakiśwaya.

wi-ća'-ki-ya-pa, *v.* See kiyapa.

wi'-ća-ki-źe, *n.* of ićakiźa; *distress, suffering.*

wi'-ća-ko-ke, *n.* of kakoka; *a rattle, a rattler.*

wi'-ća-kpe, *n. a lancet; i. q.* kaŋićakpe. See wićatpe.

wi-ća'-ksa-pa, *n. wisdom.* See wićoksape.

wi'-ća-kse, *n.* of kaksa; *an instrument to cut off with.*

wi-ća'-kte-pi, *n. killing.*

wi-ća'-kte-s'a, *n. one who kills.*

wi-ća′-ḳu-pi, *n. giving.*

wi′-ća-mde-će, *n.* of kamdeća; *an instrument to break in pieces with*, as a sledge.

wi-ća′-na-ka, *n. tremor.* See náka.

wi-ća′-na-kśe-ća-pi, *n.* of nakśeća; *the cholera.*

wi-ća′-na-su, *n. the human brain. T.*, wićanasula.

wi-ća′-ni, *v.* and *n. T. they live; life; prosperity;* used of many, as wićoni is of one.

wi-ća′-ni-to, *n. the loins.*

wi-ća′-no-ġe, *n. human ears.*

wi-ćaŋ′-ḣpi, *n a star, the stars.*

wi-ćaŋ′-ḣpi-hiŋ-ḣpa-ya, *n. the falling of the stars*—applied to 1833.

wi-ćaŋ′-ḣpi-taŋ-ka, *n. large stars.* The name given to both *Venus* and *Jupiter*, as the morning and evening stars.

Wi-ćaŋ′-ḣpi-ya-mni, *n. three stars*—the name given to *General Crook.*

wi-ća′-o-ḣaŋ-ko, *n. T.* of oḣaŋko; *dexterity.*

wi-ća′-pa-ha, *n. the human scalp.*

wi-ća′-pa-hu, *n. the human skull.*

wi-ća′-pa-kśiŋ, *n. the human kidneys, the reins. T.*, wićaśa aźoŋtka.

wi′-ća-p'e, *n.* of ćap'a; *a piercer; the spines* or *beard* of one or more species of grass or weed; *a fork, a table-fork.* See wićabwotapi.

wi′-ća-p'e-ća, *n. a kind of grass armed with a long sharp beard. T.*, mićapeća.

wi′-ća-p'e-daŋ, *n. dim.* of wićape.

wi-ća′-pi, *n. the human liver.*

wi-ća′-po, *n. a swelling.*

wi-ća′-po-ġe, *n. the human nose.*

wi′-ća-po-te, *n.* of kapota; *an instrument to rend with.*

wi′-ća-psi-će, *n.* of kapsića; *anything to make jump with.*

wi′-ća-psiŋ-te, *n. a whip.* See ićapsiŋte.

wi′-ća-saŋ, *n. a razor. T.*, putiŋićaśla. See ićasaŋ.

wi′-ća-sde-će, *n.* of kasdeća; *something to split with, a wedge.*

wi′-ća-ski-će, *n.* of kaskića; *a press.*

wi′-ća-spe-ye, *n. a weight, a balance; scales. T.; scales, weights,* etc, are witkeyute.

wi′-ća-sto, *n* of kasto; *anything to smooth with, a brush.*

wi-ća′-śa, *n. Ih.* and *T. i. q.* wićaśta.

wi-ća′-śa-i-kte, *n. T. poison.*

wi-ća′-śa-ke, *n. human nails.*

wi-ća′-śa-ya-ta-pi-ka, *n. T.* See wićaśtayatapi.

wi′-ća-śda, *n.* of kaśda; *a scythe. T.*, peźićaśle. See ićaśda.

wi′-ća-śke, *n. something to tie with, bonds.*

wi′-ća-śki-će, *n. a press.*

wi-ća′-śta, *n. man, a man; mankind*—wimaćaśta *and* wićamaśta, wiuŋćaśtapi. See wićaśa *and* waśićuŋ.

wi-ća′-śta-a-kan-tu, *n. one of human kind, a mortal,* distinguished from the dead and spirits.

wi-ća′-śta-i-hda-wa, *n. one who counts himself a man; a chief.*

wi-ća′-śta-śni, *adj. unmanly, mean, wicked*—wićamaśtaśni *and* wimaćaśtaśni, wićaniśtaśni *and* winićaśtaśni, wićauŋśtapiśni.

wi-ća′-śta-śni-yaŋ, *adv. unmanly, wickedly.*

wi-ća′-śta-taŋ-ka, *n. a middle-aged man.*

wi-ća′-śta-wa-kaŋ, *n. a minister.* (In 1871 this was applied to *Indian* ministers, as waśićuŋ wakaŋ was to *white* ministers.—J. O. D.)

wi-ća′-śta-ya-ta-pi, *n a chief, a ruler, a sachem.* The Dakota chiefs have little authority, not much honor, and no emolument. *T.*, wićaśayatapika.

wi-ća′-ta-ku-ni-śni, *n. destruction.* See wićotakuniśni.

wi-ća′-taŋ-ćaŋ, *n. the human body.*

wi-ća′-taŋ-ktaŋ-ka, *n. the gull.*

wi-ća′-taŋ-ktaŋ-ka-daŋ, *n. the gull,* somewhat larger than a pigeon.

wi-ća′-ta-wi, *n. the raccoon moon, February.*

wi′-ća-ti-će, *n. a thing to scrape with, a scraper.*

wi-ća′-to-ka, *n. a male captive; a man-servant. T.*, toka wićaśa.

wi-ća′-to-ke-ća, *n difference; things different.*

wi-ća′-to-kto-ke-ća, *n. red.* of wićatokeća.

wi′-ća-tpe, *n. a lancet.* See ićatpe *and* wićakpe.

wi′-ća-tpi, *n.* of katpi; *something to crack with.*

wi-ća′-tu-te, *n. chapping,* as of the hands.

wi-ća′-ṭa, *n. the dead.*

wi′-ća-ṭe, *n. an instrument to kill with.*

wi′-ća-ṭiŋ-ze, *n. something to make tight with, a screw* or *nail.*

wi-ća′-uŋ-pi, *n. a man's shirt.*

wi′-ća-we-ġe, *n. something to break with.*

wi-ća′-wi-ho-mni, *n. a lewd fellow, a whore-monger*—wićawimahomni. *T.*, witkowiŋ waśtelaka.

wi-ća′-wi-tko-wiŋ-la, *n. T. a man who takes many women in succession, but does not keep any of them long.*

wi-ća′-wo-ȟa, *n. a man who lives with his wife's relations,* literally *a buried man*—wicawoȟa wauŋ. See wiwayuȟa. *T., a son-in-law, i. q.* takośku.

wi-ća′-ya, *adv. manly. T.*, wićaśa taŋka se.

wi-ća′-ya-ćo-pi, *n.* of yaćo; *condemnation; pronouncing sentence. T.*, wićayasupi.

wi-ća′-ya-taŋ-pi, *n. praise, compliments.*

wi-ća′-ya-zaŋ, *n. a being sick, a sickness.*

wi-ća′-yu-he, *n. a master.*

wi-ća′-yu-wa-ȟpa-ni-ća, *n. making poor.*

w i - ć a′ - y u - w i ŋ - t a - p i, *n. honoring*, as the Dakotas do at feasts, calling the maker of the feast by some name signifying relationship or friendship. *T.*, *stroking in* or *before the face, in token of respect* or *friendly greeting.*

w i′ - ć a - z o, *n. a pen, a pencil.*

w i′ - ć a - z i - p e, *n.* of kaźipa; *something to smooth* or *shave with, a plane.*

w i - ć e′ - ś k a, *n. the hole in the top of a tent.*

w i - ć e′ - ś k a - i - p a - s i - s e, *n. the pins that fasten a tent in front.*

w i - ć i′ - a - t k u - k u, *n.* See wićaatkuku.

w i - ć i′ - ć a - ġ e, *n. a growth of men, a generation.*

w i - ć i′ - ć a - ś k e, *n. T.*, *strips of blanket*, or *ornamented strips of any thing, worn over the shoulders and trailing on the ground.*

w i′ - ć i′ - ć i ŋ - ć a, *n.* Same as wićaćiŋća.

w i′ - ć i′ - m d e - z a, *n. clearness, pleasantness.*

w i - ć i′ - n a - p ć i ŋ - w a ŋ - k a, *num. adj. the ninth. T.*, wićinapćiŋyuŋka.

w i - ć i′ - n o ŋ - p a, *num. adj. the second.*

w i - ć i ŋ′, *v. to desire women, hunt after women*—wiwaćiŋ.

w i - ć i ŋ′ - ć a, *n. a girl.*

w i - ć i ŋ′ - ć a - d a ŋ, *n. a little girl:* wićiŋćapidaŋ.

w i - ć i ŋ′ - ć a - l a, *n. T. a girl.*

w i - ć i ŋ′ - ć a - n a, *n. Ih. a girl.*

w i - ć i ŋ′ - p i, *n. desiring women.*

w i - ć i ŋ′ - ś k a ŋ, *v. T. to be flirting* or *courting while busy at some kind of work.*

w i - ć i ŋ′ - y a ŋ - n a, *n. a girl, a damsel, a little girl*, applied also to to young women: wićiŋyaŋpidaŋ, *girls*—wimaćiŋyaŋna. *T.*, wićiŋćana.

w i - ć i′ - ś a - h d o - ġ a ŋ, *num. adj. the eighth: i. q.* ićiśahdoġaŋ.

w i - ć i′ - ś a - k d o - ġ a ŋ, *num. adj. Ih. the eighth.*

w i - ć i′ - ś a - k o - w i ŋ, *num. adj. the seventh: i. q.* ićiśakowiŋ.

w i - ć i′ - ś a - k p e, *num. adj. the sixth: i. q.* ićiśakpe.

w i ć - i ś′ - n a - n a, *adj. none with one, alone.*

w i′ ć i - ś n i - y a ŋ, *adv away off, not near* anything: wićiśniyaŋ eḣpeya, *to throw off at a distance, to lose.*

w i ć - i′ - ś p a, *n. the fore-arm; the distance from the elbow to the end of the middle finger, a cubit.*

w i ć - i′ - ś t a, *n. the human eye.*

w i ć - i′ - ś t i ŋ - b e, *n. sleep; they are asleep:* wićiśtiŋbe hiyeya, *they are all asleep.* See wićoiśtiŋbe.

w i ć - i′ - t e, *n. the human face, the countenance.*

w i ć - i′ - t e - g l e - ġ a, *n. T. the raccoon: i. q.* itehdeġadaŋ.

w i ć - i′ - t e - o - w a - p i, *n. T. the picture of a face; a photograph*, etc.

w i ć - i′ - t o - k a - p a, *n. the eldest born.*

wi-ći'-to-pa, *num. adj. the fourth: i. q.* itopa.

wić-i'-tpi, *n. the human stomach. T.*, wićikpi.

wi-ći'-wi-kće-mna, *num. adj. the tenth: i. q.* iwikćemna.

wi-ći'-ya-mni, *num. adj. the third: i. q.* iyamni.

wi-ći'-ye, *pron. one's self; themselves.*

wi'-ći-ye-ća, *v. n. not to lay to heart; not to think about; it is of no use*—wimiçiyeća. This is one of the words to which we have long endeavored to attach an intelligible idea, but in vain. The meanings given are simply approximative. See wićiyeśni.

wi'-ći-ye-ća-e, *v.* Same as wićiyeća.

Wi-ći'-ye-la, *n. T.* the name applied by the Tetons to the Yankton and Yanktonnais Dakotas.

wi'-ći-ye-śni, *v. n.* winiçiyeśni ake nakuŋ den yahi, *not caring, thou hast come back again.*

wi-ći'-yo-ki-pi, *n. excellence, beauty, pleasantness.*

wić-i'-yuŋ-ka, *n. T. bed-time.* See iwaŋka.

wi-ći'-za-ptaŋ, *num. adj. the fifth.*

wi-ćo'-a-ho-pe, *n.* of ahopa; *law, custom, ceremony.*

wi-ćo'-a-i-e, *n.* of aia; *slander.*

wi-ćo'-a-yu-śtaŋ, *n.* of ayuśtaŋ; *leaving off.*

wi-ćo'-be, *n.* of obe; *a company. T*, wićowe.

wi-ćo'-bi-li-he-ća, *n. T.* See wićomniheća.

wi-ćo'-ćaŋ-ni-ye, *n.* of ćaŋniyaŋ; *anger, malice. T.*, wićoćaŋzeka.

wi-ćo'-ćaŋt-a-hde, *n.* of ćaŋtahde; *evil intention, malice.*

wi-ćo'-ćaŋ-te, *n. the human heart.* See wićaćaŋte.

wi-ćo'-ćaŋ-te-i-yu-taŋ-ye, *n. temptation.* See wowiyutaŋye.

wi-ćo'-ćaŋ-te-o-ze, *n. thought, purpose. T.*, wićoćaŋteoyuze.

wi-ćo'-ćaŋ-te-ptaŋ-ye, *n.* of ćaŋteptaŋyaŋ; *passion.*

wi-ćo'-ćaŋ-te-śi-ća, *n. sadness.*

wi-ćo'-ćaŋ-te-wa-śte, *n. gladness.*

wi-ćo'-ćaŋ-te-yu-ze, *n. disposition, wish.*

wi-ćo'-ćaŋt-i-he-ye, *n. desire, covetousness.*

wi-ćo'-ćaŋt-i-ya-hde-ye, *n. what is desired.*

wi-ćo'-ća-źe-ya-te, *n.* of ćaźeyata; *traditions.* See wićoie.

wi-ćo'-će-ya, *n.* of ćeya; *crying, weeping. T.*, wićaćeya.

wi-ćo'-ćo-koŋ, *n.* of ćokoŋ; *threatening, intending evil.*

wi-ćo'-ću-wi-ta, *n. the feeling of coldness.*

wi-ćo'-du-za-he, *n.* of duzahaŋ; *swiftness.*

wi-ćo'-e-će-tu, *n.* of ećetu; *uprightness.*

wi-ćo'-e-ki-će-tu-ye, *n.* of ekićetuya; *restoration.*

wi-ćo'-haŋ, *adv. into the crowd*—prob. wića *and* ohna.

wi-ćo'-hni-hde, *n. traveling.*

wi-ćo'-ḣaŋ, *n.* of oḣaŋ; *work, custom, habit.*

wi-ćo'-ḣta-ni, *n.* of ḣtani; *labor, work.* *T.*, wowaśi; wowaśi ećoŋpi.

wi-ćo'-i-ća-ġe, *n.* of ićaġa; *a generation*

wi-ćo'-i-e, *n.* of oie; *a word, a speech.* *T.*, also *a story, legend,* etc.

wi-ćo'-i-hda-taŋ, *n.* of ihdataŋ; *boasting.*

wi-ćo'-i-na-ḣni, *n.* of inaḣni; *haste, hurrying.*

wi-ćo'-i-śtiŋ-be, *n.* of iśtiŋma; *sleep.* See wićiśtiŋbe.

wi-ćo'-i-toŋ-pe, *n.* of itoŋpa; *carefulness.*

wi-ćo'-i-toŋ-śni, *n* of itoŋśni; *a lie, a falsehood.* *T.*, wićoowewakaŋ.

wi-ćo'-i-tu-ka-ġe, *n.* of itukaġa; *falsehood, calumny.* *T.*, wićoie otuya kaġe

wi-ćo'-i-yo-ki-śi-će, *n. sorrow.*

wi-ćo'-i-yo-pe-i-ç̣i-ye, *n. repentance.*

wi-ćo'-ka-ġi, *n.* of kaġi; *a hindrance.*

wi-ćo'-ka-ġi-ye, *n. an obstruction.*

wi-ćo'-ka-ki-źe, *n.* of kakiźa; *suffering.*

wi'-ćo-kaŋ-hi-ya-ya, *n.* *T. noon.*

wi'-ćo-kaŋ-hi-ya-ya sam i-ya-ya, *n.* *T. afternoon.* See witakiŋyaŋyaŋka.

wi'ćo-kaŋ-hi-ya-ya-yaŋ-ka, *adv.* *T. just at noon.*

wi-ćo'-kaŋ-hi-yu-i-ći-ya, *v* *T. to come in unasked: i. q.* ipasbuiyeiç̣iya.

wi'-ćo-ka'-ya, *n.* *Ih. noon.*

wi-ćo'-ki-ći-yu-wa-śte, *n. a blessing, peace*

wi-ćo'-ki-ći-ze, *n.* of kićiza; *fighting*

wi-ćo'-ki-pa-źiŋ, *n.* of kipaźiŋ; *opposition.*

wi-ćo'-koŋ-ze, *n. influence, law; a kingdom.*

wi-ćo'-ksa-pe, *n.* of ksapa; *wisdom.*

wi-ćo'-ku-źe, *n.* of kuźa; *laziness.* *T., sickness.* See wokwźe.

wi-ćo'-ku-źi-ṭa, *n. dying of laziness.*

wi-ćo'-mni-ći-ye, *n.* of mnićiya; *an assembly.*

wi-ćo'-mni-he-ća, *n.* of mniheća; *activity.* *T.*, wićobiliheća.

wi-ćo'-ni, *n.* (wića *and* oni) *life, present* but especially *to come; a life-time:* wićoni owihaŋke wanića, *eternal life.*

wi-ćo'-ni-pe-źi-hu-ta, *n. the balsam of life.*

wi-ćo'-ni-wo-wa-pi, *n. the book of life, the Bible.*

wi-ćoŋ'-ṭe, *n.* (wića, oŋ *and* ṭa) *death.*

wi-ćo'-oŋ-śi-ke, *n.* of oŋśika; *poverty.*

wi-ćo′-o-pe, *n.* *law, custom.*

wi-ćo′-o-uŋ-hda-ka, *n.* of uŋhdaka; *a moving party.* *T.*, oiglake.

wi-ćo-o-we-wa-kaŋ, *n.* *T.* *a lie, a falsehood.*—W. J. C.

wi-ćo′-o-we-wa-kaŋ-kaŋ, *n.* *Ih.* *deceit:* *i. q.* wohnaye.—J. O. D.

wi-ćo′-o-wo-taŋ-na, *n.* of owotaŋna; *righteousness.*

wi ćo′ o yu mdo ćo, *n.* *a breaking in pieces, separation.*

wi-ćo′-su-ta, *n.* of suta; *firmness, strength.*

wi-ćo′-śi-će, *n.* of śića; *evil.*

wi-ćo′-śi-ḣtiŋ, *n.* of śiḣtiŋ; *debility.* *T.*, *imperfection; badness*

wi-ćo′-śkaŋ-śkaŋ, *n.* of śkaŋśkaŋ; *moving, motion;* used for *government, reign.*

wi-ćo′-śka-te, *n.* of śkata; *play.*

wi-ćo′-śki-śke, *n.* of ośkiśke; *difficulty, distraction.*

wi-ćo′-ta, *n.* *many persons, a multitude.*

wi-ćo′-ta-ku-ni-śni, *n.* *destruction.*

wi-ćo′-ta-ku-ye, *n.* of takuya; *relationship, brotherhood.*

wi-ćo′-ta-wa-ćiŋ, *n.* *disposition.*

wi-ćo′-te-ća, *n.* of teća; *newness.*

wi-ćo′-ti, *n.* *a village, i. q.* otoŋwe; *a camp.*

wi-ćo′-to-ke-tu, *adv.* *how is it?* wićotoketu taŋiŋ śni, *how it is is not apparent.*

wi-ćo′-uŋ, *n.* *a family, all that are related by blood.* This word, and also "wićotakuye," we have used for *covenant.* See wićowazi.

wi-ćo′-uŋ-hda-ka, *n.* of uŋhdaka; *a moving.*

wi-ćo′-wa-ćiŋ, *n.* *thought.*

wi-ćo′-wa-ćiŋ-ko, *n.* of waćiŋko; *bad temper.*

wi-ćo′-wa-ḣba-daŋ, *n.* *gentleness.*

wi-ćo′-wa-kaŋ-he-źa, *n.* *debility.*

wi-ćo′-wa-mna-da-śni, *n.* *disrespect, contempt.*

wi-ćo′-wa-ś'a-ke, *n.* *human strength.*

wi-ćo′-wa-śte, *n.* of waśte; *goodness.*

wi-ćo′-wa-zi, *n.* *a family, kindred.* See waohećoŋ.

wi-ćo-we-pi, *n.* *T.* *relatives; family; ancestry.* See wićobe.

wi-ćo′-wi-ća-śta-śni, *n.* *villainy.* *T.*, wićowićaśaśni, *mischief, meanness,* etc.

wi-ćo′-wo-hda-ke, *n.* *relating stories, biography.*

wi-ćo′-wo-ya-ke, *n.* of oyaka; *declaration, narration, doctrine* We have used this word for *chapter.*

wi-ćo′-yu-ta-ku-ni-śni, *n.* *that which causes destruction.*

wi-ćo′-yu-tkoŋ-ze, *n.* *that which makes equal.*

wi-ćo′-zun-ye, *n.* of zuŋta; *connectedness, relationship.* *T.*, otakuye.

wi-ćo′-źi-će, *n.* of źića; *riches.* *T.*, wiźiće.

wi-ćo′-źu-daŋ, *n.* of oźudaŋ; *fullness; full of people.*

wi-çi′-ćaḣ, *adv.* *uneasily:* wiçićaḣ yaŋka: *according to habit, in his own way.* *T.*, iyaye kinil

wi-çi′-ćaḣ-ćaḣ, *adv. red.* of wiçićaḣ. These words are used when one, getting uneasy and wishing to leave, pulls his blanket up, rises and walks about, but says nothing.

wi′-çiŋ, *n.* of ķiŋ; *the strap which the Dakotas use in packing.*

wid′-wi-ta-ya, *adv. red.* of witaya; *in groups, assembled in different places:* widwitaya yakoŋpi.

wi′-dun-ye, *n.* *anything to color red with, cochineal.* *T.*, wilulye

wi′-ha-ha, *adj.* *jovial, good natured.*

wi′-ha-ha-ka, *n.* *one who is pleased with trifles.*

wi′-ha-ha-ya, *adv.* wihahaya iću, *to take trifles gladly.*

wi-ha′-ke, *n.* *the fifth child, if a daughter;* so called, probably, from its usually *being the last.* *T.*, wihakakta.

wi′-haŋ-mde, *v.* Same as wihaŋmna.

wi′-haŋ-mde-ś'a, *n.* *a dreamer.*

wi′-haŋ-mna, *v.* of ihaŋmna; *to dream*—wiwahaŋmna, wiuŋhaŋmnaŋpi.

wi′-haŋ-mnaŋ-pi, *n.* *a dreaming.*

wi′-hda-ḣpa, *v. pos.* *to strike* or *take down one's own tent*—wiwahdaḣpa. *T.*, glaḣpá. See kaḣpa.

wi′-hda-śta-ka, *v. pos.* *to beat one's wife*—wiwahdaśtaka. *T.*, wíkte. See hdaśtaka.

wi′-hda-wa, *v.* of ihdawa; *to count one's self*—wiwahdawa.

wi′-hdi, *n.* of ihdi; *oil, grease.*

wi′-hdu-kćaŋ, *v.* of ihdukćaŋ; *to understand one's own* or *one's self, to form an opinion*—wiwahdukćaŋ.

wi′-hi-na-pa, *n.* *the sun rising, the east.*

wi′-hi-na-pa-taŋ-haŋ, *adv.* *from the east.*

wi-hiŋ′-pa-spa, *n.* *T.* *a tent-pin.*

wi′-hi-ya-ye-daŋ, *n.* *a clock, a watch.* *T.*, mazaśkaŋśkaŋ.

wi′-hmuŋ-ke, *n.* of hmuŋka; *the rainbow; a trap, a snare.* In this latter sense, however, it is not much used. *T.*, wigmuŋke, *a rainbow;* but mas-igmuŋke, *a trap* or *snare.*

wi′-hni, *v.* of ihni; *to hunt,* as deer—wiwahni. *T.*, wigni.

wi′-hni-pi, *n.* *a chasing deer.*

wi′-hnu, *v.* of ihnu; *to murmur; to reproach, accuse; to be displeased with*—wiwahnu.

wi′-hnu-pi, *n.* *a murmuring.*

wi-ho′-mni, *n.* *turning round; a prostitute.* *T*, *turning round;* but *a prostitute* is wihomniwiŋ

wi-hu′-ta, *n.* *the lower border of a tent.*

wi-hu′-ta-i-na-ta-ke, *n.* *something used to fasten up around the bottom of a tent,* as grass.

wi-hu′-ti-pa-spe, *n.* *tent-pins.*

wi'-ḣaŋ, *v.* of iḣaŋ; *to graze, eat grass*, like cattle.

wi'-ḣaŋ-ki-ya, *v. a.* *to cause to graze; to keep cattle*—wiḣaŋwakiya.

wi'-ḣaŋ-pi, *n.* *a feeding*, as cattle, *a grazing.*

wi'-ḣaŋ-wi-ća-ki-ye, *n.* *a grazier.*

wi-ḣi'-pa, *n.* *Sisit.* See wiḣupa.

wi'-ḣmuŋ-ġe, *n.* *witch-medicine; i. q.* oŋ kićiḣmuŋġapi.

wi'-ḣpe-ya, *v. a.* *to throw away a woman; leave a wife*—wiḣpewaya. *T., to give away things after a death in the family.*

wi'-ḣpe-ya-pi, *n.* *T.* *the practice of giving away property on the death of a member of the family.*

wi-ḣu'-pa, *n.* *the flaps of a tent. T.*, wipipa.

wi-i'-ći-hni, *v.* *to scold* or *whip a woman*—wiiwećihni *and* wiiwakihni.

wi-i'-hni, *v.* *to maltreat a woman*—wiiwahni. See ihni.

wi'-i-na-ḣma, *v.* *to conceal a woman, take her off; to commit fornication*—wiinawaḣbe, wiinauŋḣmaŋpi.

wi'-i-ya-ḣpa-ya, *v.* *T.* *to commit rape, to force a woman: i. q.* wikiśleya.

wi'-i-ya-oŋ-pa, *v.* *to charge a man* or *woman with infidelity, accuse in reference to a woman*—wiiyawaoŋpa, wiiyauŋḳoŋpapi.

wi'-i-ya-oŋ-pa-pi, *n.* *charging with infidelity* or *with having had illicit intercourse.*

wi'-i-ya-pa-ḣi-će, *n.* *the fastenings of a tent at the top.*

wi'-i-ya-ta-pi, *n.* *a girl betrothed* or *given to one without his asking for her. T.*, wiŋyaŋ wićaḳupi. See iyata.

wi'-i-ya-ya, *v.* *the sun sets; sundown.*

wi'-i-ya-yu-ḣa, *v.* *to leave home and take a wife at another village and live with her friends*—wiiyamduḣa.

wi'-i-ya-yu-ḣi-ya, *adv.* *with the course of the sun, from east to west.*

wi'-kal-ye, *n.* *T.* *a tea-kettle; a coffee-pot.*

wi'-kaŋ, *n.* *Ih.* *a leather cord, a packing-strap; i. q.* teḣmiso.

wi'-ka-waŋ-ka-bu, *n.* *T. about* 7 or 8 *a. m.*

wi'-kće-kće-ya, *adv.* *T.* *for nothing; to no purpose:* wikćekćeya omani, *to walk about aimlessly.*

wi-kće'-mna, *num. adj.* *ten:* wikćemna noŋpa, *twenty*, etc.

wi'-ki-ćaŋ-ye, *n.* *tools, implements.*

wi'-ki-ći-yuŋ-ġa-pi, *n.* *T.*, of iyuŋġa; *a questioning of one another.*

wi'-ki-çuŋ, *adv.* *T.* waćiŋ wikiçuŋśni, *one who is indifferent.*

wi-ki'-kśaŋ, *v.* *to commit a rape*—wiwakikśaŋ.

wi-ki'-kśaŋ-pi, *n.* *rape.*

wi-ki'-śde, *v.* *to offer indignities to women*—wiwakiśde. *T.*, wikiśle.

wi-ki'-śde-pi, *n* *a molesting* or *taking liberties with women.*

w i - k i'- ś d e - ś d e, *v. red.* of wikiśde.

w i - k i'- ś d e - y a, *v. a. to offer insults to a woman*—wikiśdewaya. See wiiyaḣpaya.

w i - k i'- ś k a ŋ, *v. T. to play with a woman*, but not in a bad sense: *i. q.* wikiśkata.

w i - k i'- ś k a ŋ - p i, *n. T. playing* or *romping with a woman.*

w i - k i'- ś k a - t a (wi *and* kiśkata), *v. T. i. q.* wikiśkaŋ.

w i - k i'- ś l e - y a - p i, *n. T. rape.*

w i'- k i - y u - t a, *v. to beckon to, talk by signs*—wiwakiyuta.

w i - k o', *n: cont.* of wikośka.

w i'- k o - p a, *v.* of ikopa; *to fear, be afraid*—wikowapa.

w i'- k o - p e - ć a, *n. one who is to be feared.*

w i'- k o - p e - ś n i - y a ŋ, *adv. without fear, securely.*

w i - k o'- ś k a, *n. a young woman*—wimakośka, wiuŋkośkapi. This word, like kośka, had a bad meaning in *T.*, and should be avoided: wiśaŋ yazaŋ, "a woman who is kośka, or *affected with the venereal disease.*"—W. J. C.

w i - k o'- ś k a - l a - k a, *n. T. a young woman; i. q.* wikośka.

w i - k o'- ś k a - t a ŋ - k a, *n. a developed woman.*

w i'- k s a - p a, *v.* of iksapa; *to comprehend well, to have experience*—wiwaksapa.

w i'- k t e, *v. to beat a woman*—wiwakte. *T., to beat one's wife.* See wiḣdaśtaka.

w i - k u'- ć i - y e - l a, *n. T. towards sunset, late in the afternoon.*

w i - k u'- w a - y a b - y a - y a, *n. T. about three p. m.*

w i'- m a - k a - h e - y a, *n. that which tempts, that which leads* one *to kill* any thing. *T., that which enables* one *to earn* or *accomplish much.*

w i'- m a - h e l - i - y a'- y a, *n. T. sunset.*

w i'- m n a - ś n i, *adj. not having known women.* See wipemnaśni.

w i n, *cont.* of wiŋta; win uŋ, *it is creeping. T.*, slohaŋ.

w i'- n a - ḣ m a, *v.* of inaḣma; *to hide, conceal.* See wiinaḣma.

w i'- n a - ḣ o ŋ, *v.* of naḣoŋ; *to hear, to be able to hear*—winawaḣoŋ: winaḣoŋ śni, *deaf.*

w i'- n a - k a - p o, *n. T. hops; yeast.*

w i'- n a - k i - w i - ż i, *v. to be jealous* or *envious of*—winawakiwizi.

w i'- n a - p ć e, *n. T. the esophagus.*

w i'- n a - p i - ś k a ŋ - y e, *n. T. a toy, toys, playthings.* See inapiśkaŋyaŋpi.

w i'- n a - p o ḣ - y a - p i *or* wi'- n a - p o ḣ - y e, *n. T.* of napoġaŋ; *yeast.*

w i'- n a - t a - k e, *n.* of inatake; *a fastening, a lock.*

w i'- n a - w i - z i, *v. to be jealous* or *envious*—winawawizi, winauŋwizipi.

w i - n a'- w i - z i - d a ŋ, *n. the cockle-burr*, or *clot-burr, a species of Xanthium.*

w i'- n a - w i - z i - p i, *n. jealousy.*

w i - n a'- w i - z i - s' a, *n. a jealous person; of a jealous disposition.*

wi-no'-ȟća, *n.* *Ih.* and *T.* *an old woman:* In *Ih.* and *T.* wiŋyaŋ is used for *woman.* *T.*, winoȟća is never used of *a middle-aged woman.*

wi-no'-ȟća-la, *n.* *T.* *an old woman.*

wi-no'-ȟiŋ-ća, *n.* *a woman, women.*

wi-no'-na, *n.* *the first-born child, if a daughter.* *T.*, witokapa.

wi-no'-za-ta, *n.* See winuzata.

wi-nu', *n.* *a name given to a woman who is a captive from another people.* *T.*, wi-wayaka.

wi'-nu-ke, *n* *something that makes grow*, as *manure* on a field, and *food* for man. *T.*, wićaȟye.

wi-nu'-za-ta, *n.* *the lower part of a tent* or *house in the inside.*

wiŋ, *adj.* *female, woman, wife; i. q.* winoȟiŋća. This is commonly suffixed to the names of women.

wiŋ'-ġa, *v. root.* *bending.*

wiŋȟ, *cont.* of wiŋġa.

wiŋȟ-ya, *adv.* *in a bent manner.*

wiŋ'-kta, *n.* *a hermaphrodite; i. q.* wiŋyaŋićida. *T.*, wiŋkte.

wiŋ'-kta-pi, *n.* *sodomy.* *T.*, wiŋktépi.

wiŋ'-na, *adj. dim.* of wiŋ.

wiŋś, *cont.* of wiŋźa.

wiŋś-ki'-ya, *v. a.* *to make bend, bend down*—wiŋśwakiya.

wiŋś-wiŋ'-źe-daŋ, *adj.* *limber, pliant, not stiff; tender.*

wiŋ'-ta, *v. n.* *to creep, crawl*, as a child—wawiŋta, uŋwiŋtapi, See win.

wiŋ'-yaŋ, *n.* *Ih.* and *T.* *a woman;* plur. wiŋyaŋpi. See winoȟća. *T.*, wiŋyaŋ witkowiŋ se uŋ, *one who takes many wives but is constant to none*

wiŋ'-yaŋ, *adj* *female*—wimayaŋ, winiyaŋ.

wiŋ'-yaŋ-ćiŋ, *v.* *T.* *to buy a wife:* *i. q.* wiŋyaŋ opetoŋ.

wiŋ'-źa. See yuwiŋźa.

wiŋ-źa'-haŋ, *part.* *bent down*, as grass.

wiŋ-źa'-wa-haŋ, *part.* *bent down.*

wi-o'-ki-he-daŋ, *n.* See wiyokihedaŋ. *T.*, wowapi.

wi-o'-ki-ya, *v.* of okiya; *to court* or *talk with a woman; to gratify lust*—wiowakiya, wioyakiya.

wi-o'-ki-ya-pi, *n.* *courting.*

wi-o'-wa, *n.* *a painted tent.* *T.*, tiowapi.

wi'-pa-ġu-ke, *n.* of paġuka; *a bone* or *iron used for scraping down skins in the process of dressing.*

wi'-pa-ȟte, *n.* *T.* *string; any thing used for tying; a bridle.* See ipaȟte.

wi'-pa-mda-ye, *n.* of pamdaya; *something to smooth with, smoothing irons, flat-irons.*

wi'-pa-śki-će, *n.* of paśkića; *a press; a washboard.*

wi'-pa-ta, *v.* of ipata; *to ornament, work with porcupine quills*—wiwapata, wiuŋpatapi.

wi'-pa-ta-pi, *n.* *quill-work, embroidery.*

wi'-pa-tiŋ, *n.* *T.* *starch.*

w i - p a′ - z u - k a , *n.* *a species of red berry* growing on small bushes, which is good to eat: *the service berry,* sometimes called *June berry.*

w i - p a′ - z u - k a - h u , *n.* *a small bushy shrub used by the Dakotas for making arrows, arrow-wood; the service berry bush.*

w i′ - p a - ź a - ź a , *n.* of paźaźa; *soap.* *T.*, ha-ipaźaźa.

w i′ - p a - ź i ŋ , *v.* *to be prevented from succeeding in what one attempts to do by having lost a friend,* etc.—wimapaźiŋ. When the Dakotas are unsuccessful in fishing or hunting, they attribute the fact to the presence of ghosts who scare away the fish or the deer. In some instances they think it is their own spirit which is already leaving the body, and they regard it as an omen of approaching death.

w i′ - p e , *n.* of pe; *sharp instruments, arms; weapons* of any kind, *firearms.*

w i′ - p e - m n a - ś n i , *adv.* *T.* *without being wounded; dead but not wounded; dead without apparent cause.* Compare wimnaśni.

w i′ - p e - o - ḣ d o - k a , *n* *a wound made by a spear.*

wi - pe′ - ya, *v.* *T.* *to sell a woman* or *girl in marriage,* as the Dakotas do.

w i - p e′ - y a - p i , *n.* *T.* *a woman* or *girl thus* sold. See wiiyatapi.

w i′ - p i , *v. n.* *to be full of food, to be satisfied*—wimapi, winipi, wiuŋpipi.

w i - p i′ - p a , *n.* *T.* *tent-flaps: i. q.* wiḣipa.

w i′ - p i - y a , *v. a.* *to fill, cause to be full*—wipiwaya; wipiiçiya, *to satisfy one's self with eating*—wipimiçiya.

w i′ - p i - y a , *adv.* *full.*

w i′ - p u - s p e , *n.* of puspa; *a seal, a wafer.*

w i′ - s a m - y e , *n.* *any thing which gives a black hue, blacking.*

w i′ - s a ŋ - y e , *n.* *whiting.*

w i′ - s i - t e - t o ŋ - n a , *n.* *a harlot, a whore.* See witkowiŋ.

w i′ - s k u - y e , *n* *any thing which fastens colors,* such as *alum* or *cranberries.* *T.*, *anything which sweetens* or *sours* other things.

w i - s m a′ - h i , *n.* *T.* *an arrow-head.*

w i′ - s p e - y a , *v.* *to cast anchor*—wispewaya. *T*, walićaśke eḣpeya. See speya.

w i′ - s p e - y e , *n.* *an anchor.* *T.*, walićaśke.

w i - ś a ŋ′ , *n.* *the "mons veneris;" the vagina: i. q.* śaŋ.

w i′ - ś a - y e , *n.* *any thing used in coloring red.*

w i′ - ś i , *n* *Ih. and T.* *hire, pay for work, remuneration.*

w i - ś ' o′ - ś ' o , *adj.* *hasty, quick*—wimaś'oś'o.

w i - ś ' o′ - ś ' o - k a , *n.* *one who is hasty.*

w i′ - ś t e - ć a , *adj.* *modest, bashful*—wimaśteća, winiśteća

w i′ - ś t e n - k i - ć i - y a - p i , *n.* *the being ashamed of each other.* *T.*, wiśtelkićiyapi. See wiśteŋkiya.

wi′-śten-ki-ya, *v. a.* *to be bashful* or *reserved*, *to be ashamed of*, as a Dakota man is of some of his wife's relations, especially the females, and a woman of her husband's relations, especially the males. By this custom, which is universal, they are not permitted to mention the names of these connections, nor to look them in the face or communicate directly with them—wiśtenwakiya, wiśtenmakiya. *T.*, wiśtelkiya.

wi′-śten-ki-ya-pi, *n.* *the custom above spoken of.*

wi′-śten-ya, *v. n.* *to cause to be ashamed*—wiśtenwaya. *T.*, wiśtelya.

wi′-śte-śte-ća, *adj. red.* of wiśteća; *modest.*

wiś-wi′, *intj* *almost*, *nearly; oh!* *i. q.* wawateća *and* iśnikaeś.

wi′-ta, *n.* *an island.*

wi′-ta-ke, *n.* *T.* *a frying-pan.*

wi′-ta-kiŋ-yaŋ-yaŋ-ka, *n.* *afternoon.* *T.*, wićokaŋhiyaya sam iyaya *and* witaŋunaptaŋhiyaya.

wi′-ta-ki-ya, *adv.* *together*, *en masse.*

wi′-taŋ, *adj.* *proud*, *elated*—wimataŋ. See itaŋ, wowitaŋ, *and* yutaŋ.

wi-taŋ′-śna, *n* *a maiden*, *one who is without a husband*, *one who lives alone:* witaŋśna uŋ. Mr. Renville has used this word to designate *figs*, but with doubtful propriety. Witanśna taŋke, *an old maid*.

wi-taŋ′-śna-hu, *n.* a name given by Mr. Renville to the *fig-tree.*

wi′-taŋ-taŋ, *v. red.* of witaŋ; *proud*, *vain*—wimataŋtaŋ.

wi′-taŋ-taŋ-ka, *n.* *one who is proud.*

wi′-taŋ-taŋ-pi, *n.* *vain-glory*, *pride.*

wi′-taŋ-taŋ-yaŋ, *v a.* *to make proud.*

wi′-taŋ-taŋ-yaŋ, *adv.* *glorying.*

Wi′-ta-pa-ha, *n. p.* *a tribe of Indians—the Kiowas.*

wi′-ta-wa-ta, *n.* *a ship.* *T.*, miniwaŋća wata.

wi-ta′-wa-ṭen-ya, *v.* *to be willing.* See tawaṭenya.

wi′-ta-ya, *adv.* *together*, *in company.* See ptaya.

wi′-ta-ya-i-he-ya, *v.* *to assemble together*—witaya iheuŋyaŋpi.

wi′-te-ha-ka, *n.* *one who is dissatisfied with every little thing.* *T.*, wakaȟtakeka.

wi-te′-śdag-ki-toŋ, *v.* *the moon* or *sun wears a crown;* said of the halo sometimes observed. *T.*, wiaćeićiti.

wi′-tka, *n.* of itka; *an egg; a testicle.* *T.*, *a testicle* is "susu." Witka eś kaȟuġe śni, *slowly*, *gently; so as not to break even eggs.* The phrase comes from the habit of carrying eggs for long distances.

wi′-tka-toŋ, *v.* *T.* *to lay eggs*, as fowls.

wi′-tke-u-ta, *n.* *a steelyard*, *scales.* *T.*, witkeyute.

wi-tko′, *n.* *a kind of fish* with a thick short body, *the dog-fish.*

wi-tko′, *adj.* *drunk, drunken; foolish*—wimatko, winitko, wiuŋtkopi.

Wi-tko′-ka-ġa, *n.* *the fool-maker;* an imaginary being worshipped by the Dakotas, and said to visit them in dreams.

wi-tko′-koŋ-za, *v. n.* *to pretend to be drunk*—witkowakoŋza.

wi-tko′-pi, *n.* *drunkenness.*

wi-tko′-tko, *adj.* *foolish*—wimatkotko, wiuŋtkotkopi.

wi-tko′-tko-ka, *n.* *a fool*—wimatkotkoka.

wi-tko′-tko-pi, *n.* *foolishness.*

wi-tko′-tko-ya, *adv.* *foolishly.*

wi-tko′-wiŋ, *n.* *a foolish woman, a harlot.* *T.*, witkowiŋwaśtelaka, *a lewd fellow: i. q.* wićawihomni. See wisitetoŋna.

wi-tko′-wiŋ-na, *n.* Same as witkowiŋ. *T.*, witkowiŋla.

wi-tko′-ya, *v. a.* *to make drunk*—witkowaya, witkomayaŋ.

wi-tko′-ya, *adv.* *foolishly, like a drunken man.*

wi-tko′-ya-haŋ, *adv.* *foolishly, sillily.*

wi-to′-ka, *n.* *a female captive.* *T.*, toka wiŋyaŋ. See winu.

wi′-toŋ-pe-śni, *adv.* *T.* *without fear* or *regard for anything: i. q.* kaġiśniśni. See itoŋpa.

wi′-to-ye, *n.* *something that dyes blue* or *green; green* or *blue blanketing.*

wi′-wa-koŋ-za, *v. a.* *to wail for those who have gone out on a war party*—wiwawakoŋza, wiwicayawakoŋza. *T.*, wićakićilowaŋ.

wi′-waŋ-ġa, *v.* of iwaŋġa; *to ask questions, to inquire*—wimuŋġa, wiuŋwaŋġapi, wimawaŋġa. *T.*, wiyuŋġa.

wi′-waŋ-ġa-pi, *n.* *questions.*

wi′-waŋḣ, *cont.* of wiwaŋġa; wiwaŋḣ wahi, *I have come to ask questions.* *T.*, wiyuŋḣ.

wi′-waŋḣ-tu-ken, *adv.* *in an inquiring way.*

wi′-waŋḣ-ya, *v. a.* *to cause to inquire*—wiwaŋḣwaya.

wi′-waŋ-kaŋ-tu-ya, *n.* *T.* wiwaŋkaŋtuya u *or* hiyu, *about* 9 *a. m.*

wi-wa′-śte, *n.* See wiwaśteka.

wi-wa′-śte-ka, *n.* *a beautiful woman, a lady.*

wi-wa′-ya, *adj.* *boggy, marshy.* See wiwiyela.

wi-wa′-yu-ḣa, *v.* *to live with the relatives of one's husband; a woman who lives with her husband's relations*—wiwamduḣa. See wićawoḣa *and* wiwoḣa.

wi-wa′-zi-ća, *n.* *a widow.*

wi-wi′, *n.* *a bog, a quagmire.* *T.*, wiwila.

wi′-wi-ća-hnu-pi, *n.* *accusation, blaming.*

wi′-wi-ća-waŋ-ġa-pi, *n.* *questions.* *T.*, wiwićayuŋġapi.

wi′-wi-ća-źi-će, *n.* *riches.*

wi-wi′-la, *n.* *T.* *a spring, a bog: i. q.* wiwi.

wi-wi′-ya, *adj.* *T.* *springy, boggy, marshy.*

wi-wi′-ye-la, *adj.* *T.* *ditto.*

wi-wo′-ḣa, *n.* *T.* *i. q.* wiwayuḣa.

wi′-wo-śta-ke, *n.* *T.* *a blunt arrow,* such as boys use.

wi-wo′-ti-ki-ya, *v.* *T.* See wotikiya.

wi′-ya-ćiŋ, *v.* of iyaćiŋ; *to liken to, compare to* or *with*—wimdaćiŋ, wiuŋyaćiŋpi.

wi′-ya-ćiŋ-i-a-pi, *n.* *parables, similitudes.*

wi′-ya-ćiŋ-pi, *n.* *likeness, resemblance, similitude.*

wi′-ya-ćiŋ-yaŋ, *adv.* *parabolic, in the form of similitude.*

wi′-ya-haŋ, *v.* of iyahaŋ; *to alight in,* as birds.

wi′-ya-ka, *n.* *a quill, a feather of the wing* or *tail of geese,* etc.

wi-ya′-ka, *n.* *sand.* *T.*, ćasmu, ćasmuska.

wi′-ya-ka-skab-ye, *n.* *T.* *mucilage; solder.*

wi′-ya-ka-śke, *n.* *a band, i. q.* teḣmiso.

wi-ya′-kpa, *v. n.* *to shine, glisten.*

wi-ya′-kpa, *adj.* *bright, glistening.*

wi-ya′-kpa-kpa, *red.* of wiyakpa.

wi-ya′-kpa-pi, *n.* *brightness.*

wi-ya′-kpa-ya, *adv.* *brightly.*

wi′-ya-oŋ-pa, *v.* of iyaoŋpa; *to blame, charge with*—wiyawaoŋpa. See wiiyaoŋpa.

wi′-ya-pe, *v.* of iyape; *to lie in wait*—wiyawape.

wi′-ya-śpa-pi, *n.* *the moon is nibbled;* an expression used in reference to the moon when it has commenced waning.

wi-ya′-śpu-ye-daŋ, *n.* *a large species of field-mouse* with a pointed nose, which is said to eat up the moon.

wi′-ya-ta-hde, *v.* *to have exceeding much*—wiyatamahde. *T.*, iyakapeya—iyakapeya ehaś bluha, *I have more than I need.*

wi′-ya-ta-hde-ya, *adv.* *having much, surpassingly.*

wi′-ya-ta-om-ya, *n.* See wiataomya.

wi-ya′-te-ća, *n.* *a species of red, sour berry,* growing on bushes five or six feet high: *a species of cranberry.*

wi′-ya-tkaŋ, *n.* *a drinking vessel, a cup.* *T*, miniyatke, the better form.

wi′-ya-tke, *n.* Same as wiyatkaŋ.

wi-ya′-tpa, *adj.* *bright, glittering: i. q.* wiyakpa.

wi-ya′-tpa-tpa, *adj. red.* of wiyatpa.

wi-ya′-tpa-ya, *adv.* *brightly.*

wi-ya′-tpa-ya, *v. a.* *to cause to glisten.*

wi′-ya-ya, *adv.* *ready:* wiyaya hnaka, *to make ready.* See wiyeya.

wi′-ya-yu-ski-ta, *v.* *to bind around*—wiyamduskita.

wi′-ya-yu-ski-te, *n.* *a bandage.*

wi'-ye, *n.* *the female of animals.*

wi'-ye, *adj.* *female*, used only in reference to animals.

wi'-ye-daŋ, *dim.* of wiye; *the female* of animals, birds, etc.

wi'-ye-la, *n.* *T.* *a female animal: i. q.* wiyedaŋ *and* wiyena.

wi'-ye-ya, *adv.* *ready, prepared;* wiyeya maŋka, *I am ready;* wiyeya hnaka, *to make ready, prepare.*

wi-yo'-ćo-kam-tu, *n.* *the middle moon*, applied to *January* and *July.*

wi'-yo-hi, *v.* of iyohi; *to reach to, to be sufficient for.* See iyohi, etc.

wi-yo'-hi-yaŋ-pa, *n.* *the east, the sun-rising.*

wi-yo'-hi-yaŋ-pa-ta, *adv.* *at the east, eastward.*

wi-yo'-hi-yaŋ-pa-ta, *n* *the east:* wiyohiyaŋpata ećiyataŋhaŋ, *from the east.*

wi-yo'-hi-yaŋ-pa-taŋ-haŋ, *adv.* *from the east.*

wi'-yo-ḣpe-ya, *v.* of iyoḣpeya; *to put* or *throw into*, as meat into a kettle to boil—wiyoḣpewaya.

wi-yo'-ḣpe-ya-ta, *n.* *the west, where the sun sets; at the west.*

wi-yo'-ḣpe-ya-ta-ki-ya, *adv.* *westward; towards the west.*

wi-yo'-ḣpe-ya-taŋ-haŋ, *adv.* *from the west.*

wi-yo'-ḣpe-ya-ta-wi-ća-śta, *n.* *the man of the west*, a name given to the *thunder.*

Wi'-yo-ke-ze-pa-ha, *n. p.* *the Bijou Hills.* So called from the stones found there, with which arrows are marked in zigzag lines.—W. J. C. See wiyukeza.

wi-yo'-ki-he-daŋ, *n.* *wampum; a flag, a banner; a flag of peace.* Used only by the Santees. *T., a flag* or *banner* is wowapi.

wi'-yo-ki-he-he-la, *n.* *T.* *wampum*, like the wasuhula, but straight; much used by the Omahas.

wi-yo'-ki-ya, *v.* *to court a woman.* Same as wiokiya.

wi-yo'-ki-ye-daŋ, *n* Same as wiyokihedaŋ.

wi'-yo-pe-ki-ya, *v.* of iyopekiya; *to sell*—wiyopewakiya.

wi'-yo-pe-ya, *v.* of iyopeya; *to sell, trade*—wiyopewaya.

wi'-yo-pe-ye, *n.* *a seller, a merchant; something to trade for, merchandise. T., a trader;* but *merchandise* is maza.

wi-yo'-taŋ-haŋ, *n.* *noon; the south. T.,* wićokaŋhiyaya.

wi-yo'-taŋ-haŋ-i-na-śdo-ke, *n.* *afternoon, past noon.*

wi-yo'-taŋ-he-ćiŋ, *n.* *noon.*

wi'-yo-wa, *n.* *paint, something to mark* or *write with; ink*, etc.: *a pen. T., a pen,* maza wiyowa; *a pencil,* ćaŋwiyowa. See wowapiićaġe.

wi-yo'-yaŋ-pa, *n.* *the east: i. q.* wiyohiyaŋpa.

wi'-yo-źaŋ-źaŋ, *v.* of iyoźaŋźaŋ; *to shine.*

wi'-yu-ćaŋ, *n.* *a sieve; a riddle.* *T.*, wićaćaŋ. See iyućaŋ.

wi'-yu-ćaŋ-ćaŋ, *n.* *a sieve.*

wi'-yu-ha, *v.* of yuha; *to obtain, possess; to have* or *be with a woman*—wimduha.

wi'-yu-hiŋ-te, *n.* *T.* *a rake.*

wi'-yu-ȟdo-ke, *n.* *an opener, a key.* See iyuȟdoke.

wi'-yu-kćaŋ, *v.* of iyukćaŋ; *to understand, have an opinion; one who forms an opinion*—wimdukćaŋ. See wokćaŋ.

wi'-yu-kćaŋ-pi, *n.* *forming an opinion.*

wi'-yu-ke-za, *n.* *T.* *the instrument for making the zigzag* or *winding marks on arrows.*

wi'-yu-kiŋ-će, *n.* *something to scrape with, a scraper.*

wi'-yu-kpaŋ, *n.* *a mill to grind with; i. q.* iyukpaŋ.

wi'-yuŋ-ġa, *v.* *T.* See wiwaŋġa.

wi'-yu-sdo-haŋ, *n.* *a sled; a sleigh.*

wi'-yu-sdo-he, *n.* Same as wiyusdohaŋ. See iyusdohe.

wi'-yu-ski-te, *n.* *a bandage; a press.*

wi'-yu-śki-će, *n.* *a press.*

wi'-yu-śkiŋ, *v.* of iyuśkiŋ; *to rejoice, be glad*—wimduśkiŋ, wiuŋyuśkiŋpi.

wi'-yu-śkiŋ-ki-ya, *v. a.* *to cause to rejoice.*

wi'-yu-śkiŋ-pi, *n.* *rejoicing.*

wi'-yu-śkiŋ-śkiŋ, *v. red.* of wíyuśkiŋ.

wi'-yu-śkiŋ-śkiŋ-na, *n.* *the chickadeedee, the black-cap titmouse.*

wi'-yu-śkiŋ-yaŋ, *v. a.* *to cause to rejoice*—wiyuśkiŋwaya.

wi'-yu-śkiŋ-yaŋ, *adv.* *rejoicingly, gladly.* See iyuśkiŋ.

wi'-yu-śla, *n.* *T.* *an instrument for shearing; shears.* See yuśda.

wi'-yu-ta, *v.* of iyuta; *to measure; to weigh*—wimduta, wiuŋyutapi. *T.*, *to make signs; to talk by signs*—wibluta.

wi'-yu-ta, *v.* of yuta; *to eat one thing with another*—wiwata.

wi'-yu-ta-pi, *n.* *a measure.*

wi'-yu-te, *n.* *a measure; a steelyard.*

wi'-yu-tpaŋ, *n.* *a mill.* Same as wiyukpaŋ.

wi'-yu-wi, *n.* *a vine.*

wi'-yu-źa-źa, *n.* *something to wash in,* as corn; *a colander, a basket; a tub.*

wi-zi', *n.* *an old smoky tent,* or *part of one.*

wi'-zi-će, *n.* *incense,* as cedar leaves, etc. *T.*, wizilye.

wi-zi'-daŋ, *n.* *an old smoky tent.*

wi'-zin-ya, *v.* *to offer incense*—wizinwaya. *T.*, wizilya.

wi-zi'-paŋ, *n.* *Ih.* and *T.* *the rawhide sack* or *satchel* made by western Sioux. *The native trunk* or *carpet bag,* a case made from untanned hide, to serve as a trunk. A half a buffalo hide, if large, will make two small *wizipans.* The hide is fleshed and pinned to the ground to dry in the sun. Such painting as is desired is done at once on the upper side, while the hide is green. When dry the hair is scraped off, and the cases are made, folding and lacing the ends together. Usually a hide makes but two *wizipans*—a side for each. Bull's hides are commonly used.

w i - z i′ - p a ŋ - h e - ć a, *n. Ih.* and *T. a black bag; a common satchel.*

w i - z i′ - p á ŋ - s a - p a, *v. a satchel.*

w i′ - z i - y e, *n. something to color yellow with.*

w i′ - ź i - ć a, *n. T. riches.*

w i′ - ź i - ć a, *adj.* of iźića; *rich*—wimaźića. *T.*, źića.

w o, *n. food.* See woyute.

w o, *the sign of the imperat. sing.* used by men; as, ećoŋ wo. *T.*, also yo, the more common form.

w o, *a prefix.* 1. Verbs commencing with "o" make their absolute form by prefixing "w" instead of "wa," the "a" being dropped; as, oyaka, *to tell*, woyaka; woźu, etc. 2. "Wo" prefixed to verbs and adjectives generally converts them into abstract nouns; as, wowaśte, *goodness;* wokiksuye, *remembrance.*

w o, *a. T. prefix* to verbs, signifying that the action is done by *shooting, punching, pounding* with the end of a stick, or by *blowing.* It is also used when the action of *rain* is expressed. The pronoun's place is after the prefix See bo.

w o′ - a - ć a - k ś i ŋ, *n.* of aćakśiŋ; *a stepping over.* This has been used for *the Passover.*

w o′ - a - h d a, *n. a taking home.*

w o′ - a - h d i, *n. a bringing home.*

w o′ - a - h e - ć o ŋ, *n. family connexions.* See wowahećoŋ.

w o′ - a - h i, *n. a bringing*

w o′ - a - h o - p e, *n.* of ahopa; *a ceremony, a custom; a law, a commandment:* woahope wikćemna kiŋ, *the ten commandments. T.*, see, also, wowasukiye.

w o′ - a - ḣ t a̧ - n i, *n.* of aḣtani; *a transgression* of superstitious customs; *sin. T., a misfortune;* when one meets with unlooked-for trouble he is "woaḣtani akipa." Perhaps this does not mean that he has "met with misfortune," but that his "sin has found him out." See waiçiḣtani. "*A transgression* of customs, *a sin*," is woahope awaḣtanipi *and* awaiçiḣtanipi.

w o′ - a - i, *n. the act of taking to a place.*

w o′ - a - i - e, *n.* of aia; *a talking about, slander.*

w o′ - a - i - ḣ p e - y e, *n.* of aiḣpeya; *leaving to; a will, a testament; that which is left* to one, *a legacy.*

w o′ - a - k a - ġ e, *n. a making on, blasphemy.*

w o′ - a - k a - ḣ p e, *n.* of akaḣpa; *a covering.*

w o′ - a - k e - y e, *n. a curtain, a screen, something thrown up around like a tent. T.*, awakeyapi. See wakeya.

wo′-a-ki-ḣo, *n.* of akiḣo; *a habit; a trade.* *T.*, wićoḣaŋ.

wo′-a-ki-ktoŋ-źe, *n.* of akiktoŋźa; *forgetfulness.*

wo′-a-kta, *n.* of akta; *regard,* but not used without śni.

wo′-a-kta-sni, *n.* *disregard.*

wo′-a-na-ġo-ptaŋ, *n.* of anaġoptaŋ; *obedience.*

wo′-a-na-ġo-ptaŋ-yaŋ, *adv.* *obediently.*

wo′-a-na-ḣbe, *n.* of anaḣma; *concealment; a secret.* *T.*, woanaḣme.

wo′-a-na-ḣma, *n.* Same as woanaḣbe.

wo′-a-pe, *n.* of ape; *waiting for, expectation, hope.*

wo′-a-na-pte, *n.* of anapta; *a stopping, restraint; something astringent.*

wo′-a-sni, *n.* of asni; *recovery from sickness.* *T.*, woasnikiye

wo′-a-śa-pe, *n.* of aśapa; *defilement.*

wo′-a-ta-ku-ni-śni, *n.* of takuniśni; *destruction.*

wo′-a-wa-ćiŋ, *n.* of awaćiŋ; *thinking on, faith.*

wo′-a-ya-te, *n.* of ayate; *prediction.*

wo′-a-yu-pte, *n.* of ayupta; *an answer.*

wo′-ba-śpe, *n.* of baśpa; *a piece cut off.*

wo′-bi-li-he-ća, *n.* *T.* *activity; industry.*

wo′-bl̇e-ća, *n.* *T.* *a breaking open, a splitting apart.*

wo′-bo-pte, *n.* See owobopte.

wo′-ćan-śi-će, *n.* *sorrow.* See ćaŋteśića *and* ćanśinya.

wo′-ćaŋ-ḣi-ya, *v. n.* of ćaŋḣiya; *not to be prevented from succeeding in any thing by any event,* as the loss of a friend, etc.; *to be lucky*—woćaŋḣimayaŋ.

wo′-ćaŋ-ksi, *n.* of ćaŋksi; *ill humor.*

wo′-ćaŋ-ni-ye, *n.* of ćaŋniyaŋ, *malice, wrath, anger.* *T.*, woćaŋzeka.

wo′-ćaŋt-a-hde, *n.* of ćaŋtahde; *evil intention against, malice; the object of evil purpose.*

wo′-ćaŋ-te, *n.* of ćaŋte. See its use in the following words.

wo′-ćaŋ-te-i-yu-taŋ-ye, *n.* *temptation.*

wo′-ćaŋ-te-ki-ye, *n.* *love.* See woćaŋtkiye.

wo′-ćaŋ-te-ptaŋ-ye, *n.* *anger.*

wo′-ćaŋ-te-śi-će, *n.* *sorrow.*

wo′-ćaŋ-te-wa-śte, *n.* *gladness.*

wo′-ćaŋt-i-he-ye, *n.* *ardent desire.*

wo′-ćaŋt-i-yu-taŋ, *n.* *temptation.*

wo′-ćaŋt-ki-ye, *n.* *love, benevolence.*

wo′-ćaŋt-o-hna-ke, *n.* *compassion.*

wo′-ćaŋt-o-kpa-ni, *n.* *a longing for.*

wo′-ćaŋt-o-tpa-ni, *n. a.* *longing for.*

wo-ća′-źe-ya-te, *n.* *the naming* of things; in Dakota singing, *the words* that follow "hi-hi-hi."

wo′-će-ki-ye, *n.* of ćekiya; *crying to, prayer, petition.*

wo′-će-ṭuŋ-hda, *n.* of ćeṭuŋhda; *unbelief.*

wo′-će-ye, *n.* of ćeya; *crying.* See wićaćeya.

wo′-ćiŋ, *v.* of oćiŋ; *to beg, ask for; to be begging, on an errand:* woćiŋ wahi, *I have come to ask for something;* wokićiŋ *and* wokićićiŋ, *to ask of* one.

wo′-ćiŋ-pi, *n.* *T.* *begging.*

wo′-ćo-koŋ, *n.* of ćokoŋ; *a threat, a curse.*

wo′-da, *v.* *to beg food; begging.*

wo′-da-s'a, *n.* *a beggar.*

wo′-de, *v.* of ode; *to seek for*—wowade.

wo′-don, *cont.* of wodota; wodon wahi, *I have come to borrow.* *T.*, wolol.

wo′-do-ta, *v.* of odota; *to borrow, borrowing; to hire*—wowadota, wouŋdotapi. *T.*, wolota.

wo′-do-ta-pi, *n.* *borrowing.*

wo′-du-ta, *n.* *the round of an animal when dried.* See odute.

wo′-du-za-he, *n.* *swiftness;* also *one who is swift.* See wićoduzahe.

wo′-e-će-tu, *n.* of ećetu; *fulfillment.*

wo′-e-ćoŋ, *n.* *work, doing.*

wo′-e-ćoŋ-na, *n.* *gambling.* See oećoŋna. *T.*, wayékiyapi.

wo′-e-ćoŋ-yaŋ, *v.* *to do; one who is always doing*—woećoŋwaya.

wo′-e-hda-ku, *n.* of ehdaku; *deliverance.*

wo′-e-ḣpe-ye, *n.* of eḣpeya; *putting* or *throwing away.*

wo′-e-ki-će-tu, *n.* *renewal, resurrection.*

wo′-e-ye, *n.* *T.* *a speech, word,* or *saying.* See iapi.

wo′-glu-ze, *n.* *T.* *a giving and taking it back again.*

wo-gna′, *v. a.* *T.* *to shell off by shooting* or *punching.* See bohba.

wo′-gna-ka-pi, *n.* *T.* *a basket* or *receptacle.* See wohnaka.

wo′-e-ki-će-tu-ye, *n.* *restoration.*

wo′-gna-ye, *v. a.* *T.* *to miss in shooting.* See bohnayaŋ.

wo′-ġa, *v.* *to husk,* as corn—wamduġa, wauŋyuġapi.

wo′-ġaŋ, *n.* *a snow-drift.* *T.*, wáwotaikeya.

wo′-ġa-pi, *n.* *the act of husking corn.*

wo′-ġi, *n.* of ġi; *brownness.*

wo′-ġu, *n.* *scraps,* as of tallow tried out.

wo′-ha-ka-kta, *n.* *the youngest, the last:* *i. q.* wahakakta.

wo′-haŋ, *v.* of ohaŋ; *to cook, boil; to make a feast*—wowahe, wouŋhaŋpi.

wo′-haŋ-pi, *n.* *a boiling; a feast:* wakaŋ wohaŋpi, *a sacred feast.*

wo′-hda-hda-ka, *v. red.* of wohdaka.

wo′-hda-ka, *v.* of ohdaka; *to converse of* or *detail one's own* affairs; *to talk*—wowahdaka, wouŋhdakapi. *T.*, woglaka, also means *to counsel.*

wo'-hda-ka-pi, *n.* *telling one's own* affairs. *T.*, woglakapi, *counseling.*

wo'-hde-će, *n.* *an omen, a presentiment:* wohdeće mduha. *T.*, taku inihaŋwićaya.

wo'-hdu-ze, *n.* *something sacred* or *forbidden*, as the heart, etc., of animals. When a young man engages to hold anything as "wohduze" he must not eat of it until, by killing an enemy, the *taboo* is taken off. It is something abstained from and considered sacred, including the idea of *an oath* or *sacrament* or *binding of one's self.* Hence the word is used for *baptism* and the *Lord's supper*, to the partakers of which many things are forbidden to be done. *T.*, iċićoŋzapi; woićićoŋze. See wogluze.

wo'-hdu-ze-toŋ, *v. a.* *to set apart, consecrate.*

wo'-hdu-ze-ya, *v. a.* *to have for* wohduze—wohduzewaya.

wo'-he, *v.* See wohaŋ.

wo'-he-ki-ya, *v. a.* *to cause to cook: to have for a cook*—wohewakiya.

wo'-he-ki-ya-pi, *n.* *a cook:* wohewićakiyapi, *cooks.* *T.*, wohela, *a cook.*

wo'-he-yuŋ, *n.* of heyuŋ; *a package, a bundle*, as of dried meat.

wo'-hiŋ-ḣpe-ya, *v. a.* *T.* *to shoot and make fall; to punch over.* See boha.

wo'-hiŋ-yaŋs-ya, *adv.* *T.* *crossly; sternly.* See hiŋyaŋsya.

wo'-hi-ti, *adj.* *furious, terrible.*

wo'-hi-ti-da, *v a.* *to regard as furious*—wohiwada: wohitiiċida, *to think one's self terrible*—wohitimiċida. See ohitida.

wo'-hi-ti-da-ka, *v.* Same as wohitida.

wo'-hi-ti-hda, *n.* of hitihda; *something loathed.*

wo'-hi-ti-ka, *adj.* of ohitika; *terrible, furious, violent; energetic*—womahitika, wouŋhitipika.

wo'-hi-ti-ya, *adv.* *furiously, violently; energetically.*

wo'-hi-ya, *v.* *to overcome, conquer.* See ohiya.

wo'-hmuŋ-ke, *n.* *something to be trapped*, as beaver, etc.

wo'-hna, *prep.* *in.* See ohna.

wo'-hna-ka, *v.* of ohnaka; *to put* or *place in*—wowahnaka.

wo'-hna-ye, *n.* of hnayaŋ; *deceit.*

wo'-ho-da, *v.* of oḣoda; *to honor.* See woohoda.

wo'-ḣa, *n.* of ḣa; *a place to bury in, a corn-hole* or other *place of deposit in the ground, a caché; a cellar, a pit; something buried.*

wo'-ḣa-ka, *n.* of oḣaka; *something that hurts* or *injures, whether externally* or *internally; something eaten that does not agree with the stomach; poison.* See woṭa. *T.*, śupéośića.

wo'-ḣa-ka, *v.* of oḣaka; *to be poisoned*—womaḣaka. *T.*, śupéośića—śupéomaśića, etc.

wo'-ḣdo-ke-ća, *n.* *one who invents, an inventor.*

wo′-ħe-śma, *adj.* *T.* *thick,* as grass or underbrush; *dense.*

wo′-ħe-śma-śni, *adj.* *T.* *destitute of undergrowth,* as a forest; *not thick,* as grass growing thinly.

wo′-ħiŋ-yaŋ, *v.* of oħiŋyaŋ; *to be dissatisfied with, to take offence at*—wowaħiŋyaŋ.

wo′-ħiŋ-yaŋ-pi, *n.* *dissatisfaction, offence.*

wo′-ħla, *v.* *T.* *to ring,* as a bell—wowaħla. See yuħla.

wo′-ħpa, *v. a.* *to carry presents to give in exchange for a woman, to buy a wife*—wowaħpa *and* wamduħpa. Buying is the honorable way of taking a wife among the Dakotas. Usually they pay about the value of $40—a horse, four or five guns, or six or eight blankets.

wo′-ħpa-pi, *n.* *buying a wife.* *T.,* wiŋyaŋćiŋpi

wo′-ħta-ka, *v. a.* *T.* *i. q.* boħtaka.

wo′-i-ća-ġe, *n.* of ićaġa; *a growth; a creation.*

wo′-i-ćaŋ-ksi, *n.* of ićaŋksi; *ill-temper.*

wo′-i-ćaŋ-śi-ća, *n.* *T.* *sadness; a cause of sadness.* See wokaħake.

wo′-i-ća-zo, *n.* of ićazo; *debt; credit.*

wo′-i-ća-źe, *adj.* *many, very many:* wićaśta woićaźe. *T., many kinds; a great variety.*

wo′-i-ca-źe-ka, *adj.* *very many.* *T*, same as woićaźe.

wo′-i-ću, *n.* of ića; *a receiving.*

wo′-i-ç̌i-ćoŋ-ze, *n.* *T.* of koŋza; *a resolution; a sacrament; a binding* one's self *by an oath* or *resolution.* See wohduze.

wo′-i-ç̌i-hde, *n.* *one who lays up for himself; substance.* See hde.

wo′-i-en-hde, *n.* *a casting up to, charging with.*

wo′-i-haŋ-mde, *n.* *a dream.*

wo′-i-hda-ka, *v.* *reflex.* of wohdaka; *to declare one's self, declare one's purposes; to vow*—womihdaka.

wo′-i-hda-taŋ, *n.* of ihdataŋ; *boasting.*

wo′-i-hnu, *n.* *murmuring.* See wowihnu.

wo′-i-ħa, *n.* of iħa; *something laughable.*

wo′-i-ħa-daŋ, *n.* *something that causes laughter.* See wowiħadaŋ.

wo′-i-ħa-ħa, *n.* *raillery.*

wo′-i-ħa-ya, *adv.* *laughably, ludicrously.*

wo′-i-ħa-ya-ken, *adv.* *ludicrously.*

wo′-i-ki-ksa-pe, *n.* of ikiksapa; *experience.*

wo′-i-ko-pe, *n.* *T.* of ikopa; *fear;* anything *frightful* or *discouraging.*

wo′-i-ksa-pe, *n.* *something difficult.*

wo′-i-ksa-pe-ća, *n.* *that which is difficult.*

wo′-i-la-ke, *n.* *T.* *a servant; an instrument;* anything *made to serve* for a definite purpose. See wowidake.

wo-i′-le, *v. a. T. to make blaze by blowing: i. q.* boide.

wo′-i-ma-ġa-ġa, *n. T. an amusement.* See imaġaġa.

wo′-i-mnaŋ-ka, *adj. T. powerful, strong; capable.*

wo′-i-na-ḣbe, *n.* of inaḣma; *concealment.*

wo′-i-na-pe, *n.* See wowinape.

wo′-i-pu-za, *n.* of ipuza; *thirst.*

wo′-i-śtiŋ-be, *n.* of iśtiŋma; *sleep.*

wo′-i-śtiŋ-ma, *n.* of iśtiŋma; *sleep.*

wo′-i-toŋ-pe, *n. carefulness.* See wowitoŋpe. *T., a surprise; a cause for wonder.*

wo′-i-toŋ-pe-ya, *adv. T. angrily*—woitoŋpeya ia, *to speak angrily; insecurely, in danger*—woitoŋpeya egle, *to place insecurely,* as a lamp.

wo′-i-toŋ-śni, *n.* of itoŋśni; *a lie, falsehood. T.,* owewakaŋ, wićoowewakaŋ.

wo′-i-tu-ka-ġe, *n.* of itukaġa; *a falsehood.*

wo′-i-ye-će-tu, *n. fulfillment, uprightness.*

wo′-i-yo-ki-śi-će, *n. sorrow, sadness.*

wo′-i-yo-taŋ-i-ye′-ki-ye, *n. difficulty.*

wo′-i-yu-śkiŋ, *n. gladness.* See wowiyuśkiŋ.

wo-kab′-i-ye-ya, *v. a. T. to remove what has been sent into* another's *body by magic* or the wićaḣmuŋġa process,

wo′-ka-ġa, *v.* of okaġa; *to make like.*

wo′-ka-ġe, *n.* of kaġa; *anything made, forms.*

wo′-ka-ġe, *adj. stuck full of splinters* or *briers*—womakaġe. *T.,* wokaġa.

wo′-ka-ġi, *n.* of kaġi; *a hindrance.*

wo′-ka-ġi-ye, *n. one who obstructs.*

wo′-ka-ḣa-ke, *n. the cause of sadness* or *evil:* wokaḣake wanin wauŋ, *I have no cause of sadness. T.,* woićaŋśića.

wo′-kaḣ-ni-ġa, *v.* okaḣniġa; *to understand*—wowakaḣniġa. *T.,*wokićaḣniġa.

wo′-kaḣ-ni-ġe, *n.* of kaḣniġa; *choice.*

wo′-ka-kiś-ye, *n. the cause of suffering.*

wo′-ka-ki-źe, *n.* of kakiźa; *suffering, misery.*

wo′-ka-mna, *n.* of kamna; *a gathering, a hoard.*

wo′-ka-paŋ, *n. pounded meat; a meat-block. T.,* wokápaŋpi.

wo-ka′-pa-za, *n. pungency, anything pungent,* as pepper.

wo′-ka-pe, *n.* of kapa; *going beyond, transgression; one who catches a ball.*

wo′-ka-sda-ta, *v.* of okasdata; *to stick in,* as a splinter—womakasdata, wonićasdata *T.,* okásleća.

wo-ka′-sda-te, *n. a splinter. T,* wokasleće.

wo′-ka-se, *n.* of kasa; *a deposit in the snow,*

w o'-k a-ś e-y e, *n.* *something opposing, a hindrance.*

w o'-k ć a ŋ, *v.* of yukćaŋ; *to judge, understand, form an opinion, decide* — wamdukćaŋ.

w o'-k ć a ŋ, *n.* wićaśta wokćaŋ, *a prophet.*

w o'-k ć a ŋ-k a, *n.* *one who understands things.*

w o'-k e-y a, *n.* *a shelter, a cover, a booth.* See wakeya *and* keya.

w o'-k i-ć a-ḣ n i-ġ a, *v.* *T.* *to detect, see through, understand,* as the deception or untruthfulness of another. See okićaḣniġa.

w o'-k i-ć a ŋ-p t e, *n.* of kićaŋpta; *comfort, consolation.*

w o'-k i-ć i-ć i-y a-p i, *n.* *talking to each other, friendly intercourse.*

w o'-k i-ć i-z e, *n.* of kićiza; *fighting.*

w o'-k i-ć i-ź u, *n.* of woźu; *to sow* or *plant for* one—wowećiźu.

w o'-k i-ć o ŋ-ż e, *n.* *law, government, kingdom.* See kićoŋza *and* koŋza.

w o'-k i-d a-p i, *n.* *the act of requesting.*

w o'-k i-k s u-y e, *n.* of kiksuya; *remembrance.*

w o'-k i-k ś a ŋ, *n.* *rape.* See wikikśaŋ.

w o'-k i-k t a, *n.* of kikta; *watching, waking.*

w o'-k i-m n a ŋ-k a, *adj.* *liberal, large; good, wise, honored.* *T.*, *wide awake, on the alert,* as a wolf.

w o'-k i-n i, *v.* of okini; *to get a share, acquire*—wowakini, wouŋkinipi.

w o'-k i-n i-h a ŋ, *n.* of kinihaŋ; *honor, respect.*

w o-k i ŋ'-ć a, *v a.* *T.* *to make sting* or *smart by shooting.* See bokiŋća.

w o-k i ŋ t'-k i ŋ-ć a, *v. red.* of above. See botukaka.

w o'-k i-p a-ź i ŋ, *n.* *opposition, rebellion.*

w o'-k i-t a ŋ, *n.* *a little of* any thing; wokitaŋ mayaķu, *thou hast given me very little.* See kitaŋ, kitaŋna, etc.

w o'-k i-t a ŋ, *n.* of kitaŋ; *obstinacy.* *T.*, wanáḣoŋpiśni.

w o'-k i-t a ŋ-i ŋ, *n.* of okitaŋiŋ; *manifestation.*

w o'-k i-t a ŋ-i ŋ-y a ŋ, *adv.* *gloriously.*

w o'-k i-t a ŋ-y a ŋ, *adv.* *obstinately, perseveringly.* *T.*, wanaḣoŋpiśniyaŋ.

w o'-k i-u-n i, *n.* *T.* *a hurt, an injury.* See oŋtoŋyaŋpi.

w o'-k i-y a, *v.* of okiya; *to speak with, talk with; to make peace*—wowakiya, wouŋkiyapi.

w o'-k i-y a, *v.* of ókiya; *to help.* See wawokiya.

w o'-k i-y a g, *cont.* of wokiyaka; wokiyag waḣi, *I have come to announce to* one.

w o'-k i-y a-ķ a, *v.* of okiyaka; *to tell to* one, *declare to*—wowakiyaka *and* wowakimdaka, woyakiyaka *and* woyakidaka, wouŋkiyakapi.

w o'-k i-y a-p i, *n.* *making peace, peace, a covenant.* *T.*, olakol kaġapi.

w o'-k i-y e, *n.* *peace.* See wookiye. *T.*, olakota.

wo'-ki-ye-a-i-e-wi-ća-ki-ya-pi, *n.* (wokiya *and* aiekiya) *councillors.* *T.*, wakiya wićaśa.

wo'-ki-yu-ḣe, *n.* of kiyuḣa; *copulation.* *T*; kiyuḣapi.

wo'-ki-yu-śke, *n.* of kiyuśka; *setting free, deliverance.*

wo'-ki-zi, *n.* of okizi; *healing; salve.*

wo'-ki-zi-ya, *v.* *to heal*—wokiziwaya.

wo'-ki-zi-ye, *n.* *a healer; that which heals, salve.*

wo'-ki-źa, *v.* of woźa; *to make hasty-pudding for* one—wowakiźa. *T.*, wokićiźa.

wo'-ko-ki-pe, *n.* of kokipa; *fear; the cause of fear.*

wo'-ko-ki-pe-ya, *adv.* *fearfully.*

wo'-koŋ, *n.* of koŋ; *desire, something desirable.*

wo'-koŋ-ka, *n.* *something desired.*

wo'-koŋ-ze, *n.* of koŋza; *a decree, law, influence.*

wo'-ko-ya-ke, *n.* of koyaka; *clothing.* See heyake *and* oġepi.

wo'-ko-ze, *n.* of koza; *a swinging, a brandishing.*

wo'-kpaŋ, *v.* of yukpaŋ; *to grind,* as grain—wamdukpaŋ: wokpaŋ wahi, *I have come to grind.* See wotpaŋ.

wo'-kpaŋ-ti-pi, *n.* *a grinding mill.*

wo'-ksa, *v.* of yuksa; *to break off, to pull,* as corn—wamduksa, wauŋyuksapi.

wo'-ksa-pe, *n.* of ksapa; *wisdom.*

wo'-ksa-pi, *n.* *pulling corn, harvest; those engaged in harvesting, reapers.*

wo'-ksa-pi-wi, *n.* *the harvest moon, August.*

wo'-kte, *n.* of kte; *a killing.*

wo'-kte-ka, *n.* *one who kills much.*

wo'-kte-ya, *v. a.* *to have for the purpose of killing* things, as a gun or dog—woktewaya.

wo'-ku-źe, *n.* of kuźa; *idleness, laziness.* *T.*, *sickness, indisposition.*

wo'-ku-źi-ṭe, *n.* *laziness.*

wo'-ḳe, *n.* of ḳa; *a digging; a place dug to* bury in.

wo'-ḳiŋ, *n.* of ḳiŋ; *a pack; a carrying.* See waḳiŋ.

wo'-ḳiŋ-yu-ṭe-ya, *v. a.* *T.* *to overload.*

wo'-ḳu, *v.* of o**ḳu**; *to give food to; to lend*—wowaḳu.

wo'-ḳu-pi, *n.* *a lending, giving to.*

wo'-la-ko-ta, *n.* *T.* *peace; friendship.*

wo'-mdu, *v.* of yumdu; *to pulverize, to plough*—wamdumdu. *T.*, woblu.

wo'-mna, *v.* of omna; *to smell, perceive smell; to have smell*—wowamna.

wo'-mna-ka, *n.* *any thing that gives forth much odor.*

wo'-mna-śni, *adj.* *pure, clean, inodorous; i. q.* wimnaśni *and* wiŋmnaśni. Said of one who is unmarried See witaŋśna *and* wotiyemnaśni.

wo'-mna-ye, *n.* of mnayaŋ; *a collection*

w o'-m n i-ć i-y e, *n.* *an assembly.* See wićomnićiye.

w o'-m n i-h e-ć a, *n.* *activity.* *T.*, wobiliheća. See wićomniheća *and* miniheća.

w o n, *cont.* of wota: won mani, *he walks eating.* *T.*, wol.

w o'-n a-k e, *v.* of naka; *a tremor, an omen.*

w o'-n a-s e, *n.* of nasa; *a hunting of buffalo.*

w o'-n a-t e, *v.* *T.* *to beat* as in a race; *to excel: i. q.* kapa.

w o'-n a-t e, *v.* *to stop giving to* one, *to withhold*—wonawate, wonamayate. *T.*, hehaŋyela ayuśtaŋ.

w o'-n a-t e-y a, *v. a.* *not to give to* one as one has been accustomed to do—wonatewaya.

w o'-n a-t e-y a, *v. a.* *T.* *to cause to excel,* etc.

w o'-n a-t i-ć e, *v. n.* *not to have received any thing; to be disappointed*—wonamatiće. *T.*, wonatape. See iyohiśni.

w o'-n i-h i ŋ-ć i-y e, *n.* of nihiŋćiya; *fright.*

w o-n i'-y a, *n.* *spirit, life, breath:* Woniya Wakaŋ, *the Holy Spirit.*

w o n'-k i-y a, *v. a.* of wota; *to cause to eat, to feast*—wonwakiya. *T.*, wolkiya.

w o'-n u-k a, *adj.* *fertile,* as land, *producing well:* maka wonuka, *fertile land.* *T.*, owoźu waśte.

w o n'-y a, *v. a.* *to cause to eat, to make a feast:* wonwićawaya, *I cause them to eat.* *T.*, wolya.

w o'-o-h d a-k e, *n.* of ohdaka; *a declaring of one's own* rights or intentions.

w o'-o-h i-y e, *n.* of ohiya; *victory.*

w o'-o-k a-ḣ n i-ġ e, *n.* of okaḣniġa; *the understanding of things, comprehension.* wookićaḣniġa.

w o'-o-k i-h i, *n.* of okihi; *power, ability.*

w o'-o-k i-t a ŋ-i ŋ, *n.* *manifestation.*

w o'-o-k i-y e, *n.* of okiya; *peace.* *T.*, wookiye kaḣya, *at peace, quiet,* as a people not at war; *peaceably.*

w o'-o-k i-y e, *n.* of ókiya; *help.*

w o'-o-k i-z i, *n.* of okizi; *healing.*

w o'-o-m n a, *n.* *smell, that which produces smell.*

w o'-o ŋ-s p e, *n.* of oŋspe; *a precept, a lesson.*

w o'-o ŋ-s p e-k a, *n.* *something that teaches, a lesson.*

w o'-o ŋ-s p e-k i-y e, *n.* of oŋspekiya; *teaching.*

w o'-o-p e, *n.* of opa; *law, custom.* See woahope.

w o'-o-ś k i-ś k e, *n.* of śkiśka; *confusion, difficulty, complexity.*

w o'-o-t a ŋ-i ŋ, *n.* of otaŋiŋ; *manifestation, news.*

w o'-o-w o-t a ŋ-n a, *n.* of owotaŋna; *righteousness, uprightness.*

w o'-o-z i-i-ç i-y e, *n.* *rest, repose.* *T.*, woasnikiye. See oziya.

w o'-o-ź i-ź i, *n.* of oźiźi; *whispering.*

w o'-p a-ġ e, *n.* *something bulky,* for which there is no room. Compare paŋġa. *T.* See okiṭeyela.

w o′ - p a - ġ i, *n.* *something stuffed* (*T.*, opuġitoŋ); *the noise made by a blow* (*T.*, to).

w o′ - p a - ġ i - y a, *adv.* *in a stuffed manner.* *T.*, opuġitoŋyaŋ.

w o′ - p a - k a ŋ, *v. n.* of pakaŋ; *to be honored; i. q.* ohodapi—womapakaŋ. *T.*, okinihaŋ.

w o′ - p a - k i ŋ - t e, *n.* of pakiŋta; *wiping.*

w o′ - p a - m n a - y a ŋ, *adv.* *collected together.*

w o′ - p a - m n i, *n.* *a pile, a share, a distribution.* See wakipamni *and* wapamnipi.

w o′-p a - n i - ć a, *v. n.* *to be easily made angry, to be sensitive* or *irritable*—wopamanića. *T.*, waćaŋzezeka.

w o′ - p a - s m i, *n.* of pasmi; *spite, anger.* *T.* See wowićaśaśni.

w o′ - p a - s n o ŋ, *n* of pasnoŋ; *a roast, a roasting of meat*

w o′ - p a - t a, *n.* of pata; *a place for cutting up meat; the act of cutting up meat.*

w o′ - p a - ṭ o - y e, *n.* *a hindrance.*

w o′ - p a - ź i ŋ, *v. n.* of paźiŋ; *to be prevented by, to be made unsuccessful*—womapaźiŋ.

w o′ - p e - m n i, *n.* *a rolling up; an accumulation.* See pemni.

w o′ - p e - m n i - k a - ġ a - p i, *n.* *something made into a roll; a pie, pies.*

w o′ - p e - t o ŋ, *v.* of opetoŋ; *to buy, to buy and sell, to trade*—wopewatoŋ, wopeuŋtoŋpi.

w o′ - p e - t o ŋ, *n.* *a trader, a merchant.*

w o′ - p i - d a, *n.* of pida; *thanks; joy, gladness.* *T.*, pilapi. wopida ḳu, wopida ećiya, etc., have no corresponding *T.* forms. They are equivalent, I suppose, to pila kiŋ oglaka, pilayapi kiŋ oglaka (or okiyaka), and the like.—W. J. C.

w o′ - p i - d a - k i - y e, *n.* *something that makes glad.* *T.*, ipilaye.

w o′ - p i - d a - y a, *v. a.* *to make joy* or *gladness*—wopidawaya. *T*, pilaya.

w o′ - p i - d a - y e, *n.* *something that makes glad.*

w o′ - p i - k a, *adj.* *T.* *skillful in making* anything. See wayupika.

w o′ - p i - y e, *n.* of opiye; *a case, a bag, a box, a medicine sack; a storehouse; any place in which things are kept.*

w o′ - p i - y e - y a, *v. a.* *to have for a* wopiye—wopiyewaya.

w o′ - p t a, *v.* of yupta; *to cut out,* as clothes. *T.*, oyupta.

w o′ - p t e, *n.* *scraps, cuttings.* *T*, oyupte. See woptuḣa.

w o′ - p t e - ć a, *n.* *one who cuts out clothes.* *T.*, oyupte.

w o′ - p t e - ć a, *adj.* *what can be measured* or *counted* See woptećaśni.

w o′ - p t e - ć a - k a, *adj.* *immense, abundant.*

w o′ - p t e - ć a - ś n i, *adj.* *immense, innumerable, immeasurable:* taku woptećaśni.

w o′ - p t u - ḣ a, *n.* *T.* *remnants; leavings; chips; scraps,*

w o′-s a ŋ-k a, *n.* *a place where nothing can be obtained, a country destitute of game.* *T.*, wamakaśkaŋ wanića.

w o′-s a-p a, *n.* of sapa; *blackness.*

w o′-s d e-ć a, *n* *Ih.* *cracked corn.*

w o′-s d o-h e, *n.* *Ih.* *a drag, a sled.*

w o′-s d o-h e-d a ŋ, *n.* *paths made by squirrels in the grass.*

w o′-s d o n-y e, *n.* of sdonya; *knowledge.*

w o s′-i-ć u, *v. a.* *T.* *to take by force.*

w o-s k a′, *v. a.* *T.* *i. q.* boska, *to wash off*, as rain does whitewash, etc. See bożaża.

w o′-s k a, *n.* *one who makes white* *T.*, waska); *ornamental work* (*T.*, wipatapi).

w o′-s k a-k a, *n.* *one who makes white* or *works moccasins.*

w o-s k a′-p a, *v.* *T.* *to miss fire:* said when the cap explodes but does not ignite the charge. Same as boskapa.

w o′-s k a-p i, *n.* *quill-work.* *T.*, wipatapi. See oskapi.

w o′-s k u-y e, *n.* of skuya; *taste, savor.*

w o′-s m a-k a, *n.* *T.* *a valley.* See osmaka *and* kaksiza.

w o′-s p a-y e, *n.* *wetness.* See spaya.

w o′-s u-k a n-y u-z a, *v.* *to take openly when one has no right.* See osukanyuza. *T.*, owaśtekal iću; taŋiŋyaŋkel manoŋ.

w o′-s u-k i-y e, *n.* *Ih.* *completion.* See su *and* yasu.

w o′-ś a, *n.* of śa; *redness.*

w o′-ś'a-k a, *adj.* *overloaded.* *T.*, wok̇iŋyuṫeyapi. See yuś'aka.

w o′-ś a-p a, *n.* of śapa; *anything that blackens* or *defiles.*

w o′-ś i-ć e, *n.* of śića; *evil, badness, the cause of disease.*

w o′-ś i-h d a, *n* of śihda; *anger.*

w o′-ś i-ḣ a ŋ, *n.* of śiḣaŋ; *wickedness.* *T.*, śićayaoḣaŋyaŋpi.

w o′-ś i-ḣ t i ŋ, *n.* of śiḣtiŋ; *feebleness, debility.* *T.* *i q.* waśiće.

w o′-ś i-t k i-h d a, *n.* of śitkihda; *affliction, displeasure.*

w o′-ś i-t k i-h d a-y a, *v.* *to afflict; to make angry.*

w o′-ś k a-t e, *n.* of śkata; *play.* See wićośkate.

w o′-ś k i-ć a, *v.* of yuśkića; *to press.*

w o′-ś k i-ś k e, *n.* of ośkiśke; *trouble, confusion.*

w o′-ś n a, *v.* of yuśna; *to sacrifice; to drop*—wowaśna. *T.*, wauŋyaŋ; wayuḣtata.

w o′-ś n a, *n.* *something offered to the gods, a sacrifice.*

w o′-ś n a-k a-ġ a, *n.* *one who offers sacrifice, a priest.* *T.*, wauŋyaŋkaġa; wayuḣtata-kaġa.

w o′-ś n a-k i-y a, *v. a.* *to cause to sacrifice*—waśnawakiya.

w o′-ś n a-p i-k a-ġ a, *n.* *a priest.*

w o′-ś p a ŋ-k a, *n.* of śpaŋ; *something to cook in.* *T.*, wośpaŋyaŋpi.

w o′-ś p i, *v.* of yuśpi; *to pick*, as berries—wamduśpi.

w o-ś t e′, *intj.* *T.* *horrible!*

w o'-ś t e-k i-d a, *v.* *to consider difficult*—wośtewakida. *T.*, oteȟila.

w o'-ś u ŋ g-y a, *adv.* *violently; very; i. q.* nina. *T.*, ośuŋgyela.

w o'-t a, *v.* of yuta; *to eat*—wawata, wauŋtapi: aśkatuḋaŋ mawota tuka nina wawata heoŋ mataŋka, *I have been eating only a little while, but have eaten much, and therefore I am large.*

w o'-t a-k p e, *n.* of takpe; *an attack, an assault.*

w o'-t'a ŋ, *v.* of yut'aŋ; *to touch, to feel; anything that feels about* for food, as the raccoon.

w o'-t a ŋ-d a, *n.* *respect.* *T.*, yuonihaŋpi.

w o'-t a ŋ-i ŋ, *v.* of otaŋiŋ; *to be apparent.*

w o'-t a ŋ-i ŋ, *n.* *news.*

w o'-t a ŋ-i ŋ-w o-w a-p i, *n.* *a newspaper.*

w o'-t a ŋ-k a, *v. n.* *to be in need of*—womataŋka. *T.*, ićakiś uŋ.

w o'-t a ŋ-k a, *n.* *largeness, anything large*— ćaŋ waŋźi wotaŋka: *a great matter*, as, woġupi hećeena woawaćiŋ wotaŋka.

w o'-t a-p i, *n.* *eating.*

w o'-t a-t p e, *n.* *an attack.* See wotakpe.

w o'-t a-w e, *n.* *armor; weapons consecrated by religious ceremonies; whatever is relied upon in war.*

w o'-t a-w e-w o-h a ŋ-p i, *n.* *the armor feast.* This feast is usually made by young men who wish to kill an enemy. They cry and howl frightfully.

w o'-t e-ć a, *n.* *wild beasts, cattle, ruminating animals.* This term includes such as are granivorous and herbivorous. *T.*, wamakaśkaŋ. See wanuŋyaŋpi.

w o-t e'-ć a, *n.* of teća; *newness.*

w o'-t e-h n i, *v.* See wotihni.

w o'-t e-ȟ i, *n.* *something hard to be endured, difficulty, trouble.* See oteȟi.

w o'-t e-ȟ i-k e, *n.* *difficulty.*

w o'-t e-k t e-h d a, *v. n.* *to be hungry*—wotektewahda, wotekteuŋhdapi. *T*, lo'ćiŋ. See akiȟaŋ.

w o'-t e-k t e-h d a-p i, *n.* *hunger.* *T.*, loćiŋpi.

w o'-t i-ć a, *n.* of tića; *scraping* or *pawing*, as an ox or horse does snow.

w o'-t i-h n i, *v.* of ihni; *to hunt large animals*, as deer and elk—wotiwahni, wotiuŋhnipi.

w o'-t i-h n i-p i, *n.* *the hunting of deer*, etc.

w o'-t i-k i-y a, *v.* *T.* *to ask of* one *for* another; *i. q.* ikićituka: wiwotikiya, *to ask for a wife for another man*—wotiwakiya.

w o-t i'-t i, *adv.* *T.* *irresolutely; unsteadily:* wotiti mani, *to walk unsteadily* or as a blind man; wotiti ećoŋ, *to do hesitatingly;* wotiti inaźiŋ, *to stand undecided.*

w o'-t i-y e-m n a-ś n i, *adj.* *T.* *pure; clean*, as a person or a house. See womnaśni.

w o t'-k i-y a, *v.* See wonkiya.

w o-t o', *v. n.* *T.* *to miss fire.* See boto.

wo'-to-ki-ç̣oŋ, *n.* of tokiç̣oŋ; *revenge.*

wo'-toŋ, *n.* of toŋ; *property.* *T.*, woyuha.

wo'-tpaŋ, *v.* of yutpaŋ; *to grind*, as grain—wamdutpaŋ. See wokpaŋ.

wo'-tpaŋ-ti-pi, *n.* *a grist mill.*

wo'-ṭa, *v.* *to be dead of food, to have eaten too much, to be surfeited*—womaṭa. See woḣaka.

wo'-ṭe, *n.* *death.*

wo'-ṭe-ye, *n.* *the cause of death.*

wo'-wa, *v.* of owa; *to mark, to paint, to write*—wowawa, woyawa.

wo'-wa-ći, *n.* of waći; *the dance, dancing.*

wo'-wa-ćiŋ-ko, *n.* of waćiŋko; *irascibility.*

wo'-wa-ćiŋ-taŋ-ka, *n.* *patience, perseverance.*

wo'-wa-ćiŋ-yaŋ, *n.* of waćiŋyaŋ; *trusting in, reliance upon, faith.*

wo'-wa-ćiŋ-ye, *n.* Same as wowaćiŋyaŋ.

wo'-wa-hde-će, *n* *a twitching, an omen.* *T.*, taku inihaŋwićaya. See wahdeća.

wo'-wa-he-ćoŋ, *n.* *kindred, relationship; names expressing relationship.* See takukićiyapi.

wo'-wa-ho-koŋ-ki-ye, *n.* of wahokoŋkiya; *instruction, advice.*

wo'-wa-ḣba-daŋ, *n.* of waḣbadaŋ; *gentleness, meekness.*

wo'-wa-ḣpa-ni-ća, *n.* of waḣpanića; *poverty.*

wo'-wa-ḣta-ni, *n.* See woaḣtani.

wo'-wa-ḣte-da-śni, *n.* of waḣtedaśni; *dissatisfaction.*

wo'-wa-ḣte-da-śni-yaŋ, *adv.* *not pleased with.*

wo'-wa-ḣte'-śni, *n.* *a hated thing; a disgrace.*

wo'-wa-kaŋ, *n.* of wakaŋ; *something supernatural.* This word we have used for *holiness.*

wo'-wa-ka-śo-te-śni, *n.* of wakasoteśni; *purity.*

wo'-wa-ki-ćoŋ-ze, *n.* of wakićoŋza; *law, government, influence.*

wo'-wa-ki-taŋ, *n.* of wakitaŋ; *something that is contended for*

wo'-wa-ki-taŋ-ye, *n.* *that which causes obstinacy* or *determination, resolution*

wo'-wa-koŋ-ze, *n.* of wakoŋze; *determination; law, rule, justice.*

wo'-wa-kta, *n.* of wakta; *a mark, a sign; circumspection.*

wo'-wa-ma-noŋ, *n.* *theft.*

wo'-wa-mna-da, *n.* of wamnada; *respect.*

wo'-wa-ni-ki-ye, *n.* of wanikiya; *salvation*

wo'-waŋ-ya-ke, *n.* *a vision, a sight, a show.*

wo'-wa-oŋ-spe, *n.* of waoŋspe; *precept, instruction*

wo'-wa-oŋ-spe-ki-ye, *n.* *instruction.*

wo'-wa-oŋ-śi-da, *n.* of waoŋśida; *mercy; pity, kindness.*

wo'-wa-pe-tog-toŋ, *n.* of wapetogtoŋ; *a mark, a sign.*

wo'-wa-pe-to-ke-ća, *n.* *a sign, a wonder, a miracle.*

wo'-wa-pi, *n.* of owa; *a painting* or *carving in hieroglyphics; a painting* or *representation, a picture; a writing, a letter; a book.* *T., a flag, banner* or *signal:* wowapi pawoslal iyeya, *to run up a flag.* "A letter" or "book" is miniȟúowapi, though wowapi is slowly coming into use here for these also.—W. J. C.

wo'-wa-pi-i-ća-ġe, *n.* *something used to paint* or *write with, a pen* or *pencil.* See wiyowa.

wo'-wa-pi-ka-ġa, *v.* *to write, to make a book*—wowapi wakaġa.

wo'-wa-pi-ka-ġa, *n.* *a scribe, a clerk.*

wo'-wa-pi-o-hni-hde, *n.* *a newspaper.* Wotaŋiŋ-wowapi is better.

wo'-wa-pi-o-ki-źa-te, *n.* *T.* *a flag of truce.*

wo'-wa-pi-wa-kaŋ, *n.* *the holy book, the Bible.*

wo'-wa-pi-wi-ćo-ni, *n.* *the book of life.* Wićoni-wowapi is thought to be the better form.

wo'-wa-su-ki-ye, *n.* *Ih.* *a law; a prophecy.* *T., a rule;* law; *regulation; determination* to be followed as a law.

wo'-wa-ś'ag-ya, *adv.* *strongly.*

wo'-wa-ś'a-ke, *n.* of waś'aka; *strength.*

wo'-wa-śi, *n.* *Ih* and *T.* *labor, work: i. q.* woȟtani. *T.,* also *a worker* or *servant.* See wićoȟtani.

wo'-wa-śte, *n.* of waśte; *goodness.*

wo'-wa-śte-da-ke, *n.* *love, complacency.*

wo'-wa-wo-ki-ye, *n.* of wawokiya; *help.*

wo'-wa-ya-zaŋ, *n.* of wayazaŋ; *sickness, disease.*

wo'-wi-ća-da, *n.* of wićada; *belief, faith.*

wo'-wi-ća-da-ya, *v. a.* *to cause belief, to persuade*—wowićadawaya.

wo'-wi-ća-hna-ye, *n.* *deception.* See wohnaye.

wo'-wi-ća-ȟtag-ni-ća, *v. n.* (ićaȟtaka *and* nića) *to be irritable, easily provoked; to be unwilling to be touched*—wowićaȟtagmanića. *T.,* wowićaȟtake wanića.

wo'-wi-ća-ke, *n.* of wićaka; *truth:* wowićake ećiyataŋhaŋ, *of a truth, truly.*

wo'-wi-ća-ke-ya-taŋ-haŋ, *adv.* *of a truth, truly.*

wo'-wi-ća-śa-śni, *n.* *T.* *spite; mischief; meanness.*

wo'-wi-ćiŋ, *n.* See wićiŋpi.

wo'-wi-dag-ya, *v. a.* *to make a servant of, to have for a servant, to cause to serve*—wowidagwaya, wowidaguŋyaŋpi, wowidagmayaŋ.

wo'-wi-da-ke, *n.* of idaka; *a servant.* *T.,* woilake.

wo'-wi-haŋ-mde, *n* of ihaŋmna; *a dream, dreams.*

wo'-wi-haŋ-mna, *n.* *dreams.*

wo'-wi-hnu, *n.* of ihnu; *murmuring.*

wo'-wi-ȟa, *n.* of iȟa; *something laughable.*

wo'-wi-ḣa-daŋ, *n.* *fun; something laughable.*

wo'-wi-ḣa-ḣa, *n.* *laughing, making fun.*

wo'-wi-ḣa-ḣa-ki-ya, *v.* *to laugh at one's own*—wowiḣaḣawakiya.

wo'-wi-ḣa-ḣa-ya, *adv* *shamefully.*

wo'-wi-ḣaŋ, *n.* *T* of wiḣaŋ; *grazing.*

wo'-wi-ḣa-ya, *adv.* *laughably.*

wo'-wi-ḣa-ya-ken, *adv.* *ridiculously.*

wo'-wi-ma-ġa-ġa, *v. n.* of imaġaġa; *to be cheerful* or *merry*—wowimamaġaġa, wowinimaġaġa. *T.*, also *an amusement.* See woimaġaġa.

wo'-wi-ma-ġa-ġa, *n.* of imaġaġa; *something cheering.*

wo'-wi-na-ḣni, *n.* of inaḣni; *haste.*

wo'-wi-na-ki-wi-zi, *n.* of inakiwizi; *jealousy.*

wo'-wi-na-pe, *n.* of inapa; *a refuge, a retreat.*

wo'-wi-na-pe-ya, *v. a.* *to have for a refuge.*

wo'-wi-na-wi-zi, *n.* of inawizi; *jealousy, envy; the cause of envy.*

wo'-wi-ni-haŋ, *n.* of inihaŋ; *something frightful, fear.*

wo'-wi-ni-haŋ-yaŋ, *adv.* *fearfully.*

wo'-wiŋ-kta, *n.* of iwiŋkta; *gladness; glory.*

wo'-wiŋ-yuŋ-yaŋ, *v. a.* *to use as an instrument*—wowiŋyuŋwaya. See iyuŋ *and* wowiyuŋyaŋ.

wo'-wiŋ-yuŋ-yaŋ-pi, *n.* *tools, instruments.*

wo'-wi-śte-će, *n.* of iśteća; *shame.*

wo'-wi-śten-ya, *adv.* *disgracefully, shamefully:* wowiśtenya ećamoŋ, *I have acted shamefully.*

wo'-wi-śten-ye, *n.* *the cause of shame.*

wo'-wi-śu-te, *adj.* of iśute; *very much:* taku wowiśute. *T.*, lila ota.

wo'-wi-śu-te-ka, *adj.* *very much.*

wo'-wi-śu-te-ya, *adv.* *very much, abundantly.*

wo'-wi-taŋ, *n.* of itaŋ; *honor, glory; pride.*

wo'-wi-taŋ-yaŋ, *v. a.* *to glory in*—wowitaŋwaya.

wo'-wi-taŋ-yaŋ, *adv.* *honorably, gloriously.*

wo'-wi-toŋ-pe, *n.* of itoŋpa; *something to be feared* or *guarded against; danger.*

wo'-wi-yuŋ-yaŋ, *v.* See wowiŋyuŋyaŋ.

wo'-wi-yu-śkiŋ, *n.* of iyuśkiŋ; *gladness, rejoicing.*

wo'-wi-yu-śkiŋ-yaŋ, *adv.* *gladly, rejoicingly.*

wo'-wi-yu-taŋ, *n.* of iyutaŋ; *temptation.*

wo'-wi-yu-taŋ-ye, *n.* *temptation.*

wo'-wi-źi-će, *n.* of wiźića; *riches.*

wo'-ya-ćo, *n.* of yaćo; *judgment, condemnation* *T.*, woyasu.

wo'-yad-ya. See Wooŋspe Itakiḣna, p. 97, l. 8.

wo′-yag, *cont.* of woyaka; woyag waḣi, *I have come to tell.*

wo′-yag-ki-ya-pi, *n. T. a witness; one made to testify.*

wo′-ya-ka, *v.* of oyaka; *to tell, relate, declare, publish*—womdaka, wouŋyakapi.

wo′-ya-ka-pi, *n. a declaration, a narration.*

wo′-ya-ke, *n. a relation, a declaration, a vow.*

wo′-ya-pta-pi, *n.* of oyapta; *leavings, fragments of food.*

wo′-ya-pte, *n.* See woyaptapi.

wo′-ya-su, *n.* of yasu; *finishing, i. q.* yaćopi. See woyaćo.

wo′-ya-taŋ, *n.* of yataŋ; *praise.*

wo′-ya-tke, *n.* of yatkaŋ; *drink.*

wo′-ya-ṭa-ġa, *n.* of yaṭaġa; *something astringent.*

wo′-ya-wa, *n.* of yawa; *a counting.*

wo′-ya-wa-śte, *n.* of yawaśte; *blessing, praise.*

wo′-ya-wa-taŋ-ka, *n. a great count, a million. T.,* kokta śića.

wo′-ya-ya, *n. T. a skein; a bunch,* as of beads or thread; *a string,* as of beads.

wo′-ye-taŋ-iŋ, *v. n. T. there are tracks.*

wo′-yu-e-će-tu, *n.* of yuećetu; *a making right.*

wo′-yu-ha, *n.* of yuha; *possessions, property.*

wo′-yu-ḣtaŋ-yaŋ, *n. small burrs* of several varieties of plants, probably species of *Xanthium.*

wo′-yu-kćaŋ, *n* of yukćaŋ; *opinion, judgment.*

wo′-yu-o-ni-haŋ, *n. T. an honor; honor*

wo′-yu-ska, *n. ornamental work,* such as cutting strips into skin, and winding them with quills.

wo′-yu-su, *n.* of yusu; *a making right, finishing. T.,* yuećetu; waśte kaġa.

wo′-yu-su-ta, *n.* of yusuta; *a making firm.*

wo′-yu-śda-ye-hna, *n.* See śdayehna.

wo′-yu-śi-će, *n.* of yuśića; *that which makes bad.*

wo′-yu-śi-ḣtiŋ, *n. that which makes feeble. T., that which injures* or *makes bad.*

wo′-yu-śki-śke, *n.* of yuśkiśka; *that which causes difficulty.*

wo′-yu-śna, *n.* of yuśna; *missing, letting fall; sacrificing.*

wo′-yu-śtaŋ, *n.* of yuśtaŋ; *finishing, completion, perfection; putting one in another.*

wo′-yu-te, *n.* of yuta; *something to eat, food.*

wo′-yu-te-ya, *v. a. to have* or *use as food*—woyutewaya.

wo′-yu-tkoŋ-ze, *n.* of yutkoŋza; *finishing, perfecting. T.,* also *making equal.*

wo′-yu-tpaŋ, *n. T.,* woyukpaŋ. See wiyutpaŋ.

wo′-yu-wa-śte, *n.* of yuwaśte; *that which makes good.*

wo′-zaŋ-ni, *n.* of zani; *health.*

w o'- z e, *n.* of yuze; *taking out, lading out* of a kettle.

w o'- z e - p i, *part. laded out.*

w o'- z i, *n.* See zi.

w o'- ź a, *v.* of yuźa; *to mash; to stir,* as mush, *to make mush*—wowaźa *and* wamduźa.

w o'- ź a - p i, *n. something mashed and stirred up; hasty-pudding, mush:* also *a stew* of any kind mixed; ćaŋpa woźapi, kaŋta woźapi.

w o'- ź a - ź a, *v.* of yuźaźa; *to wash, do a washing*—wamduźaźa.

w o'- ź a - ź a - p i, *n. washing.*

w o'- ź i - ć e, *n.* of źića; *riches.*

w o'- ź u, *v.* of oźu; *to sow, to plant*—wowaźu, woyaźu, wouŋźupi.

w o'- ź u, *n. a sower.*

w o'- ź u - h a, *n. an empty bag, a sack, a case.* See oźuha.

w o'- ź u - h a - d a ŋ, *n. a small bag.*

w o - ź u - h a - g l a - t a - t a, *v. a. T. to exhaust, use all up,* as one's supply *by giving* to others: *i. q.* peaglatata—wozuhawaglatata.

w o'- ź u - p i, *n. seed for planting* (*T.*, iwóźu; woźupi su); *sowing* or *planting; a field* or *garden* (*T.*, woźupi).

w o'- ź u - p i - w i, *n. the planting moon, May.*

w o'- ź u - ṭ i, *n. a farm-house; a farmer.*

w o'- ź u - t o ŋ, *v.* of oźutoŋ; *to fill up into bags* or *sacks*—woźuwatoŋ.

w o'- ź u - t o ŋ - p i, *n. a bag* or *sack filled, a bag of corn.*

w o'- ź u - ź u, *v.* of yuźuźu; *to take to pieces; to demolish; to unpack*—wowaźuźu *and* wamduźuźu.

w o'- ź u - ź u - p i, *n. taking to pieces.*

w u h, *intj. T.* of surprise; *oh!*

w u h'- w u h - w u h, *intj.* Used by the Dakota women in calling a dog. *T.*, wehwehweh.

Y.

y, *the twenty-seventh letter of the Dakota alphabet,* with the common sound of "y" in English.

y a, *a prefix.*

1. It is prefixed to a large class of verbs, and signifies that the action is done *with the mouth, by biting, talking,* etc.; as, yaksa, *to bite off.*
2. It is prefixed to adjectives, and sometimes nouns, making of them verbs signifying *to speak of as such* or *to make so with the mouth;* as, waśte, *good,* yawaśte, *to call good, to bless;* wićaśta, *man,* yawićaśta, *to speak of as a man.* In these cases the different persons are formed as in ya, *to go.*

y a, *v. aux. causative; to cause, to make.* This is suffixed to verbs, adjectives, etc.; as, ećoŋya, *to cause to do;* samya, *to make black;* waś'agya, *to make strong.* The place of the pronoun is before the "ya."

y a, *v. aux. suffix* to nouns; *to have for, regard as;* as, tiyopa-ya, *to have for a door;* isaŋ-ya, *to have for* or *use as a knife.* It is also used in cases of relationship; as, ate-ya, *to have for father*—atewaya, ateuŋyaŋpi: taŋkśiwaya, *she is my sister* or *I have her for sister.*

y a, *pron. in comp. thou, you.*

y a, *v. n. to go, to start, to proceed*—mda, da, uŋyaŋpi. *T*, mla, la—*future*, mni kta, ni kta, yiŋ kta.

y a, *exclamation of scolding*, used by *T.*, women.

y a *or* y a ŋ, *an adverbial termination of adjectives* and *an adverbial* or *participial termination of verbs;* as, śića, *bad*, śićaya, *badly;* yuktaŋ, *to bend*, yuktaŋyaŋ, *bending. T.*, also yakel.

y a - a′- d o s - d o - z a, *v.* of adosdoza; yaadosdoza se iyeya, *to say something that makes another feel uncomfortable, to injure one's feelings. T.*, yaćaŋtiyap'a iyeya.

y a - a′- o - p t e - ć a, *v. a.* of aopteća; *to speak of as being small, to underrate*—mdaaopteća.

y a - a′- o - p t e n, *cont.* of yaopteća; yaaopten iyeya.

y a - a′- o - p t e n - y a, *adv. in a depreciating manner.*

y a - a′- o - p t e - t u, *v. a.* of aoptêtu; *to speak of as less, to underrate*—mdaaoptetu.

y a - a′- o - p t e - t u - y a, *adv. underrating.*

y a - a′- ś d a, *v. n. to graze*, as cattle. See aśda.

y a - a′- ś d a - y a, *v. a. to make bare*, as a falsehood; *to unfold, tell, explain; to make bare with the teeth*—mdaaśdaya.

y a - a′- ś k a - d a ŋ, *v. a.* of aśkadaŋ; *to speak of as near*—mdaaśkadaŋ. *T.*, yakiyela.

y a - a′- ś k a - ś k a - d a ŋ, *v. red.* of yaaśkadaŋ.

y a - a′- ś k a - y a - k e n, *adv. speaking of as near.*

y a - a′- ś k a - y e - d a ŋ, *v. a. to speak of as near*—mdaaśkayedaŋ.

y a - b a′- ġ a, *v. a. to turn about with the mouth, to twist; to bite* or *vex*, as one dog does another; *to vex* or *annoy by begging*—mdabaġa. *T.*, yawazeća. See yabaza, pabaġa, etc.

y a - b a′- ġ a - k a, *v. a. to annoy, to beg of*—mdabaġaka.

y a - b a′- z a, *v. a. to annoy*, as one dog does another *by biting.* See yabaġa, yubaza, etc.

y a - b a′- ź a, *v. a. to bite* or *gnaw*, as a horse does wood.

y a - b i′- l i - h e - ć a, *v. a T. to make active by talking to.* See miniheća.

y a - b o′- s d a n, *v.* of bosdan; *to set up with the mouth:* yabosdan yapa *and* yabosdan ehnaka, *to hold upright with the mouth.*

y a - b u′, *v. a* of bu; *to growl, to speak* or *sing with a hoarse voice*—mdabu. *T.*, also *to make any loud but indistinct noise* or *a disagreeable noise*, as children with horns, etc.

y a - b u′- b u, *v. red.* of yabu; *to speak with a hoarse rough voice*—mdabubu.

y a - b u'-y a, *adv. hoarsely:* yabuya ia, *to speak with a hoarse voice.*

y a - ć a ŋ' - ć a ŋ, *v. a.* of ćaŋćaŋ; *to make shake with the mouth.*

y a - ć a ŋ t - i - y a - p'a - i - y e - y a, *v. T. to say something to hurt another's feelings: i. q.* yalos iyeya. See yaadosdoza

y a - ć a ŋ' - z e - k a, *v. a. T. to make angry by talking to.*

y a - ć e' - k a, *v. a.* See yaćekćeka.

y a - ć e' - k ć e - k a, *v. a. to bite and make stagger*—mdaćekćeka.

y a - ć e' - y a, *v. a.* of ćeya; *to make cry by talking to* or *biting*—mdaćeya, mayaćeya.

y a - ć i' - ķ a - d a ŋ, *v. a.* of ćiķadaŋ; *to count small; to make small with the mouth; to undervalue*—mdaći-ķadaŋ.

y a - ć i' - s t i ŋ - n a, *v. a.* of ćistiŋna; *to speak of as small*—mdaćistiŋna. *T.*, yaćisćiyela.

y a - ć o', *v.a. to judge, condemn, fine*—mdaćo, daćo, uŋyaćopi. See yasu.

y a - ć o' - ć o, *v. a. to chew up fine*—mdaćoćo.

y a - ć o' - k a, *v.a. to judge, to condemn* (*T.*, same meaning)*; to make empty.*

y a - ć o' - k a - k a, *v. a. to empty by eating out the inside*, as dogs do a dead animal.

y a - ć o' - n a - l a, *v. a. T. to speak of as few.*

y a - ć o' - p i, *n. condemnation; i. q.* woyaćo. *T.*, yasupi.

y a - ć o' - y a, *adv. condemning. T.*, yasuya.

y a - ć o' - y a - k e n, *adv. in the way of condemning. T.*, yasuyakel.

y a - ć o' - z a, *v. a. to call warm, to make warm with the mouth*—mda-ćoza.

y a - d e m' - d e - p a, *v. a. to bite notches in*—mdademdepa.

y a d u' - z a - h a ŋ, *v.a. to call swift*—mdaduzahaŋ: also 2d pers. sing. of duzahaŋ.

y a - e' - ć a ḣ, *adv.* Same as yae-ćayaḣ. *T.*, yawićakeya se.

y a - e' - ć a - y a ḣ, *adv. deceptively; ironically:* yaećayaḣ oyaka, *to tell* a thing *not as it is, to make a statement of which the very reverse is true*—yaećayaḣ omdaka.

y a - e' - ć e - d a ŋ, *v. a. to speak of as right, to make right with the mouth*—mdaećedaŋ.

y a - e' - ć e n - y a, *adv.* yaećenya oyaka, *to tell a thing as it ought to be told.*

y a - e' - ć e - t u, *v. a. to consummate by speaking; to speak correctly*—mda-ećetu.

y a - e' - ć e - t u - y a, *adv. speaking correctly.*

y a - ġ a', *v. a. to peel off with the teeth; to husk with the mouth*—mdaġa.

y a - ġ a' - ġ a, *v. red.* of yaġa; yaġaġa iyeya.

y a - ġ a m', *cont.* of yaġapa; yaġam iyeya.

y a - ġ a n' - ġ a - t a, *v. a. to make forked with the mouth, to prevaricate*—mdaġanġata.

y a - ġ a ŋ′, *v. a.* *to suck out* or *open*—mdaġaŋ.

y a - ġ a′ - p a , *v. a.* *to bite off*, as the skin or bark from anything—mdaġapa.

y a - ġ a′ - t a , *v.* See yaġanġata.

y a - ġ e′, *v. a* *to drink up*, as water from a spring—mdaġe: *to gather with the mouth*, as an ox does grass.

y a - ġ e′ - ġ e , *v. a.* *to gather with the mouth*, as an ox does grass.

y a - ġ i′ - t a , *v.* ho yaġita, *to make the voice hoarse by speaking.* See hoġita.

y a - ġ o′, *v. a.* *to make a noise with the teeth*—mdaġo.

y a - ġ o m′, *cont.* of yaġopa; yaġom yatkaŋ, *to sip*, as water: yaġom iću.

y a - ġ o′ - p a , *v. a.* *to suck up, to make a noise with the mouth*, as in eating soup, etc.—mdaġopa.

y a - ġ u′ - k a , *v. a.* *to strain*, as one's neck, *by biting* anything—mdaġuka. See yuġuka.

y a - h a′, *v. n.* *to prick* or *run into*, as beards of rice or porcupine quills—mayaha, wićayaha. *T*, yahaŋ.

y a - h a′ - h a , *n.* See yahahadaŋ.

y a - h a′ - ħ a - d a ŋ , *v. a.* *to shake* or *move with the mouth; to move* one in his purpose *by talking to, to persuade*—mdahahadaŋ. See yuhahadaŋ.

y a - h a′ - h a - y e - d a ŋ, *v. a.* *to move by talking to, to shake in one's purpose*—mdahahayedaŋ: ćaŋte yahahayedaŋ.

y a - h a′ - i - y e - y a , *v. a.* *to throw down with the mouth, to turn aside with the mouth.*

y a - h b a′, *v. a.* *to shell with the mouth, to bite off*—mdahba.

y a - h b e′ - z a , *v. a.* *to bite and make rough*—mdahbeza See yuhbeza.

y a - h b u′ - y a - i - y e - y a, *v.* *to push into with the nose and make a noise*, as into a barrel of corn.

y a - h d a′, *v. a.* *to bite off*, as a dog does the fat from entrails: *to uncoil with the mouth.*

y a - h d a′ - h d a , *v. a.* *to uncoil*, as a dog does entrails, *with the mouth.*

y a - h d a′ - h e - y a, *adv.* yahdaheya ia, *to set in order; to lay open, explain.*

y a - h d a′ - k a , *v. a.* *to bite off and make toothed* or *notched*, as a beaver does—mdahdaka.

y a - h d a′ - k i ŋ - y a ŋ , *v. a.* of hdakiŋyaŋ; *to go across in one's speech, to contradict one's self, to tell what is false*—mdakdakiŋyaŋ.

y a - h d a′ - p i - s e, *adv.* *fluently, plainly:* yahdapise oyaka.

y a - h d o′ - k a, *v. a.* *to put out of place by means of the teeth*—mdahdoka. See yaħdoka *and* yaśdoka.

y a - h i n′, *cont.* of yahiŋta; yahin iyeya, *to eat all up.*

y a - h i ŋ′ - t a, *v. a.* *to brush away with the mouth, to eat all up*—mdahiŋta.

y a - h m i′, *v. a.* *to clear off, to bite off*, as grass, etc.

y a - h m i′ - ć a , *v.* *to catch by the hair in the mouth.*

y a - h m i'- h m a, *v. a. to roll with the mouth*—mdahmihma.

y a - h m i'- p i - s e, *adv. rounded off*, as a bunch of grass or weeds whose tops have been bitten off.

y a - h m i'- y a ŋ - y a ŋ, *v. a. to make round in the mouth*, as bullets—mdahmiyaŋyaŋ. See yamima.

y a - h n a', *v. a. to shake off*, as fruit, *with the mouth*—mdahna.

y a - h n a'- y a ŋ, *v. a. to miss with the mouth*, as in attempting to catch in it; *to miss with the mouth, tell a falsehood*—mdahnayaŋ: also 2d pers. sing. of hnayaŋ.

y a - h n u'- n i, *v. a.* of hnuni; *to cause to wander in mind by talking to, to confuse*—mdahnuni.

y a - h o'- ġ i l - y a, *adv. T. hoarsely.*

y a - h o'- ġ i - t a, *v. n. T. to become hoarse from singing*—blahoġita. *To become hoarse from speaking* is iglá-hoġita.

y a - h o'- h o, *v. a. to shake* or *make loose with the mouth*—mdahoho.

y a - h o'- h o - y a, *adv. shaking with the mouth.*

y a - h o'- m n i, *v. a. to turn* one *round by argument, to make* one *change his views, to convert*—mdahomni, mayahomni.

y a - h o'- t a, *v. to draw in with the breath, to inhale*, as cold air, dust, etc.—mdahota: sni dahota, *thou hast taken cold.*

y a - h o'- t o ŋ, *v. a.* of hotoŋ; *to bite and make cry out*—mdahotoŋ.

y a - h u'- h u s, *cont.* of yahuhuza: yahuhus iyeya. *T.*, yahuŋhuŋs.

y a - h u'- h u - z a, *v. a to shake with the mouth; to shake one's resolution by talking to*—mdahuhuza. *T.*, yahuŋhuŋza.

y a - h u'- t e - d a ŋ, *v. a. to bite off short, to wear off to a stump*, as the teeth—mdahutedaŋ.

y a - ḣ a - ḣ a, *v. a. to tangle with the teeth*—mdaḣaḣa.

y a - ḣ a'- k p a, *v. a. to bite and make rough*—mdaḣakpa; *i. q.* yaḣatpa.

y a - ḣ a m', *cont.* of yaḣapa; yaḣam iyeya, *to scare away*, as game, *by talking.*

y a - ḣ a ŋ'- h i - y a, *adv.* of ḣaŋhi; *making slow by talking to.*

y a - ḣ a ŋ'- i - ṭ e - y a, *adv. making weary by talking to.*

y a - ḣ a'- p a, *v. to frighten* or *scare up*, as game, *by talking*—mdaḣapa. See kaḣapa.

y a - ḣ a'- t p a, *v. a. to make rough with the teeth*—mdaḣatpa; *i. q.* yaḣakpa.

y a - ḣ b a', *v. a. to make sleepy by talking to*—mdaḣba.

y a - ḣ ć i', *v. a. to tear out a little piece with the teeth*—mdaḣći.

y a - ḣ ć i'- ḣ ć i, *v. red.* of yaḣći.

y a - ḣ d a', *v. a. to make rattle with the mouth*—mdaḣda.

y a - ḣ d a'- ġ a ŋ, *v. a. to enlarge with the mouth.*

y a - ḣ d a'- ḣ d a, *v. red.* of yaḣda.

y a - ḣ d a n', *cont.* of yaḣdata; yaḣdan ia, *to speak as one does who is starving to death.*

ya-ȟda'-ta, *v.* *to speak as one dying of hunger* is said to speak—mdaȟdata. *T.*, akiȟaŋ ṭiŋ kta se hotaŋiŋ śni.

ya-ȟda'-ya, *v. a.* *to bite* or *peel off the skin* or *rind* of any thing *with the teeth; to tell a lie*—mdaȟdaya, daȟdaya.

ya-ȟde'-ća, *v. a.* *to tear with the mouth, to bite to pieces*—mdaȟdeća, uŋyaȟdećapi.

ya-ȟde'-ȟde-ća, *v. red.* of yaȟdeća.

ya-ȟden', *cont.* of yaȟdeća: yaȟden iyeya.

ya-ȟdog', *cont.* of yaȟdoka: yaȟdog iyeya.

ya-ȟdo'-ȟdo-ka, *v. red.* of yaȟdoka; *to bite and tear*, as dogs do—mdaȟdoȟdoka.

ya-ȟdo'-ka, *v. a.* *to bite a hole in, to bite open, to make an impression on with the teeth*—mdaȟdoka, daȟdoka, uŋyaȟdokapi. See yahdoka.

ya-ȟem', *cont.* of yaȟepa; yaȟem iyeya, *to drink up at once.*

ya-ȟem'-ȟe-pa, *v. red.* of yaȟepa.

ya-ȟe'-pa, *v. a.* *to drink up*, as water, etc.—mdaȟepa, daȟepa, uŋyaȟepapi.

ya-ȟe'-yan, *cont.* of yaȟeyata: yaȟeyan iyeya.

ya-ȟe'-ya-ta, *v.* *to put aside with the mouth* or *in speaking, to reject*—mdaȟeyata, mayaȟeyata.

ya-ȟi'-ća, *v. a.* *to waken one up with the mouth* or *by talking*—mdaȟića.

ya-ȟin', *cont.* of yaȟića: yaȟin iyeya.

ya-ȟi'-ya-ya, *v.* *to be awkward with the mouth*, as in speaking or making a bullet round in the mouth—mdaȟiyaya.

ya-ȟle'-ća, *v.* *T.* *i. q.* yaȟdeća.

ya-ȟlo'-ka, *v.* *T.* *i. q.* yaȟdoka.

ya-ȟmiŋ', *v. a.* *to crook* or *turn aside with the mouth; to distort*—mdaȟmiŋ.

ya-ȟmiŋ'-yaŋ, *adv.* *turning aside with the mouth:* yaȟmiŋyaŋ ehnaka.

ya-ȟmuŋ', *v.* *to make a humming* or *rattling noise with the mouth:* yaȟmuŋ se yutapi.

ya-ȟpa', *v. a.* *to throw* any thing *down with the mouth*—mdaȟpa.

ya-ȟpa'-ȟpa, *v. red.* of yaȟpa.

ya-ȟpaŋ', *v. a.* *to moisten* or *soak in the mouth*—mdaȟpaŋ.

ya-ȟpaŋ'-ȟpaŋ, *v. red.* of yaȟpaŋ; *to make soft with the mouth*, as a quill or takaŋ—mdaȟpaŋȟpaŋ.

ya-ȟpe'-ya, *v. a.* *to cause to throw down with the mouth*—yaȟpewaya.

ya-ȟpu', *v. a.* *to bite off*, as any thing *sticking on, bite off in small pieces*, as gum—mdaȟpu.

ya-ȟpu'-ȟpu, *v. red.* of yaȟpu.

ya-ȟtag', *cont.* of yaȟtaka: yaȟtag iyeya.

ya-ȟtag'-ki-ya, *v. a.* *to cause to bite* anything—yaȟtagwakiya.

ya-ȟtag'-ya, *v. a.* *to cause to bite*—yaȟtagwaya.

ya-ȟtag'-ya, *adv.* *biting.*

y a - ḣ t a′ - k a, *v. a.* *to bite, to take hold of with the teeth*—mdaḣtaka, daḣtaka, uŋyaḣtakapi.

y a - ḣ u′, *v. a.* *to peel off*, as the hull or rind, *with the teeth*—mdaḣu.

y a - ḣ u′ - ġ a, *v. a.* *to bite into; to crush with the teeth*—mdaḣuġa.

y a - ḣ u′ - ġ a - p i, *n.* *T* *nuts*, because cracked with the teeth, especially *peanuts.*

y a - ḣ u ḣ′, *cont.* of yaḣuġa: yaḣuḣ iyeya.

y a - ḣ u ḣ′ - k i - y a, *v. a.* *to cause to crush* or *bite into*—yaḣuḣwakiya.

y a - ḣ u′ - ḣ n a - ġ a, *v. a* of ḣuḣnaġa; *to speak evil of, to destroy one's character*, as if *burnt up*—mdaḣuḣnaġa. *T.*, yaatakuniśni.

y a - ḣ u′ - ḣ u - ġ a, *v. red.* of yaḣuġa.

y a - ḣ u ḣ′ - y a, *v. a.* *to cause to crush with the teeth*—yaḣuḣwaya.

y a - ḣ u ŋ′ - ḣ u ŋ - t a, *v. red.* of yaḣuŋta.

y a - ḣ u ŋ′ - t a, *v. a.* *to draw through the mouth and make pliable*, as sinew for sewing and bark for tying—mdaḣuŋta.

y a - i′ - d e, *v. a.* of ide; *to make blaze by blowing with the mouth*—mdaide.

y a - i′ - ḣ a, *v.* of iḣa; *to make laugh by talking to*—mdaiḣa.

y a - i - m n i - ź a, *v. a.* *T* *to speak of as if* (it) *were a rock.*

y a - i′ - n a - ḣ n i, *v. a.* of inaḣni; *to make hasten by speaking to*—mdainaḣni.

y a - i′ - n a - ḣ n i - y a, *adv.* *hastening by speaking to.*

y a - i′ - n i n, *cont.* of yainina; yainin eḣpeya, yainin iyeya, *and* yainin ya, *to put to silence by argument.* *T.*, yainil.

y a - i′ - n i - n a, *v. a* of inina; *to put to silence by speaking to*—mdainina. *T.*, yainila.

y a - i′ - ś t e - ć a, *v. a.* of iśteća; *to make ashamed by speaking to*—mdaiśteća.

y a - i′ - ś t e l - y a, *v. a.* *T.* Same.

y a - i′ - ś t e n - y a, *adv.* *making ashamed by speaking to.*

y a - i′ - t o - k a ŋ, *v. a.* *T.* *i. q.* yaiyoka.

y a - i′ - t p i - s k a - e - ḣ p e - y a, *v.* (itpi, ska, *and* eḣpeya) *to make turn over on the back*, as a dog, *by speaking to* or *biting.*

y a - i′ - y o g, *cont.* of yaiyoka; yaiyog iyeya, *to put aside with the mouth, reject.*

y a - i′ - y o - k a, *v. a.* of iyoka; *to put aside, reject*—mdaiyoka.

y a - i′ - y o - w a, *v. a.* of iyowa; *to make yawn by speaking*—mdaiyowa. *T.*. yaiyoya.

y a - i′ - y o - w a s, *cont.* of yaiyowaza; yaiyowas iyeya.

y a - i′ - y o - w a ś, *cont* of yaiyowaźa: yaiyowaś ie śni, *he does not speak to the point.*

y a - i′ - y o - w a - z a, *v. a.* *to make echo by speaking*—mdaiyowaza.

y a - i′ - y o - w a - z a, *n* *an echo.*

y a - i′ - y o - w a - ź a, *v. a.* of iyowaźa; *to speak of as near, to speak to the point.* See yaiyowaźaśni ya-i'-yo-wa-źa-sni, *v. a. not to speak to the point*—mdaiyowaźaśni.

ya-i'-yo-yag, *cont.* of yaiyoyaka; yaiyoyag iyeya.

ya-i'-yo-ya-ka, *v. a.* of iyoyaka; *to make sad by speaking to.*

ya-ka', *v. a. to split with the mouth*, as the feather end of a quill—mdaka.

ya-ka'-ka, *v. a. to champ*, as a horse his bit.

ya-ka'-kiś-ya, *adv. making suffer by scolding:* yakakiśya ia.

ya-ka'-ki-źa, *v. a.* of kakiźa; *to make suffer by scolding* or *biting*—mdakakiźa.

ya-kam', *cont.* of yakapa; yakam iyeya. *T.*, yakab.

ya-kaŋ'-ye-la, *v T. to speak of as near: i. q.* yakiyela. See yaaśkadaŋ.

ya-ka'-pa, *v. a. to catch in the mouth* anything that is tossed—mdakapa.

ya-ka'-tiŋ, *v. a. to straighten* or *bend out straight with the mouth*—mdakatiŋ.

ya-ka'-wa, *v. a. to open* or *push back* anything *with the mouth*—mdakawa.

ya-kća', *v. a. to untie with the mouth, disentangle*—mdakća, uŋyakćapi.

ya-kel, *adv. termination* very common in *T.*

ya-ki'-ki-ta, *v. a. to make limber* or *pliable by biting*, as in making moccasins—mdakikita. *T.*, yapaŋpaŋ.

ya-kiŋs', *cont.* of yakiŋza; yakiŋs iyeya.

ya-kiŋs'-kiŋ-za, *v. red.* of yakiŋza.

ya-kiŋ'-za, *v. a. to make a grating* or *creaking noise with the teeth, to gnash*—mdakiŋza.

ya-ki'-pe-haŋ, *v. a.* of pehaŋ; *to double* or *fold up with the mouth*, so as to make the ends meet—mdakipehaŋ.

ya-ki'-pu-ski-ća, *v a. to press close together with the mouth*—mdakipuskića.

ya-ki'-pu-skin-ya, *adv. putting close together.*

ya-ki'-ye-la, *v. T. i. q.* yakaŋyela.

ya-ki'-ye-la-kel, *adv. T.* of the foregoing verb.

ya-kog', *cont.* of yakoka; yakog iyeya.

ya-ko'-ka, *v. a. to rattle with the teeth, chatter, gnash*—mdakoka.

ya-ko'-ke-daŋ; *v. a.* of kokedaŋ; *to make active by talking to*—mdakokedaŋ. *T*, yabiliheća.

ya-ko'-ki-pa, *v a.* of kokipa; *to make afraid by talking to*—mdakokipa.

ya-ko'-kog, *cont.* of yakokoka.

ya-ko'-kog-ya, *v. a to cause to make a chattering with the teeth*—yakokogwaya.

ya-ko'-kog-ya, *adv. chattering.*

ya-ko'-ko-ka, *v. a. red.* of yakoka; *to rattle the teeth, chatter, gnash*—mdakokoka.

y a - k o ŋ' - p i, *v. pl* *they are*—uŋyakoŋpi, dakanoŋpi. Perhaps the singular may be yaŋka. *T.*, uŋpi.

y a - k o ŋ' - p i - s' a, *n.* *inhabitants.* *T.*, uŋpis'a.

y a - k o' - p e - h d a, *v. a.* of kopehda; *to make one afraid by talking to*—mdakopehda.

y a - k o' - y a - ḣ a ŋ - n a, *v. a.* of koyaḣaŋna; *to make hasten by talking to*—mdakoyaḣaŋna.

y a - k p a', *v. a.* *to bite out, bite through*—mdakpa: iśta yakpa, *to bite out the eye, make blind* See yatpa.

y a - k p a' - k p a, *v. red.* of yakpa.

y a - k p a ŋ', *v. a.* *to chew fine, masticate*—mdakpaŋ, dakpaŋ, uŋyakpaŋpi: *i. q.* yatpaŋ.

y a - k p a ŋ' - k p a ŋ, *v. red.* of yakpaŋ.

y a - k p a ŋ' - y a ŋ, *adv.* *chewing fine.*

y a - k p i', *v. a.* *to crack with the teeth*, as lice, etc.—mdakpi: *i. q* yatpi.

y a - k p i' - k p i, *v. red.* of yakpi.

y a - k p u' - k p a, *v. a.* *to bite in small pieces, to crumble up with the teeth*—mdakpukpa: *i. q.* yatputpa.

y a - k s a', *v. a.* *to bite off*, as a stick—mdaksa, daksa, uŋyaksapi.

y a - k s a' - k s a, *v. red.* of yaksa; *to bite off often*—mdaksaksa.

y a - k s a' - p a, *v. a.* *to make wise by talking to*—mdaksapa: also 2d pers. sing. of ksapa.

y a - k s a' - y a, *v. a.* *to cause to bite off*—yaksawaya.

y a - k s a' - y a, *adv.* *biting off.*

y a - k ś a', *v. a.* *to bend up with the mouth*—mdakśa.

y a - k ś a' - d a ŋ, *v. a.* Same as yakśa.

y a - k ś a' - k ś a, *v. red.* of yakśa.

y a - k ś a ŋ', *v. a* *to bend with the mouth*—mdakśaŋ.

y a - k ś a ŋ' - k ś a ŋ, *v. red.* of yakśaŋ; *to bend* or *curl up.*

y a - k ś i' - k ś i - ź a, *v. red.* of yakśiźa.

y a - k ś i ś', *cont.* of yakśiźa; yakśiś iyeya.

y a - k ś i' - ź a, *v. a.* *to double up with the teeth*

y a - k t a ŋ', *v. a.* *to bend with the mouth*—mdaktaŋ. See yaoktaŋ.

y a - k t a ŋ' - k t a ŋ, *v. red.* of yaktaŋ; *to bend in several places with the mouth.*

y a - k t a ŋ' - y a ŋ, *v. a.* *to cause to bend with the mouth*—yaktaŋwaya.

y a - k t a ŋ' - y a ŋ, *adv.* *bending with the mouth.*

y a - k u' - k a, *v. a.* *to destroy with the teeth, bite to pieces*—mdakuka.

y a - k u ŋ' - t k u ŋ - t a, *v. a.* *to bite notches in*—mdakuŋtkuŋta.

y a - ķ e' - ġ a, *v. a.* *to make a grating noise with the teeth, to gnaw*—mdaķeġa. See yaķoġa.

y a - ķ e ḣ', *cont.* of yaķeġa; yaķeḣ iyeya.

y a - ķ e ḣ' - ķ e - ġ a, *v. red.* of yaķeġa.

y a - ķ e s', *cont.* of yaķeza; yaķes iyeya.

y a - ķ e s' - ķ e - z a, *v. red* of yaķeza.

y a - ķ e' - z a, *v. a.* *to make smooth with the teeth*—mdaķeza

ya-ḳo'-ġa, *v. a.* *to bite* or *gnaw off*, as something hard—mdaḳoġa.

ya-ḳoḣ', *cont.* of yaḳoġa; yaḳoḣ iyeya.

ya-ḳoḣ'-ḳo-ġa, *v. red.* of yaḳoġa.

ya-ḳos', *cont.* of yakoza; yakos iyeya.

ya-ḳos'-ḳo-za, *v. red.* of yaḳoza.

ya-ḳo'-za, *v. a.* *to make smooth with the mouth; to eat all off smooth*, as grass—mdaḳoza. See yaḳeza.

ya-los'-ye-ya, *v.* *T.* *i. q.* ya-adosdoza se iyeya.

ya-ma', *v. a.* *to gnaw*—mdama.

ya-ma'-hen-i-ye-ya, *v. a.* *to push into with the mouth.* See mahen.

ya-mdas', *cont.* of yamdaza; yamdas iyeya. *T.*, yablas.

ya-mda'-ska, *v. a.* of mdaska; *to flatten with the mouth*—mdamdaska. *T.*, yablaska.

ya-mda'-ya, *v. a.* of mdaya; *to make level with the teeth*—mdamdaya. *T.*, yablaya.

ya-mda'-za, *v. a.* of mdaza; *to tear open with the teeth*—mdamdaza. *T.*, yablaza.

ya-mde'-ća, *v. a.* *to break* or *crush with the teeth*—mdamdeća. *T.*, yableća.

ya-mde'-mde-ća, *v. red.* of yamdeća.

ya-mde'-mde-za, *v. red.* of yamdeza.

ya-mden', *cont* of yamdeća; yamden iyeya.

ya-mdes'-ya, *adv.* *cheeringly:* yamdesya ia, *to speak cheeringly.*

ya-mde'-za, *v. a.* of mdeza; *to make sober by talking to; to enlighten, cheer*—mdamdeza. *T.*, yableza.

ya-mdu', *v. a.* *to make fine by chewing*—mdamdu.

ya-mdu'-mdu, *v. red.* of yamdu.

ya-mi'-ma, *v. a.* *to make round*, as a wheel, *with the mouth*—mdamima. See yahmiyaŋyaŋ.

ya-mna', *v. a.* *to acquire by talking*, or in any way *with the mouth, to gain*—mdamna. See kamna.

ya-mna'-ki-ya, *v. a.* *to cause to gain by talking*—yamnawakiya.

ya-mna'-yaŋ, *v. a.* *to cause to gain with the mouth*—yamnawaya.

ya'-mni, *num. adj.* *three.*

ya-mni', *v.* 2d pers. sing. of mni.

ya-mni', *v. a.* *to turn* or *change the course* or *plan* of one *by speaking to* or *with*: mdamni.

ya-mni'-ġa, *v. a.* *to make shrink by biting*—mdamniġa.

ya'-mni-ki-ya, *adv.* *in three different ways.* See topakiya.

ya'-mni-mni, *adv.* *by threes, three each.* See tomtom.

ya'-mni-na, *adv.* *only three.* *T.*, yamnila. See tomnana.

ya-mni'-źa-ka, *v. a.* *to speak of* any thing *as if it were a rock*—mdamniźaka. *T.*, yaimniźa.

ya-mnu'-mnu-ġa, *v. a.* *to crunch, crush, grind, champ*, or *make a noise with the teeth*, as in eating; *to gnaw*, as a dog a bone, etc.—mdamnumnuġa.

y a - m n u' - m n u - ġ a - p i, *n.* *the hackberry tree;* so called because animals crunch its berries; *the Celtis crassifolia. Ih.*, also *black pepper. T.*, also *pepper.*

y a n, *cont.* of yata; as, ćaźeyata, ćaźeyan, *in the name of.* *T.*, yal.

y a - n a' - k e - y a, *v. a* *to turn aside with the mouth; to give a one-sided account of* any thing—mdanakeya. See kanakeya, nakeya, etc.

y a - n a' - ź i ŋ, *v. a.* of naźiŋ; *to cause to stand by speaking*—mdanaźiŋ.

y a - n m i' - n m a, *v. a.* *to roll with the mouth*—mdanminma: *i. q.* yahmihma. *T.*, yagmigma.

y a ŋ, *an adverbial* or *participial termination.*

y a ŋ, or y a, *v.* *a causative suffix to verbs.*

y a ŋ - k a', *v. n.* *to be, exist,* having reference to place—maŋká, naŋká, uŋyáŋkapi. Perhaps also yákoŋpi, uŋyakoŋpi, etc., belong to this word.

y a ŋ' - k a, *v. a.* *to weave,* as snow-shoes, or as in basket-making—mnáŋka, náŋka, uŋyaŋkapi. *T.*, kazoŋ.

y a - o' - ć i - k p a - n i, *v.* See yaoćitpani.

y a - o' - ć i - p t e - ć a, *v. a.* *to count less, make less, under-estimate*—mdaoćipteća. See yaaopteća.

y a - o' - ć i - p t e n, *cont.* of yaoćipteća.

y a - o' - ć i - p t e n - y a, *adv.* *speaking of as less* or *unequal.*

y a - o' - ć i - p t e - t u, *v. a.* *to count less*—mdaoćiptetu. See oćiptetu *and* yaaoptetu.

y a - o' - ć i - p t e - t u - y a, *adv.* *speaking of as less.*

y a - o' - ć i - p t e - t u - y a - k e n, *adv.* *speaking of as unequal.*

y a - o' - ć i - t p a - n i, *v. a.* of oćitpani; *to make unequal with the mouth*—mdaoćitpani, daoćitpani. *T.*, yaoćikpani.

y a - o' - h d a - p ś i ŋ, *v.* yaohdapśiŋ eȟpeya, *to turn over with the mouth.*

y a - o' - h d a - p ś i ŋ - y a ŋ, *adv.* of ohdapśiŋyaŋ; *turning over with the mouth:* yaohdapśiŋyaŋ iyeya.

y a - o' - h m u s, *adv.* of ohmus; yaohmus se ia, *to talk with the mouth full.* *T.*, yaogmus.

y a - o' - ȟ a ŋ - k o, *v. a.* of oȟaŋko; *to hasten* one *by speaking to*—mdaoȟaŋko.

y a - o' - ȟ l o - k a, *v. a.* *T.* *to bite a hole in.* See yaȟdoka

y a - o' - ȟ m i ŋ, *v.* yaoȟmiŋ iyeya, *to say anything sideways, to speak so as to hit* one *obliquely; to hint, insinuate.* See oȟmiyaŋ.

y a - o' - ȟ p a, *v. a.* *to bite into*—mdaoȟpa.

y a - o' - k i - n i - h a ŋ, *v. a.* of okinihaŋ; *to honor with the mouth, to praise*—mdaokinihaŋ.

y a - o' - k s a, *v.* *to bite through*—mdaoksa, daoksa.

y a - o' - k s a - k s a, *v. red.* of yaoksa.

y a - o' - k t a ŋ, *v. a.* *to bend in with the mouth.* See yaktaŋ.

ya-o′-ktaŋ-yaŋ, *adv.* *bending with the mouth.*

ya-o′-ni-haŋ, *v. a.* *to praise, honor*—mdaonihaŋ. See nihaŋ, inihaŋ, okinihaŋ, etc.

ya-o′-ni-haŋ-yaŋ, *adv.* *praising.*

ya-o′-po, *v. a.* *to compress by biting*—mdaopo.

ya-o′-poŋ, *v. T.* *to bite off and blow away,* as flowers; *to spread,* as news, *by telling it* blaopoŋ.

ya-o′-ta, *v. a.* of ota; *to speak of as many, to multiply* — mdaota, daota, uŋyaotapi.

ya-o′-taŋ-iŋ, *v. a.* of otaŋiŋ; *to make manifest, proclaim*—mdaotaŋiŋ, uŋyaotaŋinpi.

ya-o′-taŋ-iŋ-yaŋ, *adv.* *declaring.*

ya-o′-ṭiŋs, *cont.* of yaoṭiŋza; yaoṭiŋs iyeya.

ya-o′-ṭiŋ-za, *v. a.* of oṭiŋza; *to press in tight with the mouth*—mdaoṭiŋza.

ya-pa′, *v. a.* *to take in the mouth,* as a pipe in smoking; *to hold in the mouth,* as a dog does a bone; *to bite*—mdapa.

ya-pa′-ko, *v.* of pako; *to bend* or *twist with the mouth.*

ya-paŋ′-paŋ-na, *v. a.* of paŋpaŋna; *to make soft with the mouth*—mdapaŋpaŋna.

ya-pće′-će-la, *v. a. T.* *to shorten with the mouth; to speak of as short: i. q.* yapteċedaŋ.

ya-pe′, *v. a.* of pe; *to bite sharp:* yape śni, *to make dull,* as the teeth, *by biting*—mdapeśni.

ya-pe′-haŋ, *v. a.* of pehaŋ; *to fold up with the teeth*—mdapehaŋ.

ya-pe′-mni, *v. a.* of pemni; *to twist, turn,* or *make crooked with the mouth*—mdapemni, dapemni.

ya-pe′-mni-yaŋ, *adv.* *twisting with the teeth.*

ya-pe′-sto, *v. a.* *to make sharp-pointed with the teeth*—mdapesto.

ya-pi′, *v. a.* of pi; *to declare good*—mdapi, dapi. *T.*, yawaśte.

ya′-pi, *v. pl.* of ya; *they go.*

ya-piŋ′-za, *v. a.* of piŋza; *to make squeak with the mouth*—mdapiŋza.

ya-piŋ′-źa, *v. a.* of piŋźa; *to pull out long hairs from a skin with the teeth*—mdapiŋźa.

ya-pom′, *cont.* of yapopa; yapom iyeya. *T.*, yapob.

ya-pon′, *cont.* of yapota; yapon iyeya. *T.*, yapol.

ya-po′-pa, *v. a.* of popa; *to make pop,* as in blowing a leaf—mdapopa.

ya-po′-ta, *v. a.* of pota; *to tear in pieces with the mouth*—mdapota, dapota, uŋyapotapi.

ya-pot′-po-ta *or* ya-pon′-po-ta, *v. red.* of yapota.

ya-po′-wa-ya, *v. a.* of powaya; *to blow up* or *make rough,* as nap or fur—mdapowaya.

ya-psag′, *cont.* of yapsaka; yapsag iyeya.

ya-psag′-ya, *v. a.* *to cause to bite off*—yapsagwaya.

ya-psag′-ya, *adv.* *biting off,* as cords.

y a - p s a′ - k a, *v. a.* of psaka; *to bite off*, as a cord or string—mdapsaka, uŋyapsakapi.

y a - p s a′ - p s a - k a, *v. red.* of yapsaka.

y a - p s i′ - ć a, *v. a.* of psića; *to cause to skip* or *jump by biting*—mdapsića.

y a - p s i n′, *cont.* of yapsića; yapsin iyeya. *T.*, yapsil.

y a - p s o ŋ′, *v. a.* *to turn over and spill with the mouth*—mdapsoŋ.

y a - p s o ŋ′ - p s o ŋ, *v. red.* of yapsoŋ.

y a - p s u ŋ′, *v. a.* Same as yapsoŋ.

y a - p ś a′, *v. n.* *T.* *i. q.* pśamayapśa, *I sneeze.* Adage: "Some one is speaking his name," said of him who sneezes; especially if two friends or lovers are separated, and one sneezes, it means that his name is then mentioned by the other, and in recognition of it (and remembering their past happiness when together), after sneezing he says, "Haŋ, haŋ," with a long-drawn sigh.—W. J C.

y a - p ś u ŋ′, *v. a.* *to cast* or *shed*, as teeth; *to pull out by the roots with the mouth*—mdapśuŋ.

y a - p t a′, *v. a.* *to bite off around*—mdapta, dapta.

y a - p t a ŋ′ - y a ŋ, *v. a.* of ptaŋyaŋ; *to turn over with the mouth*—mdaptaŋyaŋ.

y a - p t e′ - ć e - d a ŋ, *v. a.* of ptećedaŋ; *to bite off short, to shorten with the mouth*—mdaptećedaŋ. *T.*, yapćećela.

y a - p t u′ - p t u - ź a, *v. red.* of yaptuźa.

y a - p t u ś′, *cont.* of yaptuźa; yaptuś iyeya.

y a - p t u ś′ - y a, *v. a.* *to cause to crack with the mouth*—yaptuśwaya.

y a - p t u′ - ź a, *v. a* of ptuźa; *to crack* or *split with the mouth*—mdaptuźa.

y a - p o′, *v.* of po; *to make steam with the mouth*, as in breathing in cold air—mdapo.

y a - s ' a′, *v. a.* of s'a; *to make a ringing* or *roaring noise in speaking*—mdas'a; noǧe omayas'a.

y a - s a ŋ′, *v. a.* *to whiten with the mouth*—mdasaŋ.

y a - s a ŋ′ - k a, *v.* See yasaŋ.

y a - s b a′, *v. a.* *to pick in pieces with the teeth*—mdasba.

y a - s b a′ - s b a, *v. red.* of yasba.

y a - s b u′, *v.* yasbu se yuta, *to eat in little pieces* or *strings.*

y a - s d a′, *v. a.* *to grease with the mouth*, as a dog does anything.

y a - s d e′ - ć a, *v. a.* *to split with the teeth*—mdasdeća.

y a - s d e n′, *cont.* of yasdeća; yasden iyeya. *T.*, yaslel.

y a - s d e′ - s d e - ć a, *v. red.* of yasdeća.

y a - s d i′, *v. a.* *to bite and press out*, as grease from a bag—mdasdi.

y a - s d i′ - t k a, *v. a.* of sditka; *to make knobbed* or *tapering with the teeth*—mdasditka.

y a - s d o′ - h a ŋ, *v. a.* of sdohaŋ; *to drag along with the mouth*—mdasdohaŋ, dasdohaŋ.

y a - s d o′ - h a ŋ - h a ŋ , *v. red.* of yasdohaŋ.

y a - s d u n′, *cont.* of yasduta: yasdun iyeya; yasdun iću, *to pull out with the teeth* *T.*, yaslul.

y a - s d u′ - t a , *v. a.* *to pull out with the mouth.*

y a - s k a′, *v. a.* *to make clean, to suck off*, as the women put "pahiŋ" into their mouths to prepare them for working—mdaska.

y a - s k a′ - p a , *v. a* *to make a sucking noise with the mouth, to press the mouth on and suddenly withdraw it*—mdaskapa. *T.*, *to make a noise, as in kissing.*

y a - s k e m′, *cont.* of yaskepa; yaskem iyeya. *T.*, yaskeb.

y a - s k e′ - p a , *v. a.* of skepa; *to drink up*—mdaskepa, daskepa.

y a - s k i′ - ć a , *v. a.* *to press with the mouth, to suck* or *lick*, as bones—mdaskića.

y a - s k i n′, *cont.* of yaskića; yaskin iyeya. *T.*, yaskil.

y a - s k i′ - s k i - t a , *v. a.* *to bite and make soft*, as a hard string—mdaskiskita.

y a - s k u′, *v. a.* *to bite off* or *peel off with the teeth*, as the skin from an apple or corn from the cob—mdasku.

y a - s k u′ - s k u , *v. red.* of yasku.

y a - s m a g′, *cont.* of yasmaka; yasmag iyeya.

y a - s m a g′ - s m a - k a , *v. red.* of yasmaka.

y a - s m a′ - k a , *v. a.* of smaka; *to make a hollow place with the teeth, indent*—mdasmaka.

y a - s m i ŋ′, *v. a.* *to bite off*, as meat from a bone; *to make bare with the mouth*—mdasmiŋ.

y a - s m i ŋ′ - k i - y a , *v. a.* *to cause to make bare with the teeth*—yasmiŋwakiya.

y a - s m i ŋ′ - s m i ŋ , *v. red.* of yasmiŋ.

y a - s m i ŋ′ - y a ŋ , *v. a.* *to cause to make bare with the teeth*—yasmiŋwaya.

y a - s m i ŋ′ - y a ŋ - y a ŋ , *v. a* *to make bare with the mouth; to eat off close and smooth.*

y a - s n a′, *v. a.* *to cause to ring with the mouth; to ravel with the teeth*—mdasna.

y a - s n i′, *v. a.* of sni; *to blow, cool by blowing*—mdasni.

y a - s o n′, *cont.* of yasota; yason iyeya. *T.*, yasol.

y a - s o n′ - y a , *adv.* *eating up.*

y a - s o′ - t a , *v. a.* of sota, *to expend; to use up words, finish speaking; to use up with the mouth, eat all up*—mdasota, dasota, uŋyasotapi.

y a - s p a′ - y a , *v. a.* of spaya; *to wet with the mouth*—mdaspaya.

y a - s t a ŋ′ - k a , *v. a.* *to moisten with the mouth*—mdastaŋka.

y a - s t a ŋ′ - k a - ś n i , *v. n.* *to lie, tell a lie*—mdastaŋkaśni *T.*, owewakaŋkaŋ.

y a - s t o′, *v. a.* *to lick smooth*, as hair mdasto.

y a - s t o′ - s t o , *v. red.* of yasto.

y a - s u′, *v. a.* *to make right by speaking, to judge; to decree. T., to judge; condemn; pronounce sentence on: i.q.* yaćo.

y a - s u k′ - s u - t a, *v. red.* of yasuta.

y a - s u′ - t a, *v. a.* of suta; *to make firm with the mouth, to establish*—mdasuta, dasuta.

y a - s u′ - y a, *adv. rightly:* yasuya oyaka, *to tell rightly. T., judging; condemning.*

y as - y a′ - z a ŋ, *v. red.* of yazaŋ; *to be lame* or *sick all over*, as from hard labor—mayasyazaŋ.

y a - ś ' a′ - k a, *v. a. to make no impression with the mouth; i. q.* yaȟdoke śni mdaś'aka: ia yaś'aka. See kaś'aka, yuś'aka, etc.

y a - ś a m′, *cont.* of yaśapa; yaśam iyeya. *T.*, yaśab.

y a - ś a′ - p a, *v. a.* of śapa; *to soil with the mouth*—mdaśapa.

y a - ś d a′ *v. a. to bite* or *graze off, make bare*—mdaśda.

y a - ś d a′ - ś d a, *v. red.* of yaśda.

y a - ś d a′ - y a, *adv. grazing off.*

y a - ś d a′ - y e - h n a. See yaaśdayehna.

y a - ś d o g′, *cont.* of yaśdoka; yaśdog iyeya.

y a - ś d o g′ - y a, *adv. pulling out with the teeth.*

y a - ś d o′ - i - a, *v. to speak with much saliva in the mouth. T., to make a whistling* or *hissing sound with the teeth* in talking—yaśdoiwaa.

y a - ś d o′ - k a, *v. a. to pull out with the teeth,* as a cork; *to bite out,* as an eye—mdaśdoka. See yaȟdoka.

y a - ś d u n′, *cont.* of yaśduta; yaśdun iyeya. *T.*, yaślul.

y a - ś d u′ - ś d u - t a, *v. a. to make slippery with the mouth*—mdaśduśduta.

y a - ś d u′ - t a, *v. a. to let slip from the mouth; to have the teeth slip off* from any thing—mdaśduta.

y a - ś i′ - ć a, *v. a.* of śića; *to make bad with the mouth; to speak evil of, curse*—mdaśića, mayaśića. See yaśiȟtiŋ.

y a - ś i′ - h d a, *v. a. to insult by talking to*—mdaśihda.

y a - ś i′ - ȟ t i ŋ, *v. a. to make feeble by biting,* etc.—mdaśiȟtiŋ. *T., to make bad with the mouth: i. q.* yaśića.

y a - ś i m′, *cont.* of yaśipa; yaśim iyeya. *T.*, yaśib.

y a - ś i m′ - ś i - p a, *v. red.* of yaśipa.

y a - ś i ŋ′ - ś i ŋ, *v.* Said of copulating—mdaśiŋśiŋ See yuśiŋśiŋ.

y a - ś i′ - p a, *v. a. to bite off close,* as an animal the branches or twigs of a tree—mdaśipa.

y a - ś k a′, *v. a. to untie with the mouth*—mdaśka.

y a - ś k a ŋ′ - ś k a ŋ, *v. a. to make move about by talking to*—mdaśkaŋśkaŋ.

y a - ś k i′ - ć a, *v. a. to press with the teeth* or *mouth*—mdaśkića: ćaŋdi yaśkića, *to chew tobacco.* Perhaps yaskića ma sometimes be so used.

y a - ś k i n′, *cont.* of yaśkića; ćaŋdi yaśkin uŋ. *T.*, yaśkil.

y a - ś k i′ - p a, *v. T. to bite and make full up.*

y a - ś k i' - ś k a, *v. a.* *to make rough with the mouth; to disarrange by talking to, raise objections; to make difficulty*—mdaśkiśka.

y a - ś k o' - k p a, *v. a.* *to bite out and make concave*—mdaśkokpa.

y a - ś k o m', *cont.* of yaśkopa; yaśkom iyeya. *T.*, yaśkob.

y a - ś k o' - p a, *v. a.* *to make crooked or twisting with the mouth*—mdaśkopa.

y a - ś k o' - ś k o - p a, *v. red.* of yaśkopa.

y a - ś k o' - t p a, *v. a.* *to hollow out with the mouth*—mdaśkotpa *T.*, yaśkokpa.

y a - ś n a', *v. a.* *to miss* or *let slip*, as in taking any thing into the mouth; *to blunder in speaking* or *reading*—mdaśna, uŋyaśnapi. See yaś'aka, yuśna, yahnayaŋ, etc.

y a - ś n a' - k i - y a, *v. a.* *to cause to miss with the mouth*—yaśnawakiya.

y a - ś n a' - ś n a, *v. red.* of yaśna; *to stammer.*

y a - ś n a' - y a, *v. a.* *to cause to miss with the mouth, to make stammer*—yaśnawaya.

y a - ś n a' - y a ŋ, *adv.* *mistaking, blundering with the mouth.*

y a - ś n i ś', *cont.* of yaśniźa; yaśniś iyeya.

y a - ś n i' - ś n i - ź a, *v. red.* of yaśniźa.

y a - ś n i' - ź a, *v. a.* *to make wither by biting*—mdaśniźa.

y a - ś p a', *v. a.* *to bite off a piece*—mdaśpa, daśpa, uŋyaśpapi.

y a - ś p a' - p i, *part.* *bitten off:* said of the moon when it has commenced waning.

y a - ś p a' - ś p a, *v. red.* of yaśpa.

y a - ś p e' - k i - y a, *v. a.* *to cause to bite off a piece*—yaśpewakiya.

y a - ś p e' - y a, *v. a.* *to cause to bite a piece off*—yaśpewaya.

y a - ś p i', *v. a.* *to pick off*, as birds do berries.

y a - ś p u', *v. a.* *to bite off* any thing *stuck on*—mdaśpu. See yaḣpu.

y a - ś p u' - ś p u, *v. red.* of yaśpu; *to bite in pieces*, as ice or gum—mdaśpuśpu.

y a - ś p u' - y a, *v.* *to bite*, as lice do, *make itch;* hence, *to itch*—mdaśpuya.

y a - ś t a ŋ', *v. a.* *to finish speaking* or *eating*—mdaśtaŋ, daśtaŋ, uŋyaśtaŋpi. See kaśtaŋ *and* yuśtaŋ.

y a - ś u ś', *cont.* of yaśuźa; yaśuś iyeya.

y a - ś u' - ś u - ź a, *v. red.* of yaśuźa.

y a - ś u' - ź a, *v. a.* *to crush*, as a dog does bones, *to bite* or *mash up*—mdaśuźa. See yaḣuġa.

y a' - t a, *prep. in comp.* *at, by, to;* as in ćaŋyata.

y a' - t a, *v.* 2d pers. sing. of yuta.

y a' - t a, *v.* *to speak, utter*, as in ćaźeyata *and* wićaśta-yatapi.

y a - t a', *v. a.* *to chew; to try by the taste*—mdata.

y a - t a' - k i ŋ, *v. a.* *to make leaning with the mouth*, as a dog in trying to pull down a stick.

y a - t a' - k i ŋ - y a ŋ, *adv.* *making leaning with the mouth.*

y a - t a′ - k u, *v. a.* of taku; *to make something of in relating, make up a story about*—mdataku.

y a - t a′ - k u - k a, *v. a. to make something of nothing in narration, overestimate*—mdatakuka.

y a - t a′ - k u - n i - ś n i, *v. a. to eat up, destroy with the mouth; to speak contemptuously of*—mdatakuniśni.

y a - t a′ - k u - n i - ś n i - y a ŋ, *adv. destroying with the mouth.*

y a - t a′ - k u - ś n i, *v. a. to speak of as being of no value, depreciate*—mdatakuśni. See yataku.

y a - t a′ - k u - y a, *adv. speaking of as if it were something:* yatakuya omdaka.

y a - t a ŋ′, *v. a. to speak well of, praise*—mdataŋ.

y a - t'a ŋ′, *v. a. to touch with the mouth, to pull,* as in sucking—mdat'aŋ, uŋyat'aŋpi. *T., to pull with the mouth,* as in smoking—yat'aŋ yo, *draw* or *pull* the smoke.

y a - t a ŋ′ - i ŋ, *v. a.* of taŋiŋ; *to declare* anything, *make manifest*—mdataŋiŋ.

y a - t a ŋ′ - i ŋ - y a ŋ, *adv. manifestly.*

y a - t a ŋ′ - k a, *v. a. to speak of as large*—mdataŋka.

y a - t a ŋ′ - n i, *v. a. to wear out* or *make old with the mouth*—mdataŋni.

y a - t a ŋ′ - y a ŋ, *adv. praising.*

y a - t e′ - h a ŋ, *v. a.* of tehaŋ; *to speak long, to be long finishing; to speak of as long* or *as far in the future*—mdatehaŋ. See yutehaŋ.

y a - t e′ - h a ŋ - h a ŋ, *v. red.* of yatehaŋ.

y a - t e′ - ḣ i - k a, *v. a.* of teḣika; *to make difficult with the mouth, speak of as difficult*—mdateḣika.

y a - t e m′, *cont.* of yatepa; yatem iyeya. *T.,* yateb.

y a - t e′ - p a, *v. a. to bite off short, wear off,* as the teeth—mdatepa, uŋyatepapi.

y a - t i′ - ć a, *v. a. to scrape away with the mouth,* as snow.

y a - t i n′, *cont.* of yatića; yatin iyeya. *T.,* yatil.

y a - t i′ - t a ŋ, *v. a. to pull with the mouth* or *teeth*—mdatitaŋ.

y a - t i′ - t a ŋ - y a ŋ, *adv. pulling with the teeth.*

y a - t i′ - t a ŋ - y a ŋ, *v. a. to cause to pull with the teeth*—yatitaŋwaya.

y a - t k a ŋ′, *v. a. to drink*—mdatkaŋ, datkaŋ.

y a - t k a ŋ′ - y a ŋ, *adv. drinking.*

y a - t k a′ - p a, *v a. to eat,* as something that is viscid or sticks in the mouth—mdatkapa. See yaskapa.

y a - t k e′ - k i - y a, *v. a. to cause to drink*—yatkewakiya, yatkemakiya.

y a - t k u′ - ġ a, *v. a. to bite* or *pull and break with the mouth*—mdatkuġa.

y a - t k u ŋ s′, *cont.* of yatkuŋza; yatkuŋs iyeya.

y a - t k u ŋ′ - t k u ŋ - t a, *v.* See yakuŋtkuŋta.

y a - t k u ŋ′ - z a, *v. a to bite off even*—mdatkuŋza.

y a - t k u′ - t k u - ġ a, *v. red.* of yatkuġa.

y a - t o g′ - y e, *adv.* yatogye oyaka, *to relate a thing differently.*

y a - t o' - k a ŋ, *v. a.* *to put in another place with the mouth, speak of as being in another place*—mdatokaŋ.

y a - t o' - k e - ć a, *v. a.* of tokeća; *to alter with the mouth, to speak of as different*—mdatokeća.

y a - t o' - n a - n a, *v. a.* of tonana; *to speak of as few*—mdatonana. *T.*, yaćonala.

y a - t o' - t o, *v. a.* *to eat up*, as a horse does grass: yatoto eḣpeya. *T.*, oyátoto.

y a - t p a', *v. a.* *to bite through:* noġe yatpa, *to make deaf by talking to*—mdatpa. *i. q.* yakpa.

y a - t p a ŋ', *v. a.* *to chew fine, masticate*—mdatpaŋ. *i. q.* yakpaŋ.

y a - t p a ŋ' - t p a ŋ, *v. red.* of yatpaŋ.

y a - t p i', *v. a.* *to crack with the teeth*, as lice or nuts—mdatpi. *i. q.* yakpi.

y a - t p i' - t p i, *v. red.* of yatpi.

y a - t p u' - t p a, *v. a.* *to bite in pieces, to crumble up with the teeth*—mdatputpa. See yakpukpa.

y a - t u' - k a, *v. a.* *to nibble off, spoil*, as mice do furs.

y a - t u' - t k a, *v. a.* *to bite into little pieces*—mdatutka.

y a - ṭ a', *v. a.* *to bite to death*—mdaṭa.

y a - ṭ a' - ġ a, *v. a.* *to make rough by biting*—mdaṭaġa.

y a - ṭ i ŋ s', *cont.* of yaṭiŋza; yaṭiŋs iyeya.

y a - ṭ i ŋ' - s a, *adv.* *firmly;* yaṭiŋsa oyaka, *to relate firmly* or *with authority.* See yaṭiŋza.

y a - ṭ i ŋ' - s a - s a, *red.* of yaṭiŋsa.

y a - ṭ i ŋ s' - y a, *adv.* *firmly.*

y a - ṭ i ŋ' - z a, *v. a.* *to make firm with the mouth, to affirm*—mdaṭiŋza: ćaŋte yaṭiŋza, *to strengthen one's heart, encourage one.*

y a - w a', *v. a.* *to count, say over; to read*—mdawa, dawa, uŋyawapi.

y a - w a' - ć i ŋ - h i ŋ - y a ŋ - z a, *v. a.* *to make cross* or *surly by talking to.*

y a - w a' - ć i ŋ - k o, *v. a.* *T.* *to make angry by talking.*

y a - w a' - ć i ŋ - t o ŋ, *v. a.* *to make intelligent, to instruct*—mdawaćiŋtoŋ

y a - w a' - ḣ b a - d a ŋ, *v. a.* *to make gentle by talking to, to soothe*—mdawaḣbadaŋ.

y a - w a' - ḣ b a - k a, *v. a.* *to make gentle, pacify by talking kindly*—mdawaḣbaka.

y a - w a' - ḣ t e - ś n i, *v. a.* of waḣte; *to speak contemptuously of*—mdawaḣteśni.

y a - w a' - k a ŋ, *v. a* *to consider supernatural* or wakaŋ—mdawakaŋ.

y a - w a' - n i - s t i ŋ - n a, *v. a.* *to count as little* or *few*—mdawanistiŋna. *T.*, yaćisćila.

y a - w a ŋ g', *cont.* of yawaŋka; yawaŋg iyeya.

y a - w a ŋ' - k a, *v. a.* *to throw down with the mouth*, as beavers do trees, or as a dog does a deer; *to defeat in debate*—mdawaŋka.

y a - w a ŋ' - k a n, *v.* yawaŋkan iyeya *and* yawaŋkan iću, *to raise* or *elevate the voice.*

y a - w a s', *cont.* of yawaza.

y a - w a′ - ś ' a g, *cont.* of yawaś'aka.

y a - w a′ - ś ' a g - y a, *adv.* *in a strengthening manner.*

y a - w a′ - ś ' a - k a, *v. a.* *to strengthen by talking to, to speak of as strong*—mdawaś'aka.

y a - w a′ - ś a - k a, *v.* Same as yawaśakadaŋ.

y a - w a′ - ś a - k a - d a ŋ, *v. a.* *to count cheap* or *easy, to underrate*—mdawaśakadaŋ.

y a - w a′ - ś ' a - k e - ś n i, *v. a.* *to make weak by talking to*—mdawaś'akeśni.

y a - w a′ - ś t e, *v. a.* *to call good, to bless*—mdawaśte, dawaśte, uŋyawaśtepi.

y a - w a′ - z a, *v. a.* *T.* *to bite in play,* as horses and dogs do. See yabaza.

y a - w a′ - z e - ć a, *n.* *T.* *one who annoys* others *by begging.*

y a - w a′ - z e - ć a, *v. a.* *T.* *to annoy* one *by frequent begging*—blawazeća.

y a - w e′ - ġ a, *v. a.* *to break,* as a stick, *with the mouth, but not entirely off*—mdaweġa.

y a - w e ḣ′, *cont.* of yaweġa; yaweḣ iyeya.

y a - w e ḣ′ - w e - ġ a, *v. red.* of yaweġa.

y a - w e ḣ′ - y a, *v. a.* *to cause to break with the mouth*—yaweḣwaya.

y a - w i′ - ć a, *v. a.* of wića; *to call a man, to call brave*—mdawića.

y a - w i′ - ć a - k a, *v.* of wićaka; *to speak of as true; to affirm to be true*—mdawićaka.

y a - w i′ - ć a - k e - y a - ḣ ć a, *adv.* *T.*, yawićakeyaḣća oyaka, *to try to make a thing appear true by telling it as true.* See yaećayaḣ.

y a - w i′ - ć a - k e - y a - s e, *adv.* *T.* *i. q.* yaećaḣ.

y a - w i′ - ć a - ś t a, *v. a.* of wićaśta; *to call a man*—mdawićaśta. See wićaśa.

y a - w i′ - ć a - ś t a - ś n i, *v. a.* *to call bad; to make bad by talking to, corrupt*—mdawićaśtaśni.

y a - w i′ - h n u - n i, *v. a.* *to destroy with the mouth.* See hnuni.

y a - w i′ - n o - ḣ i ŋ - ć a, *v.* of winoḣiŋća; *to call a woman, to speak to as to a woman.* *T.*, yawiŋyaŋ.

y a - w i ŋ′ - ġ a, *v. a.* *to bite* or *pull round with the teeth,* as in making moccasins—mdawiŋġa.

y a - w i ŋ ḣ′, *cont.* of yawiŋġa; yawiŋḣ iyeya.

y a - w i ŋ ḣ′ - w i ŋ - ġ a, *v. red.* of yawiŋġa.

y a - w i ŋ ś′, *cont.* of yawiŋźa; yawiŋś iyeya.

y a - w i ŋ ś′ - k i - y a, *v. a.* *to cause to bend down with the mouth*—yawiŋśwakiya.

y a - w i ŋ ś′ - w i ŋ - ź a, *v. red.* of yawiŋźa.

y a - w i ŋ′ - ź a, *v. a.* of wiŋźa; *to bend down with the mouth*—mdawiŋźa

y a - w i′ - t a - y a, *v. a.* of witaya; *to collect together with the mouth*—mdawitaya.

y a - z a′, *v. a.* *to string,* as beads—mdaza, daza. *T.*, oyaza.

ẏa-za'-haŋ, *v.* (yaza *and* haŋ?) *to continue to string*, as beads—mdazahaŋ.

ya-za'-mni, *v. a.* *to open* or *uncover with the mouth; to lay bare* or *expose by argument*—mdazamni.

ya-zaŋ', *v. n.* *to be sick, to be in pain; to be tired*—mayazaŋ, niyazaŋ, uŋyazaŋpi: pa yazaŋ, *to have the headache.*

ya-zaŋ'-hda, *v. n.* *to become sick suddenly, to be taken sick; to be in pain*—yazaŋwahda.

ya-zaŋ'-ki-ya, *v. a.* *to make* one *sick*—yazaŋwakiya.

ya-zaŋ'-ya, *v. a.* *to make* one *sick*—yazaŋwaya

ya-za'-za, *v. red.* of yaza. *T.*, oyazaza.

ya-ze', *v. a.* *to take out* food from a kettle, as a dog does, *with the mouth.*

ya-ze'-ze, *v. a.* *to make swing with the mouth.*

ya-zi'-ća, *v. a.* *to stretch* anything *with the teeth*—mdazića.

ya-zin', *cont.* of yazića; yazin iyeya. *T.*, yazil.

ya-zo'-ka, *v. a.* *to suck*—mdazoka, uŋyazokapi.

ya-zoŋ'-ta, *v. a.* *T.* *to praise* one *who ought to be reproved.*

ya-zuŋ'-ća, *v. a.* *to weave together, connect*, as language. See yazuŋta.

ya-zuŋ'-ća-ya, *adv.* *connectedly*, as in speaking.

ya-zuŋ'-ta, *v. a.* *to connect*, as words in speaking—mdazuŋta.

ya-źa'-haŋ, *adv.* yaźahaŋ ia, *to speak roughly* or *hoarsely.* *T.*, ho źahaŋ.

ya-źa'-źa, *v. a.* *to lick* or *wash with the mouth*, as a cat. See boźaźa, yuźaźa, etc.

ya-źim', *cont.* of yaźipa; yaźim iyeya. *T.*, yaźib.

ya-źim'-źi-pa, *v. red.* of yaźipa.

ya-źiŋ'-ća, *v. a.* *to snuff* anything *up the* nose: ćaŋli yaźiŋća, *to take snuff.*

ya-źi'-pa, *v. a.* *to bite* or *pinch with the teeth, bite*, as bugs or mosquitoes; *to sting*, as one's foot asleep—mdaźipa, mayaźipa. See paźipa, etc.

ya-źo', *v. a.* *to blow on an instrument, play on a fife* or *flute*—mdaźo, daźo, uŋyaźopi.

ya-źo'-ki-ya, *v. a.* *to cause to blow on an instrument*—yaźowakiya.

ya-źo'-ya, *v. a.* *to make* one *blow a fife* or *flute*—yaźowaya.

ya-źuŋ', *v. a.* *to pull up by the roots with the mouth*, as birds do corn—mdaźuŋ.

ya-źu'-źu, *v. a* *to tear down* or *tear to pieces with the mouth; to refute* or *demolish*, as an argument—mdaźuźu. See yuźuźu, etc.

ye, *intj.* *oh!* expressing fear.

ye, *intj.* *shame on you.*

ye, *a precatory form of the imperat. sing.;* used by women and not unfrequently by men also; as, ećoŋ ye.

y e, *a particle*, which often follows at the close of a sentence to give emphasis to what is said. It is used by the women as "do" is by the men; as, waŋna mduśtaŋ ye, *I have already finished.* Sometimes this is used by the men, and is not unfrequently followed by "do;" as, ećamoŋ yedo, maḳu yedo.

y e, *pron.* 2d pers. compounded of "ya" and "ki;" as in yeksuya, of kiksuya.

y e'-ġ a, *v. n.* *to shine, glitter.* *T.*, ileġa.

y e ḣ, *cont.* of yeġa. *T.*, ileḣ.

y e ḣ - y a', *v. a.* *to cause to shine, to make shine*—yeḣwaya. *T.*, ileḣya.

y e ḣ - y e'- ġ a, *v. red.* of yeġa; *to glisten, twinkle, sparkle.* *T.*, ileḣleġa.

y e - k i'- y a, *v. a.* of ya; *to cause to go, to send, drive; to extend to*, as the hand; nape yewakiya.

y e - k i'- y a, *v. a.* *to bet, to stake anything.* This is connected with the one preceding, as the Dakotas tie on to a stick the articles staked in a dance, for example: yewakiya.

y e'- l a - k a ś, *adv.* *T.* *i. q.* nakaeś; *indeed, truly*, etc.; *since; as, because.*

y e - l o', *T.* *i. q.* yedo; but after the plur. termination "pi" the "ye" is often dropped, and the "pi" becomes "pe," e. g., hećel ećoŋpe lo.

y e - ś a' *or* y e - ś a ŋ, *conj.* *T.* *i. q.* eśa; *although*

y e - ś a'- h a ŋ, *conj.* *T.* *i. q.* eśtaŋhaŋ.

y e - ś a ś', *intj.* *T.* *i. q.* eśtaś.

y e - ś i', *v. a.* *to command to go, to send*—yewaśi.

y e - y a', *v. a.* *to cause to go, to send; to extend to.*

y e - y e', *v.* *to be, exist.*

y o, *Ih.* and *T.* the sign of the imperative singular, used by men: *i. q.* wo—ćeti yo, *make a fire.*

y o - t a ŋ'- k a, *v. n.* *to sit;* śuktaŋka akan yotaŋka *and* śuŋk akan yotaŋka, *to ride on horseback*—mdotaŋka. See iyotaŋka.

y u, *a causative prefix.* It expresses the idea of causation in some way not conveyed by "ba," "bo," "ka," "na," "pa," and "ya;" as, yunaźiŋ, *to cause to stand* or *to lift up;* yukakiźa, *to cause to suffer.* Sometimes it conveys the idea of *pulling.* As a prefix to adjectives, and sometimes nouns, it forms verbs of them, and means *to make* or *cause to be;* as, yuwaśte, *to make good.*

y u *or* y u ŋ, *intj.* Said when one is hurt, *ugh!* See yuhuhu.

y u - a'- d o s - d o - z a - s e i-y e-y a, *v. a.* *to injure one's feelings in any way.* See adosdoza *and* yaćaŋtiyap'a iyeya.

y u - a'- k a - ḣ p a, *v.* of akaḣpa; yuakaḣpa iću, *to draw* anything *over* one, as a blanket turned down.

y u - a'- k a n, *v.* of akan; yuakan hiyuya, *to cause to come up to the top.*

y u - a'- k a - z a - m n i, *v. a.* of akazamni; *to open out, uncover:* yuakazamni iyeya.

y u - a' - k i - ȟ a ŋ , *v. a.* of akiȟaŋ; *to cause to starve*—mduakiȟaŋ.

y u - a' - k i - p a m , *adv.* of akipam; *separately:* yuakipam ehnaka, *to separate, divide. T.*, yuakipab.

y u - a' - k i - p a - p a m , *adv. red.* of yuakipam.

y u - a' - k i - p a ś , *cont.* of yuakipaźa; *crossing each other; in bows:* yuakipaś iću, *to tie in a bow-knot. T.*, yuwose iću, *to tie a bow-knot.*

y u - a' - k i - p a - ź a , *v. a.* of akipaźa; *to place across*—mduakipaźa. See yuakipaś.

y u - a' - m d a - y a , *v. a. to make level on*—mduamdaya.

y u - a' - o - p t e - ç a , *v. a. to make less*—mduaopteća.

y u - a' - o - p t e n, *cont.* of yuaopteća; yuaopten iyeya *T.*, yuaoptel

y u - a' - o - p t e - t u , *v. a. to make less, lessen*—mduaoptetu.

y u - a' - o - p t e - t u - y a , *adv. lessening.*

y u - a' - s n i , *v. T. i. q.* asnikiya.

y u - a' - ś a - p a , *v. a.* of aśapa; *to defile*—mduaśapa.

y u - a' - ś d a - y a , *v. a. to uncover, expose.*

y u - a' - ś k a - d a ŋ , *v. a. to make near, to bring near*—mduaśkadaŋ. See yukiyela *and* yuhaŋska.

y u - a' - ś k a - k e , *v.* See yuaśkadaŋ.

y u - a' - z i , *v. a.* of azi; *to run aground,* as a boat, *pull ashore*—mduazi.

y u - b a' - ġ a , *v. a. to twist, roll, turn,* as the hands in running—mdubaġa. See yubaza.

y u - b a s', *cont.* of yubaza; yubas iyeya.

y u - b a s' - b a - z a , *v. red.* of yubaza.

y u - b a s' - y a , *adv. in a twisting manner; vexing.*

y u - b a' - z a , *v. a. to twist* or *turn,* as the hands in running; *to vex, tease, annoy, and continue to do so*—mdubaza. See yubaġa, yabaġa, etc. *T., to twist* or *rub around,* as the hair on a horse, or the arm *against* anything when the former itches.

y u - b e', *v. a.* Same as yumaŋ.

y u - b i' - l i - h e - ć a , *v. a. T. to make active, to stimulate.*

y u - b o' - s d a n , *v.* of bosdan; yubosdan ehde, *to set up on end. T.*, yuwoslal.

y u - b o' - s d ạ - t a , *v. a. to set upright*—mdubosdata.

y u - b u', *v. a. to make a drumming noise*—mdubu.

y u - b u' - b u , *v. red.* of yubu.

y u - b u' - y a , *adv. in a drumming manner.*

y u - ć a b', *cont. T.* of yućapa.

y u - ć a b' - ć a b - k i - y a , *v. red. T. to cause to trot.*

y u - ć a b' - ć a - p a , *v. red. T.* of yućapa.

y u - ć a b' - l u - z a - h a ŋ , *v. T. to trot rapidly.*

y u - ć a b' - l u - z a - h a ŋ , *adj. fast trotting,* as a fast trotting horse.

y u - ć a ŋ', *v. a. to shift, shake in a sieve*—mdućaŋ, dućaŋ, uŋćaŋpi.

y u - ć a ŋ′ - ć a ŋ, *v. a.* *to make shake*—mdućaŋćaŋ.

y u - ć a ŋ′ - n a n, *v.* yućaŋnan iyeya, *to push out into the stream.*

y u - ć a ŋ′ - z e - k a, *v. a.* *T.* *to make angry.*

y u - ć a′ - p a, *v. T.* *to trot* as a horse.

y u - ć a p′ - ć a - p a, *v. red.* *T.* *i. q.* yućabćapa.

y u - ć e′ - k a, *v. a.* *to make stagger*—mdućeka.

y u - ć e′ - k ć e - k a, *v. a.* *to make stagger*—mdućekćeka.

y u - ć e′ - y a, *v. a.* *to make cry*—mdućeya, mayućeya.

y u - ć i′ - ķ a - d a ŋ, *v. a.* *to make small, compress*—mdućiķadaŋ.

y u - ć i′ - ķ a - y e - d a ŋ, *adv.* *in a small space, pressed together, compactly.*

y u - ć i′ - s t i ŋ - n a, *v. a.* *to make small*—mdućistiŋna. *T.*, yućisćila.

y u - ć o′, *v. a.* *to make good* (*T.*, yuwaśte); *to perfect, finish*—mdućo, dućo, uŋyućopi. See yusu.

y u - ć o′ - ć o, *v. a.* *to make soft*, as mortar—mdućoćo.

y u - ć o′ - k a, *v. a.* *to empty, make empty*—mdućoka.

y u - ć o′ - k a - k a, *v. red.* of yućoka.

y u - ć o′ - n a - l a, *v. a.* *T.* *to make few; to lessen in number* or *quantity:* *i. q.* yutonana.

y u - ć o s′ - ć o - z a, *v. red.* of yućoza.

y u - ć o′ - y a, *adv.* *finished; well.* *T.*, ayućoyakel.

y u - ć o′ - z a, *v. a* of ćoza; *to make comfortably warm*, as a house or clothes—mdućoza.

y u - d e m′ - d e - p a, *v. a.* *to make notches in*—mdudemdepa. *T.*, yuleblepa.

y u - d u′ - z a - h a ŋ, *v. a.* of duzahaŋ; *to make swift*—mduduzahaŋ.

y u - e′ - ć e - d a ŋ, *v. a.* of ećedaŋ; *to purify*—mduećedaŋ, uŋyuećepidaŋ.

y u - e′ - ć e l - y a, *adv.* *T.* *rightly, correctly*—yuećelya iću, *place it rightly.* But *less* is yuoptetuya.

y u - e′ - ć e n - y a, *adv.* *less:* yuećenya ećamoŋ.

y u - e′ - ć e - t u, *v. a.* of ećetu; *to fulfill, accomplish; to restore*—mduećetu, duećetu, uŋyuećetupi.

y u - e′ - ć e - t u - y a, *v. a.* *to cause to fulfill*—yuećetuwaya.

y u - e′ - ć e - t u - y a, *adv.* *fulfilling; making right.*

y u - e′ - ć i, *v. a.* *to turn wrong side out*, as a garment or bag—mdueći, dueći. *T.*, yuećiya.

y u - g l a′ - k śi ŋ - kśi ŋ, *adv.* *T.* *zigzag*, or in *all kinds of ways*, as children mark on the snow. See kayowedaŋ.

y u - ġ a′, *v. a.* *to husk*, as corn—mduġa, duġa, uŋġapi.

y u - ġ a′ - ġ a, *adv.* *spread out, open.*

y u - ġ a d′ - y a, *v.* *to speak out to, to worship.*

y u - ġ a d′ - y a - p i, *n.* *worshiping, worship.*

y u - ġ a′ - ġ a, *v. n.* *to spread out, open out, display.*

y u - ġ a m′, *cont.* of yuġapa; yuġam iyeya. *T.*, yuġab.

yu-ġan', *cont.* of yuġata. *T.*, yuġal.

yu-ġan'-ġa-ta, *v. red.* of yuġata.

yu-ġaŋ', *v. a.* *to open*, as a door; *to tear open*, as a corn husk, *to husk* corn—mduġaŋ, uŋyuġaŋpi.

yu-ġaŋ'-ġaŋ-na, *v. a.* *to make open* or *flimsy*—mduġaŋġaŋna.

yu-ġaŋ'-pi, *n* *a husking*. See woġaŋpi.

yu-ġaŋ'-yaŋ, *v. a.* *to cause to open, to cause to husk*—yuġaŋwaya.

yu-ġa'-pa, *v. a* *to strip* or *pull off*, as the skin from an animal, *to flay*—mduġapa.

yu-ġa'-ta, *v. a.* *to open out*, as the hand; *to open*, as a door—mduġata, duġata. *T.*, *to spread out the hands, to stretch out* or *raise the arm.* See yuwiŋta.

yu-ġat'-ġa-ta, *v. red.* See yuġanġata. *T.*, yuġalġata.

yu-ġe', *v. a.* *to take out with the hand*—mduġe. *T.*, kaġe.

yu-ġe', *n.* *T.* *a part* or *portion; some.* See uġe *and* oŋġe.

yu-ġe'-ġe, *v. a.* *to gather up in the hand, to take up by handfuls:* yuġeġe iwaću.

yu-ġi'-mna-na, *v.* *to pinch up with the fingers:* yuġimnana mduza. *T.*, yuźibyela.

yu-ġo', *v. a.* *to make marks such as are made on arrows*—mduġo. *T.*, also *to scratch, to make scratches on.*

yu-ġo', *v. n.* *T.* *to be tired, fatigued*—bluġo: *i. q.* watuka *and* mdokiṭa.

yu-ġo'-ġo, *v. red.* of yuġo.

yu-ġu'-ka, *v. a.* *to stretch, strain; to pull out*, as an arrow from the quiver—mduġuka.

yu-ha', *v. a.* *to have, own, possess*—mduha, duha, uŋhapi *and* uŋyuhapi: *to lift, be able to carry.* With this latter meaning the "a" is not changed to "e" on assuming the "kta" or "śni;" as, mduha śni.

yu-ḣa'-ḣa-daŋ, *v. a.* *to make not firm, to unsettle*—mduḣaḣadaŋ.

yu-ha'-ha-ye-daŋ, *v. a.* *to move, shake, make unstable*—mduhahayedaŋ.

yu-ha'-i-ye-ya, *v. a.* *to push down.*

yu-ḣaŋ'-ska, *v. a.* *T.* *to make longer, to prolong.* See yutehaŋ.

yu-ha'-pi, *part.* *owned, held; a servant:* yuhapi ćiŋ, *he wants to be held.*

yu-ha'-ya, *adv.* *T.* *in the manner of having; having*—yuhaya uŋ.

yu-hba', *v. a.* *to shell*, as corn; *to open*, as pods—mduhba. *T.*, yugba.

yu-hbe'-za, *v. a.* *to make rough*—mduhbeza. *T.*, yugbeza.

yu-hbu', *v. a.* *to make a noise*, as in taking hold of a bag of shelled corn; *to make rattle*, as corn—mduhbu. *T.*, pasbu.

yu-hbu'-hbu, *v. red.* of yuhbu.

yu-hbu' ya, *adv.* *making a rattling noise*, as in pushing anything into shelled corn: yuhbuya iyeya.

yu-hda', *v. a.* *to untwist, unroll, uncoil, stretch out*—mduhda. *T.*, yugla.

y u - h d a′ - h d a, *v. red.* of yuhda; *to stretch out:* yuhdahda aya, *to go one after another, to follow in Indian file.*

y u - h d a′ - k a, *v. a. to make far apart*—mduhdaka. *T.*, paóglaya egnaka.

y u - h d a′ - k a - y a, *adv. separately, singly:* yuhdakaya enaźiŋ. *T.*, paóglaya.

y u - h d a′ - k i ŋ - y a ŋ, *adv. across:* yuhdakiŋyaŋ iću, *to take across, put across.*

y u - h d a′ - k i - y a, *v. a. to cause to uncoil* or *stretch out*—yuhdawakiya.

y u - h d a′ - y a, *v. a. to cause to uncoil*—yuhdawaya.

y u - h d o′ - h d o, *v. a. to make grunt,* as a buffalo calf, by catching it—mduhdohdo.

y u - h d o′ - k a, *v. a. to sprain badly, dislocate*—mduhdoka.

y u - h e′, *v.* Same as yuha: yuhe ćiŋ, *one who owns, a master.*

y u - h e′ - k i - y a, *v. a. to cause to have; to give to*—yuhewakiya.

y u - h i′, *v. a. to drive off,* as game—mduhi. *T., to arouse, startle, stir up,* as game; *to throw into confusion,* as the wind does feathers.

y u - h i n′, *cont.* of yuhiŋta; yuhin iyeya. *T.*, yuhiŋl.

y u - h i ŋ′ - t a, *v. a. to sweep off, brush off, rake away*—mduhiŋta, uŋyuhiŋtapi. See yuhotapise.

y u - h i′ - y a - ḣ a ŋ, *v. to prolong* one's *days. T.*, tehaŋ niya.

y u - h i′ - y a - ḣ a ŋ - n a - k e - ć i ŋ - h a ŋ, *adv. waiting a little, not in haste. T.*, ćisćiyela ape.

y u - h m i′, *v. a. to clear off,* as grass, etc., from a field—mduhmi, duhmi. *T.*, yugmi.

y u - h m i′ - ć a, *v. a. to catch by the hair of the head, pull one's hair*—mduhmića, mayuhmića.

y u - h m i′ - h m a, *v. a. to roll,* as a wheel, etc., with the hand—mduhmihma. *T.*, yugmigma. See yuhomni.

y u - h m i n′, *cont.* of yuhmića: yuhmin yuza, *to take hold of the hair of the head.*

y u - h m i′ - y a ŋ - y a ŋ, *v. a. to make round,* as a ball, with the hand—mduhmiyaŋyaŋ. See yumima.

y u - h m u ŋ′, *v. a. to twist,* as a string—mduhmuŋ, duhmuŋ, uŋyuhmuŋpi. *T.*, yugmuŋ.

y u - h n a′, *v. a. to shake,* as fruit from a tree—mduhna. *T.*, yugna.

y u - h n a′ - h n a, *v. red.* of yuhna; *to take a loose hold of:* yuhnahna wakuwa. *T.*, yugnagna.

y u - h n a′ - ś k i ŋ - y a ŋ, *v. a. to make* one *crazy; to possess,* as a demon or spirit—mayuhnaśkiŋyaŋ.

y u - h n a′ - y a ŋ, *v. a. to miss,* as in attempting to grasp anything—mduhnayaŋ. *T.*, yugnayaŋ.

y u - h n u′ - n i, *v. a. to cause to wander*—mduhnuni: waćiŋyuhnuni, *to distract, bewilder. T.*, yugnuni.

y u - h o′ - h o, *v. a. to move, shake,* as something not firm—mduhoho.

yu-ho'-ho-daŋ, *v. a.* *to shake*, as something not solid—mduhohodaŋ.

yu-ho'-ho-pi-ća-śni, *adj.* *immovable.*

yu-ho'-ho-ya, *v. a.* *to cause to shake.*

yu-ho'-ho-ya, *adv.* *shaking.*

yu-ho'-mni, *v. a.* *to turn around* anything, *to turn*, as a grindstone—mduhomni, duhomni, uŋhomnipi, *and* uŋyuhomnipi: ihduhomni, *to turn one's self around.* See yuhmihma.

yu-ho'-mni-mni, *v. red.* of yuhomni.

yu-hoŋ'-hoŋ-za, *v. a.* *Ih.* *to shake; i. q.* yuhuhuza.

yu-ho'-ta-pi-se, *adv* *clearing away obstacles:* yuhotapise iyaya, *he has gone to clear the way.* *T.*, yuhiŋtapi se.

yu-hu'-hu, *intj.* Said when one is hurt, *i. q.* yuŋ. *T.*, yu.

yu-hu'-hus, *cont.* of yuhuhuza; yuhuhus wauŋ. *T.*, yuhuŋhuŋs.

yu-hu'-hus-ya, *v. a.* *to cause to shake*—yuhuhuswaya.

yu-hu'-hus-ya, *adv.* *shaking, moving.*

yu-hu'-hu-za, *v. a.* *to shake with the hand*—mduhuhuza. *Ih.*, yuhoŋhoŋza. *T.*, yuhuŋhuŋza.

yu-hu'-ku-ya, *v. a.* of hukuya; *to humble, bring down;* mduhukuya: yuhukuŋ iyeya, *to cast down.*

yu-huŋ'-ka, *v.* *to shake, to rock from side to side* (*T.*, yuŋgyuŋka)—mduhuŋka: yuhunke se mani, *to walk as a sailor* (*T.*, yuŋgyuŋka semani).

yu-hu'-te-daŋ, *v. a.* *to make short, wear off*—mduhutedaŋ. *T*, yutepa.

yu-ḣa', *v. n.* *to curl, branch out.*

yu-ḣa', *adj.* *curled, frizzled:* pa yuḣa, *a curly head*

yu-ḣa'-ḣa, *v. red.* of yuḣa; *to become curled* or *branched.*

yu-ḣa'-ḣa, *adj.* *curly, having many branches* or *prongs.*

yu-ḣa'-kpa, *v. a.* *to make curved, as the edge of a knife that has been long in use*—mduḣakpa.

yu-ḣaŋ'-hi, *v. a.* *to make slow*—mduḣaŋhi.

yu-ḣaŋ'-hi-ka, *adj.* *T.* *slow.*

yu-ḣa'-tka, *v. a.* *to ruffle*, as hair or feathers—mduḣatka.

yu-ḣa'-tpa, *v. a.* Same as yuḣakpa.

yu-ḣba', *v. a.* *to make drowsy;* mduḣba.

yu-ḣda', *v. a.* *to ring*, as a bell, *to rattle*—mduḣda, duḣda, uŋḣdapi. *T.*, yuḣla. See also woḣla.

yu-ḣda'-ġaŋ, *v. a.* *to enlarge; to separate from, leave*—mduḣdaġaŋ: ti hduḣdaġaŋ śni, *to stay always at home.*

yu-ḣda'-hda, *v. red.* of yuḣda.

yu-ḣda'-ḣda-ta, *v. red.* of yuḣdata.

yu-ḣda'-hda-ya, *v. red.* of yuḣdaya.

yu-ḣdan', *cont.* of yuḣdata; yuḣdata; yuḣdan iyeya. *T.*, yuḣlal.

yu-ḣda'-ta, *v. a.* *to scratch*, as a cat; *to scratch off*—mduḣdata.

y u - ḣ d a'- y a, *v.* *to peel off, to skin; to take off,* as a sticking plaster—mduḣdaya, duḣdaya.

y u - ḣ d e'- ć a, *v. a.* *to tear in pieces, tear up, rend*—mduḣdeća, uŋyuḣdećapi. *T.*, yuḣleća.

y u - ḣ d e'- ḣ d e - ć a, *v. red.* of yuḣdeća.

y u - ḣ d e n', *cont.* of yuḣdeća; yuḣden iyeya. *T.*, yuḣlel.

y u - ḣ d e n'- k i - y a, *v. a.* *to cause to rend*—yuḣdenwakiya.

y u - ḣ d e n'- y a, *v. a.* *to cause to tear up*—yuḣdenwaya.

y u - ḣ d o', *v.* *i. q.* yuḣdoka.—W. J. C.

y u - ḣ d o g', *cont.* of yuḣdoka; yuḣdog iyeya: yuḣdog haŋ, *to stand open.*

y u - ḣ d o g'- k i - y a, *v. a.* *to cause to open*—yuḣdogwakiya.

y u - ḣ d o'- ḣ d o - k a, *v. red.* of yuḣdoka; *to make holes in.*

y u - ḣ d o'- k a, *v. a.* *to make a hole; to bore a hole; to open,* as a door, as, tiyopa yuḣdoka; *to open,* as a box, barrel, etc.—mduḣdoka, duḣdoka, uŋḣdokapi *and* uŋyuḣdokapi. *T.*, yuḣloka.

y u - ḣ e m', *cont.* of yuḣepa; yuḣem iyeya. *T.*, yuḣeb.

y u - ḣ e m'- ḣ e - p a, *v. red.* of yuḣepa.

y u - ḣ e'- p a, *v. a.* *to absorb, empty, exhaust,* as a fluid, *by lading out*—mduḣepa, uŋyuḣepapi.

y u - ḣ e'- y a m, *cont.* of yuḣeyapa; yuḣeyam iyeya, *to put aside.* *T.*, yuḣeyab.

y u - ḣ e'- y a n, *cont.* of yuḣeyata; yuḣeyan iyeya. *T.*, yuḣeyal.

y u - ḣ e'- y a - p a, *v. a.* *to put a little back, put aside*—mduḣeyapa.

y u - ḣ e'- y a - t a, *v a.* *to put back, reject.*

y u - ḣ i', *v. n.* *to pimple; to be pimpled*—mayuḣi: hence, oyuḣi, *pimples.* *T.*, yuḣ'i.

y u - ḣ i'- ć a, *v. a.* *to waken* one *up*—mduḣića, duḣića, uŋyuḣićapi, mayuḣića.

y u - ḣ i'- ḣ i, *v. red.* of yuḣi; *to be pimpled, marked, rough.* *T.*, yuḣ'iḣ'i.

y u - ḣ i n', *cont.* of yuḣića; yuḣin iyeya. *T.*, yuḣil.

y u - ḣ i'- s e, *adj.* *like pimples; striped, figured,* as dimity or diaper. *T.*, yuḣ'ise.

y u - ḣ i'- y a - y a, *v. a.* *to do badly, bungle*—mduḣiyaya.

y u - ḣ l a', *v. a. T.* *i. q.* yuḣda

y u - ḣ l e'- ć a, *v. T.* *i q.* yuḣdeća.

y u - ḣ l o'- k a, *v. T.* *i. q.* yuḣdoka.

y u - ḣ m i ŋ', *v. a.* *to sling,* as a stone, *sidewise; to make go crooked.* *T.*, *to make crooked,* as writing.

y u - ḣ m i ŋ'- y a ŋ, *adv.* *off sidewise, crookedly;* yuḣmiŋyaŋ elinaka, *to place out of line,* or *crookedly.*

y u - ḣ m u ŋ', *v. a* *to make whizz,* as in throwing a stone from a sling—mduḣmuŋ.

y u - ḣ m u ŋ'- ḣ m u ŋ, *v. red.* of yuḣmuŋ.

y u - ḣ m u ŋ'- y a ŋ, *adv.* *making whizz.*

y u - ħ o ŋ′ - t a, *v. a.* *to make soft*, as thread, *to rub soft*, as skin—mduħoŋta. See yuħuŋta.

y u - ħ p a′, *v. a.* *to throw down*, as one's load; *to unharness* or *unload* a horse; *to shake off*, as leaves from a tree; *to buy a wife*—mduħpa, duħpa, uŋyuħpapi. *T.*, also *to put down* or *shut down*, as a window-sash.

y u - ħ p a′ - ħ p a, *v. red.* of yuħpa; *to throw over* or *down* in lumps, as in ploughing hard ground.

y u - ħ p a ŋ′, *v. a.* *to soak and make soft*, as leather—mduħpaŋ.

y u - ħ p a ŋ′ - ħ p a ŋ, *v. red.* of yuħpaŋ; *to soak and make a little soft*, as leather—mduħpaŋħpaŋ. See yuħtuta.

y u - ħ p e′ - y a, *v. a.* *to cause to throw down*—yuħpewaya.

y u - ħ p u′, *v. a.* *to pick off a piece, break off, crumble off*—mduħpu.

y u - ħ p u′ - ħ p u, *v. red.* of yuħpu.

y u - ħ t a ŋ′, *v. a.* *to make rough*. See yuħtaŋyaŋ.

y u - ħ t a ŋ′ - y a ŋ, *v. a.* *to make rough, to whet to a rough edge*—mduħtaŋyaŋ.

y u - ħ t u′ - t a, *v. a.* *to mash* or *break* a skin for dressing, *to make pliant*—mduħtuta. *T.*, yupaŋpaŋ.

y u - ħ u′, *v. a.* *to take off the hull* or *rind, to peel*, as bark with the hand—mduħu.

y u - ħ u′ - ġ a, *v. a.* *to break a hole in, to stave in; to break to pieces*—mduħuġa. See yuśuźu.

y u - ħ u ħ′, *cont* of yuħuġa; yuħuħ iyeya.

y u - ħ u ħ′ - n a - ġ a, *v. a.* *to cause to burn up*—mduħuħnaġa.

y u - ħ u′ - ħ u - ġ a, *v. red.* of yuħuġa.

y u - ħ u ŋ′ - ħ u ŋ - t a, *v. red.* of yuħuŋta.

y u - ħ u ŋ′ - t a, *v. a.* *to make soft*, as flax, *in dressing it*, or as a skin, *by rubbing*—mduħuŋta.

y u - ħ u ŋ′ - w i ŋ, *v. a.* *to make putrefy*, as flesh—mduħuŋwiŋ. *T.*, see ħuŋwiŋya.

y u - ħ w i ŋ′, *v.* See yuħuŋwiŋ.

y u - i′ - ć i - ć a - h i, *v. a.* *to mix together, to mingle.*

y u - i′ - ć i - ć a - h i - y a, *adv.* *mingling:* yuićićahiya iyeya.

y u - i′ - ć i - ć a - w i ŋ, *v. a.* *to make turn back on the same way* (*T.*, the same); *to cause to pass by*, as the two ends of anything—mduićićawiŋ. See next word.

y u - i′ - ç i - ç u - y a, *v. a.* *T.* *to cause to pass by over* or *alongside of each other*, as the two ends of anything; *to make overlap each other.*

y u - i′ - d e, *v. a.* *to cause to blaze, to kindle a fire*—mduide.

y u - i′ - d e - p i, *n.* *Ih.* *something to make a blaze—friction matches.*

y u - i′ - ħ a, *v. a.* *to make laugh*—mduiħa.

y u - i′ - l e - p i, *n.* *T.* *i. q.* yuidepi: ćaŋ kaidepi.

y u - i′ - n a - ħ n i, *v. a.* *to hasten* one mduinaħni.

y u - i′ - n a - ħ n i - k i - y a, *v. a.* *to cause* one *to hasten.*

y u - i'- n a - ḣ n i - y a ŋ, *adv. hastening.*

y u - i'- n i - n a, *v. a.* of inina; *to make still, put to silence*—mduinina. *T.*, yuinila.

y u - i'- n i n - y a, *adv. putting to silence. T.*, yuinilya.

y u - i'- p a - t k u - ġ a, *v. a.* of ipatkuġa; *to place in a row*—mduipatkuġa. *T.*, yuoweċiŋhaŋ.

y u - i'- p a - t k u ḣ - y a, *adv. placing in a row*

y u - i'- š t e - ć a, *v. a. to make* one *ashamed*—mduišteća.

y u - i'- ś t o - h m u s, *cont.* of yuiśtohmuza.

y u - i'- ś t o - h m u - z a, *v. a.* of iśtohmuza; *to make* one *shut his eyes; to deceive*—mduiśtohmuza.

y u - i'-t o-k a ŋ, *v. a. T. to put out of the way; to remove from; to reject.* See yuḣeyata, etc.

y u - i'- t p i - s k a - e - ḣ p e - y a, *v. to turn* any thing *over on its back,* as a dog, etc.

y u - i'- y a - k i - p a m, *adv. dividing, separating. T.*, yuiyakipab.

y u - i'- y a - k i - p a - p a m, *adv. red.* of yuiyakipam.

y u - i'- y o g, *cont.* of yuíyoka; yuiyog iyeya, *to put out of the way, reject. T.*, yuitokaŋ; yutokaŋ.

y u - i'- y o - k a, *v. a. to shun.* See yuiyog.

y u - i'- y o - t a ŋ, *v.* of iyotaŋ; yuiyotaŋ iyeya, *to cause* one *to do more by telling him to stop, to make more determined.*

y u - i'- y o - t a ŋ g, *cont.* of yuiyotaŋka: yuiyotaŋg eḣpeya, *to push* one *down, make sit down.*

y u - i'- y o - t a ŋ - h a ŋ, *v.* yuiyotaŋhaŋ iyekiya, *to afflict, to trouble.*

y u - i'- y o - w a s, *cont.* of yuiyowaza.

y u - i'- y o - w a ś, *cont.* of yuiyowaźa; yuiyowaś iyeye śni. See yuiyowaźaśni.

y u - i'- y o - w a - z a, *v. a. to make resound, to make echo*—mduiyowaza.

y u.- i'- y o - w a - ź a - ś n i, *v. to place afar off.*

y u - i'- ż e - n a, *v. T. to stir* or *mix together.*

y u - k a', *v. a. to strip off,* as the feather part of a quill—mduka.

y u - k a'- k i - ź a, *v. a. to cause to suffer*—mdukakiźa.

y u - k a m', *cont.* of yukapa; yukam iyeya. *T.*, yukab—yukab emayaya, *you jerk me.*

y u - k a ŋ', *v. n. to be; there is.* This verb wants the forms of the first and second persons singular; plur., uŋkaŋpi, dukaŋpi, yukaŋpi. Yukaŋ is often used with a plural signification, as, taḣiŋća yukaŋ, *there are deer;* hu mayukaŋ, *legs are to me,* i. e., *I have legs.* See yuke *and* yuki.

y u - k a ŋ', *v. to give room.* See tiyukaŋ, kiyukaŋ, *and* yukiŋ.

y u - k a ŋ', *v. a.* of kaŋ; *to make old*—mdukaŋ.

y u - k a ŋ', *v. a. to shake off,* as dew—mdukaŋ.

y u - k a ŋ'- k a ŋ, *v. red.* of yukaŋ.

yu-ka'-pa, *v. a.* *to catch*, as a ball, *in the hand*—mdukapa. *T*, *to jerk away from.* See yakapa, yukab, etc.

yu-ka'-ta, *v. a.* of kata; *to make warm by rubbing; to heat by making a fire*—mdukata.

yu-ka'-tiŋ, *v. a.* *to straighten out with the hand*—mdukatiŋ.

yu-ka'-wa, *v. a.* *to open*, as the mouth, eyes, etc.—mdukawa, dukawa, uŋyukawapi.

yu-ka'-wa-ki-ya, *v. a.* *to cause to open*—yukawawakiya

yu-kća', *v. a.* *to loose a knot, untie, unwrap, open what is tangled*—mdukća.

yu-kćaŋ', *v. a.* *to comprehend* anything, *to understand, know, guess; to have an opinion, to judge*—mdukćaŋ, dukćaŋ, uŋkćaŋpi. See iyukćaŋ.

yu-kćaŋ'-yaŋ, *v.* *comprehending, guessing.*

yu-kće'-ka, *v.* *i. q.* yućeka.—W. J. C.

yu-ke', *v. n.* *to be.* See yukaŋ.

yu-kes', *cont.* of yukeza; yukes iyeya.

yu-ke'-ya, *adv.* *T.* *being; having, possessing*—waħtani yukeya uŋ, *a sinner*, i. e., *one who is leading a sinful life.*

yu-ke'-za, *v. a.* *to make smooth*—mdukeza.

yu-ki', *cont.* *T.* of yukaŋ; tato yuki nahaŋ ćaŋli yukaŋ, *there is beef and there is tobacco.*

yu-ki'-ki-ta, *v. a.* *to make limber*—mdukikita. *T.*, yuwiŋświŋźa.

yu-kin', *cont.* of yukiŋća; yukin iwaću. *T.*, taħu akaħpe ogle.

yu-kiŋ'-iŋ-pi, *n.* *a cloak.* *T.*, yukiŋl.

yu-ki'-nu-kaŋ, *v. a.* *to divide between, to separate*—mdukinukaŋ, dukinukaŋ.

yu-ki'-nu-kaŋ, *adv.* *divided:* yukinukaŋ ehnaka, *to place out separately.*

yu-ki'-nu-kaŋ-ki-ya, *adv.* *divided, separately.*

yu-ki'-nu-kaŋ-yaŋ, *adv.* *separately.*

yu-kiŋ', *v. a.* *to give room to pass, to lean to one side*—mdukiŋ, mayukiŋ.

yu-kiŋ'-ća, *v. a.* *to scrape off with the hand*—mdukiŋća.

yu-kiŋ'-kiŋ, *adv.* *to and fro* or *from side to side*, as a sailor in walking. *T.*, *from side to side*, as in working a stick in a hole; but "as a sailor walking" is yuŋgyuŋka se.

yu-kiŋs', *cont.* of yukiŋza; yukiŋs iyeya.

yu-kiŋs'-kiŋ-za, *v. red.* of yukiŋza.

yu-kiŋ'-za, *v. a.* *to make creak*—mdukiŋza

yu-ki'-pas, *cont* of yukipaza; yukipas yuza, *to seize by the hair of the head*—yukipas mduza. *T.*, yupaŋś.

yu-ki'-paś, *cont.* of yukipaźa; yukipas iyeya: yukipaś yuza, *to double around and hold.*

y u - k i′ - p a - z a, *v.* See yukipas, the form in use.

y u - k i′ - p a - ź a, *v. a.* *to bend* any thing *around, to double over, to bend so as to make the ends meet*—mdukipaźa. See yuakipaźa.

y u - k i′ - p e - h a ŋ, *v. a.* *to fold, to lay in folds*—mdukipehaŋ: yukipehaŋ ehnaka.

y u - k i′ - p u - s k i - ć a, *v. a.* *to put close together, to press*—mdukipuskića.

y u - k i′ - p u - s k i n, *cont.* of yukipuskića; yukipuskin yuza, *to hold* one thing *close to* another. *T.*, yukipuskil.

y u - k i′ - p u - s k i n - y a, *adv.* *pressed close to.*

y u - k i′ - y e l a, *v. a.* *T.* *to make near.* See yuaśkadaŋ.

y u - k i′ - y u - t e - y a, *adv.* Said of any thing *crisped* or *drawn up. T.*, natipa.

y u - k m i′ - ć a, *v. Ih. i. q.* yuhmića.

y u - k o′, *v. a.* *to make a hole*—mduko: yuko eḣpeya, *to throw open. T., to enlarge an opening.*

y u - k o g′, *cont.* of yukoka; yukog iyeya.

y u - k o′ - k a, *v. a.* *to ring* or *rattle,* as an old kettle—mdukoka.

y u - k o′ - k e - d a ŋ, *v. a.* *to make active, to stimulate*—mdukokedaŋ. *T.*, yubiliheća.

y u - k o - k i′ - y a, *v. a.* *T.* *to make wrinkle:* ite yukokiya, *to frown* or *scowl.*

y u - k o′ - k o - k a, *v. red.* of yukoka.

y u - k o ŋ′ - t a, *v.* See yukuŋta

y u - k o′ - y a - ḣ a ŋ, *v. a.* *to cause to be quick, to hasten*—mdukoyaḣaŋ. See yuinaḣni.

y u - k p a′, *v. a.* iśta yukpa, *to make blind;* noġe yukpa, *to make deaf*—mdukpa. See yutpa.

y u - k p a ŋ′, *v. a.* *to grind,* as corn, etc., *to make fine, to pulverize*—mdukpaŋ, dukpaŋ, uŋkpaŋpi. See yutpaŋ.

y u - k p a ŋ′ - k p a ŋ, *v. red.* of yukpaŋ.

y u - k p a ŋ′ - p i, *n.* *grinding.*

y u - k p a ŋ′ y a ŋ, *v. a.* *to cause to grind*—yukpaŋwaya.

y u - k p i′, *v. a* *to crack* or *burst,* as a louse. *i. q* yutpi.

y u - k p i′ - k p i, *v. red.* of yukpi.

y u - k p u′ - k p a, *v. a.* *to make fine, to crumble up and scatter about*—mdukpukpa See yukpukpa.

y u - k s a′, *v. a.* *to break off,* as a stick, *with the hand; to pull,* as corn; *to cut off* or *out with shears*—mduksa, duksa, uŋksapi.

y u - k s a′ - k s a, *v. red.* of yuksa.

y u - k s a′ - p a, *v. a.* of ksapa; *to make wise*—mduksapa. Said also of an animal who breaks away from a trap, as he is *made wise* or *wary* by it.

y u - k s a′ - p i, *n.* *a breaking off, a gathering* of corn.

y u - k s e′ - k s e - y a, *v. red.* of yukseya.

y u - k s e′ - y a, *v. a.* *to cause to break off,* as in trapping—yuksewaya.

y u - k s e' - y a, *adv.* *broken off; straight down*, as if *broken off;* said of a bluff shore where the water is deep; *i. q.* hutotkoŋza.

y u - k ś a', *v. a.* *to bend* or *double up*, as a blanket—mdukśa.

y u - k ś a' - d a ŋ, *adv.* *bent up, crooked:* yukśadaŋ iću. See yakśadaŋ.

y u - k ś a ŋ', *v. a.* *to bend, fold up*—mdukśaŋ.

y u - k ś a ŋ' - k i - y a, *v. a.* *to cause to bend* or *fold up*—yukśaŋwakiya.

y u - k ś a ŋ' - k ś a ŋ, *v. red.* of yukśaŋ.

y u - k ś a ŋ' - k ś a ŋ, *adv.* *crooked, curled about.*

y u - k ś a ŋ' - y a ŋ, *v. a.* *to cause to bend*—yukśaŋwaya.

y u - k ś a ŋ' - y e - y a, *adv.* *bent around, in a circle.*

y u - k ś i' - k ś i - ź a, *v. red.* of yukśiźa.

y u - k ś i ś', *cont.* of yukśiza; yukśiś iyeya.

y u - k ś i ś' - y a, *v. a.* *to cause to double up*—yukśiświaya.

y u - k ś i' - ź a, *v. a.* *to double up, to bend*, as the arm at the elbow; *to double up*, as iron, etc.; *to pull the trigger of a gun*—mdukśiźa.

y u - k t a ŋ', *v. a.* *to bend with the hand*—mduktaŋ.

y u - k t a ŋ' - k i - y a, *v. a.* *to cause to bend* anything.

y u - k t a ŋ' - k i - y a, *adv.* *crookedly.*

y u - k t a ŋ' - k t a ŋ, *v. red.* of yuktaŋ; *to bend, crook.*

y u - k t a ŋ' - k t a ŋ, *adj.* or *adv.* *zigzag; bent.*

y u - k t a ŋ' - k t a ŋ - k i - y a, *adv. red.* yuktaŋkiya.

y u - k t a ŋ' - k t a ŋ - y a ŋ, *adv. red.* of yuktaŋyaŋ.

y u - k t a ŋ' - y a ŋ, *adv.* *crookedly.*

y u - k t a ŋ' - y e - y a, *adv.* *crookedly, not in a straight line:* yuktaŋyeya waŋka.

y u - k u' - k a, *v. a.* *to pull to pieces; to make rotten, to destroy*—mdukuka.

y u - k u ŋ' - t a, *v. a.* *T.* *to pick* with any thing *in a hole* or *cavity*, as to pick the ears or nose.

y u - ḳ e' - ġ a, *v. a.* *to scratch, scrape*—mduḳeġa. See yuḳoġa.

y u - ḳ e ḣ', *cont.* of yuḳeġa; yuḳeḣ iyeya.

y u - ḳ e ḣ' - ḳ e - ġ a, *v. red.* of yuḳeġa.

y u - ḳ e ḣ' - y a, *adv.* *scratching, scraping.*

y u - ḳ e s', *cont.* of yuḳeza; yuḳes iyeya.

y u - ḳ e s' - ḳ e - z a, *v. red.* of yuḳeza; *to shave off close and smooth*, as the hair of the head—mduḳesḳeza.

y u - ḳ e' - z a, *v. a.* *to make hard and smooth; to shear off close*, as the hair of the head—mduḳeza. See yuḳoza.

y u - ḳ o' - ġ a, *v. a.* *to scratch up, make rough with the nails*—mduḳoġa. See yuḳeġa.

y u - ḳ o ḣ', *cont.* of yuḳoġa; yuḳoḣ iyeya.

y u - ḳ o ḣ' - ḳ o - ġ a, *v. red.* of yuḳoġa.

y u - ḳ o s', *cont.* of yuḳoza; yuḳos iyeya.

y u - ḳ o s′ - ḳ o - z a, *v. red.* of yuḳoza.

y u - ḳ o′ - z a, *v. a.* *to make smooth and hard* by taking off the grass, etc.—mduḳoza, duḳoza. See yuḳeza.

y u - l a b′, *cont.* of yulapa.

y u - l a b′ - l a - p a, *v. red.* of yulapa.

y u - l a′ - p a, *v. a.* *T.* *to make smooth.*

y u - m a′ - h e n - i - y e - y a, *v. a.* *to push* one thing *into* something else, *to insert.*

y u - m a ŋ′, *v. a.* *to sharpen by grinding, filing,* or *whetting,* as an ax, etc.—mdumaŋ, uŋyumaŋpi.

y u - m d a′, *v. a.* *to separate,* as the layers of bark or the leaves of a book—mdumda. *T.*, yubla.

y u - m d a′ - p i, *n.* *a page* or *leaf of a book,* etc. *T.*, yublapi.

y u - m d a s′, *cont.* of yumdaza; yumdas ehnaka, *to open out,* as in dressing a cow; yumdas iyeya.

y u - m d a′ - s k a, *v. a.* *to make flat*—mdumdaska *T.*, yublaska.

y u - m d a′ - y a, *v. a.* *to open, spread out, unfold; to make level*—mdumdaya, uŋyumdayapi. *T.*, yublaya.

y u - m d a′ - y a - p i, *n.* *a spreading out; a page in a book.*

y u - m d a′ - z a, *v. a.* *to burst open,* as the bowels, or as a bag of corn; *to break open by hauling; to make a longitudinal incision*—mdumdaza. *T.*, yublaza

y u - m d e′ - ć a, *v. a.* *to break to pieces* or *crush,* as brittle ware; *to rend* or *tear open*—mdumdeća. *T.*, yubleća.

y u - m d e′ - m d e - ć a, *v. red.* of yumdeća.

y u - m d e n′, *cont.* of yumdeća; yumden iyeya. *T.*, yublel.

y u - m d e n′ - k i - y a, *v. a.* *to cause to break to pieces*—yumdenwakiya.

y u - m d u′, *v. a.* *to make mellow, to pulverize, to plough,* as ground—mdumdu, dumdu, uŋmdupi, *and* uŋyumdupi. *T.*, yublu.

y u - m d u′ - k i - y a, *v. a.* *to cause to plough*—yumduwakiya.

y u - m d u′ - m d u, *v. red.* of yumdu.

y u - m d u′ - y a, *v. a.* *to cause to pulverize*—yumduwaya. See yumdukiya.

y u - m i′ - m a, *v. a.* *to make round,* as a wheel. See yuhmiyaŋyaŋ.

y u - m i′ - m e - y a, *adv.* *T.* *in a circle; circular:* yumimeya yaŋka po, *sit round in a circle.*

y u - m n a′, *v. a.* *to rip a seam with scissors, to rip a seam in any way by pulling,* etc.—mdumna. *T.*, blumna, lumna, etc.

y u - m n a′ - k i - y a, *v. a.* *to cause to rip*—yumnawakiya.

y u - m n a′ - m n a, *v. red* of yumna.

y u - m n i′, *v. n.* *to turn round, to go round in circles.*

y u - m n i′ - ġ a, *v.* *to shrink, draw up; to cause to shrink*—mdumniġa. *T.*, *to twist,* as clothes, in wringing them; but "to shrink, draw up" is namniġa; and "to cause to shrink" is namnih̔kiya.

y u - m n i′ - m n i, *v. red.* of yumni; *to turn round and round.*

yu-mni'-mni-ġa, *v. red.* of yumniġa.

yu-mni'-mniś, *cont.* of yumnimniźa; *curled:* yumnimniś iyeya.

yu-mni'-mniś-ya, *v. a.* *to cause to curl.*

yu-mni'-mniś-ya, *adv.* *curly.*

yu-mni'-mni-źa, *adj. red.* of yumniźa; *curled*, as hair. *T.*, *wavy*, as hair; *ruffled up.*

yu-mni'-mni-źa, *v. a.* *to ruffle, to pleat*—mdumnimniźa.

yu-mni'-wa-ći-pi, *n.* *the circle dance.* In this dance a pole is set up in the center, which is encircled at a distance of twenty or thirty feet by branches of trees. By the central pole a small arbor is made, which is occupied by the high priest of the ceremonies. The young men dance around.

yu-mni'-źa, *adj.* *curled, not straight*, as hair. *T.*, *wavy.*

yu-mnu'-mnu-ġa, *v. a.* *to make a noise*, as in handling corn—mdumnumnuġa. *T.*, *to craunch, to make a noise*, as a horse in eating corn. See yamnumnuġa.

yun, *cont.* of yuta; yun mani, *he walks eating.* *T.*, yul.

yu-na'-ke, *v.* See yunakeya.

yu-na'-ke-ya, *v. a.* *to turn* anything *partly up, turn on one side*—mdunakeya. *T.*, *to tip.* See kanakeya, panakeya, etc.

yu-na'-źiŋ, *v. a.* *to cause to stand, to raise* or *lift up*—mdunaźiŋ.

yu-ni', *v. a.* *to touch* one *so as to call* his *attention to* anything—mduni, duni, mayuni. *T.*, pani. See bonini, etc.

yu-ni'-ni, *v. red.* of yuni; *to touch so as to arouse* one, or call his attention to anything—mdunini.

yu-ni'-ya-śni, *v. a.* *to put out of breath, to strangle*—mduniyaśni.

yun-ki'-ya, *v. a.* of yuta; *to cause to eat, to feed*—yunwakiya.

yu-nmi'-nma, *v. a.* *to roll with the hand*—mdunminma. *T.*, yugmigma. Same as yuhmihma.

yu-nuŋ'-ġa, *v. a.* *to make a hard* or *callous place*, by sprain or otherwise—mdunuŋġa. *T.*, yunoġa.

yun-ya', *v. a.* *to feed, cause to eat*—yuŋwaya. *T.*, yulya; yulkiya.

yuŋ, *intj.* *oh!* *O dear me!*

yuŋg-yuŋ'-ka, *v.* *T.* *to rock* or *sway from side to side*, as a sailor in walking; yuŋgyuŋka se mani. See yukiŋkiŋ.

yuŋ-ġe', *n.* *T.* *part, some:* *i. q.* uġe *and* oŋġe.

yuŋ-ka', *v.* *T.* *i. q.* waŋka; *to lie along*—muŋka.

yuŋ-ka'-he, *adv.* *T.* *lying prone*, as a tree cut down: *i. q.* waŋkahe.

yuŋ'-kaŋ, *conj.* *T.* *and; also; then:* *i. q.* uŋkaŋ.

yuŋ-kaŋś', *conj.* *T.* used only of past time; *if, provided;* *i. q.* uŋkaŋś.

yuŋś, *conj.* *T.* *i. q.* yuŋkaŋś; *if, provided:* refers to the past only. Hećoŋ śni yuŋś, *if he had not done it.*

y u - o′- ć i - k p a - n i, *v. a.* Same as yuoćitpani.

y u - o′- ć i ŋ - ś i - ć a, *v. a.* *to make cross*—mduoćiŋśića.

y u - o′- ć i - p t e - ć a, *v. a.* *to make* one *shorter* than another; *to make a difference, diminish*—mduoćipteća.

y u - o′- ć i - p t e n, *cont.* of yuoćipteća.

y u - o′- ć i - p t e n - y a, *adv.* *diminishing by degrees.*

y u - o′- ć i - p t e - t u, *v. a.* *to make of different sizes, to lessen*—mduoćiptetu.

y u - o′- ć i - p t e - t u - y a, *adv.* *lessening.*

y u - o′- ć i - p t e - t u - y a - k e n, *adv.* *of different sizes.*

y u - o′- ć i - t k o ŋ - z a, *v. a* *to make equal*—mduoćitkoŋza. See yuotkoŋza.

y u - o′- ć i - t p a - n i, *v. a.* *to make unequal*—mduoćitpani. *T.*, yuoćikpani.

y u - o′- h d a - p ś i ŋ, *v.* yuohdapśiŋ eḣpeya, *to turn* any thing *over.*

y u - o′- h d a - p ś i ŋ - y a ŋ, *adv.* *turning over.*

y u - o′- ḣ a ŋ - k o, *v. a.* *to make hasten*—mduoḣaŋko.

y u - o′- ḣ a ŋ - k o - y a, *adv.* *hastening.*

y u - o′- ḣ d a - ġ a ŋ, *v. n.* *to become loose.*

y u - o′- ḣ d a ḣ, *cont.* of yuoḣdaġaŋ; yuoḣdaḣ iću, *to become loose.*

y u - o′- ḣ p a, *v. a.* *to break into, break through*—mduoḣpa.

y u - o′- ḣ p e - y a, *v. a.* *to cause to break through*—yuoḣpewaya.

y u - o ḣ′ - y a, *adv.* *obliquely*, as the characters are placed in writing: yuoḣya ehnaka. See kaoḣya.

y u - o′- k a - h b o - k a, *v. a.* *to make float, to send afloat*—mduokaḣboka.

y u - o′- k a - ḣ p a, *v.* *to cause to float.*

y u - o′- k a - p o - t a, *v.* *to cause to be borne up*, as on water.

y u - o′- k i - n i - h a ŋ, *v. a.* *to make honorable*—mduokinihaŋ.

y u - o′- k o, *v. a.* *to make a hole*—mduoko.

y u - o′- k o ŋ - w a ŋ - ź i - d a ŋ, *v. a.* of okoŋwaŋźidaŋ; *to make one of, join one to another*—mduokoŋwaŋźidaŋ. *T.*, rather *to make alike* or *similar.*

y u - o′- k s a, *v. a.* *to break off into*—mduoksa. See oyuksa.

y u - o′- k t a ŋ, *v. a* *to bend into*—mduoktaŋ. See oyuktaŋ.

y u - o′- m d e - ć a, *v. a.* *to divide, disperse, break in pieces, scatter abroad*, as a people—mduomdeća. See oyumdeća.

y u - o′- m d e - ć a, *v. n.* yuomdeća yuza, *to hold the sharp part up*, as the edge of a bòard.

y u - o′- m d e - ć a - h a ŋ, *part.* *in a dispersed state, scattered.*

y u - o′- m d e n, *cont.* of yuomdeća; yuomden iyaya, *to go off, disperse;* yuomden iyeya, *to cause to scatter abroad.* *T.*, yuoblel.

y u - o'- m n i - n a, *v. a. to shelter from the wind, make a calm*—mduomnina. *T.*, yuoblula.

y u - o'- n i - h a ŋ, *v. a. to honor, treat with attention*—mduonihaŋ, uŋyuonihaŋpi, mayuonihaŋ.

y u - o'- n i - h a ŋ - y a ŋ, *adv. honoring, treating politely.*

y u - o'- p o, *v. a. to press out of shape, press in at the sides,* as a kettle; *to make warp*—mduopo.

y u - o'- p t e - ć a, *v. a. to make less*—mduoptećа.

y u - o'- p t e n, *cont.* of yuoptećа. *T.*, yuoptel.

y u - o'- p t e n - y a, *adv. making less.*

y u - o'- p t e - t u, *v. a. to make less*—mduoptetu.

y u - o'- p t e - t u - y a, *adv. lessening.*

y u - o'- p o ŋ, *v. to scatter, spread abroad.*

y u - o'- s e, *and* y u - o'- s e k - s e, *n. one who shoots but does not hit.* This would seem to be used ironically.

y u - o'- s e - y a, *v. T. to get into a hard knot.* See yuośiŋ.

y u - o'- s e - y a, *adv. T. tightly; in a hard knot;* yuoseya iyakaśka.

y u - o'- s'i ŋ, *v. to hate. T.*, oyus'iŋ.

y u - o'- s i ŋ - s i ŋ, *v. a. to bedaub* one with semen—mduosiŋsiŋ. See osiŋsiŋ *and* yaśiŋśiŋ.

y u - o'- ś i ŋ, *v. n. to get into a hard knot, become hard to untie. T., to tie in a bow knot* or *loosely.*

y u - o'- ś i ŋ - y a ŋ, *adv. T. loosely; tied in a bow knot.*

y u - o'- t a, *v. a. to make many, to multiply*—mduota, duota, uŋyuotapi.

y u - o'- t a ŋ - i ŋ, *v. a. to make appear, make manifest; to celebrate*—mduotaŋiŋ.

y u - o'- t a ŋ - i ŋ - y a ŋ, *adv. making manifest, celebrating.*

y u - o'- t a - p i, *n. a multiplying; multiplication.*

y u - o'- t k o ŋ - z a, *v. a. to make of equal length; to do right; to finish*—mduotkoŋza. See yuoćitkoŋza.

y u - o'- ṭ i ŋ s, *cont.* of yuoṭiŋza; yuoṭiŋs iću, *to draw in tight:* yuoṭiŋs iyeya.

y u - o'- ṭ i ŋ s - ṭ i ŋ - z a, *v. red.* of yuoṭiŋza.

y u - o'- ṭ i ŋ - z a, *v. a. to press in tight; to make firm in*—mduoṭiŋza. See oyuṭiŋza.

y u - o'- w e - ć i ŋ - h a ŋ, *v. T. to place in a row: i. q.* yuipatkuġa.

y u - o'- w i - ś n i, *v. i. q.* owikeśni; *to be unused; to accumulate without being drawn upon,* as provisions: yuowiśni mićiyaŋka.

y u - o'- w o - t a ŋ, *v.* Same as yuowotaŋna.

y u - o'- w o - t a ŋ - n a, *v. a. to make straight; to make upright, justify*—mduowotaŋna.

y u - o'- y a - ḣ e, *v. T. to absorb; to cause to absorb.* See yuḣepa.

y u - p a', *v. a. to make bitter*—mdupa.

y u - p a'- ġ a, *v. to grasp tightly.*

y u - p a ḣ', *cont.* of yupaġa; yupaḣ yuza, *to hold in a bunch;* yupaḣ nawaŋka, *to gallop slowly and with the body bent together.* See iyupaġa.

y u - p a′ - k o, *v. a.* *to make crooked*—mdupako.

y u - p a′ - k o - y a, *adv.* *making crooked, twisting.*

y u - p a ŋ′ - ġ a, *v. a.* *to tie up loosely, to make a large bundle*—mdupaŋġa.

y u - p a ŋ ḣ′, *cont.* of yupaŋġa; yupaŋḣ iyeya.

y u - p a ŋ ḣ′ - y a, *adv.* *loosely, in a large bundle.*

y u - p a ŋ - p a ŋ - n a, *v. a.* *to make soft*—mdupaŋpaŋna.

y u - p a ŋ ś′, *cont* of yu-paŋ′-źa; *v. a.* *T.* *to seize by the hair of the head: i. q.* yuhmića.

y u - p a′ - t u ś, *cont.* of yupatuźa; yupatuś iyeya.

y u - p a′ - t u - ź a, *v. a.* of patuźa; *to cause to stoop down, to bend down*—mdupatuźa.

y u - p ć e′ - ć e - l a, *v. a.* *T.* *to make short; to shorten: i. q.* yuptećedaŋ.

y u - p ć e l′ - y e - l a, *v. a.* *T.* Same meaning.

y u - p e′, *v. a.* *to make sharp*—mdupe.

y u - p e′ - h a ŋ, *v. a.* *to fold up*—mdupehaŋ.

y u - p e′ - m n i, *v. a.* of pemni; *to twist, make warp,* as a board—mdupemni.

y u - p e′ - m n i - m n i, *v. red.* of yupemni; *to warp, crook, twist.*

y u - p e′ - m n i - y a ŋ, *adv.* *crookedly.*

y u - p i′, *v. a.* *to make good*—mdupi, dupi.

y u - p i′ - k a, *v. a.* *to clothe one up well, to make look well*—mdupika. *T.*, yupiya kaġa.

y u - p i′ - k a, *n.* *one who dresses well; one who does things neatly.* *T.*, yupiyakel uŋ.

y u - p i ŋ s′, *cont* of yupiŋza; yupiŋs iyeya.

y u - p i ŋ s′ - p i ŋ - z a, *v. red.* of yupiŋza.

y u - p i ŋ ś′, *cont.* of yupiŋźa; yupiŋś iyeya.

y u - p i ŋ ś′ - p i ŋ - ź a, *v. red.* of yupiŋźa.

y u - p i ŋ′ - z a, *v. a.* *to make creak*—mdupiŋza.

y u - p i ŋ′ - ź a, *v. a.* *to pull out the coarse hair from a skin; to pull off all the hair* or *fur*—mdupiŋźa.

y u - p i′ - y a, *adv.* *T.* *well; nicely; finely; beautifully.*

y u - p i′ - y a - k e l, *adv.* *T.* Same meaning.

y u - p o′, *v. a.* *to make swell*—mdupo.

y u - p o m′, *cont.* of yupopa: yupom yuza, *to catch* or *hold with a snap* or *spring,* as a trap, *to catch round the body.* *T.*, yupob.

y u - p o n′, *cont.* of yupota; yupon iyeya. *T.*, yupol.

y u - p o n′ - p o - t a, *v. red.* of yupota. *T.*, yupolpota.

y u - p o′ - p a, *v. a.* *to cause to snap* or *burst, to make a snapping noise*—mdupopa.

y u - p o′ - t a, *v. a.* *to wear out, tear to pieces,* as a garment; *to use up, destroy*—mdupota, dupota.

y u - p o t′ - p o - t a, *v. red.* of yupota.

y u - p o′ - w a - y a, *v. a.* *to roughen up,* as fur or nap—mdupowaya.

yu-psag', *cont.* of yupsaka; yupsag iyeya.

yu-psag'-ya, *v. a.* *to cause to break*, as a string.

yu-psag'-ya, *adv.* *breaking*, as a cord.

yu-psa'-ka, *v. a.* *to break* or *pull in two*, as a string—mdupsaka, uŋpsakapi.

yu-psaŋ'-psaŋ, *v. a.* *T.* *to wag*, as a tail; *to cause to move back and forth.*

yu-psa'-psa-ka, *v. red.* of yupsaka.

yu-pse', *v.* yupse hiŋhda; yupse hiyeya.

yu-psi'-ća, *v. a.* *to make jump, to toss*—mdupsića: hoyupsića, *to fish with hook and line.*

yu-psin', *cont.* of yupsića; yupsin iyeya. *T.*, yupsil.

yu-psi'-psi-ća, *v. red.* of yupsića.

yu-psi'-psin, *cont.* of yupsipsića.

yu-psoŋ', *v. a.* *to turn over and spill*, as water, etc.—mdupsoŋ, dupsoŋ.

yu-psoŋ'-psoŋ, *v. red.* of yupsoŋ; *to turn over* on the belly, as the Dakotas do in skinning an animal; yupsoŋpsoŋ ehnaka. *T.* This refers especially, if not altogether, to the buffalo, other animals being cut down the belly after they are turned over on the back.

yu-psoŋ'-psoŋ-na, *v. a.* *to make round, to take off the corners*—mdupsoŋpsoŋna.

yu-psuŋ', *v. a.* Same as yupsoŋ.

yu-pśuŋ', *v. a.* *to pull out by the roots, to extract*, as a tooth; *to put out of joint*—mdupśuŋ, dupśuŋ, uŋyupśuŋpi.

yu-pśuŋ'-ka, *v. a.* *to double up in a round bunch:* nape ḣdupśuŋka, *to clench the fist*—mdupśuŋka.

yu-pśuŋ'-pśuŋ, *v. red.* of yupśuŋ.

yu-pta', *v. a.* *to cut out*, as a garment; *to cut off*, as the border of a buffalo-skin, etc.—mdupta, dupta, uŋyuptapi.

yu-pta'-hnag, *adv.* (yupta *and* hnaka?). *all together, collectively.* See witaya *and* yuptaya.

yu-ptaŋ'-ptaŋ, *v. a.* *to turn* or *roll back and forth with the hand, to rock*—mduptaŋptaŋ.

yu-ptaŋ'-ptaŋ-yaŋ, *v. a.* *to roll back and forth, to roll over and over*—mduptaŋptaŋyaŋ.

yu-ptaŋ'-yaŋ, *v. a.* *to roll over, to turn over*—mduptaŋyaŋ, duptaŋyaŋ.

yu-pta'-pta, *v. red.* of yupta.

yu-pta'-ya, *adv.* of ptaya; *together, collectively:* yuptaya ehnaka.

yu-pte'-će-daŋ, *v. a.* *to shorten*—mduptećedaŋ. *T.*, yupćećela.

yu-pten'-ye-daŋ, *adv.* *hastening, shortening;* yuptenyedaŋ ehnaka. *T.*, yupćelyela.

yu-ptu'-ḣa, *v. a.* *to pick in pieces*—mduptuḣa.

yu-ptu'-ptu-źa, *v. red.* of yuptuźa.

y u - p t u ś′, *cont.* of yuptuźa; yuptuś iyeya.

y u - p t u ś′- k i - y a, *v. a.* *to cause to split* or *crack*—yuptuśwaya.

y u - p t u′- ź a, *v. a.* *to make crack* or *split*, as a board, *by boring*—mduptuźa.

y u - p u′- z a, *v.* *to make dry, to wipe dry.*

y u s, *cont.* of yuza; yus naźiŋ; yus aya, *to lead.*

y u - s a′, *adv.* *prickly, knobby, sharp; i. q.* owasiŋ pepeya bosdan yaŋka. *T.*, nasa.

y u - s a′- k i m, *adv.* *both together.* *T.*, yusakib.

y u - s a′- k i m - t u, *adv.* *both together.*

y u - s a ŋ′, *v. a.* *to make brownish* or *whitish, to make fade*—mdusaŋ.

y u - s a ŋ′- p a, *v. a.* of saŋpa; *to make more, cause to increase*—mdusaŋpa.

y u - s a′- p a, *v. a.* *to blacken*—mdusapa.

y u - s b a′, *v. a.* *to ravel out; to pick to pieces*, as wool—mdusba, dusba.

y u - s b a′- s b a, *v. red.* of yusba.

y u - s b u′, *v. a.* *to make a rattling* or *rustling noise*, as in taking hold of shelled corn—mdusba. See pasbu.

y u - s b u′- p i - s e, *adv.* *with a noise;* said of one diving. *T.*, *going gradually under* (water) as a swimmer; but *with a noise* is píǵese.

y u - s b u′- s b u, *v. red.* of yusbu.

y u - s d e′- ć a, *v. a.* *to split*—mdusdeća, uŋyusdećapi. *T.*, yusleća.

y u - s d e n′, *cont.* of yusdeća; yusden iyeya. *T.*, yuslel.

y u - s d e n′- k i - y a, *v. a.* *to cause to split*—yusdenwakiya.

y u - s d e n′- y a, *v. a.* *to cause to split*—yusdenwaya.

y u - s d e′- s d e - ć a, *v. red.* of yusdeća.

y u - s d i′, *v. a.* *to press out*, as fat with the hand, *to make ooze out*—mdusdi. *Ih.*, *to milk*, as a cow: *i. q.* yuskića. See yusli.

y u - s d i′- t k a, *v. a.* *to make taper; to make small by pinching*—mdusditka.

y u - s d o′- h a ŋ, *v. a.* *to draw* or *drag along, to draw*, as a horse does a load; *to lead* a horse—mdusdohaŋ.

y u - s d o′- h a ŋ - h a ŋ, *v. red.* of yusdohaŋ.

y u - s d o′- h a ŋ - y a ŋ, *adv.* *dragging along.*

y u - s d o′- h e - k i - y a, *v. a.* *to cause to draw along*—yusdohewakiya.

y u - s d o′- s d o, *v. a.* *to make soft by pressing with the hand*, as an apple—mdusdosdo.

y u - s d u n′, *cont.* of yusduta; yusdun iću *and* yusdun iyeya. *T.*, yuslul.

y u - s d u′- t a, *v. a.* *to pull out, to draw out from under*—mdusduta, dusduta.

y u - s e m′, *cont.* of yusepa; yusem iyeya. *T.*, yuseb.

y u - s e′- p a, *v. a.* *to rub off*, as paint, *to deface; to wear off*, as the skin from the hand—mdusepa. *T.*, yutepa.

yu-ska′, *v. a.* *to whiten, cleanse; to clean up; to gather with the fingers*—mduska, duska.

yu-ska′-ki-ya, *v. a.* *to cause to bleach*—yuskawakiya.

yu-ska′-pi-daŋ-se, *adv.* *in a compact body.*

yu-ska′-pi-se, *adv.* *close together.*

yu-skem′, *cont.* of yuskepa; yuskem iyeya. *T.*, yuskeb.

yu-ske′-pa, *v. a.* *to cause to escape, make evaporate; to drain off*—mduskepa.

yu-ski′-ća, *v. a.* *to press, make tight*—mduskića.

yu-skin′, *cont.* of yuskića *and* yuskita; yuskin iyeya. *T.*, yuskil.

yu-ski′-ski-ća, *v. red.* of yuskića.

yu-ski′-skin, *cont.* of yuskiskića *and* yuskiskita.

yu-ski′-ski-ta, *v. red.* of yuskita; *to wrap round and round*, as in fastening a child on a board—mduskiskita.

yu-ski′-ta, *v. a* *to bind, bandage; to hoop*, as a barrel—mduskita.

yus-ki′-ya, *v. a.* of yuza; *to cause to hold*—yuswakiya.

yu-sku′, *v. a.* *to peel off the skin with the hand; to pare; to shave* or *cut off short*, as hair—mdusku.

yu-sku′-sku, *v. red.* of yusku; *to shave* or *cut off short*, as the hair.

yu-sku′-ya, *v. a.* *to make sweet* or *sour*, etc., *to flavor*—mduskuya.

yu-sli′, *v. a* *T.* *to press out, to milk*, as a cow: *i. q.* yusdi.

yu-smag′, *cont.* of yusmaka; yusmag iyeya.

yu-smag′-sma-ka, *v. red.* of yusmaka.

yu-sma′-ka, *v. a.* *to make a hollow place, indent*—mdusmaka.

yu-sma′-ka, *n.* *a hollow place.* See osmaka.

yu-sma′-sma-ka, *v. red.* of yusmaka.

yu-sma′-sma-ka, *n.* *hollow places.*

yu-smiŋ′, *v. a.* *to pick off*, as meat from a bone—mdusmiŋ.

yu-smiŋ′-smiŋ, *v. red.* of yusmiŋ.

yu-smiŋ′-yaŋ-yaŋ, *v. a.* *to make smooth* or *bare; to wear off smooth*—mdusmiŋyaŋyaŋ.

yu-smi′-smi, *v. red.* of yusmi; *to shave off short*, as hair—mdusmismi.

yu-sna′, *v. a.* *to ring* or *tinkle*, as little bells; *to ravel out*, as a stocking; *to shake off*, as leaves or fruit from a tree—mdusna, dusna.

yu-sna′-sna, *v. red.* of yusna.

yu-sni′, *v. a.* *to put out, extinguish*, as a fire; *to make cold*—mdusni.

yu-sni′-sni, *v. red.* of yusni.

yu-so′, *v. a.* *T.* *to cut in strings* or *strips*, as a hide.

yu-s'o′, *v. n.* *T.* Same as following.

yus-o′, *v. n.* *to swim*, as a duck or muskrat: said of a muskrat when it brings its head above the water: yusoniwaŋ.

y u s - o′ - d a ŋ - k a, *v. n.* *to be slow, to loiter:* ećen mdusodaŋka. *T.*, yus'olaŋka, *to be tired out, used up.*

y u s - o′ - k i - y a, *v. a.* *to cause to swim,* in the manner of a duck—yusowakiya.

y u - s' o′ - l a - k a, *v. n.* *T.* *to be exhausted, tired out.*

y u - s' o′ - l a - s e, *adv.* *T.* *in an exhausted manner,* as one tired.

y u - s o n′, *cont.* of yusota; yuson iyeya. *T.*, yusol.

y u - s o n′ - k i - y a, *v. a.* *to cause to use up*—yusonwakiya.

y u - s o n′ - y a, *v. a.* *to cause to use up*—yusonwaya.

y u - s' o′ - s' o, *v. red.* *T.* of yus'o.

y u s - o s′ - o, *v. red.* of yuso: *i. q.* yus'os'o.

y u - s o′ - t a, *v. a.* *to use up, make an end of, expend*—mdusota, dusota, uŋsotapi.

y u - s p a′ *and* y u - s p e′, *v. a.* *Ih.* and *T.* *to catch with the hand*—mduspa. (*T.*, bluspe): napeyuspe, *to shake hands.* See napeyuza.

y u - s p a′ - i - ć u - s e - m a - n i, *v.* *to limp; to go with a catching gait.* *T.*, huśteśteyakel mani.

y u - s t a ŋ′ - k a, *v. a.* *to moisten*—mdustaŋka.

y u - s t o′, *v. a.* *to smooth down,* as the hair, *to make smooth:* pa yusto, *to oil and smooth the head*—mdusto.

y u - s t o′ - k i - y a, *v. a.* *to cause to make smooth*—yustowakiya.

y u - s t o′ - s t o, *v. red.* of yusto.

y u - s t o′ - y a, *v. a.* *to cause to make smooth*—yustowaya.

y u - s u′, *v. a.* *to make right*—mdusu. *T.*, yuećetu; yuowotaŋla. See yućo.

y u - s u′ - t a, *v. a.* *to make firm*—mdusuta, uŋyusutapi.

y u - s u′ - y a, *v. a.* *to cause to make well*—yusuwaya. *T.*, yuwaśtekiya.

y u - ś a′, *v. a.* *to make red by touching*—mduśa

y u - ś' a g′, *cont.* of yuś'aka.

y u - ś' a g′ - y a, *v. a.* *to overburden, overload*—yuś'agwaya. *T.*, tkeya wakiŋ.

y u - ś' a′ - k a, *v. n.* *to be heavily laden, have as much as one can carry*—mduś'aka, duś'aka. *T.*, tkeya wakiŋ.

y u - ś a m′, *cont.* of yuśapa; yuśam iyeya. *T.*, yuśab.

y u - ś a m′ - y a, *v. a.* *to cause to soil*—yuśamwaya.

y u - ś a′ - p a, *v. a.* *to soil, blacken,* or *defile* any thing—mduśapa, uŋyuśapapi

y u - ś b e′, *v. a.* *to make deep*—mduśbe. *T.*, yuśme.

y u - ś b e′ - y a, *adv.* *deeply;* yuśbeya waŋka.

y u - ś d a′, *v. a.* *to make bare* or *bald; to cut off,* as hair; *to shear,* as sheep; *to pull out,* as grass or weeds, *to weed; to reap; to pick off,* as the feathers of ducks, etc.—mduśda, duśda, uŋśdapi.

y u - ś d a′ - k i - y a, *v. a.* *to cause to pull, pluck,* or *shear off*—yuśdawakiya.

y u - ś d a' - ś d a, *v. red.* of yuśda.

y u - ś d a' - y a, *v a. to uncover; to pull off*—mduśdaya.

y u - ś d a' - y e - h n a, *adv.* of śdayehna; *plainly, manifestly, openly:* yuśdayehna yuza.

y u - ś d i', *v. a. to press* or *squeeze with the hand*—mduśdi.

y u - ś d i' - y a, *adv. pressing:* yuśdiya iyakaśka, *to squeeze up and tie tight.*

y u - ś d o g', *cont.* of yuśdoka; yuśdog iyeya.

y u - ś d o g' - y a, *v. a. to cause to pull off* or *out*—yuśdogwaya.

y u - ś d o' - k a, *v. a. to pull off,* as a garment; *to pull out,* as a cork from a bottle— mduśdoka, uŋśdokapi *and* uŋyuśdokapi.

y u - ś d o' - ś d o - k a, *v. red.* of yuśdoka.

y u - ś d u n', *cont.* of yuśduta; yuśdun iyeya. *T.*, yuślul.

y u - ś d u' - ś d u - t a, *v. red.* of yuśduta; *to make smooth* or *slippery*—mduśduśduta.

y u - ś d u' - t a, *v. a. to slip out, to let slip from* one—mduśduta.

y u - ś' e', *v. a. T. to cause to fall in drops; to make drip.*

y u - ś e' - ć a, *v. a. to deaden, to make dry*—mduśeća.

y u - ś e' - k ś e - ć a, *v. red.* of yuśeća.

y u - ś e n', *cont.* of yuśeća; yuśen iyeya, *to cause to wither. T*, yuśel.

y u - ś' e' - ś' e, *v. red. T.* of yuś'e.

y u - ś i' - ć a, *v. a. to make bad; to injure, spoil*—mduśića. See yuwaȟteśni.

y u - ś i - g l a, *v. T.* yuśigla kta kuwa: *i. q.* pasmi.

y u - ś i' - h d a, *v. a. to make angry*—mudśihda.

y u - ś i' - ȟ a ŋ, *v. a.* of śiȟaŋ; *to make act badly*—mdusiȟaŋ. *T.*, yuoȟaŋśića; yuśića.

y u - ś i' - ȟ a ŋ - y a ŋ, *adv. causing to do badly.*

y u - ś i' - ȟ t i ŋ, *v. a. to enfeeble*—mduśiȟtiŋ, mayuśiȟtiŋ. *T, to make bad; to injure* in any way; *to do a thing badly.*

y u - ś i' - ȟ t i ŋ - p i, *n. feebleness. T., badness; imperfection.*

y u - ś i' - ȟ t i ŋ - y a ŋ, *adv. feebly:* yuśiȟtiŋyaŋ ećoŋpi. *T., badly; imperfectly.*

y u - ś i m', *cont.* of yuśipa; yuśim iyeya. *T.*, yuśib.

y u - ś i m' - ś i - p a, *v. red.* of yuśipa.

y u - ś i ŋ', *v. n. to wrinkle.*

y u - ś i ŋ' - p i, *n. wrinkles.*

y u - ś i ŋ' - ś i ŋ, *v. red.* of yuśiŋ; *to wrinkle.*

y u - ś i ŋ' - ś i ŋ, *v. a. to tickle*—mduśiŋśiŋ. *T.*, yuś'iŋś'iŋ; also *to amuse, make laugh.*

y u - ś i ŋ' - y a - y a, *v. n. to be afraid; to be frightened*—mayuśiŋyaya, niyuśiŋyaya, uŋuśiŋyayapi. *T., to startle, surprise.*

y u - ś i ŋ' - y e - y a, *v. a to frighten, terrify*—yuśiŋyewaya, yuśiŋyeuŋyaŋpi.

y u - ś i' - p a, *v. a. to break off close,* as the limbs of a tree, the teeth of a comb, or projecting pins—mduśipa. *T., to slip past the joint* or *bearing.*

y u - ś k a′, *v. a.* *to loosen, untie*—mduśka, duśka, uŋyuśkapi.

y u - ś k a ŋ′ - ś k a ŋ , *v. a.* *to cause to move about*—mduśkaŋśkaŋ.

y u - ś k e′ - h a ŋ , *v. a.* *to make wild*—mduśkehaŋ.

y u - ś k e′ - h a ŋ - h a ŋ , *v. red.* of yuśkehaŋ; *to make prance about*—mduśkehaŋhaŋ.

y u - ś k i′, *v. a.* *to plait, to gather*—mduśki, uŋyuśkipi.

y u - ś k i′ - ć a , *v. a.* *to press, squeeze, wring*, as clothes (*T.*, same); *to milk*, as a cow (*T.*, yusli)—mduśkića

y u - ś k i n′, *cont.* of yuśkića; pte yuśkin mda, *I go to milk the cow.* *T.*, yuśkil.

y u - ś k i′ - p i, *part.* *plaited, gathered in folds.*

y u - ś k i′ - ś k a , *v. a.* *to make rough, difficult*, or *complicated*—mduśkiśka.

y u - ś k i′ - ś k e - y a , *v. a.* *to cause to make difficult*—yuśkiśkewaya.

y u - ś k i′ - ś k i - ć a , *v. red.* of yuśkića.

y u - ś k o′ - k p a , *v. a.* *to hollow out*, as a trough—mduśkokpa.

y u - ś k o m′, *cont.* of yuśkopa; yuśkom iyeya. *T.*, yuśkob.

y u - ś k o′ - p a , *v. a.* *to bend, to make crooked* or *twisting*—mduśkopa.

y u - ś k o′ - ś k o - p a , *v. red.* of yuśkopa.

y u - ś k o′ - t p a , *v. a.* *to hollow*—mduśkotpa. *T.*, yuśkokpa.

y u - ś k u′, *v. a.* *to shell off*, as corn with the hands—mduśku.

y u - ś k u′ - ś k u , *v. red.* of yuśku.

y u - ś n a′, *v. a.* *to drop* any thing, *to let slip, to make a mistake*—mduśna, duśna, uŋśnapi.

y u - ś n a′ - k o ŋ - z a , *v.* (yuśna *and* koŋza) *to pretend to make a mistake*—yuśnawakoŋza.

y u - ś n a′ - p i , *n.* *a mistake.*

y u - ś n a′ - ś n a , *v. red.* of yuśna; *to try to catch and fail often, to miss*—mduśnaśna.

y u - ś n i′ - ś n i - ź a , *v. red.* of yuśniźa.

y u - ś n i′ - ź a , *v. a.* *to cause to wither*—mduśniźa.

y u - ś o′ - ś a , *v. a.* *to make muddy, to roil up*—mduśośa.

y u - ś p a′, *v. a.* *to break off, to separate from, to detach; to break loose from, break away, escape; to free from; to break open; to divide*—mduśpa, uŋyuśpapi: ihduśpa, *to free one's self from.*

y u - ś p a′ - p i , *n.* *fractions;* topa yuśpapi waŋźi, *one-fourth;* kiyuśpapi, *division.*

y u - ś p a′ - ś p a , *v. red.* of yuśpa; *to break in pieces*—mduśpaśpa.

y u - ś p i′, *v. a.* *to pick* or *gather*, as berries; *to pull off*—mduśpi, uŋśpipi.

y u - ś p i′ - ś p i , *v. red.* of yuśpi.

y u - ś p u′, *v. a.* *to pick off with the hand* any thing that *adheres, to pull off*—mduśpu.

y u - ś p u′ - ś p u , *v. red.* of yuśpu.

y u - ś p u′ - ś p u - p i , *n.* *pieces broken off; slugs.*

y u - ś p u′ - ś p u - y a , *v. red.* of yuśpuya.

yu-śpu′-ya, *v. a.* *to scratch,* as the skin when it itches—mduśpuya, uŋyuśpuyapi.

yu-śtaŋ′, *v. a.* *to finish* any thing; *to perfect*—mduśtaŋ, duśtaŋ, uŋśtaŋpi *and* uŋyuśtaŋpi. See yaśtaŋ, etc.

yu-śta′-śta, *v.* *to soak a skin preparatory to dressing it*—mduśtaśta.

yu-śuś′, *cont.* of yuśuźa; yuśuś iyeya.

yu-śu′-śu-źa, *v. red.* of yuśuźa.

yu-śu′-źa, *v. a.* *to crush,* as bones—mduśuźa. *T., to break in slivers,* as a tough piece of wood, by *twisting; to break,* as a bear does the bushes in getting cherries, or as a tent pole *slivered.* See yuḣuġa, yuḣdeća, yumdeća, etc.

yu′-ta, *v. a.* *to eat* any thing—wata, yata, uŋtapi: taku yutapi, *something to eat, food.*

yu-ta′-hen-la, *v. a.* *T.* *to make nearer; to put towards:* yutahenla iću, *to draw it this way* or *towards himself.*

yu-ta′-kiŋ, *v. a.* *to cause to lean*—mdutakiŋ.

yu-ta′-kiŋ-yaŋ, *adv.* *leaning.*

yu-ta′-ku-ni-śni, *v. a.* *to destroy*—mdutakuniśni.

yu-ta′-ku-ni-śni-yaŋ, *adv. destroying.*

yu-ta′-ku-śni, *v. a.* *to bring to naught; to frustrate*—mdutakuśni.

yu-taŋ′, *v. a* *to honor, glorify*—mdutaŋ. See yuwitaŋ.

yu-t'aŋ′, *v. a.* *to touch, to feel; to pull, stretch* (*i. q.* yutitaŋ)—mdut'aŋ.

yu-taŋ′-ćo-daŋ, *v. a.* *to make naked*—mdutaŋćodaŋ.

yu-taŋ′-iŋ, *v. a.* *to make manifest, to expose*—mdutaŋiŋ.

yu-taŋ′-iŋ-yaŋ, *adv.* *manifestly.*

yu-taŋ′-ka, *v. a.* *to make great* or *large, to enlarge*—mdutaŋka

yu-taŋ′-ka-ya, *adv.* *largely, greatly.*

yu-taŋ′-ni, *v a.* *to make old, to wear out*—mdutaŋni.

yu-taŋ′-ni-ka, *v. a.* *to wear out,* as clothes; *to make old*—mdutaŋnika

yu-t'aŋ′-pi, *n.* *T.* *semen: i. q.* hiyáye.

yu-t'aŋ′-t'aŋ, *v. red.* of yut'aŋ.

yu-taŋ′-toŋ, *v. a.* *to make last well, to make substantial*—mdutaŋtoŋ.

yu-taŋ′-toŋ-śni, *v. a.* *to use up, expend*—mdutaŋtoŋśni.

yu-taŋ′-toŋ-śni-yaŋ, *adv. expending.*

yu-taŋ′-yaŋ, *adv.* *praising.*

yu-ta′-om, *adv.* *leaning:* yutaom ehde, *to place leaning.* *T.,* yutaob.

yu-ta′-oŋ-pa, *v. n.* *to lean* See yutaom.

yu-ta′-ta, *v. a.* *to shake off,* as dust from a garment; *to scrape* or *brush off with the hand*—mdutata.

yu-te′-ća, *v. a.* *to make new, renew*—mduteća, duteća, uŋyutećapi.

yu-te′-haŋ, *v. a.* *to put off, prolong; to make slow, retard*—mdutehaŋ.

yu-te′-ḣi-ka, *v. a.* *to make difficult, make hard to be endured*—mduteḣika.

y u - t e m', *cont.* of yutepa; yutem iyeya. *T.*, yuteb.

y u - t e m' - t e - p a, *v. red.* of yutepa.

y u - t e' - p a, *v. a.* *to wear off short*—mdutepa. *T.*, *to rub off*, as paint.

y u - t i' - ć a, *v. a.* *to scrape away*, as snow, *with the hand; to paw*, as a horse does—mdutića.

y u - t i m', *cont.* of yutipa; yutim iyeya. *T.*, yutib.

y u - t i m' - t i - p a, *v. red.* of yutipa.

y u - t i n', *cont.* of yutića; yutin iyeya. *T.*, yutil.

y u - t i ŋ' - t a, *v. a.* *to pull out long hairs, to strip off long hairs*—mdutiŋta. *T.*, yupiŋźa.

y u - t i' - p a, *v. a.* *to cramp*, as muscles; *to make crisp* or *draw up*, as burnt leather. *T.*—See natipa.

y u - t i' - t a ŋ, *v. a.* *to pull*—mdutitaŋ, dutitaŋ.

y u - t i' - t a ŋ - y a ŋ, *v. a.* *to cause to pull at*—yutitaŋwaya.

y u - t k a ŋ' - l a, *n.* *T.* *much, abundance.*

y u - t k e' - y a, *adv.* *deeply;* said of a bluff shore where the water is deep, *i. q.* yukseya.

y u - t k i' - t k a, *v.* yutkitka yuza, *to take hold of a bunch* of any thing.

y u - t k o' - ġ a, *v. a.* *T.* *to lock* or *fasten*, as a door.

y u - t k u' - ġ a, *v. a.* *to break off square*—mdutkuġa. *T.*, *to break off;* but *to break off square* is otkoŋs yuksa.

y u - t k u ħ', *cont.* of yutkuġa; yutkuħ iyeya.

y u - t k u ŋ s', *cont.* of yutkuŋza; yutkuŋs iyeya.

y u - t k u ŋ' - t k u ŋ - t a, *v.* See yukuŋtkuŋta.

y u - t k u ŋ' - z a *or* y u - t k o ŋ - z a, *v. a.* *to cut off even*, as with shears—mdutkuŋza. *T.*, yuotkuŋza. See oyutkoŋza.

y u - t k u' - t k u - ġ a, *v. red.* of yutkuġa; *to break* or *divide in several pieces.*

y u - t o g' - y e, *v a.* *to make different.* See yutokeća.

y u - t o' - k a ŋ, *v. a.* *to put in another place, remove; to reject*—mdutokaŋ.

y u - t o' - k a ŋ - k a ŋ, *v. red.* of yutokaŋ; yutokaŋkaŋ iyeya, *to scatter abroad.*

y u - t o' - k a ŋ - y a ŋ, *adv.* *in another place, removed:* yutokaŋyaŋ iyeya.

y u - t o' - k e - ć a, *v. a.* *to make different, to alter*—mdutokeća.

y u - t o' - n a - n a, *v. a.* *to diminish*—mdutonana. *T.*, yućonala.

y u - t o' - t o, *v. a.* *to clear off*, as a field—mdutoto.

y u - t o' - t o m - y a, *v. a.* of yutotopa; *to soak and make soft*—yutotomwaya. *T.*, yutotobya.

y u - t o' - t o - p a, *v. n.* *to become soft*, as leather, *by soaking.* See yututupa.

y u - t p a', *v. a.* noġe yutpa, *to make deaf;* iśta yutpa, *to make blind:* yutpapi se haŋ *and* yutpapi se iyeya. See yukpa.

y u - t p a ŋ', *v. a.* *to mash* or *grind fine*, as corn—mdutpaŋ. See yukpaŋ.

yu-tpaŋ′-tpaŋ, *v. red.* of yutpaŋ.

yu-tpa′-tpa, *v. red.* of yutpa.

yu-tpi′, *v. a.* *to crack with the fingers*—mdutpi. See yukpi.

yu-tpi′-tpi, *v. red.* of yutpi.

yu-tpu′-tpa, *v. a.* *to crumble and throw about; to mix up together*—mdutputpa. See yukpukpa.

yu-tug′-tu-ka, *v. red.* of yutuka; *to pick to pieces*, as furs.

yu-tuḣ′-ye-la, *adv.* *T.* *bent, doubled up:* yutuḣyela mani, *to walk bent over*, as an old man. See pakśayela.

yu-tu′-ka, *v. a.* *to pull off* or *destroy*, as fur; *to spoil*—mdutuka: yutukahaŋ, *to be pulling off*, as hair, etc.

yu-tu′-ka-ka, *v. red.* of yutuka; *to bend up, to hurt*, as in a trap; *to destroy*—mdutukaka.

yu-tu′-ta, *v. a.* *to make smart*—mdututa.

yu-tu′-tka, *v. a.* *to break in small pieces*—mdututka.

yu-tu-tu-ka, *v. red.* of yutuka.

yu-tu′-tu-pa, *v. a.* *to make slimy* or *slippery*—mdututupa. See yutotopa.

yu-ṭa′, *v. a.* *to kill;* poskin yuṭa, *to choke to death* (*T.*, yuṭa), *kill by hanging* (*T.*, pa nakseya)—mduṭa.

yu-ṭiŋs′, *cont.* of yuṭiŋza; yuṭiŋs iyeya.

yu-ṭiŋs′-ṭiŋ-za, *v. red.* of yuṭiŋza.

yu-ṭiŋ′-za, *v. a.* *to draw tight, to tighten*—mduṭiŋza.

yu-wa′-ćiŋ-hiŋ-yaŋ-za, *v. a.* *to make cross*—mduwaćiŋhiŋyaŋza.

yu-wa′-ćiŋ-ko, *v. a.* *T.* *to make angry.* See yawaćiŋko, etc.

yu-wa′-ćiŋ-ksa-pa, *v. a.* *to make wise*—mduwaćiŋksapa.

yu-wa′-ćiŋ-taŋ-ka, *v. a.* *to make magnanimous; to make obstinate*—mduwaćiŋtaŋka.

yu-wa′-ćiŋ-toŋ, *v. a.* *to make intelligent*—mduwaćiŋtoŋ.

yu-wa′-ḣba-daŋ, *v. a.* *to make gentle*—mduwaḣbadaŋ.

yu-wa′-ḣba-ka, *v. a.* *to make mild* or *gentle*—mduwaḣbaka.

yu-wa′-ḣpa-ni-ća, *v. a.* *to make poor* — mduwaḣpanića, mayuwaḣpanića.

yu-wa′-ḣte-śni, *v. a.* *to make bad, do badly*—mduwaḣteśni. See yuśića.

yu-wa′-kaŋ, *v. a.* *to set apart, consecrate*—mduwakaŋ.

yu-wa′-kaŋ-yaŋ, *adv.* *consecrating*

yu-waŋg′, *cont.* of yuwaŋka; yuwaŋg iyeya. *T.*, yuuŋg.

yu-waŋ′-ka, *v. a* *to throw down, to make lie down; to demolish*—mduwaŋka. *T.*, yuuŋka.

yu-waŋ′-ka-daŋ, *v. a.* *to make soft* or *tender*—mduwaŋkadaŋ.

yu-waŋ′-kan, *v.* yuwankan iću, *to lift* or *raise up;* yuwaŋkan iyeya. *T.*, yuwaŋkaŋl.

yu-waŋ′-kan-tu-ya, *adv.* *upwards, above.*

yu-waŋ′-kaŋ′-yaŋ, *adv.* *up.*

y u - w a′ - ś ' a g, *cont* of yuwaś'aka; yuwaś'ag iyeya.

y u - w a′ - ś ' a g - y a, *v. a. to cause to make strong*—yuwaś'agwaya.

y u - w a′ - ś ' a - k a, *v. a. to make strong, strengthen* — mduwaś'aka, mduwaś'akapi.

y u - w a′ - ś a - k a - d a ŋ, *v. a. to make cheap* or *easy*—mduwaśakadaŋ.

y u - w a′ - ś ' a - k e - ś n i, *v. a. to make weak, enfeeble*—mduwaś'akeśni.

y u - w a′ - ś t e, *v. a. to make good, to bless*—mduwaśte, uŋyuwaśtepi.

y u - w e′ - ć i, *v.* See yueći.

y u - w e′ - ġ a, *v. a. to break*, as a stick, with the hands, but not entirely off; *to break*, as a bone—mduweġa, uŋyuweġapi. See yuksa, yumdeća, etc.

y u - w e ḣ′, *cont.* of yuweġa; yuweḣ iyeya.

y u - w e ḣ′ - w e - ġ a, *v. red.* of yuweġa.

y u - w e ḣ′ - w e ḣ, *cont.* of yuweḣweġa.

y u - w e ḣ′ - y a, *v. a. to cause to break*, etc., yuweḣwaya.

y u - w i′, *v. a. to wrap around, bind up, bandage*—mduwi, uŋyuwipi.

y u - w i′ - ć a - k a, *v. a. to make true; to prove, convince; to show that a cause is true, to establish it*—mduwićaka.

y u - w i′ - ć a - k e - y a - ḣ ć a, *adv. T.* yuwićakeyaḣća oyaka, *to tell a thing not as it is, to make a thing appear true by telling it as true.* See yawićakeyaḣća.

y u - w i′ - ć a - k e - y a - s e, *adv T.* Same meaning.

y u - w i′ - ć a - ś t a, *v. a. to make manly:* yuwićaśta se uŋ, *one who is bad but always wishes to be thought good.* See wićaśa.

y u - w i′ - ć a - ś t a - ś n i, *v. a. to seduce, corrupt*—mduwićaśtaśni. *T.*, yuwićaśaśni, *to make mean.*

y u - w i′ - h n u - n i, *v. a. to cause to perish, to destroy*—mduwihnuni.

y u - w i′ - h n u - n i - y a ŋ, *v. a. to cause to destroy*—yuwihnuniwaya.

y u - w i′ - n o - ḣ i ŋ - ć a, *v. a. to make a woman of, to render effeminate*—mduwinoḣiŋća. *T.*, yuwiŋyaŋ.

y u - w i ŋ′ - ġ a, *v a. to turn around, turn back*—mduwiŋġa.

y u - w i ŋ ḣ′, *cont.* of yuwiŋġa; yuwiŋḣ iyeya.

y u - w i ŋ ḣ′ - w i ŋ - ġ a, *v. red.* of yuwiŋġa.

y u - w i ŋ ḣ′ - y a, *adv. coming round:* yuwiŋḣya hdiću.

y u - w i ŋ ś′, *cont.* of yuwiŋźa; yuwiŋś iyeya.

y u - w i ŋ ś′ - w i ŋ - ź a, *v. red.* of yuwiŋźa.

y u - w i ŋ ś′ - y a, *v. a. to cause to bend down*—yuwiŋśwaya.

y u - w i ŋ′ - t a, *v. a. to spread out the hands, to worship; to salute.* The ceremony of salutation among the Dakotas consists in extending the hand towards the person saluted It is, however, I believe, confined to their feasts. *T.*, ite yuwiŋta, *to salute*, as the Dakotas do when they desire peace, etc.; *to spread both hands out toward* or *over the face* of another *in salutation; to wipe the face* of another *with the hands*, not actually, but *in gesture*—a sign of friendly salutation. *To smooth with the hands, to spread out the hands* is yuġata.—W. J. C. See yusto.

y u - w i ŋ' y a ŋ - k e - s e, *adv. T.*, yuwiŋyaŋkese uŋ, *one who is a bad woman, but who wishes to be thought good.*

y u - w i ŋ' - ź a, *v. a. to bend* or *break down*—mduwiŋźa. *T., to make limber* or *pliant.* See yukikita

y u - w i' - t a ŋ, *v. a. to honor* one, *to glorify*—mduwitaŋ. See yutaŋ.

y u - w i' - t a - y a, *v. a. to collect together, assemble*—mduwitaya.

y u - w i' - t a - y a, *adv. all together, assembled.*

y u - w i' - t k o, *v. a. to make drunk*—mduwitko.

y u - w i' - t k o - t k o, *v. a. to make foolish*—mduwitkotko.

y u - w i' - t k o - t k o - k a, *v. a. to make foolish*—mduwitkotkoka.

y u - w i' - y a - k p a *and* y u - w i' - y a - t p a, *v. a. to make shine.*

y u - w i' - y a - y a, *v. a. to make ready, prepare. T.*, yuwiyeya.

y u - w i' - y e - y a, *v. a. to make ready, prepare*—mduwiyeya.

y u - w o' - h d u - z e, *v. a. to make* wohduze—mduwohduze.

y u - w o' - h d u - z e - t o ŋ, *v. a. to consecrate, dedicate*—yuwohduzewatoŋ.

y u - w o' - s e, *v. T.* yuwose iću, *to tie in a bow knot.* See yuoseya *and* yuośiŋ.

y u' - z a, *v. a. to take hold of, catch, hold; to take a wife*—mduza, duza, uŋzapi.

y u - z a' - h a ŋ, *v. a. to make a noise,* as by tearing cloth—mduzahaŋ.

y u - z a' - m n i, *v. a. to open, uncover;* (*T., to spread out,* as a cloth); *to open out,* as a door—mduzamni: yuzamni ehde, *to set open.*

y u - z a' - m n i - h a ŋ, *adv. standing open:* yuzamnihaŋ ehde.

y u - z a' - m n i - m n i, *v. red.* of yuzamni.

y u - z a ŋ', *v. a. to part* or *separate,* as high grass; *to push aside* or *raise up,* as a curtain—mduzaŋ See kazaŋ, pazaŋ, zaŋzaŋ, etc.

y u - z a' - p a - p i - s e, *adv. with a rush, impetuously:* yuzapapise napeuŋyaŋpi. *T.*, ķosela.

y u - z e', *v. a. to dip, lade out,* as food from a kettle; *to skim*—mduze, duze, uŋzepi.

y u - z i' - ć a, *v. a. to stretch,* as a skin—mduzića.

y u - z i g' - z i - ć a, *v. red.* of yuzića; *to stretch, make pliable*—mduzigzića.

y u - z i n', *cont.* of yuzića; *stretching:* en yuzin amaupi, *they stretch it to me, they charge all upon me:* yuzin iću, *to stretch. T.*, yuzil.

y u - z o g', *cont.* of yuzoka; yuzog iću.

y u - z o' - k a, *v. a. to stretch out from one*—mduzoka.

y u - z u n'- y a, *adv.* *connectedly.* *T.*, icikoyaka.

y u - z u n' - ć a, *v. a.* *to connect.* See yuzuŋta.

y u - z u ŋ' - ć a - y a, *adv.* *connectedly.*

y u - z u ŋ' - t a, *v. a.* *to connect*—mduzuŋta.

y u - ź a', *v. a.* *to mash; to stir up*, as mush, *to make mush*—mduźa, uŋyuźapi.

y u - ź a g', *cont.* of yuźaka; yuźag iẏeya.

y u - ź a' - h a ŋ, *v. a.* *to make a jarring noise*—mduźahaŋ. See źahaŋ.

y u - ź a' - h a ŋ, *adj.* *sounding.*

y u - ź a' - h e - y a, *adv.* *sounding, harshly.* See źaheya.

y u - ź a' - k a, *v. a.* *to pull open, strain open*, as the eyes—mduźaka.

y u - ź a' - p i, *part.* *mixed up*, as mush; *i. q.* woźapi.

y u - ź a' - ź a, *v. a.* *to wash*, as clothes, etc.—mduźaźa, duźaźa, uŋźaźapi *and* uŋyuźaźapi.

y u - ź i b' - y e - l a, *adv.* *T.* *pinching up with the fingers; i. q.* yuġimnana.

y u - ź i m', *cont.* of yuźipa; yuźim iyeya. *T.*, yuźib.

y u - ź i m' - n a - n a, *adv.* *pinching a little:* yuźimnana mduza. *T.*, yuźibnala.

y u - ź i m' - ź i - p a, *v. red.* of yuźipa.

y u - ź i ŋ', *v. a.* *to stretch out*, as a skin on a board or stick—mduźiŋ.

y u - ź i ŋ' - ć a, *v. a.* *to pull* or *blow*, as the nose—mduźiŋća: poġe yuźiŋća.

y u - ź i' - p a, *v. a.* *to pinch*—mduźipa, mayuźipa.

y u - ź i p' - ź i - p a. See yuźimźipa.

y u - ź o', *v. a.* *to scratch*—mduźo. *T.*, *to whistle to; to scratch* is yuġo.

y u - ź o' - h a ŋ, *n.* *a scratch.* *T.*, yuġo.

y u - ź o' - ź o, *v. red* of yuźo; *to scratch* or *make rough*, as cats, *by clawing*—mduźoźo. *T.*, *to whistle to.*

y u - ź u ŋ', *v. a.* *to pull out by the roots*, as a tooth or quill; *to pull up*, as any thing growing—mduźuŋ.

y u - ź u ŋ' - t a, *v. a.* *T.* *to thrust into;* iśta yuźuŋta, *to thrust* something *into the eye and make it water.*

y u - ź u' - ź u, *v. a.* *to tear down, destroy, deface; to pull in pieces, undo, open*, as a bundle; *to make void*, as an agreement, etc.—mduźuźu, uŋyuźuźupi *and* uŋźuźupi.

Z.

z, *the twenty-eighth letter of the Dakota alphabet*, with the same sound as in English.

za. See yuza.

za-haŋ', *adj.* See zazahaŋ.

Za'-ke, *n. p.* *the Sac* or *Sauk Indians.*

za'-mni. See yuzamni.

za'-mni-haŋ, *part.* *uncovered*

za'-mni-wa-haŋ, *part.* *uncovered.*

za-ni', *adj.* *well, not sick*—mazani, uŋzanipi; also said of a part of the country from which the game has not been hunted, *unmolested.*

za-ni'-ka, *adj.* *healthy, sound, well*—mazanika. *T.*, taŋzanika.

za-ni'-ken, *adv.* *in health.* *T.*, taŋzani.

za-ni'-yaŋ, *adv.* *well, in health;* zaniyaŋ wauŋ. *T.*, taŋzaniyaŋ.

za-ni'-yaŋ-ken, *adv.* *in health.* *T.*, taŋzanikel.

zaŋ-zaŋ, *adv.* *separate, standing far apart*, as stalks of grass. See yuzaŋ, etc.

zaŋ-zaŋ'-na, *adv.* *scattered, standing far apart.* *T.*, zaŋzaŋla.

za'-ptaŋ, *num. adj.* *five.*

za'-ptaŋ-ki-ya, *adv.* *in five ways, in five places.*

za'-ptaŋ-na, *adv.* *only five.* *T.*, zaptaŋla.

za'-ptaŋ-ptaŋ, *adv.* *by fives, five apiece.*

za-za'-haŋ, *adj.* *ragged.* See zahaŋ, kaza, etc.; also *T.*, ḣ'eḣ'e *and* sbaka.

ze, *adj.* *disturbed* See ćanze.

ze'-ka, *adj.* *disturbed.* See ćanzeka.

ze'-ya, *v. a.* *to make angry*—zewaya, zemayaŋ. *T.*, ćaŋzeya.

ze-ze'-ya, *adv.* *swinging:* zezeya ehnaka. *T.*, also *dangling*, as earrings

zi, *adj.* *yellow.*

zib-zi'-pe-daŋ, *adj.* *thin, fine*, as silk or fine cloth.

zi'-ća. See yuzića.

zi-ća', *n* *the reddish grey squirrel*, common in the Dakota country.

zi'-ća, *n.* *the partridge* or *pheasant.*

zi-ća'-ḣo-ta, *n.* *the common grey squirrel, the grey ground squirrel.*

zi'-ća-taŋ-ka, *n.* *the turkey.* *T.*, wagleksuŋtaŋka.

zi'-ća-ti-hda-bu-daŋ, *n.* *the drumming partridge.*

zig-zi'-ća, *adj.* *flimsy, not firm; elastic.*

zin-ya', *v. a.* *to smoke, fumigate*—zinwaya. *T.*, zilya.

zi'-pe-daŋ, *adj.* *thin, fine.* See zibzipedaŋ.

zip-zi'-pe-daŋ, *adj.* See zibzipedaŋ.

zi'-ta, *v. n.* *to smoke.* See izita.

zi-tka', *n.* *a bird, birds* of all kinds.

zi-tka'-ćaŋ-ḣpaŋ-na, *n.* *a small bird with a large bill.*

zi-tka'-daŋ, *n.* *the generic name for small birds.*

zi-tka'-na, *n.* *Ih.* *i. q.* zitkadaŋ.

zi-tka'-na-i-pa-ta-pi, *n.* *Ih.* *moss; mold.*

zi-tka'-sdi-daŋ, *n.* *a kind of bird.*

zi-tka'-taŋ-ka, *n.* *the common blackbird.* *T.*, wáḣpataŋka.

zi-tka'-to, *n.* *T.* *the blue jay.*

zi-tka'-wa-kaŋ-taŋ-haŋ, *n.* *the magpie, i. q.* uŋkćekiḣa.

zi-ya', *v. a.* *to dye* or *paint yellow*—ziwaya.

zi-ya', *adj.* *yellowish.*

zi-ya'-to, *adj.* *green:* from zi *and* to.

zi-zi', *adj.* *red.* of zi; *yellow.*

zi-zi'-pe-daŋ, *adj.* *fine, thin.* See zibzipedaŋ.

zo-he'-la, *adv.* *T.* *slowly: i. q.* slohe se; iwaśtela.

zoŋ'-ta, *adj.* *T.* *honest; trustworthy.* See zuŋta.

zoŋ'-ta'-he-ća, *n.* *T.* *an honest person.*

zoŋ-ta'-he-ya, *adv.* *T.* *in close succession; connectedly.*

zu-haŋ', *adj.* *striped.* *T.*, gleglézela.

zu-haŋ'-haŋ, *adj.* *red. striped.* *i. q.* zuzuhaŋ.

zu-he'-ya, *adv.* *in a striped manner.* *T.*, gleglezela.

zun-ya', *adv.* *well, correctly; joined:* zunya ećamoŋ. *T.*, taŋyeḣćiŋ. See zuŋta.

zun-ya'-ken, *adv.* *well, correctly.*

zuŋ'-ća, *adj.* *joined together, connected; braided, woven.*

zuŋ'-ća-ya, *adv.* *connectedly.* See zoŋtaheya *and* ićikoyagya.

zuŋ'-ta, *adj.* *connected, braided, woven together.*

zuŋ'-te-śni, *adj.* *incorrect, disjoined,* as language.

zuŋ-ya'-kel, *adv.* *T.* *well; finely:* iyeś kalaka zuŋyakel woglaka, *he speaks eloquently.*

zuŋ-ziŋ'-ća, *n.* *the yellow-hammer,* a kind of bird. *T*, suŋzića.

zu-ya', *v. n.* *to go on a war party, to make war; to lead out a war party*—zuwaya, zuyaya, zuuŋyaŋpi.

zu-ye'-ćiŋ, *n.* (zuye *and* ćiŋ) *the maker* or *leader of a war party.*

zu-ze' ća, *n.* *T.* *a rattlesnake.*

zu-zu'-haŋ, *adj.* *striped.* *T.*, gleġleġa, gleglezela.

zu-zu'-he-ća-daŋ, *n.* *the common striped ground snake.*

Ź

ź, *the twenty-ninth letter of the Dakota alphabet*, having nearly the sound of the French *j* or English *zh*.

ź a . See yuźa.

ź a g , *cont.* of źata.

ź a g - ź a n′ - y a , *adv. red.* of źanya; *forkedly*.

ź a g - ź a′ - t a , *adj.red.* of źata; *forked, brushy, rough*.

ź a - h a ŋ′, *adj. rough, harsh, making a loud noise*, as an animal; ho źahaŋ. See yuźahaŋ.

ź a - h a ŋ′ - h a ŋ , *adj. rough, unpleasant, grating:* ho źahaŋhaŋ.

ź a - h e′ - s a , *adv. T. i. q.* źaheya: źahesa ap'a, *to strike and make a loud noise*.

ź a - h e′ - y a , *adv. roughly, harshly, not melodious*, as the voice: źaheya ia. See yuźaheya

ź a′ - k a , *adj. rolling* or *straining*, as the eyes. See yuźaka.

ź a l - y a′, *adv. T.* źalya wiyukćaŋ, *to be of two minds, to be undecided: i. q.* ćanźalya.

ź a n , *cont.* of źata. *T.*, źal.

ź a n - y a′, *adv. forkedly:* źanya haŋ. *T.*, źalya.

ź a ŋ - ź a ŋ′, *n. a vial, a bottle, a glass* of any kind, *window-glass:* śina źaŋźaŋ, *a red blanket*, so called by the Missouri Indians.

ź a ŋ - ź a ŋ′ - h d e - p i , *n. a window.* See oźaŋźaŋhdepi.

ź a′ - t a , *adj. forked*, as a stick, stream, etc.; *double* or *forked, lying* or *false*, as the tongue: ćeźi źata, *to lie, speak falsely.* Henok says this use of the word has been introduced by white people. See ġata.

ź a - ź a′. See yuźaźa.

ź a - ź a′ - y a , *adj. exposed; i. q.* śdayehna: *clearly, plainly; i. q.* taŋiŋyaŋ.

ź a - ź a′ - y e - l a , *adv. T. clearly, distinctly:* źaźayela waŋyaka, *i. q.* kaźaźa waŋyaka.

ź i , *adj. thin* and *briskly*, as the hair on the hands and arms, also like a young duck: pteźićadaŋ ha kiŋ he "źi."

ź i′ - ć a , *adj. rich*—maźića. See iźića *and* wiźića.

ź i - ć a′ - k a , *adj. rich*—maźićaka.

ź i - ć e′ - n a , *Ih.* and *T. i. q.* zićadaŋ. See ptezićadaŋ.

ź i′ - d a ŋ , *adj. thin* and *briskly*, as hair. See źi.

ź i n - y a′, *v. a. to make rich*—źinwaya. See wiźinya

ź i n - y a′, *adv. richly. T.*, źilya. See źića.

ź i n - y e′ - ć a , *v. a. to make rich*—zinwayeća.

ź i ŋ′, *v. n. to stand erect, stiffen up*—maźiŋ. See yuźiŋ, ćeźiŋ, etc.

ź i ŋ - ć a′, *v. n. to snuff up; to hiss*—waźiŋća, uŋźiŋćapi. *T., to blow out from the nose, to blow the nose. To snuff up* is yaźiŋća; *to hiss* is s'a. See yuźiŋća.

ź i'-p a. See kaźipa.

ź i-p a'-h a ŋ, *part.* See źipaheća.

ź i-p a'-h e-ć a, *part. becoming smooth* or *hollowed out of itself, i. q.* ḣ'apeća *T.*, źipawahaŋ.

ź i'-y a, *adv. thin and standing up*, as hair; *thin, scattered, and sparkling* in the sunbeams.

ź i-y e'-l a, *adv. T. thinly, sparsely*, as hair on the hands

ź i-ź i', *v. to whisper*—waźiźi, yaźiźi, uŋźiźipi.

ź i-ź i'-d o-w a ŋ, *v. to sing in a low, whispering, drawling manner*, as the Dakota women do when lulling their infants to sleep—źiźiwadowaŋ, źiźiuŋdowaŋpi.

ź i-ź i'-y a, *adv. red.* of źiya; *standing up*, as the hair on one's hand.

ź i-ź i'-y a-h a ŋ, *adv. whispering.*

ź o, *v. to whistle*, as a man does—waźo, yaźo, uŋźopi.

ź o-ź o', *v. red.* of źo; *to whistle, whistle for*, as for young ducks—waźoźo, uŋźoźopi. See kiźoźo.

ź o-ź o'-d o-w a ŋ, *v. to whistle a tune*—źoźowadowaŋ.

ź o-ź o'-k a, *n. a fish-hawk.*

ź o-ź o'-y a g-t o ŋ, *adv. T. in a noose:* źoźoyagtoŋ iću yo, *make it into a noose.* See śuŋgźoyake.

ź o-ź o'-y a-k e, *n. T. a noose* or *slip-knot.*

ź u, *v. a. to put, place, lay up*—waźu, yaźu, uŋźupi. See aźu, oźu, etc.

ź u ŋ. See yuźuŋ.

ź u'-ź u. See kaźuźu, etc.

ź u-ź u'-h a ŋ, *part.* See źuźuwahaŋ

ź u-ź u'-w a-h a ŋ, *part. broken, fallen to pieces, demolished*, as a house; *become loose*, etc.

APPENDIX.

While the copy for this edition of the Dictionary was in the course of preparation, some correspondence was had with Rev. W. J. Cleveland, of Rosebud Agency, in regard to furnishing on a somewhat extended scale the Titoŋwaŋ forms of the Language. But it was not known that he could undertake the task until after the work had gone into the hands of the printer. When his first installment of notes came thirty pages had been electrotyped. It was important that, in some form, these words should appear in the Dictionary. Hence these, with other words, some of them not Titoŋwaŋ, that have come from various quarters during the progress of the work, are here given in an appendix.

S. R. RIGGS.

A.

a-ba′-gla *and* a-wa′-gla, *v.* *T.* *i. q.* abahda. The Titoŋwaŋ dialect always changes "hd" of the Santee into "gl;" and generally, but not always, the prefix "ba" is changed to "wa," and "bo," to "wo."

a-ba′-śla, *v.* *T.* *i. q.* abaśda.

a-bi′-li-he-ća, *v.* *T.* *i. q.* aminiheća. Here it will be noted that "m" is changed to "b," and "n" to "l."

a-bi′-li-hel-ya, *adv.* *T.* *i q.* aminihenya.

a-bla′-ke-la, *adv.* *T.* *i. q.* amdakedaŋ.

a-bla′-ya, *adv.* *T.* *i. q.* amdaya.

a-ble′-ća, *adv.* *T.* *i. q.* amdeća.

a-bles′, *cont.* *i. q.*, amdes.

a-bles′-ya-kel, *adv.* *T.* *i. q.* amdesyaken.

a-ćaŋ′-te-śil-ya, *adv.* *T.* *i. q.* aćaŋteśinya.

a-ćaŋ′-te-śil-ya-kel, *adv.* *T.* *i. q.* aćaŋteśinyaken.

a-ćeb′-ya, *v.* *T.* *i. q.* aćemya.

a-ćeb′-ya-kel, *adv.* *T.* *i. q.* aćemyaken.

a-će′-sli, *v. and n.* *T.* *i. q.* aćesdi.

a′-e-ta-gnag-ya, *adv.* *T.* *i. q.* aetahnagya: "h" becomes "g" in the combinations "hd," "hm" and "hn."

a′-e-ta-gla-ka, *v.* *T.* *i. q.* aetahnaka.

a-gla′-gla, *adv.* *T.* *along-side of, in front of;* aglagla iŋyaŋka, *to run in front of* one.

a-gla′-haŋ, *v. n.* *T.* *to slip* or *slide out,* as a tent-pole when a number are dragged along.

a-gla′-ptus, *cont. adv.* *T.* *prone;* aglaptus iḣpaya, *to fall flat on the ground.*

a-gla′-śki-ća, *v.* *T.* *i. q.* ahdaśkića.

a-gle′-śka-la, *n.* *T.* *i. q.* ahdeśkadaŋ.

a-gli′-yu-ḣpa, *v.* *T.* *i. q.* ahdiyuḣpa.

a-gmi′-gbe-ya, *v.* *T.* *i. q.* ahmihbeya.

a-gmi′-gma, *v.* *T.* *i. q.* ahmihma.

a′-gna *and* a-gna′, *prep.* *T.* *i. q.* ahna.

a-gna′-gna, *red.* *T.* *i. q.* ahnahna.

a-gna′-ka, *v* *T.* *i. q.* ahnaka.

a-gna′-la, *adv.* *T.* *i. q.* ahnana.

a′-gna-wo-ta-pi, *n.* *T.* *i. q.* ahnawotapi.

a-ġu′-ya-pi-blu, *n.* *T.* *i. q.* aġuyapimdu.

a-ġu′-ya-pi-i-ća-śla, *n* *T.* *i. q.* aġuyapiićaśda.

a-ha′-ha-ye-la, *adv.* *T.* *i. q.* ahahayedaŋ.

a-ha′-kab, *adv.* *T.* *i. q.* ahakam.

a-haŋ′-ble, *v.* *T.* *i. q.* ahaŋmde.

a-haŋ′-ke-ye-la, *adv.* *T.* *previously, just before:* *i. q.* ećahaŋkeyela.

a-he′-ćel, *adv* *T.* *i. q.* ahećen.

a-he′-ćel-ya, *adv.* *T.* *i. q.* ahećenya.

a-hi′-pa-ni, *v.* of ahi *and* pani; *to shove with the elbow; to push* or *crowd against*—ahiwapani.

a-hi′-uŋ-pa, *v.* *T.* *to bring and place* See ahi *and* uŋpa *or* oŋpa.

a-hi′-ya-gle, *v.* *T.* *i. q.* ahiyahde.

a-hi′-yu-śtaŋ, *v.* of ahi *and* yuśtaŋ; *to come and finish; to come to the end; to say the last word in a talk.*

a-ḣaŋ′-ḣaŋ-yaŋ, *adv.* *T.* *carelessly.*

a-ḣe′-yuŋ-ka, *v.* *T* *i. q.* aḣewaŋka.

a-ḣlo′, *v.* *T.* *i. q.*, aḣdo

a-ḣwa′-ya, *adv.* *T.* *i. q* aḣbaya.

a-ḣwa′-ye-la, *adv.* *T.* *i. q.* aḣbayedaŋ.

a-i′-gla-gla, *adv.* *T.* of aglagla.

a-i′-gla-ḣpa, *v.* *T.* *i. q.* aihdaḣpa.

a-i′-glu-taŋ, *v.* *T.* *i. q.* aihdutaŋ.

a-i′-glu-za, *v.* *T.* *to refuse to give up one's own;* *i. q.* aihduza.

a-i′-kća-pta, *v.* *T.* *to talk much to, reprove, scold.* See aikapa.

a-i′-kpa-bla, *v.* T. *to talk to no purpose; to do mischief by talking*—amikpabla.

a-i′-le, *v.* T. *i. q.* aide.

a-i′-ni-la, *adv.* T. *i. q.* ainina.

a-i′-śta-gna-ka, *v.* T. *i. q.* aiśtahnaka.

a-i′-śta-gna-ke-śni, *v.* T. *i. q.* aiśtahnake śni. The use of the negative, as in words like this, for a strong affirmative, is common.

a′-i-ta-gla-ḣwe, *adv.* T. *i. q.* aitahdaḣbe.

a′-i-ta-gla-ḣwe-ya, *adv.* T. *i. q.* aitahdaḣbeya.

a′-i-to-pta, *adv.* T. *i. q.* aetopta.

a′-i-to-pte-ya, *adv.* T. *i. q* aetopteya.

a-i′-ya-gle, *v.* T. *i. q.* aiyahde.

a-i′-ya-ka-pte-ya, *adv* T. *up hill, ascending.*

a-i′-yo-ptel *and* a-i′-yo-pte-tu, *adv.* T. *towards, in the direction of.*

a-kab′, *adv.* T. *i. q.* akam.

a-ka′-bla, *v* T. *i. q.* akamda.

a-ka′-blel, *adv.* T. *i. q.* akamden.

a′-ka-ġalt-ki-ya, *adv* T. *i. q.* akaġatkiya.

a-ka′-ḣtaŋ, *v. n.* T. *to boil over on.*

a-ka′-kaŋ, *v.* T. *to shake* or *beat off on.* See kakaŋ.

a-kal′-mna, *v.* T. *i q.* akanmna

a-kaŋl′, *prep.* T. *i. q* akan.

a-kaŋl′-ta, *adv.* T. *i. q.* akaŋta.

a-kaŋl′-taŋ-haŋ, *adv.* T. *i. q.* akaŋtaŋhaŋ.

a-kaŋl′-tu, *adv.* T. *i. q.* akaŋtu.

a-kaŋl′-tu-ya-kel, *adv.* T. *i. q.* akaŋtuyaken.

a′-ka-pa, *adv.* T. *afterwards, following.*

a-ka′-pol, *cont.* T. *i. q.* akapon.

a-ka′-pol-ya, *adv.* T. *i. q.* akaponya.

a-ka′-pte-će-la, *adv* T. *i. q.* akaptećedaŋ.

a′-ka-ta, *v.* T. *to draw a bow: i. q.* ećate.

a-ka′-yuŋg, *cont.* T. *i. q.* akawaŋg.

a-ka′-yuŋ-ka, *v.* T. *i. q.* akawaŋka.

a-ke′-śa-glo-ġaŋ, *adj.* T. *i. q.* akeśahdoġaŋ.

a-ke′-waŋ-źi-la, *adv.* T. *i. q.* akewaŋźidaŋ.

a-ki′-ći-çuŋ-çuŋ-ka, *v.* T. *to overdo; to be importunate.*

a-ki′-ći-yul, *cont.* of akićiyuta; *adv.* T. *face to face, looking at each other.*

a-ki′-ći-yu-ta, *adv.* T. *face to face.*

a-ki′-gla-ski-ća, *v.* T. *to lie on one's own; i. q.* akihdaskića.

a-ki′-gla-skil, *cont.* of akiglaskića.

a-ki′-gla-skil-ya, *adv.* T. *i. q.* akihdaskinya.

a-ki′-gna, *adv.* T *i. q.* akihna.

a-ki′-gna, *v.* T. *to sit as a hen on eggs.*

a-ki′-gna-ka, *v.* T. *i. q.* akihnaka.

a-ki'-hde, *v. pos.* of ahde: *Ih.* akikde; *T.*, akigle.

a-ki'-hel-he-ća, *adv.* *T.* *i. q.* akihenheća.

a-kil', *cont.* *T.* *i. q.* akin.

a'-ki-le-ćel, *adv.* *T.* *i. q.* akidećen.

a'-ki-le-ćel-ya, *adv.* *T.* *i. q.* akidećenya.

a-ki'-nil, *cont.* *T.* *i. q.* akinin.

a-ki'-nil-ya, *adv.* *T.* *i. q.* akininya.

a-ki'-pśa-pśa, *v.* *T.* *to come home and vomit.*

a-ki'-ptaŋ, *v. n.* *T.* *to do together*—uŋkakiptaŋpi.

a-ki'-śog, *cont.* *i. q.* akiś'ag.

a-ki'-ṭe-ya, *adv.* *T.* *crowded together.*

a-ki'-ya-ta-ke-ća, *adv.* *T.* *touching;* as, hiŋyete akiyatakeća, *shoulders shrugged up;* hu akiyatakeća, *knock-kneed.*

a-ki'-ye-la, *adv.* *T.* *i. q.* akiyedaŋ.

a-ko'-ki-ya, *adv.* *T.* *beyond; from one:* akokiya eś patitaŋ yo, *push it away.*

a-ko'-źal, *adv* *T.* *i. q.* akoźan.

a-ko'-źal-ya, *adv.* *T.* *i. q.* akoźanya.

a-kpa'-spe-ya, *adv.* *T.* *patiently; out of sight.*

a-kśa'-ka, *adv.* *T.* *i. q* akśa.

a-kśu', *v.* *T.* *to pile up on, to load on.* See aźu.

a-kśu', *n.* *T.* *a load.*

al-a'-ta-ya, *adv.* *T.* *i. q.* adataya.

a-le'-tka, *n.* *T.* *i. q.* adetka.

a-li', *v.* *T.* *i. q.* adi.

a-li'-li-ya, *v.* *T.* *red.* of aliya.

a-li'-li-ya-kel, *adv.* *T.* *i. q.* adidiyaken.

a-li'-ya, *v.* *T.* *i. q.* adiya.

a-li'-ya-kel, *adv.* *T.* *i. q.* adiyaken.

a-lo'-sab-ya, *v.* *T.* *i. q.* adosya.

a-ma'-śte-ṭa, *v. n.* *to have a sun stroke.*

a-na'-ha-ha, *adv.* *T.* *slowly, carefully:* anahaha mani.

a-na'-ḣla-ta, *v.* *T.* *to hold on carefully; to crawl cautiously:* *i. q.* anaḣdate.

a-na'-ḣwe, *v.* *T.* *i. q.* anaḣbe.

a-na'-ḣwe-ya, *adv.* *T.* *i. q.* anaḣbeya.

a-na'-źi-pa, *v.* *to pinch*—anawaźipa. See naźipa.

a-o'-ći-kpa-ni, *adv.* *T.* *i. q.* oćikpani.

a-o'-ći-kpa-ni-ya, *adv.* *i. q.* oćikpaniya.

a-o'-ći-ptel, *adv.* *T.* *i. q.* oćipten.

a-o'-ći-ptel-ya, *adv.* *T.* *i. q.* oćiptenya.

a-o'-ho-mni, *adv.* *around, surrounding.* See ohomni.

a-o'-ho-mni-ya, *v.* *T.* *to go around.*

a-o'-śla, *n.* *T.* *the part behind the shoulder over* which the shoulder blade moves.

a-o'-ṭo-gnag-ya, *adv.* *T.* *daringly.*

a-pa'-ba-ġa, *v. a.* *to rub together* as two hard surfaces; *to card*, as wool.

a-pa'-la-pa, *v. T.* *to make smooth*, *to plane.*

a'-pa-ma-gle, *adv.* *T.* *i. q.* apamahde.

a'-pa-ma-gle-ya, *adv.* *T.* *i. q.* apamahdeya.

a-pa'-wa-ġa, *v.* *T.* *i. q.* apabaġa.

a-pa'-waħ-wa-ġa, *v. red.* of apawaġa.

a-saŋ'-pi-gbu-gbu *and* a-saŋ'-pi-gwu-gwu, *n.* *T.* *thick milk;* *i. q.* asaŋpinini.

a-ta'-śo-śa, *v. T.* *i. q.* ataġośa.

a-tkaŋ', *v. n.* *T.* *i. q.* atkiŋ.

a-ṭe'-ća, *adj.* *T.* *luke-warm*, as water.

a-ṭe'-ća-ħa, *adj.* *T.* *i. q.* iṭeća *and* it'eća.

a-wa'-bla-za, *v.* *T.* *i. q.* abamdaza.

a-wa'-ble-ća, *v.* *T.* *i. q.* abamdeća.

a-wa'-blel, *cont.* *T.* *i. q.* abamden.

a-wa'-gla, *v.* *T.* *i. q.* abahda.

a-wa'-ħta-ni, *v. a.* of waħtani; *to transgress a usage* or *law*, *to offend against a custom; to fail to perform a vow;* the person offending is awaħtani towards the custom, and himself awaiçiħtani. The idea seems to be that some evil is brought on one's self by the transgression.—W. J. C. See under waħtani.

a-wa'-ka, *v.* *T.* *to cut the feather from a quill, as in making arrows; i. q.* abaka.

a-wa'-ke-za, *v.* *T.* *i. q.* abakeza.

a-wa'-źal, *cont.* *T.* *i. q.* abaźan

a'-we-we-ya, *adv. red.* of áweya.

a'-we-ya, *adv* *T.* *i. q.* ábeya.

a-wo'-bla-za, *v.* *T.* *i. q.* abomdaza.

a-wo'-ble-ća, *v.* *T.* *i. q.* abomdeća

a-wo'-blel, *cont.* *T.* *i. q.* abomden.

a-wo'-blu, *v.* *T.* *i. q.* abomdu.

a-wo'-ksa, *v.* *T.* *i. q.* aboksa.

a-yu'-ćo-ya-kel, *adv.* *T.* *i. q.* ayućoya.

a-yu'-hiŋ-haŋ, *v.* of yuhiŋhaŋ; *to rake* or *harrow over.*

a-yu'-ħam, *adv.* *crawling*, *creeping on*, or *towards:* ayuħam iyaya.

B.

b o - ś o′ - k a, *adj.* *T.* *puffed out; enlarged, ending in a knob.* See ibośoka.

C.

ć a ḣ - ć a ŋ′ - ġ a, *adj.* *T.* *gristly, cartilaginous.*

ć a ŋ - g l e′ - p i, *n.* *T.* *cord-wood.*

ć a ŋ - h a ŋ l′, *adv.* *T.* *perhaps, possibly; I don't know: i. q.* naćeća.

ć a ŋ - k a′ - s k u - s k u, *v.* *T.* *to hew a log.*

ć a ŋ - n a′ - k s e - y u - h a, *n.* *T.* *one who carries a club, a policeman.*

ć a ŋ - t e′ - i - y a - p a *and* ć a ŋ t - i′ - y a - p a, *v. n.* *T.* (ćaŋte *and* iyapa) *to be flurried* or *excited; to have the heart beat unnaturally.*

ć a ŋ - t e′ - i - y a - p a - k i - y a, *v. a.* *to cause to be excited, to make one's heart beat quickly.*

ć a ŋ - t e′ - y a - p a - y a *and* ć a ŋ t - i′ - y a - p a - y a, *adv.* *T.* *excitedly.*

ć a ŋ - t e′ - i - y a - p a - p i *and* ć a ŋ t - i′ - y a - p a - p i, *n.* *T.* *heart-beating, excitement.*

ć a ŋ - t e′ - w a - k a ŋ - h e - ź a, *v.* *T.* *to be childlike; weak-hearted.*

ć a ŋ′ - y u - k t a ŋ, *n.* *bent wood:* ćaŋpagmiyaŋpi ćaŋyuktaŋ, *a wagon bow.*

ć a p - i′ - h m u ŋ - k e, *n.* (ćapa *and* hmuŋka), *a trap for catching beavers.* *T.*, ćabihmuŋke.

ć a t - i′ - p a - ś l a - y a, *v.* *T.* (ćaḣota *and* paślaya); *to hull corn with ashes; to make hominy.*

ć e ḣ - i′ - y o - k a - ś k e, *n.* *the stick* or *thong on which a kettle is hung* over the fire.

ć e - k p a′ - t a, *adv.* of ćekpa; ćekpata uŋ slolya, *to have known before birth; i. q.* hiśni itokab slolya.

ć e - p a ŋ′ - ś i, *n.* *T.* *i. q.* ićepaŋśi.

ć e - p a ŋ′ - ś i - t k u, *n.* *i. q.* ićepaŋśitku.

ć e - p a ŋ′ - ś i - y a, *v.* *i. q.* ićepaŋśiya.

ć o - k a ŋ′ - h i - y u - i - ç i - y a, *v. reflex.* *to thrust one's self into; to come uninvited.*

ć u - w i′ - g n a - k a, *n.* *T.* *a white woman's gown.* See ćuwi *and* hnaka.

ć u - w i′ - p u - s k i - ć a, *v. n.* *T.* *to be oppressed with anger.*

ć u - w i′ - p u - s k i - ć a - ṭ o - k i n i - ć a, *v.* *to be dying with pent up rage; bursting with anger.*

ç u - w i′ - y u - k s a, *adj* *cut off at the waist:* so the proper name, Mato ćuwiyuksa, *grizzly bear cut off at the waist* (or *from the waist up*). ćuwiyuksa ogle, *a vest.*

E.

e-ćè′-la, *adv.* *T.* *i. q.* ećedaŋ.

e-će′-la-kel, *adv.* *T.* *itself alone; without help.*

e-haŋ′-tu-ķe, *adv.* *just then; then, indeed.*

G.

glo-gle′-ska *and* gl̩o-glo′-ska, *n.* *T.* *the windpipe, the trachea:* not *the gullet,* which is winapće. It will be seen that these do not correspond with hdohdeska *and* dohdeska, as is supposed in the text, page 120.

gna-śka′, *n.* *T.* *a frog, frogs; i. q.* hnaśka.

gnu-gnu′-śka-sa-pa, *n.* *T.* *the black grasshopper,* or *out-door cricket: the house-cricket* is tiyoślola. See gnugnuśka.

H.

haŋ′-ţe-ya, *adv.* *T.* *wearily:* haŋţeya se ia.

ha′-yu-ħpu, *v. n.* *T.* *to be scabbed.*

ha′-yu-ħpu-ħpu, *v. red.* of hayuħpu.

he′-e-ća-śka, *adv.* *T.* *still, nevertheless.*

he′-e-ća-tu-ka, *adv* *T.* *nevertheless:* heećatuka ito miś wowaźukta, *nevertheless I will plant.*

he-i′-ća-kaŋ, *n.* *T.* *a fine comb; a louse comb.* See heya *and* ipakćasbudaŋ.

hi-na′, *T.* *intj.* of *surprise; i. q.* ina!

hi-na′-hi-na′-hi-na′, *T.* *red.* of hina!

hi-nob′-u-ye, *n.* *T.* *a two-year-old colt.* See hitobtobuye *and* makićimala.

hi-nu′, *T.* *intj.* of *gladness* and *surprise,* as when one meets a friend.

hi-nu′-hi-nu-hi-nu′, *T.* *intj. red.* of hinu!

hiŋ-yaŋs′-e-la *or* hiŋ-yaŋ′-se-la, *adv.* of hiŋyaŋza; *T.* *badly, wickedly.*

h i ŋ - y a ŋ′ - z e - k a, *adj.* *T.* *i. q.* hiŋyaŋzeća, *it storms.*

h i ŋ - y a ŋ′ - z e - ć a, *v. n.* *T.* *it storms violently; i. q.* ośićića.

h i ŋ - ź i′ - l a, *adj.* *T.* *downy; i. q* hiŋ źidaŋ.

h i - s t o′ - l a, *adv.* *T.* *without barbs.*

h i - s t o′ - l a, *n.* *T* *an arrow without barbs.*

h i - t o b′ - t o b - u - y e, *n.* *T.* *a four-year-old colt.*

h o - ḣ a′ - p a, *adj.* *T.* *i. q.* hoġata.

h o ḣ′ - e - ć e ś, *T.* *intj.* of *disbelief: i. q.* ḣoećaḣi.

h o - k ś i′ - h i - y u - y a, *v.* *T.* *to have an abortion.*

h o - k ś i′ - h i - y u - y e - k i - y a, *v. a.* *to cause an abortion.*

h o - ź i′ - l a, *intj.* *T.* *how beautiful! splendid!*

h u - i′ - n a - k e ḣ - y e, *n.* *T.* *a wagon-brake:* huinakeḣye ećel iću, *to put on the brake.*

h u ŋ′ - p e, *n.* *T.* *a stick with a crotch in one end,* used for bracing tent-poles in the inside.

h u ŋ′ - p e - p l e - ć e - l a, *n.* *T.* *a picket-pin.*

h u - p a′, *n.* *a travois; tent-poles tied together to pack on.*

h u - t i′ - n a - ć u - t e, *n.* *T.* a rib of an ox or cow cut short, polished smooth and ornamented—to throw on the ice or snow. See hutanakute *and* hutinaćute.

h u - t i′ - y a - h d e - y a, *n.* (huta *and* iyahde) *a peninsula.*

h u - w o′ - ġ a, *adj.* *T.* *i. q.* huboġa, *bandy-legged.*

Ḣ.

ḣ a ŋ - t k a ŋ′ - o - y u - z e, *n.* *T.* *an armlet; elastic bands for holding up the shirt-sleeves.*

ḣ d o′ - k a, *adj.* *hollow, decayed;* hiwićaḣdoka, *decayed teeth.*

ḣ p e′ - l a, *adj.* *T.* *weak:* ḣpela hiŋgla, *to become discouraged; to be diverted from.*

I.

i'-bo-śo *and* i'-wo-śo, *n.* *T.* *pouting lips.*

i'-bo-śo-ka, *adj.* *T.* *pouting, mouth pushed out.*

i'-bo-śo-ki-ya, *v.* *T.* *to push out the lips; to pout*—ibośowakiya.

i-ća'-ḣći, *v.* of kaḣći. *T.* *to pull out of; to break out from.* See inaḣći *and* iyuḣći.

i-ća'-kśa, *v.* of kakśa. See under payata.

i-ća'-ḳo-ġe, *n.* *T.* a scraper.

i-ća'-ḳos, *cont.* of ićaḳoza.

i-ća'-ḳo-za, *v. n.* *T.* *to be made bare by:* tate na ićaḳos iyaya, *the wind blew and it became bare.*

i-ćaŋ'-te-ni-ća, *v. n.* *T.* *to have no heart for; to be controlled by habit so that the will power is gone.*

i-ća'-slo-he, *n.* *T.* *a stick which is made to slide along on snow or ice: the game of billiards;* ićaslo ećoŋ, *to play billiards.*

i-će'-te, *n.* *T.* *the rim* or *lip* of a kettle. See ćeḣiha *and* tete.

i-ći'-ha-kta-ya, *adv.* of ihakta; *following each other.*

i-ći'-ḣmiŋ-yaŋ, *adv.* *T.* *crookedly, incorrectly, confusedly;* ićiḣmiŋyaŋ naḣoŋ, *to hear incorrectly.*

i-ći'-oŋb, *adv.* *T.* *i. q.* ićuŋom.

i-ći'-oŋb-ya, *adv.* *T.* *i. q.* ićuŋomya.

i-ći'-oŋ-pa-taŋ-haŋ, *adv.* *T.* *i. q.* ićuŋoŋpataŋhaŋ.

i-ći'-ṭe-ya, *adv.* *T.* *very close together; crowding each other badly;* ićiṭeya yaŋkapi.

i'-ći-ya-ki-gle, *adv.* *T.* *one by one, one after another; i. q.* kićihdeya.

i'-ći-ya-ki-gle-gle, *adv. red.* of ićiyakigle.

i-ću'-ḣćiŋ, *adv* *T.* *the very one, the only one:* waŋźila ićuḣćiŋ au yo, *bring it even if but one.*

i'-e-ća-daŋ, *adv.* *near to, soon, soon after.* See ećadaŋ.

i-gla'-ṭa, *v.* *T.* *to have convulsions; i. q.* ihdaṭa: hoḣpiglaṭa (of hoḣpa *and* iglaṭa), *to cough convulsively.*

i-glu'-ta, *v.* *T.* *pos.* of iyuta.

i-glu'-taŋ, *v.* *T.* *i. q.* ihdutaŋ.

i-ka'-mna, *v.* *T.* *to rip;* ogle iwakamna, *I ripped my coat.* See kamna.

i-ko'-kab, *adv.* *T.* *i. q.* itokam.

i-ku'-źa, *v. n.* *T.* *to be sick* or *indisposed on account of.* See kuźa.

i-leḣ'-ya-uŋ-pa-pi, *n.* *T.* *cigars, cigarettes.*

i-ma'-he-ća, *adj.* *T.* *inner, occult; i. q.* imahen.

i-mde'-za, *v. n.* *to be enlightened about*—iwamdeza *and* imamdeza.

i-mna′-mna-he-ća, *n.* *T.* *the fourth* or *smallest manyple* of animals.

i-na′-ḣme-ki-ći-ya-pi, *n.* *T.* *the game of hide and seek.*

i-na′-ḣu-ġa, *v.* *T.* *to mash by stepping on.*

i-na′-ki-kśiŋ, *v.* *to take shelter in* or *behind; to make a shelter of,* as of a tree.

i-ni′-ti-yu-ktaŋ, *v.* *to bend willows over for a booth.* See initi *and* yuktaŋ.

i-pa′-ḣlal-ya, *adv.* *T.* *in a row facing one way, in line,* as soldiers in platoon.

i-pa′-ḣo, *v.* *T.* *to brush up,* as hair from the forehead, *to brush into a curl*—iwapaḣo.

i-pa′-śki-ća, *v.* *T.* of paśkića; *to rub,* as clothes, *on a wash-board.*

i-pa′-ta-pi, *n.* *T.* *embroidery, ornamental work; i. q.* wipatapi.

i-pa′-wa-ġa, *v.* *T.* *to rub, scrub,* or *scour,* as a floor—iwapawaġa.

i-śiŋ′-ḣćiŋ, *adv.* *T.* *crossly, angrily;* iśiŋḣćiŋ ia.

i-śkaŋ′-ka-piŋ, *v.* *T.* *to be lazy by reason of.* See kapiŋ.

i-śta′-i-yo-ta-wa-pa, *v.* *T.* *to look in the direction* that some one else is looking. See tawapa.

i-taŋ′-a-nog, *adv.* *cont.* of itaŋanokataŋhaŋ.

i-te′-o-yus, *cont.* of iteoyuze.

i-te′-o-yus-ya, *adv.* *T.* *pleasantly.*

i-te′-o-yu-ze, *n.* *T.* *a look, cast of countenance, appearance:* ite oyuze waśte, *a pleasant face.*

i-toŋ′-pa, *v.* *T.* *to be surprised, astonished; to wonder.*

i-tu′-ma-ko-skaŋ, *adv.* *T.* *in vain; to no purpose.*

i-tu′-śi-ka, *adv* *T.* *by all means, nevertheless.*

i′-wi-ća-mde-za, *n.* of imdeza; *enlightenment.*

i-wi′-ća-mna, *adj.* *T.* of imna; *satisfying, furnishing much nourishment.*

i-wo′-ćo, *n.* *T.* *a churn: i. q.* iboćo.

i-wo′-hta-ke, *n.* *T.* *a billiard stick* or *cue.*

i-wo′-źu, *n.* of woźu; *something to plant* or *sow; garden seeds, seed of any kind.*

i-ya′-glu-ḣa, *v. pos.* of iyayuḣa; *to follow after,* as a colt its mother.

i-ya′-na-źi-ća, *v.* *T.* *to run away with,* as a horse with a wagon. See naźića.

i-yo′-hop, *intj.* *T.* used in playing hide and seek.

i-yo′-kal, *adv. cont.* *T.* iyokal śpaŋyaŋ, *to toast* or *roast by holding to the fire.*

i-yo′-kal-ya, *adv.* *T.* *by the heat.*

i-yo′-ko-gna, *adv.* *T.* *between* one place and another: *i. q.* okitahepi.

i-yu′-ho-mni, *n.* of yuhomni; *something to turn with,* as a doorknob.

i-yu′-paḣ, *adv.* *T.* *together, in a bunch:* iyupaḣ nauŋg au, *they come together on a gallop.*

K.

k a - b l a ś', *adj. cont. T. spread apart; i. q.* kamdaś.

k a - g b u', *v. T. to make a noise*, as persons in water.

k a - g l a' - g l a, *adv. red.* of kagla: *alongside of.*

k a - ġ e' - ġ e, *v. red.* of kaġe. *T. to take out by handfuls: i. q.* yuġeġe.

k a - ġ i', *v. T. to hold in esteem, to respect, honor, reverence*, or *fear*, on account of dignity.

k a - ġ i' - ś n i, *adv. T. without respect or consideration:* kaġiśni oḣaŋ, *to d without restraint.*

k a - h a ŋ l', *adv. T. i. q.* kahan.

k a - ḣ a b', *cont. T. i. q.* kaham.

k a - i' - ć o - ġ a, *v. i. q.* ićoġa.

k a - l a' - l a, *adj. T. ragged: v. i. q.* kadada.

k a ŋ - h a ŋ' - h a ŋ, *adj. T. tattered.*

k a - t i' - ć a, *v. a. to stir* or *mix up*. See katiktića.

k ć e' - y a, *v. T.* to cook by hanging over the fire: hence the side or ribs of an animal are called wakćeyapi. See pćeya.

k i - ć i' - k t e - p i, *n. T. murder.*

k i - ḣ a ŋ', *v. T. i. q.* kiḣaŋśića; *it storms: i. q.* lila ośićeća *and* hiŋyaŋzeća.

k i - n i l' *and* **k i ŋ - n i l'**, *adv. T. fully, completely:* oyasiŋ kiŋnil, *every one.*

k i ŋ - ś l e' - l a, *adv. T. whizzing*, as a bullet.

k i - ś l e' - y a, *v. T. to hold and feel, to force, to commit rape.* See wikiśleya.

k o' - k t a - ś i - ć a, *adj. T. a million; i. q.* woyawa taŋka.

k o - ś k a', *v. T. i. q.* to be affected with the venereal disease: *i. q.* će ḣli—komaśka.

k o - ś k a' - l a - k a, *n. T. a young man.*

k p a ŋ' - y a ŋ, *v. a. to tan, to dress*, as a skin. See tpaŋyaŋ.

k p e - y e' - l a, *adv. T. resounding;* kpeyela ap'a, *to strike and make resound.*

k u ś, *cont.* of kuźa; *inactive, feeble;* kuś amayaŋ, *I am growing feeble.*

L.

l e - h a ŋ l', *adv. T. i. q.* dehan.

l e - h a ŋ' - y a ŋ k *or* **l e - h a ŋ' - y a g**, *adv. T. i. q.* tokaŋ: ti lehaŋyaŋk, *at some other house.*

M.

m a - k a' - i - y u - ḣ l o - k e, *n. T. an auger to dig* post holes.

m a - k a' - i - y u - p t e, *n. T. a breaking plow; the wheel,* or *cutter of a breaker.*

m a - k a' - s i ŋ - t e - p e - ź i, *n. T. a kind of grass, skunk-tail grass,* which grows in bunches, and heads like timothy.

m a - k i' - ć i - m a - l a, *n. T. a two year old.* See hinobuye.

m a - k o' - b l a - y e, *n. T. i. q.* makomdaye.

m a - k u' - n a - s n u - z a, *n. T. the lower extremity of the breast bone.*

m a - k u' - p i ŋ - k p a, *n. T. the end of the breast, the part just above the navel.*

m a s - i' - b a - p t e, *n. T. a spade; i. q.* maza ibapte.

m a - ś t e' - ć a ŋ - h a ŋ - p a, *n. T. slippers; warm-weather shoes.*

m a - ś t i ŋ' - s a - p e - l a, *n. T. the common rabbit.*

m a - ś t i ŋ' - s k a, *n. T. the hare,* or *jack rabbit.*

m a - t o' - ć i ŋ - ć a - l a, *n. T. a bear's cub; i. q.* waćiŋćadaŋ.

m a - t o' - h a, *n. T. a bear's skin.* See waha.

m a - y a' - ś l e, *n. T. a small species of wolf, the jackal.*

m a' - z a - i - b a - p t e, *n. T. a spade.*

m a z - i' - y u - w i, *n. T. bridle bits.*

m d a - ś k a', *adj broad and flat,* as in pasumdaśka. See mdaska.

m d i - h e' - ć a, *v. n. Ih. i. q.* miniheća, etc.

m d i - h e' - y a, *adv. Ih. i. q.* miniheya.

m i' - n i - ḣ u - h a - m a - z a - s k a - i - i - ć u, *n. T. a bank check.*

m i' - n i - s a' - p a - i - p a - p u - z e, *n. T. an ink blotter.*

M n i - k a ŋ' - y e - w o - ź u, *n. p. i. q.* Minikaŋyewoźu, also Mni-ko-o-źu.

O.

o' - ġ e - y a, *adv. T. just as it is, whole, all together:* oġeya iću, *take it as it is.*

o' - ć o - ġ a *and* o' - i - c o - ġ a, *i. q.* ićoġa.

o - k a' - s o l, *cont. T.* of okasota.

o - k a' - s o - t a, *v. to use up, destroy.*

o - k a' - w a - t o ŋ - y a ŋ, *adv.* without hindrance, unobstructedly.

o - k a' - w a - t o ŋ - y a - k e l, *adv.* without hindrance, unobstructedly.

o ŋ' - t o ŋ - y a, *v.* See next.

o ŋ' - t o ŋ - i - ç i - y a, *v. refl. to injure one's self.*

P.

pa′-mnu-mnu-ga, *n.* *T.* *the gristle* or *cartilage in the end of the nose; the end of the nose*

S.

slo-he′-se *and* slo-haŋ′-se, *adv.* *T.* *slowly*, as if crawling along.

W.

wa-ya′-wa-ćiŋ-hiŋ-yaŋ-za, *v.* This differs from wayawahiŋyaŋza as "to bite" differs from "to backbite." the latter refers to wayawaćiŋhiŋyaŋza, *to make* one *cross by talking against him.*—A. L. R.

Y.

yu-ble′-za, *v. a.* *T.* *to make clear.*

o